Suggested Scope and Sequence for One-Semester Courses with Differing Emphases

Chapter	Basic Civics (16 chapters)	Civics, Economics, and Law (16 chapters)	Civics, Law, and Politics (15 chapters)	Civics and a Global Society (15 chapters)	Civics and Problems of Democracy (17 chapters)
1 A Portrait of Americans	•	•	•	•	•
2 American Society and its values	•	•	•	•	•
3 The Meaning of Citizenship	•	•	•	•	•
4 America's Political Heritage	•		•	•	•
5 Creating the Constitution	•	•	•	•	•
6 The Bill of Rights	•	•	•	•	•
7 Our Living Constitution	•	•	•	•	•
8 The Legislative Branch	•	•	•	•	•
9 The Executive Branch	•	•	•	•	•
10 The Judicial Branch	•	•	•	•	•
11 State Government	•				
12 Local Government	•				
13 What is an Economy?		•		•	
14 Basics of Our Economic System	•	•		•	•
15 Money and Banking		•			
16 Government's Role in Our Economy		•			•
17 Our Economy and You		•			
18 Laws and Our Society	•	•	•		•
19 Criminal and Juvenile Justice		•	•		
20 Civil Justice		•	•		
21 Political Parties in Our Democracy	•		•		
22 Voting and Elections	•		•		
23 Confronting Society's Problems			•	•	•
24 One Nation Among Many				•	•
25 American Foreign Policy				•	•
26 Making a Difference in the World				•	•

ADDISON-WESLEY

CIVICS

PARTICIPATING IN OUR DEMOCRACY

ANNOTATED TEACHER'S EDITION

AUTHORS

James E. Davis

Phyllis Maxey Fernlund

CONSULTANTS

Barry K. Beyer

Mabel McKinney-Browning

ADDISON-WESLEY PUBLISHING COMPANY
Menlo Park, California • Reading, Massachusetts
New York • Don Mills, Ontario • Wokingham, England
Amsterdam • Bonn • Sydney • Singapore • Tokyo
Madrid • San Juan • Paris • Seoul • Milan • Mexico City • Taipei

Project Team Acknowledgments

Editorial	Susan Hartzell, John Burner, Jeannie Crumly Cole, Eric Engles, Bobbi Watkinson
Design	Debbie Costello, Kevin Berry
Product Management	Gary Standafer
Photo Edit	Karen Koppel, Inge Kjemtrup
Production	Jenny Vodak, Steve Rogers, Don Shelonko, Kay Brown, Therese DeRogatis, Odette Thomas, Keiko Tsuyuki, Cathleen Veraldi, Ellen Williams
Manufacturing	Sarah Teutschel, Eva Wilson
Marketing Services	Greg Gardner, Christopher Lierle
Permissions	Mauren Schaeffer, Marty Granahan

ISBN 0-201-81564-8

2 3 4 5 6 7 8 9 10 -VH- 97 96 95 94 93 92

CONTENTS

PLANNING GUIDES, TEACHING STRATEGIES, AND ANSWER KEYS

Connects citizenship to the student's real world

Encourages active learning and motivates students to take action.

- ***Thought-provoking questions relate to students' lives and stimulate discussion and involvement.***
- ***Realistic vignettes written from the students' point of view invite participatory learning.***
- ***Decision-making strand teaches important practical skills.***

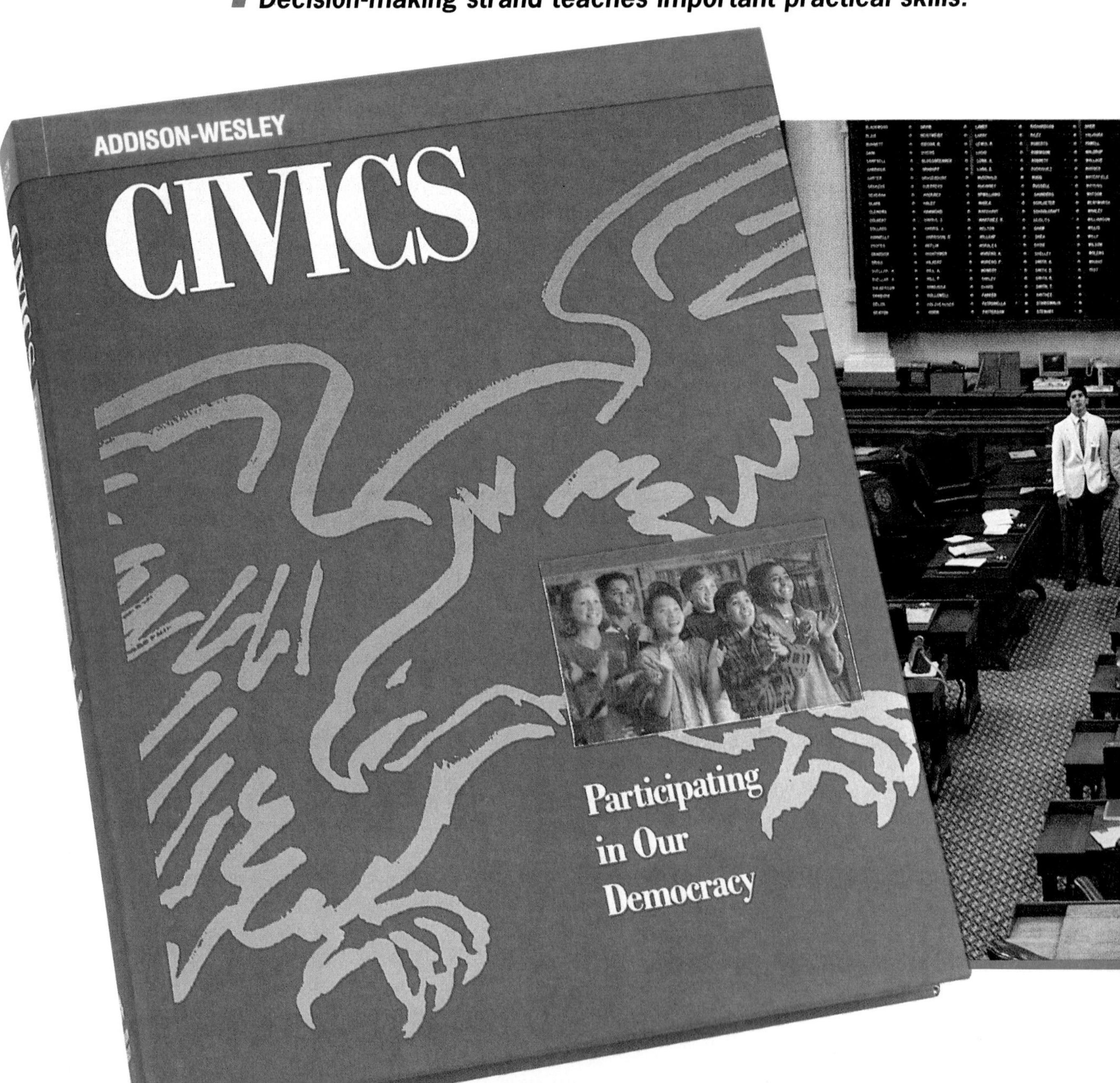

Integrated program invites students to examine society and citizenship

- Weaves together our social, legal, economic and political systems.
- Shows how these systems are organized, how they operate, and how they relate to students' lives.
- Focuses on the fundamental values of our democratic society: freedom, equality, and justice.

RELEVANT...

- ***Issues that Affect You* involve students in current real-world situations through case studies.**

- ***Compelling portrayals of contemporary issues provide students with a realistic look at how individuals, groups, and governments work together to solve problems.***

ISSUES THAT AFFECT YOU: A CASE STUDY

Banning Neighborhood Noise

Darien Mann's rock and roll band was loud. When Darien and his friends practiced in Darien's garage, many of the neighbors complained that they could not talk to each other without shouting. It made the neighbors even more angry that the four boys practiced late into the night.

Darien's next-door neighbors, the Macks, lived closest to the garage. They were disturbed by the noise more often than anyone else in the neighborhood.

One evening Mr. Mack thought the band was playing even louder than usual. He rang the Manns' doorbell and pounded on the door, but no one answered. In disgust, Mr. Mack returned home and called the police.

Los Angeles police officer Richard Hoefel and his partner answered the call at about 8 P.M. After months of complaints, the Mann house had become a regular stop on their beat. They could hear the band from half a block away.

The officers walked to the chain link fence in front of the Manns' garage and rapped on the gate with their flashlights to get the teenagers' attention. Officer Hoefel ordered the boys to meet him on the front porch.

Once they all were gathered together, Officer Hoefel explained the reason for the neighbor's complaint. He warned the group that if they did not stop making the noise he would have to arrest them for breaking the law. The Los Angeles Municipal Code has a "noise ordinance" which states that it is against the law for any person to make any "loud, unnecessary, and unusual noise which disturbs the peace and quiet of any neighborhood."

Thirteen months later, the Manns and the Macks were still arguing over the noise problem.

The officers talked wi[th] the band about ways th[ey] could avoid noise comp[laints] in the future. The offic[ers] said that the band cou[ld rent] a hall, soundproof th[e ga]rage, or agree with th[e ...] about good times to [prac]tice. Because the boy[s were] cooperative, Officer [Hoefel] decided to let them [off with] only a warning.

Thirteen month[s later,] the Manns and th[e Macks] were still arguing [over the] noise. An inform[al ...] before the city a[...] failed to end th[e] differences. Da[rien's] band wanted t[o ...] in the garage, [...] wanted the m[...] permanently.

To settle [...] and for all, [...] and his par[...] bring a law[...]

INSPIRING...

- *Views of Noted Americans* ***introduces students to the experiences and ideas of famous citizens.***
- *People Make a Difference* ***provides models of how ordinary citizens can bring about change in areas that relate to students' everyday lives.***
- ***Engaging student-oriented writing style keeps readers interested in content.***

PEOPLE MAKE A DIFFERENCE

Ice Cream Makers Share Success

Ben Cohen and Jerry Greenfield, the owners of Ben and Jerry's Homemade, Inc., have a well-known product: ice cream. Their business, which they started in a converted gas station in 1978, was an immediate success. Today, their ice cream sells in stores around the nation.

The two entrepreneurs, who have been friends since junior high school, believe

there would be
social problem
try, because th
enough money
them," says B
He and Je
helped start
1 Percent Fo
seeks to red
the nation's
to promote
understan
courages

VIEWS OF NOTED AMERICANS

Barbara Jordan

Barbara Jordan has never let difficulties keep her from achieving her goals. She has been a Texas state senator, a member of Congress, and is now a college professor. Each success has been, to Jordan, "just another milestone I have passed; it's just the beginning."

Barbara Jordan grew up in Houston, Texas in the 1940s and 1950s when there were still separate schools for blacks and whites. During her senior year in an all-black high school, she worked hard to be the best in her class. She was president of the National Honor Society, a star debater, and winner of many academic awards and honors. She also participated in a number of community projects. As a result she won her school's "Girl of the Year" award.

Jordan entered

only two women and a handful of blacks in her class. After graduating in 1959, Jordan returned to Houston to practice law, eager to use her free time in community service. After volunteering with the Democratic party in the 1960 election campaign, she declared that she "had really been bitten by the political bug."

Politics, Jordan decided, offered the best opportunity to make government

respond to the needs of the people. Therefore, she
decided to run for politica
office. In 1966, Barbara J
dan passed another mile-
stone when she was elec
to the Texas State Senat
Jordan's next goal w
seat in the United State
House of Representati
which she won in 197
There she earned resp
her hard work and th
ful decisions. In 197
was honored by bei
vited to give the op
speech at the natio
vention of the Dem
party.
In 1978 Jorda
not to run for ree
Her work in poli
ever, is far from
teacher, speaker
she continues t
ideas about po
She tells her st
every Americ
citizenship re
seriously, bec
are too high
to be a spec

PROVOCATIVE...

- **Taking a Stand challenges students to articulate their opinions on controversial issues.**
- **Up-to-date content presents key issues facing Americans today.**

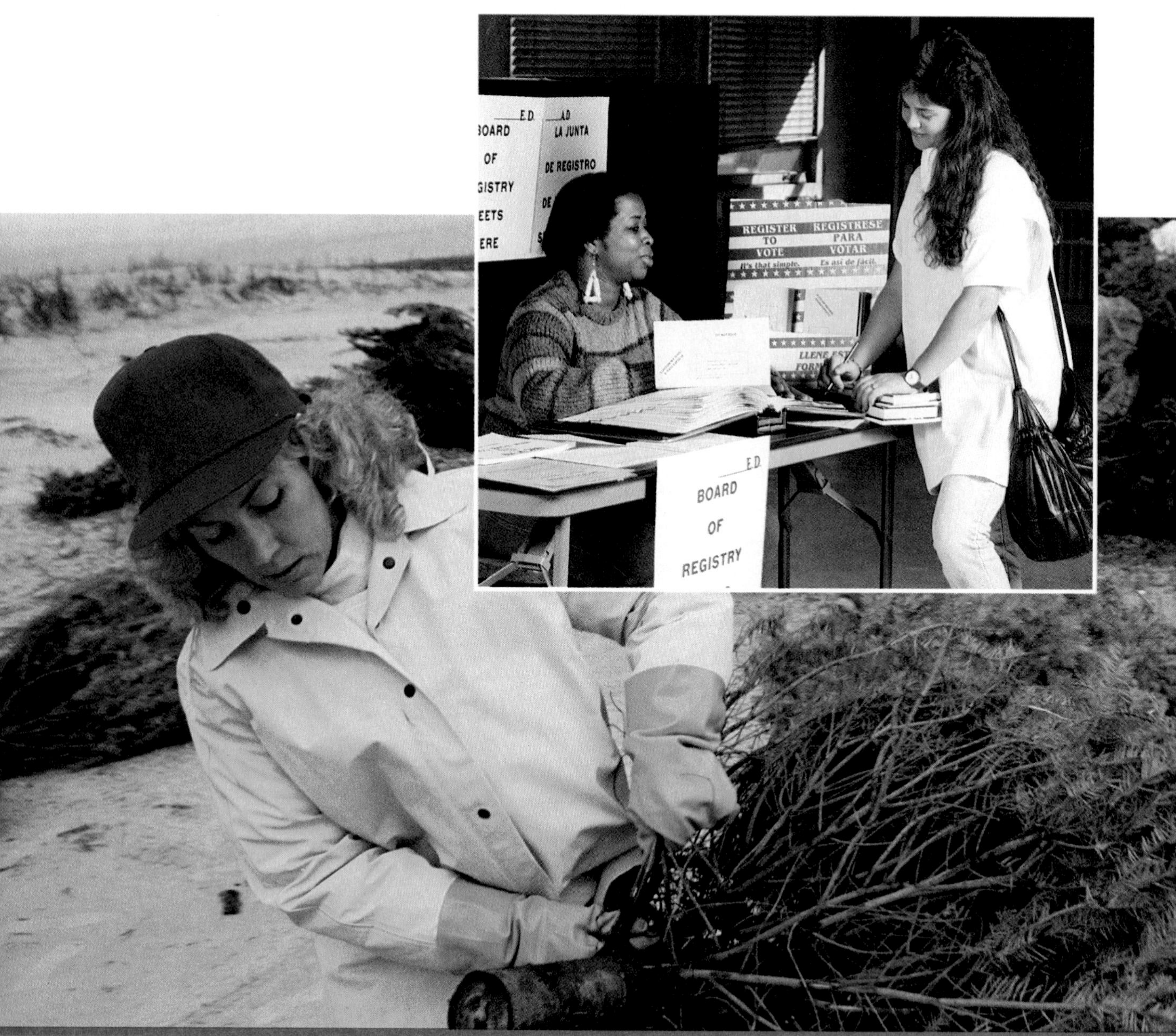

CHAPTER 23

Confronting Society's Proble

The year: 1633. The place: Dorchester, Massachusetts, now part of Boston. The trouble: cows and goats had broken through the fences and were wrecking the village green.

John Maverick, a Dorchester minister, began to worry that the village green would be destroyed. He knew that he could not take care of the matter by himself. Furthermore, in 1633 Dorchester ha no local government, no elected or appointed government officers

UNIT SURVEY

LOOKING BACK AT THE UNIT

1. Is it possible to treat another person with equal respect even if you find that he or she has opinions or values different from your own? Explain your answer, giving examples.

2. What does it mean to you now to play a citizenship role in the United States? How do you think you might answer this question when you are an adult?

3. Explain how each of the following activities contributes to the common good: **(a)** voting in an election **(b)** recycling newspapers **(c)** expressing your views in a letter to the editor **(d)** treating a person with equal respect.

4. Match each social role listed below with the social institution that *most* affects you when you are playing that role.

1. son or daughter
2. student
3. citizen
4. consumer

(a) the economy
(b) government
(c) the family
(d) education

TAKING A STAND

The Issue

Should there be laws declaring English to be the official language of the United States?

Americans have always been proud of their ... Immigrants have brought their own ... religious practices to ... who

important information, such as ba application forms, in other languag as English. Schools have set up bili grams, teaching students in both E their native language, to help the their new country.

Some people think that using other than English endangers na They want their states to pass la English the official language States. Such laws are often ca only laws." They would requir glish be used in any govern function. English-only laws c cial workers and doctors in p example, from using any lan in their work.

The groups supporting say that making English th would encourage immigra faster than they might oth grants would become pa culture more quickly. Th also save the money it n ing important informat language.

Opposing groups would discriminate ag have not yet learned E make it very difficult to receive health and cause a person has they say, is not a re equal rights.

INFORMATIVE...

- In Their Own Words **Primary source materials bring reality and relevance to the subject of civics.**
- Data Bank **provides opportunities for extended learning.**
- American Notebook **appeals to students' fascination with facts and figures.**

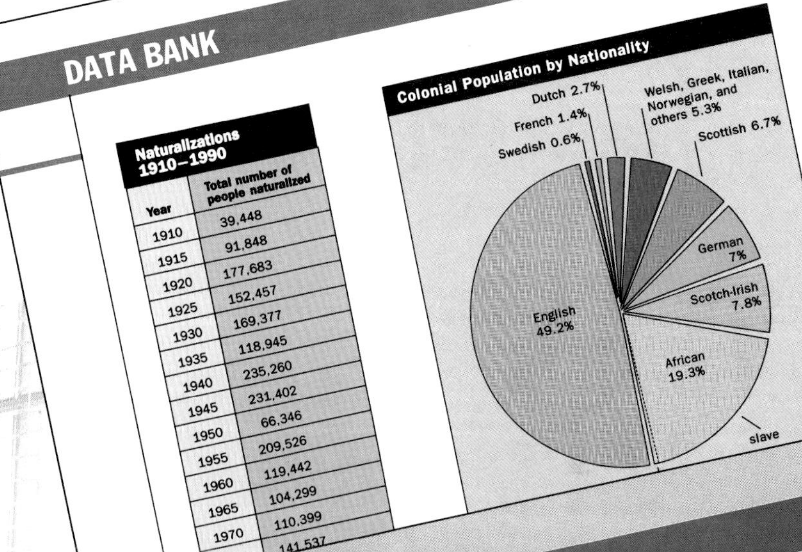

DATA BANK

Naturalizations 1910–1990

Year	Total number of people naturalized
1910	39,448
1915	91,848
1920	177,683
1925	152,457
1930	169,377
1935	118,945
1940	235,260
1945	231,402
1950	66,346
1955	209,526
1960	119,442
1965	104,299
1970	110,399
1975	141,537

IN THEIR OWN WORDS

Theodore Roosevelt: "I believe in a strong executive"

During his two terms as President, from 1901 to 1909, Theodore Roosevelt faced many challenges at home and abroad. The United States was suffering growing pains as a result of becoming an industrial giant and a world power.

Roosevelt believed that in order to lead the United States through these difficult times, he must push the powers of the presidency to their limit. In doing so, he received much criticism. Some people accused him of usurping, or taking away, power from the other two branches. On June 19, 1908, Roosevelt wrote a letter in which he defended his belief in a strong presidency.

While President I have *been* President, emphatically; I have used every ounce of ...wer there was in the office ...nd a rap for

fairs of Santo Domingo and Cuba; or as I did . . . in settling the anthracite coal strike, in keeping order in Nevada [during a strike by miners], or as I have done in [controlling] the big corporations. . . . In all these cases I have felt not merely that my action was right in itself, but that in showing the strength of, or in giving strength to, the executive, I was establishing a precedent of value.

I believe in a strong ex- ... power;

well of the Republi... most of all, I belie... whatever value m... may have comes from what I *am* ... what I *do*.

I may be mi... is my belief th... my countrym... whom Abrah... called "the p... the farmers, ... small trade... ing professi... that I am i... their Presi... sent the ... what the ... coln did ... sincere ... govern... and fo...

From ... G. O. ...

Analy...

1. A... w... i...

2.

PRACTICAL...

- **Decision-Making** program develops essential thinking skills needed to define a problem, set goals, select an alternative, make a plan of action and carry out the plan.

  - **Skills Workshop** provides opportunities to practice social studies and decision-making skills.

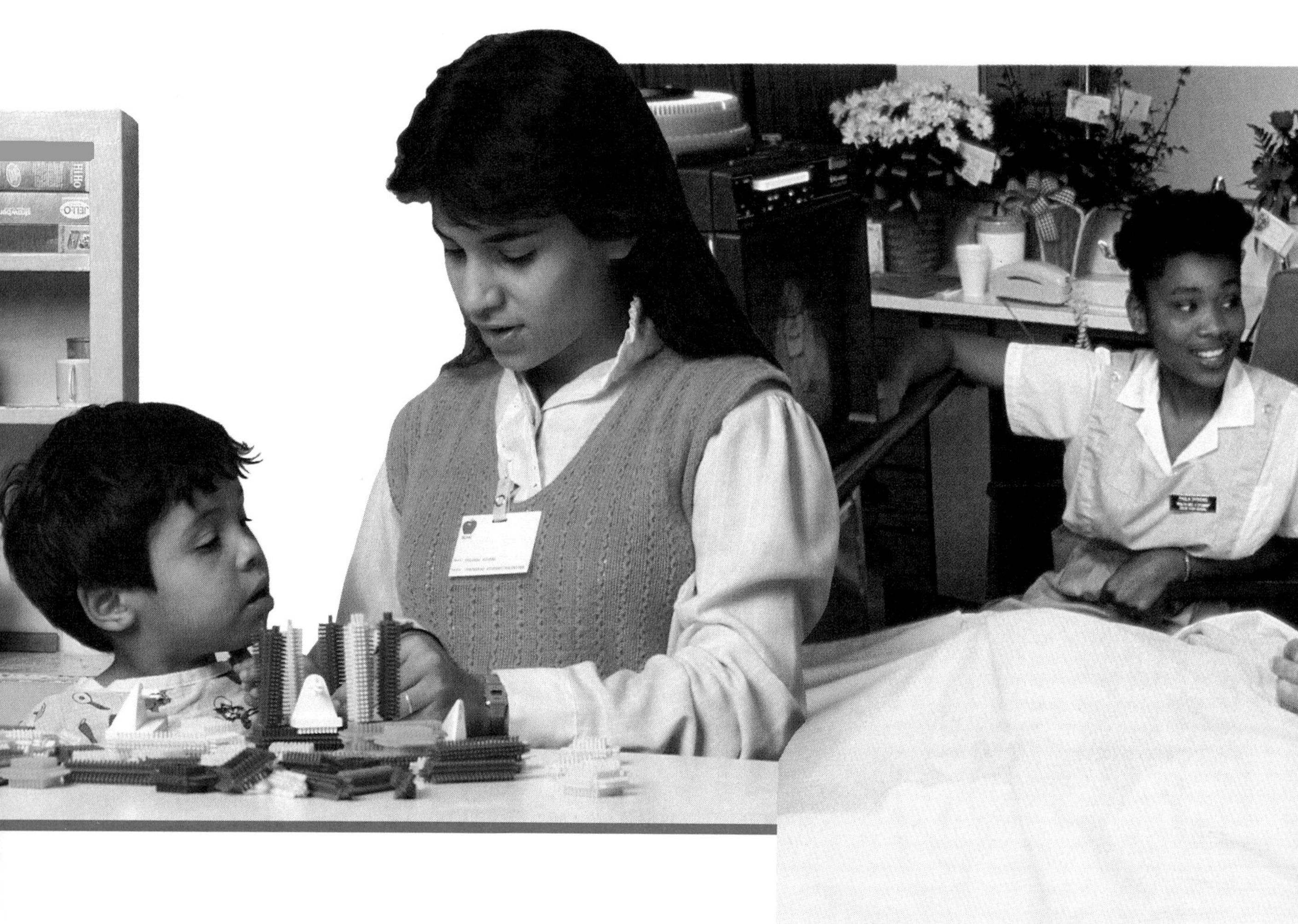

SKILLS WORKSHOP

SOCIAL STUDIES SKILLS

Reading a Newspaper

One of your responsibilities as a citizen is to inform yourself about public issues. A good way to do this is to become a regular newspaper reader. Newspapers can provide you with a wealth of information about your community, state, nation, and world.

Most newspapers are divided into sections. The front section covers major news

3. In which two secti local news story be lo

DECISION-MAKIN

Taking Action

In the profile of Ba you read about so action to achieve. tify what her goa

Decision-Making Checklist

Choosing	Critical Thinking	Taking
✓ Do I have a clear goal?	✓ Have I checked how reliable my sources of information are?	✓ Is my stated
✓ Do I know what my standards are?	✓ Do I know which kinds of information relate to my subject?	✓ Do I k reso
✓ Have I brainstormed all my options?	✓ Do I know which pieces of information are statements of fact and	✓ Do I prob
✓ Have I identified which types of information I need about each option?		✓ Do to ac

DECISION MAKING

The Process

Choosing and Taking Action

Picture yourself in the following situation: You leave school on Friday, thinking about a long report that is due Monday. Suddenly some friends remind you that the money for the school candy sale has to be turned in on Monday. When they ask if you can help sell candy, you say that you are not sure because you have homework to do. They reply, "Well, let us know when you are through making up your mind."

"Making up your mind" is another way of saying "making a decision." You make decisions, or choices, every day. Some, such as deciding what to have for breakfast or which

ANALYZING THE PROCESS

You have read that we are larg immigrants. In the following Lopez, an immigrant from La plains how he and his wife their family to the United St what specific steps they wen ing their decision.

Food was scarce in our tow going up fast. Conditions pany where I worked wer went on strike, many of u My wife, Maria, joined a protesting cruel treatme worked for my release. group killed several me

Extensive teacher support provides flexibility

- Complete Annotated Teacher's Edition provides teaching strategies, including cooperative learning activities, to accommodate varied learning styles and ability levels.
    - Comprehensive Teacher's Resource Book includes Activity Book; Issues and Decision Making Book; Citizenship Skills Book; Voices of America Readings; and Tests.
        - Additional supplements include a complete Transparency and Activity Book Package and Testing Software with Data Bank Book.

ADDISON-WESLEY

Transparencies and
Activity Book

ADDISON-WESLEY

Voices of America
A Book of Readings

ADDISON-WESLEY

CIVICS

Activity Book

Participating
in Our
Democracy

Introduction to the Student Text

Civics: Participating in Our Democracy is a comprehensive, well-balanced program that inspires students to active participation in their role as citizens. Below is an overview of how the text's organization and features will engage students in their study of civics.

UNIT ORGANIZATION

Each unit begins with a thought-provoking quotation that leads into a brief unit overview. At the end of each unit, broad **Unit Survey** questions help students draw together the content. Following the questions, a **Taking a Stand** activity asks students to make a decision on a controversial issue and then take action through a writing or speaking assignment.

Unit 1 shows students how their everyday lives relate to their roles as citizens in our diverse society and how their rights and responsibilities as citizens stem from basic American values and institutions. This unit lays the groundwork for later units in which students explore such topics as our political heritage, government on the national, state, and local levels, basic principles of our political system, and our nation's global role.

In addition to exploring basic civics content and concepts, the text responds to the nationwide call for more thorough coverage of our economic and legal systems. Practical, student-centered examples show how our political, economic, and legal systems relate to each other and to students' daily lives.

CHAPTER ORGANIZATION

Each chapter begins with an **Opening Narrative** that engages students and leads into a brief overview of the chapter. **Read to Find Out** objectives begin each section by identifying vocabulary terms and key concepts to be covered. Each section closes with **Section Review** questions that check whether students achieved the reading objectives. Section Reviews also reinforce higher-level thinking with questions labeled *Analysis, Application, Evaluation,* or *Synthesis*. These questions call for students to use analytical or critical thinking skills in Bloom's taxonomy. A Data Search question, which appears at least once per chapter, asks students to analyze specific data in the book.

At the end of each chapter, **A Broader View** puts the chapter content into perspective by comparing our society with societies in other countries or with American society in earlier times. Then a one-page **Chapter Survey** provides vocabulary activities, chapter questions that test comprehension and higher-level thinking, and activities that foster participatory citizenship and cooperative learning. In a one-page **Skills Workshop,** students apply social studies and decision-making skills to information related to the chapter.

SPECIAL FEATURES

Special features stimulate student interest and help students develop skills. A thorough **Decision-Making Program** of lessons and activities guides students in the steps of the decision-making process and related critical-thinking skills. Legal case studies called **Issues That Affect You** reinforce the law-related focus of the book and encourage students to weigh evidence and make decisions. **In Their Own Words** features give students opportunities to analyze relevant primary sources.

In keeping with the theme of participation, every chapter has a biography feature that provides an inspiring example of citizenship. Those titled **Views of Noted Americans** highlight ideas and accomplishments of famous Americans, while **People Make a Difference** features show how ordinary citizens have taken effective action. **American Notebook** features further enhance chapter content by providing interesting facts, figures, and quotations.

A reference center at the back of the book includes a 10-page **Data Bank** of graphs and charts, maps of the United States and the world, and tables listing Presidents and Vice-Presidents and facts about the states. The text of the Declaration of Independence follows Chapter 4, and an annotated text of the Constitution follows Chapter 5. Throughout the book, charts, tables, graphs, and maps complement chapter content.

Introduction to the Annotated Teacher's Edition

The Annotated Teacher's Edition provides a **Planning Guide**, a detailed **Teaching Strategy**, and a comprehensive **Answer Key** for each chapter.

Each planning guide page begins with a chapter **Overview** and major learning **Objectives.** The planning guide lists the activities in the teaching strategy and all of the teaching resources in the student text and the *Teacher's Resource Book*.

The teaching strategy for each chapter consists of five kinds of activities. The **Introducing the Chapter** activity gets students interested in the chapter. Two **Teaching Activities** focus on major themes and concepts. The **Evaluating Progress** activity assesses students' understanding of material. The **Reinforcement Activity** focuses on a difficult concept in the chapter. The **Enrichment Activity** extends a different concept than the one covered in reinforcement. Each activity is identified as an individual, cooperative, or class project. Look for the identifying symbols:

- **Individual Project**
- **Cooperative Project**
- **Class Project**

Annotations appear throughout the 26 chapters. Challenge annotations, with labels from Bloom's taxonomy, suggest discussions involving critical thinking. Decision-making annotations reinforce the decision-making lessons. Activity or discussion annotations extend special features that highlight people, primary sources, and issues. Teaching annotations indicate where teachers may want to use activities. Other annotations state themes and amplify information in the text.

The teacher's edition also includes a list of books, audio-visual materials, and computer software; a list of organizations that provide free or inexpensive civics materials; and suggested readings for students.

COURSES WITH DIFFERENT EMPHASES

A civics course is often a student's first encounter with a formal study of society. *Civics: Participating in Our Democracy* provides a comprehensive introduction, examining not only our political heritage and government, but also economics, social and legal institutions, and political systems and processes and the connections between them. Because of its extensive coverage, the text can be used for a one- or two-semester course with a variety of emphases.

Civics (26 chapters): A two-semester course in civics would include all of the chapters in *Civics: Participating in Our Democracy.*

Basic Civics (16 chapters): A one-semester course in basic civics would include Units 1, 2, 3, 4; Unit 5, Chapter 14; Unit 6, Chapter 18; and Unit 7, Chapters 21 and 22.

Civics, Economics, and Law (16 chapters): A one-semester course with this focus would include Unit 1; Unit 2, Chapters 5, 6, 7; Unit 3; Unit 5; and Unit 6.

Civics, Law, and Politics (15 chapters): A one-semester course with this focus would include Units 1, 2, 3, 6, and 7.

Civics and a Global Society (15 chapters): A one-semester course with this focus would include Units 1, 2; Unit 3, Chapters 8 and 9; Unit 5, Chapters 13 and 14; Unit 7, Chapter 23; and Unit 8.

Civics and Problems of Democracy (17 chapters): A one-semster course with this focus would include Units 1, 2, 3; Unit 5, Chapters 14 and 16; Unit 6, Chapter 18; Unit 7, Chapter 23; and Unit 8.

A Note About Citizenship and Decision Making

Of all the skills essential to effective citizenship, none are more important than decision-making skills. The quality of students' lives as individuals, as members of a school and a community, as citizens of our nation, and as inhabitants of Spaceship Earth depends largely upon their ability to make good decisions. Consequently, *Civics: Participating in Our Democracy* includes extensive instruction in decision making.

The decision-making process presented in this text combines a number of expert models. We see the process as having two basic parts: choosing and taking action. No decision has value unless action is taken, and no action is likely to be productive if the decision is poorly made. To make good decisions, young citizens must examine the quality of their thinking and the information they use. Therefore, we have included instruction in four critical-thinking skills that can help students evaluate information.

The chart below identifies key skills for evaluating information and summarizes our view of the decision-making process. To help young citizens think critically and become better decision makers, the program in *Civics: Participating in Our Democracy* is based on three principles: providing explicit instruction, helping students develop and refine skills gradually, and integrating skills with civics content.

PROVIDING EXPLICIT INSTRUCTION

The text provides direct, explicit instruction in decision making and critical thinking. Research in skill teaching, skill acquisition, and cognition suggests that in order to learn a thinking skill well, students need to: (1) concentrate on the attributes of the skill, (2) see the skill modeled, (3) apply the skill themselves with instructive feedback, and (4) reflect on and share how they carried out the skill. In addition, students need frequent guided practice in the skill.

Each decision-making and critical-thinking skill is introduced in detail in a two-page lesson. Civics content serves as a vehicle for learning each skill.

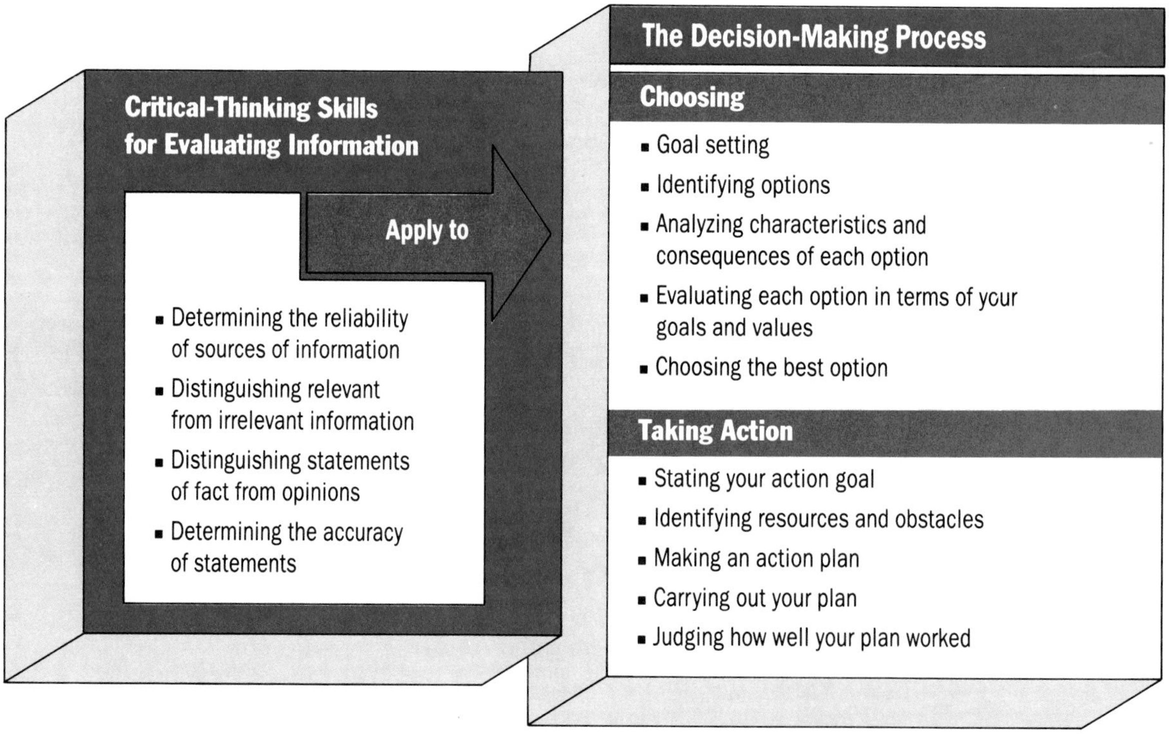

Critical-Thinking Skills for Evaluating Information

- Determining the reliability of sources of information
- Distinguishing relevant from irrelevant information
- Distinguishing statements of fact from opinions
- Determining the accuracy of statements

Apply to

The Decision-Making Process

Choosing

- Goal setting
- Identifying options
- Analyzing characteristics and consequences of each option
- Evaluating each option in terms of your goals and values
- Choosing the best option

Taking Action

- Stating your action goal
- Identifying resources and obstacles
- Making an action plan
- Carrying out your plan
- Judging how well your plan worked

Following an overview of the decision-making process in the first lesson, eleven other lessons focus in more detail on the parts of the process and on critical-thinking skills. Each of these lessons has the following components:

- An introduction that relates the process or skill to students' experiences.
- An explanation of how students might apply that part of the decision-making process or that specific critical-thinking skill to decision making.
- An opportunity for the students to apply the process or skill themsleves.
- Questions that provide students with instructive feedback on how well they applied the process or skill.
- Questions that help students review the basic components of the process or skill.

End-of-chapter activities provide opportunities for students to apply what they have learned in the lessons. These activities include questions that help students think about how they applied the process or skill and how the process or skill might be applied to other situations. Workbook activities provide additional practice.

DEVELOPING SKILLS GRADUALLY

To move students most easily toward a better understanding and more skillful application of the decision-making process, instruction is presented in stages:

- Chapters 1 through 5 introduce students to the basic steps of the decision-making process. Through guided analysis of case studies, students get an overview of the decision-making process.
- In Chapters 6 through 12, students focus on using critical-thinking skills to evaluate information.
- In Chapters 13 through 23, students put together what they have learned about decision making and critical thinking. They also refine and deepen their understanding of both by focusing on key parts of the decision-making process and applying them in making their own decisons.
- After having received detailed instruction on critical-thinking skills and the parts of the decision-making process, students review the process as a whole in Chapters 24 through 26.

INTEGRATING SKILLS WITH CONTENT

All the lessons and activities are closely related to the content of the chapters in which they appear. Thus, the content learning and skill learning reinforce each other. Each lesson also has teacher annotations that further tie decision making and critical thinking to civics content. In addition to the lesson annotations, special "Decision Making" annotations suggest other ways to relate the process to the chapter content.

The decision-making program also relates to the "content" of students' lives, showing how the process applies to both personal and public policy decisions. By focusing first on familiar personal decisions, the program helps students make the jump to broad public policy decisions. In this way, students learn how to make good decisions in their various roles as citizens, consumers, members of families, friends, and members of social groups.

In summary, the program in *Civics: Participating in Our Democracy* moves students from a relatively simple overview of the decision-making process to a more detailed understanding and practice of the process and of related critical-thinking skills. Students also move from analyzing other people's decisions to making their own, and from step-by-step practice to integrated application of the whole process. Using this approach, students can develop considerable proficiency in decision making and critical thinking in the course of their study of civics. The ultimate goal is to make students skillful, independent thinkers.

Books, Audio-Visual Materials, and Computer Software

GENERAL SOURCES

Beyer, Barry K. *Practical Strategies for the Teaching of Thinking.* Boston: Allyn & Bacon, 1987. Presents a rationale for the teaching of thinking, discusses the nature of thinking processes, and describes specific teaching strategies.

Greene, Jack P., ed. *Encyclopedia of American Political History: Studies of the Principal Movements and Ideas.* 3 vols. New York: Scribner's, 1984. Grouping of 90 scholarly essays under several broad political themes, such as civil rights, federalism, and suffrage.

Johnson, David W., and Roger Johnson. *Learning Together and Alone: Cooperative, Competitive, and Individualistic Learning.* Englewood Cliffs, NJ: Prentice-Hall, 1987. Summarizes cooperative learning research, presents a model for cooperative learning, and provides implementation strategies.

La Raus, Roger, and Richard Remy. *Citizenship Decision Making: Skill Activities and Materials.* Menlo Park, CA: Addison-Wesley Publishing Co., 1978. Provides 25 lessons for grades 4–9 on making, judging, and influencing civic decisions.

Oliver, Donald W. and James P. Shaver. *Teaching Public Issues in the High School.* Boston: Houghton Mifflin Co., 1966. Reissued through Utah State University Press, Logan, UT, 1974. A classic work providing a sound conceptual basis for issue-oriented classroom instruction.

Political Science and American Government. Resource Packet RP-1. Bloomington, IN: ERIC Clearinghouse for Social Studies/Social Science Education, n.d. Provides annotated lists of materials for social studies teachers and curriculum specialists.

Shaver, James P., ed. *Building Rationales for Citizenship Education.* Washington, DC: National Council for the Social Studies, Bulletin #52, 1977. Stresses the importance of thinking through reasons for and objectives of civic education programs.

Stanley, Harold W., and Richard G. Niemi. *Vital Statistics on American Politics.* Washington, DC: Congressional Quarterly, 1988. Presents data on national and regional politics—past and present—in more than 200 charts, tables, and graphs.

Statistical Abstract of the United States: National Data Book and Guide To Sources. Washington, DC: U.S. Government Printing Office, annual. Contains tables on all aspects of the United States, including demographics, the economy, and government.

Turner, Mary Jane, and Sara Lake. *U.S. Government: A Resource Book for Secondary Schools.* Santa Barbara, CA: ABC-CLIO, 1989. Reviews the principles of our government and provides an annotated list of classroom resources.

UNIT 1

Books

de Tocqueville, Alexis. *Democracy in America.* 2 vols. New York: Random House, 1945. Classic early nineteenth-century analysis of America's politics and national character.

Handlin, Oscar. *The Uprooted.* Boston, MA: Little, Brown, 1951. Classic study of the European immigrant experience, dealing with all aspects of coming to America.

Presno, Vincent, and Carol Presno. *The Value Realms: Activities for Helping Students Develop Values.* New York: Columbia University Teachers College Press, 1980. Describes more than 80 model values activities, usable in grades 4–12 with individuals and groups, for many subject areas.

Terkel, Studs. *The Great Divide: Second Thoughts on the American Dream.* New York: Pantheon Books, 1988. An anthology of views of ordinary Americans on the issues of the 1980s and 1990s and American beliefs.

Films and Videocassettes

Freedoms. 23 min. Barr Films.

The Girl Who Spelled Freedom. 90 min. Disney.

Making Government Work. 12 films, 30 minutes each. Films, Inc.

Rights and Responsibilities. 11 films, 20 minutes each. Agency for Instructional Technology.

Filmstrips

Accent on Ethnic America. 6 filmstrips. Multi-Media Productions.

Cultural America. 4 filmstrips. Britannica Education Corporation.

Equality in America. 3 filmstrips. Human Relations Media.

How Nations Are Governed. 4 filmstrips. Filmstrip House/United Learning.

Refugees, Immigrants, Illegal Aliens: Impact on America. 1 filmstrip. Society for Visual Education.

Computer Software

The Age of Responsibility. Apple, IBM PC, TRS-80. Aquarius Instructional.

The American People. Apple, Commodore. Focus Media.

Decisions, Decisions: Immigration: Maintaining the Open Door. Apple, IBM PC. Tom Snyder Productions.

Democracy. Apple, Commodore. Right On Programs.

UNIT 2

Books

Adler, Mortimer J. *We Hold These Truths: Understanding the Ideas and Ideals of the Constitution.* New York: Macmillan, 1987. An analysis of the Declaration of Independence and the Constitution by one of today's leading philosophers.

Glade, Mary Elizabeth. *Review of Resources: Teaching Law and the Constitution.* Boulder, CO: Social Science Education Consortium, 1987. Analyzes 160 print, nonprint, and teacher resource titles (K–12) relating to law, the Constitution, and the Bill of Rights.

Keller, Clair W., and Denny L. Schillings, eds. *Teaching About the Constitution.* Bulletin #80. Washington, DC: National Council for the Social Studies, 1987. Relates the Constitution to American life since the eighteenth century.

Ketcham, Ralph, ed. *The Anti-Federalist Papers and the Constitutional Convention Debates.* New York: New American Library Mentor Paperbacks, 1986. Illuminates the controversy surrounding the ratification of the Constitution.

Lieberman, Jethro. *The Enduring Constitution: A Bicentennial Perspective.* St. Paul, MN: West Publishing Co., 1987. Clarification of the genesis of the Constitution and the principles of our government by a law specialist.

Madison, James, Alexander Hamilton, and John Jay. *The Federalist Papers.* New York: New American Library Mentor Paperbacks, 1961. The basic arguments for ratification of the Constitution, penned by some of its principal designers.

Teaching the Bill of Rights. ERIC Digest 88-9. Bloomington, IN: ERIC Clearinghouse for Social Studies/Social Science Education, 1988. A concise overview of current teaching practice.

Films and Videocassettes

The Background of the U.S. Constitution. 20 minutes. BFA Educational Media.

The Constitution: The Compromise That Made a Nation. 27 minutes. Learning Corporation of America.

In Pursuit of Liberty. 4 films, 60 minutes each. WNET-TV.

Filmstrips

The Bill of Rights: Foundation of Our Liberties. 2 filmstrips. Guidance Associates.

The Civil Rights Movement: 20 Years Later. 1 filmstrip. New York Times.

The Constitution—A Living Document. 6 filmstrips. Guidance Associates.

The Declaration of Independence. 1 filmstrip. National Geographic.

This Precious Heritage: Civil Rights in the United States. 1 filmstrip. Anti-Defamation League.

The U.S. Constitution in Action. 8 filmstrips. Random House.

Computer Software

AppleWorks Database: The U.S. Constitution: Then and Now. Apple. Scholastic Software.

Creating the U.S. Constitution. Apple. Educational Activities.

UNIT 3

Books

American Leaders, 1789–1987. Washington, D.C.: Congressional Quarterly, 1987. Provides basic political data on all presidents, vice-presidents, state governors, Supreme Court justices, and members of Congress.

Congressional Quarterly Almanac. Washington, D.C.: Congressional Quarterly, annual. Summary of congressional activity, with a detailed explanation of issues.

Congressional Quarterly's Guide to Congress. 3d ed. Washington, D.C.: Congressional Quarterly, 1982. Covers the history and evolution of Congress, providing biographies.

Congressional Quarterly's Guide to the U.S. Supreme Court. Washington, D.C.: Congressional Quarterly, 1979. Standard reference work including biographies of all justices and clear discussion of the evolution of the Court.

The Encyclopedia Dictionary of American Government. 3d ed. Guilford, CT: Dushkin, 1986. Provides over 1,000 concise definitions of major ideas and terms.

Nelson, Michael, ed. *The Presidency and the Political System.* Washington, D.C.: Congressional Quarterly, 1986. Twenty essays examine the role of the chief executive in American politics.

The United States Government Manual. Washington, D.C.: U.S. Government Printing Office, annual. The official organizational handbook and directory of the United States government, covering all three branches in detail.

Films and Videocassettes

An Act of Congress. 58 minutes. Learning Corporation of America.

Branches of Government—A Series. 3 films, 22–23 minutes each. National Geographic.

What the Presidency Is All About. 25 minutes. Carousel Films.

Filmstrips

The Cabinet: All the President's Men. 2 filmstrips. Guidance Associates.

The Judicial System of The United States. 2 filmstrips. National Geographic.

The U.S. Government in Action. 6 filmstrips. Random House.

We the People: Aspects of American Government. 4 filmstrips. Guidance Associates.

Computer Software

American Government I-V. Apple, IBM PC. Queue.

How a Bill Becomes Law. Apple, IBM PC, Amiga. Queue.

Political Genie. Apple, IBM PC. Boring Software.

Presidency Series. Apple. Focus Media.

President's Choice. IBM PC. Spinnaker Software.

UNIT 4

Books

Beyle, Thad L., ed. *State Government: CQ's Guide to Current Issues and Activities, 1987–1988.* Washington, D.C.: Congressional Quarterly, 1988. Surveys key issues and developments in the governments of all 50 states.

The Book of the States, 1988–89 Edition. Lexington, KY: Council of State Governments, 1988. Basic statistics and current officials are listed for each state. Articles review current government and judicial actions.

The Municipal Yearbook. Washington, D.C.: International City Management Association, annual. Includes data and names of officials for cities of more than 2,500 people and reviews local issues.

Filmstrips

Local Government and the Individual. 2 filmstrips. Social Studies School Service.

State and Local Government in Action. 6 filmstrips. New York Times.

Computer Software

Decisions, Decisions: Urbanization: The Growth of Cities. Apple, IBM PC. Tom Snyder Productions.

Our Town Meeting: A Lesson in Civic Responsibility. Apple, IBM PC. Tom Snyder Productions.

Scholastic PFS: U.S. Government. Apple, IBM PC. Scholastic Software.

UNIT 5

Books

Banaszak, Ronald A., ed. *Directory of Organizations Providing Business and Economic Education Information.* New York: Joint Council on Economic Education, 1986. Describes over 200 nonprofit organizations.

Davis, James E., and Regina McCormick. *Economics: A Resource Book for Secondary Schools.* Santa Barbara, CA: ABC-CLIO, 1988. Gives secondary students and teachers a nontechnical introduction to economics and describes many learning resources.

Davis, James E. *Teaching Economics to Young Adolescents: A Research-Based Rationale.* San Francisco: Foundation for Teaching Economics, 1987. Reviews the intellectual, psychological, social, and economic development of middle level students and makes recommendations for economic education.

Economic Report of the President. Washington, D.C.: U.S. Government Printing Office, annual. This annual report to Congress reviews the status of the American economy.

The Handbook of Basic Economic Statistics. Washington, D.C.: Economic Statistics Bureau, monthly. Provides a condensation of federal economic statistics.

Heilbroner, Robert L. *The Making of Economic Society.* Revised for the mid-1980s. 7th ed. Englewood Cliffs, NJ: Prentice-Hall, 1985. One of the nation's leading figures in economics clearly explains the emergence of modern economic systems.

Hodgetts, Richard M., and Terry L. Smart. *Economics.* Menlo Park, CA: Addison-Wesley Publishing Co., 1988. Senior high textbook offering a sound conceptual presentation and useful graphics, biographies, and real-world examples.

Saunders, Phillip, et. al. *Master Curriculum Guide in Economics: A Framework for Teaching Basic Concepts.* 2d. ed. New York: Joint Council on Economic Education, 1984. Includes easy-to-understand economic principles and concepts for pre-college level students.

Silk, Leonard. *Economics in Plain English, Updated and Expanded.* New York: Simon and Schuster Touchstone Books, 1986. This simple summary of economic theory highlights current issues and the personal and social effects of economics.

The United States Budget in Brief. Washington, D.C.: U.S. Government Printing Office, annual. Designed for the general public, this booklet is a concise summary of the President's annual budget proposal to Congress.

Watkins, Alfred J. *Red Ink II: A Guide to Understanding the Continuing Deficit Dilemma.* rev. ed. Washington, D.C.: Roosevelt Center for American Policy studies, 1988. This nonpartisan report explains the federal budget-making process and the deficit problem.

Films and Videocassettes

Chickenomics: A Fowl Approach to Economics. 20 minutes. World Research.

Famous Amos: The Business Behind the Cookie. 25 minutes. Learning Corporation of America.

Give and Take. 12 films, 15 minutes each. Agency for Instructional Technology.

The Joy of Stocks. 104 minutes. MGM/United Artists.

Money. 15 minutes. Guidance Associates.

Tax Whys: Understanding Taxes. 9 films, 15 minutes each. Agency for Instructional Technology.

Filmstrips

American Business. 3 filmstrips. Encyclopedia Britannica.

Banking and Money Series. 4 filmstrips. Marshfilm.

Economic Issues in American Democracy. 5 filmstrips. New York Times.

Economics in the Marketplace. 4 filmstrips. Encyclopedia Britannica.

An Introduction to Capitalism, Socialism and Communism. 4 filmstrips. National Geographic.

Our Economy: How It Works. 6 filmstrips. Random House.

A Sound Investment. 1 filmstrip. Encyclopedia Britannica.

The Young Spenders. 4 filmstrips. Social Studies School Service.

Computer Software

Choices. Apple. Joint Council on Economic Education.

Conglomerates Collide. Apple. American Micro Media.

Enterprise Sandwich Shop: A Market Simulation. Apple, IBM PC. Gregg/McGraw-Hill.

Interactive Video Disk Minicourse: Intro to Economics. Apple. Minnesota Educational Computing Consortium (MECC).

Millionaire: The Stock Market Simulation. Apple, Atari. Blue Chip Software.

Pete's Pizzeria. Apple. Joint Council on Economic Education.

UNIT 6

Books

Coughlin, George Gordon. *Your Introduction to the Law.* 4th ed. New York: Barnes and Noble, 1983. Introduces the American legal system, explaining personal rights and obligations and the role of lawyers and courts.

Friedman, Lawrence M. *A History of American Law.* New York: Simon & Schuster Touchstone Books, 1973. Traces the development of American law from the colonial period to the twentieth century.

Law-Related Education. Resource Packet RP-10. Bloomington, IN: ERIC Clearinghouse for Social Studies/Social Science Education, n.d. This inexpensive packet includes annotated resource lists for teachers.

Thomas, R. Murray, and Paul V. Murray. *Cases: A Resource Guide for Teaching About the Law.* Glenview, IL: Scott, Foresman and Co., 1982. Over 50 actual cases of juvenile crime are included in this text on juvenile law, the justice process, and the rights of minors.

Turner, Mary Jane, and Lynn Parisi. *Law in the Classroom: Activities and Resources.* rev. ed. Boulder, CO: Social Science Education Consortium, 1984. Includes innovative teaching activities and resources for law-related education.

Films and Videocassettes

Civil Law: Understanding Your Rights, Remedies, and Obligations. 45 minutes, Human Relations Media.

In Search of Justice. 28 minutes. Barr Films.

Urban Turf: A Focus on Street Gangs. 26 minutes. United Learning.

Violence in America. 60 minutes. Close Up Foundation.

Filmstrips

Current Legal Issues II. 4 filmstrips. Random House.

Great American Trials. 6 filmstrips. Random House.

The Juvenile Justice System. 2 filmstrips. Social Studies School Service.

Street Law: A Student's Guide to Practical Law. 6 filmstrips. Random House.

Computer Software

Jury Trial II. Apple, IBM PC. Navic.

The Law. Apple. Aquarius Instructional.

You and the Law. Apple. Queue.

UNIT 7

Books

Barone, Michael, and Grant Ujifosa, eds. *Almanac of American Politics.* Washington, D.C.: National Journal, biennial. Offers review of the year in politics and profiles of legislators.

Moore, John L., ed. *Congressional Quarterly's Guide to U.S. Elections.* 2d ed. Washington, D.C.: Congressional Quarterly, 1985. Covers national elections from 1788 to 1984, popular votes since 1824, and all party conventions since 1831.

National Party Conventions, 1831–1984. Washington, D.C.: Congressional Quarterly, 1987. A detailed history and analysis of national nominating conventions, biographies of candidates, and data on votes and platforms.

Presidential Elections Since 1789. 4th ed. Washington, D.C.: Congressional Quarterly, 1987. This thorough history of presidential elections through 1984 includes primaries and party conventions.

Social Issues Resources Series (SIRS). Boca Raton, FL: SIRS, dates vary. This service offers over thirty notebooks (with annual supplements) of article and newspaper reprints on important issues.

Films and Videocassettes

By the People. 16 films, 15 minutes each. CTI.

Elections in the United States. 19 minutes. BFA Educational Media.

Political Parties in America: Getting the People Together. 20 minutes. Britannica Films.

Filmstrips

All About Voting: A Complete Election Kit. 1 filmstrip. J. Weston Walch.

Our Political System. 2 filmstrips. National Geographic.

Toxic Wastes. 2 filmstrips. Hawkhill.

Winners and Losers: Issues That Decide Elections. 2 filmstrips. Center for Humanities.

Computer Software

"And If Re-Elected . . ." Apple, IBM PC, Tandy. Focus Media.

Decisions, Decisions: On the Campaign Trail. Apple, IBM PC. Tom Snyder Productions.

President Elect. 1988 edition. Apple, Atari, Commodore, IBM PC. Strategic Simulations.

UNIT 8

Books

Albert, Cecilia A. *World Economic Data: A Compendium of Current Economic Information for All Countries of the World.* Santa Barbara, CA: ABC-CLIO, 1987. This easy-to-use reference provides country data and expanded chapters on American economic indicators.

Benegar, John, and Jacquelyn Johnson. *Global Issues in the Intermediate Classroom.* rev. ed. Boulder, CO: Social Science Education Consortium, 1988. Provides 14 lessons to help middle level students with global issues.

A Citizen's Guide to U.S. Foreign Policy, Election '88. New York: Foreign Policy Association, 1988. Reviews international issues, American foreign policy, and the UN.

The Global Resource Book. New York: American Forum for Global Education, 1989. This looseleaf bibliography (with periodic supplements) cites background materials, curricula, and audiovisuals on global topics.

Handbook of the Nations. 7th ed. Detroit: Gale Research, 1987. Provides current data on population, economics, government, and the military in 191 nations.

Reardon, Betty A., ed. *Educating for Global Responsibility.* New York: Columbia University Teachers College Press, 1987. K–12 lessons that develop global citizenship, planetary stewardship, and positive values for peace.

Remy, Richard C., and Robert Woyach, eds. *Approaches to World Studies: A Handbook for Curriculum Planners.* Boston: Allyn and Bacon, 1989. Provides a balanced approach to teaching world/global history and problems at the secondary level.

Spanier, John. *Games Nations Play.* 6th ed. Washington, DC: Congressional Quarterly, 1987. Provides a clear introduction to international politics and the world as a system.

World Commission on Environment and Development. *Our Common Future.* New York: Oxford University Press, 1988. Series of reports on current global issues and problems.

World Encyclopedia of Political Systems and Parties. New York: Facts on File, 1987. Offers objective articles on the government and politics of more than 170 nations.

The World in Figures. Boston: G.K. Hall, 1987. This superior reference work provides worldwide and country-by-country economic data, showing trends since 1970.

Films and Videocassettes

Close-Up at the United Nations. 60 minutes. Close Up Foundation.

International Relations: Understanding the Behavior of Nations. 60 minutes. Close Up Foundation.

Mother Teresa. 82 minutes. Petrie Productions.

On Common Ground: A Tour of the United Nations. 30 minutes. Social Studies School Service.

Filmstrips

The Global Community: A Unit of Study. 4 filmstrips. United Learning.

Human Rights. 1 filmstrip. Associated Press.

The Postwar Era. 6 filmstrips. New York Times.

Relations of Nations: 20th Century Intervention. 6 filmstrips. Random House.

Computer Software

Decisions, Decisions: Foreign Policy: The Burdens of World Power. Apple, IBM PC. Tom Snyder Productions.

Nationalism: Past and Present. Apple. Focus Media.

One World: Countries Database. Apple, Commodore, IBM PC. Active Learning Systems.

The Other Side: A Geopolitical Simulation. Apple, IBM PC. Tom Snyder Productions.

Who'll Save Abacaxi? A Third World Government Simulation. Apple. Focus Media.

Organizations Providing Free or Inexpensive Civics Materials

American Bar Association
Special Committee on Youth
Education for Citizenship
750 North Lake Shore Drive
Chicago, IL 60611
(312) 988-5735

American Civil Liberties Union
132 West Forty-third Street
New York, NY 10036
(212) 944-9800

Center for Civic Education
5146 Douglas Fir Road
Calabasas, CA 91302
(818) 340-9320

Center for Teaching International Relations
University of Denver
Graduate School of International Studies
Denver, CO 80208
(303) 871-3106

Close Up Foundation
1235 Jefferson Davis Highway
Arlington, VA 22202
(703) 892-5400

Constitutional Rights Foundation
601 South Kingsley Drive
Los Angeles, CA 90005
(213) 487-5590

C-SPAN in the Classroom
444 North Capitol Street NW
Washington, D.C. 20001
(202) 737-3220

Educators for Social Responsibility
23 Garden Street
Cambridge, MA 02138
(617) 492-1764

Heritage Foundation
214 Massachusetts Avenue NE
Washington, D.C. 20002
(202) 546-4400

Jefferson Foundation
1529 Eighteenth Street NW
Washington, D.C. 20033
(202) 234-3688

League of Women Voters of the
United States
1730 M Street NW
Washington, D.C. 20036
(202) 429-1965

National Coalition on Black Voter
Participation
1101 Fourteenth Street NW, Suite 925
Washington, D.C. 20005
(202) 898-2220

National Council for the Social Studies
3501 Newark Street NW
Washington, D.C. 20016
(202) 966-7840

National Institute for Citizen Education
in the Law
25 E Street NW, No. 400
Washington, D.C. 20001
(202) 662-9620

People for the American Way
2000 M Street NW, Suite 400
Washington, D.C. 20036
(202) 467-4999

Social Science Education Consortium, Inc.
855 Broadway
Boulder, CO 80302
(303) 492-8154

Social Studies Development Center/ERIC
Clearinghouse of Social Studies/Social
Science Education
Indiana University
2805 East Tenth Street
Bloomington, IN 47408-2698
(812) 855-3838

U.S. Chamber of Commerce
1615 H Street NW
Washington, D.C. 20062
(202) 463-5436

Suggested Readings for Students

UNIT 1

America's People, 1987–1988. Culver City, CA: Social Studies School Service, 1987. Fifty graphs and maps depict aspects of American demography and history, with comparisons to other nations.

Brownstone, David M., et. al. *Island of Hope, Island of Tears.* New York: Penguin Books, 1986. Immigrants tell their own stories of passing through Ellis Island.

Family: Past and Present. Sturbridge, MA: Old Sturbridge Village, 1986. Primary sources are used in activities to help students understand changes in families over time.

Kronewetter, Michael. *Are You a Liberal? Are You a Conservative?* New York: Franklin Watts, 1984. This illustrated text traces the historical evolution of two current political philosophies.

Lawrence, Bill. *A Social History of America.* Portland, ME: J. Weston Walch, 1986. Provides an anecdotal account of everyday life.

Lawson, Robert, ed. *Watchwords of Liberty: A Pageant of American Quotations.* rev. ed. Boston, MA: Little, Brown, 1986. Over 50 quotations are presented in story form, with illustrations.

Voices of Freedom. Washington, D.C.: People for the American Way, 1987. An audio tape presents short selections from such Americans as Walt Whitman and Booker T. Washington.

UNIT 2

Bartholomew, Paul C., ed. *Summaries of Leading Cases on the Constitution.* Totowa, NJ: Rowman and Littlefield, 1983. Provides a synopsis of issues in important Supreme Court cases.

Binkley, Dennis. *Great Documents That Shape American Freedoms.* Hayward, CA: Janus Books, 1986. Provides high interest/low vocabulary activities on the Magna Carta, the Constitution, and other important documents.

Chapin, June, and Rosemary Messick. *You and the Constitution.* Menlo Park, CA: Addison-Wesley Publishing Co., 1988. This supplementary text emphasizes thinking skills and cooperative learning.

Feinberg, Barbara Silberdick. *The Constitution: Yesterday, Today, and Tomorrow.* Jefferson City, MO: Scholastic, Inc., 1987. This text, with project activities, looks at the history and future of the Constitution.

Letters of Liberty: A Documentary History of the U.S. Constitution. Los Angeles: Constitutional Rights Foundation, 1987. Uses documents and pictures to trace the history of the Constitution and the Bill of Rights.

Lindrop, Edmund. *Birth of the Constitution.* Hillside, NJ: Enslo Publishers, 1987. Covers the creation of the Constitution with an emphasis on personalities.

The United States Constitution. Boston, MA: Knowledge Products, 1987. In two audiotapes, Walter Cronkite describes the Constitutional Convention and explains the Constitution and amendments.

UNIT 3

Aten, Jerry. *Presidents (A Workbook/Supplement).* Carthage, IL: Good Apple, 1985. Includes separate units on each president with research questions and some presidential trivia.

CQ's Guide to Current American Government. Washington, D.C.: Congressional Quarterly, biennial. These student resource books provide an overview of current government, plus in-depth analysis of key events or issues.

How Congress Works. Washington, D.C.: Congressional Quarterly, 1983. Introduces the workings of Congress and lobbyists.

Stinebrickner, Bruce, ed., *American Government 87/88.* 17th ed. Guilford, CT: Dushkin, 1987. This anthology, for more advanced students, reprints articles from major news and political journals.

UNIT 4

Council: A Simulation of Problem-Solving on the Community Level. Lakeside, CA: Interact, n.d. Involves a whole class in simulating the election and operations of a city council.

Eichner, James A., and Linda M. Shields. *Local Government.* New York: Franklin Watts, 1983. Explains the various forms of local government and the services they provide.

Fourteen Case Studies in Local Government. Portland, ME: J. Weston Walch, 1983. Involve students in making decisions about real-life situations in city government.

State and Local Government 87/88. Annual Edition Series. Guilford, CT: Dushkin, 1987. An anthology of current articles on various issues, suitable for advanced students.

UNIT 5

Janus Money Matters Guides. Wichita, KS: Janus Publications, 1981–1984. Consumer skills, such as money management and consumer rights, are taught in this series of eight high interest/low vocabulary worktexts.

Keenan, Diana. *Making Sense of the Deficit: A Guide for Students.* 2d ed. Culver City, CA: Social Studies School Service, 1987. This cartoon-illustrated unit with reproducible worksheets examines all sides of the federal deficit issue.

Kronewetter, Michael. *Capitalism vs. Socialism: Economic Policies of the U.S. and the USSR.* New York: Franklin Watts, 1986. Examines the history of capitalism and socialism as political theories and how these theories are exemplified in the United States and the Soviet Union.

Meltzer, Milton. *Poverty in America.* New York: William Morrow and Co., 1986. Explores who the poor really are, the myths about them, and what government programs have accomplished against poverty.

Pool, John Charles, and Ross M. LaRoe. *The Instant Economist: All the Basics of Economics in One Hundred Pages of Plain Talk.* Menlo Park, CA: Addison-Wesley Publishing Co., 1985. Written as a dialogue, this book explains basic principles of economics.

Spiselman, David. *A Teenager's Guide to Money, Banking and Finance.* New York: Julian Messner, 1987. Offers teenagers a basic introduction to our economic system and practical advice on money managment.

UNIT 6

Criminal Justice: Opposing Viewpoints. rev. ed. Culver City, CA: Social Studies School Service, 1987. This easily read volume offers experts' arguments on such issues as the fairness of the criminal justice system, victims' rights, and legal ethics.

McMahon, Edward T., Lee P. Arbetman, and Edward L. O'Brien. *Street Law: A Course in Practical Law.* 3d. ed. St. Paul, MN: West Publishing Co., 1986. This easily understood text was prepared by the National Institute for Citizen Education in the Law.

Olney, Ross R., and Patricia Olney. *Up Against the Law: Your Legal Rights as a Minor.* New York: Lodestar Books, 1985. Uses real-life cases to explain civil and criminal law.

Sullivan, John J., and Joseph L. Victor. *Criminal Justice 87/88.* Annual Edition Series. Guilford, CT: Dushkin, 1987. This anthology of reprints from major journals covers such topics as juvenile delinquency and white-collar crime.

Suter, Coral, and Marshall Croddy. *The Crime Question: Rights and Responsibilities of Citizens.* Los Angeles: Constitutional Rights Foundation, 1984. These units use active approaches, such as case studies and moot court, to examine response to crime by all levels of government.

UNIT 7

AIDS: Opposing Viewpoints. St. Paul, MN. Greenhaven Press, 1988. Presents debates by experts, such as C. Everett Koop, on the impact of AIDS on society.

Archer, Jules. *Winners and Losers: How Elections Work in America*. San Diego, CA: Harcourt, Brace Jovanovich, 1984. Describes the election process including election-winning tactics.

Current Issues. 1988 Edition. Washington, D.C.: Close Up Foundation, 1987. Provides analyses of both sides of important foreign and domestic policy issues.

Kelley, Marjorie, ed. *Participating in Government*. Castro Valley, CA: Quercus, 1987. This high interest/low vocabulary worktext seeks to spark students' political awareness.

Lindrop, Edmund. *By a Single Vote! One-Vote Decisions That Changed American History*. Harrisburg, PA: Stackpole Books, 1987. These stories of more than 30 close calls in American elections demonstrate that each vote counts.

The Think Series. New York: Walker, dates vary. These thought-provoking student texts on current issues are prepared by noted authors. Topics include space, terrorism, poverty, and drugs.

UNIT 8

Basic Facts About the United Nations. New York: United Nations, 1984. A thorough history and description of the UN and its affiliated agencies.

Cornish, Edward, ed. *Global Solutions: Innovative Approaches to World Problems*. Bethesda, MD: World Future Society, 1984. These articles from *Futurist* magazine optimistically outline alternate futures and solutions to current problems.

Global Issues. Annual Edition Series. Guilford, CT: Dushkin. This collection of journal article reprints for advanced students deals with such topics as Chernobyl and the Philippines.

Snow, Jon. *Atlas of Today: The World Behind the News*. New York: Warwick Press, 1987. Colorful maps and explanatory text illuminate current issues, such as telecommunications, famine in Africa, and endangered wilderness areas.

World Politics. Annual Edition Series. Guilford, CT: Dushkin. Almost 50 article reprints for advanced students examine United States foreign affairs and global relations.

OVERVIEW

Americans are a diverse group of people with great variation in the places they live, the work they do, their ages, and their backgrounds. The diversity of Americans creates a cultural mosaic with people's differences fitting together to make a dynamic society. The shared beliefs and values of Americans form the glue that holds this mosaic together.

OBJECTIVES

After completing this chapter, students should be able to

- identify important ways in which Americans differ from one another.
- identify important ways in which Americans are changing.
- describe the concept of the American mosaic.
- explain the American belief in equal respect and the values of equality, freedom, and justice.

PLANNING GUIDE

Teaching Strategy	Skills	Special Features	Review/Evaluation
Introducing the Chapter: Cooperative Project **Teaching Activity 1:** Cooperative Project—The United States: Melting Pot or Mosaic (Section 1-2) **Teaching Activity 2:** Class Project—American Values: What Do You Believe? (Section 1-3) **Evaluating Progress:** Individual Project (Section 1-3) **Reinforcement Activity:** Individual Project—Worksheet (Section 1-1 or 1-2) **Enrichment Activity:** Individual Project—Worksheet (Section 1-1) **Unit 1 Activity:** Taking a Census	Decision-Making Lesson: Choosing and Taking Action Social Studies Skills Workshop: Analyzing Bar Graphs Decision-Making Skills Workshop: Choosing and Taking Action **Issues and Decision Making:** Worksheet Chapter 1	American Notebook People Make a Difference: Indian Artist Keeps Traditions Alive	Section Reviews Chapter 1 Survey **Tests:** Chapter 1 Test **Testing Software** **Additional Resources** **Activity Book** **Citizenship Skills** **Transparencies and Activity Book** **Voices of America**

For reinforcement and enrichment worksheets and unit activities, see the Activity Book.

Teaching Strategy

Introducing the Chapter: Cooperative Project

Diversity is one of the central themes of Chapter 1. In order for students to appreciate diversity in America, they must first understand the diversity in their own classroom. This introductory activity gives students an opportunity to learn how their classmates are different and similar. From this experience, students will be able to expand the concept of diversity to the United States.

Divide students into groups of four. Give each group a sheet of paper, divided as shown below. Tell students to write in the inside rectangle 16 features they have in common. Encourage students to find unusual similarities beyond obvious ones like sex or race. Suggest such topics as families, rules, beliefs, and experiences.

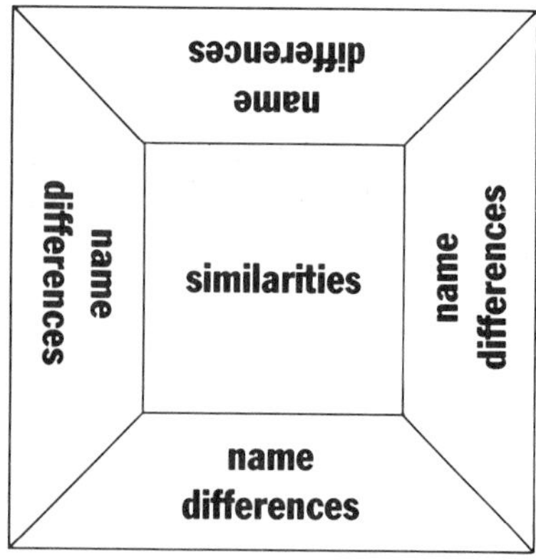

In one of the four spaces surrounding the rectangle, each student should write his or her name. In that section the student is to name four things that make him or her different from the others in the group. Encourage students to go beyond consideration of appearance and age and select examples that show special abilities and different family traditions and backgrounds.

Conclude the activity by having students discuss the following questions:

- Which were more difficult to find—similarities or differences? Why? (Answers will vary depending upon the diversity of the class. A class that had difficulty finding differences may not be very diverse.)
- How similar to or different from the rest of the United States do you think your school or community is? Why? (Encourage students to consider such factors as the diversity of residents' racial/ethnic backgrounds, the income level of the community, the diversity of job opportunities, and the average age of community residents.)
- What were some of the differences in families, beliefs, and traditions?
- What did you learn about your class in doing this activity?

Teaching Activity 1: Cooperative Project

The United States: Melting Pot or Mosaic

For many students the diversity of our nation is not obvious. In this activity, which may be used at the conclusion of Section 1-2, students analyze diversity in the United States.

Review the definitions of melting pot and mosaic. Then have each student take out a piece of paper and draw a line down the middle. On one side of the paper, students write *melting pot;* on the other, *mosaic.* Allow two to three minutes for students to write examples that show America as a melting pot and as a mosaic. Assign students to pairs and have the pairs share and add to each other's list. Direct each pair to combine with another pair to form groups of four. Have the new groups compare and add to their lists to produce a master list with as many examples as possible.

Reconvene the class and have each group mention one example from its melting pot list until all examples are exhausted. Follow the same procedure for the mosaic list. You may want to write the examples on the chalkboard.

Discuss with the class whether the examples support the view that American society can be described better as a mosaic than as a melting pot. Why or why not? Students who live in a homogeneous community may not have been exposed to diversity. Help them think about other geographical areas, economic classes, and ethnic/racial populations in the country.

Teaching Activity 2: Class Project

American Values: What Do You Believe?

After students have read the material in Section 1-3, conduct this activity. It enables students to examine their belief in equal respect and in the values of equality, freedom, and justice.

Designate an imaginary line down the middle of your classroom. Define one end of the line as the "agree" end and the other as the "disagree" end. The middle of the line is for those who "don't know."

Read some or all of the following statements and have the students stand along the imaginary line to indicate their responses.

- Everyone is created equal.
- Women should be able to do the same things men do.
- Everyone deserves equal opportunity in life.
- I can say whatever I want to say.
- Children should have the same freedoms as adults.
- All groups have the right to parade in town.
- Rich people have an advantage in the United States.
- A job should go to the best qualified person.
- The majority should rule.

After each statement is read, ask several students why they chose their place on the line. Allow for discussion since there probably will be different semantic interpretations as well as value conflicts.

Conclude the activity by asking students if they believe equal respect is an ideal or reality in our society. Students should provide evidence to support their opinions. Have students discuss who has the responsibility for equality, freedom, and justice in our society. What role do students, the legal system, schools, and adult citizens have in maintaining these basic values? (The topic of social institutions is introduced in Chapter 2.)

Evaluating Progress: Individual Project

After students have read the material in Section 1-3, use this activity to evaluate their understanding of the American ideal in everyday life.

Have students write three paragraphs describing how school life might be improved to continue to ensure equal respect and its supporting values of equality, freedom, and justice. For example, students might discuss the need for more equal treatment of girls' and boys' sports programs and recommend providing more money to girls' teams for equipment and uniforms. Have students include at least three specific examples with recommendations for improvement. Allow time in class for students to read their papers.

Criteria for evaluation should include the extent to which students' recommendations reflect the belief in equal respect and the values of equality, freedom, and justice.

Reinforcement Activity: Individual Project

Use this reinforcement activity after students have read the material in Section 1-1 or 1-2. In the activity students examine the media for evidence of diversity in the United States.

Begin by asking students to define the word *diversity* and give examples. Then assign each student the medium of newspapers, magazines, or television and ask students to find five examples of diversity. Students should keep a record of the television programs they watch or the articles they read.

After students have finished their research, have them complete Reinforcement Worksheet Chapter 1, "Diversity in America," in the Activity Book. When the assignment is finished, students can compare answers.

To conclude this activity, have students summarize how each medium—television, magazines, and newspapers—provides evidence of diversity in the United States. Discussion should include the extent of in-depth coverage, the realism of visuals, and the objectivity of the presentation. Discuss which medium best reflects students' lives. Why?

Enrichment Activity: Individual Project

Use this enrichment activity after students have read the material in Section 1-1. In the activity students create a class profile to determine how closely they and their families reflect recent trends in the movement, occupations, family size, and backgrounds of Americans.

To gather class data, have students complete Enrichment Worksheet Chapter 1, "Who We Are: A Class Survey," in the Activity Book. When students have completed the assignment, ask a pair of volunteers or a committee to compile the data and put the results on the chalkboard. Use the following guidelines for compilation.

- Determine the total number of students who have moved at least once. Does this figure represent two thirds of the class members?
- Determine the total number of employed family members. Then determine the total number of employed family members in service jobs. Do holders of service jobs represent more or less than one half of the total number of employed family members?
- Compare the size of students' families and their parents' families. Have the majority of families today decreased in size?
- Determine the total number of students or their ancestors who came from other countries or who are American Indians. Then determine the percentage from each country and from North America. Compare the percentages with the chart on text page 11.

Have students consider this profile. Then discuss how the class is similar to and different from the profile of Americans in Section 1-1.

Answer Key

CHAPTER 1

Section 1-1 Review (text page 8)

1. See definition for *diversity* on text page 7.
2. The Sunbelt (the South and the West) has grown the fastest in the last 30 years.
3. A service job is a job that involves providing a service for other people. Examples may include doctor, teacher, school secretary, car mechanic, fast food restaurant worker.
4. People are living longer, the many people born during the baby boom are getting older, and families are having fewer children today than in the past.
Analysis. Answers may include differences in Americans' ages, the places they live, the work they do, and their backgrounds.
Data Search. The West grew the most (by 22.3 percent). Answers may include better climate, more jobs, and less crowded conditions.

Section 1-2 Review (text page 15)

1. See definitions for the following terms on text pages indicated in parentheses: *immigrants* (8), *discrimination* (11), *racism* (11).
2. Reasons why people from other countries came to America may include the following: to seek religious freedom, to seek political freedom, to have an opportunity for a better life, to escape revolutions and political persecution, to make money to

send home to relatives, and because they were brought by force as slaves.
3. The five major groups of Americans are European Americans, black Americans, Hispanic Americans, Asian Americans, and American Indians. Members of each group share a common land of origin. In addition, Hispanic Americans share a common language and a common heritage from Spain.
Application. Answers may include people of varied racial backgrounds, food from different cultures, restaurants serving different kinds of food, holidays from different lands, signs or advertisements in different languages, and television programs in different languages.
Data Search. European immigration peaked around 1905 (about 1,200,000 people). On the graph, the highest point of Asian immigration is much later (1990) and involves far fewer people (about 300,000).

Section 1-3 Review (text page 19)

1. See definitions for the following terms on text pages indicated in parentheses: *beliefs* (16), *values* (16), *equality* (16), *freedom* (17), *justice* (18).
2. The three basic American values are equality, freedom, and justice.
3. Examples may include someone being treated unfairly by being denied equal rights and opportunities because of age, sex, race, religion, wealth, opinions, or background.
Synthesis. Answers may include the idea that a belief in equal respect helps different people live together because it means respecting people's worth no matter what their beliefs, race, wealth, etc.

Decision-Making Lesson (text pages 20–21)

1. Carlos and Maria's goals were for their children to live comfortably, get a good education, have opportunities to earn a good living, and enjoy peaceful lives. They set these goals because of economic problems in their community, particularly the strike and scarce food; the imprisonment of Carlos; and their fear for the safety of their children.
2. They considered the options of staying where they were, moving to the city, or moving to the United States.
3. They sold belongings to raise money, wrote to American friends for assistance, planned a trip to the United States, changed plans and left early for Mexico, and described their problem to American officials in Washington, D.C.
4. (c) The good points were that the conditions might improve and Maria would have work. The bad points were that Carlos would be unemployed and that his family would not be protected because he would not join the rebel group.
5. (b) The good point was that Carlos would have a better chance of finding a job. The bad point was that they might be killed.
6. (a) The bad points—the expense, leaving behind friends, and the challenges of learning English and finding jobs—were outweighed by the fact that Americans would be helpful and that the children would have a chance for a good education and prosperous lives.
7. (c)
8. The two main parts of decision making are choosing (setting a goal and selecting the best way to achieve it) and acting (planning how to take action and then doing what you planned).
9. Answers may include the following: Setting a goal is important to give direction to your thinking and actions. Listing options is important because you need to explore all the possibilities. Looking at both the good and bad points of each option is important in determining the best one. Planning action is important to increase your chances of achieving your goal. Changing your plans as necessary is important because something unexpected can happen. Looking back on the effects of your action is important in order to prepare for future decisions.

Chapter Survey (text page 22)

Understanding New Vocabulary

1. *Immigrants* is related to *diversity* because immigrants have made our country diverse with their varied backgrounds and customs.
2. *Freedom* is related to *values* because freedom is one of the basic American values.
3. *Discrimination* is related to *equality* because discrimination is the opposite of equality.

Putting It in Writing. Answers may include personal moral and religious beliefs, but should also connect the ideal of equal respect to the promotion of equality, justice, freedom, and national unity.

Looking Back at the Chapter

1. Answers may include the following: The population of the United States has increased because of immigration and natural growth. The population has become older because Americans are living longer and people are having fewer children than their parents did. The population has become more diverse as people from a greater variety of countries have come here. The population has moved from farms to cities and from the North and the East to the South and the West.
2. (a) European Americans all come from the same continent but speak different languages and have different customs. **(b)** Hispanic Americans all speak the same language and have ancestors from Spain but come from different countries in Latin America. **(c)** American Indians have ancestors who were all original inhabitants of North America, but they are made up of different groups, each with its own language and customs.
3. They have been denied equal rights and opportunities compared to whites. Blacks were victims of slavery, Asians were excluded from this country, and American Indians had treaties broken.
4. Each group has retained some of its unique customs and beliefs, like the individual tiles in a mosaic, rather than melting together and becoming similar to every other group.
5. To give every person an equal opportunity means to ensure that a person's race, sex, background, or beliefs are not used to deny him or her the same chances to succeed as everyone else.
6. To have freedom means to be able to choose your work, your friends, where you go, and what you do.
7. To show justice to another person means to treat him/her fairly, to judge him/her only on his/her abilities.
8. The American ideal is that every person be treated with equal respect. This ideal is supported by our basic values of equality, freedom, and justice.
9. Answers may include the idea that a diverse country is stronger or more interesting, but that diversity can lead to conflict between different groups.
10. Answers may include the idea that equality does not mean everyone is always treated the same because differences in ability should be recognized.
11. Answers may include the idea that a belief in the superiority of one race over another will not allow people to be treated with equal respect.
12. Answers may include a discussion of how exercising one's freedoms should not interfere with other people's freedoms.
13. Answers will vary.

Working Together

Answers will vary.

Skills Workshop (text page 23)

Social Studies Skills

1. The birth rate is currently at its lowest level. The birth rate during this period is about half of what it was during the peak years (1915–1924 and 1955–1964).
2. The birth rate declined from about 120 to about 80 births per year.
3. The baby boom lasted for 20 years, from 1945 to 1964.
4. Generally, the trend in birth rates has been downward since 1915 except for the baby boom.
5. Answers will vary but should be explained.

Decision-Making Skills

1. Both the Mennonite and Carlos and Maria set goals, listed options, identified consequences of each option, chose the best option, planned how to reach their goal, adjusted the plan as necessary, and evaluated the decision afterwards.
2. Decisions will vary. Some important things to remember are setting a goal, listing options, identifying consequences of each option, and comparing options to choose the best one.

OVERVIEW

Shared values make it possible for Americans to live and work together as a society. Americans learn these values through the process of socialization in five major social institutions: the family, religion, education, the economy, and government. These institutions meet people's needs and shape their values.

OBJECTIVES

After completing this chapter, students should be able to

- describe how people learn values and rules of behavior important to society.
- identify five major social institutions and describe the needs they meet.
- explain how the structure of American families is changing.
- describe freedoms that individuals have in the American economy.

PLANNING GUIDE

Teaching Strategy	Skills	Special Features	Review/Evaluation
Introducing the Chapter: Class Project **Teaching Activity 1:** Class Project—Family Ties: The Family as a Social Institution (Section 2-2) **Teaching Activity 2:** Class Project—Food for Thought: Economic Principles at Work (Section 2-3) **Evaluating Progress:** Individual Project (Section 2-4) **Reinforcement Activity:** Individual Project—Worksheet (Section 2-1) **Enrichment Activity:** Individual Project—Worksheet (Section 2-2)	Decision-Making Lesson: Choosing Social Studies Skills Workshop: Analyzing Statistical Tables Decision-Making Skills Workshop: Choosing **Issues and Decision Making:** Worksheet Chapter 2	People Make a Difference: Minister Helps Serve Neighborhood American Notebook	Section Reviews Chapter 2 Survey **Tests:** Chapter 2 Test **Testing Software** **Additional Resources** **Activity Book** **Citizenship Skills** **Transparencies and Activity Book** **Voices of America**

For reinforcement and enrichment worksheets and unit activities, see the Activity Book.

Teaching Strategy

Introducing the Chapter: Class Project

Chapter 2 focuses on our five major social institutions. Students undoubtedly have had some experience with the family, religion, education, the economy, and government but probably have not perceived them as social institutions. This introductory activity will help students see how such institutions meet their individual needs.

Ask each student to take out a piece of paper and write the following at the top: "Everybody has needs. As a teenager, citizen, and human being, some of my needs are . . ." Give examples of needs, such as food, love, and rules to live by. Allow two to three minutes for students to complete their lists. While students are doing so, write the names of the five social institutions (the family, religion, education, the economy, government) across the top of the chalkboard.

Have students take turns reading items from their lists and indicating which institutions can best meet the needs they have listed. Record students' answers on the board. Using this information, discuss which institutions have the most influence on students' lives. Ask students which institutions will have greater influence in five years. Why? Close the activity by asking students to summarize the purpose of the five institutions and define *social institution* in their own words.

Teaching Activity 1: Class Project

Family Ties: The Family as a Social Institution

The family is the most basic institution in any society, yet its structure can take many forms. In this activity, which may be used with Section 2-2, students extend the theme of diversity introduced in Chapter 1 and examine differences in family structure.

Ask students to draw illustrations of the structures of their families on blank sheets of paper. Remind students that any arrangement of children living with adults who meet their physical and emotional needs can be considered a family. Encourage accuracy but protect students' anonymity. Emphasize that artistic ability is not necessary; students are welcome to draw stick figures. Allow five to ten minutes for drawing.

While students are drawing, write headings for different family structures on the chalkboard: two parents with two or three children; two parents with fewer or more children; single parent with children; blended family; extended family (including relatives such as grandparents, aunts, or uncles); foster family; and group home (structured care facility for people with problems or without resources).

When they are finished, ask students to post their drawings with tape on the chalkboard under the appropriate headings. Create more headings if necessary. Tally the results and compare with the statistic in the text that one in twenty American families is a two-parent family with two or three children.

Have students discuss their reaction to the data. Were they surprised at the results? Why or why not? Do the class results correspond with the perception of American families created by television and movies? Encourage students to provide examples of "media families" to support their views.

Teaching Activity 2: Class Project

Food for Thought: Economic Principles at Work

Use this activity after students have read the material in Section 2-3. In the activity students apply economic principles to everyday life.

Bring in six popular but healthful snacks, such as small bags of popcorn, yogurt cups, or apples, and display them. Begin the activity by asking the class if anyone is interested in having a snack. Tell students there will be an opportunity for some of them to have the snacks later in the class.

Ask the class to define the word *good* as it applies to economics (not as in taste). Is yogurt, an apple, or popcorn a good? Have students discuss the following questions regarding the snacks:

- Who are the workers associated with making these snacks? (Appropriate workers will depend on the specific snacks but might include farmers, bakers, or food processors.)
- What services were required to get the snacks to this classroom? (delivery, sales)
- Who are the potential consumers of the snacks? (students, teachers, other people)
- Why do students want the snacks? (to satisfy the desire for food)
- Does everyone have an equal opportunity to buy the snacks? (*yes* in the sense that all do have access to the snacks; *no* in that not everyone has money to buy the snacks, and the supply is limited)
- How will the price of the snacks be determined? (The teacher can set a price, as a seller does, or the class can bid as people do at an auction.)

Invite students to buy the snacks with money. They can combine their money for a cooperative purchase. Prompt students to suggest how they might barter to get a snack. For example, students might promise to turn in a homework assignment on time in exchange for a snack. Sell the snacks to the highest bidders, give them away, or accept a trade, but use ill-defined or inconsistent criteria for the exchange.

After all of the snacks are gone, have students discuss the following questions about the activity:

- How was the situation like the real economic world? (sellers' freedom to sell and earn a profit, buyers' freedom not to buy, buyers' freedom to buy individually or cooperatively)
- How was the situation unlike the real economic world? (no competitive sellers, control of purchases by the seller, shortage of a common item, inconsistent rules of trade)
- Why are the rules of the American economy important to the way our society functions? (designed to give all Americans freedom to try to achieve their dreams)

Evaluating Progress: Individual Project

This writing activity may be used to evaluate students' understanding of the five social institutions. The activity is most effectively used at the end of Chapter 2.

Ask students to choose a recent day and describe how that day was influenced by any four of the five social institutions. Students should write one paragraph for each social institution, giving three examples of its influence and identifying one need it satisfied. For example, a student might describe how school (education) determined the time he or she arose and the time devoted to homework in the evening and satisfied the need to obey state laws or acquire certain skills.

Evaluation criteria should include the behaviors affected and the need satisfied by each social institution.

Reinforcement Activity: Individual Project

Although students will probably understand individual social institutions as they read about them in the chapter, recognizing the influence of the various institutions in everyday life is more difficult. In this activity students identify social institutions referred to in newspaper headlines. The activity may be used after Section 2-1 or at the end of the chapter.

Distribute Reinforcement Worksheet Chapter 2, "Identifying Social Institutions," in the Activity

Book. Review the directions for the first part of the worksheet with students and make certain they understand that a headline can refer to more than one social institution. Encourage students to review text material before completing the second part of the worksheet.

When students are finished, discuss the headlines that students believe refer to more than one social institution. Then call on volunteers to share the needs they identified for the five social institutions. Have students discuss which institutions seem to affect them most in their daily lives. How will the effect of these institutions change as they get older?

☐ Enrichment Activity: Individual Project

The difference in and relationship between rules and values are sometimes difficult for students to grasp. This activity is intended to help students differentiate between the two concepts while recognizing the close relationship between them. The activity is most effective after students have read the material in Section 2-2.

Enrichment Worksheet Chapter 2, "Values and Rules," in the Activity Book lists eight commonly held values; students are to write a rule that is related to each value. Introduce the worksheet by reviewing with students the difference between values and rules. If students need clarification of the task, provide the following example:

Value: Education is important.
Rule: Children must attend school until they are sixteen years old.

Review students' completed worksheets in class. Ask students which values seem to have the most legislated rules to support them. (for example, honesty and murder) Which values seem to have the fewest legislated rules? (for example, charity and friendship) Discuss why some values have been legislated and others seem to be left to the consciences of individuals.

Answer Key

CHAPTER 2

Section 2-1 Review (text page 28)

1. See definitions for the following terms on text pages indicated in parentheses: *rules* (26), *socialization* (27), *social institutions* (28).
2. People join groups in order to satisfy physical, emotional, and spiritual needs.
3. The five major social institutions are the family, religion, education, the economy, and government.
Application. Answers may include physical needs, such as food and shelter; emotional needs, such as love and companionship; and spiritual needs, such as comfort in times of sorrow.

Section 2-2 Review (text page 34)

1. The family benefits the individual by instilling a sense of security and belonging. The family benefits society by serving as a training ground for future adults, establishing rules that reflect the values held by society as a whole.
2. Religion provides comfort in times of sorrow, a sense of belonging to a community of people, a moral code for behavior, and answers to spiritual questions about the purpose of life and death.
3. Children gain skills and knowledge to earn a living, learn how to get along with others, and learn the values and rules necessary to play their roles as citizens of our democratic nation.
Analysis. The family provides the first model for functioning within a group; within this structure you learn to live by rules while developing a sense of security and independence. Religion is an extension of family, further developing a sense of belonging to a community of people with shared values. Education differs from the family and religion by supplying you with the knowledge and skills to become a working adult and a citizen. All three institutions share the ability to transmit values from generation to generation.
Data Search. In 1940, 4.6 percent of students completed four years of college; by 1990, this figure had risen to 21.1 percent.

Section 2-3 Review (text page 36)

1. See definitions for the following terms on the text pages indicated in parentheses: *goods* (35), *services* (35), *wants* (35), *economy* (35), *consumer* (35), *market* (35), *price* (35), and *money* (36).
2. Our society benefits from having an economic system by getting the goods and services needed to fulfill people's wants.
3. Americans have the economic freedom to buy and sell, to compete, to make a profit, to own property, and to choose an occupation.
Application. Answers may include freedom to buy any product that you can afford, variety in products to buy because of the freedom to compete in our economy, freedom to make a profit on any good you produce or service you provide, and freedom to choose a job.

Section 2-4 Review (text page 39)

1. See definitions for the following terms on the text pages indicated in parentheses: *monarchy* (38), *dictatorship* (38), *democracy* (38).
2. Government meets the needs for law and order (example: establishing courts to try people accused of committing crimes); security (example: maintaining armed forces to withstand an attack by another nation); public services (example: building schools to educate children of the community); and maintaining other institutions (example: providing retirement benefits).
3. In a monarchy the power to make decisions is held by a monarch, who has inherited the title; in a dictatorship it is held by an individual who has seized control through force; in a democracy the power is shared by all of the people, who elect representatives.
Synthesis. Answers will vary. Some examples of laws are having the right to vote at the age of eighteen, paying income taxes, being protected as a juvenile in the event of an arrest, having freedom of speech. Students may speculate about a society where a twelve-year-old who is accused of a crime is treated as an adult or a society in which no one pays taxes and therefore receives no government benefits such as public services.

Decision-Making Lesson (text pages 40–41)

1. They needed a more specific goal that would address the cause of the problem.
2. The goal led to rejecting the option because using guards would not be a way to get students to cooperate voluntarily.
3. (b) The members of the student council concluded that the problem was the students' attitude, not the lack of money.
4. (a) The faculty advisor raised the issue of how to weigh the options, but the students were already prepared with a method. The chart was important for comparing the options, and willingness to consider all options helped the brainstorming process. Otherwise, they might not have arrived at the button idea.
5. A clear goal gives direction to your thinking in weighing options and your actions in carrying out a decision.
6. Options may be judged by identifying which consequences are good and which are bad. Then the good and bad consequences of the options can be compared to choose the best option.

Chapter Survey (text page 42)

Understanding New Vocabulary

1. *Socialization* is related to *rules* because in order to participate in a group one must learn the rules for behavior within it.
2. *Goods* is related to *wants* because goods satisfy our wants.
3. *Money* is related to *price* because money is used to pay for a product at a specific price.
4. *Monarchy* is related to *dictatorship* because both types of government are controlled by one person.
Putting It in Writing. Answers may include the idea that in a monarchy and a dictatorship one person—usually a monarch or a military leader—has the power to make laws. In contrast, in a democracy, the people, through the election of representatives, have the power to make laws.

Looking Back at the Chapter

1. Answers may include food and shelter, a sense of security, desire for love and companionship,

moral guidance, knowledge and skills, and answers to questions about the meaning of life and death.
2. Members of a group must learn and obey the rules so that the group will continue to meet their needs.
3. A child benefits from the institution of the family by developing a sense of security and belonging, identity, and gradual independence. These benefits help to shape the future adult who can achieve personal goals and play his or her role as citizen in our democratic nation.
4. Individuals receive comfort, a sense of belonging, answers to spiritual questions, and moral guidance. Society benefits from the charity and morality practiced by members of religious groups.
5. Schools give children skills and knowledge to earn a living and teach them how to get along with others and the values and rules necessary to be citizens in our democracy.
6. The basic purpose of an economic system is to ensure that the goods and services desired by people are produced and distributed.
7. A consumer can pay for a product or service by providing another product or service in exchange or by paying with money.
8. People form governments to establish law and order, protect individuals' security, provide public services, and maintain other institutions.
9. Answers may include the idea that if the institution of the family did not exist, adults would lack a sense of security and would not understand how to participate in society or contribute to it. Society might break up or establish an institution to perform the functions of the family.
10. Answers may include one's family, school, religion, a circle of friends, or a club.
11. Answers may include the idea that loss of any of our economic freedoms would deprive us of freedom of choice. For example, if you could not choose an occupation, you might be forced to work at something that provides little or no satisfaction.
12. Answers may include the view that the family has had the greatest effect on shaping values. Examples of beliefs and values may include being considerate, sharing, trusting others, working with others, taking responsibility for maintaining things that belong to the family and oneself, and obeying rules.

Working Together

Answers will vary.

Skills Workshop (text page 43)

Social Studies Skills

1. The purpose of the table is to show how a person's level of education affects how much money he or she will earn in a lifetime.
2. Women who do not finish high school earn the least.
3. Men with five or more years of college earn the most. Their earnings are about $1 million more than or three times as much as the earnings of the lowest paid group.
4. The highest paid group of women, with five or more years of college, earn only $110,000 more than the lowest paid group of men, who did not finish high school.
5. Lifetime earnings rise with a person's level of education. Men earn much more than women with the same level of education.

Decision-Making Skills

1. Answers may vary. Most students will probably choose the pantry option, which seems to guarantee immediate help that is likely to continue on a long-term basis.
2. A clear goal helps to direct both your thinking in weighing options and your actions in working toward your goal.
3. You should consider all options because your first idea may not be the best.
4. Answers will vary.

OVERVIEW

Being a citizen of the United States, by birth or naturalization, involves rights, duties, and responsibilities. These include contributing to the common good. Throughout life, an individual plays many social roles which change, overlap, and conflict. It is important for students to understand their responsibility in the citizen role to protect the basic values that unite us as a society.

OBJECTIVES

After completing this chapter students should be able to

- describe who is a citizen and how one becomes a citizen.
- explain the importance of the "office of citizen."
- compare the rights, duties, and responsibilities of citizens.
- describe the seven social roles.

PLANNING GUIDE

Teaching Strategy	Skills	Special Features	Review/Evaluation
Introducing the Chapter: Class Project **Teaching Activity 1:** Cooperative Project—Citizenship Court (Section 3-1) **Teaching Activity 2:** Class Project—Social Roles: A Chain Story (Section 3-3) **Evaluating Progress:** Individual Project (Section 3-1 or 3-3) **Reinforcement Activity:** Individual Project—Worksheet (Section 3-3) **Enrichment Activity:** Individual Project—Worksheet (Section 3-2)	Decision-Making Lesson: Taking Action Social Studies Skills Workshop: Reading a Newspaper Decision-Making Skills Workshop: Taking Action **Issues and Decision Making:** Worksheet Chapter 3	American Notebook Views of Noted Americans: Barbara Jordan In Their Own Words: Martin Luther King, Jr.—"I have a dream"	Section Reviews Chapter 3 Survey Unit 1 Survey **Tests:** Chapter 3 Test, Unit 1 Test **Testing Software** **Additional Resources** **Activity Book** **Citizenship Skills** **Transparencies and Activity Book** **Voices of America**

For reinforcement and enrichment worksheets and unit activities, see the Activity Book.

Teaching Strategy

Introducing the Chapter: Class Project

Chapter 3 takes a broad view of the meaning of citizenship. It examines not only the rights, duties, and responsibilities of citizens, but also concepts of the "office of citizen," the common good, and social roles. Because many of these ideas will be new to students, focusing on a familiar aspect of citizenship—voting—is a good way to begin students' thinking about their role as citizens.

Introduce the chapter by having the class discuss the distinction between rights and duties. (Rights are the privileges guaranteed to citizens; duties are required by law.) Ask for examples of rights and duties in our democracy. (rights—freedom of speech, freedom to own a business; duties—obeying the laws, paying taxes)

Have students discuss this question: Is voting our right or our duty? Divide the class into two groups; designate one group to argue that voting is a right and the other that it is a duty. Encourage students to examine the role of citizens in a democracy. Stimulate conversation by asking: Should citizens be punished if they do not vote? If only 25 to 30 percent of the people vote, is the United States really a democracy? Write the arguments on the chalkboard so that students can evaluate their persuasiveness.

Conclude the activity by asking students: What should a person do in order to be a good citizen? Their answers can be compared to those presented in the introduction to Chapter 3.

Teaching Activity 1: Cooperative Project

Citizenship Court

Ten percent of the American population is composed of naturalized citizens. In this activity, which can be used with Section 3-1, students apply their knowledge of the requirements for naturalization to fictitious applicants for citizenship.

Divide the class into groups of two or three. Direct each group to write a description of an applicant for naturalization. It should include the applicant's name and country of origin and an explanation of any infectious diseases, such as tuberculosis, and any convictions for crimes involving drugs or murder. On the chalkboard, write the criteria listed below. Students must provide information about their applicant for each item.

- age of applicant
- parents' country of citizenship
- ability to read, write, and speak English
- length of stay in the United States
- behavior that reflects accepted moral standards
- loyalty to the basic values of American government
- knowledge of history and form of government of the United States
- presence of two United States citizens as witnesses

Secretly tell some groups to write a description of a person who is eligible for citizenship and others to write a description of an ineligible person.

Encourage students to write sophisticated descriptions that challenge other class members to test their knowledge of citizenship requirements. Stress that failure to meet only one or two criteria can make an applicant ineligible for citizenship. Allow 20 to 30 minutes for groups to write their descriptions.

When finished, each group should read its description to the class. The class will act as the citizenship court, deciding whether the applicant is eligible for naturalization. To conclude the activity, have students discuss how strict or lenient they believe qualifications for citizenship should be and why. Should exceptions to the rules be made in cases of political persecution? Why or why not?

Teaching Activity 2: Class Project

Social Roles: A Chain Story

After students have read the material in Section 3-3, plan for them to participate in this activity. Much like creating a chain letter, students use their knowledge of social roles to add to a continuing story about the activities of a fictitious young man or woman named Lee.

Make enough slips of paper for all class members and write one of the seven social roles (self, family member, social group member, worker, friend, citizen, consumer) on each. Have each student choose a slip of paper and then mentally create a one-minute story about Lee functioning in this role. Challenge students to create realistic, interesting stories.

After allowing time for preparation, ask for a volunteer to begin the story and proceed around the classroom. Write on the chalkboard all of the activities the students mention. After the story, ask students to identify the role exemplified by each activity. For example, if Lee helped a sister or brother do homework, the class would identify the social role of family member. Have students discuss times in which Lee's roles overlap or come into conflict. Ask them to share situations in which their roles were in conflict and to explain what choices they made.

Evaluating Progress: Individual Project

The concept of delegation of power is critical to an understanding of the "office of citizen." In this activity, which can be used at the end of Section 3-1 or at the end of the chapter, students apply their understanding of this concept to newspaper and news magazine articles. Students may complete the assignment out of class, or you can bring a collection of newspapers and news magazines for them to use in class. The assignment will require most of a class period.

Review with students the concept of delegated power, telling them that delegated powers are used by our elected and appointed government officials everyday. Challenge students to find at least five examples of the use of delegated powers in newspapers and news magazines. Direct students to cut out the appropriate articles and indicate on an attached note what delegated power is exemplified in each article (making laws, building roads, determining the guilt of an accused person, etc.) and to whom the power has been delegated.

Criteria for evaluation of student work should include correct identification of both the power delegated and the position of the person carrying out the power.

Reinforcement Activity: Individual Project

This activity can be assigned after students have read the material in Section 3-3. Reinforcement Worksheet Chapter 3, "Saturday's Project: Social Roles," in the Activity Book presents a story about three teenagers who play different roles as they engage in various activities. Students reinforce their understanding of the seven social roles by reading the story and classifying the actions of the teenagers.

To begin the activity, review the seven social roles with students. Then distribute the worksheet, making sure that students understand the directions. After students have completed the worksheet, compare answers.

Conclude the activity by collecting information about the class on the chalkboard. Write the seven social roles across the top of the board and ask each student to tell how many activities related to each role he or she participated in last Saturday. Tally all the students' responses and total each column. Discuss which roles students participated in most and least. Ask students if the totals might have been different if they had described a weekday rather than a weekend.

Enrichment Activity: Individual Project

Students will be better able to hold the "office of citizen" if they are aware of the many opportunities they have to work for the common good. In Enrichment Worksheet Chapter 3, "Citizen Action," in the Activity Book, students classify actions as rights, duties, or responsibilities of citizens. This worksheet is most effectively used after students have completed Section 3-2.

After students have classified the actions in the worksheet, ask them to read the list a second time and determine how important they think each action is for the common good. Direct students to use a five-point scale to assess importance: 1—not important; 2—somewhat important; 3—important; 4—important but not essential; 5—essential. Students should write their assessment to the left of the number of each action.

After the class has completed the activity, check answers. Ask students to share their assessment of each of the actions by a show of hands. Discuss differences. Some of the actions may not be immediately obvious as important citizen responsibilities. Discuss with the class the civic importance of being able to support oneself financially, of keeping good physical and mental health, and of being able to express oneself.

Answer Key

CHAPTER 3

Section 3-1 Review (text page 47)

1. See definitions for the following terms on the text pages indicated in parentheses: *citizen* (46), *naturalized* (46), *alien* (46), *representatives* (47).
2. You must be born in the United States or its territories; have at least one parent who was an American citizen at the time of your birth; go through the process of becoming a citizen (naturalization); or be under eighteen when your parents were naturalized.
3. The "office of citizen" is the power citizens in the United States have to decide what their government will and will not do.
Analysis. Both citizens and elected officials hold office. Elected officials hold office only as long as citizens want them to; citizens hold the "office of citizen" for life.
Data Search. More than 200,000 people were naturalized in 1940, 1945, 1955, 1985, and 1990.

Section 3-2 Review (text page 54)

1. See definitions for the following terms on the text pages indicated in parentheses: *jury of peers* (50), *witnesses* (50), *the common good* (51), *candidate* (53).
2. Answers may include the right to vote, to hold elected office, to say what you think in speech or in writing, to practice your own religion, to have a fair trial, to be protected by your government in other countries, and to privacy.
3. Answers may include obeying the laws, defending the nation, serving on a jury or as a witness in court, paying taxes, and attending school.
4. Answers may include contributing to the common good, voting, holding government office, helping with election campaigns, influencing government actions, and serving the community.
Analysis. Answers may include the idea that voting, holding office, helping with elections, and influencing the government help protect our rights and freedoms.

Section 3-3 Review (text page 59)

1. See definition for *social roles* on text page 55.
2. Answers may include the role of student in a classroom, on an athletic team, or in a club.
3. Answers may include friend-student, son/daughter-citizen, and family member-worker.
4. The person must make a choice based on the consequences of each behavior and the values in each role. Examples will vary.
5. Examples may include obeying the laws, paying taxes, voting, running for office, and influencing government actions.
Synthesis. Answers may include inadequate and/or incompetent community government.

Decision-Making Lesson (text pages 60–61)

1. The goal was to ensure that the buttons would get students to help keep the campus clean.
2. Resources included the button-making machine and free poster paper which would help keep down the cost of the plan. Obstacles included possible student complaints that the discounts were unfair. If complaints became widespread, the plan would be unlikely to succeed because it depended on voluntary help.
3. Examples may include asking for the principal's permission, contacting the Pep Club president, developing a button design, making rules for button distribution, signing up teams and clubs as sponsors, handing out buttons, making announcements, and writing articles. Students should explain why the actions were important. For instance, making rules for button distribution was important because the students would not support an unfair plan.
4. (c) The clean campus was the best sign that the students were cooperating with the plan.
5. (a) The council added a recycling program.
6. Choosing involves setting a goal and selecting the best option for achieving it. Acting involves actually taking steps to achieve the goal.
7. "Doing something" can mean actions that are not well-thought out. Acting involves careful planning and checking how well your plan is going.

Chapter Survey (text page 62)

Understanding New Vocabulary

1. (c) *Naturalized* is related to *immigrant* because it is the process by which immigrants become American citizens.
2. (a) *The common good* is related to the "*office of citizen*" because the basic responsibility of a citizen is to contribute to the common good.
3. (b) *Jury of peers* is related to *trial* because an accused person has the right to a fair trial with the final decision made by a jury of peers.
4. (d) *Candidate* is related to *election* because a candidate gains public office by winning an election.
Putting It in Writing. Answers may include the importance of acting in ways that protect the rights and freedoms of other Americans and make our communities, states, and nation good places for all of us to live.

Looking Back at the Chapter

1. See information in box on text page 47.
2. Answers may include the idea that only citizens have the power to decide what the government will and will not do.
3. Answers may include freedom—of speech, religion, the press, privacy; justice—fair trial; equality—voting and holding office.
4. Duties include obeying the laws, defending the nation, serving on a jury or as a witness in court, paying taxes, attending school. By fulfilling each of these duties, we support our government's efforts to meet the needs of society.
5. Answers may include helping with election campaigns, influencing government, and making our communities better places to live in.
6. Answers may include voting, holding government office, helping with election campaigns, influencing government, and making our communities better places to live in.
7. Answers may include friend and student, family member and citizen, and family member and consumer.
8. Answers may include the born-into role of son or daughter, the required role of student, and the chosen role of employee.
9. The basic responsibility of every citizen is to contribute to the common good.
10. Answers will vary. For example, as a driver a citizen can obey the traffic laws or disobey them, causing confusion and/or accidents.
11. Answers will vary. The values that guide behavior in each role should be compared.
12. Answers may include the idea that if you choose not to vote, you are giving up your right as a citizen to have a voice in government and to make a difference in your community.
13. Supporting answers may include the idea that a democracy can operate only if citizens actively participate in it; thus, the "office of citizen" is the most important office there is. Opposing answers may include the lack of citizen interest in government, especially in voting.

Working Together

Answers will vary.

Skills Workshop (text page 63)

Social Studies Skills

1. **(a)** B-1 **(b)** A-10 **(c)** A-5 **(d)** E-1 **(e)** B-10
2. A likely name for section D is Entertainment.
3. An important local news story could be located in either Section A or Section B.

Decision-Making Skills

1. Her goals included being the best in her class, becoming Girl of the Year, helping Democratic candidates in 1960, making government respond to the people's needs, getting elected to the Texas Senate and the House of Representatives.
2. (a) The difficulty of law school admissions tests was probably not an obstacle because Jordan was well-qualified.
3. (c) The award was based on academic and community service achievements, neither of which is a result of making friends at school.
4. (b) Her main goal in entering politics was to serve the needs of the people.
5. (a) Helping Democratic candidates did not increase her salary. Also, becoming a member of the House was a result of a conscious effort.
6. Planning involves stating the goal of your action, identifying resources and obstacles, listing actions you need to take, taking those actions, and checking how well your plan is going.
7. Answers will vary.

In Their Own Words (text page 64)

1. The Declaration of Independence and the Constitution guarantee the rights of life, liberty, and the pursuit of happiness to all, but these rights have been denied to black Americans.
2. Answers may include the idea that although opportunities in education, jobs, and housing have improved, discrimination still exists.
3. Answers may include treating all people with equal respect, writing letters to elected representatives and newspapers about injustice, and joining or creating an organization to influence government actions.

Unit 1 Survey (text page 65)

Looking Back at the Unit

1. Answers may include the idea that treating such a person with equal respect is important in order to ensure that the rights of all Americans to equality, freedom, and justice are protected.
2. Answers may include obeying the laws, attending school, possibly paying taxes, helping with election campaigns, influencing the government, and serving the community. New activities may include defending the nation, serving on a jury or as a witness in court, paying taxes, voting, and holding government office.
3. **(a)** By voting, we take part in our political process, deciding what the government will or will not do. **(b)** By recycling newspapers, we take responsibility for preserving natural resources and making our community a good place to live in. **(c)** By expressing views in a letter to the editor, we work to influence government actions. **(d)** By treating a person with equal respect, we try to ensure that the rights of all Americans to equality, freedom, and justice are protected.
4. 1. (c) 2. (d) 3. (b) 4. (a)

Taking a Stand

Answers may include arguments cited in the text and/or arguments students develop, for example, the willingness of previous immigrants to learn English without government reliance on English-only laws.

OVERVIEW

Our American heritage rises from Greek, Roman, and English traditions of government. Belief in self-government prompted colonists in England's 13 American colonies to rebel against English rule, win independence, and establish a national government dedicated to preventing tyranny and protecting the rights of citizens.

OBJECTIVES

After completing this chapter, students should be able to

- explain the significance of the concept of natural rights.
- describe what political traditions and principles influenced the colonists' ideas about government.
- summarize events that led to the creation of a permanent national government.

PLANNING GUIDE

Teaching Strategy	Skills	Special Features	Review/Evaluation
Introducing the Chapter: Cooperative Project **Teaching Activity 1:** Cooperative Project—Declaration of Children's Rights (Section 4-2) **Teaching Activity 2:** Individual Project—Locke, Montesquieu, and the American Revolution (Section 4-3) **Evaluating Progress:** Individual Project (Section 4-3) **Reinforcement Activity:** Individual Project—Worksheet (Section 4-2) **Enrichment Activity:** Individual Project—Worksheet (Section 4-3)	Social Studies Skills Workshop: Interpreting Political Cartoons Decision-Making Skills Workshop: Choosing **Issues and Decision Making:** Worksheet Chapter 4	American Notebook People Make a Difference: Citizen Seeks Memorial to Black Patriots	Section Reviews Chapter 4 Survey **Tests:** Chapter 4 Test **Testing Software** **Additional Resources** **Activity Book** **Citizenship Skills** **Transparencies and Activity Book** **Voices of America**

For reinforcement and enrichment worksheets and unit activities, see the Activity Book.

Teaching Strategy

Introducing the Chapter: Cooperative Project

It is important for students to understand and appreciate that our beliefs about freedom and self-government are carried out in our everyday lives. Every day we use the ideas of the founders of our nation, often not recognizing how these beliefs became a part of our thinking and actions.

Introduce Chapter 4 by asking students to respond to a short story. Read the following story and the accompanying questions aloud. The questions should also be written on the chalkboard.

> You and three friends play in a jazz band. The band director has made you and your friends angry too many times. You are tired of playing her type of music and practicing when she calls the rehearsals. Also, you have no say in how the band's money gets spent. The four of you quit the band and start your own group.

Divide the students into groups of four to determine answers to the following questions:

- What rules will you adopt as a group?
- How will you make decisions?
- How will you deal with conflict?
- How will you guarantee that band members understand and follow the rules?

Allow 10 to 15 minutes for the groups to work on these questions, then direct them to decide on a name for their new band. Allow only a couple of minutes for the groups to make this decision.

As a whole class, have students discuss the decisions reached in their groups. Help students focus on the following questions:

- What similarities appear in all of the bands' rules, decision-making procedures, and enforcement practices?
- What values are common to all of the groups' decisions?
- What ideas about government seem to have influenced the groups' decisions?
- Did the groups follow their agreed-upon rules when they chose their band names?
- Did the rules make the process of choosing a band name easier?

(Students' answers will vary but should reflect both a recognition of the importance of establishing rules and procedures and the difficulty of implementing them.)

To conclude this activity, ask students: From this activity, what do you think we will study in this chapter?

Teaching Activity 1: Cooperative Project

Declaration of Children's Rights

Americans take the concept of natural rights for granted, but for people in many other countries, it is still a dream. In this activity, which may be used after Section 4-2 has been completed, students explore the significance of the concept of natural rights. The activity can take an entire class period or be assigned as an out-of-class writing exercise.

To introduce the activity, ask students to define *natural rights*. (Natural rights are rights that people are born with and that no government can take away, such as the rights to life, liberty, and property.) Next discuss the following statement: Children are special and have unique rights that must be protected.

Divide the class into groups of three or four and ask the groups to brainstorm to determine the necessities a child must have in order to grow up healthy and become a contributing member of society. For example, necessities might include food, shelter, clothing, and a sense of security and belonging.

Ask each group to convert its list of necessities into a declaration of rights that all children should be guaranteed. Have one or two members of each group write an introductory paragraph that states the reason for such a declaration. Encourage students to write the declarations on unlined paper and to add a border design and/or signatures to make the document look official.

You may want to ask each group to read its declaration to the class and have students compare the rights listed. You may also want students to compare their declarations with the Declaration of Independence, after they have read Section 4-3, and/or the United Nations Declaration of the Rights of the Child.

Teaching Activity 2: Individual Project

Locke, Montesquieu, and the American Revolution

This activity can be used after students have read Sections 4-2 and 4-3. In the activity students apply their knowledge of the ideas of John Locke and Montesquieu to events in the colonies on the eve of independence. The activity can be done out of class, but some class time should be allowed for discussion.

Remind students that John Locke and Montesquieu were two European writers whose ideas about government influenced the colonists as they wrote the Declaration of Independence and created new state and national governments. Explain that Locke died in the early 1700s and Montesquieu in the mid-1700s—before the American colonists took steps toward independence. For this activity, however, students are to imagine that each writer visited the American colonies early in 1776, before the Declaration of Independence was written. While there, they observed colonial governments and talked with colonists about their views on independence.

Direct students to imagine that they are one of the two writers upon his return to Europe. As either Locke or Montesquieu, students are to write a letter of encouragement to the American colonists. In the letter the author should clearly state his political ideas—Locke on natural rights and Montesquieu on separation of powers. Reviewing the chapter, students should find examples of how the ideas were or were not being implemented in the colonies and present a persuasive argument for incorporating them in a new national government. You may want to encourage students to read more about these two writers' ideas in encyclopedias or American history reference books.

After their letters are completed, have students discuss how they think Locke's and Montesquieu's ideas fit or contrasted with the ideas of the colonists before 1776. Have students share specific examples included in their letters. Post the letters in a bulletin board display and encourage students to read their classmates' work.

Evaluating Progress: Individual Project

After completing this chapter, students should recognize that the ideas our government was founded on still function today. To evaluate students' ability to recognize these ideas at work in our society, have them collect newspaper or magazine articles that show these principles in action.

Ask each student to choose five principles from the following list: contributing to the common good, freedom of religion, freedom of the press, freedom of speech, direct democracy, republicanism, the right to a trial by jury, the right to petition, natural rights, separation of powers, and constitutionalism. Direct students to find one article that reflects each of the principles chosen. Students should then summarize in four or five paragraphs how all of the articles exemplify the founding principles at work in our country today.

Criteria for evaluating student work should include students' choice of articles and their correct explanation of how the articles illustrate founding principles.

Reinforcement Activity: Individual Project

Assign this activity after students have read the material in Section 4-2. In the activity students use a graphic organizer to outline political traditions and principles that influenced the development of American government. Completing the activity in class will require at least 30 minutes.

The information in Section 4-2 offers a good opportunity for students to use a graphic organizer. If students have worked with this study technique previously, they will probably be able to complete Reinforcement Worksheet Chapter 4, "Roots of American Government," in the Activity Book independently. If they are unfamiliar with graphic organizers, provide instruction as suggested below.

Review the directions for the first part of the worksheet with students. Explain that a graphic organizer is a type of outline that shows relationships among ideas and can be very useful in understanding and remembering some kinds of information. The information that will complete the graphic organizer is in Section 4-2.

Direct attention to the five long lines radiating out from the circle. Tell students that on these lines they are to write five sources of thinking that colonists drew on in creating the first forms of American government. If necessary, give students the hint that three of the answers are places and two are people. Next, point out that Section 4-2 describes the idea or ideas that each of these sources contributed to our form of government. Students should write these ideas on shorter lines extending out from the source lines. Point out that one source will have two ideas extending from it.

After students have completed their graphic organizers, discuss the usefulness of showing information in this form. Then direct students to the second part of the worksheet in which principles of American government are traced to the five sources shown in the graphic organizer. Students then choose one principle and explain why it is important.

Enrichment Activity: Individual Project

This project can serve as a culminating activity for Chapter 4 and as a reminder to students of the many significant events that took place in the formation of the United States before the Constitution was written. In Enrichment Worksheet Chapter 4, "Steps Leading to a National Government," in the Activity Book, students put these steps in chronological order and summarize their importance.

Introduce the activity by emphasizing to students that Chapter 4 tells a story of steps that led to the creation of a permanent national government for our country. Each step in the story was embedded in conflict, sometimes between the colonists and the English government, sometimes among colonists who had different points of view. Instruct students to list the steps named on the worksheet in the order in which they occurred and to provide a date for each. Students then explain the importance of each step.

Conclude the activity by having students discuss several possible endings for the story told in Chapter 4. Although many students will realize that the Americans went on to write an acceptable national constitution, encourage them to think about other alternatives. For example, some or all of the states could have returned to English rule or become separate countries.

Answer Key

CHAPTER 4

Section 4-1 Review (text page 74)

1. See definitions for the terms on the text pages indicated in parentheses: *heritage* (70), *legislature* (70), *charter* (70).

2. Colonial citizens were able to influence the laws that governed them because they elected representatives to their legislatures. Also, the English Parliament was too busy to pay attention to colonial laws.
3. English citizens in the colonies were similar to American citizens today in their right to self-government and in their responsibility to work for the common good. However, in the colonies only white men who owned property could vote or hold office; today, women and nonwhite Americans have these rights. English citizens in the colonies also did not have total freedom of religion or freedom of the press; American citizens today have both of these rights.
4. Freedom of religion for Christians was practiced in the colonies and this eventually led to freedom of religion for all Americans. The Zenger case made freedom of the press an issue in the colonies and this freedom eventually became the right of Americans.
Evaluation. The colonists took an important step by demanding freedom, justice, and equality for themselves. However, they did not practice these values with black Americans (who were treated as property), women, servants, and non-Christians.
Data Search. About 50 percent of the colonists were English. The information reflects the cultural mosaic by showing that even in colonial times America was made up of people with many different backgrounds.

Section 4-2 Review (text page 77)

1. See definitions for the terms on the text pages indicated in parentheses: *direct democracy* (75), *republic* (75), *natural rights* (76), *separation of powers* (77).
2. Traditions in colonial government that can be traced back to ancient Greece and Rome include the direct democracy of town meetings and the representative government of colonial legislatures.
3. From the English tradition of government, the colonists inherited the ideas of limiting the power of the monarch and giving basic rights to all citizens, such as the right to trial by jury.
4. The colonists were inspired by Locke's ideas that government existed for the people and its purpose was to protect natural rights, and by Montesquieu's idea of separation of powers so that no branch of government or government official could gain too much power.
Analysis. Answers may include the idea that in the Greek, Roman, and English traditions of government citizens had a voice in government and tyranny was prevented.

Section 4-3 Review (text page 83)

1. See definitions for the terms on the text pages indicated in parentheses: *compact* (80), *constitution* (80), *ratification* (82).
2. The colonists rebelled because they were taxed without being represented in Parliament, subjected to unfavorable trade policies, and threatened with the loss of their rights as citizens.
3. Each state legislature created a written constitution which limited government power through separation of powers and restricted the governor's term of office. Some state constitutions also included lists of citizens' rights. The Second Continental Congress created the Articles of Confederation, an alliance of independent states. The only branch of government would be a national legislature which had no power to tax or enforce laws that it made.
4. The Confederation government could not raise money to pay war debts, regulate trade with England, or force states to help put down an uprising such as Shays' Rebellion.
Analysis. Answers may include the idea that the experience of tyranny under English rule made many Americans fearful of giving too much power to a central government.

Chapter Survey (text page 84)

Understanding New Vocabulary

1. *Compact* and *constitution* are written agreements. However, a compact is a written agreement to make and obey laws for a group's welfare, and a constitution is a plan of government.
2. *Direct democracy* and *republic* are forms of government in which citizens make laws. However, in a direct democracy laws are made directly

by the citizens, and in a republic citizens elect representatives to make laws.

Putting It in Writing. Answers may include practice of direct democracy in colonial town meetings and republican government in colonial legislatures, and constitution writing by states.

Looking Back at the Chapter

1. As English citizens, the colonists had the right to elect representatives to their legislature.
2. Only white men who owned a certain amount of land had the rights of citizenship.
3. Colonial citizens participated in their government by voting and holding office and served their communities in various ways, such as being members of juries and supporting education.
4. Freedom of religion in the colonies, unlike today, did not extend to all religions.
5. (a) The direct democracy of ancient Athens was practiced by American colonists in town meetings; the republican system of government of ancient Rome gave rise to the representative government used in England and in the colonial legislatures. **(b)** The Magna Carta and English Bill of Rights influenced American state and national governments to limit the power of government and to list basic rights of citizens. **(c)** Locke's ideas of natural rights and the purpose of government were incorporated in the Declaration of Independence and in state constitutions; Montesquieu's idea of separation of powers was incorporated in state constitutions.
6. Colonists could not vote for members of Parliament, and no colonists were members themselves.
7. The Declaration of Independence states that all people have unalienable rights and that people give power to their government as long as it protects those rights. Locke's ideas of natural rights are reflected in Jefferson's reference to unalienable rights and in the view that the purpose of government is to protect those rights.
8. It was important to continue the tradition of basing government on written agreements and to spell out the limits of government power.
9. The colonists were fearful of giving power to a central government.
10. A stronger government would solve the economic problems that led to Shays' Rebellion, raise money through taxes, deal effectively with European nations, and keep law and order.
11. Answers may include the treatment of black Americans as property; lack of citizenship rights for women, black Americans, and servants; and lack of total religious freedom.
12. Answers may include English colonists' right to a voice in government, self-government in the colonies, and colonists' resistance to English efforts to weaken their legislatures, tighten control and abuse their rights.
13. Affirmative answers may include English efforts to increase control over the colonies and abuse of colonists' rights. Negative answers may include better attempts to heal differences and the creation of a system in which the colonies had more freedom but remained a part of the English empire.

Working Together

Answers will vary.

Skills Workshop (text page 85)

Social Studies Skills

1. The snake stands for the English colonies. The snake's body is divided into parts, each labeled with the abbreviation of a colony's name.
2. Franklin's message was that if the colonies did not join together against the French, they would be destroyed. Opinions on whether the cartoon is effective will vary.

Decision-Making Skills

1. A clear goal helps you to judge options.
2. If you do not consider many options, you may not find the best possible way to achieve your goal.
3. Answers may include the following: to set a clear goal, to list all options, to consider the consequences of each option, to compare the consequences and choose the best option, to identify resources and obstacles, to list what you need to do to achieve your goal, to check how well your plan is going and change it if necessary.
4. Students' goals and options will vary.

OVERVIEW

Many issues faced the Constitutional Convention. The decisions made in creating the Constitution were arrived at through debate and compromise. The result was a document that created a strong national government but also divided and checked powers and provided for flexibility and change. To assure approval of the Constitution, the Federalists promised to propose a bill of rights after ratification.

OBJECTIVES

After completing this chapter, students should be able to

- identify the major issues addressed in the Constitutional Convention.
- discuss the role of compromise in creating the Constitution.
- discuss the views of the Federalists and the Anti-Federalists.
- explain how the principles of the Constitution affect the daily life of citizens.

PLANNING GUIDE

Teaching Strategy	Skills	Special Features	Review/Evaluation
Introducing the Chapter: Cooperative Project **Teaching Activity 1:** Individual Project—Nation or State: Which Should Be Stronger? (Section 5-2) **Teaching Activity 2:** Individual Project—The Constitution: "The Supreme Law of the Land" (Section 5-3) **Evaluating Progress:** Individual Project (Section 5-2 or 5-3) **Reinforcement Activity:** Individual Project—Worksheet (Section 5-1 or 5-3) **Enrichment Activity:** Cooperative Project—Worksheet (Section 5-3)	Social Studies Skills Workshop: Interpreting a Flow Chart Decision-Making Skills Workshop: Taking Action **Issues and Decision Making:** Worksheet Chapter 5	Views of Noted Americans: James Madison American Notebook	Section Reviews Chapter 5 Survey **Tests:** Chapter 5 Test **Testing Software** **Additional Resources** **Activity Book** **Citizenship Skills** **Transparencies and Activity Book** **Voices of America**

For reinforcement and enrichment worksheets and unit activities, see the Activity Book.

Teaching Strategy

Introducing the Chapter: Cooperative Project

The delegates to the Constitutional Convention often had conflicting views of government, yet they were able to compromise on major issues in order to create the Constitution. It is important for students to appreciate the role of compromise in the Constitutional Convention and in their everyday lives. In this introductory activity, students work in groups on a task which requires compromise to complete. The activity will require most of a class period.

Write the following jobs on the board: physical therapist, computer programmer, medical assistant, data processing equipment repairer, electrical engineer, travel agent, paralegal person, computer systems analyst, electronics technician, computer operator. Ask students to rank the jobs according to demand in the next five years, with number one being the job in most demand. Explain any jobs students are unfamiliar with.

Allow time for students to complete their lists. [Actual ranking by experts in work force predictions in the Department of Labor: (1) paralegal person, (2) computer programmer, (3) computer systems analyst, (4) medical assistant, (5) data processing equipment repairer, (6) electrical engineer, (7) electronics technician, (8) computer operator, (9) travel agent, (10) physical therapist. See the chart "Career Outlook" in Chapter 17.]

Divide the class into groups of five. Ask each group to discuss its members' individual lists and then combine ideas to produce a group ranking of the jobs in demand. Allow students about 20 minutes to create a list. When students are finished, have each group read its list and write it on the board to make comparisons easier. When all groups have reported, provide the expert ranking. Have students determine if their group rankings were closer than their individual rankings to the experts' list.

After discussing the rankings, ask students the following questions about the process of making their lists:

- How did the group get started?
- Was a leader appointed or did one emerge?
- How did the group work out disagreements?
- What problems were created by the requirement to produce only one list?
- Was everyone in the group completely satisfied with the list?
- What was most difficult about working on this group task for you as an individual?
- What can be gained or lost by compromise?
- What communication skills are needed to reach a compromise?

Ask the class to discuss the meaning of the word *compromise.* (Compromise is a settlement in which both sides agree to give up a part of what each demands.) Ask for examples of compromise in the deliberations of the groups. Discuss how compromise is a part of everyday life. Explain that Chapter 5 is about the compromises that enabled the framers to create the Constitution.

Teaching Activity 1: Individual Project

Nation or State: Which Should Be Stronger?

After reading Section 5-2, give students a chance to evaluate the views of the Federalists and the Anti-Federalists. In this activity students write paragraphs in support of Federalist or Anti-Federalist beliefs and determine their persuasiveness.

Divide the class into two groups and assign students in one group to be Federalists and students in the other to be Anti-Federalists. Randomly assign the following Federalist and Anti-Federalist beliefs to students in the appropriate groups. More than one student can be assigned the same belief.

Federalist Beliefs

- A strong national government can best represent the interests of all of the people.
- A strong national government can protect all citizens against foreign nations.
- A strong national government can pay the nation's debts and keep the value of American money stable.
- Under the Constitution, a strong national government would protect citizens' rights.

Anti-Federalist Beliefs

- A central government is too removed from citizens to understand their needs.
- Vague wording in the Constitution might lead to an abuse of power by the national government.
- A strong national government might swallow up state governments.
- A bill of rights is necessary to ensure that citizens' rights are protected.

Have students write a persuasive paragraph in support of their assigned belief, much like the Federalist farmer's letter in "American Notebook" on text page 98. Students should explain their belief and provide at least one example to support their position. For example, a student might support the Federalist argument for a strong national government for protection against foreign nations by noting the inability of an individual state to repel a foreign invasion. Allow class time to complete the writing or assign it as homework.

Have students read their paragraphs to the class, alternating students from the two groups. Allow the class to ask clarifying questions, but permit no debate of the issues. After all students have read their paragraphs, call for a vote to decide whether to create a strong national government.

Discuss the arguments that were most persuasive to students. Ask students to infer what America would be like if the Anti-Federalists had won. (example: less feeling of national unity and more loyalty to states)

Teaching Activity 2: Individual Project

The Constitution: "The Supreme Law of the Land"

As citizens, students need to understand the Constitution's continuing importance as "the supreme law of the land." In this activity, which can be used after completion of Section 5-3, students use newspaper and magazine articles to evaluate the role of the Constitution in daily life.

Ask students to collect one magazine or newspaper article that describes a current event related to one of the three branches of government. Have each student write a paragraph summarizing the event and describing how it could affect his or her life. This exercise can be done as homework or an in-class assignment.

When the assignment has been completed, divide the students into groups of four. Ask each group to review all of the articles collected by its members and to choose the article that describes an event they believe has the greatest effect on their lives as teenagers. Have each group select a spokesperson to tell the class about the event described in the article and its effect on students.

Evaluating Progress: Individual Project

Only under the Constitution did Americans become united in one nation. In this activity, which may be used after Section 5-2 or at the end of the chapter, students describe the significance of the Constitutional Convention in the role of television commentators.

Ask students to imagine that television had been available during the 1780s. Explain that the Constitutional Convention would have been a major news event, dominating nightly news reports even if cameras had not been allowed in the sessions.

Tell students to assume that they are the television commentator assigned to do the wrap-up on the convention at its conclusion. Direct students to include some background information on the delegates and the convention's setting in Philadelphia. Then have students summarize the proceedings of the convention—the issues discussed and the compromises announced. Have students end their reports with an assessment of the job ahead for the supporters and the opponents of ratification of the Constitution.

Students' commentaries may be presented orally or in writing. Assess the reports in terms of students' understanding of the significance of the Constitutional Convention, identification of the major issues, appreciation of the delegates' ability to compromise, and understanding of the compromises reached.

Reinforcement Activity: Individual Project

Use this activity after students have read Section 5-1 or at the end of the chapter. In Reinforcement Worksheet Chapter 5, "The Constitution: Issues and Compromises," in the Activity Book, students describe how conflicting ideas of government were resolved at the Constitutional Convention.

Introduce the worksheet by reminding students of the many difficult issues that the framers faced at the Constitutional Convention. Explain that the worksheet lists these issues; students must describe two options for resolving each issue and the compromise which was reached. When students have completed their worksheets, review their answers. Discuss why some compromises are no longer in effect.

Enrichment Activity: Cooperative Project

It is important for students to understand how the system of checks and balances operates to control abuse of power in the federal government. In Enrichment Worksheet Chapter 5, "Checks and Balances," in the Activity Book, students describe how each of the three branches of government can limit the power of the other two. This worksheet, which can be used after students have read Section 5-3, will require most of a class period to complete.

Review the principle of checks and balances with students. Then divide the class into groups of three, distribute the worksheet, and review the instructions. Groups should decide if they want to divide the task by having individual students specialize in the legislative, executive, or judicial branch, or to research the worksheet as a group. Before students begin reviewing Section 5-3 and Articles 1-3 of the Constitution (text pages 108–117), they should read the entire worksheet to learn what information is required.

When their worksheets are finished, have the groups share their answers with the class.

Answer Key

CHAPTER 5

Section 5-1 Review (text page 95)

1. See definition for *bicameral* on text page 93.
2. If debates were reported in newspapers, delegates would not feel free to change their minds or to consider the common good of all the states rather than the narrow interests of each state.
3. The three main issues were whether the states or the national government would have more power; how many representatives each state would have in Congress; and who should elect the President and members of Congress.
4. The Great Compromise was a plan proposed by Roger Sherman for a two-house legislature with a House of Representatives elected on the basis of state population and a Senate that had two senators from each state. If both sides had not accepted this plan, the Constitutional Convention probably would have failed.
Analysis. Answers may include the idea that all views had been debated at the convention and

that each side had given up part of what it wanted in order to benefit all.

Section 5-2 Review (text page 99)

1. Answers may include the following: A central government in a distant city would not fairly represent citizens, the "necessary and proper" clause in the Constitution could allow the national government to abuse its power, and the national government could endanger people's liberties because the Constitution lacked a bill of rights.
2. The Federalist papers were written to respond to Anti-Federalist arguments against ratification of the Constitution.
3. Support for the Constitution grew as a result of the Federalists' campaign, Washington and Franklin's support, and Federalist agreement to add a bill of rights to the Constitution.
Analysis. Answers may include the framers' desire to increase support for the Constitution by having Americans in ratifying conventions study the merits of the Constitution rather than members of state legislatures, which would lose some power under the new government.
Data Search. New York's population was 340,000; Virginia's was 692,000. Answers may include Pennsylvania, North Carolina, Maryland, and Connecticut; the new government might not have survived without the support of these populous states.

Section 5-3 Review (text page 105)

1. See definitions for the following terms on the text pages indicated in parentheses: *veto* (101), *delegated powers* (101), *amendments* (103), *federalism* (104), *concurrent powers* (104), *reserved powers* (104), *checks and balances* (105), *impeach* (105).
2. The Preamble states the goals of our government.
3. Some powers belong only to the federal government; some belong only to the states; and others are shared by both.
4. The Constitution divides power between the executive, legislative, and judicial branches and gives each of the three branches ways to limit the power of the other two.
Analysis. Answers may include national unity, justice, and defense achieved through an effective national government; protection of liberty through separation of powers and checks and balances; and responsiveness to new conditions through amendments.

Chapter Survey (text page 106)

Understanding New Vocabulary

1. *Reserved powers* and *concurrent powers* refer to powers given to government in the Constitution. Concurrent powers are shared by the federal and state governments; reserved powers are granted only to the state governments.
2. *Federalism* and *checks and balances* are constitutional principles having to do with division of power. Federalism refers to division of power between the state and federal governments, while checks and balances relates to division of power within the federal government.
Putting It in Writing. Answers may include division of power between the state and federal governments, division of power within the federal government, and limiting each branch's power through checks and balances.

Looking Back at the Chapter

1. They realized that the Confederation government lacked the power to deal with the nation's debts, interstate disputes, and disorder.
2. (a) Many delegates feared that a strong national government might abuse its powers. **(b)** Large states wanted state representation by population, but small states demanded equal representation for all states. **(c)** Some delegates wanted the President and members of Congress to be directly elected by citizens; others distrusted the people's judgment and feared direct election would take away too much power from state legislatures.
3. The delegates divided power between the state and national governments; set up a two-house legislature, with each state having two members in the Senate, and the House of Representatives being elected on the basis of state population; and decided that citizens would elect members of the House, state legislatures would select senators,

and the Electoral College would select the President.
4. Federalists: The Constitution would create a national government strong enough to protect the nation, maintain order, regulate trade and the nation's finances, and guarantee citizens' rights. Anti-Federalists: A central government could not truly represent the people, vague wording in the Constitution enabled the government to abuse its power, and citizens' rights might not be respected because the Constitution lacked a bill of rights.
5. Support grew as a result of the Federalists' effective campaign, Washington and Franklin's support for the plan, and the Federalists' agreement to propose a bill of rights.
6. The six goals are to unite the states under an effective national government; establish fair ways to settle disputes between individuals, between individuals and governments, and between governments; to protect people from the unlawful acts of others; to protect citizens from foreign attack; to create conditions that will benefit all Americans; and to give people freedom to choose where they live and work, what they believe, and who shall represent them in government.
7. The first three articles divide power in the federal government among the legislative, judicial, and executive branches and give each branch ways to limit the power of the other two.
8. Article 4 reduces the possibility of conflict between states. Article 5 enables Americans to change the Constitution through amendments. Article 6 requires officials in state government to acknowledge that federal laws take priority over state laws. Article 7 establishes the procedure for ratification of the Constitution.
9. Affirmative answers may include Madison's proposal of the Virginia Plan and his efforts to gain support for ratification of the Constitution. Negative answers may include the idea that the compromises made to keep the convention from failing entitled all involved delegates to the title.
10. Answers will vary, but opinions should be supported by examples, such as opinion polls that measure public awareness of issues.
11. Evidence may include the principles of federalism, separation of power, and checks and balances; the addition of the Bill of Rights; Article 4 (respect for the rights of states); Article 5 (the states' role in the amendment process); and Article 6 (supremacy of the Constitution).
12. Answers may include prevention of abuse of power by separation of powers, checks and balances, and the Bill of Rights; and the ability to amend the Constitution to reflect changing needs.

Working Together

Answers will vary.

Skills Workshop (text page 107)

Social Studies Skills

1. Amendments can be proposed by Congress or by a national convention called by Congress at the request of two thirds of the state legislatures.
2. Amendments can be ratified by state legislatures or by special state ratifying conventions.
3. There are four ways to propose and then ratify an amendment.
4. Most amendments have been proposed by Congress and ratified by the state legislatures.

Decision-Making Skills

1. The main steps are to set your action goal, to identify resources and obstacles, to list what you have to do to achieve your goal, to carry out your plan, and to judge how well your plan worked.
2. The Federalists identified resources (patriots' support and the arguments of economic experts) and obstacles (members of state legislatures). They determined what they had to do (get a quick vote in states where a majority supported the Constitution, build support in Virginia, Massachusetts, and New York). They carried out their plan (by promising to add a bill of rights, by using Washington's support to help win Virginia, and by writing articles to win over New Yorkers).
3. You identify obstacles and resources in order to determine what you need to do and how to change your plan if necessary.

OVERVIEW

The Federalist promise to add a bill of rights to the Constitution was fulfilled in 1791 when Congress approved and the states ratified the first ten amendments. These amendments spell out individual freedoms, protections against government abuse of power, and rights of citizens accused of crimes. Since ratification, the amendments' broad descriptions of rights have required interpretation by the courts.

OBJECTIVES

After completing this chapter, students should be able to

- explain why a bill of rights was added to the Constitution.
- describe the basic rights listed in the Bill of Rights.
- describe how landmark Supreme Court cases have interpreted First Amendment rights.

PLANNING GUIDE

Teaching Strategy	Skills	Special Features	Review/Evaluation
Introducing the Chapter: Cooperative Project **Teaching Activity 1:** Cooperative Project—Debating the Bill of Rights (Section 6-1) **Teaching Activity 2:** Class Project—The Galactic Bill of Rights (Section 6-2) **Evaluating Progress:** Individual Project (Section 6-3) **Reinforcement Activity:** Individual Project—Worksheet (Section 6-2) **Enrichment Activity:** Individual Project—Worksheet (Section 6-2) **Unit 2 Activity:** First Amendment Rights: A Survey	Decision-Making Lesson: Which Sources Can You Trust? Social Studies Skills Workshop: Using Primary Sources Decision-Making Skills Workshop: Which Sources Can You Trust? **Issues and Decision Making:** Worksheet Chapter 6	American Notebook People Make a Difference: Accused Citizen Fights for Rights	Section Reviews Chapter 6 Survey **Tests:** Chapter 6 Test **Testing Software** **Additional Resources** **Activity Book** **Citizenship Skills** **Transparencies and Activity Book** **Voices of America**

For reinforcement and enrichment worksheets and unit activities, see the Activity Book.

Teaching Strategy

Introducing the Chapter: Cooperative Project

In this introductory activity, students work in groups to organize their knowledge of the rights protected in the Bill of Rights.

On the chalkboard, write the following phrases: individual freedoms, protections against government abuse of power, and rights of citizens accused of crimes.

Divide students into groups of four or five. Point out that the phrases on the board describe the three main categories of rights in the Bill of Rights. Explain that the groups have five minutes to write as many examples of the rights in each category as possible. For instance, an individual freedom is freedom of speech.

When students have completed their lists, give each group a piece of poster paper and a marker. Instruct each group to make a graphic organizer showing the categories and examples. For instance, students might draw three long lines radiating out from a circle labeled "Bill of Rights." On these lines students can write the categories. Examples can be written on shorter lines extending out from the category lines.

Display the posters and provide time for students to examine them. Assess the posters as students read the chapter and revise as necessary.

Teaching Activity 1: Cooperative Project

Debating the Bill of Rights

In this activity students write paragraphs for and against adding a bill of rights to the Constitution and then evaluate their effectiveness. The activity, to be used after Section 6-1, can be done in class or assigned as homework. Discussion will require most of a class period.

Divide students into groups of three or four. Assign each group one of the following arguments:

- The new government has more pressing needs than writing a bill of rights.
- Adding a bill of rights is a way to earn the trust of the people.
- Adding a bill of rights is a way to serve the people.
- A bill of rights is unnecessary because the Constitution protects citizens' rights.
- A bill of rights would cause a flood of new amendments.
- A specific list of rights would limit citizens' rights because some might be overlooked.

The task for each group is to write one to two paragraphs in support of its assigned argument. For example, students could list tasks facing Congress, such as passing laws concerning the nation's debt or defense, in order to show that the government had more pressing needs than preparing a bill of rights. Encourage students to review Chapters 4 and 5 to gather information.

When the students have finished the activity, ask for a volunteer from each group to read its paragraph to the class. Have students discuss why each argument is effective or ineffective.

Have students discuss why, based on the various arguments, they think the Bill of Rights was added to the Constitution. Conclude by having students speculate about how our country might be different today if the Bill of Rights had not become part of the Constitution.

Teaching Activity 2: Class Project

The Galactic Bill of Rights

In this activity students use information about the Bill of Rights to amend a fictitious constitution to include a list of rights. The activity, which will require at least a full class period, can be used after students have read the material in Section 6-2.

Ask the class to imagine that it is the year 2050. In an effort to address concern about the lack of individual rights listed in the Universal Decree of Confederation, representatives from across the galaxy meet to write a galactic bill of rights.

Have students assume they are the galactic representatives. Brainstorm some concerns that a galaxy government might have in common with the First Congress in writing a bill of rights. Concerns might include an individual's right to be protected from interplanetary laser scans or the right to be tried by a jury of peers from one's own planet.

Divide students into groups of four to write a galactic bill of rights. It should have a preamble followed by a list of rights for all galaxy inhabitants. Make sure that the document is realistic enough for people to accept its principles. Provide class time or assign as homework.

When this assignment is finished, combine groups of four into groups of eight and have these groups synthesize their statements into one master list. Ask each group of eight to read its bill of rights to the whole class. Combine similar ideas until there is one bill of rights.

When finished with the task, have students review Section 6-2 to compare the decisions they had to make in creating the Galactic Bill of Rights with those made by the creators of our Bill of Rights.

Evaluating Progress: Individual Project

To assess students' understanding of the interpretations of First Amendment rights in landmark court cases, ask each student to analyze one of the two case studies in Section 6-3. Students should use the following structure for their analyses:

- Name of the case:
- Issues in the case:
- Arguments presented by one side:
- Arguments presented by the other side:
- The Court's decision:
- Reasons given for the Court's decision:
- My evaluation of the Court's decision:

Evaluation of students' analyses should be based on a clear statement of the issues in the case, correct assessment of the Court's decision and reasoning, and a personal evaluation which reflects an understanding of the conflicting issues involved in freedom of speech.

Reinforcement Activity: Individual Project

After completing Section 6-2, students can apply their knowledge of the Bill of Rights in Reinforcement Worksheet Chapter 6, "Protecting Individual Freedoms," in the Activity Book. Students can complete the worksheet in 15 to 20 minutes.

Introduce the activity by reviewing the worksheet directions with students. Using the worksheet, students read hypothetical situations and identify the rights that are being abused and the amendments that protect those rights.

Review students' answers to the worksheet in class. Challenge students to describe other situations in which rights protected in the Bill of Rights are denied to citizens.

Enrichment Activity: Individual Project

As students study the First Amendment, it is important that they recognize situations in which their freedom of speech may be limited. In Enrichment Worksheet Chapter 6, "The Hazelwood Case: Students and Free Speech," in the Activity Book, students analyze a case involving censorship of a school newspaper. The worksheet can be used after students have read "Protections of Individual Freedoms" in Section 6-2. About 30 minutes should be allowed to complete the worksheet in class, but it can be assigned as homework.

Introduce the activity by reminding students that freedom of speech is not unlimited. Distribute the worksheet and have a volunteer read the case study. Make certain students understand that their task is to write one paragraph supporting the students' right to publish the articles and another supporting the principal's right to bar publication of the articles.

After students have completed the worksheet, have them share their reasons for supporting the students and the principal. Then use a show of hands to determine how students would have voted as Supreme Court justices.

Tell students that in January 1988 the Supreme Court ruled, 5 to 3, in favor of the principal. Justice Byron R. White, writing the majority opinion, stated, "A school needs not tolerate student speech that is inconsistent with its basic educational mission, even though the government could not censor similar speech outside the school." Encourage discussion of the decision.

Because the Tinker case, described in Section 6-3, also deals with students' freedom of speech, you may wish to compare the Court's decisions in the two cases. Commenting on them, Justice White said:

> The question whether the First Amendment requires a school to tolerate particular student speech—the question that we addressed in *Tinker*—is different from the question whether the First Amendment requires a school to promote particular student speech. The former question addresses educators' ability to silence a student's personal expression that happens to occur on school premises. The latter question concerns educators' authority over school-sponsored publications, theatrical productions, and other expressive activities that bear the imprimatur of the school.

White concluded that the student newspaper, written by the school's Journalism II class, clearly was part of the school's curriculum.

Answer Key

CHAPTER 6

Section 6-1 Review (text page 133)

1. Congress proposed all 26 amendments.
2. Amendments may be ratified by the approval of the legislatures or special conventions of three fourths of the states.
3. The Constitution did not adequately protect citizens' rights. The Constitution already limited the government's power.
Evaluation. Answers may include the importance of passing laws to get the new government started or the importance to the new government of earning the trust of its citizens.

Section 6-2 Review (text page 139)

1. See definitions for the following terms on the text pages indicated in parentheses: *separation of church and state* (134), *eminent domain* (137), *due process of law* (137), *double jeopardy* (138).
2. The First Amendment protects freedom of religion, freedom of speech, freedom of the press, freedom of assembly, and freedom to petition.
3. The Third Amendment prevents the government from placing soldiers in a home without the owner's consent; the Fourth Amendment prevents unreasonable searches and seizures; the Fifth Amendment requires the government to pay owners a fair price if their property is seized for public use, requires an indictment for serious crimes, and protects the accused from standing trial for the same crime twice (double jeopardy).
4. The Sixth and Seventh amendments guarantee a citizen's right to a speedy, public, and fair trial, and the Eighth Amendment protects accused persons from long-term imprisonment before trial by forbidding unreasonably high bail.
Synthesis. Answers may include the idea that under the Bill of Rights every citizen is guaranteed certain freedoms, protected from abuse of power by government officials, and given certain rights when accused of crimes.

Data Search. Each of the documents gave rights to people accused of crimes and/or protections for people convicted of crimes. Only the two American documents protect individual freedoms.

Section 6-3 Review (text page 145)

1. The first ten amendments are broad descriptions which do not explain how the rights apply to every situation. Also certain rights have to be weighed against other rights.
2. Case studies show the principles of the Constitution being put into action.
3. The Tinker case involved students who wore black armbands to school to protest American involvement in Vietnam and were suspended. The Tinkers' parents argued that the school board was denying the students' right to free speech. The Supreme Court ruled in favor of the students. The Skokie case involved efforts by a city government to block a parade by the American Nazi party; the Nazis declared this a violation of their First Amendment rights. The Supreme Court ruled that the Nazis had the right to march.
Application. A judge must weigh the rights of the person arrested against the need to protect the public from a possible murderer. The individual has a right to be protected from unreasonable searches and a right of due process. A judge must consider whether the arresting officers had good reason to enter the suspect's house in the interest of protecting the public.

Decision-Making Lesson (text pages 146–147)

1. Source A is likely to be more reliable because it is written by a prize-winning journalist who has included in her article viewpoints of the students and the school board members. The author of Source B is likely to be biased against the Court's decision and does not include student quotes.
2. (b) The record would be objective. The other two sources are likely to be biased.
3. (c) Reputation and background indicate the author's degree of expertise. The number of books written and the dates of publication do not indicate the author's knowledge of the subject.
4. (b) Journalism awards reflect a reputation for accuracy; mere publication does not. Neither does the fact that the person witnessed the events; an eyewitness may still present a biased account.
5. Reliability means trustworthiness.
6. You can check the qualifications of the people who prepared the source, check their reputations, check their methods of preparing the source, and check whether the source agrees with sources known to be reliable.
7. Examples may include trying to decide how to settle a conflict with another student. Students could name people whose advice they would trust and explain why.

Chapter Survey (text page 148)

Understanding New Vocabulary

1. (b) *Separation of church and state* relates to *protection of individual rights* because the Bill of Rights declares that the government may not favor any religion or establish an official religion.
2. (a) *Eminent domain* relates to *protection against abuse of power* because the Bill of Rights requires the government to pay a fair price to the owner of property taken for public use.
3. (c) *Due process of law* relates to *protection of the accused* because the Bill of Rights requires the government to treat accused persons fairly according to procedures established by law.
Putting It in Writing. Accused people are entitled to due process of law. This may include protection against double jeopardy, unfairly high bail, and "cruel and unusual punishments." Other guarantees may include being informed of one's rights; legal counsel; and a speedy, public, and fair trial.

Looking Back at the Chapter

1. An amendment may be proposed by Congress, after approval by a two-thirds vote in both houses, or by a national convention called for by two thirds of the state legislatures. It may be ratified by the approval of the legislatures or special conventions in three fourths of the states.
2. The Federalists had promised a bill of rights to gain Anti-Federalist support for ratification. Also, adding a bill of rights would help gain the people's trust in the new government.

3. Freedom of religion allows every citizen to practice his or her religion, or no religion, and prevents government from favoring any religion; freedom of speech protects the right of every citizen to speak and write freely as long as another is not slandered; freedom of the press permits citizens to criticize the government without fearing arrest; freedom of assembly allows citizens to meet together to protest government actions; freedom to petition permits citizens to call their grievances to the attention of the government.
4. Answers may include freedom from unreasonable searches and seizures, and the right to payment for property taken by the government.
5. The Sixth Amendment guarantees defendants in criminal trials the right to a speedy, public, and fair trial by jury. They cannot be kept in jail a long time awaiting trial and have the rights to a lawyer, to know what the accusations are, and to question witnesses. The Seventh Amendment guarantees the right to a jury trial in conflicts involving property worth more than twenty dollars.
6. Judges interpret the meaning of citizens' rights.
7. The Court declared that symbols can be a form of speech and thus are protected by the First Amendment. It also established that citizens under 18 have a basic right to free speech.
8. The courts ruled that the expression of all ideas—even ideas that threaten our basic principles—is protected under the First Amendment.
9. The Bill of Rights, like the Constitution, is based on the need to guard against tyranny by limiting government's power.
10. Answers may include the idea that for a democracy to work, people need to have the rights to speak and write freely, meet freely to consider public questions, and call their grievances to the attention of the government.
11. Answers will vary. One example is freedom of speech which gives students the right to express their views.
12. Answers will vary. One example is the right to have prayer in school.
13. Answers may include the crucial role the Bill of Rights has played in determining the meaning of citizens' rights. Examples may include the Miranda decision and the Tinker and Skokie cases.

Working Together

Answers will vary.

Skills Workshop (text page 149)

Social Studies Skills

1. The two judges did not agree. Justice Vinson believed that speech encouraging the overthrow of the government can be limited. Justice Black believed the decision violated the First Amendment.
2. Justice Vinson expresses the Court's ruling. He uses the word *we* because he speaks for the Court majority.
3. The reasoning for the Court's decision is expressed in Justice Vinson's statement that the threat of overthrowing the government by force was enough reason to limit free speech. He declared that the government must be able to protect itself against revolution.
4. Students opposing the decision may argue that government censorship of expressions of opposition, even violent opposition, violates a basic principle of freedom that the government was created to protect. Those agreeing with the opinion may argue that the government must maintain its security in order to protect citizens' rights.

Decision-Making Skills

1. Source C is likely to be most reliable because it includes expert commentary on the case by law professors. It also provides balanced information by including the arguments of lawyers on both sides. Source A only summarizes the decision and is unlikely to provide significant information on the issues. Source B is likely to be biased against censorship of school newspapers.
2. Students should summarize in their own words the steps outlined in the lesson on page 146.
3. The skill helps one locate trustworthy information on which to base a decision.
4. Examples of decisions will vary. Students might mention a decision-making situation such as choosing elective classes. They could name people whose advice they would trust and explain why.

OVERVIEW

The Constitution has survived because it can respond to the needs of a growing and changing society. This chapter illustrates the flexibility of the Constitution by examining the amendments that extended citizenship and suffrage to more Americans. The role of the Supreme Court in applying constitutional principles to a changing society is also examined.

OBJECTIVES

After completing this chapter, students should be able to

- describe how Americans have amended the Constitution to fit changing needs and attitudes.
- explain the constitutional amendments that extended citizenship and voting rights.
- describe the Supreme Court's role in making the Constitution a flexible document.

PLANNING GUIDE

Teaching Strategy	Skills	Special Features	Review/Evaluation
Introducing the Chapter: Class Project **Teaching Activity 1:** Cooperative Project—Equality by Amendment (Section 7-1) **Teaching Activity 2:** Individual Project—Future Amendments Survey (Section 7-1) **Evaluating Progress:** Individual Project (Section 7-2) **Reinforcement Activity:** Individual Project—Worksheet (Section 7-1) **Enrichment Activity:** Individual Project—Worksheet (Section 7-2)	Social Studies Skills Workshop: Using Primary Sources Decision-Making Skills Workshop: Which Sources Can You Trust? **Issues and Decision Making:** Worksheet Chapter 7	American Notebook Views of Noted Americans: John Marshall Harlan Issues That Affect You: A Case Study—Students' Rights In Their Own Words: Thomas Jefferson—First Inaugural Address	Section Reviews Chapter 7 Survey Unit 2 Survey **Tests:** Chapter 7 Test, Unit 2 Test, Quarter 1 Test **Testing Software** **Additional Resources** **Activity Book** **Citizenship Skills** **Transparencies and Activity Book** **Voices of America**

For reinforcement and enrichment worksheets and unit activities, see the Activity Book.

Teaching Strategy

Introducing the Chapter: Class Project

Before beginning this chapter on our living Constitution, it is important for students to understand why the Constitution required change, especially after the addition of the Bill of Rights. This activity helps students understand the need for constitutional amendments. It will take 20 to 30 minutes of class time. You may wish to assign the writing task as homework.

Begin the activity by writing "secure the blessings of liberty to ourselves and our posterity" on the chalkboard. Help students recall that this is one of the goals of the Constitution stated in the Preamble. Ask students which groups of Americans had the freedom to choose where they worked and lived and who represented them in government at the time the Constitution was ratified. Help students recall that in most colonies—and in most of the new states—only white men who owned property were granted citizenship and the right to vote.

Ask students what word is often used to describe a lack of equal rights. When *discrimination* is mentioned, write it on the chalkboard and have students define it by giving specific examples of unfair treatment. On the board list groups of people, such as African Americans and women, who were treated unfairly by the states. Then have students suggest other groups that have faced discrimination in our country and add them to the list. (Native Americans, Asians, Hispanics, Jews, Catholics)

Ask students to describe incidents of discrimination they have experienced. If students have not experienced racial, gender, or religious discrimination, they may have encountered age discrimination—not being allowed into certain events or not being treated with equity as consumers. As students relate their experiences, write on the board the words they use to describe their feelings.

Explain that students are going to write a cinquain (sin-KAYN), a five-line poem with a structure based on syllable count, on the topic of discrimination. On the board, write the following structure for a cinquain:

Line	Syllables	Content
1	two	Title
2	four	Describes title
3	six	Expresses action
4	eight	Expresses feeling
5	two	Refers to the title

Write the following cinquain on the chalkboard:

Unjust
Nothing for me
Marching, protests, riots
Hatred explodes, hopelessness boils
Unfair

Answer questions, then allow class time for students to write the poem, or assign it for homework. If you feel students need an alternative assignment, ask them to write one to three paragraphs describing an incident of discrimination they have experienced and their reactions.

After the assignment is completed, post the poems/narratives and allow time for students to read their classmates' writings. Conclude the activity by having students discuss how people who were denied citizenship might have felt.

Teaching Activity 1: Cooperative Project

Equality by Amendment

Section 7-1 discusses six amendments to the Constitution that extended citizenship and/or voting rights to more Americans. In this activity students clarify the importance of these amendments by making posters. The activity, to be used after Section 7-1, will require a full class period if students make the posters in class; however, poster creation can be assigned as an out-of-class project.

Provide poster paper and marking pens for the posters. Also provide old magazines and newspapers for clipping articles, photographs, and advertisements. Before introducing the activity, write the numbers of the amendments—13, 14, 15, 19, 24, and 26—on slips of paper, with each amendment repeated twice for a total of 12 slips.

Begin the activity by dividing students into groups of two or three and having each group select a slip of paper. Explain that each group is to make a poster illustrating and explaining the amendment chosen. Write the following instructions on the board and discuss them with students.

- Use a title and the date the amendment was ratified on the poster.
- Pictures or diagrams can be used on the poster to explain the meaning of the amendment.
- Attach advertisements or newspaper articles to the poster to show how the amendment affects everyday life.
- Add a one-paragraph summary to the poster describing how the amendment extends justice by giving more Americans citizenship and/or the right to vote.

Students may divide up the four tasks or work together. Allow time to collect the articles, draw, write, and assemble the poster. After their posters are completed, allow class time for student groups to explain their posters.

Teaching Activity 2: Individual Project

Future Amendments Survey

It is important for students to appreciate how controversial constitutional amendments often are. In this activity, to be used after Section 7-1, students interview adults about two suggested amendments and then analyze the arguments pro and con. Most of a class period should be devoted to summarizing survey results; the actual interviewing will be done out of class.

Before introducing the activity, choose two amendments that have been suggested and are currently being debated by citizens. Examples include a new equal rights amendment and proposals to allow official prayers to be said in public schools, to allow capital punishment for minors, to prohibit abortion, and to make burning of the American flag a statutory crime. Select issues that are of special interest to young people and/or residents of your community.

Introduce the activity by recalling with students proposals for amendments in Section 7-1. Explain that class members will conduct a survey to determine local citizens' views on two proposed amendments. Describe the proposals and answer students' questions about them. Then have students write brief descriptions of the proposals in their own words to use during their interviews.

Instruct students in techniques of interviewing by asking them to list the necessary formalities and procedures of an interview—introducing oneself, defining the purpose of the interview, asking structured questions, following up on answers, and thanking the interviewee at the conclusion of the interview. Write the following interview questions on the chalkboard for students to use.

- What is your opinion of a proposed constitutional amendment to ________________.
- What do you think is the strongest argument for the amendment?
- What do you think is the strongest argument against the amendment?

Explain to students that they are asking interviewees to give one argument for and another against each of the proposed amendments so that the class can compile as many different arguments as possible.

Allow several days for students to conduct the survey. Students should be encouraged to interview adults in their families, at school, in the neighborhood, and in other places where they come into contact with adults. Each student should interview at least five people.

After the interviews are completed, organize students into groups to compile the data. One group should record the number of people for and against each proposed amendment. A second group should record all of the arguments in favor of each amendment, and a third group should record all of the arguments against each amendment. Students in the "arguments" groups should edit and evaluate responses in order to compile a list without duplication. Have students write the arguments on the chalkboard, poster paper, or overhead transparencies so that all students can see the results.

Review the compiled data. Conclude the activity by asking students the following questions:

- Were people well-informed or poorly informed about the issues?
- What emotional responses to the amendments did you observe?
- What effect do you think age, sex, or religious background had on reactions to the amendments?

Evaluating Progress: Individual Project

Use this activity after students have completed the chapter in order to evaluate their understanding of the concept of the living Constitution. In the activity students trace the history of the Fourteenth Amendment and analyze how it has been interpreted in important Supreme Court cases.

Begin the activity by writing the following cases on the chalkboard: *Plessy* v. *Ferguson, Brown* v. *Board of Education of Topeka*, *University of California Regents* v. *Bakke, Phillips* v. *Martin Marietta Corporation.* Remind students that in each of these cases the Supreme Court reinterpreted the meaning of the Fourteenth Amendment in light of new situations.

Have students make a chart of the information in Section 7-2 about these cases using the following headings: *Central Issue in the Case, Court's Decision,* and *Effect of Decision on Citizens.* The cases should be listed in chronological order.

After students have completed this activity, direct them to write one paragraph explaining the Fourteenth Amendment and describing why it was added to the Constitution. Then ask students to explain how the Supreme Court's interpretation of the meaning of the amendment changed in each of the cases on the chart.

Criteria for assessment should focus on students' understanding of the principle of the Fourteenth Amendment and the changes in Supreme Court interpretations of this principle.

Reinforcement Activity: Individual Project

Use this reinforcement activity after students have read the material in Section 7-1. In the activity students trace the changes in American citizenship and voting rights that have taken place since 1787.

Introduce the activity by emphasizing to students that during the last two centuries there has been a great change in the requirements for citizenship and the right to vote. Distribute Reinforcement Worksheet Chapter 7, "A History of Citizenship and Suffrage," in the Activity Book and clarify directions for students.

After students have completed their worksheets, review answers. Ask volunteers to describe how the events listed in the worksheet have affected their lives.

Enrichment Activity: Individual Project

Use this enrichment activity after students have read the material in Section 7-2. In the activity students distinguish interpretations in three landmark Supreme Court cases involving the constitutional principle of equal protection.

Introduce the activity by reviewing with students the role of the courts, especially the Supreme Court, in determining whether constitutional principles have been correctly followed by government officials and other citizens. Distribute Enrichment Worksheet Chapter 7, "Equal Protection of the Laws," in the Activity Book and have students first write a definition and example of equal protection. Discuss and then have students follow the instructions on the worksheet.

After the worksheets are completed, review answers and then lead students in a discussion of the cases described in the worksheet. Do students think the Court's decisions have settled the issues to most citizens' satisfaction? Which decision has been most controversial? Why? Which decision has had the greatest effect on students' lives? Which decision(s) may have to be reevaluated by the Supreme Court in the future? Why?

Answer Key

CHAPTER 7

Section 7-1 Review (text page 157)

1. See definition for *suffrage* on text page 155.
2. It takes the power to grant citizenship away from the states and says "all persons born or naturalized in the United States are citizens."
3. The efforts of suffragists and the important economic role played by women factory workers convinced more and more Americans that women deserved to vote.
4. Many Americans believed that citizens old enough to fight and to die for their country should not be denied the right to vote.
Evaluation. Opinions will vary. In supporting a particular voting age, students should discuss the maturity of most people at that age.
Data Search. An average of only 39.7 percent of 18-to-20-year-olds have voted in recent presidential elections, the lowest turnout of any age group. Thus, voters in this age group have not been making very good use of their right to vote.

Section 7-2 Review (text page 163)

1. See definitions for the following terms on the text pages indicated in parentheses: *segregation* (159), *affirmative action* (161).
2. The Constitution is a framework of general principles that later generations can apply to a variety of situations.
3. The Supreme Court has the power to interpret the meaning of the Constitution, but may not add, remove, or change any of the words in it.
4. The Plessy and Brown cases show how the Court can change its interpretation of a constitutional principle as attitudes and conditions in society change. The Brown decision overturned the Plessy ruling, declaring that segregation was no longer allowed under the principle of equal protection.
Evaluation. Answers may include the idea that if the Constitution were made up of specific rules, it would not serve the needs of an ever-changing society. The Constitution would have to be changed so often to meet new situations or problems that it would be meaningless.

Issues That Affect You: A Case Study (text pages 164–165)

1. The use of trained dogs and pocket searches was constitutional under the doctrine of *loco parentis*. Faculty and school officials who stand in the position of "substitute parent" legally can take actions to maintain order and discipline.
2. The body search was unconstitutional because the court believed that the school officials went too far under the circumstances. Students do not give up their constitutional rights when they are on school property, including the Fourth Amendment right to privacy.
3. Yes. If the search was unconstitutional, it was so whether or not drugs were found. If unconstitutional, the drugs could not be used as evidence against Diane. Thus, there would be no case and charges would have to be dropped.
4. The court would have decided the case in the same way whether students were inside or outside the building. As long as the students were on school property, the doctrine of *loco parentis* applies.

Chapter Survey (text page 166)

Understanding New Vocabulary

1. (c) *Suffrage* is related to the passage of the Nineteenth Amendment because this amendment gave the right to vote to women.
2. (a) *Segregation* is related to the Plessy case because the Court ruled that segregating blacks from whites was constitutional as long as facilities for each group were of equal quality.
3. (b) *Affirmative action* is related to the case of *University of California Regents* v. *Bakke* because the Court decided that the university's affirmative action program was unconstitutional.
Putting It in Writing. Answers may include the idea that segregation violates the principle of equal protection because blacks are not being treated equally. Affirmative action programs that discriminate against whites only because of their race also violate the equal protection principle because whites are not being treated equally.

Looking Back at the Chapter

1. The framers needed to ensure that the southern states, which used slave labor, would ratify the Constitution.
2. Answers may include the North's victory in the Civil War; passage of the Thirteenth Amendment in 1865 (abolition of slavery); passage of the Fourteenth Amendment in 1868 (citizenship for African Americans); passage of the Fifteenth Amendment in 1870 (right of African Americans to vote); and passage of the Twenty-fourth Amendment in 1964 (illegality of the poll tax).
3. In the traditional view, the only proper place for women was working in the home and caring for the family. This view changed because increasing numbers of women took jobs by the late 1800s and became active in solving social problems. Also suffragists gained the public's attention, calling for women's right to vote.
4. The Twenty-sixth Amendment gave 18-year-olds the right to vote.
5. Answers may include passage of the Fifteenth Amendment in response to the abolition of slavery and citizenship for African Americans; passage of the Nineteenth Amendment in response to the growing role of women in the nation's economy and politics; and passage of the Twenty-fourth Amendment in response to the service of millions of young Americans in World War II, the Korean War, and the Vietnam War.
6. A Supreme Court decision is not necessarily permanent. It may be overturned by an amendment (overturning of Dred Scott decision by Thirteenth Amendment) or by a later Court decision (overturning of *Plessy* v. *Ferguson* by *Brown* v. *Board of Education of Topeka*).
7. The Court has the final say over whether constitutional principles have been correctly followed by government officials and other citizens.
8. *Brown* v. *Board of Education of Topeka* made all segregation laws unconstitutional.
9. The Supreme Court applies the general principles of the Constitution to new situations, reducing the need for amendments. In the Bakke and Phillips cases, the Supreme Court applied the constitutional principle of equal protection, originally intended to prevent states from denying rights to African Americans, to two new situations. In the Bakke case, the Court ruled that affirmative action programs that discriminate against white men only because of their race are unconstitutional. In the Phillips case, the Court ruled that unequal hiring policies for men and women are unconstitutional.
10. Answers may include the dissatisfaction of both northerners and southerners with the compromises made at the Constitutional Convention and the growing tension between the North and the South in the growing nation.
11. Answers may include the denial of citizenship to African Americans after the Civil War and the passage of the Fourteenth Amendment (citizenship for African Americans), the Fifteenth Amendment (suffrage for African Americans), and the Twenty-fourth Amendment (illegality of the poll tax).
12. Answers will vary. Two examples: a new equal rights amendment and a school prayer amendment.

Working Together 2

Answers will vary.

Skills Workshop (text page 167)

Social Studies Skills

1. The photo shows a girl holding a protest sign. Details may include the following: She is standing alone on a sidewalk; she is holding the sign up high; she is smiling and seems happy; she seems to be about ten to twelve years old; and her sign says "Girls demand equality. We deserve paper routes."
2. Answers may vary, but most students will infer that this girl has applied for a paper route and was rejected because of her sex.
3. Opinions may vary. Most students will probably answer that the decision in the Phillips case should apply in this situation because there is nothing about the job of delivering papers that would justify one hiring policy for boys and another for girls.

Decision-Making Skills

1. Source A is likely to be the most reliable because it provides objective information on voting patterns. Source B is likely to be biased against giving 18-year-olds the right to vote. Source C provides opinions of only a small sampling of parents, none of whom can accurately evaluate the political maturity of 18-year-olds in general.
2. Directions may vary but should be worded so that a younger student can follow them.

In Their Own Words (text page 168)

1. Jefferson states that majority rule must be reasonable and protect the rights of the minority. Answers in agreement with this principle may include examples of situations in which rights, such as freedom of speech or freedom of religion, are denied to a minority.
2. Answers will vary. Two examples: Maintaining "peace, commerce, and honest friendship with all nations, entangling alliances with none" will help the nation avoid conflict and war. Giving "equal and exact justice to all men" and "assuring trial by juries impartially selected" will help maintain the individual freedoms of Americans.
3. Answers will vary. One example: "The preservation of the general government in its whole constitutional rigor" is most important. Under this government, Americans became united in one nation. This government also has real governing power in matters of national concern and ensures that the Constitution remains a living document.

Unit 2 Survey (text page 169)

Looking Back at the Unit

1. The American tradition of representative government can be traced back to direct democracy in ancient Greece; the republic in ancient Rome; and the English tradition of government, which was based on limiting the power of the monarch and giving basic rights to all citizens.
2. The founders feared a strong national government might abuse its powers. The Constitution divides power between the states and the federal government; divides power within the federal government between the legislative, executive, and judicial branches; and sets up ways for each branch to limit the powers of the others.
3. The Bill of Rights was added to the Constitution to fulfill the Federalists' promise to the Anti-Federalists to add such a document if the Constitution was ratified. Examples of protections will vary. One example: the First Amendment's protection of the freedoms of religion, speech, the press, assembly, and petition.
4. The Constitution can be amended to meet changing needs and attitudes. Also, the Supreme Court applies general constitutional principles to new situations.

Taking a Stand

Answers may include arguments cited in the discussion and/or arguments students develop, for example, state and/or national bans on specific weapons, such as semi-automatic assault rifles.

OVERVIEW

The legislative branch of the federal government is responsible for making the nation's laws. Members of the Senate and the House of Representatives share the responsibility of balancing the needs of constituents with those of the nation. Congress has broad delegated and implied powers, but there are limits to keep these powers in check.

OBJECTIVES

After completing this chapter, students should be able to

- identify the general responsibilities of lawmakers.
- compare the specific responsibilities of and requirements for members of Congress.
- distinguish between delegated and implied powers of Congress.
- describe how a bill becomes a law.

PLANNING GUIDE

Teaching Strategy	Skills	Special Features	Review/Evaluation
Introducing the Chapter: Cooperative Project **Teaching Activity 1:** Class Project—Responsibilities and Skills of Legislators (Section 8-1) **Teaching Activity 2:** Cooperative Project—From Bill to Law: A Legislative Board Game (Section 8-4) **Evaluating Progress:** Individual Project (Section 8-2 or 8-4) **Reinforcement Activity:** Individual Project—Worksheet (Section 8-3) **Enrichment Activity:** Individual Project—Worksheet (Section 8-3) **Unit 3 Activity:** Creating Congressional Districts	Decision-Making Lesson: What Relates to Your Subject? Social Studies Skills Workshop: Analyzing Circle Graphs Decision-Making Skills Workshop: What Relates to Your Subject? **Issues and Decision Making:** Worksheet Chapter 8	People Make a Difference: Couple Gets Congress to Listen American Notebook	Section Reviews Chapter 8 Survey **Tests:** Chapter 8 Test **Testing Software** **Additional Resources** **Activity Book** **Citizenship Skills** **Transparencies and Activity Book** **Voices of America**

For reinforcement and enrichment worksheets and unit activities, see the Activity Book.

Teaching Strategy

Introducing the Chapter: Cooperative Project

Members of Congress share the responsibility of balancing the needs of the people they represent with those of the whole nation. In this introductory activity students gain understanding of the conflicting demands on legislators. The activity will take a full class period.

Begin the activity by asking students to assume that they are represented in the House of Representatives by Miriam Greenhaven. On the chalkboard, list groups that are prominent in your community, such as teachers, farmers, parents, environmentalists, businesspeople, Italian Americans, and Puerto Rican Americans. Explain that these are some of the politically active groups in your district.

Next list the following bills on the board: (1) a proposal to build a new highway which would run through property owned by people in Representative Greenhaven's district, (2) a proposal to increase the minimum wage by fifty cents per hour, (3) a proposal to lower import taxes on foreign products, (4) a proposal to increase gasoline taxes by five cents per gallon to pay for improved mass transit.

Divide the class into the groups listed on the chalkboard. Explain that the groups are to discuss each bill and decide whether to support or oppose it. Encourage students to create specific situations to explain their decisions. For example, a group of parents might oppose the new highway because it would be built near a school but support an increase in the minimum wage because their teenage children work in minimum wage jobs.

Allow 25 to 30 minutes for groups to discuss their responses, then conduct a town meeting as Representative Greenhaven to seek constituents' opinions on the bills. Discuss one bill at a time and have each group explain its position. Tally the results on the chalkboard with a plus (+) or minus (−) to indicate support or opposition.

Before concluding, have students tell how they believe Representative Greenhaven should vote on each bill. Explain that in Chapter 8 they will be reading about the legislative branch of government in which the hypothetical Representative Greenhaven serves.

Teaching Activity 1: Class Project

Responsibilities and Skills of Legislators

This activity will help students understand and appreciate the skills needed by lawmakers. The activity can be used after students have finished reading Section 8-1. Depending on the extent of students' discussion, the activity can take from 20 minutes to an entire class period to complete.

As a class, have students review Section 8-1 and describe all of the tasks required of a member of Congress, including learning about issues, debating, voting, and doing casework. Write these tasks on the chalkboard. Next, ask students to explain what kind of skills are necessary to do each of the tasks. Write the skills beside the tasks. Skills might include good listening, hiring and managing a staff, and speech making.

Conclude the activity with a discussion of the following questions:

- Why do people run for Congress?
- Is there anything about the job of representative or senator that should be changed?
- Do we expect too much from our legislators? Why or why not?
- What do you appreciate about our legislators after reading this section?

Teaching Activity 2: Cooperative Project

From Bill to Law: A Legislative Board Game

One way for students to use the information they read in Sections 8-3 and 8-4 is to design a board game that follows the process of how a bill becomes a law. Students may work in small groups or in pairs to create their games. The activity can take a class period or be assigned as homework.

Students will need heavy construction paper or poster board, crayons or markers, and materials for board pieces. Distribute these materials after students have designed their game boards.

Begin the activity by explaining that students are to design and construct a board game to demonstrate how a bill becomes a law. Ask students to decide first if they are going to show the legislative process of the Senate or the House of Representatives. Next, have students list all of the actions that can occur before a bill becomes a law, such as introducing the bill and assigning the bill to committee. The last action described should be sending the bill to the other house for approval and, if approved, sending it to the President. Students should review the chapter to identify specific actions.

Once the content for the game is decided, students can design the board. If squares are used to depict the actions, students will have to determine how many squares are necessary and their order. The game's first square should be labeled *Start.* Encourage groups to name their game, illustrate their board, perhaps invent a bill as the game's theme, and develop a set of playing rules. Remind students that if a bill is killed along the way, it can be revived by starting the process again.

After the games are completed, have students play one another's games. Ask students to critique the games for accuracy and organization. Allow time for students to revise their games after their classmates' critiques.

Evaluating Progress: Individual Project

To assess students' understanding of congressional responsibilities and powers, ask students to design a campaign brochure for a candidate for the Senate or the House of Representatives. This activity can be used after Section 8-2 or at the end of the chapter.

Begin by telling students that they are to make a brochure that "sells" their candidate. They will need to think about the powers of Congress, the tasks of representatives and senators, and how their candidate is qualified for the position. Students may use themselves as candidates or create fictitious ones. Share the following requirements for the brochure with students.

- Include the name of the candidate, the office he or she is seeking, party affiliation, and a photograph or a picture.
- Describe how the candidate meets the requirements to run for this office.
- Describe at least four responsibilities of the office and the skills of the candidate to meet those responsibilities.
- State the political beliefs of the candidate that show understanding of the delegated and the implied powers of Congress.
- List experiences that will influence the public to vote for the candidate.

Give each student a sheet of paper and have them fold it into thirds to create a brochure.

Assess the brochures on originality, students' understanding of congressional functions and legislators' responsibilities, and effectiveness in "selling" the candidate.

Reinforcement Activity: Individual Project

In this activity students use their knowledge of Section 8-3 to determine leaders in an imaginary

Congress. They also describe the responsibilities of congressional leaders.

After students have read Section 8-3, distribute Reinforcement Worksheet Chapter 8, "Choosing Congressional Leaders," in the Activity Book. Make certain students understand how to identify the majority and minority parties in Congress. When students are finished, review their worksheet answers. Discuss the differences in the number of majority and minority party members in the imaginary Congress and the current Congress.

Enrichment Activity: Individual Project

Students learn about congressional leaders and committees in Section 8-3. In Enrichment Worksheet Chapter 8, "Who's Who in Congress," in the Activity Book, students research the names of people who currently hold congressional offices. The worksheet can be done in class or as a homework project.

Distribute the worksheet and review the instructions. Help students locate almanacs and current reference books, such as the *Official Congressional Directory* or *The United States Government Manual*, in the library. In addition, students can look in the telephone directory for the local offices of their senators and representative and call to request the information.

Have students form small groups to check their answers. Ask individuals where they found their information.

Answer Key

CHAPTER 8

Section 8-1 Review (text page 179)

1. See definitions for the following terms on the text pages indicated in parentheses: *policy* (174), *constituents* (174), *bill* (174), *interest groups* (175), *lobbyists* (175), *census* (177), *congressional district* (177).
2. A member of Congress has responsibilities to constituents, the nation as a whole, his or her political party, and specific interest groups.
3. Members of Congress give information and help to constituents who have special needs or problems.
4. Representatives have shorter terms, serving for two years instead of the six-year term of senators; thus representatives must be more responsive to constituents. Senators must think about the interests of the entire state, not just one district.
Evaluation. Answers will vary.
Data Search. California, Texas, and Florida gained the most seats. Answers will vary depending on where students live.

Section 8-2 Review (text page 182)

1. See definition for *budget* on text page 180.
2. Answers may include the power to regulate commerce, collect taxes, borrow money, and decide how that money should be spent.
3. Congress has the power to conduct investigations in order to gather information needed to make laws or to find out how the executive branch is enforcing laws.
4. A bill of attainder convicts a person of a crime without a trial; an *ex post facto* law makes a particular act a crime and then punishes people who committed the act before the law was passed.
Evaluation. Answers may include the fact that control of the budget enables Congress to act as a check on the executive branch.

Section 8-3 Review (text page 186)

1. See definitions for the following terms on the text pages indicated in parentheses: *Speaker of the House* (183), *president pro tempore* (183), *majority party* (183), *minority party* (183), *floor leaders* (183), *whips* (183), *pocket veto* (186).
2. The Speaker of the House presides over congressional sessions, announces the order of business, decides who may speak from the floor, appoints members of committees, and refers bills to committees.

3. A standing committee studies a bill, holds public hearings, and decides whether to recommend that the House or the Senate vote on the bill. A conference committee, made up of members of both houses, studies a bill that has been changed in the process of passing from one house to the other and attempts to settle the differences.
Analysis. Political parties control congressional leadership positions. The majority party chooses the Speaker of the House and the president pro tem. In addition, in each committee the majority of members, as well as the chairperson, come from the majority party.

Section 8-4 Review (text page 189)

1. See definitions for the following terms on the text pages indicated in parentheses: *filibuster* (188), *cloture* (188).
2. Public hearings enable a congressional committee to hear from anyone who wants to speak for or against a bill.
3. The House has a Rules Committee that determines how long a bill will be debated. The Senate has no Rules Committee; senators must agree unanimously on the starting time of the debate, and there are fewer limits on length.
Evaluation. Answers may include the view that the filibuster encourages free discussion by allowing time for those who oppose a bill to present their case before a vote is taken, or the view that the filibuster is just a delaying tactic, designed to force withdrawal of the bill.

Decision-Making Lesson (text pages 190–191)

1. If you support an increase in the minimum wage, you would most likely vote for Mr. Smith. As governor, Mr. Smith supported efforts to reduce poverty and to raise highway workers' wages. Judging from Ms. Thickett's speech, she seems to think that the current minimum wage is adequate. She would support an increase only if it reduced the number of people on welfare.
2. Statement C is an *example* of a candidate's position on the minimum wage. Statement G is an *explanation* of why Ms. Thickett is likely to oppose an increase in the minimum wage.
3. (b) All three of these statements indicate the candidate's attitudes toward the financial needs of workers.
4. (b) Statements A, B, E, F, and I are irrelevant because they provide no insight into the candidates' views on the minimum wage.
5. The term *relevant* means "related to."
6. General kinds of relevant information consist of details, examples, explanations, evidence, and definitions.
7. It is important to note which information you need in order to judge options or to plan how to reach your goal; otherwise, you may waste time looking for unnecessary information.

Chapter Survey (text page 192)

Understanding New Vocabulary

1. *Constituents* are the people who a representative represents in his or her *congressional district.*
2. *Lobbyists* are the people who represent and promote the goals of *interest groups.*
3. The *Speaker of the House* is selected by the *majority party.*
4. Both *floor leaders* and *whips* are officers responsible for guiding bills through Congress.
5. A *cloture* is an agreement to put an end to a *filibuster.*
Putting It in Writing. Answers may include the selection of all congressional leaders except the president of the Senate by political parties. The majority party selects the Speaker of the House, the president pro tem, and the heads of committees. The majority and minority parties in each house choose floor leaders and whips.

Looking Back at the Chapter

1. The needs of a member's constituents may be in conflict with the needs of Americans in general.
2. Interest groups provide both money and votes that can help a senator or representative get reelected.
3. Each state is given a fair proportion of the 435 seats in the House of Representatives based on a census taken every ten years. With population constantly shifting, states may gain or lose repre-

sentatives; however, every state is entitled to at least one representative.

4. Personal staff help a member of Congress run his or her office at home and in Washington, D.C.; handle casework; and study bills.

5. Congress is said to have "the power of the purse" because it has final approval of the government's budget. Thus, Congress acts as a check on the executive branch.

6. The Constitution specifically says that Congress cannot take away a citizen's right to a writ of *habeas corpus* except in times of invasion or civil war and cannot pass *ex post facto* laws and bills of attainder.

7. The Speaker of the House has great influence over which bills pass and fail in the House. He or she presides over sessions, announcing the order of business and deciding who may speak from the floor. The Speaker also appoints members of committees and refers bills to committees.

8. (a) A standing committee helps make laws by studying a bill, holding public hearings, proposing changes in the bill, and deciding whether to recommend that the House or Senate vote on the bill. **(b)** A conference committee tries to settle the differences in a bill that passes one house but is changed in the other. **(c)** A select committee is formed to solve a problem that is not covered by a standing committee. Most select committees conduct investigations which can lead to the proposal of new laws.

9. Congress can override the President's veto by passing the bill again by a two-thirds vote in both houses.

10. In the Senate, the minority party can prevent a vote on a bill by not agreeing on a starting time for debate or by starting a filibuster.

11. Congress was able to establish an air force because it has the power to establish and maintain an army and a navy in order to defend the nation, and it has the power to make all laws that are "necessary and proper" for carrying out its listed powers.

12. Answers may include the idea that a member of the Senate, who must think about the interests of an entire state, cannot be as responsive to constituents as a representative, who serves constituents in one district. In addition, a bicameral legislature ensures that bills are more thoroughly studied and debated.

13. Answers may include the claim that students could influence a legislator's position on a bill even though they are not voters. As citizens they expect their Congressperson to act as their voice in government. However, they may exert little influence on a representative who is more concerned with serving the constituency that placed him or her in office than nonvoters.

Working Together

Answers will vary.

Skills Workshop (text page 193)

Social Studies Skills

1. The graphs show political party, sex, race or ethnic group, and profession.

2. The Democratic party had a majority.

3. The typical member of Congress was a white, male, Democratic lawyer.

Decision-Making Skills

1. Relevant information may include the fact that a committee reports a bill to the Senate, the full Senate can make changes in the bill, the Senate votes on the amended bill, and a conference committee works out differences between the House and Senate versions. All of these pieces of information relate to the process by which a bill works its way through Congress.

2. Examples of irrelevant information may include the fact that the farm bill required high farm prices, the bill included a soil bank plan, some senators did not like the soil bank plan, and no senator was pleased with the entire bill. These pieces of information relate to the farm bill itself but not the general procedure by which a bill becomes a law.

3. Answers will vary. Students should explain how each type of information is relevant and how it would help them to judge options or to plan how to reach the particular goal they mentioned.

OVERVIEW

The President is head of the executive branch of government which is responsible for enforcing laws. The President provides leadership by setting goals for the nation and developing policies. To help in achieving these goals, the executive branch employs over 3 million people, who form a huge bureaucracy. Presidential power is limited by the judicial and legislative branches of government.

OBJECTIVES

After completing this chapter, students should be able to

- identify the qualifications for the office of President.
- identify the roles and responsibilities of the President.
- describe the organization of the executive branch of government.
- compare points of view on presidential power.

PLANNING GUIDE

Teaching Strategy	Skills	Special Features	Review/Evaluation
Introducing the Chapter: Class Project **Teaching Activity 1:** Individual Project—A Poll on the Presidency (Section 9-1) **Teaching Activity 2:** Individual Project—A Poet's View of the Executive Branch (Section 9-2) **Evaluating Progress:** Individual Project (Section 9-2) **Reinforcement Activity:** Individual Project—Worksheet (Section 9-1) **Enrichment Activity:** Individual Project—Worksheet (Section 9-3)	Decision-Making Lesson: Opinion or Statement of Fact? Social Studies Skills Workshop: Using an Almanac Decision-Making Skills: Opinion or Statement of Fact? **Issues and Decision Making:** Worksheet Chapter 9	American Notebook Views of Noted Americans: Pierre Salinger	Section Reviews Chapter 9 Survey **Tests:** Chapter 9 Test **Testing Software** **Additional Resources** **Activity Book** **Citizenship Skills** **Transparencies and Activity Book** **Voices of America**

For reinforcement and enrichment worksheets and unit activities, see the Activity Book.

Teaching Strategy

Introducing the Chapter: Class Project

Before reading this chapter, students will have varying knowledge about the presidency. In this activity students use their knowledge in playing a variation of the game bingo. The activity will require a full class period.

Begin by explaining to students that they will be participating in a game of "executive bingo," which will help them assess how much combined knowledge of the presidency class members have. Provide each student with a piece of heavy paper. Instruct students to make a bingo card by first drawing a large square (approximately 6 inches by 6 inches) on the paper, then dividing the square into 25 equal squares with 5 horizontal and 5 vertical lines.

As students make their bingo cards, write the questions below on the chalkboard. Students are to fill each square on their bingo cards with one question, which can be abbreviated. Each question can be used only one time.

- Name of current President?
- Name of last President?
- Name of Vice-President?
- President's term of office?
- Maximum number of terms a President can serve?
- Minimum age for President?
- President's salary?
- Name of an executive department?
- A check on presidential power?
- How long must the President have lived in the United States?
- Vice-President's salary?
- Name of an advisory group to the President?
- Name of an executive agency?
- Name of a regulatory commission?
- Name of a government corporation?
- Number of people the President appoints to office?
- Number of employees in the executive branch?
- A responsibility of the President as chief executive?
- A responsibility of the President as commander in chief?
- A responsibility of the President as chief diplomat?
- A responsibility of the President as legislative leader?
- A responsibility of the President as chief of state?
- A responsibility of the President as party leader?
- A judicial power of the President?
- Role of the White House staff?

The difficulty of questions may be adapted to suit your students' abilities.

When students have completed their cards, explain that the objective of the game is to find classmates who know the answers to the questions on their cards. When they find a classmate who knows an answer, he or she must initial the square containing that question. The initialing student is not to answer the question orally at this time, but he or she must be prepared to give the answer later. Each square must be initialed by a different class member.

The game's winner is the first player to get initials on five squares in a row horizontally, vertically, or diagonally. The winner's card must be verified by having those students who initialed the boxes answer the questions. Allow students to skim Chapter 9 to verify the answers.

Once a winner has been determined, review answers to all questions with students. Direct them to save their bingo cards to use for review at the end of the chapter.

▣ Teaching Activity 1: Individual Project

A Poll on the Presidency

In this activity students compare points of view on presidential qualifications by conducting a public opinion poll. Because students will need time to collect and compile their poll data, the activity should begin after they have completed Section 9-1. At least half a class period should be reserved for compiling and discussing results of the poll.

Begin the activity by reminding students that Americans have different opinions on what background best prepares a person to be President of the United States. Have students name qualities, training, and experiences they believe are important for a President to have. List their responses on the chalkboard. Continue by explaining that the public also has widely different views on who among our past Presidents has fulfilled the job of President well. Ask students to name the five Presidents whom they consider to have best fulfilled the office. Record the list on the chalkboard and save it.

Tell students that in this activity they are to conduct a public opinion poll to determine other people's views on three questions:

- What personal qualities does a person need to have in order to be a good President?
- What experiences does a person need to have in order to be a good President?
- Who has been a good President?

To conduct the poll, each student must interview four people outside of class. Students are to record their interviewees' answers to all three questions. Set a time limit for the interviews to be completed.

When students' interview data has been collected, compile the information in class. Divide a large chalkboard area into thirds. Label the sections *Qualities, Background*, and *Good Presidents.*

Begin by having students read the qualities mentioned by interviewees, until all different qualities are listed. Follow the same procedure for the other two sections.

Compare the opinions gathered in the out-of-class poll with the opinions expressed earlier by students. Discuss similarities and differences. Ask students why differences occur and discuss whether we expect too much from our Presidents.

▣ Teaching Activity 2: Individual Project

A Poet's View of the Executive Branch

In this activity students gain more perspective on the bureaucracy of the executive branch by writing a poem that describes or pokes fun at its size and scope. If writing a poem is inappropriate for your students, have them draw a cartoon instead. This activity should be an out-of-class assignment begun after students have read Section 9-2.

Begin by explaining that although most citizens benefit from the work done by the executive branch, many people question the huge size of the branch's bureaucracy and whether all of its functions are necessary. Tell students that in our democracy there is a long tradition of citizens calling attention to problems in government through the use of humorous writing. Ask them to write a poem describing the executive branch and/or pointing out problems with the bureaucracy. Students' poems should comment on specific aspects of the executive branch, such as the roles of the President, the size of the bureaucracy, and presidential appointments.

Stimulate students' thinking about their poems by reminding them that nonhuman images are often used in humorous writing. Have students suggest animals, plants, or other symbols that might represent aspects of the executive branch. For example, an octopus might be used to suggest the growing power of this branch of government. Set a time for students to submit their completed poems.

Encourage all students to read their poems aloud to the class and have other students comment on them. With students' approval, submit some of the class favorites to the school's or local newspaper's editorial page.

• Evaluating Progress: Individual Project

Although the President is the head of the executive branch, he or she must depend on thousands of advisors and other employees to carry out the responsibilities of the office. In this activity students demonstrate their understanding of the organization of the executive branch by compiling a telephone directory the President can use to reach people in his or her administration. The activity can be used after students have finished Section 9-2.

Have students begin by naming the officials in the executive branch that the President contacts most often. Then they should name other departments and agencies that the President communicates with. Students then develop an organizational plan that will make it easy for the President to contact specific advisors and department and agency heads. Allow students to use their textbooks for reference.

Criteria for evaluating students' directories should include the number of positions and departments named and the appropriate organization of these listings.

• Reinforcement Activity: Individual Project

Students may have difficulty identifying the varied roles of the President within the context of a presidential working day. Reinforcement Worksheet Chapter 9, "The Roles of the President," in the Activity Book presents workdays for two Presidents and requires students to identify the role the President is fulfilling when he or she performs specific functions. The activity can be used after students have read the material in Section 9-1.

Introduce the worksheet to students by reading together the introductory material. Have students define each of the seven presidential roles listed. Make certain students understand that they are to identify the role being fulfilled by the President when he or she performs each of the functions that is numbered and underlined.

Check students' work by reviewing their answers in class. Discuss how the need to meet so many obligations makes the President's job more difficult.

• Enrichment Activity: Individual Project

Throughout Chapter 9, students read about presidential power and limitations. After they have finished Section 9-3, distribute Enrichment Worksheet Chapter 9, "Presidential Power and Its Limits," in the Activity Book. To complete the worksheet, students review the chapter to find examples of how the President is either free to act or limited in his or her actions. Students then write a paragraph supporting or opposing the belief that the President has too much power.

When their paragraphs are completed, divide students into two groups: those who support strong presidential power and those who oppose it. Challenge each group to list the five strongest arguments in support of its point of view and then select a spokesperson to present the arguments to the class. After the spokesperson from each group has presented the group's arguments, hold a secret ballot to see how many class members support or oppose strong presidential power.

Answer Key

CHAPTER 9

Section 9-1 Review (text page 200)

1. See definitions for the following terms on the text pages indicated in parentheses: *executive branch* (196), *executive orders* (198), *foreign policy* (198), *treaties* (198), *ambassadors* (198), *executive agreements* (198), *domestic policy* (199).
2. The framers guarded against abuse of presidential power by limiting the term of office, separation of powers, and checks and balances.
3. Answers may include brief descriptions of four of the following roles: chief executive, commander in chief, chief diplomat, legislative leader, party leader, and chief of state.
Evaluation. Opinions may vary, but most students will say that presidential roles overlap. When urging Congress to pass a foreign aid bill, the President is acting as both legislative leader and chief diplomat. Some students may note, however, that in many situations the roles may be seen as separate. When greeting a foreign leader in a formal ceremony, for instance, the President is acting as chief of state. He is not also acting as chief diplomat because he is not discussing policy issues with the other leader. Overall, though, presidential roles tend to overlap.

Section 9-2 Review (text page 208)

1. See definitions for the following terms on the text pages indicated in parentheses: *bureaucracy* (201), *administration* (201), *Cabinet* (203).
2. The Executive Office of the President is composed of the Vice-President, the inner circle of advisors that make up the White House staff, and special advisory groups such as the Office of Management and Budget and the National Security Council. The main purpose of the Executive Office is to advise the President on foreign and domestic policy issues. Each of the 13 executive departments is headed by a presidential appointee. The main purpose of the executive departments is to carry out the nation's laws and run government programs in a way that is consistent with administration goals. The independent agencies are divided into executive agencies under the direct control of the President, regulatory commissions, and government corporations. The agencies carry out government programs that do not fall under the direct jurisdiction of the executive departments.
3. Enforcing a law is often difficult because the process involves gathering relevant data while keeping in mind administration goals and the views of special interest groups. Before proposed regulations are written, agencies must consider all the factors involved and listen to various opinions on the issue. Often the regulations must be revised to make sure that they carry out the intent of the law.
Evaluation. Advantages may include an extensive pool of government employees to serve a growing population and specialized departments in a wide range of areas. Disadvantages may include the cost to taxpayers of programs that are run inefficiently and the "red tape" that sometimes delays action on problems.
Data Search. Health and Human Services and Defense had the largest budgets. Defense had many more employees (1,054,000 compared to 123,000 for Health and Human Services).

Section 9-3 Review (text page 211)

1. See definition for *executive privilege* on text page 209.
2. Presidents can hold talks with representatives of other countries, make executive agreements, negotiate treaties, and keep some information secret under the right of executive privilege.
3. Some advantages of executive freedom are the ability to take decisive action during a crisis, to take advantage of an opportunity, and to take action on an issue on which Congress is indecisive. Some disadvantages are that Presidents may do something that is unconstitutional or that is not in the best interests of the nation.
Evaluation. Opinions will vary. Students who think Presidents have too much power might point to the danger of American military involvement in such areas as Central America and the Middle

East. Decisions to use military force, they say, should not be made without consulting Congress because the consequences to the nation can be very serious. Students holding the opposing view might argue that the nation needs a leader with enough power to take decisive action in an emergency. They might point out that any serious abuse of power, as in the Watergate affair, will usually be exposed and corrected under the system of checks and balances.

Decision-Making Lesson (text pages 212–213)

1. Answers will vary. As an example, statement A could be rewritten to state the following fact: "Woodrow Wilson went to college."
2. (a) Both statements B and E can be proved either true or false. Statement A includes the subjective word *most*. Statement D states that Harding was elected because he was more handsome, which would be almost impossible to prove or disprove. Statement F includes the subjective word *actively*.
3. (c) Statement D includes the fact that Harding was elected after women were given the right to vote. Statement I only states a fact.
4. (a) Statement D includes a fact about when Harding was elected and an opinion about why. Statement G includes the fact that Johnson did not seek re-election and an opinion that he did so "selflessly." Statements B and C only state facts.
5. A fact can be either proved or disproved. An opinion cannot.
6. Once you have identified facts and opinions, you can check the accuracy of any statements of fact and determine whether any opinions are supported by good reasons, and then make a decision.
7. Examples will vary. Students might note situations such as deciding which movie to see. Comments from people who had seen the movie could be divided into factual statements of what the movie was about and opinions about the entertainment quality of the movie.

Chapter Survey (text page 214)

Understanding New Vocabulary

1. *Bureaucracy* and *executive branch* are both terms referring to the government employees under the authority of the President. The employees of the executive branch of the government form a bureaucracy.
2. *Executive agreements* and *treaties* are both agreements that the President makes with other nations.
3. *Cabinet* and *administration* are both terms referring to government officials appointed by the President.
Putting It in Writing. Answers may include the responsibilities of the President in his or her roles as commander in chief and chief diplomat.

Looking Back at the Chapter

1. The President is limited to serving no more than two 4-year terms. Also, the separation of powers among the three branches and the system of checks and balances guard against abuse of power.
2. Examples of presidential roles and how they relate to Congress will vary. For example, in the role of legislative leader the President makes speeches to Congress and meets with individual members of Congress to gather support for administration goals.
3. The executive branch has grown into a large bureaucracy because of the wide range of foreign and domestic policy issues that modern Presidents are expected to respond to.
4. A President needs an administration to direct the permanent bureaucracy of government employees toward meeting the President's goals.
5. Both the Cabinet members and the White House staff are appointed as close advisors to the President.
6. The civil service system guarantees a pool of qualified government employees who remain from administration to administration.
7. As commander in chief, the President could order a military response. As chief diplomat, the President could hold talks with the leaders of

the other country, either personally or through ambassadors.

8. Examples will vary. The most familiar examples might be the EPA, with its pollution regulations; the United States Postal Service; the FDIC, with its protection of savings accounts; the National Railroad Passenger Corporation, with its Amtrak service; and the Veterans Administration, which may have provided home loans to some students' parents.

9. Students who think the government interferes too much may point to what they regard as unnecessary regulations. Students who disagree may emphasize the many areas in which government regulations protect the well-being of people.

10. An executive branch appointee would be committed to furthering the President's policy goals. Also, an appointee is likely to lose his or her job at the end of the current President's term. A permanent employee would not necessarily be committed to the President's goals. Also, a competent permanent employee is guaranteed a job unless there are serious budget cuts.

11. Examples will vary. In fulfilling the role of chief diplomat, for instance, the President is helped by the Department of State and the Department of Defense. The Department of State helps the President carry out foreign policy through embassy staff. The Department of Defense provides the military strength that the President can use as leverage in pursuing foreign policy goals.

Working Together

Answers will vary.

Skills Workshop (text page 215)

Social Studies Skills

1. page 387; page 744. **2.** pages 630–42; page 610. **3.** page 609. **4.** pages 48, 596. **5.** page 624. **6.** pages 619–23.

Decision-Making Skills

1. Statements C, E, G, and H state only facts. Students should choose two of these statements and explain how they could be checked and proved either true or false.

2. Statements A, D, F, and I give opinions. Statement A includes the subjective words *too much*. Statement D includes the subjective word *greatest*. Statement F includes the subjective words *most active*, and statement I includes the subjective word *useful*.

3. Sentence B includes the fact that Ford pardoned Nixon and the opinion that the pardon was a mistake. (Some students might also interpret statements D, F, and I as including facts as well as opinions: the fact that Kennedy was one of the Presidents after World War II, that Carter was one of the Presidents during the past 30 years, and that cabinet meetings are held monthly.)

4. A statement of fact can be proved true or false; an opinion can neither be proved nor disproved.

5. Examples will vary.

OVERVIEW

The judicial branch of the federal government interprets the Constitution and decides if federal laws are protecting the rights of citizens. Both federal and state courts perform the same function of resolving legal conflicts in criminal and civil cases. The Supreme Court serves as the final court of appeals for both the state and federal court systems.

OBJECTIVES

After completing this chapter, students should be able to

- describe the functions and organization of our state and federal court systems.
- explain the difference between a civil case and a criminal case.
- explain the role and function of the Supreme Court.

PLANNING GUIDE

Teaching Strategy	Skills	Special Features	Review/Evaluation
Introducing the Chapter: Cooperative Project **Teaching Activity 1:** Individual Project—Make a Case: Workings of a Court (Section 10-2) **Teaching Activity 2:** Cooperative Project—Structure of Our Court Systems (Section 10-2) **Evaluating Progress:** Individual Project (Section 10-3) **Reinforcement Activity:** Individual Project—Worksheet (Section 10-2) **Enrichment Activity:** Individual Project—Worksheet (Section 10-3)	Social Studies Skills Workshop: Analyzing Newspaper Editorials Decision-Making Skills Workshop: What Relates to Your Subject? **Issues and Decision Making:** Worksheet Chapter 10	American Notebook Views of Noted Americans: Louis Brandeis Issues That Affect You: A Case Study—Jerry Gault and Juvenile Rights In Their Own Words: Theodore Roosevelt—"I Believe in a Strong Executive"	Section Reviews Chapter 10 Survey Unit 3 Survey **Tests:** Chapter 10 Test, Unit 3 Test **Testing Software** **Additional Resources** **Activity Book** **Citizenship Skills** **Transparencies and Activity Book** **Voices of America**

For reinforcement and enrichment worksheets and unit activities, see the Activity Book.

Teaching Strategy

Introducing the Chapter: Cooperative Project

Many students' perceptions about the legal system come from television programs about lawyers, courts, criminals, and police officers. The images created are often stereotyped, inaccurate, or unrealistic. In this activity students evaluate their perceptions of the legal system that stem from television. The activity will require at least 30 minutes.

Divide students into groups of three or four. Ask the groups to list television shows they watch that involve the legal system—police, criminals, detectives, lawyers, judges, etc. From their lists, have groups choose two or three of the more familiar programs.

While students are discussing the programs, write the following list on the chalkboard:

- persons employed by courts
- participants in court cases (defendants, plaintiffs, jurors)
- types of cases tried in courts
- kinds of courts
- court procedures (jury selection, trial, decision)

Direct each group to generate a list of examples for each of the categories from episodes of the television programs identified. Allow about 15 minutes for discussion.

Once their lists are complete, ask each group to identify two points from the television programs that may provide inaccurate or misleading information about the legal system. Ask groups to write their points in question form, such as, "What kinds of cases go before the Supreme Court?"

Reconvene the class and have each group share its responses with the rest of the class. Write their questions on a sheet of poster paper. Post the sheet on a bulletin board or have students copy the questions onto notebook paper. Tell students that as they read Chapter 10 they should refer to the poster sheet to answer the questions.

Teaching Activity 1: Individual Project

Make a Case: Workings of a Court

Sections 10-1 and 10-2 examine the role and organization of the federal courts. In this activity students apply information from their reading to outline a court scene for a dramatic play. The activity can be used after students have finished Section 10-2. The writing assignment can be done outside of class, but time should be allowed to let students share their outlines.

Introduce the activity by explaining that many popular dramatic plays have been based on plots involving courtroom scenes. Ask students to imagine that they have been asked by a Broadway producer to develop an outline for a new drama in which the climax is a courtroom trial. Have them record the following guidelines as you write them on the chalkboard:

- Explain the plot: What criminal or civil case is being heard in court?
- Describe the roles in the play.
- Identify the kind of court in the scene.
- Define the issues in the case.
- Reveal the outcome of the case.

Encourage students to add additional detail to their outlines to make the courtroom scene more interesting. Stress the importance of accuracy as well as creativity. Make sure students understand that they should make an outline and not write the assignment as a short story.

When the assignment is completed, divide the class into small groups and have students share their outlines with each other. Challenge the listening students to point out inaccuracies and offer suggestions for improvement. Allow students time to review their outlines before turning in their final copies.

Teaching Activity 2: Cooperative Project

Structure of Our Court Systems

In this activity students reinforce their understanding of the structure of our state and federal court systems. Use the activity after students have finished reading Section 10-2. It will require most of a class period to complete.

Before the activity, make a set of 10 cards for every three students. Each card will provide information about our legal system. Using index cards or pieces of paper, write one of the following headings per card to complete a set: *Cases Involving Federal Laws, Cases Involving a State Government or Foreign Diplomat, Cases Involving State and Local Laws, Special Federal Courts, U.S. District Courts, U.S. Courts of Appeals, State Trial Courts, State Appeals Courts, State Supreme Courts,* and *U.S. Supreme Court.*

Form groups of three students each. Explain that the task of each group is to organize the cards so that the information on them correctly reflects the organization of the state and federal court systems. Distribute the card sets and allow 10 minutes to complete the task.

When finished, have groups compare their results. Then have students compare their results with the chart, "The State and Federal Court Systems," on text page 224. If necessary, students should rearrange their cards in the correct order. Emphasize the differences in original and appellate jurisdiction.

Using their cards, direct students to answer the following questions:

- Which courts are in the federal court system? (special federal courts, U.S. district courts, U.S. courts of appeals, Supreme Court)
- Which courts have original jurisdiction? (Supreme Court, special federal courts, U.S. district courts, state trial courts)
- Which courts have appellate jurisdiction? (U.S. courts of appeals, state appeals courts, state supreme courts, Supreme Court)

Evaluating Progress: Individual Project

This activity assesses students' ability to apply what they have learned about our legal system to cases reported in newspapers and on television news. The activity can be used after students have completed the chapter.

Assign each student the task of collecting three newspaper articles or accounts from three television news stories on current court cases. At least one of the examples should be a federal case. Direct students to identify each case with a headline or title, then provide the following information:

- Describe the plaintiff and defendant or prosecutor and defendant.
- Is the case civil or criminal? Why?
- What court is hearing the case?
- What court would hear an appeal of the decision in the case?

Allow one week for students to collect cases and write their descriptions. Criteria for evaluation should include accuracy of information and completeness of answers.

Reinforcement Activity: Individual Project

Although Sections 10-1 and 10-2 focus primarily on the federal courts, jurisdiction in state courts is also discussed. In this activity students reinforce their understanding of the functions and organization of state and federal courts by applying their knowledge to specific cases or situations. The activity can be done after students have read Section 10-2 and will require about 30 minutes to complete.

Introduce the activity by reviewing with students the headings and major points in Sections 10-1 and 10-2. Distribute Reinforcement Worksheet Chapter 10, "Bringing a Case to Court," in the Activity Book and make certain students understand the directions. Encourage students to look back through the sections to verify their answers. After all students are finished, review their answers and discuss their reasons for deciding court assignments.

Enrichment Activity: Individual Project

As Section 10-3 points out, although Supreme Court justices are charged with interpreting the Constitution, their personal beliefs are evident in their court decisions. In Enrichment Worksheet Chapter 10, "Supreme Court Justice: A Job Description," in the Activity Book, students determine the kind of background needed by a person who holds this job. The activity should be used after students have completed Section 10-3. It can be assigned as homework or completed in about 30 minutes of class time.

Introduce the activity by explaining that employers often use a job description to clarify the nature of a job and the kind of skills and experience it requires. Distribute the worksheet and read the instructions to make certain students understand that they are to write a job description for the position of Supreme Court justice, not fill out an application for the job.

After students have completed their descriptions, review their answers. List on the chalkboard the experiences, skills, and traits students have identified. Discuss the difficulty of finding people who possess all the desired qualities to serve as justices.

Answer Key

CHAPTER 10

Section 10-1 Review (text page 222)

1. See definitions for the following terms on the text pages indicated in parentheses: *plaintiff* (219), *defendant* (219), *prosecution* (219), *precedent* (220), *original jurisdiction* (221), *appeal* (221), *appellate jurisdiction* (221).
2. Both courts and referees apply laws to actual situations.
3. Federal courts hear cases involving federal laws and those that are appealed from state supreme courts.
Analysis. Answers may include that court decisions establish precedents, which affect how a law is applied and interpreted in the future.

Section 10-2 Review (text page 225)

1. A federal district court has original jurisdiction. A federal court of appeals has appellate jurisdiction.
2. The major purpose of the Supreme Court is to serve as the final court of appeals for both the state and federal court systems.
3. Answers may include the following: Federal judges decide individual cases, whereas members of Congress enact broad laws; judges are appointed whereas members of Congress are elected; judges must be impartial whereas members of Congress are open to influence from a variety of groups.
Analysis. Answers may include that the appointment of judges helps preserve their impartiality.
Data Search. Answers will vary.

Section 10-3 Review (text page 231)

1. See definitions for the following terms on the text pages indicated in parentheses: *judicial review* (225), *judicial activism* (229), *judicial restraint* (230).
2. *Marbury* v. *Madison* was brought to the Supreme Court under a law that was in conflict with the Constitution, which allowed the Court to rule on the law instead of the case itself.

3. Congress can refuse to confirm the appointment of a justice and begin the process of changing the Constitution by proposing an amendment.
Synthesis. Answers may include how the Supreme Court has jurisdiction over both federal and state court systems; how its interpretation of the meaning of the Constitution is final; and how appeals can go no further than the Supreme Court.

Issues That Affect You: A Case Study (text pages 232–233)

1. Jerry was denied the Fifth Amendment rights to remain silent and not be compelled to testify against oneself and the Sixth Amendment rights to be informed of the nature and cause of all charges, to confront accusatory witnesses, and to have legal counsel.
2. The decisions of an Arizona juvenile court and the Arizona State Supreme Court were reversed.
3. Answers may include the opinion that the intention of creating a different criminal justice system for juveniles was to protect juveniles, not to punish them more severely.

Chapter Survey (text page 234)

Understanding New Vocabulary

1. *Original jurisdiction* is related to *appellate jurisdiction* because they describe whether a court has the authority to hear a case for the first time or on appeal.
2. *Plaintiff* is related to *defendant* because they are the two parties in a civil case.
3. *Prosecution* is related to *defendant* because they are the two parties in a criminal case.
4. *Precedent* is related to *judicial restraint* because judges who believe in judicial restraint are likely to rely on precedent to determine how a law should be applied.
Putting It in Writing. Answers may include that judicial review gives the Supreme Court the power to overturn laws passed by Congress and the states, and that the Court establishes precedents that determine the meaning of laws and how they will be applied.

Looking Back at the Chapter

1. The judge directs the proceedings, applies the law to the conflict, and decides which side's argument is most in keeping with the law.
2. A court is able to interpret a law only in a case where the law's meaning or constitutionality is in question.
3. The state and federal court systems are connected through the Supreme Court, the final court of appeals for both systems.
4. Trials are held in courts that have original jurisdiction.
5. An appeals court reviews the legal issues in a case and decides if the lower court's decision is just and if the law was applied fairly.
6. The Constitution established only the Supreme Court.
7. A federal district court's decision can be reviewed by a federal court of appeals.
8. The Supreme Court has original jurisdiction over cases involving representatives of foreign governments and interstate conflicts.
9. Federal judges are appointed by the President and confirmed by the Senate, whereas members of Congress are elected.
10. Many of the cases that the Court hears raise constitutional questions.
11. The power of judicial review allows the Court to overturn any law that it decides is in conflict with the Constitution. Judicial review was established in *Marbury* v. *Madison*.
12. The President appoints the members of the Supreme Court.
13. Answers may include a federal court because a federal law is in question. Susan's case will be civil, unless she was charged with a crime as well.
14. Answers may include the idea that judicial review and judicial restraint vary mainly in the extent to which judges are willing to overturn laws and thereby take a greater or lesser role in policymaking.
15. Answers may include the idea that the factual issues decided by a jury are not relevant in a court of appeals, only legal issues best decided by a judge.
16. Advantages may include making Supreme Court justices more responsive to voters, ensuring

that the Court's views reflect the views of the people. Disadvantages may include introducing politics and political influence into the work of the Court, which might endanger the impartiality of the justices. Answers will vary regarding the best selection process.
17. Supporting answers may include the view that the Court's role is to defend the constitutional rights of all Americans, regardless of popular support. Opposing answers may include the view that questions of great importance should be settled by Congress, which reflects the will of the people.

Working Together

Answers will vary.

Skills Workshop (text page 235)

Social Studies Skills

1. The writer opposed the Court's decision and reveals this by calling the decision a "tortuous bit of reasoning" and by saying the majority deserves "five whacks."
2. The writer says that it is wrong for the Court to deny students the same protection from beatings that the law gives wives and adult criminals.
3. The cause of the Court's decision is a "strongly entrenched" attitude that strict discipline is good for children.

Decision-Making Skills

1. A, C, F. Only these three statements relate to the Court's power to decide whether laws are constitutional.
2. Clearly identify the subject; identify kinds of information that might relate to the subject (examples, details, evidence, or explanations); examine each piece of information to see if it relates directly to the subject.
3. Examples of decisions will vary. Students should note how separating relevant from irrelevant information helps them make the decision.

In Their Own Words (text page 236)

1. Roosevelt said that a strong central executive is necessary for "the efficiency of this government."
2. Roosevelt believes responsibility should go along with power.
3. Roosevelt compares himself to Abraham Lincoln.
4. His personal character is more important than his actions. Answers in agreement may include that the *way* a President carries out duties, the image he or she projects as President, is most important. Answers in disagreement may include that a President's most important responsibility is to be accountable for all his or her actions.

Unit 3 Survey (text page 237)

Looking Back at the Unit

1. (e), (d), (c), (a), (g), (f), (b)
2. **(a)** executive and legislative **(b)** judicial **(c)** executive and legislative **(d)** executive
3. Examples of branches and checks will vary. Students should note how one branch can limit the power of the other.

Taking a Stand

Answers may include arguments cited in the text and other arguments students develop.

OVERVIEW

Under federalism, states carry out much of the work of meeting the needs of citizens. State governments are organized into executive, legislative, and judicial branches with powers similar to those of the federal government. Each branch acts as a check on the other two branches of state government. In addition, citizens can have a great influence on state lawmaking.

OBJECTIVES

After completing this chapter, students should be able to

- distinguish between state and federal powers.
- compare points of view about the balance between the national government and the states.
- explain how citizens can propose laws.
- describe methods of selecting judges.

PLANNING GUIDE

Teaching Strategy	Skills	Special Features	Review/Evaluation
Introducing the Chapter: Class Project **Teaching Activity 1:** Cooperative Project—State and Federal Powers (Section 11-1) **Teaching Activity 2:** Individual Project: Using the Initiative (Section 11-2) **Evaluating Progress:** Cooperative Project (Section 11-4) **Reinforcement Activity:** Individual Project—Worksheet (Section 11-4) **Enrichment Activity:** Individual Project—Worksheet (Section 11-4)	Decision-Making Lesson: Which Statements Are True? Social Studies Skills Workshop: Reading Newspaper Articles Decision-Making Skills Workshop: Which Statements Are True? **Issues and Decision Making:** Worksheet Chapter 11	American Notebook Views of Noted Americans: March Fong Eu	Section Reviews Chapter 11 Survey **Tests:** Chapter 11 Test **Testing Software** **Additional Resources** **Activity Book** **Citizenship Skills** **Transparencies and Activity Book** **Voices of America**

For reinforcement and enrichment worksheets and unit activities, see the Activity Book.

Teaching Strategy

Introducing the Chapter: Class Project

Students may have little understanding of how they are personally affected by state government. In this activity students develop an initial awareness of the powers of state government.

Remind students that although they have learned about the federal government, you would like to know how informed they are about their state's government. Ask students to tear a sheet of notebook paper into three pieces and number them from 1 to 3. On the separate pieces, ask students to respond to the following directions:

1. Name one state law that affects your life directly. (sales tax, school attendance)
2. Describe one situation that might require you to appear in a state court. (juvenile crime, child custody in divorce proceedings)
3. Name one state agency or office that you have used or may use in the future. (motor vehicles, consumer affairs)

Emphasize that there are many correct responses.

When students are finished, ask for three volunteers to sort the answer slips into piles according to numbers, consolidate similar answers, and post the responses on the chalkboard. As this task is being done, the rest of the students can preview Chapter 11.

Review students' answers. Have students discuss why they think the laws, functions, and agencies they listed fall in the domain of state government rather than federal or local government. Can they generalize from their answers about how state and federal government differ?

Leave the chalkboard list posted. Challenge students to review it as they read Chapter 11 and to cross off any answers that prove to be incorrect.

Teaching Activity 1: Cooperative Project

State and Federal Powers

Section 11-1 discusses the powers reserved for states and those shared with the federal government. In this activity, which can be used at the end of the section, students decide whether powers belong to the state governments, the federal government, or are shared by both. The activity will require most of a class period.

Write some or all of these topics on the chalkboard: (1) natural disaster; (2) graduation requirements; (3) safety standards for automobiles; (4) rehabilitation programs for juvenile offenders; (5) divorce laws; (6) health and safety issues; (7) school lunch programs; (8) operation of public parks; (9) the minimum wage; (10) no-fault auto insurance; (11) recycling laws for beverage containers; (12) good Samaritan laws (private citizens helping other citizens); (13) legal age for marriage; (14) highway speeds; (15) criteria for accused juveniles to stand trial as adults.

Divide students into groups and ask each group to decide whether laws on each topic are made by the state governments, the federal government, or by both. (Answers: state powers: 2,4,5,8,10,11, 12,13; federal powers: 7; shared powers: 1,3,6,9, 14,15.)

When the groups reach consensus about which powers belong to which governments, have students discuss which level of government they believe should have legislative power. Groups must be able to provide reasons for their opinions. Allow 30 minutes for the groups to work.

When groups are finished, have them compare their answers and opinions for each topic. When all topics have been discussed, ask for volunteers to summarize the differences in state and federal powers. Summaries should point out that because state governments are closer to the people, they have legislative power over matters involving people's everyday lives.

Teaching Activity 2: Individual Project

Using the Initiative

Use of the initiative has led to many changes in state law. In this activity students gain understanding of this process by proposing laws. Students can compile the assignment out of class after they have read Section 11-2.

Review the definition of initiative by explaining it is the process by which citizens can propose laws. Instruct each student to write a law that he or she feels is needed but not in existence. Possible topics might include school reform, environmental protection, new holidays, or changes in taxation. Direct students to write their initiatives in petition form with the proposed law at the top of the page and lines for supporters to sign under it. Discuss initiatives and have students revise if necessary.

Instruct students to ask 10 to 15 registered voters to read their petitions and indicate whether they would support the proposed law. Students are to record the names of these people and their reasons for supporting or opposing the initiative. Set a deadline for completion of the assignment.

Discuss the results and have students summarize why their proposals were or were not supported. Conclude by having students discuss whether the initiative really gives power to the people.

Evaluating Progress: Cooperative Project

In this evaluation activity students identify newspaper articles that illustrate information from Chapter 11. Two to three weeks of recent newspapers are needed to conduct the activity, which can be assigned after students have finished the chapter.

Divide students into pairs and direct them to cut out at least three articles from the newspapers that illustrate the functions of the state's legislative, executive, or judicial branch; conflict between federal and state powers; or citizen participation in state government. Require students to identify what topic the article illustrates.

In front of the class, have each pair read the articles' headlines and give a brief description of the articles. Ask the class how each article relates to state government. Criteria for evaluation of the pairs' work should include finding diverse articles and correctly labeling them.

Reinforcement Activity: Individual Project

Chapter 11 distinguishes between state and federal powers and explores the balance between the national government and the states. In Reinforcement Worksheet Chapter 11, "The States and the National Government," in the Activity Book, students organize this information in chart form. The worksheet can be used as a summarizing activity at the end of the chapter.

When students' worksheets are complete, ask for volunteers to summarize the most important differences between the state and federal governments. Have students discuss why the national government should or should not have greater power over the states in certain matters than it does now.

Enrichment Activity: Individual Project

In this activity students list arguments for and against election and appointment of judges in state courts and propose a method of selection that seems best to them. The activity, to be used after students have read the material in Section 11-4, will require most of a class period or can be assigned as homework.

Introduce the activity by reviewing "Judges in State Courts" in Section 11-4. Distribute Enrichment Worksheet Chapter 11, "Selecting Judges," in the Activity Book and review the directions.

When students' worksheets are complete, ask for volunteers to read their proposals for selecting judges. Encourage discussion of each proposal. Conclude by asking students if they think that the Missouri Plan is a good compromise for selecting judges. Why or why not?

Answer Key

CHAPTER 11

Section 11-1 Review (text page 246)

1. See definitions for the following terms on the text pages indicated in parentheses: *public assistance* (242), *constitutional initiative* (244).
2. States alone hold the power to set up local governments, conduct elections, set up public school systems, and oversee businesses.
3. The federal Constitution sets out general principles; state constitutions spell out the details of the powers of the branches of government. In addition, state constitutions are amended more often than the federal Constitution.
4. The federal government helps ensure that states provide equal services and offer equal protection to all citizens; also, it is better able to handle problems that are too expensive for states to solve or that involve more than one state.
Synthesis. The powers of the national government and state governments overlap in providing public assistance, collecting taxes, setting up courts, enforcing laws, and punishing lawbreakers.
Data Search. There are 18,171 elected officials in state governments compared to 542 for the federal government. However, the average number of officials *per* government is higher for the federal government (542 compared to 363).

Section 11-2 Review (text page 250)

1. See definitions of the following terms on the text pages indicated in parentheses: *apportioned* (248), *initiative* (248), *referendum* (248), *recall* (248), *revenue* (249), *sales taxes* (249), *excise tax* (249), *income tax* (249), *bonds* (250).
2. The job of state legislator became more complex and time-consuming, making it difficult for citizen legislators to balance legislative duties with the demands of full-time jobs.
3. Seats are apportioned on the basis of equal representation.
4. Two major sources of state revenue are taxes and federal funding.
Analysis. Citizens use the initiative, the referendum, and the recall to influence state legislatures. The initiative allows citizens to propose laws. The referendum allows voters to reject or approve laws passed by the legislature. The recall gives citizens the power to remove elected officials from office.

Section 11-3 Review (text page 254)

1. See definition for *item veto* on text page 252.
2. The governor and the President both play the roles of chief executive (overseeing the executive branch, making sure laws are enforced, using military power, appointing officials, and creating a budget) and legislative leader (proposing and vetoing legislation). They both have some judicial powers.
3. The President selects cabinet members, but most state executive officers are elected.
4. State executive agencies carry out the day-to-day work of the executive branch.
Evaluation. Affirmative answers may include the idea that governors, like Presidents, should be able to select the people who will assist them to assure their goals are the same. Negative answers may include the idea that elected officials are answerable to the people and that giving the governor the right to appoint such officers would limit democracy.

Section 11-4 Review (text page 257)

1. The three-tier structure is trial courts, appellate courts, and a supreme court.
2. The Missouri Plan is a method of selecting judges in which voters have the opportunity to vote on whether to keep in office a judge appointed by the governor.
3. The Supreme Court found for the citizens' group because California's free-speech rights overruled the private property rights recognized in the federal Constitution.

Evaluation. Answers may include gubernatorial appointment because governors are better able than voters to choose the best-qualified judges; election, because governors might be too biased; or the Missouri Plan, which combines appointment and election.

Decision-Making Lesson (text pages 258–259)

1. The school principal, the source of statement A, would have access to statistics on night-class enrollment and therefore may be reliable, as long as those statistics are broad-based rather than limited to local schools. The source of statement B may be reliable because documentaries are usually thoroughly researched and are intended to present accurate information. However, more information would be needed about where the makers of the documentary got their statistics. The dropout, the source of statement C, might be generalizing based on his or her own experience. One would want to know whether he or she has general statistics to support the statement. The talk-show host, the source of statement D, is unlikely to be a reliable source because he or she is not an expert on the subject.
2. Statement A is not supported by excerpt A, which says that fewer than half of the dropouts return to school, or by excerpt B, which provides no information on the percentage that return to school. Statement B is supported by both excerpts, which state that one fourth of all students drop out. Statement C is supported by excerpt B, which says that many states require workers under eighteen to be enrolled in school. Statement D is not directly supported by either excerpt because they do not give the percentage of dropouts who become criminals.
3. To evaluate statement A, you would need statistics on the percentage of dropouts enrolling in night classes. For statement B, you would need statistics on your school's drop-out rate. For statement C, you would need information on state and local employment regulations. For statement D, you would need statistics on the percentage of dropouts who commit crimes.
4. Some other sources might be newspaper and magazine articles on the dropout problem, school attendance records, state and county department of education records, employment regulations, and information from juvenile and criminal justice agencies. All of these sources might provide information on the drop-out rate and what happens to dropouts once they leave school.
5. Students should summarize the guidelines provided in the lesson in their own words.
6. Accurate information helps you choose the most effective option and put together an effective action plan to carry out a decision.

Chapter Survey (text page 260)

Understanding New Vocabulary

1. *Constitutional initiative* and *recall* are related because they are both ways in which citizens may play a direct role in state government.
2. *Initiative* and *referendum* are related because they are both ways in which citizens can influence state lawmaking.
3. *Revenue* is related to *sales tax* because sales tax is one method of raising revenue.
Putting It in Writing. Answers may include the power of citizens in some states to propose amendments and laws, approve or reject laws passed by the legislature, and remove elected officials from office.

Looking Back at the Chapter

1. The Constitution specifies the powers given to the national government. Powers not given to the national government, nor denied to the states, go to the state governments or to the people.
2. The federal Constitution and most state constitutions have a similar form (a preamble and a bill of rights) and describe how government should be organized. State constitutions are more detailed and are amended and rewritten more often.
3. Because federalism allows the states to handle local issues, state laws and services vary widely. As a result, opportunities in different states are not always equal.
4. In earlier times, most state legislators were citizens who took time off from full-time jobs to handle state affairs. Today, legislators are full-time professionals.

5. The decision established that seats in state legislatures had to be apportioned based on equal representation.
6. Answers may include lawmaking, approving the governor's budget and appointments, and the power to impeach executive and judicial officers.
7. State governments get more than half of their revenues from taxes.
8. The governor can propose legislation in the form of a bill, a budget, or a speech to the legislature; talk with legislators; or seek public support.
9. (**a**) Election of judges gives citizens some influence over the judicial system. However voters may not be knowledgeable enough about who the qualified candidates are, and elected judges might make politically popular decisions to get re-elected. (**b**) Appointment of judges enables the governor to choose judges based on merit, not popularity. However, the governor might appoint friends or supporters who are not well qualified.
10. Answers in agreement may include the idea that since state constitutions concentrate on details, a regular review would help remove outdated items. Answers in disagreement may include that holding regular conventions could lead to unnecessary changing of laws and that most changes can be made by amendment.
11. Answers may include the suggestion that state government would benefit from professionally trained legislators who understand state problems and could devote more time to finding solutions. Citizens would have the benefit of "expert" legislators; however, they might feel that their representatives could lose their focus on local issues if they were not employed closer to home. Qualified office-holders might be more encouraged to run for a full-time, well-paying job. On the other hand, it might be hard to return to an established career, in the event you lost a bid, or even if you won, to pick up where you left off when your term was over.
12. The case involved deciding which was supreme—the more general rights of the federal Constitution or the more specific rights of a state constitution. The case shows how our system of federalism is not always a clear-cut division of powers, and how the court system must play a role in deciding which powers are supreme.
13. Answers in agreement may include the idea that if civil and criminal laws of most states were similar, they could be under one federal court system. Answers in disagreement may include the idea that the enforcement of civil and criminal law is a local issue and should be left largely to the states.

Working Together

Answers will vary.

Skills Workshop (text page 261)

Social Studies Skills

1. The story is about a bill about drinking.
2. The article was written in Sacramento.
3. The source is Associated Press (AP).
4. The lead does not say why or how the bill was passed.

Decision-Making Skills

1. You might check where the writer got his or her information.
2. You would need information on the annual aid that states have given to local governments over the past few years.
3. You could look in books on American government, almanacs, and government budget publications.
4. The information in Chapter 11 does not support the statement. Examples may include the fact that under Reagan's "new federalism" states received less federal money which means less money for local governments. Also, each state can decide how to use its block grant money, so no local government is guaranteed the same amount of state aid every year.
5. Accurate information is needed in order to compare options and effectively plan how to carry out a decision.
6. Examples of decisions will vary.

OVERVIEW

Local governments have the greatest effect on the everyday life of citizens. These governments provide vital services, such as utilities, education, and public safety, which are funded by local taxes and fees for services. Although conflicts arise over land and revenue, local, state, and federal governments can unite to solve problems.

OBJECTIVES

After completing this chapter, students should be able to

- describe types of local government and the services they provide.
- compare strengths and weaknesses of forms of city government.
- identify problems of local governments and possible solutions.
- explain how local governments raise revenue.

PLANNING GUIDE

Teaching Strategy	Skills	Special Features	Review/Evaluation
Introducing the Chapter: Cooperative Project **Teaching Activity 1:** Class Project—A Community Services Guide for Newcomers (Section 12-2) **Teaching Activity 2:** Cooperative Project—Community Conflict over Land (Section 12-3) **Evaluating Progress:** Individual Project (Section 12-3) **Reinforcement Activity:** Individual Project—Worksheet (Section 12-2) **Enrichment Activity:** Cooperative Project—Worksheet (Section 12-1) **Unit 4 Activity:** A Community Handbook	Social Studies Skills Workshop: Interpreting an Organization Chart Decision-Making Skills Workshop: Opinion or Statement of Fact? **Issues and Decision Making:** Worksheet Chapter 12	People Make a Difference: Young Volunteers Serve Their Community American Notebook Issues that Affect You: A Case Study—Banning Neighborhood Noise In Their Own Words: George Washington Plunkitt—Honest Graft	Section Reviews Chapter 12 Survey Unit 4 Survey **Tests:** Chapter 12 Test, Unit 4 Test, Quarter 2 Test **Testing Software** **Additional Resources** **Activity Book** **Citizenship Skills** **Transparencies and Activity Book** **Voices of America**

For reinforcement and enrichment worksheets and unit activities, see the Activity Book.

Teaching Strategy

Introducing the Chapter: Cooperative Project

Although their lives are affected daily by local government, students may not be aware of its total impact. In this introductory activity students analyze the functions of local government. The activity will take about 30 minutes.

Begin the activity by writing on the chalkboard the following questions: (1) What decisions do local governments make that affect you? (2) What services do local governments provide for you? Divide students into groups of four or five to discuss answers to the questions.

After about five minutes, give students a prompt by asking them to consider how local governments affect their health, welfare, and safety. Allow them to work another five minutes, then ask students to consider the role local governments play in education, land use planning, and utilities. Groups have five minutes to complete their answers to the questions.

On a piece of chart paper, list students' responses to the questions. Ask the class if the original two questions have been answered. Is all the information accurate? Post the list so students can revise it if necessary at the end of the chapter.

To conclude the activity, ask the class to evaluate which level of government (federal, state, or local) most directly affects their daily lives. Why?

Teaching Activity 1: Class Project

A Community Services Guide for Newcomers

To help students understand the services provided by their local government, they will compile a community services directory for newcomers to the school. This activity, which can be used after students have read Section 12-2, will require one class period. Provide one or more local telephone directories for students to use.

Begin by asking for volunteers to share their experiences of moving into a new community or attending a new school. Explain that the class will be working on a project that will help new students to adjust to their school and community.

Discuss with the class what public service information would be helpful to a new student. Examples may include names of schools in the community, locations of public recreation areas and libraries, routes of public transportation, and the location of the driver's license bureau.

Divide students into teams. Using local telephone directories, each team will research a different kind of community service. For each topic, students are to gather names, telephone numbers, and addresses.

Once the data has been collected, develop a standard format to organize the information into information sheets or a booklet. Have each group prepare its information in the agreed-upon format. Combine the work of the groups into a packet. Students may want to add city maps and brochures from the chamber of commerce.

Duplicate the guide and distribute to new students. The local chamber of commerce or visitor's bureau also might like a copy.

Teaching Activity 2: Cooperative Project

Community Conflict over Land

At the heart of many community conflicts are economic issues. In this activity students engage in a role play about communities in disagreement over undeveloped land. The activity will require two class periods and is most appropriate after students have read Section 12-3.

Draw a rough diagram on the chalkboard to illustrate a large piece of undeveloped land that separates three communities from one another. Real estate developers want to build quality homes, a park, and possibly some small businesses on the land, which will generate additional taxes and bring non-polluting industries and new jobs to the area. Explain to the class that all three communities want to annex the land so they can benefit from the development.

Divide the class into three groups to represent the three communities. Describe the communities as follows: Community A has the lowest tax revenue, the fewest services, the least amount of development, and the most rapid growth among the three communities. The land in Community A is hilly and heavily forested—similar to the undeveloped land. Community B has higher tax revenue, provides about the same services, and is more developed than the other two communities. Community C, which is the wealthiest of the three communities and has the best services, wants to annex the land and leave it undeveloped.

Instruct groups to prepare arguments explaining the services its community would provide future residents, its financial strength, and the incentives it would be willing to offer developers. Encourage the use of visuals to accompany the presentations. Let the groups work together for most of a class period to develop their arguments and plan their presentation.

On the second day, have each group present its arguments to the class. List the arguments on the board. When all groups have presented, ask students what needs and concerns the developers would have. What points on the board would be of interest to them? Have students compare the needs and interests of communities and developers.

Discuss possible options to solve the competition for the land. Discuss the advantages and disadvantages and their consequences for the community that annexes the land. Ask students to decide individually which community should get the land, then call for a vote. Discuss the outcome and the reasons for students' decision.

⊡ Evaluating Progress: Individual Project

Use this activity to assess students' understanding of Chapter 12. In the activity students apply information from the chapter to issues in their own community. The activity should be assigned at the beginning of the chapter and completed at the end of it.

As they begin the chapter, ask students to bring to class newspaper articles from the editorial page and the news section and letters to the editor about local problems. Briefly discuss the kinds of issues they find, and direct students to identify a problem or issue that interests them. Encourage students to become expert on the topic by researching through individuals, the community or civic groups affected, and the government. Direct their research by providing the following questions on the chalkboard:

- What is the problem?
- What caused it?
- Who does it affect?
- Who is trying to deal with it?
- How is the local government involved?
- How can the problem be solved?
- What can you do about it?

At the conclusion of the chapter, have students bring in their information on the subject. Group students with the same problem together to discuss their solutions. Have each group choose a spokesperson to summarize the problem and the group's possible solutions for the class.

Challenge students to actually participate, if appropriate, in helping to solve the problem. You may wish to give extra credit to students who participate individually or as part of a group.

Criteria for assessment should focus on the completeness of answers to the research questions, the depth of understanding of the issue, and the thoughtfulness of the solutions.

Reinforcement Activity: Individual Project

The differences between federal, state, and local governments are sometimes unclear to students. In this activity students distinguish the various functions and responsibilities of local government. The activity can be used after students have read Section 12-2.

Introduce the activity by drawing an illustration of local government as a tree with many roots. Label one or two of the roots with sources of revenue, such as property taxes and user charges. Label one or two of the branches on the tree with services, such as education, police protection, or libraries.

Explain to students that the illustration is one way of showing how local governments are funded and what services they provide. Tell students that they may find the illustration helpful as they complete Reinforcement Worksheet Chapter 12, "Functions of Local Government," in the Activity Book. Review directions on the worksheet with students.

When students' worksheets are completed, review their answers. Encourage volunteers to display their diagrams and compare the ways local government can be depicted in visual form.

Enrichment Activity: Cooperative Project

Use this activity after students have read the material in Section 12-1. In the activity students compare the strengths and weaknesses of forms of city government. The activity will take about 30 minutes to complete.

Assign students to groups of four or five. Distribute Enrichment Worksheet Chapter 12, "Comparing City Governments," in the Activity Book and review the instructions with students. Because specific answers are not in the text, students will need to work together to identify the strengths and weaknesses of each plan. Remind students to determine why each factor is a strength or weakness before reaching a conclusion.

When groups have completed the task, review answers. To conclude the activity have students identify the local organizational plan and discuss its appropriateness for your community.

Answer Key

CHAPTER 12

Section 12-1 Review (text page 268)

1. See definitions for the following terms on the text pages indicated in parentheses: *board* (264), *ordinances* (264), *municipality* (266).
2. Counties, townships, and New England towns were formed to carry out laws and provide services in rural areas. Special districts provide single services that individual communities could not afford to provide for themselves. Cities serve people in urban areas.
3. Under the mayor-council plan, power is shared by the mayor and city council. In the weak-mayor plan most power rests with the council, which usually appoints the mayor from among its members. In the strong-mayor plan the mayor holds the most authority. Under the council-manager plan, the elected council hires a manager who oversees the budget and directs city employees. Under the commission plan, elected commissioners govern the city as a committee.
Analysis. Answers may include the idea that in a direct democracy citizens set government policies by a direct vote at meetings, which would be impractical in a large city or county.
Data Search. Special district governments are the most numerous type of local government. Examples may include special districts that supply water, control insects, provide parks, run subways, and protect people from fire.

Section 12-2 Review (text page 274)

1. See definitions for the following terms on the text pages indicated in parentheses: *utilities* (268), *zoning* (270), *property tax* (272), *intergovernmental revenue* (273).
2. Local governments provide for public education from elementary school through two-year colleges. They provide public health programs, public assistance programs, child care, job training, low-cost housing for the homeless, and enforcement of pollution laws. They provide for public safety through police and fire protection and by setting building codes.
3. A community would likely pay for an airport by selling bonds or getting a federal grant.
4. Officials must make policy decisions based on how much money is available. If there is a large drop in revenue, some services may have to be cut.
Evaluation. Answers will vary but should be supported with reasons.

Section 12-3 Review (text page 277)

1. See definition for *home rule* on text page 276.
2. Answers may include competition for new businesses and federal grants and cooperation through regional problem-solving meetings and joint efforts to provide services.
3. State and local governments cooperate in solving local problems and carrying out state programs. The governments may disagree over questions of what is a state matter and what is a local matter.
4. The three levels of government have many of the same problems, such as pollution and crime. The federal government needs cooperation at the state and local levels for national programs, and local governments need financial help from the state and national governments for large projects.
Evaluation. Answers may include the idea that competition for businesses and federal grants forces local governments to run more efficiently, but too much competition may result in public officials using dishonest methods to attract businesses and grants.

Issues That Affect You: A Case Study (text pages 278–279)

1. The ordinance prohibited "loud, unnecessary, and unusual noise which disturbs the peace and quiet of any neighborhood."
2. The Manns argued that the ordinance was not clear enough to be enforced because the acceptable noise level was not described scientifically.
3. Answers may include the idea that the ordinance is unfair because people should be allowed to play loud music as long as they are considerate of their neighbors or that people who enjoy loud music can listen to their radios in places where the noise will not bother others.
4. Answers may include the idea that the law was intended only to regulate noise level, not types of noise, so the court probably would have ruled similarly for loud classical music.

Chapter Survey (text page 280)

Understanding New Vocabulary

1. (d) County *board* members are often called commissioners.
2. (c) *Property tax* is a form of local government revenue.
3. (a) *Zoning* consists of organized plans for land use.
4. (b) A city is the most common type of *municipality*.
5. (f) Grants are a form of *intergovernmental revenue*.
6. (e) Water, gas, and electricity are all *utilities*.
Putting It in Writing. Answers may include determining needs of citizens, available land for plant, effect of plant on environment, building codes, building costs, funding, and gaining board approval of plan.

Looking Back at the Chapter

1. States grant powers to local governments.
2. Some types of local governments, such as counties, meet rural needs. Other types, such as cities, meet urban needs.
3. Traditional New England towns practice direct democracy. Large cities rely on representative

government in which city officials make most policy decisions.

4. The council-manager plan was created to try to remove party politics from city government. The commission plan was created when a mayor-council government was unable to manage rebuilding efforts after a hurricane destroyed a Texas city.

5. Students may choose and describe two of the following: education, utilities, health and welfare, land use planning, and public safety.

6. Local revenue comes from taxes (property tax, local sales taxes, and sometimes local income tax); service charges and profits from government-run businesses; borrowing (bank loans and bonds); and intergovernmental revenue (grants).

7. There are limits on local revenue, and federal programs are sometimes stopped. Also, local governments cannot increase their taxes without state approval and voters may limit revenue by cutting local taxes.

8. Local governments are involved because they can best determine local needs, but they often depend on state and federal financial help to keep local programs running.

9. Local governments compete for new businesses and federal grants and may come into conflict when one community's policies affect neighboring communities. Conflict with the state and federal governments may arise over local programs that need state or federal funding.

10. Answers may include the idea that local governments know how to use the money or that the state and federal governments should have a say in how their money is spent, especially since local programs affect both the states and the nation as a whole.

11. Since local governments have limited revenue to spend on services, they must decide which services to fund and which services to cut back or drop.

12. Answers may include the idea that state governments would have to expand to carry out local functions. States probably could not afford to tailor services to local needs. Without local government, communities would have less of a voice in setting policies.

Working Together

Answers will vary.

Skills Workshop (text page 281)

Social Studies Skills

1. There are four levels: the voters, the council, the city manager, and the department heads.

2. The council has the greatest power. That power is used to hire the city manager, who supervises department heads and other employees.

Decision-Making Skills

1. Answers may include that customers are charged higher utility fees when local governments provide the services. This statement of fact can be proved or disproved by comparing fees charged by government-run utilities with those charged by private companies. One opinion is that local governments do not run utilities as well as private companies do. The statement cannot be proved or disproved because people will have differing views on what *well* means. They will weigh factors such as cost and efficiency differently.

2. You can either prove or disprove statements of fact to determine whether they are accurate. Opinions may also be reliable, but first you have to check whether they are supported by good reasons. By evaluating opinions and statements of fact you can base your decisions on reliable information.

3. Students may refer to the guidelines on page 212 but should explain the skill in their own words in a way that a younger student can follow.

In Their Own Words (text page 282)

1. Honest graft is taking advantage of information available only to public officials as long as no laws are broken; dishonest graft is making money by blackmailing and other illegal activities.

2. Answers may include the view that the public was hurt because officials paid more attention to their own profit than the good of the general public or the opposite view that it was all right if officials benefited financially from public projects as long as the public benefited as well. Opinions will vary regarding whether the activities should be illegal. Some students may argue that it is unrealistic to require public officials not to take advantage of inside information as long as their actions do not cause harm to the public.

3. Under the council-manager plan, machines had less influence on city council elections, and councils were more accountable to the public. Also, since the manager was hired by the council rather than elected, presumably he or she did not owe political favors to anyone and could run city affairs more like an efficient business.

Unit 4 Survey (text page 283)

Looking Back at the Unit

1. "New federalism" was the name given to a plan introduced under President Reagan in the 1980s to return greater power to the state and local governments. The plan was a reaction to the growing power of the federal government since the 1930s.

2. Answers may include the initiative, referendum, and recall at state levels. At the local level, citizens can attend board and council meetings to voice their opinions and influence ordinances, and vote for or against local taxes and bond proposals.

3. Like the federal government, state governments have executive, legislative, and judicial branches. Many local governments, such as cities and towns, also have executive and legislative branches. All three levels have elected, appointed, and hired officials. They also have departments and agencies that provide services. Government employees at all three levels must pass examinations to qualify for their jobs.

4. All three are executive officials with the responsibility to enforce, rather than make, laws, and appoint officials to assist them in their duties. Some differences are that a President has more power over the national executive branch than a governor has over the state executive branch or a mayor has over city officials. The President generally has more influence in setting policies than state governors who must rely more on persuasion. In cities with weak-mayor or council-manager forms of government, the council controls most policymaking.

5. The relationships are similar in that state governments receive money from the federal government, and local governments receive money from state governments. Also, just as the federal government needs the help of the states to run federally sponsored programs, states need the help of local governments in running state programs. However, the federal government cannot take certain powers away from the state governments, but the states can take power away from local governments.

6. Advantages may include the fact that officials in state and local governments have a better understanding of issues and problems that affect their particular states or communities. Also, many state and local governments rely on federal aid for local projects. Some disadvantages are the conflicts that may occur between federal, state, and local policies or laws.

Taking a Stand

Supporters may argue that lotteries help make up shortfalls in state funding and participation is voluntary. Opponents may argue that lotteries encourage gambling and most ticket buyers cannot really afford to participate.

OVERVIEW

Societies decide how to use limited resources to produce goods and services that will satisfy people's unlimited wants. Decision makers in an economy decide what goods and services to produce, how to produce them, and who will get what is produced. The three economic systems represent different ways of making the goods and services people want.

OBJECTIVES

After completing this chapter, students should be able to

- explain the process of satisfying people's economic wants.
- explain how to make economic choices.
- identify the major economic decisions that must be made in any economy.
- explain how economic decisions are made in three types of economies.

PLANNING GUIDE

Teaching Strategy	Skills	Special Features	Review/Evaluation
Introducing the Chapter: Cooperative Project **Teaching Activity 1:** Individual Project—The Want-Satisfaction Chain (Section 13-1) **Teaching Activity 2:** Cooperative Project—A Cartoon Perspective on Economic Systems (Section 13-3) **Evaluating Progress:** Individual Project (Section 13-2) **Reinforcement Activity:** Individual Project—Worksheet (Section 13-1) **Enrichment Activity:** Individual Project—Worksheet (Section 13-3)	Decision-Making Lesson: Choosing and Taking Action Social Studies Skills Workshop: Interpreting a Diagram Decision-Making Skills Workshop: Choosing and Taking Action **Issues and Decision Making:** Worksheet Chapter 13	Views of Noted Americans: Lester Thurow American Notebook	Section Reviews Chapter 13 Survey **Tests:** Chapter 13 Test **Testing Software** **Additional Resources** **Activity Book** **Citizenship Skills** **Transparencies and Activity Book** **Voices of America**

For reinforcement and enrichment worksheets and unit activities, see the Activity Book.

Teaching Strategy

Introducing the Chapter: Cooperative Project

Young people are an influential segment of the American economic system. In this introductory activity students become more aware of their importance as consumers and producers in our economy. The activity will take approximately 25 minutes.

Have students choose partners for paired interviewing. (One student acts as the interviewer and the other the interviewee for a period of time, then exchange roles.) Explain that today's interview topic is "The impact of teenagers on the American economy." Point out that the purchasing power of teenagers in the United States is equal to the gross national product (GNP) of many countries. Explain GNP as the total value of a nation's annual output of goods and services. (GNP is discussed in Chapter 16.)

Direct interviewers to ask the following questions and record the answers. Then exchange roles and repeat the interview.

- What goods and services did you purchase in the past week? (Include even small purchases.)
- Why did you make these purchases?
- What jobs have you done in the past week for pay?
- Why did you decide to work? Why did you choose that job?
- Have you received other income in the past week from an allowance or as a gift?

When both students in each pair have been interviewed and their answers recorded, ask the pairs to summarize their last five days as consumers and producers. Then have each student anonymously record and submit the total cost of purchases and the total income received in the past week. Total the value of all of the students' purchases and their income. Discuss the results.

Record interview findings on the chalkboard. Emphasize that these purchases and jobs make students part of our economic system—in some cases a significant part. Explain that the questions and issues just discussed are part of economics, the topic of Chapter 13.

To extend this activity, you may want to have students graph the conclusions.

Teaching Activity 1: Individual Project

The Want-Satisfaction Chain

In this activity students apply the information they have read in Section 13-1 by diagraming a want-satisfaction chain. The activity requires a class period, or it can be assigned as homework.

Begin the activity by asking students to name the seven links in the want-satisfaction chain discussed in Section 13-1 and shown in the flow chart on text page 290. List the links on the chalkboard and have students copy them.

Ask students to think of four to six items they want to buy. Have them choose one of the items to use in illustrating the want-satisfaction chain. Advise students to write their item next to the first link they copied from the chalkboard. For the remaining six links, students should describe all of the different economic processes required for the item to be produced, distributed, and consumed. Students may need to do research if they are unfamiliar with how the item is produced or distributed.

When all the data has been collected, ask students to design a diagram or illustration (different from the one in the text) to show how their item is an example of the want-satisfaction chain. When finished, have students display their work or exchange information in small groups.

Teaching Activity 2: Cooperative Project

A Cartoon Perspective on Economic Systems

In this activity students create cartoons to reinforce their understanding of different types of economies. The activity is best conducted after students have finished Section 13-3 and can be completed in an entire class period, or assigned as homework. To stimulate students' thinking, you may wish to display some examples of economy-related cartoons.

Begin by reviewing how the goals and values of a society affect its economy. Emphasize that each economic system has weaknesses as well as strengths. Tell how editorial cartoons, which appear in newspapers and news magazines, call attention to important economic events, issues, or problems.

Explain to students that their task is to create cartoons that judge each of the three economic systems described in Section 13-3. They may work in pairs or individually. Remind students that cartoons can exaggerate, expose, or make fun of values, goals, or activities. Have students review the section and then engage in brainstorming to generate ideas or topics appropriate for cartoons.

Once students have decided on topics for their cartoons, point out that cartoonists often use animals or symbols in their work. For example, bulls and bears are used in the United States to indicate strong and weak economies. Emphasize that cartoons need a title and a caption.

Display students' cartoons around the room. Ask students to review the cartoons and write positive comments on a sheet of paper posted below each cartoon. Encourage everyone to look for good ideas and avoid repeating comments.

Evaluating Progress: Individual Project

As Chapter 13 points out, people in any economy face three major economic decisions about the production, distribution, and consumption of goods and services. To assess how well students understand these decisions, use this evaluation activity after students have read the material in Section 13-2.

Begin by asking students if they have ever wanted to invent a product or to start a service. Explain that this activity will give them an opportunity to do that. Have students think about a need they might have for a better tool, a food product, a fun toy or game, or a new style of clothing. Students who are more interested in creating a service can think of special help or advice they may need but have been unable to find.

Write on the chalkboard the three questions that students must answer about their product or service: (1) What and how much will be produced? (2) How will it be produced? (3) Who will get what is produced? Students should answer these questions in a narrative format. Criteria for assessment should focus on students' understanding of these economic decisions and the realistic nature of their proposals.

Reinforcement Activity: Individual Project

Use this activity after students have read the material in Section 13-1. In the activity students apply their understanding of opportunity cost to economic decision making.

Introduce Reinforcement Worksheet Chapter 13, "Making Economic Choices," in the Activity Book by explaining that students are to imagine that they have $150 to spend. Their options are shown on the worksheet. Review the directions and instruct students to complete the worksheet independently.

When their worksheets are finished, ask students to share the criteria they used in making their decisions. Have students speculate on how their choices might change if they were given three times as much money or one third as much money to spend.

Enrichment Activity: Individual Project

In Enrichment Worksheet Chapter 13, "Comparing Three Economies," in the Activity Book, students apply information from Sections 13-2 and 13-3 to describe the economies of three countries. Use the activity after students have finished reading the chapter.

Have students read the directions and the first paragraph of the worksheet and clarify any questions they have before they complete the sheet independently. Encourage students to apply information from the text. You may wish to allow library time for students to do some background reading on the three countries: Peru, Cuba, and Canada.

Conclude the activity by having students discuss which of the countries they would most like to visit and which they would prefer to live in. Have students consider the similarities and differences among the three economies and the economy of the United States.

Answer Key

CHAPTER 13

Section 13-1 Review (text page 292)

1. See definitions for the following terms on the text pages indicated in parentheses: *factors of production* (289), *capital* (289), *consumption* (290), *opportunity cost* (291), *scarcity* (291).
2. Everyone wants food, clothing, and shelter.
3. Distribution makes the good available to people who want it.
4. Two important parts are examining the benefits of each alternative and examining the costs of each alternative.
Analysis. Economic choices have to be made because scarcity always exists: wants are unlimited, but the resources used to satisfy them are limited.

Section 13-2 Review (text page 296)

1. Individuals who own or can get resources decide what and how much to produce. Deciding what to produce depends on what people want; deciding how much to produce depends on what the producer can afford and how much people are expected to consume.
2. People consider how much it will cost to produce the product.
3. Answers may include sharing equally, deciding on the basis of wants, giving a small group the power to decide, deciding on the basis of how much each person produces, and giving to those who could pay the most.
Evaluation. Answers may include free competition for goods and services, with some basic services, such as education, provided for all. People are free to try to obtain as many goods and services as they want, but some people go hungry.

Section 13-3 Review (text page 301)

1. See definitions for the following terms on the text pages indicated in parentheses: *traditional economy* (296), *command economy* (297), *market economy* (298), *profit* (299), *invest* (299), *free enterprise* (300), *capitalism* (300), *mixed economy* (300).
2. There is little change or growth because traditional ways of doing things determine economic decisions.
3. In a command economy the government controls resources and can quickly shift them from one use to another, controlling what is produced and consumed.
4. A market economy is influenced by the profit motive, what consumers want to buy, and competition among resource owners, workers, and buyers.
Evaluation. Answers may include the freedom of individuals to make basic economic decisions, the

economic security provided to all of the people, and the ability of each system to meet changing conditions.

Data Search. In the United States, there are 770 cars and 769 telephones per 1,000 people. In Japan, there are 435 cars and 556 telephones per 1,000 people.

Decision-Making Lesson (text pages 302–303)

1. Answers may include having a job that allows time for school activities and provides opportunities for advancement.
2. Examples may include the opinions that jobs at the Burger Barn are fun and that the job at King Grocery was easy. Some statements of fact are that Roy is earning $5.25 an hour and the work week at the library will be 10 to 15 hours. It is important to identify opinions because you have to judge them differently than statements of fact. Instead of proving or disproving them, you can only judge the reasons supporting them.
3. If your main goal is to have opportunities for advancement, you would find the information about promotion to a library desk job relevant. If your main goal is flexible hours, you may consider information about the friendliness of the employees irrelevant because it has no effect on your job schedule.
4. Consequences will vary. For instance, a good consequence of Job 1 is that you can do after-school activities because of your flexible hours. A good consequence of Job 2 is a possibility for promotion. A possible bad consequence of Job 3 is giving up weekend leisure activities.
5. Options will vary according to goals.
6. Some qualifications that will help include past experience, ability to interview well, and recommendations from respected people in the community. Obstacles may include a lack of experience, poor performance at a previous job, and competition from older applicants.
7. Examples may include filling out an application, learning as much as you can about the job, rehearsing for the interview, and asking for letters of recommendation.
8. Predicting consequences helps you compare options and avoid making a choice that you might later regret.
9. Answers may include the following: Recognizing relevant information helps you to make good decisions. Distinguishing between opinions and statements of fact helps you evaluate information. Determining which sources are reliable and judging the accuracy of statements help you get accurate information on which to base your decision.

Chapter Survey (text page 304)

Understanding New Vocabulary

1. *Scarcity* forces people to make decisions in which *opportunity cost* is a factor.
2. *Capital* is one of the *factors of production.*
3. In a *free enterprise* economy, individuals are free to start businesses in order to make a *profit.*
4. Under *capitalism*, individuals are free to *invest* in businesses.
5. Most *mixed economies* contain elements of a *command economy.*

Putting It in Writing. Answers may include the following: In a traditional economy, custom determines who grows wheat and makes bread, how bread is made, and how much is produced, and to whom it is distributed. In a command economy, a ruler or central authority makes those decisions. In a market economy, private individuals decide how much bread to produce, based on how much they think consumers will buy.

Looking Back at the Chapter

1. People live in different climates and different cultures, and have different interests and tastes that change over time.
2. Sample answer: For a bicycle, the land includes metal from ore, rubber from rubber plants, vinyl from petroleum, and a site for the bicycle factory; the labor includes workers who manufacture parts and assemble the bicycle; the capital includes the factory, machinery, and tools.
3. Steps in the process include production, distribution, and consumption.
4. There are never enough resources to meet all the economic wants of a society (scarcity).
5. The three basic economic decisions are what and how much to produce, how to produce, and who will get what is produced.

6. You would probably have the same job as your father if you are a boy, and as your mother if you are a girl.
7. A ruler or central authority decides how resources will be used and what will be produced.
8. The profit motive is the goal of individuals in a market economy to make a profit.
9. People who own valuable land and capital resources or who earn very high wages will be able to buy more goods and services than those who do not.
10. Answers may include such daily wants as food, clothing, and shelter. Wants that occur less often may include travel and products such as bicycles, cars, and VCRs.
11. Answers may include the choice to buy or not buy a particular product. Factors may include cost in money terms and the influence of friends and parents.
12. Answers may include the idea that every individual "owns" his or her own labor, but not everyone owns land or capital.
13. Answers will vary.
14. Production of that product will be reduced or will stop.

Working Together

Answers will vary.

Skills Workshop (text page 305)

Social Studies Skills

1. The subject is the relationship of the factors of production to the production of goods and services.
2. Goods and services are created in the production process. In the diagram, arrows lead from the boxes containing capital, labor, and land to the box labeled production.
3. Capital, labor, and land are all used in the production process.
4. It is a different shape because production is a process, whereas the other shapes contain "things."

Decision-Making Skills

1. Opinions may vary. To reach the goal of earning at least $100 per week while working no more than 15 total weekday hours, you need to earn about $7 an hour. Based on the counselor's estimate, you could probably earn that hourly rate if you provided good service.
2. The least reliable source would be the movie because you do not know whether it is based on true experiences. The counselor is probably familiar with local wages, and the *Teenage Employment Guide* seems to provide a realistic description of the challenge of running a car-care business.
3. Answers may include obtaining supplies, planning a schedule, advertising, and getting customer feedback.

OVERVIEW

America's free enterprise, market system depends on a circular flow of goods and services, factors of production, and money. The laws of supply and demand affect both prices and production of goods and services. In our market economy, businesses are either sole proprietorships, partnerships, or corporations. Conflict between business and labor has had an important impact on our economy.

OBJECTIVES

After completing this chapter, students should be able to

- describe the circular flow of economic activity in our market economy.
- explain how the laws of supply and demand affect our economy.
- compare sole proprietorships, partnerships, and corporations.
- compare the interests of unions and employers.

PLANNING GUIDE

Teaching Strategy	Skills	Special Features	Review/Evaluation
Introducing the Chapter: Class Project **Teaching Activity 1:** Individual Project—Entrepreneur for a Day (Section 14-2) **Teaching Activity 2:** Cooperative Project—Labor and Management Speak Out (Section 14-3) **Evaluating Progress:** Individual Project (Section 14-3) **Reinforcement Activity:** Individual Project—Worksheet (Section 14-1) **Enrichment Activity:** Individual Project—Worksheet (Section 14-2) **Unit 5 Activity:** The Big Apple: A Market Simulation	Social Studies Skills Workshop: Analyzing a Circular Flow Chart Decision-Making Skills Workshop: Opinion or Statement of Fact? **Issues and Decision Making:** Worksheet Chapter 14	People Make a Difference: Ice Cream Makers Share Success American Notebook	Section Reviews Chapter 14 Survey **Tests:** Chapter 14 Test **Testing Software** **Additional Resources** **Activity Book** **Citizenship Skills** **Transparencies and Activity Book** **Voices of America**

For reinforcement and enrichment worksheets and unit activities, see the Activity Book.

Teaching Strategy

Introducing the Chapter: Class Project

This activity introduces students to the American economic system by helping them to understand how their decisions as consumers affect supply and demand for certain products.

Write the following headings across the top of the chalkboard: *Product*, *Current Price*, *Stop or Continue Buying*, and *Product Substitute.*

Ask students to copy the headings, then follow these instructions:

- In the *Product* column, list five products you regularly buy.
- Under *Current Price*, list the price you pay for each product listed.
- In the third column, make a check mark beside the products that you would stop buying if the price increased. Draw a star beside the products that you would buy regardless of price.
- In the last column, list substitutes for the products you would stop buying if the price increased.

Below their chart, have students list any products that they no longer buy because of price increases. Then have students list any products they would like to buy if the product was available and the price was right.

While students read aloud the products they listed, have a volunteer write the information on the chalkboard, making tally marks for those products that are repeated. Check the items that most students would stop buying if the price increased. Star the items that most students would buy regardless of price. Discuss what maximum price students would be willing to pay for the remaining products.

Discuss the significance of the compiled information by asking the following questions:

- What effect does a price increase have on consumer purchases? (Consumers may stop buying the products or substitute different products.)
- Under what conditions will consumers continue to buy a product regardless of price? (The product is a necessity or has high value.)
- How do students' purchases affect their community's economy? (Stores must be able to provide products that students want at prices they can afford.)

Explain to students that in this chapter they will learn more about how our market economy works.

Teaching Activity 1: Individual Project

Entrepreneur for a Day

It is important for students to understand and appreciate the role of the entrepreneur in our economy. In this activity students, acting as entrepreneurs, plan new businesses. The activity can be used after students have finished Section 14-2 or at the end of the chapter. If students complete the activity in class, it will take most of a class period. However, you may wish to assign the writing task as homework.

Begin the activity by reminding students that entrepreneurs play an important role in the economy by starting new businesses that help the economy grow. However, starting a business can be risky.

Through brainstorming, have students create a list of ideas for business ventures. Allow about ten minutes for generating the list. Encourage ideas, but allow no discussion or comments. At the conclusion of the brainstorming, write the ideas on the chalkboard. Have each student choose a business to create from one of the suggestions on the board or an original idea.

Write the following questions on the board and direct students to write down the answers.

- How will you raise the money needed to start your own business?
- What factors of production will your business require, and how will you provide them?
- Who will buy your product or service?
- How large is the demand for your product or service and how much will you supply?
- How will your business be owned? Why?

When students have answered the questions, direct them to write a business plan to be presented to a bank, an individual investor, or a group of investors. Each plan should explain what the business will be, how it will be organized, why the student entrepreneur thinks it will be successful, and how it will be owned. The plan should be both specific and persuasive.

When students' plans are finished, discuss the difficulties they had in creating their business plans and what aspect of the business they believe to be most risky. Ask students if they would like to be entrepreneurs and to explain their reasons why or why not.

Teaching Activity 2: Cooperative Project

Labor and Management Speak Out

The current relationship between labor and management is characterized more by cooperation and compromise than by conflict. However, different interests and points of view remain among members of the two sectors. This role playing activity engages students in a panel discussion involving labor and management. The activity will be most effective after students have read Section 14-3 and will require most of a class period.

For the topic of discussion, choose a local issue, such as a recent strike, a disputed contract, unionizing a company, or voting the union out of a company. Describe to students the discussion topic you have chosen, emphasizing its local significance.

Appoint four students to play the roles of a union representative, a nonunion worker, a small business owner, and a corporate management representative. Divide the remaining students into four groups to help each panelist develop a position on the topic. Emphasize that the panelists' positions should reflect what actual people in those positions would probably believe.

After about 15 minutes of group work, seat the four panelists at the front of the room. Introduce the panelists by their assumed roles and invite each to make a short statement explaining his or her point of view on the topic. After all of the panelists have spoken, allow them time to question each other. Following their interaction, encourage other students to question the panelists. Conclude the panel.

To debrief the discussion, ask students if they think the panelists accurately represented the roles they were playing. Have students explain their reasons and identify the sources of their knowledge or opinions. Encourage students to talk with adults in the community to learn more about local conflicts and compromises between labor and management.

Evaluating Progress: Individual Project

This evaluation activity requires students to identify newspaper articles that relate to concepts in Chapter 14. For this end-of-chapter activity, you will need to gather numerous back issues of newspapers and/or news magazines for students to use.

Direct students to identify at least three articles that deal with the American economy. Emphasize that these articles can relate to such topics as consumerism, workers, businesses, unions, and supply and demand. Direct students to mount each article on a sheet of paper leaving space to write brief notes about the article.

Explain to students that they are to match their articles with concepts they studied in Chapter 14. Have them draw a line from the item in the article that exemplifies the concept to the margin and write a word or brief phrase to identify the concept. For example, students might use the terms *price*, *supply*, and *demand* for an article about the rising cost of oil. Most articles will exemplify several economic concepts.

When finished, ask each student to read a portion of one article to the class and identify the economic concepts that the article exemplifies. Give other students the opportunity to disagree with the reader's analysis and/or to identify other economic concepts in the article. Encourage students to group their articles by major concepts and post the groups of articles in the classroom.

Criteria for evaluation should include appropriate identification of articles and accurate labeling of economic concepts.

Reinforcement Activity: Individual Project

Reinforcement Worksheet Chapter 14, "Supply and Demand," in the Activity Book will reinforce students' understanding of the relationships between supply, demand, and price. Use the worksheet after students have read Section 14-1, but allow them to refer to the section as they work. Completing the worksheet will require about 30 minutes and should be done in class if students have had any difficulty understanding the section.

After you distribute the worksheet, ask students to define supply and demand. Next, discuss the demand graph with students to make certain they read it correctly. Have students answer the questions on demand, then move to the supply graph. Make certain students recognize how it differs from the demand graph. Direct them to answer the questions on supply.

Make certain that students understand that the last graph combines information from the previous two graphs. Review text page 311 and help students locate the market price on the graph—the point where the supply and demand curves intersect. Have students complete the remaining questions independently.

Enrichment Activity: Individual Project

The three types of business ownership discussed in Section 14-2 have similarities as well as differences. In Enrichment Worksheet Chapter 14, "How Businesses Are Owned," in the Activity Book, students distinguish between the sole proprietorship, the partnership, and corporate ownership. This activity can be done in class or assigned as homework.

Introduce the activity by reviewing the types of business ownership. Explain that in the worksheet students compare the advantages and disadvantages of each type of business ownership. When the worksheet is completed, review students' answers. Ask for volunteers to share what type of ownership might interest them in the future and explain why.

Answer Key

CHAPTER 14

Section 14-1 Review (text page 312)

1. See definitions for the following terms on the text pages indicated in parentheses: *rent* (309), *interest* (309), *demand* (310), *supply* (310), *market price* (311).
2. Answers may include a description of the flow of goods, services, labor, and money through the economy. Mention should be made of producers and individuals as the main groups, the factors of production, and the role of money in the flow.
3. A rise in the price of a product will tend to decrease demand for the product and increase

the supply of the product. However, in an ideal market, supply and demand will tend toward a balance.
Application. Answers may include such influences as advertising, a change in income, a perceived need.

Section 14-2 Review (text page 317)

1. See definitions for the following terms on the text pages indicated in parentheses: *entrepreneur* (312), *sole proprietorship* (314), *partnership* (315), *corporation* (315), *stock* (315).
2. Entrepreneurs take risks to start new businesses that help keep the American economy healthy.
3. The payment for capital is the interest on the loan; the payment for land is rent; and the payment for labor is wages.
Analysis. Corporations create most of the products, profits, and jobs in our economy. Also, corporations can raise large sums of money in order to grow, share their profits with millions of stockholders, often can produce goods and provide services most efficiently, and can afford to do research.
Data Search. Twenty (20) percent of the businesses are corporations. The average corporation must receive a greater amount of sales than the average sole proprietorship or partnership.

Section 14-3 Review (text page 323)

1. See definitions for the following terms on the text pages indicated in parentheses: *labor unions* (319), *collective bargaining* (320), *boycott* (320), and *strike* (320).
2. New machinery and manufacturing methods led to industrialization, creating a demand for workers in factories and putting craftspeople out of work. Farmhands and immigrants also turned to wage labor to support themselves and their families.
3. Unions can influence employers to improve wages and working conditions and protect members' rights.
4. Labor unions use slowdowns, sit-ins, boycotts, and strikes. Employers use strikebreakers, police, lockouts, yellow-dog contracts, and blacklists.
Application. Answers may include that students will be likely to work in the service sector as adults.
Data Search. The fastest growing group is married women with children under six. Answers may include the desire among women to have careers and to be mothers, and family need for another income due to the high cost of living.

Chapter Survey (text page 324)

Understanding New Vocabulary

1. *Demand* and *supply* are two factors that help determine price.
2. *Rent* and *interest* are payments for factors of production.
3. A *corporation* is owned by the people who hold shares of its *stock*.
4. The *strike* is one way a *labor union* forces management to meet its demands.
Putting It in Writing. The entrepreneur will have the idea for a product or service and will need to acquire land, labor, and capital to produce a product or service. Type of ownership will depend on the amount of capital required and the degree of personal involvement desired.

Looking Back at the Chapter

1. Consumers buy goods and services from producers, while workers sell their time and skills to producers.
2. At higher prices, people buy smaller quantities. Demand for an essential product is more likely to remain stable regardless of price increases.
3. The entrepreneur gains profit. He or she contributes new ideas, ability to raise capital, willingness to take risks.
4. Land, labor, capital, and entrepreneurship are the factors of production. Business pays rent for land, wages and salaries for labor, interest for capital, and profit for entrepreneurship.
5. Sole proprietors have the freedom to make decisions, earn all the profits, get all the satisfaction from success; partners can raise more money, share risks; corporations can raise large amounts of money to grow and be independent of original owners, and stockholders are not responsible for a corporation's debts.

6. Wage laborers own no land, must buy whatever they need, and have little control over working conditions.
7. Unions were formed to help workers get fair wages and working conditions.
8. Answers may include the idea that demand is affected by how important it is to own the item, by how much money one has to spend, and by advertising, peer pressure, and fashion.
9. Advice will depend on the scale of production proposed. The more money it takes to set up production and distribution, the more likely that a corporation would be the best form of ownership. For a small-scale, personally-supervised operation, a sole proprietorship might be preferable. A partnership would be useful if Maria needed to raise more money and/or wanted a partner with skills she lacked.
10. Owners' arguments may include: If I pay you more, I'll have to charge a higher price. As a result, demand will decrease, and I'll have to produce less. Then I won't need as many workers, and some of you will lose your jobs. Workers' arguments may include: If you pay us more, we will work harder and produce more, which will keep your costs down. Or, if you don't pay more, we will quit or strike, and you will be unable to produce and earn profit.

Working Together

Answers will vary.

Skills Workshop (text page 325)

Social Studies Skills

1. The two major groups are producers and individuals.
2. Individuals play the roles of owners of resources and consumers.
3. The outer circle shows the basic factors of production and the things they produce.
4. The inner circle shows the flow of money through the economy.
5. Producers get land, labor, and capital from owners of resources.
6. Consumers get goods and services from producers.
7. Consumers get the money to pay for goods and services from rent, wages, and interest.
8. Producers get the money to pay for land, labor, and capital by selling goods and services to consumers.

Decision-Making Skills

1. A and F. Both statements can be proved or disproved.
2. B, D, and E. Statement B uses the word *best.* Statement D uses the phrase *most important.* Statement E uses the word *should.*
3. C and G. The claim that only one worker in six is a union member can be proved or disproved, but calling this a "good thing" is a value judgment. The claim that three out of five new businesses fail in the first year can be proved or disproved, but saying that they were treated "very unfairly" is a value judgment.
4. A statement of fact can be proved or disproved, but an opinion cannot.
5. This skill helps you evaluate information because the reliability of statements of fact and opinions must be checked in different ways.

OVERVIEW

Money serves as a medium of exchange, a standard of value, and a store of value in all economies. Banks provide services to help people save their money and exchange it for goods and services. The Federal Reserve System regulates the banking industry so that it will be able to meet the needs of individuals and businesses. The Fed also regulates the nation's money supply to help keep the economy on a steady course.

OBJECTIVES

After completing this chapter, students should be able to

- describe the functions and characteristics of money.
- explain the services provided by banks and the way in which banks make profits.
- explain the functions and organization of the Federal Reserve System.

PLANNING GUIDE

Teaching Strategy	Skills	Special Features	Review/Evaluation
Introducing the Chapter: Cooperative Project **Teaching Activity 1:** Cooperative Project—Make Your Own Money (Section 15-1) **Teaching Activity 2:** Individual Project—Tracing Our Banking System (Section 15-2) **Evaluating Progress:** Individual Project (Section 15-3) **Reinforcement Activity:** Individual Project—Worksheet (Section 15-3) **Enrichment Activity:** Individual Project—Worksheet (Section 15-3)	Social Studies Skills Workshop: Analyzing Cause-Effect Chains Decision-Making Skills Workshop: Which Sources Can You Trust? **Issues and Decision Making:** Worksheet Chapter 15	American Notebook People Make a Difference: Students Run School Bank	Section Reviews Chapter 15 Survey **Tests:** Chapter 15 Test **Testing Software** **Additional Resources** **Activity Book** **Citizenship Skills** **Transparencies and Activity Book** **Voices of America**

For reinforcement and enrichment worksheets and unit activities, see the Activity Book.

Teaching Strategy

Introducing the Chapter: Cooperative Project

Chapter 15 will interest most students because they are familiar with money and perhaps some aspects of banking. In this introductory activity students think about the broad functions of money by imagining a society without currency. The activity can take from 30 minutes to a full class period to complete.

Begin the activity by discussing how a society without currency would function. If students mention bartering, point out that some societies still have this kind of economy. Have students describe how bartering would affect the kind of businesses people in these societies have. Ask students if they think a barter economy would limit the technological development of a society.

Tell students to imagine a society in the future with a technology so highly developed that there is no need for currency. All transactions are done by electronic communication.

Divide students into groups of four and then write the following transactions on the chalkboard: paying bus fare, using a pay telephone, getting a soft drink from a machine, paying back a friend, going to a movie, tipping a luggage carrier, buying a snack, saving money in a piggy bank. Direct groups to decide how people in a society without currency would make the transactions listed on the board. Allow ten minutes for discussion, then ask a spokesperson from each group to present his or her group's ideas for dealing with the transactions. Compare similarities and differences among the groups' responses.

Conclude the activity by asking students to list characteristics of currency that make it useful in our society. Explain that in Chapter 15 they will learn about how money functions in our economy.

Teaching Activity 1: Cooperative Project

Make Your Own Money

Section 15-1 describes six characteristics of money in our society. In this activity students apply their knowledge by inventing a new currency that meets the six requirements. To allow sufficient time for creative thinking, you may assign the activity one day, have students work on the task overnight, and conclude the activity during the following class period.

Divide students into four or five groups representing fictitious societies and ask them to give their society a name. Explain that each society must develop a currency that meets the six characteristics of money. Their currencies must be based on items which currently exist in the world and are already used for another purpose in our culture, such as toothpicks, rare stones, or bottle caps. Students may alter the item they choose and determine a way to restrict its production.

Emphasize that a society's currency cannot be paper money, nor can students use the currency of another country in today's world. Specify that societies should designate and assign names to denominations in their currencies and give some examples of how much specific items will cost using the new currency. Provide class time for each group to present its society's currency and explain how it meets the six characteristics of money.

Teaching Activity 2: Individual Project

Tracing Our Banking System

Because banks are an important part of the economy, students need to be aware of the services they provide. In this activity students use information from Section 15-2 to illustrate how money moves through the banking system. The activity, which can be done individually or in groups, will require at least 30 minutes.

Begin by asking students to name the three services banks provide (checking accounts or demand deposits, savings accounts, and loans) and write them on the chalkboard. Ask students to name other banking functions and activities studied in the section, including fractional reserve, interest, bank's profit, and withdrawals. Add these to the list.

Explain that students are to use the terms listed on the chalkboard to create a flow chart or diagram illustrating different ways that money comes into a bank and leaves a bank. The diagram or chart must also show how banks interact with individuals and businesses. All of the words listed on the chalkboard must be used, and relationships can be shown with pictures, arrows, boxes, circles, or other graphics.

Ask for volunteers to explain their diagrams and encourage discussion of the illustrations.

Evaluating Progress: Individual Project

Chapter 15 provides an overview of the many ways money and banks function in our economy. In this activity students demonstrate their knowledge from the perspective of an individual in our society. For the most effective evaluation, set a time limit of 30 minutes.

After students have read the entire chapter, tell them to imagine that they have been given $100. Their challenge is to spread the money in as many ways as possible through the economy (i.e., divide the money into small portions, deposit it in a checking account, save it, or spend it). If students use the money in a bank transaction or in a purchase, they can also list ways in which the bank or store might use the money (bank—fractional reserve or loans; store—pay interest, buy supplies, owner's profit, etc.). For example, a student could list:

- I deposit $25 in a savings account.
- I receive interest on the account.
- Bank uses $10 as a fractional reserve.
- Bank uses $15 as loan.

Explain to students that their grade will depend on the number of accurate uses they describe. The more uses they name, the higher their grade will be, but uses cannot be repeated.

Reinforcement Activity: Individual Project

Section 15-3 explains the organization and functions of the Federal Reserve System. In this activity students reinforce their understanding of both the nature of the Fed and its impact on our economy.

Distribute Reinforcement Worksheet Chapter 15, "The Federal Reserve System," in the Activity Book and explain that students are to analyze how the Fed would function in response to various fictional events. When they have completed all of the questions on the worksheet, review their answers. Conclude by discussing how the economy might be now if the Fed had never been established.

Enrichment Activity: Individual Project

As Section 15-3 points out, the most important responsibility of the Federal Reserve System is regulating the country's money supply. However, this abstract concept is sometimes difficult for students to understand.

Enrichment Worksheet Chapter 15, "Controlling the Money Supply," in the Activity Book challenges students to analyze how the Fed makes decisions in controlling the money supply. Students read about three economic situations, diagnose the problem in each, determine a remedy, and explain why the remedy will be effective. Encourage students to review Section 15-3 as they work on the activity.

When students have completed the worksheet, review their answers. Discuss why controlling the money supply is such a delicate and important balancing act.

Answer Key

CHAPTER 15

Section 15-1 Review (text page 330)

1. See the definition for *currency* on text page 328.
2. The three functions of money are to be a medium of exchange, to be a standard of value, and to be a store of value.
3. Our money is generally acceptable, can be counted and measured accurately, is durable, is convenient, is inexpensive to produce, and has a supply that can be easily controlled.
4. Our currency has value because our government says it has value.
Analysis. Answers may include that tobacco is not generally acceptable, it cannot be measured accurately, it is not very durable, it is not too convenient, and its supply cannot be easily controlled.

Section 15-2 Review (text page 336)

1. See definitions for the following terms on the text pages indicated in parentheses: *demand deposit* (332), *loan* (333).
2. The three kinds of money are currency, checks, and traveler's checks.
3. Banks offer checking accounts and savings accounts, and make loans.
4. Bank loans help businesses grow. When a business grows it helps other businesses in the economy.
Analysis. Answers may include that money in a savings account is safer than stored currency, that it earns interest, and that the bank can use it to make loans.

Section 15-3 Review (text page 341)

1. See definitions for the following terms on the text pages indicated in parentheses: *inflation* (341), *recession* (341).
2. The Federal Reserve System is divided into 12 districts so that it can stay in touch with the banking needs of each part of the country.
3. The Fed's jobs are to provide services to banks, serve as the government's bank, supervise banks, make loans to banks, help individuals and businesses, and control the money supply.
4. It is important because the money supply affects the health of the economy.
Application. Answers may include that you cannot buy as much with your $5 now as you could a year ago. Answers will vary as to how to increase your allowance.
Data Search. Answers will vary.

Chapter Survey (text page 342)

Understanding New Vocabulary

1. *Currency* and *demand deposit* are both forms of money, or parts of the money supply.
2. *Inflation* and *recession* are both economic problems that the Fed tries to keep in check.
Putting It in Writing. Answers may include how bank services help consumers manage, save, and use their money, and how bank loans help the economy grow.

Looking Back at the Chapter

1. (b) Money does not serve as the basis of wealth.
2. Gold and silver coins are inconvenient, they are expensive to produce, and their supply is not easily controlled.
3. The money in a checking account is called a demand deposit because it is available on demand, by writing a check or making a withdrawal.
4. A check can be written for any amount, but a traveler's check is worth a fixed amount.
5. People use checking accounts because they are a safe, convenient way to pay bills and make purchases, and because they provide a record of where and how much money was spent.
6. The money supply is the amount of money in the economy that can be used as a medium of exchange. It is made up of currency, demand deposits, and traveler's checks.

7. Banks get loan money from savings deposits.
8. Banks need to keep only a fraction of their deposits on reserve because during any one time period, only a fraction of the money deposited with the bank will be withdrawn by customers.
9. The Federal Reserve System was created in response to a series of financial panics in which many banks failed and the public demanded that the government make rules for how banks should operate and assist banks when they needed help.
10. The Fed clears checks, wires money, and supplies currency.
11. The Fed influences the money supply by raising or lowering the reserve requirement and the discount rate, and by buying or selling government bonds.
12. (b) The Fed would not raise the discount rate to pull the economy out of a recession.
13. Answers may include the idea that because savings funds are used by banks to make loans, the greater the savings, the more money banks can loan and the more the economy benefits.
14. Answers will vary.
15. Banks and credit unions are similar because they both make loans and maintain checking and savings accounts. They are different because banks are meant to earn a profit, and credit unions are nonprofit. Answers may also include differences in the goals of the two kinds of institutions.
16. Answers may include the idea that if chosen through elections, the Fed's leaders might make decisions that benefit only certain groups instead of Americans as a whole.

Working Together

Answers will vary.

Skills Workshop (text page 343)

Social Studies Skills

1. The first cause is the Fed either raising or lowering the discount rate.
2. The final effect is either a slowing or an increase of economic activity.
3. "Interest rates rise" is both a cause and an effect. A rise in interest rates is an effect of banks having to pay more for the money they borrow from the Fed, and, at the same time, rising interest rates cause businesses to postpone borrowing.
4. The two chains are related in that they are opposites. Each step in one chain is the opposite of the corresponding step in the other.

Decision-Making Skills

1. Source B would probably be most reliable because it includes advice from teenagers who have been successful in earning money. The fact that the book has been on the best seller list for months indicates that it has probably earned a good reputation. The other two sources are likely to be biased because both the bank and the greeting card company can profit from having you earn money in the ways they recommend.
2. You can check the qualifications and reputations of the people providing the information, check their methods of gathering information, and check whether the source agrees with other sources known to be reliable.
3. Examples of decisions and sources will vary.

OVERVIEW

Over the years, government has become increasingly involved in taking actions to try to keep the economy running smoothly. It has taken a firmer hand in regulating business and protecting consumers and workers. Government controls the amount of money collected in taxes and the amount spent. Government intervention in the economy has stirred much conflict in our society.

OBJECTIVES

After completing this chapter, students should be able to

- describe past and current economic problems.
- list actions government takes to correct or prevent economic problems.
- discuss the extent of government intervention in the economy.
- explain how government raises and spends revenue.

PLANNING GUIDE

Teaching Strategy	Skills	Special Features	Review/Evaluation
Introducing the Chapter: Cooperative Project **Teaching Activity 1:** Cooperative Project—Newspaper Search: Current Economic Problems (Section 16-1) **Teaching Activity 2:** Cooperative Project—Monopoly Power (Section 16-2) **Evaluating Progress:** Individual Project (Section 16-3) **Reinforcement Activity:** Individual Project—Worksheet (Section 16-3) **Enrichment Activity:** Individual Project—Worksheet (Section 16-3)	Social Studies Skills Workshop: Analyzing Line Graphs Decision-Making Skills Workshop: What Relates to Your Subject? **Issues and Decision Making:** Worksheet Chapter 16	View of Noted Americans: Ralph Nader American Notebook Issues that Affect You: A Case Study—A Question About False Advertising	Section Reviews Chapter 16 Survey **Tests:** Chapter 16 Test **Testing Software** **Additional Resources** **Activity Book** **Citizenship Skills** **Transparencies and Activity Book** **Voices of America**

For reinforcement and enrichment worksheets and unit activities, see the Activity Book.

Teaching Strategy

Introducing the Chapter: Cooperative Project

The purpose of this introductory activity is to stimulate students' thinking about the impact of government intervention on our economy by analyzing a hypothetical situation in which no intervention exists. The activity requires about 30 minutes.

Begin the activity by asking students to imagine it is the beginning of the school year, and they have just entered a class for the first time. The teacher describes the class as an open-learning environment. There are no rules to follow because the teacher believes that those students who want to learn will learn, and those who do not, will not. Students will learn at their own pace on topics of personal interest.

Divide students into small discussion groups. Have them write down benefits and possible problems with the open-learning approach. After about ten minutes, have groups report their opinions as you record them on the chalkboard.

Have students discuss what the teacher might do to control the problems mentioned. (Answers may include requiring assignments, calling parents, and planning more activities.) Discuss criteria for intervening. (Answers may include safety of students, parent complaints, poor attendance, and high rate of student failure.)

To conclude the discussion, tell students that as they read Chapter 16 they will see parallels between the open-learning classroom and a free enterprise economy. Challenge them to consider why the government, like a teacher, might need to intervene.

Teaching Activity 1: Cooperative Project

Newspaper Search: Current Economic Problems

Section 16-1 lists six economic problems that have caused Americans to look to government for solutions. In this activity students use newspapers to provide recent examples of government involvement in the economy. The activity can be used after Section 16-1 as a homework or in-class assignment. Current newspapers are required for this activity.

Pair up students into work teams. Explain that recently a number of major economic problems (examples: health care, crime, drug control) has prompted Americans to look to government for solutions. Challenge students to find at least three newspaper articles on these or other community, state, or national problems in which Americans believe government should intervene. Direct the work teams to describe each problem they find, identify the groups calling for government intervention, and explain what the groups want the government to do about the problem.

Reassemble the class and write the problems on the chalkboard. Discuss what students consider the most important problem listed. What problems are likely to exist when the students are adults? Why? Ask students to generalize about the types of problems the government is most likely to get involved in.

Teaching Activity 2: Cooperative Project

Monopoly Power

In this activity students analyze how a monopoly affects business, consumers, and workers. The activity, to be used after students have read Section 16-2, requires a class period to complete.

Begin by describing the following scenario to students.

> About five years ago the Crispi Microchip Company began selling microchips to computer companies. Because of the company's good product and willingness to sell it at a lower price than competitors, Crispi now makes and sells almost all of the microchips used by the major computer companies.

Tell students that a panel of concerned business people has been formed to discuss what seems to be a Crispi monopoly. Divide students into groups of four and designate a student in each group to play the role of each of these participants: an executive of Crispi, an assembly worker in another microchip company's factory, an executive of one of Crispi's major clients, and a representative of the Federal Trade Commission.

On the chalkboard, write the following discussion questions:

- Why is Crispi willing to sell its microchips for less?
- Who benefits the most from the Crispi monopoly?
- What could other microchip companies do to break the Crispi monopoly?

Have groups refer to information on ensuring fair business practices on text pages 349–350.

After 20 minutes, ask students to choose a speaker to report their group's responses. Then discuss which groups in the economy benefited from Crispi's monopoly and which did not. Why? Ask the class how antitrust laws relate to situations like that posed by the Crispi Company. Conclude the activity by asking students if they think antitrust laws are necessary.

Evaluating Progress: Individual Project

One recurring theme of Chapter 16 is the conflict between Americans' ideal of economic freedom and their belief in justice and equality for all. This writing assignment assesses students' understanding of this conflict. The activity is to be used at the conclusion of the chapter and can be assigned as homework or an in-class activity.

On the chalkboard, write the following areas in which government has played a role: (1) business practices, (2) working conditions, (3) product safety, (4) economic security, (5) monetary policy, (6) fiscal policy, (7) protection of the environment, (8) aid for important economic activities.

Recall with students that Chapter 16 describes numerous instances in which government intervenes in the economy. However, not everyone agrees that all government intervention is needed or useful. Ask students to think about whether the government should intervene in the eight areas listed on the board and then select five and write a paragraph for each, providing reasons for their opinions.

Evaluate individual student's writing on the basis of the arguments developed. You may also wish to assess the class' understanding by asking students to state why they are for or against each statement.

Reinforcement Activity: Individual Project

In this activity's worksheet students identify economic problems and describe possible government solutions. The worksheet should be assigned after students have completed Chapter 16 and will require most of a class period to complete.

Distribute Reinforcement Worksheet Chapter 16, "Government Intervention in the Economy," in the Activity Book. Explain that students will need to apply information from the entire chapter to identify the problems and government actions suggested by the situations. Then students are to create two situations on their own and state the problems and possible government action for each.

Conclude the activity by reviewing answers for the listed situations and by asking for volunteers to share the situations they created.

• Enrichment Activity: Individual Project

In this activity students extend their understanding of federal revenue and expenditures. The activity, which requires about 20 minutes to complete, can be used after students have finished Section 16-3. It can be assigned as classwork or homework.

Review with students the description of the federal budget in Section 16-3, calling attention to the revenue and expenditure pie graphs on text pages 358 and 359. Explain that because it is difficult to imagine $1.2 trillion, in Enrichment Worksheet Chapter 16, "Raising and Spending Federal Income," in the Activity Book, students will convert the percentages on the graphs into percentages for one federal tax dollar.

Distribute the worksheet and read the first set of directions regarding government income. Students who realize that the percentages on the dollar will be the same as those on the pie graph may proceed independently. For other students explain that they will need to match the percentages on the pie graph with the divisions on the dollar and label them appropriately. For government spending, students will need to mark off and also label the percentages on the dollar. Students conclude the worksheet by writing opinion paragraphs about federal income and expenditures.

You may explain that the percentages on the pie graphs can be expressed as cents of a dollar. For example, 26 percent spent on national defense can be expressed as 26¢ of every federal tax dollar.

Conclude with a review of answers and a discussion of students' opinions on the government's ways of raising and spending money.

Answer Key

CHAPTER 16

Section 16-1 Review (text page 349)

1. Congress was given the power to coin money, collect taxes, borrow money, set up a postal service, build roads, and regulate commerce.
2. Answers may include unfair business practices, dangerous and unfair working conditions, unsafe consumer products, lack of economic security, an unstable economy, and environmental damage.
3. Answers may include making a law that limits the number of hours a worker may be required to work in a day.
Synthesis. Answers will vary but should be based on the six economic problems described in this section.

Section 16-2 Review (text page 356)

1. See definitions for the following terms on the text pages indicated in parentheses: *trust* (350), *monopoly* (350), *business cycle* (354), *monetary policy* (354), *fiscal policy* (355).
2. The government has passed antitrust acts, established the Federal Trade Commission to break up monopolies, set rules for public utilities, and banned false advertising.
3. Consumers want to be sure the food, medicines, and other products they buy are safe.
4. The purpose of the Social Security Act was to give American families economic security in the event of future hardship.
5. To bring the economy out of a recession, the federal government can increase the money supply (monetary policy), reduce tax rates, and increase federal spending (fiscal policy).
Analysis. Answers may include how the Great Depression led government to create social security, provide public assistance, make laws protecting workers, and try to keep the economy stable.

Section 16-3 Review (text page 361)

1. See definitions for the following terms on the text pages indicated in parentheses: *gross*

national product (357), *deficit* (359), *national debt* (360).
2. The federal government closely watches the inflation rate because it is an important sign of the economy's health.
3. Personal income tax is the major source of federal revenue.
4. The national debt is considered to be a problem because the yearly interest payments on the debt are becoming a very large portion of the federal budget. This reduces the government's ability to pay for programs that promote the common good.
Analysis. The advantage of giving Congress the final say over determining the national budget is that it gives citizens a better chance of influencing the process, since Congress is the representative body of the federal government. A disadvantage is that the process will take longer because more people will have a say.
Data Search. Health and Human Services received the largest increase—$241.6 billion more in 1990 than in 1980.

Issues That Affect You: A Case Study (text pages 362–363)

1. The FTC lawyers claimed that the commercials created the impression that Dry Ban was clear and dry when in fact it was "wet and runny" and left a white powder when it dried.
2. The commissioners gave four reasons for their ruling. First, they said that the ads did not cause customers to think the product was dry in a literal sense. Second, they said the ads only intended to show that Dry Ban was clear when it was applied, and that it did not matter that it dries to a white powder. Third, they said there were real differences between the two products shown in the ads. Fourth, they said that if the ads were misleading, Bristol-Meyers would not have had repeat customers.
3. Answers will vary, but students should provide reasons for their opinions.
4. Answers will vary, but students should provide reasons for their opinions.

Chapter Survey (text page 364)

Understanding New Vocabulary

1. *Trust* is related to *monopoly* because both have to do with businesses that have monopoly power in a market.
2. *Monetary policy* is related to *business cycle* because monetary policy is a tool used by the government to "flatten out" the ups and downs of the business cycle.
3. *National debt* is related to *deficit* because the national debt is made up of yearly budget deficits added together.
Putting It in Writing. Answers should include a description of how the federal government may use fiscal and monetary policy actions to flatten out the business cycle, how gross national product can measure either the need for such actions or their success, and how a growing national debt threatens government's ability to manage the economy.

Looking Back at the Chapter

1. Americans have asked government to intervene in the economy because by itself the free enterprise system does not always promote the common good.
2. Government intervention limits individual freedom, has a huge price tag, and may not solve problems in the best possible way.
3. Monopolies and trusts are considered unfair because they can control prices by eliminating competition.
4. To ensure product safety for consumers, the federal government has regulated businesses by requiring all products to be safe, and clearly and honestly labeled.
5. Some ways the government provides economic security are through Social Security payments, unemployment wages, food stamps, and Aid to Families with Dependent Children.
6. Changes in fiscal policy have an effect on the economy because the federal government spends so much money in the economy and takes so much money away in the form of taxes.
7. The three major jobs of the federal government are to watch the economy's health, to use fiscal

and monetary policy to adjust how the economy is working, and to manage a huge sum of public money.

8. (b) A rising inflation rate is not good for the economy.

9. Federal budget deficits grew to enormous size when President Reagan began cutting taxes in the early 1980s.

10. Answers may include particular values, such as freedom or fairness, that students believe are most important in the issue of rent control.

11. Between 1981 and 1990, the GNP less than doubled; the national debt, however, rose faster: it more than tripled. Students may come to this conclusion in a variety of ways, the most direct of which is to compare the 1981 figure with the 1990 figure and to determine how many times larger it is.

12. Answers may include the idea that higher income taxes might slow economic growth because they would take money away from customers and thus reduce consumer spending and demand for goods and services. Alternative ideas for reducing the debt may include reducing spending on defense or public assistance.

Working Together

Answers will vary.

Skills Workshop (text page 365)

Social Studies Skills

1. Income and spending are almost the same. After 1974, spending exceeds income.

2. The spending and income lines were farthest apart during 1983–1987 and 1990–1991. The national debt grew rapidly during these years because government was spending much more than it received.

3. To stop the growth of the national debt, income would have to equal spending. Income would have to be greater than spending in a particular year to create a surplus that could be used to reduce the national debt.

Decision-Making Skills

1. A, D, and G are relevant to the sentence. All three statements have to do with taxes on various earnings.

2. Examples will vary. For instance, statement B is irrelevant because it provides no information on tax rates.

3. Students should summarize in their own words the guidelines in the lesson on page 190.

4. Examples of decisions will vary.

OVERVIEW

Planning is required to manage money effectively and to make good career choices. Determining goals and developing budgets to meet goals are all part of financial planning. Being a smart consumer includes saving as well as spending money. Career planning requires an examination of personal goals and values, the needs of the marketplace, and skills required.

OBJECTIVES

After completing this chapter, students should be able to

- describe the value of budgeting in managing money.
- identify values and pressures that affect spending decisions.
- describe ways to save money.
- identify considerations in planning a career.

PLANNING GUIDE

Teaching Strategy	Skills	Special Features	Review/Evaluation
Introducing the Chapter: Individual Project **Teaching Activity 1:** Cooperative Project—Smart Shopping (Section 17-2) **Teaching Activity 2:** Individual Project—Writing a Résumé (Section 17-3) **Evaluating Progress:** Individual Project (Section 17-1) **Reinforcement Activity:** Individual Project—Worksheet (Section 17-2) **Enrichment Activity:** Individual Project—Worksheet (Section 17-3)	Decision-Making Lesson: Choosing—Goal Setting Social Studies Skills Workshop: Using a Library Card Catalog Decision-Making Skills Workshop: Choosing—Goal Setting **Issues and Decision Making:** Worksheet Chapter 17	American Notebook People Make a Difference: Volunteering Helps Shape Career In Their Own Words: Milton Friedman—The Virtue of Capitalism	Section Reviews Chapter 17 Survey Unit 5 Survey **Tests:** Chapter 17 Test, Unit 5 Test **Testing Software** **Additional Resources** **Activity Book** **Citizenship Skills** **Transparencies and Activity Book** **Voices of America**

For reinforcement and enrichment worksheets and unit activities, see the Activity Book.

Teaching Strategy

Introducing the Chapter: Individual Project

In this introductory activity students decide how to spend a large sum of money and then analyze the financial decisions they made. The activity will require most of a class period.

Ask students to imagine that each of them has been anonymously given $10,000 with no strings attached. Summarize the ways money can be used (spent, invested, saved, and given away). Then ask students to think about what they want to do with the money and make a list of their choices and the cost of each item, rounded to the nearest hundred or thousand.

Discuss the decisions students made. Begin with a show of hands of the students who spent the money on one or two big items like a car or a boat. Ask if they accounted for the additional money needed to maintain the items. Identify hidden costs, such as software for a computer.

Next, ask how many students chose to save some money. What kind of savings plan would suit them best? Did they want their money to be liquid, in a time deposit, or invested? Discuss the complexity of the options available for saving.

Ask if anyone chose to donate money to help others. Discuss the civic importance and financial benefits of making contributions to political, charitable, or religious causes.

Explain that Chapter 17 will examine how to make effective financial and career decisions.

Teaching Activity 1: Cooperative Project

Smart Shopping

In this activity students become aware of the complexity of making good spending decisions by researching a major purchase. The activity, to be used after students have read Section 17-2, should be done as homework.

Explain to students that they will work in pairs to research the purchase of a major product. Each pair is to choose an item that is fairly expensive and sold in a variety of places. Examples include a bike, a compact disc (CD) player, furniture, a television, a car, a camera, or sports equipment.

On the board write the following instructions:

- Identify several models of the product and the price of each in three stores or catalogs.
- Describe the quality of the models.
- List similar and different features of models.
- Describe the warranty and service available for the models from different sellers.
- Describe the advertising techniques being used to sell the product. Explain how the advertising is, or is not, aimed at teenagers.
- Describe any pressure you felt from sales personnel to buy the product.
- Describe which model you will buy and why.

Allow time for students to do research, then have them share their experiences with the class. If some students researched the same products, compare their findings and conclusions. Ask how students made their final decisions. Conclude by asking students to describe the most important consumer lesson they learned from the activity.

Teaching Activity 2: Individual Project

Writing a Résumé

Many students in this age group are entering the seasonal job market. By writing a résumé for a potential employer, students identify their present abilities and recognize skills they must develop for the adult job marketplace. Use this activity after students have read Section 17-3. Explaining the activity requires about half a class period, but the résumé can be assigned as homework.

Ask students who have applied for jobs to describe their experiences. Ask if students are familiar with résumés. Explain that a résumé is a written statement of a job applicant's background. Have students identify information to include on a résumé. (employment experience, education, special abilities and training, scholastic achievement, membership in organizations, participation in community volunteer activities, personal references)

Although there is no official format for a résumé, neatness, conciseness, accuracy, and correct grammar and spelling are important. Emphasize that creativity and individuality can be impressive once all the basic information is provided.

Discuss references. Ask students to think of potential people to contact, such as teachers, clergy, or former employers, and to provide reasons for their choices. Emphasize that students must get permission from references to use their names.

Assign students the task of writing the first draft of a résumé for a part-time job they might want to have before they finish high school. When their drafts are complete, pair up students to offer constructive feedback of each other's résumés. Post the final résumés around the room for students to review, then summarize the characteristics of a good résumé.

Evaluating Progress: Individual Project

In this activity students show their understanding of money management by developing a personal budget. The activity, to be used after students have read Section 17-1, will require about 30 minutes and can be assigned as homework.

Direct students to design a budget based on their allowances. It must state the amount of the allowance and outline money to be spent on fixed and variable expenses, and money to be saved in particular kinds of savings plans. The budget should end with a paragraph summarizing the budgeter's goals and values. If students do not receive an allowance, have them set an imaginary amount that is similar to what other students receive.

Students' budgets should be evaluated on how practical they are and how well they reflect stated goals and values.

Reinforcement Activity: Individual Project

In this activity students review types of income, costs of borrowing and buying, ways to save and invest, and types of insurance. Reinforcement Worksheet Chapter 17, "Managing Your Money," in the Activity Book should be used after students have read Section 17-2. Completing the worksheet will require about 30 minutes.

Ask students why money management is necessary. Have volunteers give examples of how management is complicated by the many ways to spend and save money. Distribute the worksheet and direct students to complete it independently. They may refer to their texts.

To conclude the activity, have students discuss how they may manage their money differently based on what they have learned in this chapter.

Enrichment Activity: Individual Project

Use this activity after students have read the material in Section 17-3 so that they can do some personal career planning. Enrichment Worksheet Chapter 17, "Planning a Career," in the Activity Book will require 20 to 30 minutes to complete and can be done in class or as homework.

Ask students if anyone has had experience in setting goals. Stimulate their thinking by suggesting that goal setting can apply to such activities as training for a sport, planning a party, or making an important purchase. Ask students if they had a plan for reaching their goals and did they accomplish them. Encourage students to review the decision-making lessons in the text in order to master the process of setting and reaching goals.

Distribute the worksheet and have students complete it independently. Conclude by asking for volunteers to explain their goals and plans for meeting them. Ask students to turn in a list of personal goals for the year that they can review at the end of the term. Emphasize that changing interests and experiences often require readjustment of plans.

Answer Key

CHAPTER 17

Section 17-1 Review (text page 371)

1. See definitions for the following terms on the text pages indicated in parentheses: *fringe benefits* (369), *dividends* (369), *disposable income* (369), *fixed expenses* (370), *variable expenses* (371).
2. Four types of earned income are: salary, wage, commission, and bonus.
3. Fixed expenses stay the same from month to month, while variable expenses can change from month to month.
4. Answers may include the following: Budgets clearly show how personal income is being allocated to cover expenses. They are used to prioritize expenses. Budgets show how income is being divided between spending and saving. Budgets enable the budgeter to make conscious decisions about how to allocate financial resources.
Application. Answers will vary but should include allocation of the entire $200; ranking of budget items in order of importance; and labeling of each item as a fixed or variable expense.

Section 17-2 (text page 377)

1. See definitions for the following terms on the text pages indicated in parentheses: *warranty* (373), *liquidity* (375), *time deposit* (375), *insurance* (376), *liability insurance* (377).
2. Factors may include price, quality, features, warranty and service, sales and discounts. These factors are important because you want to get the greatest return for your money.
3. Three factors to consider when choosing a savings plan are liquidity, income earned from the money saved, and the safety of the money. The more liquid a plan is, the lower the income. Also, the safer a plan is, the lower the income.
4. Insurance helps protect people in the case of injury or loss.
Application. Answers will vary. Students should match a savings plan with their financial situation considering liquidity, income, and safety.
Data Search. Unpaid credit owed in 1989 was $778.0 billion. Consumers have become more willing to use credit.

Section 17-3 (text page 381)

1. Employees will be required to have more specialized training and skills. Many more jobs will require a college education.
2. Answers may include how career decisions are based on concrete goals and values: where people want to live, the kind of work they want to do, the sort of environment they wish to work in.
3. Answers may include talking to people working in the computer industry, reading computer trade magazines, consulting career manuals, arranging a summer or part-time job with a computer company, taking computer classes at school.
Evaluation. Answers may reflect the quotes from the employers in the text.
Data Search. People who have completed twelfth grade made an average of $28,060 per year, which is $15,364 more than people who have only completed eighth grade or less. People who have completed four or more years of college made an average of $49,180 per year, which is $36,211 more than people who only completed eighth grade or less, and $21,120 more than people who have completed twelfth grade.

Decision-Making Lesson (text pages 382–383)

1. Examples of decisions will vary.
2. Examples of good qualities will vary. Some

possibilities are a certain color or brand in clothing and certain features on a stereo system.

3. Examples of values will vary. For instance, one value might be loyalty to "buying American." Ranking of values will vary.

4. Goals will vary. An example might be to buy a pair of low-priced but durable jeans.

5. Explanations will vary. Generally, a clear goal will help narrow down the options.

6. A clear goal points you in a direction by giving you a measure to compare your options.

7. Students should explain the guidelines in a way that a peer would understand.

Chapter Survey (text page 384)

Understanding New Vocabulary

1. *Fringe benefits* are indirect payments for work that people do not receive as income, while *earned income* is the pay people receive for their work.

2. *Interest* is the money either charged or given to people as payment for the use of money for loans and investments, while *dividends* are the profits earned by corporations that are passed on to stockholders.

3. A *salary* is what an employer pays a worker for a certain period of time, while *disposable income* is the income people have left after they have paid their taxes.

Putting It in Writing. Answers may include the relationship between liquidity and income, the difference between investing and saving, and the role of insurance in planning for the future.

Looking Back at the Chapter

1. Her problem was that she was spending more than she was making. She did not think about how this would affect her future. She also did not understand the cost of credit.

2. First, you should understand your income. Are you paid a wage or a salary? Do you receive a commission or bonus? Do you receive interest or dividends? How much money in taxes is taken out? Using this information, you can figure your disposable income. Next, you should understand your fixed and variable expenses. Ranking these in terms of importance can help you to see where you might save money. Your final budget should reflect your saving and spending goals.

3. Consumers might feel peer pressure and pressure from advertising or salespeople.

4. Answers may include doing research, using consumer magazines, and talking to salespeople.

5. Answers may include questions about price, quality, features, and warranty.

6. One advantage is that credit allows people to buy costly items like houses and pay them off gradually. A disadvantage is that credit costs money, in the form of interest, and can greatly increase the cost of an item. Credit can also limit your future spending power by committing to large payments over a period of time.

7. Insurance is based on the idea that if many people pay some money into an insurance plan, all the money will be enough to pay the large costs of the few who will need it.

8. There are fewer farming and factory jobs than before, and service jobs are on the rise.

9. Answers may include questions about working conditions, salary, job tasks, and possibilities for promotion.

10. Answers will vary. *Aerospace human resource director:* Employees need to have good basic skills, and must be willing to learn to keep up with a changing industry. *Restaurant manager:* Customers come first; employees need to understand this and keep a positive attitude. *Photo copy manager:* Employees must be involved with their job and show that they care about it.

11. Answers will vary. See if students can differentiate between disagreeing/agreeing as a matter of personal opinion, and actually evaluating his money management choice.

12. A budget might not be necessary in instances where spending and savings decisions are simple or where very small sums of money are at stake.

13. Answers will vary.

Working Together

Answers will vary.

Skills Workshop (text page 385)

Social Studies Skills

1. (a) *How to Win the Job You Really Want* **(b)** Janice Weinberg **(c)** 1989 **(d)** 290 pages **(e)** 650.14 WEI.

2. The book covers job hunting, career development, and vocational guidance.

3. Yes, it has illustrations and an index.

4. This book would be useful for people looking for information on careers or on how to find a job. It could also be used by career counselors.

Decision-Making Skills

1. You have to decide whether to keep enough extra money to buy the sweatshirt or to spend that extra money to get a meal that costs at least $15.

2. Both options, getting the sweatshirt and getting the more expensive meal, are "extras" which you do not really need, and both will help you show that you are not poor or cheap. Values may include being respected by teammates and being honest by using the money the way you said you were going to use it.

3. Goals will vary. One example is: to do what will help me gain the most respect from my teammates in the long run. Explanations will vary.

4. A clear goal helps you to identify and judge options better.

5. Explanations will vary.

In Their Own Words (text page 386)

1. The best way to keep one person's greed from harming the rest of society is to spread out power, giving everyone plenty of opportunities.

2. Answers may include the reliance in our economic system on competition to prevent too much economic power from falling into the hands of one greedy individual and the opportunities in our government system for citizens to ask for protection against greed in the form of trusts, monopolies, etc. Answers may also include inequalities of wealth and opportunities in the United States as evidence that some people are more successful in satisfying their greed than others.

3. Friedman would be likely to oppose government intervention because it takes away the freedom of the individual to pursue self-interest.

Unit 5 Survey (text page 387)

Looking Back at the Unit

1. Both budgets are plans for how money is received and spent and include estimates of the total amount of money spent in a particular time period and the total amount received from various sources. However, a personal budget is made by one person, while the federal budget is the result of work by many people in the executive and legislative branches who debate and vote on it.

2. (a) A customer pays for the haircut with currency. **(b)** A bank customer deposits money in a savings account. **(c)** Government provides the citizen with services. **(d)** The bank lends money to the consumer. **(e)** The worker's employer pays the worker an hourly wage.

3. (a) Consumers consider the price of the food and their taste preferences. **(b)** Congress considers the advice of the President and other members of the executive branch, interest groups, citizens, and the effect on the economy. **(c)** Business owners consider the value of the labor being provided, costs, and profits. **(d)** Entrepreneurs consider how responsible they want to be for business debts, if they want to run the business with others, and how much they want the business to grow. **(e)** Career-oriented people consider what kind of skills are going to be in demand, how different jobs fit their personalities and life goals, and what resources are necessary to start a particular career. **(f)** The Fed considers whether inflation or recession may be a problem in the economy. **(g)** Most people consider how much return they will get on a particular investment or savings plan, and how much risk each involves.

Taking a Stand

Answers may include arguments cited in the discussion and/or arguments students develop, for example, the negative impact of a higher tax on the individual student.

OVERVIEW

All laws encourage people to cooperate in living peacefully together. Our laws grow out of common values and beliefs through rules written by legislators and decisions made by judges. Americans are affected by criminal law and civil law. Both help bring order to society and protect people's rights.

OBJECTIVES

After completing this chapter, students should be able to

- describe the purpose of laws.
- explain the relationship between morals and laws.
- identify the sources of laws.
- explain the importance of legal codes.
- distinguish between criminal law and civil law.

PLANNING GUIDE

Teaching Strategy	Skills	Special Features	Review/Evaluation
Introducing the Chapter: Individual Project **Teaching Activity 1:** Class Project—Protecting People's Safety, Property, and Rights (Section 18-1) **Teaching Activity 2:** Cooperative Project—Writing a Legal Code (Section 18-2) **Evaluating Progress:** Cooperative Project (Section 18-3) **Reinforcement Activity:** Individual Project—Worksheet (Section 18-2) **Enrichment Activity:** Individual Project—Worksheet (Section 18-1)	Decision-Making Lesson: Choosing—Identifying and Judging Options Social Studies Skills Workshop: Interpreting Symbols Decision-Making Skills Workshop: Choosing—Identifying and Judging Options **Issues and Decision Making:** Worksheet Chapter 18	American Notebook Views of Noted Americans: William Hastie	Section Reviews Chapter 18 Survey **Tests:** Chapter 18 Test **Testing Software** **Additional Resources** **Activity Book** **Citizenship Skills** **Transparencies and Activity Book** **Voices of America**

For reinforcement and enrichment worksheets and unit activities, see the Activity Book.

Teaching Strategy

Introducing the Chapter: Individual Project

This introductory activity gives students an opportunity to examine rules of society in a familiar setting—a local shopping area. From this experience students will better understand the need for laws. This out-of-class assignment will require about an hour of observation. Allow 20 to 30 minutes for class discussion.

On the chalkboard write the following purposes of laws: (1) bring order to society, (2) protect people's safety, (3) protect people's property, (4) protect individual freedoms, (5) promote the common good. Ask students to give examples of each purpose, then copy the list.

As a homework assignment, ask students to visit a local shopping mall or shopping area to find examples of laws that illustrate the five purposes. Students can observe actions of people, read signs, and ask merchants for information. Examples might include smoking, littering, shoplifting, and trespassing laws. Point out that any one law may serve more than one purpose. Students are to identify a minimum of two laws per purpose.

Conclude the activity by having students compile a list of all of the laws discovered. Have students explain why the laws are necessary and why everyone is expected to obey laws.

Teaching Activity 1: Class Project

Protecting People's Safety, Property, and Rights

In this activity students analyze the impact of law on our society. The activity can be used after students have completed Section 18-1 and will require about 30 minutes to complete.

Write the following laws on the chalkboard and ask students to rank them from the least important to the most important. Number 1 should be most important and number 10 least important.

- Eighteen-year olds have the right to vote.
- Computer hacking is illegal.
- Murder is against the law.
- Parking in a no parking zone is illegal.
- Americans have the right to freedom of speech.
- Shoplifting is against the law.
- Discrimination in hiring is against the law.
- Driving under the influence of alcohol or drugs is illegal.
- Robbery is against the law.
- Vandalism is against the law.

When their lists are complete, have students put a *P* beside the laws that protect property, an *S* beside the laws that protect people's safety, and an *R* beside those that protect rights. Some laws may have more than one code. Direct students to analyze their rankings and then discuss whether property, safety, or rights are more important to them.

Teaching Activity 2: Cooperative Project

Writing a Legal Code

Many students are unaware of the importance of legal codes as a way to keep track of laws and as reflections of the values and morals of societies. In this activity, which may be used at the conclusion of Section 18-2, students work in groups to create a legal code for a hypothetical field trip.

Divide students into groups of four or five. Have each group assume that it is responsible for making rules of behavior for a weekend ecology field trip with a science class. Write the following subjects for the rules on the chalkboard: keep order, protect students' safety, protect students' property, protect individual freedoms, and provide a way to settle disputes.

Direct students to write at least one rule for each subject and to describe a value or a moral that each rule reflects. Have students organize their law code in the following format: subject, rule, value or moral. For example: subject—protect students' property; rule—no stealing; belief or moral—stealing is wrong.

Conclude the activity by having the groups share their law codes. Discuss how a rule in one category can be in conflict with a rule in another. Identify recurring values and morals.

Evaluating Progress: Cooperative Project

After students have read the material in Section 18-3, use this activity to evaluate their understanding of criminal law and civil law. The activity will require most of a class period.

Pair students into work teams and have the teams count off by two. Teams numbered 1 will work on criminal law for their assignment and teams numbered 2 will work on civil law. Direct each team to design, write, and illustrate a cartoon strip that will generate interest in criminal law or civil law in seventh grade students. The strip should contain terms, concepts, and examples from Section 18-3. Once students have a rough draft for the cartoon, provide poster paper and marking pens for their final products.

Evaluate the cartoons on their content rather than artistic quality. Display the cartoons and invite younger students as well as members of the class to read and assess them.

Reinforcement Activity: Individual Project

Use this reinforcement worksheet after students have read the material in Section 18-2. In the first part of the worksheet students identify sources of laws and provide examples of each kind. In the second part students determine how a current law may need to be changed in the future. The worksheet will require about 30 minutes to complete.

Before distributing the worksheet, ask students to list kinds of laws that they are familiar with. Give a couple of examples, such as leash laws for dogs or the speed limit on interstate highways. Have students discuss who makes these laws and who is responsible for following them.

Distribute Reinforcement Worksheet Chapter 18, "Where Our Laws Come From," in the Activity Book. Review the directions for the first part of the activity. Explain that examples of all of the laws can be found in Section 18-2.

If students need an example to stimulate their thinking for the second part of the worksheet, suggest that cars in the future might be equipped with sensing devices that adjust the car's speed to road conditions. This equipment would make speed limits unnecessary but might require strict regulation.

To conclude the activity, ask students to summarize sources of laws. Invite volunteers to share their ideas on future changes of laws.

Enrichment Activity: Individual Project

This enrichment activity can be used after students have read the material in Section 18-1. In the activity students analyze situations involving moral and legal issues.

Have students complete Enrichment Worksheet Chapter 18, "Laws and Morals," in the Activity Book. When students have completed the assignment, discuss the relationship between moral and legal issues. Ask students which situation posed the most difficult moral issue for them. Have students share the action they described for each situation.

Answer Key

CHAPTER 18

Section 18-1 Review (text page 395)

1. See definitions for the following terms on the text pages indicated in parentheses: *laws* (392), *morals* (394), *civil disobedience* (394).
2. Answers may include the following reasons for having laws: to bring order to society; to protect people's safety by protecting their lives and the quality of their lives; to protect property, including ideas and inventions; to protect individual freedoms and rights; and to promote the common good.
3. Laws reflect the morals shared by most people. However, laws are not the same as morals. Sometimes people find that certain laws do not agree with their own moral beliefs.
Synthesis. Examples of laws will vary.

Section 18-2 Review (text page 398)

1. See definitions for the following terms on the text pages indicated in parentheses: *statutes* (395), *common law* (396), *legal code* (397).
2. We have laws made by legislatures (statutes and ordinances) and laws made as a result of judges' decisions (common law).
3. Constitutions and legal codes are both collections of laws. However, unlike a legal code, a constitution also includes a basic plan for a government and tells how laws can be made under that government.
4. People's beliefs, values, and customs may change. Also, their ideas about what is fair or reasonable may change.
Evaluation. Opinions will vary but should be supported with reasons.

Section 18-3 Review (text page 403)

1. See definitions for the following terms on the text pages indicated in parentheses: *crime* (399), *criminal law* (399), *felony* (400), *misdemeanor* (400), *civil law* (400).
2. Criminal law protects society as a whole by taking action against people who commit crimes. Civil law is needed to help settle disagreements between people.
3. Both criminal and civil law have statutes. However, criminal law is entirely based on statutes, while civil law is largely based on the decisions of judges.
Evaluation. Opinions will vary but should be supported with reasons.
Data Search. Examples of felonies and misdemeanors will vary.

Decision-Making Lesson (text pages 404–407)

1. Standards will vary. Some examples are: to listen carefully to each friend and to respect each friend's feelings.
2. Clear goals and standards provide ways to narrow down your options and common guidelines against which to measure each option.
3. Options will vary. Some examples are: to go to the location of the fight and try to talk them out of fighting, to talk with each friend over the phone, or to arrange to meet with both friends together before the fight.
4. Explanations will vary and should be in student's own words.
5. Types of information will vary. Some possibilities are: physical effects on the friends, time required. You might want to predict the physical effects on your friends because one of your goals is to prevent people from being seriously hurt. Knowing about how much time it would take for each option would help you decide which options are workable.
6. Examples of consequences and characteristics will vary.
7. Examples of unreliable information will vary. The piece of information might contradict the student's own experience or might come from a source the student does not trust.
8. Examples of positive and negative consequences or characteristics will vary but should be explained in relation to the stated goals and standards.
9. Choices will vary but should be explained in relation to the stated goals and standards.
10. Goals will vary.

11. One option is to meet with each friend before the fight. The other two options will vary.
12. Kinds of information include effects on friendship and physical risk to you. Other kinds of information will vary.
13. Consequences will vary.
14. Choices will vary. Again, answers should be explained in relation to the goals and standards.
15. The goals help you decide which types of information you really need. This saves you time in gathering information.
16. You should brainstorm further because other options may be even better than the first.
17. Students should present the lesson guidelines in their own words.

Chapter Survey (text page 408)

Understanding New Vocabulary

1. *Laws* and *morals* both relate to principles of proper behavior. However, morals are unwritten beliefs about right and wrong, while laws are written rules made by governments.
2. *Common law* and *statutes* are both sources of law. However, statutes are written laws made by legislatures, while common law is unwritten law reflected in decisions made by judges.
3. A *felony* and a *misdemeanor* are both types of crimes. However, a felony is a more serious crime for which the penalty is imprisonment for more than a year, a fine, or a combination of both. A misdemeanor is punishable by a jail sentence of not more than a year, a fine, or a combination of both.
4. *Criminal law* and *civil law* are both made by government officials and both protect the well-being and rights of individuals. However, criminal law protects society as a whole, while civil law provides a way for people to settle disagreements in court.
Putting It in Writing. Answers may include the need to bring order to society by telling people what they may and may not do, by setting standards, by telling how certain things should be done, and by telling how to settle conflicts; the need to protect people's safety, property, and individual freedoms; and the need to promote the common good.

Looking Back at the Chapter

1. Unlike other rules in society, laws are made by governments.
2. Purposes of laws include to bring order to society, to protect people's safety, to protect people's property, to protect individual freedoms, and to promote the common good. Examples of laws will vary.
3. Laws are based on people's beliefs and values, which may vary somewhat from state to state and community to community.
4. The two main sources of American law are legislatures and judges' decisions. Laws made by legislatures are specific written rules, while judges' decisions reflect basic principles of common law.
5. Constitutions provide the basic rules by which governments are run. Legal codes help organize laws so that they are up to date and easy to find.
6. Laws may be changed to reflect changing beliefs and customs. They may also be changed if they are unclear or unenforceable.
7. Before an act can be called a crime, a statute must be passed making the act illegal and specifying how the act may be punished.
8. The main purpose of criminal law is to protect society, while the main purpose of civil law is to settle conflicts in an orderly way. Both types of law help protect the rights of individuals and help society to run smoothly.
9. Answers may include that the moral standards of most individuals are more demanding than the requirements set by laws. Students might give examples of acts that are legal but considered immoral by many people, such as lying and refusing to help people in need.
10. Examples of laws will vary.
11. Examples of new laws will vary.
12. **(a)** This is covered by civil law. There is a disagreement between the seller and the buyer, who must prove that the defects existed before the car was bought. **(b)** This is covered by criminal law because the person has broken a specific criminal statute. **(c)** This is covered by civil law. There is a disagreement between the landlord and the tenant, who must prove that the landlord had no right to evict him or her.

13. Answers may include that without law, order might break down and people's safety, rights, and property would be threatened.

Working Together

Answers will vary.

Skills Workshop (text page 409)

Social Studies Skills

1. The blindfold represents the fact that judges and juries should be impartial, "blinding" themselves to any biases.
2. The balance scale represents the fact that judges and juries must carefully weigh the evidence for each side in a case.
3. The sword represents the fact that the government has the power to enforce laws.

Decision-Making Skills

1. Goals will vary. Some possibilities are: to avoid hurting your family's feelings, to avoid hurting your friend's feelings, and to have a good time on Saturday. Standards will vary. One possibility is to be honest with both family and friends.
2. Options will vary. Some possibilities are: to go on the camping trip, to go to the concert, to try to convince your friends to go to a different concert, to try to convince your family to postpone the trip, and to go to the concert but join your family on Sunday for the rest of the camping trip.
3. Kinds of information will vary. Some possibilities are: emotional effects on your family, emotional effects on your friends, long-range effects on your friendship, long-range effects on family relationships, and things you will enjoy about each option.
4. Choices will vary but should be explained in relation to the goals and standards.

OVERVIEW

One of our greatest national concerns is crime. There are different kinds of crime: crime against people, property, and the government; white-collar crime; and victimless crime. The criminal justice system protects society against criminals and protects the rights of the accused. Juvenile offenders are dealt with differently than adults in the courts.

OBJECTIVES

After completing this chapter, students should be able to

- identify different types of crimes, their causes, and possible solutions.
- describe criminal and juvenile court procedures.
- evaluate points of view on crime prevention and rehabilitation.

PLANNING GUIDE

Teaching Strategy	Skills	Special Features	Review/Evaluation
Introducing the Chapter: Class Project **Teaching Activity 1:** Individual Project—Fighting Crime: Television Style (Section 19-1) **Teaching Activity 2:** Cooperative Project—Criminal Justice: A Chronology (Section 19-2) **Evaluating Progress:** Individual Project (Section 19-3) **Reinforcement Activity:** Individual Project—Worksheet (Section 19-1) **Enrichment Activity:** Individual Project—Worksheet (Section 19-3)	Social Studies Skills Workshop: Analyzing Area Graphs Decision-Making Skills Workshop: Which Statements Are True? **Issues and Decision Making:** Worksheet Chapter 19	American Notebook People Make a Difference: Teen Court Shows Both Sides of the Law	Section Reviews Chapter 19 Survey **Tests:** Chapter 19 Test **Testing Software** **Additional Resources** **Activity Book** **Citizenship Skills** **Transparencies and Activity Book** **Voices of America**

For reinforcement and enrichment worksheets and unit activities, see the Activity Book.

Teaching Strategy

Introducing the Chapter: Class Project

In this introductory activity students examine their opinions on crime prevention and solutions. The activity will require most of a class period.

Designate an imaginary line down the middle of your classroom. Define one end of the line as the "agree" end and the other as the "disagree" end. The middle of the line is for those who "don't know."

Read some or all of the following statements. After each statement have students stand along the imaginary line to indicate their responses.

- Crime is one of our nation's biggest problems.
- Criminals should be locked up longer so they do not commit more crimes.
- I would spend more money on improving schools so we would not need prisons.
- The criminal justice system is too easy on criminals.
- Crime is a result of poverty and other social problems.
- The death penalty should be used for serious crimes such as murder.
- Television violence causes people to be more violent.
- To stop crime, we need more police.

When all students are in line, ask them to observe their classmates' positions and to discuss reasons for their viewpoints. Continue this procedure with the remaining statements.

Conclude the activity by asking students to summarize their beliefs on the causes of crime and on the best solutions to the crime problem.

Teaching Activity 1: Individual Project

Fighting Crime: Television-Style

In this activity students use information from Section 19-1 to analyze television crime shows. The activity is to be done as homework, but in-class discussion time should be allowed.

Ask students to list current television crime shows they watch, and select three for research and discussion. On the chalkboard write the following viewing guide for each program for students to copy and complete:

- What type of crime was committed? (See descriptions in Section 19-1.)
- What caused the criminal to break the law? (See causes in Section 19-1.)
- How were the criminal(s) and the police portrayed?
- On a scale of 1 (low) to 5 (high), how realistic was the program?

To conclude the activity, ask students to share their answers. Discuss how they might think differently about television crime programs after reading this chapter.

Teaching Activity 2: Cooperative Project

Criminal Justice: A Chronology

In this activity students construct a picture chronology of the criminal justice process based on their reading of Section 19-2. The activity will require at least 30 minutes and can be assigned as paired homework.

Before class prepare slips of paper, each with one of the following steps: the arrest (including probable cause and warrant); the Miranda warning; police station (including official record and phone call); jail; the preliminary hearing; right to the help of a lawyer; entering a plea; bail or recognizance; grand jury; arraignment; pretrial motions;

jury selection; jury trial; sentencing; prison or freedom.

Describe the following situation to students:

> When a coworker stopped by to give Rosa Hughes a ride to work, she found Rosa's body in the living room. Blood stains suggested that Rosa had died of gunshot wounds. When police arrived, neighbors described a history of violent fights between Rosa and her former husband, Charlie Hughes. The police identified Charlie as a suspect in the murder of his ex-wife.

Ask a volunteer student artist to draw a sketch of Charlie Hughes on the chalkboard. Pair up students, and have each pair choose one of the slips of paper. (If you have more than 32 students, assign 3 students to some steps. If you have fewer than 32 students, have pairs take more than one step.)

Distribute drawing paper and marking pens. Explain that each pair is to illustrate the step in the criminal justice process on their slip. If their illustration includes Charlie, they should copy the sketch on the chalkboard. Pairs can divide their paper to show substeps.

When students' pictures are complete, post them in sequence to make an accurate timeline of the judicial events Charlie may have experienced. Allow pairs to answer questions about their illustrations.

Evaluating Progress: Individual Project

To evaluate students' awareness of criminal court procedures, have class members analyze local crime reports. This activity can be used after students have completed the chapter and requires a supply of recent local newspapers.

Direct students to look through the newspapers you have provided to find articles on local criminal court proceedings. Direct each student to select one article, cut it out, and mount it on a separate sheet of paper. Remind students to identify the name and date of the newspaper in which the article appeared. Have students give the following information below the article:

- Describe the kind of criminal law involved.
- State the charge.
- Describe highlights of testimony if reported.
- Give the verdict if stated.
- Describe the sentence if known.

Display the articles and have students discuss the most frequent types of crime and penalties. Do students think newspapers do a good job of covering trials or do they influence public opinion by the way the cases are reported?

Reinforcement Activity: Individual Project

This activity, to be used after Section 19-1, will reinforce students' understanding of kinds of crime.

Begin by asking students if they have ever seen a crime report or "police blotter" in the newspaper. Explain that many newspapers print summaries of crime in the community. With students, read the instructions on Reinforcement Worksheet Chapter 19, "Name the Crime," in the Activity Book. Provide time, about 20 minutes, for students to complete the worksheet in class or as homework.

To conclude the activity, ask students to identify slang names for crimes such as shoplifting (ripping off), vandalism (trashing), and assault (wailing on). Explain that using the legal name shows the seriousness of the crime, while slang can make an offense seem less serious or "criminal."

☐ Enrichment Activity: Individual Project

Use this enrichment activity after students have read the material in Section 19-3. In Enrichment Worksheet Chapter 19, "Juvenile Court Procedure," in the Activity Book, students identify steps in the juvenile justice system.

Distribute the worksheet and review the instructions with students. Allow them about 15 minutes to complete the sheet independently.

When their worksheets are completed, pair up students and ask them to arrange the steps in the order in which they would actually happen in a court proceeding. Ask a volunteer to read the sequence and have the class verify its accuracy.

Answer Key

CHAPTER 19

Section 19-1 Review (text page 416)

1. Americans consider crime to be a major problem because it costs society billions of dollars each year, causes victims pain, makes people afraid, and changes the way we would like to lead our lives.
2. Crimes against people may include aggravated assault, murder, manslaughter, rape, and robbery. Crimes against property may include larceny, burglary, robbery, arson, and vandalism.
3. Answers may include poverty and unemployment, rapid social change, bad parenting, violence in the media, permissive courts, and not enough money for police.
Analysis. No, Kate's mother was not correct. The family had been a victim of burglary, not robbery. Robbery involves taking something from a person, whereas burglary involves entering someone's property illegally with the intention of committing a crime inside.
Data Search. The most crimes were reported in 1989; the fewest in 1984. The data does not conclusively indicate either an increase or decrease in crime; however, students could correctly argue either conclusion.

Section 19-2 Review (text page 423)

1. See definitions for the following terms on the text pages indicated in parentheses: *probable cause* (417), *warrant* (417), *bail* (418), *indictment* (418), *arraignment* (418), *plea bargaining* (419), *parole* (421).
2. A police officer must make split-second decisions, face dangers, and protect citizens from crime while respecting the rights of those suspected of committing crimes.
3. The prosecutor must prove that there is probable cause to believe the suspect committed the crime.
4. A jury must decide that the defendant is guilty beyond a reasonable doubt. In other words, the jurors can have no important reasons to doubt the guilt of the defendant.
5. Answers may include preventing crime through neighborhood watch or by attacking social problems, being tougher on criminals through mandatory sentencing laws and capital punishment, and doing a better job of rehabilitating criminals.
Analysis. Answers may include the following: Police must have probable cause to perform an arrest; prosecutor must show probable cause at the preliminary hearing; a grand jury decides if there is probable cause to charge someone with a serious crime; witnesses can be cross-examined at a trial; members of a jury must decide guilt beyond a reasonable doubt.
Data Search. In 1989, 27 percent of the people arrested for serious crimes were under age 18.

Section 19-3 Review (text page 427)

1. See definitions for the following terms on the text pages indicated in parentheses: *delinquent* (424), *status offender* (424), *probation* (426).
2. Unlike a regular criminal trial, there is no jury in an adjudicatory hearing, and the proceedings are not public. The two are similar in that defendants are entitled to be represented by attorneys in both cases, and the purpose of both is to determine guilt or innocence.

3. Wilderness programs can help juvenile delinquents by taking them away from the environments in which they committed crimes, by increasing self-esteem, and by giving them a sense that they can change their environments in positive ways.
Evaluation. Answers may include the point that the juvenile justice system is designed to help offenders, not to punish them. Or, they may include the point that there is no jury in a juvenile courtroom and that as a result juvenile judges have too much power.

Chapter Survey (text page 428)

Understanding New Vocabulary

1. Both *arraignment* and *indictment* have to do with the process by which a person is charged with a serious crime. However, an arraignment is the court appearance during which the defendant is charged, and the indictment is the charge itself, made by the grand jury.
2. Both *probable cause* and *warrant* have to do with how a criminal suspect may be legally arrested. However, probable cause refers to having enough evidence to believe that a suspect has been involved in a crime, whereas a warrant is the order to arrest a suspect based on probable cause.
3. Both *probation* and *parole* are procedures that free a person found guilty of a crime. However, parole lets a prisoner serve the rest of his or her sentence outside of prison, whereas probation lets a person be supervised instead of going to jail or prison.
4. Both *delinquent* and *status offender* describe juvenile offenders. However, a delinquent is a juvenile found guilty of a crime, whereas a status offender is a juvenile found guilty of an act that is illegal only for juveniles, such as running away from home.
Putting it in Writing. Answers should show that *probable cause* means that the government has enough evidence to reasonably believe that the suspect burglarized the property. This may be shown through examples.

Looking Back at the Chapter

1. Urban and poor communities are most likely to have a high crime rate.
2. Robbery is a crime against property because it involves theft, or taking someone else's property. It is a crime against a person because the property is taken by force or threat of force from a person's immediate possession.
3. Embezzlement is a white-collar crime because it is illegal but not violent and is committed by a white-collar worker for personal gain.
4. People believe that those who commit victimless crimes hurt innocent people because they are a bad influence and commit other crimes in order to pay for their habits.
5. The criminal justice system must balance the responsibility to protect society from criminals with the responsibility to protect the rights of those accused of crimes.
6. A grand jury determines if the government has enough evidence to charge someone with a serious crime.
7. When deciding on a sentence, a judge keeps in mind the degree of harm done and the defendant's age, attitude, and criminal record.
8. Suppressing illegally-obtained evidence can allow people who have committed crimes to go free.
9. A preliminary hearing comes before a trial and is the time when a judge decides whether a crime has been committed and if there is enough evidence against a defendant to go ahead with the case. A trial is the public proceeding to determine if the defendant is guilty or not guilty.
10. The goal of the juvenile justice system is to help children in trouble and to work in their best interests—not to punish them.
11. Answers may include the following: The goals of the two systems are different—criminal courts are designed to punish lawbreakers and protect society from criminals, whereas juvenile courts are designed to help juvenile lawbreakers. The procedures are different—criminal courts use trials whereas juvenile courts use hearings. The terms used in each system are different.
12. Answers should show that students are thinking about all the factors that influence crime

rates. If students think that the crime rate would drop with an increase in police, they should explain why. If they think an increase in police will have no effect, they should explain why other factors would outweigh the increase.

13. Answers should show a clear understanding of plea bargaining. An argument in favor may include the idea that plea bargaining helps to move cases along in a system that is already overcrowded. An argument against may include the idea that plea bargaining lets criminals get off with lighter sentences.

14. Answers may include the idea that abuse or neglect by parents can cause emotional pain that makes it hard for the children to control their behavior.

15. Arguments for treating some juveniles as adults may include the following points: juveniles can be as serious a threat to society as adults; juveniles who commit serious crimes deserve punishment, not help. Arguments against may include the following points: treating juveniles as adults will only make them worse criminals when they become adults; even juveniles who commit serious crimes do so because they are troubled emotionally, and it is more effective to treat this cause than to punish.

Working Together

Answers will vary.

Skills Workshop (text page 429)

Social Studies Skills

1. In 1987, 3 percent of all serious crimes resulted in the suspect being convicted.

2. About 25,500,000 serious crimes would have been committed if 13,500,000 were reported.

3. For every person imprisoned for a crime, 50 serious crimes are committed.

Decision-Making Skills

1. Source A is probably most reliable because it was recently done by a government agency. Source C is probably not as reliable because it was done in 1983–1985, and the statistics may have changed since then. Sources B and D are least reliable. Source B, the student, can speak only from personal experience. The statement from Source D, the police officer, seems somewhat emotional and may reflect a bias.

2. Questions will vary. Students may want to ask the student why he thinks that no one can be scared into obeying the law. The police officer might be asked what statistics back up his or her generalization.

3. To check the student's statement, you would need statistics on the number of juveniles who become repeat offenders after serving time in juvenile detention centers. To check the officer's statement, you would need statistics on the types of cases handled by juvenile courts. You might get statistics from state juvenile justice officials, almanacs, encyclopedias, statistical abstracts, and books on crime.

4. You need accurate information in order to accurately compare your options. Inaccurate information may lead you to make a poor decision.

OVERVIEW

The civil justice system provides an orderly way to settle disputes through compensation and equity. However, civil procedure is often an expensive and lengthy process. As a result, alternative methods of resolving disputes are often used.

OBJECTIVES

After completing this chapter, students should be able to

- identify different types of civil cases.
- explain the procedures of a civil trial.
- compare alternative methods of settling conflicts out of court.

PLANNING GUIDE

Teaching Strategy	Skills	Special Features	Review/Evaluation
Introducing the Chapter: Individual Project **Teaching Activity 1:** Cooperative Project—Contracts: Reading the Fine Print (Section 20-1) **Teaching Activity 2:** Cooperative Project—Resolving Disputes Through Mediation (Section 20-3) **Evaluating Progress:** Individual Project (Section 20-2) **Reinforcement Activity:** Individual Project—Worksheet (Section 20-2) **Enrichment Activity:** Individual Project—Worksheet (Section 20-3) **Unit 6 Activity:** A Mock Trial	Social Studies Skills Workshop: Interpreting Comic Strips Decision-Making Skills Workshop: Which Sources Can You Trust? **Issues and Decision Making:** Worksheet Chapter 20	American Notebook People Make a Difference: Mediation Centers Provide Missing Links Issues that Affect You: A Case Study—Personal Injury Suits In Their Own Words: Justice Richard Neely—Court As the Last Resort	Section Reviews Chapter 20 Survey Unit 6 Survey **Tests:** Chapter 20 Test, Unit 6 Test, Quarter 3 Test **Testing Software** **Additional Resources** **Activity Book** **Citizenship Skills** **Transparencies and Activity Book** **Voices of America**

For reinforcement and enrichment worksheets and unit activities, see the Activity Book.

Teaching Strategy

Introducing the Chapter: Individual Project

It is important for students to be aware of the broad range of civil cases. In this introductory activity students first review eight civil cases that require varying amounts of court time and then rank them in order of their importance. The activity will require about 30 minutes to complete.

Write the following brief descriptions of civil cases on the chalkboard or on an overhead transparency. Do not include the words in parentheses.

- A man trips on an uneven sidewalk in front of a store, breaks his hip, and sues the store. (personal injury case)
- Neighbor X sues her neighbor because the addition to neighbor Y's house covers neighbor X's solar collectors. (property case)
- Mrs. A sues Mega Polish Wax Company for destroying her plants after the company's product produced a toxic fume. (consumer case)
- The X family sues a football helmet company for head injuries incurred by their son during a football game in which he was wearing one of the company's helmets. (personal injury or consumer case)
- Mr. A sues Mr. B for not paying him for a job he did. (consumer case)
- Sister A believes she should get more money than sister B from their mother's estate. (probate case)
- A couple is divorcing, and each person wants the house they own jointly. (domestic relations case)
- A tenant refuses to pay his rent because the landlord will not fix the broken shower, and the landlord sues for past rent. (housing case)

Explain to students that each statement describes a type of civil case. Direct students to read the statements, then describe in a word or two the kind of case. (Do not expect students to use legal terms.)

Explain that although all of these cases are eligible to be heard in civil courts, the courts are very crowded. Have students rank the cases from most serious (1), where much is at stake, to least serious (8).

Discuss students' rankings. Ask them to summarize which cases they think are most and least important and explain why. Tell them that in this chapter they will learn more about how civil courts handle this wide range of cases and how alternative methods are helping to lighten the caseload in civil courts.

Teaching Activity 1: Cooperative Project

Contracts: Reading the Fine Print

In this activity students analyze how contractual conflicts arise by studying actual contracts. The activity can be used after students have read Section 20-1 and will require 30 to 40 minutes to complete.

Before class begins, collect a variety of personal contracts, such as rent or lease agreements, credit agreements, or employment contracts. You may also want to collect school-related contracts concerning rental of school facilities; employment; work-for-hire agreements with individuals or groups, such as bands to play for school dances; and/or student-teacher contracts.

Display the contracts you have collected and explain to students that throughout their lives they will deal with contracts. Although many contracts are written in legal jargon, it is important to read them carefully and be aware of what is expected of all parties involved.

Divide students into groups of three or four and have each group read a different contract. Ask groups to identify the purpose of the contract, the different parties mentioned in the contract, the obligations specified for each party, and problems that could arise from the contract.

After the groups have reviewed their contracts, have representatives report their observations to the class. Discuss problems that could arise without the use of contracts.

Teaching Activity 2: Cooperative Project

Resolving Disputes Through Mediation

In Section 20-3, students learn how mediation is used to help settle disputes without a trial. In this activity, which will require a full class period, students practice this skill by settling common school conflicts.

Begin by describing the process of mediation: The mediator asks each party to define the problem, then restates the problem in order to clarify it. Then the mediator asks each party to describe a solution, states the options presented, and helps each party to agree with the other or to develop a solution that is acceptable to both.

Have the class brainstorm a list of common student conflicts, such as locker problems, property issues, and disputes about borrowing/lending money. Write the list on the chalkboard.

Divide students into groups of three and have each group choose three conflicts from the list. (Different groups can choose the same conflict.) Direct two students in each group to role play the defendant and the plaintiff while the third student acts as mediator. Have students switch roles for the second and third conflicts.

When the groups finish, have the class reconvene to discuss the skills needed to be a mediator and the difficulties of the role. Close the activity by helping students identify the advantages and disadvantages of using mediation for solving disputes.

Evaluating Progress: Individual Project

This activity evaluates students' understanding of civil procedure and can be used as homework after they have read Section 20-2.

Review with students the variety of civil cases noted in Section 20-1. Explain that students are to choose one of the cases mentioned in this section—or create a case of their own—and write a lawyer's closing statement to the judge or jury about the case. They may argue the plaintiff's or the defendant's case. Their closing statement should include a summary of the case, an explanation of who is responsible for the dispute, and an opinion on a fair settlement.

Students' work should be evaluated on the correct use of terminology, the logic of their conclusions, and the reasonableness of the settlements they propose.

Reinforcement Activity: Individual Project

In this activity students reinforce their understanding of civil procedure by analyzing a personal injury case. The activity can be used after students have read the material in Section 20-2. The worksheet can be completed in class or as homework.

With students, read the scenario in Reinforcement Worksheet Chapter 20, "Civil Trial Procedures," in the Activity Book and clarify directions. Make certain students understand that they must create the court documents (complaints, answers, evidence, judge's decision) that will provide a history of the case.

When students have completed the activity, review their documents. Ask them to describe the evidence that they thought would be most influential in the case. Have them discuss the difficulty judges must have in making decisions in these kinds of cases.

Enrichment Activity: Individual Project

Use this activity after students have read the material in Section 20-3. In Enrichment Worksheet Chapter 20, "Methods of Settling Civil Disputes," in the Activity Book, students compare alternative methods that are used to resolve disputes in the civil justice system.

When students have finished the worksheet, ask them in which type of case they would be willing to use methods of conflict resolution other than civil trial. Conclude by discussing careers in mediation, arbitration, and law.

Answer Key

CHAPTER 20

Section 20-1 Review (text page 436)

1. See definitions for the following terms on the text pages indicated in parentheses: *lawsuits* (432), *compensation* (432), *damages* (432), *equity* (432), *injunction* (433), *contracts* (434).
2. According to the principle of compensation, a person has a right to be "made whole" for harm caused by another person's acts. The emphasis is on making up for past wrongs. The principle of equity also stresses fairness but focuses on preventing future harm.
3. The main types of civil cases are personal injury, property, consumer, housing, domestic relations, and probate cases.
Analysis. The civil justice system holds people accountable for their actions by making it possible for people to be sued and by requiring people to pay damages for past harm caused or to refrain from taking harmful actions in the future.

Section 20-2 Review (text page 439)

1. See definitions for the following terms on the text pages indicated in parentheses: *complaint* (436), *answer* (436), *discovery* (437), *subpoena* (437), *deposition* (437).
2. Trial evidence is gathered through "discovery." In this process, subpoenas are issued requiring witnesses to appear in court or to send information. Witnesses may also be asked questions orally in depositions and may be asked to respond in writing to a list of questions.
3. The burden of proof in a civil trial is less difficult than that in a criminal trial. In a criminal case, guilt must be proved "beyond a reasonable doubt," while in a civil case the plaintiff only has to prove the case "with a preponderance of the evidence," which basically means "probably so" or "more likely than not."
4. Civil trials are often long because of court delays caused by judges' growing caseloads, the time needed to gather evidence and select a jury, and court rules that allow lawyers to use delaying tactics. Trial costs are often high because of the need to hire lawyers and pay expert witnesses.
Analysis. Answers may include that state courts want to reduce the length of trials. Jury trials take longer than nonjury trials because of the extra time needed for jury selection. Also, answers may include that the time and expense involved in a jury trial is only warranted in the more serious cases where much is at stake.
Data Search. The chart "Civil Cases in U.S. District Courts 1945–1989" shows the dramatic increase in the number of cases begun each year.

Section 20-3 Review (text page 445)

1. See definitions for the following terms on the text pages indicated in parentheses: *mediation* (440), *arbitration* (440), *small claims court* (443).
2. Answers may include two of the following methods: mediation, arbitration, "rent-a-judge" programs, and mock trials. In mediation, a third party helps both sides to come to an agreement. With arbitration, a third party listens to both sides and makes a binding judgment. In "rent-a-judge" programs, a retired judge is hired by the parties to conduct a quick, informal trial. In a mock trial, a judge gives the parties in a case a preview of how the case would likely be settled. The purpose of a mock trial is to convince the parties to settle their case quickly out of court.
3. To reduce court costs, people might try to see if their case can be heard in small claims court.

They might also reduce the cost of legal services by using prepaid legal plans or comparing fees at storefront legal offices.
4. Some people argue that large awards hurt the average person by increasing insurance rates and causing some services to be eliminated because the insurance risk is too high.
Evaluation. Examples will vary but should be explained.

Issues That Affect You: A Case Study (text pages 446–447)

1. The Mets argued that people who attend a sporting event "assume the risk" that they could be hurt by a flying object. They also argued that they could not reasonably be expected to put up safety screens everywhere and that people knew this fact when they attended a game.
2. In the Akins case, the court held that the owner of a baseball field must provide a safety screen only in the most dangerous place, the area behind home plate. It also held that the screen must be in good repair so that people sitting behind it are protected.
3. Opinions will vary but should be supported with reasons.
4. Answers may include that the Mets should still be responsible because they should have used a stronger screen, that the Mets had done all that could be reasonably expected, or that the Mets should pay in any case because they have insurance.

Chapter Survey (text page 448)

Understanding New Vocabulary

1. *Damages* and *injunction* are both remedies that courts use to settle civil disputes. However, damages are payments of money to make up for past acts, while injunctions are court orders to do or not do particular acts in the future.
2. The *complaint* and the *answer* are both written legal documents filed with a court at the beginning of a civil case. However, the complaint is the document filed by the plaintiff charging someone with having caused harm. The answer is the defendant's reply to the complaint.
3. *Arbitration* and *mediation* are both methods of settling conflicts out of court. However, only in arbitration is there a decision that is binding on both parties. In mediation, the two sides are not legally required to abide by the agreement.
Putting It in Writing. Answers will vary but must include the terms *compensation, damages, equity,* and *injunction.*

Looking Back at the Chapter

1. With compensation, people know that a court can force them to pay money to make up for harm they have caused to other people. With equity, people know that a court can require them to treat other people fairly in the future by doing or refraining from doing certain actions.
2. Compensation requires people to make up for past actions by paying money, while equity requires people to act fairly in the future.
3. Answers may include discussion of conflicts in property cases, consumer cases, housing cases, domestic relations cases, and probate cases.
4. Discovery is the process of gathering evidence before a trial. The process is needed to make sure that the plaintiff, the defendant, and the lawyers know of any evidence to be presented so that the trial proceeds in a straightforward manner with no unfair surprises.
5. In both civil and criminal trials, evidence is gathered, witnesses are questioned in court, and a judge makes sure that the trial proceeds in an orderly manner. However, usually more is at risk in a criminal trial and therefore the defendant always has a right to a twelve-member jury, which must reach a unanimous verdict in order to have a conviction. A civil defendant's right to a jury depends upon the amount of money involved in the conflict. Juries in civil cases do not always have to reach unanimous verdicts and may be made up of as few as six members. Furthermore, the burden of proof is less difficult in civil cases than in criminal cases.
6. Civil courts are overcrowded mainly because the number of cases has increased greatly over the years, while the number of judges and courts has not. Also, many cases take months or even years to decide.

7. Answers may include two of the following alternatives to regular civil trials: mediation, arbitration, "rent-a-judge" programs, and mock trials. These methods enable the two sides to have a third party hear their case without having to file court papers or gather evidence according to formal court procedures. Also, by using alternative methods, the people involved in the conflict are less likely to need lawyers.
8. If the conflict is over a small amount of money, the parties can save time and money by going to small claims court. Another money-saving step is to sign up for prepaid legal plans or to shop around for low-cost legal services from storefront law offices.
9. Answers will vary. Compensation would be involved in cases concerning property damage, personal injury, and other matters that require making up for harm or losses. Equity would be involved in cases concerning probate, child custody, trespassing, and other matters that may be settled by requiring someone to do or not do something in the future. Both compensation and equity might be involved in cases concerning pollution, trespassing, personal injury, and other matters that may require someone to make up for past harm and to refrain from causing such harm in the future.
10. All three are methods of settling civil conflicts out of court. However, mediation, unlike arbitration and "rent-a-judge" programs, is not binding. Also, unlike the other two methods, in mediation the third party is not expected to make a judgment. Another difference is that "rent-a-judge" programs make use of trial procedures, while mediation and arbitration do not.
11. Answers may include hiring more judges and building new courtrooms to enable more cases to be heard; monitoring trial lengths to find ways in which trials may be speeded up; and passing laws to make it more difficult for lawyers to use delaying tactics.
12. Answers may include the argument that large awards are needed to compensate victims for pain, suffering, medical bills, and lost wages or that large awards serve as a deterrent. Answers may also include the argument that people who ask for large amounts for pain and suffering are being unrealistic and trying to take advantage of a jury's sympathy to get as much money as they possibly can.

Working Together

Answers will vary.

Skills Workshop (text page 449)

Social Studies Skills

1. The cartoonist creates a situation in which a couple is being sued by a mail carrier who tripped on their front step.
2. This situation is extreme because it is ridiculous for someone to sue for $50 million over a skinned knee.
3. The cartoonist thinks that the couple being sued, especially the wife, are the innocent victims in this situation. The cartoonist shows this by making it clear that she was very kind to the mail carrier after he tripped and hurt his knee.
4. The cartoon suggests that one reason why the courts are overcrowded is that people are suing each other for ridiculous or trivial reasons.

Decision-Making Skills

1. Source A is likely to be most reliable because it is written by a legal expert. Also, the fact that the book is in its tenth edition indicates that it has been popular over the years and therefore is probably reliable. Source B is less reliable because the manager has taken only one course in business law. Also, just being in charge of the payroll does not qualify her as an expert because she may never have encountered this issue. Source C is even less reliable because the friend got the information from a person who read a magazine article, and we know nothing about the qualifications of the author of the article.
2. Students should summarize in their own words the procedure for determining the reliability of sources, which is described on page 146.
3. You should check the reliability of your sources so that your decision is based on accurate information.

In Their Own Words (text page 450)

1. He means that people should take steps to avoid legal conflicts.
2. One method is burglar alarms, which can frighten away potential burglars. Another method is organizing a neighborhood crime watch, which can discourage criminals by making them aware that people in the community are watching each other's homes.
3. Answers may include the argument that because most conflicts can be settled out of court, the parties should at least try the out-of-court options first, or that some cases are too complex to try to settle out of court.
4. The court system would probably be less burdened because there would be fewer cases for judges to hear.
5. Questions will vary. For example, students may want to know why Judge Neely thinks that court should always be the last resort for settling conflicts. What examples can he give from his own experience as a judge to support his generalization?

Unit 6 Survey (text page 451)

Looking Back at the Unit

1. Answers may include two of the following purposes of laws: to bring order to society, to protect people's safety, to protect property, to protect individual freedoms and rights, and to promote the common good. Criminal law relates to these purposes because it punishes people who threaten the lives or property of others. Civil law helps to protect people's individual rights, including property rights. It also helps bring order to society by providing peaceful means for settling conflicts.
2. Criminal law protects society by punishing people whose acts or failures to act harm others or society as a whole. The purpose of civil law is not to punish, but rather to settle disagreements fairly and compensate people for losses they have suffered.
3. Problems in the criminal and juvenile justice systems include overcrowding in courts and prisons. Because of the increase in cases and the lack of judges, speedy trials cannot be guaranteed. Overcrowding in prisons leads to increased chance of violence. Another problem is that the public is losing confidence in the system. Critics of the juvenile justice system say that crowded courts lead to hasty and poor decisions by overworked judges. They also argue that the system is too easy on offenders and thereby contributes to an increase in crime.
4. According to lawyers and judges, the two biggest problems in the civil justice system are that lawsuits take too long and cost too much. There are not enough judges to keep up with the increasing number of lawsuits. Lengthy trials also contribute to the logjam of cases. Lawsuits can remain unsettled for months or even years. Also, the high cost of hiring lawyers and paying expert witnesses makes it difficult for most people to use the system.

Taking a Stand

Answers may include arguments cited in the text and/or arguments students develop.

OVERVIEW

Political parties are formed to influence and control government. They also provide opportunities for citizens to take part in the political process. Although our political system is dominated by two parties, third party influence has been significant historically. Major functions of political parties are nominating candidates and writing party platforms.

OBJECTIVES

After completing this chapter, students should be able to

- describe ways that political parties help government and citizens.
- explain the purpose of party platforms.
- explain the nomination and election processes.
- distinguish between Democratic party and Republican party philosophies.

PLANNING GUIDE

Teaching Strategy	Skills	Special Features	Review/Evaluation
Introducing the Chapter: Class Project **Teaching Activity 1:** Cooperative Project—The Student Party Platform (Section 21-1) **Teaching Activity 2:** Individual Project—Third Party Cartoons (Section 21-2) **Evaluating Progress:** Individual Project (Section 21-3) **Reinforcement Activity:** Individual Project—Worksheet (Section 21-3) **Enrichment Activity:** Individual Project—Worksheet (Section 21-2)	Social Studies Skills Workshop: Analyzing Election Results Decision-Making Skills Workshop: What Relates to Your Subject? **Issues and Decision Making:** Worksheet Chapter 21	American Notebook People Make a Difference: Party Commitment Begins Early	Section Reviews Chapter 21 Survey **Tests:** Chapter 21 Test **Testing Software** **Additional Resources** **Activity Book** **Citizenship Skills** **Transparencies and Activity Book** **Voices of America**

For reinforcement and enrichment worksheets and unit activities, see the Activity Book.

Teaching Strategy

Introducing the Chapter: Class Project

In this introductory activity, students do brainstorming about political parties and identify areas that are unclear. The activity will require about 30 minutes to complete.

Begin the activity by writing across the chalkboard the following topics: names of political parties, beliefs of political parties, activities of political parties, and people in political parties. For each topic, allow students to brainstorm for three minutes to list all the facts and opinions they have about the topic.

When the brainstorming is over, have students edit the lists by discussing, clarifying, and deleting ideas. Keep the final list posted for reference throughout the chapter.

Ask each student to write on a piece of paper one to three questions about political parties left unanswered in their minds. Collect the papers and use the questions to guide future discussions or to test student learning at the end of the chapter.

Teaching Activity 1: Cooperative Project

The Student Party Platform

In this activity students write platforms for a new political party. The activity can be used after students have completed Section 21-1 and will require about two class periods.

Before class, write the following political concerns on the chalkboard: crime, drug use, the environment, education, children and families, space, technology, AIDS, terrorism, nuclear war, toxic waste, animal rights, and the homeless.

Explain to the class that they are going to organize a new political party made up of students their age. Divide students into groups of three and direct each group to identify core beliefs, create a name, and develop a platform for their party. Remind students that a platform is a party's official stand on major public issues.

Call students' attention to the list of political concerns on the board. Instruct members of each group to choose five topics and write a plank for each, outlining beliefs about the issue and goals for government. Have students refer to "Selected 1988 Party Platform Statements" in Section 21-2 (text page 462) for examples of platform language and style.

Have groups read their completed platforms to the class and vote on whether students would support each platform. Discuss similarities and differences in the platforms. Challenge the class to consider compromising on one party name and one platform. Conclude by asking students if the activity represents the real world of political parties. Why or why not?

Teaching Activity 2: Individual Project

Third Party Cartoons

As pointed out in Section 21-2, third parties play an important role in our political process. In this activity students draw a cartoon about third parties. The activity, to be used after students have completed Section 21-2, can be assigned as in-class or out-of-class work. Students will need at least 30 minutes to create the cartoon. This activity requires a collection of newspaper or magazine political cartoons.

Introduce the activity by having students look at the political cartoons you have provided. Point out that cartoons generally contain three elements: characters, symbols, and captions or titles. Emphasize that a cartoon can use satire, stereotypes, or caricatures to make fun of its intended subject. Help students identify characteristics of cartoons in the examples provided.

Ask students to create a cartoon about third parties and suggest one of the following subjects: a reason why third parties form, a problem faced by third parties, or the importance of third parties. Emphasize that the content of the cartoon is more important than skillfulness in drawing it.

When students have completed their cartoons, display them. Have the class look for cartoon characteristics in the products. Invite students to read and critique their classmates' work.

Evaluating Progress: Individual Project

At the completion of Section 21-3, use this activity to evaluate students' understanding of the nomination process. The activity, which can be completed in class or assigned as homework, will take about 45 minutes.

Have students assume that they are the current President's speech writer. The President is going to speak to a civics class on the election process, and the speech writer must prepare the speech. Explain that the speech must have an introduction, a body, and a conclusion. The body should include explanations of the nomination procedure, primaries, raising money, and the national convention. The conclusion should encourage students to participate in a political party.

Ask for volunteers to deliver their speeches to the class. Evaluate students' speeches on content. Does the speech have a realistic introduction, a comprehensive description of the campaign process, and a persuasive conclusion?

Reinforcement Activity: Individual Project

This reinforcement activity can be used to help students identify the functions fulfilled by political parties. Reinforcement Worksheet Chapter 21, "Functions of Political Parties," in the Activity Book can be used after students have finished Section 21-3. The worksheet will require about 30 minutes to complete.

Before distributing the worksheet, ask students to share experiences they have had working for a political party or to describe events held by political parties in their neighborhoods. Remind students that political parties help the government as well as individual citizens. Distribute the worksheet and review the directions.

When students have completed the assignment, ask them to identify activities mentioned in their opening discussion that were not covered by the worksheet. Have students discuss political party jobs and activities that interest them.

Enrichment Activity: Individual Project

In this enrichment activity students interview adults about our two-party system and analyze the results. Use the activity after students have completed Section 21-2 and allow out-of-class time to conduct the interviews. Reserve at least 30 minutes for class discussion.

Introduce the activity by telling students that Americans have varying views on the differences between the Democratic party and the Republican party. To examine these views, students are to interview three adults about the two parties. Distribute Enrichment Worksheet Chapter 21, "Views on Our Two-Party System," in the Activity Book. Review the directions and the interview questions. Set a date for completion of the interviews. You may also want students to get literature from the local headquarters of each party.

Have students share the results of their interviews. List on the chalkboard the characteristics of each party identified by interviewees. Compare these characteristics with those noted in Section 21-2 and in party literature if obtained. Conclude by asking students if they think the parties have more characteristics in common than they have differences.

Answer Key

CHAPTER 21

Section 21-1 Review (text page 459)

1. See definitions for the following terms on text pages indicated in parentheses: *political party* (456), *nominate* (456), *platform* (457), *planks* (457), *canvass* (458).
2. Political parties help government by choosing candidates, setting goals, providing leadership, and monitoring the other party.
3. Political parties help citizens get involved by giving them a voice in government, keeping them informed so that they can make better political decisions, and providing ways for them to participate in the political process.
Analysis. Like oil in machinery, political parties can make the political process run more smoothly. They are a link between citizens and government and provide leadership and a means for selecting candidates for office.

Section 21-2 Review (text page 466)

1. See definitions for the following terms on the text pages indicated in parentheses: *precincts* (463), *patronage* (465), *straight ticket* (465), *split ticket* (465), *independent voters* (465).
2. Third parties often voice concerns about issues that the major party has not addressed. Often the major parties adopt these ideas if they have public support. Also, third parties can influence election results by taking votes away from the candidate of a major party.
3. Our two major political parties hold the same basic beliefs and values and try to appeal to a wide variety of voters by not taking extreme stands on issues. Also, both parties have national, state, and local organizations and hold national conventions every four years.
4. The decrease in patronage has weakened political parties because parties are not as able to reward loyal members with jobs or other favors.
Evaluation. Answers may include the decision to support one or the other party based on the party's views as stated in the excerpts or the opinion that there is not enough information to decide. Answers may also include that the two parties, in fact, are quite similar in their platform statements.
Data Search. In 1939, 1953, and 1977, the majority in Congress and the President were of the same party. In the 1980s, a Republican President had to face a Democratic majority.

Section 21-3 Review (text page 469)

1. See definitions for the following terms on the text pages indicated in parentheses: *self-nomination* (466), *write-in candidate* (466), *caucus* (466), *direct primary* (466), *closed primary* (467), *open primary* (467).
2. Candidates can be nominated by self-nomination, through a nominating petition, or through party conventions and caucuses. Finally, voters can select candidates at primaries.
3. Answers will vary but should show a basic understanding of the process, from a candidate's decision to run to the national convention.
Evaluation. Answers may include the following arguments: Candidates should be able to raise and spend as much money as they would like on their campaigns. Unlimited spending would make campaigns less democratic, as certain candidates might not have access to as much money as others. Some of the campaign money—government matching funds—is taxpayers' money, and therefore should be limited.

Chapter Survey (text page 470)

Understanding New Vocabulary

1. Both a *platform* and a *plank* tell a party's positions. Platforms are made up of planks, or position statements on each specific issue.
2. *Straight ticket* and *split ticket* are two ways of casting ballots for party candidates. Straight-ticket involves voting for the candidates of only one party, while split-ticket involves voting for the candidates of more than one party on the same ballot.
3. Both *closed primaries* and *open primaries* are elections held to determine a party's candidates. To vote in a closed primary, a voter must already

have registered with a party and can vote only in that party's primary. In an open primary, a voter can vote in either party's primary, but not both.
Putting It in Writing. Answers should explain how candidates are nominated by their political party through a variety of methods, including the caucus and various types of primaries, and the difference between the different types of primaries.

Looking Back at the Chapter

1. In partisan elections, candidates run as members of a political party. In nonpartisan elections, candidates do not declare their parties as part of their candidacy.
2. Party members and leaders meet to discuss issues and decide on a stand. Party leaders meet at the national convention and write a platform. These positions and goals are often turned into government programs by elected party members.
3. The party out of power checks to see that the party in power is living up to its election promises. The party out of power also may report any wrongdoing by elected or appointed officials.
4. Political parties inform citizens about political issues through mailings, in the newspapers, on radio and television, through canvassing, and by arranging meetings with candidates.
5. Third parties form to support a cause or idea or to support a certain candidate, sometimes one who breaks off from one of the main parties.
6. The core of committed supporters of each party is small and there are a growing number of voters who are independents. These voters often pay more attention to specific issues and candidates than they do to the candidates' party. Hence, they often vote a split ticket.
7. Direct primaries allow all party members to vote directly for party candidates, whereas earlier caucuses allowed only party leaders to decide who would represent the party in elections.
8. Tasks accomplished at a national convention include choosing presidential and vice-presidential candidates, and writing and approving the party's national platform.
9. Answers may include the argument that most people do not have time to keep up on all the issues and candidates, and party recommendations can help simplify their decision making. An opposing argument is that simply following a party's stand can lead to uninformed political choices.
10. Answers will vary but should express what students think is important for government to accomplish.
11. Answers will vary.
12. Answers may include that similar parties make our political system stronger because they represent all Americans. An opposing argument is that two similar parties could never represent the wide diversity of Americans. Therefore, democracy is weakened.

Working Together

Answers will vary.

Skills Workshop (text page 471)

Social Studies Skills

1. Four parties ran candidates.
2. The other parties either disappeared or endorsed another party's candidates.
3. None of the third parties were able to win 5 percent of the vote in more than one election.
4. Third parties that held popular support in one election either lost that support, disappeared, or merged with a major party after that election.

Decision-Making Skills

1. Statement C is relevant because it tells you where to find how the parties stand on some issues. Statement E is relevant because it alerts you to one of the issues on which the parties disagree.
2. Statements A , B, and D are irrelevant because they provide no information that can help you determine the differences between the parties.
3. Answers may include the party positions on various issues and opinions of trusted friends or relatives regarding the parties.
4. The skill is important because you need to focus only on information that will help you make your decision. Irrelevant information will not provide a good basis for comparing options.
5. Examples of decisions and information will vary.

Chapter 22 Voting and Elections

OVERVIEW

Through elections, voters have the opportunity to choose candidates for offices and make decisions on ballot issues. Candidates and interest groups try to influence voters through a variety of campaign methods. Campaigns are organized and carried out by a vast network of volunteers and professional managers.

OBJECTIVES

After completing this chapter, students should be able to

- describe how a citizen can become an informed voter.
- analyze problems and possible solutions in voter participation and election procedures.
- explain the role of interest groups in politics.
- describe various campaign methods.

PLANNING GUIDE

Teaching Strategy	Skills	Special Features	Review/Evaluation
Introducing the Chapter: Individual Project **Teaching Activity 1:** Cooperative Project—Improving Voter Participation (Section 22-1) **Teaching Activity 2:** Cooperative Project—Creating Interest Groups (Section 22-2) **Evaluating Progress:** Individual Project (Section 22-3) **Reinforcement Activity:** Individual Project—Worksheet (Section 22-3) **Enrichment Activity:** Individual Project—Worksheet (Section 22-2)	Decision-Making Lesson: Taking Action Social Studies Skills Workshop: Evaluating Public Opinion Polls Decision-Making Skills Workshop: Taking Action **Issues and Decision Making:** Worksheet Chapter 22	Views of Noted Americans: Curtis Gans American Notebook	Section Reviews Chapter 22 Survey **Tests:** Chapter 22 Test **Testing Software** **Additional Resources** **Activity Book** **Citizenship Skills** **Transparencies and Activity Book** **Voices of America**

For reinforcement and enrichment worksheets and unit activities, see the Activity Book.

Teaching Strategy

Introducing the Chapter: Individual Project

Students need to be aware of how voters decide on candidates. In this introductory activity students use specific criteria in analyzing two candidates in a city council election. The activity requires about 20 minutes to complete.

Discuss with students what qualifications they would look for in a candidate running for city council. Be sure to include the candidate's experience, stand on important issues, and past performance as an elected official. Consider whether the criteria for a city council candidate would be the same as for a presidential or United States Senate candidate.

As you read the following candidate descriptions aloud, ask students to write down the qualifications of each candidate.

> **Candidate 1:** Mark Shapiro is married, 34 years old, and an accountant. He believes in promoting economic development, lowering the city sales tax, and cutting the budget, especially in the area of social services. He is a member of the Lions Club. Mark has lived in the community for ten years. He is an avid duck hunter and motorcyclist.

> **Candidate 2:** Angelina Castro is single, 42 years old, and a lawyer. She is interested in slowing down land development to preserve the environment. Castro supports raising taxes to buy land for open space and believes the city should be more responsive to citizens' health needs. She has worked for United Way and is past president of the local American Civil Liberties Union. The candidate has lived in the community for three years. She likes to hike and read.

Ask students to compare the two candidates' qualifications and stands on issues and identify information that is irrelevant to the campaign. Have students discuss what other information could help them make a more informed choice.

Teaching Activity 1: Cooperative Project

Improving Voter Participation

Some political scientists believe that the low voter participation in the United States could be improved by changing voting procedures. In this activity, which can be used after Section 22-1, students propose changes in the current voting laws. The activity will require about one and a half class periods to complete.

Begin the activity by reviewing the reasons why people do not vote. In the discussion include the suggestion of changing registration procedures and the timing of elections. Divide the class into groups of three or four. Direct each group to brainstorm alternative voting procedures that might increase voter participation. Have each group write a bill proposing their best suggestion.

Allow time for each group to read its bill to the class and discuss the positive and the negative aspects of each. When all bills have been critiqued, have the class vote for the one they think would best accomplish the goal.

You may want to have students read "A Broader View" on page 489 and evaluate voting procedures in other democratic countries.

Teaching Activity 2: Cooperative Project

Creating Interest Groups

In this activity students learn about the role of interest groups in politics by creating their own interest groups. The activity, which can be used after students have read Section 22-2, requires most of a class period to complete.

Begin the activity by having students clarify the role of interest groups in elections. Ask students to generate a list of interest groups they have heard about, such as the AFL-CIO, Chamber of Commerce, National Organization of Farmers, National Education Association, National Organization of Women, and Greenpeace.

To form interest groups, divide the class into groups of four and allow time for group members to decide upon a shared interest. They can model themselves after existing interest groups or choose other issues that are important to them. Once groups have reached a decision, have them write a position paper stating the groups' goals, membership, and plans to influence the public.

Allow time at the end of class for groups to read their position papers. Post the papers and have students sign their names on the ones they support. Conclude by analyzing which interest groups could actually influence elections or policies.

• Evaluating Progress: Individual Project

A presidential campaign requires the skills and hard work of many people, especially the campaign manager. This activity evaluates students' understanding of the campaign process. The activity can be used after students have completed the chapter and will require about 30 minutes.

Introduce the activity by reminding students of the role of campaign managers described in Section 22-3. Tell students they are to create a graphic organizer to show the jobs of a campaign manager. If students have worked with graphic organizers, they can design their own. If they are unfamiliar with this study technique, review the information on graphic organizers in the Reinforcement Activity for Chapter 4 (page T 52).

Students' work should be evaluated on the accuracy of the activities they name and the completeness of information they provide.

• Reinforcement Activity: Individual Project

In this reinforcement activity students analyze concerns about our election system. The activity can be used after students have read the chapter. The worksheet, which can be assigned as an in-class or out-of-class activity, will require at least 30 minutes.

With students, read the list of topics on Reinforcement Worksheet Chapter 22, "Analyzing Election Campaigns," in the Activity Book and clarify directions. Make certain students understand that first, they are to explain why some people think these are problems in our election system, and then pose one or more solutions. Encourage students to be creative in considering solutions.

When students have completed the activity, have them share their responses with the class. Ask for comments on whether the election process should be changed and, if so, how. Have the class decide on the one change in electoral procedure they think would be most effective in increasing voter participation.

• Enrichment Activity: Individual Project

This activity will be most effective after students have read the material in Section 22-2. In Enrichment Worksheet Chapter 22, "Creating a Campaign Advertisement," in the Activity Book, students create the storyboard for a television advertisement launching the campaign of a presidential candidate. Most students will need an hour or more to complete the assignment.

Review the directions for the worksheet, making certain students understand the description of a storyboard. When students have finished the activity, ask them to display their storyboards around the room. Have the class identify the propaganda techniques used. Summarize the effectiveness of the various techniques.

Answer Key

CHAPTER 22

Section 22-1 Review (text page 478)

1. See definitions for the following terms on the text pages indicated in parentheses: *general election* (474), *registration* (474).
2. Besides the names of candidates, ballot measures (initiatives, referenda, recalls) may appear on the ballot in a general election.
3. You must be 18 years of age, a United States citizen, and a resident of the state in which you intend to vote. In addition, 49 states require that you register to vote.
4. You should find out candidates' qualifications, their stands on the issues, and their past performances as elected officials.
Evaluation. Answers may include agreement that if people do not review the qualifications of candidates and fail to vote for the best-qualified in the election, bad candidates might be elected. Or answers may include the point that bad candidates are sometimes elected even when there is a very good voter turnout, or question whether those who do not vote—and thereby fail to perform an important civic duty—are good citizens.

Section 22-2 Review (text page 484)

1. See definitions for the following terms on the text pages indicated in parentheses: *direct mail* (479), *media* (479), *propaganda* (481), *bias* (482).
2. Candidates get their messages to voters by distributing posters, buttons, bumper stickers, and leaflets; making personal appearances; sending direct mail; making media advertisements.
3. Interest groups aim to help elect candidates who support their views and defeat candidates who have taken stands against them. Interest groups also work to pass or defeat ballot measures.
4. Propaganda techniques used in political messages include: "just plain folks," name-calling, bandwagon, transfer, testimonial, glittering generalities, and card-stacking.
5. Opinion polls may affect the outcome of an election by causing some people to vote for the leading candidate. They may also cause people not to vote.
Evaluation. Answers may include the view that Lincoln would have a bad TV image and would not get elected as a result, or the view that Lincoln's qualities as a leader would come across anyway, even though he might not look good on TV.
Data Search. PAC contributions to House candidates have increased dramatically, from about $38 million in 1980 to over $100 million.

Section 22-3 Review (text page 489)

1. See definition for *incumbent* on text page 487.
2. The campaign manager is in charge.
3. Most of the campaign money comes from individuals, who can give up to $1 of their income tax, which is then put in a fund for each candidate.
4. A presidential candidate who receives the most popular votes in a state wins all of that state's electoral votes.
Evaluation. Answers may include the idea that public funding is good because getting elected to even a local office can cost a great deal of money, discouraging able candidates from running. Also, the high cost of running for office may mean that candidates have to turn to wealthy individuals and PACs for funding, thus giving these people undue influence over the elected officials. Answers may also include the idea that public funding is bad because controls on campaign contributions limit individuals' right to free speech.
Data Search. In House elections over 75 percent of all PAC contributions go to incumbents.

Decision-Making Lesson (text pages 490–491)

1. The action goal is to run a campaign to convince the city to make the area an official park.
2. Resources will vary. In addition to the help of other friends, they might include such things as paint and paper for posters. Perhaps some friends have parents who are on the city council or who know someone who is. If so, this might help you gain access to the council members.

3. Obstacles will vary. One problem is that there is little time before the vote. This obstacle could be overcome by quickly organizing a campaign. Another obstacle is that the housing developers have more money to put up signs in favor of the housing project. They might also point to the benefits new houses would bring to the city, such as new property taxes. You might overcome this obstacle by pointing to long-term benefits of the park, such as providing a good place for recreation.
4. The steps and their order will vary. Steps may include such actions as calling a meeting to organize the campaign, painting signs, and writing letters to council members.
5. Examples of steps will vary.
6. Ways of checking the plan will vary. One possibility is to ask a third party who knows council members to find out what effect the campaign is having.
7. Reactions to the changing situation will vary but should be explained.
8. A decision has little value if it is not carried out.
9. Explanations will vary but should be worded so that a seventh grader would understand.
10. Examples of decisions will vary.

Chapter Survey (text page 492)

Understanding New Vocabulary

1. *General election* and *registration* are both part of the electoral process. Registration makes people eligible to vote, and in a general election, registered voters may cast their ballots.
2. *Media* and *direct mail* can both be used to carry messages from candidates or interest groups to voters.
3. *Propaganda* and *bias* both have to do with information that is slanted or represents only one point of view. Propaganda is information meant to influence how people think, and bias is a point of view that shows favoritism for one candidate or issue over another.
Putting It in Writing. Answers may include the fact that informed voters are smarter voters. There is usually so much biased publicity before an election—through the media or direct mail—that if a voter does not know the truth about a candidate or the issues, he or she may be influenced by propaganda.

Looking Back at the Chapter

1. In voting for officeholders, people select representatives to make political decisions for them. In voting on initiatives and referenda, people play a direct role in government decision making.
2. Voter registration was introduced to prevent noncitizens and other ineligible people from voting and to stop dishonest voting practices.
3. People do not vote because the candidates appear pretty much the same; they feel that none of the candidates really represent them or understand their problems; or they think their vote could not affect the outcome of the election.
4. Direct mail has become popular because it allows a candidate to target specific groups of voters with specific messages.
5. PAC involvement in elections worries some people because most PACs are formed by special interest groups, each of which represents only a small percentage of citizens or cares about only one issue, yet they have a strong influence on the outcome of elections.
6. The bandwagon technique tries to play on people's fear of being left out of a popular movement or activity.
7. An editorial expresses the writer's or publisher's opinion, whereas a news report presents objective information and facts about what a candidate says and does.
8. For an opinion poll to be accurate, the sample must be chosen at random, or by chance.
9. Television has made it more important for a candidate to look good on the screen and perform well in front of a camera. TV has also increased the cost of campaigning and encouraged candidates to give short, simple messages rather than discussing issues in depth.
10. A campaign manager helps decide the campaign's direction and strategy, and coordinates the work of everyone else working on the campaign.
11. Presidential campaigns hire their own poll takers to find out how the voters are responding

to their campaign and what issues they think are important.

12. Because a network television report or a magazine cover story is a good source of free publicity, candidates always have the media present when "making news."

13. Laws were passed to limit the campaign funds because people were worried that individuals, businesses, and interest groups that made large contributions would have too much influence on the candidates.

14. Answers may include the view that voting should be required because this may be the only way to involve all eligible voters in the electoral process. Answers in disagreement may include the view that in a democracy people should have the right not to vote as well as the right to vote, or that compulsory voting does not mean that people will cast their votes wisely.

15. The results would not be very reliable because the sample was not random or representative of Americans. It did not include people who live in rural areas, people from states other than those of the four cities, or people who might not be found on a busy downtown street (such as senior citizens, many workers, and people working at home).

16. Answers will vary, but students should identify each propaganda technique and its purpose.

17. Answers in agreement may include the point that it is possible for a candidate to win the popular vote nationwide yet still lose the election on the basis of electoral votes. Opposing answers may include the view that since the system has worked well for more than 200 years, it should be left unchanged, or that the Electoral College vote almost always reflects the popular vote, so the system is not undemocratic.

Working Together

Answers will vary.

Skills Workshop (text page 493)

Social Studies Skills

1. On the first poll, 19 percent thought too little was spent on welfare, whereas on the second poll, 63 percent thought too little was spent on assistance to the poor.

2. Answers may include the conclusion that the wording used in a poll can have a significant effect on the results.

3. You would use the results of Poll B, which shows more support for increasing spending on assistance to the poor than Poll A.

4. Answers may include that you need to examine how the question is worded, and then decide if the words used are causing positive or negative feelings in the people who are being asked the question.

Decision-Making Skills

1. The action goal is to have the curfew abolished by getting enough people who oppose it to vote.

2. Steps may include such actions as organizing a planning meeting, conducting a poll to determine which voters are likely to oppose the curfew, and recruiting people to go door-to-door to encourage those voters to vote in the referendum.

3. Resources may include volunteer workers and paper for flyers to distribute to voters. Another resource is time, since you will have a whole month to recruit voters.

4. Obstacles will vary. One problem could be negative attitudes that some voters might have toward teenagers. Such an obstacle might be overcome by convincing voters that the curfew for teenagers is not the best way to reduce vandalism and drug abuse.

5. Methods will vary. One way is to follow up initial voter contacts with polls checking how many are still planning to vote.

6. By judging while you carry out your plan, you can make necessary changes to ensure its success. Judging after completion helps you face similar situations in the future and learn from mistakes.

7. Answers may include at least two of these skills: determining the reliability of sources, distinguishing relevant from irrelevant information, distinguishing statements of fact from opinions, and determining whether statements of fact are true. All of these skills help you evaluate information so that you can base your decision on accurate information.

OVERVIEW

Citizens have a responsibility to participate in finding solutions to public problems. Solutions to such problems generally require government action. Because we all have different values, deciding what action government should take often creates controversy. AIDS and waste management are two public problems which affect our lives.

OBJECTIVES

After completing this chapter, students should be able to

- identify public problems and potential solutions to them.
- discuss the role citizens can play in solving the problems of waste management and AIDS.

PLANNING GUIDE

Teaching Strategy	Skills	Special Features	Review/Evaluation
Introducing the Chapter: Class Project **Teaching Activity 1:** Cooperative Project—Solving Society's Problems (Section 23-1) **Teaching Activity 2:** Cooperative Project—Trash Analysis: Creating School Statistics (Section 23-3) **Evaluating Progress:** Individual Project (Section 23-3) **Reinforcement Activity:** Individual Project—Worksheet (Section 23-3) **Enrichment Activity:** Individual Project—Worksheet (Section 23-2) **Unit 7 Activity:** Petitioning the School Board	Social Studies Skills Workshop: Using a Magazine Index Decision-Making Skills Workshop: Opinion or Statement of Fact? **Issues and Decision Making:** Worksheet Chapter 23	People Make a Difference: Youth Helps the Homeless American Notebook Issues that Affect You: A Case Study—Cleaning Up the Air In Their Own Words: Davy Crockett—"Promises cost nothing"	Section Reviews Chapter 23 Survey Unit 7 Survey **Tests:** Chapter 23 Test, Unit 7 Test **Testing Software** **Additional Resources** **Activity Book** **Citizenship Skills** **Transparencies and Activity Book** **Voices of America**

For reinforcement and enrichment worksheets and unit activities, see the Activity Book.

Teaching Strategy

 Introducing the Chapter: Class Project

To stimulate students' thinking about public issues, this introductory activity involves them in brainstorming. The activity requires 20 to 30 minutes of class time.

Introduce the chapter by asking students to brainstorm for ten minutes generating a list of problems facing the United States, their state, their community, or their school. On the chalkboard list the problems without categorizing them.

When ten problems have been listed, ask each student to write down the three problems he or she considers most serious. Then identify the three most serious problems through a show of hands. Determine if students are more worried about school, community, state, or national problems, and discuss the overlap among them.

Close the activity by asking students to identify possible actions individual citizens could take to correct each of the problems listed. Save the list of problems to use with Teaching Activity 1.

Teaching Activity 1: Cooperative Project

Solving Society's Problems

This activity will help students develop an understanding of public issues. The activity can be used after students have read Section 23-1 and will require a class period to complete.

Begin the activity by listing on the chalkboard five to six problems identified in the Introducing the Chapter activity or other current issues, such as homelessness and family violence, which may not have been identified. Direct students to choose the problem that most interests them. Have students form small groups made up of classmates who chose the same problem.

Write on the chalkboard the following questions:

- What makes the situation a public problem?
- Who is troubled? Why?
- What are some possible solutions?
- What values are involved in the solutions?
- What solutions does the group favor? Why?
- How could students help to solve the problem?

Provide 30 minutes for the groups to discuss answers to the questions. Instruct the groups to designate one person to record responses and one person to act as a spokesperson in a class discussion. When the groups are finished, have each group share with the class their answers to the questions. Allow time for the class to respond.

The activity can be extended by having groups exchange their written answers and add to the solutions proposed by the first group. Groups also could develop a list of volunteer organizations that are dealing with the problems. Extra credit can be given to individual students who volunteer their services to help solve one of the problems.

Teaching Activity 2: Cooperative Project

Trash Analysis: Creating School Statistics

This activity helps students to better understand the public waste problem by having them analyze sample household trash. The activity will be most effective after students have read Section 23-3 and will require most of a class period to complete.

This activity requires five trash bags filled with common household trash to be available in class for student analysis. The trash should consist of such items as aluminum cans, glass containers, plastic items, newspaper, junk mail, computer paper, cardboard food containers, and plastic tableware. The activity also requires a scale for students to use in their analysis.

Show students the five trash bags. Divide students into five groups and give each group a bag. Direct the groups to follow this procedure: (1) weigh the bag and record the weight on the chalkboard, (2) dump the trash onto newspapers, (3) separate the trash that is recyclable in your community into a separate pile, (4) record the weight of the recyclable items, (5) compare the weight of the recyclable materials with the total weight of the bag of trash.

Ask students to record the number of bags of trash removed from their homes in one week and, if possible, the weight of each bag. At the end of a week, ask student volunteers to collect the data and figure out the average amount of trash per student family. Find out how many families are in your school and using that figure have students estimate how much trash is produced by the families of students. To extend the activity, you may want students to get information on how much trash schools, the city, or the county produce.

Challenge students to prepare a display showing the collected data. Use the data from analyzing the five trash bags to illustrate how much household trash can be recycled locally.

Evaluating Progress: Individual Project

To evaluate students' understanding of public policy issues, have them follow a public policy issue in the news and put together a scrapbook to inform other students about the problem. This activity can be assigned at the beginning of the chapter and completed after reading Section 23-3.

Write the following criteria for the scrapbook on the chalkboard and direct students to copy it.

- Title page: title of problem
- Summary page: (1) explain the situation, (2) describe who is troubled and why, (3) define the issues that arise from proposed solutions, (4) identify values involved in the proposed solutions
- Interview page: report two peoples' opinions on the problem
- Solution page: (1) list several solutions, (2) identify the best solution, (3) state your reasons for favoring that solution
- Appendix of pertinent news stories.

Evaluate each assignment for how well the student has met the major criteria and the thoughtfulness of responses. Allow time for students to view each others' work.

Reinforcement Activity: Individual Project

To promote student awareness of wastefulness in our society, this activity has students identify waste in particular situations and offer alternative practices. The activity can be used after students have read Section 23-3.

Introduce the activity by reminding students that each day every American throws away an average of 4 pounds of trash; during a full year each American disposes of 600 pounds of packaging material. Explain that this activity focuses on the wasteful practices that lead to these statistics. Review the directions on Reinforcement Worksheet Chapter 23, "Waste in Our Society," in the Activity Book.

When students have completed the worksheet, divide them into groups and have them discuss their responses. Direct each group to share with the class one creative solution to one of the problems that emerged from their group's discussion.

Enrichment Activity: Individual Project

The AIDS crisis raises many issues for schools. In this activity students read a scenario and determine responses to dilemmas created by the situation described. The activity can be used after students have read Section 23-2. It requires about 30 minutes to complete.

Having the health teacher, physician, or school nurse act as a resource during the follow-up class discussion of AIDS may be helpful in dealing with the medical aspects of the disease.

Begin the activity by having students recall any instances they have heard or read about in which students with AIDS were denied admission to school. Explain that confronting AIDS has been difficult for some school administrators and parents. Distribute Enrichment Worksheet Chapter 23, "AIDS in School," in the Activity Book and review directions with students.

When students are finished, have them discuss the questions that were the most difficult for them to answer. Make certain students base their answers on facts as stated in the chapter rather than on myth or hysteria.

Answer Key

CHAPTER 23

Section 23-1 Review (text page 499)

1. See definitions for the following terms on text pages indicated in parentheses: *issue* (496), *public policy* (497).
2. A situation becomes a problem when it troubles someone.
3. Issues come up when people disagree about how to solve a problem.
4. People first recognize that a situation is troubling. Then they propose solutions and issues arise. People can be directly involved in solving a problem and also turn to government to help solve it. When people turn to government, the issues that arise become matters of public debate. Government response to the public issues is public policy.
Application. Answers will vary but should show a clear understanding of the difference between a private and a public problem and explain why situations are problems.
Data Search. Kidnapping concerns young people most. Sixty-five percent of young people are "very concerned" about AIDS. Answers will vary about how concerned students are.

Section 23-2 Review (text page 505)

1. AIDS is a private problem for those who have the disease. Persons with AIDS must make many difficult choices, endure much suffering, and often face the emotional pain of rejection. AIDS is also a private problem for the families of AIDS patients, as they face emotional and financial hardship. AIDS is a public problem because it is a health threat to many people. The public also faces the problems of how to pay for patient care and research. Also, some people's fear of AIDS can cause discrimination.
2. Answers may include the following: People who place a high value on a person's right to privacy might oppose government testing programs. On the issue of government spending, some people's values tell them that there are more important social problems to attend to. Measures to stop the spread of the disease can raise the issue of the civil rights of AIDS patients. Some people feel that these rights might put others at risk. Some people believe that AIDS education can have a negative effect on the learner.
3. Answers may include becoming more informed, vounteering to help care for patients, and affecting public policy through voting and other political action.
Evaluation. Answers may include that AIDS education leads to either more careful behavior or to more risky behavior, or that individual states should have the freedom to make their own choices regarding AIDS education.

Section 23-3 Review (text page 511)

1. The "purchase-consume-dispose" mentality means that Americans often value convenience over concern for the environment. The NIMBY attitude says that people do not want dumps or incinerator sites near them, thus making it hard to find new places to dispose of waste.
2. Free enterprise is an issue in reducing waste because some people think that the government should restrict the type of packaging that busi-

nesses can use. Others think that such restrictions interfere with free enterprise.
3. People have made individual efforts to reduce waste and to recycle the waste they do generate, entrepreneurs have started recycling businesses, and consumers have put pressure on producers not to use expensive, wasteful packages.
Evaluation. Answers may include that people should have free choice, that such a law discriminates against large households, or that the only way to make real progress in the situation is to change people's habits using the force of the law.

Issues That Affect You: A Case Study (text pages 512–513)

1. The Clean Air Act can be enforced by the EPA or a "citizen's suit" if the EPA fails to act.
2. The city wanted the court to delay enforcement of the law because it was negotiating with the EPA to develop a new, less strict clean air plan.
3. Answers will vary.

Chapter Survey (text page 514)

Understanding New Vocabulary

1. A *problem* is an event or situation that troubles an individual or society, while an *issue* is a point of conflict or matter to be debated. Issues arise out of proposed solutions to problems and involve opposing values.
2. *Public issues* are matters that involve many people in a community; *public policy* is the government response to these issues.
Putting It in Writing. Answers should show a general understanding of the waste problem in America. Answers may include examples of how issue and public policy are related and steps being taken—including recycling—to solve this problem.

Looking Back at the Chapter

1. A private problem affects an individual and must be solved by that individual, whereas a public problem affects many people and may lead to many, sometimes conflicting, solutions. Solving public problems often involves government, community, and individuals working together.
2. There are no "right" solutions to public problems, and people often have different ideas about what should be done. Public debate involves looking at many solutions, but individuals and government must make trade-offs in deciding what to support.
3. AIDS is killing thousands of Americans every year and currently has no cure. It is extremely expensive to treat AIDS patients, as well as to conduct AIDS research and to educate the people.
4. Answers may include quarantine, which raises the issue of the civil rights of AIDS patients, and AIDS education, which may affect learner behavior.
5. If an individual's HIV test result was positive and this information was made public, this person might be barred from school or have trouble getting a job.
6. AIDS is not spread by the casual contact that takes place in the workplace or at school.
7. While people want the convenience of disposable products and low rates for trash collection, they do not want new dump sites in their "backyards."
8. The main issue is freedom of choice. Supporters of recycling laws think that laws are the only way to make significant progress in solving the waste problem. Opponents claim that recycling laws infringe on people's freedom to decide whether or not to recycle.
9. Some states have bottle bills that pay consumers to return used glass bottles. Others provide funds to help local communities set up recycling programs. Many businesses make profits from recycling.
10. Packaging accounts for about one third of the weight of trash and one half of the volume. Some packaging is not biodegradable and cannot be recycled. In addition, the purpose of much of this packaging is simply to attract consumer attention.
11. Waste-to-energy plants produce electricity or steam and can reduce waste volume by 90 percent. However, they can create dioxins and poisonous ash, which threaten people's health.
12. In the first case, the issue may include whether it is fair to apply the rule to all students, even those who already get good grades. In the second, the issue may include whether searching students

at school dances imposes on their personal rights.
13. For some uninfected Americans, AIDS is mostly a public issue, because it has not infected someone they know. Others, however, have friends or a relative infected with the virus, making it a private issue.
14. Answers will vary. Students should discuss the balance between free enterprise and serving the common good.

Working Together

Answers will vary.

Skills Workshop (text page 515)

Social Studies Skills

1. The article was published in January 1989.
2. You might have looked under the subject "the homeless" to find this listing.
3. A librarian would need to know the name of the magazine, its volume number, and its date of publication (month and year).

Decision-Making Skills

1. Statements A, E, and H are statements of fact. Statements A and E could be checked by looking at statistics in medical publications. Statement H could be checked in federal accounting records.
2. Statements B, C, D, F, and G are all opinions. Statement B uses the subjective phrase "far greater health threat." The word *threat* can mean different things to different people. Some might measure the degree of threat in terms of number of deaths, while others might place greater weight on the effect on people's quality of life. Statements C and D are opinions because people have differing views on how much money is "enough." Statement F is an opinion because estimates cannot be proved or disproved without accurate data. Statement G is an opinion because people have differing views regarding how terrifying something is.
3. Examples will vary. For instance, questions about Statement B might include the following: What standards are you using to compare the health threat of the two diseases? Why do you think the threat of cancer will grow faster than that of AIDS?
4. With statements of fact, you know that you can search for information to either prove or disprove them. With opinions, you must focus on how reasonable the supporting arguments are.

In Their Own Words (text page 516)

1. Answers may include visiting as many constituents as possible as the election nears; trying to appear like a "good old boy"; appealing to women by fussing over their children; promising all that is asked, and more; making long, high-sounding speeches; and supporting charities as long as doing so will give you good publicity.
2. Answers may include visiting constituents, kissing babies, making promises, making high-sounding speeches, and supporting charities or other kinds of special interest groups.
3. Answers may include that Crockett would advise politicians to get on television as much as possible. He might also mention specific interests to which politicians should appeal.

Unit 7 Survey (text page 517)

Looking Back at the Unit

1. The correct order of events is c, e, b, a, d.
2. **(a)** An environmental interest group could sponsor the campaign, provide funds, ask for donations, produce ads, and help get out the vote. **(b)** A candidate for governor could endorse the ballot measure. **(c)** As a citizen, you could help with the campaign by working at headquarters, canvassing, putting up posters, raising money; vote if old enough; and give money to help pay for the campaign. **(d)** A political party could endorse the measure and get candidates and elected officials to follow suit. The party could include that issue on its platform and nominate candidates who support the issue.

Taking a Stand

Answers may include arguments cited in the discussion and/or arguments students develop.

OVERVIEW

Our planet is politically divided into more than 160 developed and developing nations. Political and economic differences, as well as differences in economic goals, can lead to conflict and competition between nations. However, these differences can also lead to a world system characterized by interdependence and international cooperation.

OBJECTIVES

After completing this chapter, students should be able to

- identify characteristics of nations.
- describe how nations relate to each other.
- recognize ways in which nations are interdependent.
- identify political and economic difficulties faced by developing nations.

PLANNING GUIDE

Teaching Strategy	Skills	Special Features	Review/Evaluation
Introducing the Chapter: Cooperative Project **Teaching Activity 1:** Individual Project—Characteristics of Nations (Section 24-1) **Teaching Activity 2:** Cooperative Project—Relations Between Nations (Section 24-2) **Evaluating Progress:** Individual Project (Section 24-3) **Reinforcement Activity:** Individual Project—Worksheet (Section 24-1) **Enrichment Activity:** Individual Project—Worksheet (Section 24-3) **Unit 8 Activity:** Economic Interdependence: An Audio-Visual Presentation	Decision-Making Lesson: Choosing and Taking Action Social Studies Skills Workshop: Analyzing Systems Diagrams Decision-Making Skills Workshop: Choosing and Taking Action **Issues and Decision Making:** Worksheet Chapter 24	Views of Noted Americans: Condoleezza Rice American Notebook	Section Reviews Chapter 24 Survey **Tests:** Chapter 24 Test **Testing Software** **Additional Resources** **Activity Book** **Citizenship Skills** **Transparencies and Activity Book** **Voices of America**

For reinforcement and enrichment worksheets and unit activities, see the Activity Book.

Teaching Strategy

Introducing the Chapter: Cooperative Project

International travel, whether for pleasure or work, has broadened many Americans' view of the world. In this introductory activity students consider topics they would explore if they had the opportunity to spend time abroad. The activity requires one class period to complete.

Begin the activity by having students read the introduction to Chapter 24 on text page 521. Focus students' attention on the statement by Julie's grandfather that his view of the world changed when he joined the navy in World War II.

Encourage students to think about what it would be like to live in a foreign country for a period of time. Direct them to choose one of four countries—England, West Germany, Italy, or France—and then make a list of five aspects of life in that country that they would be interested in exploring. Sample student lists and discuss why those topics were chosen.

Have students imagine that they are going to live in Poland for a year and to list five aspects of life they would like to investigate. Next, have students consider living in Japan and then make a similar list.

Finally, have students locate Malawi (in southeastern Africa) on the world map on text pages 594–595. Tell them to imagine that they are going to live in that country for a year and to list five aspects of life they would like to explore.

When the lists are complete, ask students in what ways they would expect their experiences to be different in Poland, Japan, and Malawi than in the Western European country they had chosen. What would they want to know about life in Poland, Japan, and Malawi before leaving? Who would they ask about each country? Conclude the discussion by explaining that in Chapter 24 students will be learning about the nations of the world and the range of differences between them.

Teaching Activity 1: Individual Project

Characteristics of Nations

This activity is designed to help students identify the characteristics of nations. The activity can be used after students have read Section 24-1 and will require 15 to 20 minutes to complete.

Across the top of the chalkboard write the following characteristics: *shared language, shared identity, shared history, government, territory, national interest, nationalism,* and *sovereignty.* Down the left side of the board list the following places and groups: *your school district, South Africa, your state, the United Nations, Hungary, Native Americans.*

Have students copy the two sets of headings. Direct them to determine whether each place or group meets the characteristics necessary to qualify as a nation. If it meets a particular characteristic, students should mark a plus sign under that category. If it does not meet that characteristic, students should place a minus sign under the category. For example, your school district should have a plus sign under *shared language, shared identity, government,* and *territory,* and a minus sign under *shared history, national interest, nationalism, and sovereignty.*

Allow time to complete the charts. Then select several students to share their answers. Conclude the activity with a discussion of the following questions:

- Can a nation exist without one or more of these characteristics? How? Which characteristics are expendable? Why?
- How could such characteristics as sovereignty and nationalism hinder cooperation between nations?

Teaching Activity 2: Cooperative Project

Relations Between Nations

In this activity students describe how nations relate to each other. The activity, to be used after students have read Section 24-2, requires a class period to complete, or it can be assigned as homework.

Begin the activity by writing the following products on the chalkboard: foodstuffs, weapons, automobiles, music, clothing, computer programs, furniture, and seaweed. Divide students into groups of three and instruct each group to select a different product so that all products are covered. Before they continue their assignment, have students listen and take notes as you describe two imaginary nations.

> Gosbark is a small developing nation located in the Southern Hemisphere. The government is actively seeking trade with other nations to improve its weak economy. At the same time, Gosbarkians are fiercely nationalistic and will not tolerate being treated as inferiors by anyone. The government has recently been studying an economic partnership with the country of Banturan.
>
> Banturan is a modern developed nation. While not the largest, nor the most powerful nation in the world, Banturan is proud of its political, military, and economic accomplishments. Located north of the equator, far from Gosbark, the Banturan government is aware that Gosbarkian agents have been gathering information about their nation.

Inform each group that the nations of Banturan and Gosbark are beginning to contact each other about an economic partnership based on the product they selected. As reporters for an international newspaper, students are to write three news articles about the interactions between the two nations. One student should describe how the nations are planning to cooperate. A second student should describe how the countries are in competition over the product, and the third student should describe how the product led to conflict between the two countries. Instruct students to review cooperation, competition, and conflict in Section 24-2.

When finished, have groups share their articles. Discuss the effects each interaction had on the two nations involved and on the rest of the world. Ask the following questions:

- Depending on the product selected, is one way of interacting more likely than others to emerge?
- How do governments decide on ways to interact? Who decides in the United States? How do citizens contribute to the decision?
- What are some advantages and disadvantages of each way of interacting?

Evaluating Progress: Individual Project

A recurring theme in Chapter 24 is the variety of ways in which nations are connected. This activity evaluates students' understanding of these connections. The activity is to be used at the conclusion of the chapter and can be assigned as homework or as an in-class activity.

Across the top of the chalkboard write the following categories: *personal, technical, scientific, political, military,* and *economic.* Down the left side of the board write these categories: *United States, Tondoc, world.* Direct students to copy the headings. Begin the activity by asking students to listen as you read this scenario:

> The President of the United States has just announced that since the government of Tondoc continues to abuse the human rights of its citizens, he is recommending that all American companies stop purchasing Tondoc's only export, Aloc nuts. Although these nuts are crucial to American candy and soft drink industries, the President feels that the United

States can no longer ignore the suffering of the Tondoc people.

Direct students to write a brief description for each heading of the effects the ban on Aloc nuts will have on the United States, Tondoc, and the world as a whole. Conclude by having students write a hypothetical letter to the President of the United States or the President of Tondoc concerning the international implications of the Aloc nut ban.

Evaluate each student's writing on clarity of reasoning and thoroughness.

• Reinforcement Activity: Individual Project

Students may need practice in identifying the characteristics of nations within the context of the actions of a country. In this reinforcement activity, to be used after Section 24-1, students read descriptions and identify the characteristic of nations that each one reflects. The activity will require about 15 minutes to complete in class, or it can be assigned as homework.

Begin the activity by distributing Reinforcement Worksheet Chapter 24, "The Characteristics of Nations," in the Activity Book and review the directions. Students may use the text if necessary.

When students have finished with their worksheets, review their answers. Conclude by having students discuss how the level of economic development of a nation might affect its authority to act as a nation—to make and carry out laws, deal with other nations, and protect its national interests.

• Enrichment Activity: Individual Project

In this activity students create a graphic organizer to illustrate the interconnectedness of the world. The activity can be used after students have completed the chapter.

Before distributing Enrichment Worksheet Chapter 24, "Making Connections," in the Activity Book, read aloud some of the words on the worksheet and ask students to suggest connections between them. Distribute the worksheet and review the directions. Students who are familiar with graphic organizers can work independently. For help in using this study technique, see the Reinforcement Activity in Chapter 4 (page T 52).

Allow 15 to 20 minutes for students to complete the activity. Then have students discuss their methods of connecting the terms and their reasoning for making the connections. Invite two or more students to duplicate their work on overhead transparencies to share with the entire class.

Answer Key

CHAPTER 24

Section 24-1 Review (text page 526)

1. See definitions for the following terms on the text pages indicated in parentheses: *sovereignty* (522), *nationalism* (522), *colony* (523), *standard of living* (524).
2. Nations share the following characteristics: a defined territory with borders, a government, sovereignty, the duty to protect and promote the national interest, and nationalism.
3. Reasons developing nations find it difficult to meet the needs of their people include: Their economies are weak; they have few people trained in engineering, banking, business, or government service; there is political conflict between groups within the nation. Many of these factors are legacies of colonialism. Natural factors, such as poor soil and droughts also contribute to the problem.
Analysis. Nationalism and school spirit are both based on loyalty to a larger group. Both are encouraged by the group through slogans and songs, which may produce a feeling that "we're the best."
Data Search. Answers may include a per capita GNP between about \$750 and about \$2,000.

Section 24-2 Review (text page 532)

1. See definitions for the following terms on the text pages indicated in parentheses: *communism* (528), *cold war* (529), *alliance* (530), *détente* (531).
2. Conflict occurs when one group thinks that another group opposes its interests. Four causes of conflict are a longstanding quarrel between nations, unrest or disorder within a country, one nation thinking it is stronger than another and can get what it wants by force, and fear of being attacked.
3. The Soviets feared the United States because it was more powerful and it had the atomic bomb, and also because the Soviet Union had been invaded many times by Western nations.
4. Superpower tensions were eased by signing agreements limiting some nuclear arms, entering into trade agreements, and taking part in joint space ventures.
Synthesis. Answers may include the suggestion that nations try to focus more on common goals rather than opposing interests.

Section 24-3 Review (text page 535)

1. In a global economy, nations are dependent on each other for products they cannot make or grow themselves. The global economy has increased trade between nations.
2. Technology has been a foundation of our growing interdependence because it has improved transportation and communication between people and nations. It has made the world seem like a smaller place.
3. The world is an example of a system because the earth is a whole, and nations, organizations, and people are its interconnected parts.
Application. Answers may include that students' choice of products to purchase affects people in the nations where the products were produced or grown.

Decision-Making Lesson (text pages 536–537)

1. Goals will vary. One possible goal is "To buy the most economical car."
2. Standards will vary. One might be "Avoid making a choice based only on loyalty to American products."
3. Types of information will vary. Some possibilities are sticker price, gas mileage, and effects on American business.
4. Examples of characteristics and consequences will vary. For instance, under the category of gas mileage students could note that the foreign car gets 34 miles per gallon on the expressway.
5. Examples of skills will vary. One possibility is distinguishing relevant from irrelevant information. By applying this skill, students might identify the car dealers' interest rates as being irrelevant to the decision because local banks offer a rate that is lower than both. Students might also determine the reliability of the sources of information. For example, the foreign trade official's statement about the quality of American cars might reflect a bias.
6. Choices and reasons will vary, depending upon the students' goals and standards.
7. Resources will vary but might include such things as cash for a down payment and a good ability to negotiate with salespeople. Obstacles will vary, but might include such things as credit problems or inability to negotiate effectively with salespeople. Ways to overcome obstacles will vary. For example, you might consult a consumer's magazine for tips on how to negotiate effectively.
8. The order of the steps may vary. For example, the first step might be to set a limit for what you are willing to pay. The next step might be to rehearse how you are going to make your initial offer to the salesperson, and so on.
9. Adjustments to the plan may vary, depending on how reasonable you think the salesperson is being. If you think the salesperson is bluffing, you might call his or her bluff by saying you will stop the negotiations and go to another dealer.
10. Students should summarize in their own words the steps described in the lesson on pages 404–407.
11. You should check your action plan in order to make any necessary adjustments.
12. Critical thinking helps you to evaluate the information about each option.

Chapter Survey (text page 538)

Understanding New Vocabulary

1. Both *sovereignty* and *nationalism* are characteristics of nations. Sovereignty is the authority of a nation to make and enforce laws within its borders, and nationalism is a feeling of loyalty to a nation shared by its citizens.
2. Both *cold war* and *détente* have to do with relations between the United States and the Soviet Union. The cold war was the nonviolent struggle between these nations, and détente was a lessening of tensions in that struggle.
Putting It in Writing. Answers should describe the cold war, détente, and the end of the cold war. The cold war was shaped by the American fear of communism and featured the formation of alliances on both sides. Détente, which began in 1972, lessened tensions between the two nations. The end of the cold war brought a spirit of cooperation.

Looking Back at the Chapter

1. National power can come from control of valuable resources, building a strong military, and having a strong economy.
2. Nationalism can be based on having a common language, religion, or set of political beliefs. It can also be based on having a shared history and experiences.
3. The colonial powers grew rich by taking raw materials from the colonies and by forcing the native people to work for low wages. As a result, ways of life in the colonies were upset, and when the colonies became independent they had badly developed economies, little money, and few citizens trained in science, engineering, business, or government service.
4. Because developing nations have low standards of living, often there is no refrigeration, indoor plumbing, running water, or good medical care. Hunger is common. Few people learn how to read or write. Many people work in agriculture.
5. Competition leads to conflict when the interests of the competitors come into opposition, or when one group's interests are being promoted at the expense of the other.
6. The Soviets wanted control of nations on their western border because they feared invasion from the West and hoped the nations they controlled would provide a "territorial cushion" against invasion.
7. The United States and the Soviet Union came into conflict after World War II because both nations feared and distrusted each other. Americans saw communism as a threat, and the Soviet Union feared the atomic bomb and invasion from the West. Basically, the two nations had different political and economic visions of what was good for the people of the world.
8. Nations cooperate by agreeing to limit arms, promoting trade and economic growth, exchanging products and technology, helping control pollution and protect wildlife, and stopping aggression. Sometimes they form regional organizations to promote cooperation.
9. Two nations are interdependent when they depend on each other for things they do not produce or grow themselves. An example could be stated along the following lines: Nation A has oil but no farmland. Nation B has farmland and no oil. So, nation A supplies oil to nation B, and nation B supplies food to nation A.
10. The world is a smaller place than it was before because time and distance no longer separate people as much as they did before. Advances in communication and transportation have connected people and places much more closely.
11. The environment makes nations interdependent because we all live on the same planet, sharing the same air and water. Pollution in one nation can affect every person and living thing on earth.
12. A nation could not remain a nation if it lacked sovereignty. Without sovereignty, a nation could not enforce its laws, could not make decisions about how to deal with other nations, and would be vulnerable to other nations taking advantage of it.
13. Answers may include that developing nations are poor because they have weak economies. As colonies, they existed for the benefit of other nations. As a result, when they become independent, they lacked factories, wealth, and educated citizens, and have had unequal relations with developed nations ever since. In addition, some de-

veloping nations are poor because they cannot grow enough food to feed their people, cannot provide enough jobs for those who need work, and lack money and teachers to educate their children and to help adults improve their lives.
14. **(a)** Developed nations have a higher standard of living than developing nations; their citizens are more likely to have good medical services, indoor plumbing, refrigeration, and running water. **(b)** The majority of people in developed nations are better educated than people in developing nations. **(c)** Developed nations are industrialized, whereas developing nations have less industry.
15. Answers may include that open warfare between the two nations would involve use of nuclear weapons, and neither nation has been willing to pay the price of letting conflict get to that point. Also, the two countries have worked together since the 1970s to promote trade and slow down the arms race.
16. Answers should include examples that clearly show each kind of relationship.
17. Answers may include the dangers of relying on other nations for something as important as oil, or the benefits of interdependency.

Working Together

Answers will vary.

Skills Workshop (text page 539)

Social Studies Skills

1. Nations shown are the United States and Japan; regions shown are the European Economic Community and the Middle East.
2. The width of the lines indicates the relative value of the total amount of goods exported from one nation or region to another.
3. The European Economic Community is the major trading partner of the United States.
4. What Japan sent to the United States in trade was worth about twice as much as what the United States sent to Japan.
5. Trade between the United States and the European Economic Community is most balanced.

Decision-Making Skills

1. Answers may include preventing the installation of nuclear missiles in Cuba, stopping a nuclear war from happening, and giving the Soviet Union a chance to peacefully change its course of action.
2. Standards will vary. One possible standard might have been to avoid alarming the public unnecessarily. Another might have been to carefully consider the opinions of his advisors.
3. Options will vary. One possibility would have been an air strike against the missile sites. Another would have been to allow the missiles to be delivered but to start negotiations with the Soviets for their removal.
4. Consequences will vary. For example, a possible good consequence of the blockade is that the Soviets would turn back. A possible bad consequence is that the ships would try to run the blockade, perhaps forcing a naval battle that could lead to war.
5. Resources may include American ships stationed near Cuba, information on the positions of the Soviet ships, and communication links with Soviet leaders. A possible obstacle might be an unforeseen delay in communicating the President's orders to the ships in the blockade.
6. One way of checking would be to closely monitor the position of the Soviet ships and to try to intercept radio transmissions between the ships and the Soviet Union.
7. Answers will vary but should be supported with reasons.
8. Answers may include the importance of making every effort to talk with the Soviet leaders about the situation to ensure that no conflict occurs because of a misunderstanding.

OVERVIEW

Foreign policy is the plan used by a government to outline the goals it hopes to meet in its relations with other countries. The President is responsible for formulating and enacting our country's foreign policy but seeks advice from many governmental and nongovernmental groups. As the history of the United States shows, foreign policy changes over time.

OBJECTIVES

After completing this chapter, students should be able to

- identify the basic foreign policy goals of the United States.
- explain how foreign policy goals are achieved.
- describe influences on our foreign policy.
- identify foreign policy challenges facing the United States today.

PLANNING GUIDE

Teaching Strategy	Skills	Special Features	Review/Evaluation
Introducing the Chapter: Class Project **Teaching Activity 1:** Cooperative Project—Diplomatic Negotiation (Section 25-1) **Teaching Activity 2:** Individual Project—Influences on Foreign Policy (Section 25-2) **Evaluating Progress:** Individual Project (Section 25-2) **Reinforcement Activity:** Individual Project—Worksheet (Section 25-3) **Enrichment Activity:** Individual Project—Worksheet (Section 25-3)	Social Studies Skills Workshop: Interpreting Graphics Decision-Making Skills Workshop: What Relates to Your Subject? **Issues and Decision Making:** Worksheet Chapter 25	American Notebook People Make a Difference: Youth Gain Understanding Issues that Affect You: A Case Study—Becoming a Political Refugee	Section Reviews Chapter 25 Survey **Tests:** Chapter 25 Test **Testing Software** **Additional Resources** **Activity Book** **Citizenship Skills** **Transparencies and Activity Book** **Voices of America**

For reinforcement and enrichment worksheets and unit activities, see the Activity Book.

Teaching Strategy

Introducing the Chapter: Class Project

In determining foreign policy goals, the President of the United States must consider many competing interests. In this introductory activity students become aware of the President's responsibility to select and balance the goals and methods of foreign policy. The activity will take 20 to 30 minutes of class time.

Begin the activity by writing the following terms on the chalkboard: *national security, world peace, trade, human rights, democracy*. Explain to students that these are the foreign policy goals of our nation that they will be learning about in Chapter 25. Instruct students to rank the goals from the most important to least important for the President of the United States to pursue in his contacts with other nations. Allow five minutes for the ranking.

At the end of the time period, record the results and have students briefly discuss how closely their ranking seems to parallel the current policies of the United States. During the time they will be studying Chapter 25, leave the goals posted and challenge students to find and clip news articles that illustrate how American foreign policy seems to support or undermine the goals.

Teaching Activity 1: Cooperative Project

Diplomatic Negotiation

In this activity students practice diplomacy by negotiating a trade agreement. The activity, which will take an entire class period, is most effective after students have read Section 25-1.

Begin by dividing students into groups of four to six, then subdivide the groups into two sides. One side is to represent Country A and the other Country B. Inform students that the two nations are engaged in trade negotiations. Instruct students to take notes on their country as you read the following scenarios.

> The tiny but proud nation of Country A wants to improve its struggling economy. The country has an abundance of natural resources which other countries would like to buy. If industrialized, these resources could improve the economy and provide jobs for the country's growing population. However, government leaders would like to avoid bringing in heavy industry, such as mining, which would destroy the landscape, because many citizens want to increase the country's prosperity by promoting tourism.
>
> The tiny but proud nation of Country B is well known for its advanced technology in mining. Until recently, the state has been able to sell its engineers' expertise in gravel and open-pit mining to other countries. These contracts were a major source of wealth for the nation. However, the current negative world opinion on open-pit mining is hurting the economy, and Country B is looking for new sources of income.

Instruct students to discuss in their country groups the situations you described and identify their foreign policy goals. After they have reached consensus, Country A and Country B should begin negotiations. Country B should try to negotiate a mining contract, while Country A should try to improve its economy without damaging its appeal as a tourist spot.

Allow 20 minutes for students to negotiate and then call the class to order and have selected groups share their agreements. Help students recognize that the most effective agreements should provide clear benefits for each country. To conclude the activity, ask the following questions:

- What made the negotiations difficult?
- How did you resolve those difficulties?
- Was the agreement beneficial to each country?

- Did each country realize the foreign policy goals it had set? Explain.

Teaching Activity 2: Individual Project

Influences on Foreign Policy

This activity helps students understand and appreciate the complex process of making foreign policy decisions. The activity can be used after students have read Section 25-2. Depending on the extent of the suggested student discussion, the activity can take from 20 minutes to an entire class period to complete.

Begin by having students review the whaling case described in Section 25-2. When students are familiar with the information, ask them to take out a sheet of paper and list all of the government groups, nongovernment groups, and individuals that exerted influence in this case.

After students have made their lists, have them rank the groups and individuals to show their probable degree of influence on the case. Their ranking should start with the most influential group or individual and end with the least influential. (In general it can be assumed that government agencies close to the President have the most influence and individuals the least influence.)

Conclude the activity with a discussion of the following questions:

- Why do organized groups have more influence than individuals?
- How can individuals strengthen their influence in the process of making foreign policy?
- Can the President make decisions that go against the advice of his advisors? Why does the President generally follow his advisors' counsel?
- How would you describe the amount and variety of information involved in making a foreign policy decision?

Evaluating Progress: Individual Project

Use this activity to assess students' understanding of the process of making foreign policy. The activity can be used after students have read Section 25-2 and will require at least a class period.

Tell students to imagine that they have just been appointed advisors to the President of the United States, who wants advice on recent developments in Africa. Explain to students that a new nation has just been formed out of territory once shared by several African nations. This nation has requested recognition by the United States.

Instruct each student to develop a plan for the President to use to determine approval or denial of recognition. The plan should be in the form of a short paper in which students (1) outline the steps they would take in determining American interests in the area, (2) describe the pros and cons of recognition for the United States, (3) describe the pros and cons of American recognition for the new nation, (4) list questions to be considered in the process of making the decision, (5) identify government agencies that would be interested in the case, (6) speculate on what interest groups might react to the situation, and (7) state how they would research their plan. Students do not need to take a position on the question.

Assess the papers on coverage of the required information, accurate understanding of foreign policymaking, and perception of problems that might arise.

Reinforcement Activity: Individual Project

The United States' foreign policy changes with the flow of world events. In Reinforcement Worksheet Chapter 25, "Foreign Policy in Action," in the Activity Book, students summarize current situations in other countries or regions and describe the response of the United States. The worksheet can be used after students have finished Section 25-3 and will require about 30 minutes to complete.

Introduce the activity by asking students to recall the first news event involving the United States and a foreign country that they can remember. Have students describe the event and how they felt about it. Relate students' recollections to the historical events described in Section 25-3.

Distribute the worksheet and review the directions with students. Encourage them to review the goals and tools of foreign policy explained in Section 25-1.

When students have completed the assignment, discuss which areas of the world concern them most and why. Have students describe the foreign policy goals they believe are most important for the United States to pursue in the future.

Enrichment Activity: Individual Project

In this activity students apply goals and tools of foreign policy to a real situation. They will need about 20 minutes of class time to complete the worksheet, or it can be assigned as out-of-class work.

Begin the activity by asking students how they would respond if a foreign country wanted to build a military base next to their community. Have students discuss the consequences for them personally and for their community. Assign students to "pro-base" or "anti-base" positions. Distribute Enrichment Worksheet Chapter 25, "A Foreign Policy Issue," in the Activity Book, clarify instructions, and have students work on their own.

When students have finished the activity, pair up "pro-base" and "anti-base" students. Have them discuss each other's answers.

Answer Key

CHAPTER 25

Section 25-1 Review (text page 546)

1. See definitions for the following terms on the text pages indicated in parentheses: *aggression* (543), *deterrence* (543), *diplomacy* (544), *summit meeting* (544), *foreign aid* (544), *intelligence* (546).
2. Even if the United States is not directly involved in a war, war anywhere in the world is a threat to all nations. Only when all countries work together can we attain world peace.
3. The United States uses diplomacy to talk through and settle disagreements peacefully. It also uses diplomacy to meet other goals that both countries want to meet or to make alliances.
Synthesis. Trading countries avoid war because they depend on one another more and more for survival. Few countries have all the raw materials and manufactured goods they need, so trade can foster a spirit of cooperation.
Data Search. The chart and map do not support the statement. The United States gives most of its foreign aid to nations in the Middle East, specifically Israel and Egypt.

Section 25-2 Review (text page 551)

1. The President plays a key role in foreign policy as commander in chief of the armed forces and as chief diplomat. The President, with counsel from others, makes treaties and agreements, sets policies, appoints ambassadors, and has budget-making powers.
2. Congress must approve presidential diplomatic appointments, treaties, and the budget for defense and foreign aid. Its members also hold hearings and write and study bills involving foreign policy issues. Also, only Congress can declare war.
3. Foreign policy can affect the demand for American goods, the supply of raw materials and goods from other countries, and the American job market.

Synthesis. Answers may include that increasing interdependence means that our relations with foreign countries affect more and more aspects of American life. Examples could range from jobs to the air we breathe.

Section 25-3 Review (text page 557)

1. See definitions for the following terms on the text pages indicated in parentheses: *isolationism* (551), *neutrality* (552), *containment* (553).
2. The United States was young and wanted to stay as isolated as possible from other nations to avoid European conflict and also to continue trade with both sides in any war.
3. The United States is no longer the leader in world trade. It faces the challenge of how to establish a more favorable balance of trade with Japan, how to maintain positive trade relations with Western Europe, and how to assure its supply of oil from the powerful oil-rich nations.
Evaluation. Answers may include the argument that interdependence makes isolationism impossible, or the argument that the United States should be less involved in the internal affairs and conflicts of other countries and, except for trade, should be more isolationist.

Issues That Affect You: A Case Study (text pages 558–559)

1. Beatrice depended on the Immigration and Nationality Act to allow her to remain in the United States.
2. The law requires this information in order to follow Congress's intention to limit annual immigration into the United States. If the law did not require such "proof" of danger, then anyone with a general concern for his or her safety could become a refugee and stay in the United States.
3. Answers may include the opinion that if the INS makes it difficult for everyone to prove they should be refugees, it could be unfair because not every alien can afford an attorney as Beatrice could. Answers may also include support for the INS's policy on the grounds that if it were easier, too many aliens could qualify as refugees.

Chapter Survey (text page 560)

Understanding New Vocabulary

1. *Aggression* is an attack or threat of attack by another country, while *deterrence* is keeping a strong defense to discourage aggression by other nations. Both involve the military and can involve threats.
2. *Diplomacy* is usually used by members of the State Department to conduct relations between nations, while a *summit meeting* is a meeting between the heads of nations to further diplomatic relations. Summit meetings are a particular way of carrying out diplomacy.
3. *Isolationism* is a foreign policy that seeks to limit a country's relations with other countries. *Neutrality* is a foreign policy of not taking sides in wars between other countries. Neutrality can be a part of isolationism, but countries can be neutral without being isolationist.
4. *Containment* is a foreign policy of using military power and money to prevent the spread of communism. *Deterrence* is keeping a strong defense to discourage aggression by other nations. Deterrence can be a part of containment, but countries can practice deterrence without containment.
Putting It in Writing. Answers may include the use of deterrence to help protect national security; the use of diplomacy to promote world peace and trade; and the use of foreign aid to promote trade, world peace, and democracy.

Looking Back at the Chapter

1. Trading creates foreign markets for American goods and services, and supplies American consumers with goods from other countries.
2. Because the United States has built up its supply of arms and troops, foreign countries know that if they attack the United States, they risk severe military retaliation. This knowledge should deter them from attacking.
3. Alliances can protect national security and world peace, and promote trade, human rights, and democracy.
4. The United States uses military aid to help nations defend themselves and remain independ-

ent and to encourage democracy. Economic aid fosters world peace through building healthy economies and creating stronger trading partners.
5. Opponents of military aid claim that the United States has helped governments that violate human rights. Critics of economic aid claim that certain types of aid give the United States too much control over how other countries develop.
6. Countries work hard to gather intelligence to help meet their national security goals. They try to learn ahead of time if countries are unfriendly and what these countries intend to do.
7. The Department of State advises the President on foreign policy, represents the United States in diplomatic meetings, runs the diplomatic corps, and assists Americans abroad.
8. The Senate has the power to approve or reject treaties and appointments. Congress also approves money spent on defense and foreign aid. The President, therefore, needs the approval of Congress on most key foreign policy moves.
9. Private groups influence foreign policy by putting pressure on Congress and executive branch policy makers. Some encourage citizens to write letters to members of Congress or vote for certain candidates. Other groups form organizations that lobby toward certain goals.
10. Washington chose neutrality to keep America out of wars and to allow America to continue trading with both sides in the conflicts.
11. Expansion brought the United States into contact and conflict with nations that held claims to the land the United States sought to control.
12. Japan has become a dominant world economic power and has tipped the balance of trade in its favor. Additionally, Western European nations have gained economic strength. Oil-rich nations have also demonstrated their economic power by withholding oil from Western nations.
13. Answers will vary but should be based on how students prioritize foreign policy goals.
14. Answers will vary but should include criteria for determining if military force is defensive or aggressive.
15. Much of foreign policy revolves around defense and foreign aid. These two areas account for a large part of the federal budget and require the support of Congress to be implemented.
16. The United States may refuse to sell to a certain country, may refuse to buy from a certain country, or may establish tariffs.
17. Without *perestroika* and *glasnost* the cold war competition would have continued to influence political and economic relations between the superpowers and between the superpowers and countries seeking aid from them. Specific examples will vary.

Working Together

Answers will vary.

Skills Workshop (text page 561)

Social Studies Skills

1. The center dot represents the total weapon power used in World War II.
2. The other dots represent the weapon power of all nuclear weapons in the 1980s.
3. Answers will vary.
4. Answers will vary.
5. Answers may include the view that concern over national security caused the buildup of nuclear weapons, or the view that the existence of so many destructive weapons may have forced nations to put a higher priority on the goal of promoting world peace.

Decision-Making Skills

1. Statements A, C, D, and G are relevant because they concern interaction with other nations.
2. Statement B is irrelevant because being drafted is not a choice and therefore does not imply a view on American involvement in the war. Statement E is irrelevant because favoring a tax cut does not indicate either candidate's priorities for government spending in the area of foreign policy. Statement F is irrelevant because drilling off the California coast is a domestic issue.
3. Kinds of information may include statements made by the candidates regarding nonmilitary aid to foreign countries.
4. Decisions and information will vary.

OVERVIEW

Global problems related to the environment, health, peace, and human rights concern Americans as well as citizens of other countries. Nations can cooperate in solving global problems through international governmental and nongovernmental organizations. Individuals can also make a difference in the state of the world by using their skills, money, connections, and time.

OBJECTIVES

After completing this chapter, students should be able to

- identify problems facing our world and possible solutions.
- explain how organizations are dealing with global problems.
- describe ways that individuals can help solve global problems.

PLANNING GUIDE

Teaching Strategy	Skills	Special Features	Review/Evaluation
Introducing the Chapter: Cooperative Project **Teaching Activity 1:** Individual Project—Making Others Aware of Global Problems (Section 26-1) **Teaching Activity 2:** Individual Project—Global Interdependence in the News (Section 26-2) **Evaluating Progress:** Individual Project (Section 26-1) **Reinforcement Activity:** Individual Project—Worksheet (Section 26-2) **Enrichment Activity:** Individual Project—Worksheet (Section 26-3)	Social Studies Skills Workshop: Interpreting Maps Decision-Making Skills Workshop: Choosing and Taking Action **Issues and Decision Making:** Worksheet Chapter 26	American Notebook Views of Noted Americans: Ginetta Sagan In Their Own Words: Carl Sagan—"One more step is needed now"	Section Reviews Chapter 26 Survey Unit 8 Survey **Tests:** Chapter 26 Test, Unit 8 Test, Quarter 4 Test **Testing Software** **Additional Resources** **Activity Book** **Citizenship Skills** **Transparencies and Activity Book** **Voices of America**

For reinforcement and enrichment worksheets and unit activities, see the Activity Book.

Teaching Strategy

Introducing the Chapter: Cooperative Project

In this introductory activity students brainstorm in the area of global problems and possible solutions. The activity will require most of a class period.

Before class prepare five pieces of poster paper by writing one of the following headings at the top of each: *Worldwide Environmental Problems, Problems of Global Peace, Organizations That Deal with Global Problems, Ways That Individuals Can Help Solve Global Problems,* and *Reasons to be Optimistic About the World's Future.* Post the papers at stations around the room and provide additional writing sheets.

Begin the activity by calling students' attention to the stations of the five poster sheets. Explain that groups will do brainstorming about global problems or solutions at each station.

Divide the class into five groups and send each group to a "brainstorm station." Give the groups three minutes to list everything they know about the topic posted at their station. Have groups move to a new station, read the list written by the previous group, then add new information about the topic. Allow three minutes for their additions. Continue this process until each group has been to all five stations.

Reconvene the class and have students read the lists of environmental and global peace problems. Help students rank the problems on each list to determine which are the most serious. Review the organizations that are dealing with global problems and have students discuss whether more organizations are needed. Discuss ways that individuals can help solve global problems and have students share personal experiences. Finally, focus on reasons to be optimistic about the world's future. Have students discuss what needs to be done to make young people more optimistic about the future.

Conclude by explaining that the last chapter in the text will discuss the topics on the poster sheets.

Teaching Activity 1: Individual Project

Making Others Aware of Global Problems

In this activity students make others aware of global problems by writing public service announcements. The activity can be used after students have completed Section 26-1 and will require about two class periods to complete in class. The announcement can be written out of class.

On the chalkboard write the following topics: renewable and nonrenewable resources, toxic chemicals, acid rain, the greenhouse effect, weakened ozone layer, arms buildup, terrorism, violations of human rights, and deforestation.

Begin by asking students what a public service announcement (PSA) is. Encourage them to describe examples they have heard on the radio or seen on television (drug prevention, automobile safety, AIDS). Explain that radio and television stations broadcast PSAs free of charge; organizations or individuals prepare PSAs as one form of citizen participation.

Tell students that a PSA must inform the public about a problem and offer a solution or a partial solution. Listeners or viewers are usually asked to participate in solving the problem. Often a PSA attempts to catch the public's attention with a shocking statement, picture, or catchy slogan.

Tell students that their assignment is to prepare and present a radio or television PSA on one of the topics listed on the chalkboard. The PSA must include a statement of the problem, a solution, and a call for public participation. The PSAs should be no longer than one minute. Students who do a television PSA should include one or more pictures, symbols, or other graphics to illustrate the message.

On presentation day, have the class give feedback to students as they read their PSAs. You may also want to arrange for some or all of the students to read their PSAs on the school intercom system during announcements.

⊡ Teaching Activity 2: Individual Project

Global Interdependence in the News

In this activity students analyze news articles on world problems and problem solving efforts in order to assess global interdependence. The activity can be used after students have read Section 26-2. Allow out-of-class time for students to collect news articles. Discussion in class will require most of a class period.

Introduce the activity by asking students to name current international events that pose problems for the world and organizations or people working to solve them. Direct students to read the newspaper for the next week and clip articles that deal with such global problems as environmental damage, the arms buildup, and human rights violations. Instruct students to bring their articles to class on a specific day.

On the assigned day, have students display and discuss their articles. List the problems on the chalkboard and challenge students to create different ways to categorize them. Categorizations might include regions of the world; money or policy solutions; short-term or long-term solutions; or action by governments, nongovernmental organizations, or individuals. Have students discuss how conflicts between interests and changes in the nature of these problems over time make problem solving more complex.

End the activity by asking students to what extent the nations of the world are interdependent. What news articles support the idea of a Spaceship Earth? Discuss what responsibilities the United States has to other countries.

⊡ Evaluating Progress: Individual Project

After students have read Section 26-1, use this activity to evaluate their understanding of the problems that threaten our planet. The activity, which can be completed in class or assigned as homework, will take about 45 minutes.

Remind students about the Universal Declaration of Human Rights which is mentioned in Section 26-1. Emphasize that the declaration was written to protect people's basic rights. Tell students that they are to write a universal declaration of rights for the Planet Earth.

Students' declarations should have an opening paragraph stating their beliefs about the environmental dangers facing the planet. Next, there should be a list of rights and rules for citizens to follow in order to protect Earth. Students can use wording common to declarations, such as "Earth has the right to . . ." and "No one shall. . . ." The declarations should conclude with a summary paragraph asking for support.

Evaluate students' writing on content. Does the declaration have an introductory paragraph, specific statements of action, and a conclusion asking for support? Encourage volunteers to read their declarations.

⊡ Reinforcement Activity: Individual Project

This activity can be used to help reinforce students' understanding of the organizations working to solve global problems. Use Reinforcement Worksheet Chapter 26, "Organizations That Make a Difference," in the Activity Book after students have finished Section 26-2. It will require about 30 minutes to complete.

Before distributing the worksheet, ask students to list organizations they would use to help solve a problem at school, in the community, or in the state. Remind students of the organizations that help solve global problems that are described in Section 26-2. Encourage students to use the information in that section to help complete the worksheet.

When students have completed the assignment, ask them to share and explain their answers. Then have them discuss other ways global problems might be solved.

▣ Enrichment Activity: Individual Project

As pointed out in Section 26-3, individuals can make a difference in solving international problems. In this enrichment activity students analyze how they might solve global problems. The activity is best used at the chapter's conclusion and can be assigned as in-class or out-of-class work. Students will need at least 30 minutes to thoughtfully complete the assignment.

Introduce the activity by having students name people who try to solve local, national, or international problems. Ask them to think about how the role of citizen requires us to take responsibility for the welfare of others. Direct students to imagine themselves helping to solve a global problem.

Distribute Enrichment Worksheet Chapter 26, "You Can Make a Difference," in the Activity Book and review the directions. Make certain students understand that the information they provide would be used in a press release. Encourage students to see themselves as making a difference in an area that is of concern to them.

When students have finished their worksheets, post them around the room and let the class read about themselves as future problem solvers.

Answer Key

CHAPTER 26

Section 26-1 Review (text page 570)

1. See definitions for the following terms on the text pages indicated in parentheses: *renewable resource* (564), *nonrenewable resource* (564), *deforestation* (566), *terrorism* (567).
2. Answers may include the following: Some resources are nonrenewable, resources are not spread evenly around the world, the world's population is growing rapidly, life-styles in developed nations use up a lot of resources, and developing nations are using up resources to improve their economies.
3. Toxic chemicals, acid rain, the greenhouse effect, and the weakened ozone layer are all global issues because their effects are not confined to a single nation or a small number of nations.
4. The arms buildup is a global issue because some countries have the power to wage nuclear war which could destroy life on the planet. Terrorism has a global impact because terrorists can strike anywhere in the world. Human rights is a global issue because many people throughout the world believe that everyone has certain basic rights. Also, violations of human rights in one country can affect other countries as refugees flee across borders.
5. Nations often do not cooperate because they place their short-term goals ahead of the long-term goals for the earth, blame each other for global problems rather than sharing responsibility, and have different views on such issues as human rights and the use of resources. Nations might cooperate more if they looked at what is best for the world rather than just their own needs, respected each other's sovereignty, recognized each other's need to develop economically, and understood factors that can lead to terrorism and violations of human rights.
Evaluation. Answers may include the opinion that developed nations bear more responsibility because they have greater financial resources and are primarily to blame for pollution and the arms buildup.

Data Search. Resources that will likely run out during students' lifetime include aluminum, copper, gold, lead, natural gas, petroleum, silver, and tin. Resources that are not likely to run out during their lifetimes are coal and iron.

Section 26-2 Review (text page 574)

1. The UN plays a peacekeeping role through the Security Council. It also works to improve standards of living throughout the world by providing food, health care, education, and economic aid. In addition, the World Court gives nations a way to settle conflicts peacefully.
2. Answers may include the work of CARE, the Red Cross, Amnesty International, the World Council of Churches, and the Roman Catholic Church in supporting human rights; environmental work by Greenpeace; and support of arms control by Physicians Against Nuclear War.
3. Cooperation is fostered by the need for countries to help each other grow economically or deal with natural disasters. Countries are also more likely to cooperate when they are in the same region and share economic and political interests. Among the barriers to cooperation is each nation's concern over its own security.
Evaluation. Answers may include the view that the UN cannot work effectively as a democratic organization if its resolutions are not binding on every member nation, or the view that a government's first duty is to look after the needs of its own citizens.

Section 26-3 Review (text page 577)

1. Answers may include using singing, speaking, or writing talents to inform people of global problems and to raise money to deal with those problems. Also, scientific and medical skills can be used to help deal with environmental, economic, and health problems.
2. Raoul Wallenberg used his Swedish diplomatic connections to protect human rights by helping Jews escape Nazi-occupied Hungary. Armand Hammer used his business connections to help the Chinese and Soviet people improve their economies. Also, he used his money to help with disaster relief.
3. Through volunteering her time and effort, Mother Teresa has helped many of the poor in India and has inspired people throughout the world to help the sick and needy.
Analysis. By dealing with the problem of hunger, Mother Teresa has helped to protect human rights, especially economic rights. Armand Hammer's efforts improved American relations with the Soviet Union and China, thereby reducing the threat of world war. He also faced the issue of human rights, especially economic rights, by helping disaster victims.

Chapter Survey (text page 578)

Understanding New Vocabulary

1. Both are natural resources, the resources we depend on for life. A *renewable resource* can be replaced after being used, but a *nonrenewable resource* cannot be replaced once it has been used.
2. Both are global problems. *Terrorism* is a political problem, while *deforestation* is an economic and environmental problem.
Putting It in Writing. Answers should show a general understanding of the relationship between resource use and environmental destruction.

Looking Back at the Chapter

1. People in developed nations use up more resources because they use more gasoline and electric power for cars, factories, and households.
2. Answers may include lack of information about dangerous effects of pollution, the months or years it may take to discover and undo the damage caused by some products, and the view held by many people that it is too costly or difficult to fight pollution.
3. Each country wants to protect its own security and is careful about reducing its military arms.
4. Examples may include violation of the right of free speech when governments arrest people who criticize them and denial of the right to vote to nonwhite people in South Africa.
5. The General Assembly is best suited for open debate because it includes representatives of all member nations.

6. Membership in the UN is voluntary, and the UN does not have sovereignty over member nations. It can only make proclamations and can assist countries in settling disputes only if the parties involved agree to accept this help.
7. Countries are usually more eager to accept economic aid than to consider giving up political power through compromise. Nations usually do not see economic aid as a threat to their sovereignty.
8. The UN is an organization that has been set up by the governments of the world and in many ways is similar to a government in structure. Organizations such as the International Red Cross and CARE are nongovernmental groups.
9. Answers may include writers, musicians, scientists, and medical workers' use of their skills to get information about causes of problems, to inform people about problems, and to find solutions. People can also use business and government connections to deal with problems. Another way people can help is by volunteering time.
10. Answers will vary but should demonstrate an understanding of the difference between renewable and nonrenewable resources. Examples of materials that can be recycled will vary.
11. Supporting answers may include the opinion that machines and other products that can cause pollution are created to meet human demands; unless people change their life-styles, the technology and products that cause pollution are unlikely to change significantly. Opposing answers may include the argument that through new technology people can find ways to reduce pollution without requiring major changes in life-styles.
12. Answers may include the following suggestions: Developed nations could provide technical assistance in helping other nations incorporate pollution controls in factories, use farming techniques that do not harm the environment, and so on. Developed nations could also provide loans to developing nations.
13. Opinions will vary but should be supported with examples and reasons.

Working Together

Answers will vary.

Skills Workshop (text page 579)

Social Studies Skills

1. The maps cover the years between 1979 and 1984.
2. The subject is the hole in the ozone layer over Antarctica.
3. The maps show that the ozone-depleted area over Antarctica increased greatly.

Decision-Making Skills

1. Answers may include such goals as avoiding another world war, helping nations to settle disputes, and encouraging economic cooperation between nations.
2. Answers may include the following options: There might have been no Security Council, and instead the General Assembly would be the only body voting on political issues. The Security Council might exist, but members would not have veto power. The nations might have decided that a World Court was not practical.
3. Answers may include the following positive consequences: Nations would find the structure somewhat familiar because most national governments also have a legislative branch, a judicial branch, and a bureaucracy. A familiar structure might make it easier for representatives of different nations to work together. Also, the most powerful nations, the Big Five, would continue to support the UN, knowing that they could veto any UN proposal that they disliked. A negative consequence may include the inability of the UN to take decisive action on many political issues because of the veto power of the Big Five.
4. Answers may include the economic strength of the United States and other developed nations as a major resource. These nations could provide money to construct UN buildings, hire staff, and set up economic programs. Another resource was translators to facilitate communication between representatives of member nations.

5. Answers may include the difficulty the Big Five faced in trying to support the new organization financially while recovering economically from the effects of World War II and the resentment of many nations of the veto power of the Big Five.
6. Answers may include selecting a location for UN headquarters, getting financing for the construction of the buildings, and hiring staff.
7. Answers may include making World Court decisions binding on all members to strengthen the role of the Court and doing away with the veto power to make the UN a more democratic organization.

In Their Own Words (text page 580)

1. According to Sagan, we must decide whether humankind has a future, given the greed, hatred, and shortsightedness that people have shown throughout history.
2. He is optimistic because of the love people show for their children and people's willingness to learn from history. He also notes signs of a growing awareness among people of our common humanity, including the abolition of slavery, the growth of women's rights, and the efforts by citizens of aggressor nations to stop their countries from going to war.
3. The next step is to think about a complete reorganization of our societies.
4. Answers may include such goals as ensuring that no one goes without food or shelter and guaranteeing low-cost medical care to everyone.

Unit 6 Survey (text page 581)

Looking Back at the Unit

1. Developed nations are heavily industrialized, with most citizens living in urban areas, working at service jobs, and having a fairly high standard of living. In developing nations, the majority of the people are poor. The economies of developing nations rely more heavily on farming than on industry, and technology is behind that of the developed nations. Tensions arise between developed and developing nations over global issues, especially the environment and the arms buildup. In trying to catch up economically and militarily with industrial nations, developing nations add to the pollution problem and use up resources quickly. However, they believe that developed nations have no right to ask them to slow down their efforts.
2. Answers may include relations with communist nations, relations with developing nations, and trade policies. In dealing with these issues, our government must consider the needs of other nations because countries are increasingly interdependent. American policies that harm other countries economically, socially, or politically may also hurt the United States.
3. Examples of global problems and possible responses by the United States will vary. One possibility is that the United States can support human rights by restricting trade with countries that deny basic rights to their citizens.
4. Like many nations, the UN has a government with a legislative branch, a judicial branch, and a bureaucracy. Unlike nations, however, the UN does not have sovereignty.

Taking a Stand

Answers may include arguments cited in the text and/or arguments students develop.

ADDISON-WESLEY

CIVICS

PARTICIPATING IN OUR DEMOCRACY

AUTHORS

James E. Davis

Phyllis Maxey Fernlund

CONSULTANTS

Barry K. Beyer

Mabel McKinney-Browning

ADDISON-WESLEY PUBLISHING COMPANY
Menlo Park, California • Reading, Massachusetts
New York • Don Mills, Ontario • Wokingham, England
Amsterdam • Bonn • Sydney • Singapore • Tokyo
Madrid • San Juan • Paris • Seoul • Milan
Mexico City • Taipei

Authors

James E. Davis, a consultant and developer of curriculum in the social sciences, received his Ed.D. in social science education from the University of Colorado, Boulder. Davis has taught at both the secondary and college levels. Between 1968 and 1984 he was a staff member and associate director of the Social Science Education Consortium, a research and development organization. An active NCSS member for over 20 years, he has developed curriculum materials and teacher resources for elementary and secondary levels.

Phyllis Maxey Fernlund is Professor of Education at California State University, San Bernardino. She holds a Ph.D. in education from Northwestern University and received her B.A. and M.A.T. degrees in history from the University of Illinois, Urbana. A former high school social studies teacher, she has conducted many workshops on civic education, middle school education, and K–12 social studies articulation. She is co-author of *Teaching Social Studies in the Elementary Schools.*

Consultants

Barry K. Beyer is Professor of Education at George Mason University. He received an M. Ed. in social studies education from Syracuse University and a Ph.D. in history from the University of Rochester. He is a widely recognized expert on teaching thinking skills and has been a consultant to school systems across the nation. A former junior and senior high school teacher, he has edited *Social Education* issues on writing and critical thinking. He is the author of several books on teaching thinking skills.

Mabel McKinney-Browning is Staff Director of the American Bar Association's Committee on Youth Education for Citizenship. She holds an Ed.D. in curriculum development and teacher education from the University of Illinois, Urbana and has taught social studies and language arts methods at the University of Illinois, Chicago. Specializing in law-related education, she has conducted teacher workshops and has written articles for *Social Education, Today's Education,* and other education journals.

Contributing Writers

Toni Dwiggins is coauthor of a United States history textbook and has contributed to numerous texts in the social studies and sciences.

Diane Hart, a Woodrow Wilson Fellow, is the author of a number of books in the social studies. She has taught social studies at both elementary and high school levels.

Roberta M. Jackson, a social studies and language arts teacher at Lake Ridge Middle School, Woodbridge, Virginia, is working on a doctorate in education at George Mason University.

James McTighe, a former Foreign Service Reserve officer, has written books and articles on American history.

Robert Silver, J.D., is an assistant professor at Lincoln University in San Francisco, California, and writes social studies materials and articles on business and law.

ISBN 0-201-81563-X

2 3 4 5 6 7 8 9 10 - VH - 95 94 93 92

Content Review

Jeffrey J. Blaga is Director of Social Studies Education for the Racine Unified School District, Racine, Wisconsin.

Walter D. Christofferson is a social studies teacher in the Kenosha Unified School District #1, Kenosha, Wisconsin.

Edward J. Erler is Professor and Chair, Department of Political Science, California State University, San Bernardino.

Thomas L. Ilgen is Jones Professor of Political Studies at Pitzer College and Faculty Associate, Center for Policy and Politics, Claremont Graduate School, Claremont, California.

Barbara Norrander is Associate Professor of Political Science at San Jose State University, San Jose, California.

Charles P. Osborn holds an M.B.A. from Cornell University. He is a former economist with the Department of Justice Anti-Trust Division.

Judith B. Rhodes is chair of the social studies department at Phillips Junior High School, Chapel Hill, North Carolina.

Charles Schierloh is chair of the social studies department at Lima South Junior High School, Lima, Ohio.

Ron Schukar is Director of the Center for Teaching International Relations at the University of Denver and former social studies consultant for the Colorado Department of Education.

Donald Schwartz, who holds a Ph.D. in diplomatic history, is a member of the history department at California State University, Long Beach, and is Social Studies Credential Coordinator there.

Barton H. Thompson, Jr., an associate professor at Stanford Law School, is a former law clerk to Supreme Court Justice William H. Rehnquist.

Field Test

Bob Brogden, social studies teacher, Culbreth Junior High School, Chapel Hill, North Carolina.

Robert K. DeVorse, social studies teacher, Riverside University High School, Milwaukee, Wisconsin.

Dada T. Dye, civics teacher, Tazewell Middle School, Tazewell, Virginia.

Terry Erickson, social studies teacher, Sylvan Middle School, Citrus Heights, California.

Donna S. Humberd, civics teacher, Worley Junior High School, Westwego, Louisiana.

Robert J. Sivak, civics teacher, Washington High School, Milwaukee, Wisconsin.

Student Review

Parts of this book were read and reviewed by the following students at Centennial Junior High School in Boulder, Colorado:

Chad Fletemeyer, Angela Gomez, Michael Greene, Angélica Lozano-A., Nathan Uhlir, and Amanda Wallen.

TABLE OF CONTENTS

UNIT 1 FOUNDATIONS OF CITIZENSHIP 1

JUSTICE
FREEDOM
DEMOCRACY

WHY PUT A HELIPORT IN OUR TOWN? YOU'LL DESTROY THE PEACE ALL AROUND!
DON'T LET NATURE BE DESTROYED WITH HELICOPTERS

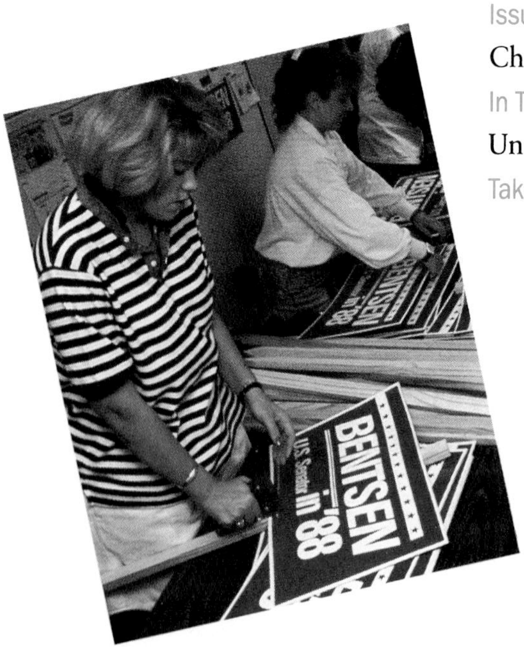
BENTSEN
U.S. Senate in '88

SKILLS

Decision-Making Skills

Social Studies Skills

CHARTS, TABLES, AND GRAPHS

MAPS

AUTHORS' NOTE TO STUDENTS

When we began planning this book, we asked ourselves lots of questions—about citizenship, about students, and about teaching. Here are three major questions that guided our thinking as we wrote.

- How can knowledge about citizenship be presented so it appeals to students?
- How can we help show connections between our political system, our economy, our society, and students' lives?
- How can we help students develop the skills they will need to take action in solving problems and improving their own communities?

Every day, American citizens—"We the People"—come together to govern themselves. To help you see how this process works, we have included stories about real people as they pursue life, liberty, and happiness. Our student reviewers liked the idea of reading about real people. We hope that you, too, find these stories interesting and that they help you understand the meaning of United States citizenship.

Our society is very complex, and so are our individual lives. It is often difficult to sort things out—to "get a handle on the world." Being a citizen is just one role you play in our complex world. You have other very important roles to fulfill as a family member, a friend, a member of social groups, a consumer, a worker, and by just being yourself. Citizenship applies to all the roles you play in life. Understanding your social roles will help you make connections between our political system, our economy, and our society.

It is our belief that good citizenship means taking effective action. Each day, people throughout the United States express their concerns about problems in our society. They try to figure out what has gone wrong. They get together to right those wrongs. They ask elected leaders for help. They run for office. They vote. They work on political campaigns and on environmental cleanup projects. To take effective action, people must develop skills. They must be able to define problems, set goals, think through options and their consequences, plan what to do, and carry out their plans. Throughout the book we provide many opportunities for you to develop such skills. We present biographies of people who have been—and are—good decision-makers. We also confront you with challenges and problems that you will need to solve.

As a citizen, you are the real source of power in our society. When you finish this book, we hope you understand the nature of that power, the rights it gives you, and the responsibilities that go with it. Above all, we hope you will have enjoyed learning from *Civics: Participating in Our Democracy*.

James E. Davis
Phyllis Maxey Fernlund

UNIT 1

Unit Quotation: Stephen Vincent Benét (1898–1943) thought a great deal about what it means to be an American. In such poems as *John Brown's Body* and *Western Star*, Benét vividly described America's history and its unique legends, ideas, and ways of living. Personal freedom is a recurrent theme.

FOUNDATIONS OF CITIZENSHIP

Democracy Is a Trust

Let us say this much to ourselves, not only with our lips but in our hearts. Let us say this: I myself am a part of democracy—I myself must accept responsibilities. Democracy is not merely a privilege to be enjoyed—it is a trust to keep and maintain. I am an American. I intend to remain an American . . . I will sustain my government. And through good days or bad I will try to serve my country.

—Stephen Vincent Benét

As you read these words written by the twentieth-century American poet Stephen Vincent Benét, do they make you think about what it means to be an American? As Americans, what do we believe about our country, our government? Where do our ideas come from? How do we know what to expect from our government? How do we know what is expected of us?

In Unit I you will be taking a look at American society and at the ideas and beliefs that Americans share. You will begin to learn what it means to be an American citizen and what rights and responsibilities citizens share.

Chapter Themes: Americans are a diverse group of people with great variation in where they live, the work they do, their ages, and their family backgrounds. The diversity of Americans creates a dynamic society which is held together by shared beliefs and values.

CHAPTER 1

A Portrait of Americans

My name is Peter Ky. I am fifteen years old. I was born in Vietnam, and I came to the United States with my family in 1981. In 1987 we all became American citizens. We have a family-owned restaurant in San Francisco, California. My mother and father do the cooking. My older brother, who is twenty-three, orders supplies, plans the menus with my parents, and handles the finances. With my twin sisters, who are seventeen, I work in the restaurant when I am not going to school.

I am Bernice Kelman. I am seventy-one years old. I grew up on a farm in western Kansas. My father, who came to this country from Scotland, and my mother, who was born in Germany, homesteaded a farm near Dodge City, Kansas, in 1918. I live nearby in the small town of Sublette where, until I retired, I was a secretary for the superintendent of schools. My brother Jack and his youngest son, Roger, now manage our family farm, where we grow wheat, corn, and soybeans.

My name is Doris Hollingsworth. I am forty-one. My great-grandparents were slaves on a plantation near Augusta, Georgia, and my father was a construction worker in Atlanta. I graduated from Spelman College, and now I work for a large company as a computer analyst. At night I go to Emory University where I am studying for my masters degree in business administration. My husband is a high school science teacher and a basketball coach. With our sixteen-year-old daughter, we live in Tucker, Georgia, a suburb of Atlanta.

Think for a moment about Peter, Bernice, and Doris. What do they have in common? They are all American citizens—members of a very large group of people who live in this country we call the United States of America. In this chapter you will read about the many different kinds of people who are Americans and about some of the important ideas and values that bind us together as a nation and as a people.

Teaching Note: Use the Introducing the Chapter activity, page T 32.

Teaching Note: Use the Reinforcement Activity, page T 33, and accompanying worksheet in the Activity Book with Section 1-1 or 1-2.

1-1

WHO AMERICANS ARE

Read to Find Out

- what the term *diversity* means.
- where Americans live.
- how Americans' jobs are changing.
- why there are more older Americans today.

What if a visitor from another country asked you, "Who are Americans?" How could you go about answering that question? What kinds of information do you think you would want to give?

As you can see from reading about Peter, Bernice, and Doris, not all Americans are alike. We live in different places and work at different jobs. We are different ages. We come from different backgrounds. Gathering information about all these different characteristics can help to make a portrait of the American people.

Where We Live

Americans live in almost every kind of terrain the world has to offer. We live in high mountains and on broad prairies. We live in warm, tropical climates and in areas with frigid winters. From Alaska to Texas, and from the Hawaiian Islands to the coast of Maine, the United States is a vast and varied land.

When Peter Ky goes home, he climbs three flights of stairs to his family's apartment in San Francisco, a city of 700,000 people on the shore of the Pacific Ocean. Doris and her husband and daughter live in a condominium in Tucker, Georgia, a suburb of Atlanta with a population of about 20,000. Bernice's home is in Sublette, Kansas, a small farming town of 1,800 people.

Americans on the move. In the early days of our country's history, most people lived on farms or in small towns that hugged the eastern seacoast. Gradually, as more and more people came to the New World seeking land and jobs, our population spread out across the continent.

When Bernice was a little girl in the 1920s, one out of three Americans lived on a farm, as she did. Gradually, people began to concentrate in urban areas, or cities, where jobs were available in factories and offices. Today, three out of four Americans (about 180 million) live in urban areas, as do Peter and Doris.

Americans have not only moved from farms to cities. They also have been moving from the North and the East toward the South and the West, settling in warm-weather states such as Georgia, Florida, Texas, Arizona, and California. This region, which is called the Sunbelt, has been the fastest growing area in the nation in the last thirty years.

What Work We Do

Americans have always worked hard. The first settlers from Europe supported themselves by scratching farms out of the wilderness in Virginia and Massachusetts. Since then, we have

AMERICAN NOTEBOOK 

We recognize our country in the words of Woody Guthrie's famous folk song:

> ***This land is your land, this land is my land,***
> ***From California, to the New York Island,***
> ***From the redwood forests to the Gulf Stream waters,***
> ***This land was made for you and me.***

The westward movement of Americans is reflected in the nation's shifting center of population—the point around which the population is evenly balanced. In 1790, the center was near Baltimore, Maryland. By 1880, it had moved to the Indiana-Ohio border and by 1980 to eastern Missouri.

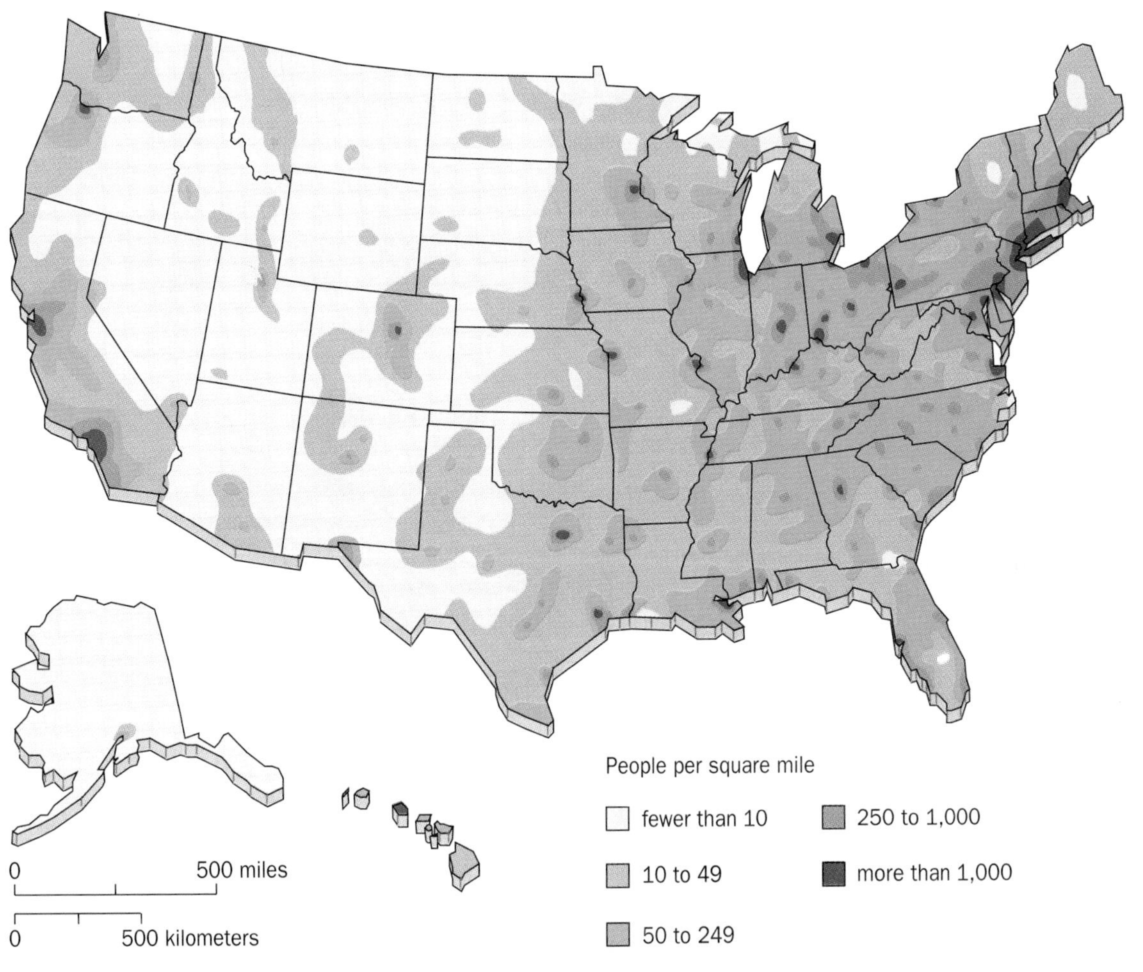

Population Density in 1990. *Although the population of the South and West has been growing, the Northeast remains heavily populated.*

cultivated land on both coasts and in the fertile plains and valleys across the continent. We have built houses, stores, factories, and office buildings. We have laid out roads, canals, railroads, and airports. We have manufactured a vast array of products and sold them at home and in countries around the world. We have founded banks, insurance companies, colleges, and hospitals.

The American work force. Our work force is made up of about 55 million women and 65 million men working in nearly 30,000 different occupations. Recently, an increasing number of people in your age group have been joining the work force by taking jobs. Before they graduate from high school, four out of five of today's students will have had the experience of working at part-time and summer jobs.

A hundred years ago, most Americans worked in farming and manufacturing. The development of modern farm machinery and the increasing use of electronic technology in our factories, however, has brought about a change.

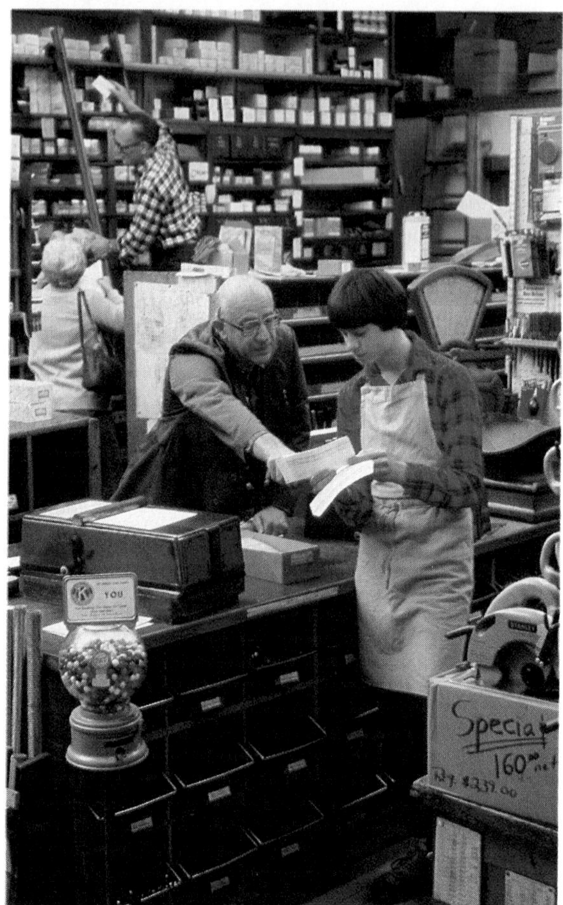

Many teenagers enter the work force for the first time when they take part-time or summer jobs. A large percentage of these jobs are service jobs.

Since 1980, more than half of American workers have held service jobs. In a service job, a person makes a living by providing a service for other people. Your doctor, your teacher, the school secretary, and the person who fixes your family's car are all engaged in service jobs.

How Old We Are

To answer the question, "Who are Americans?" you will need to include some information about how old we are. At different times in our history, the percentage of people in different age groups has varied. The bar graph on this page illustrates this point.

In 1850 more than half of Americans were children or were just beginning to help support themselves and their families, while a very small percentage were of retirement age. How had those statistics changed by 1990?

Why there are more older Americans. There are several reasons for the changes in the percentage of the population in each age group. One reason is that improvements in medical care have increased our life expectancy. More and more Americans are living past age sixty. The average person in your age group today can expect to live to be seventy-five.

Another reason for the changes in the age of our population is the "baby boom" that occurred between 1946 and 1966. During these years, many American couples had three or more children. Today, the large number

The Ages of Americans

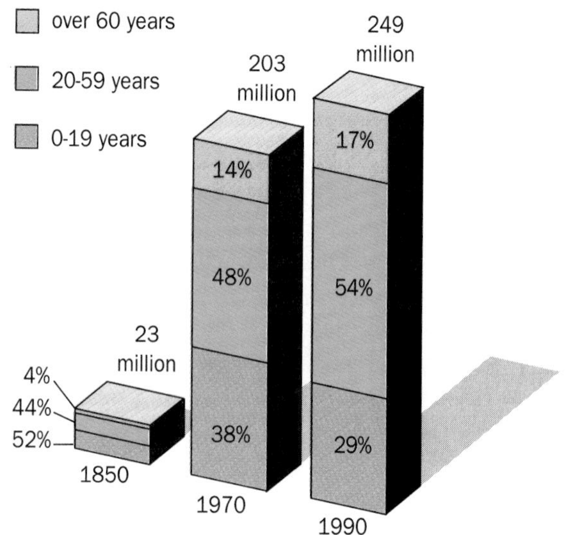

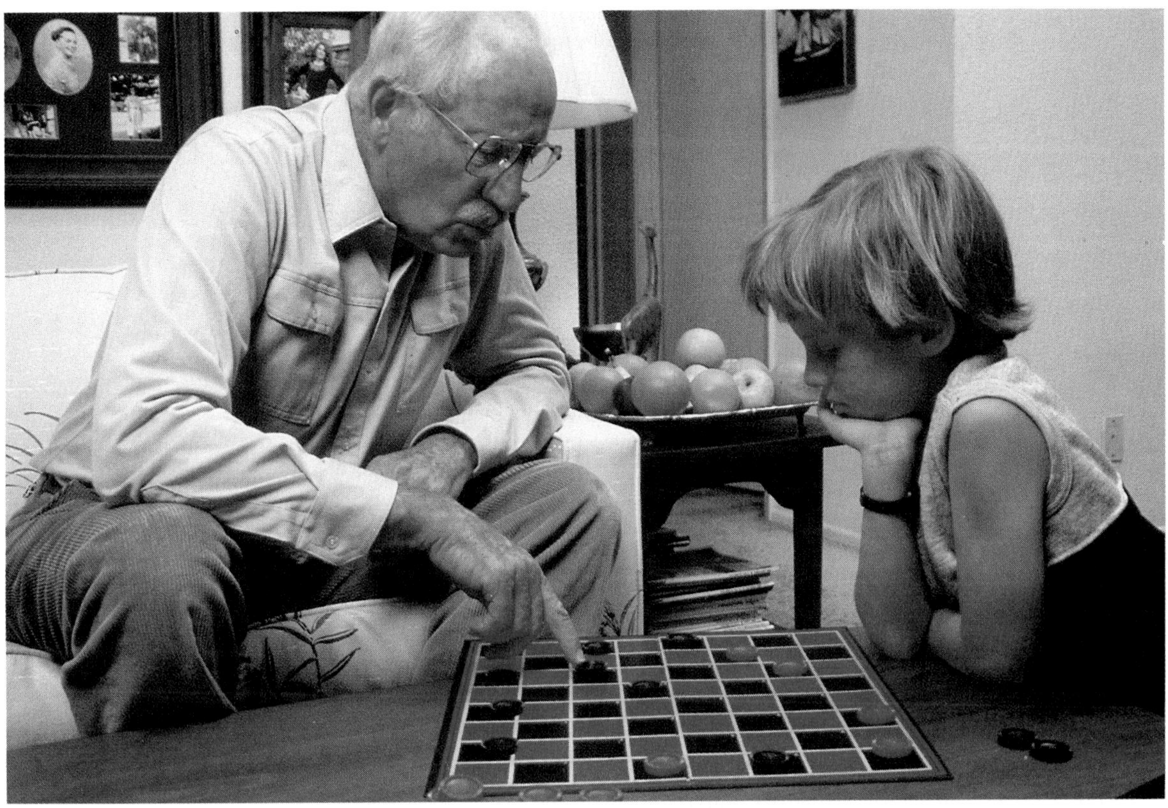

Older Americans make up an increasingly large part of our population. At the same time, the number of children per family is going down.

of people born during the baby boom have swelled the ranks of Americans in the 20 to 59 age group. Your parents, in fact, are likely to be baby boomers. Although there are more adults of child-bearing age than ever before, they are having fewer children than did people of their parents' generation. This is one reason why the percentage of younger people in our population has declined.

Population experts predict that by the year 2030, when the members of the baby boom generation will be senior citizens, the number of people over age sixty will have doubled. That means that one in five Americans will be age sixty-five or older. A description of the age of Americans will be very different then than it was in 1850 or in 1990. How do you think our country might change as a result of the aging of our population?

Where We Have Come From

Americans are a people who are known for their ***diversity***, or differences, from each other. Our diversity is reflected in our different jobs, home towns, and ages—and especially in our backgrounds. Our backgrounds differ because we are from many different countries and belong to different races.

Peter Ky and his family have been Americans for only a few years. Like their ancestors,

Challenge (Analysis): Have students discuss what impact a large senior population will have on their lives in 2030.

Teaching Note: Use the Enrichment Activity, page T 34, and accompanying worksheet in the Activity Book after students have read Section 1-1 or 1-2.

the Kys were born in the Southeast Asian country of Vietnam and grew up speaking a Vietnamese language, eating Vietnamese food, and observing the customs of that country. The Kys now think of themselves as Americans whose background is Vietnamese.

Doris's ancestors lived in Africa and were brought to this country as slaves to work on cotton and tobacco plantations. Doris's family has lived in America for almost 300 years, so she considers herself to be an American of African background.

Bernice has a mixed background. Her father was born in Scotland and her mother, in Germany. Bernice is not unusual. Many Americans have ancestors from more than one country or of more than one race.

As you explore what it means to be a citizen of this nation called the United States, it will be useful to look more closely at the diversity of our backgrounds and learn how that diversity contributes to who we are as a people.

Answers will be found on page T 34.

Section Review

1. Define *diversity.*
2. What region of our country has grown the fastest in the last 30 years?
3. What is a service job? Give five examples of service jobs.
4. Why do older Americans now make up a greater percentage of our population than they did in the past?

Analysis. What are some of the important ways in which Americans are diverse?

Data Search. Look on page 582 in the Data Bank. Which region of the country grew the most between 1980 and 1990? Why do you think people wanted to move there?

1-2 AMERICA: A CULTURAL MOSAIC

Read to Find Out

- what the terms *immigrants, discrimination,* and *racism* mean.
- why people from other countries came to America.
- in what lands the five major groups of Americans originated.

America was built by a nation of strangers. From a hundred different places they have poured forth . . . joining and blending in one mighty and irresistible tide. The land flourished because it was fed from so many sources—because it was nourished by so many cultures and traditions and peoples.

—*President Lyndon B. Johnson, 1965*

America has often been called a nation of ***immigrants***, people who move from one country to make their homes in another. Immigrants brought to America the customs and traditions of their homelands as well as their hopes and dreams for a better life in the New World. You will be taking a closer look at the different backgrounds of these newcomers, the reasons they immigrated, and the places they have made for themselves in our society. As you read, think about some of the ways in which diversity has both strengthened our nation and caused difficulties.

European Americans

The first immigrants to the lands that became the United States were Europeans seeking religious freedom, political freedom, and opportunities to have their own farms and busi-

Until 1954, Ellis Island in New York Harbor was the "Gateway to the New World" for hundreds of thousands of European immigrants.

nesses. In the 1600s and 1700s they came mostly from England, Ireland, and Scotland, bringing their language—English—and their traditions of government, which would deeply influence the future nation.

Many settlers also arrived from Germany, France, the Netherlands, and Scandinavia. A majority of these immigrants were Protestants, although Catholics and Jews also found a haven in the New World.

The years between 1830 and 1920 saw the arrival of waves of Central and Eastern Europeans, including Germans, Slavs, and Russians. Denied political and economic freedom at home, these immigrants, many of them Jews, sought new opportunities in the United States. Meanwhile, Irish, Italians, Greeks, and others suffering from crop failures and lack of adequate farm lands also immigrated in large numbers.

Differences among European Americans. Although European Americans came from the same continent, these immigrants were in many ways more diverse than they were alike. For example, they had grown up under

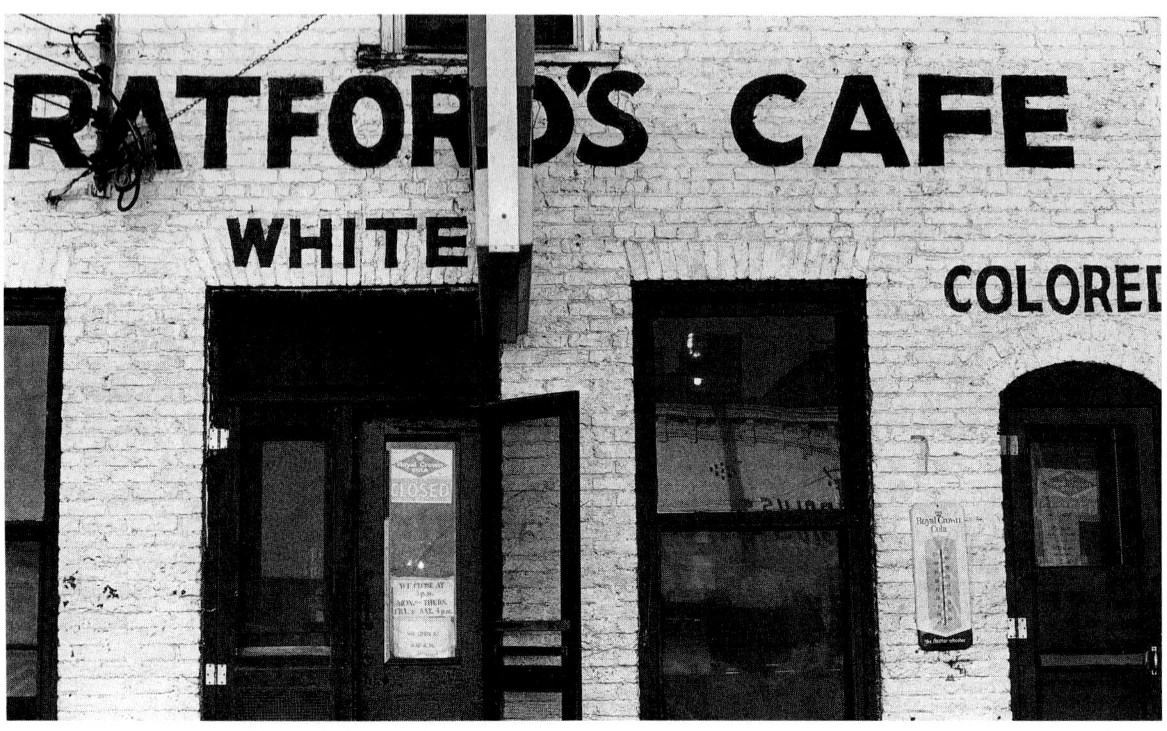

Separate doorways for blacks and whites are a thing of the past. However, blacks still suffer from other forms of discrimination today.

different forms of government, and they spoke many different languages. They ranged from highly educated to unable to read or write, and they were accustomed to very different kinds of food, music, and clothing styles. They had different forms of worship. They celebrated different holidays—or the same holidays in different ways.

Furthermore, immigrants from different European countries tended to settle in different parts of the United States. That is why you may still hear German spoken in Pennsylvania farm towns, attend a Norwegian church in Minnesota, and sit down to a Polish dinner in Chicago.

Although the waves of immigrants from Europe have dwindled to a mere trickle in recent years, European Americans still make up the largest segment of our population. Today, about 80 percent of Americans, or about four out of five, are of European ancestry.

African Americans

The second largest group in the United States today is made up of African Americans. Unlike immigrants who came to America by choice, this group of people did not come here voluntarily. Their African ancestors were brought to this country as slaves, beginning in early colonial times and continuing until the slave trade was ended in 1808.

Struggle for equality. The burden of two hundred years of slavery has been a difficult one. Although slavery was ended legally in 1865, it has taken a long time to change the way African Americans are treated.

Slavery flourished in the South, where plantations grew tobacco, cotton, and other crops on such a large scale that many laborers were needed. Large-scale slavery was impractical in the North, where economic activity centered around small farms, trade, and sea-based industries.

Teaching Note: For highlights of Martin Luther King, Jr.'s speech "I Have a Dream," see "In Their Own Words" on page 64.

Both by law and by custom, black Americans have suffered from ***discrimination***, the unfair treatment of a group of people compared with another group. Because of discrimination, black Americans have not always had the same rights and opportunities as white Americans.

For many years, in various communities and states, African Americans were barred from voting, from attending schools with white students, and from living in neighborhoods with whites. Many restaurants, hotels, and theaters had signs warning "For Whites Only." Even public buses had seats reserved for whites, with black riders having to sit or stand in the back.

Discrimination is the result of ***racism,*** the belief that members of one's own race are superior to those of other races. Even though laws and practices that discriminate against blacks have been outlawed in the United States, less visible kinds of discrimination persist in our society because of racism.

Since the era of slavery, courageous African Americans have struggled against racism and sought to obtain equal treatment for their people. During recent years, inspired by the example of leaders like the Reverend Dr. Martin Luther King, Jr., African Americans in all parts of the United States have been calling attention to the unequal treatment that their people have received. As a result, opportunities in education, jobs, and housing have been improving.

There have always been notable black scientists, educators, and politicians in the United States. Today, an increasing number of black Americans are using their training and talents to make careers in business, politics, athletics, and the arts.

However, equal treatment for all is a goal that has not yet been completely achieved. Many African Americans live in poverty due to lack of opportunities.

U.S. Population by Group, 1990 Census

Group	Population (in millions)	Approximate percent of total
European Americans	200	80%
African Americans	30	12%
Asian Americans	7	3%
Native Americans	2	1%
Other races	10	4%
Hispanic origins, any race	22	9.0%

Hispanic Americans

Hispanic Americans share a common heritage from Spain and a common language, Spanish. (The Latin name for Spain is *Hispania.*) Many also share a common religion, Catholicism. Hispanic Americans can be of any race.

As our nation expanded in the 1800s, it added areas that had been settled mostly by Spaniards and later by people from Mexico, then a Spanish colony. The inhabitants of these regions—the present-day states of Florida, Louisiana, Texas, Arizona, New Mexico, and California—became American citizens.

Today, people from Mexico and the Spanish-speaking countries of Central and South America and the Caribbean make up the largest group immigrating to the United States. Fleeing revolutions and political persecution at home, they have come seeking better jobs and lives for themselves and their families.

Finding opportunities. Making a place for themselves in this country has been easier for some Hispanics than for others. Those with training in business or the professions have often made the quickest adjustment.

Martin Luther King, Jr., a Baptist minister, believed that nonviolent protest, such as sit-ins and boycotts, was the best way to end discrimination. This philosophy was widely adopted in the civil rights movement of the 1950s and 1960s.

Other Hispanic immigrants find the transition to a new land difficult. Like many European immigrants who came before them, many of these newcomers do not speak English and do not have the skills they need to support themselves in our complex, technologically oriented economy. Furthermore, like black Americans, they often feel the effects of racism. As a result, many Hispanic Americans can find only low-paying jobs.

Like immigrant groups in the past, and like blacks, Hispanics are beginning to work together to improve their opportunities. Hispanic labor leaders are pressing for better working conditions, while voters are electing Hispanics to political offices, where they can represent the interests of these new Americans.

Asian Americans

Among the first Asians to come to America were young men from farm villages in southern China. They had heard tales of the discovery of gold in California in 1849 and came to America to make money to send home to their families.

Like others lured by the gold rush, many Chinese set up small businesses to supply the miners' needs. Later arrivals found work building the roads and railroads of the West and working on farms and in fisheries. As Japanese workers began to arrive, they also prospered in farming and business.

Exclusion of Asians. The success of these Asian immigrants bred resentment and racism among other groups, who accused the Asians of taking away jobs by working for lower wages. As a result of such protests, laws were passed in 1882 and 1907 prohibiting any further immigration from China and Japan.

The last of these Asian "exclusion" laws were repealed in 1952. Since then, Asians have been coming to the United States in increasing numbers, especially from the Philippines, South Korea, India, and China. After 1972, immigrants from the Southeast Asian countries of Vietnam, Laos, and Cambodia began arriving, driven from their homes by the effects of wars and revolutions.

At present there are over seven million Asian Americans living in the United States. Their numbers have more than doubled in the last ten years. They speak many different languages and practice a number of different religions—including Christianity, Buddhism, Hinduism, and Islam.

Like Hispanic and black Americans, Asian Americans vary greatly in their educational backgrounds, and thus in the kinds of jobs they can hold. Trained scientists and engineers have made significant contributions to the nation's progress in medicine, physics, and electronics. Meanwhile, other Asian immigrants often struggle to find ways to support their families.

Native Americans

Not all Americans are immigrants or descendants of immigrants. People had been living on the North American continent thousands of years before Columbus and later explorers "discovered" America. Today, descendants of these original inhabitants of our country call themselves Native Americans or American Indians.

These people were themselves very diverse, made up of many groups with differing languages and traditions. Some groups relied on farming, while others hunted, fished, and gathered wild plants to feed and clothe themselves. A few groups built large cities, and others lived in villages or moved from place to place. Different groups had different religious beliefs, and they cultivated different art forms, including pottery, painting, wood carving, and basketry.

Hispanics are the fastest growing group in the United States. Their median age is 26.1 years compared to 32.6 years for the general population.

PEOPLE MAKE A DIFFERENCE

Indian Artist Keeps Traditions Alive

Geronima Cruz Montoya is an American Indian artist known both for her own paintings and for the influence she has had on many other American Indian artists. She signs her work with her Indian name, P'otsunu', which means "White Shell."

As a child, P'otsunu' was surrounded by the rich heritage of her tribe, the O'ke Pueblo Indians of San Juan near Santa Fe, New Mexico. She spoke the Tewa language of her tribe and danced in their religious and cultural ceremonials.

At a boarding school for Indians in Santa Fe, P'otsunu' excelled in arts and crafts. She was given the award for outstanding student when she graduated in 1935.

P'otsunu' was invited to teach at her school after she graduated, and was soon promoted to be head of the art department. There she encouraged the artistic talent she found among her Indian students. It was not long before P'otsunu' and many of her students had become nationally known for their fine artwork.

After over 20 years of teaching at the school, P'otsunu' returned to her own village of San Juan to begin an educational program for local artists and craftspeople. By 1968, this program had developed into a center of American Indian art, where artists could exchange techniques and ideas.

Out of the program also sprang a successful cooperative business designed to sell the arts and crafts of the local people. Then one year P'otsunu' organized a show of crafts from several local villages. The show is now an annual event at which Indians from all over the country sell their crafts.

P'otsunu' believes that "Indian art has a distinct and important contribution to make to the art world." She has taught art in the true tribal tradition because she believes it is a way for her people to "put their heritage down in a form which could not be distorted by outsiders."

P'otsunu's dedication to tribal traditions has helped focus national attention on the unique quality of Indian art and culture.

Based on an unpublished biography by Jeanne Shutes and Jill Mellick.

When the first European settlers came to our shores, Indians often welcomed them and helped them adapt to the unfamiliar conditions they found. As more and more settlers arrived, they began to compete with the Indians for farm land and hunting grounds.

Although Indians fought for their lands in many bloody battles, they were gradually pushed west, often onto land that was not suitable to their traditional way of life. By the late 1800s, wars with settlers and the effects of the unfamiliar diseases the settlers brought

Discussion: Have students discuss the methods P'otsunu' has used to keep traditional American Indian art alive. Why are her methods also an effective way to create change?

Just as thousands of tiles fit together to form a mosaic, so all the diverse individuals and groups in the United States fit together to form our nation.

with them had taken their toll, and many thousands of Indians had died. Today, about two million people are Native Americans, a very small percentage of the population of what was once their homeland.

Living in modern America. Trying to balance their religious and social traditions with efforts to support themselves in our modern society poses a great challenge to Indians today. They are meeting this challenge in a number of ways. For example, some groups are developing oil and other mineral resources on their lands. Others are pressing the government to pay them for lands illegally taken from them when treaties were broken.

Many Native Americans realize that to prepare themselves for the future, they must overcome the handicaps of poverty and lack of education. Thus, there has been a marked increase in Indians seeking higher education in business, medicine, law, education, and other professions, through which they can contribute to the progress of their people and their nation.

The American Identity

In this description of Americans, you have again seen that we are a very diverse people. Perhaps you have heard America called a "melting pot." This term reflects the idea that people from all over the world came here and, like butter and other ingredients, melted into American society, giving up the heritage of their native lands.

Teaching Note: You may wish to use the Unit 1 Activity, "Taking a Census," in the Activity Book after students have read the material in Section 1-2.

Teaching Note: Use Teaching Activity 1, page T 32, as a culminating activity after students have read the material in Section 1-2.

It is true that some immigrants have worked very hard at shedding their native traditions and "becoming Americans." They have learned English, adopted American customs of dress, food, and entertainment, and celebrated American holidays.

However, many immigrants have continued to speak their native language in their homes and with friends, and to follow their native customs. You can see evidence of these diverse customs in the wide variety of foods we can buy: Mexican tortillas, Italian spaghetti, Chinese eggrolls, German sausage. Throughout the year, parades celebrate the special days of different nationality groups: St. Patrick's Day for the Irish, Columbus Day for the Italians, Chinese New Year. Radio and television stations broadcast in a variety of languages and play salsa, soul, reggae, and rumba music.

Such examples of our cultural differences make clear that Americans have not melted together to form one identity. Instead of giving up our separate cultures, we have retained parts of them and, in the process, have enriched American culture as a whole.

The American mosaic. Have you ever seen a piece of mosaic (moh-ZAY-ik) artwork? A mosaic is made of small tiles of different sizes, shapes, and colors. When they are all fitted together, these diverse tiles create a whole picture.

Like mosaic tiles, all the diverse individuals and groups in the United States—Irish and Iranian, farmer and factory worker, grandmother and grade schooler, Baptist and Buddhist—fit together to form a whole nation. Thus, when we ask ourselves, "Who are Americans?" we may answer that they are part—not of a melting pot—but of a mosaic in which each different tile is an essential part of the picture. That picture is American society.

Answers will be found on page T 34.

Section Review

1. Define *immigrants, discrimination,* and *racism.*
2. List and explain four reasons why people from other countries came to America.
3. What are the five major groups of Americans? What do members of each group have in common?

Application. Think about your school and community and what you see in newspapers and magazines and on television. What evidence can you find that American society is a mosaic made up of contributions from many cultures?

Data Search. Look on page 583 in the Data Bank. Compare European immigration at its highest point to Asian immigration at its highest point.

1-3

THE VALUES THAT UNITE US

Read to Find Out

- what the terms *beliefs, values, equality, freedom,* and *justice* mean.
- what three basic values unite Americans as a nation.
- how our society may not always reflect our ideals.

Each American is part of the cultural mosaic that makes up American society. As you have learned, we are a diverse people. We take pride in thinking and acting independently, in "knowing our own minds," as Doris Hollingsworth might say.

Despite our differences, we have survived as a nation for more than two hundred years. What unites us as one people, one nation?

Challenge (Application): Have students examine the names of cities, counties, and geographic features in the area where they live. Can they determine from the place names who the area's first inhabitants or settlers from other countries were?

What is the glue that holds together all the pieces of our cultural mosaic?

Americans are held together by certain shared beliefs and values. ***Beliefs*** are certain ideas that we trust are true. ***Values*** are our standards of behavior. Values help us decide how we should act and how we should live our lives. They are the guidelines for how we should treat each other. Shared beliefs and values form the glue that keeps our cultural mosaic together.

Equal Respect: The American Dream

The beliefs and values on which our nation was founded have attracted many of the immigrants who have chosen to make their homes in the United States. Peter Ky remembers when his father first spoke of leaving Vietnam:

> *My father was discouraged by how hard life was for us in Vietnam. We had so little freedom and so few opportunities to improve our lives. My father said that in America, people were treated with respect and dignity. We would have a chance to make a good life for ourselves there.*

Mr. Ky's dream of a better life in America is based on a basic American belief: that everyone, regardless of age, sex, race, wealth, opinions, or education, has worth and importance. We believe that all people—unique tiles in our cultural mosaic—deserve the same chance to realize their full potential and to contribute their talents and ideas to society. In other words, every person has the right to be treated with equal respect.

AMERICAN NOTEBOOK

Throughout our history, Americans have cherished the three basic American values. We read about them. We recite them. We even sing songs about them. Here are some lines that may be familiar to you. Do you know where they come from?

1. "let *freedom* ring"
2. "all men are created *equal*"
3. "with *liberty* and *justice* for all"
4. "the land of the *free*"
5. "sweet land of *liberty*"
6. "to establish *justice* and secure the blessings of *liberty*"

Answers: 1. "My Country 'Tis of Thee," 2. Declaration of Independence, 3. Pledge of Allegiance, 4. "The Star-Spangled Banner," 5. "My Country 'Tis of Thee," 6. Preamble to the Constitution

Basic American Values

The American belief that all people deserve equal respect is supported by three basic values: equality, freedom (sometimes called liberty), and justice. To see what these values mean, consider the experiences of Doris Hollingsworth. Doris, a black woman, often relied on these three values to support her efforts to gain equal respect as a computer analyst, which is traditionally a white, male occupation.

Equality. Equal respect is based on the belief that every person can contribute to society. In order to make this contribution, each person must have the same rights and opportunities in life as any other person. The condition of everyone having the same rights and opportunities is called ***equality***.

Doris Hollingsworth learned that even though equality is one of our basic values, equal opportunity is not always available in America. She recalls:

> *Job hunting was tough at first. I thought I'd never get that first interview. Then, when I walked into the room, the interview committee—all white men—looked at me and then at each other as if to say, "We knew she was a woman, but black, too?" I didn't get the job, and I have a strong feeling that my being a black woman had something to do with it.*

Doris's experience is not uncommon. Even though discrimination because of race or sex is against the law, it still affects the lives of many people.

In this chapter you have learned just how varied the backgrounds, lifestyles, and occupations of Americans can be. Everyone has different skills and abilities. You may be a natural at math, for example, while your friend's greatest talent is on the soccer field.

Our opportunities in life may be limited by our abilities. Your friend may be less likely to get a job as a math teacher than you are. Our opportunities may also be limited by our energy and interests. Although your friend could have a career as a soccer player, he or she might not like training so hard and traveling so much. However, our race, sex, religion, background, and opinions should not be used to deny us an equal chance to succeed in life.

Doris, confident of her ability and training, knew she had the right to an equal opportunity. Says Doris:

> *I didn't give up. I had interviews at many companies. Then I finally landed a job with a company that judges me by the quality of my work, not by the color of my skin or by my sex. It feels good to work where I'm treated as an equal.*

Working and playing together on the football field, these athletes have an equal opportunity to develop their talents and skills.

Freedom. When you try to define ***freedom***, you may explain that it means having the ability to say what you want, go where you want, choose the friends you want. Doris knows that freedom also means being able to choose where you want to work and with whom. She says:

> *Thinking back on that first interview, I know I wouldn't have accepted the job even if it had been offered to me. I just didn't feel comfortable with the men on that committee. It was good to know that I was free to look for a job that I felt better about.*

Protection of the right of all Americans to equality has been expanded over the past 200 years. For example, the "equal protection clause" of the Fourteenth Amendment, ratified in 1868, prevents states from passing laws to discriminate unreasonably against any group of people. (See Chapter 7.)

If you believe in equal respect, you give the same freedoms to others that you expect for yourself. However, you must not be so free in your actions or beliefs that you interfere with someone else's freedom.

For example, you are free to listen to music you like. However, if you walk down the street playing your favorite tape at full volume, you may interfere with the right of other people to stroll quietly or listen to their own music. Can you think of another situation in which your freedom is limited because of respect for others' freedom?

Justice. The third basic value, ***justice***, can also be thought of as fairness. Equal respect includes the idea that every person deserves to be treated fairly. For example, you should not be paid more or get better grades or a better job because of your race, sex, or connections to powerful or well-known people.

Justice, however, does not require that people always be treated the same. In the work place, for example, people with greater skills and experience are rewarded with more pay or responsibility than those with fewer skills or less experience. Differences in pay are considered fair if they are based on differences in skill and experience.

When Doris was hired, she became the newest employee in the company. She made less money than employees who had worked there longer and were more experienced. As Doris continued to work for the company, she gained experience and showed her ability to do a good job. Her pay was then raised to match that of people with equal experience and performance.

Citizens and the American Ideal

The glue that holds American society together is our shared belief in equal respect and in values such as equality, freedom, and justice. These beliefs and values form an ideal, or model, of the kind of nation we want the United States to be. We judge our society by how well we are living up to this ideal.

An imperfect society. Our history and the headlines in our daily newspapers show that we do not always achieve our ideal. Peter Ky found that his first few years in the United States were sometimes difficult. In Vietnam he had been told that everyone in America enjoyed freedom and equality. However, he found out that this statement did not always represent the truth.

Peter recalls something that happened when he was nine years old and had been in his new homeland for only one year.

> *I was out in the street playing with some kids. Two older boys began choosing teams for kickball. The other kids begged to be picked. My English wasn't so good, so I kept quiet. Finally, I was the only one left to be picked—and I was the only Asian in the bunch. The two boys stared*

Although the society around them is imperfect, young people like these can live the American ideal by treating each other with equal respect.

Challenge (Synthesis): Have students discuss what everyday life would be like in an ideal society in which everyone believed in and practiced equality, freedom, and justice.

Teaching Note: Use Teaching Activity 2, page T 33, to assess students' understanding of the chapter.

at me. "You take him," one said, pointing at me. "Forget it," the other replied. "I don't want him on my team." He looked at me. "What's the matter?" he jeered, "Don't you speak English?" Then he pulled at the corners of his eyes, to make them slanted, and laughed. I ran home crying. That was my first experience with racism. I'll never forget it. Never.

Peter Ky's story illustrates that, while our nation is held together by the belief in equal respect for all, everyone does not live according to this ideal. The difference between the ideal of equal respect and its reality shows us the work that still needs to be done to ensure that the rights of all Americans to equality, freedom, and justice are protected.

Answers will be found on page T 35.

Section Review

1. Define *beliefs, values, equality, freedom,* and *justice.*
2. What are the three basic American values?
3. Give an example that shows someone not being treated with equal respect.

Synthesis. How does the ideal of equal respect make it possible for the diverse individuals and groups in the United States to live together as one nation?

A BROADER VIEW

Americans represent a mosaic of peoples from nearly every land on earth. If each of us traces our roots back in time, we may end up in a Chinese city, an Italian seaport, an African village, a Mexican town, or any of a thousand other places. Compared to American Indians, who have called this country home for over 10,000 years, the rest of us are relative newcomers. Whether our ancestors arrived here four centuries ago or four years ago, most of us came from somewhere else.

No other country in the world is both as varied as ours and as shaped by immigrants and their descendants. Though our diverse backgrounds have often been a cause of conflict, we have been held together remarkably well by a set of shared values and ideals. We have achieved unity as a country because most immigrants to America, while retaining some of their native customs and beliefs, have gladly accepted many of the values shared by those who came before.

Today, people in many parts of the world are still packing up their belongings and leaving their homelands in search of freedom and opportunities for better lives. They are settling in a variety of foreign countries, including Great Britain, France, Australia, and the United States.

Like the United States throughout its history, the countries accepting large numbers of immigrants today face the difficult challenge of including in their societies people with values and beliefs very different from those of the native population. These countries are finding that immigrants do not always willingly give up the values, traditions, and languages they have lived with all their lives. Unity, therefore, can be difficult to achieve, and conflict often occurs between a country's native citizens and the immigrants.

Despite the problems that may arise, worldwide immigration may have a positive result as well. As more people all over the world learn to accept and even to welcome the differences between themselves and others, they will recognize the benefits of equal respect.

Teaching Note: Use the Evaluating Progress activity, page T 33.

The Process

Teaching Note: For reinforcement of decision-making skills, use Decision-Making Worksheet Chapter 1.

Choosing and Taking Action

Picture yourself in the following situation: You leave school on Friday, thinking about a long report that is due Monday. Suddenly some friends remind you that the money for the school candy sale has to be turned in on Monday. When they ask if you can help sell candy, you say that you are not sure because you have homework to do. They reply, "Well, let us know when you are through making up your mind."

"Making up your mind" is another way of saying "making a decision." You make decisions, or choices, every day. Some, such as deciding what to have for breakfast or which movie to see, are not very important and usually do not involve much thinking. Others, as in the situation above, should be carefully thought out. Unfortunately, people sometimes put little thought into making important decisions. They might choose friends or school activities almost as quickly as they pick a cereal for breakfast.

Important decisions should be carefully thought out because the quality of your life may depend on them. Good decision making is a process that includes two main parts:

Choosing: Setting a goal—what it is that you want, and then selecting the best way to achieve it.

Taking Action: Planning how to take action and then doing what you planned.

The lessons in this text will help you understand and master the process of decision making. Making good decisions is an important part of being a citizen because your choices may affect your family, friends, relatives, neighbors, fellow students, and other people in your community.

ANALYZING THE PROCESS

You have read that we are largely a nation of immigrants. In the following account, Carlos Lopez, an immigrant from Latin America, explains how he and his wife decided to move their family to the United States. Think about what specific steps they went through in making their decision.

> Food was scarce in our town, and prices were going up fast. Conditions at the sugar company where I worked were very bad. When we went on strike, many of us were put in prison. My wife, Maria, joined a group that was protesting cruel treatment of prisoners and worked for my release. After opponents of this group killed several members, Maria was terrified. She feared that our house was being watched and that our children might be hurt.
>
> We wanted our children to live comfortably, to get a good education, to have opportunities to earn a good living, and to enjoy peaceful lives. We had to decide how to achieve these things. After I was released from prison, we listed options and carefully considered each one.
>
> One option was to stay where we were, hoping that conditions would change. Maria could earn money by washing clothes. However, there was no work for me. I could have joined a group fighting against the government, but I refused. Even though they promised to provide food and protection for my family, I did not believe in using violence.
>
> If we moved to the city, I would have a better chance of finding a job. However, in the city people who protested cruel treatment of prisoners were threatened and often killed. We had already received death threats.
>
> A third option was to move to the United States. The journey would cost us our home and all our savings, and we would leave behind our friends. Also, our children might have dif-

Have students give examples of typical situations they face that require decisions. List some examples on the board. Then have students identify which decisions they think are particularly important and should therefore be carefully thought out. Have them explain why these decisions are important.

Answers will be found on page T 35.

ficulty learning English, and we might have trouble finding jobs. Still, we knew that Americans were friendly to people like us. Also, Maria and I already knew some English, and our children would have a chance for a good education and a prosperous life. We decided to move to America.

After deciding what to do, we had to plan how to do it. To get money, I sold our furniture. Maria wrote to some American friends who agreed to help us get permission to enter the United States. We figured out how to travel to America and where to live there.

We thought we could stay in our country while waiting to hear from our American friends. However, when we were questioned about our protests, we feared that any delay would cost us our lives. Therefore we traveled to Mexico.

After many weeks our permits to stay in Mexico were about to run out, and we still had not received permission to enter the United States. I contacted our American friends, who arranged for us to meet government leaders in Washington, D.C. After describing our problem, we were granted permission to live in the United States.

Now that we are living in America, we have looked back at how we decided to come here. We realize now that we did not think about the possible effects on our relatives. We worry that the same people who threatened our lives might threaten theirs. Our relatives face a long struggle for equal respect and justice.

If we had to make the decision over again, we would consider the effects on our relatives. However, we would probably still make the same choice. In the United States we have the best chance of being treated equally and fairly. We have found jobs and are living with friends until we can find a place of our own. School is hard for our children, but they are learning quickly. Our goal of giving our children productive, peaceful lives has been achieved.

CHECKING YOUR UNDERSTANDING

Now that you have examined how Carlos and Maria Lopez made their decision, answer the following questions.

1. What goals did they set? What caused them to set these goals?

2. What options did they consider as ways to achieve their goals?

3. What actions did they take to achieve their goals?

4. In considering the first option, Carlos and Maria identified **(a)** only good points, **(b)** only bad points, **(c)** good and bad points. Explain your answer.

5. In considering the second option, Carlos and Maria identified **(a)** only good points, **(b)** good and bad points, **(c)** only bad points. Explain your answer.

6. In considering the third option, Carlos and Maria decided that **(a)** the good points outweighed the bad points, **(b)** they would automatically choose it because the other options were unacceptable, **(c)** they should seek the advice of their relatives. Explain your answer.

7. In taking action to achieve their goals, Carlos and Maria did all of the following *except* **(a)** adjust their plan when the situation changed, **(b)** decide what they needed in order to get out of the country, **(c)** postpone making plans about where to live in the United States.

REVIEWING THE PROCESS

8. Describe the two main parts of decision making.

9. To make good decisions, there are a number of steps you should take. Name one of them and explain why it is important.

Have each student give examples of two important decisions: a good choice and a bad one. Examples may come from their own experiences or from those of fictional characters. Have students discuss the examples in order to understand what can make the difference between good and bad decisions.

CHAPTER SURVEY

Answers to Survey and Workshop will be found on page T 35.

UNDERSTANDING NEW VOCABULARY

Seeing Relationships

The vocabulary terms in each pair listed below are related to each other. For each pair, explain how the two terms are related.

Example: *Freedom* is related to *justice* because both are basic American values.

1. *immigrants* and *diversity*
2. *freedom* and *values*
3. *discrimination* and *equality*

Putting It in Writing

Suppose someone asked you, "Why is it important to treat each person with equal respect?" Write an answer to this question. Use at least four of the following terms, making sure that you make your meaning clear: *freedom, justice, equality, immigrants, diverse.*

LOOKING BACK AT THE CHAPTER

1. Describe three ways in which the population of the United States has changed over the years. Explain why each type of change has occurred.

2. Explain how the people in each of the following groups are both similar and diverse: **(a)** European Americans **(b)** Hispanic Americans **(c)** American Indians.

3. What are some ways that blacks, Asians, Hispanics, and American Indians have been treated unfairly?

4. Why can American society be described better as a mosaic than as a melting pot?

5. What does it mean to give every person an equal opportunity?

6. What does it mean to have freedom?

7. What does it mean to show justice, or fairness, to another person?

8. Explain what the American ideal is. How does it relate to our basic values?

9. *Evaluation.* What do you think are some advantages of being a diverse people? What are some of the problems that arise from diversity?

10. *Application.* Does the value of equality mean that anyone who wants to should be allowed to play in the school band? Explain.

11. *Synthesis.* Why is racism in conflict with the ideal of equal respect?

12. *Evaluation.* "One person's freedom ends where another person's freedom begins." Do you agree? Discuss your answer in terms of the three basic American values.

13. *Evaluation.* Of the three basic American values, which do you think is the most important? Explain your answer.

WORKING TOGETHER

1. In groups of three or four, discuss what evidence you can find that the students in your school reflect the cultural mosaic of America. What evidence can you find that people from different cultures have adapted to "American" customs?

2. Collect materials and prepare a collage that shows the diversity of Americans.

3. Visit your local supermarket or grocery store and find the international or foreign foods section. Make a list of all the foods you see that are associated with a different country. Group these foods according to their country of origin.

4. With two or three other students, prepare a skit that presents a situation in which a basic American value is—or is not—being put into practice. Some possible situations might be a job interview, a tryout for a school team, or a group of friends making plans. Afterwards, discuss with the class what effects such a situation might have on the people involved.

SKILLS WORKSHOP

SOCIAL STUDIES SKILLS

Analyzing Bar Graphs

The bar graph below shows changes in the nation's birth rate since 1915. The birth rate is the number of babies born each year per 1,000 women of childbearing age. Each bar represents the yearly birth rate averaged over a 10-year period. From 1915 to 1924, for example, an average of almost 120 babies were born each year for every 1,000 women aged 15 to 44.

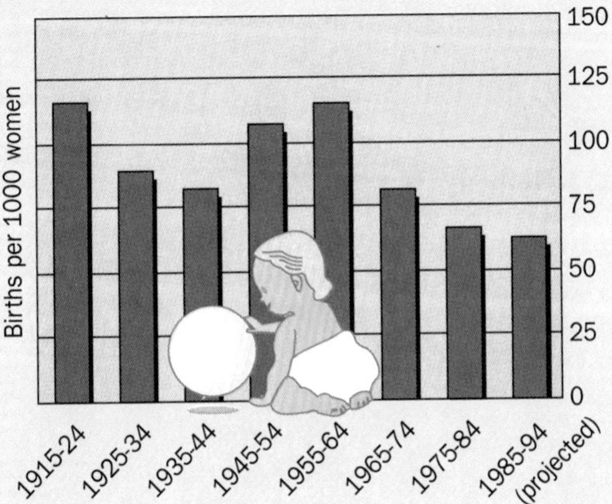

The following questions will help you analyze the graph.

1. When did the birth rate fall to its lowest level? How does the birth rate during this period compare with the highest rate?

2. Between 1930 and 1945 the United States went through the Great Depression and World War II. How did these events affect the nation's birth rate?

3. After World War II ended in 1945, the United States experienced a baby boom. About how long did the baby boom last?

4. Looking at the graph as a whole, would you say that the birth rate has generally gone up or gone down since 1915?

5. Do you think this trend will continue in the next 10 years? Why or why not?

DECISION-MAKING SKILLS

Choosing and Taking Action

Compare the decision-making steps taken by Carlos and Maria Lopez, on pages 20–21, with the following decision by a Mennonite, a member of a particular Christian church that believes in living a simple, peaceful life.

> Our rural church community was facing problems. Public school officials had said that we were not qualified to teach our children at home. Therefore, they had to attend public schools with city children. Contact with the city was hurting our community. Already some of the children were starting to use drugs.
>
> I wanted my family to grow up in a land where we could preserve our way of life. I had to do something. I could have stayed in the United States, taking the school officials to court and arguing for the right to educate our children at home. However, I avoid conflict, even in courtrooms. Also, a court case might take months, and I did not want my children to be exposed to any more drugs and violence.
>
> I learned that Paraguay welcomed immigrants, and that many Mennonites had already settled there. They had their own schools and did not have to serve in the military. Therefore, I decided to move to Paraguay.
>
> I wrote to the Mennonites in Paraguay and received permission to move. Finding a way to get there was difficult, but we adjusted our plans to meet the changing situations.
>
> Now that we are in Paraguay, our way of life is secure. My only regret is that my friends in the United States are not with me.

1. What steps described above were also taken by the Lopezes? Explain.

2. Think of a decision that you will have to make soon. What are some important things you should remember when deciding? Explain.

THANX
MOM

Chapter Themes: People belong to groups, and groups influence how we think and act. Five social institutions—the family, education, religion, the economy, and government—determine how our society is organized to meet people's needs and shape their values.

CHAPTER 2

American Society and Its Values

Doris Hollingsworth did not always have plans to be a computer analyst for a large corporation.

The idea that I could go to college and learn about computers never occurred to me. Some of my friends were talking about quitting school and getting jobs at the Snack Shack so we could hang out together and have fun. My parents were urging me to finish high school. They said I should think about how I could support myself and, later, if I got married and had my own family, how I could help support it. I had always been an average student. Doing well in school didn't really matter to me. But I had always thought I'd finish high school and then get a job in town.

In my junior year, my plans changed. Early in the year, Mrs. Hansen, my math teacher, took me aside. She said she saw a lot of potential in me. With some hard work, I could be an "A" student. She offered to help me a couple of days a week after school.

I agreed to the help, but I didn't really think I'd do any better. I was wrong. By the end of the semester, I was getting A's in math and finding that I really liked it. My other grades started improving, too. I guess the rest is history. I don't know where I'd be today if Mrs. Hansen hadn't pushed me to see that doing well in school could make a big difference in my life.

When Doris Hollingsworth was in high school, she was getting advice from several different groups to which she belonged—from her family, from her friends, and from her school, as represented by Mrs. Hansen. Like Doris, everyone belongs to many groups.

In this chapter you will read about why people belong to groups and how groups influence what we believe and how we act. You will also learn about how our society is organized to meet the needs and shape the values of its members through the family, education, religion, the economy, and government.

Teaching Note: Use the Introducing the Chapter activity, page T 38.

2-1

GROUPS AND INSTITUTIONS: MEETING NEEDS AND SHARING VALUES

Read to Find Out

- what the terms *rules, socialization,* and *social institutions* mean.
- why people form groups.
- what the five major social institutions are.

Everybody has needs. For example, people have physical needs for such things as food and shelter. They have emotional needs such as the desire for love and companionship. They have spiritual needs for answers to questions about the purpose of life and what happens after death.

People form groups to satisfy many of their physical, emotional, and spiritual needs. Of course, simply being born makes you a member of some groups, such as your family, a particular religion, and a nation. You are required to join other groups, such as a school, and you choose some groups, such as clubs and circles of friends. In any case, groups meet particular needs in people's lives. By looking at an informal group—a group of friends—it may be easier to understand how groups meet our needs and how they influence our values.

As you read, it is important to remember the difference between values and rules. Values are standards that guide our behavior, whereas ***rules*** are specific expectations about what our behavior should be. Rules are based on values. Because our society holds the value that education is important, for example, our schools have made certain rules that help students become educated. Doris accepted the value that education is important, and chose to follow the rules of her school, such as getting to class on time and finishing homework every night.

A Group of Friends

Peter Ky's best friends are Alex and Carol. The three of them spend a lot of time together. Alex drives Peter and Carol to the beach, to concerts, and to school. They share the latest school gossip and give each other advice. They have this to say about their friendship:

> Peter:
> *I trust Carol and Alex. They've helped me when I've been really down. They listen to me and let me be myself.*
>
> Carol:
> *These guys make me laugh. But I also know that when things get bad at home or in school, they'll be there to help me out.*
>
> Alex:
> *Without Peter and Carol, I'd have no one to go to the beach with or to call for biology notes. They help with gas money and usually cover doughnuts in the morning.*

As a group, Carol, Alex, and Peter's goal is to provide each other with companionship and a sense of belonging. This goal can be expressed as a value: it is important to be a good friend. The group has two other values: it is important to help your friends, and you should let members be themselves.

These values are the basis of unwritten rules—friends take time to listen to each other, and friends share expenses. These rules guide the behavior of the group's members. Following these rules ensures that Alex, Carol, and Peter remain friends and thus continue to meet their needs for companionship and a sense of belonging.

Many rules have roots in religious tradition. For example, in Judeo-Christian societies, many laws are based on the Ten Commandments; in Islamic societies, many laws are based on the Koran, the holy book of Muslims.

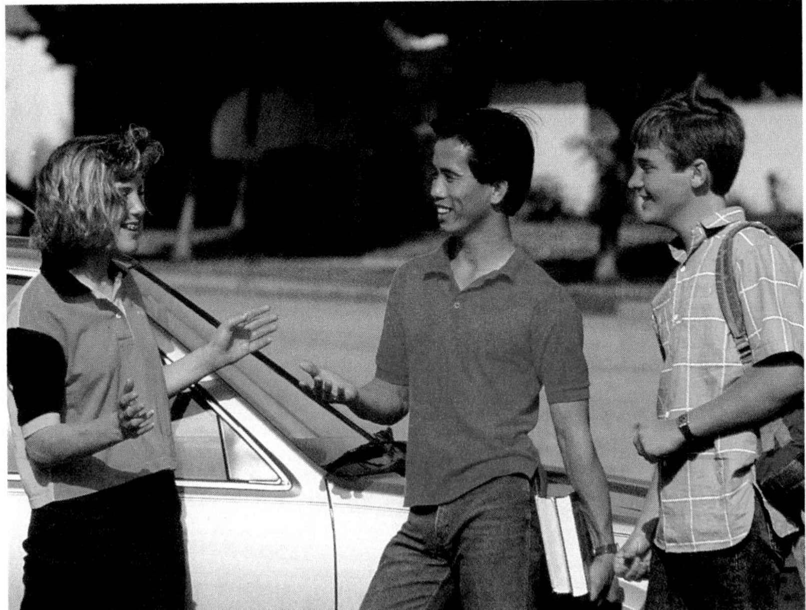

A group of friends shares common values and rules of behavior. A new member will need to learn these rules.

Becoming a group member. The process of learning how to participate in a group is called ***socialization***. Socialization also means learning to accept the values of a group and learning the rules for behavior within it. A new girl in school, Melissa, went through the process of socialization when she joined Peter, Alex, and Carol's group.

Melissa met Peter, Alex, and Carol in biology class, and she quickly became a regular in their group. The friendship ran into trouble in one area, however. "I was kind of thoughtless when they first met me," remembers Melissa.

On one occasion, Melissa agreed to meet her new friends at the beach at two o'clock. She did not take the meeting time seriously and finally showed up just before four. Alex tells what happened next:

> *She was so cool about being late, it really got us mad. We had been worried about her. Peter had to be back at work by five o'clock. Our afternoon was ruined. We told her that if she was going to be late, for no good reason, she could go to the beach alone next time. Then she got mad and stormed off.*

Without realizing it, Melissa had run into one of the group's important values: being a good friend means being considerate. One of the rules based on this value is that everyone should show up for activities on time. Melissa had broken this rule, which brought her into conflict with the group.

Melissa moped around for a few days, but she missed her friends. "I called them," relates Melissa. "I told them that I was sorry and that I would really try to watch the clock better." Melissa's need for friendship led her to accept the group's values and to agree to change her behavior. In other words, Melissa went through the process of socialization.

By socializing new members, groups can continue to meet their members' needs. Imagine what would happen if everyone in Peter's group began showing up late for activities. Soon Alex, Peter, Carol, and Melissa would be angry at each other, perhaps angry enough

Sociology is a social science that deals, in part, with the formation, structure, and function of human groups. Some sociologists work with small groups, observing such behavior as conformity. They also study the way members of a group respond to each other and to other groups.

Teaching Note: Use the Reinforcement Activity, page T 39, and accompanying worksheet in the Activity Book after students have read the material in Section 2-1 or at the end of the chapter.

to break up their friendship. Then they would no longer have a group to satisfy their need for friendship.

Groups, then, have a powerful influence over your behavior and beliefs. Think of all the groups to which you belong, such as friends, teams, and clubs. Much of your life is shaped by these groups.

Institutions That Affect Us All

Although groups are important, they do not satisfy all of our needs. For example, they do not provide food or products such as clothing and houses. They do not make laws or help govern our society. In addition, groups themselves need a source of values and expected ways of behaving.

These functions, which groups are unable to perform by themselves, are taken care of by ***social institutions,*** systems of values and rules that determine how our society is organized. Five major social institutions in our society are the family, religion, education, the economy, and government.

Every society needs these five institutions in one form or another. Social institutions not only satisfy needs and teach values, they also provide a framework within which groups and organizations can exist.

Your family, for example, is a group. This group is part of the institution of the family, which provides the framework for how a family is set up and how it works in our society. Parents do not just make up the ideas that they will raise their children and that they will have the power to make rules for their children's behavior. These ideas come from the institution of the family.

In Chapter 1 you learned that shared values make it possible for Americans to live and work together as a society. It is through the process of socialization in our five social institutions that we learn those values.

Answers will be found on page T 40.

Section Review

1. Define *rules, socialization,* and *social institutions.*
2. What are some of the reasons that people join groups?
3. What are the five major social institutions?

Application. Think of several groups to which you belong. What needs of yours does each group meet?

2-2

FAMILY, RELIGION, AND EDUCATION: SOCIETY'S TRAINING GROUNDS

Read to Find Out

- how the family meets needs.
- why some people belong to religious groups.
- why our society provides schools.

The institutions of the family, religion, and education play very important parts in shaping the behavior and the values of the members of society. As you read this section, think about how these institutions affect you and the people you know.

The Family: Your First Institution

The family is the most basic institution in any society. From birth you depend on your family to provide you with food, clothing, and shelter, and to give you a sense of security and belonging. Your family also teaches you many of the values you need to participate in society and contribute to it.

What is a family? Many Americans think of the typical family as a husband at work and

Challenge (Application): Have students use their knowledge of socialization to describe an experience they have had in being socialized.

Teaching Note: You may want to use Teaching Activity 1, page T 38, as an introduction to Section 2-2 or as a culminating activity after students have read the material.

a wife at home with two or three children. Today, however, only about one in twenty American families fits that picture.

Many changes have taken place in the American family in the past 20 or 30 years. Families are now smaller. As the cost of raising and educating children rises, and as more women work outside the home, couples are deciding to have fewer children.

Even the typical family structure of father, mother, and children is changing. Because divorce is increasingly common, and more unmarried mothers are choosing to raise their babies alone, many families consist of a single parent—either a mother or a father—and one or more children. Some families are "blended families" made up of adults and their children from previous marriages. Children whose parents are not able to care for them may become part of other families through adoption or foster care.

Almost any arrangement of children living with adults who meet their physical and emotional needs can be considered a family. That family plays a very important part in preparing the children to take their place in society.

The Changing American Family

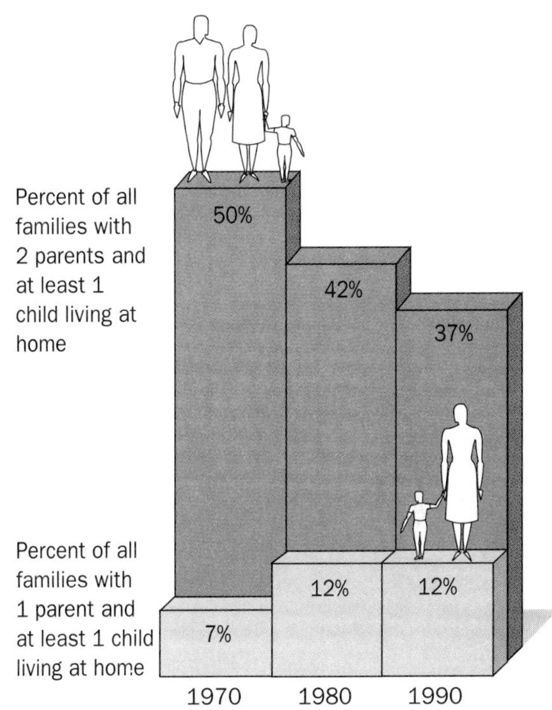

Source: U.S. Census Bureau

Meeting needs. Imagine moving to a distant country where the people speak a language you do not understand. You cannot read the billboards, street signs, or newspapers; they are written in a language that uses an alphabet completely different from your own. The air is filled with strange sounds and smells. You feel completely confused.

Peter Ky had this experience when he arrived in San Francisco in 1981. "Coming to America from Vietnam terrified me at first," Peter remembers. "Everything was so strange. I couldn't talk to anyone. I didn't know how to act." Luckily, he was not alone. "I had my family. We gave each other a lot of support. And we made it. We survived."

Peter's comments illustrate that your happiness depends on whether or not you feel secure. Feeling secure includes believing that you are safe and that you will be protected and cared for. You also need to have a sense of belonging, which is the knowledge that you are important and that no one else could take your place.

Your family can meet these needs. It can provide you with a safe, secure environment in which to grow and learn. It can act as an "anchor point"—a support base—while you learn to become an independent, contributing member of society.

Rules of daily life. The family is the first group to which you belong and from which

United States Census Bureau statistics for 1990 show that one out of six families is headed by a single female.

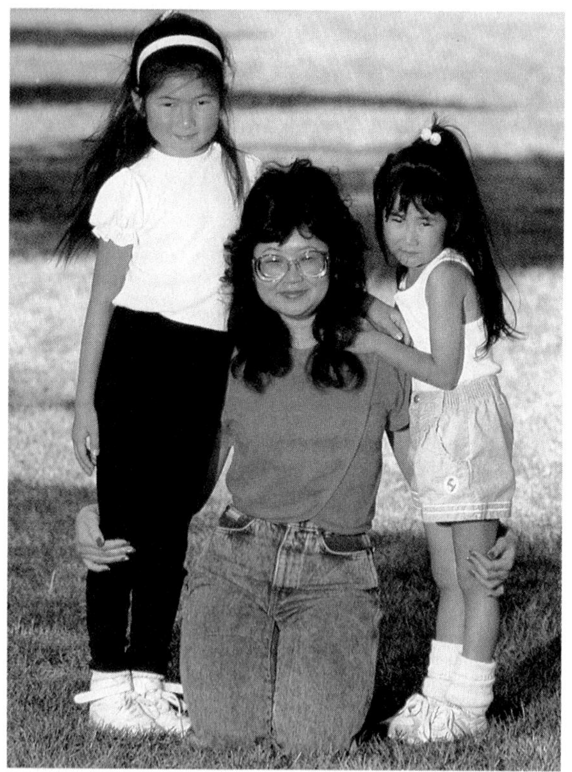

There are many types of families in the United States. A growing number of families are made up of one parent with several children.

you learn many of the rules that govern daily life. Here is a list of some of the rules that a teenager might learn at home:

Do take out the garbage.
Do keep your room clean.
Do be polite to adults.
Do finish your homework.

Do not use bad language.
Do not leave the kitchen a mess.
Do not let the dog loose.
Do not use the phone too much.

Such rules reflect a set of values that parents think their children ought to live by: being responsible, clean, and respectful of others.

Every teenager has experienced punishments for breaking such rules. Being "grounded" for staying out too late is probably a familiar one. Of course, there are rewards for following the rules, too, such as praise from your parents, and being given more freedom.

How the family benefits society. The rules of conduct you learn at home do not disappear when you step out the door. For example, your parents have taught you to put trash in the garbage can rather than let it pile up on the floor. Society has created similar rules called laws. If you toss your soda can out of the car window, for instance, you are breaking the rule against littering.

This simple example makes the point that the rules established within the family often reflect the values held by society as a whole. In a real sense, the family benefits society by serving as a kind of training ground for adults-to-be.

Religion: A Source of Support and Guidance

Although not everyone in America belongs to a religious group, the institution of religion plays an important part in our society, as it has in societies throughout history. Religion meets important individual needs, such as the need for comfort in times of sorrow, and the need to find answers to spiritual questions about the meaning of life and death.

Like the family, religious groups can also give people a sense of belonging—in this case a feeling of being part of a community of people who have similar goals and similar ways of looking at life. Religions provide people with moral standards that they can use to judge right from wrong and to decide how they should live their lives.

Comfort and a sense of community. Bernice Kelman cannot imagine life without her

PEOPLE MAKE A DIFFERENCE

Minister Helps Serve Neighborhood

Henry Vellinga, a Protestant minister, is a well-known figure in his urban Chicago neighborhood. His energy and commitment to helping solve the problems of his community have inspired church members and non-church members alike.

In 1983, Vellinga became executive coordinator of the Beverly-Morgan Park Protestant Cluster of Churches. Members of 15 churches have agreed to share their time, knowledge, and resources with each other and with citizens in need. Their goal is to improve the quality of life for everyone in their community.

Beverly-Morgan Park is a community of contrasts. Its 55,000 residents include the wealthy and the poor.

"Our community has many needs," Vellinga points out. "There are people who do not have adequate housing, enough food, or medical treatment when needed." Vellinga is also

aware that new people moving into the neighborhood bring new cultures and traditions that the older residents are not used to.

Henry Vellinga's leadership in the Cluster has been a key element in helping the community confront some of its problems. Among the most successful programs of the Cluster are the Food Pantry, the Beverly-Morgan Senior Services, and an orientation program for high school students.

The Pantry, staffed entirely by volunteers, provides free food to people who otherwise might go hungry. Seniors in the area benefit from home-delivered meals, social and educational activities, and visits from volunteers. The orientation program teaches local students the skills they will need to be successful in high school.

Vellinga is seen as the guiding light of the Cluster's programs. "Whenever [we need] food or money, we go to Henry," says a volunteer. "He goes to merchants, he goes to churches, he plans fundraisers to see that the Pantry and our other programs survive."

Henry Vellinga believes that "churches do not simply provide once-a-week opportunities to think about spiritual life. It is part of our American values to help our neighbors," he declares. "We all feel better about ourselves when we can give back to our community."

church. It helps to draw the members together, giving them a sense of belonging to a community that can support them in times of trouble. Bernice says:

Church keeps us busy. We have services on Sunday and on Wednesday evening. We have youth groups for the kids, women's circles, even a men's choir.

We know we can count on each other, too. Last year the Smith family lost everything—their house, barn, and crops—in a tornado. At church the following Sunday, we took up a collection. The next

Activity: Have students find out about a church or synagogue in their community that provides outreach programs. Ask students to report on how the program is helping to solve a problem in the community.

week, members of the church rebuilt the Smith's barn.

Bernice Kelman's church provides its members with support. It is a place where members can meet to observe their faith together as one community. The church community gives each member a place to turn when times are bad.

Bernice recalls how religion has helped members of her church cope with unexpected tragedies by giving them comfort and a deeper understanding of life and death:

I remember when the Ramsey boy died of cancer. The whole congregation was upset. Our minister, Reverend Williams, showed us that the Ramsey boy had lived a good life, and that we should remember this more than his death. Reverend Williams helped us see that his death had brought us all closer together.

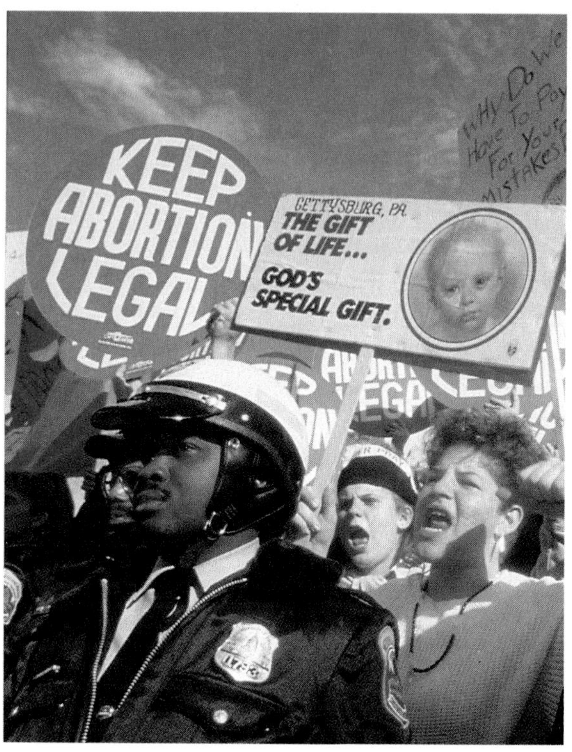

Demonstrators express their opinions about abortion. Differing religious values can cause conflict in our diverse society.

Rules to live by. Every religion has a moral code that establishes expectations for people's behavior and helps them judge right from wrong. These moral codes can be general guides for behavior, such as the Golden Rule: "Do unto others as you would have them do unto you." They can also include very specific rules, such as "Thou shall not kill," and "Thou shall not steal," two of the Ten Commandments found in the Bible.

A religious group can exert a powerful influence on its members to live according to its rules. Each religion has punishments for those who stray from its moral path. One form of punishment is to withdraw the emotional and spiritual support the group provides. An individual can also be threatened with punishment after death.

People who follow the rules of their religion are rewarded by the acceptance and approval of the group. Most religions promise faithful members some kind of reward after death. Obeying religious rules and embracing the values they reflect also give people confidence that they are "living right": living lives that are moral and good.

How religion affects society. Many of the rules that guide people's behavior in our society are written into laws. However, the members of Bernice's church were not required by law to give money and to work to replace the Smiths' barn. They acted out of their belief that charity—helping others who are less fortunate—is good.

Charity, sympathy, and loyalty to friends and family are values that cannot be written into laws. However, when people live their lives according to such values, the whole society benefits. By teaching values, and by pass-

Challenge (Application): Have students give examples of moral standards they use to judge right from wrong and to decide how they should live their lives.

ing them on from generation to generation, the institution of religion makes an important contribution to American society.

Conflicting religious values. The diverse people who make up the cultural mosaic described in Chapter 1 belong to many religious groups. In fact, more than a thousand different religious groups can be found in the United States today.

Not all of these religious groups share the same values and rules. If one religious group tries to impose its values on the rest of society and make everyone follow its rules, serious conflicts can arise. In America today, disagreements about such issues as abortion and the teaching of evolution are often based on the values of different religious groups.

As we debate such issues, we face the challenge of balancing two of our most important rights: freedom of speech and freedom of religion. One test of whether or not we as Americans are living up to our ideal of equal respect is whether members of religious groups can act according to their own beliefs and values while still respecting the right of others to hold different beliefs.

Education: More Than ABC's

Think back to your first days in elementary school. There were dozens of new rules to learn. You had to come on time, raise your hand to be called on, stand in line, and sit quietly at your desk. There were new names to remember and new games to learn. Soon you were practicing your ABC's, counting, and learning to write with a pencil.

Many of the rules and skills were new to you. You had not needed to know them to get along in your family and your neighborhood. However, as you moved into the larger world outside family and neighborhood, your needs began to change. To fit into that larger world, you needed to learn new skills and rules. The institution of education exists to meet those needs.

Why people need education. When Doris Hollingsworth was a little girl, she dreamed of growing up to be a firefighter and riding on a big red fire truck with its siren screaming. At age ten, Peter Ky could not decide between being a fisherman and an astronaut. Bernice Kelman was sure that nursing would be the best job for her.

Whatever your dreams might be, you, like every young person, have hopes for a career that uses your skills and talents, that provides you with a comfortable life, and that gives you a sense of being a worthwhile person. To achieve this goal, you will need at least a high school education.

Education is increasingly important in our society. Because we live in a time of rapid technological change, more and more of the available jobs require a great deal of knowledge or a special skill. It is in school that you will learn most of the skills and knowledge that will prepare you for your life as a working adult.

The institution of education has another important effect on you. School is one of the first places where you meet people from different backgrounds and with different values. As a member of a family, you are exposed mostly to people who share your values and live by the same rules you do. In school you begin to recognize the importance of listening to others' opinions and respecting their ideas and abilities.

Meeting society's needs. While the institution of education is meeting the needs of individual students, it is also serving our society. Society needs to train its citizens to do work. Without trained workers, how could our businesses and industries provide the products that we

In the mid-1800s, disagreement about the abolition of slavery in the United States was so strong that the issue divided the Protestant churches. Baptists, Methodists, and Presbyterians all set up separate northern and southern organizations.

Teaching Note: Use the Enrichment Activity, page T 40, and accompanying worksheet in the Activity Book as a culminating activity after students have read the material in Section 2-2.

AMERICAN NOTEBOOK

Dropping out of high school before graduating can seriously interfere with your opportunities for leading a satisfying life. Here are some facts about high school dropouts:

- **Nearly one in three dropouts is unemployed.**
- **Over half of Americans living in poverty are dropouts.**
- **More than half of convicted criminals are dropouts.**
- **In a lifetime, a high school dropout will earn much less money, on average, than a high school graduate.**

want? Who would run the banks, insurance companies, hospitals, and all the other services of our complex society?

In addition, our society needs to prepare its citizens to live together as a nation. The children who enter our schools are as diverse as American society itself. The values and customs they bring from home often differ from those of their classmates and are sometimes in conflict with them.

Society has entrusted the schools with the task of teaching young citizens the rules and values by which Americans are expected to live. Our schools offer us a knowledge of our history, culture, and government. They teach us a common language by which we can communicate with our fellow citizens. Our schools transmit society's ideal of equal respect and the values of freedom, equality, and justice that support it.

Schools also teach us how to think, form opinions, make judgments, and solve problems. The institution of education gives us the opportunity to examine our own beliefs while exposing us to new ideas.

As you have learned, any group that wants to continue to exist must teach its values and rules to its members. It is through the institution of education—our schools and colleges, our teachers, our textbooks—that American society assures that this country will continue to be a free, democratic nation.

More than grades, more than a paycheck. What are the rewards offered by the institution of education? Getting good grades can be rewarding and so can getting a satisfying job. However, the rewards of your education can go far beyond grades and paychecks.

By the time you finish high school, you may have spent the better part of 13 years in school. As you walk across the stage to pick up your diploma, what rewards will you recognize? You will probably have some good memories and close friendships as well as some practical and academic skills. Perhaps, too, you will leave school with a better sense of who you are and how you can contribute to American society.

Answers will be found on page T 40.

Section Review

1. How does the family benefit the individual and society?
2. What needs do religious groups meet for the people who belong to them?
3. What do children gain from the institution of education?

Analysis. How do the institutions of the family, religion, and education differ in the needs they meet and the ways they help society? What do they have in common?

Data Search. Americans are better educated today than they were 50 years ago. Refer to the appropriate chart on page 583 to find out the percentages of students who completed at least four years of college in 1940 and in 1989.

In 1989, the median amount of money earned by a worker with a high school diploma was $28,060. In contrast, the median amount earned by a college graduate was $49,180.

2-3

THE ECONOMY: SATISFYING WANTS

Read to Find Out

- what the terms *goods, services, wants, economy, consumer, market, price,* and *money* mean.
- what needs the institution of the economy meets in our society.
- what freedoms individuals have in our economy.

Imagine that one day you are baking desserts for a party and you experiment by combining two recipes. The brownie-like bar that comes out of the oven is incredibly delicious. You are pleased with your discovery, but you remember that you are out of eggs, you need some new clothes, the TV is broken, and your bicycle has a flat tire.

You get an idea: why not make a huge batch of these bars and then trade them for what you need? Surely no one could resist the taste of your new creation, which you call the Wonderbar.

Filling a box with Wonderbars, you take off for Jane's farm. Jane tries a Wonderbar sample and agrees to exchange a dozen eggs for one of your Wonderbars. Then you are off to the tailor to trade him thirty Wonderbars for a pair of pants.

You have provided yourself with food and clothing. Such physical products are called ***goods.***

Your next stop is at Danny's Handyman Shop. You ask Danny to fix your broken television and patch your bicycle tube. Danny agrees to perform these ***services***—work you will pay to have done—in exchange for two dozen Wonderbars.

You have just exchanged, or bartered, your Wonderbars to satisfy your ***wants,*** or desires for goods and services. Some of your wants, such as food, clothing, and shelter, are essential for your survival. Others, such as a television or bicycle that work, may not be essential, but they make your life more enjoyable.

The American Economy

Just as you, Danny, and Jane found a way to get what you wanted, every society has a system for producing and distributing goods and services to fulfill people's wants. This system is called an ***economy.*** Like the other institutions you have been learning about, the institution of the economy is organized to meet needs, which in this case means responding to people's wants. It also has a set of rules and expectations for its members.

Characteristics of our economy. We see evidence of our economy all around us every day. In addition to goods and services we see people, markets, prices, and money.

As participants in our economy, we play several roles. Each of us is a ***consumer,*** a person who uses, or consumes, goods and services to satisfy his or her wants. Most people are also workers. They provide the skills and the labor necessary to produce goods such as Wonderbars and televisions, or to provide services such as television repair and Wonderbar shipping.

A place or situation in which an exchange of goods or services takes place is called a ***market.*** In some markets, such as stores or shops, people meet face-to-face to exchange what they have for what they want. In other markets, such as stock exchanges, buyers and sellers never meet, but make transactions using complicated accounting systems.

The amount you must pay for a good or service in a market is its ***price.*** You used the

Teaching Note: Use Teaching Activity 2, page T 38, as a culminating activity after students have read the material in Section 2-3.

barter system when you exchanged your Wonderbars for eggs, pants, and repair services. Although bartering is one way to pay for what you want, people usually use money. ***Money*** is anything, from beads to coins to checks, that is generally accepted as payment for a good or a service.

Rules of the American Economy

Like all institutions, our economy has rules that its participants must follow. These rules reflect some of the important values that Americans have agreed upon. One value, freedom, forms the cornerstone of our economy, or economic system. Built into this system are rules protecting five important freedoms.

Freedom to buy and sell. You have the freedom to sell your Wonderbars to anyone you wish. You are also free to charge whatever price you think you can get for them. In addition, every person has the freedom to buy or not to buy your Wonderbars.

Freedom to compete. You are free to make and sell Wonderbars. At the same time, other people are free to compete with you, trying to make and sell more or better dessert bars than you do.

Freedom to make a profit. If people are willing to pay more for your Wonderbars than it costs you to make them, then you will earn a profit. Freedom to earn a profit on what they make and sell encourages people to produce goods and services.

Freedom to own property. Your Wonderbars are your property, and you own them until you agree to sell them. The right to own your own property and to buy and sell and use it as you wish is a basic rule of the American economic system.

Freedom to choose an occupation. You are free to pursue any career you wish. Of course whether you are successful will depend on whether there are jobs available in that career and on whether you have provided yourself with the proper training and skills.

In addition to protecting freedom, the rules of our economic system are based on the idea of fairness. If you make an agreement to do a job, sell a product, or pay a worker, for example, you may not break it. Furthermore, you may not make a product that does not work and claim that it does.

You and America's Economy

Not everyone has the job he or she wants, and most people cannot buy all the goods and services they would like. There are also people in our country who are very poor. On the whole, however, our economic system succeeds. The goods and services we desire are produced, distributed, and sold. We have the freedom to try to achieve our dreams—to have careers and lifestyles of our own choosing. In these ways, we benefit from the institution of the economy in the United States.

Answers will be found on page T 41.

Section Review

1. Define *goods, services, wants, economy, consumer, market, price,* and *money.*
2. How does our society benefit from having an economic system?
3. Make a list of the economic freedoms Americans have.

Application. Think of a recent day in your life. Did you have wants for goods and services? Were they fulfilled? How? Did you act as a producer or consumer? Describe how our economic system affected you on that day.

Challenge (Analysis): Have students name countries that have different economic systems than the United States and then compare the rules of these economies with our economic freedoms and limitations. (Types of economies are discussed in Chapter 13.)

2-4

GOVERNMENT: MEETING SOCIETY'S NEEDS

Read to Find Out

- what the terms *monarchy, dictatorship,* and *democracy* mean.
- why a society needs a government.
- who has the power to make decisions in each of the three most common forms of government.

Do you think the following scenes could take place in the United States?

- Suddenly, in the middle of the night, soldiers rush into your home and arrest your parents. You never see them again.
- A president and other officials appoint themselves to office and stay in power as long as they want.
- Religion is outlawed. Churches and temples are locked and barred.

These scenes are an everyday reality for people in many countries. Individuals live in constant fear because their rights are not protected. For them, government is the enemy.

Life in the United States is different. Our government was formed to protect our rights and to ensure that events such as the ones just described do not occur. Like the other institutions you have been reading about, America's institution of government reflects the shared values of its members.

The Need for Government

Without government, life would be disorganized. There would be no order to the way roads were built or towns and cities planned.

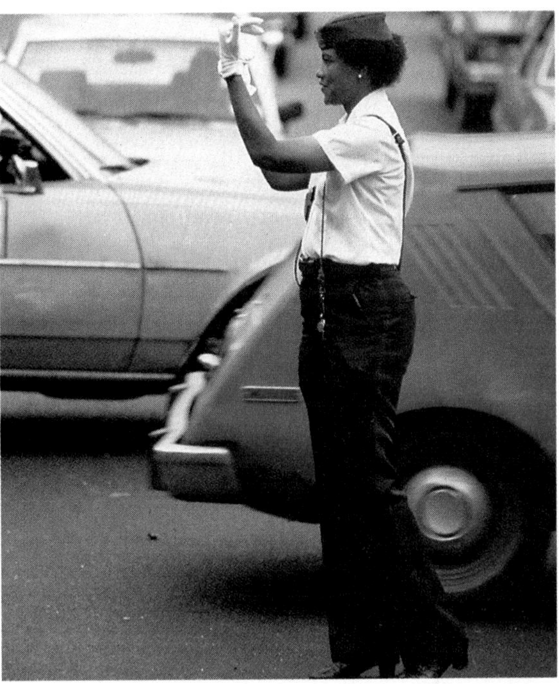

By preventing crime and protecting community safety, police officers help government maintain law and order in our society.

People would disagree about ways to settle arguments and deal with crime. We would have no proper way to defend our nation from attack.

The institution of government helps people solve such problems. It satisfies important needs of society by establishing law and order, protecting individuals' security, providing public services, and maintaining other institutions.

Law and order. Government makes and enforces laws that protect rights and ensure that people's lives can proceed in a peaceful, orderly way. Through courts, our government can also settle disputes and punish law breakers.

Security. Government provides for our common defense against outside attack by maintaining armed forces and weapons. Our government makes treaties with other countries in which both sides agree to keep the peace or to help each other in case of attack.

Public services. Government provides services we need but cannot depend on private businesses to provide. Such services include building and maintaining roads, sewers, and schools.

Maintaining other institutions. Government can help to maintain the other institutions in society. For example, in the United States, government protects our freedom of religion, pays for our schools, and provides hundreds of services for families, from health care to issuing marriage licenses.

Forms of Government

There are many forms of government that can provide the order, security, and services that a society needs. In the world today, monarchy, dictatorship, and democracy are the three most common forms of government.

Monarchy. A *monarchy* is a form of government in which all or most of the power is in the hands of one individual, the monarch. The monarch's authority is hereditary; it stays in the family, usually being passed down to a son or daughter. King, queen, and emperor are some of the titles that have been given to monarchs.

Monarchies were once the most common type of government in the world. Today, however, real monarchies—in which the monarch holds all the power—are rare. An example of such a modern-day monarchy is the kingdom of Saudi Arabia.

Dictatorship. A *dictatorship* is a government controlled by one person, called a dictator. A dictator is different from a monarch because a dictator usually takes power by force, rather than by inheriting it. Historically, dictators have usually come to power when an existing government is weak or has lost the support of the people.

Dictators are frequently military leaders. They rely heavily on the support of the armed forces and the police to maintain them in power. Their actions are not limited by laws or legislatures. Recent military dictatorships include Germany under Adolf Hitler and Libya under Colonel Qadhafi (kah-DAH-fee).

Democracy. A third form of government is a *democracy,* a system in which the power is shared by all the people. Democracy means "government by the people." By voting and by choosing representatives, the people decide how their government will meet their needs and protect their rights and freedoms.

The United States was the first modern democracy. Since our nation was founded in 1787, countries in all corners of the world have adopted democratic forms of government. Many countries that were once monarchies have become democracies. Most of these countries, such as Great Britain and Japan, still have monarchs with ceremonial duties, but real power is held by democratically elected representatives. Countries with this form of democratic government are often called constitutional monarchies.

Laws: The Rules of Government

Laws are the formal rules that govern our behavior in society. The most basic and important laws of our nation are written down in a document called the Constitution. The Constitution tells what the government can and cannot do, and lists the rights guaranteed to states and to citizens. In the United States, governments at the town, county, state, and national levels can make laws, as long as these laws are not in conflict with the basic laws in the Constitution.

Challenge (Synthesis): Have students discuss what our society might look like if we depended on private companies to provide roads, police and fire protection, and sewers.

Teaching Note: Use the Evaluating Progress activity, page T 39.

Laws influence nearly everything we do, from driving a car and voting in elections to getting a fishing license and disposing of garbage. By following our laws, we ensure that rights are protected and order maintained in society. What are some of the laws that affect how you ride your bicycle or skateboard?

Breaking laws can lead to very specific punishments. The seriousness of the punishment depends on the seriousness of the crime. For example, if you were to break the speed limit or litter, you would probably have to pay a fine. If you were to rob a bank, you could spend years in jail.

Changing the laws. In a democracy, the citizens have a right to express their opinions and work with others to try to make laws they think are needed. They can also try to change laws they think are unfair or harmful to society.

Our government responds to our demands, but only when it hears them. The opinions of the people do make a difference when they are made known to lawmakers and government officials.

Answers will be found on page T 41.

Section Review

1. Define *monarchy, dictatorship,* and *democracy.*
2. What are four important needs that the institution of government meets? Give an example of how each need is met.
3. In each of the three most common systems of government, who has the power to make decisions?

Synthesis. Think of four laws that affect you. How would society be different if those laws did not exist?

A BROADER VIEW

Social institutions provide the framework for our lives. They meet our most important physical, emotional, spiritual, and economic needs. Their values shape our own personal values, and their rules determine how we behave much of the time.

Because they reflect a society's most basic values, the institutions of the family, education, and religion change very slowly if at all in most societies. Forms of government and economic systems, however, can sometimes change very quickly.

A sudden, drastic change in a government is called a revolution. In a revolution, a government is overthrown by force and a new government is established. Often the new government orders major changes in the economy. Revolutions often occur when many people in a society believe that the government and economy are not meeting their needs. In this century, revolutions have occurred in the Soviet Union, China, and many African and Latin American countries.

As you know, the United States was created as a result of a revolution in 1776. Since then, however, our government and economy have changed only gradually. Even though many Americans have at times sharply disagreed with the way the government and the economy were working, we have never had to face another revolution. We are fortunate that our government was carefully designed to be flexible and responsive to the demands of its citizens.

The Process

Teaching Note: For reinforcement of decision-making skills, use Decision-Making Worksheet Chapter 2.

Choosing

"I don't know. What do *you* want to do?" "I can't make up my mind. You decide." "What a boring day. I can't think of anything to do."

Do those statements sound familiar? At times we rely on other people to make choices for us, or we wait for something to happen so that we do not have to make a choice. Although frequently we must let others make decisions that affect us, sometimes we let them decide simply because it is "easier" or "safer." Unfortunately, the more we do this, the less control we have over our lives.

Often people let others decide because they feel that they cannot make good decisions themselves. Making good decisions, though, is mainly a matter of taking your time and following a careful process. This lesson will help you understand the first part of that process: choosing.

EXPLAINING THE PROCESS

The following guidelines will help you choose a way to achieve your goal.

1. State your goal clearly. Determine exactly what you want to happen. That is, set a clear goal that points you in a direction, rather than a fuzzy goal that will not help you make a decision. Decide how you will be able to tell whether you have reached your goal.

2. Identify options, or possible ways of achieving your goal. Brainstorm a list of as many options as you can. Do not judge each option right away. Remember, one idea may lead to another.

3. Think about the possible consequences, or effects, of each option. For each option ask, "If I do this, what will probably happen?"

4. Judge each option. Identify which consequences are good and which are bad.

5. Choose the best option. Compare the good and bad points of each option to determine which option is best.

ANALYZING THE PROCESS

The following account describes how a student named Janice worked with other student council members to choose a way to achieve a goal. As you read, look carefully at how they followed some specific steps of the decision-making process.

> I was angry. Our school was looking like a garbage dump. Students wrote all over the desks and left wads of paper on the classroom floors. The bathroom mirrors and walls were covered with graffiti. Lunch tables were littered with wrappings and leftover food.
>
> I brought my complaint to the other members of the student council, who agreed that the messiness of the school campus was a big problem. We talked about what we wanted to achieve. "We want to have a clean campus," said one council member. "Obviously, that is our goal." Soon we realized, however, that our goal was more specific than that. We wanted to deal with the *cause* of the problem, that is, to get students to recognize the importance of keeping the school clean. Therefore, we stated our goal more clearly. Chris, the student council president, wrote it on the chalkboard: *Goal: To get most students to willingly help keep the school clean.*
>
> Next we considered what we could do to achieve that goal. We made a list of possibilities. No one judged any of the options while we brainstormed. Chris made a chart on the blackboard listing them.
>
> After that we looked closely at each option and considered what might happen if we tried

Later decision-making lessons will discuss more specific criteria for judging options, such as taking into account personal values, costs, benefits, and long-term and short-term effects.

it. For instance, we thought that Jerry's suggestion of having student monitors might work for a while. However, in the long run we would probably have trouble finding enough volunteers to go on patrol. I found it hard to sit through the discussion on each option because I thought it was obvious that giving out spirit buttons was the best choice. But, as you will soon see, I am glad that I was patient.

GOAL: To get most students to willingly help keep the school clean.

Option	Consequences
Student Monitors	Will not cost money + Might quit soon —
Professional Guards	Will be expensive — Will be effective + Students will resent them —
Spirit Buttons	Will not cost much money + Having a reward will get students to volunteer +
Detentions	Will not cost any money + Will be difficult to assign fairly —

Our faculty advisor said that we had an impressive list but wanted to know how we were going to determine which option was best. We told her that we would look at the possible results of each option, using plus and minus signs to rate each consequence.

In looking at the options, we kept our goal in mind. Some possibilities, such as hiring guards, would help keep the campus clean but would not encourage students to take responsibility themselves. Our goal was to have the students keep the campus clean because they *wanted* to, not because they were forced to.

Most council members liked my idea of handing out spirit buttons as a reward to students who help keep the school clean. However, some thought that buttons were not enough of a reward. Then Karen came up with a clever idea: letting students cash in the buttons to get discounts at the cafeteria or on tickets for dances, athletic events, and other activities. We decided that passing out buttons that students could cash in was the best option.

CHECKING YOUR UNDERSTANDING

1. Why did the students decide that their goal should not be only "to have a clean campus"?

2. How did the student council's goal lead them to reject the option of hiring guards?

3. In making their choice, the members of the student council were *not* influenced by **(a)** the importance of students taking responsibility, **(b)** the need to raise money for cleaning up the school, **(c)** the long-term effects of the option they chose. Explain your answer.

4. Which of the following was *not* an important part of the process the student council went through in making their choice? **(a)** the advice they received from the faculty advisor, **(b)** the chart they created, **(c)** their willingness to consider all the options. Explain your answer.

REVIEWING THE PROCESS

5. Why is it important to define your goal clearly?

6. Explain how to judge options when making a decision.

Have students brainstorm other options and consequences that could be added to the list shown in the lesson. Students might also apply the five steps described in the lesson to a problem their own school faces. The goal, options, and consequences may be listed on the board and discussed.

CHAPTER SURVEY

Answers to Survey and Workshop will be found on page T 41.

UNDERSTANDING NEW VOCABULARY

Seeing Relationships

The vocabulary terms in each pair listed below are related to each other. For each pair, explain how the two terms are related.

Example: *Social institution* is related to *economy* because the economy is a social institution which meets the needs of individuals.

1. *socialization* and *rules*

2. *goods* and *wants*

3. *money* and *price*

4. *monarchy* and *dictatorship*

Putting It in Writing

Using the terms *monarchy, dictatorship*, and *democracy*, write a paragraph describing who has the power to make laws under each form of government.

LOOKING BACK AT THE CHAPTER

1. What are some of the needs that groups meet in our lives?

2. Explain the reasons that members of a group must learn and obey the group's rules.

3. How does a child benefit from the institution of the family?

4. What benefits do individuals and society receive from the institution of religion?

5. Why does our society need to have schools?

6. What is the basic purpose of an economic system?

7. Describe two ways that a consumer can pay for a product or service.

8. What are the four major reasons that people form governments?

9. *Synthesis*. How might society be different if the institution of the family did not exist?

10. *Application*. Think of a group to which you belong. What needs of yours does it meet? What are some of its rules, rewards, and punishments? Describe your process of socialization into that group.

11. *Synthesis*. Pick one of the economic freedoms (freedom to buy and sell, to compete, to make a profit, to own property, and to choose an occupation). How might your life be different if you did not have that freedom?

12. *Evaluation*. At this point in your life, which of the five social institutions has had the greatest effect on shaping your values? Explain your choice and give examples of beliefs and values you have learned from that institution.

WORKING TOGETHER

1. With three or four classmates, choose a recent day and analyze your activities as consumers in our economic system. Make a chart like the one below listing the wants for goods and services that you each experienced during that day. Note which wants you were able to fulfill. Which wants could you not fulfill? Why?

Wants	Fulfilled? yes no
Goods	
Services	

2. Collect newspaper and magazine articles about the American family or about religions in America. For each article, underline references to the needs the institution meets and the rules and values it enforces for its members.

SKILLS WORKSHOP

SOCIAL STUDIES SKILLS

Analyzing Statistical Tables

Statistics are collections of information in the form of numbers. Once statistics are collected, they are easier to analyze if they have been organized and displayed in some way. Sometimes statistics are displayed as graphs, but often the numbers are arranged in a statistical table such as the one below.

Education and Lifetime Earnings

Level of education	Average lifetime earnings of full-time workers in 1981 dollars	
	Men	Women
High school dropouts	$845,000	$500,000
High school graduates	1,041,000	634,000
1–3 years of college	1,155,000	716,000
4 years of college	1,392,000	846,000
5 or more years of college	1,503,000	955,000

The following questions will help you analyze the table.

1. What is the purpose of the table?

2. Which group earns the least over a working lifetime?

3. Which group earns the most over a lifetime? How do the earnings of this group compare with the earnings of the lowest-paid group?

4. Compare the highest-paid group of women with the lowest-paid group of men. What do you notice?

5. What two conclusions can you draw from this statistical table?

DECISION-MAKING SKILLS

Choosing

Create a chart with two labels at the top: *Options* and *Consequences*. Then imagine that you are considering the options in the following account. List the options and consequences. Mark each good consequence with a plus and each bad one with a minus.

Your goal is to get food for needy people quickly and to prevent the problem of hunger in the future. You consider writing letters to local newspapers asking for help. You also think of writing to your representative in Congress, requesting government aid. Another option is to have local people organize a food pantry.

If you write to local newspapers, hundreds of readers might send donations. A lot of these people, though, might make only one or two donations and then lose interest.

If you choose to write to your representative in Congress, you might get some long-term aid. However, you would be competing with other communities that need assistance. Also, you might have to wait months for the money.

If the aid is provided through a food pantry, you would not have to rely on outside money. Also, local volunteers would be available soon and could help for as long as they are needed. However, there would be less money than you might receive from the government.

1. After referring to your chart, state which of the above options is best. Explain your choice.

2. Why is having a clearly stated goal important in making decisions?

3. In decision making, why should you consider all options rather than choosing your first idea?

4. Think of a recent decision you made. Name two options you had and identify two consequences of each one.

VICTORY
MICHIGAN
AFL
CIO
STATE
Dukakis
Bentsen
We're The Duke
We're The Duke

Chapter Themes: Citizens of the United States are privileged to have many rights. Accompanying those rights are duties and responsibilities which citizens fulfill as they participate in several social roles.

CHAPTER 3

The Meaning of Citizenship

Some students in American schools were asked the following questions:

- What is citizenship?
- What does it mean to be an American citizen?
- What should a person do to be a good citizen?

As you read the answers the students gave, decide which ones you agree with. How do these responses compare to the answers that you might give?

There are rights and responsibilities when you are a citizen. They go together. It's like a family, only on a larger scale. —*Girl, age 16*

Citizenship means to help to make the country better without being paid. —*Boy, age 15*

Being a citizen means you are a good person. —*Girl, age 9*

A good citizen obeys all laws, pays taxes, and is kind to others. —*Boy, age 14*

Being a citizen means that I don't have to go back to my old country. —*Girl, age 15*

If there is something wrong with the government, a citizen should get involved and should try to fix it. —*Boy, age 15*

Although these definitions of citizen and citizenship are not exactly alike, there is some truth in each of them. They show that each of us has his or her own way of thinking about what it means to be a citizen. In this chapter you will learn about citizenship: who has it, what rights and duties it involves, and how Americans of all ages can fulfill its responsibilities.

Teaching Note: Use the Introducing the Chapter activity, page T 44.

Teaching Note: Use Teaching Activity 1, page T 44, as a culminating activity after students have read the material in this section.

3-1 WHAT IT MEANS TO BE A CITIZEN

Read to Find Out

- what the terms *citizen, naturalized, alien,* and *representatives* mean.
- who can be a citizen of the United States.
- how each citizen holds an "office" just as important as that of an elected official.

Bernice Kelman lives in Sublette, Kansas, in the United States. She is a citizen of her town, her state, and her nation. A ***citizen*** is a person with certain rights and duties under a government. Citizens' rights include the right to express an opinion and the right to protection of the laws. Duties include obeying laws and paying taxes. Each of us is a citizen of the town, state, and nation in which we live.

The word *citizen* also has a special meaning. Our Constitution says that a citizen of the United States is a person who by birth or by choice owes allegiance to this nation.

Who Is a Citizen?

You are legally an American citizen if any of these statements are true:

- You were born in the United States or its territories. (This is true even if your parents were not citizens, unless they were living in the United States as representatives of a foreign government.)
- At least one of your parents was a United States citizen when you were born.
- You have been ***naturalized***, which means you have gone through the process of becoming a citizen.
- You were under age eighteen when your parents were naturalized.

Naturalized citizens. When the Ky family first came to this country from Vietnam, they were considered aliens. An ***alien*** is a citizen of one country who lives in another country. As aliens, the Kys had many of the same rights and duties as American citizens. However, they could not vote or hold government office.

In order to become American citizens, Peter's parents went through the process called naturalization, which is described in the box on the next page. They learned English, studied the history of the United States, and learned the important values, laws, rights, and duties of citizens.

In Chapter 2 you learned that socialization is the process of learning the rules of a group or institution to which you belong. You might think of the process of naturalization as our government's way of socializing aliens who want to become American citizens.

Because Peter was less than eighteen years old at the time his parents became naturalized citizens, he automatically became a citizen, too. The history, civics, and government classes he takes in school will socialize him as they are socializing you: teaching you the rules and the benefits of being a citizen.

Naturalized citizens have all the rights and duties of citizens by birth except the right to be President or Vice-President. Once you are a citizen, you will always be a citizen except in a few special cases. For example, a person can decide to give up citizenship, or become a citizen of another country. In addition, citizenship may be taken away from a person who is convicted of trying to overthrow the United States government by force.

The Office of Citizen

Being a United States citizen has a unique meaning. In this country, each citizen holds a very important position of authority. As Abraham Lincoln observed, ours is a govern-

The Fourteenth Amendment, ratified in 1868, defines state as well as national citizenship to prevent states from setting up their own definitions of citizenship in order to exclude blacks or other groups. This amendment is discussed in Chapter 7.

Teaching Note: Use the Evaluating Progress activity, page T 45, after students have read the material in Section 3-1 or at the end of the chapter.

The Naturalization Process

Application:
You must fill out an application form and submit it with biographical information and fingerprints.

Examination:
You must make a request for naturalization to a naturalization officer and bring two U.S. citizens as witnesses. You must prove that you have the following qualifications for citizenship:

1. You are at least eighteen years of age.
2. You have lived in the U.S. legally for the previous 5 years (3 years if your husband or wife is a United States citizen) and in your state for 6 months.
3. Your character and behavior reflect accepted moral standards.
4. You are loyal to the basic values of the American government and have not supported any group seeking to overthrow the government by force.
5. You can read, write, and speak English and know the history and form of government of the United States.

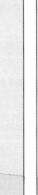

Final Hearing:
After at least 30 days, during which the Naturalization Service may obtain more information, an officer will present a report to a judge in a citizenship court, recommending that you be granted citizenship.
The judge will ask you to take an oath of loyalty to the United States and will give you a certificate of citizenship.

ment "of the people, by the people, and for the people." He meant that our government can operate—make laws, build roads and bridges, collect taxes, fight wars, make agreements with other countries—but only if we citizens want it to. When we say that the power of our government is based on "the consent of the governed," we mean that the citizens have the power to decide what our government will and will not do.

As citizens, we elect ***representatives***, people who are chosen to speak and act for their fellow citizens in government. We elect members of Congress as well as city council members, mayors, Presidents, governors, and many of our judges. They have the power to make decisions and to pass laws.

However, our representatives hold office only as long as we want them to. We delegate—or lend—our power to them. The real power belongs to us. In a way, therefore, each of us holds an office, too—the "office of citizen." In our society, that is the most important office there is. As citizens we hold it for life.

Answers will be found on page T 46.

Section Review

1. Define *citizen, naturalized, alien,* and *representatives.*
2. What are the qualifications to be a citizen?
3. What is the "office of citizen"?

Analysis. How is the office of citizen similar to that of an elected official? How is it different?

Data Search. Look on page 584 in the Data Bank. In which years since 1910 have more than 200,000 people been naturalized?

Challenge (Evaluation): Have students discuss the following question: Should the ability to speak English be required of all citizens? Students should provide reasons for their opinions. (For a discussion/activity on this issue, see "Taking a Stand" on page 65.)

3-2

THE RIGHTS, DUTIES, AND RESPONSIBILITIES OF CITIZENS

Read to Find Out

- what the terms *jury of peers, witnesses, the common good,* and *candidate* mean.
- what the important rights of American citizens are.
- why citizens have duties, and what those duties are.
- what responsibilities citizens can choose to fulfill.

Here is a riddle: How is holding the "office of citizen" like having a driver's license? If you do not know the answer, think for a minute about what it means to have a driver's license.

Having a license gives you certain rights. Your rights include the right to drive on public roads and highways, and the right to park where the law allows.

Of course, you also have duties. Your duties, which are required by law, include observing traffic signals and signs and obeying the speed limit and other rules of the road. You must park only in legal places and for the legal amount of time, and when you park where there are parking meters, you must put money in them.

In addition to your duties, you will have responsibilities. They can be summed up this way: You will be expected to drive in a way that will not endanger others and that will protect the safety of other drivers, cyclists, and pedestrians.

Have you figured out the answer to the riddle? Holding the "office of citizen" is like being a licensed driver because in both situations you have important rights, duties, and responsibilities.

Rights of Citizens

Can you name some of the rights of American citizens? Here are some that may be most familiar to you:

- the right to vote and to hold elected office
- the right to say what you think in speech or in writing
- the right to practice your own religion
- the right to have a fair trial
- the right to be protected by your government when you are working or traveling in other countries
- the right to privacy in your home and your personal life

These rights, and our other rights as citizens, are based on the fundamental beliefs and values we Americans share: equal respect, freedom, equality, and justice. Our rights are guaranteed to us by our Constitution and protected by our laws and our courts.

Duties of Citizens

Just as a licensed driver has certain duties that go with the right to drive, citizens have duties, too. These duties include:

- obeying the laws
- defending the nation
- serving on a jury or as a witness in court
- paying taxes
- attending school

By performing each of these duties, we, as citizens, support our government's efforts to meet our needs as a society.

Obeying the laws. Your family and your classroom have rules that keep them running in

The concept of the citizen as a person with certain rights and duties developed in the cities of ancient Greece in about 700 B.C. The Greeks believed that men who owned property deserved citizenship. Slaves and women were excluded.

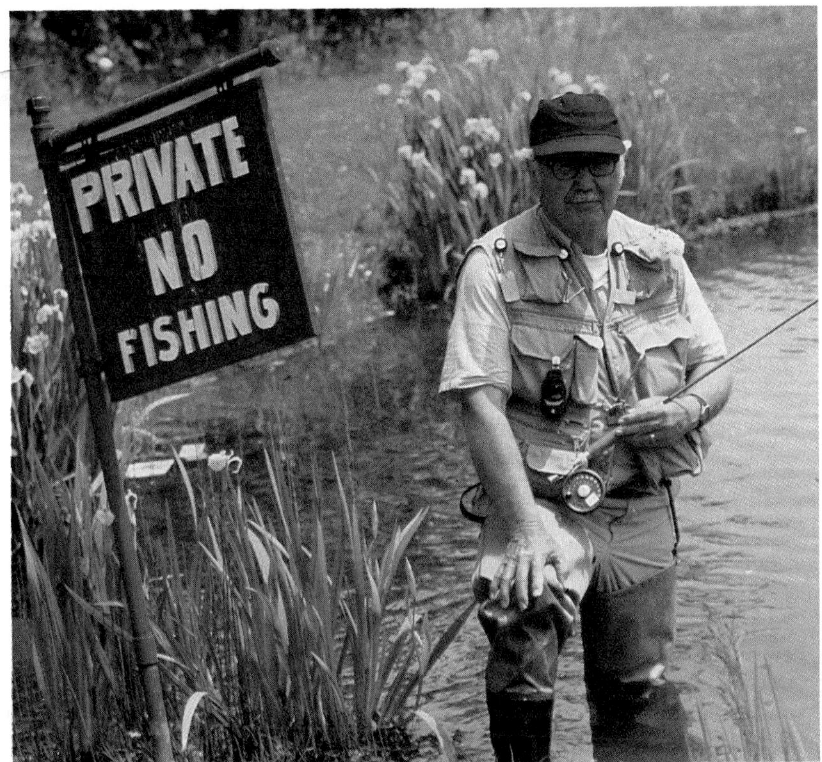

When we obey laws we respect the rights of others. Some laws protect the right of individuals to determine who can use their private property.

an orderly way. As you know, a society's formal, or written, rules are called laws. Some laws are to keep us from hurting each other. They range from laws requiring drivers and bicycle riders to stop at stop signs to laws against murder and armed robbery.

Other laws establish the rules for making agreements and for settling disagreements in a fair and peaceful way. If Bernice Kelman hires Mr. Carey to paint her house, they might draw up and sign a written contract. A contract is a document that states how much Bernice will pay and how long it will take Mr. Carey to finish the job. Both Bernice and Mr. Carey have a legal duty to live up to the contract. If either of them thinks the other has broken the contract, the law gives them the opportunity to take the case to court.

We also must obey laws that protect citizens' rights. For example, the right of equal opportunity is protected by laws. Do you remember when Doris Hollingsworth was applying for a job? If an employer refused to hire her because of her race or religion, the employer would be breaking the law.

It would be impossible to know all the laws of your city, state, and nation. However, it is up to you to know the ones that affect your life and your actions. If you plan to go fishing, for instance, you must know the laws covering fishing licenses and the limit on the number of fish you may catch in a day. If you break those laws, the fish and game warden may use the famous expression, "Ignorance of the law is no excuse," and may make you pay a fine.

Defending the nation. Helping our country defend itself against threats to our peace and security is another important duty of citizens. The United States maintains armed services even in peacetime. In this way, the nation can defend itself in case of attack and can help other countries protect themselves.

When you are eighteen years old or older, you may volunteer to serve in the army, navy,

The navy is one of the armed forces that defend our nation. Men and women who volunteer for the armed forces can learn valuable skills.

air force, or marines. In addition, all young men must register for military service when they reach age eighteen. Registering does not mean that they will have to serve in the armed forces, but it does mean that they can be called to serve when there is a national emergency. A man whose moral beliefs prohibit him from fighting may ask to be considered a conscientious (kahn-shee-EN-shush) objector. If his request is approved, he will be assigned to some other kind of public service, such as working in a hospital.

Serving on a jury or as a witness in court. One of the basic rights of citizens is the right to a fair trial. In our legal system no person may be found guilty of a crime unless that guilt can be proved "beyond a reasonable doubt." We believe that the best way to determine a person's guilt or innocence is to conduct a trial in an open manner, with citizens participating in the process.

Experts, such as lawyers, police officers, and psychologists, may play an important part in a criminal trial—the process of trying to prove that an accused person did or did not commit a crime. However, experts do not make the final decision as to innocence or guilt.

A judge does not make the final decision, either, unless the accused person gives such permission. Instead, our Constitution guarantees that anyone accused of a crime may have the case decided by a ***jury of peers***, a group of ordinary citizens who hear the case and decide whether the accused person is innocent or guilty.

During the trial, the lawyers may need the help of ***witnesses*** to prove their case. Witnesses are people who have seen events or heard conversations related to the crime, or who have special information that may help determine the guilt or innocence of the person on trial.

Criminal trials are not the only ones that use witnesses and juries. People may also ask a court to decide cases in which they think their rights have been violated or they have been treated unfairly. If Bernice Kelman and Mr. Carey cannot settle their dispute over the housepainting job, for example, they have the right to ask for a jury to hear the case. They may also call witnesses to help them—such as a neighbor who can testify that Mr. Carey did not finish painting the house when he agreed to.

As you can see, juries and witnesses play an important part in assuring that a trial is fair. Because Americans have a right to a fair trial, our law requires that all adult citizens serve as jurors and act as witnesses when they are called to do so.

Paying taxes. Are you a taxpayer? A few students your age earn enough money at part-time jobs or through savings accounts or investments that they must pay income tax

The Sixteenth Amendment, ratified in 1913, enabled the federal government to levy a tax on individual incomes. During the early 1900s, the income tax became the main source of revenue for the government. (See Chapter 16.)

to the government. Many more of you pay sales taxes on items you buy, such as books, clothes, and cassette tapes.

As an adult, you will probably pay other taxes as well, such as property taxes on land and a house or building that you may own. Through taxes our local, state, and national governments raise money to pay for the services that citizens ask them to provide.

Attending school. Did it ever occur to you that every time you go to school you are performing one of your duties as a citizen? Although age requirements vary from state to state, children are usually required to attend school from age five or six to at least age sixteen.

As you discovered by reading about the institution of education in Chapter 2, our society depends on our schools to teach young citizens the knowledge and skills they need as they are growing up and when they become adults. One purpose of school attendance laws is to make sure that young people are prepared to support themselves and to contribute to our economy.

Another important task of the schools is to give students the knowledge, skills, and experiences they need to carry out the duties and responsibilities of the "office of citizen." If we, as citizens, are to continue to govern ourselves, uphold our values, and protect our rights, each of us must be educated about our history, our government, and the workings of our society. It is to the schools that our society has entrusted this important task.

Responsibilities of Citizens

As citizens of this democracy, we not only have duties, but responsibilities as well. Unlike duties, responsibilities are fulfilled by choice—they are voluntary. However, even though we are not required by law to fulfill our responsibilities, doing so is just as important a part of being a citizen as performing our duties.

The common good. The basic responsibility of a citizen is to contribute to ***the common good***, or the well-being of all members of society. Contributing to the common good means acting in ways that protect the rights and freedoms of other Americans and that make our communities, our states, and our nation good places for all of us to live.

All the other responsibilities of citizenship are part of contributing to the common good. They include the many ways we participate in

AMERICAN NOTEBOOK

Being a responsible citizen is not always easy. A black mother in New York City's Harlem neighborhood explains why she has made the effort:

> **I'm not like all these other[s] you see in the neighborhood, . . . doing nothing for their community, doing nothing for nobody. That's not for me. When I see something wrong, I speak up. I get involved. . . . That's why I ran for the school board. . . . I couldn't let [them close our schools]. I had to do something about it. Some'll tell you I'm a bigmouth, and maybe I am. But the way I see it, people who don't look out after anything, who only think of themselves, are really missing out on life. . . . It's hard being involved. The meetings are long, and it takes you away from your kids. . . . [But] while I was looking out for me, I was looking out for everybody else, too. Especially those kids.**

From *Best Intentions* by Robert Sam Anson

VIEWS OF NOTED AMERICANS

Barbara Jordan

Barbara Jordan has never let difficulties keep her from achieving her goals. She has been a Texas state senator, a member of Congress, and is now a college professor. Each success has been, to Jordan, "just another milestone I have passed; it's just the beginning."

Barbara Jordan grew up in Houston, Texas, in the 1940s and 1950s when there were still separate schools for blacks and whites. During her senior year in an all-black high school, she worked hard to be the best in her class. She was president of the National Honor Society, a star debater, and winner of many academic awards and honors. She also participated in a number of community projects. As a result she won her school's "Girl of the Year" award.

In 1956 Jordan entered Boston University School of Law, where she met the challenge of being one of only two women and a handful of blacks in her class. After graduating in 1959, Jordan returned to Houston to practice law, eager to use her free time in community service. After volunteering with the Democratic party in the 1960 election campaign, she declared that she "had really been bitten by the political bug."

Politics, Jordan decided, offered the best opportunity to make government respond to the needs of the people. Therefore, she decided to run for political office. In 1966 Barbara Jordan passed another milestone when she was elected to the Texas State Senate.

Jordan's next goal was a seat in the United States House of Representatives, which she won in 1972. There she earned respect for her hard work and thoughtful decisions. In 1976 she was honored by being invited to give the opening speech at the national convention of the Democratic party.

In 1978 Jordan decided not to run for re-election. Her work in politics, however, is far from over. As a teacher, speaker, and writer, she continues to present her ideas about political issues. She tells her students that every American should take citizenship responsibilities seriously, because "the stakes are too high for government to be a spectator sport."

our political process. For example, as citizens we vote for people who will represent us in government, and some of us agree to hold elected or appointed office ourselves. We also work alone or with others to influence government policies and decisions.

Voting. The right to vote is one of the basic rights of American citizens. It is also one of our most important responsibilities. We vote for representatives at all levels of government, from President of the United States to members of the local school board.

Discussion: Barbara Jordan ran for political office so that she could make the government respond to the needs of the people. Have students discuss other ways citizens can make the government respond to needs.

In addition, in our states and our local communities citizens are often asked to vote on issues. We may be asked to make decisions about such public issues as building schools, changing taxes, or protecting wilderness areas.

To make good decisions and vote wisely, citizens have the responsibility to inform themselves. You can get information by reading, asking questions, and discussing the candidates and issues with other people. It is always important, when preparing to vote, to try to separate facts from opinions, and to try to base your decisions on reasons and not on personal likes and dislikes.

Holding government office. The people who agree to hold government office are fulfilling another important responsibility of citizenship. They have accepted the responsibility of learning about the issues and trying to make decisions that are in the best interests of the people they represent.

Citizens who hold office include our elected city council members, mayors, governors, and state and national representatives and senators. They also include appointed officials, such as members of local water boards and planning commissions, as well as advisors to the President.

Helping with election campaigns. Although there are age requirements for voting and for holding political office, most of the voluntary responsibilities of the "office of citizen" do not depend on age. One of the important ways to fulfill the responsibilities of a citizen is to help a ***candidate***—a person running for office—with his or her election campaign.

You may be aware that getting elected to government office is not always easy. Often the candidate must face stiff competition. Listen to Bernice:

> *When my father ran for election to the Kansas state House of Representatives, our neighbors really helped out. They wrote letters, made phone calls, and knocked on doors, telling people about my father and what a good representative he would be for our area.*
>
> *When my father gave speeches, his campaign workers were there, handing out information. And on election day they went around, reminding people to vote and even driving them to their voting place. Thanks to them he was elected.*

There are a number of ways that, as a teenager, you might help a candidate. They include carrying a campaign sign at a rally, stuffing envelopes with information to send to voters, and going door-to-door to encourage people to vote for your candidate.

Influencing government. Another way you can fulfill the "office of citizen" is to work to get the government to take action in a cause you believe in. Citizens of any age can influence the government by expressing their opinions in letters to elected representatives and to newspapers, and by speaking at city council and school board meetings.

You can also join or create an organization with a goal of influencing government actions. Here is Peter's experience:

> *At home and in our restaurant, my family has always been very careful to recycle bottles, cans, and newspapers. We have read that if we don't save our resources, the earth may run out of them.*
>
> *Last year some friends and I noticed that the trash cans in the school lunchroom were overflowing with cans and bottles that kids had thrown away. We talked to the principal about it. He suggested that we organize a committee and look into ways to set up recycling at the school.*

Eighteen-year-olds were given the right to vote by the Twenty-sixth Amendment, ratified in 1971. However, in the 1988 presidential election, only 33.2 percent of 18- to 20-year-olds voted—the fewest number of actual voters for any age group.

Teaching Note: Use the Enrichment Activity, page T 46, and accompanying worksheet in the Activity Book after students have read the material in Section 3-2.

We talked to kids at other schools in the city, and they organized recycling committees, too. Then we went to the school board and asked them to provide special bins for cans and bottles. The committees are working out details with the school board now, and we hope to have our recycling project underway soon.

Peter and his friends convinced their government representatives—in this case, the members of the school board—to take an action the students thought was important for their community. They did it by forming an organization and working together.

Serving the community. Not all of the responsibilities of citizenship are directly connected with government. Each of us is responsible for doing whatever we can to make our communities better places to live in.

When you listen with respect to the opinion of a person who disagrees with you, and when you make a new student feel welcome in your school or pick up a candy wrapper someone else dropped on the sidewalk, you are acting as a responsible citizen. You are fulfilling the "office of citizen" by contributing to the common good.

Answers will be found on page T 46.

Section Review

1. Define *jury of peers, witnesses, the common good,* and *candidate.*
2. List at least four rights of American citizens.
3. What are four duties that every American is required to fulfill at some time?
4. What are three of the responsibilities of citizenship?

Analysis. Choose one of the responsibilities of citizenship and explain how fulfilling it helps contribute to the common good.

3-3

CITIZENSHIP AND OUR OTHER ROLES IN SOCIETY

Read to Find Out

- what the term *social roles* means.
- how roles can change in different situations and at different times.
- how each of us plays more than one role at a time.
- why you sometimes have to choose between roles, and how you make such choices.
- in what ways you can play the citizen role.

Doris Hollingsworth leads a busy life. Here is how she described a typical day:

This morning at breakfast I was looking through the newspaper to find out what the mayor had had to say about the need for more stop signs at the intersections near the school. Then my daughter rushed in, asking if I would drill her for her French vocabulary test. I barely had time to rinse out my coffee cup before I heard a horn tooting outside. It was my car-pool. I really had to dash.

At work I had a conference with my boss and then sat down with three co-workers to decide how to organize our new project. Luckily, by noon, things had calmed down, and I had time for lunch with two old college friends.

After work I picked up a few groceries at the supermarket. When we finished dinner, my husband and I watched a ballgame on TV. Then I finished the reading assignment for my class tomorrow evening. Finally, the two of us took a stroll around the neighborhood before we turned in for the night.

Challenge (Evaluation): Have the class agree or disagree with the following statement: Students should do one year of service to their country after graduating from high school. Students should provide reasons for their opinions and identify the services a teenager could perform.

In the course of her day, Doris acted as a citizen, a family member, a member of a social group, a worker, a friend and a consumer. She also acted as her own person—her self—in making choices throughout the day.

Playing Social Roles

When you think of the word *role*, you may think of an actor playing a role in a film or play. Doris plays roles, too. However, her roles are called ***social roles***, which are roles people play in real life.

When Doris helped her daughter with her homework, she was playing the mother role. Having dinner, watching television, and taking a walk with her husband were part of her wife role. The roles of mother and wife are both part of Doris's family member roles.

As a carpool member and a student, Doris was playing social group roles. The social groups of which we are members can range in size from small to large. Two people painting a poster for the school dance make up a social group. Other examples of social groups are all students, all workers, and all women.

When she was reading the newspaper, Doris was playing the citizen role by informing herself on a government issue. She played a worker role when meeting with her boss, a friend role at lunch with old friends, and a consumer role when she shopped for groceries. Finally, as she played all her roles, Doris was also playing the self role. She was guided by a sense of who she is as a person.

Our many social roles. Like Doris, you play many different social roles in the course of a day and in the course of your life. Some roles you play because you were born into them. Some you play because you are required to play them. Some roles you choose for yourself.

You were born into your family, where you may play several roles: son or daughter, sister or brother, grandchild, cousin, and so on. At this point in your life, you are required to be a student. Therefore, you are playing a role as a member of that social group. Later, you may be required to pay taxes and serve as a juror, which are citizen roles. Roles you choose now may include being a friend, being a member of a club, and being a consumer.

Roles as expected behaviors. In each of your roles you behave differently. What causes you to act the way you do when you are playing a certain role? Partly, your behavior is determined by a set of expectations that people have of how someone in that role should act.

A cheerleader, for example, is expected to wear school colors and to jump, dance, and lead the crowd in school cheers. A member of the marching band is expected to wear a uniform and to know the music and the marching formation. If you want to be a member of a group, you will make an effort to learn the expected behaviors for that group.

The Seven Social Roles

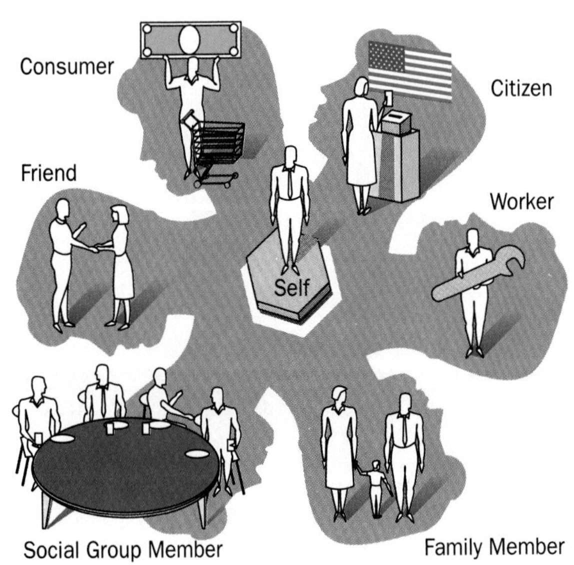

The way you play a role also depends on how you want to play it, and on the kind of person you are. People who know you begin to expect certain behaviors from you when you play your roles. A brother may always grumble when it is his turn to do the dishes. On the other hand, he may be the kind of brother who volunteers to do the dishes for his sister when he sees that she has too much homework.

Changing Roles

You may notice that sometimes a person plays the same role in different ways, depending on the situation. In Chapter 2 you read about Peter Ky and three of his friends. For Peter, playing the role of friend to Carol, Alex, and Melissa includes acting sympathetic, sharing biology notes, and going to the beach. Peter plays the friend role differently with Jerry. Jerry and Peter both like to read science fiction novels, and when these two friends get together, it is often to swap books and talk about their favorite authors.

Roles can also change over time. Bernice Kelman has been a daughter and a wife. However, since the death of her parents and her divorce, she no longer plays those roles.

The way Bernice plays her role as a mother has changed, too. Once she fed her babies and changed their diapers. Later she helped them make Halloween costumes, attended their track meets and school plays, and made sure they had finished their homework. Today her children are adults, living in other states. She now writes them letters, sends them presents on their birthdays, and gets together with them for family reunions.

Overlapping Roles

As you think about your many roles, you will realize that sometimes you are playing more than one at the same time. In such cases, you can say that two or more of your roles overlap.

When Peter gets together with Carol, Alex, and Melissa to study for a biology test, he is playing two roles, friend and student, at the same time. When he fulfills his father's expectation that he will recycle their restaurant's bottles and cans, he is performing the son's role in his family. At the same time, he is playing a citizen role, serving the common good by protecting the environment.

Bernice's roles of daughter and citizen overlapped when she helped her father in his election campaign. In Doris's job as computer programmer she fulfills roles as both a worker and a family member since her salary helps support her family.

Conflicting Roles

Sometimes it is easy to play more than one role at a time. At other times, however, you find that the demands of your roles are in conflict with each other. Consider the following situations:

- You want to go to the school dance, but you have already agreed to take a babysitting job that night.
- Your best friend manages to get tickets to a rock concert tomorrow, but your stepmother reminds you that your grandmother is arriving for a visit.
- It is your night to cook dinner for the family, but your big term paper is due in the morning.
- You do not need a new pair of jeans, but everyone you know is buying the latest brand.

In each of these cases, two of your roles are in conflict, forcing you to make a difficult de-

Challenge (Synthesis): Have students discuss which social roles have the greatest importance in their lives now. Then have them discuss which roles will have greatest importance in their lives in 20, 40, and 60 years.

cision. In the first case, your social group role is in conflict with your worker role. What roles are in conflict in the other situations? How will you decide what to do?

Making choices in situations like these is not easy. It requires you to think about the consequences of each possible behavior. Often, being aware of the values that guide your behavior in each role can be helpful. For example, it may help you to choose whether or not to buy the popular jeans if you realize that you are weighing the value "it is not good to spend money on items I do not really need" against the value "being accepted by the social group that wears the latest fashions is important to me."

Many teenagers volunteer as part of their citizen role. This girl works with a group that provides information and advice to other teenagers.

Level of Participation

As you play your social roles, you will often have to make choices about how actively you want to participate in a role at any given time. These choices, too, are based on your values and your sense of what is most important to you at the time. If you think that there are not enough social activities at your school, what can you do? You can do nothing, or you can get a group of students to help you plan a dance, hire a band, sell tickets, and decorate the gym. The course of action you choose will depend on how much time and energy you are willing to devote and how important it is to you to achieve a certain result.

You have a choice about your level of participation. However, you must realize that you will have to take the consequences of participating or deciding not to participate. In the case of the school dance, if you do nothing, you will have no activity, or perhaps someone else will plan an activity you do not enjoy. If you choose to take an active role, you are likely to have the kind of school activity you enjoy. Most people find that when they participate fully in a role, they feel satisfaction and get a better sense of who they are as a person.

Playing the Citizen Role

Earlier in this chapter, you learned the importance of the "office of citizen" in American society. In fulfilling that office, you are playing a very important role: the citizen role.

Some of the behaviors that people expect of citizens in our society include obeying the laws and paying taxes. These are the required duties of citizenship. The rest of the behaviors we expect of citizens are the voluntary activities, such as voting, running for office, and organizing to influence government actions.

Choosing citizen activities. For some people, playing the citizen role has high priority. When faced with a conflict between roles, they choose to devote more of their time and energy to the "office of citizen." These people, when they are students, are the ones who take

Teaching Note: There are more than 500,000 elected officials in all levels of government. For a breakdown, see page 586 in the Data Bank.

leadership roles in student government. They plan the school activities and work with the administration and the school board to solve school problems, as Peter Ky did with the recycling program.

Adults for whom the citizen role has high priority may run for government office. They may volunteer to serve on boards and committees that study government problems or plan for parks and recreation. They may devote much of their time to helping with political campaigns or working for organizations that try to influence government decisions.

Other people spend less time playing the citizen role. Some are satisfied simply to keep informed, to vote, or perhaps to give money to support candidates and issues.

As with your other roles, you cannot always participate in citizenship activities as actively as you might want to. For example, Peter Ky would like to be more active in student government. However, he knows that at this stage in his life, he needs to spend most of his time studying and helping in his family's restaurant.

Doris Hollingsworth has her hands full as a wife, mother, worker, and student. She says that she has very little time to devote to political activities just now.

AMERICAN NOTEBOOK

According to a study by the Independent Sector of Washington, D.C.:

- **80 million American adults participate in some form of volunteer work.**
- **45% of all Americans spend an average of 4.7 hours a week in volunteer work.**
- **Almost 50% of volunteers have full-time jobs outside the home.**
- **37% of volunteers report that they are spending more time as volunteers than they did three years ago.**
- **Women make up the largest group of volunteers, but the number of men who do volunteer work is increasing rapidly.**
- **There are four major reasons why people volunteer:**
  1. **They like the opportunity to do something useful.**
  2. **They enjoy the work.**
  3. **The work helps a family member.**
  4. **Volunteering supports their religious values.**

Contributing to the common good. Being a responsible citizen is not limited to participating in political activities, however. Earlier in this chapter you learned that the overall responsibility of every citizen in the United States is to contribute to the common good. Many people are making such a contribution to the common good when they play roles that they may not think of as citizen roles.

For example, Bernice Kelman helps at the church thrift shop. The money the shop raises goes to buy medicine and food for elderly people in the community. In this way, Bernice is contributing to the common good while playing a role in a social group in her church. In addition, helping others makes Bernice feel good about herself.

When Bernice was secretary to the superintendent of schools, she was playing a worker role. However, the work she did supported the town's efforts to educate its children. Therefore, Bernice was contributing to the common good in her role as worker. Although neither of these activities is political, they both make Bernice's community a better place to live.

Setting priorities for citizenship. How much time and energy will you devote to fulfilling

A famous contributor to the common good was Jane Addams, who founded Chicago's Hull House with Ellen Gates Starr in 1889. Hull House helped improve life in the slums by providing residents with medical care, education, and financial help.

Teaching Note: Use Teaching Activity 2, page T 45, as a culminating activity after students have read the material in this section.

your responsibilities as a citizen? This decision is one that you will make again and again in your life. Each time, that decision will be influenced by the other roles you are playing and how important they are to you. It will also be influenced by the stage of your life, by your values, and by your particular talents and interests.

Playing the citizen role in a political way may not always be a high priority for you. However, as a citizen you share the responsibility of all Americans to protect the basic values that unite us as a people and as a society. Therefore, if you choose *never* to play the citizen role, you are giving up your right to have a voice in your government and to make a difference in your community.

Answers will be found on page T 46.

Section Review

1. Define the term *social roles*.
2. Describe two different situations in which you play the role of student differently.
3. Give an example of a situation in which you play two overlapping roles.
4. What happens when a person's roles come into conflict with each other? Give an example.
5. Give two examples of how people behave when playing the citizen role.

Synthesis. What do you think might happen in your community if no one chose to perform the voluntary activities of the citizen role?

A BROADER VIEW

In this chapter you have been learning about what it means to be an American citizen. Do citizens of other nations have the same rights, duties, and responsibilities as we do? The answer to that question depends upon the type of government a nation has.

You might be a citizen of a nation governed by an absolute monarch, such as Saudi Arabia; by a dictator, such as Libya; or by a group or political party that has complete authority to make and enforce the laws, such as the Soviet Union. The government of that nation might provide the services you and its other citizens need. It might protect the rights it thinks its citizens should have.

As a citizen of such a nation, you might be loyal to it and willing to defend it against its enemies. However, the nature of your citizenship would be very different than it is in the United States. You would be a subject—a citizen who must abide by the government's decisions but who has no legal power to try to change them or to choose different government officials.

The United States is the first modern nation in which the citizens deliberately took the power into their own hands. They created a government system in which the people, rather than a monarch or dictator or ruling party, have the final power.

Therefore, as citizens we must take the responsibility to be well informed and to participate in government by holding office, by voting, and by working to make sure that everyone's rights are protected and that everyone's voice is heard.

In a speech he gave in 1952, Adlai E. Stevenson, a candidate for President said:

> *As citizens of this democracy, you are the rulers and the ruled, the lawgivers and the law-abiding, the beginning and the end.*

With these words, he summed up the meaning of American citizenship.

Teaching Note: Use the Reinforcement Activity, page T 45, and accompanying worksheet in the Activity Book.

The Process

Teaching Note: For reinforcement of decision-making skills, use Decision-Making Worksheet Chapter 3.

Taking Action

"Well, did you do what you said you were going to do?" Often, many of us have to answer "No" to this question.

Good decision making is not just a matter of choosing *what* to do. You have to plan *how* to do it and then *do* it. Otherwise you will be like someone who goes bowling and aims well but does not follow through. Your good decisions will roll into the gutter.

The lesson in Chapter 2 showed you the steps involved in the first part of the decision-making process: *choosing* which way to reach your goal. This lesson will focus on the second part of the decision-making process: *taking action*—doing what needs to be done to reach your goal. Creating a plan of action and following through with it are necessary in good decision making.

EXPLAINING THE PROCESS

One way to make an action plan is to follow these steps:

1. State your action goal. Your action goal is to carry out the decision you just made.

2. Identify resources (what will help you) and obstacles (what you will have to overcome). Knowing what you can use and what problems you might face will help you decide what has to be done.

3. List what you have to do to achieve your goal. Think about who will do what and when it will be done.

4. Carry out your plan. Check each step you take to see if what you are doing is getting you toward your goal. If necessary, change your plan.

5. Judge how well your plan worked. Identify the results of what you did, including any unexpected results. Determine what you might do differently if you used the plan again.

ANALYZING THE PROCESS

On page 40, you read about how the student council at Janice's school chose a way to achieve a clean campus. Now you will see how the members of the student council put their choice into action.

> Everyone was pleased with our decision to give buttons as rewards to students for helping to keep the school clean. However, before we had finished congratulating ourselves, the student council president reminded us that we were not done yet. "I know this button idea looks great," Chris said. "But we still have to make it work. We have to make sure that the buttons will get most students to keep the campus clean." So with that the student council got down to business.
>
> First, we thought of what might help us in putting our idea into action. Debbie thought that we could use the Pep Club's button-making machine and get free poster paper from the art teacher. But there were also some possible problems to deal with. For instance, as Rob warned, students might complain that exchanging buttons for ticket discounts was unfair to people paying full price. If enough students thought that the plan was unfair, it would fall apart very quickly.
>
> Now that we knew what would be useful and what might get in the way, we were ready to list things we needed to do, including using the available help and dealing with problems. Sharon and Raul would ask the principal for permission. Then Debbie would talk with the Pep Club president about using the button-making machine. Karen would develop a colorful button design.

Have students list other resources and obstacles that the student council might have found. Also, students might choose an option for dealing with a particular problem at school. Then they can identify resources and obstacles, as well as list what steps might be taken to achieve their goal.

To get students to support the idea of exchanging buttons for discounts, Tim and Rob would make rules showing that the buttons could be easily earned by any student. Eventually, our list of tasks covered everything from signing up teams and clubs as clean-up sponsors to recruiting students who would hand out buttons.

As our plan went into effect, we held several meetings to discuss our progress. Chris kept everyone's job flexible. For example, at first my task was to make morning announcements encouraging students to keep the campus clean. As the clean-up campaign got rolling, however, I began writing weekly reports for the school paper on the progress of the clean-up.

After a few weeks we knew that our plan was a success. The campus was free of litter, and the bathroom mirrors shone. Students were taking more pride in the school. There were also some results we had not expected. For example, instead of losing money by giving discounts to button holders, the school actually made *more* money. People who had complained about high ticket prices were now going to more dances and athletic events. The crowds were bigger than ever! We had helped school spirit in more ways than one.

One day Chris called us all together for another meeting and said, "Okay, our plan is working. Now what can we do to make it even better?" Diane suggested using several different button designs for variety. Then Ken came up with the idea of earning money for the school by recycling drink cans instead of throwing them in the trash. Right away we began thinking about how to include those suggestions in our clean-up plan.

CHECKING YOUR UNDERSTANDING

Now that you have read about the students' plan, answer the following questions.

1. What was the student council's action goal?

2. What did the students think might help them? What was one of the problems they expected? Explain.

3. Name at least three actions the student council took. Explain why each action was important.

4. The main sign of the plan's success was **(a)** attendance at dances and athletic events, **(b)** the support of the principal and teachers, **(c)** the clean campus. Explain your answer.

5. After judging how well their plan worked, the student council **(a)** made changes in it, **(b)** decided that it was no longer necessary, **(c)** started a new project. Explain.

REVIEWING THE PROCESS

6. How does the *acting* part of the decision-making process differ from the *choosing* part?

7. Explain why *acting* in decision making means more than just "doing something."

Have each student give examples of two decisions that he or she has carried out. For each decision ask the student to analyze what went right and why and what went wrong and why. Students may share their examples in small discussion groups.

CHAPTER SURVEY

Answers for Survey and Workshop will be found on page T 47.

UNDERSTANDING NEW VOCABULARY

Seeing Relationships

Match each numbered vocabulary term with the lettered word or phrase most closely related to it. Then explain how the items in each pair are related.

Example: *Social roles* is related to *friend* because being a friend is one social role you might play.

1. *naturalized*	**(a)** "office of citizen"
2. *the common good*	**(b)** trial
3. *jury of peers*	**(c)** immigrant
4. *candidate*	**(d)** election

Putting It in Writing

Explain why contributing to *the common good* is an important responsibility of citizenship.

LOOKING BACK AT THE CHAPTER

1. Describe the process of becoming a naturalized American citizen.

2. Explain what is meant by "government of the people, by the people, and for the people."

3. Choose three rights of citizens. Which basic values do they reflect?

4. Choose one of the five duties of citizens and explain why we are required to fulfill it.

5. Describe two ways that a person under age eighteen can fulfill the voluntary responsibilities of citizenship.

6. List five voluntary citizen activities that adults you know participate in.

7. Give two examples of situations in which you have played more than one role at the same time.

8. Give an example of a role you were born into, a role you are required to play, and a role you have chosen for yourself.

9. What is the basic responsibility of every citizen?

10. *Application.* As people play their social roles, they can contribute to the common good, and they can also interfere with the common good. Give two examples of each kind of behavior.

11. *Application.* Describe a situation in which you had to make a decision about which of two conflicting roles to play. What values did your choice reflect?

12. *Synthesis.* Imagine that someone said to you, "Why should I bother to vote? My one vote won't make a difference." How would you answer that person?

13. *Evaluation.* "In a democracy, the 'office of citizen' is the most important office there is." Do you agree with this statement? Explain why or why not.

WORKING TOGETHER

1. With three or four classmates, make a chart like the one below, listing all the social groups each of you is a member of. Which social group memberships do all the people in your group have in common?

Name	Social Groups
Peter Ky	males teenagers Asian Americans students recycling committee

2. Among a group of four or five classmates, choose one person who you will imagine is going to run for student president of your school. The rest of the group will serve as the candidate's campaign committee. Working together, create a plan for how you will get your candidate elected.

SOCIAL STUDIES SKILLS

Reading a Newspaper

One of your responsibilities as a citizen is to inform yourself about public issues. A good way to do this is to become a regular newspaper reader. Newspapers can provide you with a wealth of information about your community, state, nation, and world.

Most newspapers are divided into sections. The front section covers major news stories. This section may also include the editorial pages. Editorials express points of view on events and issues. Readers' opinions appear here in the form of letters to the editor.

Other sections may cover local news, sports, business, entertainment, life styles, food, and gardening. The classified section has listings of job openings, housing for sale and rent, and items for sale.

The front page of most newspapers has an index like the one below to help readers find specific information. In this index the letters and numbers refer to sections and to page numbers in a section. The comics, for example, are on D-7, or on page 7 in section D.

Index

Business	C-1	Sports	F-1
Classified ...	E-1	Local News . .	B-1
Comics	D-7	Television ...	D-5
Editorials . . .	A-10	Weather ...	B-10
Movies	D-2	World News . .	A-5

1. Where would you look for information about the following topics? **(a)** a new plan to improve parking in your city, **(b)** what readers think about the parking plan, **(c)** racial problems in South Africa, **(d)** where to buy a used bicycle, **(e)** how cold it will be tonight.

2. What is a likely name for section D?

3. In which two sections could an important local news story be located?

DECISION-MAKING SKILLS

Taking Action

In the profile of Barbara Jordan on page 52, you read about some goals that Jordan took action to achieve. Reread the profile to identify what her goals were and what were some of the steps she took toward reaching those goals. Consider what steps she might have taken that are not mentioned in the profile.

1. Name three goals that she set for herself.

2. Which of the following was probably NOT an obstacle for Jordan in her effort to become a lawyer? **(a)** the difficulty of law school admissions tests, **(b)** the fact that few women attended law school, **(c)** the fact that few blacks attended law school. Explain.

3. Which of the following was probably NOT an action that helped Jordan become Girl of the Year? **(a)** joining the debate club, **(b)** participating in community projects, **(c)** making as many friends as she could. Explain.

4. By serving in the Texas State Senate and in the United States House of Representatives, Jordan was *mainly* trying to achieve her goal of **(a)** using the training she had received in law school, **(b)** making government respond to the people's needs, **(c)** earning respect for blacks and women. Explain.

5. Which of the following was an unexpected result of Jordan's decision to help the Democratic party's candidates in 1960? **(a)** "being bitten by the political bug," **(b)** becoming a member of the House of Representatives, **(c)** earning a greater salary as a lawyer. Explain.

6. What are some useful steps to take in planning how to carry out a decision?

7. What is a step in action-planning that you think is particularly useful? Explain.

Martin Luther King, Jr.: "I have a dream"

Answers will be found on page T 48.

On August 28, 1963, more than 200,000 Americans gathered in Washington, D.C., to demand fair and equal treatment for black Americans. They assembled in front of the Lincoln Memorial to hear speeches by black leaders. One speaker was the Reverend Dr. Martin Luther King, Jr.

Inspired by the philosophy and achievements of Mahatma Gandhi of India, King had become a leader of nonviolent campaigns for black civil rights. Dr. King's speech has become a lasting statement of the civil rights movement. Here are highlights of that speech:

> Five score years ago, a great American . . . signed the Emancipation Proclamation [to free the slaves]. This momentous decree came as a great beacon light of hope to millions of Negro slaves. . . .
>
> But one hundred years later, we must face the tragic fact that the Negro is still not free. . . . The life of the Negro is still sadly crippled by . . . segregation and . . . discrimination. . . .
>
> When the architects of our republic wrote the magnificent words of the Constitution and the Declaration of Independence, they were signing a . . . promise that all men would be guaranteed the unalienable rights of life, liberty, and the pursuit of happiness.
>
> It is obvious today that America has [not kept her promise]. So we have come to . . . demand the riches of freedom and the security of justice. . . .
>
> We can never be satisfied as long as the Negro is the victim of the unspeakable horrors of police brutality . . . as long as the Negro's basic mobility is from a smaller ghetto to a larger one. . . .
>
> I say to you today, my friends, that in spite of the difficulties and frustrations of the moment I still have a dream . . . I have a dream that one day this nation will rise up and live out the true meaning of its creed: "We hold these truths to be self-evident; that all men are created equal."
>
> I have a dream that one day . . . the sons of former slaves and the sons of former slaveowners will be able to sit down together at the table of brotherhood . . . that my four little children will one day live in a nation where they will not be judged by the color of their skin but by the content of their character. . . .
>
> And if America is to be a great nation this must become true. . . . When we let freedom ring . . . from every state and every city, we will be able to speed up that day when all [people] . . . will be able to join hands and sing in the words of the old Negro spiritual, "Free at last! free at last! thank God Almighty, we are free at last!"

Abridged from I Have a Dream *by Martin Luther King, Jr. Reprinted by permission of Joan Daves.*

Analyzing Primary Sources

1. According to Dr. King, in what ways has the promise of the Declaration of Independence and the Constitution not been fulfilled?
2. Has Martin Luther King's dream been realized today? Explain.
3. How can individuals like you help make Dr. King's dream come true?

Activity: Martin Luther King, Jr. was well known for his great oratorical style. Play a recording of his "I Have a Dream" speech and ask for students' reactions. Play the recording again and have students discuss what makes this speech a lasting statement of the goals of the civil rights movement.

UNIT SURVEY

Answers will be found on page T 48.

LOOKING BACK AT THE UNIT

1. Is it possible to treat another person with equal respect even if you find that he or she has opinions or values different from your own? Explain your answer, giving examples.

2. What does it mean to you now to play a citizenship role in the United States? How do you think you might answer this question when you are an adult?

3. Explain how each of the following activities contributes to the common good: **(a)** voting in an election **(b)** recycling newspapers **(c)** expressing your views in a letter to the editor **(d)** treating a person with equal respect.

4. Match each social role listed below with the social institution that *most* affects you when you are playing that role.

1. son or daughter	**(a)** the economy
2. student	**(b)** government
3. citizen	**(c)** the family
4. consumer	**(d)** education

TAKING A STAND

The Issue

Should there be laws declaring English to be the official language of the United States?

Americans have always been proud of their diversity. Immigrants have brought their own languages, customs and religious practices to their new home. Yet each immigrant who wants to become a citizen of the United States has also needed to learn English in order to fulfill the requirements for naturalization.

Since 1980, the United States has had the second largest wave of immigration in its history. More than 14 million people have come to this country, and many of them did not know English when they arrived.

To help people who do not yet speak English, some states provide services and print important information, such as ballots and application forms, in other languages as well as English. Schools have set up bilingual programs, teaching students in both English and their native language, to help them adapt to their new country.

Some people think that using a language other than English endangers national unity. They want their states to pass laws that make English the official language of the United States. Such laws are often called "English-only laws." They would require that only English be used in any government-supported function. English-only laws could prohibit social workers and doctors in public clinics, for example, from using any language but English in their work.

The groups supporting English-only laws say that making English the official language would encourage immigrants to learn English faster than they might otherwise. Thus immigrants would become part of the American culture more quickly. The government would also save the money it now spends on providing important information in more than one language.

Opposing groups say English-only laws would discriminate against immigrants who have not yet learned English. Such laws would make it very difficult for non-English speakers to receive health and social services. Just because a person has not yet learned English, they say, is not a reason to deny that person equal rights.

Expressing Your Opinion

What do you think? Should English be made the official language?

Look in a newspaper to see how a letter to the editor is written. Then write your own letter to the editor stating your opinion on the issue. Give convincing reasons for your viewpoint.

UNIT 2

Unit Quotation: Experience with injustice led English-born Thomas Paine (1737–1809) to become a passionate believer in political freedom. His pamphlet *Common Sense* was the first clear call for separation of the American colonies from England and for the creation of a federal union.

CREATING A LASTING GOVERNMENT

A Government of Our Own

A government of our own is our natural right. It is infinitely wiser and safer to form a constitution of our own in a cool, deliberate manner, while we have it in our power, than to trust such an interesting event to time and chance.

—Thomas Paine, *Common Sense*, 1776

You have already read about our values, rights, and responsibilities as American citizens. One of our most basic values is freedom. Unlike the millions of people who live under the iron fists of dictators, our lives and the future of our nation lie in our own hands. To echo the words of the American patriot Thomas Paine, we truly have a "government of our own." However, as you know, our nation was not born without a struggle.

Unit 2 will explore the origins of our government. You will see how the colonists' beliefs about citizenship and government led to the creation of the Constitution that guides our nation today.

Chapter Themes: The American political heritage is rooted in the belief in government by consent of the people. That belief, based on Greek, Roman, and English traditions of government and the concept of natural rights, led to the American War of Independence.

CHAPTER 4

America's Political Heritage

The date was November 11, 1620. A lone ship, the *Mayflower,* had just anchored off the rugged Massachusetts coast. Aboard the vessel were 102 weary passengers. About half of them were Pilgrims seeking religious freedom. The others, whom the Pilgrims called "strangers," had made the stormy two-month voyage from England mainly to seek wealth.

Now, as they surveyed the bleak winter landscape, they faced a shocking fact: they were not where they were supposed to be! They had set sail for the colony of Virginia, but rough weather had driven their ship hundreds of miles northward to a rocky, unexplored coast.

Some of the "strangers" were glad not to have to obey the laws of the Virginia colony, and they therefore threatened to separate from the group. These threats frightened the Pilgrim leaders, who knew that everyone would need to work together to survive the harsh winter. Order had to be established—but how? Who would make the laws?

The men were called to an urgent meeting in the main cabin of the *Mayflower.* When they emerged from the cramped room, 41 of them had signed an agreement to make and obey "just and equal" laws for the "general good of the colony." This famous agreement is now known as the Mayflower Compact.

In a world in which most people had laws imposed upon them, the *Mayflower* passengers had made a written agreement to govern themselves. Over 150 years later, this agreement set an example for the founding of a nation—the United States of America.

This chapter will explore the origins of our American belief in government by consent of the people—a rare form of government in the history of the world. You will see how that belief grew in the colonies and eventually sparked the American Revolution. After reading this chapter, you will have a better understanding of where our American ideas about government and citizenship came from.

Teaching Note: Use the Introducing the Chapter activity, page T 50.

4-1
THE COLONIAL EXPERIENCE

Read to Find Out

- what the terms *heritage, legislature,* and *charter* mean.
- why the colonists had a voice in their government.
- what were the characteristics, rights, and responsibilities of colonial citizens.
- why religious freedom and freedom of the press became important issues in the colonies.

Many of the American traditions you read about in Unit 1—government by elected representatives, contributing to the common good, the love of freedom—took root during the colonial period. The values and experiences of the settlers in the 13 English colonies make up an important part of our ***heritage,*** the traditions passed down to us from generation to generation.

A Voice in Government

From the beginning, citizens in the 13 colonies were used to having a voice in their government. It was one of their rights as citizens of England. In each colony, citizens could elect representatives to the ***legislature***, a group of people chosen to make the laws. This gave them a degree of self-government that was rare in the world at that time. Unlike citizens of the Spanish and French colonies in the New World, they had a hand in making the laws that governed them.

The beginning of representative government in America can be traced back to the year 1619, when the colonists of Virginia elected representatives called burgesses. This first colonial legislature, the Virginia House of Burgesses, was soon followed by other legislatures as more colonies were founded.

The right to elect members of their legislature, however, did not give colonial citizens complete control of their government. They were still subject to the authority of England, whose monarch established each colony through a ***charter,*** a document giving permission to create a government. Any colony that seriously challenged England's authority might be stripped of its charter and become a royal colony under the control of the monarch, who appointed a royal governor.

In theory, England had final authority over the colonies, and the English legislature—called Parliament—could reject laws passed by colonial legislatures. However, throughout the 1600s and early 1700s England was busy fighting wars, and Parliament had little

AMERICAN NOTEBOOK 

A colonist did not cast his vote in the privacy of a voting booth as voters do today. Instead, he voted in full view of the candidates and other voters. One historian gives a picture of voting day at a county courthouse in Virginia:

> **At a table sat the sheriff, the candidates, and the clerk. The voters came up one at a time to announce their choices, which were recorded publicly. Since anyone present could always see the latest count, a candidate could at the last minute send supporters to bring in additional needed votes. As each voter declared his preference, shouts of approval would come from one side and hoots from another. The favored candidate would rise, bow, and express thanks to the voter.**

The London Company, a joint-stock company that received a charter to colonize North America, brought settlers to Virginia in 1607 and acted as government until 1619. Then company leaders, suggesting that settlers "have a hand in the governing of themselves," set up the House of Burgesses.

time to pay attention to colonial laws. Left on a loose leash, the colonists played a large role in governing themselves.

Preserving Rights

Used to having a voice in government, colonial citizens resisted any efforts to ignore their rights or to weaken their legislatures. Typically those efforts were made by colonial governors, who were usually appointed to their posts rather than elected, and who generally represented England's interests rather than those of the colonists. Some also represented proprietors—wealthy nobles or merchants who had been granted charters.

From time to time, the legislatures became involved in power struggles with colonial governors and proprietors. For instance, in 1624 the Virginia House of Burgesses declared that the governor could not tax citizens without the legislature's consent. In 1639 Lord Baltimore, the proprietor of Maryland, tried to make the Maryland Assembly approve all his proposed laws, but the legislature reacted by insisting that he respect citizens' rights. Similarly, in 1641 the Massachusetts legislature passed laws protecting basic rights, such as trial by jury.

Citizenship in the Colonies

Many of our American rights and traditions can be traced back to the colonial period. However, being an English citizen in the 1600s and 1700s differed in some important ways from being an American citizen today.

First of all, most people who can now vote in our country would have been denied that right in the English colonies. Usually only white men who owned a certain amount of land—typically 50 acres or a town lot—were allowed to vote or hold office. A common belief was that they were the people most affected by the laws. Also, only a wealthy man was thought to have enough education and free time to become involved in politics.

Colonial Settlement by Nationality in 1770. *America's cultural mosaic can be traced back to the colonial period. Over half of the colonists were non-English.*

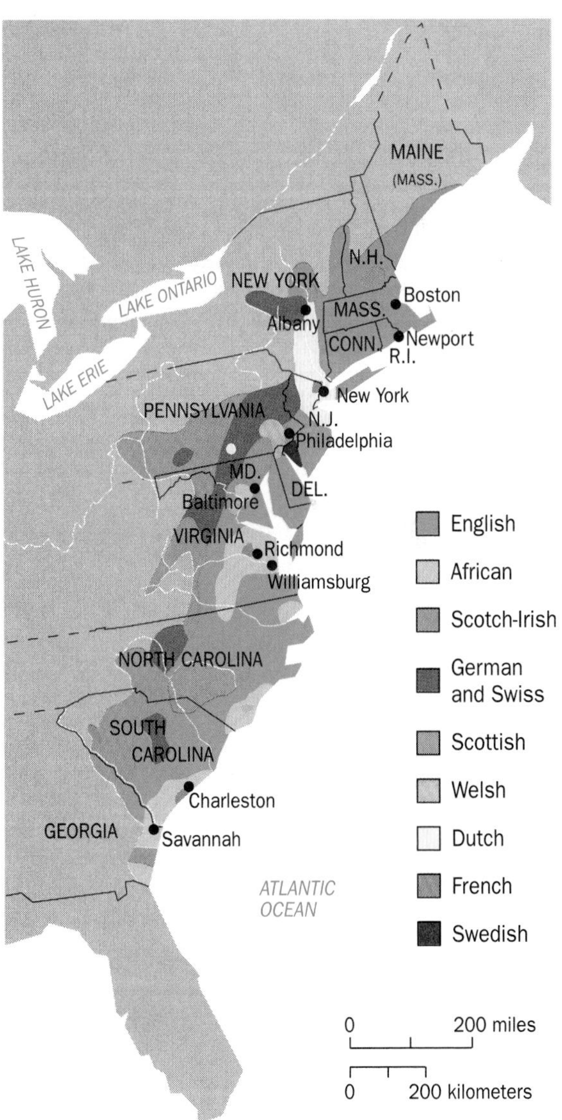

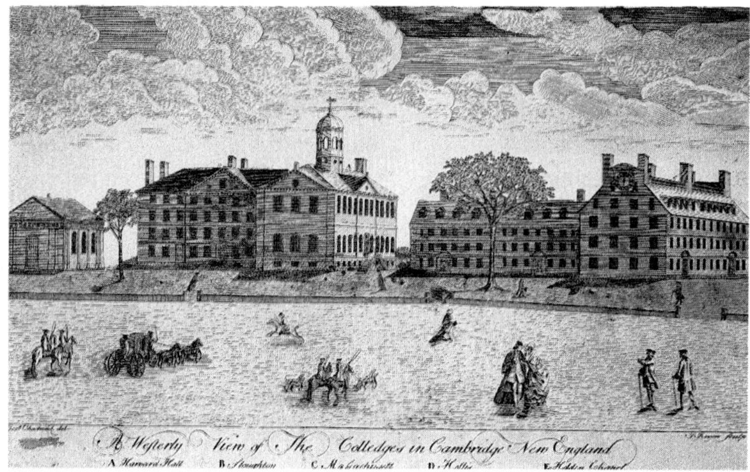

This metal engraving of Harvard College was made in 1767 by Paul Revere, who later became one of America's most famous patriots.

In no colony could enslaved persons vote. Colonial laws not only denied them the right to vote, but also treated them as property rather than as people. The European colonists wanted rights for themselves, but they denied rights to the Africans who were forced to come to the colonies as slaves.

Although it is important to recognize that relatively few people in the colonies were allowed to vote, we should also remember that citizens in most nations and colonies during the 1600s and early 1700s did not have any rights. Their lives were controlled by their governments. The English colonies in America were among the few places in the world where citizens actually participated in their government.

Contributing to the common good. Colonial citizens, like citizens today, had a responsibility to work for the common good. They helped their communities in various ways, such as constructing community buildings, serving on juries, and becoming members of the local militia, or volunteer army.

Citizens also served their communities by supporting education. For instance, the Puritans in New England set up a public school system to make sure that people could read and understand the Bible and colonial laws. Harvard College, the oldest university in the United States, was founded by the Puritans in 1636. In the middle and southern colonies, where there were few public schools, parents usually sent their children to private schools or taught them at home.

Some Roots of Freedom

We Americans have many freedoms. Among these are freedom of the press, freedom of speech, and freedom of religion. Such individual freedoms, however, were unknown for most of human history. They became part of our heritage mainly through the efforts of the colonists.

Toward greater religious freedom. The colonists lived at a time when religion was closely tied to government in most parts of the world. All English citizens, for instance, had to pay taxes to support the Anglican church as the official Church of England. Many colonists, including the Pilgrims on the *Mayflower* and the Puritans who founded the Massachusetts Bay Colony, had left England because they were persecuted for disagreeing with the Anglican church.

Although the Puritans had fled persecution in England, they denied religious freedom to

Challenge (Analysis): Colonists believed one of the purposes of government was to protect individual property rights; thus, the right to vote was limited to men who owned property. Have students discuss what arguments could be used to support or oppose this policy.

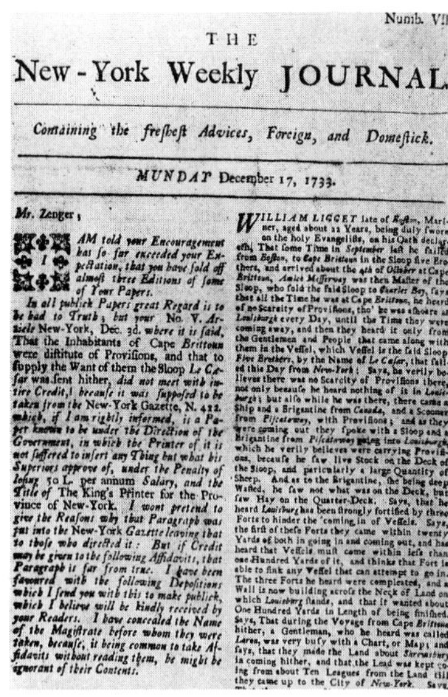

Numb. VII

THE

New-York Weekly JOURNAL

Containing the freſheſt Advices, Foreign, and Domeſtick.

MUNDAY December 17, 1733.

Mr. Zenger,

I *AM told your Encouragement has ſo far exceeded your Expectation, that you have ſold off almoſt three Editions of ſome of Your Papers.*

In all publick Papers great Regard is to be had to Truth; but your No. V. *Article* New-York, Dec. 3d. *where it is ſaid,* That the Inhabitants of Cape *Brittoun* were diſtitute of Proviſions, and that to ſupply the Want of them the Sloop *Le Caſar* was ſent hither, *did not meet with intire Credit, because it was ſuppoſed to be taken from the* New-York Gazette, N. 422. *which, if I am rightly informed, is a Paper known to be under the Direction of the Government, in which the Printer of it is not ſuffered to inſert any Thing but what his Superiors approve of, under the Penalty of loſing* 50 L. per annum *Salary, and the Title of* The King's Printer for the Province of New-York. *I wont pretend to give the Reaſons why that Paragraph was put into the* New-York *Gazette leaving that to thoſe who directed it: But if Credit may be given to the following Affidavits, that Paragraph is far from true. I have been favoured with the following Depoſitions which I ſend you with this to make publick, which I believe will be kindly received by your Readers. I have concealed the Name of the Magiſtrate before whom they were taken, becauſe, it being common to take Affidavits without reading them, he might be ignorant of their Contents.*

WILLIAM LIGGET late of *Boſton*, Mariner, aged about 22 Years, being duly ſworn on the holy Evangeliſts, on his Oath declareth, That ſome Time in *September* laſt he failed from *Boſton*, to *Cape Brittoun* in the Sloop five Brothers, and arrived about the 4th of *October* at Cape *Brittoun*, *Amice Mefferway* was then Maſter of the Sloop, who ſold the ſaid Sloop to *Charles Bay*, ſays that all the Time he was at Cape *Brittoun*, he heard of no Scarcity of Proviſions, tho' he was aſhoare at *Louisburgh* every Day, until the Time they were coming away, and then they heard it only from the Gentlemen and People that came along with them in the Veſſel, which Veſſel is the ſaid Sloop *Five Brothers*, by the Name of *Le Caſar*, that failed this Day from *New-York*: Says, he verily believes there was no Scarcity of Proviſions there, not only becauſe he heard nothing of it in *Louisburgh*; but alſo while he was there, there came a Ship and a Brigantine from *Canada*, and a Scooner from *Piſcataway*, with Proviſions; and as they were coming out they ſpoke with a Sloop and a Brigantine from *Piſcataway* going into *Louisburgh*, which he verily believes were carrying Proviſions, becauſe he ſaw live Stock on the Deck of the Sloop, and particularly a large Quantity of Sheep. And as to the Brigantine, ſhe being deep Waſted, he ſaw not what was on the Deck, but ſaw Hay on the Quarter-Deck. Says, that he heard *Louisburg* has been ſtrongly fortified by three Forts to hinder the coming in of Veſſels. Says, the firſt of theſe Forts they came within twenty Yards of both in going in and coming out, and has heard that Veſſels muſt come within leſs than one Hundred Yards of it, and thinks that Fort is able to ſink any Veſſel that can attempt to go in. The three Forts he heard were compleated, and a Wall is now building acroſs the Neck of Land on which *Louisburg* ſtands, and that it wanted about One Hundred Yards in Length of being finiſhed. Says, That during the Voyage from Cape *Brittoun* hither, a Gentleman, who he heard was called *Laren*, was very buſy with a Chart, or Map; and ſays, that they made the Land about *Shrewsbury* in coming hither, and that the Lead was kept going from about Ten Leagues from the Land till they came up to the City of *New-York*. Says,

An engraving (right) shows Andrew Hamilton boldly defending freedom of the press. Also shown is an early issue of John Peter Zenger's paper.

those who disagreed with them. They forced a minister named Roger Williams to leave their colony after he criticized church leaders. In 1644, Williams founded the colony of Rhode Island, promising that no colonist would be punished "for any differences in opinions in matters of religion." Before long, other colonies were following Rhode Island's example of allowing religious freedom.

Actually, the colonists' definition of "religious freedom" differed from our definition today. They usually meant that a person could belong to any Christian church, such as the Presbyterian or Anglican churches. They did not mean freedom for members of non-Christian religions. Nevertheless, considering the world in which they lived, the colonists were taking an important step—one that would eventually lead to freedom of religion for all Americans.

A call for freedom of the press. When the first colonial newspapers appeared in the early 1700s, they quickly became an important source of information. Freedom of the press, however, did not exist in England or in the English colonies. Under English law, a publisher was not allowed to criticize the government. A colonial governor could shut down a newspaper that criticized him and could even put the publisher in jail.

One of the earliest arguments for freedom of the press was made in 1735 in a crowded New York City courtroom. On trial was John Peter Zenger, the publisher of a four-page newspaper called the *Weekly Journal*. Zenger had printed articles accusing the New York governor of abusing his power by accepting bribes and interfering with elections. Furious, the governor had burned copies of the newspaper and had jailed Zenger, accusing him of trying to stir up rebellion against the government.

Zenger's lawyer, Andrew Hamilton, argued that Zenger was innocent if what he had written was true. The jury listened intently as Hamilton declared that freedom of the press was a basic right:

Religious freedom may have resulted from religious pluralism. During the colonial period, no religious group constituted a majority of the population. Therefore, it was impractical for any group to seek to establish itself as a national religion.

> The question before the court is not of small nor private concern. . . . It may in its consequence affect every free person that lives under a British government. It is the best cause. It is the cause of liberty, the liberty both of exposing and opposing arbitrary power by speaking and writing truth.

After hearing Hamilton's argument, the jury left the room to discuss the case. When the 12 jurors returned, the spectators leaned forward in their chairs. A member of the jury stood to announce the verdict. "Not guilty," he declared. Loud cheers filled the packed courtroom. Zenger was released from jail and went back to publishing his newspaper.

Although the verdict freed Zenger, it did not change English law and therefore it did not actually guarantee freedom of the press in America. However, the Zenger case did inspire other colonists to continue the fight for freedom of the press and to criticize governors who abused their power.

Signs of Discontent

By the mid-1700s, England had tightened its control over the colonies, making most of them royal colonies. Like Zenger, many colonists were angry at royal governors who used power without regard for citizens' rights. Some governors ordered citizens' homes to be searched without warning and kept accused persons in jail without a trial.

Zenger's lawyer had spoken of "arbitrary power," or abuse of power—which was more frequently called tyranny. As people complained about royal governors, the word *tyranny* was increasingly used throughout the colonies. A growing number of colonists began to wonder whether England might eventually try to strip them of their rights and silence their voice in government.

Answers will be found on T 52.

Section Review

1. Define *heritage, legislature,* and *charter.*
2. Why were colonial citizens able to influence the laws that governed them?
3. How were English citizens in the colonies similar to American citizens today? How were they different?
4. How are some of our freedoms rooted in the colonial period?

Evaluation. How well do you think the colonists practiced the values of freedom, justice, and equality? Explain.

Data Search. Look on page 584 in the Data Bank to answer the following questions. Approximately what percentage of the colonists were English? How does the information in the chart reflect the American cultural mosaic?

4-2

ROOTS OF AMERICAN GOVERNMENT

Read to Find Out

- what the terms *direct democracy, republic, natural rights,* and *separation of powers* mean.
- which roots of American government are found in ancient Greece and Rome.
- how the English tradition of government influenced American government.
- which European writers greatly influenced the colonists' ideas about government.

To understand how our country began, we must recognize that the American colonists had the benefit of other people's experiences and ideas about government. They learned much from the history of earlier societies that

Zenger remained in jail for eight months before his case came to trial. His *Weekly Journal*, however, continued to appear. It was printed by his wife, Anna Catherine, who managed to talk business with her husband through a hole in the jailhouse door.

This Roman coin, minted in 137 B.C., shows a citizen voting by dropping a ballot into a box. Roman ballots were wooden or stone tablets.

had tried to prevent tyranny. John Adams, who eventually became one of the founders of our nation, urged his fellow colonists to look to the past for inspiration:

> Let us study the law of nature; search into the spirit of the British constitution; read the histories of the ancient ages; [think about] the great examples of Greece and Rome; set before us the conduct of our own British ancestors.

Looking to Ancient Greece and Rome

What did John Adams mean by "the great examples of Greece and Rome"? First of all, he was thinking of the ancient Greek city of Athens. For hundreds of years, Athens and other Greek cities had been ruled by all-powerful kings. In time, the Athenians came to believe that the wisdom of all the citizens together was superior to the wisdom of one ruler.

Around 500 B.C., the Athenians created the world's first ***direct democracy***, a form of government in which laws are made directly by the citizens. The citizens of Athens met twice a year to discuss ways to make life better for their community. Centuries later the American colonists practiced direct democracy by holding town meetings to vote on local issues.

While town meetings mirrored Athenian-style direct democracy, the colonial legislatures resembled a representative form of government established in ancient Rome. In 509 B.C., the Romans founded a ***republic,*** a government in which citizens elect representatives to make laws. Instead of being ruled by a monarch, citizens of the Roman republic elected representatives called senators, who conducted the business of government.

As in Athens, citizenship in Rome was limited to wealthy men. However, because Rome had a large population spread over a vast area, representative government made more sense than direct democracy. This same practical reason gave rise to the representative government later used in England and in the colonial legislatures.

The English Tradition

The people in the English colonies saw the democracy of Athens and the republic of Rome as noble examples of governments designed to prevent tyranny. Unfortunately, those governments eventually gave way to government by force. The voices of citizens were replaced by the commands of monarchs, who often abused their power.

After the end of the Roman republic, government by the people disappeared for hundreds of years. Then, in the year A.D. 1215, a dramatic conflict took place in England—a conflict that changed the course of English history and laid the groundwork for the type of government we have today.

The Magna Carta. For centuries, monarchs had ruled with complete authority over the English people. Instead of being citizens with rights, the people were subjects—they were subject to the monarch's command. Although some monarchs used their powers in a wise

Challenge (Evaluation): With future inventions in telecommunication, people may be able to vote by computer or telephone. Have students discuss whether direct democracy could be possible with these inventions. Would direct democracy be positive for our society? Why or why not?

King John is surrounded by nobles and church leaders who forced him to sign the Magna Carta. A monument stands at the site of the signing.

and just manner, other monarchs were tyrants who stirred resentment among their subjects.

By the early 1200s, English nobles had become strong enough to challenge royal power. In 1215 they forced King John to sign the Magna Carta, or Great Charter, which listed rights that even the English monarch would not have the power to take away. Among these rights were the right to a fair trial and the right to travel freely.

The Magna Carta was an important step in gaining basic freedoms for all English people. For the first time the monarch's power had been limited. Although the document was intended to protect only nobles, the rights it listed were eventually given to all English citizens—including the colonists.

The English Bill of Rights. Once the monarch's power had been limited, a representative government soon followed. By the late 1200s, a legislature called Parliament was well established in England. Over the centuries, Parliament gradually became more powerful than the monarch.

In 1689, Parliament passed the English Bill of Rights, which has been called the "second Magna Carta" because it further limited the power of the monarch. For example, the king or queen would no longer be able to limit free speech in Parliament or to collect taxes without Parliament's approval.

The English Bill of Rights listed the rights of all English citizens, not just nobles. It included ideas that would later find a place in our government. One is that everyone, even government leaders, must obey the law. Another is that all people have the right to a trial by jury and the right to make a formal petition, or request, to the government.

By stating the rights of English citizens, both the Magna Carta and the English Bill of Rights provided protections against tyranny. The colonists in America treasured these protections of their rights.

Relying on Reason

After reading the quotation from John Adams at the beginning of this section, you may have wondered what he meant by urging his fellow colonists to "study the law of nature." Actually, he was echoing what a number of European writers were saying during the 1600s and 1700s: that people have the power of reason, the ability to think clearly. By using reason, these writers argued, people can recognize their ***natural rights,*** rights they are born with and that no government can take away.

One writer who particularly inspired the colonists was the Englishman John Locke. He argued that representative government is the only reasonable kind—that government exists for the people, not people for the government.

The English Bill of Rights also declared that excessive bail and fines and "cruel and unusual punishment" were illegal. A monarch could not keep a peacetime standing army without Parliament's consent, and Parliament was to meet regularly, not simply when a monarch called it into session.

Teaching Note: Use Teaching Activity 1, page T 50, as a culminating activity after students have read the material in Section 4-2.

According to Locke, the purpose of government is to protect natural rights—the rights to life, liberty, and property. Any government that abuses its power by interfering with those rights should not be obeyed.

Many colonial leaders were also inspired by the ideas of the French writer Montesquieu (mon-tes-KYOO). Since they knew that power could lead to tyranny, they liked his proposal for ***separation of powers***, dividing government power among legislative, executive, and judicial branches. The legislature would only make the laws; the executive, such as a governor, would only enforce the laws; the judges would only interpret the meaning of the laws. Such a system would guard against tyranny because no government official or branch of government could gain too much power.

The writings of John Locke (1632–1704) had so much influence that he has sometimes been called "the intellectual ruler of the eighteenth century."

Answers will be found on T 53.

Section Review

1. Define *direct democracy, republic, natural rights,* and *separation of powers.*
2. Describe which traditions in colonial government can be traced back to ancient Greece and Rome.
3. What did the colonists inherit from the English tradition of government?
4. What ideas of Locke and Montesquieu were important to the colonists?

Analysis. What similarities do you think the colonists saw in the Greek, Roman, and English traditions of government?

4-3 MOVING TOWARD NATIONHOOD

Read to Find Out

- what the terms *compact, constitution,* and *ratification* mean.
- why the colonies united in opposing English rule.
- how Americans established state and national governments after independence.
- why many Americans wanted a stronger national government.

If the colonists had inherited their tradition of representative government from England, why did they become dissatisfied with English rule? Why did relations between the colonies and England get worse, eventually exploding into the war that led to American independence? Answering these questions involves looking first at how tensions developed between England and the colonies over the issue of representation in government.

Teaching Note: Use the Reinforcement Activity, page T 52, and accompanying worksheet in the Activity Book after students have read Section 4-2.

A Clash of Views

England believed that Parliament represented all English citizens—including the colonists. The colonists, on the other hand, believed that they were only represented by their own legislatures. The colonists pointed out that they could not vote for members of Parliament and that no colonists were members themselves. They also noted that, unlike the colonial legislatures, Parliament had little understanding of the colonists' needs.

The colonists and the English government also had opposing views on colonial trade. Parliament permitted the colonies to trade only with England, and it tried to control prices of trade goods. The colonists wanted the freedom to sell their products to any country.

A 1765 tax on stamped paper, which had to be used for official documents, enraged colonists. Here they burn stamped paper in protest.

Despite these sharply differing views, many colonists still considered themselves loyal English citizens. In fact, they helped England defeat France in a war that lasted from 1754 to 1763. The colonists celebrated the victory, not knowing that their loyalty would soon be tested by new taxes forced on them by the English government.

"No Taxation Without Representation"

Facing huge war debts, Parliament decided to squeeze money out of the colonies through taxes, mainly on trade goods. Outraged, the colonists protested that they should not be taxed unless their own representatives approved such taxes. The colonists believed, following the ideas of John Locke, that taxation without representation was taking people's property without their consent. Soon the cry of "no taxation without representation" was heard throughout the colonies.

To make people pay the taxes, Parliament gave the governors greater power. Colonists accused of breaking tax laws were thrown in jail. Parliament ignored petitions protesting the taxes and the governors' actions, claiming that it had the power to make laws for the colonies "in all cases whatsoever." The cloud of tyranny seemed to be growing darker.

Steps Toward Independence

At first the colonies did not join together in protesting Parliament's actions. Having quarreled with each other in the past over boundaries and trade, they were not used to working toward a common goal. To inspire cooperation, some colonists organized Committees of Correspondence to pass news from colony to colony about how England was violating colonists' rights. Eventually many of the colonial legislatures saw the need for a united response to Parliament's threats. They called

The war between the French and the English, which the colonists called the French and Indian War, spread beyond North America to the Caribbean, Europe, Africa, and Asia. With the English victory, the French were driven from North America. England became the most powerful nation in the world.

Thomas Jefferson, at age 33, was chosen to draft the Declaration of Independence. He is shown here, presenting the document to the members of the Second Continental Congress.

for a congress, or formal meeting, of representatives from all the colonies.

In 1774, delegates from 12 colonies met in Philadelphia for the First Continental Congress. The delegates hoped to convince the English government to respect colonists' rights. To pressure Parliament, they pledged to cut off all trade with England. Then they agreed to meet the following year if the situation did not improve.

Far from improving, the situation got worse. By the time the Second Continental Congress met in 1775, colonists in Massachusetts were already fighting English soldiers. Some delegates argued for independence, stating that the war had already begun and that there was no turning back.

Many colonists feared independence, however. No European colony had ever separated from its parent country. Even if they fought and won, they thought, what future would they face without the security of being part of a strong nation like England?

The writings of Thomas Paine changed many people's minds. In 1776, Paine published a pamphlet titled *Common Sense*, in which he presented his argument:

> To be always running 3,000 or 4,000 miles with a tale or a petition, waiting four or five months for an answer which, when obtained, requires five or six more [months] to explain it in, will in a few years be looked upon as folly and childishness—there was a time when it was proper, and there is a proper time for it to cease. There is something absurd in supposing a continent to be perpetually governed by an island. England [belongs] to Europe. America to itself.

The Declaration of Independence

With popular support for separation from England increasing, the delegates to the Second Continental Congress finally voted for independence. However, they still had to convince some Americans of the wisdom of a break with England. The delegates also wanted to tell European countries why the colonies deserved to be free. Therefore, they appointed a committee to write a declaration of independence. Among the committee members were Thomas Jefferson, Benjamin Franklin, and John Adams. Jefferson was asked to do the actual writing.

The name "United States of America" was first used officially in the Declaration of Independence. During the revolution, "United Colonies" was used rather than "United States." George Washington wrote "U.S." in 1791, and within a few years "U.S.A." came into use.

The ringing phrases of the Declaration of Independence capture many of the colonists' beliefs about natural rights:

> We hold these truths to be self-evident, that all men are created equal, that they are endowed by their Creator with certain unalienable rights, that among these are life, liberty, and the pursuit of happiness.

As did John Locke, Jefferson described these rights as "unalienable"—meaning that no government has the power to take them away.

Further reflecting Locke's views, Jefferson described the purpose of government:

> . . . to secure these rights, governments are instituted among men, deriving their just powers from the consent of the governed.

In other words, the people give power to their government as long as it protects their rights. If a government abuses its powers, the people may change it or do away with it:

> . . . whenever any form of government becomes destructive of these ends, it is the right of the people to alter or to abolish it, and to institute [create] a new government.

Jefferson then listed the ways in which England had ignored the colonists' rights as English citizens—proof that England was trying to rule the colonies with "absolute tyranny."

The Declaration concludes with the signers pledging to support it "with our lives, our fortunes, and our sacred honor." Adopted by representatives of the colonists in Philadelphia on July 4, 1776, the Declaration of Independence proclaimed that "these united colonies are and of right ought to be free and independent states."

The full text of the Declaration of Independence will be found on pages 86–87.

Organizing a New Government

Now that the colonies had become "free and independent states," each of them had to organize a government of its own. Because the colonies had been established by charters, people were used to the idea of having a written plan of government. People also remembered that the *Mayflower* passengers had made a ***compact***, a written agreement to make and obey laws for the welfare of the group.

State constitutions. The newly independent states wanted to continue this tradition of basing governments on written agreements. Therefore each state legislature created a ***constitution***, or plan of government. By creating written constitutions, the states were clearly spelling out the limits on government power. Some state constitutions also included a list of citizens' rights, such as trial by jury and freedom of religion. A few even provided for ways to change the constitution if necessary.

To help guard against tyranny, each state constitution limited the number of years a governor could hold office. The states wanted to make it clear that a governor could not be like a king who holds office for life. As a further protection against abuse of power, each state used Montesquieu's idea of separating government into legislative, executive, and judicial branches. Of the three branches, the legislature was given the most power because it most directly represented the interests of citizens.

The Articles of Confederation. Although the states were united in opposing England, they were still 13 separate governments. During the war against England, the delegates to the Second Continental Congress debated about how to form a national government.

The delegates faced a difficult task. Conflicts with the English king and Parliament

Challenge (Analysis): Have students discuss what rights the colonists had claimed as English citizens. Why would these rights still be important after independence was gained?

PEOPLE MAKE A DIFFERENCE

Citizen Seeks Memorial to Black Patriots

Maurice Barboza has an ambitious goal. Since 1984 he has led an effort to establish a memorial to African Americans who fought in the Revolutionary War and to the thousands of black slaves seeking freedom at that time. Gathering support for his idea, he started a volunteer organization—the Black Revolutionary War Patriots Foundation in Washington, D.C.

In working toward his goal, Barboza has been particularly inspired by his own heritage, having traced his family's roots back 11 generations to a Revolutionary War soldier. He wants to make sure that present and future generations will not ignore or forget the many African Americans who gave their lives to create our nation.

Black soldiers fought in every major battle from Lexington and Concord to Yorktown because they viewed the Declaration of Independence as a crucial opportunity to attain freedom and equality. "These black patriots fought a dual battle for independence," Barboza says. "They fought for American independence from the British . . . but they were also fighting for their own independence from slavery."

The quest for the memorial has been a long one. Even after he won support from Congress and the President in 1986, Barboza's work had just begun. He still had to get government officials to approve a location for the memorial.

After nearly two years of discussions, he finally received approval for his first choice: a special place of honor between the Washington Monument and the Lincoln Memorial in Washington, D.C.

Now Barboza is tackling his next challenge: raising the $4 million needed to build the memorial. He is confident, however, that the memorial will become a reality, one which will remind all Americans that blacks "participated in the Revolution and struggled for freedom and the principles on which this nation was founded."

had made the colonists fearful of giving power—especially the power to tax—to a central government. Also, the states disagreed on how many representatives each one should have in the government. Large states like Virginia wanted the number of representatives to be based on population. Small states like Rhode Island were afraid that the large states, with more representatives, would then have too much power. They argued that each state should have the same number of votes.

In 1777, after long and heated debate, the Continental Congress drew up a plan for a loose confederation, or alliance of independent states. This compact, known as the Articles of Confederation, called for a national legislature in which each state would have one vote. There would be no executive or judicial branches of government, mainly because the state legislatures feared that these branches might try to take power away from them.

Activity: Have students find out about public memorials in their community and then discuss how accurately these memorials represent the community and the nation. What memorials do students feel should be added? Why?

In 1787, Shays' army of farmers marched on a government arsenal in an attempt to get guns. The Massachusetts state militia opened fire, forcing the farmers to retreat.

The national legislature, known as Congress, was given power to declare war, make treaties with foreign countries, and work out trade agreements between states. However, it was *not* given the power to tax or to enforce any laws it made. Therefore, most of the power would remain with the states.

Before the Articles of Confederation could go into effect, they needed the ***ratification,*** or approval, of all 13 states. At first it seemed the states would reject the plan because many state legislatures still did not trust a central government. Even though the Revolutionary War was raging, it took four years for the states to agree on a plan of government. Finally, the states realized that they had to cooperate or lose the war. The Articles were ratified in 1781.

A Limping Government

You know the story of how the patriots under General George Washington won our independence in the Revolutionary War. However, after winning the war the new government had to face another challenge: a struggling economy. Congress and the states had borrowed money to buy war supplies. Now they could not pay off these huge debts because they did not have enough gold and silver to back up their printed money. Many Americans and foreigners lost confidence in the value of American money.

Another problem was that the new Congress had no power to regulate trade with England. Americans were buying most of their manufactured goods from England because prices were low. American merchants could not sell their goods as cheaply as the English. Congress could not help because it did not have the power to raise the prices of English goods by taxing them. Furthermore, England no longer allowed Americans to trade with English colonies in the Caribbean, one of the most important markets for American crops and manufactured goods.

Shays' Rebellion. Many farmers slid into debt, largely because they could not sell their crops to the Caribbean colonies. Farmers in Massachusetts faced an added problem. To pay its war debts, the state legislature had sharply raised taxes on land. Many farmers who were unable to pay the taxes faced loss of their farms. Local courts threatened to sell the farms and use the money to pay the taxes.

Decision Making: Have students place themselves in the position of American leaders trying to decide on a type of national government. Have them list options and discuss the possible consequences of each option.

Teaching Note: Use Teaching Activity 2, page T 51, after students have read the material in this section.

In 1786, hundreds of angry Massachusetts farmers, led by a former war hero named Daniel Shays, stormed into courthouses to disrupt court business. In some cases they set fire to the buildings. Congress did not have the power to force other states to help put down the uprising. Massachusetts had to use its own state militia to crush the rebellion.

Newspapers quickly spread word of the violent clash, which shocked people throughout the states. Many Americans called for a stronger national government, one that would keep law and order and solve the economic problems that had led to Shays' Rebellion. George Washington thought that the Articles of Confederation had crippled Congress, leaving it unable to keep order, raise money through taxes, or deal effectively with European nations. What he saw was a "half-starved, limping government, always moving on crutches, and tottering at every step."

Most Americans agreed that the 13 proud and independent states would have to face the challenge of establishing a stronger government. Their future was at stake.

Answers will be found on page T 53.

Section Review

1. Define *compact, constitution,* and *ratification.*
2. Why did the colonies rebel against England?
3. After declaring independence, how did the Americans organize their state and national governments?
4. Why did many Americans think that the national government under the Articles of Confederation was too weak?

Analysis. How did the experience under English rule make it difficult for Americans to form a strong national government?

A BROADER VIEW

Building on the English tradition, our ancestors established a government that was unique in its time. Nowhere else was there a government so dedicated to protecting the rights of citizens. The American example inspired other revolutions against tyranny, most notably the French Revolution in 1789. The days of powerful monarchs were numbered.

Although the nineteenth and twentieth centuries have seen the decline of powerful monarchs, they have not seen the end of tyranny. Monarchs are not necessarily tyrants and tyrants are not necessarily monarchs. Tyranny simply refers to any cruel and unjust use of power by a government. Hitler's Nazi dictatorship is an example of a tyrannical government of the twentieth century.

More recent examples of tyranny have been the governments of military dictators in a number of Latin American, African, and Asian countries. Over the past 20 years, perhaps the most notorious dictators were Idi Amin of Uganda and Pol Pot of Cambodia, both of whom brutally killed hundreds of thousands of citizens who opposed their governments.

The success of our representative government in the United States continues to demonstrate that government by consent of the people provides the best protection of citizens' rights and the best defense against abuse of power. As long as citizens control their government by carefully electing its leaders, they can prevent it from ever controlling them.

Teaching Note: Use the Evaluating Progress activity, page T 51, to assess students' understanding of the chapter and the Enrichment Activity, page T 52, and accompanying worksheet in the Activity Book.

CHAPTER SURVEY

Answers to Survey and Workshop will be found on page T 53.

UNDERSTANDING NEW VOCABULARY

Seeing Relationships

The vocabulary terms in each pair listed below are related to each other. For each pair, explain what the two terms have in common. Also explain how they are different.

Example: A *legislature* and a *monarch* are similar because they both make laws. They are different because a legislature is elected and a monarch inherits power.

1. *compact* and *constitution*

2. *direct democracy* and *republic*

Putting It in Writing

Write a paragraph explaining how each of the following is part of our heritage as Americans: *direct democracy*, *republic*, and *constitution*.

LOOKING BACK AT THE CHAPTER

1. How did self-government become part of our heritage as Americans?

2. Explain why few people in colonial America had the rights of citizenship.

3. What are some ways in which colonial citizens were similar to citizens today?

4. Explain how freedom of religion in the colonies differed from freedom of religion in the United States today.

5. Explain how each of the following influenced American government: **(a)** the governments of ancient Athens and Rome, **(b)** the history of English government, **(c)** the ideas of Locke and Montesquieu.

6. Why did many colonists think that Parliament did not provide them with representative government?

7. Describe the view of government expressed in the Declaration of Independence. In your explanation, note how Locke's ideas influenced the Declaration of Independence.

8. Explain why the legislatures of the newly independent states thought that it was important to write state constitutions.

9. Why did the national government under the Articles of Confederation have little power?

10. Why did many Americans want a stronger government?

11. *Analysis.* Why can it be said that the colonists were more committed to the value of freedom than to the values of justice or equality?

12. *Analysis.* Explain how the American Revolution resulted from the ideas colonists brought from England and from their experiences after settling in America.

13. *Evaluation.* Do you think that the American Revolution was unavoidable? Explain your answer.

WORKING TOGETHER

1. Work in a group to write a dialogue between a citizen of colonial America and a citizen today. The dialogue should show the similarities and differences between citizenship then and now.

2. Work in a group to put on a mock trial of John Peter Zenger. Members of your group should play the following roles: Zenger, Andrew Hamilton, the governor of New York, the governor's lawyer, witnesses, and a judge. The rest of the class will play the role of the jury.

3. Work in teams to prepare a debate on Shays' Rebellion. One side can argue in favor of the farmers, explaining why they had a right to rebel. The other side can argue in favor of the government, explaining why it had a right to put down the rebellion. Both sides of the debate should make comparisons between Shays' Rebellion and the Revolutionary War.

Teaching Note: For reinforcement of decision-making skills, use Decision-Making Worksheet Chapter 4.

SOCIAL STUDIES SKILLS

Interpreting Political Cartoons

Freedom of the press extends not only to words but also to political cartoons, pictures that make a point about events in the news. Political cartoons, which are usually found on the editorial pages of newspapers, are often funny but also communicate serious messages. They usually get their point across through symbols—drawings of people, animals, or objects that stand for something else. Therefore, to understand a political cartoon, you need to know what event or problem the cartoonist is illustrating.

Below is a cartoon created by Benjamin Franklin in 1754, shortly after war had broken out between French and English colonists. Most historians think that this was the first political cartoon to appear in an American newspaper. The cartoon was printed in the *Pennsylvania Gazette* shortly before representatives from many of the English colonies gathered to discuss whether they should fight together against the French.

1. In this cartoon, what does the snake stand for? How can you tell?

2. What do you think Franklin's message was? Do you think this cartoon communicates his message effectively? Why or why not?

DECISION-MAKING SKILLS

Choosing

Imagine that you are a farmer in Massachusetts in 1786. Because you are unable to pay your taxes, a local court has threatened to sell your farm. Some of the farmers in your area are becoming desperate. Already you have heard a rumor that a man named Daniel Shays is trying to organize a farmers' rebellion against the government. You are worried about your family's future, and you need to decide what to do about your situation.

Copy the following chart and use it as a guide in making your decision. After you have filled in the chart and made your decision, answer the questions that follow.

Goal: ______________________	
Options	Consequences
1.	
2.	
3.	
Decision: ______________________ Reasons for decision:	

1. Why is it important to set a clear goal?

2. Why is it important to consider many options?

3. What do you think are two rules that anyone should follow when making a decision?

4. Name a goal that you have now and state two possible ways to achieve it.

The Declaration of Independence

When, in the course of human events, it becomes necessary for one people to dissolve the political bands which have connected them with another, and to assume, among the powers of the earth, the separate and equal station to which the laws of nature and of nature's God entitle them, a decent respect to the opinions of mankind requires that they should declare the causes which impel them to the separation.

We hold these truths to be self-evident, that all men are created equal, that they are endowed by their Creator with certain unalienable rights, that among these are life, liberty, and the pursuit of happiness. That, to secure these rights, governments are instituted among men, deriving their just powers from the consent of the governed. That, whenever any form of government becomes destructive of these ends, it is the right of the people to alter or to abolish it, and to institute new government, laying its foundation on such principles, and organizing its powers in such form, as to them shall seem most likely to effect their safety and happiness.

Prudence, indeed, will dictate that governments long established should not be changed for light and transient causes; and, accordingly, all experience has shown that mankind are more disposed to suffer, while evils are sufferable, than to right themselves by abolishing the forms to which they are accustomed.

But when a long train of abuses and usurpations, pursuing invariably the same object, evinces a design to reduce them under absolute despotism, it is their right, it is their duty, to throw off such government, and to provide new guards for their future security. Such has been the patient sufferance of these colonies; and such is now the necessity which constrains them to alter their former systems of government. The history of the present King of Great Britain is a history of repeated injuries and usurpations, all having in direct object the establishment of an absolute tryanny over these states. To prove this, let facts be submitted to a candid world.

He has refused his assent to laws the most wholesome and necessary for the public good.

He has forbidden his governors to pass laws of immediate and pressing importance, unless suspended in their operation till his assent should be obtained; and when so suspended, he has utterly neglected to attend to them.

He has refused to pass other laws for the accommodation of large districts of people, unless those people would relinquish the right of representation in the legislature; a right inestimable to them and formidable to tyrants only.

He has called together legislative bodies at places unusual, uncomfortable, and distant from the depository of their public records, for the sole purpose of fatiguing them into compliance with his measures.

He has dissolved representative houses repeatedly, for opposing with manly firmness his invasions on the rights of the people.

He has refused for a long time, after such dissolutions, to cause others to be elected; whereby the legislative powers, incapable of annihilation, have returned to the people at large for their exercise; the state remaining in the meantime exposed to all the dangers of invasion from without, and convulsions within.

He has endeavored to prevent the population of these states; for that purpose obstructing the laws for naturalization of foreigners; refusing to pass others to encourage their migrations hither, and raising the conditions of new appropriations of lands.

He has obstructed the administration of justice, by refusing his assent to laws for establishing judiciary powers.

He has made judges dependent on his will alone, for the tenure of their offices, and the amount and payment of their salaries.

He has erected a multitude of new offices, and sent hither swarms of officers to harass our people, and eat out their substance.

He has kept among us, in times of peace, standing armies, without the consent of our legislatures.

He has affected to render the military independent of and superior to the civil power.

He has combined with others to subject us to a jurisdiction foreign to our constitution, and unacknowledged by our laws; giving his assent to their acts of pretended legislation:

For quartering large bodies of armed troops among us;

For protecting them, by a mock trial, from punishment for any murders which they should commit on the inhabitants of these states;

For cutting off our trade with all parts of the world;

For imposing taxes on us without our consent;

For depriving us, in many cases, of the benefits of trial by jury;

For transporting us beyond seas to be tried for pretended offenses;

For abolishing the free system of English laws in a neighboring province, establishing therein an arbitrary government, and enlarging its boundaries, so as to render it at once an example and fit instrument for introducing the same absolute rule into these colonies;

For taking away our charters, abolishing our most valuable laws, and altering fundamentally the forms of our governments;

For suspending our own legislatures, and declaring themselves invested with power to legislate for us in all cases whatsoever.

He has abdicated government here, by declaring us out of his protection, and waging war against us.

He has plundered our seas, ravaged our coasts, burnt our towns, and destroyed the lives of our people.

He is at this time transporting large armies of foreign mercenaries to complete the works of death, desolation, and tyranny already begun with circumstances of cruelty and perfidy scarcely paralleled in the most barbarous ages, and totally unworthy the head of a civilized nation.

He has constrained our fellow citizens, taken captive on the high seas, to bear arms against their country, to become the executioners of their friends and brethren, or to fall themselves by their hands.

He has excited domestic insurrections among us, and has endeavored to bring on the inhabitants of our frontiers, the merciless Indian savages, whose known rule of warfare is an undistinguished destruction of all ages, sexes, and conditions.

In every stage of these oppressions, we have petitioned for redress in the most humble terms. Our repeated petitions have been answered only by repeated injury. A prince, whose character is thus marked by every act which may define a tyrant, is unfit to be the ruler of a free people.

Nor have we been wanting in attentions to our British brethren. We have warned them from time to time of attempts by their legislature to extend an unwarrantable jurisdiction over us. We have reminded them of the circumstances of our emigration and settlement here. We have appealed to their native justice and magnanimity, and we have conjured them by the ties of our common kindred to disavow these usurpations, which would inevitably interrupt our connections and correspondence. They too have been deaf to the voice of justice and of consanguinity. We must, therefore, acquiesce in the necessity, which denounces our separation, and hold them, as we hold the rest of mankind, enemies in war, in peace, friends.

We, therefore, the representatives of the United States of America, in General Congress assembled, appealing to the Supreme Judge of the world for the rectitude of our intentions, do, in the name and by authority of the good people of these colonies, solemnly publish and declare, that these united colonies are and of right ought to be free and independent states; that they are absolved from all allegiance to the British Crown, and that all political connection between them and the state of Great Britain is and ought to be totally dissolved; and that, as free and independent states, they have full power to levy war, conclude peace, contract alliances, establish commerce, and to do all other acts and things which independent states may of right do. And for the support of this declaration, with a firm reliance on the protection of Divine Providence, we mutually pledge to each other our lives, our fortunes, and our sacred honor.

Chapter Themes: A product of compromise, the Constitution set up limited government by dividing power between the state and federal governments and within the federal government. The amendment process gave the new government flexibility.

CHAPTER 5

Creating the Constitution

Imagine that you have traveled back in time to witness the historic gathering that will lead to the birth of our nation. It is May 1787. Delegates are arriving in Philadelphia for the Constitutional Convention.

As you walk along busy Market Street, you see one of the first delegates arrive in a carriage. He wears a bright blue and beige coat, knee-length pants, and white stockings. His hair is powdered and tied back. The people who pass James Madison cannot know that he will go down in history as "the architect of the Constitution."

Madison's suitcases are stuffed with books and papers. He has come prepared for an uphill battle, knowing that many delegates will oppose his plan for a more powerful central government.

Several days later you see another carriage arrive, this time welcomed by clanging church bells, a cannon salute, and cheering. George Washington, tall and dignified, greets the crowds. Someone near you whispers that his concern for the nation has caused him to leave his quiet Virginia plantation and attend the convention.

Like Madison, Washington sees the need for a stronger national government. Having seen "one head gradually turning into thirteen" during the war, Washington hopes to restore unity.

Later, outside the red-brick Pennsylvania State House, you see Washington with a short, plump man wearing wire-rimmed glasses. You recognize this person as Benjamin Franklin, governor of Pennsylvania and the convention's host. At the age of eighty-one, he is also its oldest delegate. His wit and good nature will be needed at the convention, as the debates are sure to be tense.

By late May, enough delegates have arrived so that the convention can begin. Some of the most brilliant people in the country are preparing to debate its future.

In this chapter you will visit the Constitutional Convention to see how our nation's plan of government was created. You will also see why it was so difficult to get the Constitution approved by the states. Finally, you will examine the principles that have formed the basis of our government for over 200 years.

Teaching Note: Use the Introducing the Chapter activity, page T 56.

5-1

THE CONSTITUTIONAL CONVENTION

Read to Find Out

- what the term *bicameral* means.
- why the convention debates were kept secret.
- what key issues the delegates disagreed on.
- what compromises were made at the convention.

As you saw in Chapter 4, Shays' Rebellion raised doubts in the minds of many Americans about the young government under the Articles of Confederation. With no power to tax or to enforce laws, Congress seemed almost powerless to deal with the country's debts or to settle disputes between the states. Therefore, in 1787 Congress approved a convention "for the sole and express purpose of revising the Articles of Confederation."

Even before the convention began, most delegates agreed that a national government was needed, not just an alliance of states. Also, they recognized the need to guard against abuse of power. Many delegates agreed with Montesquieu's principle of separation of powers among three branches of government: legislative, executive, and judicial. In addition, they agreed that the government's power must be limited by dividing power between the states and the national government.

Despite these areas of agreement, the delegates were sharply divided on other important questions, such as how many representatives each state should have in the national government and how much power the government should be given. As the delegates packed their bags and left for Philadelphia, they braced themselves for a long convention.

Getting Organized

The site of the Constitutional Convention was the Pennsylvania State House, where the Declaration of Independence had been signed in July 1776. Summer in Philadelphia meant heat, humidity, and flies, prompting Thomas Jefferson to joke that the Declaration was signed quickly because flies were biting the signers. Actually, the Declaration had been signed only after long, heated debate, and the convention of 1787 promised more of the same.

On Friday, May 25, the business of the convention began with the unanimous selection of George Washington as the presiding officer. However, the delegates realized that it would take more than Washington's popularity to keep the convention on course. Without clear rules, the meeting could end in confusion, and the young country might fall apart.

Setting the rules. Several of the rules the convention adopted were aimed at keeping the discussions secret. It was feared that if their debates were reported in the newspapers, delegates would not feel free to change their minds or to consider the common good of all the states rather than just the narrow interests of people back home. With these concerns in mind, they decided that no one should remove notes from the meeting room. They also agreed that conversations about the proceedings should take place only inside the State House, and that doors and windows were to be kept shut at all times.

Other rules covered voting procedures and behavior during meetings. Each state had one vote, regardless of its number of delegates. The debate rules allowed for each person's opinion to be heard. Each delegate could speak twice on a subject. Additional comments had to wait until all others had been

The 55 delegates to the Constitutional Convention were well equipped for their task. More than half had served in one or another of the Continental Congresses. Many had helped write their state constitutions, and most had served in their state legislatures. Seven had been state governors.

Today "sunshine laws" require government agencies to hold open meetings when public policies are discussed. By opening the meetings "to let the sunshine in," the laws discourage secrecy in government.

given an opportunity to speak. No one was to whisper, pass notes, or read while another delegate was speaking.

The delegates met six days a week from 10:00 A.M. until 4:00 P.M., without stopping for a meal. They also met with each other before and after the formal sessions. Although some of the 55 delegates left Philadelphia for brief times, an average of 40 were present on any given day.

Madison's Plan

As one of their first acts, the delegates voted not to revise the Articles of Confederation. Most of them believed that government under the Articles was so ineffective that a new plan was needed. Few delegates, though, had specific ideas about how to organize the new government.

One person who did have some definite ideas was Virginia's James Madison, who proposed a framework for a strong national government with legislative, executive, and judicial branches. The legislative branch would have two parts: a House of Representatives and a Senate. Members of the House would be elected directly by the people. Senators would be chosen by members of the House. The number of seats in the House and the Senate would be based on each state's population.

Madison's proposal, known as the Virginia Plan, dominated discussion for the entire convention. Madison was calling for the alliance of independent states to be replaced by a strong national government. Many of the delegates, however, feared that under Madison's plan the national government would be too strong, snatching away important powers of the state legislatures.

Sharing Power with the States

The states had become used to controlling all their own affairs. Many delegates feared that a strong national government might

Convention delegates meet in the Pennsylvania State House. Standing at center is Washington, with James Madison on his right.

Decision Making: Have students analyze the delegates' decisions regarding representation in Congress, executive leadership, and selection of government officials. Have them list options and the possible consequences of each option.

VIEWS OF NOTED AMERICANS

James Madison

If asked to name the persons most responsible for the founding of our nation, most Americans would quickly recite the familiar names of Washington, Jefferson, and Franklin. Few would mention the name of James Madison. Yet Madison played the leading role in building the lasting framework of our government, becoming known as the "architect of the Constitution."

Madison's role is not well known because much of his work was done out of the public eye. Convinced that good government is the result of careful thought, he spent years studying political ideas. After deciding which ideas he thought would best serve the American people, he was determined to put those ideas into the Constitution. No one at the Constitutional Convention presented proposals more persuasively or persistently.

Madison's studious habits can be traced back to his childhood. Born on March 16, 1751, in Port Conway, Virginia, young "Jemmy" often suffered from illnesses, but his mind remained healthy and inquisitive. By the time he was eleven, he had read all of his father's books. A dedicated student, he graduated from the College of New Jersey at Princeton in only two years, often studying by candlelight late into the night.

Sparked by the colonists' growing dissatisfaction with British rule, Madison entered politics in 1774. He helped write Virginia's constitution and represented his state in the Continental Congress.

Madison's experience in the Virginia legislature confirmed his belief that the states should be united under a strong government. At the Constitutional Convention, his proposed plan for a republic was based on the ideas of many thinkers whose writings he had studied over the years.

Crowning a career devoted to the new nation, Madison served as President from 1809 to 1817. Upon leaving public office, he returned home to edit the detailed notes he had taken at the convention. Madison left the most complete record we have of the meeting that led to the birth of our American government.

abuse its powers, treating the states in much the same way England had treated the colonies. Throughout much of the long, hot summer, delegates argued over how power would be shared between the national government and the states.

One issue was whether each state would have the power to either protect or abolish the slave trade. Several northern states wanted the national government to regulate all trade and to outlaw slavery. The southern states objected to this proposal because their plantations depended upon slave labor. Eventually the delegates compromised because they saw

Discussion: Have students discuss the skills that made James Madison a good student as well as a good constitution maker.

the urgent need to form a new government. They agreed that the national government could regulate trade in general but that it could not interfere with the slave trade until 1808.

Some delegates hoped that a national government might end slavery at a later time, but first that national government had to be created. Eventually, the delegates decided which powers would be given to the national government, which would be kept by the states, and which would be shared by both.

Representation in Congress

Reaching agreement on the powers of the national government was only part of the struggle. The delegates also had to decide how that government would be organized. Since the core of a representative government is the legislature, the delegates focused mainly on issues relating to representation in Congress.

The major question was how many representatives each state would have in the legislature. In Madison's Virginia Plan each state's population would determine the number of its representatives. Objecting that they would always be outvoted by the large states, the small states supported a different plan proposed by William Paterson of New Jersey. Known as the New Jersey Plan, it called for a one-house legislature in which each state would have an equal number of votes.

As supporters of each plan argued back and forth, tempers flared in the June heat and some delegates went home in disgust. The convention seemed to be going nowhere.

The Great Compromise. Realizing that they were making no progress, the delegates considered a plan proposed by Roger Sherman of Connecticut. Like the Virginia Plan, it called for a ***bicameral***, or two-house, legislature. The House of Representatives would be elected on

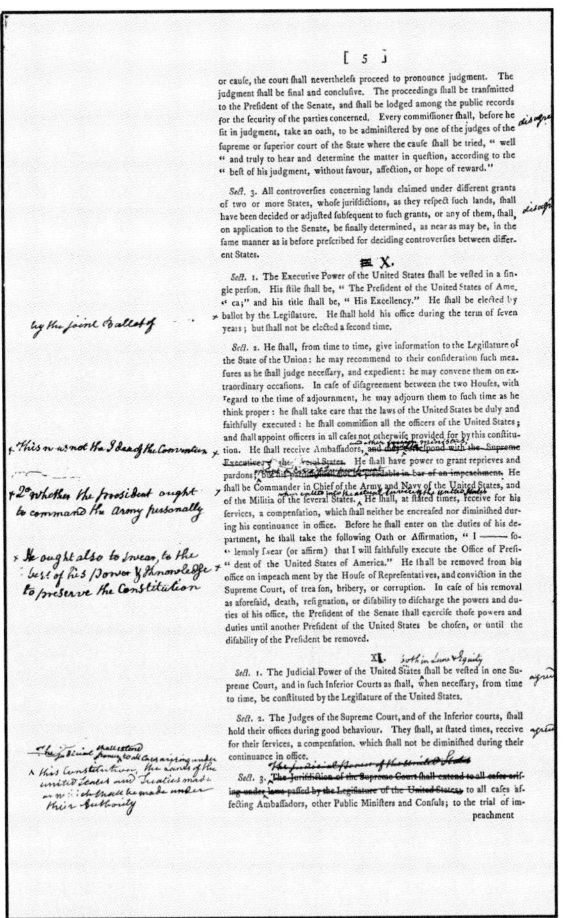

[5]

or cauſe, the court ſhall nevertheleſs proceed to pronounce judgment. The judgment ſhall be final and concluſive. The proceedings ſhall be tranſmitted to the Preſident of the Senate, and ſhall be lodged among the public records for the ſecurity of the parties concerned. Every commiſſioner ſhall, before he ſit in judgment, take an oath, to be adminiſtered by one of the judges of the ſupreme or ſuperior court of the State where the cauſe ſhall be tried, "well "and truly to hear and determine the matter in queſtion, according to the "beſt of his judgment, without favour, affection, or hope of reward."

Sect. 3. All controverſies concerning lands claimed under different grants of two or more States, whoſe juriſdictions, as they reſpect ſuch lands, ſhall have been decided or adjuſted ſubſequent to ſuch grants, or any of them, ſhall, on application to the Senate, be finally determined, as near as may be, in the ſame manner as is before preſcribed for deciding controverſies between different States.

X.

Sect. 1. The Executive Power of the United States ſhall be veſted in a ſingle perſon. His ſtile ſhall be, "The Preſident of the United States of America;" and his title ſhall be, "His Excellency." He ſhall be elected by ballot by the Legiſlature. He ſhall hold his office during the term of ſeven years; but ſhall not be elected a ſecond time.

Sect. 2. He ſhall, from time to time, give information to the Legiſlature of the State of the Union: he may recommend to their conſideration ſuch meaſures as he ſhall judge neceſſary, and expedient: he may convene them on extraordinary occaſions. In caſe of diſagreement between the two Houſes, with regard to the time of adjournment, he may adjourn them to ſuch time as he think proper: he ſhall take care that the laws of the United States be duly and faithfully executed: he ſhall commiſſion all the officers of the United States; and ſhall appoint officers in all caſes not otherwiſe provided for by this conſtitution. He ſhall receive Ambaſſadors, ~~and may correſpond with the Supreme Executives of the ſeveral States.~~ He ſhall have power to grant reprieves and pardons; ~~but his pardon ſhall not be pleadable in bar of an impeachment.~~ He ſhall be Commander in Chief of the Army and Navy of the United States, and of the Militia of the ſeveral States. He ſhall, at ſtated times, receive for his ſervices, a compenſation, which ſhall neither be encreaſed nor diminiſhed during his continuance in office. Before he ſhall enter on the duties of his department, he ſhall take the following Oath or Affirmation, "I —— ſolemnly ſwear (or affirm) that I will faithfully execute the Office of Preſident of the United States of America." He ſhall be removed from his office on impeach ment by the Houſe of Repreſentatives, and conviction in the Supreme Court, of treaſon, bribery, or corruption. In caſe of his removal as aforeſaid, death, reſignation, or diſability to diſcharge the powers and duties of his office, the Preſident of the Senate ſhall exercise thoſe powers and duties until another Preſident of the United States be choſen, or until the diſability of the Preſident be removed.

XI.

Sect. 1. The Judicial Power of the United States ſhall be veſted in one Supreme Court, and in ſuch Inferior Courts as ſhall, when neceſſary, from time to time, be conſtituted by the Legiſlature of the United States.

Sect. 2. The Judges of the Supreme Court, and of the Inferior courts, ſhall hold their offices during good behaviour. They ſhall, at ſtated times, receive for their ſervices, a compenſation, which ſhall not be diminiſhed during their continuance in office.

Sect. 3. ~~The Juriſdiction of the Supreme Court ſhall extend to all caſes ariſing under laws paſſed by the Legiſlature of the United States;~~ to all caſes affecting Ambaſſadors, other Public Miniſters and Conſuls; to the trial of impeachment

A page from a draft of the Constitution has notes by Virginia's George Mason. He suggested that the President take an oath to obey the Constitution.

the basis of state population. In the Senate, however, each state would have two senators, regardless of its population. This plan gave the large states more power in the House of Representatives, but each state had equal power in the Senate.

Although no one was completely satisfied with Sherman's plan, the delegates finally approved it by the narrow margin of one vote. The plan became known as the Great Compromise because each side gave up part of what it wanted in order to benefit all. If both sides had been unwilling to give and take, the convention probably would have failed.

By the time of the Constitutional Convention, slavery was being abolished in the northern states. Many delegates believed that abolition societies and competition from immigrant white labor would eventually end slavery elsewhere in the nation.

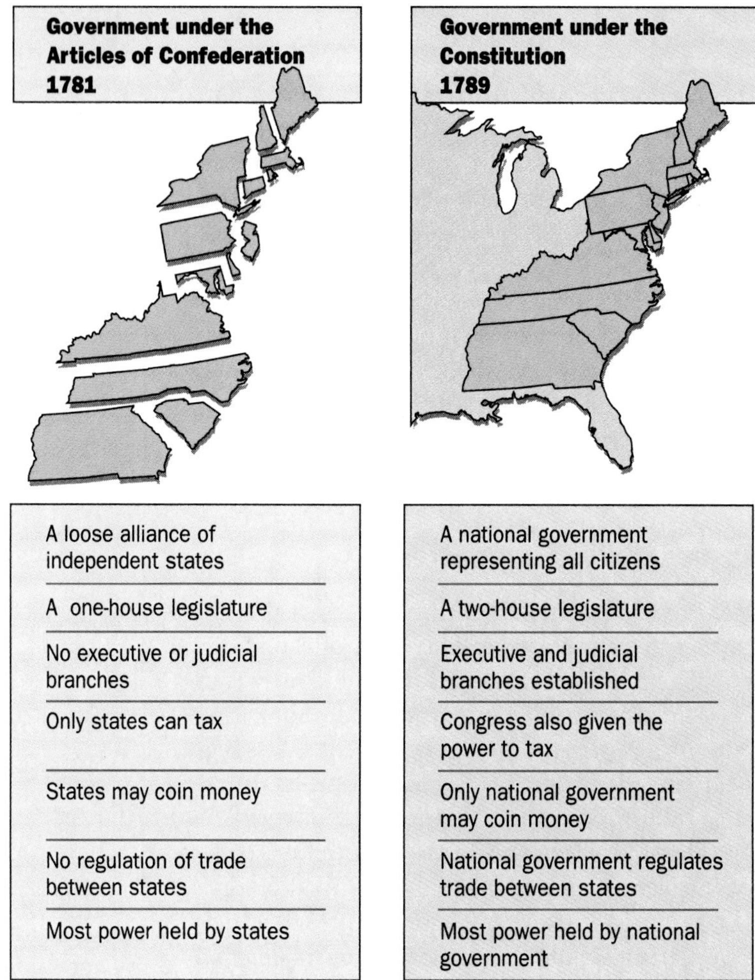

Government under the Articles of Confederation 1781
Government under the Constitution 1789
A loose alliance of independent states
A one-house legislature
No executive or judicial branches
Only states can tax
States may coin money
No regulation of trade between states
Most power held by states
A national government representing all citizens
A two-house legislature
Executive and judicial branches established
Congress also given the power to tax
Only national government may coin money
National government regulates trade between states
Most power held by national government

From the Articles of Confederation to the Constitution. *As this chart shows, the Constitution created a much stronger national government than had existed under the Articles of Confederation.*

Although they had argued over the number of representatives, most of the delegates agreed that a two-house legislature was a good idea. It would help ensure that fair laws were passed because each proposed law would have to be approved by both houses.

Jefferson, who was out of the country serving as ambassador to France, later asked Washington why the delegates had established a Senate in addition to a House of Representatives. Washington replied by asking, "Why do you pour your coffee into a saucer?"

"To cool it," Jefferson answered.

Washington replied, "Even so, we pour legislation into the senatorial saucer to cool it."

The three-fifths compromise. The Great Compromise kept the convention alive, but it did not settle the question of how to count state populations when determining representation in the House. Although slaves were treated as property, the southern states wanted to count each slave as a person when figuring state populations. The northern states objected that this would give the southern states more members in the House of Representatives and therefore more power.

Once again the delegates compromised. They agreed to count each slave as three fifths of a person when a state's population was calculated.

Teaching Note: Use the Reinforcement Activity, page T 58, and accompanying worksheet in the Activity Book after students have read the material in Section 5-1 or at the end of the chapter.

The Executive and Judicial Branches

As you recall, under the Articles of Confederation there had been no executive branch to enforce the laws and no judicial branch to interpret the laws. The delegates agreed that these branches would be needed to provide for separation of powers.

The delegates decided that executive power should be given to one President rather than to a committee of leaders. They broadly defined the powers and duties of the President. In establishing the judicial branch, they created a Supreme Court that would have authority to interpret laws and would thus be able to settle conflicts between different states.

A Government by the People?

Although there was general agreement on the functions of each branch of government, the delegates argued about who should elect the President and the members of Congress. Should they be chosen by all the citizens or just by the members of the state legislatures?

Some delegates argued for direct election by the citizens because it would take into account the opinions of a wide variety of people. Madison wrote, "If the will of the majority cannot be trusted [in America], . . . it can be trusted nowhere." Gouverneur Morris of Pennsylvania agreed, stating that "if the people should elect, they will never fail to prefer [someone] of distinguished character."

Many delegates, however, distrusted the people's judgment. Roger Sherman stated that average citizens "will never be sufficiently informed." Elbridge Gerry of Massachusetts declared that the people were easily swayed and not very thoughtful. Many delegates also worried that direct elections would take too much power away from the state legislatures.

As part of the Great Compromise, the delegates decided that all eligible citizens—that is, white men with property—would elect members of the House, but state legislatures would select senators. The delegates determined that a group of electors known as the Electoral College would select the President. Each state legislature could determine how that state's electors would be chosen.

The Signing

In mid-September the convention finally drew to a close, with 38 delegates signing the Constitution on September 17, 1787. Benjamin Franklin was impressed that the debate and the compromises had produced such a strong plan. On the final day of the convention, he stated, "Thus I consent, Sir, to this Constitution because I expect no better, and because I am not sure that it is not the best."

The delegates to the Constitutional Convention are often called "the framers" because they framed, or shaped, our form of government. Over the years changes have been made in the Constitution, as the framers expected there would be. However, if they could see their work today, they would still recognize the basic plan of government they created over 200 years ago.

Answers will be found on page T 58.

Section Review

1. Define *bicameral*.
2. Why did the delegates decide to keep their discussions secret?
3. Identify and explain the three main issues that arose during the debates at the Constitutional Convention.
4. What was the Great Compromise? Why was it important?

Analysis. Why do you think Benjamin Franklin stated that he could "expect no better" plan of government?

Challenge (Evaluation): Have students discuss Roger Sherman and Elbridge Gerry's view of the people's judgment in the context of today's citizenry. Do people have the necessary judgment to elect the President directly? Students should provide reasons for their opinions.

5-2

THE STRUGGLE FOR RATIFICATION

Read to Find Out

- why the Federalists supported the Constitution and why the Anti-Federalists opposed it.
- how the Federalists worked to get the Constitution approved by the states.
- why the states finally ratified the Constitution.

The next step in forming a new government was for the states to vote on the plan. To go into effect, the Constitution had to be ratified, or accepted, by at least nine state conventions. Only those states that ratified the new Constitution would be part of the new nation.

By calling for ratifying conventions, the framers bypassed the state legislatures. They suspected that most members of the state legislatures would vote against a Constitution that stripped away some of the states' power. The framers felt that ratifying conventions would give more people an opportunity to study the merits of the Constitution and might increase support for ratification.

While all discussions had been secret during the Constitutional Convention, the issues were now out in the open. When the Constitution was published in newspapers, a storm of debate arose. People argued in churches, meetinghouses, roadside inns, and town squares. Some strongly supported the plan while others loudly opposed it.

The Federalists

The supporters of the Constitution were known as Federalists because they supported a strong federal, or national, government. The Federalists argued that individual states might not be able to protect themselves against foreign nations. A strong national government, they declared, would provide protection, maintain order, regulate trade, and guarantee the rights of citizens. It would also ensure that the nation's debts were paid and

In this 1788 cartoon, each state that ratifies the Constitution is shown as a "pillar" supporting a new national government.

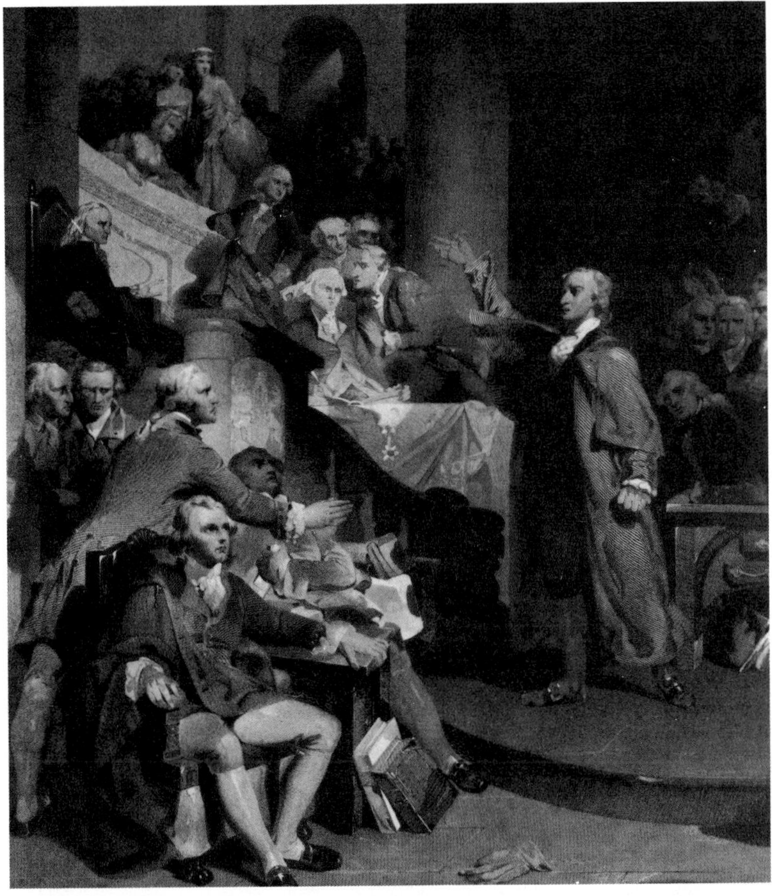

Patrick Henry addresses a session of the Virginia House of Burgesses. A person familiar with Henry's speeches once declared, "He is by far the most powerful speaker I ever heard."

that American money had a stable value at home and abroad.

The Anti-Federalists

The opponents of the Constitution, who were called Anti-Federalists, feared that a strong central government would endanger the people's liberties. According to them, a central government that met so far away from local communities could not truly be called a government by consent of the people. The Anti-Federalists believed that representatives should meet in a location close to the people whose interests they sought to protect.

What especially worried those who feared a strong national government was the statement in the Constitution giving Congress power to make laws "necessary and proper" to carry out its stated powers. Anti-Federalists argued that this wording left the door open to an abuse of power. A strong national government, they said, might eventually swallow up the state governments.

The Bill of Rights Issue

The Anti-Federalists were also troubled by what was left out of the Constitution: a bill of rights. They feared that a strong national government might not respect citizens' rights. The Federalists responded that it was unnecessary to list the rights of citizens because the Constitution already carefully limited the government's powers.

The strongest Anti-Federalist voice in this debate was that of Virginia's Patrick Henry. During the colonial period he had raised the

Challenge (Analysis): Have students discuss how the arguments of the Anti-Federalists have stood the "test of time." Were their concerns justified? Students should give reasons for their opinions.

Teaching Note: You may want to use Teaching Activity 1, page T 56, as a culminating activity after students have read the material in this section.

cry: "Give me liberty or give me death!" His reputation as a fiery speaker and a Revolutionary War hero made him a tough opponent of the Federalists. Calling the Constitution "horridly defective," he led the fight in Virginia against ratification. At the Virginia ratifying convention he warned:

> Mr. Chairman, the necessity for a Bill of Rights appears to me to be greater in this government than ever it was in any government before. . . . All rights not expressly reserved to the people are relinquished [given up] to rulers.

The Federalist Papers

Some leading Federalists responded to Patrick Henry and other Anti-Federalists in a series of pro-Constitution newspaper articles. James Madison, Alexander Hamilton, and John Jay wrote the articles, which became known as the Federalist papers.

In the Federalist papers, Madison argued that the Constitution would protect the liberty of every citizen. With a national government representing all the people, no group would be able to ignore the rights of everyone else. Instead, to reach some of its goals, each group would have to compromise with other groups.

The Federalist papers also emphasized the problems America faced as a weak, young nation on a large continent. If the states did not unite under a strong national government, the forces of Spain, England, and France might overpower them.

Ratification

Support for the Constitution grew as many Americans were persuaded by the Federalists' effective campaign. Washington's and Franklin's support swayed people who admired those two great leaders. Many were won over after the Federalists agreed to propose a bill of rights if the Constitution was ratified.

Still, the debates in many state conventions dragged on for months. In many cases the Constitution was approved by only a few votes. Finally, in June 1788, the new government was officially born when New Hampshire became the ninth state to ratify the Constitution.

AMERICAN NOTEBOOK

At the Massachusetts ratifying convention, a farmer named Josiah Smith spoke for the Federalist cause:

> **I am a plain man and get my living by the plow. I am not used to speaking in public, but I beg your leave to say a few words. . . . I have lived in a part of the country where I have known the worth of good government by the want [lack] of it. There was a black cloud [Shays' Rebellion] that rose in the east last winter and spread over the west. . . .**
>
> **When I saw this Constitution, I found that it was a cure for these disorders. I got a copy and read it over and over. I had been a member of the convention to form our own state constitution, and had learnt something of the checks and balances of power, and I found them all there.**
>
> **Some gentlemen say, don't be in a hurry. Take time to consider, and don't take a leap in the dark. I say gather fruit when it is ripe. There is a time to sow and a time to reap. We sowed our seed when we sent men to the Federal Convention. Now is the harvest. Now is the time to reap the fruit of our labor. And if we don't do it now, I am afraid we shall never have another opportunity.**

George Mason, framer of Virginia's bill of rights and a delegate to the Constitutional Convention, campaigned against ratification of the Constitution, insisting on the addition of a bill of rights. Mason's Virginia bill of rights became the basis of the first ten amendments to the Constitution.

Teaching Note: You may want to use the Evaluating Progress activity, page T 57, after students have read the material in this section or at the end of the chapter.

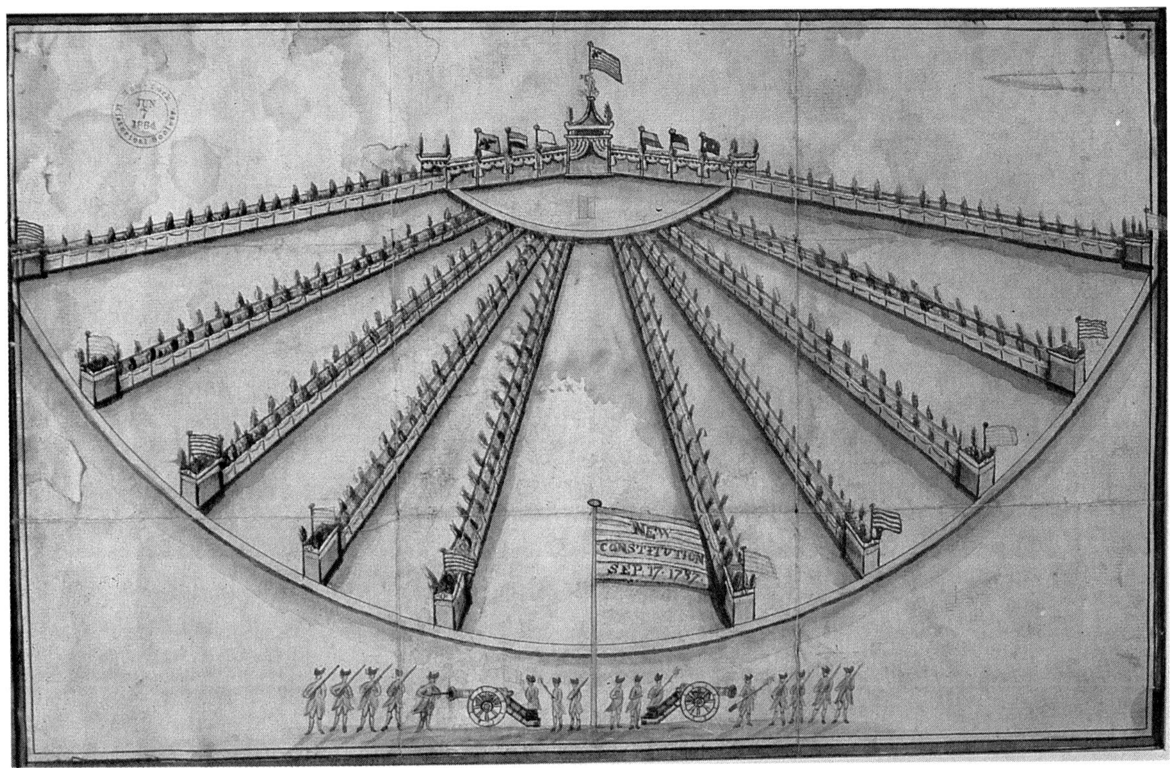

Over 6,000 citizens of New York City attended an outdoor banquet to celebrate their state's ratification of the Constitution in July 1788.

The government would not last long, however, without the support of the remaining four states, which included nearly half of the nation's people. The two key states were Virginia and New York. After bitter debate, Virginia ratified the document by only ten votes (89–79) and New York approved by the slim margin of three votes (30–27). By the spring of 1790, all 13 states had ratified the new Constitution.

The birth of our nation is really marked by the ratification of the Constitution, not by the signing of the Declaration of Independence. Only under the Constitution did Americans become united in one nation. What had once been a loose union of independent states had become the United States of America.

Answers will be found on page T 59.

Section Review

1. What were the key arguments against the Constitution?
2. Why were the Federalist papers written?
3. State three reasons why the Constitution was ratified.

Analysis. Why do you think the framers decided that the Constitution needed to be approved by the state conventions?

Data Search. Look on page 584 in the Data Bank to find the populations of New York and Virginia in 1790. Which other states do you think the Federalists particularly needed the support of? Explain.

Delaware was the first state to ratify the Constitution in December 1787. Rhode Island, which had not sent delegates to the Constitutional Convention and was reluctant to join the Union, finally ratified the Constitution in May 1790, when the Bill of Rights was ready to be added to the Constitution.

5-3

THE SUPREME LAW OF THE LAND

Read to Find Out

- what the terms *veto, delegated powers, amendments, federalism, concurrent powers, reserved powers, checks and balances,* and *impeach* mean.
- what the goals of our government are.
- how power is divided between the federal and state governments.
- how the principles of separation of powers and checks and balances are evident in the Constitution.

The full text of the Constitution will be found on pages 108–129.

The Constitution establishes our form of government, a republic. As you recall from Chapter 4, a republic is a government in which citizens elect their representatives. As the "supreme law of the land," the Constitution protects the rights of citizens by providing general rules that the national government and the state governments must follow.

The Goals of Our Government

The Constitution begins by stating the goals of our government. Just as the signers of the Declaration of Independence explained why they were seeking freedom from England, the framers declared why they were replacing the Articles of Confederation with a new form of government. In the Preamble, or introduction, they listed six goals:

1. *"to form a more perfect union"*: The framers were seeking a better government than the one under the Articles of Confederation. Their main concern was to unite the 13 separate states under an effective national government.

2. *"establish justice"*: We have a legal system that seeks fair ways to settle disputes between individuals, between individuals and the government, between states, and between the national and state governments.

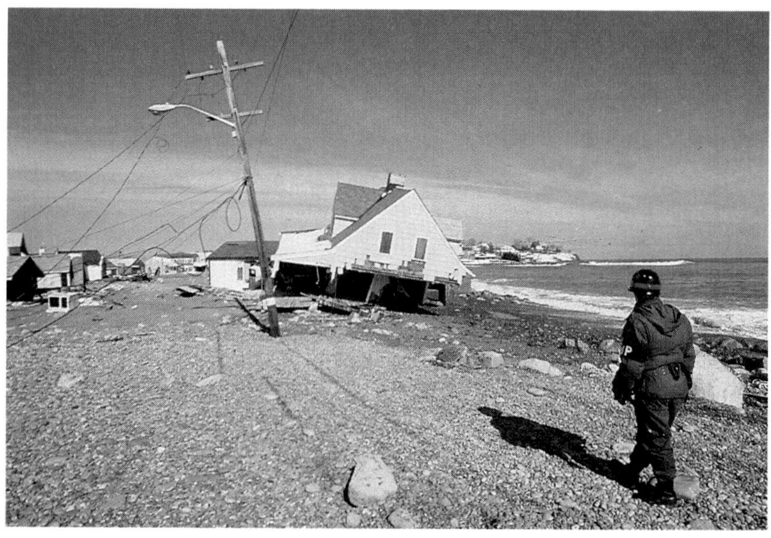

Providing relief from hurricanes and other disasters is one of the many ways in which our government promotes the general welfare of citizens.

Teaching Note: For Thomas Jefferson's description of the principles of American government, see "In Their Own Words" on page 168.

3. *"insure domestic tranquility"*: Our government tries to establish a peaceful society in which people are protected from the unlawful acts of others.

4. *"provide for the common defense"*: Our government seeks to protect citizens from attacks by other countries.

5. *"promote the general welfare"*: Our government tries to create conditions that will benefit all Americans.

6. *"and secure the blessings of liberty to ourselves and our posterity"*: Our government seeks to give people the freedom to choose where they work, where they live, what they believe, and who shall represent them in government. Few people in history have enjoyed such blessings of liberty.

However, our liberty as Americans does not leave us free to do whatever we want. Our actions should not interfere with the rights of others. The government protects the liberty of *all* citizens. It also protects future Americans—our posterity, or descendants.

The Articles

Following the Preamble, the framers laid out the plan for our government. This plan is organized into seven parts called articles. Most of the articles are divided into sections according to topic, and the main points on each topic are stated in clauses. Some of the key ideas in the articles are described in the following paragraphs.

Article 1: The Legislative Branch. In a republic, the direct representatives of the people are the most important part of the government. Therefore, it is not surprising that the legislative branch is discussed in the first—and longest—article.

Article 1 describes the organization and powers of the national legislature, called the Congress of the United States. Congress is divided into two houses: the House of Representatives and the Senate.

The most important power of Congress is to make laws. A proposed law, called a bill, must gain a majority vote in both houses of Congress before it goes to the President for approval. If the President signs the bill, it becomes law. The President may ***veto,*** or reject, the bill; however, Congress has the final word. A vetoed bill can still become a law if Congress votes on it again, with two thirds of the members of each house approving it.

The powers given, or delegated, to Congress are known as ***delegated powers.*** Look at the chart on page 102. Most of these delegated powers—such as the power to coin money, to declare war, and to regulate trade—are specifically listed in Article 1, Section 8. However, not all of Congress's powers are listed. Congress may also make laws that are "necessary and proper" for carrying out the powers that are listed.

By using the words "necessary and proper," the framers wanted to give the government flexibility to carry out its work and change with the times. However, this flexible wording—sometimes called "the elastic clause"—troubled the Anti-Federalists and continues to bother Americans who worry that Congress might abuse its powers. It is important to note, however, that Article 1 also limits the government's power by stating which actions Congress may not take.

Article 2: The Executive Branch. While the powers of the legislative branch are shared by hundreds of members of Congress, the framers gave the power of the executive branch to one person—the President. By establishing the office of President, they created something very new in the world: a leader who has some

Challenge (Application): Have students discuss current events that illustrate how the six goals of the Constitution are still important in our country.

of the strengths of a monarch, but whose authority is based on the consent of the people. In order to continue in office after their four-year term, both the President and the Vice-President have to be re-elected.

Sharing the Power

•Maintain army and navy
•Declare war
•Coin money
Powers of National Government
•Regulate trade between states and with foreign nations
•Make all laws necessary for carrying out delegated powers
•Enforce Laws
•Establish courts
•Borrow money
Shared Powers
•Protect the health and safety of the people
•Build roads
•Collect taxes
•Conduct elections
•Establish schools
Powers of State Governments
•Regulate businesses within the state
•Establish local governments
•Regulate marriages
•Assume other powers not given to the national government or denied to the states

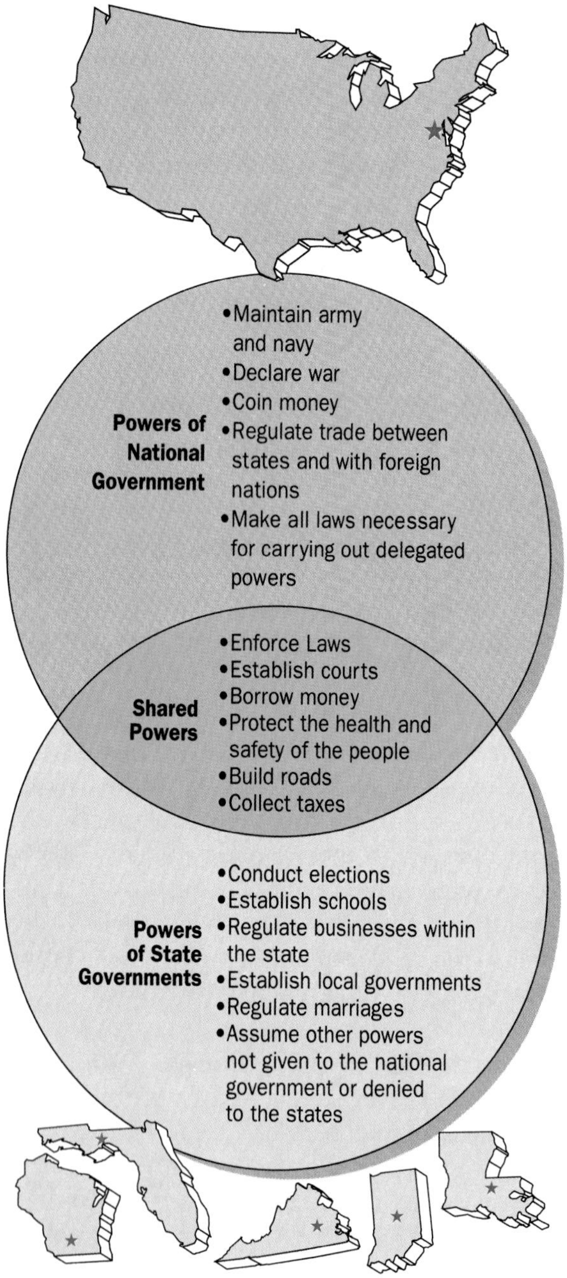

The painful memory of the colonies' experience with King George of England was still fresh in the framers' minds. To avoid having another monarch, they made it clear that the President's job is to execute, or carry out, the laws—not to make them. The President may make treaties, but they are only binding if approved by the Senate. The President may also nominate judges, but the Senate has the right to reject the President's nominees.

The Constitution is far less specific on the office of President than it is on the national legislature. There had never been a President before. Most delegates to the Constitutional Convention believed that George Washington would be elected as the first President and that he could best create the office, setting an example for later Presidents.

Article 3: The Judicial Branch. Although each state had its own courts, the framers wanted a national court system to settle disputes between states. The framers agreed that neither Congress nor the President should control the national courts. Accordingly, the President nominates judges, but the Senate must approve the nominations. Once appointed, judges may serve for life as long as they demonstrate "good behavior."

One of the most important contributions of the framers was the creation of the Supreme Court. This court has the final say in all cases involving the Constitution. Important cases on which lower courts disagree can be appealed to the Supreme Court for a final decision, thus ensuring that legal issues affecting the nation will not be left unsettled.

Article 4: The States. To ensure that the rights of the states are respected, each state must honor the laws of other states. A New York marriage license, for instance, is valid in any

The framers of the Constitution took special care to define treason in Article 3 as an overt act, one that can be seen. Merely talking about treason is not a federal crime. Thus, the government cannot use this charge to punish critics.

In 1987, parades, speeches, and a shower of balloons over Philadelphia's Independence Hall marked the 200th anniversary of the signing of our Constitution.

other state. Requiring states to respect each other's laws helps preserve each state's rights and reduces the possibility of conflict between states.

Article 5: Amending the Constitution. The framers knew that future Americans might want to change the Constitution. Therefore, they included in the Constitution instructions for making ***amendments,*** or changes. To ensure that each change reflects the will of the people, three fourths of the states must approve an amendment. In Chapter 6 you will learn more about the amendment process.

Article 6: The Supremacy of the Constitution. Since both state and national governments may pass laws, the framers wanted to avoid any uncertainty about which laws take priority. Therefore, Article 6 requires officals in state and national government to take an oath to support the Constitution as "the supreme law of the land." No state law may violate the Constitution. Also, if a state law conflicts with a federal—or national—law, the federal law takes priority.

Article 7: Ratification. The last article of the Constitution establishes the procedure for ratification, or approval, of the Constitution.

Amendments to the Constitution

When you read the Constitution, you will see that a series of amendments follow the seven articles. The first ten amendments, ratified in 1791, are called the Bill of Rights and were added in response to the concerns of the Anti-Federalists. Since the approval of the Bill of Rights, only sixteen other amendments have been added. Clearly the Constitution has stood the test of time. You will read more about the Bill of Rights and the other amendments in Chapters 6 and 7.

Main Principles of the Constitution

Most of the Constitution declares what the state governments and the branches of the national government are allowed to do and what they are not allowed to do. These rules are based on three principles: federalism, separation of powers, and checks and balances.

Federalism. The Constitution establishes a principle of ***federalism,*** the division of power between the states and the federal, or national, government. Under federalism, some powers belong only to the national government, some belong only to the states, and some are shared by both. The chart on page 102 shows how the powers are divided and shared.

Article 1 describes the delegated powers, those that belong to Congress. A number of these powers, such as the power to coin money or declare war, are denied to the states.

Some of the powers given to Congress are not denied to the states. For instance, the states, too, can collect taxes, establish courts, and borrow money. The powers shared by the federal and state governments are known as ***concurrent powers.***

The Tenth Amendment declares that the states have ***reserved powers,*** those powers that the Constitution neither gives to Congress nor denies to the states. For example, two of the powers not mentioned in the Constitution which are reserved to the states are the authority to establish schools and to form police organizations.

By dividing power between the federal and state governments, the system of federalism gives the federal government the authority it needs but also helps to protect each state's rights. This system also allows the federal government to deal with issues affecting all citizens, while each state government can better serve the particular needs of its people.

Separation of powers. Under our Constitution, power is not only divided between the

Checks and Balances

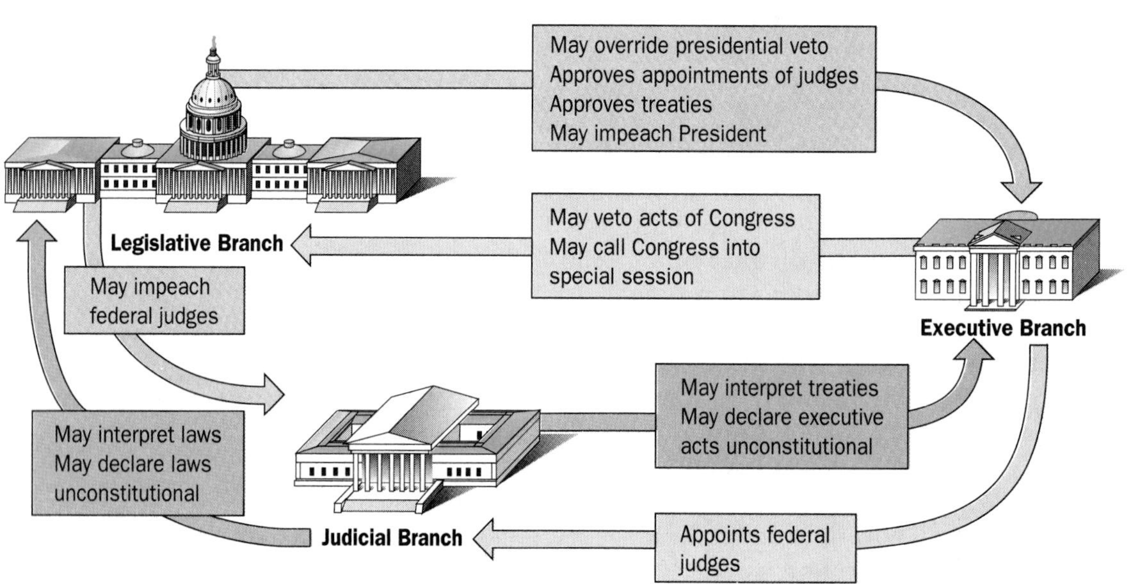

The Constitution creates five categories of powers: powers delegated to the federal government, powers denied to the federal government, powers retained by states, powers denied to the states, and concurrent powers.

Teaching Note: You may want to use Teaching Activity 2, page T 57, as a culminating activity after students have read the material in this section.

state and federal governments; it is also divided within the federal government. Dividing power among the executive, legislative, and judicial branches helps prevent any one branch from abusing its power.

Checks and balances. Another way the Constitution protects against abuse of power in the federal government is through ***checks and balances***, the system that gives each of the three branches of government ways to limit the powers of the other two. For instance, the House can ***impeach***, or accuse the President or other high officials of serious wrongdoing. If found guilty in a trial in the Senate, the official will be removed from office.

The President can check the actions of Congress by vetoing bills that are not in the best interest of the nation. Meanwhile, the judicial branch checks the power of the other two branches by determining whether laws passed by Congress or actions taken by the President are constitutional. By checking and balancing each other, the three branches of government ensure that they work together for the welfare of citizens.

Answers will be found on page T 59.

Section Review

1. Define *veto, delegated powers, amendments, federalism, concurrent powers, reserved powers, checks and balances,* and *impeach.*
2. What is the purpose of the Preamble to the Constitution?
3. Explain how power is divided between the national government and the states.
4. How does the Constitution provide for separation of powers and the principle of checks and balances?

Analysis. How are the goals of the framers reflected in the Constitution?

A BROADER VIEW

The United States Constitution has been called "the most wonderful work ever struck off at a given time by the brain and purpose of man." Although the framers' plan was not the world's first constitution, up until then most governments had unwritten constitutions based on custom or on the will of monarchs. Therefore, to the rest of the world it was quite remarkable that American citizens were using their knowledge and past experience in order to write their own plan of government.

The framers saw themselves as setting an example for self-government. Madison proclaimed, "We are teaching the world the great lesson that men do better without kings and nobles than with them." Hamilton declared that the Constitution was a model of "establishing good government by reflection and choice" rather than by "accident and force."

Indeed, the Constitution has set an example for many countries, particularly for former colonies in Latin America and Africa when they gained their independence. A number of countries have modeled their constitutions after the American document, spelling out rights and responsibilities of the government and the citizens. For many nations a written constitution has been a useful "rule book" that everyone must follow—from the highest government official to the "average citizen."

Teaching Note: Use the Enrichment Activity, page T 58, and accompanying worksheet in the Activity Book.

CHAPTER SURVEY

Answers to Survey and Workshop will be found on page T 59.

UNDERSTANDING NEW VOCABULARY

Seeing Relationships

The vocabulary terms in each pair listed below are related to each other. For each pair, explain what the two terms have in common. Also explain how they are different.

Example: *Impeach* and *veto* both refer to the system of checks and balances. However, the first is a check on the executive branch by the legislative branch, while the second is a check on the legislative branch by the executive branch.

1. *reserved powers* and *concurrent powers*

2. *federalism* and *checks and balances*

Putting It in Writing

Write a paragraph briefly explaining how power is divided in our form of government. In your explanation, use each of the following vocabulary terms: *federalism, delegated powers, reserved powers, checks and balances.*

LOOKING BACK AT THE CHAPTER

1. Why did many delegates to the Constitutional Convention think that a new form of government was needed?

2. Explain why the delegates strongly disagreed on these three main issues: **(a)** the powers of the state and national governments, **(b)** representation in the national legislature, **(c)** the election of the President and members of the national legislature.

3. Explain how the delegates at the Constitutional Convention were able to settle each of the three main issues.

4. What were the Federalists' main arguments in favor of the Constitution? What were the Anti-Federalists' main arguments against it?

5. Explain why the Constitution was finally ratified.

6. Describe in your own words the six goals stated in the Preamble.

7. Explain how the first three articles of the Constitution ensure that no part of the government abuses its power.

8. Explain the importance of each of the last four articles of the Constitution.

9. *Evaluation.* Do you think the title "architect" of the Constitution is appropriate for James Madison? Explain.

10. *Evaluation.* Some framers of the Constitution believed that average citizens are not well enough informed to vote on candidates and issues. Do you agree? Explain.

11. *Analysis.* What evidence is there that the Constitution resulted from debate between strong supporters of a powerful national government and strong supporters of states' rights?

12. *Evaluation.* Why do you think that our Constitution has lasted for over 200 years?

WORKING TOGETHER

1. Working in groups of four, put together a skit illustrating the Constitutional Convention. Choose people to play the roles of James Madison, George Washington, William Paterson, and Roger Sherman. Prepare arguments on the main issues facing the convention: dividing power between the states and the national government, representation in Congress, and the procedure for selecting government officials.

2. Work together to stage a debate between the Federalists and the Anti-Federalists on the issue of ratification of the Constitution.

3. With a group, make a scrapbook of articles from newspapers and news magazines that illustrate principles outlined in the Constitution. Write a short paragraph for each article telling how it shows the Constitution in action.

Teaching Note: For reinforcement of decision-making skills, use Decision-Making Worksheet Chapter 5.

SOCIAL STUDIES SKILLS

Interpreting a Flow Chart

Often it is not enough to have someone tell you the steps in a process. You may want to *see* those steps, perhaps in a flow chart, one that uses arrows and lines to show movement.

A good example is the flow chart below, which illustrates the amendment process described in Article 5 of the Constitution. The chart shows the different paths that can be followed to propose and then ratify an amendment. Study the flow chart and then answer the questions that follow.

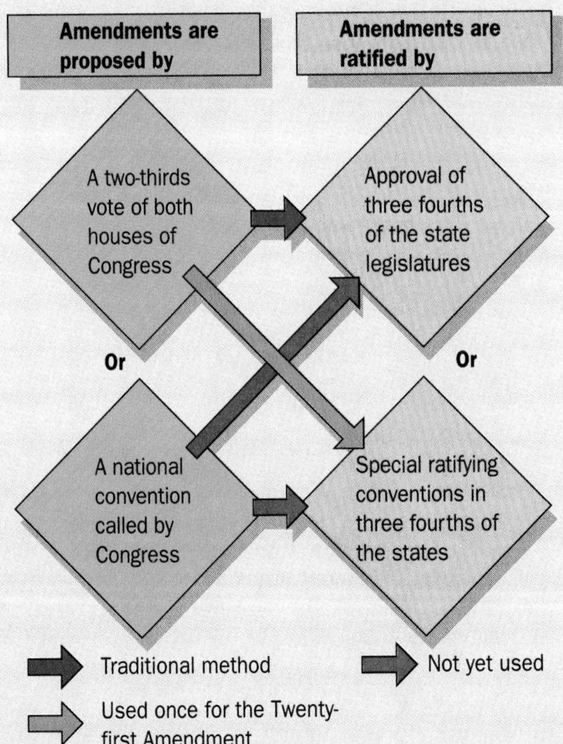

1. Who can propose amendments?

2. Who can ratify amendments?

3. How many different ways are there to propose and then ratify an amendment?

4. Which way has been most often used?

DECISION-MAKING SKILLS

Taking Action

Read the following description of how the Federalists worked to get the Constitution ratified. Identify the steps they went through in taking action to reach their goal. Then answer the questions.

The Federalists knew that their greatest obstacle was the state legislatures, whose members wanted to protect states' rights. On the positive side, the Constitution was supported by many patriots, including George Washington, who could take the Federalists' message directly to the voters. Also, economic experts like Alexander Hamilton could convince people that a strong government would help the country's ailing economy.

The approval of nine states was needed to ratify the Constitution. In states where the majority of the people supported the Constitution, the Federalists tried to get a vote taken quickly. They did not want to give the Anti-Federalists in those states time to get organized. However, in Virginia, Massachusetts, and New York, the Federalists needed more time to build support.

In Massachusetts the Federalists faced unexpected criticism from the popular patriot Samuel Adams. To win his support, they promised to add a bill of rights. Washington's support helped win over Virginia, but it looked like New York would probably reject the Constitution. To prevent this, James Madison, Alexander Hamilton, and John Jay wrote a series of articles for New York newspapers. Their convincing arguments tipped the scale in favor of the Constitution.

1. What are the main steps in taking action?

2. Which steps are evident in the above account? Explain.

3. Why is it important to identify obstacles and resources when planning and taking action in decision making?

The Constitution of the United States

The text of the Constitution appears to the left below. In this version, spelling, capitalization, and punctuation have been modernized. Blue lines in the text mark passages that have been changed or voided by amendments. The words to the right below are comments on the meaning and history of the Constitution.

PREAMBLE

We the people of the United States, in order to form a more perfect Union, establish justice, insure domestic tranquility, provide for the common defense, promote the general welfare, and secure the blessings of liberty to ourselves and our posterity, do ordain and establish this Constitution for the United States of America.

PREAMBLE

The Preamble lists the purposes of the new government, based on the will of the people. Following the Preamble are the first three articles of the Constitution. They divide the powers of government among three distinct branches. They create a system of checks and balances.

ARTICLE 1

Section 1

All legislative powers herein granted shall be vested in a Congress of the United States, which shall consist of a Senate and House of Representatives.

ARTICLE 1. The Legislative Branch

Section 1. A Two-Part Congress

The legislative branch is empowered to make laws. Its powers are given to both the Senate and the House of Representatives.

Section 2

Clause 1. The House of Representatives shall be composed of members chosen every second year by the people of the several states, and the electors in each state shall have the qualifications requisite for electors of the most numerous branch of the state legislature.

Section 2. The House of Representatives

Clause 1. Elections and Voters. All the members of the House are elected every two years. Voters for House members must be qualified to vote in certain state elections.

Clause 2. No person shall be a representative who shall not have attained to the age of twenty-five years, and been seven years a citizen of the United States, and who shall not, when elected, be an inhabitant of that state in which he shall be chosen.

Clause 2. Qualifications of Representatives

Clause 3. Representatives and direct taxes shall be apportioned among the several states which may be included within this Union, according to their respective numbers, ~~which shall be determined by adding to the whole number of free persons, including those bound to service for a term of years, and excluding Indians not taxed, three fifths of all other persons.~~ The actual enumeration shall be made within three years after the first meeting of the Congress of the United States, and within every subsequent term of ten years, in such manner as they shall by law direct. The number of representatives shall not exceed one for every thirty thousand, but each state shall have at least one representative; ~~and until such enumeration shall be made, the state of New Hampshire shall be entitled to choose three, Massachusetts eight, Rhode Island and Providence Plantations one, Connecticut five, New York six, New Jersey four, Pennsylvania eight, Delaware one, Maryland six, Virginia ten, North Carolina five, South Carolina five, and Georgia three.~~

Clause 3. Apportionment of Representatives. The number of Representatives from each state is based on the state's population. Originally, indentured servants ("those bound to service") were counted as if they were free. But slaves ("all other persons") were counted as three fifths of a person. Thus it took 500 slaves to equal 300 free persons in deciding numbers of Representatives. When slavery was ended by the Thirteenth Amendment in 1865, the three-fifths rule became meaningless.

The "actual enumeration," or census, was first made in 1790. It has been repeated every ten years since. Today there is no worry that the number of Representatives might exceed one for every thirty thousand persons. A typical House member now represents about five hundred thousand persons.

Clause 4. When vacancies happen in the representation from any state, the executive authority thereof shall issue writs of election to fill such vacancies.

Clause 4. Filling Vacancies. The "executive authority" refers to a state governor. If a House seat becomes vacant between regular elections, the governor is empowered to call a special election to fill the seat.

Clause 5. The House of Representatives shall choose their speaker and other officers, and shall have the sole power of impeachment.

Clause 5. Officers; Power of Impeachment. The Speaker of the House is the leading officer of the House. Only the House can bring impeachment charges. (See Section 3, Clauses 6 and 7, below.)

Section 3

Section 3. The Senate

Clause 1. The Senate of the United States shall be composed of two senators from each state, ~~chosen by the legislature thereof,~~ for six years; and each senator shall have one vote.

Clause 1. Elections. Senators were elected by state legislatures until the Seventeenth Amendment, ratified in 1913. Since then, Senators have been chosen directly by the voters of each state.

Clause 2. Immediately after they shall be assembled in consequence of the first election, they shall be divided as equally as may be into three classes. The seats of the senators of the first class shall be vacated at the expiration of the second year, of the second class at the expiration of the fourth year, and of the third class at the expiration of the sixth year, so that one third may be chosen every second year; ~~and if vacancies happen by resignation, or otherwise, during the recess of the legislature of any state, the executive thereof may make temporary appointments until the next meeting of the legislature, which shall then fill such vacancies.~~

Clause 2. Overlapping Terms of Office; Filling Vacancies. By dividing Senators into three classes, or groups, the Constitution set up a system of overlapping terms in office. Every two years, one third of the Senators must leave office or stand for reelection. Thus the Senate changes somewhat every two years, even though Senators are elected to six-year terms.

The method of filling vacancies in the Senate was changed by the Seventeenth Amendment. It gave the power of choosing replacements to the voters of each state.

Clause 3. No person shall be a senator who shall not have attained to the age of thirty years, and been nine years a citizen of the United States, and who shall not, when elected, be an inhabitant of that state for which he shall be chosen.

Clause 3. Qualifications of Senators

Clause 4. The Vice-President of the United States shall be president of the Senate, but shall have no vote, unless they be equally divided.

Clause 4. President of the Senate. The Vice-President serves as president of the Senate, but votes only in case of a tie.

Clause 5. The Senate shall choose their other officers and also a president pro tempore, in the absence of the Vice-President, or when he shall exercise the office of President of the United States.

Clause 5. Election of Senate Officers. The Senate elects officers, including a temporary president of the Senate. The president pro tempore, or pro tem, leads meetings when the Vice-President is absent.

Clause 6. The Senate shall have the sole power to try all impeachments. When sitting for that purpose, they shall be on oath or affirmation. When the President of the United States is tried, the Chief Justice shall preside. And no person shall be convicted without the concurrence of two thirds of the members present.

Clause 6. Impeachment Trials. The Senate serves as a jury in impeachment cases. A conviction requires a two-thirds vote of the members present. In 1868 the House impeached President Andrew Johnson, but the Senate acquitted him. In 1974 the House considered impeaching President Richard M. Nixon. Nixon resigned before the House made a final decision about impeachment.

Clause 7. Judgment in cases of impeachment shall not extend further than to removal from office, and disqualification to hold and enjoy any office of honor, trust, or profit under the United States; but the party convicted shall nevertheless be liable and subject to indictment, trial, judgment, and punishment, according to law.

Clause 7. Penalty for Conviction. If an impeached person is convicted, the person will be removed from office (see Article 2, Section 4) and barred from other federal office. The Senate cannot impose further punishment, but the convicted person can then be tried in a regular court. The Senate has convicted only four persons, all judges. They were removed from office but not tried in regular courts.

Section 4

Clause 1. The times, places, and manner of holding elections for senators and representatives shall be prescribed in each state by the legislature thereof; but the Congress may at any time by law make or alter such regulations, ~~except as to the places of choosing senators.~~

Clause 2. The Congress shall assemble at least once in every year, ~~and such meeting shall be on the first Monday in December, unless they shall by law appoint a different day.~~

Section 4. Times of Elections and Meetings

Clause 1. Elections. Each state regulates its own congressional elections, but Congress can change the regulations. In 1872 Congress required that every state hold congressional elections on the same day.

Clause 2. Meetings. Congress must meet once a year. The Twentieth Amendment, ratified in 1933, changed the first day of the meeting to January 3, unless Congress specifies a different day.

Section 5

Clause 1. Each house shall be the judge of the elections, returns, and qualifications of its own members, and a majority of each shall constitute a quorum to do business; but a smaller number may adjourn from day to day, and may be authorized to compel the attendance of absent members, in such manner and under such penalties as each house may provide.

Clause 2. Each house may determine the rules of its proceedings, punish its members for disorderly behavior, and, with the concurrence of two thirds, expel a member.

Clause 3. Each house shall keep a journal of its proceedings and from time to time publish the same, excepting such parts as may in their judgment require secrecy; and the yeas and nays of the members of either house on any question, shall, at the desire of one fifth of those present, be entered on the journal.

Clause 4. Neither house, during the session of Congress, shall, without the consent of the other, adjourn for more than three days, nor to any other place than that in which the two houses shall be sitting.

Section 5. Basics of Organization

Clause 1. Members; Attendance. Each house can judge whether new members have been elected fairly and are qualified to serve. A quorum is the minimum number of members who can act for all. Discussion and debate can go on without a quorum. A quorum is required for voting by either house, however.

Clause 2. Determining Procedures. Each house can set up its own rules of conducting business.

Clause 3. Written Records. Since 1873 the journals of the House and Senate have been published together in the *Congressional Record*. It appears each day when Congress is meeting. A member of either house may insert a speech in the published *Record* even though the speech was not actually delivered on the floor of the House or Senate.

Clause 4. Adjournment. Both houses must agree to any adjournment longer than three days.

Section 6

Clause 1. The senators and representatives shall receive a compensation for their services, to be ascertained by law, and paid out of the Treasury of the United States. They shall in all cases, except treason, felony, and breach of the peace, be privileged from arrest during their attendance at the session of their respective houses, and in going to and returning from the same; and for any speech or debate in either house, they shall not be questioned in any other place.

Clause 2. No senator or representative shall, during the time for which he was elected, be appointed to any civil office under the authority of the United States which shall have been created, or the emoluments whereof shall have been increased, during such time; and no person holding any office under the United States shall be a member of either house during his continuance in office.

Section 6. Special Rights and Restrictions

Clause 1. Salaries and Privileges. The members of Congress can by law set their own salaries. When Congress is in session, members cannot be arrested except on certain criminal charges. Thus the work of Congress cannot be disrupted by lawsuits against Senators and Representatives. In particular, the members of Congress cannot be sued for "any speech or debate in either house." While taking part in the work of Congress, members can write or say anything about anyone without fear of being sued for libel or slander.

Clause 2. Employment Restrictions. Members of Congress cannot create new federal jobs or increase the "emoluments," or payments, for old ones and then leave Congress to take those jobs. Nor can anyone holding a federal job outside Congress serve at the same time as a member of Congress. This restriction prevents the members of Congress from simultaneously working for other branches of the federal government.

Section 7

Clause 1. All bills for raising revenue shall originate in the House of Representatives; but the Senate may propose or concur with amendments as on other bills.

Clause 2. Every bill which shall have passed the House of Representatives and the Senate shall, before it becomes a law, be presented to the President of the United States. If he approve he shall sign it, but if not, he shall return it, with his objections, to that house in which it shall have originated, who shall enter the objections at large on their journal and proceed to reconsider it. If, after such reconsideration, two thirds of that house shall agree to pass the bill, it shall be sent, together with the objections, to the other house, by which it shall likewise be reconsidered, and, if approved by two thirds of that house, it shall become a law. But in all such cases the votes of both houses shall be determined by yeas and nays, and the names of the persons voting for and against the bill shall be entered on the journal of each house respectively. If any bill shall not be returned by the President within ten days (Sundays excepted) after it shall have been presented to him, the same shall be a law, in like manner as if he had signed it, unless the Congress by their adjournment prevent its return, in which case it shall not be a law.

Clause 3. Every order, resolution, or vote to which the concurrence of the Senate and House of Representatives may be necessary (except on a question of adjournment) shall be presented to the President of the United States; and before the same shall take effect, shall be approved by him, or being disapproved by him, shall be repassed by two thirds of the Senate and House of Representatives, according to the rules and limitations prescribed in the case of a bill.

Section 8

The Congress shall have power:

Clause 1. To lay and collect taxes, duties, imposts, and excises, to pay the debts and provide for the common defense and general welfare of the United States; but all duties, imposts, and excises shall be uniform throughout the United States;

Clause 2. To borrow money on the credit of the United States;

Clause 3. To regulate commerce with foreign nations, and among the several states, and with the Indian tribes;

Clause 4. To establish a uniform rule of naturalization and uniform laws on the subject of bankruptcies throughout the United States;

Clause 5. To coin money, regulate the value thereof, and of foreign coin, and fix the standard of weights and measures;

Section 7

Clause 1. Tax Bills. All tax bills must begin in the House. The Senate, however, can thoroughly revise such bills.

Clause 2. Submitting Bills to the President. After Congress passes a bill, it goes to the President. The bill can then become a law in one of three ways. First the President may approve the bill and sign it. Second, the President may veto the bill and return it to Congress with objections. If Congress is able to override the President's veto by a two-thirds vote of both houses, the bill becomes law. Third, the President may do nothing. In that case the bill becomes law after 10 days (not counting Sundays), provided Congress is in session at that time.

The bill can fail to become a law in two ways. First, the President may veto it. If Congress is unable to override the veto, the bill dies. Second, the President may do nothing. If Congress adjourns within 10 days, the bill dies. This method is called a pocket veto. A President may use it to avoid an open veto of a controversial bill.

Clause 3. Submitting Other Measures to the President. If other measures require agreement by both houses and are in effect bills, they must go to the President. Thus Congress cannot avoid submitting bills to the President by calling them orders or resolutions. When such measures reach the President, they are treated as bills.

Section 8. Powers Granted to Congress

Clause 1. Taxation. Congress can impose "duties," taxes on imported goods. But Congress cannot tax exports. (See Section 9, Clause 5, below.) "Excises" are taxes on making, selling, or using items such as cigarettes within the nation. "Imposts" are taxes of any sort.

Clause 2. Borrowing.

Clause 3. Regulating Interstate Trade. This is the "interstate commerce clause," the basis of many federal regulations.

Clause 4. Naturalization; Bankruptcy

Clause 5. Coining Money. The federal government's power to print paper money derives from this clause.

Clause 6. To provide for the punishment of counterfeiting the securities and current coin of the United States;

Clause 6. Punishment of Counterfeiting. The "securities" referred to are government bonds.

Clause 7. To establish post offices and post roads;

Clause 7. Providing Postal Service

Clause 8. To promote the progress of science and useful arts, by securing for limited times to authors and inventors the exclusive right to their respective writings and discoveries;

Clause 8. Encouraging Authors and Inventors. Through this clause authors receive copyrights and inventors receive patents.

Clause 9. To constitute tribunals inferior to the Supreme Court;

Clause 9. Establishing Lower Courts. Federal courts "inferior to the Supreme Court" include district courts and the United States Court of Appeals.

Clause 10. To define and punish piracies and felonies committed on the high seas and offenses against the law of nations;

Clause 10. Punishment of Crimes at Sea

Clause 11. To declare war, grant letters of marque and reprisal, and make rules concerning captures on land and water;

Clause 11. Declaring War. "Letters of marque and reprisal" authorize private ships to attack and seize enemy ships.

Clause 12. To raise and support armies, but no appropriation of money to that use shall be for a longer term than two years;

Clause 12. Raising Armies

Clause 13. To provide and maintain a navy;

Clause 13. Maintaining a Navy

Clause 14. To make rules for the government and regulation of the land and naval forces;

Clause 14. Regulating the Armed Forces

Clause 15. To provide for calling forth the militia to execute the laws of the Union, suppress insurrections, and repel invasions;

Clause 15. Calling Out the Militia. Congress can empower the President to call out state militia units, now known as the National Guard.

Clause 16. To provide for organizing, arming, and disciplining the militia, and for governing such part of them as may be employed in the service of the United States, reserving to the states respectively the appointment of the officers and the authority of training the militia according to the discipline prescribed by Congress;

Clause 16. Maintaining the Militia. The federal government and each state government share in providing funds for the National Guard.

Clause 17. To exercise exclusive legislation in all cases whatsoever over such district (not exceeding ten miles square) as may, by cession of particular states and the acceptance of Congress, become the seat of the government of the United States, and to exercise like authority over all places purchased by the consent of the legislature of the state in which the same shall be for the erection of forts, magazines, arsenals, dockyards, and other needful buildings; and

Clause 17. Control of Federal Property. Congress makes laws for the District of Columbia and for federal land on which forts, naval bases, and other federal structures stand.

Clause 18. To make all laws which shall be necessary and proper for carrying into execution the foregoing powers and all other powers vested by this Constitution in the government of the United States, or in any department or officer thereof.

Clause 18. Carrying Out Granted Powers. This clause, known as the "necessary and proper" clause, gives Congress a basis for dealing with matters not specifically named in the Constitution. The clause is also known as the "elastic clause."

Section 9

Section 9. Powers Denied to Congress

Clause 1. The migration or importation of such persons as any of the states now existing shall think proper to admit shall not be prohibited by Congress prior to the year 1808, but a tax or duty may be imposed on such importation, not exceeding ten dollars for each person.

Clause 1. Ending the Slave Trade. Congress was forbidden to end the importing of slaves before 1808. In that year, Congress declared that further importing of slaves was illegal.

Clause 2. The privilege of the writ of habeas corpus shall not be suspended, unless, when in cases of rebellion or invasion, the public safety may require it.

Clause 2. Suspending the Writ of Habeas Corpus. A writ of habeas corpus is a legal order saying that a person who is held in custody must be brought into court so that a judge can decide whether the person is being held illegally.

Clause 3. No bill of attainder or ex post facto law shall be passed.

Clause 3. Imposing Certain Penalties. A "bill of attainder" allows a person to be punished without a jury trial. An "ex post facto law" allows a person to be punished for an act that was not illegal when it was committed.

Clause 4. No capitation ~~or other direct~~ tax shall be laid, unless in proportion to the census or enumeration herein before directed to be taken.

Clause 4. Taxing Individuals Unfairly. A "capitation tax," also known as a "head tax," is paid by individuals directly to the government. This clause requires that any such tax be divided fairly among the states according to their population. The Sixteenth Amendment, ratified in 1913, prevents this clause from being applied to income taxes.

Clause 5. No tax or duty shall be laid on articles exported from any state.

Clause 5. Taxing Exports. Here "exported" means sent out of a state, whether to another state or to another country.

Clause 6. No preference shall be given by any regulation of commerce or revenue to the ports of one state over those of another; nor shall vessels bound to or from one state be obliged to enter, clear, or pay duties in another.

Clause 6. Taxing Trade Unfairly; Allowing Ships to Be Taxed in Trade Between States

Clause 7. No money shall be drawn from the Treasury but in consequence of appropriations made by law; and a regular statement and account of the receipts and expenditures of all public money shall be published from time to time.

Clause 7. Unlawful Spending. The federal government can spend money only when Congress authorizes the spending. Federal spending and receipts must be recorded and published.

Clause 8. No title of nobility shall be granted by the United States. And no person holding any office of profit or trust under them shall, without the consent of the Congress, accept of any present, emolument, office, or title of any kind whatever from any king, prince, or foreign state.

Clause 8. Creating Titles of Nobility; Allowing Gifts from Foreign Countries Without Permission. Congress cannot give anyone a title such as duchess or count. Congress has passed laws letting federal officials accept small gifts from foreign countries. Larger gifts become the property of the United States government.

Section 10

Section 10. Powers Denied to the States

Clause 1. No state shall enter into any treaty, alliance, or confederation; grant letters of marque and reprisal; coin money; emit bills of credit; make anything but gold and silver coin a tender in payment of debts; pass any bill of attainder, ex post facto law, or law impairing the obligation of contracts, or grant any title of nobility.

Clause 1. Certain Foreign, Financial, and Legal Dealings. Some of these powers are given exclusively to the federal government. Others are denied to any government, state or federal.

Clause 2. No state shall, without the consent of the Congress, lay any imposts or duties on imports or exports, except what may be absolutely necessary for executing its inspection laws; and the net produce of all duties and imposts laid by any state on imports or exports shall be for the use of the Treasury of the United States; and all such laws shall be subject to the revision and control of the Congress.

Clause 2. Taxing Imports or Exports Without Permission. Except with the consent of Congress, a state cannot tax any goods entering or leaving the state. The state can charge a small fee, however, to pay for inspection of the goods.

Clause 3. No state shall, without the consent of Congress, lay any duty of tonnage; keep troops or ships of war in time of peace; enter into any agreement or compact with another state or with a foreign power; or engage in war, unless actually invaded, or in such imminent danger as will not admit of delay.

Clause 3. Taxing Ships or Making Military or Diplomatic Arrangements Without Permission. States need permission of Congress to tax ships' cargo ("tonnage") or to prepare for or wage war, except in a military emergency.

ARTICLE 2

Section 1

Clause 1. The executive power shall be vested in a President of the United States of America. He shall hold his office during the term of four years, and, together with the Vice-President, chosen for the same term, be elected as follows:

Clause 2. Each state shall appoint, in such manner as the legislature thereof may direct, a number of electors, equal to the whole number of senators and representatives to which the state may be entitled in the Congress; but no senator or representative, or person holding an office of trust or profit under the United States, shall be appointed an elector.

~~**Clause 3.** The electors shall meet in their respective states and vote by ballot for two persons, of whom one at least shall not be an inhabitant of the same state with themselves. And they shall make a list of all the persons voted for and of the number of votes for each; which list they shall sign and certify, and transmit sealed to the seat of the government of the United States, directed to the president of the Senate. The president of the Senate shall, in the presence of the Senate and House of Representatives, open all the certificates, and the votes shall then be counted. The person having the greatest number of votes shall be the President, if such number be a majority of the whole number of electors appointed; and if there be more than one who have such majority, and have an equal number of votes, then the House of Representatives shall immediately choose by ballot one of them for President; and if no person have a majority, then from the five highest on the list the said house shall in like manner choose the President. But in choosing the President, the votes shall be taken by states, the representation from each state having one vote; a quorum for this purpose shall consist of a member or members from two thirds of the states, and a majority of all the states shall be necessary to a choice. In every case, after the choice of the President, the person having the greatest number of votes of the electors shall be the Vice-President. But if there should remain two or more who have equal votes, the Senate shall choose from them by ballot the Vice-President.~~

Clause 4. The Congress may determine the time of choosing the electors and the day on which they shall give their votes, which day shall be the same throughout the United States.

ARTICLE 2. The Executive Branch

Section 1. The Offices of President and Vice-President

Clause 1. The President as Executive; Term of Office. As chief executive, the President is responsible for executing, or carrying out, the laws passed by Congress.

Clause 2. Choosing Electors. This clause set up the electoral college, the group of people who elect the President and Vice-President. At first the electors were chosen mainly by state legislatures. After 1800 the electors were chosen increasingly by popular vote. Today all electors are chosen in this way.

Clause 3. Voting by Electors. Originally each elector voted for two candidates. Either might become President. As a result, the Republican candidate for President in 1800, Thomas Jefferson, received the same number of electoral votes as the Republican candidate for Vice-President, Aaron Burr. The choice was then left to the House of Representatives, which finally chose Jefferson.

To prevent similar ties between candidates for President and Vice-President, Congress passed the Twelfth Amendment in 1803. The amendment was ratified in June 1804, before the next presidential election. It required electors to cast one ballot for President and a separate ballot for Vice-President.

Clause 4. Time of Elections. Congress has decided that presidential elections are to be held every four years. The people vote on the Tuesday following the first Monday of November. Electoral votes are cast on the Monday after the second Wednesday in December.

Clause 5. No person except a natural-born citizen, or a citizen of the United States at the time of the adoption of this Constitution, shall be eligible to the office of President; neither shall any person be eligible to that office who shall not have attained to the age of thirty-five years and been fourteen years a resident within the United States.

Clause 5. Qualifications of the President

Clause 6. In case of the removal of the President from office, or of his death, resignation, or inability to discharge the powers and duties of the said office, the same shall devolve on the Vice-President, and the Congress may by law provide for the case of removal, death, resignation, or inability, both of the President and Vice-President, declaring what officer shall then act as President, and such officer shall act accordingly until the disability be removed or a President shall be elected.

Clause 6. Presidential Succession. In 1886 Congress specified that the line of succession would go from the Vice-President to members of the cabinet. In 1947 Congress changed the line of succession to go from the Vice-President to the Speaker of the House, then to the president pro tempore of the Senate, and then to the cabinet. The Twenty-fifth Amendment, ratified in 1967, prevents a long vacancy in the office of Vice-President. The amendment also establishes procedures in case the President is disabled.

Clause 7. The President shall, at stated times, receive for his services a compensation, which shall neither be increased nor diminished during the period for which he shall have been elected, and he shall not receive within that period any other emolument from the United States or any of them.

Clause 7. Presidential Salary

Clause 8. Before he enter on the execution of his office, he shall take the following oath or affirmation: "I do solemnly swear (or affirm) that I will faithfully execute the office of President of the United States, and will, to the best of my ability, preserve, protect, and defend the Constitution of the United States."

Clause 8. The Oath of Office. The Constitution does not say who will administer the oath. Ordinarily it is the Chief Justice of the Supreme Court. Federal Judge Sarah Hughes administered the oath of office to Lyndon Johnson after President John F. Kennedy's assassination in 1963.

Section 2

Section 2. Powers Granted to the President

Clause 1. The President shall be commander in chief of the army and navy of the United States, and of the militia of the several states when called into actual service of the United States. He may require the opinion, in writing, of the principal officer in each of the executive departments upon any subject relating to the duties of their respective offices. And he shall have power to grant reprieves and pardons for offenses against the United States, except in cases of impeachment.

Clause 1. Military Powers; Executive Powers; Reprieves and Pardons. Together, the military powers of the President and of Congress assure civilian control of the armed forces.

The President may grant a reprieve to stop punishment after a trial or a pardon to prevent a trial. In 1974 President Gerald R. Ford issued a pardon to Richard M. Nixon. Nixon then could not be tried on federal charges related to the Watergate scandal.

Clause 2. He shall have power, by and with the advice and consent of the Senate, to make treaties, provided two thirds of the senators present concur; and he shall nominate, and by and with the advice and consent of the Senate, shall appoint ambassadors, other public ministers and consuls, judges of the Supreme Court, and all other officers of the United States whose appointments were not herein otherwise provided for, and which shall be established by law; but the Congress may by law vest the appointment of such inferior officers as they think proper in the President alone, in the courts of law, or in the heads of departments.

Clause 2. Treaties and Appointments. The President may make treaties and appointments. This power can be checked by the power of the Senate to reject them.

Clause 3. The President shall have power to fill up vacancies that may happen during the recess of Senate, by granting commissions which shall expire at the end of their next session.

Clause 3. Temporary Appointments. When the Senate is not in session and cannot confirm appointments, the President may fill vacancies on a temporary basis.

Section 3

He shall from time to time give to the Congress information of the state of the Union, and recommend to their consideration such measures as he shall judge necessary and expedient; he may, on extraordinary occasions, convene both houses, or either of them, and in case of disagreement between them with respect to the time of adjournment, he may adjourn them to such time as he shall think proper; he shall receive ambassadors and other public ministers; he shall take care that the laws be faithfully executed, and shall commission all the officers of the United States.

Section 3. Duties of the President

The President delivers a State of the Union message to Congress each January. On many occasions, especially in the 1800s, the President has called Congress into special session. No President has needed to adjourn Congress.

The duty of receiving ambassadors fits the President's power to make treaties. The duty to "take care that the laws be faithfully executed" places the President in charge of federal law enforcement.

Section 4

The President, Vice-President, and all civil officers of the United States shall be removed from office on impeachment for, and conviction of, treason, bribery, or other high crimes and misdemeanors.

Section 4. Impeachment

Among the "civil officers" who can be impeached are cabinet members and federal judges.

ARTICLE 3

Section 1

The judicial power of the United States shall be vested in one Supreme Court, and in such inferior courts as the Congress may from time to time ordain and establish. The judges, both of the Supreme and inferior courts, shall hold their offices during good behavior, and shall, at stated times, receive for their services a compensation which shall not be diminished during their continuance in office.

ARTICLE 3. The Judicial Branch

Section 1. Federal Courts

Congress has established district courts and appeals courts under the Supreme Court.

Congress also has decided from time to time how many justices serve on the Supreme Court. But Congress can neither abolish the Supreme Court nor remove any federal judges unless they are impeached and convicted. Nor can Congress put pressure on judges by lowering their "compensation," or salaries.

Section 2

Clause 1. The judicial power shall extend to all cases, in law and equity, arising under this Constitution, the laws of the United States, and treaties made, or which shall be made, under their authority; to all cases affecting ambassadors, other public ministers and consuls; to all cases of admiralty and maritime jurisdiction; to controversies to which the United States shall be a party; to controversies between two or more states; ~~between a state and citizens of another state;~~ between citizens of different states; between citizens of the same state claiming lands under grants of different states; and between a state, or the citizens thereof, and foreign states, ~~citizens, or subjects.~~

Section 2. Jurisdiction of Federal Courts

Clause 1. Types of Cases. This clause names the types of cases that federal courts can rule on. These include "all cases . . . arising under this Constitution." Therefore the Supreme Court can exercise the right of judicial review, as asserted by Chief Justice John Marshall in the case of *Marbury v. Madison*. Thus the Court can declare a law unconstitutional. First, though, a case that involves the specific law must be brought before the Court. The Court cannot review a law unless it is presented to the Court as part of a case.

Clause 2. In all cases affecting ambassadors, other public ministers and consuls, and those in which a state shall be party, the Supreme Court shall have original jurisdiction. In all the other cases beforementioned, the Supreme Court shall have appellate jurisdiction, both as to law and fact, with such exceptions and under such regulations as the Congress shall make.

Clause 2. Original Cases and Appeals Cases. Cases of "original jurisdiction" go directly to the Supreme Court. Cases of "appellate jurisdiction" go first to lower courts. Then, if the lower court proceedings are appealed, the cases go to the Supreme Court. Congress sets the rules for appeal. Nearly all cases heard by the Supreme Court begin in the lower courts.

Clause 3. The trial of all crimes, except in cases of impeachment, shall be by jury; and such trial shall be held in the state where the said crimes shall have been committed; but when not committed within any state, the trial shall be at such place or places as the Congress may by law have directed.

Clause 3. Cases Requiring Trials by Jury. This clause covers trials involving federal crimes. The clause does not require juries in civil cases, which involve individual rights, or in criminal cases under state laws.

Section 3

Section 3. Treason

Clause 1. Treason against the United States shall consist only in levying war against them or in adhering to their enemies, giving them aid and comfort. No person shall be convicted of treason unless on the testimony of two witnesses to the same overt act, or on confession in open court.

Clause 1. Limits of the Crime. To be convicted of treason against the United States, a person must commit an overt act, one that can be seen. Merely talking or thinking about treason is not a crime.

Clause 2. The Congress shall have power to declare the punishment of treason, but no attainder of treason shall work corruption of blood or forfeiture except during the life of the person attainted.

Clause 2. Limits of the Punishment. "Attainder of treason" and "corruption of blood" refer to punishing the family of a traitor. Such punishment is banned by this clause.

ARTICLE 4

ARTICLE 4. Relations Among the States, the Territories, and the United States

Section 1

Section 1. Official Acts of the States

Full faith and credit shall be given in each state to the public acts, records, and judicial proceedings of every other state. And the Congress may by general laws prescribe the manner in which such acts, records, and proceedings shall be proved, and the effect thereof.

Every state must recognize and honor the official acts of other states. Congress can decide what official proofs (for example, marriage certificates) must be accepted from state to state.

Section 2

Section 2. Privileges and Liabilities of Citizens

Clause 1. The citizens of each state shall be entitled to all privileges and immunities of citizens in the several states.

Clause 1. Privileges. No state can discriminate against a citizen of another state except in special cases, such as residence requirements for voting or entrance requirements for state colleges.

Clause 2. A person charged in any state with treason, felony or other crime, who shall flee from justice and be found in another state, shall, on demand of the executive authority of the state from which he fled, be delivered up to be removed to the state having jurisdiction of the crime.

Clause 2. Liabilities of Fugitive Criminals. If a person commits a crime in one state and then flees to another state and is caught, the governor of the state where the crime took place can demand the person's return.

~~**Clause 3.** No person held to service or labor in one state under the laws thereof, escaping into another, shall, in consequence of any law or regulation therein, be discharged from such service or labor, but shall be delivered up on claim of the party to whom such service or labor may be due.~~

Clause 3. Liabilities of Fugitive Slaves or Servants. The phrase "held to service or labor" refers to slavery or to service as an indentured servant. The Thirteenth Amendment nullified this clause.

Section 3

Section 3. Admitting New States and Regulating Territories

Clause 1. New states may be admitted by the Congress into this Union; but no new state shall be formed or erected within the jurisdiction of any other state; nor any state be formed by the junction of two or more states, or parts of states, without the consent of the legislatures of the states concerned as well as of the Congress.

Clause 1. New States. Congress can add new states to the Union. New states cannot be formed by dividing existing states (as when Maine separated from Massachusetts in 1820) or by combining parts of existing states unless both Congress and the states involved consent to the changes.

Clause 2. The Congress shall have power to dispose of and make all needful rules and regulations respecting the territory or other property belonging to the United States; and nothing in this Constitution shall be so construed as to prejudice any claims of the United States, or of any particular state.

Clause 2. Territories. Besides having power over federal property of various kinds, Congress has the power to govern federal land. This land includes territory not organized into states and also federal land within states.

Section 4

The United States shall guarantee to every state in this Union a republican form of government, and shall protect each of them against invasion, and, on application of the legislature or of the executive (when the legislature cannot be convened), against domestic violence.

Section 4. Protection of the States

The federal government promises that each state will have some form of representative government. The federal government also promises to protect each state from invasion. It will send help, when requested, to stop rioting within a state.

ARTICLE 5

The Congress, whenever two thirds of both houses shall deem it necessary, shall propose amendments to this Constitution or, on the application of the legislatures of two thirds of the several states, shall call a convention for proposing amendments, which, in either case, shall be valid, to all intents and purposes, as part of this Constitution when ratified by the legislatures of three fourths of the several states, or by conventions in three fourths thereof, as the one or the other mode of ratification may be proposed by the Congress; provided ~~that no amendment which may be made prior to the year 1808 shall in any manner affect the first and fourth clauses in the ninth section of the first article; and~~ that no state, without its consent, shall be deprived of its equal suffrage in the Senate.

ARTICLE 5. Methods of Amending the Constitution

There are two ways to propose amendments to the Constitution. One is by a two-thirds vote of both the House and the Senate. The other way—which has not yet been used—is by a special convention demanded by two thirds of the states.

Once an amendment is proposed, there are two ways to ratify it. First, three fourths of the state legislatures may vote to approve it. Second, special conventions in three fourths of the states may approve the amendment. This way has been used only once, to ratify the Twenty-first Amendment. Congress decides which method of ratification to use.

The three-fourths requirement for ratification means that 38 states must now approve a proposed amendment before it becomes law.

ARTICLE 6

ARTICLE 6. Federal Debts and the Supremacy of Federal Laws

Clause 1. All debts contracted and engagements entered into before the adoption of this Constitution shall be as valid against the United States under this Constitution as under the Confederation.

Clause 1. Federal Debts. This clause promises that all debts incurred by Congress under the Articles of Confederation will be honored by the United States under the Constitution.

Clause 2. This Constitution and the laws of the United States which shall be made in pursuance thereof, and all treaties made, or which shall be made, under the authority of the United States, shall be the supreme law of the land; and the judges in every state shall be bound thereby, anything in the constitution or laws of any state to the contrary notwithstanding.

Clause 2. Supremacy of the Constitution and of Federal Laws. The Constitution and federal laws or treaties made under it are the highest laws of the nation. When federal laws are in conflict with state laws or constitutions, state judges must follow the federal laws.

Clause 3. The senators and representatives beforementioned, and the members of the several state legislatures, and all executive and judicial officers, both of the United States and of the several states, shall be bound by oath or affirmation to support this Constitution; but no religious test shall ever be required as a qualification to any office or public trust under the United States.

Clause 3. Oaths to Support the Constitution. All federal and all state officials must promise to support the Constitution. But federal officials must not be required to meet any religious standards in order to hold office.

State officials may be required to meet religious standards, but since the 1840s no state has set such requirements for its officials.

ARTICLE 7

The ratification of the conventions of nine states shall be sufficient for the establishment of this Constitution between the states so ratifying the same.

Done in convention by the unanimous consent of the states present the seventeenth day of September in the year of our Lord one thousand seven hundred and eighty-seven, and of the independence of the United States of America the twelfth. In witness whereof we have hereunto subscribed our names,

George Washington,
President and deputy from Virginia

New Hampshire
John Langdon
Nicholas Gilman

Massachusetts
Nathaniel Gorham
Rufus King

Connecticut
William Samuel Johnson
Roger Sherman

New York
Alexander Hamilton

New Jersey
William Livingston
David Brearley
William Paterson
Jonathan Dayton

Pennsylvania
Benjamin Franklin
Thomas Mifflin
Robert Morris
George Clymer
Thomas FitzSimons
Jared Ingersoll
James Wilson
Gouverneur Morris

Delaware
George Read
Gunning Bedford, Jr.
John Dickinson
Richard Bassett
Jacob Broom

Maryland
James McHenry
Dan of St. Thomas Jenifer
Daniel Carroll

Virginia
John Blair
James Madison, Jr.

North Carolina
William Blount
Richard Dobbs Spaight
Hugh Williamson

South Carolina
John Rutledge
Charles Cotesworth Pinckney
Charles Pinckney
Pierce Butler

Georgia
William Few
Abraham Baldwin

ARTICLE 7. Ratification of the Constitution

"Conventions" refers to special conventions held in the states to approve or disapprove the Constitution. Nine state conventions voted their approval by June 21, 1788. The Constitution was signed on September 17, 1787, in the 12th year of the country's independence. George Washington signed first as the president of the Philadelphia convention. He was not elected President of the United States until 1789. Of the 55 delegates to the Philadelphia convention, 39 signed the Constitution and 16 did not.

Amendments to the Constitution

The first ten amendments, called the Bill of Rights, were proposed as a group in 1789 and ratified in 1791. Other amendments were proposed and ratified one at a time. The dates in parentheses below are the years of ratification.

AMENDMENT 1

Congress shall make no law respecting an establishment of religion or prohibiting the free exercise thereof, or abridging the freedom of speech or of the press, or the right of the people peaceably to assemble and to petition the government for a redress of grievances.

AMENDMENT 1 (1791). Religious and Political Freedoms

Congress cannot establish an official religion or interfere with freedom of worship. It cannot prohibit free speech or other political freedoms.

These freedoms are not absolute, though. They are limited by the rights of others. For example, the right of free speech does not include slander—the spreading of false stories to damage another person's reputation. Nor does the right of free speech include words that present what the Supreme Court has termed a "clear and present danger," such as screaming "fire" in a crowded theater.

AMENDMENT 2

A well-regulated militia being necessary to the security of a free state, the right of the people to keep and bear arms shall not be infringed.

AMENDMENT 2 (1791). The Right to Bear Arms

For the purposes of maintaining a state militia, citizens may keep and bear arms. Congress has prohibited the possession of certain firearms, however, such as sawed-off shotguns and machine guns.

AMENDMENT 3

No soldier shall, in time of peace, be quartered in any house without the consent of the owner, nor in time of war but in a manner to be prescribed by law.

AMENDMENT 3 (1791). The Quartering of Soldiers

In peacetime, soldiers cannot be quartered, or given lodging, in any private home unless the owner consents. In wartime, soldiers can be quartered in private homes, but only as directed by law.

AMENDMENT 4

The right of the people to be secure in their persons, houses, papers, and effects against unreasonable searches and seizures shall not be violated, and no warrants shall issue, but upon probable cause, supported by oath or affirmation, and particularly describing the place to be searched and the persons or things to be seized.

AMENDMENT 4 (1791). Freedom from Unreasonable Searches and Seizures

People and their homes and belongings are protected against unreasonable searches and seizures. As a rule, authorities must go before a court and obtain a search warrant before seizing evidence. They must get an arrest warrant before arresting someone. To obtain a legal warrant, the authorities must explain why it is needed, where the search will take place, and who or what will be seized.

AMENDMENT 5

No person shall be held to answer for a capital or otherwise infamous crime unless on a presentment or indictment of a grand jury, except in cases arising in the land or naval forces, or in the militia, when in actual service in time of war or public danger; nor shall any person be subject for the same offense to be twice put in jeopardy of life or limb; nor shall be compelled in any criminal case to be a witness against himself, nor be deprived of life, liberty, or property without due process of law; nor shall private property be taken for public use without just compensation.

AMENDMENT 5 (1791). Rights Regarding Life, Liberty, and Property

A person cannot be placed on trial in a federal court for a crime punishable by death or for any other major crime without a formal written accusation by a grand jury. This rule does not apply if the person is a member of the armed services during war or a time of public danger.

A grand jury can decide that there is not enough evidence to accuse a person of a crime. Or the jury can make a formal accusation. The charge can be based on evidence the jury gains on its own (a presentment) or on evidence presented by a prosecutor (an indictment). The accused person can then be held for trial before a trial jury.

If a person is found not guilty of a certain crime, the person cannot be tried again for the same offense (double jeopardy) in a federal court.

A person accused of a federal crime cannot be forced to give evidence against himself or herself. Nor can a person lose his or her life, liberty, or property in federal proceedings except as specified by law. When the government takes private property for public use, the government must pay a fair price.

AMENDMENT 6

In all criminal prosecutions, the accused shall enjoy the right to a speedy and public trial by an impartial jury of the state and district wherein the crime shall have been committed, which district shall have been previously ascertained by law, and to be informed of the nature and cause of the accusation; to be confronted with the witnesses against him; to have compulsory process for obtaining witnesses in his favor, and to have the assistance of counsel for his defense.

AMENDMENT 6 (1791). The Right to a Trial by Jury in Criminal Cases

A person accused of a crime has the right to a prompt, public trial. The case will be heard by a jury selected from the district in which the crime was committed. That district must be one that already has been described by law, such as an established city or county.

Accused persons must be informed of the exact charges against them. They must be allowed to face and question witnesses. Any accused person has the power to force witnesses to appear in court and has the right to a defense lawyer.

AMENDMENT 7

In suits at common law, where the value in controversy shall exceed twenty dollars, the right of trial by jury shall be preserved, and no fact tried by a jury shall be otherwise reexamined in any court of the United States than according to the rules of the common law.

AMENDMENT 7 (1791). The Right to a Trial by Jury in Civil Cases

Common law is based on customs and on decisions made by judges in previous cases. (Statute law, in contrast, is established by legislatures.)

When suits involve more than $20 and are tried in federal courts, either side can insist on a jury trial. If both sides agree, they can choose not to have a jury.

A jury's decision cannot be overturned merely because a judge disagrees with the jury's findings.

AMENDMENT 8

Excessive bail shall not be required, nor excessive fines imposed, nor cruel and unusual punishments inflicted.

AMENDMENT 8 (1791). Bail, Fines, and Punishments

Bail is money or property that an accused person gives temporarily to a court as a guarantee that he or she will appear for trial. The more serious the crime, usually the higher the bail. The amount also depends on the reputation and circumstances of the accused person. Unreasonably high bail is forbidden. So are unreasonably high fines and cruel and unusual punishments.

AMENDMENT 9

The enumeration in the Constitution of certain rights shall not be construed to deny or disparage others retained by the people.

AMENDMENT 9 (1791). Further Rights of the People

The naming of certain rights in the Constitution does not mean that people are limited to those rights only. People may claim other rights as well.

AMENDMENT 10

The powers not delegated to the United States by the Constitution, nor prohibited by it to the states, are reserved to the states respectively, or to the people.

AMENDMENT 10 (1791). Powers Reserved to the States and to the People

The federal government is granted certain powers under the Constitution. All other powers, except those denied to the states, belong to the states or to the people.

AMENDMENT 11

The judicial power of the United States shall not be construed to extend to any suit in law or equity commenced or prosecuted against one of the United States by citizens of another state, or by citizens or subjects of any foreign state.

AMENDMENT 12

The electors shall meet in their respective states and vote by ballot for President and Vice-President, one of whom at least shall not be an inhabitant of the same state with themselves; they shall name in their ballots the person voted for as President, and in distinct ballots the person voted for as Vice-President, and they shall make distinct lists of all persons voted for as President and of all persons voted for as Vice-President and of the number of votes for each, which lists they shall sign and certify and transmit sealed to the seat of government of the United States, directed to the president of the Senate. The president of the Senate shall, in the presence of the Senate and House of Representatives, open all the certificates and the votes shall then be counted. The person having the greatest number of votes for President shall be the President, if such number be a majority of the whole number of electors appointed; and if no person have such majority, then from the persons having the highest numbers not exceeding three on the list of those voted for as President, the House of Representatives shall choose immediately, by ballot, the President. But in choosing the President the votes shall be taken by states, the representation from each state having one vote; a quorum for this purpose shall consist of a member or members from two thirds of the states, and a majority of all the states shall be necessary to a choice. And if the House of Representatives shall not choose a President whenever the right of choice shall devolve upon them, ~~before the fourth day of March next following,~~ then the Vice-President shall act as President, as in the case of the death or other constitutional disability of the President. The person having the greatest number of votes as Vice-President shall be the Vice-President, if such number be a majority of the whole number of electors appointed, and if no person have a majority, then from the two highest numbers on the list the Senate shall choose the Vice-President; a quorum for the purpose shall consist of two thirds of the whole number of senators, and a majority of the whole number shall be necessary to a choice. But no person constitutionally ineligible to the office of President shall be eligible to that of Vice-President of the United States.

AMENDMENT 11 (1795). Lawsuits Against the States

This amendment came about because the states feared a loss of authority if they could be sued in federal courts by foreigners or by citizens of other states. The amendment prevents such lawsuits from taking place in federal courts.

AMENDMENT 12 (1804). Separate Voting for President and Vice-President

In each presidential election before 1800, the two leading candidates received differing numbers of electoral votes. The candidate with the higher number became President. The second-place candidate became Vice-President.

In 1800, electors voted along party lines. The Republican candidates for President and Vice-President received equal numbers of electoral votes. To prevent similar ties in later elections, this amendment requires separate electoral voting for President and Vice-President.

If no single candidate for President has a majority of the electoral votes for President, the House of Representatives must choose, by ballot, from the three leading candidates. In the balloting, each state may cast only one vote, no matter how many Representatives it has. If no single candidate for Vice-President has a majority of the electoral votes for Vice-President, the Senate must choose between the two leading candidates.

AMENDMENT 13

Section 1

Neither slavery nor involuntary servitude, except as a punishment for crime whereof the party shall have been duly convicted, shall exist within the United States or any place subject to their jurisdiction.

Section 2

Congress shall have power to enforce this article by appropriate legislation.

AMENDMENT 14

Section 1

All persons born or naturalized in the United States and subject to the jurisdiction thereof are citizens of the United States and of the state wherein they reside. No state shall make or enforce any law which shall abridge the privileges or immunities of citizens of the United States; nor shall any state deprive any person of life, liberty, or property without due process of law; nor deny to any person within its jurisdiction the equal protection of the laws.

Section 2

Representatives shall be apportioned among the several states according to their respective numbers, counting the whole number of persons in each state, ~~excluding Indians not taxed.~~ But when the right to vote at any election for the choice of electors for President and Vice-President of the United States, representatives in Congress, the executive and judicial officers of a state, or the members of the legislature thereof is denied to any of the ~~male~~ inhabitants of such state, being ~~twenty-one years of age and~~ citizens of the United States, or in any way abridged, except for participation in rebellion or other crime, the basis of representation therein shall be reduced in the proportion which the number of such ~~male~~ citizens shall bear to the whole number of ~~male~~ citizens ~~twenty-one years of age~~ in such state.

Section 3

No person shall be a senator or representative in Congress, or elector of President and Vice-President, or hold any office, civil or military, under the United States, or under any state, who, having previously taken an oath as a member of Congress or as an officer of the United States or as a member of any state legislature or as an executive or judicial officer of any state to support the Constitution of the United States, shall have engaged in insurrection or rebellion against the same, or given aid or comfort to the enemies thereof. But Congress may by a vote of two thirds of each house remove such disability.

AMENDMENT 13 (1865). Abolition of Slavery

Section 1. Abolition

The Emancipation Proclamation, which took effect in 1863, applied only to the area then controlled by the Confederacy. This amendment bans slavery throughout the United States. The amendment also bans forced labor—"involuntary servitude"—except as legal punishment for crimes.

Section 2. Power of Enforcement

Congress has the power to pass laws to enforce this amendment.

AMENDMENT 14 (1868). Citizenship and Civil Rights

Section 1. Citizenship

This section defines state citizenship. It prevents states from setting up their own definitions of citizenship in order to exclude blacks or other groups.

The section also applies the due-process clause of the Fifth Amendment to actions by state governments. Since all citizens have "equal protection of the laws," states may not pass laws to discriminate unreasonably against any group.

Section 2. Representation and Voting Rights

Before 1865, each slave was counted as three fifths of a free person in determining the number of Representatives a state could send to Congress. This section does away with the three-fifths rule and sets up a different rule. If a state denies the right to vote to male citizens age 21 or over—excepting those who have taken part in a rebellion or other crimes—that state would lose a proportional number of Representatives in Congress.

The rule was meant to force former slave states to allow black men to vote. It has never been enforced. Instead, the Fifteenth Amendment, ratified in 1870, has been used in lawsuits concerning voting rights for blacks.

Section 3. Disqualification of Former Confederate Leaders

Former state and federal officials who had served in the Confederacy were disqualified from holding state or federal office again, unless Congress voted otherwise. Congress did not completely remove this disqualification until 1898.

Section 4

The validity of the public debt of the United States, authorized by law, including debts incurred for payment of pensions and bounties for services in suppressing insurrection or rebellion, shall not be questioned. But neither the United States nor any state shall assume or pay any debt or obligation incurred in aid of insurrection or rebellion against the United States or any claim for the loss or emancipation of any slave; but all such debts, obligations, and claims shall be held illegal and void.

Section 4. Legal and Illegal Debts

The payment of the federal debt cannot be questioned, according to this section. This referred to debts that the Union incurred during the Civil War. Payment of the Confederate debt by any state or by the United States is illegal. Former slave owners have no legal claim to payment of any kind for their loss of slaves.

Former Confederate states were not allowed back into the Union until their legislatures ratified the Thirteenth and Fourteenth Amendments.

Section 5

The Congress shall have power to enforce, by appropriate legislation, the provisions of this article.

Section 5. Power of Enforcement

Congress has the power to pass laws to enforce this amendment.

AMENDMENT 15

Section 1

The right of citizens of the United States to vote shall not be denied or abridged by the United States or by any state on account of race, color, or previous condition of servitude.

AMENDMENT 15 (1870). Suffrage for Blacks

Section 1. The Right to Vote

Race, color, or "previous condition of servitude"—status as an ex-slave—cannot be used by any state or by the United States to deny a person's right to vote. For a long time, states were able to use literacy tests and other devices to prevent many blacks from voting, despite this amendment.

Section 2

The Congress shall have power to enforce this article by appropriate legislation.

Section 2. Power of Enforcement

Congress has the power to pass laws to enforce this amendment.

AMENDMENT 16

The Congress shall have power to lay and collect taxes on incomes, from whatever source derived, without apportionment among the several states, and without regard to any census or enumeration.

AMENDMENT 16 (1913). Income Taxes

Before this amendment, Congress could not levy an income tax. Article 1 of the Constitution (Section 2, Clause 3, and Section 9, Clause 4) says that federal taxes collected, state by state, must be in proportion to the states' population. This amendment allows an income tax to be levied on individuals and corporations without regard to the populations of the states.

AMENDMENT 17

Section 1

The Senate of the United States shall be composed of two senators from each state, elected by the people thereof for six years; and each senator shall have one vote. The electors in each state shall have the qualifications requisite for electors of the most numerous branch of the state legislatures.

AMENDMENT 17 (1913). Direct Elections of Senators

Section 1. Regular Elections

Article 1 of the Constitution (Section 3, Clause 1) says that Senators are to be elected by state legislatures. This amendment gives the power to elect Senators to the voters of each state.

Section 2

When vacancies happen in the representation of any state in the Senate, the executive authority of such state shall issue writs of election to fill such vacancies, provided that the legislature of any state may empower the executive thereof to make temporary appointments until the people fill the vacancies by election as the legislature may direct.

Section 2. Special Elections

Any vacancy in the Senate must be filled through a special election called by the state governor. The state legislature may let the governor appoint someone to fill the vacancy temporarily, until an election can be held.

Section 3

This amendment shall not be so construed as to affect the election or term of any senator chosen before it becomes valid as part of the Constitution.

Section 3. Time of Effect

This amendment takes effect only when it is ratified as part of the Constitution, and not before.

~~AMENDMENT 18~~

~~Section 1~~

~~After one year from the ratification of this article the manufacture, sale, or transportation of intoxicating liquors within, the importation thereof into, or the exportation thereof from the United States and all territory subject to the jurisdiction thereof for beverage purposes is hereby prohibited.~~

AMENDMENT 18 (1919). National Prohibition

Section 1. The Ban on Alcoholic Beverages

Manufacturing, selling, and transporting alcoholic beverages are to be illegal in the United States and its territories. The ban takes effect one year after the ratification of this amendment. Exporting and importing alcoholic beverages are to be illegal at the same time. This amendment was repealed in 1933 by the Twenty-first Amendment.

~~Section 2~~

~~The Congress and the several states shall have concurrent power to enforce this article by appropriate legislation.~~

Section 2. Power of Enforcement

Both Congress and the states have the power to pass laws to enforce this amendment.

~~Section 3~~

~~This article shall be inoperative unless it shall have been ratified as an amendment to the Constitution by the legislatures of the several states, as provided in the Constitution, within seven years from the date of the submission hereof to the states by the Congress.~~

Section 3. Time Limit for Ratification

This amendment is not to take effect unless it is ratified by state legislatures within seven years.

AMENDMENT 19

Section 1

The right of citizens of the United States to vote shall not be denied or abridged by the United States or by any state on account of sex.

AMENDMENT 19 (1920). Suffrage for Women

Section 1. The Right to Vote

Women and men have an equal right to vote in the elections of the United States and of all the states.

Section 2

Congress shall have power to enforce this article by appropriate legislation.

Section 2. Power of Enforcement

Congress has the power to pass laws to enforce this amendment.

AMENDMENT 20

Section 1

The terms of the President and Vice-President shall end at noon on the 20th day of January, and the terms of senators and representatives at noon on the 3rd day of January, of the years in which such terms would have ended if this article had not been ratified; and the terms of their successors shall then begin.

AMENDMENT 20 (1933). Terms of the President, Vice-President, and Congress

Section 1. Ending Dates of Terms

The terms of the President and Vice-President end on January 20 in their final year. The terms of Senators and Representatives end on January 3.

Before this amendment, the terms of the President, Vice-President, and Congress ended on March 3. Defeated officeholders had to serve until March as "lame ducks," with little political power. This amendment, known as the "lame duck amendment," greatly reduces the time during which defeated officeholders remain in office.

Section 2

The Congress shall assemble at least once in every year, and such meeting shall begin at noon on the 3rd day of January, unless they shall by law appoint a different day.

Section 2. Meetings of Congress

Congress must meet at least once a year, beginning on January 3. Congress, however, can choose a different day.

Section 3

If, at the time fixed for the beginning of the term of the President, the President-elect shall have died, the Vice-President-elect shall become President. If a President shall not have been chosen before the time fixed for the beginning of his term, or if the President-elect shall have failed to qualify, then the Vice-President-elect shall act as President until a President shall have qualified; and the Congress may by law provide for the case wherein neither a President-elect nor a Vice-President-elect shall have qualified, declaring who shall then act as President, or the manner in which one who is to act shall be selected, and such person shall act accordingly until a President or Vice-President shall have qualified.

Section 3. Death or Lack of Qualification of a President-elect

If a President-elect dies before taking office, the Vice-President-elect will become President. If there is a deadlocked election and no President-elect has been qualified to take office, the Vice-President-elect will become President temporarily. If neither a President-elect nor a Vice-President-elect has been qualified to take office by the start of the term, Congress will decide on a temporary President.

Section 4

The Congress may by law provide for the case of the death of any of the persons from whom the House of Representatives may choose a President whenever the right of choice shall have devolved upon them, and for the case of the death of any of the persons from whom the Senate may choose a Vice-President whenever the right of choice shall have devolved upon them.

Section 4. Death of a Likely President-elect or a Likely Vice-President-elect

If no candidate for President receives a majority of the electoral votes, then, under the Twelfth Amendment, the House of Representatives must choose a President from among the three leading candidates. If one of those three dies before the House makes a choice, Congress can decide how to proceed, under this section.

Similarly, Congress can decide how to proceed in case a vice-presidential election goes to the Senate and one of the two leading candidates dies before the Senate makes its choice between them.

Section 5

Sections 1 and 2 shall take effect on the 15th day of October following the ratification of this article.

Section 5. Time of Effect

The first two sections of this amendment take effect on October 15 after the amendment is ratified.

Section 6

This article shall be inoperative unless it shall have been ratified as an amendment to the Constitution by the legislatures of three fourths of the several states within seven years from the date of its submission.

Section 6. Time Limit for Ratification

This amendment is not to take effect unless it is ratified by state legislatures within seven years.

AMENDMENT 21

Section 1

The eighteenth article of amendment to the Constitution of the United States is hereby repealed.

AMENDMENT 21 (1933). Repeal of Prohibition

Section 1. Repeal

National prohibition is no longer required by law.

Section 2

The transportation or importation into any state, territory, or possession of the United States for delivery or use therein of intoxicating liquors, in violation of the laws thereof, is hereby prohibited.

Section 2. Carrying Alcohol into "Dry" States

If a state is "dry"—if it prohibits alcoholic beverages—then carrying alcoholic beverages into that state is a federal crime.

Section 3

This article shall be inoperative unless it shall have been ratified as an amendment to the Constitution by conventions in the several states, as provided in the Constitution, within seven years from the date of submission hereof to the states by the Congress.

Section 3. Method and Time Limit for Ratification

This amendment must be ratified by special state conventions. The amendment is not to take effect unless it is ratified by the state conventions within seven years.

AMENDMENT 22

Section 1

No person shall be elected to the office of the President more than twice, and no person who has held the office of President or acted as President for more than two years of a term to which some other person was elected President shall be elected to the office of the President more than once. But this article shall not apply to any person holding the office of President when this article was proposed by the Congress, and shall not prevent any person who may be holding the office of President or acting as President during the term within which this article becomes operative from holding the office of President or acting as President during the remainder of such term.

Section 2

This article shall be inoperative unless it shall have been ratified as an amendment to the Constitution by the legislatures of three fourths of the several states within seven years from the day of its submission to the states by the Congress.

AMENDMENT 22 (1951). The Ban on Third Terms for Presidents

Section 1. Limit on Presidential Terms

No person can be elected President more than twice. If a Vice-President or someone else succeeds to the presidency and serves for more than two years, that person cannot then be elected President more than once. This ban does not apply to the person who is President at the time of proposal of this amendment.

Harry S. Truman was President in 1947, when this amendment was proposed.

Section 2. Time Limit for Ratification

This amendment is not to take effect unless it is ratified by state legislatures within seven years.

AMENDMENT 23

Section 1

The district constituting the seat of government of the United States shall appoint in such manner as the Congress may direct: A number of electors of President and Vice-President equal to the whole number of senators and representatives in Congress to which the district would be entitled if it were a state, but in no event more than the least populous state; they shall be in addition to those appointed by the states, but they shall be considered, for the purposes of the election of President and Vice-President, to be electors appointed by a state; and they shall meet in the district and perform such duties as provided by the twelfth article of amendment.

Section 2

The Congress shall have power to enforce this article by appropriate legislation.

AMENDMENT 23 (1961). Electoral Votes for the District of Columbia

Section 1. The Number of Electors

The District of Columbia can have the same number of electors it would be entitled to if it were a state. But that number cannot be greater than the number of electors from the state with the smallest population. Since each state has at least one Representative and two Senators, the smallest number of electors possible is three. The District of Columbia may therefore have three electors.

The effect of this amendment is to let residents of Washington, D.C., vote in presidential elections.

Section 2. Power of Enforcement

Congress has the power to pass laws to enforce this amendment.

AMENDMENT 24

Section 1

The right of citizens of the United States to vote in any primary or other election for President or Vice-President, for electors for President or Vice-President, or for senator or representative in Congress, shall not be denied or abridged by the United States or any state by reason of failure to pay any poll tax or other law.

Section 2

The Congress shall have power to enforce this article by appropriate legislation.

AMENDMENT 24 (1964). Abolition of Poll Taxes

Section 1. Abolition

Neither the United States nor any state can require a citizen to pay a poll tax—a tax per head, or individual—in order to vote in a presidential or congressional election. The effect of this amendment is to prevent states from using poll taxes to keep poor people, especially blacks, from voting.

Section 2. Power of Enforcement

Congress has the power to pass laws to enforce this amendment.

AMENDMENT 25

Section 1

In case of the removal of the President from office or of his death or resignation, the Vice-President shall become President.

Section 2

Whenever there is a vacancy in the office of the Vice-President, the President shall nominate a Vice-President who shall take office upon confirmation by a majority vote of both houses of Congress.

Section 3

Whenever the President transmits to the president pro tempore of the Senate and the speaker of the House of Representatives his written declaration that he is unable to discharge the powers and duties of his office, and until he transmits to them a written declaration to the contrary, such powers and duties shall be discharged by the Vice-President as Acting President.

Section 4

Whenever the Vice-President and a majority of either the principal officers of the executive departments or of such other body as Congress may by law provide, transmit to the president pro tempore of the Senate and the speaker of the House of Representatives their written declaration that the President is unable to discharge the powers and duties of his office, the Vice-President shall immediately assume the powers and duties of the office as Acting President.

Thereafter, when the President transmits to the president pro tempore of the Senate and the speaker of the House of Representatives his written declaration that no inability exists, he shall resume the powers and duties of his office unless the Vice-President and a majority of either the principal officers of the executive department or of such other body as Congress may by law provide, transmit within four days to the president pro tempore of the Senate and the speaker of the House of Representatives their written declaration that the President is unable to discharge the powers and duties of his office. Thereupon Congress shall decide the issue, assembling within forty-eight hours for that purpose if not in session. If the Congress, within twenty-one days after receipt of the latter written declaration, or, if Congress is not in session, within twenty-one days after Congress is required to assemble, determines by two-thirds vote of both houses that the President is unable to discharge the powers and duties of his office, the Vice-President

AMENDMENT 25 (1967). Presidential Disability and Succession

Section 1. Replacement of the President

If the President is removed from office or dies or resigns, the Vice-President becomes President.

Section 2. Replacement of the Vice-President

When the vice-presidency becomes vacant, the President will choose a Vice-President. The choice must be confirmed by both houses of Congress.

Section 3. Temporary Replacement of the President with the President's Consent

If the President sends Congress notice in writing that he or she is disabled from performing official duties, the Vice-President becomes Acting President. The President may resume office when he or she sends Congress written notice of renewed ability to serve.

Section 4. Temporary Replacement of the President Without the President's Consent

If a President is disabled and cannot or will not send written notice to Congress, the Vice-President and a majority of the cabinet (or some other group named by Congress) can send such notice. The Vice-President will then become Acting President.

The Vice-President will step down when the President sends Congress written notice of renewed ability to serve, unless the Vice-President and others disagree. If they disagree, they must send written notice to Congress within four days.

Congress then must meet within 48 hours to decide whether the President is still disabled. Within 21 days they must vote. If two thirds or more of both houses vote that the President is disabled, the Vice-President remains in office as Acting President. If they do not, the President resumes official duties.

shall continue to discharge the same as Acting President; otherwise, the President shall resume the powers and duties of his office.

AMENDMENT 26

Section 1

The right of citizens of the United States, who are eighteen years of age or older, to vote shall not be denied or abridged by the United States or by any state on account of age.

Section 2

The Congress shall have power to enforce this article by appropriate legislation.

AMENDMENT 26 (1971). Suffrage at Age Eighteen

Section 1. The Right to Vote

Neither the United States nor any state can deny the vote to citizens of age 18 or older because of their age. The effect of this amendment is to lower the voting age from 21, the former minimum in federal and most state elections, to 18.

Section 2. Power of Enforcement

Congress has the power to pass laws to enforce this amendment.

765
ERDI'S
FOOD NOT BOMBS
Penguins for Dis-armament
BENNINGTON VERMON
Stop Arms Race Not the Human Race
THOU SHALT NOT KILL!
ARLINGTON VERMONT VOTED FOR A NUCLEAR ARMS FREEZE
SANDGATE VERMONT VOTED FOR A NUCLEAR ARMS FREEZE 177 OUT OF 195 TOWNS
ANTARCTICA WANTS A FREEZE
EVERYONE CARES
Penguins Prefer PEACE
POWNAL VERMONT VOTED FOR A NUCLEAR ARMS FREEZE 177 OUT OF 195 TOWNS
MANCHESTER VERMONT
THEREFORE CHOOSE LI
NOT TO BE
PAX
BRIDPORT VERMONT VOTED FOR A NUCLEAR ARMS FREEZE
MONKTON VERMONT
NO
PEACE-NOT
BETHEL VERMONT VOTED FOR A NUCLEAR ARMS FREEZE 177 OUT OF 195 TOWNS
Stop Arms Race Not the Human Race
RUPERT VERMONT VOTED FOR A NUCLEAR ARMS FREEZE 177 OUT OF 195 TOWNS
A TIME TO CHOOSE
READING VERMONT VOTED FOR A NUCLEAR ARMS FREEZE 177 OUT OF 195 TOWNS
BROOKFIELD VERMONT VOTED FOR A NUCLEAR ARMS FREEZE 177 OUT OF 195 TOWNS
STAMFORD VERMONT VOTED FOR A NUCLEAR ARMS FREEZE 177 OUT OF 195 TOWNS
The Earth is the L
END THE ARMS RACE SAVE THE HUMAN RACE
NO
VOTED FOR A NUCLEAR ARMS FREEZE 177 OUT OF 195 TOWNS
Mutual Nuclear Weapons Freeze
CHINA STOP NUCLEAR TESTS IN

Chapter Themes: The Bill of Rights sets specific limits on the power of the federal government. These ten amendments spell out individual freedoms, protections against governmental abuse of power, and the rights of the accused. Interpreting the meaning of these rights is the role of the courts.

CHAPTER 6

The Bill of Rights

"What is so great about being an American?" Mr. Walker's question surprised all of his students.

Finally Sharon raised her hand. "Well, we have rights," she said. "We live in a free country."

"Okay, but suppose someone from another country asked you what 'free' means. What would you say?"

Sharon thought a moment. "For one thing, we have freedom of speech."

"Does that mean it is okay to falsely accuse a classmate of stealing your money?"

"Well, no," Sharon replied. "I guess we really don't have a right to say anything we want. We still have to be fair."

"So perhaps freedom of speech has limits," said Mr. Walker. "We will explore that point later. Your answer raises another question: How do you know that people have to be treated fairly?"

Juan raised his hand. "There are laws. The police can't just say someone is guilty of a crime and then throw the person in jail. People have a right to a trial—with lawyers, a judge, and a jury."

"Why do we have laws about how to treat a person who has been accused of a crime?" asked Mr. Walker.

"Probably to make sure that an innocent person isn't punished," answered Juan.

"That's true," said Mr. Walker. He leaned against his desk and addressed the whole class. "Sharon and Juan have mentioned two basic rights of United States citizens: freedom of speech and trial by jury. I'd like each of you to jot down other rights you think you have as an American."

If you were asked to list your rights as a United States citizen, what would you write? As Americans we have many rights—more than most of us can name. These rights are listed in a part of the Constitution called the Bill of Rights. How did the Bill of Rights become part of "the law of the land"? This chapter will answer that question and help you understand the value of your rights. You will see that the story of the Bill of Rights is really an unfinished play in which you have an important part.

Teaching Note: Use the Introducing the Chapter activity, page T 62.

Article 1, Section 9, of the Constitution lists specific limits to the powers of Congress which protect the rights of citizens. These limits are discussed in Chapter 8.

6-1

ADDING THE BILL OF RIGHTS

Read to Find Out

- what two methods may be used to propose an amendment.
- what two methods may be used to ratify an amendment.
- what were some arguments for and against adding a bill of rights to the Constitution.

To understand how the Bill of Rights became part of the Constitution, you need to recall why a list of citizens' rights was left out of the original document. Quite simply, the framers thought that it was unnecessary. They believed that the Constitution already guarded against tyranny by limiting the government's power.

The Anti-Federalists disagreed and put up a stiff fight against ratification. If James Madison and other Federalists had not promised that a bill of rights could be added later, in the form of amendments, the Constitution might not have been ratified.

After the ratification, Madison was determined to fulfill his promise to the Anti-Federalists. Adding a bill of rights would be an important step toward gaining their support for the new government. The stage was set for the first changes in the Constitution and therefore the first test of the amendment process.

The Amendment Process

The Constitution requires that any amendment must be approved at both the national and state levels. First an amendment is approved at the national level—usually by Congress—and proposed to the states. Then the states either ratify it or reject it.

There are two ways to propose an amendment to the states. Congress may propose an amendment if it has been approved by a two-thirds vote in both the Senate and the House of Representatives. The 26 amendments that are part of our Constitution today were all proposed this way.

An amendment may also be proposed by a national convention called for by two thirds of the state legislatures. This method, however, has not yet been used.

Once an amendment is proposed, there are two ways for the states to ratify it. The usual route is approval by the legislatures of three fourths of the states. The other method is approval by special conventions in three fourths of the states. Congress chooses which method will be used. The amendment process can take months or even years to complete because any proposed change in the Constitution must gain such widespread support.

The Debate in Congress

In the case of the Bill of Rights, the amendment process began in Congress. Speaking to fellow members of the House in June 1789, Madison declared that many Americans believed that the articles of the Constitution did not adequately protect their rights. By proposing a bill of rights, he argued, Congress would be responding to the people's will and earning their trust, thereby laying a solid foundation for the new republic.

The newly-elected Congress, however, was impatient to begin passing laws that would set the young government firmly on its feet. Therefore, Madison agreed that a bill of rights could wait. He urged Congress, though, to prepare a bill of rights as soon as possible. By doing so, he declared, Congress would "make the Constitution better in the opinion of those who are opposed to it without weakening its

The states have a great deal of power in the process of amending the Constitution. States can propose amendments, and both methods of ratification give the states the authority to make the final decision. For a graphic look at the amendment process, see page 107.

Teaching Note: Use Teaching Activity 1, page T 62, as a culminating activity after students have read the material in this section.

George Mason wrote Virginia's Declaration of Rights, which became a model for the Bill of Rights added to the Constitution in 1791.

frame in the judgment of those who are attached to it."

Two months later, in August, members of Congress began preparing the amendments that they hoped would become the bill of rights. After some debate, they produced a list which drew on many earlier statements of individual rights, such as the Magna Carta, the English Bill of Rights, colonial charters, and state constitutions.

The next issue was where in the Constitution to place the bill of rights. The Anti-Federalists had wanted to have the rights listed at the beginning to serve as standards for judging the government. Madison, however, thought that the rights belonged within the articles to show their relationship to limits already placed on the government.

As it turned out, a majority of members of Congress voted to attach the list of rights to the end of the document to show that it was not needed. They believed that the articles of the Constitution already protected citizens' rights and that the amendments were just being added to satisfy the Anti-Federalists. In the long run, they thought, history would prove that a bill of rights was unnecessary.

The Proposal and the Ratification

Following the debates, a committee of Congressmen wrote final versions of twelve amendments, including ten which protected citizens' rights. Congress approved the amendments and proposed them to the states in September 1789.

The amendments were welcomed by people who had not trusted the new government. Only two failed to gain enough support: proposals to limit the size of the House and to limit when Congress might raise its salaries. By December 15, 1791, the states had ratified ten amendments protecting citizens' rights. The Bill of Rights had become part of the Constitution.

Answers will be found on page T 64.

Section Review

1. Describe the method by which all 26 amendments have been proposed.
2. What is one method of ratifying an amendment?
3. What was the main argument in favor of a bill of rights? What was the main argument against a bill of rights?

Evaluation. If you had been a member of Congress in 1789, which would you have considered more important: getting the new government organized or proposing a bill of rights? Explain.

Challenge (Evaluation): Have students discuss whether the Bill of Rights was a necessary addition to the Constitution. Students should give reasons for their opinions.

Teaching Note: Use the Enrichment Activity, page T 63, and accompanying worksheet in the Activity Book after students have read "Protections of Individual Freedoms."

6-2

PROTECTIONS IN THE BILL OF RIGHTS

Read to Find Out

- what the terms *separation of church and state, eminent domain, due process of law,* and *double jeopardy* mean.
- what specific freedoms are protected by the Bill of Rights.
- how the Bill of Rights helps prevent the government from abusing its power.
- how the Bill of Rights protects people who are accused of crimes.

When the first ten amendments were added to the Constitution, they were intended to protect citizens' rights against actions by the national government. Madison had suggested another amendment protecting citizens' rights against the actions of state governments, but his proposal was rejected because many Americans believed that the national government posed the greatest threat. As you will see in Chapter 7, though, today the Bill of Rights applies to the state governments as well as to the national government.

The Bill of Rights did not change any basic principles in the Constitution. Instead, these ten amendments spell out basic rights that are protected under our form of government. These rights fall into three main categories: (1) individual freedoms, (2) protections against government abuse of power, and (3) rights of citizens accused of crimes.

Protections of Individual Freedoms

Imagine what your life might be like if the following were true: you could be arrested for criticizing a government official; the government could decide which books or magazines may be published and which movies or television shows you may watch; daily newspapers could publish no articles critical of the government and no political cartoons that poke fun at government officials; a person could be jailed because of religious beliefs.

Perhaps you are asking yourself, "What is the point of supposing things that could never happen?" The answer is that they do happen. Millions of people in the world today are denied the rights that we Americans often take for granted. These rights include a number of freedoms protected by the First Amendment.

Freedom of religion. The First Amendment provides for freedom of religion. Every American is free to follow the religion of his or her choice, or not to practice any religion at all. Also, the First Amendment establishes ***separation of church and state***, the situation in which the government may not favor any religion or establish an official religion. This was the first time in history that a government had taken such a step. With separation of church and state, religion may never be used as a test for deciding who may hold office or who may vote.

Freedom of speech. When people say, "This is a free country, so I can say what I want," they are referring to freedom of speech, another right protected by the First Amendment. As an American you have the right to speak and write freely, to say what you believe.

Does freedom of speech mean that you may say anything, whenever and wherever you please? No. You are not free to slander another person, telling lies that damage his or her reputation. However, you are free to express opinions, no matter how unpopular, and to write articles, stories, and poems, no matter how much other people may dislike them or disagree with them.

Teaching Note: You may wish to use the Unit 2 Activity, "First Amendment Rights: A Survey," in the Activity Book after students have read the discussion of the First Amendment.

The Bill of Rights 1791	
Amendment	Subject
1st	Guarantees freedom of religion, of speech, and of the press; the right to assemble peacefully; and the right to petition the government
2nd	Guarantees the right to possess firearms in a state militia
3rd	Declares that the government may not require people to house soldiers during peacetime
4th	Protects people from unreasonable searches and seizures
5th	Guarantees that no one may be deprived of life, liberty, or property without due process of law
6th	Guarantees the right to a trial by jury in criminal cases
7th	Guarantees the right to a trial by jury in most civil cases
8th	Prohibits excessive bail, fines, and punishments
9th	Declares that rights not mentioned in the Constitution belong to the people
10th	Declares that powers not given to the national government belong to the states or to the people

The full text and an explanation of these amendments will be found on pages 120–121.

Freedom of the press. As you read in Chapter 4, the belief in freedom of the press took root during the colonial period, especially through the Zenger case. That belief became a reality with the First Amendment, which prevents the government from deciding what may be printed.

Together with freedom of speech, freedom of the press guarantees that people may criticize the government without fearing arrest. In many countries today, the government controls newspapers and radio or television stations. In the United States, the First Amendment helps guarantee that citizens can get information and hear different opinions.

Like freedom of speech, freedom of the press has its limits. For instance, a newspaper is not free to libel, or print lies about, a person because this would unfairly damage his or her reputation. Also, both freedom of speech and freedom of the press may be limited when what is said or written endangers the lives of citizens, as when a person falsely shouts "Fire" in a theater and causes a panic. Furthermore, any spoken or written statement that presents a danger to the nation in a time of war may be forbidden.

Freedom of assembly. Under the First Amendment, citizens also have the right to assemble, or meet together. For instance, a group may hold a demonstration to protest a new law as long as their demonstration is peaceful and does not violate the rights of other citizens.

Freedom of petition. Perhaps you have heard people make statements such as, "I don't like that law, but there is nothing I can do about it." According to the First Amendment, there *is* something they can do about it. Any citizen or group of citizens has the right to ask a

Freedom of speech has been limited in time of war. In 1919, the Supreme Court ruled in *Schenck* v. *United States* that Charles Schenck's protest against the draft during World War I presented a "clear and present danger" to the nation and was, thereby, not protected by the First Amendment.

Teaching Note: For a discussion/activity on the issue of handgun control, see "Taking a Stand" on page 169.

Freedom of the press applies not only to writings but also to political cartoons. This 1975 cartoon pokes fun at President Gerald Ford.

government representative to change a law, to make a new law, or in other ways to solve problems that arise. A citizen may make such a request by writing a letter, by telephoning, or by sending a petition—a request signed by many citizens—to a representative in Congress.

Protections Against Abuse of Power

The Second, Third, Fourth, and Fifth amendments all help protect citizens from abuse of power by police and judges, or by any other government officials. These amendments stem from the colonists' experience under the rule of England.

The right to bear arms in a state militia. The Second Amendment supports the right of citizens to "keep and bear arms" as part of a state militia. This amendment was intended to protect state governments against abuse of power by the national government. After all, the Revolutionary War was still fresh in the minds of Americans. Many remained suspicious of a strong central government and wanted to guard against leaving all military power in its hands.

Throughout our nation's history, some have argued that the Second Amendment gives citizens the right to own guns for personal use. The Supreme Court and lower courts, however, have consistently ruled that it only guarantees the right of states to keep militia, now known as National Guard units. In other words, the courts have declared that individual citizens do not have a constitutional right to possess guns. Congress can regulate the interstate sale of guns, and states can limit the sale and use of guns within their borders.

The housing of soldiers. During the colonial period, England had allowed English soldiers to use colonists' homes as living quarters. The Third Amendment states that the government must obtain the owner's consent first. During wartime a citizen may have to provide soldiers with lodging, but only if Congress passes laws requiring it.

Freedom from unreasonable searches and seizures. "Open up! This is the police. We have a warrant to search your house!" You have probably seen movies in which police officers say this when entering the home of a suspect. Under the Fourth Amendment, officers need a search warrant—written permission from a judge—to search citizens, their homes, or their belongings. To obtain a warrant, the police must convince a judge that they are likely to find evidence of a crime. The warrant must

With the use of electronic surveillance, freedom from unreasonable searches and seizures had to be reinterpreted by the courts. In 1972, the Supreme Court ruled that law enforcement agencies can search for and seize evidence by electronic means if a federal or state court issues a search warrant.

Teaching Note: For a discussion of students' rights and freedom from unreasonable searches and seizures, see "Issues that Affect You: A Case Study" on pages 164–165.

describe the place to be searched and the property that might be seized, or taken.

During much of the colonial period, English law protected citizens' privacy by strictly limiting search warrants. Judges granted warrants only if authorities were looking for stolen goods. As tensions between England and the colonies increased, however, Parliament allowed officers to make unlimited searches and seizures. Through the Fourth Amendment, Americans were guarding against any such abuse of power by the new government.

Protecting property rights. May the government take away your property to build a freeway, subway, or other public project? Yes, it may. The government has the power of ***eminent domain*** (EM-eh-nehnt do-MAYN), the power to take private property for public use. However, the Fifth Amendment protects citizens from an abuse of this power by requiring the government to pay owners a fair price for their property.

Protections of the Accused

When arresting a person suspected of a crime, a police officer makes the following statement:

> You have the right to remain silent. Anything you say can and will be used against you in a court of law. You are entitled to have an attorney present when you are questioned. If you cannot afford an attorney, one will be provided for you at public expense.

This statement is part of the Miranda warning, which is named after a man who was arrested without being informed of his rights. As a result of a Supreme Court decision in 1966, police officers must state the Miranda warning to anyone they arrest.

The rights of the accused are spelled out in the Fifth, Sixth, Seventh, and Eighth amendments. These amendments reflect English legal tradition dating back to the Magna Carta, which stated that no person could be deprived of life, liberty, or property except by "the law of the land." The Constitution continues English tradition by stating that citizens are entitled to ***due process of law***, a process by which the government must treat accused persons fairly according to rules established by law. People accused of crimes have rights under the Constitution.

Rights under the Fifth Amendment. The Miranda warning mentions the right to remain silent because the Fifth Amendment says that nobody may be forced to "be a witness against himself." This is why accused persons sometimes say, "I take the Fifth" or "I refuse to answer on the grounds that it may incriminate me [make me appear guilty]." In some countries, police use torture or other methods

AMERICAN NOTEBOOK

George Washington spoke of the future of a government that protects the rights of its citizens:

> **If we have wisdom to make the best use of the advantages with which we are now favored, we cannot fail, under the just administration of a good government, to become a great and happy people. The citizens of the United States of America have a right to applaud themselves for having given to mankind examples of a policy worthy of imitation. All possess alike liberty of conscience and immunities [protections] of citizenship.**

Challenge (Application): Ask students which amendment offers them protection if a law enforcement officer insists they tell what they know about a crime. (Fifth)

PEOPLE MAKE A DIFFERENCE

Accused Citizen Fights for Rights

In 1961 Clarence Gideon was charged with stealing food and money from a vending machine in a Florida pool hall. When brought to trial in a Florida court, he pleaded innocent. However, he could not afford a lawyer, and the court refused to provide him with one. He was found guilty and sentenced to five years in prison.

Although most people involved in the trial thought the case was closed, it was later reopened—by the highest court in the land. Gideon's case would eventually affect the rights of accused citizens throughout the nation.

A seemingly insignificant case came to the attention of the Supreme Court because Clarence Gideon was determined to prove that his rights had been violated. As he later wrote, "I always believed that the [main] reason of trial . . . was to reach the truth. My trial was far from the truth."

Gideon spent hours in the

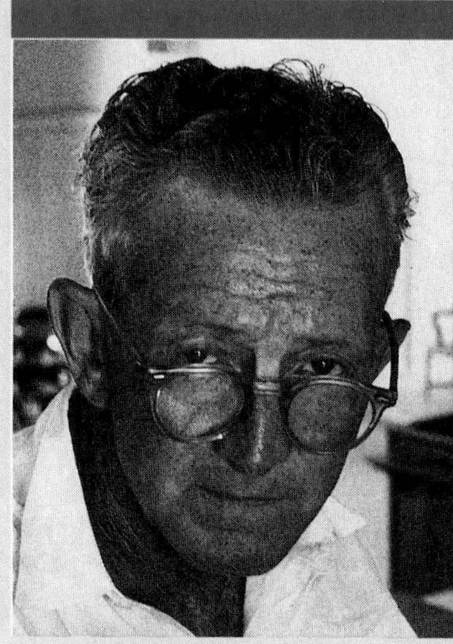

prison library studying law books and the Constitution. He learned that the right to have a lawyer is stated in the Sixth Amendment. However, books about previous cases revealed disagreement over whether the right applied in state courts. Believing that it should apply in *any* court, Gideon wrote a letter asking the Supreme Court to hear his case.

The issue of whether state courts should provide lawyers to represent the poor had already come before the Court several times. The Court had ruled that this right to a lawyer applies only to special circumstances. Gideon's situation did not seem special, but the Court agreed to re-examine the issue.

When the case came before the Court on January 14, 1963, all of the justices concluded that no court should deny a citizen the right to have a lawyer because he or she is too poor to afford one. It was a victory not only for Gideon but also for thousands of other Americans.

In winning his case before the Court, Gideon also won the right to a new trial in Florida. This time the court paid for a lawyer to represent him, and he was found not guilty. In learning about his rights and taking action to defend them, Gideon stands as an example that every citizen's voice can be heard.

to pressure citizens into confessing to crimes. Under the Fifth Amendment, any confessions must be freely given, not forced.

The Fifth Amendment also states that persons suspected of committing serious crimes such as murder must be indicted (in-DĪ-ted), or accused, by a grand jury. A grand jury determines whether there is enough evidence to put the person on trial. In addition, citizens are protected from ***double jeopardy*** (JEP-erd-ee), being placed on trial twice for the same crime. Thus, a person who has been found "not guilty" of a certain crime in a federal court is protected from being put on trial again.

Activity: Have students find out who represents the poor in court in their community. Does the local justice system have a public defender or are private lawyers appointed by the courts? Do legal aid agencies exist in the community?

Teaching Note: Use Teaching Activity 2, page T 62, as a culminating activity after students have read the material in this section.

Right to trial by jury. A key element of due process of law is trial by jury. The Sixth Amendment guarantees a citizen's right to a speedy, public, and fair trial in any case involving a crime. A person may not be tried in secret or kept in jail for a long time awaiting trial. An accused person has the right to the advice of a lawyer. An accused person also has the right to know what the accusations are and the right to ask questions of any witnesses during the trial.

The Seventh Amendment permits jury trials in cases where there are conflicts over property or money—as long as the value in dispute is over twenty dollars. The Sixth and Seventh amendments reflect the belief that trial by jury is important if people are to have trust and confidence in the law. The work of the courts is open to public view and public participation. When people serve as jurors, they help to make sure that their fellow citizens are treated fairly.

Limits on bail, fines, and punishments. The Eighth Amendment protects accused persons from unfair treatment both before and after a trial. Instead of having to stay in jail until the trial, an accused person may deposit with the court a certain amount of money—called bail. This money is a pledge that the person will appear at the trial.

The Eighth Amendment forbids the amount of bail from being unfairly high. When the person appears at the trial, the bail is returned. This system protects the accused person from long-term imprisonment before being convicted of a crime. The Eighth Amendment also protects people from "cruel and unusual punishments" such as whipping and branding, which were common in England and America during the 1700s. The debate continues today over whether the death penalty should be considered "cruel and unusual punishment."

Protections of Other Rights

One of the objections to adding a bill of rights had been that all rights could not possibly be included. James Madison, however, had provided a solution to this problem. Madison had suggested an amendment stating that citizens' rights are not limited to the ones listed in the Constitution. This proposal became the Ninth Amendment.

The Tenth Amendment settles a question arising from Article 1 of the Constitution. Article 1 describes which powers Congress has and does not have, and which powers are denied to the states. But who has the powers that the Constitution does *not* mention? The Tenth Amendment declares that those powers belong to the state governments or to the people.

Answers will be found on page T 64.

Section Review

1. Define *separation of church and state, eminent domain, due process of law,* and *double jeopardy.*
2. List the freedoms protected under the First Amendment.
3. Explain how the Third, Fourth, and Fifth amendments protect citizens from government abuse of power.
4. Explain how the Bill of Rights guarantees that the government cannot suddenly arrest a person and put him or her in prison without a reason.

Synthesis. In what ways does the Bill of Rights reflect our American belief in freedom, justice, and equality?

Data Search. Look on page 585 in the Data Bank to find ways in which the Bill of Rights and the Virginia Declaration of Rights were similar to and different from the Magna Carta and the English Bill of Rights.

Teaching Note: Use the Reinforcement Activity, page T 63, and accompanying worksheet in the Activity Book.

6-3

INTERPRETING THE BILL OF RIGHTS

Read to Find Out

- why it is often difficult to interpret the meaning of citizens' rights.
- why case studies are helpful in understanding citizens' rights.
- what issues often have to be considered in cases involving freedom of expression.

What happens when people disagree about the meaning of our rights under the Constitution? Consider freedom of the press and freedom of speech as examples. Is a school principal violating students' rights when he or she censors an article written for the school newspaper? Does a person have the right to make a speech that causes listeners to riot, injuring others and damaging property?

The rights of citizens are often difficult to interpret. One reason is that the first ten amendments are broad descriptions of rights. They were not intended to explain how those rights apply to every situation. Another reason is that sometimes certain rights have to be weighed against other rights. For example, suppose a person wants to make a speech that may cause a violent reaction. The right of free speech must be weighed against the importance of providing for the safety of other citizens.

The Role of the Courts

The people who tackle the difficult job of interpreting the meaning of citizens' rights are the judges in our nation's courts. As legal experts, they decide whether people's rights are being violated by the actions of other citizens. They also decide whether rights have been violated by any laws.

Usually cases involving citizens' rights are first brought before local judges. If necessary, the decisions of these judges may be examined by higher courts, such as state courts. A few cases that start out in local courts eventually reach the United States Supreme Court. Perhaps you have seen movies in which a person says, "I'm taking this all the way to the Supreme Court!" Actually, few cases reach the highest court in the land. Those that do usually have far-reaching consequences for the nation.

The value of case studies. You will now be reading about two challenging cases that reached the Supreme Court. Both cases involve First Amendment rights. The decisions of the Court are presented as case studies, which are descriptions of situations or conflicts, the issues involved, and the decisions made.

Case studies can help you see principles of the Constitution being put into action. You can see how an ideal, such as freedom of speech, applies to a real situation. As you read each case study, imagine that you are one of the nine justices, or judges, of the Supreme Court. Think about how you would decide the case.

The Tinker Case: Students and Free Speech

On December 16, 1965, two students in Des Moines, Iowa—13-year-old Mary Beth Tinker and 16-year-old Christopher Eckhardt—came to school wearing black armbands. The next day John Tinker, Mary Beth's 15-year-old brother, also wore a black armband to school. The students were protesting American involvement in the Vietnam War. Their small protest would eventually cause the Su-

Mary Beth and John Tinker display the black armbands that the Supreme Court ruled were a form of speech protected by the First Amendment.

preme Court to wrestle with two questions: What is meant by "speech" in freedom of speech, and what rights do students have under the Constitution?

The case. When the Des Moines school board first learned of the students' plan to protest, it announced that armbands would be forbidden. When the students wore armbands anyway, they were suspended. The Tinkers' parents argued that the school board was denying the students' right to freedom of speech. They declared that the students had not disrupted classes or interfered with other students' rights. School officials defended the armband rule, stating that it preserved discipline. They argued that schools were not places for political demonstrations.

The Court's decision. The case first came before a local court, which ruled that the armband rule was necessary to avoid disruption of classes. After a higher court also agreed with the school board, the students had one last hope: the Supreme Court.

The Supreme Court heard the case and ruled in favor of the students. It held that armbands were a form of "speech" because they were symbols representing ideas. The justices also said that the protest was protected by the First Amendment because it had not interfered with other students' right to an education.

Most importantly, the Court emphasized that citizens under the age of eighteen *do* have a basic right to free speech. The Court declared:

The Court affirmed students' right to freedom of speech in the Tinker case but warned that conduct that "materially disrupts class work or involves substantial disorder or invasion of the rights of others is, of course, not [protected] by the constitutional guarantees of freedom of expression."

> It can hardly be argued that students shed their constitutional rights to freedom of speech or expression at the schoolhouse gate. . . . Students in school as well as out of school are persons under our Constitution.

Take a moment to think about the Court's ruling. Why do you think it is important for students to have freedom of speech? What responsibilities go along with that freedom?

The Skokie Case: Freedom for Nazis?

When may freedom of expression be limited? What other rights must be considered? What if a person or group expresses ideas that are very unpopular? All of these questions were involved in the Skokie case, one of the most controversial in our nation's history.

The case. The year was 1938. Members of dictator Adolf Hitler's Nazi party attacked the homes of Jews throughout Germany. Between 1938 and 1945, the Nazis forced millions of Jews and other people into camps to be starved, tortured, and killed.

The year was 1977. The place was Skokie, Illinois. The town's residents included 40,000 Jews. Many of these people had survived the horror of Nazi camps, but many of their relatives had not. In May a small group of uniformed men applied for a permit to march through Skokie. Each man's uniform displayed a large black swastika—the symbol of the Nazi party.

Shocked and enraged by the plans of these members of the American Nazi party, Skokie officials wanted to prevent the march. They passed laws forbidding any demonstrator to wear a military-type uniform or distribute material that stirred up racial or religious hatred. Also, anyone wanting to make a speech or demonstration would have to pay $350,000 for insurance to cover possible property damage.

When the Nazis planned a rally to protest these laws, the county court stated that the group could not hold a demonstration. The court forbade anyone to march in a Nazi uniform, display the swastika, or distribute material promoting hatred.

When the Nazis challenged the court order and the Skokie laws, a long and painful court battle began. From the Illinois courts to the United States Supreme Court, judges faced a challenging question: does the First Amendment protect even Nazis and their message of hatred?

The case stirred nationwide interest. Many people argued that the First Amendment does not protect people who want to destroy freedom and spread violence. As one citizen stated, "Freedom of expression has no meaning when it defends those who would end this right for others." Another said, "In Germany they also started with a bunch of crazies. . . . Anybody who advocates killing should not be allowed to rally."

Those who argued that Nazis do have a right to freedom of expression included members of the American Civil Liberties Union (ACLU), an organization devoted to defending citizens' rights under the First Amendment. ACLU lawyers asked a basic question: if the government may deny freedom of expression to one group, what will prevent it from denying that right to any other group? A Jewish member of the ACLU summed up this argument by saying, "The First Amendment has to be for everyone—or it will be for no one."

Clearly, the Skokie case presented a major challenge for the courts. There were powerful arguments and strong feelings on both sides.

The Court's decision. Because they were unwilling to accept the county court order, the

Decision Making: Suppose that members of a group holding controversial views want to have a demonstration or give a speech on a school campus. Have students decide how they would respond to the group's request. They should list options and discuss the consequences of each option.

When should freedom of speech be limited? Courts have faced this difficult question in cases involving the American Nazi party and other groups that promote hatred.

Nazis took their case to the Illinois Supreme Court. However, that court refused to overrule the county court order or to rule on the fairness of the Skokie laws. Therefore, the Nazis asked the United States Supreme Court to hear their case.

On June 15, 1977, the Supreme Court ruled that the Nazis did have the right to freedom of expression under the First Amendment. The Court did not discuss either the county court order or the Skokie laws, but its decision led the Illinois courts to examine those laws closely in light of the First Amendment.

For almost a year, the Illinois courts struggled with the issue of limits on the Nazis' right to freedom of expression. The courts finally decided that the Skokie law requiring insurance violated the First Amendment. The courts stated that the insurance was too costly for most groups and therefore limited free speech and assembly. Also, the law had not been applied equally. The town officials required the Nazis to pay for insurance, but other groups were allowed to hold rallies without insurance.

The courts also concluded that the Nazis had a right to distribute material expressing hatred. The First Amendment protects the expression of all ideas—even beliefs that threaten the basic principles of our nation. As Justice Oliver Wendell Holmes said, over 50 years before the Skokie case, our Constitution protects "the principle of free thought—not free thought for those who agree with us but freedom for the thought we hate."

The courts discussed whether the Nazi uniform and swastika symbol were protected by the First Amendment. Earlier court decisions, particularly the Tinker case, had established that symbols were a form of speech. The issue was whether the hated swastika symbol would cause a violent reaction, threatening public safety. By planning to wear their swastikas in Skokie, were the Nazis guilty of trying to start a fight?

The courts heard strong testimony from Jews in Skokie about the meaning of the swastika to them. One concentration camp survivor angrily declared, "I do not know if I could control myself if I saw the swastika in a parade." Skokie attorney Harvey Schwartz argued that for Jews, seeing the swastika was just like being physically attacked.

The Illinois Supreme Court deeply sympathized with the Skokie residents but decided that the swastika could not be banned. Otherwise, the mere possibility of violence could be used to keep anyone from exercising the right to freedom of expression. The court reluctantly concluded that the Nazis could wear their symbol, just as war protestors could wear black armbands. The United States Supreme Court let the Illinois court's decision stand, thereby removing the last roadblock to the Nazi rally.

In the summer of 1978 the Nazis finally held two rallies, but not in Skokie. Both rallies were in Chicago, and the Nazis faced thousands of people demonstrating against them. Over 2,000 Chicago police officers were assigned to prevent any violence.

A marketplace of ideas. The Skokie case showed that the First Amendment protects not only views that most citizens support but also unpopular beliefs. The First Amendment makes possible what Justice Holmes called "a marketplace of ideas," in which all views may be expressed. Holmes believed that people should be allowed to hear many different ideas. Then they can accept, or "buy," the good ones and reject the bad. According to Justice Holmes, the test of a good idea is "the power of the thought to get itself accepted in the competition of the market."

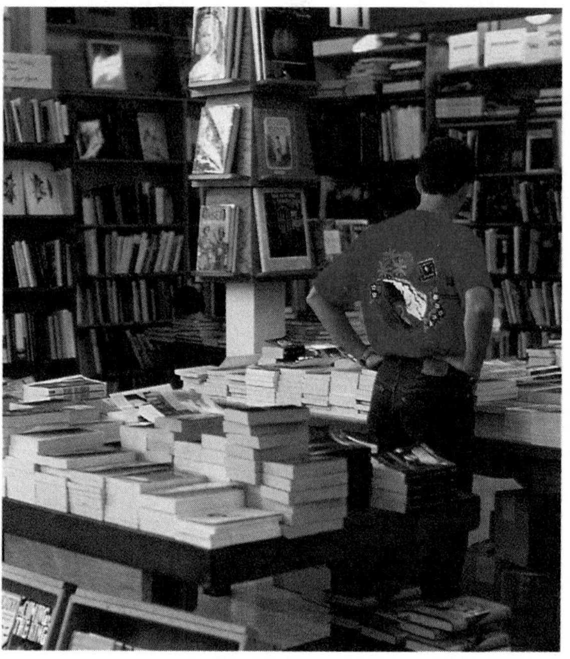

In our marketplace of ideas, a bookstore like this one invites people to read the opinions of many different authors on a wide range of subjects.

What do you think? Should any person be allowed to state his or her beliefs, even when those beliefs are very unpopular or encourage hatred and prejudice?

The Continuing Challenge

Protecting the rights of citizens is not just the responsibility of judges and laws. It is a continuing challenge that we all share. Another famous American judge, Learned Hand, made this point in the following way:

> I often wonder whether we do not rest our hopes too much upon constitutions, upon

Sometimes citizen advocacy groups try to influence the "marketplace of ideas" directly. In the mid-1980s, the Parents Music Resource Center persuaded record companies to warn consumers of recordings containing explicit messages about sex, violence, or drug and alcohol abuse.

Teaching Note: Use the Evaluating Progress activity, page T 63, to assess students' understanding of the chapter.

> laws, and upon courts. These are false hopes. . . .
>
> Liberty lies in the hearts of men and women; when it dies there, no constitution, no law, no court can ever do much to help it. While it lies there it needs no constitution, no law, no court to save it.

As Judge Hand emphasizes in his statement, the rights of citizens are not protected just because they have been written down in the Constitution. We as citizens play a key role in protecting our rights. By respecting each other's rights, we help guarantee that the Bill of Rights survives—not just as dry ink on faded parchment but as beliefs that we Americans live by.

Answers will be found on page T 65.

Section Review

1. Why is it often difficult to interpret the meaning of citizens' rights?
2. How do case studies help you understand the meaning of citizens' rights?
3. Describe the issues involved in the Tinker and Skokie cases, and explain how the cases were decided.

Application. You have looked at some of the issues judges have to deal with in cases involving freedom of expression. What issues would be involved when police arrest a murder suspect without obtaining permission to enter the suspect's home?

A BROADER VIEW

The Bill of Rights reflects our American belief that there are human rights which no government should take away. In many countries today governments ignore such basic rights as freedom of speech and trial by jury. People who criticize the government may be imprisoned without a trial. Many prisoners are tortured and killed.

Imagine living your entire life in prison. Amonissa Issa of Ethiopia does not have to imagine; he was born in a prison. In 1980 his parents were imprisoned without a trial. Before Amonissa was born, his father was transferred to a different prison. The two have never seen each other.

What is being done to fight the injustice suffered by Amonissa, his parents, and thousands of other people throughout the world who are being denied their basic human rights? A number of human rights organizations, such as Amnesty International, help political prisoners by writing petitions to government officials, protesting against the use of torture, and sending medicine, food, and clothing to prisoners. These organizations promote worldwide observance of the United Nations Universal Declaration of Human Rights, an international agreement on human rights.

The United Nations declaration lists many of the rights found in our Bill of Rights. The declaration shows that most nations acknowledge certain basic rights, such as freedom of speech, freedom of religion, and freedom from unfair arrest or imprisonment. However, the treatment of prisoners in some countries shows that their governments only claim to support human rights.

We are fortunate to live in a country that is dedicated to respecting human rights. However, human rights are not preserved only by words in documents such as the United Nations declaration or the Bill of Rights. People must be willing to abide by those agreements, treating each other with respect as fellow human beings.

Challenge (Evaluation): Have students agree or disagree with the following statement: "The First Amendment has to be for everyone—or it will be for no one." Students should provide reasons for their opinions.

Critical Thinking

Teaching Note: For reinforcement of decision-making skills, use Decision-Making Worksheet Chapter 6.

Which Sources Can You Trust?

"John was right again! That movie I saw last night was super." Many of the decisions you make, such as choosing what movie to see or selecting a summer job, are frequently based on information you get from other sources. Often, however, you do not have enough time to check the accuracy of every single piece of information. Therefore, you often base your decisions on information from sources you trust, such as a particular friend or a reference book.

Making good decisions involves knowing how to determine which sources of information are reliable, or trustworthy. A reliable source is one that you can depend on to provide accurate information. For instance, you think that John is a reliable source because his recommendations about movies have been good in the past.

Of course, information can come not only from what friends tell you but also from many other sources, such as books, magazines, newspapers, radio, television, and movies. Suppose that you have to form your own opinion about the Tinker case described on page 140. You want to get more information about the facts of the case and the legal issues before deciding. Imagine also that among the available sources is the one described here:

> A movie about the Tinker case, made in 1970, portrays the students challenging the rule against armbands. The writers of the script interviewed the students' parents and the lawyers representing the students. The film credits list the writers and producers as members of an organization that opposed the Vietnam War.

How might you determine the reliability of the Tinker movie as a source? Here is one procedure you could follow.

EXPLAINING THE SKILL

One method to determine a source's reliability is to follow these steps. Notice how the steps relate to the example of the Tinker movie.

1. Check the qualifications of the people providing the information. Do they have training or knowledge that qualifies them to write or speak about the topic? Sometimes background on them may be found in the source itself. You can also check to see if the library has information about them. [We have no evidence that the writers of the Tinker movie are legal experts.]

2. Check the reputations of the people providing the information. Do they have a past history of being accurate? Have they received or won any awards? Might their beliefs or goals affect how they write or speak about this topic? [We do not know whether the writers have a record of accuracy. As opponents of the war, they might be presenting a one-sided story. They might not be accurately describing the legal issues involved in the case.]

3. Check the methods the people used in preparing the source. How did they get their information? Did they provide enough evidence to support their statements? Were their sources reliable? [The information in the movie is probably incomplete because no one seems to have interviewed the students. Also, it is probably one-sided because the school board and the principal do not seem to have been consulted.]

4. Check to see if this source agrees with other sources known to be reliable on the topic. When two or more sources agree with what your source says, you can be fairly certain that the source you are using is reliable. [You could

Remind students that there are degrees of reliability and that reliability is always in reference to a certain subject. They should also note that checking the reliability of sources will save time in the future. Whenever they need information on a subject, they can then turn to a "bank" of sources.

Answers will be found on page T 65.

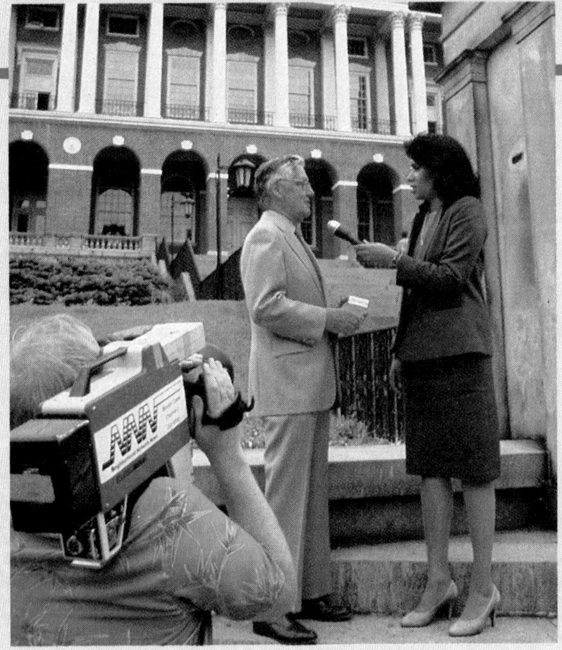

check records on the Tinker case, as well as articles that legal experts have written about the case.]

APPLYING THE SKILL

Suppose the following sources on the Tinker case were available. Determine which source would be more reliable.

A. A collection of newspaper articles written in 1969 by a Pulitzer Prize-winning journalist. Her articles about the Tinker case include interviews with the three students and with members of the school board. She also relied on quotes from the minutes of school board meetings and on information from local newspapers. In addition, she examined the effect of the Supreme Court's past rulings on individual freedoms. Her explanation of the rulings refers to her sources throughout.

B. A book published in 1970 and written by a past president of the Des Moines school board. The author has also written several books calling for tougher discipline in public schools. The book includes quotes from board members, parents, and teachers regarding the armband protest. Interviews with the superintendent and the principal are included. The book contains summaries of lower court decisions in the case.

CHECKING YOUR UNDERSTANDING

1. Which one of the two sources is likely to be more reliable on the topic of the Tinker case? Explain your answer.

2. Which of the following would be the best source to use to check the accuracy of information about issues in the Tinker case? **(a)** an interview with Mary Beth Tinker, **(b)** the written record of the court proceedings, **(c)** letters written by the school principal to a principal in another school district.

3. Of the following characteristics, which one is the best indicator of a reliable source? **(a)** being written by a person who is the author of more than one book, **(b)** the date of publication, **(c)** the reputation and background of the author. Explain your answer.

4. Of the following, which one is the best sign of reliability? **(a)** being published in a book, **(b)** being written by someone who has received awards for journalism, **(c)** being written by a person who observed the events being described. Explain your answer.

REVIEWING THE SKILL

5. What is meant by reliability?

6. What are four things you can do to check the reliability of a source?

7. Describe two situations in which you could use the skill of determining the reliability of a source.

Have students choose a particular subject, list possible sources, and compare the reliability of each source. Have them also give examples of decision-making situations in which they would have to determine the reliability of sources.

CHAPTER SURVEY

Answers to Survey and Workshop will be found on page T 65.

UNDERSTANDING NEW VOCABULARY

Seeing Relationships

Each of the following vocabulary terms is related to a general type of protection provided by the Bill of Rights. Match each term with the appropriate type of protection. Then explain how the term relates to that type of protection.

Example: *Double jeopardy* relates to *protection of the accused* because the Bill of Rights protects a person from being tried more than once for the same crime.

1. *separation of church and state*

2. *eminent domain*

3. *due process of law*

(a) protection against abuse of power

(b) protection of individual rights

(c) protection of the accused

Putting It in Writing

Write a paragraph explaining how the Bill of Rights protects people who have been accused of crimes. In your paragraph use the terms *due process of law* and *double jeopardy* in a way that shows you understand their meaning.

LOOKING BACK AT THE CHAPTER

1. Explain how the amendment process works.

2. Why did James Madison think that Congress should add a bill of rights to the Constitution as soon as possible?

3. Describe the freedoms protected under the First Amendment and briefly explain why each one is important.

4. Discuss two ways in which the Bill of Rights guards against unjust use of power by the government.

5. Explain how the Bill of Rights guarantees that a person accused of a crime will receive fair treatment.

6. How do judges play an important role in protecting the rights of citizens?

7. Explain the importance of the Tinker case.

8. Explain the importance of the Skokie case.

9. *Analysis.* Why can it be said that the Bill of Rights did not change any of the basic principles of the Constitution?

10. *Analysis.* Why are the individual freedoms listed in the First Amendment important in a democratic government?

11. *Evaluation.* Which two of your rights as a citizen do you consider most important? Explain your answer.

12. *Evaluation.* Supose that you could add a specific right of citizens to the Constitution. What right would you add? Explain your choice.

13. *Synthesis.* Most members of Congress in 1789 thought that history would prove a bill of rights unnecessary. What do you think would be their view if they were alive today? Support your answer with examples.

WORKING TOGETHER

1. In groups of three or four, prepare a skit in which one or more of the rights listed in the Bill of Rights is being violated. Following the skit, the class should identify the right or rights being violated and discuss what actions should have been taken to avoid violating those rights.

2. Working with two or three other students, make a collage of newspaper or magazine articles relating to a particular right, such as freedom of speech or the right to due process of law. Present your collage to the class, explaining the significance of each article you included.

SOCIAL STUDIES SKILLS

Using Primary Sources

Primary sources are historical records left by people who directly observed the events being described. If you wanted to learn more about the Tinker case, for example, some primary sources would be written statements by the Supreme Court justices who judged the case. Such statements help citizens understand how the Court arrives at its decisions and why justices often disagree with each other.

Consider a Supreme Court case that occurred in 1951. A lower court had convicted 11 people of violating a law forbidding anyone to "teach the duty of overthrowing or destroying any government of the United States by force or violence." The Court had to decide whether these people had been denied freedom of speech.

After the Court's ruling, Justice Fred M. Vinson wrote the following statement:

> Overthrow of the government by force and violence is certainly a substantial enough interest [reason] for the government to limit speech. . . . We reject any principle of governmental helplessness in the face of preparation for revolution.

Justice Hugo Black also commented on the Court's ruling:

> No matter how it is worded, this is . . . censorship [limitation] of speech and press, which I believe the First Amendment forbids.

1. Did Justice Vinson and Justice Black agree with each other? Explain your answer.

2. What was the Court's ruling on the case? How can you tell?

3. Explain why the Court decided the case the way it did.

4. If you were a Supreme Court justice, how would you have decided this case? Explain.

DECISION-MAKING SKILLS

Which Sources Can You Trust?

Can school officials decide what students may and may not write in school newspapers? The Supreme Court has heard a number of cases on school newspaper censorship. One case in 1988 involved Hazelwood East High School, near St. Louis, Missouri. Below are three sources. Determine which would be most reliable on the issues in the case.

A. A reference book designed as a quick guide to the work of the United States Supreme Court. Each Court decision is briefly summarized. Notes on each summary indicate where the full explanation of the Court's decision may be found in official government reports.

B. An article written by the 1988 High School Journalism Teacher of the Year and published in a collection of articles criticizing censorship in the United States. The articles are recommended by several university professors and by editors from major newspapers.

C. The script of a television program that includes interviews with lawyers for the Hazelwood School Board and with lawyers representing the students. Several professors of law comment on the arguments presented by the school board's lawyers and those presented by the students' lawyers.

1. Which one of the sources described above would be most reliable on the issues in the Hazelwood case? Explain your answer.

2. What is one way to determine the reliability of a source?

3. Why is the skill of determining the reliability of a source useful for decision making?

4. Think of a decision you might have to make. Where might you get reliable information to help you decide? Explain why those sources of information would be reliable.

SUPPORT THE
ERA

Chapter Themes: The Constitution's greatest strength is its flexibility. Amendments have enabled the Constitution to reflect changing needs and attitudes regarding citizenship and voting rights. Supreme Court interpretations have applied principles of equality in the Constitution to new situations.

CHAPTER 7

Our Living Constitution

One Monday morning Mrs. Taylor made a surprise announcement to her government class: they were going to elect a student committee to recommend rules for the class. At first the students responded enthusiastically, but then Mrs. Taylor stunned them by saying: "In order to vote for committee members, you must be a boy and you must be white."

Immediately students began to protest. Why were the girls not allowed to vote? Why could the black, Hispanic, and Asian students not vote?

After listening to the objections, Mrs. Taylor replied, "Actually, I agree with you. It *is* unfair. But I wanted to make a point about our nation. For much of our history, most states allowed only white males to vote. Fortunately, this is no longer the case because the Constitution has been changed."

Our Constitution has survived for over two centuries because it is a "living" document that can respond to the needs of a growing and changing society. Despite changes in attitudes and conditions over the years, Americans have not had to create a whole new Constitution. This chapter gives you a chance to explore the reasons our Constitution has lasted so well. First you will read about the amendments that have brought our nation closer to the ideal of treating all people with equal respect. Then you will see the role the Supreme Court has played in making the Constitution a "living" document.

Teaching Note: Use the Introducing the Chapter activity, page T 68.

7-1

CHANGING THE LAW OF THE LAND

Read to Find Out

- what the term *suffrage* means.
- why the Constitution was changed to give citizenship and voting rights to African Americans.
- why women were denied the right to vote for so long and how they eventually gained that right.
- why the voting age was eventually lowered to eighteen.

As you can see from the chart on the next page, since the Bill of Rights became part of the Constitution, 16 other amendments have been made for a variety of reasons. Most of these amendments reflect efforts by the people to change the Constitution to meet changing needs and attitudes. For example, over time there has been a great change in the attitude of Americans about who can be a citizen and who has the right to vote.

Originally, the Constitution let the states decide who was qualified to be a citizen, and most states granted citizenship only to white men who owned property. Today, however, anyone born or naturalized in the United States is a citizen, and any citizen who is at least eighteen years old may vote.

As you know, the Constitution begins with the words "we the people of the United States." Why is the meaning of "we the people" so much broader today than it was in 1787? In the following pages you will step back into history to trace the changes in citizenship and voting rights that have taken place in this country over the years. In the process, you will see how the amendment process helps the Constitution adjust to changing times.

Abolishing Slavery

Among the people denied citizenship from the beginning were the enslaved African Americans. Why did a country founded in the name of freedom permit slavery? Why was slavery eventually abolished by an amendment to the Constitution? The answers involve looking at the history of slavery in our nation.

Slavery and the framers. You may recall from Chapter 5 that the Constitutional Convention probably would have failed without a compromise on slavery. Southerners believed that their farming economy would collapse without slave labor. To ensure that both the northern and southern states would ratify the Constitution, the framers avoided making a decision on whether to abolish slavery. Nowhere in the Constitution is the word *slavery* even mentioned.

To avoid angering the southern states, the framers even made slavery seem acceptable. They agreed that slaves could be counted as part of a state's population and that runaway slaves had to be returned to their owners. However, neither the northern nor southern states were completely satisfied by the compromises at the convention. Many Americans wondered whether a nation so divided over slavery could survive.

Growing tension between North and South. As new states joined the nation during the early 1800s, the North and the South competed for power in Congress. Although the more-populous northern states controlled a majority in the House, the North argued that the three-fifths compromise gave southern states more representatives than they deserved. The South, in turn, feared that the North might use its political power to abolish slavery.

In 1820 Congress tried to head off serious conflict by passing the Missouri Compromise.

Although slavery is not specifically mentioned in the Constitution, acknowledgment of slavery appears in Article 1, Section 2, which details the three-fifths compromise; in Article 1, Section 9, which alludes to the slave trade; and in Article 4, Section 2, which concerns fugitive slaves.

Amendments 11–26		
Amendment	Year Ratified	Subject
11th	1795	Lawsuits against the states
12th	1804	Separate voting for President and Vice-President
13th	1865	Abolition of slavery
14th	1868	Citizenship and civil rights
15th	1870	Voting rights for black men
16th	1913	Income taxes
17th	1913	Direct election of senators
18th	1919	Prohibition of alcoholic beverages
19th	1920	Voting rights for women
20th	1933	Terms of the President, Vice-President, and Congress
21st	1933	Repeal of prohibition
22nd	1951	Presidents limited to two terms
23rd	1961	Electoral votes for the District of Columbia
24th	1964	Abolition of poll taxes
25th	1967	Presidential disability and succession
26th	1971	Voting age lowered to eighteen

The full text and an explanation of these amendments will be found on pages 122–129.

This law divided new lands into "slave" territories and "free" territories. It also tried to balance power in the Senate by keeping the number of "slave" and "free" states equal. Nevertheless, Americans increasingly saw slavery as an "all or nothing" issue. On one side were those who defended the right to own slaves anywhere; on the other were those who wanted slavery banned everywhere.

Since further efforts at compromise seemed hopeless, Congress tried the principle of majority rule, allowing settlers in each territory to vote on whether to allow slavery there. However, this action only sparked conflict between pro-slavery and anti-slavery settlers.

A controversial Court decision. In 1857 a tense nation awaited a Supreme Court decision on a case that many hoped would finally settle the slavery issue. A slave named Dred Scott had traveled with his owner to the territory of Minnesota, where slavery was illegal. After they returned to Missouri, Scott argued that his residence in a free territory had made him a free person. Now the Court had to decide whether or not Scott was free according to the Constitution.

The Court's decision created an uproar among opponents of slavery. It ruled that according to the Constitution slaves were property and that Congress could not prevent owners from taking slaves anywhere they wished. This decision showed that, as a result of the compromises made by the framers, the Constitution could be interpreted as allowing slavery.

On August 28, 1963, more than 200,000 Americans of all races gathered in Washington, D.C., to show their support for the struggle to guarantee African Americans the right to vote and other basic civil rights.

The Thirteenth Amendment. Although the defenders of slavery rejoiced at the Dred Scott decision, many Americans feared for the nation. In 1858, Abraham Lincoln warned, "I believe this government cannot endure permanently half slave and half free. . . . It will become all one thing, or all the other."

Lincoln's warning proved true, but only after a civil war that took the lives of over 600,000 Americans. The North's victory paved the way for the Thirteenth Amendment, which abolished slavery in 1865.

African Americans and the Right to Vote

Although the Constitution now banned slavery, the struggle for citizenship and voting rights for African Americans had only begun. Even those who had been free long before the Civil War knew that freedom did not mean equality. For one thing, the states still had the power to decide who could be a citizen, and most states—both northern and southern—continued to deny citizenship to blacks.

The Fourteenth Amendment. This amendment, adopted in 1868, ensured citizenship for African Americans. It takes the power to grant citizenship away from the states by providing that "All persons born or naturalized in the United States . . . are citizens of the United States and of the state wherein they reside." It also declares that no state may "deprive any person of life, liberty, or property without due process of law" or "deny to any person . . . the equal protection of the laws."

Why were these statements added when there was already a Bill of Rights? Actually, the first ten amendments say only that Congress must respect citizens' rights. The Fourteenth Amendment specifically requires the states to do so. Therefore, it has often been called the "second Bill of Rights."

The Fourteenth Amendment did not automatically ensure equal treatment. Although the Supreme Court ruled that state governments could not treat African Americans unfairly, it did not prevent private citizens, such as employers, from continuing to discriminate against them.

In matters of equal protection and justice, proponents of constitutional amendments believed that amendments rather than federal laws were needed to ensure that treatment of citizens would be consistent across the nation.

Challenge (Application): Ask students to provide other examples of situations in which freedom does not mean equality. Examples can come from history or student's personal life.

The Fifteenth Amendment. In some states being a citizen did not guarantee the right to vote. To keep states from denying voting rights to African Americans, the Fifteenth Amendment, added in 1870, declares that states may not deny the vote to any person on the basis of "race, color, or previous condition of servitude."

The Twenty-fourth Amendment. Despite the Fifteenth Amendment, some states found a number of ways to prevent African Americans from voting, such as requiring citizens to pay a poll tax, or fee for voting. Many were unable to vote because they were too poor to pay the tax.

Not until the passage of the Twenty-fourth Amendment in 1964 were poll taxes declared illegal. This amendment, together with civil rights laws passed by Congress in the 1960s, was an important step toward protecting the rights of African Americans.

As you have just seen, changes in the Constitution do not guarantee that attitudes and conditions in society will change completely and immediately. It has taken more than 100 years for the nation to make real progress toward ending discrimination against African Americans and other racial groups.

Women and the Right to Vote

African Americans were not the only group left out of "we the people" in 1787. Women, too, faced a long struggle for full citizenship rights. Unlike slavery, women's rights did not even seem to be an issue in the minds of the framers. Traditional ideas about the role of women help to explain why most states denied them voting rights for many years.

Traditional ideas about women. Since long before the founding of our country, the only proper place for women was thought to be working in the home and caring for the family. Women were believed to be unable to handle many of the jobs that men performed. Even after large numbers of women took factory jobs during the 1800s, laws still treated them differently from men. Some laws allowed women to do only certain—usually low-paid—jobs.

People who held the traditional view disapproved of women voting or holding political office. They argued that politically active women would leave their family responsibilities behind, upsetting the stability of family life. They also thought that women were less intelligent than men and therefore less able to make political decisions.

Challenging the traditional view. By the late 1800s, the tide had begun turning against the traditional view of women. Increasing numbers of women took jobs. Many women also became active in social problems in the cities and factories.

As women became more politically involved, they insisted on the right to vote, also known as ***suffrage.*** A declaration from a women's rights convention stated, "We hold these truths to be self evident: that all men *and women* are created equal." Nevertheless, by the turn of the century only a handful of states had granted suffrage to women.

During the late 1800s and early 1900s, supporters of women's right to vote, known as suffragists, gained the public's attention by marching, giving speeches, writing to government officials and newspapers, and even going on hunger strikes. The important economic role played by women factory workers also helped convince more and more Americans that women deserved to vote. A proposed amendment giving suffrage to women was introduced—but failed to pass—in every session of Congress for 40 years, from 1878 to 1918.

In 1989, women represented 45 percent of the work force. The majority of women entering the work force were married. Only 7 percent of American families had a father who worked outside the home and a mother who stayed home with the children.

Suffragist Carrie Chapman Catt (center) leads a march in New York City in 1918. She was a leader in the campaign that resulted in the Nineteenth Amendment, giving women the right to vote.

The Nineteenth Amendment. Finally, the suffragists' determination paid off. A breakthrough came in January 1918 at an emotional session of the House of Representatives. The visitors' galleries were packed as the House prepared to vote. Several congressmen voted despite illness—one was even brought in on a stretcher. Another left his gravely ill wife, at her request, to cast his vote. This time the House overwhelmingly approved the amendment.

After the Senate approved it the following year, the Nineteenth Amendment was ratified by the states in 1920. Women were now truly part of "we the people." However, as you will see later in this chapter, other issues relating to women's rights remained unsettled.

Youth and the Right to Vote

The most recent voting rights amendment lowered the voting age to eighteen. From colonial times through the middle of this century, the voting age was twenty-one. However, as millions of young people served in World War II, and in the Korean and the Vietnam wars, many Americans came to believe that citizens old enough to fight and to die for their country should not be denied the right to vote.

Spurred on by growing public support for lowering the voting age, Congress passed a law in 1970 giving eighteen-year-olds the right to vote in national, state, and local elections. However, the Supreme Court later ruled that Congress could set the voting age only for national—not state or local—elections.

The Twenty-sixth Amendment. After the Court decision, it seemed that the only way to guarantee eighteen-year-olds the right to vote in all elections was by changing the Constitution. Aware of widespread public support for such an amendment, Congress overwhelmingly approved it in March 1971. The vote was 401–19 in the House and 94–0 in the Senate. It took just three months and seven days for the states to ratify the proposed change, making it the Twenty-sixth Amendment.

The Voice of the People

The voting rights amendments illustrate that the Constitution can be changed in response to new attitudes and conditions in society. Although the Thirteenth, Fourteenth, and Fifteenth amendments came about largely as a result of the Civil War, all the other changes in the Constitution were made through peaceful efforts of citizens. The United States is

Decision Making: Have students decide whether they would support or oppose a particular amendment that has been either proposed by Congress or suggested by citizens. Have them list positive and negative consequences of the amendment before deciding.

Teaching Note: Use Teaching Activity 1, page T 68, as a culminating activity for this section.

truly a government by the people because the citizens decide what will be "the law of the land."

Any citizen or group of citizens may propose a change in the Constitution. More than 10,000 amendments have been proposed, and efforts continue to this day. One recently proposed change is the Equal Rights Amendment (ERA), which would require men and women to be treated equally. The proposal gained the support of both the Senate and the House but has not been approved by enough state legislatures. So far, neither supporters nor opponents of the amendment show signs of giving up their struggle.

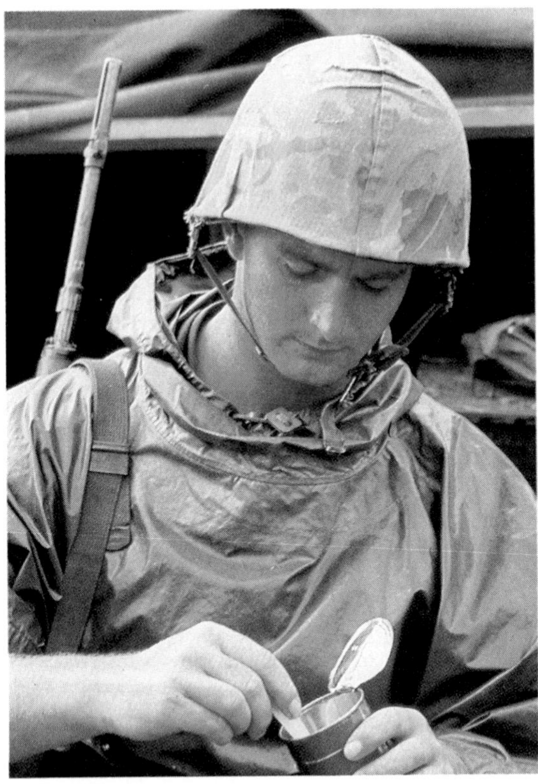

The voting age was lowered to 18 when people decided that citizens old enough to fight for their country are old enough to vote.

Another recent proposal is to amend the Constitution to allow official prayers to be said in public schools. However, this proposal has yet to be approved by Congress, and it faces stiff resistance from citizens who argue that church and state should remain separate. As debates over ERA and school prayer continue, other ideas for amendments continue to emerge.

Since not a year goes by without amendments being suggested and debated by citizens, you might be tempted to ask, "Is our Constitution truly a good plan of government?" A quick look back at history will provide the answer. If the framers had written a poor plan, we would have had hundreds, maybe thousands, of amendments by now—perhaps even a whole new constitution. Instead, we have had only 26 amendments. The voice of the people has been heard, and they have remained satisfied with the basic framework of the Constitution.

Answers will be found on page T 71.

Section Review

1. Define *suffrage.*
2. How did the Fourteenth Amendment guarantee citizenship to African Americans?
3. Explain why a women's suffrage amendment was finally added to the Constitution.
4. Why was the voting age lowered to eighteen?

Evaluation. Do you think that the voting age should be higher or lower than eighteen? If so, what age do you think it should be? Support your opinion with reasons.

Data Search. Look at the graph on page 476 showing voter turnout in recent presidential elections. What can you say about how 18-year-olds have used the right to vote that the Twenty-sixth Amendment gave them?

Teaching Note: Use the Reinforcement Activity, page T 70, and accompanying worksheet in the Activity Book. Use Teaching Activity 2, page T 69, to extend the information in this section.

7-2
A FLEXIBLE FRAMEWORK

Read to Find Out

- what the terms *segregation* and *affirmative action* mean.
- why few changes have been needed in the Constitution.
- how the Supreme Court plays a role in making the Constitution a "living" document.
- how specific Supreme Court cases can show the flexibility of constitutional principles.

You have seen how amendments enable the Constitution to change with the times. Now you will take a closer look at why, in fact, very few changes have been needed over the years. Our Constitution endures today largely because of the way it is written.

The framers realized that specific instructions for running a government in 1787 might not work years later. By providing general principles instead, they gave later generations of Americans freedom to fill in the details. In this way, the Constitution does not have to be changed to meet every new situation or problem the government might face.

The Role of the Supreme Court

You may be wondering, "If the Constitution does not spell out in detail how to follow the principles, who makes sure that they are being followed correctly?" This is where the courts, especially the Supreme Court, enter the picture. The Supreme Court has the final say over whether constitutional principles have been correctly followed by government officials and other citizens.

It is important to remember, however, that the Court may only interpret what the Constitution means; it may not add, remove, or change a single word in the document. By deciding whether a certain action violates the Constitution, the Court makes that action either legal or illegal. Supreme Court decisions must be obeyed, not only by private citizens but also by the President and by Congress.

However, a Court decision is not necessarily permanent. It may be overturned by an amendment that changes, removes, or adds a constitutional principle. For example, the Dred Scott decision was overturned when the Thirteenth Amendment abolished slavery.

A decision may also be overturned by a later Court decision. New evidence or new ideas may lead the Court to change an earlier interpretation of a constitutional principle.

Interpreting a principle. How has the Supreme Court applied broad constitutional principles to a changing society? One way to answer this question is to see how the Court's interpretation of one principle changed in the course of several important cases. A good example is the Fourteenth Amendment principle that each state must provide citizens with "equal protection of the laws."

Equal protection does not mean that everyone must be treated in exactly the same way, but only that people must be treated *fairly*. For instance, a bank does not have to lend money to every customer, but it must be fair in deciding who will receive loans. It may base its decision on a customer's ability to repay the money, but not on a customer's racial background.

Denying a loan to a person because of his or her race is, of course, an example of discrimination. Human history has been scarred by many forms of discrimination. The following cases focus on two forms that have been particularly common: racial discrimination and discrimination against women. As you read, think about the Supreme Court's impor-

New evidence may invalidate Supreme Court decisions. In 1944, the Court upheld the legality of the government's wartime internment of Japanese Americans. Evidence found in 1983 showed that government officials had falsely testified to "military necessity" to win the Court's approval of the policy.

tant role in applying the general principles of our Constitution to these situations.

Equality and Segregation

The principle of equal protection was originally intended to prevent states from denying rights to African Americans. Over the years the Court has interpreted the meaning of equal protection in many situations that might involve racial discrimination.

***Plessy* v. *Ferguson* (1896).** Although the Fourteenth Amendment had given blacks citizenship, many states passed laws requiring *segregation*, or separation, of blacks and whites in public places such as hotels, schools, restaurants, and trains. Did segregation violate the principle of equal protection?

The Court faced this question in 1896, when it heard a Louisiana case involving Homer Plessy, a black man who had refused to leave a "whites only" railroad car. Plessy argued that the Louisiana law requiring segregation violated his right to equal protection. In a famous decision, *Plessy* v. *Ferguson*, the Court ruled that the Louisiana law did not violate the Fourteenth Amendment as long as the cars for blacks and for whites were of equal quality. For more than 50 years after the decision, this "separate but equal" standard was accepted as a justification for laws that segregated blacks from whites.

Growing opposition to segregation. Not everyone, however, agreed that "separate but equal" facilities truly guaranteed "equal protection of the laws." Many schools and other facilities for blacks were not as good as those for whites. Furthermore, even when the facilities were equal in quality, the fact of being separated by law made many blacks feel that they were inferior to whites. Could it really be said, then, that they were being treated equally?

By the early 1950s, many Americans were questioning the fairness of segregation. Among them was Thurgood Marshall, a lawyer for the National Association for the Advancement of Colored People (NAACP). He and other NAACP lawyers brought before the Court several cases involving facilities that were segregated but equal in quality. They knew that such cases would force the Court to decide whether "separate but equal" facilities truly represented "equal protection." At the center of one of these cases was a schoolgirl from Topeka, Kansas. Eight-year-old Linda Brown was about to play a role in overturning a Supreme Court ruling that had permitted segregation for over half a century.

***Brown* v. *Board of Education of Topeka* (1954).** Linda Brown lived only 5 blocks from a

AMERICAN NOTEBOOK

Thomas Jefferson stressed that a plan of government must be able to change with the times:

> Some men look at Constitutions with reverence and deem them, like the ark of the covenant, too sacred to be touched. They ascribe [give credit] to the men of the preceding age a wisdom more than human, and suppose what they did to be beyond amendment. . . . Laws and institutions must go hand in hand with the progress of the human mind. As that becomes more developed, more enlightened, as new discoveries are made, new truths disclosed, and manners and opinions change with the change of circumstances, institutions must advance also and keep pace with the times.

VIEWS OF NOTED AMERICANS

John Marshall Harlan

John Marshall Harlan, who served on the Supreme Court from 1877 to 1911, was a man ahead of his time. Once a defender of slavery, he became a strong advocate for the rights of black Americans at a time when few other judges shared his view. He was famous for having strong opinions that differed from the majority of the justices, becoming known as "The Great Dissenter."

Born on June 1, 1833, in Boyle County, Kentucky, Harlan grew up in a slave-owning family. For many years a slaveowner himself, Harlan had opposed freedom and citizenship for blacks.

When the Civil War broke out, however, Harlan was forced to make a difficult decision. Although he had believed in the rights of slaveowners, he had also developed a deep respect for the Constitution as the protector of freedom. He had come to realize that the nation's survival depended on ending slavery. Since preserving the nation was more important to him than defending slavery, he joined the Union army.

After the war he opposed the Thirteenth Amendment but later came to believe that blacks should have the same rights as whites. In 1871, he publicly stated his change of opinion, declaring that he would "rather be right than consistent."

As a Supreme Court justice, Harlan often differed from the majority of the justices in cases involving individual rights. Criticizing the "separate but equal" decision in *Plessy* v. *Ferguson*, he declared, "Our Constitution is color-blind, and neither knows nor tolerates classes among citizens." In later cases, he argued for equal protection for other minority groups, such as American Indians and Chinese Americans.

People who disagreed with Harlan's opinions often strongly criticized him. However, Justice Harlan was a person who had a deep faith in his sense of what was right, and he stuck to it despite opposition.

school for white children, but by law she was required to attend a school for black children 21 blocks away. Linda's parents thought she should be able to attend the neighborhood school. Therefore they took the school board to court, with the help of the NAACP. In arguing the case before the Supreme Court, Thurgood Marshall presented evidence that separate schools had a harmful effect on both black and white children. Black children were made to feel inferior to whites, he argued, while white children learned to feel superior to blacks. Therefore, Marshall concluded, "separate but equal" schools could never be equal.

All of the justices on the Supreme Court were convinced by Marshall's reasoning. The Court agreed that segregation of blacks creates "a feeling of inferiority as to their status in the community that may affect their hearts

Discussion: John Marshall Harlan declared that he would "rather be right than consistent." Have students discuss what he meant. Do students admire a person who changes his or her mind? Under what conditions? Have they ever changed their mind about an important issue?

and minds in a way unlikely ever to be undone." Separate educational facilities, the Court ruled, were "by their very nature, unequal" and therefore violated the principle of equal protection.

The decision in *Brown* v. *Board of Education of Topeka* overturned the decision in *Plessy* v. *Ferguson* and made all segregation laws unconstitutional. Thus, it is a significant example of how Supreme Court rulings can keep the Constitution flexible.

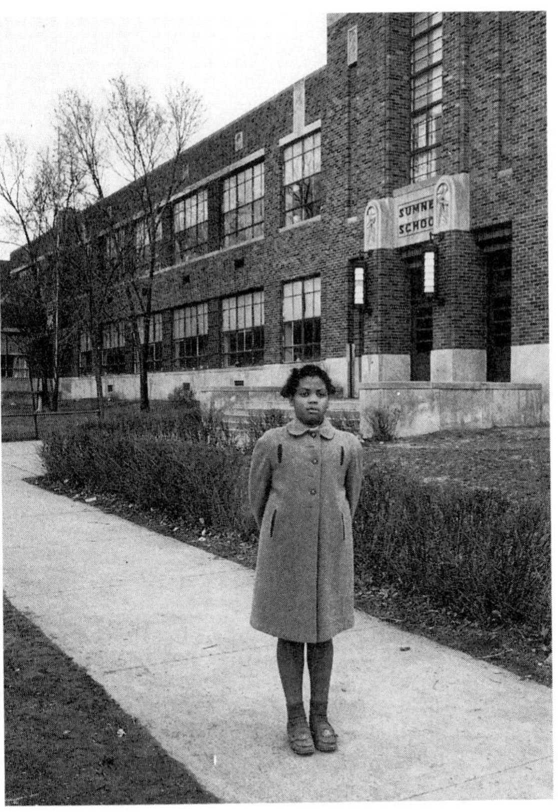

Linda Brown's case led to the Supreme Court's landmark decision declaring that school segregation was illegal.

Equality and Affirmative Action

The Court's ruling gave a powerful constitutional weapon to Americans who were fighting racial discrimination. Spurred on by the Brown case and by increasing public pressure during the 1960s, Congress passed a series of laws—known as civil rights laws—to guard against racial discrimination. However, these laws did little to make up for years of discrimination against African Americans, Hispanic Americans, Asian Americans, and Native Americans, particularly in the workplace.

Over the years, many companies have discriminated against job applicants because of race. In these companies the racial background of employees has not reflected the mixture in the local population. An example would be a business whose employees are all white, even though half of the workers in the community are African Americans, Hispanic Americans, and Asian Americans.

Since the late 1960s, as a result of the civil rights movement, the government has worked to correct the effects of unfair hiring practices. It has required companies to take ***affirmative action***, steps to counteract the effects of past racial discrimination and discrimination against women. Meanwhile, colleges and universities that in the past seemed to favor white males when hiring staff and admitting students have been required to take similar steps.

Some people have argued that affirmative action does not result in equal treatment but instead involves reverse discrimination. In other words, they say that affirmative action leads to discrimination against white male applicants. Faced with the question of whether affirmative action programs really do lead to fair treatment of applicants, the Court took another close look at the meaning of "equal protection."

***University of California Regents* v. *Bakke* (1978).** One school with an affirmative action program was the medical school of the University of California at Davis. The school reserved places in each entering class for African-American, Hispanic-American, Asian-American, and Native-American students. In 1973,

In its decision in *Brown* v. *Board of Education of Topeka,* the Court ruled that desegregation should occur "with all deliberate speed." However, in a review of Topeka schools in 1989, the United States Court of Appeals ruled that Topeka schools were still not appropriately integrated.

Traditional views on women's roles and rights have changed as more women, like this firefighter, have taken jobs previously held only by men.

and again in 1974, a white applicant named Allan Bakke applied for admission and was rejected, although some members of other racial and ethnic groups were admitted with lower grade-point averages, test scores, and interview ratings. Bakke took the university to court, arguing that he was a victim of reverse discrimination.

The Bakke case posed a challenge for the Supreme Court. Unlike the Brown case, the justices were sharply divided. Some thought the admissions program was a reasonable way to overcome effects of discrimination. The majority, however, agreed with Bakke.

The Court ruled that under the equal protection principle it was unconstitutional for an admissions program to discriminate against whites only because of their race. However, the Court stated that race could be *one* of the factors considered if the school wished to create a more diverse student body while treating white applicants fairly.

Women and Equality

Recently, the Court has applied the equal protection principle to other issues, particularly to the debate over whether companies may treat male employees differently from female employees. May a company hire only males for certain jobs? May a company have rules that treat women differently from men? The following case illustrates how the Court has applied the principle of equal protection to such questions.

***Phillips* v. *Martin Marietta Corporation* (1966).** In 1966 Ida Phillips applied for a position with the Martin Marietta Corporation in Florida. Part of the corporation's screening process was to find out whether female applicants had young children. In the corporation's view, young children take up a lot of a woman's time and energy, thus interfering with her work performance. Women such as Ida Phillips, who had two pre-schoolers, were denied jobs for that reason.

When Ida Phillips was rejected for the job, she decided to take the corporation to court, where her lawyers argued that she had not been treated equally. She charged the company with discriminating against women because male applicants were not questioned about their children and were hired whether they had young children or not.

After studying the case, the Court concluded that the corporation's lawyers had not proved that family responsibilities of a mother with young children would get in the way of job performance. Therefore, the Court ruled in favor of Ida Phillips, declaring that the company could not have "one hiring policy for women and another for men."

Challenge (Synthesis): Have students discuss what other ways, beside affirmative action, our society can overcome the effects of past discrimination.

Teaching Note: Use the Enrichment Activity, page T 70, and accompanying worksheet in the Activity Book.

A Framework for the Future

The cases you have just examined all show how the Supreme Court applies general principles of the Constitution to new situations or issues. A hundred years ago, most Americans could not have imagined that racial discrimination against a white man would ever become an issue, as happened in the Bakke case. However, the equal protection principle can be applied just as well to racial discrimination of any type.

Similarly, the question of whether men and women should be treated equally in the workplace did not become a major issue until relatively recently. However, as more women have taken jobs outside the home, they have called attention to cases of unequal treatment. In response, the Supreme Court has applied the old principle of equal protection to this new situation.

The general principles of our living Constitution have guided our nation for over two centuries and can be expected to do so in the future. Judging from past history, amendments may be required from time to time, but the Constitution's sturdy framework of principles will most likely remain intact.

Answers will be found on page T 71.

Section Review

1. Define *segregation* and *affirmative action.*
2. How has the way the Constitution is written helped to keep it flexible?
3. What powers does the Supreme Court have regarding the Constitution? What is the Court not allowed to do to the Constitution?
4. Explain how the cases of *Plessy* v. *Ferguson* and *Brown* v. *Board of Education of Topeka* show the flexibility of the Constitution.

Evaluation. What do you think would happen if the Constitution were a list of specific rules for the government to follow?

A BROADER VIEW

Here is an item that you might find in a trivia quiz or a book of world records:

Question: What is the oldest written plan of government in the world today?
Answer: The United States Constitution.

That question and answer are far from trivial, though. They speak for the strength of our plan of government. Because it is limited to setting forth general principles and because it can be amended, our living Constitution has endured while constitutions of many other nations have been struck down by revolution or have been completely rewritten. For instance, since the French Revolution of 1789, France has had five different constitutions. By comparison, the basic framework of the United States Constitution remains the same.

The American Constitution is similar to a building constructed to withstand earthquakes. Such a building is designed to move *with* the motion of the earth, not against it. It can adjust to fairly strong movement without collapsing. In the same way, the American Constitution adjusts to the force of changing conditions and attitudes. Our Constitution stands as a tribute to the framers' foresight—their ability to plan for the future of our great nation.

Teaching Note: Use the Evaluating Progress activity, page T 70, to assess students' understanding of the chapter.

Students' Rights

The dogs arrived without warning. The students sat quietly at their desks while the dogs sniffed up and down the aisles. Anyone who knew the school gossip guessed what the dogs were looking for.

People were saying that drug use at the junior and senior high schools in Highland, Indiana, had increased dramatically. Over a 20-day period, 13 students had been found with drugs or under the influence of drugs.

Concern among parents, faculty, and school officials had increased as each new incident became known. Furthermore, many students were saying that they felt pressure from friends to use drugs at school.

To fight what he believed to be a serious drug problem, Omer Renfrow, the superintendent of schools, decided to use trained dogs to conduct a drug investigation in March, 1979. The aim was to rid the junior and senior highs of illegal drugs and to discourage further drug use on campus.

Although the police were to be present during the procedure, they had agreed not to step in if drugs were found. Instead, they would allow school officials to discipline any students found with drugs.

Teachers were informed of the inspection that morning. Just before the end of first period, dogs trained to detect the odor of marijuana were brought into each classroom. The dogs spent about five minutes in each room, sniffing near every student. When a dog found a suspicious odor, it alerted the trainer. With each alert, that student was asked to empty his or her pockets or purse.

The dogs spent about five minutes in each room, sniffing near every student.

The purse of one student, Diane Doe (not her real name), was searched, but no drugs were found. Because the dog continued to react, Diane was taken to the nurse's office where a more thorough "body search" was conducted. Still no drugs were found.

Diane sued those involved in the investigation. She claimed they had violated her Fourth Amendment right to be free of "unreasonable searches and seizures." Using drug-sniffing dogs in the schoolroom and searching her body without a search warrant was illegal, said Diane.

The United States District Court agreed that the body search, although done privately in the nurse's office, violated Diane's rights under the Fourth Amendment. However, the court also held that using drug-detecting dogs in a schoolroom and asking students merely to empty their pockets and

Activity: Have students find out their school's policy concerning student rights, *loco parentis*, and search and seizure. You may want to invite an administrator to class to be interviewed by students on this subject.

Answers will be found on page T 71.

purses if the dogs reacted was *not* unconstitutional.

The court explained that students do not "shed at the schoolhouse door rights guaranteed by either the Fourth Amendment or any other constitutional provision." However, said the court, a student's right to be free from unreasonable searches must be balanced against a school's responsibility to maintain order and discipline. Thus, a school may limit a student's rights in certain circumstances.

According to the court, a student's rights may be limited whenever school administrators or teachers are acting *in loco parentis*. Under this legal doctrine, school officials take on the rights and responsibilities that parents have in relation to their children.

There is "no question," the court said, that school officials have the authority of parents and thus have the duty to keep schools "free from activities harmful to [education] and to the individual students." Therefore, using trained dogs in the school and ordering students suspected of having drugs to empty their pockets or purses are allowable actions under the doctrine of *loco parentis*.

On the other hand, said the court, the more thorough search of Diane was an invasion of privacy forbidden by the Fourth Amendment because it caused more than the "mild inconvenience" of a pocket search. According to the court, "there is a core of privacy so vital to the student's personhood that it must be respected by a school official standing *in loco parentis*." Before such a search can be done without a search warrant, there must be additional reasons to suspect that a person possesses drugs. Diane Doe was a good student and had never been in trouble before, so there was not good cause to suspect her.

Students do not "shed at the schoolhouse door rights guaranteed by either the Fourth Amendment or any other constitutional provision."

Analyzing the Case

1. Why did the court decide that it was allowable to use trained dogs in the school?
2. Why was the body search of Diane unconstitutional even though the school officials were acting *in loco parentis*?
3. If drugs had been found on Diane during the body search, do you think the court would have decided the case the same way? Explain.
4. Do you think that the court would have reached a different decision if the dogs had been used outside in the school yard rather than inside the building? What if the students had been across the street from the school? Explain.

The Supreme Court has said that the Fourth Amendment "protects people not places." Under that theory, drug-detecting dogs have been used at airports, courts, and in other public places.

CHAPTER SURVEY

Answers to Survey and Workshop will be found on page T 72.

UNDERSTANDING NEW VOCABULARY

Seeing Relationships

Match each vocabulary term with the event to which it relates. Explain the connection between the term and the event.

Example: *Segregation* is related to the case of *Brown* v. *Board of Education of Topeka* because in that case the Supreme Court decided that any laws permitting segregation are not allowed by the Constitution.

1. *suffrage*

2. *segregation*

3. *affirmative action*

(a) the case of *Plessy* v. *Ferguson*
(b) the case of *University of California Regents* v. *Bakke*
(c) the passage of the Nineteenth Amendment

Putting It in Writing

Write a paragraph explaining how *segregation* and *affirmative action* relate to the principle of equal protection of the laws under the Fourteenth Amendment.

LOOKING BACK AT THE CHAPTER

1. Explain why slavery was not forbidden by the original Constitution.

2. Describe how African Americans gained citizenship and the right to vote.

3. Describe the traditional view of women and then explain why that view has changed over the years.

4. How did eighteen-year-olds gain the right to vote?

5. Explain how the voting rights amendments show that the Constitution can be changed in response to a changing society.

6. Is a Supreme Court decision permanent? Explain your answer.

7. How does the Supreme Court help ensure that our Constitution continues to apply to a changing society?

8. What was the importance of the Supreme Court's decision in *Brown* v. *Board of Education of Topeka*?

9. How have the general principles of the Constitution helped to reduce the need for amendments? Explain how the Supreme Court decisions in the Bakke and Phillips cases illustrate this point.

10. *Analysis.* Why do you think the nation had to finally settle the issue of slavery?

11. *Analysis.* As you already know, the Constitution alone cannot guarantee citizens' rights. The people themselves must cooperate by respecting each other's rights. How does the struggle for African-American rights after the Civil War reflect this fact?

12. *Evaluation.* What is one amendment that you think will be proposed in the future? Explain why.

WORKING TOGETHER

1. Working in a group of three or four students, create two "constitutions" for your class, one a list of very specific rules and the other a list of general principles. (An example of a specific rule would be: "No student will call a classmate 'stupid'." An example of a general principle would be: "No student will insult a classmate.") Predict and compare the possible effects of each constitution. Be sure to look at the advantages and disadvantages of each type of constitution.

2. With two or three other students, make a collage of recent newspaper and magazine articles to illustrate one of the following facts: **(a)** the importance of the Supreme Court's role in interpreting constitutional principles or **(b)** the continuing possibilities for new amendments.

SOCIAL STUDIES SKILLS

Using Primary Sources

Not all primary sources are written documents. Objects such as photographs, paintings, and recordings are also direct sources of information about people, places, and events. The following photograph, for example, reveals one person's experience with discrimination in employment. Look at the photograph carefully and then answer the questions that follow.

1. Describe what you see in the photograph.

2. What do you think led the girl in the photograph to do what she is doing?

3. Do you think the Supreme Court's decision in *Phillips* v. *Martin Marietta Corporation* applies to the girl in this picture? Explain your answer.

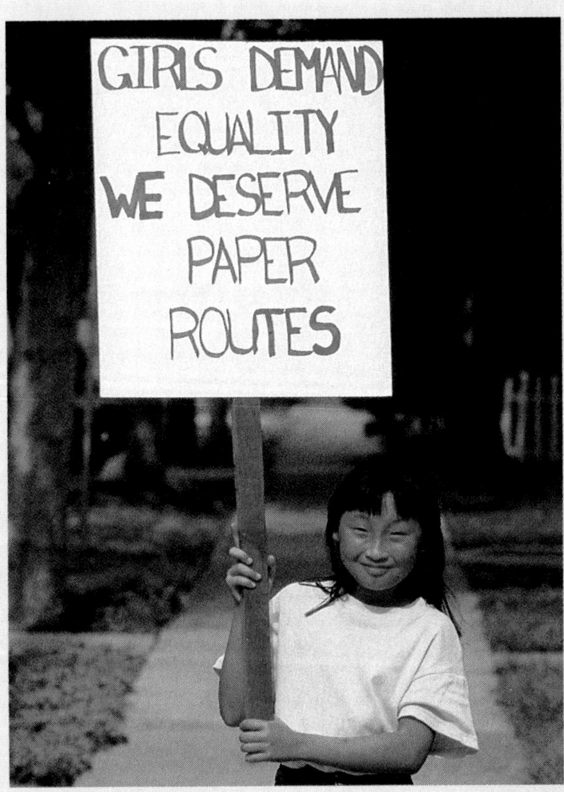

Teaching Note: For reinforcement of decision-making skills, use Decision-Making Worksheet Chapter 7.

DECISION-MAKING SKILLS

Which Sources Can You Trust?

Suppose some Americans have started a campaign against the amendment that grants voting rights to eighteen-year-olds. These people are urging Congress to propose that the amendment be removed from the Constitution. You are not sure what stand to take on the issue. Your search for information leads you to the following sources. Determine which source would be most reliable on the issue of voting rights for eighteen-year-olds.

A. A book of statistics on American voters. The information was provided by election officials, and the book was published by the federal government. The statistics are divided according to age brackets, showing percentages of eligible voters who vote, as well as how different age groups have voted on various issues over the past several national elections.

B. A book about teenagers and the right to vote. The book was published in 1984 by an organization called Mothers Against Drunk Driving. The author, a professor of child psychology, has written several books on the effects of teenagers "growing up too fast" in America.

C. A collection of interviews with ten parents of eighteen-year-olds, who stated whether their sons and daughters were mature enough to vote. Half of the parents were Republicans, and half were Democrats. Most of them regularly voted in national elections.

1. Which one of the sources described above is likely to be most reliable on the topic of whether eighteen-year-olds should keep the right to vote? Explain your answer.

2. Suppose you had to explain to a seventh grader how to determine the reliability of a source. What specific directions would you give?

IN THEIR OWN WORDS

Thomas Jefferson: First Inaugural Address

Answers will be found on page T 73.

In 1800 Thomas Jefferson defeated John Adams in a close and bitterly contested campaign for the presidency. Afraid that bad feelings might linger among voters who had supported Adams, Jefferson was determined to keep political fighting from tearing the young nation apart. Therefore, in his first speech as President he reminded the American people of their shared goals and values.

Below are some excerpts from the inaugural address that Thomas Jefferson delivered in March 1801. As you read, think about the importance of each principle Jefferson mentions.

> Friends and Fellow-Citizens: This [election] now being decided by the voice of the nation, announced according to the rules of the Constitution, all will of course arrange themselves under the will of the law and unite in common efforts for the common good. All too will bear in mind this sacred principle, that, though the will of the majority is in all cases to prevail, that will, to be rightful, must be reasonable; that the minority possess their equal rights, which equal laws must protect, and to violate would be oppression. . . .
>
> Let us then, fellow citizens, unite with one heart and one mind. . . . Every difference of opinion is not a difference of principle. . . . If there be any among us who would wish to dissolve this Union, or to change its republican form, let them stand undisturbed as monuments of the safety with which error of opinion may be tolerated where reason is left free to combat it. . . .
>
> It is proper you should understand what I [consider to be] the essential principles of our Government. . . . Equal and exact justice to all men; . . . peace, commerce, and honest friendship with all nations, entangling alliances with none; the support of the state governments; . . . the preservation of the [federal] Government in its whole constitutional vigor; . . . care of the right of election by the people; . . . [complete obedience] to the decisions of the majority; . . . a well-disciplined militia; . . . the supremacy of the civil over the military authority; economy in the public expense; . . . the honest payment of our debts; . . . encouragement of agriculture and of commerce; . . . freedom of religion; freedom of the press, . . . and trial by juries impartially selected.
>
> These principles form the bright constellation which has gone before us and guided our steps through an age of revolution and reformation. The wisdom of our sages and blood of our heroes have been devoted to their attainment. They should be the creed of our political faith, the text of our civic instruction, . . . and should we wander from them in moments of error or of alarm, let us hasten to retrace our steps and to regain the road which alone leads to peace, liberty, and safety.

Analyzing Primary Sources

1. What points does Jefferson make regarding majority rule? Do you agree? Explain your answer.
2. Pick three of the principles that Jefferson mentions. Then explain how they help lead to "peace, liberty, and safety."
3. Which one of the principles mentioned by Jefferson do you think is most important to our nation? Explain your answer.

Activity: Ask students to imagine that they have just been elected President of the United States after a long, bitter campaign. Have them list five points they would make in their inaugural speech to try to gain the support of all of the American people.

UNIT SURVEY

Answers will be found on page T 73.

LOOKING BACK AT THE UNIT

1. Discuss the roots of our American tradition of representative government.

2. Why did the founders of our nation want to limit the powers of the national government? In what ways does the Constitution limit the government's powers?

3. Explain why the Bill of Rights was added to the Constitution. Describe at least four protections provided in the Bill of Rights.

4. Explain how our Constitution has been able to adjust to changing attitudes and conditions in society.

TAKING A STAND

The Issue

Should handguns be harder for people to buy?

On March 30, 1981, a gunman fired shots that seriously wounded President Ronald Reagan. This attempted murder fueled an already fierce debate between those who argue that citizens have the right to own handguns and those who want the sale of handguns to be tightly controlled.

People who oppose tight control of handgun sales argue that handguns are necessary for self-defense, allowing people to protect their families and homes and offering the only real protection against crimes like mugging and rape. In an emergency, they say, a time-consuming call to the police would probably be useless. Opponents of gun control also argue that "if guns are outlawed, only outlaws will have guns." They want the government to concentrate on locking up criminals rather than preventing law-abiding citizens from purchasing guns. Furthermore, they say, the mere possibility that homeowners have deadly weapons discourages criminal break-ins, thereby controlling crime.

Those who want tight control of handgun sales argue that protecting communities against criminals is the job of the police, and that citizens should not take the law into their own hands. Furthermore, they point out, far from protecting families and homes, handguns add to the threat. Loaded guns in the home are within reach of people who may be drunk, depressed, or angry. They note that murders by handgun happen less often between strangers than between married couples or family members. Of the over 20,000 deaths by handgun in the United States each year, over half are suicides and about 1,200 are accidental. On average, one child a day is killed in a handgun accident. Supporters of gun control argue that to decrease these tragedies laws should be passed to severely limit handgun sales.

Expressing Your Opinion

Decide how you stand on the issue of gun control. Should laws be passed making it more difficult for the average citizen to buy a gun? State your opinion and your reasons in a letter to one of your United States senators, urging him or her to support your point of view. Begin your letter "Dear Senator" and address it as follows:

The Honorable (name of senator)
Senate Office Building
Washington, D.C.
20501

To obtain the names of your senators, ask your librarian.

UNIT 3

Unit Quotation: President Roosevelt's concern for the welfare of Americans during the Great Depression of the 1930s led him to use the power of the federal government more than ever before to help restore prosperity. His policies sparked controversy about the federal government's power.

THE FEDERAL GOVERNMENT

A Three Horse Team

I describe the American form of government as a three horse team provided by the Constitution to the American people so that their field might be plowed. The three horses are, of course, the three branches of government—the Congress, the executive, and the courts.

—President Franklin D. Roosevelt

The Constitution established a federal government made up of the legislative, executive, and judicial branches. The framers divided power among these branches in order to prevent any one branch from abusing its power. The three branches also limit each other's power through a system of checks and balances. These checks and balances ensure that the branches work "as a three horse team" for the welfare of citizens.

Unit 3 will examine the three branches of the federal government. You will see how each branch works and how it checks and balances the power of the others.

Chapter 8 The Legislative Branch

Chapter 9 The Executive Branch

Chapter 10 The Judicial Branch

Chapter Themes: As lawmakers and servants of the people, members of Congress must balance many responsibilities and handle conflicting pressures. Congress uses its broad powers to meet the goals of the Preamble to the Constitution. Committees and congressional leaders facilitate lawmaking.

CHAPTER 8

The Legislative Branch

At first, Anne Petrini thought little about the hourly wage she received working at the muffin shop. It was her first real job, and she was happy just having some extra spending money.

Then she got to know one of her co-workers, Diana Perez. Diana was the mother of three children, and she had to pay all the family bills with the money she made at the shop. Diana often spoke about how hard it was to get by. "That minimum wage," Diana would say, "is much too low. Who can support a family on $3.35 an hour?" As Anne got to know Diana better, her respect for the woman grew. So did her feeling that the minimum wage—the lowest amount certain workers can be paid—was unfair.

When Anne arrived at work one day in March, Diana was talking with Denise and Elena, who also worked at the muffin shop.

"My sister-in-law told me that Congress might raise the minimum wage this year," Denise was saying. "She heard that a new law was proposed in the Senate and that everyone should write their senators."

"Do you really think a letter from us would help?" asked Diana. "My senator doesn't even know who I am."

"Anyway," added Elena, "the boss says that she can't afford to pay us more. If Congress raises the minimum wage, some of us might lose our jobs."

Anne was puzzled by what she had heard. Could Congress pass laws about how much a worker should be paid? Would a senator—or a representative—pay attention to letters from citizens? It would be worth a try, she decided. But how did members of Congress make up their minds about laws when people had strong feelings for and against them?

In this chapter, you will read about the members of Congress and the lawmaking powers given to Congress by the Constitution. Then you will find out how Congress is organized. Finally, you will learn how a proposal to increase the minimum wage made its way through the Senate.

Teaching Note: Use the Introducing the Chapter activity, page T 75.

8-1
THE MEMBERS OF CONGRESS

Read to Find Out

- what the terms *policy, constituents, bill, interest groups, lobbyists, census,* and *congressional district* mean.
- what groups a member of Congress is responsible to.
- what it means for a member of Congress to be a servant of the people.
- how the jobs of senator and representative compare.

Congress is the legislative, or lawmaking, branch of the national government. It is made up of two houses, the Senate and the House of Representatives.

The most important job of Congress is to make laws. Laws are the life blood of the nation. They do not simply state what you can and cannot do. A law can establish a national ***policy***, a plan of action designed to achieve a certain goal. Laws, for example, spell out how the government raises and spends its money. They protect the environment, provide money for school lunches, and send astronauts into space. Laws, as Anne Petrini learned, can also determine how much workers are paid.

The Responsibilities of Lawmaking

We are often faced with important decisions in our lives. Can you remember a time when you had to make a decision? Your parents wanted you to decide one way, your friends wanted you to decide a different way, and you were caught in the middle trying to make up your mind what to do.

This is the kind of situation members of Congress face every day. A member has responsibilities to different groups of people. Often these groups make different demands. Lawmaking involves balancing many responsibilities and handling conflicting pressures.

Local versus national needs. Each member of Congress represents a group of citizens much smaller than the nation as a whole. One of a member's major responsibilities is to his or her ***constituents*** (kun-STICH-oo-ents), the people he or she represents. Constituents expect senators and representatives to listen to their ideas about problems and issues and to be their voice in Congress.

In addition, a member of Congress has a responsibility to the whole nation. The laws Congress makes often affect all Americans. Sometimes, the needs of a member's constituents are in conflict with the needs of Americans in general. For example, a representative from a wheat-growing region may have to vote on a law that would please local wheat farmers but would anger the nation's consumers by raising the price of bread.

Political parties. A member of Congress also has a responsibility to his or her political party. A party is an organization of people who share certain ideas about what government should do. Most members of Congress today belong to either the Republican party or the Democratic party. Each party works to elect its candidates to Congress. In return, the party expects its members to support the party's position on an issue before Congress.

This responsibility may present a member of Congress with a difficult choice. The senator who received Anne Petrini's letter about the ***bill***, or proposed law, to increase the minimum wage was pressured from two sides. As a Republican, he felt he should follow his party's position and oppose the bill. However, most of the letters he had received from constituents were in support of the bill.

Constituents and interest groups send approximately 196 million letters and postcards to members of Congress each year. A representative receives an average of about 365,000 letters and a senator receives about 360,000.

PEOPLE MAKE A DIFFERENCE

Couple Gets Congress to Listen

No one can tell David and Reba Saks that being in your mid-seventies is too old to make a difference. Both David and Reba were nearing retirement when they started Organization for Use of the Telephone (OUT).

Reba Saks has difficulty hearing and uses a hearing aid. One day in 1973, Reba tried to use a pay telephone. Instead of normal sounds, she heard a loud squeal.

The Sakses contacted American Telephone and Telegraph (AT&T) about the incident. AT&T told them that new telephones were being placed across the nation to improve the phone system. Unfortunately, with certain hearing aids the new telephones caused the high-pitched squeals.

David Saks was very upset. He knew that if AT&T continued its program, nearly 3 million hearing-aid users would be unable to use the new telephones.

The Sakses wrote letters to telephone company officials and newspapers. They formed OUT and encouraged others to join. Their motto became All Telephones Must Work with All Hearing Aids Everywhere.

At first, AT&T refused to change the telephones. Later, AT&T agreed to make the changes, but other phone companies did not. The Sakses decided to ask Congress to support their cause. As a result of their lobbying, in 1982 Congress passed a law requiring some telephones to work with hearing aids. Not satisfied, the Sakses and OUT continued to lobby. In 1988, Congress finally passed a law banning companies from making or importing telephones that cannot be used with hearing aids.

The Sakses say, "It is our government, and if we do not petition it to address our grievances, we are shirking our duty, we are not good citizens." With a lot of work, the Sakses and OUT achieved their goal.

Interest groups. A member of Congress may well want to run for re-election when his or her term of office ends. For this reason, members try to gain support and raise money for campaigns. They often get help from ***interest groups***, groups of people who work together for similar interests or goals. Interest groups can supply both votes and money. Examples of well-known interest groups are the American Medical Association, the American Farm Bureau, and the National Rifle Association.

An interest group works to convince senators and representatives to support bills that help its members and to oppose bills that hurt them. This is done by hiring ***lobbyists***, people who represent interest groups. For example, hotel and motel owners form one interest group that opposed the minimum wage bill. They argued that it would increase their costs by forcing them to pay their workers more. Their lobbyists tried to convince members of Congress to oppose the bill.

Activity: As students go about their daily lives in the community, have them record other examples of how society meets the special needs of citizens with handicaps.

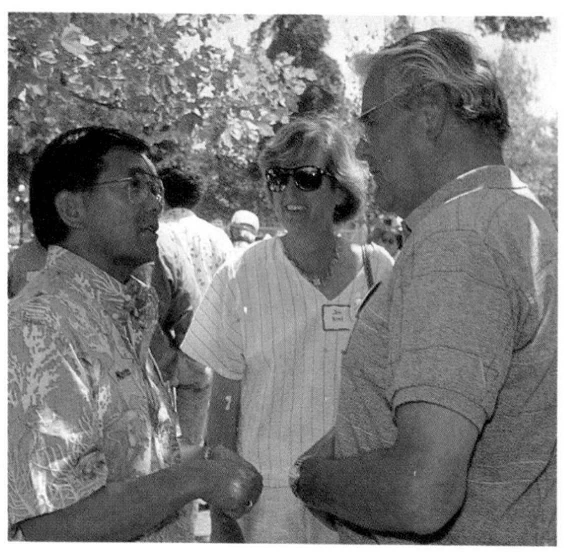

Like other representatives, Norman Mineta, left, keeps in touch with constituents, as at this picnic in his California district.

Often a member of Congress supports the goals of a particular interest group. In return, that group encourages its members to vote for him or her in the next election.

Factors in decision making. A member of Congress votes on hundreds of bills every year. Each vote represents a decision the member must make. He or she must weigh conflicting information and arguments presented by constituents, fellow party members, and lobbyists.

A member must also search his or her own conscience and values. Predicting what the result of a bill will be in the long run can be difficult, but the member must consider that, too. All of these factors are part of the responsibilities of lawmaking.

Servants of the People

In addition to being a lawmaker, a member of Congress plays a second important role as servant of the people. In this role, a member gives information and help to individual constituents who have special needs or problems. The owner of a small business, for example, may want to know the latest government rules that apply to her business. An elderly person may want his social security checks to come on time.

Solving the problems of individual constituents is called casework. Many members of Congress place a great deal of emphasis on casework because it makes the member's constituents happy—and more likely to vote for him or her for re-election.

Members of Congress at Work

In 1899, one senator joked, "God made a day 24 hours long for the ordinary man. After a man becomes a United States senator, he requires a day 48 hours long." These words still ring true for senators as well as for representatives. Although they work hard, it is almost impossible for them to do all that is required of them.

Members of Congress spend a great deal of time learning about the issues on which they must vote. In 1987 and 1988, for example, members needed to know about trade between the United States and Canada and the effect of a serious dry spell on ranchers and farmers. Members also had to know about medical costs of the elderly, drug use in the nation, and the government's treatment of Japanese Americans during World War II. Congress passed legislation, or laws, in each of these areas in 1988.

Members of Congress also try to be present on the floor of the House or Senate chamber as much as possible. There, they listen to speeches, give speeches, and vote on bills.

Every day, members of Congress go to meetings. Every day, dozens of people compete for their time—a fellow member with

It is estimated that there are between 10,000 and 20,000 lobbyists in Washington, D.C. They call themselves political consultants, foreign representatives, legislative specialists, consumer advocates, trade association representatives, and government affairs specialists.

Teaching Note: You may wish to use the Unit 3 Activity, "Creating Congressional Districts," in the Activity Book after students have read the discussion of congressional districts.

questions about a bill, a lobbyist with arguments against one, a constituent visiting the Capitol. Between meetings, members prepare bills, study reports, and read many letters from constituents. One senator, Jacob Javits of New York, reported receiving 4,000 letters a week between 1957 and 1981.

Congressional staff. Members of Congress rely heavily on their personal staffs—about 12,000 workers who help them do their jobs. Administrative assistants run a member's offices at home and in Washington, D.C. Legislative assistants study bills. The caseworkers handle requests from constituents.

Members and their staffs try to make their home offices a link between citizens and the government. Former Representative Ella Grasso of Connecticut, for example, installed in her home office a toll-free "Ella-Phone," which gave around-the-clock service to her constituents. "It's my way," she said, "of bringing government closer to the people and the people closer to the government."

Members and their staffs also make special efforts to learn what the constituents are thinking. Some home offices set up regular neighborhood meetings so that people can talk about issues which concern them. These opinions will be taken into account when bills are proposed and voted upon.

Representatives

You read in Chapter 5 that the House of Representatives is elected on the basis of population. The Constitution requires a ***census***, an official count of the population made every ten years to find out how many representatives each state should have. Then Congress gives each state a fair proportion of the 435 seats in the House of Representatives. For example, the 1990 census determined that California, with the biggest population, should have 52 representatives. Vermont and Wyoming, with very small populations, have only one representative each. States can gain or lose representatives after each census, but each state must have at least one representative.

The area that a member of the House represents is called a ***congressional district***. Each state is divided into as many congressional districts as it has representatives in the House. By law, all congressional districts must have about the same number of people. Today, districts contain about 570,000 people.

The process of drawing district boundaries can lead to controversy. Sometimes certain areas in a state have greater percentages of voters from one political party. Then districts can be created to favor one party over another. For example, if the Democratic party

In her Washington office, Senator Nancy Kassebaum of Kansas studies bills, meets constituents, and discusses issues with members of her staff.

Challenge (Analysis): Have students discuss the possibility of increasing the number of senators and representatives in order to decrease the workload and job expectations that currently burden members of Congress. What disadvantages might such an increase have?

Manipulating the shape of legislative districts in order to favor one party over another is known as gerrymandering. This term came into use in 1812 when such a district, shaped like a salamander, was created by the Massachusetts legislature during the governorship of Elbridge Gerry.

controls a state's legislature, it can draw boundaries in such a way that Democrats will be in the majority in most of the state's districts. Another strategy would be to place most of the state's Republicans into a small number of districts. Either strategy might be used to make sure that a majority of representatives from the state will be Democrats.

Term of office. Representatives serve for two years. All 435 representatives end their terms of office at the end of every even-numbered year. They must run for re-election or retire. There is no limit to the number of times a representative can be re-elected.

If they wish to stay in office for more than two years, representatives must constantly work to earn the approval of the people in their districts. For this reason, a typical representative spends more than one fourth of his or her time working for constituents—writing letters, receiving visitors, and doing casework.

Senators

In the Senate each state is represented by two senators. Thus, a senator pays attention to the interests of the state as a whole, not just one district. For example, a representative from a congressional district in central Illinois will be very interested in farm policies because most of the constituents grow crops and raise livestock. A senator from Illinois, in contrast, is concerned not only with farming, but also with all other parts of the state's economy, including manufacturing, banking, mining, and shipping.

Term of office. Senators are elected for terms of six years. One third of the senators are elected every two years. Unlike the terms of representatives, the terms of senators overlap. As a result, at any one time, there are a number of experienced senators in the Senate.

The framers of the Constitution hoped that longer, overlapping terms would make senators less sensitive to the shifting moods of the people than representatives, who face re-election every two years. As a more stable body, the Senate was expected to prevent quick, unwise changes in the law.

Requirements. The requirements for being a senator or a representative are similar. Senators and representatives must live in the states in which they are elected. Representatives must be at least 25 years old, and senators must be at least 30 years old. A representative must have been a citizen of the United States for at least seven years, but a senator must have been a citizen for at least nine years.

Salary and Benefits

A member of Congress received an annual salary of $125,000 in 1991. In addition, a member receives benefits to help him or her do the job. For example, a member can have two offices, one in Washington, D.C., and one in his or her congressional district or state. A member receives allowances for running both offices and paying staff salaries, as well as money to travel home to meet with constituents.

Members also have free use of the postal service to send mail, such as newsletters, to constituents. This benefit is known as the franking privilege because the member's printed signature, or "frank," is placed on the envelope instead of a stamp. Congressional newsletters tell constituents about important events and what their member of Congress is doing. Many members send constituents questionnaires asking their opinions about issues. The franking privilege, like other benefits, helps a member of Congress serve his or her constituents.

The term *frank* comes from the Latin word *francus*, which means "free."

Teaching Note: Use Teaching Activity 1, page T 75, as a culminating activity after students have read the material in Section 8-1.

Answers will be found on page T 77.

Section Review

1. Define the terms *policy, constituents, bill, interest groups, lobbyists, census,* and *congressional district.*
2. Describe the groups to which a member of Congress has responsibilities.
3. How do members of Congress help their constituents?
4. What are some major differences between the jobs of senators and representatives?

Evaluation. Based on what you know about the area you live in, what do you think are some local needs your representative should take into account?

Data Search. Look on page 585 in the Data Bank. Which three states gained the most seats in the House of Representatives after the 1990 census? What happened in your state?

8-2

THE POWERS OF CONGRESS

Read to Find Out

- what the term *budget* means.
- how Congress uses its powers to meet the goals stated in the Preamble to the Constitution.
- what nonlegislative powers Congress has.
- how limits on the powers of Congress protect the rights of citizens.

Each year, our cities, states, and nation face many problems. Congress has the power to try to solve some of these problems. Others must be left to local and state governments or to individuals and groups. For example, fixing the potholes in a street is the responsibility of a city. However, repairing the interstate highway, which runs between states, must be done by the national government.

Which problems Congress can try to solve is determined in part by the powers given it in the Constitution. As you will see, these powers are broad, but they have their limits.

Powers Given to Congress

In Chapter 5 you learned that the powers given to Congress are known as delegated powers. Most of these powers are listed in the Constitution, in Article 1, Section 8. In deciding which powers to give to Congress, the framers had the goals of the Preamble in mind. These goals are "to form a more perfect union, establish justice, insure domestic tranquility, provide for the common defense, promote the general welfare, and secure the blessings of liberty." Each power reflects one or more of these goals.

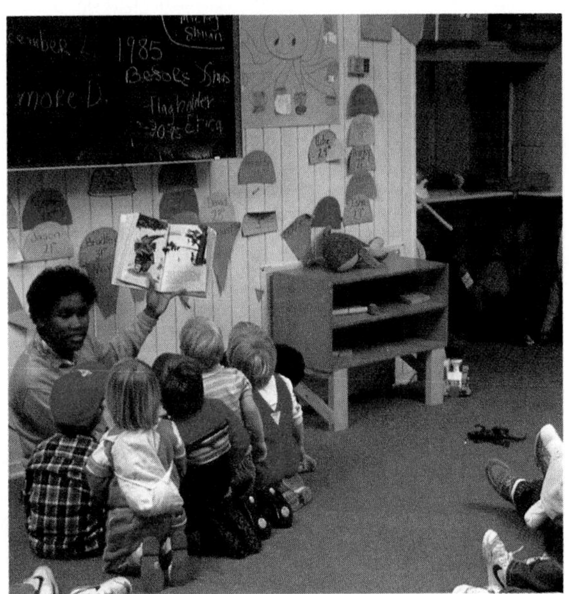

Many think that in its responsibility to promote the general welfare, Congress should provide more funds for nursery schools and day care.

Teaching Note: See Article 1, Section 8 of the Constitution on page 111.

Liberal interpretation of congressional powers and the demands of our times enable Congress to do what it considers necessary and proper to promote the general welfare. As a result, the national government has far more power than most of the framers would have imagined.

Promoting the general welfare. The term *general welfare* refers to the needs of all the people of a nation. Congress promotes the general welfare by making laws that help people live better.

Many of these laws are based on the power of Congress to regulate commerce, or business, with foreign nations and between states. For example, a law sets up an agency which controls air traffic in the nation and writes and enforces rules for air safety. Another agency approves or disapproves increases in interstate telephone rates.

Congress can limit commerce in order to promote the general welfare. In 1808, Congress passed a law forbidding traders to bring African slaves into the United States. Today, a law says that companies that do not pay all their workers minimum wages may not ship their goods to other states.

Congress also has the power to collect taxes and to borrow money. Without money the government could not function. Any bill that has to do with raising money must begin in the House of Representatives. After a money bill has been introduced in the House, the Senate may then act on it.

In addition, Congress has the power to decide how the money it collects will be spent. In this difficult task, Congress determines how much money will go to education, space programs, medical research, and so on.

Congress is said to have the "power of the purse" because it has final approval of the government's ***budget***, or plan for raising and spending money. With this power, Congress acts as a check on the executive branch, which can do very little unless Congress provides the money.

Providing for the common defense. Congress has the power to establish and maintain an army and a navy to defend the nation. Congress also has the sole power to declare war. The last time Congress used this power was in 1941, when the United States declared war on Japan.

In the 1960s and early 1970s, Presidents Lyndon B. Johnson and Richard M. Nixon sent American troops into battle in the Vietnam War even though Congress did not declare war. In 1973, Congress passed a law known as the War Powers Act. That law limits the President's power to send troops into combat without approval by Congress.

Establishing justice. Congress has the power to create federal courts below the level of the Supreme Court. In addition, the appointment of judges to these courts and to the Supreme Court must be approved by the Senate.

Another power of Congress that helps to establish justice is the power to impeach, or accuse an official, such as the President or a federal judge, of serious wrongdoing. Only the House can impeach. The Senate, however, has the power to put the impeached official on trial. If found guilty, the official is removed from office. Only 15 officials have ever been impeached. Of these, 7 officials—all judges—were found guilty.

Unlisted powers. Not all powers of Congress are specifically listed. A clause in the Constitution, often called the elastic clause, allows Congress to make all laws that are "necessary and proper" for carrying out the listed powers. For example, in order to coin money, Congress must set up a mint. The mint has power to design coins and bills, buy metal and paper, hire workers, and distribute the money to banks. None of these powers are listed in the Constitution. The elastic clause gives Congress room to stretch its powers. It makes the government flexible enough to carry out its work and change with the times.

Nonlegislative powers. Fulfilling the goals of the Preamble involves more than making

In 1868, the House impeached President Andrew Johnson for violating a federal law, but the Senate acquitted him. In 1974, the House Judiciary Committee recommended that President Richard Nixon be impeached. However, before the House could vote, Nixon resigned. (See Chapter 9.)

Teaching Note: See Article 1, Section 9 of the Constitution on page 112.

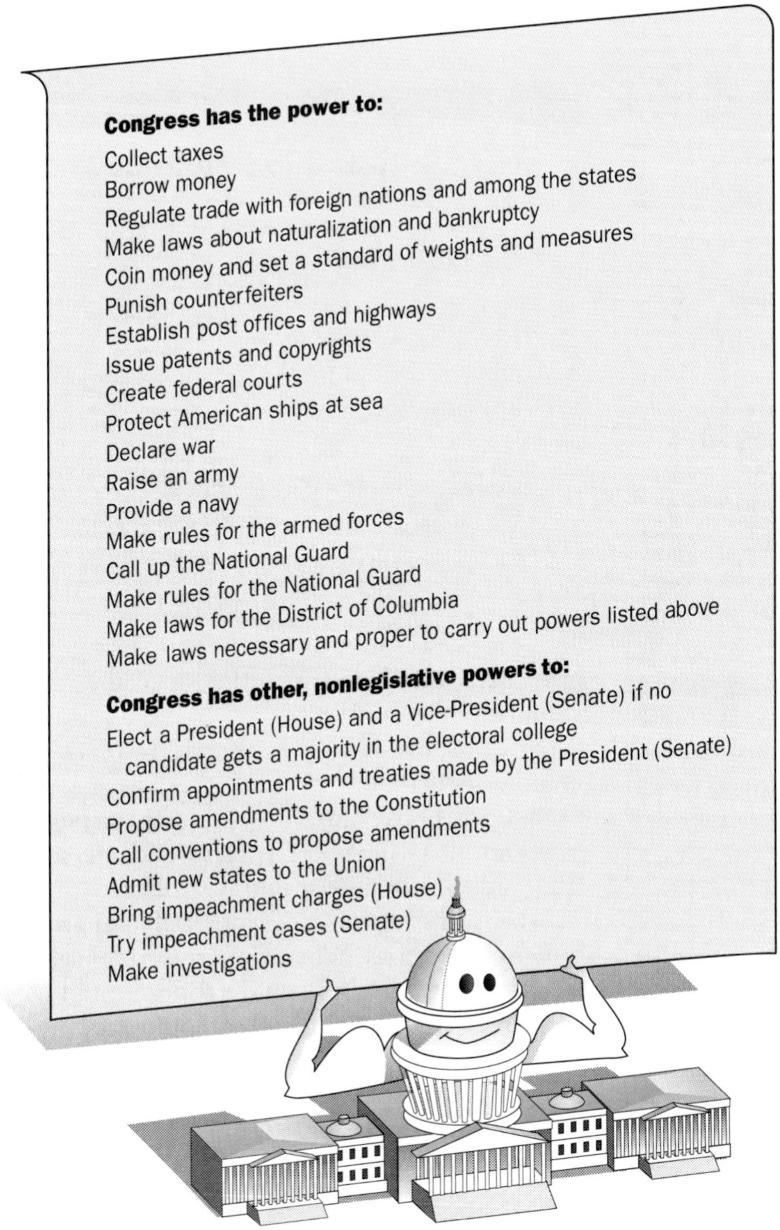

Congress has the power to:

Collect taxes
Borrow money
Regulate trade with foreign nations and among the states
Make laws about naturalization and bankruptcy
Coin money and set a standard of weights and measures
Punish counterfeiters
Establish post offices and highways
Issue patents and copyrights
Create federal courts
Protect American ships at sea
Declare war
Raise an army
Provide a navy
Make rules for the armed forces
Call up the National Guard
Make rules for the National Guard
Make laws for the District of Columbia
Make laws necessary and proper to carry out powers listed above

Congress has other, nonlegislative powers to:

Elect a President (House) and a Vice-President (Senate) if no candidate gets a majority in the electoral college
Confirm appointments and treaties made by the President (Senate)
Propose amendments to the Constitution
Call conventions to propose amendments
Admit new states to the Union
Bring impeachment charges (House)
Try impeachment cases (Senate)
Make investigations

Powers of Congress. *This chart shows the lawmaking powers granted to Congress by the Constitution. It also shows additional powers that do not involve making laws.*

laws. The Constitution grants Congress several important nonlegislative powers. You have already learned about the power to impeach, the power to approve treaties and appointments of federal judges, and the power to propose amendments to the Constitution. Congress also has the power to conduct investigations. It can gather information to help it make laws and it can find out how the executive branch is enforcing laws.

Limits on the Powers of Congress

There are both general and specific limits to the powers of Congress. The general limits come from the system of checks and balances you read about in Chapter 5. The executive branch can veto proposed laws, and the judicial branch can declare laws unconstitutional.

The specific limits are listed in Article 1, Section 9 of the Constitution. The most

Challenge (Analysis): Have students discuss why the framers devoted a large part of the Constitution to the legislative branch.

Teaching Note: Use the Evaluating Progress activity, page T 76, after students have read the material in Section 8-2 or at the end of the chapter.

important of these limits protect the rights of citizens.

In some countries, a person can be held in jail without having been charged with a crime and given a trial. In the United States, if you are held in jail without a charge, a lawyer or friend can get a writ of *habeas corpus* (HAY-bee-uhs KOR-pus). This paper orders the police to bring you into court. The court then decides if the police have enough evidence to hold you. If not, you must be released. The Constitution says that Congress cannot take away a citizen's right to a writ of *habeas corpus* except in times of invasion or civil war.

The Constitution also prevents Congress from passing bills of attainder. A bill of attainder is a law that convicts a person of a crime without a trial. In addition, Congress cannot pass *ex post facto* laws. Such a law makes a particular act a crime and then punishes people who committed the act before the law was passed. For example, you cannot be punished for something you do in April if a law against the act was not made until May.

These specific limits to the power of Congress were originally looked on as a kind of bill of rights. Together, they help to protect the rights of citizens in dealing with the police and the courts.

Answers will be found on page T 77.

Section Review

1. Define the term *budget*.
2. Describe two powers that help Congress "promote the general welfare."
3. Why does Congress have the power to conduct investigations?
4. Why are bills of attainder and *ex post facto* laws unfair?

Evaluation. Do you think the framers were right in giving the power of the purse to Congress rather than to the President? Explain.

8-3 HOW CONGRESS IS ORGANIZED

Read to Find Out

- what the terms *Speaker of the House, president pro tempore, majority party, minority party, floor leaders, whips,* and *pocket veto* mean.
- what the major congressional leadership posts are and how they are filled.
- what purpose each kind of congressional committee serves.

The terms, or meeting periods, of Congress have been numbered in order since the first Congress met in 1789. The 101st Congress began in 1989. Each two-year term of Congress is divided into two sessions, one for each year. Each house stays in session from January 3 until its members vote to end the session. Sessions often last until October.

The Constitution does not tell Congress how to make laws. When Congress first began meeting, any member could propose a bill at any time. Any other member could stop action on it by nonstop talking. There were no rules to control or stop debate. The result, one observer said, was "no agreement, no division of duties, no compromise."

Over time, Congress developed better ways to consider bills. One important way was to divide the work of preparing bills among committees, or small working groups. Another way was to choose leaders to oversee the process of committee work.

Leadership in Congress

The Constitution gives only a few directions about congressional leadership. First, it states that the House of Representatives must choose

Challenge (Evaluation): Have students discuss what communication skills would be necessary for floor leaders to have. Students should provide reasons for their opinions.

a presiding officer called the ***Speaker of the House.*** Second, it says that the Vice-President of the United States is to serve as the presiding officer, or president, of the Senate. Finally, it directs the Senate to choose an officer called the ***president pro tempore*** (pro TEM-puh-REE), who will preside over the Senate when the Vice-President is absent. This officer is also called president pro tem, for short.

The Constitution does not describe how the Speaker of the House or the president pro tem should be chosen. Early in the history of Congress, however, political parties gained control over who was elected to these positions.

Today the Democratic and Republican parties make the decisions about leadership in Congress. In both the House and the Senate, the party with more members is called the ***majority party.*** The one with fewer members is called the ***minority party.***

Before a new Congress begins, members of each party hold meetings to select congressional leaders. The majority party in the House chooses the Speaker of the House. Likewise, the majority party in the Senate chooses the president pro tem. In addition, each party in each house chooses ***floor leaders***, officers who guide through Congress the bills the party supports.

AMERICAN NOTEBOOK 

The United States Congress celebrated its 200th anniversary in April 1989. The members of the 1st Congress probably would be amazed by the size and budget of the 101st Congress.

	1st Congress	101st Congress
Members of House	65	435
Members of Senate	26	100
Standing Committees	0	38
Staff*	13	18,000
Budget	$374,000	$3 billion

*Includes committee staff as well as members' personal staff.

Speaker of the House. The Speaker is the most powerful member of the House. The Speaker presides over sessions, announcing the order of business and deciding who may speak. The Speaker also appoints members of committees and refers bills to committees. These powers give the Speaker great influence over which bills pass or fail in the House.

President of the Senate. As presiding officer of the Senate, the Vice-President is in charge of sessions but cannot take part in debates and can vote only in case of a tie. Because the Vice-President often is busy with executive duties, the president pro tem usually acts as the Senate's presiding officer.

Floor leaders. The chief officers of the majority and minority parties in each house are the floor leaders. They are responsible for guiding bills through Congress. Floor leaders work closely with committee leaders and party members to persuade them to accept compromises or trade-offs in order to win votes on bills. Lyndon B. Johnson of Texas, when he was Senate majority leader between 1955 and 1960, described the job this way:

> First, you must know what is in the bill. Second, you must understand how it is related to the various states and the various personalities in the Senate. And, third, you have to be sure that it will command the respect of a majority.

Assistant floor leaders, called ***whips***, aid floor leaders in each house. Whips try to persuade members to support the party's position on key issues and to be present when it is time to vote. On important issues, when close votes

The Speaker of the House is in a unique position of influence. The Speaker is the recognized leader of his or her political party in the House as well as the presiding officer. He or she also ranks next after the Vice-President in order of presidential succession.

are expected, much depends on the skill of a party's floor leader and whip.

Working in Committees

More than 10,000 bills are introduced in a term of Congress. Of course, it would be impossible for a member to study each bill and decide how to vote. To help handle this work, both the Senate and the House have set up a system of committees. Much of the most important work of lawmaking is done in the committees.

Introducing bills. Most bills start as ideas for solving problems. Many ideas for bills begin in Congress. Others come from individual citizens, special interest groups, and the executive branch. A group interested in wildlife may want a law to protect mountain lions. People who live near an airport may ask for a law to reduce noise. The President may call for a special police force to solve drug problems facing the nation.

Citizens, interest groups, and the executive branch can draw up bills. However, only a senator or a representative can introduce bills in Congress. A representative introduces a bill in the House by dropping it in a special box called a hopper. A senator introduces a bill by reading it aloud from the Senate floor. All bills introduced during a term are marked *HR* in the House and *S* in the Senate. They are given numbers in the order in which they are introduced. For example, when the minimum wage bill was introduced in the Senate in 1987, it was marked S.837.

Standing committees. In both houses of Congress, a bill is sent to a standing committee for action. There are 16 permanent standing committees in the Senate and 22 in the House. Each committee deals with a certain area, such as education or banking. You will find a list of the standing committees in the Data Bank on page 585.

Committees control the fate of bills. First, a standing committee carefully studies a bill. Next, it holds hearings, or public meetings, at which anyone can speak. The committee may propose changes in the bill. Finally, the committee decides whether to recommend that the entire House or Senate vote on the bill. If the committee does not recommend it, the bill dies, or goes no further.

Every committee has both Democratic and Republican members, but the majority of the members come from the majority party. The chairperson of every committee belongs to the majority party. These leaders have great power over bills because they decide which bills their committees will study. They also decide when and if the committees will meet and whether or not hearings will be held.

Select committees. Sometimes the House or Senate will form a select committee to deal with a problem not covered by any standing committee. Select committees often conduct investigations. For example, in 1972 the Senate formed the Select Committee on Presidential Campaign Activities to look into whether or not President Richard Nixon and his staff had broken the law during the presidential campaign of 1972. The findings of this committee led the House Judiciary Committee to vote to impeach President Nixon in 1974.

Joint committees. A joint committee is made up of members of both the House and the Senate. Joint committees are usually select committees, formed to conduct investigations. Congress also has created a few standing joint committees, such as the Joint Committee on Atomic Energy.

Conference committees. Before a bill can go to the President to be signed, it must be passed

Standing committees have been called "the eye, the ear, the hand, and very often the brain of Congress." President Woodrow Wilson called them "little legislatures" because the fate of most bills is decided in committee rather than on the floor of the House or the Senate.

How a Bill Becomes a Law

Except for money bills, a bill may be started in either house. It will then pass through each house before going to the President. The diagram shows the process for a bill started in the House (red arrow) and a bill started in the Senate (blue arrow). In practice, a bill is often started in both houses at the same time.

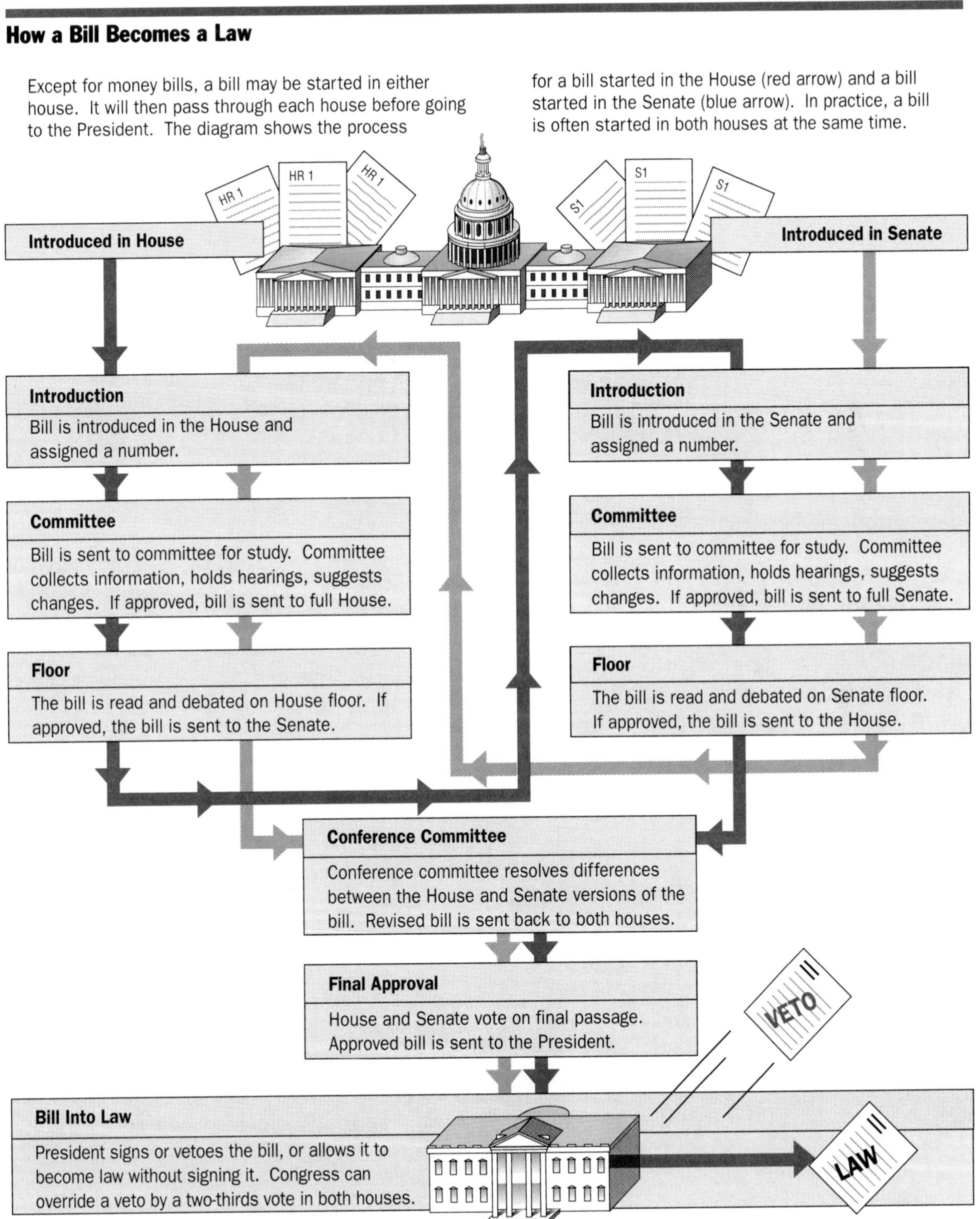

HR 1
HR 1
HR 1
S1
S1
S1
Introduced in House
Introduced in Senate
Introduction
Bill is introduced in the House and assigned a number.
Committee
Bill is sent to committee for study. Committee collects information, holds hearings, suggests changes. If approved, bill is sent to full House.
Floor
The bill is read and debated on House floor. If approved, the bill is sent to the Senate.
Introduction
Bill is introduced in the Senate and assigned a number.
Committee
Bill is sent to committee for study. Committee collects information, holds hearings, suggests changes. If approved, bill is sent to full Senate.
Floor
The bill is read and debated on Senate floor. If approved, the bill is sent to the House.
Conference Committee
Conference committee resolves differences between the House and Senate versions of the bill. Revised bill is sent back to both houses.
Final Approval
House and Senate vote on final passage. Approved bill is sent to the President.
VETO
Bill Into Law
President signs or vetoes the bill, or allows it to become law without signing it. Congress can override a veto by a two-thirds vote in both houses.
LAW

Teaching Note: Use the Reinforcement Activity, page T 77, and accompanying worksheet in the Activity Book after students have read the material in Section 8-3.

by both houses. Sometimes a bill passes one house but is changed in the other. If the two houses cannot agree, a temporary joint committee—called a conference committee—is formed. This committee, made up of an equal number of senators and representatives, tries to settle the differences. The conference committee's version of the bill must then be passed by both houses.

The President's Role

After the same bill has been passed by majority vote in both houses of Congress, it is sent to the President. The President can sign the bill, making it "the law of the land." The bill will also become law if, while Congress is in session, the President holds the bill for ten days without either signing or vetoing it.

A President may veto, or reject, a bill in one of two ways. The first way is to send the bill back to Congress unsigned. Congress can override the veto by passing the bill again by a two-thirds vote of both houses. The second way a President can veto a bill is called a ***pocket veto***. If the President pockets, or keeps, the bill for ten days, during which Congress ends its session, the bill will not become law.

Answers will be found on page T 77.

Section Review

1. Define the terms *Speaker of the House, president pro tempore, majority party, minority party, floor leaders, whips,* and *pocket veto.*
2. What powers and responsibilities does the Speaker of the House have?
3. What is the difference between standing committees and conference committees?

Analysis. How have political parties influenced the organization of Congress?

8-4 FOLLOWING A BILL IN CONGRESS

Read to Find Out

- what the terms *filibuster* and *cloture* mean.
- how a committee conducts hearings on a bill.
- when and how bills are debated.

Imagine that you are a newly elected senator watching a bill move through the Senate. This bill is S.837, the Minimum Wage Restoration Act, which was introduced in 1987 during the 100th Congress.

Introducing the Bill

On March 25, Senator Edward Kennedy of Massachusetts, a Democrat, is going to introduce an important bill. You make a point of being present in the Senate chamber when he speaks. The chamber is unusually quiet. Senator Kennedy rises to speak:

> Today I am introducing legislation to make the minimum wage a living wage. Our bill will increase the minimum wage from its present level of $3.35 an hour to $3.85 in 1988, $4.25 in 1989, and $4.65 in 1990.

The senator says that the minimum wage has not been increased for six years. With rising prices, the minimum wage now buys 27 percent less than it did in 1981. A person who works full time earning the minimum wage will make only $7,000 a year. According to government figures, this is not enough money to buy the goods and services a family of four needs.

Curious to learn more about the minimum wage, you ask a member of your staff to prepare a report on Kennedy's bill. You read:

Teaching Note: Use the Enrichment Activity, page T 77, and accompanying worksheet in the Activity Book to extend the information in Section 8-3.

Decision Making: Have students describe what steps they would go through in deciding how to vote on a bill if they were members of Congress.

The first minimum wage bill was passed in 1938. It was part of the Fair Labor Standards Act, which also made rules about child labor and the length of the work week.

Workers who earn the minimum wage today work mostly in restaurants, motels, and food processing plants. The minimum wage was increased in 1981 to $3.35 an hour. Between 1983 and 1986, bills were introduced in the House and the Senate to raise the minimum wage. None became law.

Skipping ahead to find out why people are opposed to the bill, you read:

> Those opposed to raising the minimum wage say that it would have two bad effects on the economy. First, there would be fewer jobs because employers would not be able to afford to hire as many workers. Second, it would force employers to raise the prices of their products, thus hurting consumers.
>
> Opponents of raising the minimum wage point to figures that show that few people who earn the minimum wage work full time and support a family. They claim that the typical minimum wage worker is a teenager from a family that is not poor. Most people earning the minimum wage are on their first job and will go on to earn higher wages later. Therefore, it is not true that minimum wage workers are poor and that today's minimum wage keeps them poor.

The Bill in Committee

The minimum wage bill goes to the Labor and Human Resources Committee headed by Senator Kennedy. On July 23, you attend the committee's public hearings on S.837. You listen to Walter Ellis, president of the American Farm Bureau, speak out against the bill. He says that a higher minimum wage would increase costs for the 750,000 ranchers and farmers who hire minimum wage workers.

A lobbyist from the American Hotel and Motel Association also argues against the bill. He says the jobs in the hotel industry that pay the minimum wage are "entry level" jobs which give people a start in the business world. If the minimum wage is raised, he claims, hotel costs would increase. To keep costs down, hotel owners would have to cut the number of people they hire.

You also hear testimony from supporters of the bill, such as Lane Kirkland, president of the American Federation of Labor and the Congress of Industrial Organizations (AFL-CIO). He speaks for many workers:

> These workers who have so little and already have difficulty making ends meet were particularly hurt by the rising prices of the past decade. I believe that most low-wage employers would pay a living wage if they were confident that their competition would do the same.

Reporting the Bill

The Labor and Human Resources Committee continues to study S.837. Finally, in July 1988, the committee sends S.837 to the full

Senator Edward Kennedy's 1987 bill to raise the minimum wage had strong support as well as strong opposition in Congress and the nation.

The Fair Labor Standards Act of 1938 set a minimum wage of twenty-five cents an hour and provided that the wage be raised to forty cents by 1945. The minimum wage has since been increased in 1949, 1955, 1961, 1966, 1974, 1977, 1981, 1990, and 1991.

Hispanics may be of any race and therefore are not listed as a single racial group in the government statistics on minimum wage earners.

Profile of Minimum Wage Earners

About 3.2 million people worked for the minimum wage of $3.80 an hour in January 1991.

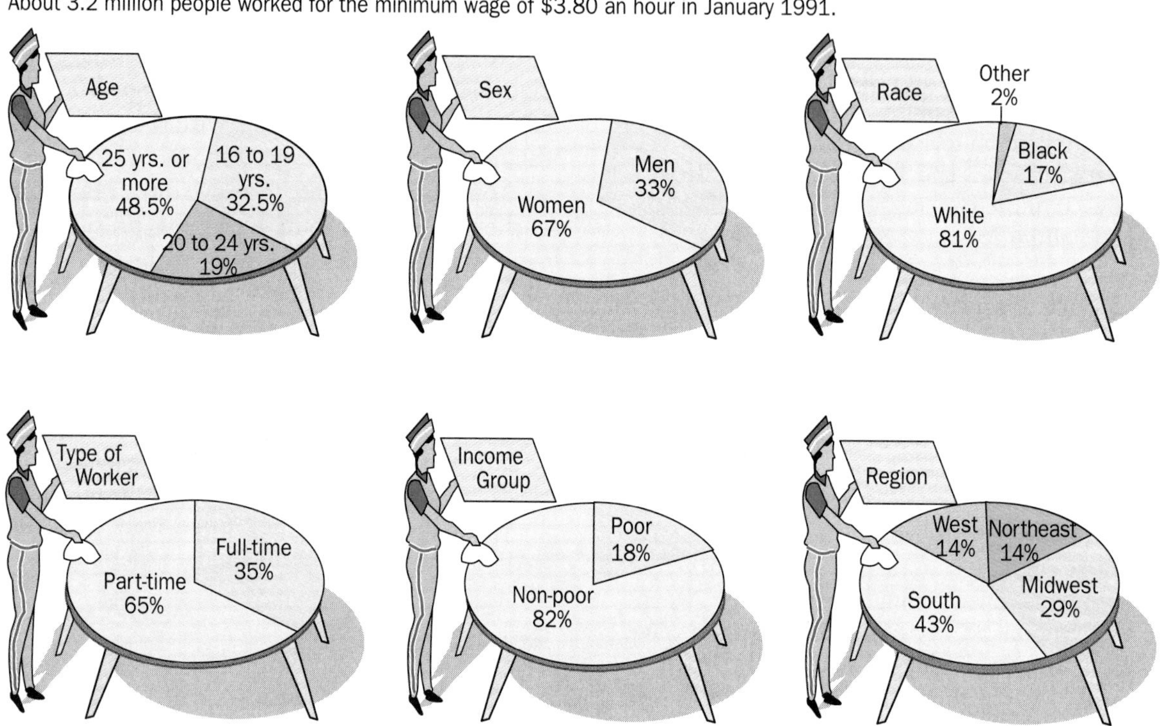

Source: Bureau of Labor Statistics, Congressional Budget Office

Senate. It recommends that the bill be approved. This is called reporting the bill.

In the House, the Rules Committee decides when and for how long a bill will be debated. In the Senate, however, there is no Rules Committee. The senators must agree on the starting time of debate. In addition, the Senate has fewer limits on the length of debate.

In the case of S.837, debate of the bill is delayed. Finally, in September, the Senate majority leader gets approval from the Republican senators who had opposed it, and he calls up the bill for debate.

When debate begins, Senator Orrin Hatch of Utah is the bill's main opponent. Fearing that the bill will be passed, Senator Hatch and some fellow Republicans start a ***filibuster***, which is the use of long speeches to prevent a vote on a bill. Filibusters cannot happen in the House, where time limits are set for debates.

On September 22, the Democrats try to stop the filibuster by calling for ***cloture*** (KLŌ-chur), or agreement to end the debate on a bill. Cloture requires a three-fifths vote. As voting begins, you wonder if they can gather the 60 votes needed. At the final count only 53 senators vote in favor of cloture. The next day, the Democrats try again but fail. The Republicans have killed the bill. It will not be acted upon during this term of Congress.

S.837 failed to become a law, but the idea of raising the minimum wage does not die. In January 1989, you hear Senator Kennedy introduce a minimum wage bill again. This

Over the years, the filibuster or the threat of it has caused the death of many important bills. Senator Strom Thurmond of South Carolina holds the record for the longest individual filibuster, speaking for more than twenty-four hours against enactment of civil rights legislation in 1957.

Teaching Note: Use Teaching Activity 2, page T 76, to apply information from Sections 8-3 and 8-4.

time, some changes are made in the bill. The Republicans like it better, and in April the Senate passes it.

Meanwhile, the House has also passed a minimum wage bill. Because the two bills are not exactly alike, a conference committee is formed to write a compromise bill. This bill is passed by both houses and sent to the President. President George Bush thinks a minimum wage of more than $4.25 an hour will hurt the economy. He vetoes the bill.

After failing to override the veto, Congress works out a compromise bill that satisfies the President, who signs it in November. The new law boosts the wage to $3.80 in April 1990 and $4.25 in April 1991.

Advantages of the Lawmaking Process

In your first two years as a senator you have learned a great deal about lawmaking. It seems to you that a bill must overcome many hurdles before becoming a law. You realize, however, that the framers wanted Congress to take its time. They wanted every bill to be studied and debated carefully. Any bill that makes it through this process has an excellent chance of being a good law.

Answers will be found on page T 78.

Section Review

1. Define the terms *filibuster* and *cloture*.
2. What is the purpose of holding public hearings for a proposed law?
3. How do the House and the Senate differ in their methods for scheduling and limiting debate?

Evaluation. Do you think senators should be allowed to hold filibusters to prevent bills from coming to a vote? Explain.

A BROADER VIEW

The United States Congress is not the only body of its kind in the world today. There are many other democratic nations with legislatures that represent citizens in government. In many of these nations the legislature is called a parliament. Like Congress, a parliament has two houses.

In some parliaments, such as the Spanish Cortes and the Japanese Diet, all the representatives are elected. In others, such as the British Parliament and the Canadian Parliament, some members are appointed or inherit their seats.

In the British Parliament, for example, one house—the House of Lords—is made up mainly of members with inherited titles of nobility. The other house of Parliament, which is called the House of Commons, is made up of representatives elected by the citizens. This house, which is subject to control by the voters, has the greater power.

Unlike the American system of government, a parliamentary system has no clear separation between the legislative and executive branches. The executive leaders, including the prime minister, are members of Parliament. They have a great deal of power because they both propose the laws and carry them out. The members of Parliament, however, must approve the laws. The Parliament also can force these leaders to resign by defeating their programs.

Challenge (Evaluation): Have students explain their opinions on increasing the minimum wage, using arguments cited in the text and other arguments they develop. (For a discussion/activity on this issue, see "Taking a Stand" on page 237.)

Critical Thinking

Teaching Note: For reinforcement of decision-making skills, use Decison-Making Worksheet Chapter 8.

What Relates to Your Subject?

Suppose you wanted to buy a cassette for a friend, a cassette that he or she would be likely to keep. To make a good decision, what would you need to know? You might think about your friend's favorite group or type of music, as well as which cassettes he or she already has. This information relates to your decision. However, you would not need to know which brand of cassette player your friend has or which cassettes are least expensive. These last two pieces of information would not help you choose the right cassette.

Whenever you need to make a decision, some types of information are *relevant*, or related, to your subject. Others are not. To make a good decision, you need to determine which information is clearly connected to your subject. Stick to the subject. Do not get sidetracked by information that is *irrelevant*, or not clearly linked to your subject. If you start relying on irrelevant information, you will probably make a poor decision. In short, always ask yourself, "Does this information relate directly to my subject?"

Imagine that you are eighteen years old and have just taken a part-time job. You think your hourly pay is too low and want a new law to be passed that will raise the minimum wage. As you prepare to vote in your first national election, you look over the information on the candidates who want to represent your state in the Senate. Below is some information available to you:

> Democratic candidate Bill Smith is a former governor who is popular with voters, partly because of his good sense of humor.
>
> Republican candidate Jane Thickett has a nineteen-year-old daughter who supports raising farm workers' wages.
>
> Mr. Smith actively campaigned for the Democratic presidential candidate, who supported an increase in the minimum wage.

You want to know which candidate is more likely to support an increase in the minimum wage. How might you determine whether each statement is relevant to the decision you must make?

EXPLAINING THE SKILL

One way to distinguish relevant information from irrelevant information is to follow these steps. As you examine the steps, notice how they might be applied to the three pieces of information you just read.

1. Identify clearly the problem or issue you are examining. Ask yourself, "What do I want to know or do?" [You want to know which candidate is more likely to support an increase in the minimum wage.]

2. Identify the kinds of information that might relate to your chosen subject. Such information might consist of details, examples, explanations, evidence, or definitions. [Examples of a candidate's position on the minimum wage and explanations of why a candidate either supports or opposes increasing the minimum wage would be relevant to the subject.]

3. Examine each piece of information to determine whether it is relevant. Judge whether each piece relates, or connects directly, to the subject. [The first two statements are not relevant. Neither the fact that Mr. Smith was a popular governor nor that Ms. Thickett's daughter supports higher farm worker wages is connected with the candidates' views. However, Mr. Smith's support of the Democratic candi-

Have students give their own examples of types of information that would be relevant and irrelevant to particular decisions.

Answers will be found on page T 78.

date *is* relevant. It shows that he probably agrees with that candidate's view on the minimum wage.]

APPLYING THE SKILL

Below are more pieces of information. Examine each one to determine whether it is relevant to the subject of the candidates' views on the minimum wage.

A. Ms. Thickett has never been elected to any public office.

B. One of the current senators from your state, who is going to retire, consistently voted against increases in the minimum wage.

C. During an unsuccessful campaign for a seat in the House, Ms. Thickett declared that she would support an increase in the minimum wage only if it reduced the number of people on welfare.

D. As governor, Mr. Smith introduced a bill to raise the wages of workers in the state highway department.

E. Governor Smith's bill to increase highway workers' wages was rejected by the state legislature.

F. Most business leaders argue that a wage increase would force many stores out of business.

G. In a speech, Ms. Thickett pointed out that the minimum wage for American workers is much higher than wages in many other countries.

H. As governor, Mr. Smith wrote an article calling for greater efforts to reduce poverty in the state.

I. Both Ms. Thickett and Mr. Smith went to well-known law schools and later worked as lawyers.

CHECKING YOUR UNDERSTANDING

When you have determined whether each piece of information is relevant to the candidates' views on the minimum wage, answer the following questions.

1. Given your concern, which candidate would you vote for? Explain why.

2. Identify a piece of information that is an *example* of a candidate's position on the minimum wage. Identify a piece of information that is an *explanation* of a candidate's position on the minimum wage.

3. Which statements are most relevant to helping you decide which candidate is more likely to support a minimum wage increase? **(a)** A, F, E; **(b)** C, G, H; **(c)** B, H, A. Explain your answer.

4. Which statements were irrelevant to your decision? Explain your answer.

REVIEWING THE SKILL

5. What does the term *relevant* mean?

6. What are some general kinds of information that might be relevant to any subject?

7. How do you think recognizing relevant information helps you to make good decisions?

Have students explain how the skill of identifying relevant information would help them in both the choosing and the acting phases of decison making.

CHAPTER SURVEY

Answers to Survey and Workshop will be found on page T 78.

UNDERSTANDING NEW VOCABULARY

Seeing Relationships

The vocabulary terms in each pair listed below are related to each other. For each pair, explain how the two terms are related.

Example: *Impeach* is related to *delegated powers* because impeachment is one of the delegated powers of Congress.

1. *constituents* and *congressional district*

2. *interest groups* and *lobbyists*

3. *Speaker of the House* and *majority party*

4. *floor leaders* and *whips*

5. *filibuster* and *cloture*

Putting It in Writing

Write a paragraph briefly explaining how political parties affect congressional leadership. In your explanation, use each of the following vocabulary terms: *Speaker of the House*, *president pro tempore*, *majority party*, *minority party*, *floor leaders*, and *whips*.

LOOKING BACK AT THE CHAPTER

1. Why must a member of Congress balance the needs of the nation as a whole with those of his or her constituents?

2. Why do senators and representatives pay attention to the opinions of members of interest groups?

3. How are the 435 seats in the House of Representatives divided among the states?

4. Describe two ways in which personal staff help a member of Congress do his or her job.

5. Explain why Congress is said to have the "power of the purse."

6. Describe two ways in which the Constitution specifically limits the powers of Congress.

7. Why is the Speaker the most powerful member of the House of Representatives?

8. Explain how each of the following committees helps Congress make laws: **(a)** standing committees, **(b)** conference committees, **(c)** select committees.

9. How can Congress pass a law despite the President's veto?

10. Describe two ways in which the minority party can prevent a vote on a bill in the Senate.

11. *Synthesis.* The Constitution does not give Congress the power to establish an air force. How, then, was Congress able to do this?

12. *Analysis.* If the House of Representatives were abolished and the Senate was left as our only lawmaking body, would our government be less democratic? Why or why not?

13. *Application.* If you wrote a letter to your representative or to one of your senators, do you think it could influence his or her position on a bill? What factors might work in your favor? What factors might work against you?

WORKING TOGETHER

1. With a group, make a scrapbook of articles from newspapers and news magazines that describe actions of Congress. Write a short paragraph for each article explaining which powers of Congress are being used.

2. Work together to stage a debate between senators and representatives on the issue of the fairness of the filibuster.

3. With members of a group, collect political cartoons about Congress or lawmaking from magazines and newspapers, or draw your own cartoons. Then meet to choose several of these cartoons to act out in front of the class. Make sure the cartoons you choose need only props you can make yourselves, such as signs or hats. After you act out one of these "cartoons," ask other class members to explain its message.

SKILLS WORKSHOP

SOCIAL STUDIES SKILLS

Analyzing Circle Graphs

Circle graphs are used to show statistical information as parts or percentages of a whole. These parts should always add up to 100 percent. The circle graphs below are one way of showing statistics about the 102nd Congress, which took office in January 1991.

The following questions will help you analyze the graphs.

1. What statistics do these graphs show?

2. Which party had a majority in the 102nd Congress?

3. How would you describe the typical member of the 102nd Congress?

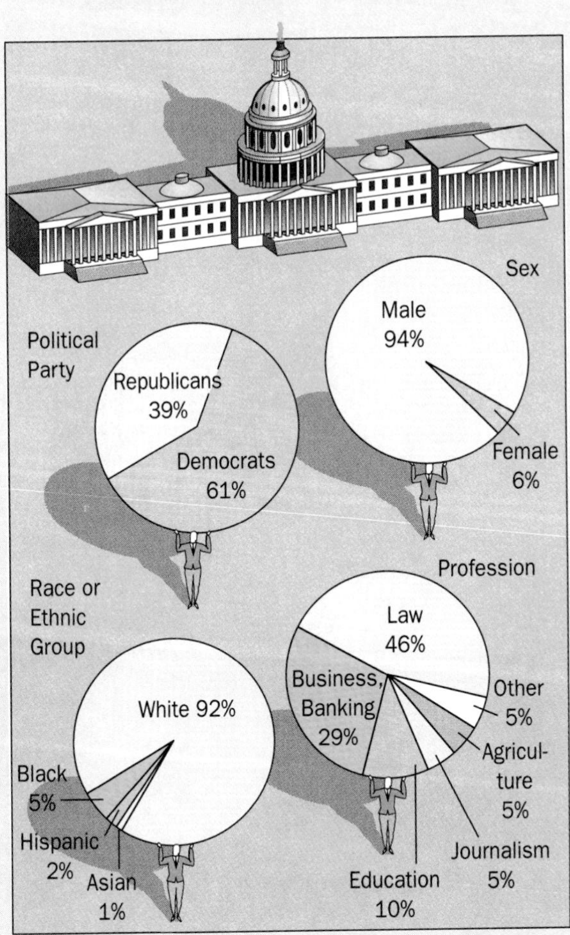

DECISION-MAKING SKILLS

What Relates to Your Subject?

Suppose you are looking for information about the subject of how a bill becomes a law. Read the following description and determine which information is relevant to the subject. Also, be prepared to explain why some of the information is irrelevant to the subject.

> The Senate Committee on Agriculture and Forestry sent a farm bill to the full Senate. Before voting, the senators made changes in it. The bill had required the federal government to help keep the prices of *all* farm products high. The Senate changed the bill to list fewer products.
>
> The bill also included a soil bank plan, under which farmers are paid for not growing crops on some of their land. This plan helps keep prices of crops from falling too low. The Senate added an amendment to the bill requiring all farmers to take part in the plan. Some senators did not like this amendment. Since the plan is an experiment, they thought that farmers should not be required to participate. Even so, the Senate approved the bill by a vote of 93–2.
>
> No senator was pleased with the entire bill, but everyone hoped for a miracle in the conference committee. In that committee, members of the House and Senate would iron out differences between the Senate bill and a similar House bill.

1. Identify three pieces of information that are relevant to the subject of how a bill becomes a law. Explain why each one is relevant.

2. Identify two pieces of information that are *not* relevant to the subject of how a bill becomes a law. Explain why each one is irrelevant.

3. Think of a decision that you will have to make soon. What kinds of information would be relevant to that decision? Explain your answer.

Chapter Themes: Presidential roles have changed and expanded over the years. The executive branch is a huge bureaucracy that helps the President enforce the law and provide national leadership. Presidential power is limited by separation of powers and checks and balances.

CHAPTER 9

The Executive Branch

The President of the United States holds a position of great responsibility. How is that responsibility reflected in the President's everyday life? Here is a look at a day in the life of Lyndon B. Johnson, who was President from 1963 to 1969.

President Johnson's day begins at 7:00 A.M. He reads the stack of newspapers next to his bed. At the same time, he has three television sets turned on so that he can keep track of the news reports on NBC, CBS, and ABC. In response to a news item, he grabs the phone to talk with a leader in Congress about a key bill.

After breakfast, the President walks down the hall to the Oval Office. He sifts quickly through his mail before leaving for a meeting in a nearby room. Twenty advisors seated around the table rise as he enters the room. He spends an hour with them, discussing a variety of concerns about the armed forces.

At 11:00 the President meets with the leaders of the major government departments, who report to him on their activities. Following the two-hour meeting, he looks over a speech he will give to a group of state governors. After meeting with the governors, the President calls together his top advisors to discuss the upcoming election.

By 3:00 the President has been working for eight hours without a break. He joins Mrs. Johnson for a late lunch before returning to his office to meet with advisors, make phone calls, and read reports. At 7:00 he dresses for a dinner and dance in the White House ballroom, held in honor of the visiting president of the Philippines.

Late in the evening the President returns to his bedroom. Casting a weary glance at a stack of reports, he decides to read them in the morning. As he starts to climb into bed, the phone rings. Fortunately, the conversation is brief. Shortly after midnight the President finally falls asleep.

In this chapter you will read about the duties of the President. You will also see how the executive branch is organized to help the President fulfill those duties. Finally, you will explore some of the ways in which Presidents have used their power.

Teaching Note: Use the Introducing the Chapter activity, page T 81.

9-1

THE ROLES OF THE PRESIDENT

Read to Find Out

- what the terms *executive branch, executive orders, foreign policy, treaties, ambassadors, executive agreements,* and *domestic policy* mean.
- how the framers of the Constitution limited the power of the President.
- what duties and powers the President has.

Who is the leader of the United States? To most of us the answer seems clear: the President. As our highest elected official, the President represents all Americans, not just citizens of one state or congressional district. It is the President who usually meets with leaders of other nations and whose daily activities are closely followed by the television networks, newspapers, and news magazines. Just about everyone knows who the President of the United States is.

How many Americans, though, have a clear picture of what the President does? The President is the head of the ***executive branch***, the branch of government responsible for executing, or carrying out, the laws. However, carrying out laws passed by Congress is only part of the President's job. The most important duty is to set goals for the nation and to develop policies, which are methods for reaching those goals. In spite of having many advisors, the President alone is responsible for making the final decisions about many important issues facing the nation.

Presidents have often tried to describe the burden of this responsibility. William Howard Taft, President from 1909 to 1913, called the presidency the "loneliest place in the world." Lyndon Johnson noted:

> The real horror was to be sleeping soundly about three-thirty or four o' clock in the morning and have the telephone ring and the operator say, "Sorry to wake you, Mr. President."

This heavy responsibility goes with an office that many think is the most powerful in the world. The office of President also has limits, though, which are set by the Constitution. To understand the powers and responsibilities of the presidency, as well as its limits, you need to look first at how the office was created.

AMERICAN NOTEBOOK

Of the 41 Presidents in the history of our nation:

- 40 were Protestant
- 34 were at least 50 years old when they took office
- 30 were college-educated
- 25 were lawyers
- 14 had previously served as Vice-President
- 17 were Republicans
- 13 were Democrats

Creating the Office of President

In creating the presidency, the last thing the framers wanted was a leader with unlimited powers. The memory of the tyranny of the English king was fresh in the minds of many Americans. During the Constitutional Convention the framers announced to the public: "Tho' we cannot tell you what we are doing, we can tell you what we are not doing—we never once thought of a king." To calm the people's fears, the framers gave very few specific powers to the President. They also included ways to prevent abuse of power.

Teaching Note: For information on our Presidents and Vice-Presidents, see page 596.

Term of office. One limit on the President's power is the term of office. The President is elected for a term of four years and must run for re-election in order to serve a second term. The Twenty-second Amendment says that no President may hold office for more than two terms.

Limited power. Another protection is the separation of powers among the three branches of government. The President may only carry out the laws. It is Congress that makes the laws. The Supreme Court has the power to decide if a law is constitutional.

The system of checks and balances also limits the President's power. Many presidential decisions must be approved by Congress. In cases of serious wrongdoing, Congress may remove the President from office. Furthermore, the Supreme Court can decide whether actions taken by the President are allowed by the Constitution.

Qualifications and salary. To be President, a person must be at least 35 years old and a natural-born citizen of the United States. He or she must have lived in the United States for at least 14 years. The President's yearly salary is set by Congress, rather than by the Constitution. That salary is $200,000.

A leader with many roles. The framers knew that the nation needed a leader who could both carry out laws and represent the nation in meetings with leaders of other countries. However, the office of President was new in a world of nations led by monarchs.

Therefore, the framers did not describe exactly how the President should fulfill the duties of this new office. Expecting that George Washington would be elected as the nation's first leader, they trusted that he would become a model of what a President should be. As Washington himself noted:

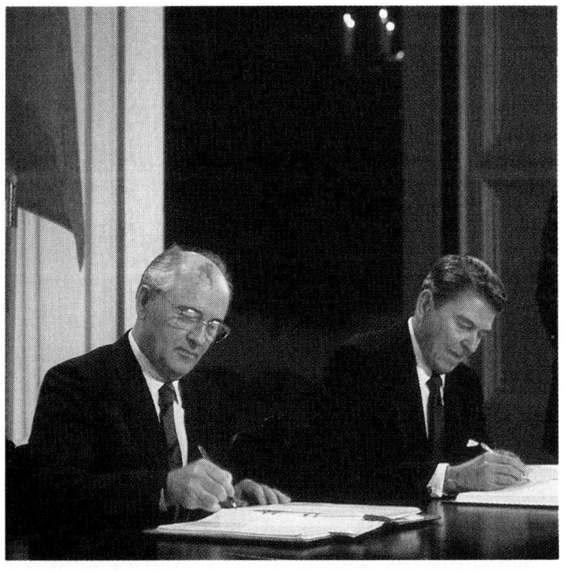

Acting as the nation's chief diplomat, President Reagan signed a weapons reduction treaty with Soviet leader Mikhail Gorbachev in 1987.

> My station is new; . . . I walk on untrodden ground. There is scarcely any part of my conduct which may not hereafter be drawn into precedent [made an example of].

Through the examples of Washington and the Presidents who followed him, the roles of the President have become more clearly defined over the years. As you read about these roles, you will see how the President alone may make decisions in some areas, but must work closely with Congress in other areas.

The President as Chief Executive

The President serves as chief executive, or head of the executive branch. The Constitution states that the President must "take care that the laws be faithfully executed." To execute laws means to make sure that they are carried out. Although Congress makes the laws, it is up to executive branch officials to decide just how to carry out laws and other policies.

Challenge (Evaluation): Some people have proposed that the President serve one seven-year term instead of serving, at most, two four-year terms. Have students discuss advantages and disadvantages of this proposal. Students should provide reasons for their opinions.

As leader of the executive branch, the President usually makes only the broadest decisions, leaving the details to other officials. One way in which the President gives direction is through ***executive orders***, which are rules or regulations that executive branch employees must follow. For example, President Harry Truman (1945–1953) gave an executive order to end segregation in the armed forces. After that, people of all races served together instead of in separate units.

The power to make executive orders, however, is limited. The President's orders may not violate the Constitution or laws passed by Congress.

As chief executive, the President also has the power to appoint about 2,000 executive branch officials. As a check on that power, Congress must confirm, or approve, many top appointments.

The President as Commander in Chief

The Constitution says that "the President shall be commander in chief of the army and navy of the United States." This statement points to the President's important role as leader of the armed forces. When the nation is at war, the President makes the most important decisions.

To protect American interests, the President may send troops to a foreign country even if Congress has not declared war. However, the War Powers Act, passed after the Vietnam War, says that such troops may not remain for more than 60 days without the approval of Congress.

The President as Chief Diplomat

The President is also our chief diplomat, the most important representative of the United States in relations with other nations. The President leads in making ***foreign policy***, plans for guiding our nation's relationships with other countries. In general, foreign policy involves deciding how to support or oppose actions of other nations. Although they usually seek advice on foreign policy, Presidents must make the final decisions. President Truman made that point when he said, "*I* make foreign policy."

Foreign policy is clearly the President's "territory," but Congress may set limits. For instance, the President may make ***treaties***, or formal agreements with other countries, but the Senate may reject any treaty. The President's appointments of ***ambassadors***, the official representatives to foreign governments, must also be approved by the Senate.

The President does have freedom, though, to make ***executive agreements***, agreements with other countries, which do not need Senate approval. Executive agreements may have a wide range of purposes. They may set goals for trade or make promises to give aid to other countries. To prevent abuse of this power, a law was passed in 1972 requiring the President to tell Congress within 60 days of making an executive agreement.

The President as Legislative Leader

You have read many times that Congress makes our nation's laws. The President, however, has a good deal of power to influence what those laws will be. The Constitution states that the President may recommend to Congress "such measures as he shall judge necessary and expedient." This means that Congress is expected to consider the President's ideas rather than act alone in making laws.

Every year in early February, the President gives a speech to both houses of Congress. In this State of the Union message, the President sets forth ideas about what America's foreign policy should be. The President also talks about problems here at home, such as taxes,

The President also has the power to use the armed forces to end domestic riots, provide help during natural disasters, and enforce federal laws and court orders. In 1957, President Dwight D. Eisenhower used this power to enforce court-ordered school integration in Little Rock, Arkansas.

Officials of all three branches of government gather to hear the President set forth his policies in his yearly State of the Union address to Congress.

day care, and pollution. By describing these problems and giving ideas for solving them, the President helps to set ***domestic policy***, plans for dealing with national problems.

How does a President get Congress to turn foreign and domestic policy into laws? One way is by getting individual members of Congress to write bills. Another is by calling and meeting with members of Congress, urging them to support the President's program. Speeches to interest groups and to the public also help gain support for bills the President wants passed.

A powerful tool for influencing Congress is the veto. Often just the threat of a veto is enough to get Congress to change a bill to make it more to the President's liking. Congress has overridden fewer than 4 percent of the more than 2,400 vetoes in our nation's history.

Another way in which the President acts as legislative leader is in making the budget. To put policy ideas into action costs money. Every year the President prepares a budget, a plan for how to raise and spend money to carry out the President's programs.

Of course, Congress does not pass all the laws the President asks for, and it almost always makes changes in the President's budget. However, Congress cannot ignore the President's power as legislative leader.

Finally, the President has the power to call special sessions of Congress if problems arise when Congress is not meeting. Today, however, Congress meets for almost the whole year, and the power is not much used.

The President's Judicial Powers

As part of the system of checks and balances, the President has several powers that affect the judicial branch. Most importantly, the President chooses Supreme Court justices and other federal judges. Of course, the President's power is balanced by the Senate which must confirm all appointments.

The President may limit the power of the judicial branch by putting off or reducing the punishment of someone convicted of a crime in federal courts. The President may even do away with the punishment by granting a pardon.

Teaching Note: Use Teaching Activity 1, page T 82, after students have read the material in Section 9-1.

As chief of state, President George Bush, with Mrs. Bush, entertains visiting foreign leaders, such as Jordan's King Hussein and Queen Noor.

Roles Created by Tradition

Over the years, the President has taken on two other roles: party leader and chief of state. Neither role is mentioned in the Constitution, yet both are natural results of the President's position and power.

The President is a member of a political party, typically either the Democratic party or the Republican party. As our highest elected official, the President is seen as the leader of that party. The President's power and prestige can be used to support party goals or candidates.

As chief of state, though, the President speaks for the whole nation, expressing the values and goals of the American people. In this role, the President carries out many ceremonial duties, such as greeting visiting leaders, giving medals to citizens, and tossing out the first baseball of the season. As chief of state, the President stands for a national unity that overshadows differences between the political parties.

Answers will be found on page T 84.

Section Review

1. Define *executive branch, executive orders, foreign policy, treaties, ambassadors, executive agreements,* and *domestic policy.*
2. In creating the office of President, how did the framers guard against abuse of power?
3. Briefly describe four of the President's roles.

Evaluation. Do you think the President's roles overlap, or are they separate from each other? Explain your answer, giving examples.

Teaching Note: Use the Reinforcement Activity, page T 83, and accompanying worksheet in the Activity Book.

Challenge (Evaluation): Many political analysts worry that key members of the White House staff may be too powerful. Have students discuss whether these advisors should be subject to Senate approval as a check on their power. Students should provide reasons for their opinions.

9-2

THE ORGANIZATION OF THE EXECUTIVE BRANCH

Read to Find Out

- what the terms *bureaucracy, administration,* and *Cabinet* mean.
- how the three parts of the executive branch are organized and what they do.
- why enforcing the laws can be difficult.

As our nation has grown, the President's duties have grown, too. Each year hundreds of laws must be carried out. Decisions must be made on a wide range of foreign and domestic policy issues. To fulfill their many duties, Presidents have needed more and more help. The executive branch has grown from a handful of officials in George Washington's time to over 3 million employees today. It is now the largest branch of government.

As it has grown, the executive branch has become a huge bureaucracy. A ***bureaucracy*** (byoo-RAH-kru-see) is an organization of government departments, agencies, and offices. Most people who work in the bureaucracy are not chosen to work just for one President. They are hired as permanent employees.

To help direct the bureaucracy, the President appoints an ***administration***, a team of executive branch officials. The nearly 2,000 members of the administration lead the three main parts of the executive branch: (1) the Executive Office of the President, (2) the executive departments, and (3) the independent agencies.

The Executive Office of the President

The Executive Office of the President is largely made up of people the President chooses to help make foreign and domestic policy. Unlike the other parts of the executive branch, the main job of the Executive Office is not to carry out laws directly, but to advise the President on important matters relating to the many presidential roles.

The White House staff. At the center of an administration is the White House staff. It includes the President's inner circle of trusted advisors and assistants. Some of these people see the President every day. They give advice and information about national security, the economy, and other subjects.

The staff includes a chief of staff and other key advisors, press secretaries, legal experts, speechwriters, office workers, and researchers. The White House staff may truly be called "the President's people" because all of its members are appointed or hired by the President and do not need Senate approval.

The White House staff helps guide the bureaucracy toward meeting the President's goals. Some Presidents like having several staff people report directly to them on issues relating to the executive departments and independent agencies. In this way the President may become closely involved in a broad range of issues.

Other Presidents have depended on one powerful chief of staff to whom other staff members report. This approach allows the President to be involved only in major issues, leaving the details to assistants.

The Vice-President. The Constitution gives the Vice-President no clear duties aside from presiding over the Senate. It is the President who decides what the Vice-President will do. Some Presidents ask the Vice-President to play an active role, heading special commissions, making trips to other countries, and working closely with Congress. More often, however, the Vice-President has been almost

The Executive Office of the President was first created in 1939 in response to the growing role of the federal government during the Great Depression. (See Chapter 16.)

VIEWS OF NOTED AMERICANS

Pierre Salinger

On October 22, 1962, Pierre Salinger watched from behind the television cameras as President John F. Kennedy told the nation that the Soviet Union was delivering missiles to the island nation of Cuba, just 90 miles off the coast of Florida. The United States would block any Soviet ships sailing to Cuba, Kennedy said. If the Soviets did not remove the missiles, a nuclear war could result. It was the worst crisis the nation had faced since World War II.

As President Kennedy's press secretary, Salinger had a difficult part to play during the next five days. He had to give the press all the information necessary to tell the public what was happening. Yet he also needed to protect national security by not telling information that might help the Soviet Union.

Salinger wrote that "no two institutions in the country have a more important relationship than the government of the United States and the press." During the Cuban missile crisis, the press, using information that Salinger gave out, played an important role in speeding up communication between President Kennedy and Soviet Chairman Nikita Khrushchev. On October 28, Khrushchev agreed to remove all missiles from Cuba. The crisis was over.

Salinger was born June 14, 1925, in San Francisco, California. As a student, he worked part-time for the *San Francisco Chronicle* and became a full-time reporter for the paper in 1946. Before becoming President Kennedy's press secretary in 1961, Salinger had also worked as a political speechwriter and as an investigator for a Senate committee.

As press secretary, Salinger created a more open relationship between the President and the press. News conferences were held often and were carried on television for the first time.

Since 1968 Salinger has lived mostly in Europe. He is well known for explaining American life and government to European audiences. Throughout his life, Pierre Salinger has been able to combine his love of journalism and of politics into a successful career.

invisible. Fearing this fate, some leaders have refused to run for Vice-President. In 1848, Daniel Webster declared, "I do not choose to be buried until I am really dead."

If the President dies, though, the Vice-President may become President. Our nation's first Vice-President, John Adams, said, "In this I am nothing, but I may be everything." Eight times in our nation's history the Vice-President has risen to the highest office in the land because of the death of the President. The Vice-President may also be asked to serve as "acting President" if the President falls seriously ill.

Since the Vice-President may become President, the qualifications for the two offices are the same. Currently the Vice-President's salary is $115,000.

Discussion: Pierre Salinger pioneered the use of presidential news conferences on television to create a more open relationship between the President and the press. Have students compare the job of press secretaries today with that of press secretaries before the invention of television.

In addition to executive department heads, the President's Cabinet includes other advisors, such as the head of the Office of Management and Budget and the ambassador to the United Nations.

Special advisory groups. The Executive Office of the President also includes several special groups that help the President make decisions on domestic and foreign policy. The two most important groups are the Office of Management and Budget (OMB) and the National Security Council (NSC).

The OMB decides how much the President's policy goals will cost. As one person put it, "You have to decide how to spend the money, in what departments, and at what rate. If you don't, you end up throwing the taxpayers' money at problems without getting real solutions." The President may change the goals in light of the price tags provided by the OMB. Then the OMB prepares the budget that is sent to Congress.

The National Security Council plays a major role in helping the President make foreign policy. The NSC includes top military officers and advisors from other government agencies and departments concerned with foreign affairs and national defense.

The Executive Departments

The Constitution refers to "executive departments" but does not tell how many or what they should do. Over the years, the number of executive departments has grown, and they have been given many duties. Today they form the largest part of the executive branch. As the chart on page 204 shows, they do much of the "nuts and bolts" work connected with carrying out the nation's laws and running government programs.

Each executive department helps fulfill one or more of the President's duties. The Department of State, for example, handles relations with other countries. It helps put the President's foreign policy decisions into action. The Department of Defense helps the President fulfill the duty of commander in chief by running the armed forces.

The duties of each department are huge, needing many workers and much money to carry out. The Department of Defense, for instance, has a budget in the billions of dollars and over a million workers. Its headquarters is a huge five-sided building in Washington, D.C., called the Pentagon.

Executive department leadership. The President appoints the head of each executive department. As a check on presidential power, each appointment must be approved by the Senate. The head of the Department of Justice is called the Attorney General. The other department heads are called secretaries, such as the Secretary of State and the Secretary of the Treasury. The department secretaries and the Attorney General form the core of the ***Cabinet***, an important group of policy advisors to the President.

Political battlegrounds. Although the heads of the executive departments are chosen by the President, the departments are not simply tools for putting presidential policies into action. First of all, Congress has a say in how the departments are run because it votes on how much money each will receive. Furthermore, only Congress can set up or get rid of an executive department. Interest groups also play a role in the work of executive departments.

When the goals of Congress or of interest groups are at odds with the President's goals, executive departments can be settings for political battles. Early in President Ronald Reagan's first term, for instance, a battle was fought over the very existence of a department.

President Reagan, as part of his policy of cutting back the size of government, tried to get rid of the Department of Education. His effort was strongly fought by the National Education Association (NEA). Lobbyists for the NEA and other interest groups convinced

Several Presidents have created unofficial cabinets of highly trusted advisors which met outside the structure of the official Cabinet. President Andrew Jackson, who served from 1829 to 1837, began this practice with his Kitchen Cabinet.

Main Duties of the Executive Departments

Department of State (created in 1789): 25,000 employees

- Carries out foreign policy.
- Supervises ambassadors and other U.S. diplomats.
- Represents the United States at the United Nations.

Department of the Treasury (1789): 164,000 employees

- Collects federal taxes through the Internal Revenue Service (IRS).
- Prints money and postage stamps; makes coins.
- Protects the President and Vice-President through the Secret Service.

Department of Defense (1789, reorganized in 1947): 1,054,000 employees

- Maintains the Army, Navy, Marine Corps, and Air Force.
- Does research on military weapons.
- Builds and maintains military bases.

Department of the Interior (1849): 76,000 employees

- Manages national parks and other federal lands.
- Protects fish, wildlife, and other natural resources.

Department of Justice (1870): 82,000 employees

- Investigates and prosecutes violations of federal laws.
- Operates federal prisons.
- Runs the Federal Bureau of Investigation (FBI).
- Represents the federal government in lawsuits.

Department of Agriculture (1889): 119,000 employees

- Provides assistance to farmers.
- Inspects food processing plants.
- Runs the food stamp and school lunch programs.
- Works to control animal and plant diseases.

Department of Commerce (1903): 53,000 employees

- Provides assistance to American businesses.
- Conducts the national census every 10 years.
- Issues patents and trademarks for inventions.
- Maintains official weights and measures.

Department of Labor (1913): 18,000 employees

- Enforces laws on minimum wage, job discrimination, and working conditions.
- Helps run job training and unemployment programs.
- Provides statistics on prices and levels of employment.

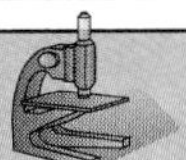

Department of Health and Human Services (1953): 123,000 employees

- Directs the Social Security and Medicare programs.
- Runs the Food and Drug Administration (FDA).
- Runs the Public Health Service.

Department of Housing and Urban Development (1965): 13,000 employees

- Helps provide housing for low-income citizens.
- Assists state and local governments with urban problems.

Department of Transportation (1966): 67,000 employees

- Helps state and local governments maintain highways.
- Enforces transportation safety standards.
- Operates the United States Coast Guard.

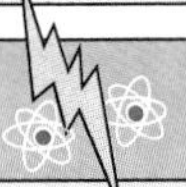

Department of Energy (1977): 17,000 employees

- Conducts research on sources of energy.
- Promotes the conservation of fuel and electricity.

Department of Education (1979): 5,000 employees

- Provides assistance to elementary, high school, and college education programs.
- Conducts research and provides statistics on education.

Department of Veterans Affairs (1988): 247,000 employees

- Gives medical, educational, and financial help to people who have served in the armed forces.
- Provides financial help to veterans' families.

Department of Environmental Protection (1992): 15,000 employees (proposed)

- Makes and enforces pollution regulations.
- Conducts research on environmental problems.

Today, the President leads a government that is much larger than the one headed by George Washington. In 1790, the national legislature was made up of 26 senators and 65 representatives. Only four executive departments existed: the state, treasury, war, and justice departments.

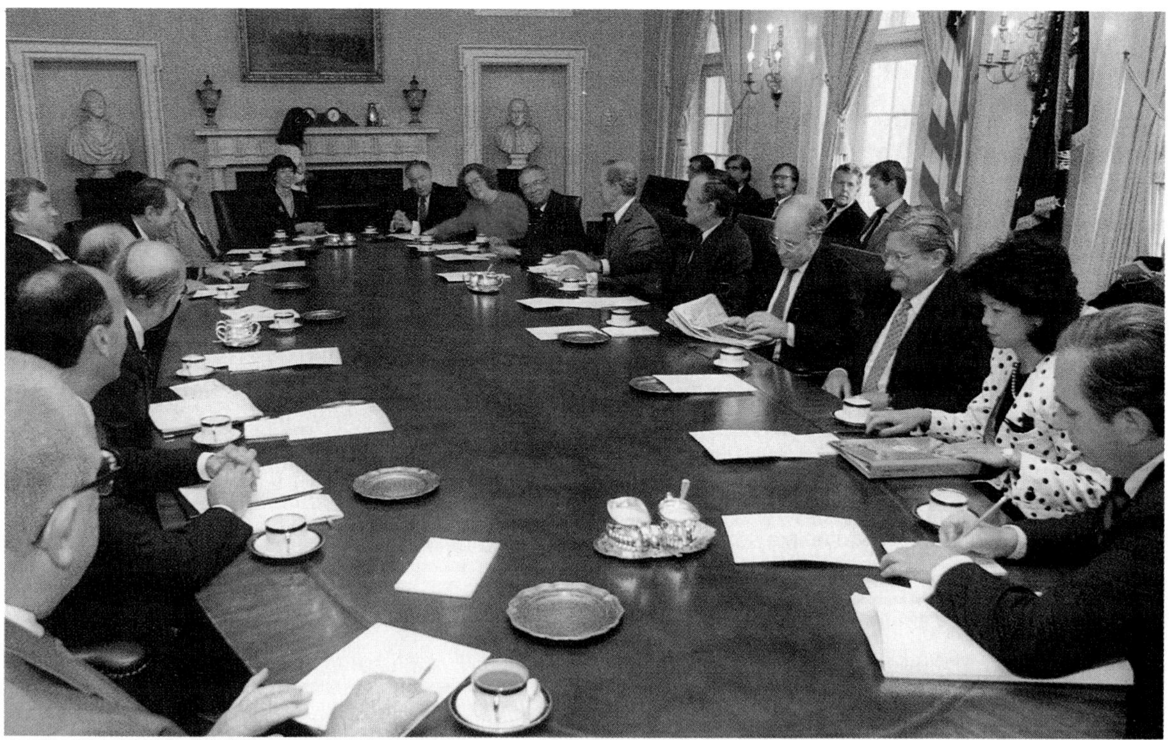

The President often meets with members of the Cabinet and other key advisors to discuss foreign and domestic issues.

Congress to block Reagan's attempt. Conflicts like this show that a President must take into account the strength of Congress and of interest groups when making policy decisions.

The Independent Agencies

The executive departments do not carry out all the duties of today's executive branch. Many tasks, from making rules about nuclear energy to providing farm loans, are carried out by over 70 independent agencies. There are three types of agencies: executive agencies, regulatory commissions, and government corporations.

Executive agencies. Executive agencies are under the direct control of the President, who can choose or remove their directors. They have many different jobs. Among the most important agencies are the National Aeronautics and Space Administration (NASA) and the General Services Administration (GSA).

Regulatory commissions. Congress has formed 12 regulatory commissions. Each one makes and carries out rules for a certain business or economic activity. The Federal Communications Commission (FCC), for instance, makes rules for radio and television stations. The Consumer Product Safety Commission (CPSC) sets safety standards for products you might find around the house. The regulatory commissions also settle disputes between businesses they regulate.

The regulatory commissions are meant to be fairly free from political influences. The President chooses members of the boards which run the commissions. Each member has a long term so that no single President can choose all of a board's members.

Government Corporations. Government corporations are like private businesses in that they try to make a profit. However, most of them provide public services that may be too risky or expensive for a private business to undertake. The United States Postal Service is the government corporation you are most likely to know about.

The Civil Service System

As you might imagine, the executive branch includes a wide variety of employees, from budget experts at the OMB to rocket engineers at NASA. The President chooses only

Independent Agencies

Selected Executive Agencies	
Central Intelligence Agency (CIA) (established 1947)	Gathers political, economic, and military information on other nations.
General Services Administration (GSA) (1949)	Buys supplies for the government, manages federal buildings, and keeps public records.
National Aeronautics and Space Administration (NASA) (1958)	Operates the space program. Conducts research on flight both within and beyond the earth's atmosphere.
Federal Election Commission (FEC) (1974)	Enforces rules on campaigns for federal offices.
Selected Regulatory Commissions	
Interstate Commerce Commission (ICC) (1887)	Regulates transportation between states.
Federal Reserve System (FRS) (1913)	Directs the nation's banking system by managing the money supply.
Federal Trade Commission (FTC) (1914)	Protects consumers from unfair or misleading business practices.
Securities and Exchange Commission (SEC) (1934)	Enforces laws that regulate the sale of stocks and bonds.
National Labor Relations Board (NLRB) (1935)	Works to correct or prevent unfair labor practices by either employers or unions.
Equal Employment Opportunity Commission (EEOC) (1964)	Enforces laws against job discrimination based on race, color, religion, sex, national origin, age, or disability.
Selected Government Corporations	
Federal Deposit Insurance Corporation (FDIC) (1933)	Insures deposits at banks that are members of the Federal Reserve System.
Tennessee Valley Authority (TVA) (1933)	Develops the natural resources of the Tennessee Valley by controlling flooding and creating electric power.
National Railroad Passenger Corporation (Amtrak) (1970)	Operates intercity passenger trains.
United States Postal Service (1971)	Provides mail service.

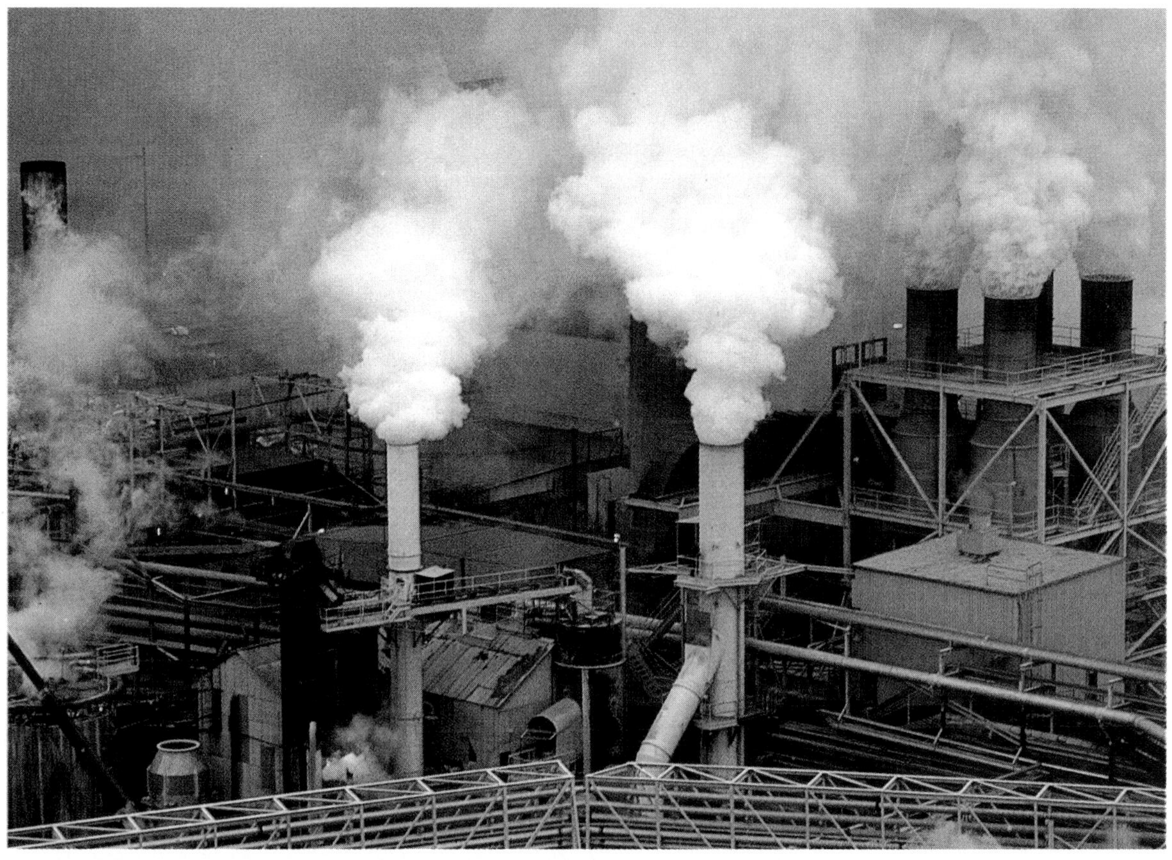

Once Congress had passed the Clean Air Act of 1990, the Environmental Protection Agency had to decide how to make the new law work.

about 1 percent of the workers in the executive branch. How do all the others get their jobs?

For many years, government jobs were likely to go to friends and supporters of the President. Loyalty to the President was more important than knowing how to do the job.

In 1883, however, Congress set up the civil service system. Under this system government workers, called civil servants, are hired on the basis of merit. There are tests for each kind of job, and workers are hired from among those with the highest scores. The civil service system provides for a group of trained workers who stay on the job from administration to administration.

The Executive Branch in Action

As you have seen, the executive branch has a big, complex job. The President and the administration, Congress, and the bureaucracy each has a major role in its operation. In addition, individual citizens and groups outside the government often play roles. The following example helps show what all these groups and individuals can do to help decide how to carry out a law.

When Congress passed the Clean Air Act of 1990, the Environmental Protection Agency had to find ways to carry out the new law. The agency had to keep in mind the President's policy: to control pollution without

Each state has a Federal Job Information Center which announces openings for civil service positions. Interested people submit applications and take an examination. Results are published, and the applicants with the top three scores are considered for the job.

Teaching Note: For more information on pollution control, see Chapters 23 and 26 and "Issues That Affect You: A Case Study" on page 512.

raising industry's costs too high. The EPA also had to decide how much pollution cars and industries could be allowed to put into the air and still be within the law.

The EPA studied pollution-control technology and how much it would cost businesses to install. The EPA also held hearings. It listened to all parties involved, including representatives from industries, city governments, and wildlife protection groups.

A first draft of the rules was checked to see whether they met the goals of the Clean Air Act. Then the draft was read by members of Congress, administration officials, and interest groups. The EPA also got letters from citizens. When the EPA had reviewed all the comments, the final rules were published. At last, the law was ready to be carried out.

Now you have an idea of the work needed to carry out a single law. Of course, there are hundreds of other laws that the executive branch must carry out. It must also make many decisions about domestic and foreign policy. Can you see why the executive branch has become a huge bureaucracy?

Answers will be found on page T 84.

Section Review

1. Define *bureaucracy, administration,* and *Cabinet.*
2. Briefly describe how each of the three main parts of the executive branch is organized. What is the major purpose of each part?
3. Explain why enforcing a law can be difficult.

Evaluation. What do you think are the advantages and disadvantages of having a large executive branch bureaucracy?

Data Search. Look on page 586 in the Data Bank and at the chart on page 204 in the text. Which two executive departments had the largest budgets in 1990? Of these, which had the most employees?

9-3 PRESIDENTS AND POWER

Read to Find Out

- what the term *executive privilege* means.
- what are some ways in which Presidents are able to act on their own.
- what are some possible advantages and disadvantages of Presidents acting on their own.

As our first President, George Washington was the leader of a small nation of about 4 million people struggling to survive in a wilderness. Today, the President's actions affect our nation of over 250 million people. They also affect nations and peoples around the world.

In setting up the office of President, the framers could not have known how much the power and duties of the office would grow. Today, many people fear that too much power is in the hands of one leader. How much power should a President have? How free should a President be from checks and balances by Congress and the judicial branch?

Freedom to Take Action

In fact, the President has a good deal of freedom to take action to meet goals. For example, the President and presidential advisors do not need permission from Congress to hold talks with representatives of other countries. Many talks result in executive agreements, which do not need Senate approval. Other talks lead to treaties. Even though the Senate has the power to reject any treaty, once the President has committed the United States to a treaty, it is hard for the Senate to say no.

Teaching Note: Use Teaching Activity 2, page T 82, after students have read the material in Section 9-2. Use the Evaluating Progress activity, page T 83, to assess students' understanding of the section.

Teaching Note: For President Theodore Roosevelt's view of presidential leadership, see "In Their Own Words" on page 236.

Another way the President can take independent action is by ***executive privilege***, the right to keep some information secret from Congress and the courts. Executive privilege is based on the idea of separation of powers. It helps keep the other branches from interfering with the President's job. Sometimes, too, the nation's safety depends on secrecy. If the President has to tell Congress, the information is more likely to leak out and ruin the plan.

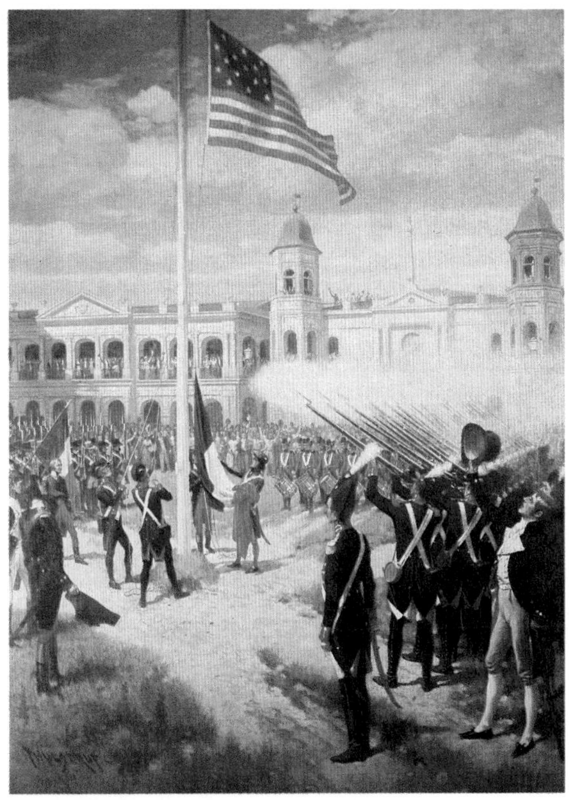

The American flag is raised over the Louisiana Territory, purchased from France by President Thomas Jefferson in 1803.

Seeking a Balance

Given the fact that the President has a good deal of freedom, an important question to ask is, "When should the President's powers be limited?" The answer depends on the situation and on the President's goals. In any situation, the possible advantages of the President acting independently have to be weighed against the possible disadvantages.

What are some reasons the President should be able to take action without talking with the other branches of government? One is that the President can act quickly in a crisis or take an opportunity that might be lost while waiting for approval by Congress. Furthermore, in some situations Congress may be seriously divided and not able to arrive at a decision.

Suppose, however, that a President often made important decisions without asking Congress or thinking about whether the actions were constitutional. How could we be sure that the President was acting in the best interests of the nation? Clearly, the need for strong presidential leadership must be balanced against the need to protect ourselves against abuse of power.

Using Presidential Power

The following examples show how three Presidents have used their powers at certain times. As you read, think about the effects of each President's action. Was the President right to take that action?

Jefferson and the Louisiana Purchase. In 1803, President Thomas Jefferson had a great opportunity. Napoleon, the emperor of France, had offered to sell the huge Louisiana territory for $15 million. By buying Louisiana, Jefferson could double the size of the United States.

Although Jefferson thought that the purchase would be good for the young nation, he was troubled because the Constitution did not

Challenge (Evaluation): Executive privilege, the right of the President to keep some information secret from Congress and the courts, is a significant freedom of the presidency. Have students discuss when, if ever, this freedom allows the President to be "above the law."

Faced with possible impeachment, President Nixon resigned. Here he and his family bid farewell to Vice-President Gerald Ford, who replaced him.

say that the President or Congress could buy territory. Jefferson thought that a constitutional amendment might solve the problem, but time was short. Napoleon was showing signs of changing his mind.

Knowing that he had to act quickly, Jefferson turned to his advisors, especially James Madison, who was then Secretary of State. Madison believed that the President's power to make treaties gave Jefferson the right to buy Louisiana. After carefully thinking about Madison's advice, Jefferson accepted Napoleon's offer. The Senate ratified the treaty, and Congress agreed to pay France for the territory.

Truman and the steel mills. In 1952, during the Korean War, President Harry Truman faced a problem. The steelworkers said they would not work unless they were given higher pay. The steel-mill owners would not agree to their demands.

President Truman knew that steel was needed to make weapons for the soldiers in Korea. He gave an executive order placing the Secretary of Commerce in control of the mills for the time being. The steel companies said that the President had no right to take control of private property. Truman said that he was acting as commander in chief to protect American troops.

The case came before the Supreme Court. The Court ruled that the President had no power to take private property, even in a national emergency. His duty, the Court said, was to carry out laws passed by Congress, not to use executive orders to make his own laws.

Nixon and Watergate. On August 9, 1974, President Richard Nixon left office as a result of the Watergate scandal. Nixon and members of his staff were accused of approving a break-in at the Democratic Committee National Headquarters in the Watergate office building in Washington, D.C. Their aim was to help get Nixon re-elected by finding out about the Democrats' campaign plans.

After the burglars were caught in the act, newspaper reporters discovered that members of the White House staff had helped plan the burglary and later tried to cover up the crime. The House Judiciary Committee began an investigation. The major question became, "Did the President know about the break-in?"

The investigation found that the President had taped all of his White House conversations. The committee asked him for the tapes, which might have important information. When Nixon said no, claiming executive privilege, Congress asked the Supreme Court

Decision Making: Have students imagine themselves in the position of the President and describe what steps they would take in handling a crisis, such as the taking of American hostages.

Teaching Note: Use the Enrichment Activity, page T 83, and accompanying worksheet in the Activity Book after students have read the material in this section.

to rule on the matter. The Court ordered Nixon to turn over the tapes. It said that executive privilege is not an unlimited power, particularly if used to hide possible criminal actions.

Based on the tapes and other facts, the House Judiciary Committee recommended that Nixon be impeached. Before the House could vote, however, Nixon resigned.

Sharing the Power

The stories you have just read show that the President does not govern alone. Instead, power is shared among the three branches of government—the "three horse team" as President Franklin D. Roosevelt described them.

Franklin Roosevelt also said that "the greatness of America is grounded in principles and not on any single personality." One of those principles is, of course, that the power of each branch must be limited by the other two, as happened in the steel mill and Watergate cases. The system of checks and balances helps to make sure that the government acts in the best interests of the people. In this way the "three horse team" works together for the good of the nation.

Answers will be found on page T 84.

Section Review

1. Define *executive privilege.*
2. Describe three ways in which Presidents can take action on their own without consulting the other branches of government.
3. What are some advantages and disadvantages of the power of Presidents to take action on their own?

Evaluation. Do you think our system of government places too much power in the hands of the President? Support your opinion with reasons and examples.

A BROADER VIEW

As you know, ours is not the only nation with a representative government that includes both a legislature and a leader. However, just as there are differences between Congress and many other legislatures, there are also differences between the presidency and the role played by leaders of many other nations.

One difference lies in the fact that the President is both our chief of state and the leader of the government. In a number of other nations, each of these roles is filled by a different person. For instance, in Great Britain the chief of state is the king or queen, who represents the nation at ceremonies but holds little political power. It is the British prime minister who leads the government, making decisions on foreign and domestic policy.

Another difference is in the way the leaders are chosen. In many parliamentary governments, such as Great Britain, West Germany, Israel, and Japan, the leader of the government is chosen by the legislature, not elected directly by the people. Such leaders usually stay in power only as long as their party has a majority in the legislature. They may be voted out of office at any time. Our Presidents, on the other hand, stay in office for a fixed term during which they may be removed from office only if convicted of crimes. Thus, in our government the chief executive is more independent of the legislature.

Critical Thinking

Teaching Note: For reinforcement of decision-making skills, use Decison-Making Worksheet Chapter 9.

Opinion or Statement of Fact?

"Today Carol made a speech about school spirit in her campaign for student body president. It was a great speech."

Suppose you were trying to decide whom to vote for in a school election, and you overheard a comment like the one above. That information might influence your decision, but you would probably want to check it out first.

You could find out whether Carol really talked about school spirit by asking students who heard the speech. The statement that the candidate talked about school spirit is a *statement of fact*, a statement that can be either proved or disproved to everyone's satisfaction. In this case, the statement is true. However, suppose you were to say to someone, "Hi, my name is Mickey Mouse. I am over 60 years old." These statements of fact could easily be proved false.

The statement that the candidate's speech was "great," however, is a statement that is neither true nor false. Instead, it is an *opinion*, a personal belief that cannot be either proved or disproved. If you asked other students whether the speech was great, you would get different answers because people have different ideas about what is "great." There will always be disagreement about opinions.

Being able to tell the difference between statements of fact and opinions helps you judge the information you use in making decisions. When making a decision, you should have good reasons for trusting the information you use, whether that information is fact, opinion, or a combination of both.

Suppose you have an assignment to rate the Presidents of the United States, deciding which ones were good, average, and below average. In order to make your decision, you have gathered information on the Presidents. Among the pieces of information are the following:

> Thomas Jefferson's most important accomplishment was the purchase of the Louisiana Territory.
>
> Andrew Johnson is the only President who was ever impeached.

How might you decide what is a statement of fact and what is opinion?

EXPLAINING THE SKILL

One way to separate statements of fact from opinions is to follow these steps. Notice how the steps apply to the information that you just read.

1. Recall the definitions of a fact and an opinion, as described above.

2. Apply the definitions of fact and opinion to each piece of information. When in doubt about whether a piece of information is a fact or an opinion, ask yourself, "Could it be proved or disproved to any reasonable person?" [Jefferson's purchase and Johnson's impeachment are statements of fact that can be checked in history books. In both cases the statements are true. However, saying that the purchase was "most important" is an opinion because there will always be disagreement about what is "important."]

3. Determine the extent to which each piece of information fits the definition of fact or opinion. Does it contain only fact, only opinion, or a combination of both? [The information about Jefferson is a combination of fact and opinion. The information about Johnson is a statement of fact.]

Have students identify which dictionary definition of *fact* applies to the use of the term in this lesson. Have them explain the difference between the uses of the term in the following sentences: "I've got the facts." "Get your facts straight."

Answers will be found on page T 85.

APPLYING THE SKILL

Examine the following information in order to identify statements of fact and opinions.

A. Woodrow Wilson was the most well-educated President.

B. During President Wilson's illness, his wife took on some of his duties as President.

C. William Howard Taft was the only person to hold the offices of President of the United States and Chief Justice of the Supreme Court.

D. After women were given the right to vote, Warren G. Harding was elected President because he was more handsome than his opponent.

E. Andrew Johnson was the only President who never spent a single day in a schoolroom.

F. Abraham Lincoln is the only President who actively took on the role of commander in chief.

G. President Lyndon Johnson selflessly gave up his political career in the interest of the nation's welfare by not running for re-election in 1968.

H. Richard Nixon would have been impeached if he had not resigned first.

I. John Tyler was the first Vice-President to become President through the death of a President.

J. Approving the purchase of the Alaska Territory was the most important action that Andrew Johnson took as President.

K. When Ronald Reagan was re-elected to a second term, he was the oldest person to serve as President of the United States.

CHECKING YOUR UNDERSTANDING

After you have identified the statements of fact and the opinions, answer the following questions.

1. Pick one of the statements that includes an opinion and rewrite it so that it only states facts.

2. Which of the following sentences include only statements of fact? **(a)** B and E, **(b)** A and D, **(c)** F and I. Explain your answer.

3. Which of the following sentences include only opinion? **(a)** D, **(b)** I, **(c)** A. Explain your answer.

4. Which of the following sentences include both statements of fact and opinion? **(a)** D and G, **(b)** A and B, **(c)** C and H. Explain your answer.

REVIEWING THE SKILL

5. What is the difference between a statement of fact and an opinion?

6. How does identifying facts and opinions help you in making good decisions?

7. Identify two times when it would be helpful for you to identify statements of fact and opinions. Explain why.

Students should recognize that accurate statements of fact are not the only information one can rely on. Opinions may also be reliable, as long as they come from trustworthy sources and are supported by good reasons.

CHAPTER SURVEY

Answers to Survey and Workshop will be found on page T 85.

UNDERSTANDING NEW VOCABULARY

Seeing Relationships

The vocabulary terms in each pair listed below are related to each other. For each pair, explain how the two terms are related.

Example: *President* is related to *executive order* because it is the President who has the power to make an executive order.

1. *bureaucracy* and *executive branch*

2. *executive agreements* and *treaties*

3. *Cabinet* and *administration*

Putting It in Writing

Write a paragraph explaining the President's role in shaping the relationships between the United States and other countries. In your paragraph use the terms *treaties*, *ambassadors*, *executive agreements*, and *foreign policy*.

LOOKING BACK AT THE CHAPTER

1. Explain how the President's power is limited.

2. Describe three of the President's roles, and explain how the duties and powers of each role require the President to work with Congress.

3. Why has the executive branch grown into a large bureaucracy?

4. Why does a President need an administration?

5. What do members of the Cabinet and the White House staff have in common?

6. Why is the civil service system important for the smooth operation of the bureaucracy?

7. *Application.* Another country has just attacked a United States Navy ship. As commander in chief and as chief diplomat, what actions does the President have the power to carry out?

8. *Application.* Pick two of the independent agencies and explain how they affect your life.

9. *Evaluation.* Some people argue that our federal government interferes too much with the lives of citizens by enforcing so many regulations. Do you agree or disagree? Support your opinion.

10. *Analysis.* If you were an executive branch official appointed by the President, how would your job differ from that of a permanent employee in the bureaucracy?

11. *Analysis.* Pick two of the President's roles. For each role, choose two executive departments or agencies that help the President carry out that role. Then explain how they help the President.

WORKING TOGETHER

1. Working with a group of three or four, collect clippings of recent newspaper and magazine articles and pictures describing the President's activities. Arrange your clippings and pictures on a large board. Present this display to the class, explaining which different roles of the President these activities reflect.

2. Create your own trivia game on the presidency and various Presidents and Vice-Presidents by writing questions on small index cards and putting the answers on the backs of the cards. Some sources of interesting facts are encyclopedias, almanacs, and the table on page 596 of this book.

3. Working in groups of three or four, imagine that you are members of a particular executive department or independent agency and that the rest of the class is Congress. Present them with a report on why you need more money. In order to convince them, explain your duties and the challenges you face. To illustrate your points, you may use pictures and refer to recent magazine or newspaper articles.

SOCIAL STUDIES SKILLS

Using an Almanac

What are a President's powers and duties? How many Presidents have been assassinated? Who is in the President's Cabinet? The quickest way to answer factual questions such as these is to look in an information almanac. Information almanacs are published each year. These books are filled with information on an amazing range of subjects from AIDS and astronomy to ZIP codes and zoos. Here are just some of the topics listed in the index of a recent almanac under the subject of U.S. Presidents.

Presidents, (U.S.). 609–11, 619–23, 630–42
- Assassinations and attempts, 624
- Biographies, 630–42
- Burial places, 610
- Cabinets, 619–23
- Elections, 614–17
- Families, 611
- Mount Rushmore carvings, 744
- Oath of Office, 596
- Portraits on currency, 387
- Powers, duties, 595–96
- Qualifications, 595
- Religious affiliations, 609
- Salary, 48, 596

On which page or pages would you look in this almanac to find answers to the following questions?

1. Which Presidents appear on our money? Which ones are carved on Mount Rushmore?

2. Which Presidents, if any, were born in your state? Buried in your state?

3. Have there been any Catholic Presidents? Jewish Presidents?

4. How much is a President paid?

5. How many of our Presidents have been assassinated?

6. What are the names of the officials who serve in the President's Cabinet?

DECISION-MAKING SKILLS

Opinion or Statement of Fact?

Below are pieces of information about the presidency and various Presidents. Examine the information to identify the opinions and the statements of fact.

A. The President has too much responsibility.

B. President Gerald Ford made a mistake in pardoning Nixon after the Watergate scandal.

C. Franklin D. Roosevelt vetoed more bills than any other President.

D. John F. Kennedy was the greatest President since World War II.

E. Most Presidents have been Republicans.

F. Jimmy Carter was the most active President in the past 30 years.

G. Most Presidents have served previously as members of Congress.

H. Under the Constitution the President may be either a man or a woman.

I. Monthly Cabinet meetings are not a useful method for advising the President.

1. List the letters of the sentences that contain only fact. Choose two and explain how you can tell that they are statements of fact.

2. List the letters of the sentences that contain only opinion. Choose two and explain how you can tell that they are opinions.

3. Identify a sentence from the list that includes both fact and opinion. Explain how it includes both.

4. How can you tell the difference between a statement of fact and an opinion?

5. Give an example of a decision in which you might rely on both fact and opinion. What types of facts might you rely on? Whose opinions might you rely on? Explain.

Chapter Themes: Our legal system is made up of two separate but interconnected court systems. At both the state and federal levels, trial courts have original jurisdiction and appellate courts hear appeals. The Supreme Court is the final court of appeal for both systems.

CHAPTER 10

The Judicial Branch

Just before 10 o'clock in the morning you enter a large white building in Washington, D.C.,on which the words "Equal Justice Under Law" are carved in stone. You are ushered into a spacious room with high ceilings supported by marble columns. As you sit facing a long bench with nine dark leather chairs behind it, a man suddenly pounds a gavel and declares:

> The Honorable, the Chief Justice and the Associate Justices of the Supreme Court of the United States. Oyez! Oyez! Oyez! All persons having business before the Honorable, the Supreme Court of the United States are admonished to draw near and give their attention, for the Court is now sitting. God save the United States and this Honorable Court!

Everyone in the courtroom stands as nine justices in black robes enter through a thick red velvet curtain and take their seats behind the bench. You sit down quietly along with the rest of the audience.

A lawyer steps forward to the lectern and begins arguing the first case of the day. Her client has been found guilty of first degree murder by a state court. Under the laws of his state he was sentenced to death. When he committed the crime, however, he was under the age of eighteen. The lawyer argues that a law allowing the death penalty for a person who has not yet reached adulthood is cruel and unusual punishment and therefore unconstitutional.

She speaks for a half hour, and then the lawyer for the state presents his argument, justifying the state's law. Later, you watch other lawyers present arguments for their cases, and you wonder how the justices will decide the difficult questions presented.

In this chapter you will read about the judicial branch of the federal government. Led by its most important body—the Supreme Court—the judicial branch judges federal laws and interprets the Constitution. In doing so, it helps protect the rights of American citizens.

Teaching Note: Use the Introducing the Chapter activity, page T 88.

Teaching Note: For a fuller discussion of civil and criminal law and the function of the courts, see Unit 6.

10-1

THE ROLE OF THE FEDERAL COURTS

Read to Find Out

- what the terms *plaintiff, defendant, prosecution, precedent, original jurisdiction, appeal,* and *appellate jurisdiction* mean.
- what courts do.
- what cases are heard by federal courts.

The judicial branch of the federal government is made up of the Supreme Court and over 100 other federal courts. The most important members of the judicial branch are judges, most of them appointed to their offices for life. Although they work quietly, away from the hubbub of politics that surrounds the President and members of Congress, the judges of the judicial branch have a very important role in our government.

In Chapters 6 and 7 you read about many cases in which decisions by the Supreme Court had a lasting effect on our society and on our lives. Although it makes the important final decisions about what the Constitution means, the Supreme Court does not work alone. It is part of both a larger federal court system and an overall system of laws and courts.

Laws and Courts

Laws, as you know, are created by legislatures to help society work effectively for all of its citizens. Laws guide people's behavior, set limits, and protect our rights and freedoms. Even though laws exist in our society, however, people have conflicts. Laws are broken, and people feel that they have been wronged by others. As a result, society needs a fair and reasonable way of settling conflicts.

In our society, disputes involving laws are resolved in the legal system. If you have watched police dramas on television and seen movies about crime, you have some idea of what our legal system is. It includes judges, juries, lawyers, and police officers, all working with a huge body of laws. The federal courts are an important part of this legal system.

To understand the need for a legal system, consider the following example. A legislative body makes a law prohibiting one person from purposely damaging another's property. If a junior high student is then accused of throwing a baseball through someone else's window, several issues may have to be decided. Was the ball thrown on purpose? Has the law been broken? Is the accused person innocent or guilty? How shall the person who threw the baseball repay the person whose window was broken? These questions may be

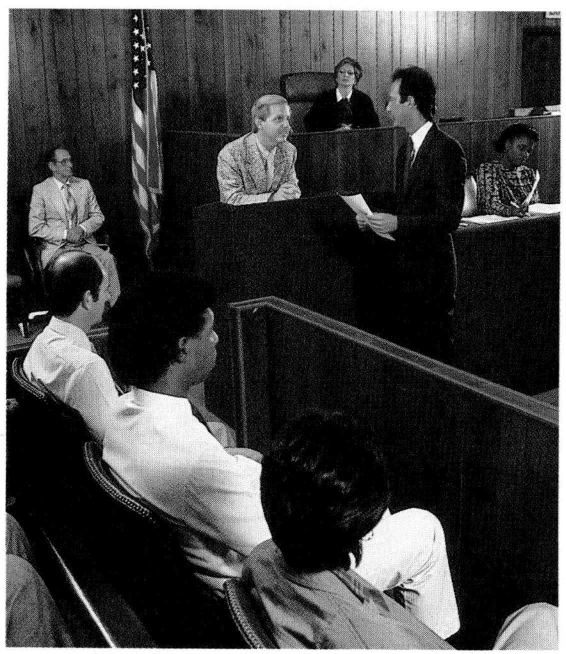

The federal courts are part of a legal system that includes all the courts and laws in the United States. In this picture a trial is in progress.

The term *judicial* comes from the Latin word *judex* which means "a judge," literally "one who points out the right."

decided by the people involved in the incident, but if the matter is serious enough, it may have to be decided within the legal system.

What Courts Do

Legal conflicts in our country are resolved by courts of law. Both the Supreme Court and the court you see in a television police drama are courts of law. All courts perform the same basic function: to apply the law to an actual situation. In a way, a court is like a referee in a ball game, who applies the rules of the game to what happens on the field.

Courts in our legal system resolve two kinds of legal conflicts. In a criminal case, a court determines whether a person accused of breaking a law is innocent or guilty. If the person is found guilty, the court also decides what the punishment will be.

In a civil case, a court settles a disagreement. The disagreement can arise over such issues as who caused an auto accident or broke a contract, over a divorce, or over possible violations of constitutional rights. The federal courts hear both civil and criminal cases, and both kinds of cases can find their way to the Supreme Court.

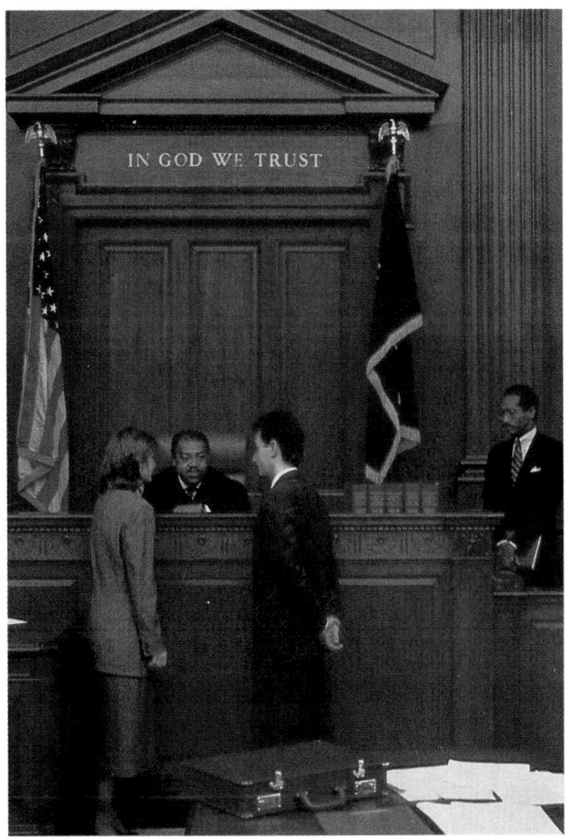

Usually each party in a court case is represented by a lawyer. Here, two lawyers discuss their case with the judge.

The parties in the conflict. Every court case involves two opposing sides, or parties. Who these parties are depends on whether the case is civil or criminal.

The typical civil case is brought to court by a party called the ***plaintiff***, an individual or a group of people who bring a complaint against another party. The party who answers a complaint and defends against it is called the ***defendant***. The defendant may be an individual, a group, or a government body.

Imagine that Mabel Edwards brought the Techno Corporation to court, claiming that the company had denied her a job because of her race. She would be the plaintiff in this civil case, and the company would be the defendant. The case would be called *Edwards* v. *The Techno Corporation.*

In contrast, a criminal case is always brought to court by the ***prosecution***, a government body that brings a criminal charge against a defendant who is accused of breaking one of its laws. The prosecution is referred to as "The People" and is represented by a government lawyer known as a prosecutor.

What if Arlo Ashley was accused of robbing a convenience store in Lima, Ohio? The state of Ohio would bring him to court on charges of theft. In a criminal case, called *The People of the State of Ohio* v. *Ashley*, Arlo Ashley would be the defendant.

Challenge (Evaluation): In our society, disputes involving laws are resolved in a legal system. Have students consider what other ways a society could resolve legal conflicts.

The members of the court. In a court the job of a judge is to apply the law to the conflict between the plaintiff or prosecution and the defendant. This means determining which side's argument is most in keeping with the law. The judge directs the proceedings but must remain neutral and not take sides in the conflict.

Many legal cases also involve a jury, which decides the facts of a case—such as what happened and who did it. You may remember that a trial by jury is one of the rights guaranteed by the Constitution to a person accused of a crime.

Interpreting the law. In the process of hearing a case, a court may have to decide what the law in question means. For example, does a law banning "motor vehicles" in a park also ban radio-controlled model cars? A court may also have to decide if the law is allowed by the Constitution. This process of interpretation is an important job of the courts.

Interpreting the law, however, can only occur when a court is hearing a specific case. In other words, no court—not even the Supreme Court—can just decide to interpret a particular law or a part of the Constitution. Instead, the court must wait for someone to bring a case that questions that law's meaning or constitutionality.

Although the legal system deals with individual cases, a court's decision in a case can have very broad effects. This is because a court's decision can establish a ***precedent***, a guideline for how all similar cases should be decided in the future. A precedent makes the meaning of a law or the Constitution clearer. It also determines how the law should be applied, both inside and outside the legal system. For example, the Court's decision in *Brown* v. *Board of Education* established a precedent that made *any* law segregating blacks and whites unconstitutional.

State Courts and Federal Courts

Our legal system is made up of two separate but interconnected court systems—those of the states and that of the federal government. Although decisions that establish the broadest precedents are made in the highest federal courts, most legal cases begin in a lower court, often at the level of state government. To understand the federal court system, it helps to know about the state court system.

Each state has courts at different levels of government and courts for different purposes, such as traffic courts and juvenile courts. All of these courts are considered part of the state court system. Since most of the laws that govern our everyday actions are state and local

A Typical Court System

Teaching Note: The origin of the legal tradition of being guided by earlier court decisions (common law) is discussed in Chapter 18.

laws, most legal disputes and violations of the law are decided in state courts.

Jurisdiction. The court to which a legal case first goes has ***original jurisdiction***, the authority to hear a case first. A court with original jurisdiction determines the facts in a case. Often this occurs during a trial conducted with a jury, but in certain cases a judge hears the case alone. Because they hold trials to resolve cases, courts with original jurisdiction are also called trial courts. There are many kinds of trial courts in a state court system, hearing different kinds of cases.

What happens if the court of original jurisdiction makes a decision that the plaintiff or defendant in the case believes is unjust? Then he or she has the right to ***appeal***, to ask a higher court to review the decision and determine if justice was done. In each state, there are appeals courts set up just for the purpose of hearing cases appealed from lower state courts. These courts have ***appellate jurisdiction***, the authority to hear an appeal.

An appeals court does not hold a trial, nor does it determine the facts in a case. Its purpose is to review the legal issues involved, to determine if the law was applied fairly and if due process of law was followed.

An appeals court may decide to affirm, or let stand, the lower court's decision. However, if it decides that the trial was unfair for some reason, it may reverse the lower court's decision. When that happens, the appeals court may order another trial, which is held in the court of original jurisdiction. When a plaintiff is declared innocent, however, the prosecution may not appeal because the Constitution prohibits double jeopardy.

The appeals process may go beyond the first appeals court. In most states, the final court of appeals is the state supreme court. Although state court systems differ, most have three levels: trial courts, appeals courts, and a court of final appeals. You will learn how state courts work in Chapter 11.

Cases Heard by Federal Courts

- Cases that raise constitutional questions
- Cases involving federal laws, such as treason and tax evasion
- Cases in which the federal government is the defendant
- Disagreements between states
- Disagreements between people from different states when more than $10,000 is in dispute
- Cases involving a foreign government and a state
- Cases involving treaties signed by the United States
- Cases involving American ships at sea
- Cases involving ambassadors and other foreign representatives

The cases heard by federal courts. If state courts have original jurisdiction over most legal disputes that occur in the United States, then what is the purpose of federal courts?

Federal courts hear two kinds of cases:

- *Cases involving federal laws and issues beyond the authority of individual states.* In these cases, the federal courts have original jurisdiction. See the box on this page for a list of these kinds of cases.
- *Cases appealed from state supreme courts.* These cases must involve a federal law or a constitutional issue. They are heard only by the Supreme Court.

The authority to hear cases appealed from the state court systems gives the United States Supreme Court and the federal judicial branch the leadership role in our legal system. In this role, the Supreme Court sees that all 50 state court systems interpret the Constitution in the same way and that the rights of all Americans are protected.

Some trial courts specialize in only one type of case. Small claims courts hear disputes involving small amounts of money. Probate courts handle wills and disputes over inheritances. Juvenile courts hear cases of children accused of crimes. (See Chapters 19–20.)

Answers will be found on page T 90.

Section Review

1. Define *plaintiff, defendant, prosecution, precedent, original jurisdiction, appeal*, and *appellate jurisdiction.*
2. How is a court of law like a referee in a game of sports?
3. What two kinds of cases are heard by the federal courts?

Analysis. Explain how a court's decision about an individual case can affect our society as a whole.

10-2

THE ORGANIZATION OF THE FEDERAL COURTS

Read to Find Out

- what relationship exists between the two levels of lower federal courts.
- what role the Supreme Court plays in the federal court system.
- how the role of federal judges differs from that of members of Congress.

The organization of the federal court system is similar to that of the state court systems. At the lowest level are the United States district courts, with original jurisdiction over most of the cases that enter the federal court system. At the next level are the United States courts of appeals. These federal courts handle appeals from the district courts. Finally, at the highest level is the Supreme Court, the highest court in the land.

The Constitution creates the framework for the federal court system in Article III:

> The judicial power of the United States shall be vested in one Supreme Court, and in such inferior courts as the Congress may from time to time ordain and establish.

As you can see, the Constitution did not spell out how the inferior, or lower, courts would be set up. Congress, however, wasted no time in establishing a complete federal court system. The very first act passed by the First Congress in 1789 was the Judiciary Act, which created the district courts and courts of appeals. Although many of the details of the Judiciary Act have since been changed, the federal court system it created is much the same 200 years later.

The District Courts

The workhorses of the federal court system are the 95 district courts scattered across the United States. Each state has at least one district court, and some larger states have as many as four. The number of judges in one district court ranges from 1 to 27, depending on the size of the district and its workload.

As courts of original jurisdiction, the district courts are the first to hear cases such as those involving kidnapping or a city's failure to obey federal air pollution standards.

A federal district court is similar to a state trial court. Witnesses are called, a jury normally decides the facts in the case, and one judge directs the proceedings and applies the law.

The Courts of Appeals

At the next highest level of the federal court system are the 12 United States courts of appeals, which handle appeals from the federal district courts. Each court of appeals takes cases from a group of district courts within a particular geographic area called a circuit. In

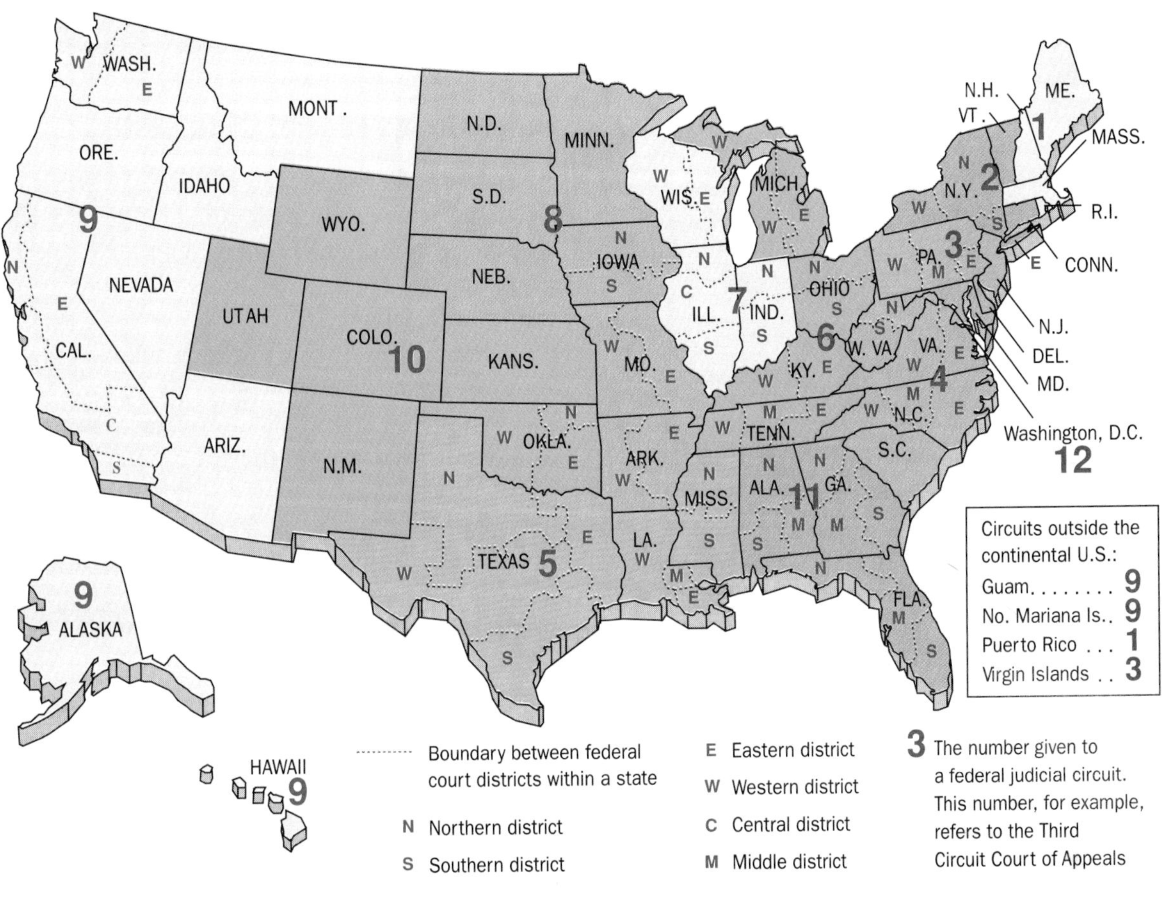

Federal Court Districts and Circuits. *Some states make up one federal court district. Other states are divided into two or more districts.*

fact, the courts of appeals are often called circuit courts. A thirteenth court of appeals has appellate jurisdiction over cases appealed from certain special federal courts and agencies of the executive branch. It is called the court of appeals for the federal circuit.

A court of appeals has no jury, calls no witnesses, and does not examine any evidence. Instead, lawyers for the defendant and the plaintiff or prosecution make arguments in front of a panel of three judges. After reviewing the case, the judges decide either to affirm the lower court's decision or to reverse it. Like state appeals courts, the courts of appeals are not concerned with guilt or innocence—only with whether the original trial was fair and whether the law was interpreted correctly.

The Supreme Court

The Supreme Court is the highest court in the federal court system. The major purpose of the Supreme Court is to serve as the final court of appeals for both the state and federal court systems.

The Judiciary Act of 1789 required Supreme Court justices to ride circuits to hear cases in courts of appeals for nine months of the year. This system was changed when more states joined the Union and the Supreme Court had more than a few months of work to do.

Teaching Note: Use Teaching Activity 1 and Teaching Activity 2, pages T 88 and T 89, as culminating activities after students have read the material in Section 10-2.

The Supreme Court, however, does have original jurisdiction over a few special kinds of cases, including those involving representatives of foreign governments and disputes between state governments. The role of the Supreme Court in the legal system and in the federal government is so important that it will be discussed in more detail later in this chapter.

Special Federal Courts

The chart on this page shows additional federal courts. These special courts include the Court of Claims, the Court of Customs and Patent Appeals, and the Tax Court. Each of these courts was established by Congress for a special purpose. Appeals from some of these courts are sent directly to the Supreme Court; others must first pass through a court of appeals or a higher special court.

Judges in the Federal Court System

Just as members of Congress do the work of the legislative branch, federal judges do the work of the judicial branch. A judge's role in government, however, is very different from that of a legislator.

A legislator is open to the influence of citizens, interest groups, other legislators, and the President. A judge, in contrast, must be impartial, favoring neither one party nor the other. A legislator seeks to solve broad problems by making laws, whereas a judge can only settle individual cases. By applying the law to specific cases, however, judges help define and clarify the work of legislators.

The State and Federal Court Systems

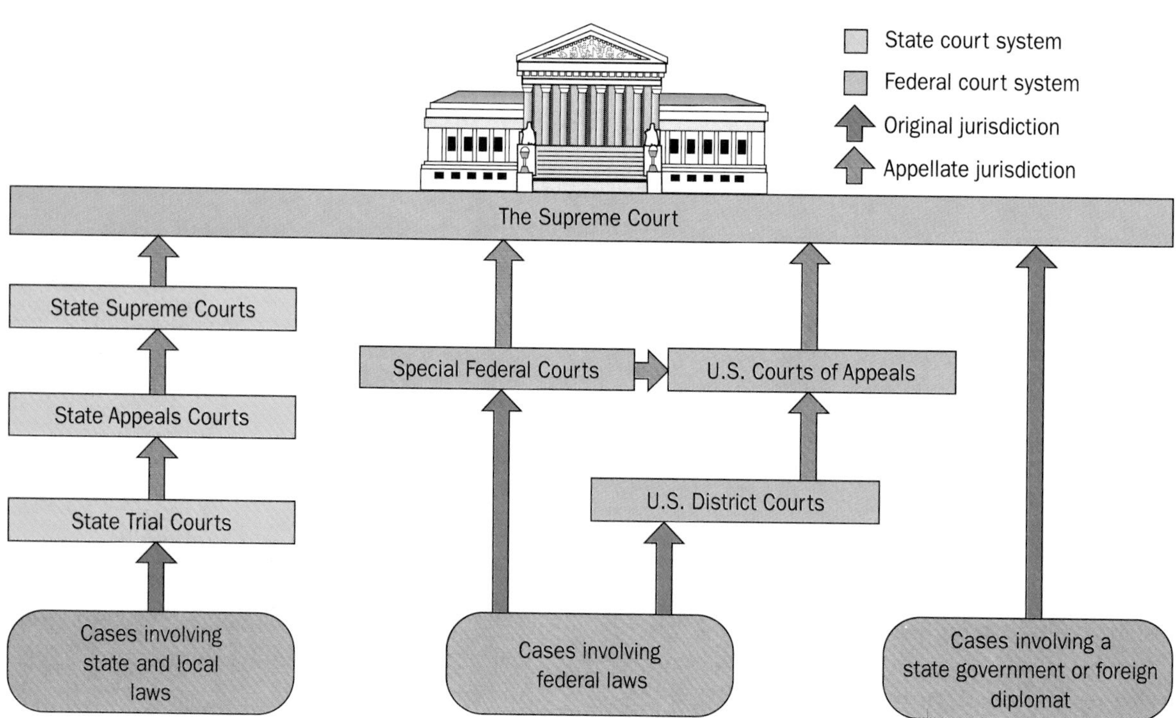

Teaching Note: Use the Reinforcement Activity, page T 89, and accompanying worksheet in the Activity Book to reinforce students' understanding of Sections 10-1 and 10-2.

In part because judges' jobs are different from those of legislators, judges are selected in a very different way. All federal judges in the district courts, courts of appeals, and Supreme Court are appointed by the President and confirmed by the Senate. They serve life terms and can be removed from office only by the impeachment process.

Federal judges shoulder great responsibility. They must balance the rights of individuals with the interests of the nation as a whole. Often they are forced to make decisions which seem fair to one side but unfair to the other. The Honorable Irving Kaufman, a federal judge from New York, has noted, "When we judges get a question, it is almost always a) very important, and b) a tough case that is close enough to drive one mad."

Of all federal judges, the nine Supreme Court justices have the most responsibility. From time to time the entire nation waits in anticipation for them to make a decision. Although they are only deciding a specific case, perhaps involving just one or two people, their decision may have very important consequences for the nation.

Answers will be found on page T 90.

Section Review

1. What kind of jurisdiction does a federal district court have? A federal court of appeals?
2. What is the major purpose of the Supreme Court?
3. Describe two major differences between a federal judge and a member of Congress.

Analysis. Why are federal judges appointed instead of being elected?

Data Search. Look at the map on page 223. Which federal court district do you live in? Which federal court circuit?

10-3 THE SUPREME COURT

Read to Find Out

- what the terms *judicial review, judicial activism,* and *judicial restraint* mean.
- how the Court asserted its power to declare laws unconstitutional.
- how the Court's power is checked by the other branches of government.

The Constitution means what the judges say it means.

—*Chief Justice Charles Evans Hughes*

What are the rights of people accused of crimes? What kinds of punishment are "cruel and unusual"? What activities are protected by the right of free speech? When the Supreme Court is asked to decide cases that raise such constitutional questions, Americans can see the importance of the Court's role in our federal government.

Lower state and federal courts make rulings in cases that involve constitutional issues, but their rulings are not necessarily final. Only the Supreme Court has the final say about what the Constitution means and what laws it will allow. A Supreme Court decision establishes the broadest and longest-lasting kind of precedent in our legal system.

Judicial Review

One of the most important powers of the Supreme Court is ***judicial review***, the power to overturn any law which the Court decides is in conflict with the Constitution. Judicial review gives the judicial branch final say over the validity of any law. Judicial review, however, is not spelled out in the Constitution.

Challenge (Evaluation): Federal judges are appointed for life. Have students discuss the advantages and disadvantages of this system. Should the terms of office be changed? Why or why not?

The Supreme Court asserted this power for itself early in its history.

As you have learned, every court of law is limited to dealing with individual cases. The Supreme Court could not simply declare one day that it had the power of judicial review. It had to do so in relation to a particular case.

***Marbury* v. *Madison*.** In 1803, William Marbury sued James Madison, then serving as Secretary of State. Marbury demanded that Madison grant him a government job he had been promised by the previous President, John Adams. Marbury brought his case directly to the Supreme Court because the Judiciary Act of 1789 gave the Court original jurisdiction in such matters. Rather than decide whether Marbury should be given the job, the Supreme Court instead focused its attention on the law that had allowed Marbury to bring his case before the Court in the first place.

John Marshall, Chief Justice for 34 years, helped to shape the Supreme Court we know today. He wrote the opinion in Marbury *v.* Madison.

The problem, said the Court, was that Congress, in the Judiciary Act, had given the Court original jurisdiction in cases involving government officials. The Constitution, however, clearly gave the Supreme Court only appellate jurisdiction in such cases. Therefore, the Court decided, the part of the Judiciary Act that gave the Court original jurisdiction in Marbury's case was unconstitutional.

Chief Justice John Marshall wrote the Court's opinion on this decision. He argued that because the Supreme Court had a sworn duty to uphold the Constitution, it also had a responsibility to declare unconstitutional any law that violated the Constitution.

The Court's decision in *Marbury* v. *Madison* established a precedent that gave the Supreme Court one of its most important powers. Judicial review was extended in later cases to cover acts of the executive branch and of the states. Since 1803, over 1,000 state and local laws and over 100 federal laws have been overturned as a result of the Supreme Court's use of judicial review.

The Justices

If the justices of the Supreme Court are to use the power of judicial review in a way that defends the Constitution and promotes the common good, they must have the highest moral standards. They must also have a thorough knowledge of the law, the Constitution, and American history.

Although the Constitution lists no qualifications for the position of Supreme Court justice, the way justices are selected helps ensure that they will be qualified for the job. The President chooses a justice from among

In *United States* v. *Nixon*, 1974, the Supreme Court, citing *Marbury* v. *Madison*, ruled that the Court, not the President, is the judge of the Constitution. The Court also ruled that Nixon could not use executive privilege to hide evidence of possible criminal actions in the Watergate scandal.

The Supreme Court justices in a 1991 portrait: (back row, left to right) David Souter, Antonin Scalia, Anthony Kennedy, Clarence Thomas; (front row, left to right) John Paul Stevens, Byron White, Chief Justice William Rehnquist, Harry Blackmun, Sandra Day O'Connor.

the most respected judges, lawyers, and legal scholars in the country. Then the Senate must approve the President's appointment.

Of the 106 justices who have served on the Court, all but three have been white men. The exceptions are Thurgood Marshall and Clarence Thomas, African-American men appointed in 1967 and 1991, and Sandra Day O'Connor, a white woman appointed in 1981. The Chief Justice's salary is $160,600 a year. Associate justices earn $153,600 a year.

The Work of the Supreme Court

The decisions of the nine justices of the Supreme Court can affect the lives of millions of people. How do the justices go about their work so that their decisions are as carefully reasoned and as fair as possible?

Selecting cases. Each year, the Court hears about 200 cases. By law, it must hear certain kinds of appeals from federal and state courts that involve the federal government or federal laws. It must also hear the few cases over which it has original jurisdiction. The remainder of the cases it hears each year are chosen from among the more than 4,000 requests for appeal it receives from lower courts in both the state and federal court systems. The cases the Court chooses are generally those that raise the most important constitutional issues.

Hearing arguments. When a case is put on the Court's calendar, each side in the case submits briefs, or written arguments. The justices study the briefs and other records of the case carefully. Then attorneys for each side present oral arguments before the Court. There are strict time limits on these arguments: each attorney is given half an hour. The justices usually ask many questions of the attorneys to challenge and clarify their arguments.

Making a decision. After hearing oral arguments for a case, the Court meets in conference to discuss that case and vote on it. Only the justices are allowed to attend. The Chief Justice leads the discussion of each case, summarizing it and offering an opinion. Then each justice has an opportunity to comment. Finally, the Chief Justice calls for a vote, with a simple majority deciding the case.

Writing opinions. Every Supreme Court decision is accompanied by an opinion, a written statement explaining the reasons for the decision. A Supreme Court opinion shows exactly

Teaching Note: For a discussion of a Supreme Court decision that affected the rights of children in juvenile courts, see "Issues that Affect You: A Case Study" on pages 232–233.

The Supreme Court lacks the power to enforce its own rulings, yet the President, Congress, other government officials, and private citizens comply with the Court's interpretation of the law. The Court is an embodiment of the ideal that ours is a "government of laws, not men."

how the law must be applied, or how the Constitution must be interpreted in a specific situation.

The Court's opinion in a case, called the majority opinion, is written by one of the justices in the majority—the winning side of the vote. A draft of the opinion is circulated among the justices and often modified to keep the support of the other justices in the majority.

A justice who agrees with the majority opinion but has different reasons for supporting it may write a concurring opinion. A justice who does not agree with the majority's decision may write a dissenting opinion.

After all opinions have been written and finalized, the justices announce their decision. Then copies of the opinions are distributed to news reporters.

Influences on Judicial Decision Making

What factors can influence how the justices vote when they decide a case? Like any judge, a justice is most concerned with the law and how it has been applied up to that point. The justices firmly believe that laws and the Constitution reflect the will of the people.

The justices, therefore, carefully review the laws involved in each case. They must consider all related precedents that have been established by any court. Precedent is always a factor in a justice's decision because a basic principle of the American legal system is to respect past judicial decisions. In this way we develop a consistent body of law.

The justices also try to determine the intentions of lawmakers at the time they made a particular law. For a constitutional question, for example, the justices may read historical documents such as the Federalist papers to try to determine the intent of the framers.

However, it is not always clear how the law should be applied to a particular case. The cases you read about in Chapter 7, for example, involved complex issues in which arguments for either side could be seen to be most in agreement with the Constitution.

The issues the Court must decide—such as abortion, discrimination, and prayer in the schools—tend to be those about which people feel strongly. Although Supreme Court justices try to be impartial and to respect precedent, it can be difficult for them to put aside their personal views completely. The justices, after all, are only human.

Knowing that the personal views of Supreme Court justices can affect their decisions, Presidents will naturally try to appoint to the Court people who agree with their political views. A President hopes that if the appointee becomes a justice, he or she will favor the President's position on important issues.

AMERICAN NOTEBOOK

Before the justices meet to hear a case or to discuss a decision, each justice shakes hands with the other eight. This traditional practice, called the "conference handshake," was begun by Chief Justice Melville Fuller in the late 1800s. Its purpose is to remind the justices that differences of opinion do not mean that the Court cannot carry out its mission to promote "equal justice under law."

A Changing Court

Throughout its history, the Supreme Court has gone through important changes in how it views its role in government and how it interprets the Constitution. These changes have been the result of shifts in public opinion and in the justices' own personal beliefs.

Decision Making: Have students explain why the justices would need to use the following critical-thinking skills in deciding cases: determining the reliability of sources, identifying relevant information, and distinguishing statements of fact from opinions.

Louis Brandeis

Rarely has a Supreme Court justice been as outspoken an advocate of poor people and workers as was Justice Louis Brandeis. During his 22 years on the Supreme Court, Brandeis worked for social and economic reform, often dissenting from the majority vote to stand up for what he saw as being morally and legally correct.

Louis Dembitz Brandeis was born in 1856 in Louisville, Kentucky, the son of Jewish immigrants from what is now Czechoslovakia. A brilliant student, Brandeis entered Harvard Law School when he was 18. He graduated in 1877 with the highest average in the law school's history.

With a friend, Brandeis began a successful law practice in Boston, which soon made him wealthy. However, Brandeis chose to protect the rights of the average American, often arguing cases without charging fees for his services. He supported public causes so actively that he soon became known throughout the nation as the "people's attorney."

In 1916, President Woodrow Wilson nominated Brandeis to the Supreme Court. Brandeis became the first Jewish Supreme Court justice in the nation's history.

As a justice, Brandeis's commitment to protecting the rights of working people was reflected in his decisions on cases. Brandeis supported unions and small business, and he argued for a balance of economic power between owners and employees.

Above all, Brandeis was committed to promoting individual liberty. He believed that liberty is "the secret of happiness, and courage [is] . . . the secret of liberty." Freedom of speech was especially important to Brandeis. He held that "freedom to think as you will and to speak as you think are means indispensable to . . . political truth."

In Chapter 7 you read about cases that showed how the Supreme Court's decisions have changed over time. The Court's view of citizenship and voting rights, for example, has changed greatly in the past 150 years.

Since the 1950s, the Court has seemed to have had three different "personalities," each reflecting the views of the Chief Justice at the time. From 1953 to 1969, the Supreme Court was called the "Warren Court" after its Chief Justice, Earl Warren. The Warren Court was known for its active defense of the rights of people accused of crimes.

One of the Warren Court's noted decisions was in the case of *Miranda* v. *Arizona*. In this case, the Court ruled that when a person is arrested, police must inform him or her of the constitutional rights to remain silent and to have the advice of a lawyer. The decisions of the Warren Court are examples of what is called ***judicial activism***, an effort by judges to take an active role in policymaking by overturning laws relatively often.

From 1969 to 1986, Warren Burger was Chief Justice. The decisions of the "Burger Court" differed from those of the Warren

Discussion: William Howard Taft, 27th President of the United States and 9th Chief Justice of the Supreme Court, called Louis Brandeis a "radical." Have students discuss which of Brandeis's beliefs might have caused Taft to use this label.

Court in that they were more likely to uphold existing laws. The Burger Court, however, made one of the most controversial decisions of this century when it overturned a state law in the case of *Roe* v. *Wade*. In this case the Supreme Court said that no state could make a law that forbids a woman to have an abortion.

The Court today is often called the "Rehnquist Court," after Chief Justice William Rehnquist. The Rehnquist Court has shifted even more than the Burger Court towards ***judicial restraint***, an effort by judges to avoid overturning laws and to leave policy-making up to the other two branches of government.

The Senate rejected Robert Bork's nomination as Supreme Court justice. He is shown during confirmation hearings in the Senate.

The Court and the Other Branches of Government

Judicial review gives the Supreme Court an important check on the power of the legislative and the executive branches. Although some people argue that appointed judges should not have what amounts to veto power over laws passed by elected legislators, nearly everyone agrees that the overall system of checks and balances prevents even the most active Court from abusing its power.

The President's power. One of the checks on the Supreme Court is the President's power to appoint justices. This extremely important power, however, can be exercised only when a justice dies or retires, creating an opening on the Court. President Carter, for example, was not able to appoint a single Supreme Court justice. President Reagan, in contrast, appointed three justices and promoted one to Chief Justice. President Reagan's appointments have had a marked influence on the Court. They have increased the chances that many of his policy goals will be carried out, even though he has left office.

The power of Congress. The Senate can check the power of both the President and the Supreme Court by refusing to confirm presidential appointments to the Supreme Court. In this way, Congress can weed out appointees who, it believes, are unsuited for the job, or who have beliefs contrary to those of the majority of Americans.

Public opinion can play an important role in the Senate's confirmation process because senators must be responsive to their constituents. Out of the 144 people who have been nominated by a President to be a Supreme Court justice, 28 have not been confirmed.

Occasionally, a Supreme Court appointee becomes the focus of a political battle between the other two branches of government. Such a battle occurred in 1987 when President Reagan appointed Robert Bork. After four months of hearings, the Senate refused to confirm Bork. His opponents convinced many Americans and a majority of senators that his views were outside of the mainstream.

In 1991 Clarence Thomas, appointed by President Bush, also faced intense questioning

Challenge (Evaluation): In 1987, a nominee for the Supreme Court withdrew his name from consideration after admitting that he had smoked marijuana earlier in his life. Have students discuss the importance of past behavior in determining a nominee's worthiness to be a Supreme Court justice.

Teaching Note: Use the Enrichment Activity, page T 90, and accompanying worksheet in the Activity Book after students have read the material in this section.

by the Senate Judiciary Committee. Thomas, however, was confirmed in a close vote.

Another important way that Congress can check the power of the Court is to begin the process that could result in a constitutional amendment. If ratified by the states, an amendment proposed by Congress can nullify, or cancel out, a Supreme Court decision. When the Thirteenth Amendment was ratified in 1865, for example, it nullified the Supreme Court's decision in the Dred Scott case.

Citizen participation. Because of the system of checks and balances, no branch of government has final, or ultimate, power over another. Citizens, therefore, always have at least one avenue through which they can try to influence policies. If the Supreme Court, for example, makes a decision that goes against the wishes of a majority of Americans, citizens can always turn to Congress and the amendment process, or they can elect a President who promises to appoint justices whose ideas they like. If citizens wish to make such changes happen, however, they must do more than hold a view—they must participate in government.

Answers will be found on page T 90.

Section Review

1. Define *judicial review, judicial activism,* and *judicial restraint.*
2. How did the case *Marbury* v. *Madison* allow the Supreme Court to assert the power of judicial review?
3. What two checks does Congress have on the power of the Supreme Court?

Synthesis. What does it mean when we say the Supreme Court is the "highest court in the land"?

A BROADER VIEW

The government of every nation in the world makes use of some kind of judicial system to apply and interpret its laws. Not every nation, however, has given its highest national court the kind of power exercised by the Supreme Court of the United States.

One hundred and fifty years ago, the Supreme Court was the only court of its kind in the world. It was then that the French writer Alexis de Tocqueville traveled to the United States to observe how our government worked. Later he wrote about the Supreme Court he had studied in America:

> I am unaware that any nation of the globe has heretofore [up to now] organized a judicial power in the same manner as the Americans. . . . A more imposing judicial power was never constituted by any people.

Since de Tocqueville's time, many nations have used our Supreme Court as a model for creating their own national high court. Today, about 60 nations, including Japan and Australia, have high courts with the power of judicial review—the authority to overturn laws made by legislatures.

In the remainder of the world's countries, in contrast, the final authority for deciding the validity of laws belongs to the legislature that creates the laws. This is true in Great Britain and many of the world's other democracies. Courts in these countries apply the laws and interpret them, but they cannot declare a law invalid.

Teaching Note: Use the Evaluating Progress activity, page T 89, to assess students' understanding of the chapter.

Jerry Gault and Juvenile Rights

On June 15, 1964, fifteen-year-old Jerry Gault was sentenced to six years of confinement in the Arizona Industrial School for juvenile delinquents. If Jerry had been over eighteen, his punishment would have been no greater than a fifty dollar fine or two months in jail.

Jerry's experience with the legal system had begun earlier that month. Jerry's neighbor, Mrs. Cook, reported to the police that Jerry and a friend had made "lewd and indecent" remarks to her over the telephone. Jerry was arrested, and after two hearings a juvenile court judge decided that Jerry had violated an Arizona law. The law prohibits anyone from using "vulgar, abusive, or obscene language" in the hearing of a woman or a child.

Neither Jerry nor his parents, however, had received official notice of the two hearings at which Jerry's guilt and punishment were determined. Mrs. Cook was not present at either hearing and was never questioned. Jerry confessed at his hearings that he was involved in the incident, but no lawyer was present to plead Jerry's case before the judge.

Mr. and Mrs. Gault filed a petition with the Arizona State Supreme Court asking that Jerry be released. They argued that their son had been denied the due process of law guaranteed by the Constitution. Jerry had not been told of his right to remain silent, said the Gaults, nor had he been properly informed of the charges against him. He was also denied both the right to question the person who accused him and the right to have the help of a lawyer.

Mrs. Cook was not present at either hearing and was never questioned about the incident.

The Arizona Supreme Court, however, denied the Gaults' request for Jerry's release. The court explained that ever since special courts for juveniles were established, "wide differences have been tolerated—indeed insisted upon—between the . . . rights [given] to adults and those of juveniles."

What the court was referring to was an established policy of treating juveniles in the criminal justice system differently from adults. This policy had developed out of a concern in the late 1800s that youths were being given long prison terms and mixed in jails with hardened adult criminals. Legal reformers had called for special juvenile courts and procedures to protect youngsters from such treatment. Concluding that the existence of a special juvenile justice system allowed youths to be treated differently, the court ruled that Jerry had not been de-

Jerry and his parents received only informal notice of the two hearings. In one case, Jerry was told about the hearing orally; in the other case, a court officer gave him a note written on a plain piece of paper.

Answers will be found on page T 91.

nied his constitutional rights to due process.

Still convinced that their son had been treated unfairly, the Gaults appealed the Arizona court's decision to the United States Supreme Court. After reviewing the record, the Supreme Court reversed the Arizona court's decision. It said that Jerry had indeed been deprived of his constitutional rights in the juvenile court hearings. The Court stated that "neither man nor child can be allowed to stand condemned by methods that flout [ignore] constitutional requirements of due process."

The Court first of all rejected the state court's decision that proper notice, as required by the Sixth Amendment, had been given to the Gaults. The Court declared that due process "does not allow a hearing to be held in which a youth's freedom and his parents' right to custody are at stake" without official notice of all charges being given in advance.

The Court also concluded that Jerry had been deprived of his Fifth Amendment right to remain silent when questioned by authorities. The Court said that "it would be surprising if the privilege against self-incrimination were available to hardened criminals but not to children." Because Jerry had not been informed of this right to remain silent, any confession he may have made could not be used as evidence against him, said the Court.

"Neither man nor child can be allowed to stand condemned by methods that flout constitutional requirements of due process."

In addition, the Court ruled that Jerry had been denied his Sixth Amendment right to face and cross-examine all witnesses. In this case, Mrs. Cook, who had made the accusations, was not even present at either of Jerry's hearings in juvenile court. Due process, said the Court, requires that the right to cross-examine be given to juveniles as well as to adults.

Finally, the Supreme Court ruled that Jerry had been deprived of his Sixth Amendment right to have a lawyer assist him in his defense. The Court concluded that where freedom is in question, "a juvenile requires the guiding hand of counsel at every step of the proceedings against him."

Analyzing the Case

1. According to the Supreme Court decision, which due process rights was Jerry denied?
2. Which two lower courts had their decisions reversed by the decision of the United States Supreme Court?
3. In your opinion, if Jerry had been given all of his due process rights but still had been found guilty of violating the law, should he have been given a six-year sentence? In general, do you think juveniles should be treated differently from adults?

Discussion: The Supreme Court declared that official notice of all charges in advance, as required by the Sixth Amendment, had not been given to the Gaults. Have students discuss why such advance notice is necessary.

CHAPTER SURVEY

Answers to Survey and Workshop will be found on page T 91.

UNDERSTANDING NEW VOCABULARY

Seeing Relationships

The vocabulary terms in each pair listed below are related to each other. For each pair, explain how the two terms are related.

Example: The *plaintiff* and the *prosecution* both bring cases to court—the plaintiff to civil court and the prosecution to criminal court.

1. *original jurisdiction* and *appellate jurisdiction*

2. *plaintiff* and *defendant*

3. *prosecution* and *defendant*

4. *precedent* and *judicial restraint*

Putting It in Writing

Using the terms *precedent* and *judicial review,* write a paragraph or two explaining how the Supreme Court, through its decisions, is able to have an important effect on our society.

LOOKING BACK AT THE CHAPTER

1. What job does the judge perform in a court of law?

2. When is a court able to interpret a law?

3. How are the state and federal court systems connected?

4. Trials are held in courts with what kind of jurisdiction?

5. Describe the job of an appeals court.

6. Which federal courts were established by the Constitution?

7. If appealed, a federal district court's decision is reviewed by which kind of federal court?

8. Over what kinds of cases does the Supreme Court have original jurisdiction?

9. Compare the way federal judges and members of Congress are chosen.

10. What is true about many of the cases that the justices of the Supreme Court choose to hear?

11. Explain the power of judicial review. In which Supreme Court case was it established as a precedent?

12. What check does the President have on the power of the Supreme Court?

13. *Application.* Susan claims that her First Amendment rights have been violated. Will she bring her case to a federal or to a state court? Will her case be civil or criminal?

14. *Analysis.* What is the difference between judicial activism and judicial restraint?

15. *Analysis.* Why is there no jury in a federal court of appeals?

16. *Evaluation.* What advantages would there be to electing Supreme Court justices instead of having Presidents appoint them? What would the disadvantages be? Which selection process do you believe is best?

17. *Evaluation.* Do you think the framers of the Constitution would have approved of a Supreme Court that was guided by judicial activism?

WORKING TOGETHER

1. If the Supreme Court is in session, collect newspaper articles and editorials about current Supreme Court decisions. Then, in a small group, select a recent decision and make a report to the class about it. Tell what the issue is, who the parties in the conflict are, and what effects the Court's decision will have or may have.

2. With two or three other students, prepare a wall chart showing the sixteen Chief Justices who have served on the Supreme Court. Include the dates they served and the Presidents who appointed them. This information can be found in most encyclopedias.

SKILLS WORKSHOP

Teaching Note: For reinforcement of decision-making skills, use Decision-Making Worksheet Chapter 10.

SOCIAL STUDIES SKILLS

Analyzing Newspaper Editorials

Newspapers cover the Supreme Court on both their news pages and editorial pages. Editorials express the opinion of the newspaper editors on the Court's decisions.

In 1977 the Supreme Court was asked to rule whether corporal punishment, or paddling, of students by school officials violates the Eighth Amendment ban on "cruel and unusual punishment." The Court ruled that it did not, saying, "The schoolchild has little need for the protection of the Eighth Amendment." The *New York Times* commented on this decision in an editorial entitled "Paddling Justice."

> The Supreme Court, by a 5-to-4 majority and a tortuous [twisted] bit of reasoning, has decided that school children enjoy no constitutional protection against paddling or corporal punishment, no matter how severe or arbitrary. . . . Each member of the errant majority deserves at least five whacks. . . .
>
> The Court's reluctance to bring children under the cloak of the Constitution—denying them the rights afforded adult criminals—tells much about a strongly entrenched American attitude that [strict discipline is good for children]. A judge of the Indiana Supreme Court posed the proper question as long ago as 1853, when he noted that it had become illegal for a husband to beat his wife . . . and asked, "Why the person of the schoolboy should be less sacred . . . is not easily explained." Indeed it is not.

1. What is the editorial writer's opinion of the Court's decision? How does the writer reveal his or her point of view?

2. How does the writer support this viewpoint?

3. According to the writer, what caused the Court to decide the way it did?

DECISION-MAKING SKILLS

What Relates to Your Subject?

Suppose you wanted to learn more about the subject of the judicial branch's power. Determine which of the following statements contain information that is relevant to your subject. If necessary, refer to the procedure described on page 190.

A. The Supreme Court may declare a law unconstitutional only as a result of hearing a specific case.

B. Sam Ervin of North Carolina had been a state supreme court judge before coming to the Senate. He was considered to be the Senate Judiciary Committee's expert on the Constitution.

C. Since 1803, over 1,000 state and local laws, as well as more than 100 federal laws, have been overturned by the Supreme Court's use of judicial review.

D. Of the 104 justices who have served on the Supreme Court, all but two have been white men.

E. The Chief Justice receives a salary of over $100,000 a year.

F. Three new justices appointed by Ronald Reagan in the 1980s all showed a tendency toward judicial restraint.

G. Oliver Wendell Holmes was one of the most famous justices in the history of the Supreme Court.

1. Which of the above statements contain information that is relevant to the subject of judicial power? Explain your answer.

2. Explain how to determine whether information is relevant to a given subject.

3. Name a decision that you might make soon where you could use the skill of recognizing relevant information. Explain how the skill would help you make a good decision.

IN THEIR OWN WORDS

Theodore Roosevelt: "I believe in a strong executive" Answers will be found on page T 92.

During his two terms as President, from 1901 to 1909, Theodore Roosevelt faced many challenges at home and abroad. The United States was suffering growing pains as a result of becoming an industrial giant and a world power.

Roosevelt believed that in order to lead the United States through these difficult times, he must push the powers of the presidency to their limit. In doing so, he received much criticism. Some people accused him of usurping, or taking away, power from the other two branches. On June 19, 1908, Roosevelt wrote a letter in which he defended his belief in a strong presidency.

> While President I have *been* President, emphatically; I have used every ounce of power there was in the office and have not cared a rap for the criticisms of those who spoke of my "usurpation of power;" for I knew that the talk was all nonsense and that there was no usurpation.
>
> I believe that the efficiency of this Government depends upon its possessing a strong central executive, and wherever I could [I established] a precedent for strength in the executive, as I did . . . in the case of sending the fleet around the world, taking Panama, settling affairs of Santo Domingo and Cuba; or as I did . . . in settling the anthracite coal strike, in keeping order in Nevada [during a strike by miners], or as I have done in [controlling] the big corporations. . . . In all these cases I have felt not merely that my action was right in itself, but that in showing the strength of, or in giving strength to, the executive, I was establishing a precedent of value.
>
> I believe in a strong executive; I believe in power; but I believe that responsibility should go with power. . . . Above all and beyond all I believe as I have said before that the salvation of this country depends upon Washington and Lincoln representing the type of leader to which we are true.
>
> I hope that in my acts I have been a good President, a President who has deserved well of the Republic; but most of all, I believe that whatever value my service may have comes even more from what I *am* than from what I *do*.
>
> I may be mistaken, but it is my belief that the bulk of my countrymen, the men whom Abraham Lincoln called "the plain people"—the farmers, mechanics, small tradesmen, hard-working professional men—feel that I am in a peculiar sense their President, that I represent the democracy in somewhat the fashion that Lincoln did, that is . . . with the sincere effort to stand for a government by the people and for the people.

From a letter written in 1908 to G. O. Trevelyan.

Analyzing Primary Sources

1. According to Roosevelt, what is the value of having "a strong central executive"?
2. What does Roosevelt believe should go along with power?
3. Which President does Roosevelt compare himself to?
4. Roosevelt says that his value as a President "comes even more from what I *am* than from what I *do*." What does he mean by this? Do you agree?

Activity: Have students compare the current President's actions with President Roosevelt's actions. Does the current President use "every ounce of power" there is in the office? Do students think that today's executive branch is too strong? Why or why not?

UNIT SURVEY

Answers will be found on page T 92.

LOOKING BACK AT THE UNIT

1. The following are events in the life of a law. Write them in the correct time order.

(a) The President signs the bill into law.

(b) The citizen appeals the court decision to a federal court of appeals.

(c) Both houses of Congress pass the bill.

(d) A senator writes the proposed law as a bill.

(e) The President proposes the law.

(f) A federal district court finds a citizen guilty of violating the law.

(g) The President gives an executive department authority to enforce the law.

2. For each of the following events, tell which branches of the federal government play an *active* role.

(a) A Supreme Court justice is appointed and confirmed.

(b) A law is declared unconstitutional.

(c) A treaty is signed and approved.

(d) War has not been declared, but troops are sent to a foreign country for two weeks.

3. Choose two of the three branches of the federal government. Describe the checks each branch has on the power of the other. What is the importance of each of these checks?

TAKING A STAND

The Issue

Should the minimum wage be increased every year?

Many people with little training or education can get only low-skilled jobs. As you learned in Chapter 8, a new minimum wage law raised the pay of such workers to $3.80 an hour. That law, however, has not ended the debate on the issue. Some people are pushing to increase the minimum wage every year, while others oppose raising it.

Supporters of raising the wage point out that between 1981 and 1987 it remained at $3.35 an hour, but the cost of living soared 27 percent. If the wage does not increase every year, they point out, minimum wage workers with families to support may be forced into poverty. A full-time worker who earns $3.80 an hour makes about $8,000 a year. This may be less than a family of four needs for basic food, clothing, shelter, and health care.

Opponents, however, warn that yearly increases in the minimum wage would throw more people out of work. Employers could not afford to have as many employees. Some people estimate that an increase of a dollar in the minimum wage could mean that half a million jobs would be lost. Or perhaps businesses would pass the higher labor costs on to consumers in the form of higher prices.

Opponents also claim that only 25 percent of minimum wage workers are heads of families. A full 37 percent are teenagers working only for pocket money to buy movie tickets, music cassettes, and so on.

Teenagers reply that they depend on their jobs for a lot more than pocket money. Some help support their families, and some are saving for college. Even if you work 20 hours a week and save every penny, they say, earning $3.80 an hour means you can save only about $3,500 in a year—barely enough to pay for one semester at a state college.

Expressing Your Opinion

How do you stand on this issue? Imagine that you are a representative. You must make a one-minute speech in the House of Representatives, arguing either that the minimum wage should be raised or that it should stay the same. Write down your main points on a sheet of paper or file cards so you can glance at them while you speak. Practice your speech until it goes smoothly, so you will feel confident in front of your fellow representatives.

UNIT 4
TOWN HALL
TOWN OFFICES

Unit Quotation: Under federalism, the federal government deals with issues affecting all citizens, while each state government serves the particular needs of its people. The Tenth Amendment confirms that the states or the people retain all powers not given to the national government.

STATE AND LOCAL GOVERNMENT

Sharing the Powers of Government

The Powers not delegated to the United States by the Constitution, nor prohibited by it to the states, are reserved to the states respectively, or to the people.

—Tenth Amendment to the United States Constitution

The three branches of the federal government make and carry out many of the policies that affect you as a citizen. However, the federal government is only one level of government that responds to the needs of Americans. On another level, each of the 50 states has its own government. The states have also set up over 83,000 local governments. All three levels of government—federal, state, and local—share the costs and responsibilities for the many programs and services they provide for their citizens.

In Unit 4 you will learn about how state and local governments are organized and what powers they have. You will also see that they offer you many opportunities to participate directly in the process of government.

Chapter 11 State Government

Chapter 12 Local Government

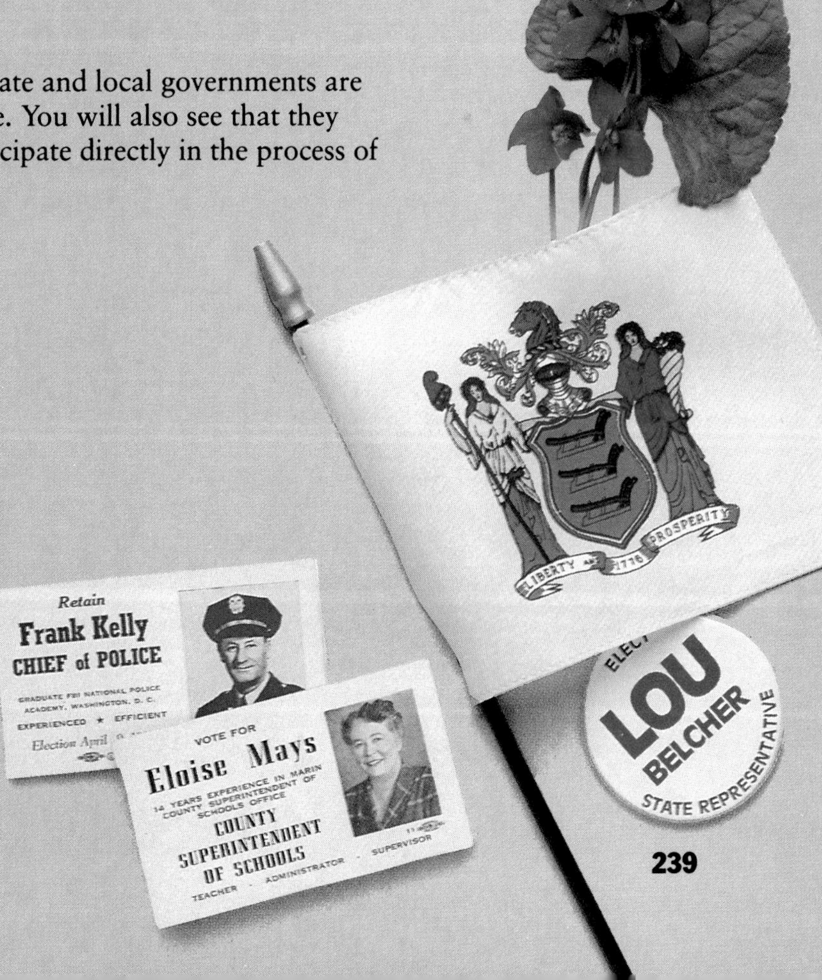

Chapter Themes: States carry out much of the work of meeting the needs of citizens. The three branches of state government not only have separate powers but also limit each other's powers through checks and balances. In addition, citizens can have a great influence on state lawmaking.

CHAPTER 11

State Government

In recent years, the public school system in Chicago, Illinois, has received a lot of bad publicity. William Bennett, a former United States Secretary of Education, labeled it "the worst in the country." Test scores, while not completely proving Bennett's claim, showed that the system had major problems. In many schools, students were reading two or three grades below the national average, and math scores were far below the national average. The drop-out rate in some high schools was above 50 percent.

Educational experts and the general public agreed: if Chicago's schools were to improve, the Illinois state government would have to make major changes in the system. Throughout 1988, state legislators and government officials met in Springfield, the state capital, to try to put together a reform plan to help the schools. However, state legislators could not agree on certain points in the plan, nor did they agree with the governor's ideas on reform. By November, the chances that the plan would become law seemed slim.

Then a group of about 50 Chicago students decided to take the matter into their own hands. They traveled to Springfield to lobby legislative leaders for reform. "I think we need to remind the legislators what this means to us," said one student. They reminded the governor, too, by delivering to his office a huge stack of handwritten letters supporting the reform plan. Their action had the desired effect. The following day the governor announced that all sides had settled their differences. By the end of the week the state legislature had approved the plan.

In this chapter you will learn about state governments, their powers, and how they are organized. You will discover that you, like the students in Chicago, can make a difference in the policies that affect your everyday life.

Teaching Note: Use the Introducing the Chapter activity, page T 94.

Teaching Note: For information on the 50 states, see page 597.

11-1

FEDERALISM: ONE NATION AND FIFTY STATES

Read to Find Out

- what the terms *public assistance* and *constitutional initiative* mean.
- what powers the states have.
- how state constitutions are similar to and different from the federal Constitution.
- what some strengths and weaknesses of the federal system are.

The national government is only one level of our government. Each of the 50 states also has its own government. If your public school system had problems like those in Chicago, would you write a letter to the President? Probably not, because most of the laws and policies that affect the public schools are made by state and local governments, not by the government in Washington, D.C.

In fact, our state governments carry out much of the work of meeting the needs of citizens. These governments have major responsibility for public education, transportation, and health and safety. How do you know which tasks and services belong to the national government and which belong to the states? The answer to this question will give you a better picture of the role of state governments.

Powers of the States

Some delegates at the Constitutional Convention of 1787 argued that only a strong national government could handle the problems facing the country. Other delegates wanted the states to keep most of the power.

In trying to bring together these points of view and "to form a more perfect union," the framers settled on the system of federalism. Federalism divides some powers between the national and state governments while allowing them to share other powers. The Constitution lists what the powers of the national government are. They include the power to declare war, make treaties with other countries, and coin money.

The Constitution does not specifically list the powers of the states. Instead, the Tenth Amendment gives to the states or to the people all powers not given to the national government nor denied to the states. Powers that the states alone hold include the power to set up local governments, conduct elections, set up public school systems, and oversee businesses. The states also make laws protecting the health and safety of their residents, such as traffic laws.

The national government and state governments also share many powers. They both collect taxes, borrow money, set up courts, enforce laws, and punish lawbreakers. Both levels of government may also provide ***public assistance***, government programs that

AMERICAN NOTEBOOK 

Every state has a motto. Here are a few examples.

Alaska: *North to the Future*
Illinois: *State Sovereignty–National Unity*
Maryland: *Fatti Maschii, Parol Femine (Manly Deeds, Womanly Words)*
New Hampshire: *Live Free or Die*
New York: *Excelsior (Ever Upward)*
North Carolina: *Esse Quam Videri (To Be Rather Than to Seem)*
Texas: *Friendship*
West Virginia: *Montani Semper Liberi (Mountaineers Are Always Free)*
Wyoming: *Equal Rights*

John Dickinson of Delaware, a delegate to the Constitutional Convention, declared that the system of federalism would be like the solar system. "The states," he said, "were the planets and ought to be left to move freely in their proper orbits."

give help to people in need. Often called welfare, this help can include money for people below a certain income level, food for the hungry, and services such as health care.

State Constitutions

Before the United States Constitution was written, each state already had its own constitution. In fact, those early constitutions became models for our national Constitution.

New states joined the union under rules stated in the Northwest Ordinance of 1787. Under those rules, when a territory wants to become a state, it must prepare a constitution, setting up its own plan of government. The constitution then has to be approved by the people of the territory and by Congress. Finally, Congress votes on whether to admit the state.

In 1954, citizens of Hawaii showed their desire for statehood by signing this petition, which they rolled up and sent to Washington.

Content and structure. The federal Constitution contains a little over 7,000 words. The constitution of the state of Alabama has about 174,000 words. Why this great difference? One reason is that state constitutions are more detailed. For example, the federal Constitution simply states that the legislative branch of government has the power to levy and collect taxes. In contrast, many state constitutions list exactly what kinds of taxes may be levied and how they may be collected.

Although different in length, most state constitutions are similar in form to the United States Constitution. All state constitutions begin with a preamble, describing the purposes of the state government. Each state constitution also includes a bill of rights, similar to the federal Bill of Rights, listing the freedoms guaranteed to all the state's citizens. However, some state constitutions offer fuller protection for individual rights and freedoms. The Illinois constitution, for example, guarantees equal rights for women.

Like our federal Constitution, all state constitutions establish legislative, executive, and judicial branches of government. The powers of these state branches are much the same as those of the national government. However, state constitutions describe these powers in great detail.

Changes. Because state constitutions are so detailed, they are often less flexible than the federal Constitution. Therefore, they are more likely to be changed as conditions and needs change.

The most common way to change a state constitution is by amendment, usually proposed by the state legislature. In all states but Delaware, the amendment must be approved by a majority of voters.

In 17 states, citizens may initiate, or begin, change by ***constitutional initiative***, a process in which citizens propose an amendment by gathering a required number of signatures on a petition. When enough people have signed the petition, the amendment goes to the voters for approval.

A state can also rewrite its constitution. Rewriting a constitution most often requires a constitutional convention, which must first be approved by the voters. The rewritten constitution must also go to the people for a vote. Of more than 230 state constitutional conventions in our nation's history, a little more than half have resulted in new constitutions.

Federalism in Action

Some people think of federalism as being like a layer cake. In this view, "layers" of government—national and state—are seen as separate, with different powers. In action, however, federalism is more like a marble cake, with the powers mixed and overlapping.

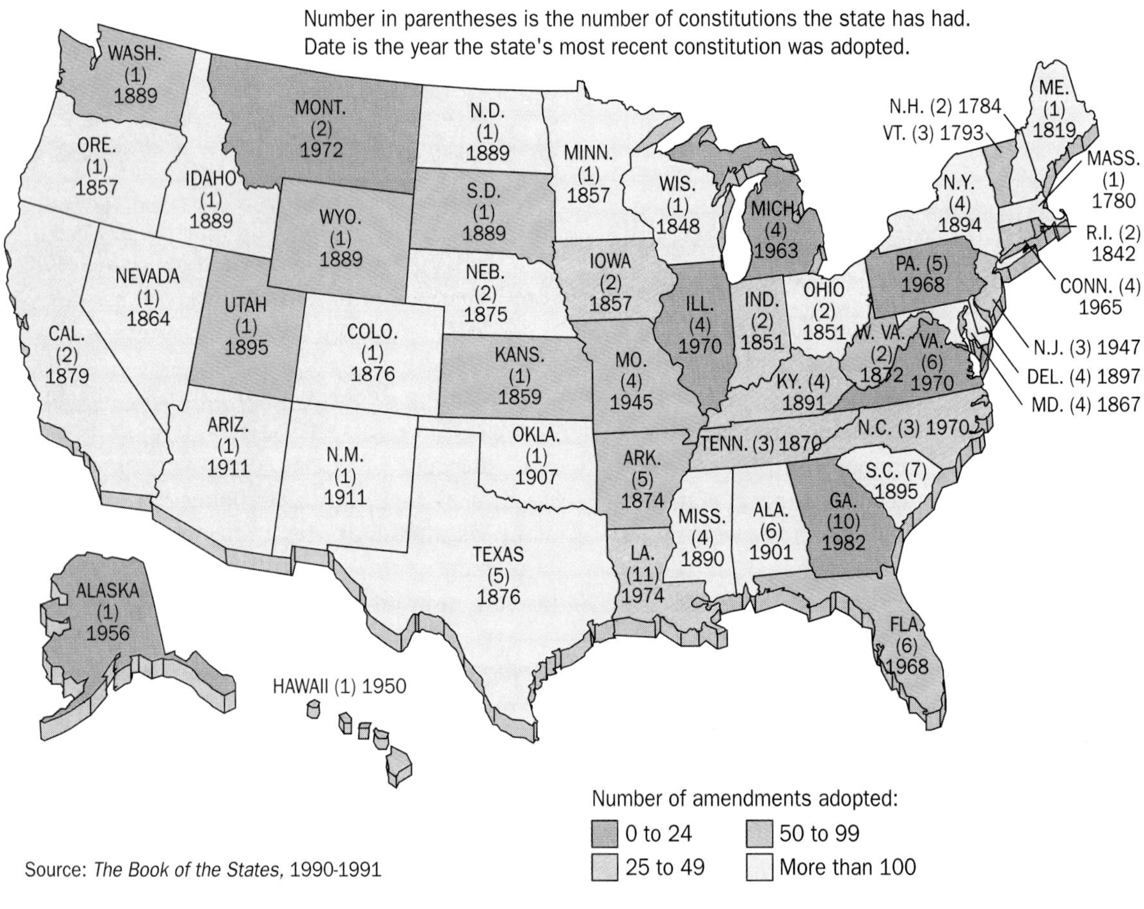

State Constitutions. *Unlike the United States Constitution, the constitutions of most states have been changed many times.*

The initiative process is an important device for citizens to use if legislatures do not respond to their demands. However, initiative power can be abused by interest groups.

This photograph shows an example of federalism in action. When a tanker spilled millions of gallons of oil off the coast of Alaska in 1989, the state asked the federal government to help with the clean up.

The way the powers of national government and state governments mix and overlap is not set, but continues to change. Some people press to keep the national government out of what they see as the states' business. Others think that the national government should have greater power over the states in certain matters.

Power to the states. Those in favor of states' rights point out that the states differ greatly, and therefore state governments can serve their people better than the national government can. State governments, they argue, should be allowed to fit laws and programs to the particular needs of their states. For example, states with large cities need more low-cost housing, health care, and public transportation than do states with mostly farmland.

People who favor states' rights also point out that citizens often feel closer to their state governments than to the federal government. James Madison recognized this point of view when he wrote that "the first and most natural attachment of the people will be to the governments of their respective States."

Dividing power can also make it easier for each level of government to do its job. When states take responsibility for local issues such as education, job training, and transportation, the national government can then focus its attention on its major responsibilities.

Finally, state governments can experiment with new programs which may later be adopted by other states or even by the national government. North Carolina Senator Terry Sanford said, "States are much more innovative [able to try new ideas] and able to get things going faster than the national government." For example, a job-training program in California has seen success in meeting one of the toughest problems facing government—unemployment. Other states might choose to start similar programs.

Power to the national government. Those who favor a strong role for the national government point out that state laws and services vary widely. As a result, the opportunities in different states are not always equal. In the past, as you read in Chapter 7, some states denied blacks the right to vote and to attend school with whites.

Today some states might spend more money per student on education or offer more special programs, such as computer education, than other states. Thus, critics of states' rights argue, the national government needs to play a stronger role to ensure equal opportunity for people in all the states.

Challenge (Analysis): Have students discuss what the United States would be like if the government operated under a unitary rather than a federal system. Under the unitary system, the state governments have only those powers that the central government gives them.

Teaching Note: Use Teaching Activity 1, page T 94, as a culminating activity after students have read the material in Section 11-1.

In addition, most citizens see that some problems are too big for individual states to solve. Building a dam to control floods or to provide electric power may cost more than a state can afford. Sometimes, too, a problem involves several states. One example is in environmental issues. If one state's factories are causing acid rain in another state, the national government might have to step in.

"New federalism." In general, the power of the national government has grown as our nation has grown. Beginning in the 1930s, the national government took on added responsibilities in response to economic problems, wars, and the growth of big business.

In the 1980s, President Reagan asked Congress to support a plan returning greater power to state and local governments. He called his plan "new federalism." He argued that citizens had lost control over basic decisions about "schools, welfare, roads, and even garbage collection." He stated that there were too many federal programs, making the national government "more unmanageable, more ineffective, more costly."

Reagan's plan involved giving states more responsibility for running programs such as public assistance. It also involved giving less federal money to the states. As you will see, many states have had difficulty making up this loss of money.

This attempt to create a new balance between the national government and the states raises questions for the future. Is it possible to change the trend toward a stronger national government? Should this trend be changed even if it means cutting back programs for the poor and the sick? Do the problems facing the nation in the 1990s require the national government to act, or are they better handled by the states? You can see that the conflicts over federalism are not just past history, but important issues today.

Answers will be found on page T 96.

Section Review

1. Define the terms *public assistance* and *constitutional initiative.*
2. Which powers do the states alone hold?
3. Why are most state constitutions longer than the federal Constitution?
4. What are some arguments for the federal government playing a strong role?

Synthesis. What evidence is there to support the "marble cake" view of federalism?

Data Search. Look on page 586 in the Data Bank. Compare the number of elected officials in state governments with the number in the federal government.

11-2

STATE LEGISLATURES

Read to Find Out

- what the terms *apportioned, initiative, referendum, recall, revenue, sales taxes, excise tax, income tax,* and *bonds* mean.
- how state legislatures are organized and what powers they have.
- how citizens can influence state lawmaking.
- how state government is paid for.

Because your state legislators usually get less news coverage than members of Congress do, you might be less aware of the activities of lawmakers in your state. However, state legislators make most of the laws that affect your day-to-day life.

Who Are State Legislators?

For much of the first 100 years of our nation's history, the states were mostly rural, with small populations. The demands on state gov-

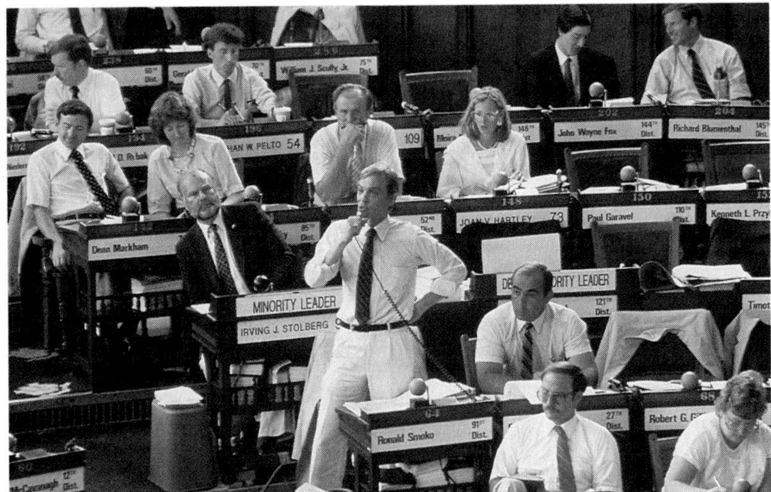

Members of the Connecticut House of Representatives debate a bill. Serving in a state legislature can be a full-time job.

ernments were not great. Legislators were citizens who would leave their jobs for a few weeks each year to go to legislative sessions. Most of these citizen legislators had jobs as farmers, lawyers, or business people.

Over time, however, the job of a state legislator grew more complex. The rapid growth of industries and cities led to new responsibilities for state government. As legislatures met more often and for longer sessions, citizen legislators found it difficult to balance their government duties with the demands of their jobs.

Today, most state legislators are full-time lawmakers. The typical legislator has studied political science, law, or public administration and has spent time in government service before running for office. Often state legislators plan on a life-long career in politics.

Qualifications and terms. Whether they serve full time or part time, state legislators have to meet certain qualifications. In all states, legislators must be United States citizens and live in the state and district they represent. Most states set the minimum age for representatives at 21, and for senators at 25. Some states have lowered these ages to 18 and 21.

In most states, senators serve four-year terms while representatives serve two-year terms. There is no limit on the number of terms a state legislator may serve. For example, L. Marion Gressette served for 35 years in the South Carolina legislature.

Organization of State Legislatures

All states except Nebraska have a bicameral, or two-house, legislature with the upper house called the senate. The lower house is usually known as the house of representatives, although in some states the lower house is called the assembly, general assembly, or house of delegates.

As with Congress, the upper house of state legislatures is smaller than the lower house. However, in the lower house, the proportion of representatives to the state's population varies widely. For example, the lower house in New Hampshire has 400 members to serve a population of about 920,000, while California has 80 members to represent more than 24 million people.

Sessions. State governments, like the national government, divide legislative terms into sessions. Most states hold annual sessions, while a few meet every other year. The majority of states limit the length of these sessions—anything from 20 days to 6 months.

In addition to being the only state with a unicameral legislature, Nebraska is the only state in which the state legislators are chosen in nonpartisan elections. Ballots for members of the legislature have no political party labels.

Decision Making: Have students imagine that they have an opportunity to use the initiative process. Have them choose an issue and develop an action plan for getting signatures to place it on the ballot.

However, the governor may call special sessions to handle urgent business.

Representation. Seats in state legislatures are ***apportioned***, or divided among districts, on the basis of equal representation. That is, state legislators represent districts that are roughly equal in population.

Apportionment was not always determined according to equal representation. Seats in upper houses used to be apportioned on a geographical basis, like the United States Senate. Apportionment of many lower houses was also geographical. As a result, one legislator might have represented a rural district with a few hundred people, while another represented all the people in a large city.

The United States Supreme Court set up the present system of apportionment in the case of *Reynolds* v. *Sims* (1964). Pointing out that legislators should "represent people, not trees or acres," the Court ruled that the apportionment of both houses of state legislatures must be based on population. Today, most states reapportion seats in their legislatures every ten years, based on the results of the United States census.

What State Legislatures Do

The major job of a state legislature is to make laws. By and large, the process is the same as in Congress. Bills are introduced, discussed in committees, and debated on the floor. Both houses must agree on the final bill, which the governor must then approve.

Powers of the people. A major difference between lawmaking in Congress and in state legislatures is that in some states citizens have a greater voice in the laws that are made. At the turn of the century, reformers known as "progressives" saw that powerful interest groups were having too much influence over state legislatures. The progressives wanted to "return the government to the people."

One of the progressives' ideas for giving lawmaking power to citizens is called the ***initiative***, the process by which citizens can propose laws. In this process, which is similar to the constitutional initiative, citizens gather signatures on a petition. When enough people have signed the petition (usually 5 to 10 percent of the registered voters), the proposed law is put to a vote in a statewide election.

If a majority of the voters approve the proposal, it becomes state law. Sometimes just knowing that people are preparing an initiative is enough to make a state legislature pass a law. The initiative is now permitted in 23 states.

Another way that citizens in some states can participate in lawmaking is the ***referendum***, the process by which a law proposed or passed by the state legislature is referred to the voters to approve or reject. Almost every state requires a referendum on constitutional amendments proposed by the legislature.

Both the initiative and referendum are ways that citizens can take lawmaking into their own hands. If enough people believe that a certain law is needed, or that a bad law should be removed, they can use the initiative or referendum.

Citizens in 12 states also have the power of ***recall***, a process for removing elected officials from office. A recall effort is usually begun by a group of citizens who believe that an official is not doing a good job. They may think the official is dishonest, or they may simply disagree with his or her policies.

Citizens begin a recall by gathering voters' signatures on a petition. If, in the recall election that follows, a majority of voters agree with the recall, the official must leave office. The recall, like the initiative and the referendum, is an important way that citizens can directly influence state governments.

The progressives, as their name suggests, believed in progress. They were certain that problems such as government corruption and poverty could be—and should be—solved. Many of their ideas were put into practice at the city, state, and national levels.

Checking the other branches. In keeping with the principle of checks and balances, state legislatures have the power to oversee, or to check, the activities of the executive and the judicial branches. In many states, the legislature must approve officials and judges who are appointed by the chief executive, the governor.

State legislatures also must approve the governor's budget. In this process, the legislature examines how well executive agencies—the departments, committees, boards, and offices that carry out the work of the executive branch—are doing their jobs. State legislators also review how federal funds are spent in their state.

Legislatures in every state except Oregon have the power to impeach, or bring charges against, executive and judicial officers and to determine their guilt or innocence. By and large, the impeachment process in the states is much the same as the process that is followed in Congress.

How the Fifty States Spend Their Money

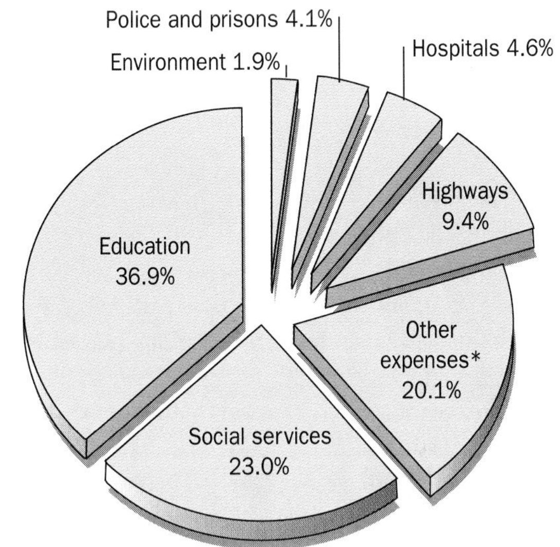

*Includes administration and insurance
Source: *The Book of the States,* 1990-1991

Financing State Government

State governments need money to meet the needs of citizens for such services as education, highways, health care, and environmental protection. In 1988 the cost of government in the 50 states was more than $432 billion. Since then, costs have been rising. The cost of state universities and colleges alone almost tripled in one ten-year period. Where does the money come from?

Taxes. States raise more than 50 percent of their ***revenue***, or income, from taxes. Most of state tax revenue comes from two sources: sales taxes and income taxes.

Most states have two kinds of ***sales taxes***, or charges made on purchases of goods and services. The general sales tax places a charge on almost all goods sold in a state. This charge usually is a percentage of the price of a product. For example, if you buy a $15 book in a state with a 6 percent sales tax, you will have to pay a tax of 6 percent of $15, or 90 cents. Therefore, you will pay a total of $15.90.

A second kind of sales tax is the ***excise tax***, a charge on certain goods, such as alcoholic beverages, gasoline, and tobacco. Most states also have an ***income tax***, a tax on what individuals and businesses earn. The income tax is a percentage of the money a person or business makes.

Other types of taxes also help states raise the money they need. For example, lumber and mining companies often must pay what is known as a severance tax on the timber, coal, gas, and oil they take from the land. All states also levy one or more of the taxes known as user fees. Charges for drivers' licenses and fees for fishing and hunting permits are examples of such fees.

Challenge (Analysis): Have students discuss why paying taxes is an important duty of citizens.

Teaching Note: Use Teaching Activity 2, page T 95, as a culminating activity after students have read the material in Section 11-2. For a discussion/activity on the issue of state use of lotteries, see "Taking a Stand" on page 283.

States choose which taxes they wish to use. New Hampshire depends on local property taxes, rather than on income taxes or sales taxes. Washington state voters have rejected an income tax, while voters in a neighboring state, Oregon, strongly oppose a sales tax.

Federal funds. Over time, state and local governments have increasingly turned to Congress for money. Federal money comes to the states in several forms. Two of the most widely used forms are categorical grants and block grants.

Categorical grants are given for specific purposes, such as a job training program or a special health program for pregnant women. These grants come with "strings attached"—certain conditions that must be met before the state may use the funds. For example, in the 1970s Congress wanted all the states to set a 55-mile-per-hour speed limit. To urge the states to go along with the plan, Congress threatened not to give highway funds to states that did not set this speed limit.

Block grants, on the other hand, are given for more general purposes. While a categorical grant might be for a special program such as health care for the homeless, a block grant might cover a broad area such as health care in general. The state can then decide which programs to use the block grant funds for.

As you learned earlier, in the 1980s the national government wanted to cut its spending. It also wanted to reduce its responsibility for making sure that state programs were running smoothly. Many categorical grants were combined into a few block grants, and the level of federal funding was greatly reduced.

Between 1981 and 1987, for example, the share of state funds that came from the national government fell from 25 percent to 17 percent. Hard pressed for money, many states raised their taxes in order to keep their programs running.

Other sources of revenue. Sometimes states borrow money by selling ***bonds***, certificates that people buy from the government. The government agrees to pay back the cost of the bond, plus interest, after a set period of time. States often use this method of raising revenue for such projects as building a school or convention center.

Some states also raise money through legalized gambling, most often lotteries. About 60 percent of the money from lottery ticket sales goes toward prizes. The remaining 40 percent goes to the state, usually to help pay for educational programs.

States with lotteries hope that the income they produce will fill the gap between tax revenues and the cost of state programs. However, even though you may hear about people winning multi-million-dollar prizes, lotteries have not fulfilled the states' dreams. No state receives more than 5 percent of its total revenue from a lottery. Further, some critics complain that any form of gambling is wrong, and the state should not encourage it. Others argue that the majority of lottery players are the people who can least afford to gamble—the poor. In spite of these criticisms, more and more states are using lotteries.

Answers will be found on page T 96.

Section Review

1. Define the terms *apportioned, initiative, referendum, recall, revenue, sales taxes, excise tax, income tax,* and *bonds.*
2. Why have citizen legislators been replaced by professional legislators in most states?
3. On what basis are seats in state legislatures apportioned?
4. Name two major sources of state revenue.

Analysis. In what ways are state legislatures more directly responsive to citizens than is Congress?

At least 75 percent of all federal aid to state and local governments is given in the form of categorical grants.

11-3

THE STATE EXECUTIVE BRANCH

Read to Find Out

- what the term *item veto* means.
- what roles the governor plays.
- how executive officials assist the governor.
- how state executive agencies operate.

The executive branch of state government is led by a governor and a group of executive officials. These officials help run the many agencies that enforce the laws and carry out the state's programs. Early state constitutions greatly limited the power of the governor. Over the years, however, many state constitutions have been changed in order to give the governor more power to take on the growing responsibilities of state government.

Ann Richards of Texas is one of a number of women who have been elected to serve as the governors of states.

The Roles of the Governor

If the state and federal executive branches are similar, would it be correct to describe the governor as the "president of the state"? Presidents and governors do play similar roles. However, there are differences between the two offices, as well.

Chief executive. The governor's role of chief executive is similar to that of the President. He or she oversees the executive branch and makes sure laws are enforced. The governor is commander-in-chief of the state militia, or National Guard, and can call on it in the event of a riot or disaster.

As chief executive, the governor has the power to appoint hundreds of officials to carry out the state's day-to-day work. However, as you will see, limits on governors' powers of appointment can greatly affect their ability to achieve their goals.

Perhaps the greatest source of executive power is the governor's budget-making role. Of course, the legislature must approve the governor's budget, and no state money may be spent without the legislature's approval. However, because the governor writes the budget, he or she still has a good deal of control over how much money various agencies get.

Legislative leader. Like the President, the governor also has legislative powers. To begin with, the governor may propose legislation in the form of a bill, a budget, or a speech to the state legislature. The governor can also influence lawmaking by talks with legislators or by whipping up public support, thus making clear what programs he or she wants lawmakers to set up and provide funds for.

Like the President, many governors, especially of states that have undergone recent reorganization, deliver or send to the legislature annual or biennial budget messages.

Another legislative power of the governor is the veto. In every state but North Carolina, the governor may veto any bill. Further, in 43 states governors have the ***item veto***, the power to reject particular parts, or items, of a bill. Presidents do not have this power. If they object to a part of a bill, they must reject the whole bill.

A state legislature may override the governor's veto. However, the veto, or even the threat of a veto, gives the governor a good deal of power over the legislature.

Judicial role. Like the President, a governor has certain judicial powers. For example, some state governors appoint certain state judges. The governor can also reduce or overturn the sentences of people convicted of crimes.

Qualifications and terms. In most states, a governor must be at least 25 or 30 years old, an American citizen, and a resident of the state. Terms of office are usually four years, and about half the states limit the number of terms a governor may serve in a row.

Other Executive Officials

A team of executive officials assists the governor. These officials include the lieutenant governor, a role similar to Vice-President; the secretary of state, who has charge of official records and documents and supervises

The Duties and Powers of the Governor

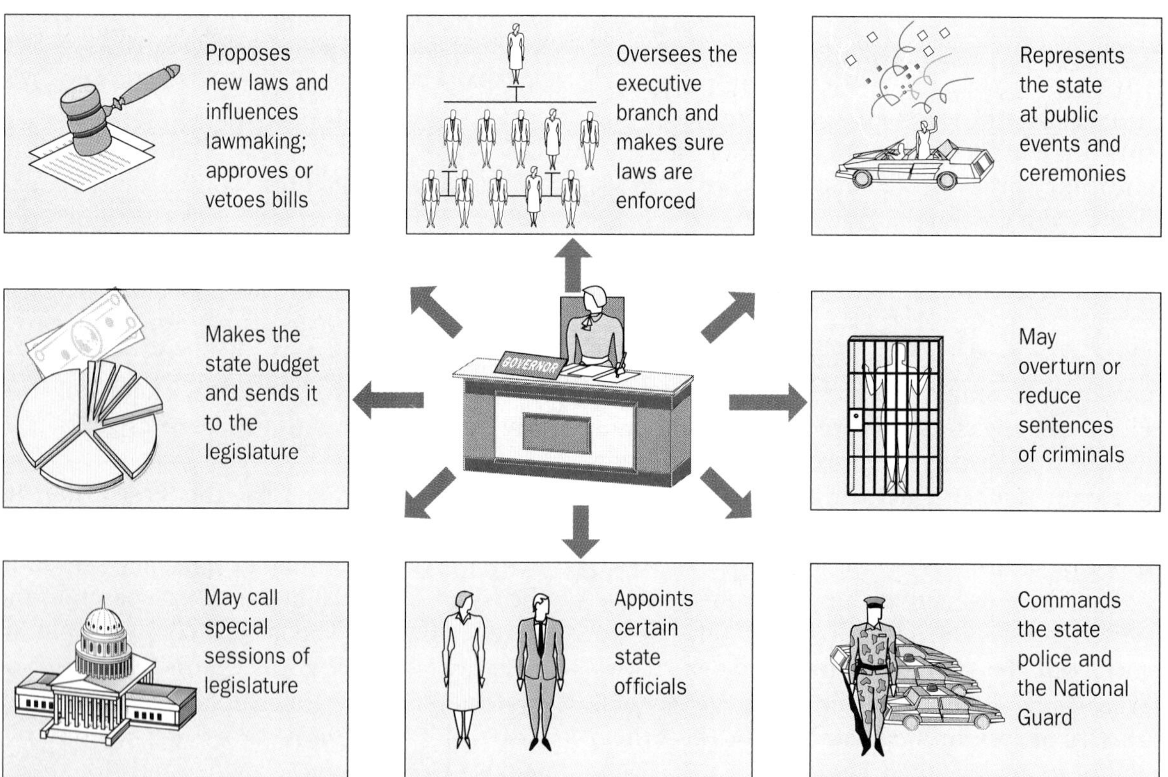

Challenge (Analysis): Have students discuss what problems might arise if the President had the power to use the item veto.

VIEWS OF NOTED AMERICANS

March Fong Eu

"If you want to have a say in your own future, you've *got* to get involved with your government." So says March Fong Eu, and she has followed this advice herself. Throughout her life, Dr. Eu has been "getting involved"—a path that led to her position as Secretary of State of California. Now she does all she can to encourage others to get involved in government.

March Fong Eu was born in the back room of her parent's hand laundry. She grew up speaking Chinese at home. Partly because her family was poor, she was determined to get a good education to increase her opportunities in life. In addition to studying, she got involved in cheerleading, sports, and student government. She also edited the school paper.

After college and a career in dental hygiene, Eu went back to school and earned a Doctor of Education degree.

In the 1950s, Dr. Eu left her career in health education to raise her children. She plunged into activities supporting the schools and soon was elected to the school board. Thus began many years of lobbying the California legislature about educational issues.

In 1966, having learned the importance of state government in the lives of citizens, Dr. Eu ran for a seat in the state assembly, the lower house of the California legislature. She was reelected four times before being elected Secretary of State in 1974.

As Secretary of State, Dr. Eu has the responsibility for all federal and state elections in California. She thinks that her most important contribution in office has been making it possible for voters to register by mail. Making registration easier for people, she claims, encourages more people to vote.

Dr. Eu believes in the federal system. "It makes sense for an overall federal government to handle national interests," she says. "Similarly, it's logical to leave the specifics . . . up to the states to manage where there can be more flexibility to meet the needs of their citizens."

As California's first elected state official of Asian ancestry, March Fong Eu knows that she is a role model for both women and Asians. Her advice to any student? "Study hard, . . . keep alert to the possibilities around you, keep your goals in sight, and believe in yourself."

elections; the attorney general, the state's chief legal officer; and the state treasurer, who oversees the state's financial affairs.

Some people have compared state executive officials to the President's Cabinet. However, Presidents can select their own Cabinet members, while most state executive officers are elected by the voters. Therefore, the governor may have to work with executive officials who do not share the same goals and may belong to a different political party.

Former Oregon governor Tom McCall describes the governor's problem: "We have to run our government like a pick-up orchestra,

Discussion: March Fong Eu declared, "If you want to have a say in your own future, you've *got* to get involved with your government." Have students discuss what Eu meant.

where the members meet at a dance, shake hands with each other, and start to play." You can see that the executive branch might not play in harmony. For example, the elected state superintendent of schools might favor a certain program that the governor has promised to eliminate.

State Executive Agencies

State executive agencies carry out the day-to-day work of the executive branch. Departments of health, revenue, and natural resources are examples of executive agencies.

To better understand what executive agencies do, take a look at one of the largest in every state—the agency in charge of education. This agency's major responsibility is to make sure that the state's education laws are carried out. One such law sets the number of school days in a year. Laws also set the subjects you have to study and how many classes you must take to graduate.

The state education agency works with local school districts to make sure that they meet these requirements. It also sets standards for teachers. Some states have laws that tell how funds for education may be raised and spent. The education agency makes sure that funds are being spent as the law requires.

State employees. The work of the executive agencies is done by people from many trades and professions—carpenters, painters, typists, accountants, lawyers, nurses, doctors, and so on. Most of these people are hired through a system like that of federal agencies. A civil service commission sets qualifications and makes rules for hiring, promotion, and firing.

As you have seen, keeping our states running takes many people, whether they be elected, appointed, or hired. In fact, our states employ millions of people.

Answers will be found on page T 96.

Section Review

1. Define the term *item veto.*
2. In what ways are the roles of governor like those of President?
3. In what ways is the governor's team of executive officials unlike the President's Cabinet?
4. What is the purpose of the state executive agencies?

Evaluation. Do you think governors should be allowed to appoint all other state executive officers? Why or why not?

11-4 STATE COURTS

Read to Find Out

- what functions the state court system fulfills.
- what methods are used to select state court judges.
- how federalism is applied in the state judicial system.

We are all subject to two levels of law: state law and federal law. Just as federal courts interpret the United States Constitution and apply federal laws, state court systems interpret state constitutions and laws. State courts handle cases that are close to people's everyday lives, such as divorces, wills, drunk driving, robberies, and murders.

The organization of courts, and even their names, varies from state to state. The way judges are selected and the terms they serve vary, too. As you read about the state courts, keep in mind that this is a general description. As a citizen, you will want to know more

Most education agencies are answerable to a state school board which is the governing body for education in the state. Members of the board are elected or appointed by the governor.

about the special features of the court system in your own state.

What State Courts Do

Most state judicial systems have three levels. On the first level, the state's trial courts hear both civil cases and criminal cases. On the second level, state appeals courts review cases appealed from the trial courts. Cases that go beyond the first appeals court are heard in the state's supreme court, the highest court in the state system.

Like the federal judiciary, state courts act as a check on the two other branches of state government. For example, state courts may decide that a law passed by the state legislature violates the state constitution. Also like the federal judiciary, state courts have the duty of protecting the rights and freedoms guaranteed to each citizen by the state constitution.

Perhaps the best known tasks of the state courts involve hearing civil and criminal cases. State courts hear more than ten million cases each year. You will learn more about our civil and criminal courts in Unit 6.

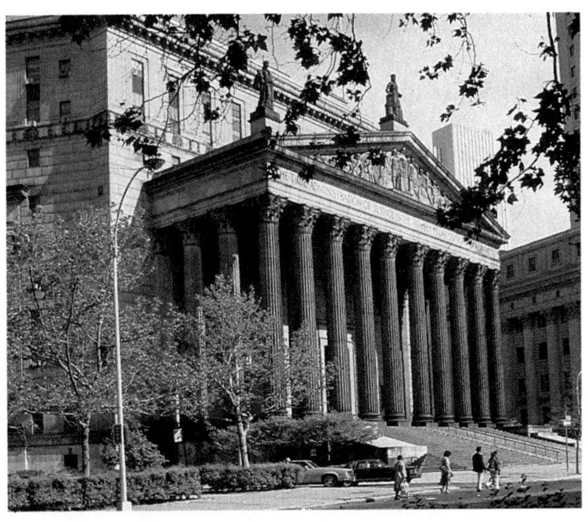

The state court systems handle heavy loads of civil and criminal cases. They also hear appeals and rule on the constitutionality of laws.

Judges in State Courts

Judges are the foundation of the state court system. State court judges perform many of the same duties as federal judges. However, the way judges are selected and the lengths of their terms vary, depending on the state and on the level of court. The main differences, and the major debates, center on whether judges are elected or appointed, and whether they serve for life or for a fixed term.

Selection of judges. There are several advantages of having judges run for election. First, an elected judge is responsible to the public, whose lives and property may be directly affected by the judge's decisions. Second, election checks the power of a governor, who might want to appoint friends and supporters even if they are not well qualified.

Opponents of electing judges paint a different picture. They say that a judge must make decisions based on the law and the facts of the case, not on what might please the voters during an election campaign. Many people who hold this view believe that judges should be chosen on merit, or ability, alone, and should not have to face election.

Some states have adopted a method of choosing judges known as the Missouri Plan. Under this plan, the governor appoints a judge from a list prepared by a commission of judges, lawyers, and ordinary citizens. Then, in the next election, voters cast a "yes" or "no" vote on whether they want the judge to stay in office.

Although the Missouri Plan does not satisfy the people who want strict merit selection, many people feel that it combines the best qualities of appointment and election. The governor is able to appoint judges from

Challenge (Analysis): Have students consider the effects of making efficiency the primary goal in processing court cases.

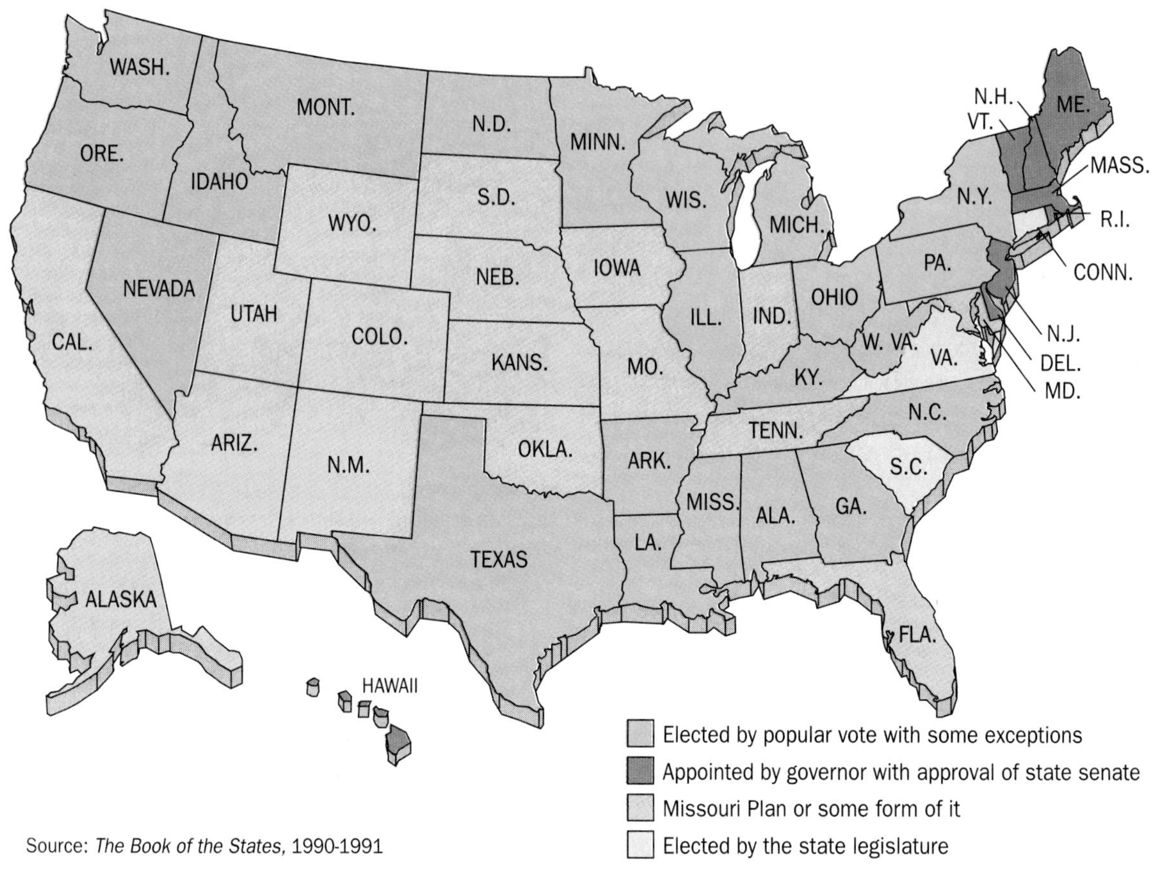

How States Select Judges. *The best way to select qualified judges is a matter of disagreement among the states.*

the best-qualified people, while the yes-or-no election gives the voters a voice.

Terms of service. The length of time judges spend in office depends on the state and on the level of the court. Most terms run from 4 to 14 years. In Rhode Island, though, judges have life appointments, while in some states judges serve until age 70.

Most judges may be removed by the voters at the end of their terms. State constitutions in most states also allow for judges to be impeached, and seven states allow for the recall of judges. These powers, however, have rarely been used.

Most states have judicial action commissions to handle situations in which a judge might not be doing his or her job well. Such a commission looks into complaints against the judge, holds hearings, reports on the judge's guilt or innocence, and decides penalties. Depending on how serious the act, a judge found guilty may face penalties ranging from a few days suspension to removal from the bench.

Case Study: Federalism and the Courts

As you may recall, some state constitutions offer greater rights and freedoms than the federal Constitution. This difference presents an

Teaching Note: Use the Enrichment Activity, page T 95, and accompanying worksheet in the Activity Book after students have read the material in this section.

interesting question about federalism. When an individual rights case comes up in one of these states, which applies—the federal Constitution or the state constitution?

Two United States Supreme Court cases, one in Oregon and one in California, will help answer this question. In each case, the owners of a shopping mall took to court members of citizens' groups who had passed out leaflets and gathered signatures on petitions at the mall. The owners claimed that it was their right not to allow such political activity on their private property. In response, the citizens' groups stated that they were simply exercising their First Amendment rights to freedom of speech and to petition the government.

In its review of the Oregon case, the Supreme Court found that the owners of the shopping mall had a right to use their private property as they wanted. The Supreme Court, therefore, found in favor of the owners.

In the California case, *Pruneyard Shopping Center* v. *Robins*, on the other hand, the Supreme Court found for the citizens' groups. The Court pointed out that California's constitution offers greater protection of free speech than does the federal Constitution. Therefore, the decision in the Oregon case did not apply to California. Thus, the federal Constitution was applied in the Oregon case, while in California the state constitution, with its greater rights, was applied.

As you have seen in this chapter, the line between federal power and state power is not always easy to draw. These two court cases show the important role the judicial branch plays in deciding questions of federalism.

Answers will be found on page T 96.

Section Review

1. What is the basic structure of state court systems?
2. What is the Missouri Plan?
3. Why did the Supreme Court find for the citizens' group rather than the mall owners in *Pruneyard Shopping Center* v. *Robins*?

Evaluation. What method of selecting judges do you support? Why?

A BROADER VIEW

Our system of federalism, although not unique, is quite unusual. The most common form of government in the world is the unitary system, in which practically all political power lies with a central government.

To see how a unitary system operates, consider the government of Japan. In the area of education, for example, the Japanese national government makes most of the decisions, even deciding the subjects to be taught in school nationwide. Such an approach suits Japan. Geographically, it is a small country, and its people lack the diversity of backgrounds found in the United States.

The size of the United States and the diversity of its people would be difficult to serve with a unitary central government. A unitary government might not be able to manage all the problems now handled by the states. Therefore, the system of federalism suits our country. Federalism also gives citizens direct access to various levels of government. As a result, government can better serve individuals and the communities of which they are a part.

Teaching Note: Use the Reinforcement Activity, page T 95, and accompanying worksheet in the Activity Book as a summarizing activity at the end of the chapter. Use the Evaluating Progress activity, page T 95, to assess students' understanding of the chapter.

DECISION MAKING

Critical Thinking

Teaching Note: For reinforcement of decision-making skills, use Decision-Making Worksheet Chapter 11.

Which Statements Are True?

Imagine yourself in the following situation: You are sixteen, and your family will soon be moving to another state. You are trying to decide whether to take a driver's education class before you move. A friend says, "You might as well wait because in that state you must be eighteen to get a driver's license." Therefore, you decide not to take the class. After you move, you find out that you made the wrong decision. The driving age in your new state is sixteen, too. You call your friend to complain: "If I hadn't listened to you, I would have been driving by now!"

To make good decisions, you need accurate, or true, information. That is why you should check the accuracy of any statements of fact before you rely on them. Remember, statements of fact are ones that can be proved either true or false.

Suppose that you are on a committee that is trying to decide how to prevent students from dropping out of school. Before the first committee meeting, you read the following information in two magazine articles by educators who have done extensive research on the dropout problem:

Excerpt from Article A

High school dropouts pose a growing problem for American education. About one million students—nearly one in every four—now quit before graduation. In some urban areas the rate reaches 65 percent. Less than 50 percent of the high school students who drop out ever return to school.

Dropouts who do manage somehow to find employment tend to work at low-paying, unskilled jobs. Many of the other teenagers who drop out turn to crime. An estimated 60 to 75 percent of prison inmates failed to complete high school.

Excerpt from Article B

According to a recent study published by the Public Television Outreach Alliance, one fourth of all students who start school will not finish. It is estimated that 700,000 students across the nation drop out of high school each year.

Many dropouts do not realize that most states require persons under eighteen to be enrolled in school in order to get a work permit. Between October 1985 and October 1986 more than 250,000 teenage girls dropped out of high school. Only a little more than half had jobs by October 1986. Those who found work discovered how little is available to them: low-paying, dead-end, no-room-for-growth jobs.

At the committee meeting, a school counselor makes the following statement: "A dropout has a poor chance of getting a skilled job." Your committee is trying to decide how to convince students to stay in school. The counselor's statement might help, but first you have to determine whether it is accurate. How might you check it out?

EXPLAINING THE SKILL

One way to check the accuracy of a statement is to follow these steps. As you read the steps, notice how they might be applied to the statement made by the counselor.

1. Check whether the source of the statement is reliable, or trustworthy. Is the person qualified to write or speak about the subject? Where did he or she get the information? [The counselor has experience in giving students advice on school problems and has probably done a lot of research on dropouts. You might ask the counselor what information he or she based the statement on.]

Explain to students that for the purposes of this lesson, the excerpts from articles A and B will be considered reliable sources.

Answers will be found on page T 97.

"You need a C average to play sports."
"Biff's Burgers pays the highest wages."
"Linda cannot be trusted."

2. Identify the general types of information that you would need in order to prove or disprove the statement. Some types of information are statistics, descriptions, dates, names, and events. [You would look for statistics on unemployment and percentages of dropouts and graduates who hold skilled and unskilled jobs.]

3. Identify reliable sources where these types of information might be found. Determine which sources are likely to have accurate information on the subject. Some sources are encyclopedias, almanacs, textbooks, dictionaries, magazines or newspapers, teachers, librarians, businesspeople, and government officials. [You could refer to the two articles you read, other articles or books, and businesspeople, who might have statistics on who is hired for skilled jobs.]

4. Check two or more reliable sources to find information that either proves or disproves the statement. Your final step is to look for specific information that either supports or disagrees with the statement. If two or more reliable sources support or agree with the statement, it is probably accurate. [Articles A and B agree with the counselor's statement. Article B provides job statistics on teenage girls. You would still want to look for additional statistics, but the statement appears to be accurate.]

APPLYING THE SKILL

Assume that you are gathering information to convince students not to drop out. Using the excerpts from articles A and B, tell how accurate each of the following statements is.

A. Most dropouts return to earn a diploma by attending night classes.
(Source: a school principal)

B. Twenty-five percent of your classmates will drop out of school before graduation.
(Source: a television documentary)

C. Dropouts are not allowed to work until they are eighteen.
(Source: a dropout who was denied a job)

D. Three fourths of students who drop out of school become criminals.
(Source: a television talk-show host)

CHECKING YOUR UNDERSTANDING

After determining whether each statement is accurate, answer the following questions.

1. For each statement, tell whether you think its source is likely to be reliable. Explain.

2. To what extent does each statement seem to be supported by excerpts A and B? Explain.

3. For each statement, explain what information you would need to prove or disprove it.

4. In addition to excerpts A and B, what sources would you use to check the accuracy of the statements? Explain why.

REVIEWING THE SKILL

5. Explain how to check whether a statement is accurate.

6. Why is it important to check whether your information is accurate?

Have students discuss what additional information they would want in order to better evaluate the reliability of the principal, the documentary, the dropout, and the talk-show host as sources of information.

CHAPTER SURVEY

Answers to Survey and Workshop will be found on page T 97.

UNDERSTANDING NEW VOCABULARY

Seeing Relationships

The vocabulary terms in each pair listed below are related to each other. For each pair, explain how the two terms are related.

Example: *Amendment* is related to *constitutional initiative* because the constitutional initiative is a process by which citizens propose an amendment to their state constitution.

1. *constitutional initiative* and *recall*

2. *initiative* and *referendum*

3. *revenue* and *sales taxes*

Putting It in Writing

Suppose someone asked you, "How can voters play a direct role in state government?" Write an answer to this question. Use at least three of the following terms, making sure that you make your meaning clear: *constitutional initiative, initiative, referendum, recall.*

LOOKING BACK AT THE CHAPTER

1. How does the national Constitution set up our system of federalism?

2. How do state constitutions compare with the federal Constitution?

3. How might federalism help create inequality in the United States?

4. How has the role of state legislator changed over the years?

5. Why was the Supreme Court decision in *Reynolds* v. *Sims* (1964) important for democracy?

6. What are some powers state legislatures have over the executive and judicial branches of state government?

7. From what source do state governments get more than half of their revenues?

8. What are some ways in which a governor can influence lawmaking?

9. Give the main arguments for and against **(a)** election of judges and **(b)** appointment of judges.

10. *Evaluation.* "States should hold constitutional conventions at least every ten years." Do you agree or disagree? Why?

11. *Synthesis.* Suppose that your state has made being a state legislator a full-time job. What would be the advantages and disadvantages for the state government? For the legislators? For the citizens? What effect might it have on who decides to run for office as a state legislator?

12. *Synthesis.* How can the case of *Pruneyard Shopping Center* v. *Robins* be seen as a case involving ideas of federalism?

13. *Evaluation.* "Because we have a federal judicial system, we do not need a state court system." Do you agree or disagree? Explain your answer.

WORKING TOGETHER

1. In groups of three or four, either follow the debate on a bill in your state legislature or track newspaper reports of one week of a session of your state legislature. Each group should present its findings in an oral report to the rest of the class.

2. With two or three other students, write letters to your state legislator, to a judge in the state court system, and to the governor or another member of the state executive branch asking them what they think is the most important aspect of their jobs. Share the replies you receive with the rest of the class.

3. With a group, choose two states to compare and contrast. Use an encyclopedia to help you. You may wish to look for similarities and differences in climate, geographical size, population, sources of revenue, constitutions, executive agencies, court system, and so on. Present your findings to the class.

SOCIAL STUDIES SKILLS

Reading Newspaper Articles

B4 METRO/ State News

Bill would lower level for drunks

SACRAMENTO (AP) - In a move that could result in more drunk driving convictions, the state senate voted Thursday to lower the alcohol level at which a motorist is presumed to be intoxicated.

The upper house, by a 24-3 vote th

So begins an article that appeared in the *San Jose Mercury News*, a local newspaper in California, on April 14, 1989. Most Americans depend on local newspapers to keep them informed about their state government.

News stories follow a pattern. A headline tells what the story is about. The dateline shows where it was written. If a story was not written by the newspaper's own reporters, the source appears on or above the dateline, or at the end of the article. The source might be a news-gathering service such as United Press International (UPI) or Associated Press (AP), or perhaps another newspaper.

The lead, or first paragraph of an article, summarizes the main facts of the story. The body, or remainder of the article, includes the rest of the details. Good articles answer the basic questions Who? What? When? Why? and How? Reread the headline and lead of the article above to answer these questions.

1. What does the headline say the story is about?

2. Where was the article written?

3. What is the source of the article?

4. Which of the following questions were not answered by the lead: What bill was passed? Who passed it? When? Why? How was it passed?

DECISION-MAKING SKILLS

Which Statements are True?

Suppose that you and other students are trying to deal with this problem in your community: there is no longer a summer job program for teenagers. Last year local officials ran a program with money from the state, but it was dropped this year. You are trying to decide how to bring the program back.

Before you can decide what to do, you have to find out why the program was stopped. In looking for information, you read a letter to the editor of your local newspaper. According to the writer, a student at your school, local officials have enough money for the program. The writer says, "*Local governments get the same amount of money from the state every year.*" You need to determine whether this statement is true.

1. How might you determine whether the writer of the statement is a reliable source?

2. What types of information would you need to determine whether the statement is true?

3. In what sources, other than this textbook, might you find information that would prove or disprove the statement?

4. Does the information in Chapter 11 support the writer's statement? Explain, giving at least two specific examples from the chapter.

5. Why is it important to check the accuracy of information when making decisions?

6. Think of a decision that you might make soon. What kinds of information would you want to check out before deciding? Why?

Chapter Themes: Local governments have the greatest effect on the everyday lives of citizens. Such governments provide vital services but face problems in paying for them. Both conflict and cooperation exist between local, state, and federal governments.

CHAPTER 12

Local Government

"No one has the right to force you to breathe smoke," says a New York City government official. The city backs up these words with a law that bans cigarette smoking in many public places. New York City is not alone in its stand against smoking. More than 400 anti-smoking laws have been made by local governments across the nation.

Not all local government officials view anti-smoking laws in the same way, however. A county official in North Carolina says, "We don't need to make a bunch of rules as to what people do with their private lives." Indeed, many local officials are torn between protecting each person's right to smoke and protecting public health.

When deciding if anti-smoking laws and other laws should be passed, officials in towns, cities, and counties must think about the needs and wishes of local citizens. Sometimes these citizens make their wishes known in a powerful way. Citizens in Aspen, Colorado organized the Group Against Smoking in Public (GASP). They asked the city to pass a law that would ban smoking in nearly all enclosed places. Restaurant and store owners did not want the law. They said it would drive business away. However, 1,000 of the 3,800 people who lived in Aspen signed a petition, and the city passed the law. Six months later, business was still good in Aspen, and nonsmokers breathed easier.

Most local officials agree that laws about smoking and many other acts in public places should be set by local governments. Governments at this level have the best idea of what their citizens want. In fact, local governments were first formed to meet people's everyday needs—from police protection to garbage collection. Often, however, local matters are also of nationwide concern. Then all levels of government must work together to handle them.

In this chapter, you will take a look at different kinds of local government. You will find out what they do and how they work with each other and with the state and federal governments for the good of our communities.

Teaching Note: Use the Introducing the Chapter activity, page T 100.

Teaching Note: Assign the Evaluating Progress activity, page T 101, and complete it at the end of the chapter.

12-1

TYPES OF LOCAL GOVERNMENT

Read to Find Out

- what the terms *board, ordinances,* and *municipality* mean.
- how counties, townships, special districts, and cities came to be created.
- what are some different plans for city government.

You already know that the Constitution gives powers to the federal and state governments. What you may not know, though, is that it does not give any power to local governments, such as counties, cities, and towns. Local governments are created by the states and have only those powers that state governments give them.

The powers that state governments give to local governments help meet the many needs of thousands of communities throughout the nation. In fact, there are more than 83,000 separate local governments in the United States.

Nearly every day you see people who work for local governments—teachers, librarians, bus drivers, police officers, and others. Your daily life runs on the services of local governments, such as garbage collection, road repair, and water supply. Perhaps your family takes part in local government. They may vote in local elections or serve on committees. Local government is the level that is closest to you. It has the greatest effect on your everyday life.

In this chapter you will be looking at the most common forms of local government: counties, townships, New England towns, special districts, and cities. Most of these types of government existed long before our nation was born.

Counties and Townships

Our oldest unit of local government is the county. Rooted in England, the county form of government came to America with the English colonists. Colonies were divided into counties to carry out laws in rural areas. Because farmers lived far apart, county business was done at a place most people could reach within a day's wagon journey. This distance to the "county seat" set the boundaries of many counties.

Today, every state but Connecticut and Rhode Island has county governments. Counties are called "parishes" in Louisiana and "boroughs" in Alaska. Counties are different sizes. For example, Arlington County in Virginia is only 24 square miles, while California's San Bernardino County is 20,131 square miles. Most counties help state governments keep law and order and collect taxes. Counties may also offer many other services, from libraries to health care.

County officials. Most counties are governed by county boards. A ***board*** is a group of people who manage the business of an organization. Most county boards have three to five elected members, called commissioners or supervisors. Board members set up county programs and pass ***ordinances***, which are local laws. The county board shares its power with other boards, which run hospitals, libraries, and other special programs.

Perhaps the best-known elected county official is the sheriff. The office of sheriff has its roots in England, just like the county form of government itself. The sheriff, with the help of deputies, runs the county jail and makes sure people obey the law. Sheriffs often work in rural areas not covered by city or state police. Other county officials may include the assessor, who figures property values; the treasurer, who sends the property tax bill; and the

County government can serve urban counties like Los Angeles County in California, Cook County in Illinois, and Dade County in Florida, or the 2,400 rural counties in the United States.

county clerk, who keeps official records such as marriage certificates.

Townships. In the Middle Atlantic states and in the Midwest, counties are often divided into townships. At first, townships were needed to help carry out duties such as setting up schools and repairing roads in rural areas far from the county seat. Over the years, though, cities have grown larger and transportation has improved, so most of these duties have been taken over by county and city governments. In many urban areas, townships just elect representatives to serve on the county board.

New England Towns

In New England, another form of rural government grew up—the town. When people from other countries came to the New England colonies, they were given land. Groups of settlers started a town by building villages with homes, a church, and a school. They also planted crops in the nearby farmlands. The town was made up of both the village and the farmlands.

Citizens took an active part in local government in the early New England towns. All the voters met once a year at town meetings to pass laws, set taxes, and decide how the money should be spent. This kind of town meeting still takes place today in some small New England towns. It is the closest thing we have to direct democracy.

At the yearly town meeting in a New England town, citizens elect a board of three to five members. The board carries on town business during the year. Other officials, such as the school board members, the town clerk, the assessor, and the treasurer, are chosen by the town board or elected by the voters. As you can see, towns in New England have most of the duties that counties have in other regions.

Like townships, New England towns have changed over the years. Because some towns have become large, it is not easy for all the citizens to gather together to decide things. Therefore, in many large towns the voters choose representatives to attend town meetings. Some towns have hired managers to take care of the town's business.

Special Districts

Sometimes it does not make sense for a community to handle certain matters alone. For example, it would not make sense for each community in a dry region to build its own water supply system. It would be too much work and cost too much money. In such a case, all the communities in the region ask the state to make a special water district to supply water to the whole region.

A special district is a unit of government that provides a single service. It can serve one community or cover parts or all of several communities. Special districts serve many

Running a large city poses very different challenges to local government leaders than does meeting the needs of a small town.

needs. In cities, they provide subways and parks. Rural special districts protect people from fires or control insects. Most such districts are run by a board. One special district that you know about is your school district.

Cities

A government that serves people who live in an urban area is called a ***municipality***. Most municipalities, especially those that serve large populations, are called cities. In some states, municipalities that serve small populations are called towns or villages.

As the population of the United States has grown, so also have the sizes of our cities. Today a mid-sized American city has between 25,000 and 250,000 citizens. Several cities have millions of people. Governments of large cities must meet many different needs, including services not heard of in earlier times, such as pollution control and drug abuse programs.

The boundaries and powers of a municipality—which can be a city, town, or village—are set by the state. Some communities write charters, or plans of government, that must be approved by the state. In other communities, the plan of government is set by state laws. No matter how they are formed, the governments of most municipalities follow one of three plans: mayor-council, council-manager, or commission.

The mayor-council plan. Like so much else in local government, the mayor-council plan comes from England. The mayor, like the English prime minister or the American President, is the executive. The council, like the English Parliament or the American Congress, is the legislative branch. More than half of the cities in the United States use the mayor-council plan.

In a city that has a mayor-council plan, people elect the mayor and city council members. Other city officials, such as court judges, the police chief, and the city attorney, may also be elected. The duties of your city officials depend on whether they work under a weak-mayor plan or a strong-mayor plan.

Under the weak-mayor plan, the mayor does not have special executive powers. In fact, most of the power rests with the council, which acts as both a legislative and executive body. Often the council chooses the mayor from among its members. The council also

The charter of a city can be compared to the constitution of a nation or a state. A charter outlines the structure of the government, determines the power of officials, and establishes election procedures.

Teaching Note: For an organization chart of the council-manager plan, see "Social Studies Skills" on page 281. For a description of "honest graft" by Tammany Hall politician George Washington Plunkitt, see "In Their Own Words" on page 282.

chooses other officials, makes ordinances, and decides how money should be spent.

The weak-mayor plan dates back to the colonies. The early settlers did not trust the English government. When they formed their own city governments, they did not want to give too much power to one person.

During the first century of our nation's history, most cities used the weak-mayor plan. As cities grew in size, however, stronger leadership was needed in city hall. By the late 1800s, most large cities had switched to a strong-mayor plan. In this plan, the relationship between the mayor and the council is more like that between the President and Congress. The council makes ordinances, but the mayor is elected by the voters and is in charge of the budget, makes policies, and chooses city officials.

The council-manager plan. By the early 1900s, many cities were in the grasp of political groups called "machines." City officials did favors for the machine, such as giving jobs to politicians and friends. In return, the machine helped the officials get elected again. This arrangement often led to corruption. Officials looked after their own interests instead of looking after the interests of the public.

In an effort to create honest government, some people came up with the council-manager plan. The goal of the plan is to run government like a business.

In the council-manager plan, the council is chosen through an election in which candidates have no political ties. The council makes ordinances and hires a city manager to handle day-to-day city business. It is the manager, not the mayor, who prepares the budget and is in charge of people who work for the city. Because the manager is not elected, he or she is supposed to be free from political pressures. The council-manager plan is used in some 3,000 cities today.

Mayor-Council Plans

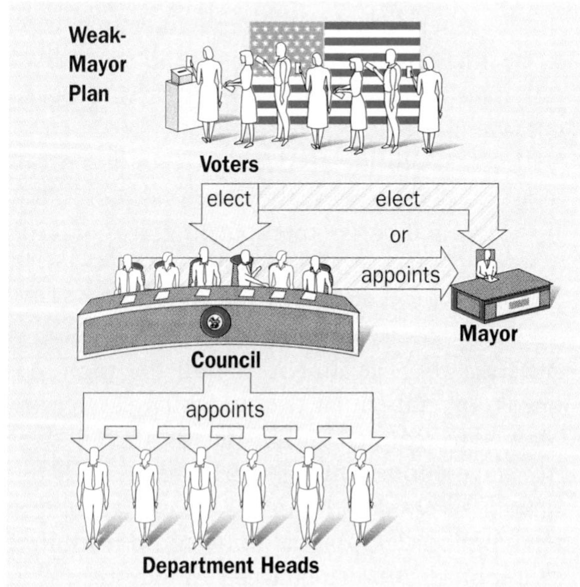

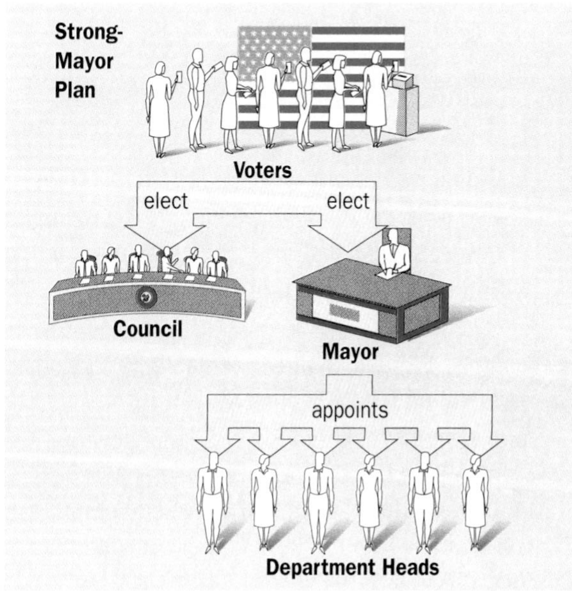

Challenge (Analysis): A city manager is supposed to be free from political pressures, yet he or she serves at the pleasure of the council and may be subject to its influence. In reality, how political is the job of manager?

Teaching Note: Use the Enrichment Activity, page T 102, and accompanying worksheet in the Activity Book after students have read the material in Section 12-1.

The commission plan. Another reform of city government took place in Galveston, Texas, in 1900. The city was destroyed by a hurricane. The weak-mayor government that Galveston had at that time could not manage the rebuilding. Local citizens convinced the state to approve a new form of government called a commission plan. Under this plan, voters choose several commissioners who together make ordinances. In addition, each commissioner directs one of the city's departments, such as finance or public assistance.

The commission plan worked so well in rebuilding Galveston that hundreds of other cities decided to try it. However, the plan does not provide for a single leader to control the budget and make the departments work together. In the past few years Galveston and most other cities that tried the plan have decided not to use it any more.

No matter what the strengths and the weaknesses are of a plan of local government, its success or failure lies in the hands of its citizens. Today, most cities seek advice from groups made up of people who live there. Citizens *can* be heard in city hall.

Answers will be found on page T 102.

Section Review

1. Define *board, ordinances,* and *municipality.*
2. Why were counties, townships, New England towns, special districts, and cities created?
3. Briefly describe the three plans of city government.

Analysis. Why would direct democracy not work well in a large county or city?

Data Search. There are 83,186 local governments in the United States. Look on page 586 in the Data Bank. What is the most numerous type of local government? Give an example of this type of government.

12-2

LOCAL GOVERNMENT SERVICES AND REVENUE

Read to Find Out

- what the terms *utilities, zoning, property tax,* and *intergovernmental revenue* mean.
- what services local governments provide.
- where local governments get their revenue.
- how revenue affects local policymaking.

"Skateboarding is dangerous!" said the mother of a child who had been run into by a skateboarder. She asked the city council to ban skateboards in public places. "That's not fair," said a teenager at the council meeting. "Then we'd have no place to skate." He asked the city to build a bowl for skateboarders.

We ask local governments to help us in many ways. They provide ***utilities***, or services needed by the public, such as water, gas, and electricity. They build parks, schools, and roads. They plan for community growth. Officials make hundreds of decisions in delivering these services. For example, they may have to decide whether a hole in a road that serves only two houses should be fixed or whether to cut water use during a dry spell.

Every time officials decide to handle a problem in a certain way, they are making policy. If the council bans skateboarding, it is making a public safety policy. Another policy might be to build a skateboard bowl.

Policy decisions often depend on money. Because no government has all the money it needs, officials must decide which services to offer. The council might decide that it does not have enough money to build a bowl, but it will allow skateboarders to use an empty parking lot. Perhaps the bowl could be built if skateboarders were charged money to use it.

Teaching Note: For a discussion of one local government's policy on neighborhood noise, see "Issues That Affect You: A Case Study" on pages 278–279.

You will be reading about the most common services of local governments. As you will see, local officials decide how best to give services to their communities. They get the money to pay for those services in a number of ways.

Education

The service that local governments spend the most money on is education. Local governments—counties, cities, and school districts—are in charge of providing all public education from elementary school through high school. Some also are in charge of two-year colleges. Local school boards build schools and hire teachers and staff to run them. Many local boards have a strong say in what courses will be taught.

The federal and state governments are also important in public education. State officials set standards for school employees and buildings. State governments have a strong say in how schools are run because they pay about 44 percent of schooling costs. The federal government pays another 8 percent. It helps to pay for buildings, school lunch programs, and programs for children with special needs.

Local vs. state control. Local and state governments often do not agree about which of them should have greater control over how to spend state education money. State officials feel that they must make sure state standards are met and that children in all school districts have equal opportunities.

On the other hand, local control can be good for schools because local citizens know what the students need. In the East Harlem part of New York City, for instance, teachers, parents, and students thought of having "magnet" schools. The schools were to attract students interested in certain subjects, such as art or science. Ideas for the schools came from teachers and citizens, and the district carried them out. As a result, the schools—and the students' test scores—improved.

Utilities

You may not even notice some local government services. However, you would certainly notice if you no longer had them. These government services are the utilities: water, gas, electricity, sewage treatment plants, and garbage collection.

In many cases, water and sewage treatment plants are owned and run by local governments. Communities often arrange for private companies to supply gas and electricity and to pick up garbage. The state makes rules to make sure the companies deliver good services at fair rates.

Local Government Spending, 1989

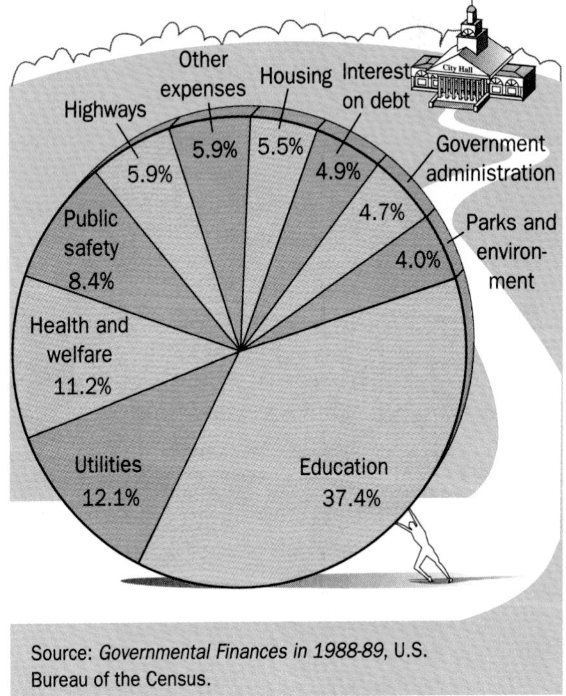

Source: *Governmental Finances in 1988-89,* U.S. Bureau of the Census.

There are more than 15,000 school districts in the United States. Each district has an elected or appointed board of education which decides school policy, finances, and other matters. The board also appoints a superintendent of schools, who supervises school operation.

One purpose of land-use planning is to prevent uncontrolled growth from destroying existing neighborhoods.

Utilities are best provided at the local level, where they can be planned to fit a community's needs. In Emmonak, a village in Alaska, the ground freezes in winter. Sewer pipes are not put underground because they would freeze, too. Instead, sewer pipes made of materials that will not freeze are laid above ground —a method that fits the Arctic climate.

Health and Welfare

Millions of Americans are poor, too ill to work, or unable to find jobs or homes. Many people help the needy, but it is a very big job. Local governments play a part by giving health and child care, training people for jobs, and providing low-cost places to live. New York City, for instance, spends about $200 million each year to shelter 18,000 people who have no homes.

Most programs giving public assistance, or welfare, are paid for by federal, state, and local governments together. However, local officials carry out the programs. One of the largest welfare programs is Aid to Families with Dependent Children (AFDC). It gives money to poor families in which only one parent takes care of the children.

Communities also look after public health. In many cases, local officials carry out state health laws. Local health officials inspect restaurants, markets, hotels, and water to be sure that state and federal standards are met. Many communities also make sure that federal and state laws to control pollution are obeyed.

Land Use

Have you ever noticed that homes and businesses are in separate areas of your community? This is the result of ***zoning***, local rules

Teaching Note: You may wish to use the Unit 4 Activity, "A Community Handbook," in the Activity Book after students have read the discussion of local government services.

Decision Making: Have students pick a local zoning issue and discuss how the decision-making process would apply to that issue.

that divide a community into areas and tell how the land in each area can be used. For example, zoning may keep a factory from being built next to your home. Zoning is a tool used by local governments to plan and control the growth of their communities.

The people who plan communities think about where roads, parks, factories, and homes should be built. They must also think about how a new factory will affect the lives of people in the community. They must think about who will be using a park and whether it will need a playground or picnic tables. Will a new road bring too much traffic into downtown? Are there enough low-rent houses and apartments for families with low incomes? Planners must also look at how development affects the environment. Will the new factory have anti-pollution controls?

The planning process. Planning is made up of many steps. A local government appoints a planning commission to set goals and get information about the community, such as its growth rate and types of businesses. Most commissions are made up of interested citizens, such as builders, environmentalists, and business leaders.

Commissioners work with a staff that looks at requests from builders and reads reports about what building will do to the environment. The staff tells the commission what they think should be done about each request. Once the commission decides what to do, it presents the matter to the city council or county board, which makes the final decision.

Some of the most heated battles in planning are over how fast communities should grow. New businesses mean more jobs and more tax money. However, new businesses may bring in more people, who will need water, schools, and parks. New businesses may also bring more traffic and pollution.

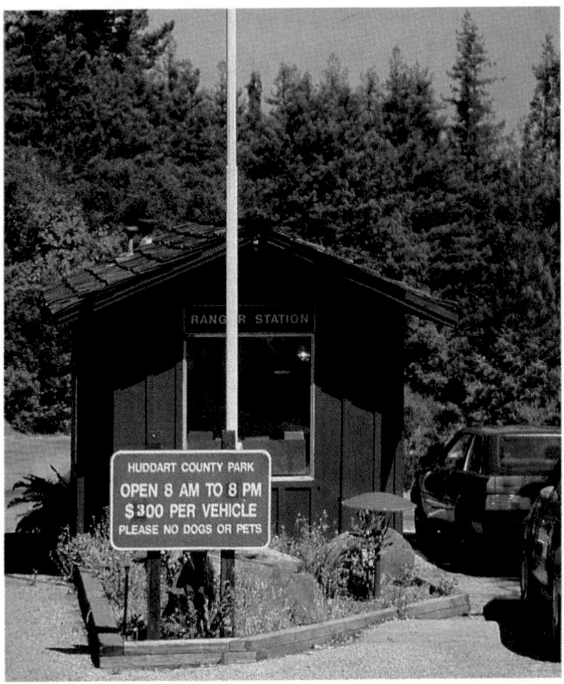

By setting aside land for public parks, local governments help to meet the recreation needs of communities.

In Reno, Nevada, government and business leaders got more than 40 companies to move to their city between 1983 and 1985. This growth brought thousands of new jobs and lots of tax money to Reno. Local officials pointed out, however, that quick growth meant the city would also need more water. Reno gets its water from melting snow from the nearby Sierra Nevada mountains. The city could make land-use plans, but it could not make more snow fall. Planners must think about the resources they have as well as the short-term and long-term needs of citizens.

Public Safety

If you had an emergency, what would you do? You might call the police or fire department, or dial 911. Police officers and firefighters also look after the public safety in non-emergencies. The police help citizens stop

Challenge (Application): Choose a six-block area surrounding the school and have students compile a list of the different types of land use within the area. Have students discuss types of land use that would be inappropriate for this area.

Local Government Revenue, 1989

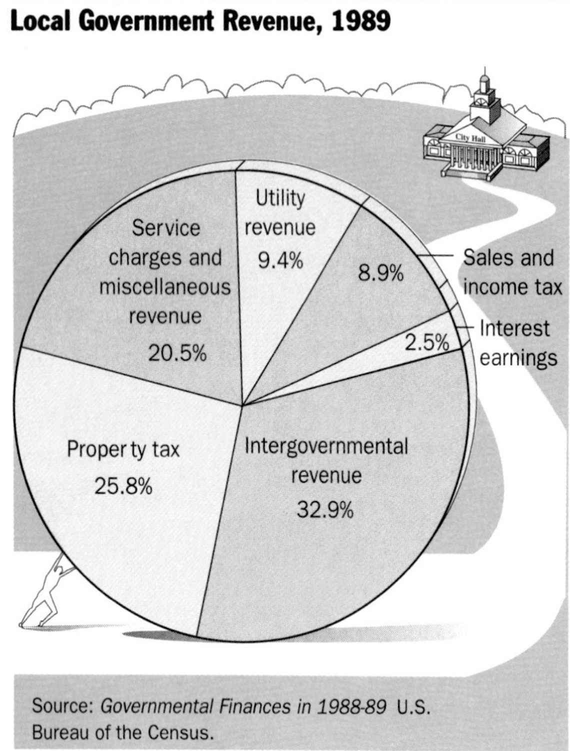

Source: *Governmental Finances in 1988-89* U.S. Bureau of the Census.

crime by teaching them how to keep people from breaking into their homes. The fire department checks for fire hazards, such as too many weeds, and teaches safety rules to children.

Local governments also hire people to make sure that safety rules, called codes, are followed. A fire code may say that all buildings must have smoke alarms. Building codes make sure that new buildings are built safely.

Revenue: Paying for Services

To provide services to citizens, local governments need money. Like state governments, local governments depend on several sources of revenue.

Taxes. About 25 percent of local government revenue comes from ***property tax***, a tax on land and buildings. The county assessor decides how much the property is worth and charges the property owner a fixed percentage of that value. Sometimes cars and other forms of property are taxed as well.

Property tax was developed more than 200 years ago. At that time, wealth was held mainly in land and buildings, which were called "real" property. It was easy to judge people's wealth by the houses, barns, and farmlands they owned, and to decide what their share of taxes should be. Many people still feel the tax is fair because the more property that citizens own, the more services they use, such as water and fire protection.

Some communities bring in money through other taxes. About 5,000 cities and counties charge a local sales tax. A few cities put an income tax on the salaries of people who work there. The idea is to collect money from "daytime citizens" who use city services during the work day but live somewhere else.

Service charges and business profits. Cities often charge money for services such as inspecting buildings to see that they meet safety codes. Communities also get money from bridge tolls, park entrance fees, and parking meters.

Some local governments make money by running businesses. For instance, the city of Naperville, Illinois, runs a parking garage. It brings in money while providing parking spaces for people who work and shop in the city. Government-owned utilities, such as electric companies, also bring in money and give low-cost service to local citizens and businesses.

Borrowing. When revenue from taxes, fees, and city-owned businesses is not enough to cover their costs, local governments can borrow money. For short-term needs, they borrow from banks. To pay for big projects,

In 1972, Congress established a revenue-sharing program which gave state and local governments a share of the tax money collected by the federal government. Communities could use this money for such general purposes as environmental protection, health, public safety, and transportation.

PEOPLE MAKE A DIFFERENCE

Young Volunteers Serve Their Community

More than 500 young people between the ages of 16 and 21 are members of the City Volunteer Corps (CVC) of New York City. Mayor Ed Koch set up the organization in 1984 to involve young people in the local community. For the volunteers, CVC provides good experience and money that they can use for their education. For the city, it supplies a dedicated group of workers for social programs that need their help.

The volunteers receive uniforms and a small monthly allowance for food and transportation. They work in teams for up to a year on projects such as helping disabled children or turning vacant lots into neighborhood parks. After the first six months, a volunteer may do a special project of interest.

Some volunteers are high-school or college students who work part-time after school and full-time during the summer. Others are taking time off from college.

Most of the volunteers, however, are former dropouts who work for CVC while studying for their high-school diplomas. After completing the year-long program, each full-time volunteer chooses between a $5,000 scholarship for college and $2,500 in cash. Part-time volunteers also receive scholarships.

CVC volunteer Jerry Michel has worked on eight projects, including teaching English to Cambodian and Vietnamese refugees. "I see CVC as a hallway with a lot of doors opening off it," Jerry says. "Behind each door is a new experience."

Fabeula Trimmingham learned that being involved in community projects requires teamwork and responsibility. "You have to be there for people—they need you," says Fabeula. "You learn to cooperate and understand each other."

Adenike Coore, who wants to study nursing and psychiatry, worked at the Bronx Children's Psychiatric Hospital. Adenike says that she has grown in self-confidence and has learned more about the city. "I've learned about the social services the city supplies. And in CVC you know something is being done—you're doing it."

such as school buildings, communities borrow money by selling bonds.

Sharing revenue. Local governments also receive ***intergovernmental revenue***, money given by one level of government to another. Federal and state governments often give money to local communities. This money is called a grant. Grants are a way to make sure that services of national or state importance are provided at the local level.

Some grants are for special uses, such as summer job programs for youth, or large building projects. Others are block grants for general uses such as education. Block grants allow local officials to decide how best to use the money.

Limits on revenue. Most communities face problems in paying for services. Sources of

Discussion: For the volunteers, the City Volunteer Corps provides money and good experience. Have students discuss what other benefits volunteering offers.

Teaching Note: Use Teaching Activity 1, page T 100, as a culminating activity after students have read the material in Section 12-2.

money may "run dry." In the 1980s, when the federal government was deeply in debt, it reduced the amount of money it gave to local governments.

Another problem is that the power to tax is controlled by the state. The state spells out what kinds of taxes may be collected and what the money may be used for.

The voters can also cut back on money for local government. In the 1970s, citizens in more than half of the states voted to cut property tax rates. With less money from taxes, many local governments had to cut services. In some Maryland schools, for instance, the libraries got almost no money to buy or replace books.

Although some communities managed to cut waste and become more efficient, by the 1980s many could barely keep up their services. Many communities began increasing revenue through such means as higher sales taxes and user fees. "People want more services and no waste and lower taxes," said one official. "Who doesn't? But services cost money." One of the hardest tasks of local government is balancing the community's need for services with the money in its treasury.

Answers will be found on page T 103.

Section Review

1. Define *utilities, zoning, property tax,* and *intergovernmental revenue.*
2. How do local governments help provide for public education, health and welfare, and safety?
3. What are two ways by which a community might pay for a major project such as building an airport?
4. How do limits on revenue affect policy-making?

Evaluation. Which two local government services do you think are most important? Explain.

12-3 CONFLICT AND COOPERATION BETWEEN GOVERNMENTS

Read to Find Out

- what the term *home rule* means.
- how local governments cooperate and come into conflict.
- how state and local governments cooperate and come into conflict.
- how the federal and state governments affect local governments.

Look in your phone book and see how many levels of government are listed that serve you. Like most citizens, you probably live under at least four layers of government. Almost every town, city, and township lies inside a county. All these local governments must answer to their state governments. Of course, the nation as a whole is guided by the federal government. As the layers overlap, governments both cooperate and come into conflict.

Relations Between Local Governments

In 1954 a county official in the Detroit area became alarmed that the region's services were not keeping up with its growth. He met with officials of neighboring counties to figure out how to meet area-wide needs. Soon other regions were holding meetings, too. These groups became known as "councils of governments."

Other groups, such as the United States Conference of Mayors, are also ways of linking local governments. Officials from these groups talk about matters that affect them all, and they work together to look for solutions. Since cooperation would seem to help everyone, what causes conflicts between local governments?

Teaching Note: Use the Reinforcement Activity, page T 102, and accompanying worksheet in the Activity Book after students have read Section 12-2.

Conflict. One big cause of conflicts between local governments is economics. Communities often compete to attract new businesses, which pay new property taxes. Communities also compete to get federal money.

Another cause of conflicts is the effect of one community's policies on neighboring communities. One city may zone an area for new factories. However, when the pollution from that factory zone blows into a neighboring city, the stage is set for conflict.

Cooperation. Problems can also lead to cooperation. Citizens of Aurora, Colorado, were angry about noise from the nearby Denver airport. Officials from the two communities worked together to find a way to quiet the noise. Denver paid to put thicker walls, doors, and windows in Aurora homes. "The thought of being able to hear their televisions and talk on the phone is making the program quite popular," said one official.

AMERICAN NOTEBOOK 

In 1989, the city of Chicago and the state of Illinois had almost finished an underground walkway between the city hall and the state government building. City workers had tunneled from one direction, and state workers from the other. As it turned out, though, the part of the walkway coming from the city hall was nine inches higher and eight inches to the side of the part leading from the state building. This shows that even when state and local governments agree on projects or issues, they do not always meet each other halfway.

Federal and state government relief workers pitch in with sandbags to help a local community protect itself against flood waters.

Sometimes communities work together to provide services that would cost too much for each to provide for itself. Six townships in Ohio have teamed up to answer emergency calls. Each township's fire department offers something different, such as clothing that protects people from fire or training for emergencies.

Small communities may also turn to counties for help. A county can build a jail or hospital to serve several small towns. In fact, more than half of the counties in this country have contracts to deliver services to the towns and cities within their borders.

Relations Between Local and State Governments

Many states have a strong voice in deciding how local governments will be set up. Other states have granted cities and some counties

Challenge (Analysis): Have students discuss conflicts that are presently occurring between your community and other communities or the state. How can the issues be resolved by cooperation?

Most cities of more than 200,000 residents and almost 40 percent of cities with a population of 5,000 or more have some measure of home rule. This right gives voters the power to decide for themselves the general structure of municipal government.

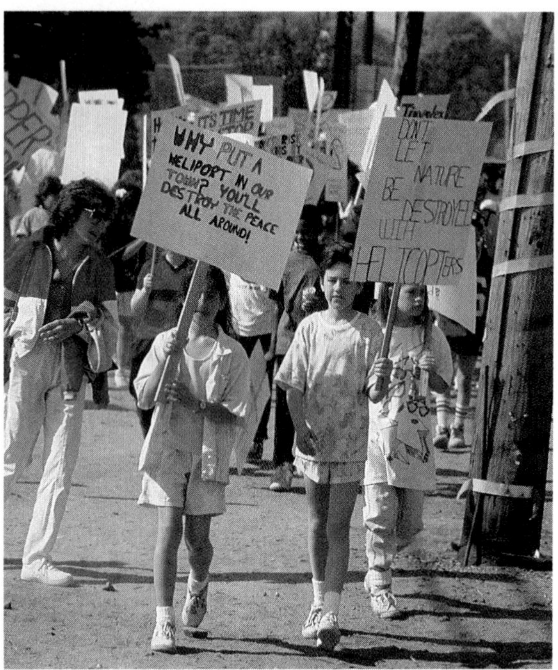

Citizens of a local community are sometimes unhappy with federal and state decisions that affect their area.

home rule, the right to choose their own form of government. Whether or not they grant home rule, most states give communities some freedom to handle local matters.

Conflict. The question of what is a local matter and what is also a state matter, however, can lead to conflict. For example, California wanted to build a sewage plant for the city of Arcata. The state had received federal money for the plant, but Arcata would have had to pay millions of dollars, too. Arcata came up with a plan for a cheaper sewage system, but the state said no. A city councilman spent two years going to meetings with state officials. Finally, Arcata won the right to build the system it wanted. When local and state laws come into conflict, however, state law is almost always enforced.

Cooperation. Many state governments work directly with local governments to solve local problems. The city of Evanston turned to the Illinois Environmental Protection Agency for help in building a park over what had been a garbage dump. The job was hard because rotten garbage is not a stable surface and makes a gas that can blow up if trapped. Together, city and state officials worked out plans to cover the garbage with a layer of clay and to build a vent for the gas to escape.

States often work with local governments to carry out state programs. When a state highway commission plans a road that will cut through a city it asks the advice of the city council. States also help local programs run smoothly. State officials help local officials in finance, law enforcement, health, and education. Also, states test and license local government workers such as teachers and doctors to be sure that they can do their jobs.

Relations Between Local, State, and Federal Governments

Money is the key to the relations of local governments to state and federal governments. The federal government gives grants and loans for housing, public assistance, and other uses. The idea is to use federal money at the local level to meet national goals.

For example, the federal government wants to help poor people, so it gives grants for job-training programs. Such grants are often given to the states. Then the states decide how to divide up the money among local governments that run the programs.

Conflict. Sometimes local officials come into conflict with federal and state officials over how to spend grant money. Most federal money for local governments can be used only in certain ways. Grants given to help meet a national goal may not match local needs. The states often have the power to decide who gets federal grants.

Conflict can occur when federal programs impose uniformity on diverse areas. For example, federally funded highways are required to have white center and side lines, but officials in Wyoming have argued without success that yellow lines are easier to see in blizzards.

Teaching Note: Use Teaching Activity 2, page T 100, as a culminating activity after students have read the material in this section.

If local governments want the freedom to set their own policies, they may have to do without federal money. Yet most communities do not have enough money to do big projects without some federal help.

Cooperation. Many problems affect all levels of government and are best solved by cooperation. If one factory dumps poisonous wastes, it is a local matter. However, poisonous wastes have polluted ground water, lakes, and rivers across the nation, so pollution has also become a nationwide concern. Federal, state, and local governments must all work together to clean up and stop pollution.

Local, state, and federal governments also cooperate in providing services, such as law enforcement. The Federal Bureau of Investigation (FBI) trains local police in the latest ways of fighting crime. Local police turn to the FBI for records of suspected criminals. Local, state, and federal officers work together to solve crimes like bank robbery and kidnapping.

The federal-state-local partnership is a good way to deal with nationwide issues. It also brings local problems to national attention because local officials can tell state and federal officials what their citizens want. Even though there are conflicts, they can lead to creative solutions. If you want to take part in finding solutions, local government is a good place to start.

Answers will be found on page T 103.

Section Review

1. Define *home rule.*
2. What are some ways in which local governments compete and cooperate?
3. In what ways do state and local governments cooperate? How do they sometimes come into conflict?
4. Why do federal, state, and local governments often have to work together?

Evaluation. Do you think competition between local governments is bad? Explain.

A BROADER VIEW

Local government powers vary from nation to nation. There are three main systems of city government outside the United States: the English, French, and Soviet systems. The English system is used in Great Britain, Australia, Canada, and New Zealand. It is similar to ours in that mayors and councils are voted for locally. They have broad power to deal with local issues.

The French system is found not only in France but also in many Latin American, African, Middle Eastern, and Asian countries. Local governments have much less power in the French system. Local officials provide services such as water, electricity, and fire protection, but it is the national government that controls the money, education, and the police.

The Soviet Union and other Eastern European countries have tight control over local government. For instance, in the Soviet Union local councils called *soviets* are really just representatives of the national government. Compared with local governments in most other countries, our cities, towns, and counties have more freedom to set policies on local matters.

Teaching Note: Complete the Evaluating Progress activity, page T 101, to assess students' understanding of the chapter.

Banning Neighborhood Noise

Darien Mann's rock and roll band was loud. When Darien and his friends practiced in Darien's garage, many of the neighbors complained that they could not talk to each other without shouting. It made the neighbors even more angry that the four boys practiced late into the night.

Darien's next-door neighbors, the Macks, lived closest to the garage. They were disturbed by the noise more often than anyone else in the neighborhood.

One evening Mr. Mack thought the band was playing even louder than usual. He rang the Manns' doorbell and pounded on the door, but no one answered. In disgust, Mr. Mack returned home and called the police.

Los Angeles police officer Richard Hoefel and his partner answered the call at about 8 P.M. After months of complaints, the Mann house had become a regular stop on their beat. They could hear the band from half a block away.

The officers walked to the chain link fence in front of the Manns' garage and rapped on the gate with their flashlights to get the teenagers' attention. Officer Hoefel ordered the boys to meet him on the front porch.

Once they all were gathered together, Officer Hoefel explained the reason for the neighbor's complaint. He warned the group that if they did not stop making the noise he would have to arrest them for breaking the law. The Los Angeles Municipal Code has a "noise ordinance" which states that it is against the law for any person to make any "loud, unnecessary, and unusual noise which disturbs the peace and quiet of any neighborhood."

Thirteen months later, the Manns and the Macks were still arguing over the noise problem.

The officers talked with the band about ways they could avoid noise complaints in the future. The officers said that the band could rent a hall, soundproof the garage, or agree with the Macks about good times to practice. Because the boys seemed cooperative, Officer Hoefel decided to let them off with only a warning.

Thirteen months later, the Manns and the Macks were still arguing over the noise. An informal hearing before the city attorney failed to end the neighbors' differences. Darien and his band wanted to keep playing in the garage, and the Macks wanted the music to stop permanently.

To settle the matter once and for all, Darien Mann and his parents decided to bring a lawsuit against the

People frequently go before the court to request that a statute be declared "void for vagueness." They are seeking a declaratory judgment—an order issued by the court that a law is not enforceable and, therefore, is null and void.

Answers will be found on page T 103.

City of Los Angeles. They wanted the municipal court to remove the noise ordinance from the municipal code. If the ordinance were removed from the books, Darien and his band would not be breaking the law when they played their music late into the night.

The Manns said that the wording of the law was not clear enough.

In court, the Manns said that the wording of the law was not clear enough to tell if the law was being broken. They pointed out that because the level of noise banned by the law was not described in a scientific way, no one could tell how loud was too loud.

The Manns then said that if the law was not clear about what noise level was illegal, then the law could not be enforced. If this was true, the court had the power to remove the law from the municipal code.

The city attorney defended the city's law. He pointed out that most laws are not scientifically exact. They must be flexible enough to be used in many different cases.

After thinking about both sides, the court ruled against the Manns. It agreed with the city attorney that it takes "common sense," not scientific measurement, to be able to know what is a "loud, unnecessary, and unusual" noise.

The court explained that it is often asked to decide if a law can be enforced. In such cases, it uses the "reasonable man test" to see if people can understand the law the way it is written.

When the court uses the reasonable man test, it puts itself in the shoes of an ordinary person. If the court believes that a reasonable man can understand what a particular law requires him to do or not to do, then the law is clear enough to be enforced.

The court also noted that the noise ordinance stated several factors for courts to think about when deciding what the law means. Some of those factors were the time of night at which the noise occurred and how near the noise was to other people's homes.

Based on the reasonable man test and the wording of the law, the court ruled that the law was clear enough to be enforced against Darien and his band.

Analyzing the Case

1. What activities were made illegal by the Los Angeles Municipal Code noise ordinance?
2. What reasons did the Manns give to the court when they argued that the noise ordinance should be removed from the municipal code?
3. Do you think that it is fair for the City of Los Angeles to pass a noise ordinance that means people cannot play loud music in the privacy of their homes? Support your opinion.
4. Do you think the court would have ruled in the same way if the band had been playing loud classical music late at night? Support your opinion.

Activity: Have students try to write laws that describe infractions in a scientific way. Have students discuss what a society with a scientifically exact legal system would be like.

CHAPTER SURVEY

Answers to Survey and Workshop will be found on page T 103.

UNDERSTANDING NEW VOCABULARY

Seeing Relationships

Match each vocabulary term with the lettered word or phrase most closely related to it. Then explain how the items in each pair are related.

Example: *Home rule* relates to *government structure* because cities and counties with home rule can choose their own government structure.

1. *board*	**(a)** land use
2. *property tax*	**(b)** city
3. *zoning*	**(c)** revenue
4. *municipality*	**(d)** commissioners
5. *intergovernmental revenue*	**(e)** water, gas, and electricity
6. *utilities*	**(f)** grants

Putting It in Writing

Write a paragraph explaining how a county might plan, build, and pay for a new sewage treatment plant. In your paragraph use the terms *board*, *zoning*, and *intergovernmental revenue*.

LOOKING BACK AT THE CHAPTER

1. How do local governments get their powers?

2. Why are there different types of local government?

3. How do the governments of traditional New England towns differ from those of large cities?

4. Why were the council-manager and commission plans created?

5. Pick two types of local government services and describe them.

6. How do local governments get the money they need to provide services?

7. What are some difficulties local governments face in trying to provide services?

8. Why do federal, state, and local governments all become involved in meeting the needs of local communities?

9. Why do conflicts arise between local governments and between a local government and other levels of government?

10. *Evaluation.* Do you think local governments should have complete freedom to decide how to use intergovernmental revenue? Support your opinion with reasons.

11. *Analysis.* Why must local governments decide which services are most important?

12. *Synthesis.* Suppose that local governments no longer existed. How would state governments be affected? How would communities be affected?

WORKING TOGETHER

1. Act out a city council meeting. Some students will be council members, and others will be citizens presenting various opinions on a particular issue, such as the skateboarding example in the chapter. After listening to the arguments of the citizens, the council members will make a decision and give reasons for their decision.

2. Bring to class a local newspaper. Find all the articles that involve local government and explain how each article is related to one or more of the services provided by local government.

3. Pick one local issue that you are concerned about. Write a letter to your local government expressing your views on the issue.

4. Look in the government listings of your phone book. List at least four services provided by your county or township that are not mentioned in the chapter. Then list at least four services provided by your city or town that are not mentioned in the chapter.

Teaching Note: For reinforcement of decision-making skills, use Decision-Making Worksheet Chapter 12.

SOCIAL STUDIES SKILLS

Interpreting an Organization Chart

Organization charts are often used to illustrate how different forms of city government work. Such charts show the parts of an organization. They also show how those parts relate to one another. In most organization charts, the official or group with the most power and authority is shown at the top. The following organization chart shows how the council-manager plan of city government works.

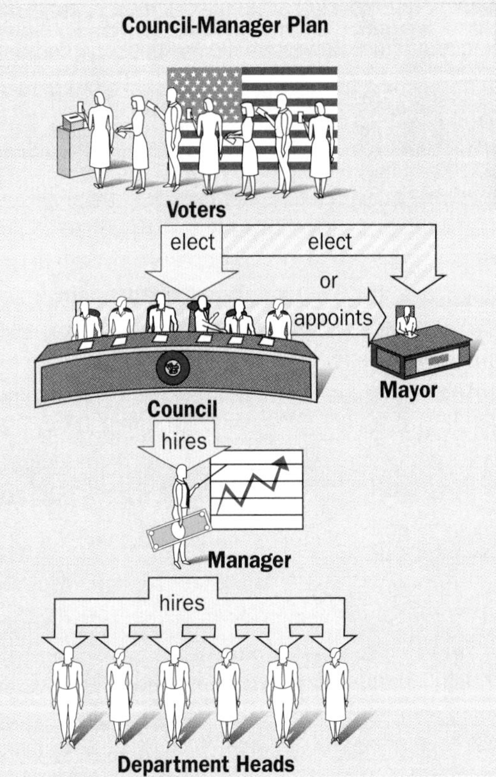

1. Each level on the chart represents a level of organization. How many levels are there in this form of city government?

2. The arrows show how authority flows from one level to another. Which city official or officials have the greatest power in this form of government? How is that power used?

DECISION-MAKING SKILLS

Opinion or Statement of Fact?

Suppose that you have been given a writing assignment to explain how your local government could improve its services. As part of your assignment, you have to decide whether utilities, such as water, gas, and electricity, should be supplied by your local government or by private companies.

In looking for information on the issue, you run across the following editorial in your local newspaper. Study the editorial to separate statements of fact from statements that give opinions. If necessary, review page 212.

> Local governments do not operate utilities as well as private businesses do. Whenever a local government tries to provide its own water, gas, and electricity service, customers are always charged higher utility fees.
>
> Let's face it, businesspeople are more talented than government officials. Most government officials do not have college training in business management, especially in managing utilities. Also, it is clear that utility workers are treated more fairly by owners of private companies than they are by government officials. The workers will be happier if they work for private companies rather than working for local governments.

1. List two statements of fact and two opinions from the editorial above. For each statement of fact, explain how it might be proved or disproved. For each opinion, explain why it can neither be proved or disproved to everyone's satisfaction.

2. Why is it important to be able to distinguish between opinions and statements of fact when making decisions?

3. Suppose you had to explain to a seventh grader how to tell the difference between an opinion and a statement of fact. What procedure would you tell that person to follow?

IN THEIR OWN WORDS

George Washington Plunkitt: "Honest Graft"

Answers will be found on page T 104.

At the turn of the century many American cities were controlled by corrupt politicians. New York City, for example, was run by a political organization known as Tammany Hall. Many of the Tammany Hall politicians became millionaires.

Reformers charged that the Tammany politicians were getting rich through such illegal activities as bribery, blackmail, and stealing money from the city treasury. These kinds of activities are known as *graft*.

In 1905, Tammany Hall politician George Washington Plunkitt gave an interview to William Riordan. He explained that he thought there was a difference between honest graft and dishonest graft.

> Everybody's talkin' these days about Tammany men growin' rich on graft, but nobody thinks of drawin' the distinction between honest graft and dishonest graft. There's all the difference in the world between the two. Yes, many of our men have grown rich in politics. I have myself. I've made a big fortune out of the game, and I'm gettin' richer every day, but I've not gone in for dishonest graft—blackmailin' gamblers, saloon-keepers, disorderly people, etc.—and neither has any of the men who have made big fortunes in politics.
>
> There's an honest graft, and I'm an example of how it works. I might sum up the whole thing by sayin': "I seen my opportunities and I took 'em."
>
> Just let me explain by examples. My party's in power in the city, and it's goin' to undertake a lot of public improvements. Well, I'm tipped off, say, that they're going to lay out a new park at a certain place.
>
> I see my opportunity and I take it. I go to that place and I buy up all the land I can in the neighborhood [while it is still cheap]. Then the board of this or that makes its plan public, and there is a rush to get my land, which nobody cared particular for before.
>
> Ain't it perfectly honest to charge a good price and make a profit on my investment and foresight? Of course it is. Well, that's honest graft.

In 1901 Tammany Hall was defeated by reformers who charged that the political bosses were robbing the city. Plunkitt insisted that "all they can show is that the Tammany heads of departments looked after their friends, within the law, and gave them what opportunities they could to make honest graft."

From Plunkitt of Tammany Hall *by William L. Riordan, 1905.*

Analyzing Primary Sources

1. According to Plunkitt, what is the difference between honest and dishonest graft?

2. Who, if anyone, was hurt by what Plunkitt called "honest graft"? Do you think such activities should be legal? Why or why not?

3. How did the council-manager plan of city government make it harder for politicians to make money through graft?

Activity: Have students read newspaper or news magazine accounts of current illegal activities in government. Discuss what opportunities were seen and taken by the people involved.

UNIT SURVEY

Answers will be found on page T 105.

LOOKING BACK AT THE UNIT

1. Explain what "new federalism" is and why it came about.
2. What are some of the ways that citizens can influence state and local government?
3. In what ways are the federal, state, and local governments similar in their organization?
4. Compare the powers and responsibilities of the President, the governor of a state, and the mayor of a city. How are they similar? How are they different?
5. How is the relationship between local and state governments similar to the relationship between the states and the federal government? How do the two relationships differ?
6. What are some advantages of having federal, state, and local levels of government? What are some disadvantages?

TAKING A STAND

The Issue

Should states have lotteries?

Have you heard the story that there is a pot of gold at the end of every rainbow? In recent years many states have passed laws that have the effect of rainbows, turning the average corner store into a shimmering pot of gold. Stirring up get-rich-quick excitement and bringing in money to support government programs, state lotteries offer payoffs worth millions of dollars for the price of a single ticket.

Lotteries are nothing new in this country. Some early colonies had them, and even Thomas Jefferson said that a lottery "is a wonderful thing. . . . It is a taxation on the willing." Modern-day supporters agree. They point out that, unlike a tax, no one is forced to buy a lottery ticket, and that in recent years state lotteries brought in more than $11 billion a year.

The money that lotteries bring in helps to pay for highways, parks, and schools in 22 states. At a time when many citizens are opposed to paying higher taxes, supporters say that a lottery is a painless and entertaining way to raise revenue.

People who disapprove of lotteries say that chasing the pot of gold is far from painless. Winners are few, and the millions of losers are mostly people with low incomes, desperate for a miracle. Lottery opponents say that the money collected is a kind of tax, paid mainly by the poor. In New Jersey, a survey showed that over one third of people earning less than $10,000 a year spend more than one fifth of their income on the state lottery.

It is wrong for states to encourage gambling, lottery opponents say. Walking into a grocery store and buying lottery tickets could become an expensive habit. For too many people, opponents argue, the lottery is an addiction, like alcohol or cigarettes.

Lottery supporters reply, "Let's stop telling other people how to run their lives! If poor people and the young have fun playing the lottery, let them. It's their money." For 96 percent of the population, lottery supporters claim, gambling is a harmless and healthy form of recreation, and of the 4 percent who are hooked on gambling, only a fraction are addicted to lotteries.

Expressing Your Opinion

Should states have lotteries? Take a position on this issue and get ready to debate with someone who supports the opposing point of view. Make notes of your main arguments, which you will give in a one-minute opening statement. After hearing your opponent's arguments, you will respond in a half-minute rebuttal. (A rebuttal is simply a reply that explains why your opponent is wrong.) Try to guess what your opponent will say, and make notes on how you will reply.

UNIT 5

Unit Quotation: President Hoover believed that government should be "an umpire instead of a player in the economic game." However, faced with the beginning of the Great Depression of the 1930s, he became the first President to use the power of the federal government to fight a depression.

THE AMERICAN ECONOMIC SYSTEM

The Economy is a Foundation

Our economic system is . . . an instrument by which we add to the security and richness of life of every individual. It by no means comprises the whole purpose of life, but it is the foundation upon which can be built the finer things of the spirit.

—President Herbert Hoover

You have been learning about how governments at different levels protect our rights as citizens. Our freedom as individuals, however, depends on more than our democratic form of government. As Herbert Hoover reminds us, our economic system is a basic part of our free society.

What is an economic system? How does our economy work? Why is money so important? What is the role of government in the economy? What role will you play in the economy? These are some of the questions you will explore as you read Unit 5.

Chapter Themes: Every society must decide how to use limited resources to produce goods and services that will satisfy people's unlimited wants. Depending on the goals and values of the society, such economic decisions will be made in different ways and produce different economic systems.

CHAPTER 13

What Is an Economy?

"Mom, guess what!" exclaimed Josh Epstein. "The manager of Burger Barn just offered me a job. I'd work three hours every day after school and ten hours on weekends. I figure I'd be making a hundred dollars a week! With that kind of money I could start saving for a computer, I could pay for movies, I could even buy my own clothes."

"That sounds wonderful, Josh," replied his mother, "but what effect would the job have on other parts of your life? You worked so hard to make the soccer team. Wouldn't this job interfere with after-school practices?"

"Wow! I was so excited, I didn't think of that," said Josh.

"And what about your computer club meetings on Saturdays? Wouldn't you miss the meetings if you worked at Burger Barn?"

"That's true. Boy, this is going to be a tough decision!"

Josh Epstein has a problem. He wants to be on the soccer team and to go to computer club meetings. He wants to work so that he can pay for movies, buy his own clothes, and save for a computer. However, Josh does not have enough time to do all these things.

Josh's problem, then, is that he has a limited amount of time compared with his many wants. Josh's time is the major resource he has for satisfying his wants. However, because that resource is limited, Josh simply cannot satisfy all his wants. Therefore, Josh will have to make a choice about whether or not to take the job.

Societies also have limited resources with which to satisfy their many wants. To solve this problem, they must make decisions. As you learned in Chapter 2, the system through which people in a society make choices about how to use their resources to produce goods and services is called an economy.

In this chapter you will read about economic wants, resources, and the decisions that must be made about using resources to satisfy wants. You will also find out about three different kinds of economic systems through which societies make those decisions.

Teaching Note: Use the Introducing the Chapter activity, page T 107.

13-1 WHY SOCIETIES HAVE ECONOMIES

Read to Find Out

- what the terms *factors of production, capital, consumption, opportunity cost,* and *scarcity* mean.
- what economic wants people have.
- how human wants for goods and services are satisfied.
- what factors people consider when making economic choices.

In reading about Josh Epstein, you came across the basic economic facts of life: in any society, people must make choices about how to use their resources to produce goods and services to satisfy their wants. Notice that there are several elements to think about when looking at these economic facts—wants, resources, production of goods and services, and choices. By looking at how each of the elements is related to the others, you will gain a clearer understanding of what an economy is and why every society has one.

People's Many Wants

Think about the first element: wants. Everyone has wants. Our most basic wants are for food, clothing, and shelter. However, people are rarely satisfied to have just their basic wants met. People also want to be able to move from place to place, to be entertained, to be educated, and to have health care when they are sick. In fact, people have an almost endless number of wants.

How wants differ. Of course, your wants will differ from those of other people, depending on where you live and who you are. One important influence on your wants is your environment. If you live in Alaska, you will want to have warm clothes to wear and good heating for your house. In the warm weather of Phoenix, Arizona, are you likely to have the same wants?

Wants are also influenced by the societies in which we live and their cultures. Americans usually want to live in houses or apartments, while the nomads of Tibet think that tents best fit their way of life.

Even when they live in the same environment and the same culture, different people want different things. Some people choose a vacation in the mountains, while others choose to go to the beach. You may favor white running shoes, while your best friend wants black ones.

People's wants can also change. Think of the toys you wanted when you were a baby. How do they compare with the goods you want to have now?

Another important characteristic of wants is that many of them can be satisfied only for

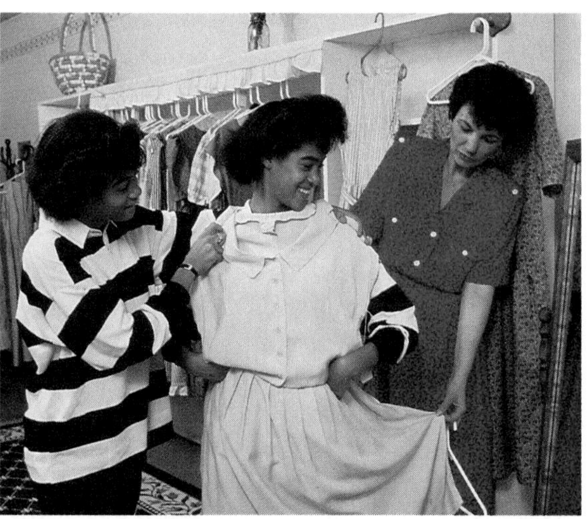

In shopping for a dress that she likes and that she can afford, this young woman is fulfilling an "economic want."

Challenge (Analysis): Wants differ depending on who you are, where you live, and the cultural influences you experience. Have students discuss how satisfying wants can create conflict and cooperation both within a nation and between nations.

a short time. Do the blue jeans you wore last year still fit you, or do you need to buy a new pair? Understanding that many wants occur again and again is basic to learning what an economy is.

Using Resources

The resources people have for producing goods and services to satisfy their wants are called ***factors of production***. According to economists—the people who study how economies work—the three basic factors of production in an economy are labor, land, and capital.

Labor. One factor of production, labor, includes time and energy. If Josh Epstein takes the job at Burger Barn, he will be using his time and energy to help produce hamburgers. His labor will also include the knowledge and skills he uses in his job.

Land. Another factor of production, land, is made up of the natural resources that are needed to produce goods and services. Such resources include soil, minerals, water, timber, fish and wildlife, and energy sources.

Capital. Finally, there is the factor of production called capital. ***Capital*** is anything produced in an economy that is saved to be used to produce other goods and services.

Capital includes any tools, machines, or buildings used to produce goods and services. When goods such as tools and factories are used as capital, they are called capital goods. For example, a griddle for frying hamburgers and a cash register for ringing up sales are capital goods to the manager of Burger Barn. Money can also be capital. However, it is capital only when it is not used for buying something now but is saved to be used for production sometime in the future.

The skills and training as well as the time and energy a person puts into a job are part of the factor of production called labor.

Production, Distribution, and Consumption

To produce the goods and services people want, the resources of labor, land, and capital must be combined in a process called production. That is why these resources are called factors of production. Farmers produce food by combining soil, water, and sunlight (land) with seeds and machinery (capital). They also use their knowledge, skills, time, and energy, as well as that of their workers (labor).

Production is followed by distribution, the process by which goods and services are made available to the people who want them. The truck that delivers bread to your market is part of the distribution process.

Finally, when goods and services have been produced and distributed, they are ready for consumption. ***Consumption*** is the act of buying or using goods and services.

The want-satisfaction chain. Satisfying people's economic wants can be a very complex process. In our economy, millions of people work in hundreds of thousands of businesses that produce and distribute many different goods and services.

The steps in the process of satisfying wants can be thought of as links in a chain of activities. As you read the following description, look at the picture of the want-satisfaction chain on this page.

The process begins with a want. Suppose, for example, that you and some of your friends decide to get together one evening for a spaghetti dinner. Among the supplies that you will want to buy and cook are the noodles. The first link in this want-satisfaction chain, then, is your want for noodles.

The next link is made up of people who combine the resources of land, labor, and capital. In the case of your noodles, farmers use soil, water, seeds, farm machinery, and labor to produce wheat, which they sell to a grain milling company. The company combines labor and machinery to turn the wheat into flour, which it sells to a noodle maker. The noodle maker adds other ingredients—water, salt, and eggs—and uses labor and machines to mix, roll, and cut the dough. This production process results in the noodles that you and your friends want.

The Want-Satisfaction Chain

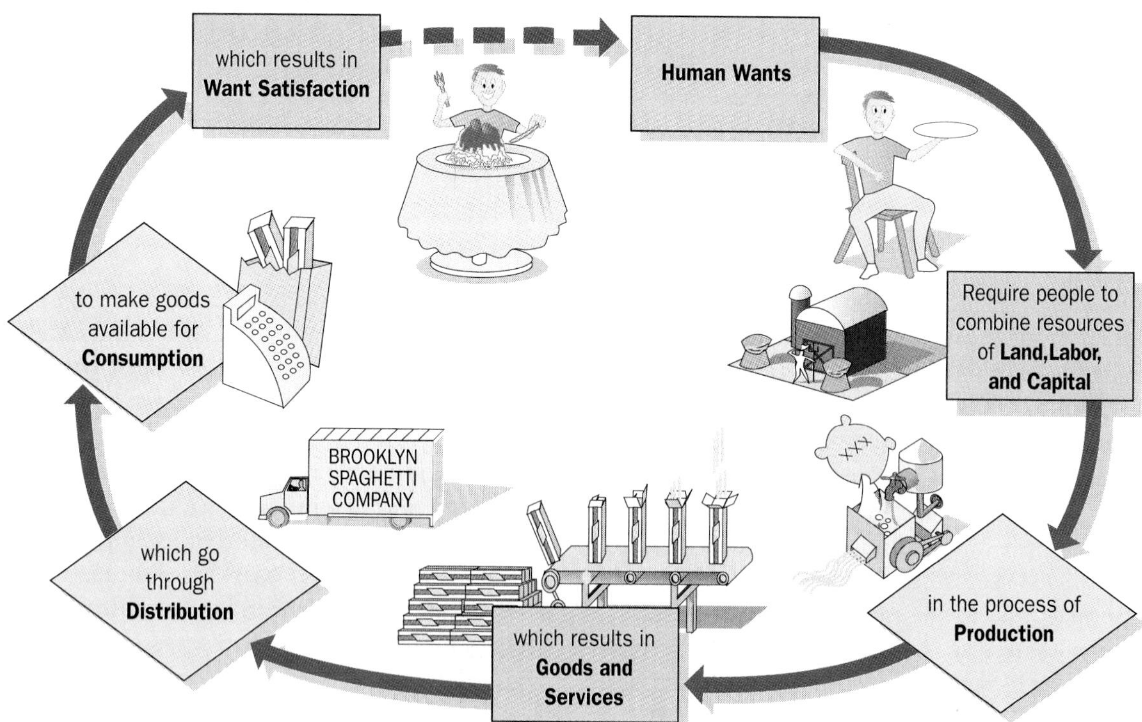

Source: Suzanne Wiggins Helburn, University of Colorado at Denver

Americans spend more than 90 percent of their after-tax income on consumption. The remainder is used for savings, frequently with consumption in mind: retirement, vacations, and so on.

Decision Making: Have students give examples of economic decisions in which they have to weigh the opportunity cost and benefits of each option.

However, your want is not yet satisfied. Once the noodles have been made, they must be sold to a grocery wholesaler who then sells and delivers them to a grocery store. This is the distribution link in the chain.

After the noodles have been distributed, you and your friends buy, cook, and eat them—the consumption link in the chain. At this point, you have achieved want satisfaction.

However, your want may be satisfied only for the time being. If you want to eat noodles another time, the chain will have to repeat itself. The want-satisfaction chain is arranged in a circle to show that the process of satisfying wants happens over and over again.

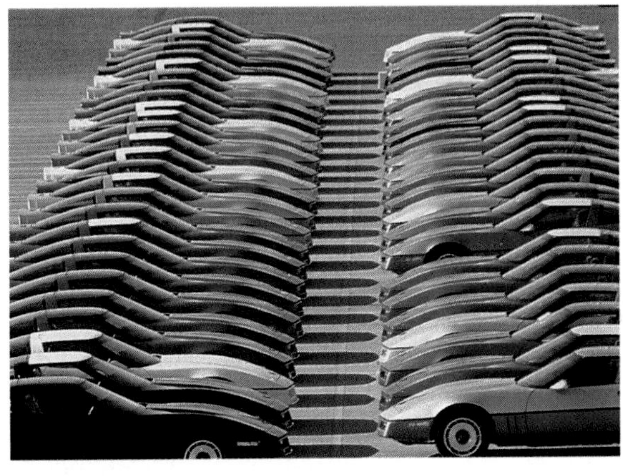

The production process completed, these automobiles are awaiting distribution to dealers, who will sell them to consumers.

Making Choices

A basic truth about all societies is that there are never enough resources to produce all the goods and services people want and go on wanting. As a result of this situation, people in all societies must make choices about which of their wants will be satisfied and which will not. These choices are economic choices, and the process of making them is what an economy is all about.

You will remember that Josh Epstein is trying to decide whether or not to take a job at Burger Barn. Josh has to make a choice because the job will use up the time, a limited resource, that he would otherwise use to satisfy his desire to play soccer and attend the computer club meetings at his school. In order to decide, Josh will have to think about how he wants to use his time.

Benefits and costs. One part of making an economic decision is looking at the benefits you will receive from each of your possible choices. Josh's benefits from the Burger Barn job will include one hundred dollars a week plus work experience and the satisfaction of having some money of his own to spend.

A second part involves looking at the costs of your choices. The major cost of any decision is giving up the benefits you would have received from the next best alternative. If Josh takes the job, for example, he will give up the benefits he would have received from using his time to play soccer and learn about computers.

Like Josh's decision, every economic decision has an ***opportunity cost***, the benefit given up when scarce resources are used for one purpose instead of the next best purpose. If Josh decides that the opportunity cost of taking the job would be greater than its benefits, then Josh should refuse the Burger Barn offer.

Scarcity

Societies have always faced, and will continue to face, a problem like Josh's problem. This problem is known as ***scarcity***, which means that resources are always limited compared with the number and variety of wants people have. Scarcity is a problem in both rich societies and poor ones. The idea of scarcity is based not on the total amount of resources in a society, but on the relationship between

Opportunity costs are clearly seen during wartime. A country's resources can be used to make weapons for soldiers or consumer goods for civilians. The opportunity cost is the consumer goods not made because of the demands of a wartime economy.

Teaching Note: Use Teaching Activity 1, page T 107, as a culminating activity after students have read the material in Section 13-1.

wants and the resources available to satisfy them.

The following example may help you understand scarcity. Society A does not have enough good farm land to grow the food its people want. Society B has plenty of good farm land. However, that land, which could be used to grow food, is also in demand for factories, houses, and shopping malls. You can see that in both Society A and Society B, land resources are scarce compared with the ways people want to use them.

Choices about resource use. In any economy, each decision to use resources to produce one kind of good or service is, at the same time, a decision not to use the same resources to produce something else that people want. The farmers who grew the wheat for the noodles chose to use their limited resources of land, labor, and capital to grow wheat instead of some other crop such as corn, oats, or barley.

In a large economy such choices are made by businesses as well as by individuals. For example, a company that makes cars and trucks with a limited number of factories, machines, and workers will have to make choices about how many cars and trucks of each model to produce.

Governments also have to make choices about the use of resources. For example, how much of the federal government's resources should be used to build defense systems in space and how much to improve the schools or to build housing for families with low incomes?

Although the choices that individuals, businesses, and governments must make are different in many ways, they all have one thing in common. They involve making economic decisions about how to use limited resources to produce goods and services to satisfy people's unlimited wants.

Answers will be found on T 109.

Section Review

1. Define *factors of production, capital, consumption, opportunity cost,* and *scarcity.*
2. What are some of the economic wants that everyone has?
3. After a good has been produced in the want-satisfaction chain, which process makes it available to people who want it?
4. What are two important parts of making an economic decision?

Analysis. Explain why even in a wealthy society economic choices have to be made.

13-2

BASIC ECONOMIC DECISIONS

Read to Find Out

- who makes the decisions about what and how much to produce in our society.
- how decisions are made about how to produce goods and services.
- how societies may decide who gets what is produced.

As you look around you, you can see goods and services being produced, distributed, and consumed. What you are seeing is the result of many economic decisions people have made and are making.

Have you ever thought that a pizza is the result of an economic decision? A restaurant owner knows that people want to be able to buy pizza. The owner makes a choice to open a pizza business. The owner decides how many pizzas to make in a day, and how many people to hire to make the pizza and serve it to customers.

Teaching Note: Use the Reinforcement Activity, page T 108, and accompanying worksheet in the Activity Book after students have read Section 13-1.

Like the restaurant owner, people in any economy face three major economic decisions:

- *What* goods and services should be produced, and *how much* of them?
- *How* should these goods and services be produced?
- *Who* will get the goods and services that are produced?

Every day, these decisions are being made in every part of the economy.

What and How Much to Produce

In any economy, people must decide what to produce with the scarce resources they have. In our economy, this first major economic decision is made by the people who own or can get resources.

A farmer who owns land and machinery may decide to produce wheat instead of barley. You might decide to use a resource you own—your labor—to mow lawns instead of serve hamburgers. Any decision about what goods or services to produce is based on a prediction of what people will want to consume.

As an owner of resources decides what to produce, he or she also decides how much to produce. The amount of a good or a service that is produced will depend on a number of factors. For instance, farmers' decisions will be based on the amount of land they own or can rent, the amount of labor and machinery they can afford, and the amount of wheat or barley they think they can sell.

How to Produce Goods and Services

The second major economic decision is how to produce goods and services. In other words, in what way will land, labor, and capital be combined to produce the goods and services people want?

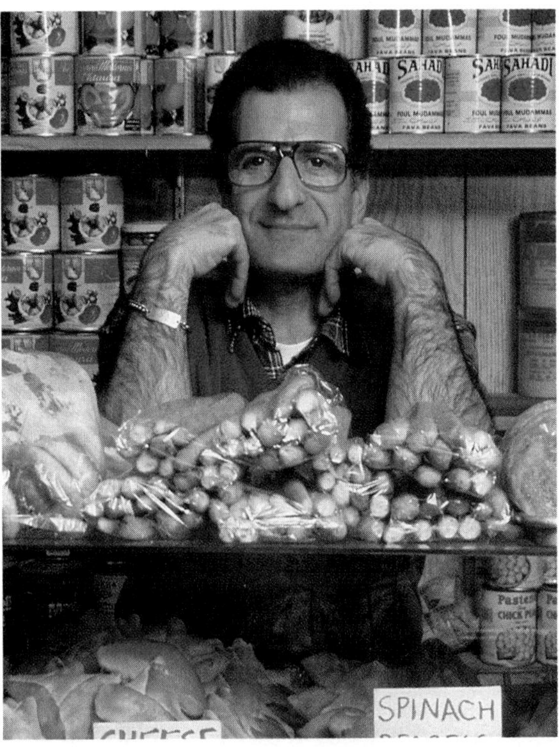

If his business is to succeed, this Armenian-American shopkeeper must make good decisions about what and how many pastries to bake.

Farmers who produce wheat must make several choices about how to do it. Should they do all the work themselves, or should they hire workers to plant and care for the wheat? Should they rely more on workers or on machinery? Should they buy the farm machinery they decide to use, or should they rent it?

In making decisions about how to produce, people want to choose the combination of resources that will be the least costly. A farmer who finds that it will cost less to hire workers than to use expensive machinery will hire workers to harvest the wheat.

The role of technology. In our economy, the desire to find the least costly way to produce goods and services has led to the growth of technology. In the early 1800s, cloth makers

Challenge (Analysis): Teenagers spend a sizable amount of money in the American economy. Have students discuss the impact of the purchasing power of teenagers on decision making by manufacturers and service providers. What impact do teenagers have on their families' buying decisions?

eagerly began using power looms. Although the new looms cost a lot of money, they could produce much more cloth much faster than the old handlooms could. Therefore, the cost of producing cloth soon dropped.

Since those early beginnings, technology has played an increasingly important part in decisions that people make about how to produce goods and provide services. For example, researchers have developed seeds that produce larger crops. Advances in electronics have given us robots to use in factories. Computers now keep records, make calculations, and speed up many jobs.

Changes in technology not only affect the way things are produced. They also make it possible to produce new goods and services. As a result, people's wants often change. For example, the speed and convenience of cars and planes has made people prefer to go places by car or airplane rather than by horse and buggy or train.

Who Will Get What Is Produced

Deciding who will get what is produced is the third basic choice that must be made in an economy. In other words, people must find a way to decide how all the goods and services will be divided up. Because wants are always greater than the resources available to satisfy them, this choice is an important one and sometimes a hard one.

Suppose you took all the goods and services produced in our economy in a year and shared them equally. Everyone would get the same number of T-shirts and the same number of jars of peanut butter. Do you think this would be a good way to divide up what has been produced?

On the other hand, suppose everyone listed everything they wanted, and then all the goods and services were given out according to the lists. How do you think that plan would work?

Using robots and other new technology can speed the production process. It also changes the training that workers need, as well as their responsibilities on the job.

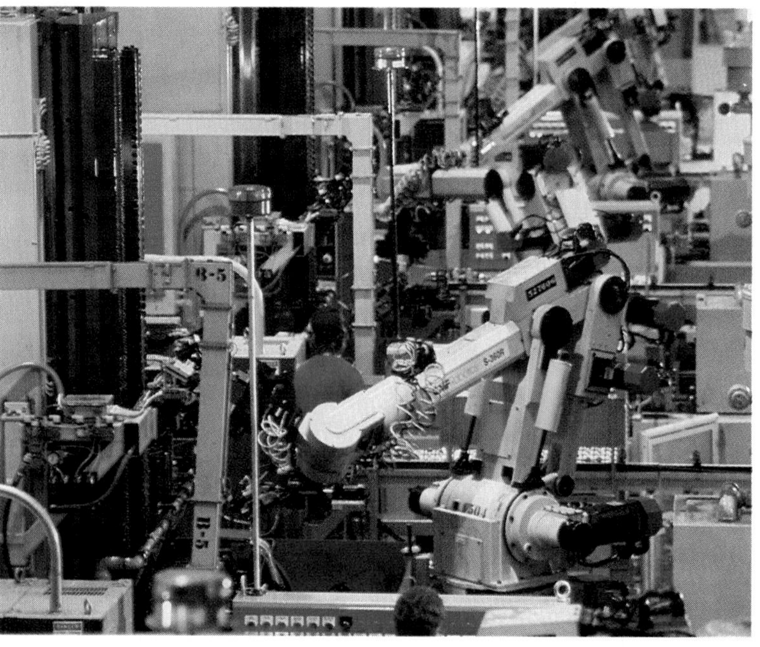

One disadvantage of improved technology is technological unemployment, which results when new products or methods of production make jobs obsolete or change the type of labor required. For example, the invention of the diesel locomotive eliminated the need for stokers on trains.

Lester Thurow

When Lester Thurow first became interested in economics in the 1960s, his goal was not to be a person who only thinks about economics and teaches it to university students. Instead, he wanted "somehow . . . to make the world better." Today, as an economist, teacher, writer, and speaker, he is known for his efforts to apply his knowledge of economics to real-world problems.

Despite his original goal, Thurow is no stranger to the academic world. He has taught economics at both Harvard University and the Massachusetts Institute of Technology.

However, Thurow has also done his part in trying to make the world a better place. Having worked as a miner before earning his degrees from Oxford and Harvard universities, Thurow understands what the economy means to the average working person.

Thurow believes that when people make decisions about working, buying, and saving, they consider more than just how to make as much money as possible. "Teamwork, motivation, envy, and cooperation" are always part of economic decision-making, he says. They are the human factors that many economists ignore. Changing our economy for the better is a "political process," Thurow says. The government has an important part to play in making our market economy more responsive to the needs of citizens.

Thurow argues that planning for long-term success rather than short-term profit is necessary for maintaining a healthy economy. "This calls for a change not in business behavior but in social behavior," says Thurow. "Our society of consumers must become a society of savers."

Here is another idea. Suppose that ten people were appointed to the Who-Gets-What Council. The task of the council would be to decide how all the goods and services produced in the United States would be divided among all the citizens. What do you think of that way of deciding who gets what?

Finally, think about this plan. The people who could pay the most would be the ones who got what they wanted. Would that be a fair way to decide how goods and services should be distributed?

In the debate over who gets what goods and services, a number of questions arise. Should everyone share and share alike, as in the first plan? Should they, as in the second plan, receive goods and services on the basis of what they say they want? Should a small group of people decide who is to receive which goods and services? Or, as in the fourth plan, should people who own more resources and produce more products get more goods and services than people who own and produce less?

The role of goals and values. Different societies have solved this problem in different ways, depending on their goals and values.

Discussion: Lester Thurow wants our society to plan for "long-term success rather than short-term profit." Have students compare the values and behaviors of individuals who plan for long-term success with those who want short-term profit.

Teaching Note: Use the Evaluating Progress activity, page T 108, to assess students' understanding of Section 13-2.

A society that wanted to achieve complete equality among all of its people might develop a system for sharing its products equally among its citizens, even if it meant that some people worked harder than others for the same reward.

On the other hand, a society in which freedom was the highest value might solve the problem by letting citizens compete freely among themselves to try to get the goods and services they want, even if it meant that some people got more than they needed while others went hungry.

How goods and services will be distributed has been the subject of much conflict throughout history. Often, wars have been fought because one group in a society believed that another group had too much control over who got what in the economy.

In fact, the goals and values of a society have a great influence on how that society makes all three basic economic decisions. In the next section you will read about three different economic systems that societies have developed for organizing their resources to produce and distribute the goods and services people want.

Answers will be found on page T 109.

Section Review

1. In our society, who decides what and how many goods and services to produce? What factors influence those decisions?
2. When making a decision about how to produce a product, what factors do people consider?
3. Describe three possible ways to determine who gets what is produced.

Evaluation. How do you think our society decides who gets what is produced? What are some of the advantages and disadvantages of that method?

13-3 THREE TYPES OF ECONOMIES

Read to Find Out

- what the terms *traditional economy, command economy, market economy, profit, invest, free enterprise, capitalism,* and *mixed economy* mean.
- how the three types of economic systems differ.
- what influences decision making in our economy.

People do not make economic decisions all by themselves. Almost every economic task, from raising wheat to providing hospital services, requires that people work together.

Also, people can rarely meet all their economic needs by themselves. Most people do one kind of work. They depend on the work of other people for most of the products and services that they use.

The three major economic decisions you have learned about in this chapter, then, are made by people who work and live together in a society. In human history, there have been three types of economic systems: the traditional economy, the command economy, and the market economy. These systems are three different ways a society can organize production, distribution, and consumption to solve the economic problem of scarcity.

A Traditional Economy

In a ***traditional economy***, the basic economic decisions are made according to long-established ways of behaving that are unlikely to change. These customs are passed along from elders to youths.

For example, a tribe of nomads may follow certain hunting customs. They will make camp at the same places and hunt the same game year after year. The roles that fathers, sons, mothers, and daughters play as they help each other in the hunt remain the same over the years.

Tradition answers the question of what and how much to produce. The people who belong to the tribe want to produce game, and they want to produce enough of it to feed the whole tribe.

There are also customs that have to do with how to "produce" the game. Year after year the men use the same weapons and methods to hunt the game, and the women use the same methods to prepare and cook it.

The tribe's customs also determine who gets what is produced. When sharing the kill, each member might get an amount based on his or her role in the hunt. In another tribe, shares might be divided according to the number of members in a family.

Because individuals or families in a traditional economy usually own their own resources, such as land, tools, and labor, they have some freedom to make their own day-to-day decisions about when and how to use their resources. They may decide, for example, not to go on a hunt one day, but to gather fruit instead. They have little freedom, however, when it comes to making the basic economic decisions already set by tradition. As a result, there is very little change in the economy over time.

Values and economic decisions. Many of the values of people in traditional economies are different from our own and may be hard for us to understand. A traditional economy is closely connected to the religious beliefs and family organization of the society and reflects the values of those institutions. Any major change in the economy would upset what people think of as a perfectly balanced relationship between people and nature.

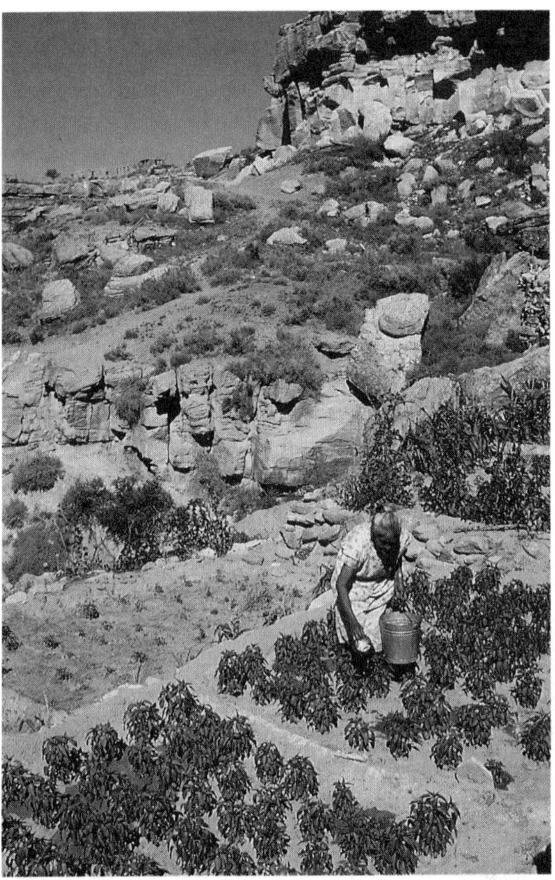

Watering her pepper plants, this member of the Hopi people of Arizona plays a traditional role in her society's farming economy.

Today, no purely traditional economy remains in the world. A few societies in parts of Central and South America, Africa, and Asia, however, still have economies that are mostly traditional.

A Command Economy

In a ***command economy***, the government or a central authority owns or controls the factors of production and makes the basic economic decisions. In such a system, the government usually has charge of important parts of the economy, such as transportation, communication, banking, and manufacturing. Farms

Even in highly industrialized societies, traces of a traditional economy can be seen in the occupations chosen by successive generations. Sons and daughters often follow their parents and grandparents into law, banking, medicine, teaching, farming, and factory work.

In the command economy of ancient Egypt, the pharaoh had the power to decide that pyramids and monuments would be built and that slaves would build them.

and many stores are government-controlled. The government may also set wages and decide who will work at which jobs.

Economic systems based on command principles have existed for thousands of years. From Egyptian pharaohs and medieval lords to some modern nations such as China, powerful rulers and governments have controlled the economies of their societies.

When you think of a command economy, you may think of a tyrannical form of government. However, it is important to know that democracies, too, can have command systems if the citizens, through elections, give their government the power to make the basic economic decisions.

Government decision making. In a command economy, a central planning group makes most of the decisions about how, what, and how much to produce. The result is that only those products that the government chooses will be available for people to consume.

Who gets what is produced in a command system depends on the goals and values of the central authority. A greedy dictator, for example, might choose to make himself and his friends rich. On the other hand, if the government's goal were to satisfy wants based on individual need, then each person might get food, clothes, and housing no matter how much or how little he or she earned.

Unlike traditional economies, command economies can make changes quickly to meet changing conditions because the government controls the resources. In the case of a dry spell, for instance, the government can decide to drill wells and use the water to irrigate crops, even if irrigation is not traditional in that society.

A Market Economy

The third kind of economic system is the ***market economy***, a system in which private individuals own the factors of production and are free to make their own choices about production, distribution, and consumption. The economy of the United States is based on the market system.

In a market economy, all economic decisions are made through a kind of bargaining

Challenge (Analysis): Have students discuss the advantages and disadvantages that a command economy might have for individuals.

process that takes place in markets. As you learned in Chapter 2, a market is a place or situation in which buyers and sellers agree to exchange goods and services. In a market, the value of what you have to offer sets the value of what you can get. Therefore, no one person or group runs a market economy. Instead, everyone takes part in running it by freely making economic decisions.

Decision making by individuals. In a market economy, people are not only free to decide how to use land, labor, and capital. They are also free to start their own businesses and to choose what jobs they want to work at. The major economic decisions about what and how much to produce and how to produce it are made by individuals, not by government command or by tradition.

In a sense, individuals also make the economic decisions about who will get what is produced in a market economy. People who make desirable products or who earn high wages for the work they do will be able to buy more goods and services than people who produce less desirable products or earn lower wages. People who own land and capital will also be able to afford more goods and services than people who do not.

AMERICAN NOTEBOOK

A market economy has been basic to the United States since our beginnings as a country. Here is what one noted American economist has said about the importance of markets:

> **The market is not some magical process, but merely a system that allows trial and error—rewarding success and punishing failure—as a daily event.**
>
> —Robert Samuelson, quoted in *Newsweek*, January 9, 1989.

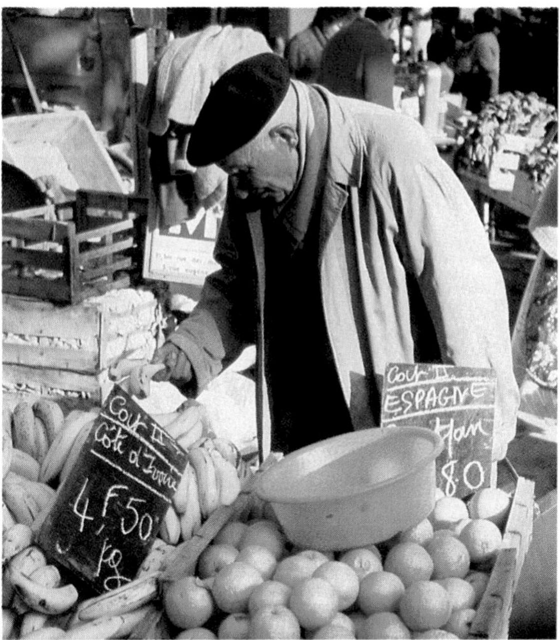

In a market economy, the wants of individuals like this French shopper play a major role in determining what will be produced.

Competition and profit seeking. Competition plays an important part in a market economy. Producers compete to satisfy the wants of consumers. Buyers compete to get the products they want. Workers compete for jobs. These individuals are all part of the process of making decisions in a market economy.

Another important influence on the way people make decisions is what is called the "profit motive." One of the chief goals of people in a market economy is to make a profit. ***Profit*** is the difference between what it costs to produce something and the price the buyer pays for it. In a market economy, people base their decisions about what and how much to produce largely on how much profit they think they will make.

The desire to make a profit also leads people to invest in a business. To ***invest*** means to use your money to help a business get started or grow, with the hope that the business will earn a profit that you can share.

Teaching Note: Buying stock in corporations is discussed in Chapter 14.

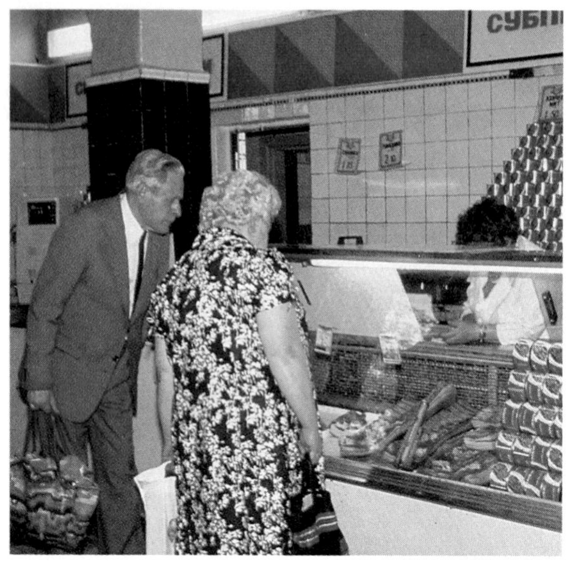

The greater choice now available to these Russian shoppers reflects their government's decision to produce more consumer goods.

Free enterprise and capitalism. It is important to get to know two other names for the market economy. One of these is *free enterprise.* The word *enterprise* comes from a French word that means "to undertake." The term ***free enterprise*** refers to the system in which individuals in a market economy are free to undertake economic activities with little or no control by the government.

The other name for the market system is *capitalism.* ***Capitalism*** is a system in which people make their own decisions about how to save resources as capital, and how to use their capital to produce goods and provide services. The term *capitalism* calls attention to the fact that in a market economy capital is privately owned.

Modern-Day Economies

Describing economic systems as traditional, command, or market can be useful for understanding the way people in different societies make economic decisions. In today's world, however, every economy is a ***mixed economy,*** an economy that is a mixture of two or more of the three basic systems. Looking at the economies of the People's Republic of China and the United States will help you understand what a mixed economy is.

The economy of China. The economy of China is mostly a command economy. A central, one-party government has charge of the major resources and makes many important economic decisions.

The government of China makes economic plans, in which it sets goals for what goods and how many of each will be produced during a certain period of years. These plans also set forth how resources will be used in production.

In the late 1980s and early 1990s, the Chinese government took steps toward making a more mixed economy by adding some features of free enterprise to its economic system. In cities, privately owned shops sell consumer goods, and new hotels abound in the free-enterprise hotel business.

Change in industry has been slower because some government officials are reluctant to release control of factories. Nonetheless,

Basic Characteristics of the Three Economic Systems	
Traditional	Decisions based on long-standing customs. Jobs passed down from generation to generation. Change occurs slowly if at all. Little individual freedom.
Command	Government or other central authority makes decisions and determines how resources will be used. Change can occur relatively easily. Little individual freedom.
Market	Resources owned and controlled by individuals. Economic decisions made by individuals competing to earn profits. Individual freedom is considered very important.

Teaching Note: For economist Milton Friedman's views on the advantages of capitalism, see "In Their Own Words" on page 386.

Teaching Note: Use Teaching Activity 2, page T 108, as a culminating activity for this section.

some factories have had more freedom in hiring and firing and in marketing goods, and this change has been working well.

The economy of the United States. The United States economy is considered a market—or free enterprise—system. Business owners are free to compete with each other to produce and distribute any goods and services they think they can sell. Americans are also free to buy and consume any goods and services they want and can afford.

However, there are elements of command in our economy as well. As you have seen in earlier chapters, our government provides, or "commands" the economy to provide, certain services such as education, mail services, and an army and navy for defense. Government also provides such goods as highways and airports. In the following chapters, you will read about many other ways in which citizens have asked government to help take charge of and guide the American economy.

Answers will be found on page T 109.

Section Review

1. Define *traditional economy, command economy, market economy, profit, invest, free enterprise, capitalism,* and *mixed economy.*
2. Why is there little change or growth in a traditional economy?
3. Why can a command economy respond quickly to changing conditions?
4. What are some of the influences on decision making in a market economy?

Evaluation. Imagine that you had lived in each of the three kinds of economic systems. Describe some of the major advantages and disadvantages that each of them would have had for you.

Data Search. Look on pages 586–587 in the Data Bank. Find data that supports the following statement: "Citizens of the United States have more consumer goods than citizens of Japan."

A BROADER VIEW

In this chapter you have learned many of the important ideas of economics. Economics is a social science. It is "social" because it studies people. It is a science because it calls for carefully looking at, explaining, and predicting how people will act and what choices they will make.

Economics was born at about the same time as the United States. In fact, many people trace its beginnings back to 1776, when Adam Smith published *The Wealth of Nations*. Adam Smith was the first to describe and study the market economy. In the market system, Smith said, competition acts like an "invisible hand" that guides the economy.

When Adam Smith's book came out, the market system he wrote about was a fairly new way to solve the problem of scarcity. For thousands of years, traditional and command economies had decided how people would produce and consume goods and services. However, as the market system came into being, people were excited by the new freedom it offered. They also wanted to know more about how the market system worked.

It is no accident, then, that economics was born in the same year that the colonies declared their independence. Both the new economic system and the new country were based on the idea that individuals should be free to make choices.

Teaching Note: Use the Enrichment Activity, page T 109, and accompanying worksheet in the Activity Book.

DECISION MAKING

The Process

Teaching Note: For reinforcement of decision-making skills, use Decision-Making Worksheet Chapter 13.

Choosing and Taking Action

This is a test. Your grade on the test will be determined by how fast you make the following decisions.

> Will you take a part-time job during the school year?
> Which sport or school club will you get involved in next year?

If you are thinking, "Stop! I need more information before I can choose," then you have passed the test. You have avoided making a snap decision.

Decision making, as you know, involves two main parts: choosing and taking action. You also know that to make a good decision you need good information. That is why you need to think critically—to judge which information is useful and accurate. Snap decisions, which are made without careful thinking, are often wrong and often regretted. The more serious the decision, the more time you should take to gather and judge information before making up your mind.

EXPLAINING THE PROCESS

The lessons on pages 40 and 60 gave you some guidelines for choosing and taking action. One way to direct your thinking when making a decision is to change those guidelines into questions that you ask yourself. As you ask the questions, also ask yourself whether you have been thinking critically about the information available to you. The chart on this page is an example of a checklist of questions for decision making.

APPLYING THE PROCESS

Suppose that you are looking for a part-time job. Determine what your goal or goals are in seeking a job. Then imagine that you have gathered the following information about three possible jobs. Use the guidelines on page 40 and the checklist questions in this lesson to help you choose which one of the three jobs to apply for.

A Decision-Making Checklist

Choosing	Critical Thinking	Taking action
	Do I know . . .	
✔ Do I know my goal or goals?	✔ which sources I can trust?	✔ Do I know my action goal?
✔ Have I listed all the possible options?	✔ what relates to my subject?	✔ Do I know what the resources and obstacles are?
✔ Have I predicted the consequences of each option?	✔ what are opinions and what are statements of fact?	✔ Have I listed what actions I will take?
✔ Can I list the good and bad points of each option?	✔ which statements are true?	✔ Have I made changes in my plan as necessary?
✔ Have I chosen the best option?		✔ Have I judged how well my plan worked?

Have students discuss how the four critical-thinking skills discussed in the text are important in both choosing and taking action.

Answers will be found on page T 110.

Information on Job 1

You see a flyer on the counter at the Burger Barn with a title that catches your attention: "Earn Money and Make New Friends." The flyer explains that jobs at the Burger Barn are fun. The employees are friendly and enjoy their work. They choose the hours that they will work and get free meals and uniforms.

The starting pay is $4 an hour. Every three months you will be eligible for a raise. If your performance is good for a year, you may be promoted to assistant manager.

Information on Job 2

Your best friend's older brother, Roy, works for King Grocery. He tells you that the grocery business is the best place to start because of the opportunities for advancement. He started out as a courtesy clerk, making $4.50 an hour bagging groceries. Once in a while he was asked to sweep the aisles. He says that the job was easy. His only problem was that he had to be available for work at any time. He missed some parties because his boss called up and said, "We need some extra help tonight."

However, after only a year Roy was promoted to service clerk and is now earning $5.25 an hour. He has been promised a position as food clerk when he turns eighteen, and he hopes that the company will later send him to management training school. His goal is to be a store manager by the time he is thirty.

Information on Job 3

When you ask the librarian at the local library about the Help Wanted sign at the checkout desk, he tells you that if you take the job, you will have a fixed schedule. Your work week will be 10 to 15 hours, including two or three hours on Saturday. Once in a while you will have to work on Sunday, for which you will get paid time and a half. The beginning salary will be $4.45 an hour.

Your duties will include putting the book carts in order and placing the books back on the shelves. You must know the Dewey decimal system of classifying books. Promotion to a job at the desk would add 35¢ to the hourly wage, more responsibilities, and a dress code. The librarian mentions that full-time summer jobs are available, too.

After you have chosen the job you prefer, imagine yourself applying for that job. Write down your action goal. List your resources and the obstacles. Then list the steps you would take to reach your action goal.

CHECKING YOUR UNDERSTANDING

1. What goal or goals did you set?

2. Write down two opinions and two statements of fact about the jobs. Why is it important to know which statements are opinion?

3. Give an example of some information that was relevant to your goal or goals. Explain how it was relevant. Give an example of some information that was irrelevant to your goal. Explain how it was irrelevant.

4. List the consequences of each job.

5. Which job option did you consider to be the best? Explain why.

6. What resources might help you reach your goal? What obstacles might you face?

7. What would you do to reach your goal?

REVIEWING THE PROCESS

8. Why is it important to predict the consequences of each option before deciding?

9. In making decisions, you need to use thinking skills to judge information. Name a skill and explain why it is important.

Have students give examples of unexpected situations that might arise when applying for a job. How would they adjust their action plans accordingly?

CHAPTER SURVEY

Answers to Survey and Workshop will be found on page T 110.

UNDERSTANDING NEW VOCABULARY

Seeing Relationships

The vocabulary terms in each pair listed below are related to each other. For each pair, explain how the terms are related.

Example: *Capitalism* is related to *free enterprise* because both terms are used to describe a market economy.

1. *scarcity* and *opportunity cost*
2. *factors of production* and *capital*
3. *free enterprise* and *profit*
4. *capitalism* and *invest*
5. *command economy* and *mixed economy*

Putting It in Writing

Using the terms *traditional economy*, *command economy*, and *market economy*, describe how decisions about making a loaf of bread might differ in those three economic systems.

LOOKING BACK AT THE CHAPTER

1. People's wants differ. Give at least three reasons why this statement is true.
2. Think of an item you have recently bought or used. Give an example of each of the factors of production (land, labor, capital) that went into producing it.
3. Pick a product that you might want. Then describe the steps in the process of satisfying your want.
4. Why do people in any economy have to make choices about what to produce and consume?
5. What are the three basic economic decisions being made in any society?
6. If you lived in a traditional economy, how would you be likely to decide on a job or career?
7. In a command economy, who decides how resources will be used and what goods and services will be produced?
8. What is the "profit motive"?
9. In a market economy, what determines who gets the goods and services that are produced?
10. *Application.* Give three examples of economic wants that occur every day. Give three examples of wants that occur less often.
11. *Application.* Think of a difficult economic choice you have had to make. What was the most important factor you considered when you made your decision? Why?
12. *Synthesis.* In a market economy, how is labor different from the other two factors of production?
13. *Application.* Imagine that you are the ruler in a society with a command economy. How would you make the three basic economic decisions for your society? Why?
14. *Analysis.* In a market economy, if consumers decide they no longer want a particular product, what will happen to production of that product?

WORKING TOGETHER

1. With a group of classmates, put on a skit that shows how economic decisions are made in one of the three basic economic systems. The skit should show goods being produced, distributed, and consumed in that kind of economy. Other groups may put on skits that show how the other two economic systems work.
2. With two or three other students, interview the manager or owner of a small restaurant. Find out what kinds of decisions the manager must make about how, how much, and what to produce. Ask how he or she makes those decisions. As a group, make a short oral report to the rest of the class about what you learned.

SKILLS WORKSHOP

SOCIAL STUDIES SKILLS

Interpreting a Diagram

Diagrams are often used to show information about the relationships between ideas. They can show, for example, the order of steps in a process or how the parts of something are related to each other.

To interpret a diagram, you need to figure out why the parts of the diagram are arranged in the way that they are. Notice whether any arrows show movement from one part of the diagram to another. Also, be aware that diagrams often use a number of different shapes. For instance, one shape could stand for an action, while another could stand for a result of an action.

The diagram below shows the relationships between some of the major concepts you learned about in this chapter. The questions will help you interpret the diagram.

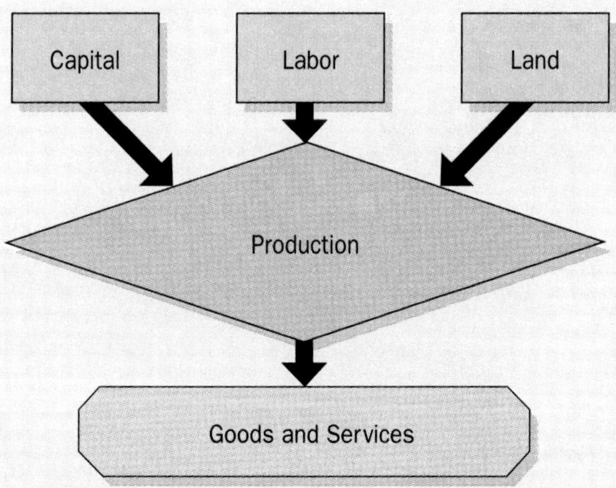

1. What is the subject of this diagram?

2. What is created in the production process—capital, labor, and land, or goods and services? How can you tell by looking at the diagram?

3. According to the diagram, how are capital, labor, and land related to each other?

4. Why is the shape containing the word *production* different from the other shapes?

DECISION-MAKING SKILLS

Choosing and Taking Action

Suppose you are trying to decide whether to try your hand at running your own part-time business during the school year. Your goals are to earn at least $100 a week and to work no more than three hours every weekday with weekends off.

Below is some information about one of your options: starting your own custom car-care business. Determine whether this option would meet your goals. If necessary, refer to the checklist of questions on page 302.

> An ad in the Sunday paper for a professional car wash notes that the charge is $20 for a basic wash and $125 for washing, waxing, and buffing. Your school counselor thinks that you might earn between $5 and $10 an hour doing at-home car cleaning in your neighborhood. However, you would have to be fast and pay careful attention to detail.
>
> You saw a movie once where the star had a similar business, and he was swamped with work. However, his customers were always complaining about one thing or another that he had forgotten to do. He never had much free time because he stayed so busy.
>
> You read in the *Teenage Employment Guide* that you could charge between $12 and $20 a car if you also checked the tire pressure, oil, windshield washer solution, battery, and radiator. However, the *Guide* noted that customers are picky. To stay in business, you would have to do a better job than your customers would do themselves.

1. Do you think that the custom car-care business would meet your goals? Explain your answer.

2. Which source of information on car-care businesses is probably *least* reliable? Explain.

3. If you decided to start a custom car-care business, what are some actions you would have to take to reach your goal?

TOMATOES
175
49
3/125
69
119
2/100
2/100
35
175
75
KING CROW
Westside
CANTALOUPES
FRESH PACKED GRAPES
HANDLE WITH CARE
BANANAS

Chapter Themes: Our market economy depends on a steady flow of resources, goods, and services, with basic decisions influenced by supply and demand. Most production is carried out by privately owned businesses. Business-labor conflict has had a vital effect on the economy.

CHAPTER 14

Basics of Our Economic System

The farmers' market is alive with activity today. People from miles around are gathered to buy apples, lettuce, tomatoes, beans, and dozens of other kinds of fruits and vegetables from the farmers who grow them.

Eric and his friends are at the farmers' market because they love fresh strawberries, and it is now the middle of strawberry season. Many farmers are selling the sweet red berries in small paper or plastic baskets.

Eric notices that the prices for a basket of strawberries are almost all the same—50 cents a basket. One farmer, however, is charging 40 cents a basket. People are crowding around his stall, buying whole flats of 12 baskets each. Another farmer is selling her strawberries for 60 cents a basket. Eric notices she has slightly fewer customers than the other farmers. He walks up to her stall and asks why her prices are higher.

"It costs me more to grow my strawberries," she answers. "I grow them without insecticides and I use organic fertilizer. I have to charge more to make a profit. But I think my strawberries taste better and are better for you."

Eric wonders which strawberries he and his friends should buy. He knows that choices made by individuals are what control a market economy. He sees that farmers make choices about how to grow their crops, and consumers make choices about what and how much to buy.

Eric then considers what would happen if more farmers lowered their prices to 40 cents a basket. Would they still make a profit? Would they sell more strawberries?

This chapter will help you to answer questions such as these. You will also find out what it means to own a business in the United States, and what it means to be a worker. As you learn more about how our market economy works, you will better understand how it affects you and your community.

Teaching Note: Use the Introducing the Chapter activity, page T 113.

14-1

THE PRINCIPLES OF OUR MARKET ECONOMY

Read to Find Out

- what the terms *rent, interest, demand, supply,* and *market price* mean.
- how goods, services, resources, and money flow through the economy.
- how the market determines the prices of goods and services.

In Chapter 13 you learned that the United States has a mixed economy that is based on the principles of a free enterprise, market system. In order to understand the American economy, then, it is important to take a closer look at the basic ways in which a market economy works.

The Circular Flow of Economic Activity

You rely on a steady flow of blood throughout your body to remain healthy. In a similar way, a healthy market economy depends on a steady flow of resources, goods, and services. An example will show how this flow occurs in our economy.

Suppose that your bicycle has a flat tire. At the bike shop you hand the clerk four dollars and receive a new inner tube. This simple kind of exchange is repeated millions of times each day by millions of Americans.

Buying something, however, is only one kind of exchange. Suppose that you also work part time for the bicycle shop. You exchange your labor for an hourly wage. These two exchanges—money for an inner tube and work for wages—are connected because you buy inner tubes with the money you earn from working.

By being a part of both exchanges, you have created a "flow" of labor, inner tubes, and money. This is an example of what economists call the circular flow of economic activity. The outside circle of the diagram below shows the flow of labor and inner tubes. The

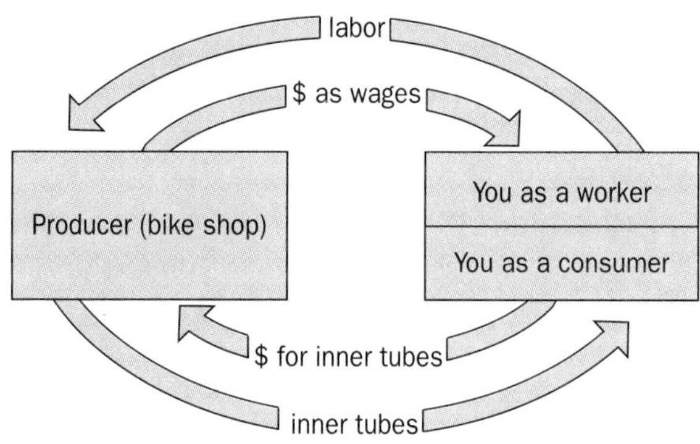

money (wages and cash) flowing in the inner circle only makes it easier for the exchange of labor and inner tubes to occur.

The exchange of labor, money, and bicycles that takes place in this bicycle shop is part of the circular flow of economic activity.

Challenge (Analysis): Have students describe how holding a part-time job makes them participants in the circular flow of economic activity.

Expanding the circular flow. This example of the circular flow of labor, inner tubes, and money involves just you and one business. In real life, people exchange their labor to buy goods and services from many businesses. The entire American economy, however, is based on a circular flow that is very similar to the one involving you and the bike shop.

Imagine, instead of the bike shop, every American business that produces goods or services. Together, all these businesses can be called producers. Then imagine, instead of you, all individuals in our society. The diagram below shows how goods, services, labor, and money flow through the United States economy.

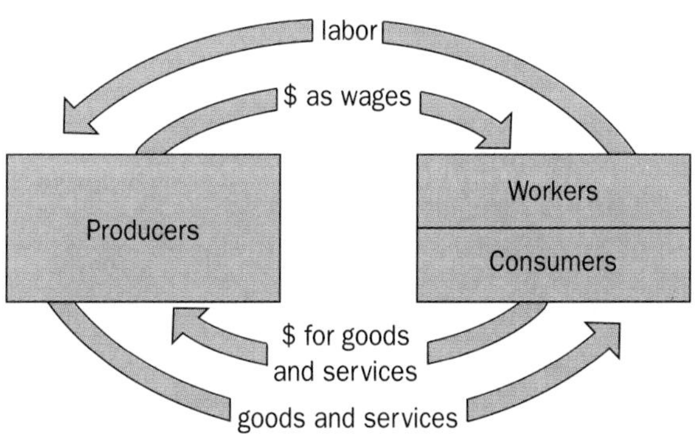

This circular flow diagram is not quite complete, however. Labor is only one of the resources that producers need to create goods. Producers also need land, which includes raw materials, and capital, which includes tools and machines used in production.

Producers exchange a certain kind of payment for the use of land and capital. ***Rent*** is the payment for the use of land. ***Interest*** is the payment for the use of capital. The payment for the use of labor is called wages. The diagram on the right above shows the complete picture of the circular flow of economic activity.

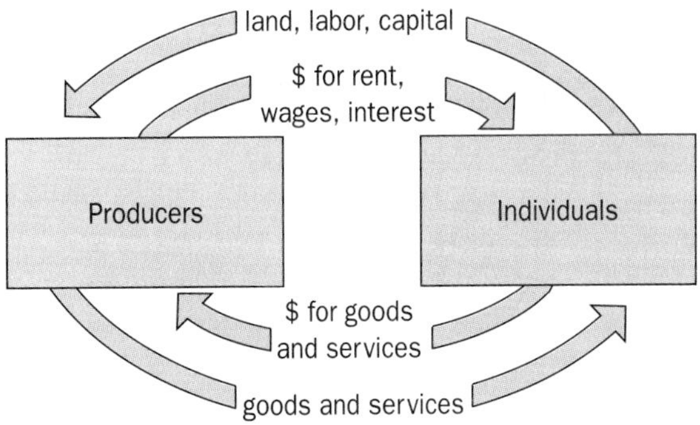

Supply and Demand

As goods, services, and money flow through the economy, producers and individuals act both as buyers and as sellers. You may recall that when buyers and sellers come together to exchange goods and services, they do so through what is called a market. Markets determine how much will be produced in a free enterprise economy. Markets also determine prices. How are markets able to do this?

When there is free competition among sellers and among buyers, a market works according to what are called the laws of supply and demand. These "laws" are not made by legislatures. They are descriptions of what happens when many people make choices in a market.

Through the process described by the laws of supply and demand, consumer choices help producers know what and how much to produce. The easiest way to understand these laws is to consider demand separately from supply. You will see, however, that supply and demand always work together.

The law of demand. Have you noticed that when the price of something is low, people will often buy more of it? Eric saw this happening at the farmers' market. People bought many strawberries from the farmer who was selling them for 40 cents a basket. In other

Teaching Note: You may wish to use the Unit 5 Activity, "The Big Apple: A Market Simulation," in the Activity Book after students have read the discusson of supply and demand.

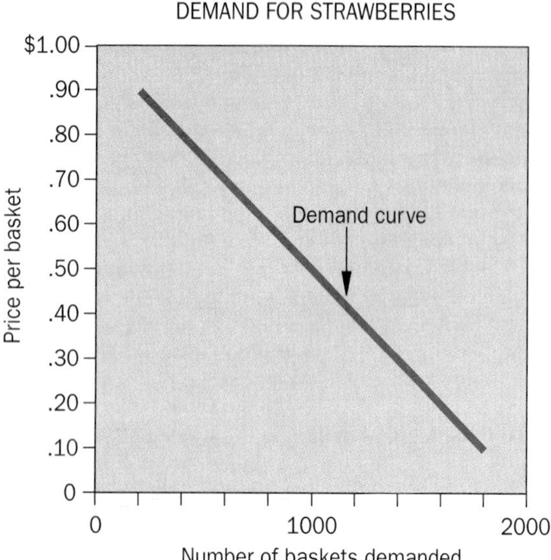

words, people were demanding large amounts of strawberries at that price. ***Demand*** is defined as the amounts of a product or service buyers are willing and able to buy at different prices.

In deciding whether or not to buy an item, you balance its cost to you with the benefit you think you will receive from it. Will you enjoy the strawberries enough to buy a basket at 40 cents? Would the benefit be great enough for you to pay 80 cents? The lower the price of an item, and thus its cost to you, the more likely you are to decide to buy it.

At a low price, more people will want baskets of strawberries, and more people will be able to afford them. Also, more people will decide to buy more than one basket. In short, the quantity demanded by buyers will be high. At a high price, fewer people will decide to buy strawberries, and the quantity demanded will be low.

The way the law of demand works for a particular product can be shown on a graph. The graph above, for example, shows what the quantity of strawberries demanded at the farmers' market is likely to be at different prices. The demand is described by the line on the graph, called the demand curve.

The law of supply. A producer, like a buyer, balances costs and benefits when making decisions in a market. A producer's cost is determined by how much it costs to produce an item, such as a basket of strawberries. The price a buyer pays determines a producer's benefit. The higher the price, the higher the benefit to the producer.

Supply is defined as the amounts of a product that producers are willing and able to offer at different prices. When the price is high, more producers are willing to supply the product and to supply more of it. As a result, the amount supplied by producers as a whole will be high. When the price is low, fewer producers are willing to supply the product, and the quantity supplied will be low.

The way the law of supply works for a particular product can also be shown on a graph. The line on the graph below is the supply

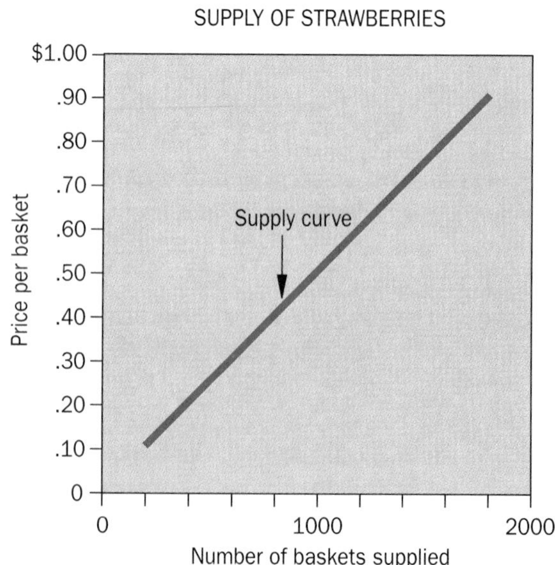

Buyers must be able to afford the good or the service in addition to being willing to purchase it. A buyer who is willing to purchase three lobsters but can only afford cod is not counted in the demand for lobster.

curve. It shows what the quantity of strawberries supplied at the farmers' market is likely to be at different prices.

Supply and demand. Think for a moment about the farmers' market. Farmers want to sell at a high price. Buyers want to buy at a low price. You may be wondering how the price gets decided.

The law of demand and the law of supply work together in determining both the price of a product and the quantity that will be offered. As you have seen, price affects the amounts demanded and the amounts supplied in opposite ways. Another way of saying this is that the demand curve slopes down and the supply curve slopes up.

At higher prices, more of a product will be supplied but less will be demanded. At lower prices, less will be supplied but more demanded.

The quantity supplied and the quantity demanded, however, will tend to equal each other in an ideal market. This balance takes place at a particular price called the market price. The ***market price*** is the price at which buyers and sellers agree to trade. If the demand and supply curves are placed on the same graph, the market price will be where the demand and supply curves intersect, or cross. The graph on the left shows supply, demand, and market price.

Colorful displays and advertising are aimed at increasing consumer demand for certain products, such as these athletic shoes.

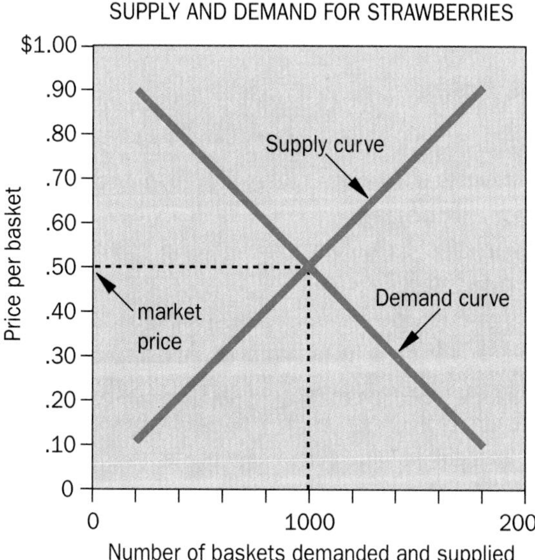

At the farmers' market today, the market price for strawberries is 50 cents a basket. At this price, all the producers together are supplying about 1,000 baskets, and consumers are demanding about 1,000 baskets. A market price of 50 cents, however, does not prevent some farmers from charging less than the market price and other farmers from charging more.

If all the farmers raised their price for strawberries to 90 cents a basket, many buyers would decide the price was too high. The quantity demanded would fall, and farmers would find they could not sell all their strawberries at that price. They would have to

Factors other than price affect supply. These include the cost of labor and raw materials, the level of technology in the industry, expectations of future price increases, and the prices of other goods the business can produce.

Teaching Note: Use the Reinforcement Activity, page T 115, and accompanying worksheet in the Activity Book after students have read the material in Section 14-1.

lower their prices in order to encourage a higher demand. If all other factors remained the same, the price would settle back to 50 cents a basket.

Other influences. Of course, demand can be influenced by factors other than price. For example, the demand for basic products, such as milk and penicillin, will not change very much when the price changes, because people believe that they need milk and medicine at almost any price.

Advertising, styles of fashion, and the way consumers perceive a certain product can also have very important effects on the demand for that product. You might decide to buy a higher-priced pair of jeans, for instance, because that brand is more popular than a lower-priced brand.

Having different but competing products on the market also affects demand. For example, what do you think the invention of running shoes has done to the demand for sneakers?

Even though supply and demand can be affected by forces other than prices, the laws of supply and demand form one of the foundations of our market economy. They have an influence on all the basic economic decisions that Americans make.

Answers will be found on page T 115.

Section Review

1. Define *rent, interest, demand, supply,* and *market price.*
2. Describe in your own words the circular flow of economic activity.
3. What effect will a rise in the price of a product have on its demand and its supply?

Application. Think about the choices you have made as a consumer in the last week. What factors affected you?

14-2

THE ROLE OF BUSINESSES IN THE AMERICAN ECONOMY

Read to Find Out

- what the terms *entrepreneur, sole proprietorship, partnership, corporation,* and *stock* mean.
- why people who take risks in starting a business are important to the economy.
- how businesses use and pay for economic resources.

Production and consumption are basic to any economy. As you have learned, people participate in production in order to be able to consume a variety of goods and services.

The production of goods and services is a complex process. In a market economy, most production is carried out by privately owned businesses. A business is any organization that combines labor, land, and capital in order to produce goods or services. Farms, supermarkets, law firms, and the company that manufactured your family's car are all businesses.

The Role of the Entrepreneur

Because businesses are so important in our economy, the people who start businesses play a very important role. A person who starts a business is called an ***entrepreneur*** (AHN-truh-preh-NOOR).

An entrepreneur begins with an idea for a new product, a new way of producing something, or a better way of providing a service. The entrepreneur then raises money for capital goods to start the business. This money can be the entrepreneur's own, or it can be borrowed from people or banks willing to invest in the business.

The word *entrepreneur* comes from a French word meaning "one who undertakes." Some twentieth-century economists consider the entrepreneur's competitive drive for innovation and improvement to be a motivating force behind free enterprise.

PEOPLE MAKE A DIFFERENCE

Ice Cream Makers Share Success

Ben Cohen and Jerry Greenfield, the owners of Ben and Jerry's Homemade, Inc., have a well-known product: ice cream. Their business, which they started in a converted gas station in 1978, was an immediate success. Today, their ice cream sells in stores around the nation.

The two entrepreneurs, who have been friends since junior high school, believe that being successful means more than making a good product. To them, success also means helping the community. Ben and Jerry call it the "community-oriented" approach to business. They believe a business can be "socially responsible," sharing profits with employees and the community.

They take this approach in running their Vermont-based ice cream company.

No one working for the company earns more than seven times the pay of the lowest-paid employee. Furthermore, part of the profits go into The Ben and Jerry's Foundation, which supports local community causes.

"If every company contributed the same percentage of profits to the community that we and a few others do, there would be virtually no social problems in the country, because there would be enough money to solve them," says Ben.

He and Jerry have also helped start an organization, 1 Percent For Peace, which seeks to redirect 1 percent of the nation's military budget to promote peace through understanding. It also encourages businesses and individuals to give 1 percent of their pre-tax profits to peace and education groups.

Ben and Jerry are successful entrepreneurs who see business as not simply an opportunity to make money. They see business as an opportunity to help their fellow citizens. As the company continues to grow, Ben notes, "our company will change. . . . We just have to make it a good change."

By deciding to start a business, the entrepreneur is usually taking a major risk. What if the business fails? The entrepreneur could lose all the money he or she invested in it. If the business does well, however, the entrepreneur stands to make a profit. This profit will be the income earned by the business, minus the costs of the resources it uses. The hope of earning a profit—the profit motive—is what motivates people in a capitalist economy to start and to run businesses.

Using the Factors of Production

In Chapter 13 you learned about three basic factors of production: labor, land, and capital. Some entrepreneurs are able to provide some factors of production themselves. Scott Sullivan, for example, is launching a small pie-baking business. He provides the labor by baking the pies himself. He provides the capital by using the pans and ovens in his own kitchen. All he needs to buy, with money

Discussion: Have students discuss the meaning of *community oriented*. Ask students to describe other ways that people and businesses can be responsible for their community.

he has saved, are ingredients such as fruit, flour, sugar, and shortening.

Payments for resources. Other entrepreneurs and business owners obtain the factors of production from other sources. Alice Ling is starting a larger pie-baking business. To set up a commercial kitchen, Alice borrows money from a bank to buy capital goods such as large ovens. In exchange for this loan, she pays the bank interest. Alice's kitchen is located on land owned by someone else. In exchange for the use of this land, Alice pays the owner rent. Finally, Alice hires workers as labor and pays them hourly wages. If she needs help in running her business, she will hire managers and pay them monthly salaries.

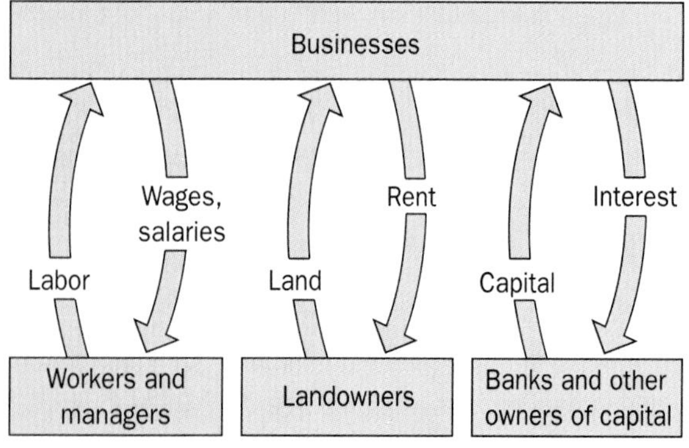

Through this example, you can see how businesses get each factor of production in exchange for a particular kind of payment. The diagram above shows these exchanges between businesses and the owners of resources. The payments for the use of resources make up the major costs of running a business. Any money left over after all the costs have been paid is the entrepreneur's profit.

Some economists consider entrepreneurship to be a fourth factor of production. They point out that entrepreneurs provide ideas and take risks in return for payment in the form of profit.

How Businesses are Owned

When entrepreneurs such as Scott and Alice are planning their businesses, they must make an important decision. How will their businesses be owned? There are three basic types of business ownership in the United States: the sole proprietorship, the partnership, and the corporation. Each type has advantages and disadvantages.

The sole proprietorship. Many entrepreneurs starting a small business, like Scott Sullivan, will establish a ***sole proprietorship***, which is a business owned by an individual. Sole proprietorships are the most common form of business in the United States. About 70 percent of the businesses in this country are sole proprietorships. Most are small businesses

Opening a sole proprietorship like this family-run Thai restaurant is a way many newcomers to the United States enter the economy.

The floor of the New York Stock Exchange is a tangle of telephones, TV monitors, and traders buying and selling shares in corporations.

such as restaurants, television repair shops, and small grocery stores.

The advantages of a sole proprietorship are many. The owner, or sole proprietor, has the freedom to decide how to run the business, and the profits belong to the owner alone. The owner also has the personal satisfaction of knowing that he or she made the business succeed.

There are also several disadvantages of a sole proprietorship. First, the owner has the whole responsibility for paying off loans and other business debts. Second, it can be hard for one owner to borrow enough money to expand the business beyond a certain size. Third, as a business grows it becomes increasingly difficult for one owner to handle all the responsibilities and decision making.

The partnership. A ***partnership*** is a type of business in which two or more people share ownership. Alice, for example, could set up her pie-baking business as a partnership if she knew someone who wanted to share the costs and help her run the business. In the United States, many law firms, medical groups, and accounting businesses are set up as partnerships.

The advantages and disadvantages of a partnership are similar to those of a sole proprietorship. The main difference is that risks and benefits are shared by more than one person. An additional disadvantage of a partnership is the possibility of serious differences arising between the partners, which could damage or ruin the business.

The corporation. Sole proprietors and partners are closely linked to the businesses they own. The debts of their businesses, for example, are their personal debts. In contrast, a ***corporation*** is a business that is separate from the people who own it and legally acts as a single person. A corporation can have debts, hire workers, and make profits.

The ownership of a corporation is shared by more than one person. The shares of ownership in a corporation are called its ***stock***, and people who buy stock are called stockholders.

AMERICAN NOTEBOOK

In 1987, women owned nearly one third of all businesses (not including corporations) in the United States. These 4.1 million businesses brought in $278.1 billion, or 14 percent of all money businesses received. California had the most businesses owned by women, with a total of nearly 560,000.

Under the principle of unlimited liability, sole proprietors and partners are legally responsible for all of the debts of the business they own. If the business fails, the owner(s) may lose personal property in order to pay its debts.

By forming corporations and selling stock, early entrepreneurs could raise enough money to build factories like this cash register factory.

Many corporations offer their stock for sale to the public. By selling stock, a corporation raises the money that is necessary to start, run, and expand the business. Millions of Americans buy stock as an investment because, as stockholders, they share the corporation's profits.

Stockholders also have a voice in important business decisions of the corporation, such as choosing the board of directors that runs the company. Each share of stock entitles its owner to one vote. In many corporations, however, a relatively small group of people own enough stock to give them effective control over the corporation.

A corporation has unique advantages. It can raise large quantities of money—mainly through selling stock—to help it grow. Furthermore, stockholders are not responsible for the corporation's debts. If the corporation

Challenge (Analysis): Have students explain how the relationship between a business and its owners in a corporation differs from that in a sole proprietorship and in a partnership.

fails, a stockholder loses only the value of his or her stock.

Corporations also have several disadvantages compared to the two other forms of business ownership. Corporations are more difficult and more expensive to start. In addition, they are more limited by government regulations.

Corporations are the most important form of business in our economy today. Although there are many more sole proprietorships, corporations create more of the products, profits, and jobs in our economy than the other two forms of businesses combined. It is important to realize, however, that although most large businesses are corporations, not all corporations are large. Even some small businesses can benefit from the advantages of being a corporation.

The Rise of Big Business

Large businesses organized as corporations dominate our economy today. They make about 90 percent of the total sales in the

The Importance of Corporations

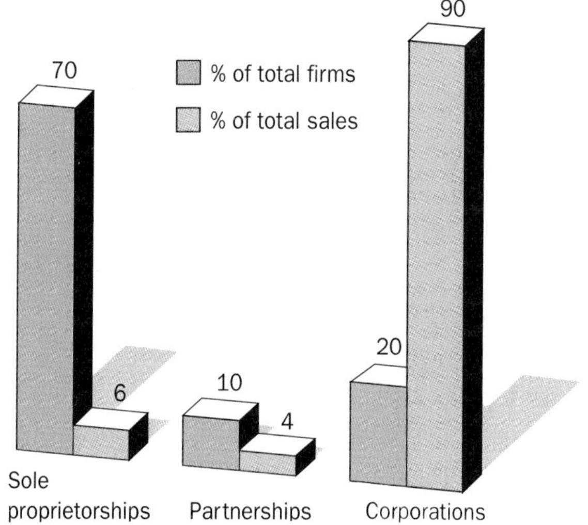

About 19 percent of Americans own shares of stock. The profile of the average stockholder is a person in his or her mid-forties who lives in a metropolitan area, is well educated, uses a broker, and owns approximately $6,200 in stocks.

Although many farms are still family owned, corporations have been playing a growing role in American agriculture.

American economy and pay about 70 percent of the total wages earned by American workers. However, large corporations did not always have such an important role in our economy.

In our country's early years, most businesses were small sole proprietorships. The economy was also very different. Many families were nearly self-sufficient, producing much of what they needed for themselves.

This situation changed dramatically during the 1800s. New inventions and manufacturing methods spurred growth and industrialization. Factories sprang up, producing more goods at lower prices. The population grew rapidly as immigrants poured into the country. People settled in cities, attracted by jobs in new industries.

People who lived in cities depended on businesses for the goods and services they wanted, and businesses did well. Successful sole proprietors turned their businesses into corporations in order to grow. Corporations could raise money more easily by selling stock and borrowing from banks. By the end of the 1800s, large corporations dominated the railroads, key manufacturing industries, and mining.

In the past 100 years, large corporations have become a major force in nearly every industry. Today, large corporations own most supermarkets and fast-food chains. They make all of our computers and automobiles. Corporations publish most of the books you read, including this textbook. They own the telephone lines and the airlines. Large corporations even own many of America's farms.

One reason large corporations have grown in importance is that they can produce goods and provide services more efficiently than smaller firms. Large firms can better afford the expensive machinery needed to produce more goods in less time. They also have the resources to do scientific research to develop new products and production methods.

In the future, large businesses organized as corporations will probably continue to grow in importance. However, sole proprietorships, partnerships, and small corporations will always have an important role to play in our economy.

Answers will be found on page T 116.

Section Review

1. Define *entrepreneur, sole proprietorship, partnership, corporation,* and *stock.*
2. Why are entrepreneurs important to the American economic system?
3. What is the payment a business makes for the use of each factor of production?

Analysis. Why are corporations the most important kind of business today?

Data Search. Look at the bar graph on page 316. What percent of the businesses in the United States are corporations? What must be true of the average corporation to account for the fact that corporations make 90 percent of the sales in the economy?

Teaching Note: Use Teaching Activity 1, page T 113, and the Enrichment Activity, page T 115, and accompanying worksheet in the Activity Book after students have read the material in this section.

14-3

LABOR IN THE AMERICAN ECONOMY

Read to Find Out

- what the terms *labor unions, collective bargaining, boycott,* and *strike* mean.
- how wage labor became common in the 1800s.
- why workers formed unions.
- what methods unions and employers have used to get what they want.

Labor, as you know, is one of the factors of production. However, labor is different from the other factors of production in that it is provided by human beings who care about their working conditions and the rewards they receive for their labor.

Workers have a built-in conflict with entrepreneurs and business managers. On the one hand, business owners want to keep costs low and profits high. One way to do this is to keep wages low. Workers, on the other hand, want to earn the highest possible wages.

You will see how this conflict between business and labor has had an important impact on the American economic system. Workers have organized to gain higher wages and better working conditions. In the process, they have had major influence on the development of the American economy.

The Growth of Wage Labor

As you recall, many Americans were farmers when our country was young. Most of what they needed they produced themselves. They could do this because they owned a productive resource—land.

Many other Americans were skilled craftspeople, such as shoemakers, blacksmiths, and tailors. Craftspeople either worked for themselves or for someone they knew personally. They also generally owned their own capi-

Unsafe working conditions and long hours, even for young children, led workers in the late nineteenth century to band together in labor unions.

tal—the tools of their craft. Most Americans, therefore, had control over the conditions of their work.

Between 1800 and 1860, however, great changes began to occur. First, improvements in farm machinery meant there was less demand for workers on farms. Second, new machinery and manufacturing methods caused rapid industrialization. Because machines could produce more goods and could do it more cheaply than people making goods by hand, many craftspeople found themselves out of work.

As a result of these changes, more and more former craftspeople and farmhands, as well as arriving immigrants, turned to wage labor to make a living. Wage laborers worked in mines, in factories, and in smaller manufacturing workshops. They owned no land or tools. Instead, they exchanged their labor for payments called wages, and their employers controlled the conditions of their work.

Poor working conditions. Many wage laborers were faced with a grim choice: to do whatever work was available at any wage or to starve. Business owners took advantage of this situation by paying very low wages. If a worker complained, he or she was fired. There were plenty of other people wanting to take that worker's place.

The numbers of wage laborers grew steadily during the 1800s as factories increased in number. In large factories, these workers no longer had personal relationships with the people they worked for. Compared with farm and crafts work, most factory jobs were monotonous, low-paid, and dangerous. Wage laborers, many of them children as young as six years old, worked six days a week, 12 to 16 hours a day. Workers were sometimes threatened, beaten, or fired if they did not work as hard as their employer wished.

The Rise of Labor Unions

Compared to the power of the owner of a large business, an individual worker had little power over wages and working conditions. Workers began to realize that they could influence their employers only if they organized into groups fighting for common goals. As a result, workers began to form ***labor unions***, which are organizations of workers that seek to improve wages and working conditions and to protect members' rights.

The first American unions began sprouting up in the 1790s. The movement grew, and by the early 1880s there were many small unions across the country. Most were organized as trade unions, made up of workers in one particular trade such as carpentry or cigar-making. These were generally skilled workers, whose jobs required some special know-how. Because such workers could not be easily replaced, their employers were more likely to listen to them to keep them from leaving.

Membership in American Labor Unions

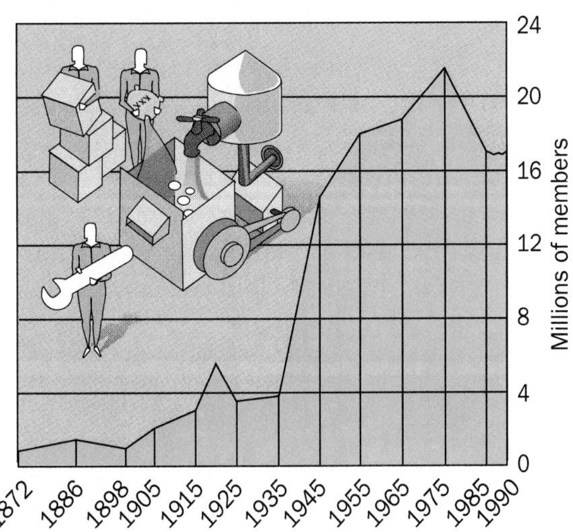

Source: Bureau of the Census, Bureau of Labor Statistics

The first wage laborers were primarily women and children from poor farm families. Because they were eager to earn money, they worked for lower wages than men demanded. Later, in the 1830s, a good source of cheap labor was found in the immigrants coming to America from Europe.

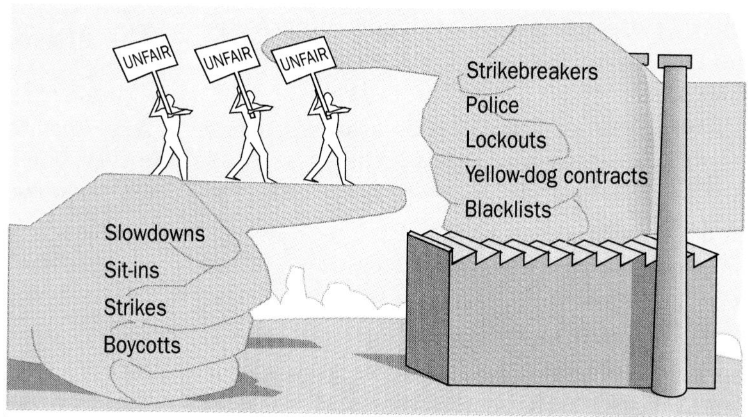

Methods that Employers and Unions Use in Disputes. *Over the years, workers and businesses have used a number of weapons in disputes over wages and working conditions.*

The first important national union was The Noble Order of the Knights of Labor, which reached its height in 1886. The Knights of Labor tried to bring together the entire working class, both skilled and unskilled. However these two groups of workers often disagreed, and finally the union broke up.

Soon after, a new union, the American Federation of Labor (AFL), gained power. Founded by Samuel Gompers in 1886, the AFL united smaller trade unions, made up of only skilled workers, into a more powerful national organization. A goal of the AFL was to force employers to agree to participate in ***collective bargaining***, the process by which representatives of a union and of a business discuss and reach agreement about wages and working conditions.

The following years were a period of intense and often bloody conflict between unions and business owners. Unions demanded an eight-hour day and higher wages, but the owners were not about to give in.

Labor's weapons. In the early days, unions used several methods to try to force reluctant employers to meet their demands. In a slowdown, workers stayed on the job but did their work much more slowly. In a sit-in, workers stopped working but refused to leave the factory, so the employer could not replace them with non-union workers. Sometimes union members would urge their members and the public to ***boycott***, or refuse to buy, an employer's products.

Through the years, however, the major weapon of the unions has been the ***strike.*** In a strike, workers refuse to work unless employers meet certain demands. Hundreds of strikes occurred between 1886 and 1920. Some of the longest strikes involving the most unions were by textile, steel, and railroad unions. Most of these strikes were organized by AFL unions, but other unions had important roles as well.

The weapons of business. Business owners responded to strikes in various ways. Typically they used strikebreakers, or "scabs"—non-union workers hired to replace the striking workers. If union workers tried to keep strikebreakers from entering the factory, business owners often hired private police to stop them. These private police also broke up union meetings and bothered union members in other ways. Often the business owners had

Challenge (Evaluation): Have students discuss which labor weapons might be most or least effective in trying to get a wage increase: negotiating for improved work conditions, or forming a union. Students should give reasons for their opinions.

the support of local police or state militias. Violence broke out during some strikes, causing many deaths.

In their struggle with the unions, employers used other methods as well. In lockouts, management refused to let union members enter the factory, and replaced them with scabs. Some employers forced workers to sign "yellow-dog contracts" in which they promised never to join the union. Finally, some employers circulated blacklists containing the names of union members and supporters, so that other employers would not hire them.

Gains and losses. The weapons used by both labor and management were basically economic. Sit-ins, slowdowns, boycotts, and strikes were all intended to interrupt production and reduce business profits. When employers used yellow-dog contracts, lockouts, blacklists, and strikebreakers, they took away union members' jobs and thus their ability to make a living.

By 1920, labor unions had achieved some important victories. A few industries had reduced the working day to 8 or 10 hours. Wages had increased for some workers. The federal government had established the Department of Labor to protect the rights of workers. In spite of these gains, however, labor suffered many crushing defeats and broken strikes.

Labor Unions Since 1930

After suffering setbacks in the 1920s, unions made important gains during the 1930s because the government began to fully recognize the right of unions to exist and to strike. In 1935, Congress passed the National Labor Relations Act, or Wagner Act. It required employers to bargain with unions. This act also outlawed several methods business owners had used to weaken unions.

More recent laws, such as the Taft-Hartley Act of 1947 and the Landrum-Griffin Act of 1959, have put limits on the powers of unions and union leaders. However, the Wagner Act marked a turning point in the history of American labor. Unions felt that their rightful place in the American economy had finally been recognized.

Meanwhile, a new kind of union was gaining strength: the industrial union. An industrial union includes all workers in a particular industry—both skilled and unskilled. Some labor leaders saw advantages to including workers in an industry-wide union rather than sticking to the traditional trade unions.

Soon, workers in such industries as steel, coal, and rubber had their own industrial unions. Some industrial unions formed within the AFL, but in 1938 these unions split off and joined together as the Congress of Industrial Organizations (CIO).

The Wagner Act and the creation of the CIO set the stage for the development of the

Percentage of Labor Force that Belongs to Unions

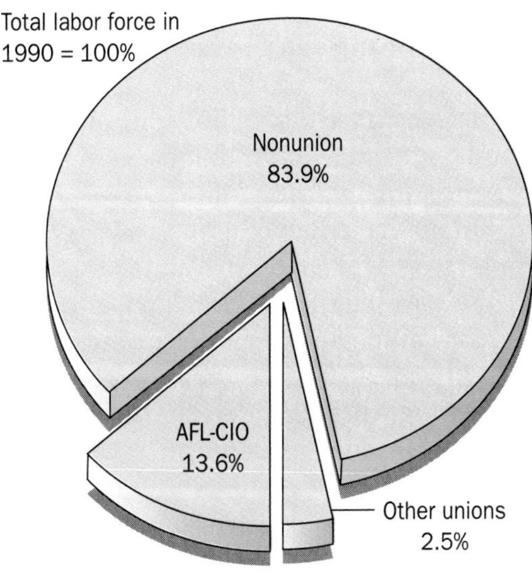

Decision Making: Have students discuss what consequences workers might have to consider when deciding whether or not to go on strike.

At the end of a successful collective bargaining session, union and business representatives sign an agreement, or contract.

modern labor movement. At first the AFL and the CIO were rivals, competing for members. In 1955, however, the two unions united to form the AFL-CIO.

Today, the AFL-CIO is the most powerful voice of organized labor in the United States. It has over 13 million members. Among its other activities, it plays an important political role, lobbying in Congress and working to elect pro-labor candidates to office.

Labor's accomplishments. In spite of setbacks and opposition, labor unions have made many gains for workers. Since the early 1930s, unions have helped win fairer wages for workers. They have been a major force in getting the government to pass laws creating social security, unemployment insurance, and a minimum wage. They have also worked for laws protecting workers' safety, banning child labor, and providing retraining for workers who have lost their jobs.

Today, only about one worker in six is a union member, and union membership has declined in recent decades. Still, labor unions have played a key role in improving the lives of all workers.

Common interests. Unions today still go on strike and encourage boycotts. However, both workers and employers have learned to see their shared interests as well as their differences. Employers see that workers need safe working conditions. They also know that workers who are paid fairly produce more and are more likely to buy goods and services, thus contributing to a healthy economy.

Unions, on the other hand, recognize that members' jobs depend on businesses making profits. They have seen that when wages rise too high, profits may decline. Then businesses may fail or move to other states or foreign countries where labor costs are lower.

Today's Labor Force

As you have seen, the composition of the labor force—the number of people working at each type of job in the economy—has changed a great deal since the birth of our country. For example, farmers, who outnumbered any other kind of worker in 1776, today make up only 3 percent of the American labor force.

There are also more women in the labor force than ever before. Since the 1940s, women have been entering the labor force in ever-increasing numbers. They make up about 44 percent of the labor force today.

Another important change in the labor force has occurred over the last several decades. Manufacturing industries such as steelmaking, once the foundation of our economy, have declined in importance. As a result, these industries are employing a decreasing percentage of America's workers.

At the same time, businesses that offer services have grown in importance. These

If collective bargaining fails, an outside party often steps in to solve the problem. In conciliation a third party encourages both sides to keep negotiating. In mediation a third party suggests solutions to the problem. In arbitration both sides agree to abide by a third party's decision.

Teaching Note: Use Teaching Activity 2, page T 114, as a culminating activity after students have read the material in this section.

service-oriented businesses, such as banks, insurance companies, computer software firms, restaurants, movie theaters, and resorts, now employ a large and growing majority of American workers. These businesses make up what is called the service sector of the economy.

The change in focus of our economy, from manufacturing to service, has caused many problems for workers. When a steel factory closes, for example, its workers do not always have the training to find new jobs in the computer industry. Furthermore, service-sector businesses are often located in different parts of the country than the factories that are closing. Americans, therefore, face personal and economic change as our country shifts from an industrial economy to a service economy.

Answers will be found on page T 116.

Section Review

1. Define *labor unions, collective bargaining, boycott,* and *strike.*
2. What changes caused the growth of wage labor in the 1800s?
3. How can unions help workers?
4. Describe the major weapons that unions and employers have used in their disputes.

Application. What are some of the ways the changes taking place in today's labor force may affect you as an adult?

Data Search. Look on page 587 in the Data Bank. What is the fastest growing group of women in the labor force? Why do you think more of these women are joining the labor force?

A BROADER VIEW

In this chapter you have learned about the American economic system. Our economy, however, does not exist alone in the world. It influences, and is influenced by, a larger economy that spans the globe.

Evidence of a global economy is all around you. Many of the products you eat, use, and wear were grown or produced in another country. The global economy makes it possible for consumers all over the world to have a widening choice of goods and services to buy.

A global economy also means that the countries of the world are interconnected. Economic events in one country can have results far beyond that country's borders. For example, if farmers in Brazil produced less coffee, coffee drinkers in Europe and the United States would feel the effect in the form of a shortage of coffee and higher coffee prices.

Similarly, your choices as an American consumer can affect the workers, farmers, and environments of other countries. Demand for a certain product in the United States, for example, can provide jobs for people who produce that product in other countries. However, American demands can sometimes have negative effects. A demand in the United States for jewelry made of ivory has encouraged the slaughter of elephants in Africa.

To avoid such problems, the nations of the world will have to work together more closely than they often have in the past. We must learn that a global economy means that we are all dependent on each other for our economic well-being.

Teaching Note: Use the Evaluating Progress activity, page T 114, to assess students' understanding of Chapter 14.

CHAPTER SURVEY

Answers to Survey and Workshop will be found on page T 116.

UNDERSTANDING NEW VOCABULARY

Seeing Relationships

The vocabulary terms in each pair listed below are related to each other. For each pair, explain how the terms are related.

Example: *Consumer* is related to *worker* because both terms describe roles individuals play in the economic system.

1. *demand* and *supply*

2. *rent* and *interest*

3. *stock* and *corporation*

4. *labor union* and *strike*

Putting It in Writing

Describe how you might set up your own business. Use the term *entrepreneur* and at least one of the following terms: *sole proprietorship*, *partnership*, *corporation*. What product or service would you offer? Describe what land, capital, and labor you would need to start your business.

LOOKING BACK AT THE CHAPTER

1. Compare and contrast the relationship between consumers and producers with the relationship between workers and producers.

2. For a particular product, why does the quantity demanded usually decrease when the price increases? When is a higher price less likely to affect demand?

3. What does an entrepreneur hope to gain by starting a business? What does he or she contribute to the business?

4. Describe each of the factors of production and name the payments that a business makes for them.

5. What are the main advantages of each form of business ownership: sole proprietorship, partnership, and corporation?

6. In what ways does a wage laborer differ from a self-sufficient farmer?

7. Why did workers form labor unions?

8. *Application.* Describe four purchases you have made and the prices you paid. Which items would you buy even if the price were higher? At what price would you no longer be willing to buy each item? What can you conclude about how price affected demand in each case? What factors other than price influenced your decisions to buy?

9. *Evaluation.* Maria Jackson has invented a new type of sugar-free, fruit-flavored soft drink. She wants to start a business to make, bottle, and sell her drinks. What form of business ownership would you advise her to set up? Explain your choice and tell why that form would be better for Maria than the other two forms.

10. *Synthesis.* A group of factory workers goes to the factory owner to ask for a pay raise. The owner does not want to give it to them. What arguments might the owner use? What arguments might the workers make?

WORKING TOGETHER

1. With a group, make a survey of a business in your community. Identify the producers and what goods or services they produce, the resource owners and the resources they contribute, and the consumers. Make a circular flow diagram to show the information you have collected. Indicate which of the three forms of business organization the business represents.

2. Look at the labels in your clothes and on other items you have purchased recently. With a group of four or five, make a chart of the products and the countries where they were made. Write a paragraph describing what evidence you found that we live in a global economy.

SKILLS WORKSHOP

Teaching Note: For reinforcement of decision-making skills, use Decision-Making Worksheet Chapter 14.

SOCIAL STUDIES SKILLS

Analyzing a Circular Flow Chart

The purpose of a flow chart is to show the steps in a process. On page 185 you looked at a flow chart that shows how a bill becomes a law. In this chapter you have been studying flow charts like the one below. Economists use circular flow charts to explain how an economy works. Such charts illustrate how money, goods, and services flow through an economy.

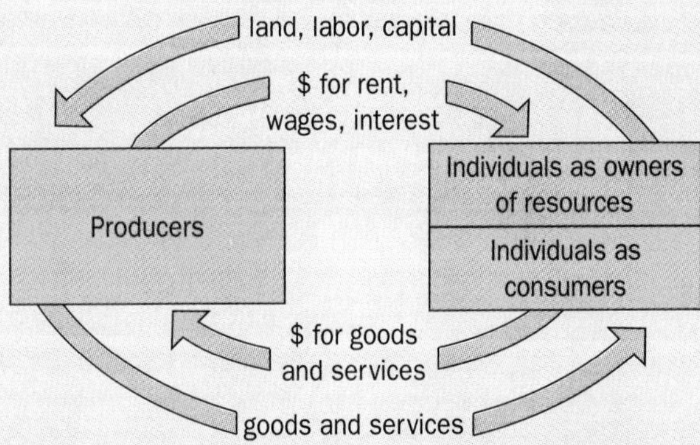

The following questions will help you analyze the chart.

1. What two major economic groups are shown on this circular flow chart?

2. What two roles do individuals play?

3. Which circle shows the basic factors of production and what gets produced?

4. Which circle shows the flow of money through the economy?

5. Where do producers get the land, labor, and capital needed to produce goods and services?

6. Where do consumers get the goods and services they need?

7. Where do consumers get the money they need to pay for goods and services?

8. Where do producers get the money they need to pay for land, labor, and capital?

DECISION-MAKING SKILLS

Opinion or Statement of Fact?

Examine the sentences below to distinguish opinions from statements of fact. Remember, a single sentence may contain both opinion and statement of fact.

A. The AFL-CIO is a labor organization that has 13 million members.

B. The AFL-CIO is the best labor organization in the United States.

C. It is a good thing that only one worker in six in the United States has decided to become a union member.

D. Corporations are the most important form of business in the United States today, far more important than small businesses.

E. Americans should buy only products made in the United States.

F. Henry Ford and Andrew Carnegie were American entrepreneurs who eventually became millionaires.

G. Three out of five new businesses fail before the third year of operation, mainly because the owners are treated very unfairly by other businesses.

1. List the letters of the sentences that give only fact. For each of those sentences explain how you were able to tell that it was a statement of fact.

2. List the letters of the sentences that give only opinion. Explain how you can tell that they are opinions.

3. Identify two sentences from the list that include both fact and opinion. Explain how each sentence includes both.

4. How can you tell the difference between a statement of fact and an opinion?

5. Explain how distinguishing between opinions and statements of fact can help you in making decisions.

Chapter Themes: Money serves as a medium of exchange, a standard of value, and a store of value in all economies. Banks help individuals and businesses manage their money. The federal government regulates banks and the nation's money supply.

CHAPTER 15

Money and Banking

Carmella reminded her older brother, Francisco, that their grandmother's birthday was coming up. "I think she'd like a sweater," said Carmella.

"Let's go to the mall and look for one, then," Francisco replied.

On the way to the mall, they stopped at a bank. Francisco walked up to the automated teller machine (ATM) and pulled a plastic card out of his pocket. Carmella watched as he put the card into a slot in the machine and punched some keys. The machine beeped, whirred, and spit out two $20 bills.

"Where does that money come from?" asked Carmella, who had never seen an ATM in action before.

"It comes from my checking account," answered Francisco. Seeing the puzzled look on Carmella's face, he began to explain what a checking account is. "I put money in the bank," said Francisco, "and the bank keeps track of how much. Whenever I want some of that money back, I use my ATM card or write a check."

"Why don't you just keep the money yourself to begin with?" wondered Carmella.

"It's safer to keep my money in a checking account," said Francisco. "I won't lose it, and the bank pays me interest on it."

At the mall they visited several stores. Carmella found three different sweaters she thought their grandmother would like. They compared the prices of all three and decided that one was too expensive. Out of the other two, Carmella picked the one with the best colors. Francisco agreed that their grandmother would like it.

As they passed the bank on their way home, Carmella decided that she, too, would get a checking account at the bank when she got her first job and started earning money.

In this chapter you will read about money and banking. Like Carmella, you will learn about what money is and does, and how banks help us save and use it. Then you will be introduced to the way our banking system is supervised by the federal government.

Teaching Note: Use the Introducing the Chapter activity, page T 119.

15-1
MONEY

Read to Find Out

- what the term *currency* means.
- what functions money serves in an economy.
- what characteristics our money has.
- why our money has value.

Our market economy could not work without money. Like the blood in your body, money flows throughout our economic system, connecting and feeding all the vital parts. You learned in the last chapter that money aids the circular flow of economic activity by making the exchange of goods and services quick and efficient. Without money, we would have to rely on bartering—exchanging goods and services. Such trading would be inconvenient in the economy we have today.

The Functions of Money

Money has three basic functions no matter what kind of economy it is used in. When you go to the store to buy a can of soda or a pen, why does the person behind the counter accept your money in exchange for real goods? After all, money is just some pieces of metal or paper. Your money is accepted because the owner of the store can spend it elsewhere to buy something he or she wants.

Exchanging money for cans of soda, pens, and other goods and services is an everyday event. It illustrates the first and most basic function of money. Money is a medium of exchange between individuals in an economy.

Money's second basic function is not as easy to see. Suppose you visit a shopping mall and discover a jacket on sale for $30. You know that this price is a "good deal," because you have checked the price of the same kind of jacket in other stores. You can compare the cost of the jacket in this store with its cost elsewhere because the price is expressed in the same way in every store—in terms of dollars and cents. Would it be as easy to know if the jacket was a good deal if the store owner offered to sell it to you for three cows, and other stores were charging six sheep?

Prices stated in money terms provide a standard which allows you to compare values of goods and services. The prices that you see every day reflect the second basic function of money. Money is a standard of value for goods and services.

The third function of money can be recognized when you decide to keep it instead of spending it. If you save money by hiding it in a dresser drawer or putting it in a bank, you are storing it for use in the future. Saving shows the third basic function of money. Money serves as a store of value, allowing you to buy goods or services sometime in the future.

The Characteristics of Our Money

The coins and paper bills used as money in an economy are called ***currency***. Other kinds of objects have been used as money in the past such as salt, furs, grains, and gold. It is said

AMERICAN NOTEBOOK 

In 1787, the United States government issued the first American coin—the Fugio penny. On the front of this large copper coin, a chain made up of thirteen links encircles the words "We Are One." On the other side is stamped the advice "Mind Your Business."

Because a good such as salt, a fur, or a cow can be consumed and satisfy a want directly, it can be used either for barter or as money. It is money if it serves the three functions stated in the text.

Our economy could not work well without money. Unlike this French fur trapper and Indian fisherman in Canada during the 1600s, we would find it hard to get what we want only by trading goods.

that in Iceland several hundred years ago three dried fish could buy a pair of shoes.

These kinds of money all worked well in the economies in which they were used. None of them, however, could function very well as money in our economy today. Each of them lacks one or more of the six characteristics that make our currency the ideal kind of money for our economy.

1. *Our money is generally acceptable.* If you tried to pay for a can of soda with some salt, grain, or dried fish, would the clerk accept it? In our society, none of these goods can serve as a medium of exchange because they are not acceptable to everyone.

2. *Our money can be counted and measured accurately.* Consider the problem of pricing everything in terms of dried fish. One small dried fish might buy one hamburger. Two large dried fish might buy a T-shirt. This pricing is not a very accurate way of establishing standard values of products, because the size of dried fish is not standard. Imagine the arguments people would have over the size of the fish used as payment for a good.

3. *Our money is durable and not easily destroyed.* Dried fish may be made into soup, and furs may be eaten by moths. These and many objects used for money in the past did not always hold their value because they could be easily destroyed. They could not always be trusted to serve as a store of value.

4. *Our money is convenient and easy to carry and use.* For hundreds of years, gold and silver in the form of standard-weight coins served as money all over the world. This kind of money worked well in an economy based on ocean trade. Unlike goods such as dried fish, gold and silver coins are durable and can be measured and counted accurately. However, gold and silver are not the ideal form of money in our economy because large amounts are very heavy and not easily transported.

5. *Our money is inexpensive to produce.* Today, gold and silver have a very high value because they are expensive to find. The value of gold and silver as metals, in fact, is greater than their value as money.

6. *The supply of our money is easily controlled.* In a growing economy, there must be

Challenge (Analysis): In his play *Major Barbara*, George Bernard Shaw states, "The universal regard for money is the one hopeful fact in our civilization." Have students discuss what Shaw meant.

Teaching Note: Use Teaching Activity 1, page T 119, as a culminating activity after students have read the material in Section 15-1.

a continuous supply of money, with just the right amount available. It is difficult, however, to control gold and silver supplies to meet the demands for them, because new discoveries of these metals are hard to predict.

Think about the coins and bills you may have in your pocket. Are they generally acceptable, durable, and convenient? Are they easily measured and counted, and inexpensive to produce? Can their supply be controlled? You will find that our currency has all six of these characteristics.

The Value of Our Currency

The coins we use are made of a mixture of 25 percent copper and 75 percent nickel. The metal in each coin is worth less than the coin's face value. Our bills are just paper. Why, then, is this currency generally acceptable?

For the answer, look closely at a dollar bill. On the side with George Washington's picture on it, you will see the words, "This note is legal tender for all debts, public and private." This means that our money is money because the government says it is. The fact that our government stands behind our money gives us confidence that it will continue to have value in exchange for goods and services.

Answers will be found on page T 121.

Section Review

1. Define *currency.*
2. What are the three functions of money?
3. What are the six characteristics of the money we use in our economy today?
4. Why does our currency have value?

Analysis. Tobacco was used as money in parts of the South during colonial times. Which characteristics of our money today are *not* shared by tobacco?

15-2

OUR BANKING SYSTEM

Read to Find Out

- what the terms *demand deposit* and *loan* mean.
- what kinds of money we use besides currency.
- what services banks offer.
- how loans from banks help businesses and the economy.

Even though the money we use in our economy is durable and convenient, it can be easily lost or stolen. To overcome this limitation of currency, societies have created banks. Banks help us to save money and to exchange it for goods and services safely and conveniently. In this way, banks help businesses and individuals manage their money.

The Beginnings of Banking

Merchants and goldsmiths in Europe created the first banks during the Middle Ages. Banks became necessary as more goods were exchanged and larger amounts of money were needed in the growing European economy.

In a similar way, banks sprang up as they were needed in the young United States. The following story about the creation of a bank in the 1860s is fictitious. However, it shows how banks developed over time into institutions that could meet the needs of consumers and producers in a modern economy.

Hiram Wakefield was a goldsmith in Denver, Colorado, when he heard about the gold strike near Gemstone City, 50 miles to the west. He moved to the frontier town with his gold-weighing scale and his large safe. There he set up a new shop.

Until the late 1800s, paper money in the United States was backed by silver and gold and could be exchanged for these precious metals. Today paper money is no longer convertible. Nothing makes it valuable except the government's decree that it is valuable.

Soon Hiram's business was booming. Miners from the Gemstone City region brought their gold to be weighed, valued, and stored. When a miner brought in some gold for safekeeping, Hiram gave him a receipt which noted the value of that amount of gold. Then Hiram stored the gold in the safe.

The miners discovered that they could give any shopkeeper one of Hiram's receipts in exchange for the goods they wanted to buy. Business owners accepted these receipts because they could exchange them for gold if they wished.

Hiram further influenced the way his receipts were used in Gemstone City. He gave each miner both a receipt for the total value of the miner's gold stored in the safe and several "blank" receipts with which the miner could easily buy things. A miner completed a blank receipt by writing in a person's name and the amount of gold Hiram was to give to that person. The blank receipts became a form of money in Gemstone City.

Hiram soon discovered that miners only rarely came to exchange their receipts for all the actual gold they had on deposit in his safe. He also knew that some miners needed more gold than they had so they could buy supplies and continue to mine. Hiram decided, therefore, that he could safely lend some of the gold in his safe to miners who needed it. Miners who received these loans signed a note saying they would pay back the gold along with an added fee for borrowing it.

Hiram Wakefield had become the Gemstone City banker. His system of issuing blank receipts and loans is very similar to what banks do today.

The Kinds of Money

When you think of money, you picture currency, such as quarters and dollar bills. Hiram Wakefield, however, had created a second kind of money—checks. The merchants of Gemstone City accepted the miners' checks—the

Bankers in gold-mining communities such as Nome, Alaska, weighed and stored the gold that miners brought to them for safekeeping.

Remind students that banks are part of the institution of the economy. Refer students to Chapter 2, Section 3, for a review of the economy as an institution organized to respond to people's needs.

Demand deposits include regular checking accounts at commercial banks and checking-type accounts at savings and loan associations, mutual savings banks, and credit unions.

blank receipts Hiram gave them—in exchange for goods and services, just as if they were currency.

Checks have all the characteristics of currency. They are generally accepted in exchange. By writing a specific amount on a check, a person states exactly how much money is to be paid. Although checks are not as durable as currency, the records banks keep for each check *are* durable. Checks are also easy to use and inexpensive to produce, and their supply can be controlled.

Checks can only exist in an economy if there are banks. In our economy, checks are used by people who have deposited money in a checking account at a bank. The money in a checking account is called a ***demand deposit.*** A person with a checking account can withdraw money from the bank "on demand" by writing a check.

Traveler's checks are a third kind of money we have in our economy today. Most traveler's checks are issued by banks. Printed on a traveler's check is the exact amount of money for which it can be cashed, usually $20, $50, or $100. Traveler's checks are generally acceptable as payment for goods and services and can be easily changed into cash.

Banks and the Money Supply

Traveler's checks, demand deposits, and currency are the kinds of money that make up the United States' money supply. The money supply is the total amount of money available for use as a medium of exchange. As you will learn later in this chapter, the money supply goes up and down. It does, however, stay within certain bounds. In 1989, the money supply was about $783 billion.

Look at the money supply table on this page. Over 70 percent of our nation's money supply is in demand deposits. Knowing that demand deposits are managed by banks, you can see how important banks are to the economy. Banks not only hold a great deal of our currency, they also have a role in every transaction that is made using a check.

Bank Services

Think back to the story of Hiram Wakefield. Hiram provided checking accounts for the miners, kept their gold safe, and made loans. Today, offering these same three services is the major function of banks in our economy.

Bill and Wilma Kowalski do business with the Central National Bank in their community. They visit the bank nearly every week, either to deposit checks or to get some cash to spend. Over the years, they have made use of all the bank's services.

Checking accounts. When Bill and Wilma first got married, they opened a checking account at Central National Bank by depositing money there. They found that using checks to pay for goods and to pay bills was an easy way to do business.

Using checks was also safe. The Kowalskis did not want to carry a lot of cash because it could be stolen. Checks, on the other hand, were useless to a thief because no one will accept a check unless it is written by the person whose name is printed on it.

The Parts of the Money Supply, 1990

Kind of money	Approximate value (in billions)	Percent of money supply
Currency	$246	30%
Demand deposits*	$571	69%
Traveler's checks	$8	1%
Total	$825	100%

*Includes all checking accounts

Automated teller machine (ATM) cards are similar to checks. They both provide access to demand deposits. Economists consider credit cards a means of making a purchase (installment buying), not a kind of money. (Credit cards are discussed in Chapter 17.)

Decision Making: Have students discuss what factors they would have to consider when trying to decide which type of savings account to open.

Loans from banks provide businesses with the money to put together big projects like this housing development.

Bill and Wilma also liked the fact that the checks provided a good record of how they spent their money. Each month the bank sent back their cancelled, or paid, checks. It also sent a statement telling how much money was in their account.

Savings accounts. Bill and Wilma also decided to save for the future. They opened a savings account at Central National Bank because they knew it was a safe place to keep their money. Unlike their checking account, the Kowalskis' savings account was not a demand deposit. They could not withdraw the money on demand. The bank reserved the right to require advance notice of a large withdrawal.

However, the bank paid the Kowalskis for keeping their money in a savings account because they were in effect lending the bank money it could use for other purposes. The payment the Kowalskis received from the bank is called interest. This kind of interest, received for the use of money, is not the same as the payment for the use of capital you learned about in Chapter 14.

People save for many reasons. The Kowalskis wanted to save for their daughter's college education and to have money in case of an emergency. Savings are an important source of funds in our economy. With savings funds, banks can make loans to help people in the economy buy goods and services and to help businesses produce goods and services.

Loans. To make some extra money, Bill and Wilma began washing windows on weekends. Soon they got so many requests for their services that they decided to quit their jobs and start their own business. To start their business Bill and Wilma had to borrow money.

The Kowalskis scheduled a meeting with Marcia Slatterly at Central National Bank to talk about getting a loan. A ***loan*** is an amount of money borrowed for a certain time period. The borrower agrees to pay back the amount of money borrowed plus a certain amount of interest.

Before their meeting with Marcia, Bill and Wilma developed a plan for the new business, which they wanted to call Willy's Window Washing. Based on their plan, Bill and Wilma thought they needed to borrow $25,000.

At the meeting, Marcia looked over their business plan. "Your plan looks good," she said. "I think a window-washing service is needed here. How will you use the $25,000 loan?"

Even though savings accounts are not demand deposits, restrictions on withdrawals vary depending on the interest rate and term of account. Some banks offer interest on checking accounts.

In addition to the services described in the text, banks provide safe-deposit boxes and life insurance to people who take bank loans. Banks also manage trust funds and provide financial advice to individuals and businesses.

Wilma answered, "We'll buy a truck, ladders, and cleaning supplies, which will amount to $12,000. We'll need $3,000 for a phone line and advertising. And we'll need $10,000 to pay ourselves, to pay bills, and to pay part-time employees until our business begins earning enough money."

"That sounds reasonable," said Marcia. "I'll approve your loan to help you begin your business, and I wish you success."

The beginning of Willy's Window Washing is the kind of story that takes place every day in banks throughout the United States. The home builder relies on bank loans for money for lumber and plumbing supplies. A factory owner may borrow money from a bank to buy new computers. People also take out loans to buy a new car or to put braces on their children's teeth. People who take out loans have decided that the benefit of having money now is greater than the cost of paying it back with interest later.

By making loans, banks serve an important function. They help businesses make use of productive resources, which causes the economy to grow. When a business gets a loan, that business often creates more jobs by hiring new workers. Bill and Wilma, for example, may create after-school and summer jobs for teenagers.

A business that gets a loan may also help other businesses grow. When Bill and Wilma buy window-washing supplies, the makers of the supplies will benefit. If enough new window-washing businesses are started up, the makers of supplies may want to hire more workers to expand *their* businesses.

Fractional Reserve Banking

Making loans is perhaps the most important role of banks in our economy. The money banks lend comes from the deposits made by other customers.

Hiram Wakefield knew that what a miner cared about was that he could get back the correct amount of gold for his deposit. He also learned that all the miners would not want all their gold at the same time. At any particular time some miners would withdraw their deposits and others would make new deposits. These withdrawals and new deposits were just about equal, so the total amount of gold in his safe stayed about the same.

Hiram found that he needed to keep only a fraction of the miners' total deposits in his vault to meet the demands for withdrawals. Therefore, he could loan out a certain amount of the gold in his vault as long as he kept—or reserved—enough gold to pay depositors who demanded it.

Modern banking operates on the same principle of fractional reserve banking. Banks keep a percentage of checking and savings deposits in reserve. The rest of the money is available for loans and investments.

When bankers learned that they needed to keep only a fraction of their money on hand, it was an important discovery. Banks could then make the money they received from depositors do useful work instead of letting it sit in a dark vault. When the money deposited in banks is loaned to businesses and individuals, it helps those who need to borrow money. It also generates economic growth and creates an income for the bank in the form of interest payments on the loans.

The Business of Banking

Like other businesses in our economy, banks exist to make a profit. Most banks are corporations with stockholders who want a return on their investment. That is, they want their investment to grow, or become more valuable.

The largest source of revenue for most banks is interest on loans. Although banks pay customers interest on savings accounts, the

Challenge (Analysis): Have students discuss the impact on the economy if people chose not to save money, or if they chose to save 30 percent of their income.

PEOPLE MAKE A DIFFERENCE

Students Run School Bank

Have you ever wondered what it would be like to work for a bank and handle other people's money? Some students in Marlborough, Massachusetts, are finding out by working at a bank at their high school.

The Marlborough High School bank is a branch of St. Mary's Credit Union. It was set up in 1987 by business teachers Joan Ledoux and Mary Egan.

Eight students are chosen each year to run the bank. The students take an eight-week training program during the summer to learn about their responsibilities as bank tellers.

When school begins, the students work as tellers during the lunch hour. They set up bank accounts, handle transactions, and complete loan applications. They use a computer connected to

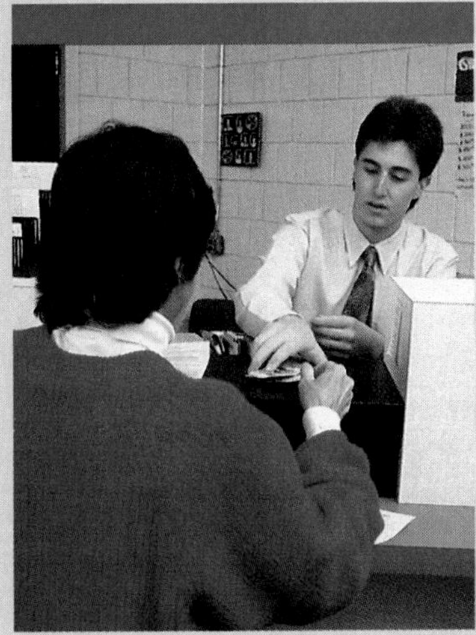

the bank's main office to keep track of loan payments and the amounts of money customers have in their accounts.

The school bank is a busy place. "We've got a lot of kids using the bank," says Joanne Sharon, the bank's supervisor. "They're enthusiastic and they're learning."

Craig Belmore, one of the students who works at the bank, is well aware of the responsibility he has as a student teller. "You're dealing with hundreds of dollars of other people's money," says Craig. "If you make a mistake, it could be their loss or the bank's loss."

The job also requires that student tellers protect the privacy of the bank's customers. "The students have shown a great deal of responsibility and professionalism," says Joanne Sharon. "More teachers are banking with us now because of the trust they have in the student tellers."

The students who run the bank at Marlborough High School are very pleased with the opportunities it gives them. They can learn about money and banking and at the same time provide a useful service to teachers and fellow students.

amount of interest banks pay on savings is less than the amount of interest banks charge on loans. The difference in the interest paid out on savings and the interest paid to a bank by borrowers is a major part of a bank's income.

Other Financial Institutions

Banks are only one kind of financial institution. Three others are savings and loan associations, mutual savings banks, and credit unions. Each was created for a particular purpose. In recent years, however, all three of these financial institutions have become more and more similar to banks.

Savings and loan associations were meant to accept savings deposits and to make loans to families for buying land and houses. Today, most savings and loan associations also offer checking accounts, like banks.

Activity: Have students prepare a list of interview questions that the Marlborough High School Bank supervisors might ask a student who is applying for a job.

Teaching Note: Use Teaching Activity 2, page T 119, as a culminating activity after students have read the material in Section 15-2.

Financial Institutions in the United States in 1989

Type of institution	Number	Total value of deposits (in billions)
Banks	12,710	$2,360
Savings and loan associations	2,880	$ 830
Mutual savings banks	490	$ 220
Credit unions	13,370	$ 170

A mutual savings bank is owned by its depositors, and any profits are paid to them. Mutual savings banks accept deposits, make loans, and allow checking accounts.

A credit union is a non-profit banking institution which serves only its members. The members often work for one organization such as a large company or a unit of government. Credit unions accept savings deposits and lend money. Credit unions also offer checking accounts called share drafts.

Our financial institutions provide important services to both producers and consumers. In this way they form a strong foundation for a healthy economy.

Answers will be found on page T 121.

Section Review

1. Define *demand deposit* and *loan.*
2. What are the three kinds of money in our economy?
3. Name three services offered by banks.
4. Explain how loans made by banks help the economy grow.

Analysis. What are the advantages of depositing money in a savings account instead of hiding it somewhere?

15-3 THE FEDERAL RESERVE SYSTEM

Read to Find Out

- what the terms *inflation* and *recession* mean.
- how the Federal Reserve System is organized.
- what functions the Federal Reserve System has as the nation's central bank.
- why the Federal Reserve regulates the money supply.

The economy of the United States, as you know, is a mixed economy, with the government playing a significant role in the way it works. One important way in which the federal government affects the economy is to regulate the banking industry and the nation's money supply. It performs these functions through the Federal Reserve System.

The Need for Government Regulation

Several times in the late 1800s and early 1900s, the economy stopped growing for a period of time. There was widespread hardship as businesses closed and workers lost their jobs.

During these periods, people who had money deposited in banks began to panic because they feared that the banks, too, would go out of business. They wanted all their money in cash. Because banks operated on the fractional reserve principle, many did not have enough money on hand to meet such a great and sudden demand. Some banks ran out of money and had to close down, and many of their customers lost all their money.

After one of these financial panics occurred in 1907, the public demanded that the

Most financial experts use the term *bank* to refer only to commercial banks, which provide a full range of services to businesses and the general public. Credit unions, savings and loan associations, and mutual savings banks are usually called *thrifts*.

To protect depositors, most money deposited in banks is insured. The Federal Deposit Insurance Corporation (FDIC) insures most commercial deposits. The Federal Savings and Loan Insurance Corporation (FSLIC) insures most deposits in savings and loan associations.

government step in and make rules for how banks should operate. They also thought that there should be a way for the federal government to assist banks when they needed help.

In 1913 Congress passed a bill creating the Federal Reserve System, which became the central bank of the United States. Often called "the Fed," the Federal Reserve System provides important services to banks all over the United States and regulates their activities.

How the Federal Reserve System is Organized

The Federal Reserve System is an independent agency of the federal government. It is organized to remain beyond the reach of political influence so it can serve the needs of the nation as a whole.

Federal Reserve districts. The lawmakers who created the Federal Reserve System wanted to keep the central bank in touch with the business needs of the country. Since the economic problems of one region may be different from those of another, Congress divided the United States into twelve geographic regions called Federal Reserve districts.

In each district there is a Federal Reserve Bank that supervises banking in that district and can pay attention to the economic problems of the area it serves. For example, the

Federal Reserve Districts

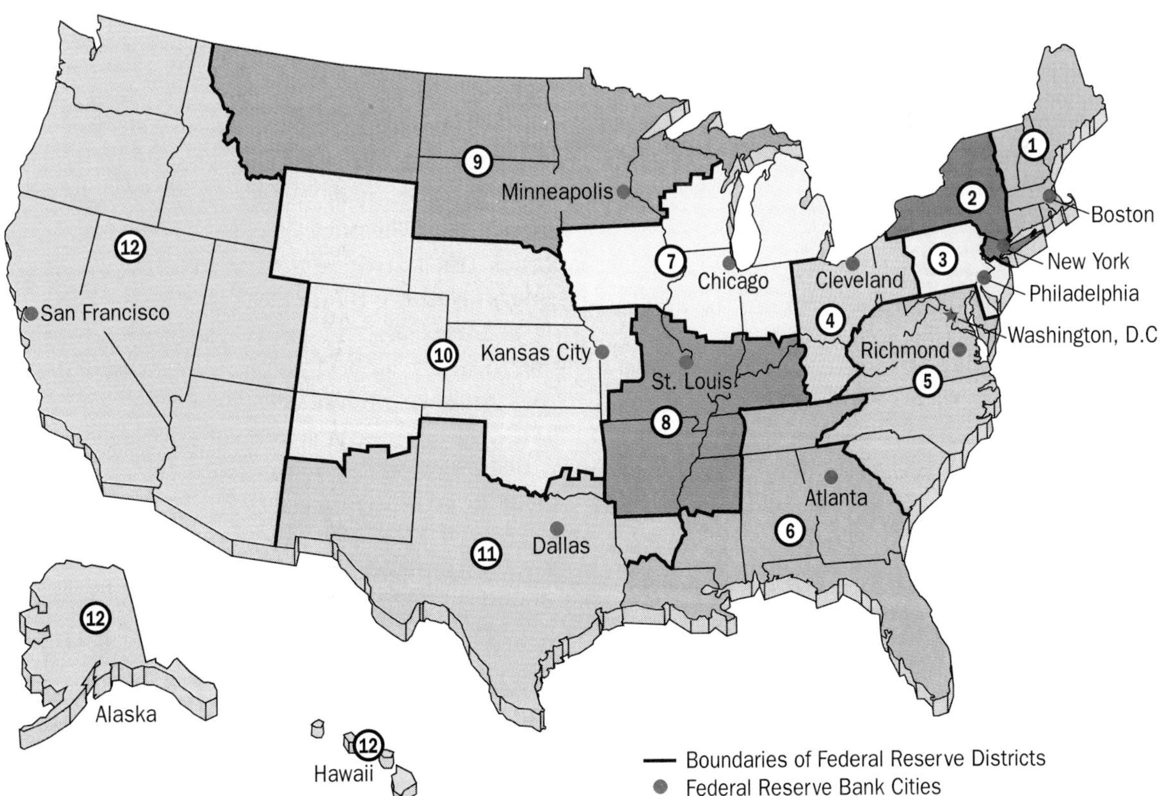

In 1815, 1837, 1873, 1893, and 1929, the United States experienced severe depressions interspersed with periods of prosperity. Milder depressions occurred in 1847, 1857, 1867, 1883, and 1907. (The business cycle is discussed in Chapter 16.)

tenth district Federal Reserve Bank in Kansas City, which serves a farming region, is aware of farmers' problems and of banks in the district that make loans to farmers.

Running the Federal Reserve System. The most powerful people in the Fed are the seven members of the Board of Governors. They are appointed by the President for 14-year terms. The Board of Governors is responsible for running the Federal Reserve System as a whole.

Two other groups are also important to the operation of the Federal Reserve System. They are the Open Market Committee and the Federal Advisory Council. The Open Market Committee includes the seven members of the Board of Governors and the presidents of five Federal Reserve Banks. Its job is to regulate our nation's money supply.

The Federal Advisory Council is made up of twelve bankers from the private banking industry, one from each Federal Reserve district. The job of the council is to give advice to the Board of Governors and the Open Market Committee on our country's business and banking problems.

The Functions of the Federal Reserve System

The Fed is not like any other bank. You cannot save money at the Fed; you cannot get a loan from the Fed; you cannot have a checking account at the Fed. The Fed, however, is important to you and to the value of your money. It is often called "the bankers' bank."

Providing services. The most important day-to-day job of the Fed is to collect and to clear checks. If you pay for your new clothes with a check, the clothing store owner deposits the check in the store's bank. The store's bank then sends the check to the Fed, which sends it on to your bank. In this process, money is taken from your checking account and put into the clothing store's checking account. In a year, the Fed will process over 15 billion checks. The diagram on page 339 shows how checks are collected and cleared.

The Fed can also wire money, which means to transfer bank funds electronically. The Fed has created "Fedwire," a nationwide communications system that sends information and transfers money. Billions of dollars are sent over Fedwire in a year.

The Fed also supplies currency to banks. If a bank needs currency to pay customers who are making withdrawals, it orders currency from the nearest Federal Reserve Bank. Look at a dollar bill. At the top of the side with George Washington's picture are the words "Federal Reserve Note." Each federal reserve note comes from one of the twelve Federal Reserve Banks.

Serving as the government's bank. The Fed has the job of keeping the federal government's checking accounts. When people pay their taxes, the money is deposited in a government account at a Federal Reserve Bank. When the government pays for highways, airplanes, and astronauts, it writes checks on its Federal Reserve Bank accounts.

The Fed also keeps track of the federal government's debts. If the government borrows money, the lender—who may be an individual, a bank, or a business—receives a certificate called a government bond. This certificate tells how much money the government borrowed. The Federal Reserve System keeps records of all government bonds.

Supervising banks. The Federal Reserve makes rules that govern the business of banking. One of the most important regulations sets a minimum on the amount of reserves a bank must keep on deposit with a Federal Reserve Bank. This rule ensures that banks will always have

Have students examine a dollar bill to identify which of the 12 Federal Reserve Banks issued the bill. Direct students to look at the circle with the large letter in the center to the left of George Washington's picture.

enough money available to meet the demand for withdrawals. To enforce its regulations, the Fed has a staff of bank examiners who visit banks from time to time to be sure they are following all the Fed's rules.

Making loans to banks. Banks sometimes need extra money. Usually this happens when bank customers want to borrow or withdraw large sums of money. The Fed will make loans to help out banks in these situations. Banks pay a special low rate of interest, called the discount rate, on funds borrowed from the Fed.

Helping individuals and businesses. Congress has passed several laws that protect businesses and individuals doing business with banks. The Fed's job is to help put these laws into effect. One of the laws enforced by the Fed is the Truth in Lending Law, which requires banks and other financial institutions to tell you the full cost of borrowing money.

Controlling the money supply. The most powerful job of the Fed is to regulate the nation's money supply—the amount available for spending. The size of the money supply has a great influence on the health of the economy.

The largest and most changeable part of the money supply is made up of demand deposits. The amount of money in demand deposits is directly affected by the amount of money that banks lend to individuals, businesses, and governments. Because of this relationship, the Fed can control the money supply indirectly—by influencing the amount of

The Story of a Check

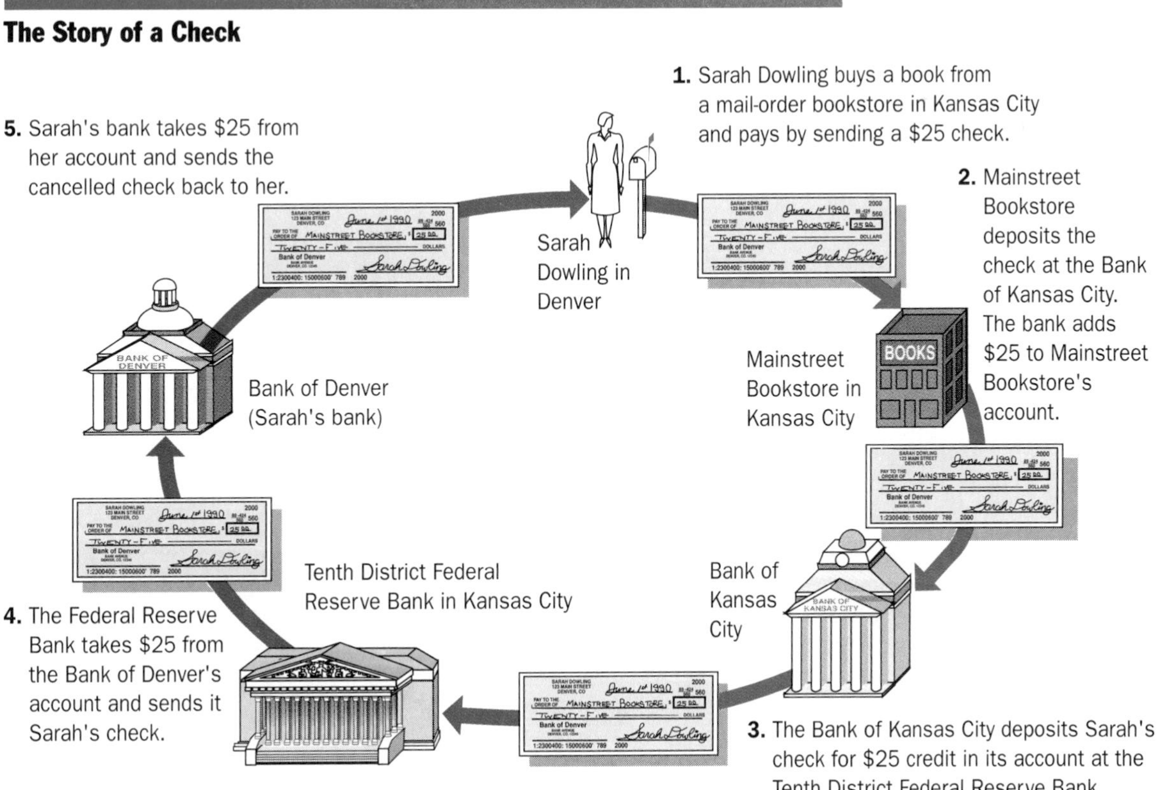

1. Sarah Dowling buys a book from a mail-order bookstore in Kansas City and pays by sending a $25 check.
2. Mainstreet Bookstore deposits the check at the Bank of Kansas City. The bank adds $25 to Mainstreet Bookstore's account.
3. The Bank of Kansas City deposits Sarah's check for $25 credit in its account at the Tenth District Federal Reserve Bank.
4. The Federal Reserve Bank takes $25 from the Bank of Denver's account and sends it Sarah's check.
5. Sarah's bank takes $25 from her account and sends the cancelled check back to her.
Sarah Dowling in Denver
Mainstreet Bookstore in Kansas City
BOOKS
Bank of Kansas City
Tenth District Federal Reserve Bank in Kansas City
Bank of Denver (Sarah's bank)
BANK OF DENVER

The Six Jobs of the Federal Reserve System

1. To provide services to banks, including clearing checks, wiring money, and supplying currency.
2. To serve as the bank for the federal government.
3. To supervise banks and other financial institutions.
4. To make loans to banks.
5. To help individuals and the business community.
6. To control the nation's money supply.

money banks can lend and the amount that individuals, businesses, and governments will choose to borrow. The Fed can use three different methods to influence the amount of money loaned by banks.

First, the Fed can change its reserve requirement. If the Fed lowers the reserve requirement, banks have to keep less money on reserve at the Fed and will have more money available to make loans. In contrast, banks can make fewer loans if the reserve requirement is raised.

Second, the Fed can change the discount rate. If the Fed lowers the discount rate, banks pay less interest on money they borrow and can therefore charge a lower rate of interest to their borrowers. Lower interest rates will encourage more people to borrow more money. On the other hand, if the Fed raises the discount rate, banks will raise the rate of interest they charge their borrowers. In this case, people will tend to borrow less money.

Third, the Fed can buy and sell government bonds. Government bonds are certificates that the federal government issues in exchange for lending it money. A government bond can be bought or sold. It represents money owed to the holder of the bond certificate. If the Fed buys government bonds from banks, banks have more reserves and thus more money to lend. If the Fed sells government bonds to banks, banks pay for them from their reserves and thus have less money to lend.

Money and the Economy: The Delicate Balance

The money supply affects our economy in important ways because it is directly related to the amount of money people can spend in the economy. In order for the economy to be healthy, spending must be approximately equal to the economy's ability to produce

How the Fed Affects the Money Supply and the Economy

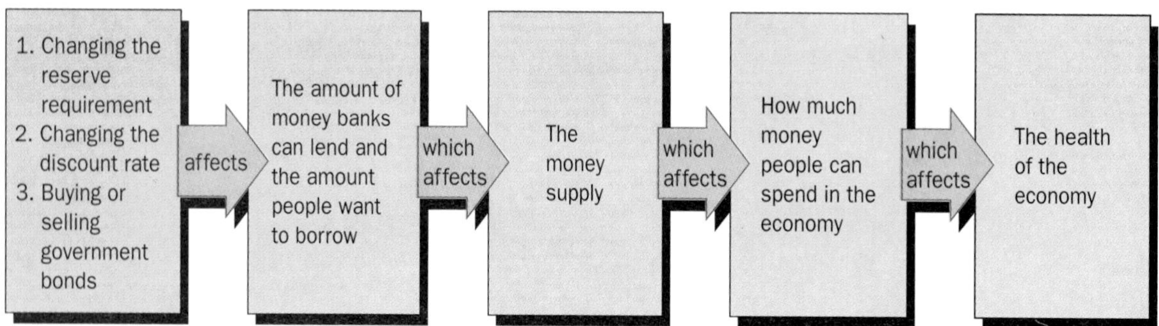
1. Changing the reserve requirement
2. Changing the discount rate
3. Buying or selling government bonds
affects
The amount of money banks can lend and the amount people want to borrow
which affects
The money supply
which affects
How much money people can spend in the economy
which affects
The health of the economy

Challenge (Analysis): Have students assume that they want to start a business. How might they be affected by the Fed's actions in raising or lowering the reserve requirement?

Teaching Note: Use the Reinforcement and Enrichment activities, page T 120, and accompanying worksheets in the Activity Book after students have read the material in this section.

goods and services. If this balance is not maintained, two different problems may result.

When there is more money in the economy than there are goods and services to spend it on, increased demand for goods and services will cause prices to rise. A general rise in the prices of goods and services throughout the economy is called ***inflation.*** Inflation reduces the buying power of people's money. If your income stays the same, you can buy less because of inflation.

When there is less money in the economy than goods and services to spend it on, the demand for goods and services decreases. This situation can cause businesses to cut back on production. Such a slowdown in economic activity and production is called a ***recession.*** A recession is bad for the country because it results in lower production, lower profits for businesses, and increased unemployment.

Controlling the money supply is therefore a delicate—and very important—balancing act. When prices begin to rise, the Fed may decide to discourage loans. With less money being loaned, spending slows and prices are less likely to rise. If a recession threatens to occur, the Fed will likely make it easier for banks to make loans. Increased lending will stimulate spending and increase production.

Through its ability to affect the money supply, the Fed can help keep the economy on a steady course. At the same time, the Fed helps keep our banking system safe and able to meet the needs of businesses and individuals.

Answers will be found on T 121.

Section Review

1. Define *inflation* and *recession.*
2. Why is the Federal Reserve System divided into districts?
3. Name three of the Fed's jobs.
4. Why is controlling the money supply important?

Application. Suppose you have an allowance of $5 a week. After a year of high inflation, your allowance is still $5 a week. What problem do you have? How will you try to convince your parents that you need a larger allowance?

Data Search. Look at the map on page 337. What is the number of the Federal Reserve District in which you live? In what city is your district's Federal Reserve Bank?

A BROADER VIEW

Banks fill important needs in our economic system and in those of other countries. The services that banks can offer are so important, in fact, that several international organizations much like banks have been created to help countries participate in the global economy. The two most important international "banks," the International Monetary Fund and the World Bank, were created just after World War II.

The International Monetary Fund (IMF) was established mainly to promote better international trade. Every country has its own kind of currency, and so when countries buy goods from each other they must exchange different currencies. One of the jobs of the IMF is to help keep the rates of exchange between currencies stable and orderly.

The World Bank, officially called the International Bank for Reconstruction and Development, is closely linked to the IMF. The major job of the World Bank is to make loans to developing countries to help them improve their economies.

Teaching Note: Use the Evaluating Progress activity, page T 120, to assess students' understanding of the chapter.

CHAPTER SURVEY

Answers to Survey and Workshop will be found on page T 121.

UNDERSTANDING NEW VOCABULARY

Seeing Relationships

The vocabulary terms in each pair listed below are related to each other. For each pair, explain how the terms are related.

1. *currency* and *demand deposit*

2. *inflation* and *recession*

Putting It in Writing

Banks are important in our economy. Using the terms *demand deposit* and *loan*, write a paragraph that supports this statement.

LOOKING BACK AT THE CHAPTER

1. Which of the following is *not* a function of money?

- **(a)** standard of value
- **(b)** basis of wealth
- **(c)** medium of exchange
- **(d)** store of wealth

2. What characteristics of today's currency do gold and silver coins lack?

3. Why is the money a person keeps in a checking account called a demand deposit?

4. What is the difference between a check and a traveler's check?

5. Why do people use checking accounts?

6. What is the money supply? What makes up the money supply?

7. Where do banks get the money to make loans?

8. Why do banks need to keep only a fraction of their deposits on reserve?

9. What were the reasons for the creation of the Federal Reserve System?

10. What services does the Fed provide to banks?

11. In what three ways can the Fed influence the money supply?

12. Which of the following actions would the Fed *not* take to bring the economy out of a recession?

- **(a)** buy government bonds
- **(b)** raise the discount rate
- **(c)** lower the reserve requirement

13. *Analysis.* Many economists say that Americans should save more money than they do. What do you think is the argument behind this point of view?

14. *Application.* Suppose you want to start a business in your neighborhood, such as a lawn-mowing or housecleaning service. Where could you go to get a loan to start the business? How would you use the money that was lent to you?

15. *Analysis.* How are banks and credit unions similar? How are they different?

16. *Evaluation.* The leaders of the Federal Reserve System are appointed so that they will not be influenced by political pressures. What problems do you think might arise if these leaders were elected instead of being appointed?

WORKING TOGETHER

1. With a group of classmates, visit the banks in your area. Find answers to the following questions at each bank: Does the bank charge a fee for its checking accounts? Does it pay interest on checking deposits when they are greater than a certain amount? What rate of interest does it pay on savings accounts? What is its rate of interest on loans? Compare the fees and interest rates of each bank you visit. Which bank would you do business with?

2. Meet with one of the employees at a local bank who opens new accounts. Ask him or her to explain what it means to receive *compound* interest. If you start with $100 in a savings account at that bank, how much interest will you earn in 3, 6, 9, and 12 months?

Teaching Note: For reinforcement of decision-making skills, use Decision-Making Worksheet Chapter 15.

SOCIAL STUDIES SKILLS

Analyzing Cause-Effect Chains

In this chapter you have read that the Federal Reserve Board can affect the nation's economy by taking three kinds of actions. If the Federal Reserve Board's final goal, for example, is to bring the nation's economy out of a recession, it may decide to lower the discount rate. The Federal Reserve's action of lowering the discount rate, however, does not affect the recession directly. Instead, this action ripples through the economy, like falling dominoes, until the final goal is achieved.

Diagrams called cause-effect chains are often used to show the steps in such a process. An example is the diagram below. The questions that follow will help you analyze the double cause-effect chain shown here.

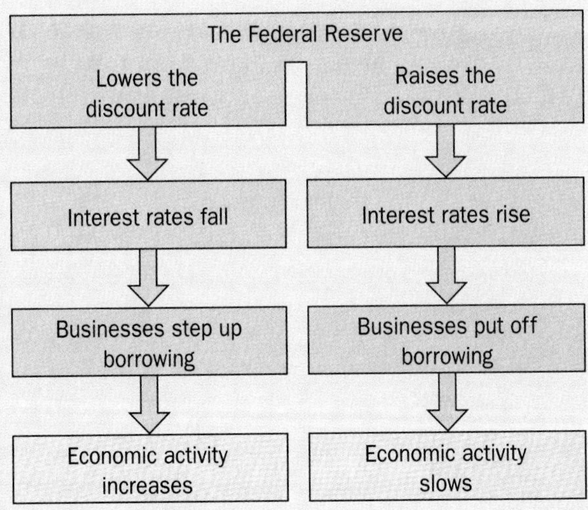

1. What is the the first action, or cause, in each of the cause-effect chains?

2. What is the final effect in each cause-effect chain?

3. Is "interest rates rise" a cause, an effect, or both? Explain your answer.

4. How are the two chains in this diagram related?

DECISION-MAKING SKILLS

Which Sources Can You Trust?

Suppose you need to decide the best way to earn some money. Below are descriptions of three sources of information that might help you. Determine which one of these sources would provide the most reliable information on earning money.

A. A booklet called *Stash Your Cash*, which has been put out by a bank in your community. The booklet provides information on the interest rates that this local bank offers. It shows that those interest rates are the same or better than the rates offered by several other banks in your state.

B. A book called *Teenage Entrepreneurs*, which gives advice from successful teenagers, ranging from a twelve-year-old owner of a gardening service to a seventeen-year-old owner of a rent-a-disc-jockey business. The book was on the best seller list for five months.

C. A letter you received this week from a nationally-known greeting card company. The letter explains how you can earn money in your spare time by selling greeting cards door-to-door in your neighborhood. For each $10 package of greeting cards that you sell, the company will pay you 50 cents. The letter quotes a teenager who earned an average of $500 a month selling cards over the past year.

1. Which one of the sources would probably provide the most reliable information on earning money? Explain why you think this source is more reliable than the others.

2. What is one way to determine how reliable a source is?

3. Think of a decision you might have to make soon. In which sources would you look for reliable information to help you decide? Explain.

Chapter Themes: The federal government shapes our economy. It must help solve economic problems to promote the common good without limiting individual freedom. The government also manages our economy in an effort to keep it running smoothly.

CHAPTER 16

Government's Role in Our Economy

At the electronics plant where Laura works, she cleans manufactured parts by dipping them into a chemical called a solvent. As she gets ready to dip a new batch of parts, she notices a man with a clipboard. Soon he walks up to her work station.

"I'm from a federal agency that protects the safety of workers," he says. "May I ask you some questions?"

"Sure," replies Laura. "Go ahead."

"How do you feel when you're working with this solvent?" asks the man.

"Well," Laura replies, "almost every day I get a headache—but it goes away pretty quickly. Sometimes I feel dizzy, too. Some of the other people I work with complain about the same things."

The man asks Laura questions about how she uses the solvent. Then Laura, curious, asks him why he is here. She finds out that his agency thinks that the solvent she works with may increase her chances of getting cancer. Laura feels a sudden rush of fear. No one ever told her the solvent was dangerous. She thinks about her friend Dorothy, who worked at the plant for 15 years and now is sick with cancer.

The man says the federal government is thinking of making rules that require businesses to protect workers who use the solvent. It is even possible, he says, that the government will ban the use of the solvent.

Making rules that protect workers is one of the many ways that local, state, and federal governments take actions that affect the economy. The word *intervention* is used to describe such government actions. Government intervention is what makes our free enterprise system a mixed economy. In this chapter, you will learn why and how government intervention occurs.

Teaching Note: Use the Introducing the Chapter activity, page T 124.

16-1

GOVERNMENT INTERVENTION IN THE ECONOMY

Read to Find Out

- how the government provides a foundation for economic growth.
- what economic problems Americans have asked government to solve.
- what governments can do to affect the economy.

The government plays an important role in the American economy. In Chapter 15, for example, you learned how the Federal Reserve System controls the supply of money and regulates banks. Government shapes and controls our economy in other ways, too. It makes rules for how businesses should operate, spends over $1 trillion each year, and taxes individuals and corporations.

The federal government is both the largest consumer in the economy and the biggest employer. How and why did government's role in our economy become so important?

American Values and Economic Goals

Individual freedom is one of the basic values upon which our government is built. The framers of our Constitution believed that economic freedom, like political freedom, is a basic right of citizens. They held that producers and consumers should be free to own property, to make a profit, and to make their own choices about what to produce, buy, and sell. In writing the Constitution, they had in mind a country with an economy based on a market system.

To make sure that the economy of the new nation would be strong and be able to grow, Article 1, Section 8 of the Constitution gave Congress the power to coin money, collect taxes, borrow money, set up a postal service, build roads, and regulate commerce. In other words, Congress was to lay a foundation on which a market economy could flourish.

The Constitution also gave Congress and the states the power to make "ground rules" for a market economy. These rules include laws that protect private property against theft and laws that say how corporations may be set up.

Once the foundations had been laid and the rules set, citizens expected government to play only a small role in the economy. Like the framers, they wanted businesses to be able to operate freely in our market economy.

At the same time, Americans believed strongly in the basic values of equality and justice. They hoped free enterprise would promote the common good and provide opportunities for all Americans to prosper.

The Limits of Free Enterprise

As the economy has developed, however, Americans have become increasingly aware that the free enterprise system does not always serve the common good. True, it has made the United States one of the wealthiest countries in the world. However, it has also led to problems that cannot be solved by letting the market system work entirely on its own.

The United States has experienced a number of major economic problems that have caused Americans to look to government for solutions. Six of these problems are listed below to help you understand why government has become involved in our economy. Later in this chapter you will read more about these problems and what government has done about them.

1. *Businesses have sometimes earned profits unfairly.* They have driven competitors

The federal government performs other basic economic functions which do not constitute intervention. Such functions include providing loans and information to help owners of small businesses get started and supporting scientific and agricultural research.

This famous photograph by Lewis Hine shows children working in a coal mine in 1910. Unsafe working conditions and the use of child labor led to increasing demands for government regulation.

out of business or made secret agreements with competitors to fix prices at high levels. Businesses have also fooled consumers through false or misleading advertising.

2. *Conditions for workers have sometimes been unsafe and inhumane.* As you learned in Chapter 14, workers have sometimes been badly treated. Some have been required to work long hours with low pay, while others have had to use dangerous machinery or chemicals without protection.

3. *Unsafe products have harmed consumers.* Foods have sometimes spread diseases and caused other health problems. Household products have injured people, and toys have hurt children.

4. *Not all Americans have had economic security.* People who lose their jobs or cannot work due to sickness, injury, or old age have faced hunger and homelessness. Discrimination has made it hard for others to get jobs to support themselves.

5. *The economy has been unstable.* Periods of economic slowdown have put many people out of work and caused great hardship. Periods of inflation have reduced the buying power of the dollar.

6. *The environment has been damaged.* Businesses and consumers have polluted the air, water, and land upon which we depend for our basic life needs. Many animals and plants are also in danger.

Because government is the institution most responsive to the needs of all citizens, Americans have called on government to help solve each of these problems. As a result, governments at various levels have become increasingly involved in our market economy.

Methods Governments Use

What can governments do to correct or prevent economic problems? Later in this chapter you will study examples of America's economic problems. You will see that governments at all three levels regularly take the following kinds of actions to make changes in the way the economy works.

1. *Governments regulate businesses.* They pass laws that set rules for business conduct. For example, they can limit the number of hours workers are required to work in one day, or set rules that make sure airplanes are safe to fly. They can also set up regulatory agencies to enforce these laws.

Challenge (Analysis): Have students discuss which economic problems they think will have the most impact on their future.

Setting air traffic control standards is one way government regulates business to protect the public.

2. *Governments make direct payments to individuals.* They can give money to people who need help to pay for food, shelter, medical care, and other basic needs.

3. *Governments own resources and produce goods and services.* They can own land, such as the national forests. They also can run businesses that promote the common good, such as providing hydroelectric power from a government-built dam.

4. *Governments help pay for important economic activities.* They can give a sum of money to a private business to help it provide an important product or service. For example, the federal government has given money to help farmers, airlines, and builders of housing for the poor.

5. *Governments control the amount of money they spend and the amount they receive in taxes.* Taxes take money from the economy, and spending puts it back. By controlling the in-and-out flow of taxes and spending, governments can influence how the economy performs. In addition, the federal government can control the total supply of money.

6. *Governments make tax rules and collect special taxes.* They can change the rates at which people's incomes are taxed, and they can make tax rules that reward certain economic activities and punish others.

The Debate Over Government Intervention

A majority of Americans agree that government should have some role in the economy. We see that the market system alone does not always promote the common good. However, most people also see that there is a negative side to government intervention. Government regulations, for example, usually put some limits on individual freedom. They affect our

There are two basic views about government intervention in the economy. Liberals often favor government action to protect equality, justice, and the health of people. In contrast, conservatives believe most problems are best solved by individuals, private business, and the market.

Teaching Note: Use Teaching Activity 1, page T 124, as a culminating activity after students have read the material in Section 16-1.

freedom to buy and sell, to make a profit, and to do as we wish with our property.

Government intervention also has a huge price tag. The taxes that pay for government programs take large parts of most citizens' incomes. In addition, government does not always solve economic problems in the best way possible. People often complain that the government uses more time, more money, and more paperwork than necessary.

Because government intervention can both solve problems and cause problems, it often stirs great conflict. The question of how much to regulate business, for example, involves our most basic values. When freedom comes into conflict with equality and justice, as well as with the health of the public and the environment, people disagree about which values are more important to protect.

In our democratic society, there will always be debate over how much the government should get involved in the economy. Will a government rule do what it was meant to do? Who will gain or lose if government takes a certain action? What is the cost to taxpayers of a government action? These are questions you will have to ask yourself as you play your citizen role. Think about them as you read the rest of this chapter.

Answers will be found on page T 126.

Section Review

1. What basic economic powers did the Constitution give to Congress?
2. Name three economic problems that have caused citizens to ask government to become involved in the economy.
3. Give an example of government intervention in the economy.

Synthesis. How might your life be different today if there were little government intervention in the economy?

16-2

GOVERNMENT'S EFFORTS TO SOLVE ECONOMIC PROBLEMS

Read to Find Out

- what the terms *trust, monopoly, business cycle, monetary policy,* and *fiscal policy* mean.
- how government has regulated businesses.
- how government has protected workers, consumers, and the environment.
- how government has provided economic security for Americans.
- how government tries to keep the economy stable.

The economic problems you have just read about have one thing in common. They raise a conflict in our basic values. On the one hand, we believe that individuals should have economic freedom. On the other hand, we believe that our economy should be fair and should promote the common good.

These economic problems also differ in many ways. Each has different causes and each affects different groups. Through the democratic process, citizens have asked government to solve each problem in a way that balances freedom with equality and justice.

Ensuring Fair Business Practices

The free enterprise system itself has no rules for how businesses should operate. Competition and the law of supply and demand are supposed to keep prices fair.

Many business owners in the late 1800s, however, learned how to get rid of competition and thus make bigger profits. Large companies gathered greater and greater shares of the markets in which they operated.

Challenge (Evaluation): Some people believe that mergers harm the economy by reducing competition. Others, however, claim that mergers create more efficient businesses that offer lower prices. Which view do students agree with? Why?

By 1890, the steel, oil, sugar, meat, flour, and sewing machine industries were no longer competitive. In some industries, all but one or two large corporations were forced out of business. Other industries were controlled by a ***trust***, a group of several companies organized to benefit from the high prices they all agree to charge. A trust or a single corporation that controls a market has what is called monopoly power—the power to control prices in a market. A single business with monopoly power is often called a ***monopoly***.

Controlling monopolies. During the 1870s and 1880s, Americans became angry about the growth of monopoly power. People demanded fairness—reasonable prices and the chance for small businesses to compete in any market. In response to public pressure, Congress passed the Sherman Antitrust Act in 1890. This act outlaws any agreements that limit competition.

In 1914, the Clayton Antitrust Act was passed to strengthen the Sherman Act. It outlaws many of the practices used by monopolies and trusts. In the same year, Congress created the Federal Trade Commission and gave it the power to break up companies with monopoly power.

The antitrust laws have prevented large businesses from keeping or gaining monopoly power in any one industry. However, these laws have not prevented corporations from growing larger and more powerful. Today, many large corporations are buying out and merging, or combining, with other large corporations, gaining big shares of several markets at once.

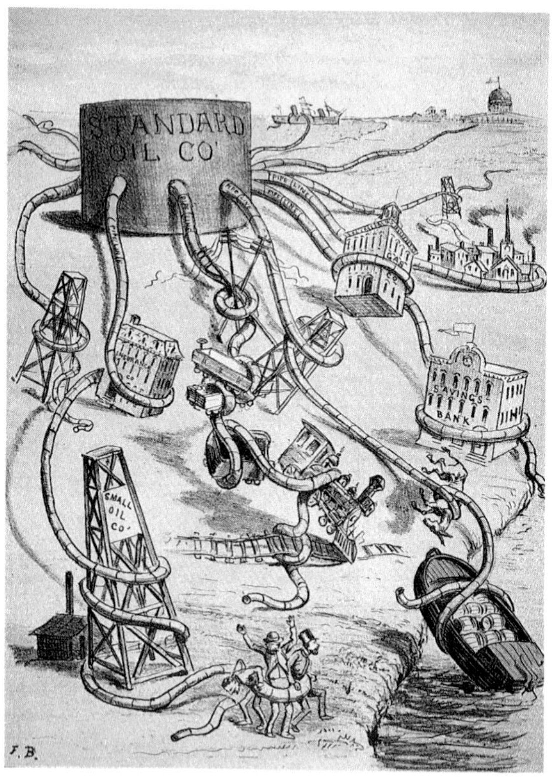

An 1884 cartoon, "The Monster Monopoly," attacked the Standard Oil Company, which almost completely controlled the oil industry.

Legal monopolies. Monopoly power is not always a problem. Businesses that provide services people need to have, such as electricity, water, and local phone service, are often allowed to have legal monopoly power. Such a business is called a public utility.

Governments allow public utilities to be monopolies because competition by many small businesses in these service industries would be inefficient. Can you imagine ten different companies each putting up electrical lines in your neighborhood and competing for customers? To make sure that the prices public utilities charge for their services are fair, state and local governments often set the rates by law.

Banning false advertising. In 1938, Congress outlawed "unfair or deceptive practices" in the way products are labeled and advertised.

Teaching Note: For a discussion of false advertising and the case of Dry Ban deodorant, see "Issues That Affect You: A Case Study" on pages 362–363.

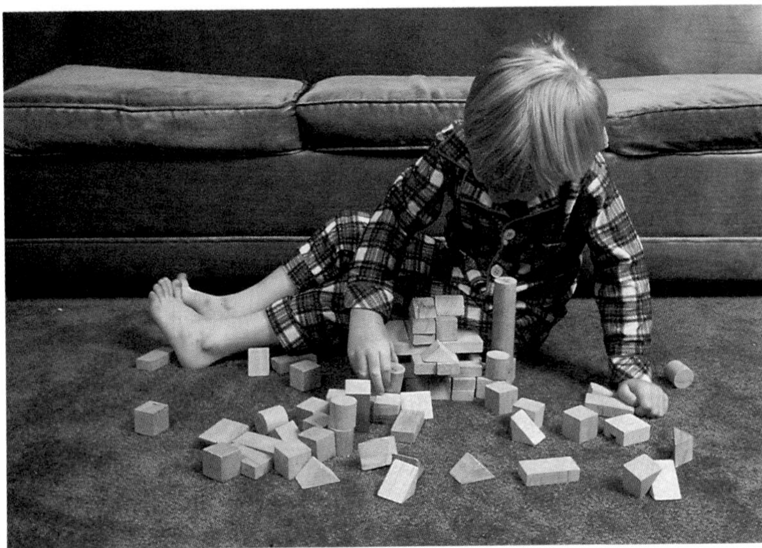

To protect consumers, the government sets safety standards for many products—from fireproof pajamas for children to power tools for the home workshop.

Ads, for example, may not say that a medicine can cure a disease when in fact it contains only sugar and alcohol. Because makers must use truthful labels and honest advertisements, consumers are better able to make good choices.

Protecting Workers

Although the growth of industries made our economy strong, workers were often treated unfairly, as you read in Chapter 14. From the 1870s on, labor unions fought for shorter hours, higher wages, and safer conditions. When unions could not force employers to meet their demands, they looked to government for help.

You have learned that in the 1930s the federal government finally began to take an active role in protecting workers. Beginning with the National Labor Relations Act in 1935, and the Fair Labor Standards Act in 1938, the government has passed laws to limit working hours, set minimum wages, and require employers to bargain with unions.

Safe working conditions. Workplace dangers, such as unprotected cutting blades on power tools, toxic chemicals, and disease-causing dust in the air, can threaten workers' health and lives. For over 100 years, labor unions have argued that business owners had a duty to make sure that working conditions were safe. Businesses, however, did not want to pay the extra costs of safe equipment.

At last, under strong union pressure, Congress created the Occupational Safety and Health Administration (OSHA) in 1971. This agency sets and enforces safety and health standards in the workplace.

Protecting Consumers

When you go the supermarket or department store, can you be sure the products you buy are safe to use or consume? Ninety years ago, the answer to that question was very different than it would be today. In 1906, Upton Sinclair published a novel called *The Jungle*, which described the meat-packing industry. Americans read about such horrors as sausage being made with dead rats, rat poison, and old, moldy meat.

Shocked citizens demanded that the government take action to make sure that all food products were safe. Congress quickly passed the Meat Inspection Act, which regulated the production of meat products.

Government intervention to protect workers began at the state level. In the early 1900s, many states passed laws to make factories safer and cleaner, provide income for workers disabled on the job, and limit or ban the hiring of children in factories and mines.

VIEWS OF NOTED AMERICANS

Ralph Nader

Many citizens work to convince Congress to pass laws that protect consumers. Ralph Nader, however, has done more for consumers' rights than any other single American.

Nader first entered the public spotlight in 1965 when he published *Unsafe at Any Speed.* In this book, he charged that the American automobile industry was paying more attention to style than it was to safety. Alarmed by Nader's book, the public demanded that the government require automobile makers to make safer cars. In 1966, Congress responded by passing the Traffic and Motor Vehicle Safety Act. Overnight, Ralph Nader became a hero to American consumers.

Nader then began working for the public interest in other areas. He helped improve safety standards in mines and other dangerous workplaces. He helped establish rules for safer food products. He also pushed for laws that would protect the environment.

In the course of his work, Nader began encouraging ordinary citizens to get involved protecting their rights as consumers. Nader helped start several citizens' groups that gather information and work for changes in consumer and political affairs. These groups include Public Interest Research Group; Public Citizen, Inc.; and Congress Watch. Over the years Nader has built a large network of supporters known as "Nader's Raiders."

Nader believes in "citizen empowerment," the idea that individuals should have more say in government and in the marketplace. "The highest status of an educated person," he says, "is one who knows how to be an effective citizen."

Since 1906, several laws have been passed to protect consumers from unsafe and harmful food and drug products. A federal agency, the Food and Drug Administration (FDA), was created in 1938. The FDA sees that foods, cosmetics, and drugs are safe and labeled correctly. It requires that new drugs be tested before they go on the market.

In 1972, the federal government took yet another step to protect consumer safety by creating the Consumer Product Safety Commission (CPSC). This government agency makes safety rules for products other than food and drugs, such as toys, tools, children's clothes, and household appliances.

Providing Economic Security

In 1929, the United States fell suddenly into a long period of economic hardship called the Great Depression. Factories closed down and banks failed. Farmers plowed under the crops they were unable to sell because of the near collapse of the market system. Within three years, 12 million people—24 percent of the workforce—were out of work.

Activity: Have students devise a strategy for complaining about a faulty product or unacceptable service that was purchased locally.

America was faced with what seemed to be the failure of the free enterprise system. At that point, the voters turned to a new leader who promised that government could save the economy and the country.

In 1932, Americans elected a new President, Franklin D. Roosevelt. Keeping his promises to the voters, he began a broad government program called the "New Deal." The New Deal was designed to get the economy moving again and help people in need. Roosevelt created agencies such as the Works Progress Administration (WPA), through which government put millions of unemployed people to work building bridges, roads, and public buildings.

The New Deal marked a turning point in our history. It greatly expanded the government's role in the economy. Ever since, Americans have been increasingly likely to turn to government to solve economic problems.

Social security. In addition to giving people immediate help, a major goal of the New Deal was to give American families economic security. In other words, families were to have a minimum level of income in case of future hardship. The Social Security Act, passed in 1935, provides a monthly payment to workers or their families to replace the income lost when a person retires, becomes injured, or dies. It also provides for unemployment insurance. Through this program, workers who lose their jobs receive payments while they look for new jobs.

Public assistance. The Social Security Act was just the beginning. Since then, local, state, and federal governments have expanded their efforts to help people in need through public assistance programs. Public assistance helps poor families—not just people unable to work—by providing cash payments and various services.

There are several important forms of public assistance today. Food stamps, for example, are given to people with low incomes to help them buy food. These stamps are paid for with federal funds. Aid to Families with Dependent Children (AFDC) provides

Soup kitchens fed unemployed workers and their families during the Great Depression of the 1930s. Scenes like this pointed to the need for government to provide jobs to help rebuild the economy.

monthly cash payments to needy parents to help them feed and clothe their children. AFDC money comes from local, state, and federal sources.

Maintaining Economic Stability

The hardships of the Great Depression—soup lines, unemployment, poverty, the breakup of families, the failure of businesses—were not easily forgotten. Following World War II, citizens asked government to find ways to prevent future depressions. The Employment Act of 1946 was one result.

This act committed the federal government to promote "maximum employment, production, and purchasing power." Government was now to play a major role in trying to keep the economy stable and growing.

Economic instability has always been a part of the free enterprise system. Like a roller coaster ride, the economy goes through what is called the ***business cycle***, a repeated series of "ups" of growth and "downs" of recession. During a period of economic growth, businesses increase their production of goods and services, and new jobs are created. Each period of growth is followed by a recession, or period of economic slowdown. In a recession, fewer goods are produced and unemployment increases. The Great Depression of the 1930s was a long, bad recession.

Because Americans want a stable economy, government tries to "flatten out" the ups and downs of the business cycle. It uses two major methods to reach this goal: monetary policy and fiscal policy.

Monetary policy. In Chapter 15 you learned that the Federal Reserve System regulates the money supply. Regulation of the money supply by the Federal Reserve System is called ***monetary policy***.

If the economy is slowing down and a recession is feared, for example, the Fed may take action to increase the money supply. It may lower interest rates, lower the reserve requirement, or buy bonds from banks. Any of these actions will provide more money for banks to lend, encouraging consumers to spend more. Spending will cause businesses to produce more goods and services.

The Business Cycle 1930–1990

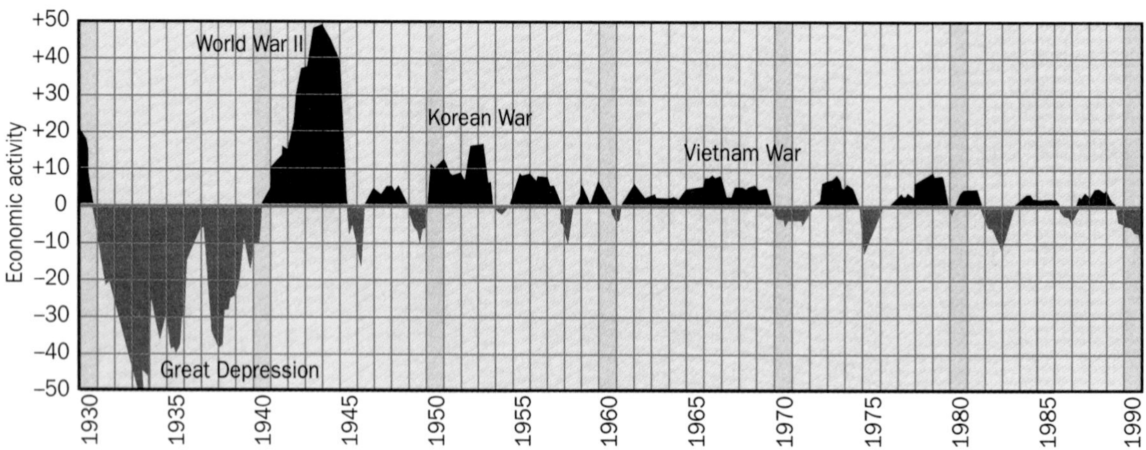

The business cycle graph illustrates periods of recession, depression, recovery, and prosperity. The graph was computed from indexes of business activity and production, commodity prices, imports and exports, government income and expenditures, banking, and stock prices.

Teaching Note: The EPA is discussed in greater detail in Chapter 9.

Government workers protect the environment by inspecting dump sites to see whether toxic waste is being disposed of properly.

Fiscal policy. A government's decisions about the amount of money it spends and the amount it collects in taxes are called its ***fiscal policy.*** Although state governments have fiscal policies, the federal government's fiscal policy has a far greater effect on the economy.

Fiscal policy affects the economy because the role of the federal government as a spender and a taxer is so important. The federal government spends billions each year on highways, public assistance, employee salaries, weapons, and thousands of other products and services. Most of this money goes straight into the economy. Federal taxes, on the other hand, take 25 percent or more of most people's income.

If the economy is entering a recession, the government may cut tax rates. Then people can spend more of their incomes on goods and services. This increased spending will stimulate production and may bring the economy out of the recession. The same goal may be achieved if government increases its spending. Increased government spending will help to create more jobs, also giving people more money to spend.

Protecting the Environment

By the 1960s, years of pouring toxic wastes into the rivers, the lakes, and the air had begun to cause big problems. Thick smog hung over cities and fish were dying. Our drinking water had poisons in it. Scientists warned that we were not just changing our environment but were rapidly destroying it as well. They said we were causing damage that could threaten our health and all life on earth.

Businesses were slow to take responsibility for the pollution they caused. They feared that trying to control or clean up their pollution would increase their costs and put them at a disadvantage compared to their competitors. As a result, citizens turned to the government because government has the power to require *every* business to control pollution. Laws can force all businesses to recognize pollution control as one of the costs of production.

Faced with growing citizen pressure, Congress passed the Environmental Protection Act in 1970. This act, though not the first to protect the environment, was certainly the most important. It created the Environmental Protection Agency (EPA). The EPA controls pollution by making rules about what and how much can be dumped into our air, water, and soil.

Stepping in to protect the environment is one of the many ways you have seen in which government plays a role in our free enterprise economy. Most Americans value the freedom a market economy gives them. However, when faced with an economic problem—such as pollution, depressions, or unfair business practices—citizens ask our government to help promote the common good.

Timing is critical in fiscal policymaking. By the time the government becomes aware of a recession, the President and Congress agree to cut taxes, and the tax cut really takes effect, the economy may be out of the recession, and new spending may cause inflation.

Teaching Note: Use Teaching Activity 2, page T 124, as a culminating activity after students have read the material in Section 16-2.

Answers will be found on T 126.

Section Review

1. Define *trust, monopoly, business cycle, monetary policy,* and *fiscal policy.*
2. What are two methods government has used to ensure fair business practices?
3. Why have consumers asked the federal government for protection?
4. What was the purpose of the Social Security Act of 1935?
5. What can the federal government do to try to bring the economy out of a recession?

Analysis. Explain how the Great Depression helped to greatly increase government intervention in the economy.

16-3 MANAGING THE ECONOMY

Read to Find Out

- what the terms *gross national product, deficit,* and *national debt* mean.
- how the federal government watches the economy's health.
- how the federal government raises money.
- why we have a national debt.

You have seen that the federal government has become deeply involved in solving problems in the economy. At the same time, American citizens have come to expect the federal government to keep our economy running smoothly. As a result, the federal government has taken on a role the framers of the Constitution could not have imagined. In addition to being the economy's biggest consumer and employer, the federal government has become the economy's chief manager.

As manager of the economy, the federal government has three major jobs. First, it keeps track of the economy's health. Second, it tries to adjust the economy's performance, using the fiscal and monetary policies you have already been introduced to. Third, it manages a huge sum of public money, deciding how to spend it and how to raise more of it from taxes. Like the manager of a large corporation, the government in its role as economic manager must be responsive to its "stockholders"—the citizens of the United States.

The Nation's Economic Health

The federal government is constantly checking on the health of the economy. Government agencies keep track of the number of people employed and unemployed, the number of new jobs created, the amount of money spent on imported goods and the amount received from exports. These figures, and many others like them, can be used to measure the economy's health. Like a doctor taking a patient's pulse and blood pressure, the government needs to measure the economy's health before it can decide how to maintain and improve it.

Inflation. One of the most closely-watched signs of the economy's health is the rate of inflation. You may remember that inflation is a general rise in the price level of goods and services. The rate of inflation describes how fast prices are rising. During a period of inflation, money loses its buying power. If your income stays the same, you can afford to buy less and less. For this reason, inflation is one of the biggest worries of government, businesses, and consumers.

The rate of inflation is usually given as a yearly, or annual, percentage. If a set of goods cost $100 at one point, an annual inflation rate of 5 percent will increase the price of these goods to $105 a year later.

Pensioners and most salaried workers live on a fixed income and are badly hurt by inflation. Workers in expanding industries or industries with strong labor unions often are somewhat protected from inflation by an automatic increase in wages based on changes in the cost of living.

Inflation has been a problem for the past 30 years. It is difficult to control because as prices rise, workers demand higher pay to keep up. Businesses then spend more on labor costs and raise their prices even higher so they can still make a profit. A high rate of inflation is dangerous to the economy because it always threatens to skyrocket out of control.

The federal government mainly uses monetary policy to keep inflation in line. When the inflation rate gets too high, the Fed often raises the interest rate.

Gross national product. One of the government's major goals is to keep the economy growing. The most important way the government measures the economy's growth is by calculating the ***gross national product*** (GNP), the total dollar value of all final goods and services produced in the country in a year. Final goods are those that are complete and ready for sale. Goods that are used to make other goods, such as the rubber, steel, and glass used to make automobiles, are not counted in the GNP because their values will be included in the value of the final product, the car.

In general, a rising GNP means that more goods and services are being produced and the economy is growing. A falling GNP calls for measures that will help the economy, such as increasing federal spending. In 1990, our GNP was about \$5.25 trillion.

Gross National Product 1981–1990

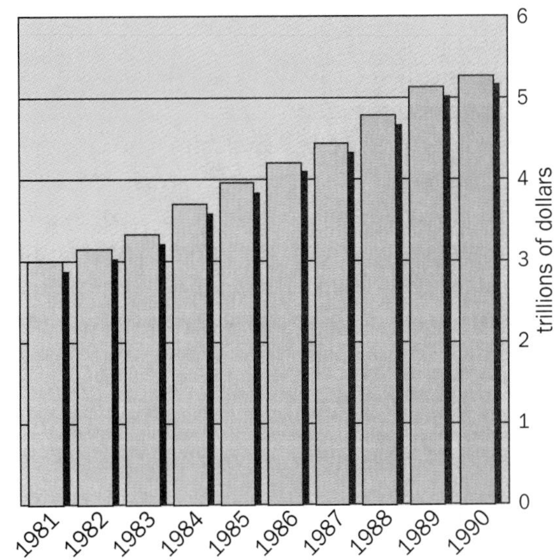

AMERICAN NOTEBOOK

Federal spending on national defense has a huge impact on the economy. In 1991, the federal government spent over \$300 billion on defense. Most of this money was paid to private businesses in exchange for such products as planes, ships, missiles, and computers. In addition, the federal government employs nearly 4 million people in defense-related jobs.

The Federal Budget

Each year the federal government spends over \$1 trillion—about 20 percent of the GNP. Much of this money is spent correcting and preventing economic problems, as you learned in the first section of this chapter. In addition, money is needed to pay for other government functions, such as national defense. Federal spending has a big effect on the economy no matter what the money is used for.

All federal spending is planned ahead of time in great detail. The amount of money that each federal program, agency, department, and office will receive during a year is set by the federal budget. The federal budget is the government's plan for how it will raise and spend money. The budget includes estimates of both the total amount of money to be spent in a particular year and the total income.

To counteract the effect of inflation on the gross national product, economists determine what the GNP would have been if prices had not risen during a particular period. The value of all final goods and services produced in a year, adjusted for inflation, is called the real GNP.

The pie graph on this page shows the spending side of the federal budget for 1991. It is divided into the five largest kinds of spending. Benefit payments to individuals include social security payments and public assistance, such as food stamps. Interest is what the government pays for using money that it has borrowed.

Although $1.4 trillion is a huge sum of money, the federal government faces the same problem that individuals and businesses face in our economy—scarcity. People's wants for goods and services provided by the government are much greater than the government's resources. As a citizen, when you vote for elected representatives, you help make decisions about the quantity and quality of goods and services that the government will provide.

The Federal Budget for 1991: Spending $1.4 Trillion

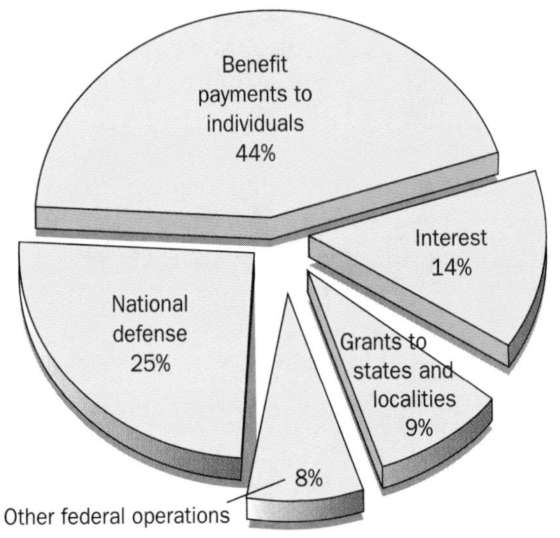

Sources of Federal Income

How does the federal government raise the money it spends? The pie graph on the next page shows that the federal government receives revenue, or income, from a variety of sources.

Income taxes. Governments at every level depend on taxes as a major part of their revenue. State and local governments, you may remember, receive most of their revenue from sales and property taxes. In contrast, the largest part of the federal government's revenue comes from income taxes.

Individuals pay two kinds of federal tax on their incomes: personal income tax and social security tax. The amount of personal income tax you pay is based on a percentage that increases as your income grows. In other words, the more money you earn, the greater the percentage of your income you pay in income tax.

The amount of social security tax you pay is also based on a percentage of your income. However, this percentage does not vary according to income. Everyone's income is taxed at the same rate, except that any amount of income over $42,000 is not taxed.

Personal income taxes make up the single most important source of federal revenue. Your personal income tax dollar goes to pay for a wide variety of government spending. Social security taxes, in contrast, pay for a specific kind of government spending—mainly the benefit payments established by the Social Security Act.

AMERICAN NOTEBOOK

Over 200 years ago, Benjamin Franklin said, "Nothing is certain but death and taxes." Most Americans would agree that taxes are the kind of government intervention that affects us most directly. In 1991, the average American family paid $15,000 in local, state, and federal taxes.

Challenge (Synthesis): Have students invent a new kind of tax for the government to use to raise revenue to improve education.

Teaching Note: For a discussion/activity on the issue of raising the federal excise tax on gasoline, see "Taking a Stand" on page 387.

The Federal Budget for 1991: Raising $1.1 Trillion

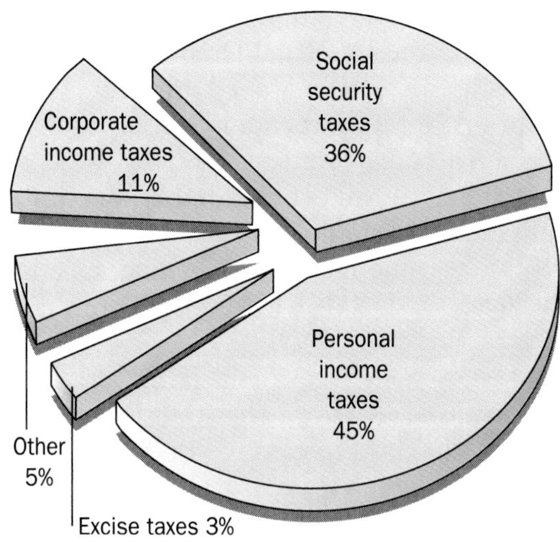

Social security and federal income taxes make up the largest part of most people's total tax bill. For this reason, income taxes are often the subject of conflict and debate. No one likes to pay taxes, yet everyone wants the services and the protections that taxes pay for. As a result, there are always arguments about who should pay how much tax.

Corporations must also pay income tax. Corporate income tax makes up about 11 percent of federal revenue.

Excise taxes. Taxes charged on specific products such as cigarettes, alcohol, gasoline, jewels, and furs are called excise taxes. Many excise taxes have two main purposes. In addition to raising money, they are intended to regulate certain kinds of consumption. For example, the excise tax on liquor is designed to discourage drinking by making liquor more expensive.

Tariffs, fees, and sales. The federal government collects about four percent of its revenue from various other sources. The most important of these are tariffs, fees, and sales of government-owned land or resources. Tariffs are taxes on imported products. Fees are charges to users of certain services, such as visitors to national parks. The resources the government may sell to make money include trees on national forest land, which are sold to lumber and paper companies.

Borrowing. Since 1970, the federal government has run a deficit. A ***deficit*** is the amount

Tax Deductions From Your Paycheck

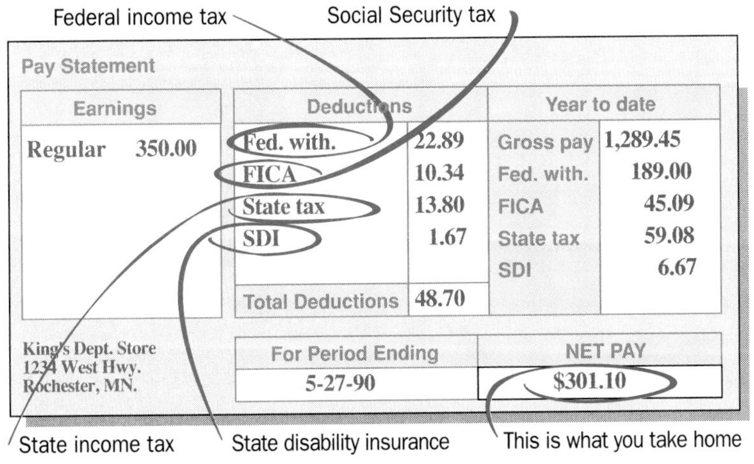

Pay Statement

Earnings		Deductions		Year to date	
Regular	350.00	Fed. with.	22.89	Gross pay	1,289.45
		FICA	10.34	Fed. with.	189.00
		State tax	13.80	FICA	45.09
		SDI	1.67	State tax	59.08
				SDI	6.67
		Total Deductions	48.70		

King's Dept. Store
1234 West Hwy.
Rochester, MN.

For Period Ending	NET PAY
5-27-90	$301.10

The National Debt 1981–1990

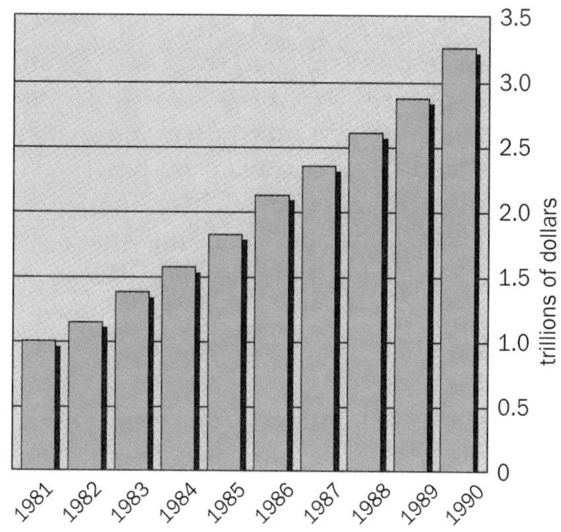

by which government spending is greater than government income. A deficit occurs when a government spends more money in a year than it takes in from taxes, tariffs, fees, and sales. To make up the deficit, the government borrows money. In 1990, the federal government had to borrow over $90 billion.

Borrowing and the National Debt

Budget deficits have occurred because government spending keeps rising faster than tax revenues. Why has government spending increased? One major reason has to do with the way in which the federal government makes the budget.

The executive branch, the Congress, interest groups, and the general public all play a role in the federal budget-making process. The demands of all these groups taken together create enormous pressure for increasing spending. Everyone wants a bigger share of the budget pie, and so the pie as a whole gets larger.

For example, retired people may demand higher social security benefits to keep up with the higher cost of living, and the President may want to build up the armed forces to better defend the country. Members of Congress may vote more money for both of these programs. As a result, spending increases.

Increased government spending did not cause huge budget deficits until President Reagan started cutting taxes in the early 1980s. As tax revenue fell further behind spending, the yearly budget deficits suddenly grew much larger.

The national debt. The total amount of money the government owes to lenders is called the ***national debt.*** Because the federal government borrows money every year to cover the deficit, the national debt keeps adding up. It is now over $3 trillion.

The size of the national debt worries many people. It is one of the major problems faced by government today because it threatens government's ability to manage the economy.

IF HE'S REALLY WORRIED—THERE'S A SIMPLE WAY OUT

Decision Making: Have students compare options for reducing the national debt, noting positive and negative consequences of each option.

Teaching Note: Use the Enrichment Activity, page T 126, and accompanying worksheet in the Activity Book after students have read the material in this section.

Like any borrower, the federal government must pay interest on money it has borrowed. One danger of such a large debt is that the interest that must be paid on it is taking a larger and larger bite out of our federal budget. Today, about 15 cents of every federal tax dollar, over $150 billion per year, goes to pay the interest on the debt. This huge amount of money—which buys nothing useful—reduces government's ability to pay for programs that promote the common good.

Many proposals have been and will be made to try to reduce the national debt. These plans include raising taxes, cutting benefit payments to individuals, and cutting defense spending. Each plan has its supporters and its critics. Like any economic problem, the national debt requires citizens to become involved in deciding the best course of action for government and the economy.

Answers will be found on page T 126.

Section Review

1. Define *gross national product, deficit,* and *national debt.*
2. Why does the federal government closely watch the rate of inflation?
3. What is the major source of federal revenue?
4. Why is the national debt considered to be a problem?

Analysis. What is an advantage of giving Congress, rather than the President, the final say in determining the federal budget? What is a disadvantage?

Date Search. Look on page 586 in the Data Bank. Which executive branch department received the largest increase in its budget between 1980 and 1990?

A BROADER VIEW

Government's role in our economy has grown over time. Today, the importance of its role is shown by the many ways in which the federal government helps manage the economy. The role of our government in our economy, however, is not nearly as important as the role government plays in many other countries.

You have already learned that in countries with command economies, the government has nearly complete control over the economy. In the world today, there are also countries in which the government has more control than in a market economy like ours, but less control than in a command economy. The economic system of many of these countries is called democratic socialism.

In a democratic socialist system, such as in Sweden, Iceland, and Canada, the government owns or controls at least some of the basic industries, such as transportation and banking. Businesses in the rest of the economy are privately owned. Under this system, individuals make many of the basic economic decisions, but a democratically elected government has some power to decide who gets what is produced. For example, in many democratic socialist countries, health care and college educations are provided free, and every citizen is guaranteed both housing and a minimum income.

Democratic socialist economies reflect a strong belief in economic fairness and equality. In these societies, having one's basic needs met is considered a right. However, to achieve this goal, citizens in these countries must give up some freedom to make their own economic decisions.

Teaching Note: Use the Evaluating Progress activity, page T 125, to assess students' understanding of the chapter. Use the Reinforcement Activity, page T 125, and accompanying worksheet in the Activity Book.

A Question About False Advertising

Two women and a man are riding in an elevator. One woman turns to the other and says, "Guess what I happen to have."

"What?" asks the second woman.

"A leading anti-perspirant spray," says the first woman.

"Me, too," the second woman says, "but mine's Dry Ban."

"Mine helps keep me dry," says the first woman.

"So does my Dry Ban," claims the second. "Watch. Yours goes on like this."

The second woman takes off the man's glasses. He is very surprised. She sprays the first woman's deodorant on one of the lenses. A white, creamy deposit appears. Then she says, "Mine goes on like this." She sprays Dry Ban on the other lens and you see that the lens remains clear and dry.

"Uh . . . hmm . . . I see the difference," says the first woman. "I'll try it on my boss's glasses."

The commercial closes as an announcer says, "Clear Dry Ban helps keep you feeling clean and dry."

This commercial and four others like it ran on national television for 14 months during 1969 and 1970. Each of the ads showed that Dry Ban went on "clear and dry" instead of wet and creamy like the "leading spray." These television spots cost the Bristol-Meyers Company, makers of Dry Ban, $5.8 million.

In 1972 the Federal Trade Commission (FTC) brought a lawsuit against Bristol-Meyers for showing the Dry Ban commercials. It wanted to prevent Bristol-Meyers from showing similar commercials in the future.

The FTC lawyers claimed that the product was actually "watery, wet, and runny."

The FTC is responsible for protecting the public from "false, misleading, and deceptive" activities in the advertising and sale of products. It may act as both a

prosecutor and a court. The FTC's lawyers can bring legal actions against companies who break certain federal laws. Such cases are then decided by five FTC commissioners who act as judges.

The FTC lawyers claimed that although the product appeared to be clear and dry when shown in the television ads, it was actually "watery, wet, and runny" and left a white deposit when it dried.

The FTC lawyers supported their conclusions about the product in two ways. First, during the trial, the deodorant was sprayed on glass and on a person's arm. In both cases, a wetness appeared that soon dried, leaving a white powder.

Second, the FTC lawyers looked at the results of consumer surveys about the Dry Ban commercials. The FTC

The FTC can stop deceptive advertising by issuing a cease and desist order or making a voluntary agreement, called a consent order, with the offending advertiser. The FTC can also fine or imprison the advertiser or order repayment of money obtained as a result of illegal activities.

Answers will be found on page T 127.

lawyers argued that the surveys showed that people who saw the ads came away thinking that Dry Ban was a *dry* spray and that it left no visible residue. These impressions, they said, were false and misled people who saw the ads.

The FTC commissioners, however, ruled that the Dry Ban commercials were not false, misleading, or deceptive. Bristol-Meyers, they said, had operated within the law when it showed the ads on television.

The commissioners explained that they interpreted the consumer surveys differently than the FTC's lawyers. The commissioners believed that consumers did not think of Dry Ban as "dry" in a literal, or actual, way. They said that "consumers understood the commercials' message to be that Dry Ban was drier than the comparison product or that Dry Ban was relatively dry."

Moreover, said the commissioners, the commercials were meant to show only that Dry Ban "goes on" clear. It did not matter that the product did not stay clear after it dried.

The commissioners went on to say that there were real differences between the two products shown in the ads. Dry Ban is an alcohol-based product that does appear clear and dry when it is first sprayed on, although it dries to a powder after two or three minutes. In contrast, the "leading spray" in the commercials, Arrid, is oil-based and goes on as a white cream. Arrid was "ideally suited to play the role of a brand X," said the commissioners.

If the commercials were misleading, customers would try Dry Ban but never buy it again.

The commissioners also made the point that if the commercials were misleading, customers would try Dry Ban but never buy it again. A Dry Ban customer "standing in front of his TV set with a dripping armpit," said the commissioners, "is not likely . . . to go out and buy a second can of the stuff if . . . it is a *literally* dry antiperspirant that he wants."

The commissioners said that because Dry Ban had $7.4 million in sales during the period the commercials ran, it was obvious that most customers were satisfied with the product and were buying it again and again. They reasoned that any customer who bought the product more than once was not being misled by the ads, but was getting what he or she expected.

Analyzing the Case

1. Why did the FTC's lawyers claim that the commercials were "false, misleading, and deceptive"?
2. Why did the commissioners decide that the commercials were not misleading?
3. Do you agree with the commissioners' opinion about the commercials? Explain.
4. If the FTC decides that a commercial is misleading, do you think the company should have to run another ad to set the record straight? Explain.

Discussion: Have students describe television commercials that they think are "false, misleading, and deceptive." Students should provide reasons for their opinions.

CHAPTER SURVEY

Answers to Survey and Workshop will be found on page T 127.

UNDERSTANDING NEW VOCABULARY

Seeing Relationships

The vocabulary terms in each pair listed below are related to each other. For each pair, explain how the two terms are related.

1. *trust* and *monopoly*

2. *monetary policy* and *business cycle*

3. *national debt* and *deficit*

Putting It in Writing

Write a paragraph explaining the basic ways in which the federal government manages the economy. Use the terms *business cycle*, *national debt*, *monetary policy*, *fiscal policy*, and *gross national product*.

LOOKING BACK AT THE CHAPTER

1. Why have Americans asked government to intervene in the economy?

2. What problems are caused by the negative side of government intervention?

3. Why are monopolies and trusts considered unfair?

4. What has the federal government done to make sure products are safe for consumers?

5. What are some major ways in which the federal government provides economic security for Americans?

6. Why do changes in the government's fiscal policy affect the economy?

7. What are the three major jobs of the federal government as manager of the economy?

8. Which of the following is *not* good for the economy? Why?

- **(a)** a rising GNP
- **(b)** a rising inflation rate
- **(c)** the creation of new jobs

9. When did federal budget deficits begin to grow to an enormous size?

10. *Evaluation*. An issue in many cities is whether local governments should be able to control rents. Compare the rights of landlords with people's rights to affordable housing. Whose rights do you think are more important? Is rent control a good idea or not?

11. *Analysis*. Compare the graph on page 357 showing the rise in the GNP with the graph on page 360 showing the rise in the national debt. Which rose faster between 1981 and 1990, the GNP or the debt? How can you tell?

12. *Application*. Suppose that a proposal has been made to increase income taxes in order to reduce the budget deficit and the national debt. What other effects might higher income taxes have on the economy? What else might be done to reduce the debt?

WORKING TOGETHER

1. With several classmates, go to a bicycle store in your community. Ask what features on bicycles are required by the Consumer Product Safety Commission, and why. Then write a short report about the regulations the federal government makes for the bicycle industry in order to protect consumers.

2. Form a group in which each member finds a different newspaper article about government intervention in the economy. Read your article carefully and ask questions of your teacher, librarian, or parents until you understand it. Then give a short explanation of the article to the members of your group so that they can understand it, too. Find out how the issue in the article may affect your life.

3. Suppose that your representative in Congress has proposed a law requiring producers of apple juice to warn consumers if the apples used were grown using harmful chemicals. With a group, put on a debate between apple growers, who oppose this government intervention, and consumers, who favor it.

Teaching Note: For reinforcement of decision-making skills, use Decision-Making Worksheet Chapter 16.

SOCIAL STUDIES SKILLS

Analyzing Line Graphs

When the federal government spends more money than it takes in as income, the result is a deficit. Yearly deficits add up to form the national debt. Since 1974, the national debt has grown rapidly. In 1991, the national debt was increasing at the rate of about $10,000 per second.

The graph below shows both federal spending and federal income from 1974 to 1991. The line for federal income includes money from taxes, fees, sales, and tariffs, but not from borrowing.

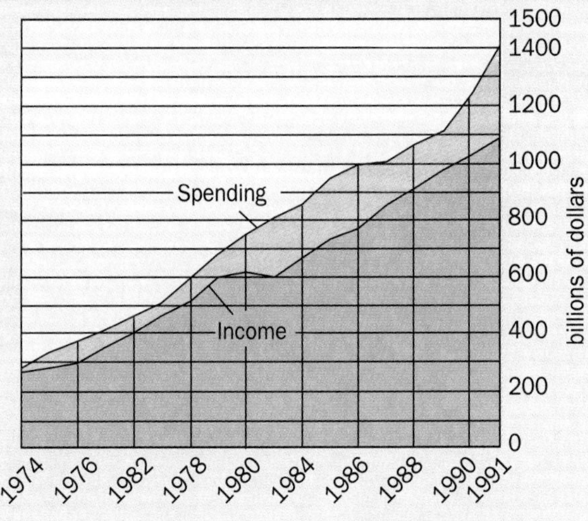

1. What do you notice about income and spending in 1974? What happens to the income and spending after 1974?

2. During what period were the income and spending lines farthest apart? What do you think happened to the national debt during these years? Why?

3. What would have to happen to income and spending to stop the growth of the national debt? What would have to happen to income and spending to create a surplus that could be used to reduce the debt?

DECISION-MAKING SKILLS

What Relates to Your Subject?

Suppose that you are deciding which side to take in a debate over the fairness of the social security system. Determine which of the statements below are relevant to the following sentence: *Social security taxes are not applied fairly.* If necessary, refer to the procedure for identifying relevant information described on page 190.

A. Social security taxes take the same percentage from the paycheck of a worker earning $15,000 as from the paycheck of a worker earning $40,000.

B. To receive social security benefits, every worker must have a social security number.

C. Social security helps to provide you with some income if you are unable to work.

D. Any additional amount of income above $42,000 is not taxed for social security.

E. Some other types of federal taxes are personal income taxes and excise taxes.

F. The social security system started in 1935.

G. Employers take the same percentage for social security out of each paycheck, no matter how much each employee is earning.

H. The social security system not only provides benefits for retired people but also provides unemployment insurance.

1. Which of the above statements are relevant to the sentence? Explain why each of these statements is relevant.

2. Pick one of the statements that is irrelevant and explain why it is irrelevant.

3. Explain how to determine whether information is relevant to a given subject.

4. Name a decision that you might make soon where you could use the skill of recognizing relevant information. Explain how the skill would help you make a good decision.

yum
GOURMET PASSAGE
Boots
Drug Stores

Chapter Themes: Personal money management requires understanding income and expenses and making decisions about goals for spending and saving. To make effective career decisions, individuals must assess their own values, interests, and abilities as well as career options.

CHAPTER 17

Our Economy and You

Have you ever listened to a radio talk show? The following is a short segment from a show called "Managing Your Money." Kathy Clarke, a twenty-four-year-old travel agent, has called in to share her financial story with the talk show host:

Kathy: *My trouble began when I started using credit cards just after I moved out of my parents' house and into my own place.*

Host: *I gather that you used them a lot?*

Kathy: *Yes. You name it, I bought it—new clothes, a color TV, some luggage. I kept telling myself that I needed the stuff I was buying, and that I could save later.*

Host: *But later you had bills?*

Kathy: *Right. At first I thought I could handle them because I was expecting a raise at work. But the raise never came. Now I'm stuck with a growing pile of bills. I'm really in a panic.*

Kathy's story shows that people, acting as workers and consumers, make choices about money that dramatically affect their lives. Kathy made decisions about her income that included how to spend or save it. Not all of these choices were good ones. She ended up in financial trouble.

As you become an adult, you will find that managing your money and making career choices take careful planning. In this chapter, you will look at personal money management. You will read about how to become a smart consumer and learn some methods for saving money. Finally, you will learn about planning for your future by exploring career options.

Teaching Note: Use the Introducing the Chapter activity, page T 130.

17-1

MANAGING YOUR MONEY

Read to Find Out

- the meaning of the terms *fringe benefits, dividends, disposable income, fixed expenses,* and *variable expenses.*
- what forms personal income can take.
- what the different types of expenses are.
- how a budget can help you make good choices about managing your money.

Learning how to manage your money involves several steps. Understanding your income, knowing what your expenses will be, and determining your goals and values are all important steps in financial planning. Kathy Clarke got in trouble because she did not give enough thought to what her income and expenses were. Also, she did not understand credit well enough to see how using credit cards would affect her.

Making a budget, or a plan for spending and saving, can help you to set your goals and reach them. Kathy realizes that in order to pay the money she owes on her credit cards, she needs to come up with a plan for managing her money.

Income: Knowing What You Have

There are many forms of income. You can earn income directly by working. If you own stock in a corporation, or have money in a savings account, you will earn income from these sources. Gifts of money and money earned by renting or selling property are also income.

Earned income. The pay that people receive for their work is known as earned income. Earned income comes in several forms: salary, wage, commission, and bonus.

At the time Kathy got into debt, she was earning $18,000 per year at the travel agency. Kathy received a salary, or payment at regular intervals, of $1,500 a month.

Others in Kathy's office are paid in different ways. Mark Aguilar, a college student, works part time for a wage of $6 per hour. Mark's weekly income changes depending on how many hours he works.

Joe Pelligrino has been a travel agent for 20 years. In addition to his salary, he gets a commission, or a percentage of money taken in on sales. Joe's commission is 20 percent of his sales. If he sells five or more tours in a month, he also receives a bonus, extra income as a reward for excellent work.

Kathy decides to look at her salary to see what she is making per hour. She discovers

This grocery store clerk works part time and receives an hourly wage. Many after-school and summer jobs are paid by the hour.

The government taxes personal income to raise revenue. It also taxes gifts that exceed $10,000 in value because such gifts are considered a form of income. As with other personal income, the rate of taxation increases with the value of the gift.

Types of Income			
Type	Description	Advantages	Disadvantages
Salary	Employee receives a fixed payment at regular intervals, usually once a month	Guaranteed pay whether business thrives or is slow	No extra pay for extra hours worked
Wage	Employee paid by the hour	Paid for all time worked	May face loss of income if business is slow and hours are cut back
Commission	Employee receives a percentage of the price of a good or service as payment for making the sale	Hard work rewarded with increased pay	Income not guaranteed; if business is slow, income could fall sharply
Bonus	Employee given additional money for excellent work performance	Good work rewarded with additional income	None
Piecework	Employee paid for each unit of a product he or she makes	Faster workers make more money—income limited only by speed	Income can vary widely depending on work speed and availability of work

that because she is working many extra hours each month, she is actually making a low wage. Based on this information, Kathy manages to convince her boss to give her a raise.

Fringe benefits. In addition to salaries or wages, people often receive ***fringe benefits***, or indirect payments for their work. Medical and dental care, sick leave, and vacation with pay are examples of fringe benefits provided for employees. These benefits mean that workers do not need to set aside part of their incomes to use for such purposes.

Other income. Kathy has a savings account at a local bank. She earns income in the form of interest on money in the account. People who own stock receive ***dividends***, or payments from the profits of companies in which they own stock. People can also receive income from the sale or rental of their personal property, from gifts, and from money they inherit when a relative or friend dies.

To understand her income, Kathy now starts with her new, higher salary. She adds the interest on her savings account. Then she subtracts what she pays in taxes. The result is her ***disposable income***, the amount of money left after taxes have been paid. Once Kathy knows how much money she has, she can make some choices about what to do with it.

Making Financial Choices

Choosing how to use your money involves making trade-offs, giving up one want in order to satisfy another. To make these choices wisely, you must look at your disposable income and at your current and future needs.

When Kathy was piling up credit card bills, she did not think about the future. She used her credit cards like cash to buy things she wanted. When the bills came at the end of the month, she could not pay them all. Then Kathy learned that there was an interest charge on the amount of money that she

Economists distinguish between nominal income, the actual number of dollars earned, and real income, the amount of goods and services that you can buy with a given income. Unless nominal income rises at the same rate as prices, inflation causes the real income of individuals to fall.

Paying for goods and services with credit cards is a common practice in stores, restaurants, and other businesses around the world.

owed. Thus, she would actually have to pay more than the original cost of the things she bought.

Although she did not realize it, Kathy was making a trade-off when she used the cards. She was trading her future buying and saving power to satisfy her immediate wants.

Goals and values. The choices people make about money are based on their goals and values. For Kathy, spending money on consumer goods was her goal. Consumer spending—buying clothes, a TV, and luggage—was more important to her than financial planning.

Some people choose to plan carefully in order to stay out of debt. Some plan to save for a particular goal, such as buying a house or going to college. Many people also choose to give money away. They may choose to give money to friends or family or people in need, or they plan to give to a cause or organization. All of these decisions reflect individual goals and values.

Kathy's credit card troubles have made her think about her values and her goals. She now sees the importance of good spending and saving habits. She knows she needs to take a look at her income and expenses and to make some decisions about what is most important.

Making a budget. Making a budget is a good way to decide how you want to spend and save. It helps you to be sure you set aside enough money for the things you need. It also helps keep you from buying more than you can afford.

Armed with good information about her income and with clear financial goals, Kathy sets out to make her personal budget. To do this, she asks herself the following questions:

- What time period will my budget cover?
- How much income will I be making during this time?
- What will my expenses be during this time?
- How much money should I set aside for each expense, and for savings and personal spending?
- What expenses are most important to pay first?

Kathy decides that her first budget will cover one month. With her new raise, her disposable income is $1,600 a month.

Next, Kathy looks at her expenses. Some are ***fixed expenses***, expenses that remain the

Challenge (Analysis): Have students discuss the human weaknesses that make it difficult for people to stick to a budget. What can people do to stay within their budgetary limits?

Consumers make many choices about how to spend their disposable income. Entertainment, such as movies, is a variable expense.

same from month to month, such as rent and car payments. Unless Kathy moves into a cheaper apartment or sells her car, she cannot change those fixed expenses.

Kathy also has ***variable expenses***, expenses that change from month to month. For Kathy, these variable expenses include food, clothes, entertainment, and her telephone bill. Cutting back on her variable expenses is a good way for Kathy to make progress in paying off her debt.

Finally, Kathy figures how much money she can save each month and how much she can put towards paying off her credit card debt. She then arrives at the following budget for the month:

rent	$650
car payment	$170
car insurance	$ 40
food	$160
personal (clothes, entertainment, etc.)	$100
utilities (electricity, gas, water)	$ 50
gasoline/transportation	$ 50
telephone	$ 50
savings	$125
credit card debt	$205
	$1,600

Making a budget gives Kathy a sense of confidence. She has made the choice to plan her spending and saving. If Kathy sticks to her current plan, she will be able to pay off her credit card debt. At that point she may want to take a new look at her budget. Budgets are not carved in stone. Whenever your income, expenses, or goals change, you can change your budget as well.

Answers will be found on page T 132.

Section Review

1. Define *fringe benefits, dividends, disposable income, fixed expenses*, and *variable expenses.*
2. What are four types of earned income?
3. What are the two types of expenses and how do they differ?
4. Explain how a budget can help you to make good money management choices.

Application. Imagine that you earn $200 a month at an after-school job. You are still living at home. Make a budget showing how you would spend or save this money. Indicate whether each item is a fixed or a variable expense. Rank each budget item from most to least important.

Teaching Note: Use the Evaluating Progress activity, page T 131, to assess students' understanding of Section 17-1.

17-2

SPENDING AND SAVING

Read to Find Out

- the meaning of the terms *warranty, liquidity, time deposit, insurance,* and *liability insurance.*
- what factors to consider when deciding whether or not to purchase a product.
- what factors to consider when deciding on a savings plan.
- how insurance can be a part of financial planning.

You have seen that a budget is a plan of how much you will spend on goods and services, and how much you will save to use in the future. Even after you have created a budget, however, your decisions are not over. You will have many choices to make about which goods and services to buy. You will also need to think about what savings plan will be the best for you. Just as personal goals and values affect budget-making, goals and values will also affect your spending and savings decisions.

Making Spending Decisions

Mark Aguilar, the college student who works part time in Kathy's office, has to make a

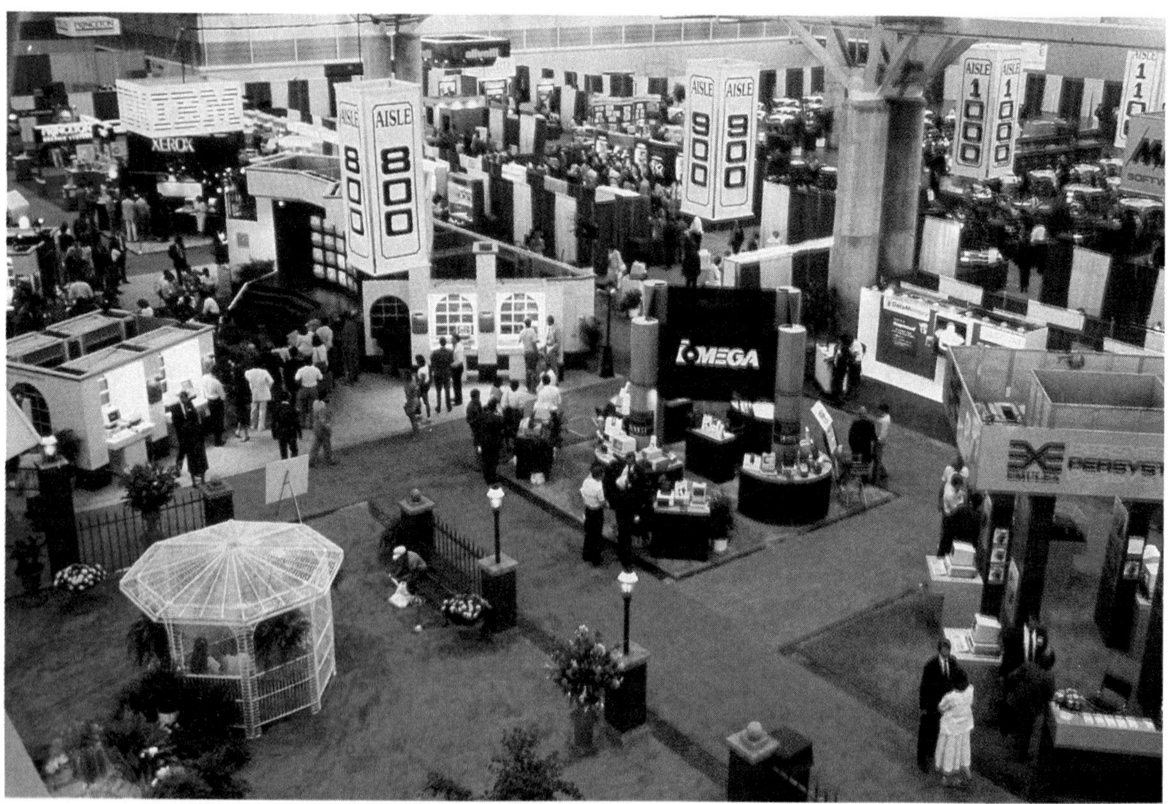

A trade show, such as this exhibition by the computer industry, is one place to compare products and make buying decisions.

Underwriters Laboratory (UL) is a group that tests electrical products for safety. Consumers should look for the UL seal of approval before buying an electrical product.

spending decision. He is trying to decide between buying a compact disc (CD) player and a new printer for his computer.

Mark listens to a lot of music. He knows that the sound quality of CDs is better than that of records or tapes. However, the computer printer he has now is old and breaks down often. He uses the printer both for school work and for his work at the travel agency, so he needs a printer he can count on.

Values and pressures. Values have a strong influence on a person's decisions about what to buy. Mark is faced with a conflict in values. Music is an important part of his life. However, he also values his education and his work, and he uses his computer for both.

To decide between a CD player and a printer, Mark must also be aware of factors other than his values. All consumers face certain pressures to buy. Being aware of these pressures can help Mark to weigh whether or not they should influence his decision.

Mark knows that his desire to buy a CD player is influenced by what his friends think. Most of his friends have CD players. They see this "high tech" piece of stereo equipment as an important part of a good sound system.

Mark also realizes that salespeople and advertisements have an influence on him. He says, "When I talk to salespeople, I get the feeling that tapes and records are from the Stone Age, and that music worth listening to comes from a CD." Mark has learned that a common sales method is to make consumers think that items they now own are not good enough.

Finally, Mark makes a decision. He would like to have a CD player, but he knows that there is nothing really wrong with the stereo system he has now. On the other hand, his printer is nearly past repair. If he does not replace it, he will not be able to do as good a job in school or at the travel agency. Mark decides to buy a printer instead of a CD.

Choosing what to buy. Once you have decided to buy an item, the next decision is which one to buy. Often there is a wide selection of brands and models from which to choose. Wise shoppers consider a variety of factors when making buying decisions. Considering the following factors can help you choose.

1. *Price.* Can you afford the product? Is its price about the same as the prices of other models of similar quality?

2. *Quality.* Will the product last? Is it well made? Does its quality match its price?

3. *Features.* Does the product have the features you need? Will you be paying for features you do not need?

4. *Warranty and Service.* Does the product have a ***warranty***—a manufacturer's promise to repair the product if it breaks within a certain time from the date of purchase? Will the store repair or replace the product or give you your money back if it breaks down?

5. *Sales/Discounts.* Can you buy the same product at a lower price at a discount store or a special sale?

When Mark goes shopping he thinks about all these factors. He talks to salespeople at several stores and compares printers that have similar prices. He reads ads in the local paper to see if any printers are on sale. He also goes to the library to look at a consumer magazine, *Consumer Reports*, put out by a group called Consumers' Union. It lists the major products, their features, and their prices. It also gives the results of product tests.

Finally, Mark narrows his choices to two printers. Both are well made and have good warranties. One model costs about $400, the highest price that Mark had thought he would be willing to spend. The other model costs $500, but it has extra print features.

Consumer credit. Mark is about to decide in favor of the less expensive printer. Then the salesperson suggests that Mark buy the more expensive printer. After all, it does have more features. She tells him that he will not have to pay the whole price at once. He can make a down payment, or pay part of the price. Then he can finance the rest through a credit arrangement with the computer store.

Personal Consumption 1989

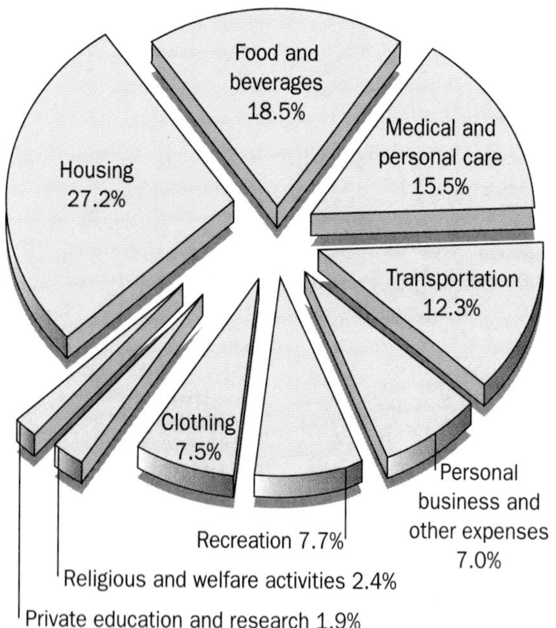

Source: *Statistical Abstract of the United States*, 1991

AMERICAN NOTEBOOK 

At the end of 1988, American consumers owed $728.9 billion in unpaid credit. This personal debt is more than five times greater than it was in 1970.

This credit plan—getting a loan from the store to cover the rest of the printer's cost—sounds good to Mark. However, he finds out that he would be paying 20 percent interest on the borrowed money. If he takes a year to pay this money back, he will end up spending nearly $600 on the printer, once interest payments are added in. Mark decides to buy the cheaper printer to avoid the cost of credit.

People often borrow money to pay for large purchases. Some borrow from banks, savings and loans, or credit unions. Others use a store credit plan, like the one the store offered Mark. Still others, like Kathy, use credit cards to pay off costs over time.

In borrowing money for purchases, it is important to pay attention to the real cost of the item—the purchase price plus interest. Consumers often "shop" for a loan. Sometimes a bank loan will cost less than a store's credit plan. In that case, a person might choose to borrow money from a bank for the purchase rather than use the store's plan.

Making Savings Decisions

People save for all sorts of reasons. Many save for that "rainy day" that comes along without warning. They want to have money set aside

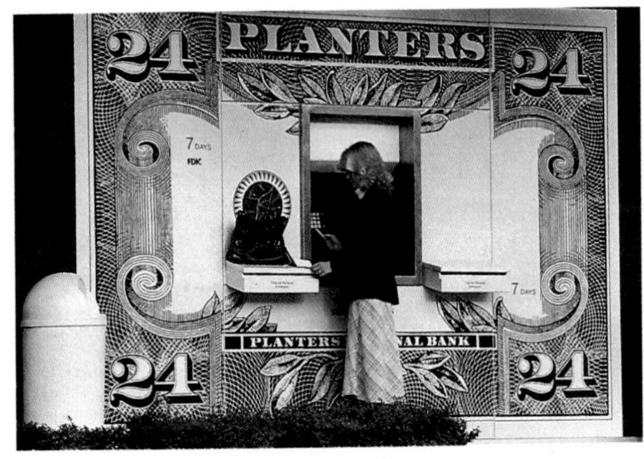

Automatic teller machines make it possible for people to deposit and withdraw money from their accounts at all hours.

for car repairs or a long illness, for example. People save to buy homes, to finance vacations, or to pay for education. Saving can be an important way to help plan for the future. There are many ways to save money. When you are deciding which method would be best for you, think about the following factors: liquidity, income, and safety.

Liquidity. One of the first questions to ask yourself when you begin to plan for savings is "How quickly do I need to be able to get at my money?" The ability to turn savings back into cash is called ***liquidity***. Some savings plans are very "liquid." For example, if your savings are in a passbook account at a savings bank, you can withdraw part or all of the money immediately. However, if you have used your money to buy a house or a piece of land, you will not be able to use that money until you have sold the property.

Income. Another factor to consider is the overall income you will earn from the money you save. If you choose to put your money in a savings account, your income will be the interest you earn on your deposit. You can also earn income from money you have set aside to invest—to buy property, such as a piece of land or stock in a corporation, with the hope of earning income from the profits.

Banks offer a number of savings plans, each with different possibilities for income. In general, banks pay higher interest rates on accounts that require you to leave your money in for a certain minimum amount of time. A ***time deposit*** is a savings plan with a set length of time that you must keep your money in the account. The bank charges a fee, called a penalty, if you withdraw money early.

As you have seen in earlier chapters, you can also earn income by buying bonds. Government bonds and bonds issued by corporations pay a fixed rate of interest. With bonds, as with savings accounts, you can know ahead of time what income your savings money will earn.

People whose main goal is to make as much income as possible are more likely to invest their savings than to put them in a bank. They may buy stocks or invest in mutual funds. A mutual fund is a collection of money from many small investors, which experts invest in stocks and bonds. Another way to invest money is to buy real estate—land and buildings—in the hope that its value will increase.

When you are thinking about a savings or investment plan, you will have to make a trade-off between income and liquidity. In general, the higher the interest rate on a savings plan, the longer you will have to leave your money on deposit. Thus your savings will be less liquid. Investments in stock and real estate are usually hard to turn back into cash. Thus you will want to be sure that money you save or invest for a long period of time is not money you will need for that "rainy day."

Safety. Of course you want your money to be safe. However, sometimes there is a trade-off between safety and income. Most deposits

Individuals are rated as a credit risk based on income, financial reliability, and records of previous credit transactions. These ratings establish how much a person can buy on credit or borrow. Credit bureaus compile credit ratings and provide this information to stores and lending institutions.

in banks and savings and loans companies are insured by the federal government. As long as your account does not have more than $100,000 in it, it is safe even if the bank or savings and loan fails. Government bonds are also considered safe investments. However, savings accounts and bonds have relatively low interest, and therefore low income.

Common Savings Plans	
Passbook savings	Pays a fixed interest rate; money can be withdrawn at any time.
Interest-bearing checking	Called NOW (Negotiable Order of Withdrawal) accounts; the owner can write checks on the account, which also earns interest.
Time deposit	Funds deposited for a set period of time; usually a penalty for early withdrawal. Interest rate dependent upon time limit on deposit.
Savings bond	Sold by the government. Common for bonds to be sold for half their full value, reaching their full value in 10 years.
Stock	Shares in corporations. Owners of stock earn income from dividends. They make profits when they sell their stock for a higher price than they paid for it.
Mutual fund	Pooled funds of small investors, managed by professionals. Funds usually invested in stocks and bonds.
Real estate	Purchase of land and/or buildings. Income earned from rent. Profit made when real estate is sold for a higher price than was paid for it.
Insurance	Investment can be made in an insurance policy such as life insurance. After a set number of years, it is "surrendered" for its cash value, plus interest.

In contrast, buying stocks in a corporation can be a risk. If the corporation makes big profits, your share of those profits, called dividends, may be higher than the amount you could earn from a savings account. The price of the stock may go up, too, and you could make money by selling it. However, if the corporation has a bad year, or if the economy has a recession, you could lose money on your stocks. Real estate investments involve a similar trade-off: safety against income.

Savings and you. As a teenager, you may find that a passbook savings account best meets your needs. It is safe. It is also liquid: you can get money whenever you need it. Not having your money tied up for long periods of time is probably more important to you at this stage in your life than earning higher interest.

However, your life will be changing and so will your financial needs. Your income and expenses will most likely increase. Your goals may change as well. You may decide you want to do some long-term financial planning. It is always possible to change your savings plan to suit these changes in your life.

Insurance

Most people find it impossible to save enough money to cover a serious emergency. In order to protect themselves, people buy ***insurance***, a plan by which a company gives protection from the cost of injury or loss. In return, the insured person makes regular payments, called premiums, to the company.

Insurance is based on a simple idea. If many people pay some money into an insurance plan, all the money, taken together, will be enough to pay the large costs of the few people who will need it. Many kinds of insurance are available. The four major kinds of insurance are described on the next page.

Challenge (Application): Have students imagine that they inherited $20,000 while they were juniors in high school and wanted to use the money to help pay for a college education. Where would students put the money? Why?

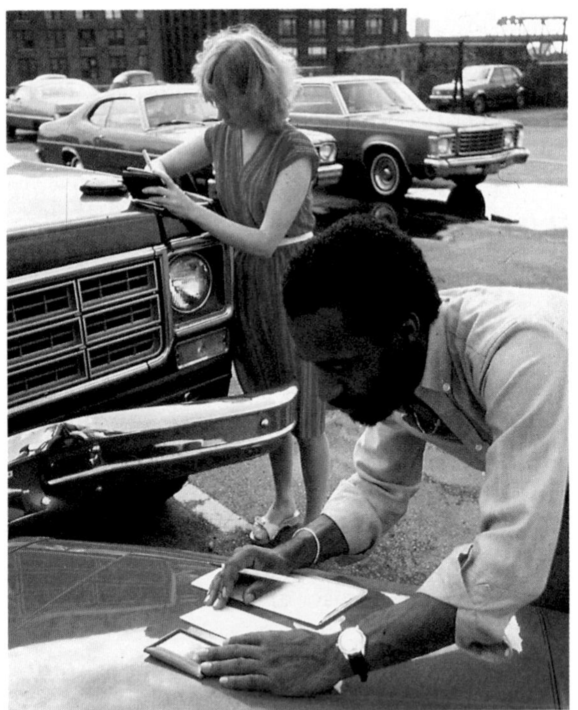

Car accident damages can amount to thousands of dollars. These drivers are exchanging names of their insurance companies.

1. *Life insurance.* People buy life insurance to protect their families from loss of income. If the insured person dies, the money from the life insurance policy can help support his or her family.

2. *Property insurance.* Property insurance protects houses, cars, and other property. It pays to rebuild a house after a fire or to repair or replace a car after an accident. In some cases, property insurance pays for lost or stolen items.

3. *Liability insurance.* Many people carry ***liability insurance***, which is insurance that protects a person from the costs of damage or injury to others. For example, if a tree in your yard falls onto a neighbor's roof, you are legally responsible for the damage. Liability insurance will pay to fix the roof. Most car insurance includes liability coverage.

4. *Health insurance.* Medical care can be very costly. The average worker would find it almost impossible to pay the bills for doctors, hospitals, and medicine out of salary and savings. Health insurance pays all or part of these costs.

Health insurance plans are included in the fringe benefits of many working people. The government gives health insurance, through the Medicaid system, to many people who cannot afford it, and to senior citizens through Medicare.

Having insurance, like saving and investing, is a way to set aside money from current income in order to meet needs you may have in the future. Making decisions about insurance will be part of the way you manage your money as an adult.

Answers will be found on page T 132.

Section Review

1. Define *warranty, liquidity, time deposit, insurance*, and *liability insurance.*
2. List some factors to consider when buying a product. Explain why these factors are important.
3. Gives three factors to consider when choosing a savings plan, and tell how they are related.
4. Why is insurance a part of the financial plan of many people?

Application. Decide on one savings plan that would be the best for you now and one that would be the worst. Give arguments to support each of your choices.

Data Search. Look on page 588 in the Data Bank to find out how much unpaid credit consumers have owed. What conclusion can you draw about changes in consumers' willingness to use credit?

Teaching Note: Use Teaching Activity I, page T 130, and the Reinforcement Activity, page T 131, and accompanying worksheet in the Activity Book after students have read the material in this section.

17-3

CAREERS: PLANNING FOR THE FUTURE

Read to Find Out

- why educational requirements for jobs will increase in the future.
- how personal goals and values affect career choices.
- how to learn about career possibilities.

In this chapter you have read about the importance of personal economic planning. You have learned about planning a budget and about making spending and saving decisions. Perhaps the most important planning you will do will be planning your career. How you choose to earn a living will affect all the other economic decisions you make in your life.

Thinking About Careers

Think for a moment about people who work in your community. How many ways do you see that people are making a living? Then think of all the people in the United States who are working at different jobs. Some of these people have had the same job for their whole working lives. Others have had several different careers.

There are thousands of careers for people to choose from. Furthermore, as our economy changes, career options change, too. When you begin to think about careers, it will be helpful to know what the changes in our economy may mean for you. Thinking about what you will have to offer to the working world will also help you to choose a career.

The changing economy. In Chapter 14 you learned that the economy of the United States is changing dramatically. Most Americans used to work in farming and factory jobs. Today, however, over 70 percent of our work force performs service jobs.

New technology is also changing the career outlook. Computers, lasers, robots, and communication satellites are taking the place of some jobs and creating others. Many of these new jobs demand a much higher level of education than farm and factory jobs did.

In fact, an increasing amount of special training is needed for many careers, such as engineering, accounting, computer programming, law, and medicine. Jobs in management and sales also call for education and training.

According to a 1987 report by the United States Department of Labor, between now and the year 2000

> the amount of education and knowledge [needed] to make a productive contribution to the economy [will become] greater. . . . A majority of all new jobs will require [college] education. Many professions will require nearly a decade of study following high school.

This report shows the importance of education in finding a job in tomorrow's economy.

Asking yourself questions. Evaluating your interests, talents, and personality can be an important step in finding your place in the job market. The school subjects you enjoy and do well in might give you some clues. What you like to do outside of school can also indicate things to look for in a career. Mark Aguilar's interest in music and in technology has led him to consider being a sound engineer.

In addition to looking at your interests and abilities, thinking about your life goals and personal values is an important part of a career search. Do you want to make a lot of money? Do you like a fast pace? Do you want

Service and information industries are expected to grow in coming years. Skills that are especially important in these industries are language and communication, information processing and evaluating, and interpersonal relations.

PEOPLE MAKE A DIFFERENCE

Volunteering Helps Shape Career

For four years, Lorena Sanchez worked as a Peace Corps volunteer, helping farmers in the South American nation of Ecuador. When she returned to the United States, she faced a decision: what career would she choose?

Sanchez's parents wanted her to go into business, like her two sisters. Instead, she decided to apply for a job at Families in Transition, a non-profit organization in East Palo Alto, California.

After her time in Ecuador, Sanchez knew that she wanted to help poor families learn to support themselves. Sanchez decided that to her, success meant helping those who most needed her skills. "I wanted to directly serve a population that was needy, impoverished, and Hispanic," says Sanchez. She found that she could reach that goal at Families in Transition.

Lorena Sanchez can understand the struggles of the families she serves. She herself was born in the United States to immigrant parents. Her family moved back to Mexico, and Sanchez lived there until she was eleven. She then returned to California, finished school, and graduated from college before deciding to go to Ecuador as a volunteer.

Sanchez now spends each day working with Hispanic pre-school students and their parents. Some families speak very little English. Furthermore, says Sanchez, "Many of the children had never been exposed to a learning environment." Sanchez helps the children feel good about themselves. Then they are more likely to be successful in school.

Sanchez also helps the families learn about their community. Many of the parents have become more aware of what their rights and responsibilities are. Through the help of Sanchez and Families in Transition, these Hispanic families are able to take part in the community around them.

When asked what she likes about her career, Sanchez replied, "We're helping to empower people to help themselves. There's a lot of satisfaction in that."

to live in the country? Do you want your work to involve helping people? Answering these questions will help to guide your search by pointing you to careers that agree with your outlook on life and your personal goals.

Career Research

Once you have an idea of where your interests and abilities lie, you can begin to look at career fields. One way to learn about the possibilities is to do some research. Reading about career fields, the types of jobs they include, and the skills and abilities they require can help give you direction.

The library has information about careers. One example is the *Occupational Outlook Handbook*, which tells about hundreds of jobs, their requirements, and their future possibilities.

Discussion: In her job Lorena Sanchez fulfills both worker and citizen social roles. Have students discuss how Sanchez takes her role as citizen seriously. How does her job help others become responsible citizens?

Challenge (Analysis): Some states require students to work in community businesses, agencies, or schools before graduation. Have students discuss the pros and cons of such work as a graduation requirement and as a way to learn about careers.

When you find a career field that interests you, try talking to someone who works in that field. Some questions you might ask are:

- What do you actually do in this job?
- What training and education does it require?
- What do you like most about your job? What do you like least?
- What job opportunities are available in this field now and in the future?
- What is the salary range for this job?
- Would I have to live in a certain region or city in order to get work in this field?

On-the-job experience can be a good way to find out whether or not a career is for you. Perhaps you can get a part-time or summer job in a field that interests you. You might work in an office, for example, to see what goes on day-to-day in a certain business. Many students volunteer in hospitals and day-care centers to see what careers in medicine and teaching are like.

Career Outlook

Fastest-growing jobs through 1995	Percent of increase
Paralegal personnel	97.5
Computer programmers	71.7
Computer systems analysts, electronic data processing	68.7
Medical assistants	62.0
Data processing equipment repairers	56.2
Electrical and electronics engineers	52.8
Electrical and electronics technicians and technologists	50.7
Computer operators	46.1
Travel agents	43.9
Physical therapists	42.2
Fastest-declining jobs through 1995	**Percent of decrease**
Stenographers	−40.3
Shoe sewing machine operators and tenders	−31.5
Railroad brake, signal, and switch operators	−26.4
Rail car repairers	−22.3
Furnace, kiln, or kettle operators	−20.9
Shoe and leather workers and repairers	−18.6
Private household workers	−18.3
Telephone installers and repairers	−17.4
Sewing machine operators	−16.7
Textile machine operators	−15.7

Source: *Monthly Labor Review,* United States Department of Labor.

Satisfying Employers

While you may be hunting for just the right job, employers are on the lookout for just the right employees. Understanding what an employer expects can help you prepare yourself to be successful in your work.

Three employers were asked what they expect from their employees. A personnel director at an aerospace company said:

> You have to know the basic skills of reading, writing, and calculating. I want someone who is willing to learn—both on the job and outside of it. Our business is changing very fast, and we need people who are willing to learn new things—new computer programs, new management ideas, new uses of metals. We provide training, but we can't teach unwilling learners.

A restaurant manager said:

> My customers come first. They are not always right, but I need to treat them as if they are, or else they won't come back. People who work for me have to understand this and be able to maintain a positive attitude no matter what customers say and do.

Decision Making: Have students compare careers they might be interested in, noting possible positive and negative consequences of each career.

Teaching Note: Use the Enrichment Activity, page T 131, and accompanying worksheet in the Activity Book after students have read the material in this section.

The manager of a photocopy sales and rental company said:

> People who work for me have to get engaged in the job. They need to know customers' names. They need to know whom we buy supplies and equipment from. I have had to fire people who didn't seem to care very much. You can't do a good job if you don't care.

Most employers say that they want employees with a positive outlook and a "can do" approach. Persistence and effort are two important qualities for making a successful career.

Your Career Future

Doing career research can help you to feel more confident about your future. However, any decision you make today is not final. You will probably change career goals a number of times. In fact, most people change careers—or at least jobs within a career field—more than once. Planning a career is ongoing. It involves continuing to look at your interests, goals, skills, and experiences.

Answers will be found on page T 132.

Section Review

1. How are the educational requirements for jobs going to change in 20 or 30 years?
2. Describe how personal goals and values affect career decisions.
3. Describe three ways to find out about a career in the computer field.

Evaluation. Which qualities are most important for employees to have? Explain.

Data Search. Look on page 588 in the Data Bank. Compare the average annual incomes of people who have completed the following levels of education: eighth grade or less, twelfth grade, four or more years of college.

A BROADER VIEW

Americans have not always had the wide range of career choices that exist today. The work most Americans did around 1900 was decided by family tradition and geography. If you were a male born in eastern Kentucky, you mined coal. If you were born in the steel towns of Ohio or Pennsylvania, you went to work in a steel mill. In Oklahoma or Kansas you were a farmer.

Meanwhile, job opportunities for women were few. Women did not enter the work force in great numbers until World War II. Today, women make up 44 percent of the work force, and an increasing number of management jobs are held by women. These changes could hardly have been imagined at the turn of the century, when most women spent their lives doing housework and raising children.

Many factors have contributed to the increase in career opportunities for Americans. The service sector has been growing, opening up new jobs. Education, including college, is much more widely available. People are more willing to move to other parts of the country to find jobs they like. Finally, barriers based on race and sex have been breaking down. All these changes have combined to give Americans career options and opportunities not even dreamed of at the turn of the century.

Teaching Note: Use Teaching Activity 2, page T 130, as a culminating activity after students have read the chapter.

The Process

Teaching Note: For reinforcement of decision-making skills, use Decision-Making Worksheet Chapter 17.

Choosing: Goal Setting

Suppose your gym teacher led everyone out to a field and said, "Run a race." The class would be puzzled. No one would know where to go. In a way, making a decision is like running a race. You need a finish line—a clear goal to reach. In this lesson you will take a closer look at how to set clear goals.

Imagine that you have to decide which jacket to buy. With a fuzzy goal like "to buy a jacket," you could be in the store all day. However, a clear goal like "to buy an inexpensive blue jacket" points you in a direction and gives you a way to identify and judge options. It helps you limit your options to a reasonable number. In this case, you would look only at blue jackets.

Choosing a jacket is a decision in which you already have a goal. Many times, though, you are faced with options before you can think about a goal.

You are offered a part-time job. Should you take it or not? You see a bike you like. Should you buy it or keep your money in the bank? Friends invite you to a party on the same night that your family is planning a special dinner. What should you do? Whether you start out with a fuzzy goal or with no goal at all, the first thing you need to do in decision making is to set a clear goal or goals.

EXPLAINING THE PROCESS

The following steps can help you set clear goals. Notice how the steps relate to Mark Aguilar's decision in Section 2 of Chapter 17.

1. Recognize your opportunity to make a decision. Ask yourself, "What do I have to make a choice about?" You might begin your answer with "I have to decide whether . . ." or "I have to decide what . . ."

[Mark might describe his situation in this way: "I have to decide whether to buy a compact disc player or a new printer. I do not have enough money to buy both. I would like to have better quality music, and my friends are pushing me to buy a CD player. However, my classes and my job are important, too, and I need a good printer for both."]

2. Think of the qualities and values that are important to you.

(a) Suppose your problem is that you have a fuzzy goal. You need a better idea of what you want. Think of what qualities you might look for. For example, if you need to choose a bike, you could say to yourself: "I would like a bike that is black, costs less than $150, is a 10-speed, etc." The qualities you list will help you state a clearer goal.

(b) Suppose your problem is that you have two or more options, and you do not know your goal yet. To identify a clear goal, you might ask yourself what good qualities each option has. Then ask yourself what good qualities the options have in common. You could start by saying, "What I like about all the options is that they are inexpensive, enjoyable, useful, easy to do, etc." The qualities that come to mind will help you state a goal by helping you identify what is important to you.

Also, think about how your values and feelings might affect how you look at the options. Some might be pulling you toward one option, while others might be tugging you toward another one. Suppose one of your values is honesty, and another one is loyalty to friends. If you see a friend cheating on a test, these conflicting values might make it hard for you to decide what to do. To help you state

Have students give their own examples of fuzzy goals and then have them revise each goal to make it clear.

your goal, think about which values and feelings are most important to you.

[Mark has two options but no goal. Mark might ask what qualities he likes about both machines. For instance, both are useful and are better than the machines he has. Mark also considers his values and feelings. His love of music and respect for his friends' opinions pull him toward the CD player, but the value he places on education and on his job pulls him toward the printer. He decides that his education and his job are most important in the long run.]

3. Use the qualities and values to help you state your goal. Look at the qualities and values that are most important to you. Your goal should be to choose whichever option most closely reflects them. Word your goal carefully so that later you can clearly tell if you achieve it.

[Usefulness and improved performance were two qualities that Mark wanted. He especially valued anything that would help his education and his job. Therefore, his goal might be "to buy the machine that will be more useful and more of an improvement on what I already have." The new CD player will not be much of an improvement because his stereo is in good condition. However, the new printer will be a big improvement over the old one. Also, the printer will be more useful because he can use it for activities that he values more highly than listening to music.]

Answers will be found on page T 132.

APPLYING THE PROCESS

Imagine that you are faced with a big spending decision. There are two or more things that you want to buy, but you only have enough money to buy one. Make a chart in which you include the following:

A. A description of what you will have to decide about.

B. A list of the qualities and values you think are important to keep in mind when choosing which thing to buy.

C. A clear statement of your goal.

CHECKING YOUR UNDERSTANDING

After you have set your goal, answer the following questions.

1. What did you have to decide about?

2. What good qualities did the things you wanted to buy have in common?

3. What values did you consider? Which of these values was most important to you? Explain why.

4. What goal did you set? Explain why.

5. How would your goal help you in making a decision about which thing to buy?

REVIEWING THE PROCESS

6. Why is it important to set a clear goal?

7. Tell in your own words how to set a clear goal in decision making.

Before the students do "Applying the Process," have them work in small groups, each with a different situation requiring a decision. Each group should state several clear goals for that decision.

Answers to Survey and Workshop will be found on page T 133.

CHAPTER SURVEY

UNDERSTANDING NEW VOCABULARY

Seeing Relationships

For each pair below, explain how the first term is different from the vocabulary term that follows.

Example: A *passbook savings* account is different from a *time deposit* because a passbook savings account allows withdrawal at any time, while a time deposit specifies a length of time the money must be in the bank.

1. *earned income* and *fringe benefits*

2. *interest* and *dividends*

3. *salary* and *disposable income*

Putting It in Writing

Using the terms *liquidity*, *invest*, *time deposit*, and *insurance*, discuss some different ways to plan for the future.

LOOKING BACK AT THE CHAPTER

1. Summarize Kathy Clarke's financial problem, and tell why she had it.

2. Explain the steps involved in making a budget. What factors should you consider in making this plan?

3. Describe some pressures to buy that consumers should be aware of.

4. What steps might you take in choosing which model of a certain product to buy?

5. Make a list of the questions you would want to ask a car salesperson to ensure that you were choosing the right car.

6. Describe some advantages and disadvantages of using credit.

7. Explain in your own words the idea on which insurance is based.

8. What kinds of jobs are vanishing from the American job market? What sort of jobs are replacing them?

9. Create a list of questions you would want to ask an employer at a job interview.

10. *Analysis.* Choose two of the quotes from employers on pages 380 and 381. Compare and contrast their viewpoints and what they expect from employees.

11. *Evaluation.* Do you think Mark Aguilar made a good money management choice when he decided to purchase a printer instead of a CD player? Give reasons why or why not.

12. *Application.* Can you think of instances in which people might not need a budget in order to spend and save wisely? If you can, give examples. If not, state why.

13. *Application.* Think of a career that interests you now. How does it fit your goals, values, and talents?

WORKING TOGETHER

1. Turn to Kathy's budget on page 371. List her expenses in order from most to least important. Share your list with others in your group. Compare the order in which you listed Kathy's expenses, and why.

2. Collect different advertisements for a product. Which statements in the ads give you facts that could help you decide whether or not to buy the product? Which statements are just putting pressure on you to buy the product? Organize the statements in a chart like the one below.

Information I Can Use to Make a Decision	Attempts to Pressure Me to Buy

3. Choose three banks in your local area. Find out what savings plans each bank offers. Present each of these plans to the class. As a group, decide which plan would be best for students.

SOCIAL STUDIES SKILLS

Using a Library Card Catalog

One of the best places to look for information about careers is in your public library. There you will find a number of books with up-to-date information on careers and job-hunting. You might begin your search by looking in the library's card catalog under the subject heading *Careers*.

Every book in a library is listed in the card catalog in three ways—by its title, by the author's name, and by the book's subject. Traditionally this information has been put on paper cards and arranged alphabetically in special drawers. Today many libraries have switched to computerized catalogs. Library users gain access to these catalogs through computer terminals. As the sample card below shows, you can find a lot of information about a book by looking at its card.

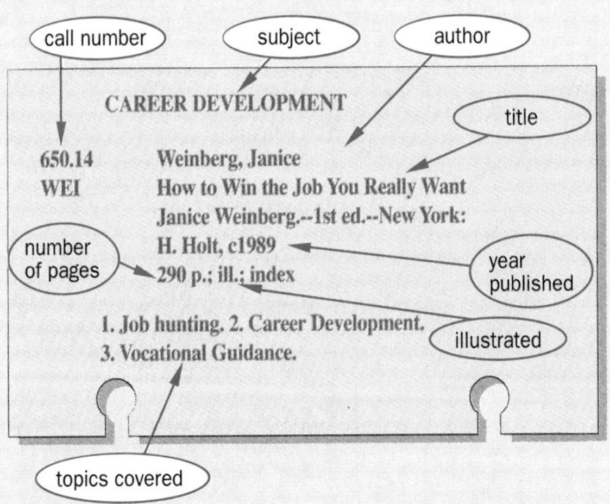

Use the sample card to answer these questions:

1. Find the following information about the book:

(a) Title
(b) Author
(c) Year published
(d) Number of pages
(e) Call number

2. What topics does the book cover?

3. Does it have illustrations? Does it have an index?

4. Who might find this book useful?

DECISION-MAKING SKILLS

Choosing: Goal Setting

Sometimes you have to make a decision soon, so you have to quickly figure out what your goal is. Imagine that you are in the situation described below. Determine what your goal would be.

> Your team has just won the championship. You and your teammates have gone to a restaurant to celebrate. You have $30 in your pocket.
>
> You did not take an after-school job last fall so that you could practice with the team. Since you have not had a job, all of your spending money comes from your parents. Out of the money in your pocket, you are supposed to spend $20 to buy a team sweatshirt. After a long argument, you had finally convinced your mother to give you the money for the sweatshirt. She had agreed only because all the other players have them.
>
> You are the youngest member of the varsity squad. You have not yet made good friends with the other players on the team. You hear your teammates discussing what to order. Everyone is choosing meals that cost $15 or more. You do not want them to think that you are cheap. What should you do?

1. Describe what decision has to be made in the above situation.

2. What qualities do the options have in common? In this situation what values did you consider to be important?

3. What goal did you set? Explain why.

4. Why is it important to set a clear goal?

5. Explain in your own words some important steps a person should take when setting a goal in decision making.

IN THEIR OWN WORDS

Milton Friedman: The Virtue of Capitalism

Answers will be found on page T 134.

The American economist Milton Friedman is known for his appreciation of the freedom we enjoy in our economic system. In 1976 Friedman was awarded the Nobel Prize in Economics for his work in economic theory.

A few years earlier, Friedman gave an interview. The interviewer pointed out one of the major criticisms of capitalism: that it is based on individuals pursuing their own self-interest. In a pure market system, there is no protection to make sure that economic freedom does not interfere with justice and equality.

The interviewer asked, "How would you answer those who claim that capitalism can't [encourage] a just and orderly society, since it's based on greed?" Here is Friedman's answer:

> What kind of society isn't [based] on greed? As a friend of mine says, the one thing you can absolutely depend on every person to do is to put his own interests ahead of yours. Now, his interests may not be greedy in a narrow, selfish sense. Some people's self-interest is to do good for others. Florence Nightingale [the founder of the Red Cross] pursued her self-interest through charitable activities. But for most

> people, most of the time, self-interest is greed.
>
> So the problem is how to set up an arrangement under which greed will do the least harm. It seems to me that the great virtue of capitalism is that it's that kind of system. Because under capitalism, the power of any one individual over his fellow man is relatively small. You take the richest capitalist in the world; his power over you and me is trivial. . . .
>
> We want the kind of world in which greedy people can do the least harm to their fellow men. That's the kind of world in which power is widely [spread out] and each of us has as many [opportunities] as possible . . .
>
> Only [a very few people], whether in a communist society or in a capitalist society, are concerned with nonmaterial [goals]. . . . Say I'm in a [communist] society and I want to save an endangered species; I want to save the heron. I have to persuade the people in charge of the government to give me money to do it. I have only one place I can go; and with all the bureaucratic red tape that [I would have to go through], the heron would be long dead before I ever saw a dollar, if I ever did. In a free-enterprise capitalist society, all I have to do is find one crazy millionaire who's willing to put up some dough and I can save the heron.

Adapted from Milton Friedman, "The Great Virtue of Capitalism," in Bright Promises, Dismal Performance. *3rd ed. (Sun Lakes, Arizona: Thomas Horton and Daughters, 1983.)*

Analyzing Primary Sources

1. According to Friedman, what is the best way to keep one person's greed from harming society?
2. Do you think the economic and government systems of the United States protect people from the greed of others? Explain.
3. Based on the ideas presented here, do you think Friedman would be likely to favor or to oppose government intervention in the economy? Why?

Discussion: Milton Friedman declared that "for most people, most of the time, self-interest is greed." Have students discuss what Friedman means by "greed." What does he mean by "nonmaterial goals"?

UNIT SURVEY

Answers will be found on page T 134.

LOOKING BACK AT THE UNIT

1. If you were to compare the federal government's budget with a personal budget you might make, how would they be alike? How would they be different?

2. Each situation below describes half of an exchange. For each, describe the other half.

- **(a)** a barber gives a haircut
- **(b)** a bank pays interest
- **(c)** a citizen pays taxes
- **(d)** a consumer pays interest to a bank
- **(e)** a worker works for an hour

3. Describe who in our society makes each of the following economic decisions. Also, describe what factors must be considered when each decision is being made.

- **(a)** whether to buy pizza or a hamburger
- **(b)** how much to spend on national defense
- **(c)** what wages to pay
- **(d)** whether to set up a business as a sole proprietorship or a corporation
- **(e)** what career to choose
- **(f)** whether or not to raise the reserve requirement for banks
- **(g)** how to save or invest money

TAKING A STAND

The Issue

Should the tax on gasoline be raised?

Whether it is a family piling into the station wagon for a weekend trip, or teenagers cruising Main Street on Friday night, few activities give Americans the sense of freedom they feel when driving their cars. Having to pay more for gas can be seen as taking away that freedom. Therefore, proposals to raise the federal gasoline tax are sure to fuel a hot dispute.

However, the federal excise tax on gasoline is seen by some as a handy tool for helping the economy. Many think this tax should be increased. Under some proposals, it would be raised by as much as 50 cents a gallon.

Supporters of a higher tax say that every 1-cent rise in the gas tax would wipe $1 billion off the national debt every year. They say Americans are spoiled. Our gas is cheaper than gas in other countries. Even if we increased the gas tax by 50 cents, we would still be paying only one third the price that Europeans and Japanese pay.

Tax supporters say that if gas cost more, Americans would take much-needed steps to save it—by building fuel-saving cars, using public transportation, and joining car pools. Less driving would result in less air pollution. In addition, using less gas would reduce our need to buy foreign oil. In 1990, we imported 45 percent of the oil we consumed.

Opponents say that a higher gasoline tax would hurt some Americans more than others. The rich, they say, could easily pay a higher tax, but poor Americans would suffer. They point to a study showing that families earning under $5,000 a year spend eight times as much of their disposable income on gas taxes as those earning over $50,000.

Also, opponents say, a higher tax would be unfair to people who must drive great distances and cannot use buses, subways, or car pools. One study shows that increasing the gas tax 50 cents per gallon would cost a typical Wyoming driver $412 a year, while a New Yorker would pay only $282 more.

Expressing Your Opinion

Imagine that a newpaper has invited you to write an editorial giving your opinion on whether the gasoline tax should be raised. Look at some editorials. Notice how they combine the facts with a call for action. In your editorial, you may want to stress the well-being of the whole economy or to focus on the results of an increase for you as an individual.

UNIT 6

Unit Quotation: A system of justice provides a framework within which groups and organizations in society can exist. It is essential, as Judge Wilson declared, "to whatever else people accomplish." Influenced by traditional ideas of right and wrong, every society has recognized the need for law.

THE AMERICAN LEGAL SYSTEM

An Orderly Society

When you reflect on it, the only thing that allowed the human race to stop living as animals and start living as human beings was by adopting a set of rules—a system of justice. Maintaining a system of justice in an orderly society is essential to whatever else people accomplish.

—Frank W. Wilson, U. S. District Judge, 1964

Perhaps no duty of our federal, state, and local governments is more important than the duty to make and enforce laws. However, do you ever stop to think about why we need laws? Do laws, as Judge Wilson says, make the difference between living as human beings and living as animals? Why are the words *law* and *order* so often linked together?

In Unit 6 you will be considering the role laws play in our society. The first step will be to explore some of the basic purposes and origins of our laws. Then you will examine how the criminal and juvenile justice systems deal with people who are accused of breaking the law. Finally, you will read about the ways our civil justice system helps people to settle conflicts in an orderly manner.

Chapter Themes: The purpose of laws is to keep order; protect people's safety, property, and individual freedoms; and promote the common good. Laws are made by legislatures and judges in court decisions. The two main types of laws that affect us are criminal law and civil law.

CHAPTER 18

Laws and Our Society

You have probably seen the movie or read the book. People who have lived through a shipwreck or plane crash are stranded on an island, struggling to survive until help arrives. Why do authors and moviemakers find such situations interesting?

Imagine yourself in such a situation. You and the rest of the survivors face many problems that you must solve at once. Who will make decisions? Will the group need leaders during this emergency? How much power should the leaders have? What should be done with people who act selfishly and do not think about the needs of others? What responsibilities will each person have?

Books and movies have often used this dramatic setting to explore one of the necessities of society, the need for rules or laws. The survivors must make rules about how to live together. They must make laws to help handle conflicts and bring about order.

In this chapter you will read about laws and their importance to your life. You will take a closer look at why we have laws, where laws come from, and what basic kinds of laws affect your daily life.

Teaching Note: Use the Introducing the Chapter activity, page T 136.

18-1

WHY WE HAVE LAWS

Read to Find Out

- what the terms *laws*, *morals*, and *civil disobedience* mean.
- what purposes laws serve.
- how laws are related to our ideas about right and wrong.

Throughout this book you have read about ***laws***, rules of society that are enforced by governments. In some ways laws are like other rules, such as family, sports, or class rules. Rules set standards, or requirements. They also set penalties, or punishments, for failing to meet standards. A coach might have a rule that anyone who skips practice may not play in the next game.

Governments also set standards of behavior. An example is the law that requires drivers to stop at red lights. People who break this law usually must pay a fine.

Laws are different from other types of rules, however. Laws are the only rules that everyone in your community has to follow. A family rule against playing the stereo after 9:00 P.M. applies only to your family, and your family decides what should be done if you break the rule. However, what if you broke a local law against playing loud music after midnight? You could be fined by your local government for disturbing the peace.

Why do governments make rules? In the following pages, you will explore some of the reasons why we have laws.

The Need for Order

One of the most basic purposes of laws is to bring order to society. One way laws bring order is by telling people what they may or may not do. Some of the most familiar do's and don'ts are traffic laws. Every driver must drive on the right side of the road and obey traffic signs. What would happen if people could drive on either side of the road? What if everyone tried to go through an intersection at the same time?

Another way laws help bring order is by setting standards in many areas. Some laws help make sure that supermarket scales, gasoline pumps, and other measuring devices are accurate. Others set standards for education, including the length of the school year and graduation requirements.

In many ways laws help bring order by telling people how something should be done. They tell how public officials should be elected, how evidence should be presented in trials, how building permits should be obtained, and so on.

Laws also spell out the proper ways to settle serious conflicts. Suppose a bicycle rider runs into you, knocking you down and causing you to break your leg. You and your family ask the rider's family to pay your medical bills, but they refuse. Laws help bring order by providing peaceful ways of settling such conflicts in court.

The Need to Protect People's Safety

Another purpose of laws is to protect people's lives. No society can run smoothly if people live in constant fear. Therefore, physical attacks such as murder and rape are against the law. These actions are punished by prison or even death.

Laws also protect the quality of people's lives. They especially look after the lives of people who are less able to protect themselves, such as children and the elderly. Laws hold parents responsible for the care of their children, including food, clothing, housing,

Challenge (Analysis): Have students discuss what characteristics of human nature make government and laws necessary.

One purpose of laws is to protect people's safety. For example, there is a law requiring that new cars be put through crash tests.

and medical care. Laws help protect the elderly in many ways, such as guaranteeing retirement income and low-cost medical care.

The Need to Protect People's Property

Imagine what would happen if people were allowed to take anything that they wanted from each other. Laws against stealing are one way in which the government protects your property, whether it be money or anything else you own. If your bike is stolen, you can tell the police. They will try to find your bike and arrest the thief so that he or she can be punished.

Laws also give you rights if your property is damaged. Suppose you lend your video game player to a friend who knocks over a can of soda onto it. You ask him to pay for the damage, but he refuses. Laws give you the right to take him to court. A judge may order him to pay for the damage.

Property also includes ideas and inventions. Ideas for a new cereal, a board game, a new style of skateboard, or a labor-saving invention for the home are the property of the person or company who thought of them. A person also owns any work of art, music, or literature that he or she creates.

Any creation or invention can be protected by law. Examples of this protection are all around you. Books, cassettes, videotapes, and games display the copyright symbol: ©. Brand names have the ® symbol standing for "registered trademark." Patent numbers are stamped on many products, from sports shoes to computers. Copyrights, trademarks, and patents are all warnings that it is against the law to copy creations or inventions without permission.

The Need to Protect Individual Freedoms

Americans have always treasured individual freedoms. As you know, these freedoms are protected by the Constitution—the highest law in the land. The Constitution, in the Bill of Rights, makes it illegal for the government or for any person or group to deny freedom of religion, freedom of speech, freedom of the press, and other basic freedoms.

The Constitution protects the basic rights and freedoms of individuals by limiting the government's power. The Constitution also guarantees, through the Fourteenth Amendment, that laws will be applied fairly and equally to all people.

The Need to Promote the Common Good

The Preamble of the Constitution declares that one of the goals of our government is to

The Constitution gives Congress the power to grant copyrights and patents. Copyright covers original literary, dramatic, musical, artistic, or audio-visual works as well as sound recordings and computer programs. Patents cover inventions and discoveries or improvements of useful processes.

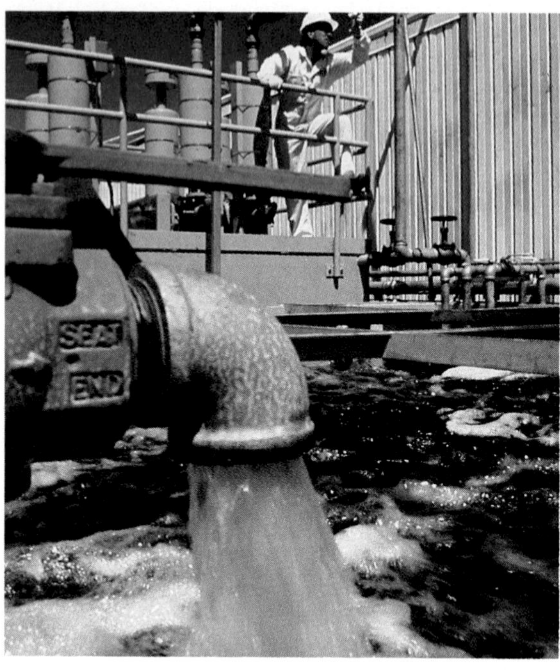

To guard public health, laws require that waste water be cleaned at treatment plants before being released into rivers, lakes, or the ocean.

promote the general welfare, which means the common good of the people. Therefore, laws do not just protect the safety, property, and freedoms of each individual. They also protect society as a whole.

Some laws protect the environment and everyone's health. Laws limit pollution to improve the quality of the air we breathe. They also regulate the safety of the water we drink, the food we eat, and the products we use. Laws cover everything from how restaurants prepare food to how nuclear power plants get rid of their wastes.

Laws also make sure that help is given to people who need it. Laws set up unemployment insurance and job-training programs that help people who have little or no income. Laws allow the government to give aid to victims of floods and other disasters. These and many other laws remind people of their responsibilities toward each other.

A Common Goal

You have just looked at several purposes of laws: to keep order; to protect the safety, property, and freedoms of individuals; and to promote the common good. However, any law may serve more than one purpose.

Laws that set speed limits, for instance, help preserve order and also protect people's safety. Laws that regulate the quality of food protect the safety of the individual. They also serve the common good by protecting everyone in our society. The purposes of law are closely tied to each other because all laws have a common goal: to encourage people to live together peacefully.

Laws and Morals

Most of us do not consciously think about the purposes of laws. However, we know that laws reflect many of the basic values and beliefs we share. Beliefs about what is fair and what is right or wrong are called ***morals***. Most of us have similar morals. Our values and morals, rather than our laws, are the real glue that holds our nation together.

Most Americans obey laws because they want to. Theft and murder are against the law, but most people believe those actions are wrong anyway. Even if there were no laws, most people would never steal or commit murder. Laws are necessary, however, so that the government can take action against people who do act wrongly.

What happens, though, if a law goes against your beliefs? In a situation like that, some people disobey the law. Breaking a law because it goes against personal morals is called ***civil disobedience***. For example, a person might refuse to pay income tax because he or she opposes government spending on nuclear weapons.

People who take part in civil disobedience

Teaching Note: Use Teaching Activity 1, page T 136, and the Enrichment Activity, page T 137, and accompanying worksheet in the Activity Book after students have read the material in Section 18-1.

willingly accept the punishment for breaking the law. In this way, they follow their morals while recognizing the need for order in society. There could be no order if everyone decided to disobey certain laws but was unwilling to accept the punishments. If people want to change a law, our democratic government provides ways to do so. In the meantime, we have a responsibility to each other to live by the laws we have.

Answers will be found on page T 138.

Section Review

1. Define *laws, morals,* and *civil disobedience.*
2. Describe four of the main reasons we have laws.
3. Explain how laws are related to morals.

Synthesis. Choose a law that you consider to be particularly important and predict what would happen if that law no longer existed.

18-2

WHERE OUR LAWS COME FROM

Read to Find Out

- what the terms *statutes, common law,* and *legal code* mean.
- how laws made by legislatures differ from judges' decisions.
- how laws are collected and organized.
- why laws are sometimes changed.

Where do our laws come from? Basically, they grow out of common values and beliefs in two ways: through rules written by legislatures and through decisions made by judges. Both of these sources of law have a long history, and both have played an important role in the development of American law.

Laws Made by Legislatures

When a certain need or problem arises, people often say that "there ought to be a law" to deal with it. If littering is a problem, your town or city council may pass a law setting a $500 fine for littering. Are too many people being injured in motorcycle accidents? Your state legislature may pass a law that riders must wear helmets. When the price of food goes up, Congress may pass a law increasing Social Security payments to the elderly.

All of these are ***statutes***, written laws made by legislatures. Usually the term *statute* refers to laws made by Congress or by state legislatures. Laws made by city or town councils are typically called ordinances.

In making laws, elected officials are guided by the morals, values, beliefs, and customs shared by most of the people served by the government. Laws passed by Congress reflect basic values shared by most Americans. Whenever you see the words *federal law* or *federal statute,* you know that everyone in the nation has to obey that law.

Laws passed by a state or local government, however, only apply within that state or local community. Since customs and beliefs in one state or community may differ somewhat from those in another, their laws may differ, too. For instance, one state may allow lotteries while another does not.

The relationship between laws and common beliefs has always been a close one. For example, in ancient Rome, where most people believed in witchcraft, statutes made it illegal for anyone to "cast an evil spell or put a spell upon crops." Laws against witchcraft were even found in the American colonies. Today we have no such laws because most people do not believe in witchcraft.

A major difference between constitutional provisions and statutes is that statutes can be changed more easily. Provisions and statutes are similar in that both may be interpreted by the courts.

However, there are some behaviors that almost every society has outlawed. For example, the idea that murder is wrong is set down in laws as ancient as those of the Babylonians, who lived almost 4,000 years ago.

Judges' Decisions

When people talk about "laws," they are usually referring to statutes and ordinances. However, "obeying the law" also means obeying decisions made by judges. Unlike legislatures, judges do not write laws. Instead, they wait for cases to come to them, and they decide each case based on laws that already exist. Those laws may be statutes and ordinances, or they may be earlier decisions made by judges in similar cases.

American judges have inherited from England a strong tradition of being guided by earlier court decisions. Hundreds of years before the colonists came to America, a system of laws had developed in England. Some of these laws were statutes made by Parliament, the English legislature. However, the English people also relied greatly on ***common law***, a body of law based on judges' decisions.

Here is how common law worked. In making a decision on a case, an English judge would always consider general community customs and beliefs about what was fair. However, a judge would also need specific guidelines to follow in deciding each case. To find those guidelines, he looked at written records of how other judges had decided similar cases. If those decisions reflected the current beliefs of the community, the judge would follow them as a precedent, or guide.

Suppose, however, that community beliefs changed. Or perhaps a case came up that had no precedent. A judge would then make a new decision that reflected current beliefs and customs. The new ruling would be a precedent for future cases that were similar.

When the tradition of common law came to America, judges still followed many of the decisions of English judges. However, conditions and customs were not always the same in the United States as in England.

Under English common law, for example, cattle owners had to fence in their animals to keep them from trampling other farmers' crops. This law made sense in England, where most land holdings were small and close together. In the American West, however, ranchers could not be expected to fence in huge cattle-grazing areas. American judges, therefore, changed the common law by ruling that farmers had to fence in their crops instead.

In short, judges' decisions reflect the customs and beliefs of the majority of the people. Since most of those beliefs do not change, many precedents are followed by judges year after year. However, decisions may change to reflect new beliefs and customs or to deal with new problems.

AMERICAN NOTEBOOK

Over the years legislatures have passed some unusual laws. Try to guess why each of the following laws was made.

A Maine law declared that "whoever acts as an umpire in any fight between rats shall be punished by a fine of not more than $200."

A California city passed a law forbidding roosters to crow within the city limits.

A Kentucky law said, "No female shall appear in a bathing suit on any highway within this state unless she is escorted by at least two officers or unless she be armed with a club." An amendment was later added: "This statute shall not apply to females weighing less than 60 pounds; nor shall it apply to female horses."

Many legal disputes concern the application of precedents. Opposing lawyers try to persuade the court that precedents support their side of the case or that related precedents should not be followed. The judge weighs the precedents and makes a decision.

Judges spend hours studying previous cases. Here Supreme Court Justice Harry A. Blackmun does research in one of the Court's libraries.

Legal Codes

As you might imagine, thousands of laws have been made over the years. To help keep track of laws, lawmakers have organized many of them into legal codes. A ***legal code*** is a written collection of laws, often organized by subject. Traffic laws, for instance, are collected in your state's motor vehicle code, while laws relating to schools will be found in the state education code. Codes provide a way to organize laws so that they are up-to-date and easy for people to find.

Legal codes have a long history. One of the earliest codes was made almost 4,000 years ago when the Babylonian king Hammurabi collected the laws of his people. The Code of Hammurabi was carved on stone tablets. It contained almost 300 laws. Some of these ideas we share today, such as the belief that "the strong shall not injure the weak."

Another ancient legal code was the Justinian Code, created under the orders of the Roman emperor Justinian. This collection of Roman laws influenced the development of laws in Europe, particularly in France. In the early 1800s, the French ruler Napoleon had France's laws organized into what became known as the Napoleonic Code. Many ideas of Roman law live on in that code and in the laws of a number of countries today, including our own.

Legal codes played a key role in the growth of American government. When the colonies were being formed, there was a need for order. Codes such as the *Laws and Liberties of Massachusetts* provided lists of laws that everyone could know and follow.

American legal codes mainly show the influence of English law, but there are other influences as well. Some parts of the United States started out as colonies of France and Spain. Laws in those states reflect the influence of French and Spanish law. Louisiana's laws are based largely on the Napoleonic Code. California has traces of Spanish law.

Legal codes adopted by each state legislature have reflected the traditions and beliefs of the people of that state. Legal codes adopted by Congress, of course, reflect the beliefs and traditions shared by Americans as a nation.

Constitutions

Our United States Constitution and the constitutions of the states are also collections of laws. We do not usually think of constitutions as "laws" in the sense of rules or regulations,

Challenge (Analysis): Rules for living also have come from religious sources, such as the bibles of Jews and Christians. Have students discuss these rules and explain how they have influenced the laws we have today.

Government agencies decide how smog tests on cars should be carried out to meet the goals of anti-pollution laws.

yet they include the basic rules by which our governments are run.

Constitutions tell how laws may be made and what the government can and cannot do. They also list the rights of citizens. As you know, state laws must follow the state constitution. Local, state, and federal laws must all follow the United States Constitution.

Regulations by Government Agencies

When Congress and the state legislatures make statutes, those laws usually set very general requirements. Government agencies then spell out how those requirements are to be met. Suppose that Congress passes a law requiring school cafeterias to provide healthy lunches. Officials of the Department of Agriculture set regulations about what should be in those lunches. If cafeteria workers do not follow those rules, they are breaking the law.

Decision Making: Have students discuss how they would go about deciding whether a law should be changed.

Agency regulations are reviewed by the legislature that made the laws. Any regulations that do not carry out the laws are changed.

Changing the Law

In our country citizens have the final say on all laws. Through elected representatives, we can add, change, or remove any law. Changes might be as major as amending the Constitution or as minor as doing away with a local ordinance.

As you have already seen, sometimes laws become out of date as beliefs, values, or customs change. People may also change their ideas about what is fair or reasonable. If the majority of the people disagree with laws, the government will usually change them. One example, of course, was the change in the laws about voting rights for women.

Sometimes laws are changed because they were not written in a clear way. If government officials cannot understand a law, it will be impossible for them to figure out how to enforce it. And, needless to say, if people do not know what a law means they cannot obey it. In short, the laws that last are those that are seen as fair, reasonable, and understandable by the majority of the people.

Answers will be found on T 138.

Section Review

1. Define *statutes, common law,* and *legal code.*
2. What are the two main ways that our laws are made?
3. How are constitutions and codes similar and different?
4. Why do laws made by our legislatures sometimes become out of date?

Evaluation. What is one law that you think should be changed? Explain why.

Teaching Note: Use Teaching Activity 2, page T 136, and the Reinforcement Activity, page T 137, and accompanying worksheet in the Activity Book after students have read the material in Section 18-2.

18-3

KINDS OF LAWS

Read to Find Out

- what the terms *crime, criminal law, felony, misdemeanor,* and *civil law* mean.
- how the main purposes of criminal and civil law differ.
- what are the sources of criminal and civil law.

Laws affect your life in many ways. You are reminded about laws even when you rent a videotape. Before the movie begins, a message in big letters pops up on the screen:

> WARNING
>
> Federal law provides severe civil and criminal penalties for the unauthorized reproduction, distribution, or exhibition of copyrighted motion pictures, videotapes, or video discs.
>
> Criminal copyright infringement is investigated by the FBI and may constitute a felony with a maximum penalty of up to five years in jail and/or a $250,000 fine.

Why do you think the government might punish people for copying or selling videotapes? What does the warning mean by civil and criminal? You have probably heard the word *felony,* but what does it mean?

This section will explore the answers to these and other questions by looking at the two main types of law that affect you: criminal law and civil law. Both types help people live together peacefully.

Criminal Law

When people refer to "breaking the law," they are usually talking about crimes. If you were asked to name some crimes, which ones would you think of first? At the top of your list might be murder, robbery, and kidnapping. But do you know that running a stoplight and littering are also crimes?

A ***crime*** is any behavior that is illegal because the government considers it harmful to society. A crime may be an act, such as stealing. It may also be a failure to do something required by law, such as refusing to pay income taxes. Something cannot be a crime unless there is a specific written law against it. Each law must define a behavior and state how it may be punished. ***Criminal law*** refers to the group of laws that tell which acts are crimes, how accused persons should be tried in court, and how crimes should be punished.

The purpose of criminal law. The main purpose of criminal law is to protect society as a whole. Suppose that you catch a burglar leaving your home. The burglar returns the stolen money, and you agree not to tell the police. You might be satisfied just to get your money back. However, the government is not satisfied because it sees the burglar as a threat to the community's safety. That is why the act is a crime and must be reported.

To see how crimes harm society, imagine what would happen if the government did not punish people who commit them. If stealing was not against the law, there would be little to discourage some people from taking the property of others. Society would be harmed because everyone's property would be threatened. Suppose that people were allowed to copy and sell products made by businesses, such as videotapes. Society would be hurt because businesses could not make a fair profit.

Penalties for crimes. Criminal laws must set fair and reasonable penalties. Some crimes deserve greater penalties than others. Also, most crimes have maximum and minimum penalties. This range allows people guilty of the

Challenge (Evaluation): Have students discuss the following question: Will tougher penalties curb crime? Students should provide reasons for their opinions. (This issue is discussed in Chapter 19.)

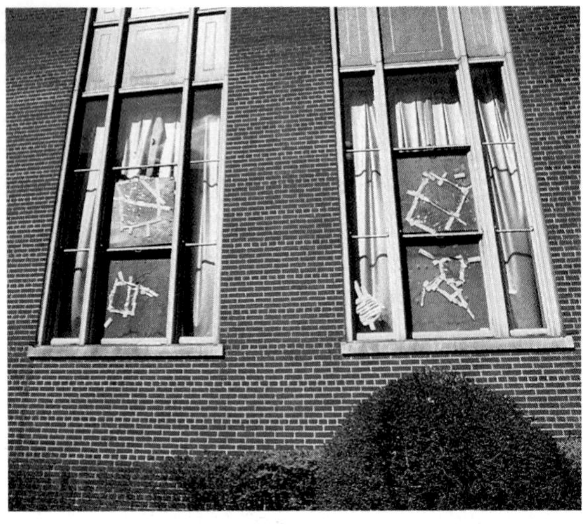

Under criminal law, people who purposely damage the property of others may be punished by fines or jail terms.

same crime to receive different punishments, depending on the case. For instance, a first-time offender will probably receive a lighter penalty than someone who has committed many crimes.

Crimes are divided into two categories: felonies and misdemeanors. A ***felony*** is a crime for which the penalty is imprisonment for more than one year, a fine, or a combination of both. Felonies include such crimes as kidnapping and murder. A ***misdemeanor*** is a crime for which the penalty is a jail sentence of not more than one year, a fine, or a combination of both. Littering and driving without a license are examples of misdemeanors.

Sources of criminal law. Would you feel comfortable if a single government leader could decide which types of behavior should be punished as crimes? Probably not. Too much power would be in the hands of one person. In the United States, no President, state governor, or judge may make a law declaring that a certain act is a crime.

When people talk about "the government" making an act a crime, they are referring either to Congress, to state legislatures, or to local lawmakers such as city councils. At all three levels of government, criminal laws are passed, written down, and organized into codes. They are numbered and listed by subject so that they can be looked up easily.

Congress decides which types of behavior will be considered crimes anywhere in the United States. Each state legislature, though, can make its own criminal laws as long as they do not come into conflict with federal statutes or the Constitution.

Some types of behavior, such as gambling, may be illegal in one state but legal in another. Punishments may also differ. Drunk driving may be a felony in one state but a misdemeanor in another. Each state legislature takes into account the needs and beliefs of the majority of people in the state.

Some actions are crimes only within a particular town, city, or county. You may be reminded of this on the Fourth of July. Some cities allow fireworks because they do not see them as a serious fire danger. However, others might post notices like this: "No Fireworks Allowed!—Tindertown Municipal Code, Ordinance 451." In short, criminal laws can reflect local beliefs and needs.

Civil Law

As you have seen, criminal law includes all the laws that the government can punish people for breaking. ***Civil law*** is the group of laws that help settle disagreements between people. Americans are used to the idea that conflicts can be settled in court. That is why statements like "I'll sue you" or "I'm taking you to court" sound so familiar.

The purpose of civil law. Civil law provides a way for people to settle disagreements in court if they cannot or will not settle them privately. In civil cases, the government will not automatically get involved, as it does with

The word *suit* is generally used to refer to civil cases, and the word *trial* is used for most criminal cases. Sometimes the terms are used interchangeably.

VIEWS OF NOTED AMERICANS

William Hastie

Equality for all Americans under the law—such was the goal inspiring William Hastie when he graduated from Harvard Law School in 1930. At that time, segregation laws were glaring signs that the nation fell far short of that ideal. Indeed, in some cities African-American lawyers like Hastie had to enter the courthouse by the back door.

Having felt the sting of segregation, Hastie sought to change a legal system that allowed racial discrimination. He made his views known throughout a distinguished career as a lawyer, law professor, and federal judge.

As a young attorney, Hastie argued ground-breaking civil rights cases in the early 1930s, including that of a black student applying to a university that had been open only to white students. He also questioned the constitutionality of paying black teachers less than white teachers.

Earning respect for his legal skills, Hastie was appointed as a federal judge in the Virgin Islands and then as a professor at Howard University Law School. In 1940 he became a civilian aide to the Secretary of War, with the hope of ending segregation in the armed forces. He later resigned in anger, though, after the military showed little interest in changing its policies.

Some of Hastie's friends thought that by resigning he had closed the door to further opportunities in government. However, his reputation for courage and integrity led to his being appointed as Governor of the Virgin Islands and later as a judge on the U.S. Circuit Court of Appeals. Both achievements were "firsts" for an African American, but they meant less to him than the goal of equal legal treatment for all.

In serving on the Circuit Court from 1949 until his retirement in 1971, Judge Hastie showed keen insight into legal issues and gave his complete effort to every case. Since he had experienced injustice himself, he worked faithfully to carry out the heavy responsibility of applying the law fairly.

crimes. An individual or group involved in the conflict must first ask for help by suing, or taking the matter to court.

By providing a system of civil law, the government is in effect saying, "If you disagree with someone and think you have been treated unfairly, first try to work it out yourselves. If that fails, there are laws that judges and juries may use to help settle the conflict."

Suppose, for example, you buy a cassette player that breaks down the first time you use it. The store owner refuses to replace the machine, saying that you must have broken it. Under civil law, you have the right to sue the owner. That is, you may file a complaint with a court stating why you think the owner has been unfair to you. Both you and the owner might then tell your stories to a judge or jury, who will make a decision based on rules of civil law.

When you set out to make a major purchase, it is reassuring to know that one purpose of civil law is to help make sure that buyers and sellers treat each other fairly.

Sources of civil law. In criminal cases, the main question is, "Did the accused person commit a crime?" Judges and juries must compare the facts of the case with the statute that defines the crime. In civil cases, however, the main question is, "What is a fair way to settle this type of disagreement?" To answer that question, judges and juries often refer to earlier decisions that have been made in similar cases.

Decisions in civil cases may also be based on statutes. Most civil statutes sum up the unwritten laws on which judges have based their decisions over the years. For instance, in case after case judges have ruled that a seller has a duty to deliver goods and that a buyer must pay for them. Eventually, legislatures decided that this basic unwritten law should be spelled out as a written statute: "The obligation of the seller is to transfer and deliver and that of the buyer is to accept and pay in accordance with the contract."

Some civil statutes are collected and organized into legal codes. The example just mentioned comes from the Uniform Commercial Code, which includes many laws that protect consumers.

Where Criminal Law and Civil Law Meet

Criminal law gives government the power to protect society as a whole by taking action against individuals who commit crimes. Civil law provides a way for individuals or groups within society to settle their conflicts in an orderly manner. Both types of laws help bring order to society and protect people's rights.

Sometimes situations involve both criminal and civil law. Suppose a drunk driver who has no insurance severely injures someone. Criminal law protects society by punishing the driver for drunk driving. However, it does not require the driver to pay the injured person's medical bills. That is where civil law

Teaching Note: Use the Evaluating Progress activity, page T 137, to assess students' understanding of this section.

enters the picture. If the driver refuses to pay, the injured person can sue. Under civil law, a court can force the driver to pay.

Think back to the warning that appears on videotapes. Criminal law protects society by fining or imprisoning a person who illegally copies and sells a company's tapes. However, punishing the criminal does not completely solve the company's problem. It has lost money it could have earned by selling tapes itself. Under civil law, the company can ask a court to force the criminal to pay the company the amount lost in sales.

Together, criminal and civil law look after our needs and rights. In Chapters 19 and 20 you will look at how our systems of criminal law and civil law work.

Answers will be found on page T 138.

Section Review

1. Define *crime, criminal law, felony, misdemeanor,* and *civil law.*
2. Explain why we have both criminal law and civil law.
3. How are the sources of criminal and civil law similar? How are they different?

Evaluation. Which group of laws do you think is more important—criminal law or civil law? Explain your answer.

Data Search. Look on page 589 in the Data Bank to identify two felonies and two misdemeanors. Why do you think they are classified as such? If necessary, look up definitions of the four crimes you picked.

A BROADER VIEW

Laws in our society have changed as Americans' beliefs about what is right and wrong have changed. Up until the early 1900s, for example, there were few child labor laws.

The change from a rural society to an urban one, however, brought changes in attitudes toward child labor. Instead of working at home or on a farm, many children worked in large factories. Eight-year-olds might work ten hours a day. As more people began to object to child labor, state legislatures passed laws limiting the hours children could work. The goal was to protect the health and safety of children and to ensure time for schooling.

The growth of industry has also brought changes in laws on pollution. Until recently, few Americans worried about pollution of the air, water, and land. Now, however, the public has demanded that some forms of pollution be made crimes for which companies may be fined.

Another example of change is in laws protecting consumers. For many years American courts upheld laws based on the idea "let the buyer beware." If buyers bought a bad product, it was their fault for making a poor decision. Today, consumers expect the government to take action against sellers who make defective products, use false advertising, or fail to deliver the promised services. Changes in consumer law have given the buyer more protection than in the past.

As our society changes, our laws will also change. In most cases, new laws will be added. In some cases, acts that were previously crimes may be "decriminalized." For example, during the 1920s and early 1930s the sale and manufacture of alcoholic beverages was a federal crime. However, people found that prohibiting alcohol created more problems than it solved, and the law was changed. As you look to the future, what changes in our laws do you think lie ahead?

The Process

This four page lesson is best taught over three periods: (1) "Explaining the Process," (2) "Applying the Process," and (3) "Checking Your Understanding" and "Reviewing the Process."

Choosing: Identifying and Judging Options

Suppose that two of your friends have gotten into an argument. They plan to meet to fight it out. You know where and when the fight will take place. You worry that one or both of them might be seriously hurt. How will you decide what to do?

Decision making, as you know, has two main parts: choosing and taking action. The lesson in Chapter 17 provided some guidelines for the first step in choosing: goal setting. This lesson will help you with identifying and judging options.

EXPLAINING THE PROCESS

Suppose that in deciding how to deal with the planned fight you have set two goals: to prevent anyone from getting seriously injured and to preserve your friendship with both friends. Copy the chart that appears on page 405. Allow plenty of space between the options. As you read the following guidelines for identifying and judging options, you will be answering questions and filling in the chart.

Have a clear idea of what you want. Identify qualities and values that you think you should consider when deciding what to do. You will usually include the most important ones in the statement of your goal or goals. You can also list some qualities and values separately as other standards, or requirements, that your final choice must meet.

Suppose, for example, that you are deciding which people to invite to a party. You might look for certain qualities in guests, such as friendliness and a good sense of humor. You could also consider values, such as kindness, that might guide you in choosing guests. For example, your goal might be: "To invite people who are friendly and have a good sense of humor." This goal already includes two standards. If you value kindness, you might add: "I will try to include some people who are not usually invited to parties."

[Your goals in deciding how to deal with the planned fight might be to prevent anyone from getting seriously injured and to preserve your friendship with both friends. These goals already include some standards, such as the value of friendship. If you also value fairness, you might add another standard: "Do not play favorites." If you value honesty, you might add: "Do not lie to either friend." Whatever you finally decide to do would have to measure up to these goals and standards.]

1. Write down another standard that you might use in deciding what to do about the fight. Add it to your chart.
2. How do clear goals and standards help you identify and judge options?

Identify your options. Keeping in mind your goals and standards, identify ways to meet them. You can identify options by brainstorming. When you brainstorm, be sure to:

- Quickly list as many options as you can.
- Avoid criticizing the options you think of.
- Piggy-back options. In other words, use options you have already thought of to help you think of even more options.

[One option is to meet with each friend and try to talk them out of the fight.]

3. State at least two other options and add them to your chart. Leave plenty of space between options.
4. If you were to tell another student how to brainstorm, what advice would you give?

Teaching Note: For reinforcement of decision-making skills, use Decision-Making Worksheet Chapter 18.

Decision to be Made: I need to decide what to do about the fight that my friends are planning to have.

My Goals: To prevent anyone from getting seriously injured. To preserve my friendship with both friends.

My Standards: Do not play favorites. Do not embarrass either friend.

Add another standard.

	Kinds of Information I Need		
Options	Effects on Friendship	Physical Risk to Me	**Add another kind of information.**
1. Meet with each friend.	+ Friends might appreciate my efforts. ~~– Friends may get angry with me.~~ + probably will not embarrass either friend	+ probably none	
2. Add another option.			
3. Add another option.			

Get useful information about each option. To choose the best option, you need information that is relevant, or related, to your decision. That information must also be reliable. Your search for useful information has three parts: (a) identifying which kinds of information you need, (b) finding that information, and (c) checking whether it is accurate.

Identify which kinds of information you need. To compare options, you will need certain types of information about each one. This might include *characteristics* of each option and *consequences,* or effects, of each option.

Look for information that relates to the type of decision you are making. In deciding which part-time job to take, for example, you might look at characteristics such as wages and schedules, and consequences such as effects on school activities. Ask yourself, "What do I need to know about each option?"

[You might consider consequences such as physical risks to you and effects on your friendship.]

5. Name one other kind of information you might want. Explain how it would help you make a good choice. Then list it.

You may wish to have students work together in groups when answering questions 1–8 and filling out the chart. Students might also suggest other possible formats for an options chart.

If necessary, students should review key critical-thinking skills for evaluating information, which are discussed on pages 146, 190, 212, and 258.

Collect the information you need. Find reliable sources of information about the characteristics and consequences of each option. Perhaps you can rely on some of your own ideas and experiences. You can also get information from other sources that you trust. Suppose, for instance, that you are deciding which school activity to sign up for, and you want to know how much time each one will take. You might check with team or club members about practice schedules and meeting times.

[You might recall that you once talked some friends out of fighting. They had agreed that it was a poor way to settle their disagreement. Therefore, you think that meeting with each friend might have a good effect.]

6. For each of the options you listed in the chart, name at least three specific consequences or characteristics. Then add these pieces of information to your chart. Make sure that you have put at least one piece of information in each section of your chart.

Check whether the information is accurate. Even though you have collected information from reliable sources, take a closer look to make sure it is accurate. First, separate the statements of fact from the opinions because you will need to judge them differently.

In judging statements of fact, check whether they are true. Suppose you are deciding which video game to buy, and a friend who recently bought a game tells you prices from several stores. You might call the stores to check whether prices have changed.

In judging opinions, check whether they are reasonable. Suppose that a friend tells you a certain video game is "great." Does your friend have good reasons to back up that opinion? Keep in mind that statements about consequences are often opinions. When you look at a possible consequence, always ask yourself, "How likely is this to happen?"

[Suppose your brother tells you that trying to talk friends out of fighting will just make them angry. How reliable is his opinion? Based on your experience, you might consider this opinion unreliable and ignore it.]

7. Give an example of information that you would *not* rely on when deciding what to do about the planned fight. Explain why you would not trust this information. Then look at your chart and cross out any information that you do not consider reliable.

Judge each option. Identify the good and bad points of each option. Put a plus (+) next to each characteristic or consequence that meets one or more of your goals or standards. Put a minus (–) next to each one that does not.

You might think that some characteristics and consequences are more important than others and therefore give them greater weight. Next to important good points you might put two pluses. Next to important bad points you might put two minuses.

Give each option a fair look. If you are leaning toward one before carefully examining the others, look for any bad points you may have overlooked. This will help you to be as objective as possible.

[In judging the option of meeting with each friend, you could put a plus next to "friends might appreciate my efforts."]

8. Name one characteristic or consequence that you would consider positive and one that seems negative. Explain why. Then put a plus and a minus next to them on your chart. Judge the other pieces of information on your chart and mark each with a plus or minus.

Have students give examples of decisions relating to their various social roles (page 55). For which decisions would an options chart be useful? For decisions that have to be made more quickly, what steps do they think should be followed?

Answers will be found on page T 138.

Let's Make a Snap Decision!
OPTION 1
OPTION 2
OPTION 3
Try to avoid guessing games.
Judge your options carefully.

Choose the best option. Decide how best to reach your goal or goals by comparing the good and bad points of each option. In choosing the best option, keep in mind that some characteristics or consequences may be more important to you than others.

You might also consider how your choice could affect goals you have not listed, especially long-range goals. Suppose you have a goal to buy a car and are trying to decide whether to take a part-time job during the school year. If college is a long-range goal, you might consider the effect on your grades.

[In judging the options for dealing with the fight, you might consider the effect on friendship to be most important.]

9. Which option would you choose? Why?

Now that you have filled out your chart, you can see that it would not be practical to use a chart like this every time you make a decision. After all, many decisions have to be made quickly. However, whenever you have enough time to think over an important decision, a chart can be a useful tool. Of course, whether or not you use a chart, you should always consider a number of possible options and think of their good points and bad points.

APPLYING THE PROCESS

Picture yourself in the following situation: You are standing in the lunch line at the cafeteria. An older student comes up to you and demands that you hand over your lunch money. You do not want to get hurt, so you hand over the money. "Thanks for the donation," the student says. "I'll be back tomorrow for another one."

First, describe exactly what it is you have to make a choice about. You might begin by saying, "I have to decide whether . . ." or "I have to decide what. . . ." Next, set clear goals and standards. Then brainstorm and judge at least three options. Make a chart like the one on page 405 and fill it in as you move through the process. Finally, choose the best option. Be prepared to explain your choice.

CHECKING YOUR UNDERSTANDING

After you have completed your chart and have chosen an option, answer these questions.

10. What goal or goals did you set?

11. What were three options you identified?

12. What kinds of information did you collect about each option?

13. Pick one of the options and tell what consequences you predicted.

14. Which option did you choose and why?

REVIEWING THE PROCESS

15. Why is it helpful to know your goals before collecting information about options?

16. Suppose that one of the first options you think of seems to be a good one. Why is it useful to continue to think of other options?

17. Explain how to identify and judge options when making a decision.

After students have completed "Applying the Process" and "Checking Your Understanding," have them discuss in groups how they arrived at their decisions.

CHAPTER SURVEY

Answers to Survey and Workshop will be found on page T 139.

UNDERSTANDING NEW VOCABULARY

Seeing Relationships

The vocabulary terms in each pair listed below are related to each other. For each pair, explain what the two terms have in common. Also explain how they are different.

1. *laws* and *morals*
2. *common law* and *statutes*
3. *felony* and *misdemeanor*
4. *criminal law* and *civil law*

Putting It in Writing

In a paragraph explain why society sets rules for everyone to follow. Use the terms *laws, morals, criminal law,* and *civil law.*

LOOKING BACK AT THE CHAPTER

1. How do laws differ from other types of rules found within society?

2. Describe five purposes of laws. For each purpose give your own example of a law that meets that purpose.

3. Why might laws in one city or state differ from those in another city or state?

4. Describe the two main sources of American law and explain how those sources differ.

5. Explain the importance of constitutions and legal codes.

6. Explain why laws are sometimes changed.

7. What must happen before an act can be called a crime?

8. How does the purpose of criminal law differ from the purpose of civil law? How are criminal law and civil law similar in their purposes?

9. *Synthesis.* Suppose that someone says, "To be a moral person, you only have to avoid breaking any laws." What would you say to try to prove this person wrong?

10. *Application.* Give an example of a law that applies in your state but not necessarily in other states. Give an example of a law that applies in your city or town but not necessarily in other cities or towns.

11. *Synthesis.* If you could pass a new law, what would it be? Explain why. Keep in mind the general purpose of all laws: to encourage people to live together peacefully.

12. *Application.* Identify whether each of these situations is covered by criminal or civil law. Explain each answer. **(a)** A person buys a car that turns out to have defects, but the dealer will not fix them. **(b)** A person is caught stealing items from a store. **(c)** A landlord evicts a tenant without proper notice.

13. *Synthesis.* Imagine a world without laws. Predict how your life would be different.

WORKING TOGETHER

1. With a group of three or four classmates, make a list of five school rules that you consider to be very important. Prepare an explanation of why those rules are necessary and make proposals for how they should be enforced. Each group should present its findings to the class.

2. Prepare a report on how laws are organized in your state's education code or motor vehicle code. Give several examples of laws found in the code and explain how those laws affect the lives of teenagers.

3. In groups of three or four, discuss what you think are appropriate penalties for each of the following crimes. Include a minimum and maximum penalty for each crime. The penalties might include prison terms, fines, public service hours, and so on. Be prepared to explain your penalties.

murder	car theft
armed robbery	drunk driving
shoplifting	writing bad checks

SKILLS WORKSHOP

SOCIAL STUDIES SKILLS

Interpreting Symbols

A symbol is something that stands for something else. For example, the flag and Uncle Sam both stand for the United States, a dove and an olive branch stand for peace, and a lion stands for courage.

Some of the symbols we use go back to ancient times. The Greek goddess Themis, for example, is a very old symbol of justice. Statues of Themis can be found on courthouses across the United States. The symbol of justice usually looks like this:

1. Why do you think that the symbol of justice is usually shown with a blindfold over her eyes?

2. Why do you think that the symbol of justice is shown holding a balance scale in one of her hands?

3. For hundreds of years, the sword has been a symbol of the power and authority of government. Why do you think that the symbol of justice carries a sword?

DECISION-MAKING SKILLS

Choosing: Identifying and Judging Options

Suppose that your friends have invited you to go to a concert next Saturday. You tell them that you will have to think about it. You are hesitating because you know that a family camping trip is already scheduled for that weekend. The rest of your family wants you to go along. What will you do?

Make a chart like the one below. List your goal or goals and your standards. Then list at least two options. List the characteristics and consequences of each option and mark each one with a plus or minus to indicate good points and bad points. Finally, choose the best option.

Decision to be Made:
Goals: 1.
2.
Standards: 1.
2.

Options	**Kinds of Information Needed**		
1.			
2.			

Choice:
Reasons:

1. What were your goals? What standards did you set?

2. What were two options you identified?

3. What kinds of information did you collect about each option?

4. Which option did you choose? Explain why.

Chapter Themes: The job of our criminal justice system is to protect people against crime and to find and punish lawbreakers. Criminal and juvenile justice procedures differ, but both systems share the challenge of protecting society against lawbreakers while protecting the rights of the accused.

CHAPTER 19

Criminal and Juvenile Justice

When Kate arrived home with her family after their vacation, something felt odd to her, but she couldn't figure it out. Then she walked into the family room.

"Mom, where's the VCR?" she called back into the kitchen, her heart beginning to pound.

"Isn't it where it always is?" replied her mother, walking in with a worried look. She stared at the blank spot next to the television and said in a shaky voice, "Kate, I think we've been robbed. Call your father."

Kate's father and brother ran to see for themselves. Then everyone rushed to a different part of the house to see what else might be missing.

"Look at the mess they made of my dresser!" moaned Kate's mother. "And they took my pearl necklace!"

"My camera's gone," yelled Kate's brother from his room.

Kate turned her doorknob slowly. She looked into her room and burst into tears. Her computer was gone, too.

Kate's mother called the police, and an officer arrived soon after. He asked what had been taken and then started checking each window in the house.

"Looks like the burglar got in through here," said the officer, looking up at the half-open window above the kitchen sink. A muddy footprint could be seen at the edge of the sink.

"Will I get my computer back?" asked Kate.

"We'll do our best," said the officer, "But don't count on it. We don't recover many stolen items. And many burglars aren't caught."

Crime may have already touched your life. If you have never been a victim of a crime, you may know someone who has been. In this chapter you will study the problem of crime in our society. You will also learn about how governments deal with adult criminals and with children who break the law.

Teaching Note: Use the Introducing the Chapter activity, page T 142.

Teaching Note: For more information on the occurrence of crime in the United States, see the crime clock on page 589.

19-1

CRIME IN AMERICAN SOCIETY

Read to Find Out

- why crime is a problem in the United States.
- what the major types of crime are.
- what some of the causes of crime are.

A jogger is mugged in the park. A four-year-old is kidnapped from his front yard. A bank president flees the country, having stolen millions of dollars from depositors. These are the kinds of crimes you hear about all too often on the news. Other crimes take place every day. Cars are stolen, purses snatched. Crime is certainly a major problem in the United States today.

Crimes are acts or failures to act that break the law. They can range from stealing a bar of candy to murder. When Americans talk about the "problem" of crime, however, they mean crimes such as murder, rape, and burglary.

The Problem of Crime

Crime touches many Americans every year. According to the Department of Justice, there was a violent crime or theft in one of every four American households in 1988. A violent crime happens in the United States about every 25 seconds, and a property crime takes place about every 3 seconds.

Crimes take place in the United States more often than in most other countries. An American is from seven to ten times more likely to be murdered than a citizen of most European countries or Japan. Americans are six times more likely to be robbed than West Germans.

Americans believe that crime is one of our nation's biggest problems. Crime costs people, businesses, and governments billions of dollars every year.

Crime also makes people afraid. Because they fear crime, they change the ways they lead their lives. They put extra locks on their doors and do not go out at night. They are suspicious of strangers in their neighborhoods. When people and property are not safe, everyone becomes a victim of crime.

Although crime is a problem for all Americans, some places have more crime than others. In general, there is more crime in urban areas than there is in suburban or rural communities. In addition, poor neighborhoods have more crime than wealthy ones. For ex-

When people fear crime, they look for ways to protect themselves. Putting bars on windows is one way to try to prevent burglary.

Reporting a crime to the police can benefit the victim by leading to compensation for medical expenses and property damage. Reporting can benefit the police and society by bringing a criminal to justice.

ample, compare the crime rates in two cities of about the same size in southern California. The city of Compton is in an urban area and has many poor families. Thousand Oaks is a suburb, and many of its families are wealthy. In 1983, Compton had 50 murders per 100,000 residents and over 1,300 reported robberies. Thousand Oaks, on the other hand, had no murders and 55 robberies.

The Types of Crimes

Serious crimes fall into several major groups. In the following paragraphs you will read about the kinds of crimes that cause the most concern among Americans.

Crimes against people. Acts that threaten, hurt, or end a person's life are crimes against people. They are also called violent crimes. Murder, rape, and assault are examples of violent crimes.

The most common violent crime is assault. Assault is an attack on a person for the purpose of causing injury to that person's body. Most people who assault another person use a weapon, such as a knife or gun.

Killing someone is known as homicide. When a killing is planned ahead of time, it is called murder. A killing that happens by accident or in a fit of anger is called manslaughter. Not all killings are crimes. Killing someone in self-defense is not against the law, if that is the only way to save your life.

Crimes against property. Crimes against property happen more often than any other crimes. Most involve stealing.

There are three kinds of stealing. Larceny is taking anything of value that belongs to another person without using violence. Examples include shoplifting and stealing a car.

Robbery is a special kind of stealing. A robber takes something of value from another person by force or by threat of violence. Robbery is therefore both a crime against property and a crime against a person.

When a person breaks into a building and plans to do something illegal inside, that person is committing burglary. Burglary is a crime against property, but it may or may not involve stealing.

Other kinds of crimes against property include arson and vandalism. Arson is the act of setting fire to someone's property—such as a house, factory, or store—on purpose.

Police sometimes draw lines around the body of the victim as part of their investigation at the scene of the crime.

There are four types of homicide: criminally negligent homicide, or unintentional killing; manslaughter; second-degree murder, which involves malice; and first-degree murder, which involves malice and premeditation.

Vandalism is purposely damaging property. Breaking windows and painting graffiti on walls are examples of vandalism.

White-collar crime. White-collar crimes are illegal but nonviolent acts by white-collar, or professional, workers for personal or business gain. One white-collar crime is fraud, or taking someone else's property or money by cheating or lying. Another is embezzlement, stealing money that has been trusted to your care. If a bank employee put money from other people's bank accounts into his or her own account, that would be embezzlement. Stealing company secrets and not paying your taxes are other white-collar crimes.

Victimless crimes. Drug use and gambling are victimless crimes, acts that hurt no one, except possibly the people who commit them. Our society calls them crimes because they go against common values or because people believe they hurt society as a whole.

There is disagreement over whether some victimless crimes should be crimes at all. Should there be laws against acts that do not hurt any innocent people?

On one side are people who say that making laws against activities such as gambling and using drugs only cuts down on the freedom of individuals. On the other side are people who argue that such acts really do hurt innocent people. They warn that gamblers and drug users are a bad influence, that their families suffer, and that they often turn to violent crime to pay for their habits.

Crimes against government. Crimes against government include treason and terrorism. Treason is the betrayal of one's country by helping its enemies or by making war against it. Terrorism is a crime in which people or groups of people use, or say they will use, violent acts in order to get what they want. Terrorists have kidnapped and sometimes murdered people, hijacked airplanes, and set off bombs, causing injury and death to hundreds of innocent people.

The Causes of Crime

In the United States crimes are committed by millions of people each year. What causes so many people to break our society's rules?

Poverty. Poverty and unemployment are closely connected to crime. When people cannot earn enough money to support themselves and their families, they often feel that society is not working very well for them. People who feel this way are more likely to break society's rules.

Poverty does not fully explain the crime problem, however. Many countries that are poorer than ours have less crime. Also, crime rates are rising in some wealthy communities in the United States.

Rapid social change. New technology and changes in the economy are bringing about great changes in the United States. Many Americans must learn new job skills or move to different parts of the country. Values are changing, too. It can be hard to get used to these changes. In the process, some people lose their sense of right and wrong.

Poor parenting. Some studies show that an unhappy family life can make a person much more likely to break laws. Children who have been hurt or neglected by their parents may suffer great emotional pain. As a result, some find it hard to control their behavior as adults.

Violence on television. Every day, millions of children and adults watch violent acts on television. They see gangsters, police, and soldiers

Challenge (Analysis): Because white-collar crime does not involve assault or robbery, judges and juries sometimes are lenient in punishment of offenders. Have students discuss the consequences other members of society may suffer as a result of such leniency.

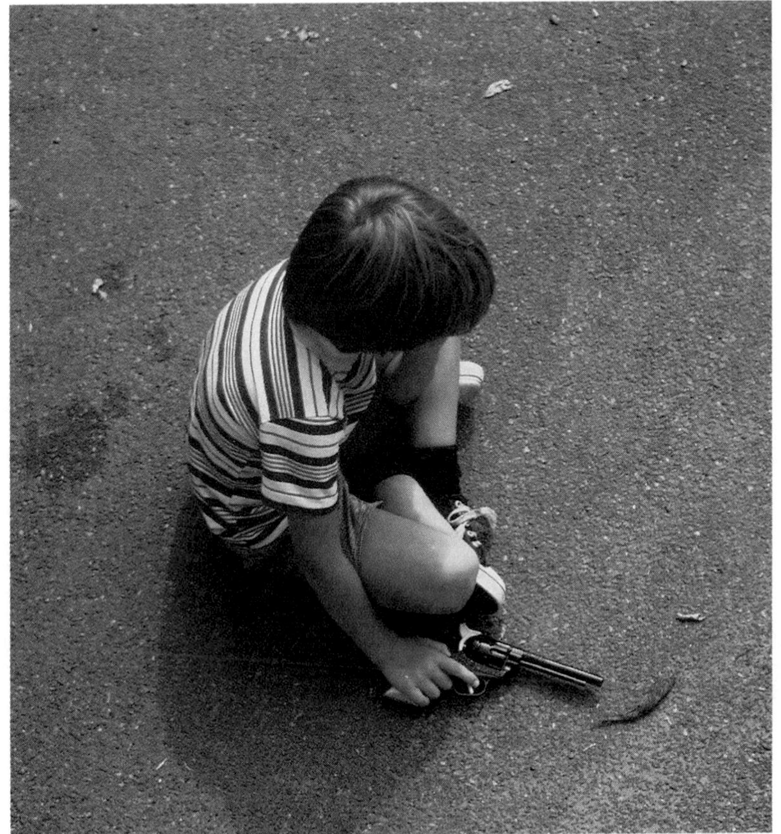

Experts disagree over whether playing with guns and watching violence in movies and on TV encourages children to violent behavior.

hurting and killing people. The same happens in movies and video games. Many people believe that watching a great deal of violence causes people to be more violent themselves.

Drug abuse. More and more of the crimes committed each year are drug-related. That is, the people who commit them are under the influence of drugs, are stealing to support their habit, or are selling drugs. Many people think that solving the drug-abuse problem in our society will also help solve the crime problem.

Permissive courts. Some people place much of the blame for crime on the way our courts treat criminals. Too few criminals are sent to prison, they say. Also, those criminals who do go to prison are let out too soon and go right back to committing crimes.

Not enough money for police. Crime will not be reduced, say many people, until the chances of getting caught are much higher. However, the police say that they do not have enough money to do a good job of catching criminals. Money for police departments has been cut in recent years. Many cities cannot hire as many police officers as they need.

No single cause. These and many other aspects of our modern society have been blamed for causing crime. People do not agree about which of these causes are most important. Experts do agree, however, that no single cause can explain our crime problem.

By the time a student graduates from high school, he or she may have watched as many as 15,000 hours of television. A survey in the late 1980s indicated that violence occurs from 13 to 37 times during a typical television episode.

Teaching Note: Use Teaching Activity 1, page T 142, and the Reinforcement Activity, page T 143, and accompanying worksheet in the Activity Book after students have read the material in Section 19-1.

Answers will be found on page T 144.

Section Review

1. Why do Americans consider crime to be a major problem?
2. Name a kind of crime against a person and a kind of crime against property.
3. List three possible causes of crime.

Analysis. In the beginning of this chapter, was Kate's mother correct in saying they had been robbed? Explain.

Data Search. Look on page 589 in the Data Bank. In which year between 1980 and 1989 were the most crimes reported? The fewest? Looking at the statistics in this table, would you say crime is increasing or decreasing?

19-2 THE CRIMINAL JUSTICE SYSTEM

Read to Find Out

- what the terms *probable cause, warrant, bail, indictment, arraignment, plea bargaining,* and *parole* mean.
- what the responsibilities of police officers are.
- what happens to someone who is arrested.
- what happens during a criminal trial.
- how people have proposed we fight crime.

Police and other law enforcement agencies, courts, and jails and prisons make up our criminal justice system. Together, their job is to protect people against crime and to find and punish lawbreakers.

The criminal justice system faces a challenge. On the one hand, it must protect society against those who break the law. On the other hand, it must protect the rights of people who have been accused of crimes. Americans often disagree about how to balance these responsibilities. As a result, there is an ongoing debate about how best to solve our crime problem.

The Role of the Police

All levels of government have police officers. Most of them work for city police departments. A large city may have over 10,000 officers. A local police officer patrols neighborhoods, finds stolen property, investigates complaints, arrests lawbreakers, helps solve disputes, and writes traffic tickets.

The job of state police varies from state to state. In many states their major job is to protect automobile drivers and enforce traffic laws on state highways.

Federal law enforcement agencies such as the Federal Bureau of Investigation (FBI) help local police with such problems as gang wars and drug dealing. The FBI also enforces federal laws such as those against bank robbery and kidnapping.

Can you imagine yourself as a police officer? Officers must know the law and what steps to follow when arresting people. They must be able to protect themselves and others from dangerous people. They have to make many quick decisions. Police officers come face to face with many of society's problems—child abuse, street fights, and drug dealing.

The police have great power. They can use weapons as part of their job. It is important, therefore, that they be trained to use their power wisely and legally.

What Happens to Someone Who is Arrested

The purpose of our criminal justice system is to find and punish people who have committed crimes. In order to make sure that

Nearly all police departments require police officers to have a high school education; some departments require a college education. Generally, candidates must be 21 years old and pass an intelligence test and a strict physical examination. Recruits receive training in a police academy.

Teaching Note: For the text of the Miranda warning, see page 137.

Arrests for Serious Crimes in 1989

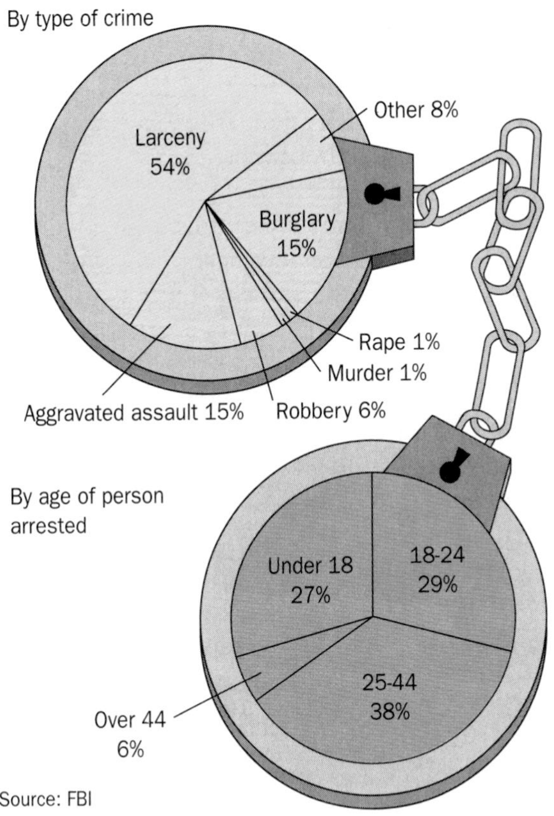

Source: FBI

people's rights are protected, there are many steps to be taken in deciding whether a person is guilty. To follow those steps, suppose that Jack Jones broke into a radio store and stole calculators and portable radios.

The arrest. Jack Jones enters the criminal justice system when he is arrested by a law enforcement official. When Jack is arrested, it means that he is no longer free to go. The police must have ***probable cause***, a good reason to believe that a suspect has been involved in a crime. If the police see Jack commit the crime, or if someone reports that a person looking like Jack has committed the crime, then the police have probable cause.

A person can also be arrested if the police have a warrant for his or her arrest. A ***warrant*** is a legal paper, issued by a court, giving police permission to make an arrest, seizure, or search. To get a warrant the police must give evidence to a judge.

During the arrest, the officers must tell Jack that he has the constitutional right to remain silent and to have a lawyer present during questioning. This is called the Miranda warning.

After the arrest, Jack is taken to a police station. The police record Jack's name, the time of the arrest, and the charges, or reason for the arrest. At this time, Jack has the right to make a phone call to a lawyer or to a friend who can arrange for a lawyer. Then he is placed in a jail cell.

Soon after this process has taken place, the case is given to a prosecuting attorney, or prosecutor. In the state court systems, the prosecutor will be the district attorney (DA) or an attorney on the DA's staff. The prosecutor will lead the government's case against Jack Jones. If the prosecutor decides that the case against Jack is too weak, the charges may be dropped, and the suspect released.

The preliminary hearing. On the day of his arrest or soon after, Jack appears in court for a preliminary hearing. The suspect, Jack Jones, is now called the defendant. At this hearing, the prosecutor must show the judge that a crime has been committed, and that there is enough evidence against Jack to go ahead with the case. The judge may decide to dismiss the case if the prosecutor cannot show that there is probable cause to believe that Jack committed the crime.

If the crime could lead to a jail or prison sentence, Jack has a right to the help of a lawyer, or attorney. If he does not have enough money to pay for a lawyer, the court will appoint one at this hearing. The lawyer may be

About 80 percent of the people arrested for crimes are male. During the mid-1980s, the number of women arrested for serious crimes increased 10 percent, and the number of men arrested rose 5 percent.

Challenge (Analysis): Have students discuss the saying that a person is innocent until proven guilty. Why is our criminal justice system not based on the belief that a person is guilty until proven innocent?

either a private attorney whom the government will pay or a public defender. Public defenders are lawyers who work full time for the government defending criminal suspects who cannot afford to pay. The defendant's lawyer is called the defense attorney.

In a misdemeanor case, the defendant may enter a plea of guilty or not guilty at this first court hearing. For a felony, which is a crime that could send a person to prison for more than one year, a plea is entered later.

At this first appearance in court, the judge may set bail. ***Bail*** is money that a defendant gives the court as a kind of promise that he or she will return for the trial. If the defendant does not return, the court keeps the bail. The judge may also simply let the defendant go on his or her "own recognizance." This means that the defendant is considered to be a good risk to appear at the trial. A defendant who the judge decides is dangerous to society can be held in jail without bail.

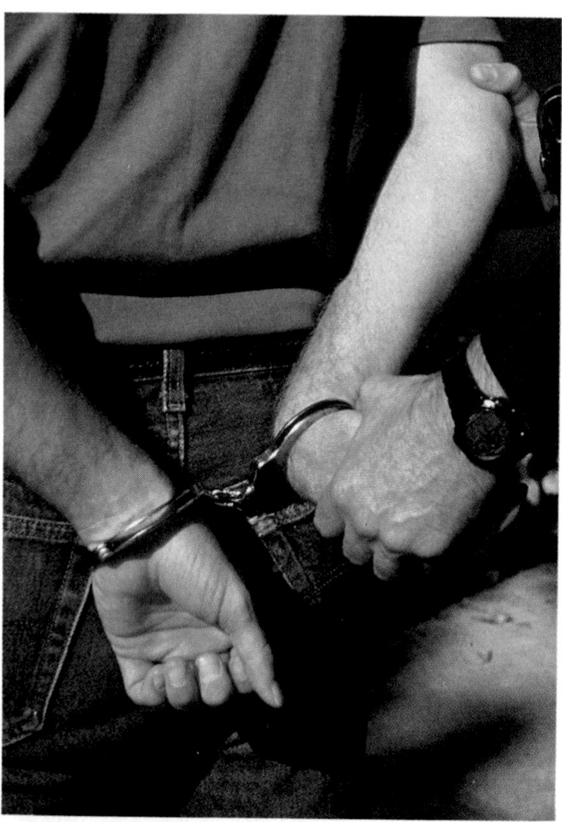

At the time of an arrest, the police must tell the suspect of the right to remain silent and to have the help of a lawyer.

Grand jury. The Constitution says that a grand jury must review cases involving serious federal crimes. Some states use grand juries, too. The grand jury is a group of from 16 to 23 citizens. Their job is to decide if there is probable cause for believing that the defendant committed the crime. The grand jury acts as a check on the government. It protects the rights of the individual, making sure there is enough evidence against him or her.

The grand jury may either return an indictment [in-DĪT-ment] or refuse to indict. An ***indictment*** is a formal charge against the accused.

A defendant who is indicted must appear in court for a felony arraignment [uh-RAIN-ment]. An ***arraignment*** is a court hearing in which the defendant is formally charged with a crime and enters a plea of guilty or not guilty. If the defendant pleads guilty, no trial is needed. If the defendant pleads not guilty, the defense attorney will take the next step.

Pretrial motions. Suppose that Jack Jones has pleaded not guilty to the charges against him. There are important steps, called pretrial motions, that may be taken by Jack or his attorney before the actual trial begins.

One of the most important motions is the motion to keep evidence from being presented in court. Evidence may be kept back for many reasons. Sometimes the defense attorney may say that the other side got the evidence through an illegal search. If the judge rules that key evidence cannot be used in the

The selection process for a grand jury is the same as that for a trial jury. A list of residents is compiled from sources that ensure a cross section of the community. Names of jurors are drawn from that list.

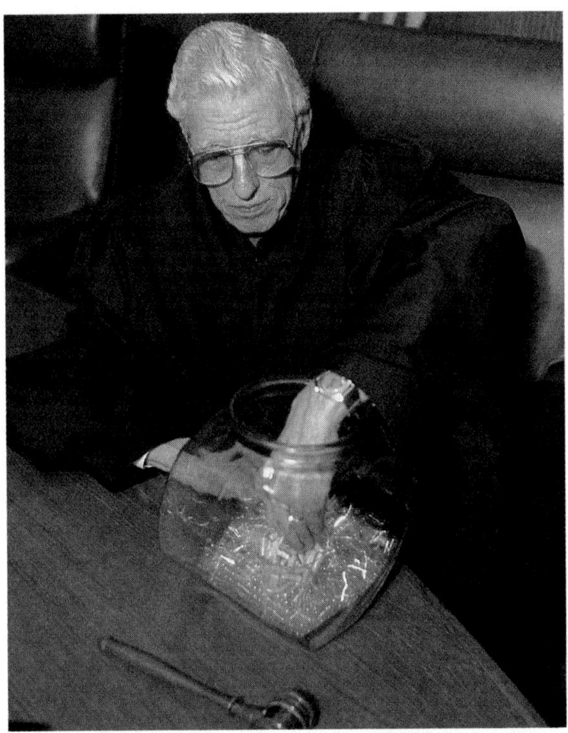

In a Maryland court, the names of people to be called to jury duty are drawn by lot. From that large group, trial juries will be selected.

trial for this reason, the prosecution may have to drop the charges.

Some people believe it is wrong for the courts to throw out evidence that clearly shows a defendant's guilt. Although this rule protects the constitutional rights of the accused, it may result in people who have actually broken the law being set free.

Plea bargaining. Did you know that most criminal cases never go to trial? As you have seen, some are dropped by the prosecutor or the grand jury, and some are dismissed by the judge. However, the main reason cases do not go to trial is that the defendant pleads guilty, and a trial is not needed.

Why would a defendant plead guilty? If you knew that you had broken the law and that the evidence against you was strong, you might want to make a deal with the prosecutor. Such a deal is called ***plea bargaining***, agreeing to plead guilty in exchange for a lesser charge or a lighter sentence. As a result of plea bargaining, the defendant gets a milder punishment than he or she would probably have received in a trial. Meanwhile, the government saves the time and cost of a trial.

Although plea bargaining can be good for both sides, many people do not like it. Some people, including victims of crimes, think that because of plea bargaining, criminals get off with lighter punishments than they should. Other people, however, point out that prosecutors often "overcharge" defendants in the first place. Overcharging means to charge the accused person with more crimes or a more serious crime than he or she could probably be found guilty of.

Going to Trial

Suppose that, after all of these steps, Jack's case makes it to trial. What happens in the courtroom?

Jury selection. Citizens are called to serve on the jury. First they are questioned by both attorneys in the case. The attorneys are looking for people who will listen carefully to the evidence presented in court and then make up their minds fairly. Sometimes many people must be questioned before the attorneys agree on a group of jurors.

The trial. The rights of due process granted by the Constitution determine how a trial is run. The trial must be speedy and public. The defendant—Jack—has the right to call witnesses and to question witnesses called by the prosecution. He has the right to be present in the courtroom, but he does not have to answer questions. The purpose of the trial is to decide upon the truth: is Jack innocent or

Judges instruct jurors not to discuss the trial with anyone until it is over because such discussions could influence their opinions. In cases that have received much publicity, jurors may be sequestered and may not be allowed to read or hear anything on television about the trial.

guilty? This important question is answered by carefully studying the evidence.

Usually, statements made by witnesses are the most important evidence in a trial. A witness may be a person who saw the crime take place. A witness may also be anyone who knows anything about the defendant, the victim, or the crime.

The attorneys in the trial each call their own witnesses, asking them questions in court. After one attorney questions a witness, the other attorney may question that same witness.

The Constitution and the Criminal Justice System

Our Constitution gives many protections to those accused of crimes. These protections form the basis of our criminal justice system.

Article 1, Section 9
Forbids taking away the right of *habeas corpus*. Forbids bills of attainder and *ex post facto* laws.

Article 3, Section 2
Guarantees a trial by jury for those accused of federal crimes.

Amendment 4
Forbids unreasonable searches and seizures.

Amendment 5
Guarantees review and indictment by a grand jury and due process of law. Forbids double jeopardy and self-incrimination.

Amendment 6
Guarantees a speedy and public trial by jury, the right to confront witnesses, the right to be informed of charges, the right to counsel, and the right to force witnesses to appear in court.

Amendment 8
Forbids excessive bail, excessive fines, and cruel and unusual punishments.

Amendment 14
Guarantees due process of law in state courts, and equal protection of the laws in the states.

At the end of the trial, the attorneys for each side make closing arguments. The judge then gives directions to the jury and sends it out to make its decision.

A jury must decide if the defendant is guilty "beyond a reasonable doubt." In other words, the jurors must have no important reasons to doubt that the defendant is guilty. If they are not sure beyond a reasonable doubt, they must find the defendant "not guilty." If the jury cannot agree, it is called a "hung jury," and the case may be tried again before another jury.

Sentencing. If Jack is found guilty or pleads guilty, the final step in the courtroom is sentencing. Sentencing is deciding how the defendant will be punished.

In most cases, the law sets both the maximum and minimum sentences for each crime. Inside that range, the judge has the power to decide the exact sentence. In deciding on a sentence, the judge thinks about many factors, such as how much harm was done by the crime.

The judge also considers factors such as the criminal record, age, and attitude of the offender. For example, if the law calls for a sentence of five to ten years in prison for armed robbery, the judge may give a first-time offender who regrets the crime the lowest—or five-year—sentence.

Correctional Institutions

Having been convicted, Jack now enters what is called the corrections system. He may be sentenced to a community treatment program, a jail, or a prison.

Jails are run by cities and counties. They are used to hold people waiting for trial. People convicted of misdemeanors may also serve time in a jail. Prisons are run by both state and federal governments. People convicted of

Decision Making: Provide students with information about a criminal case, including evidence for and against the defendant. Then have them act as a jury and decide the case.

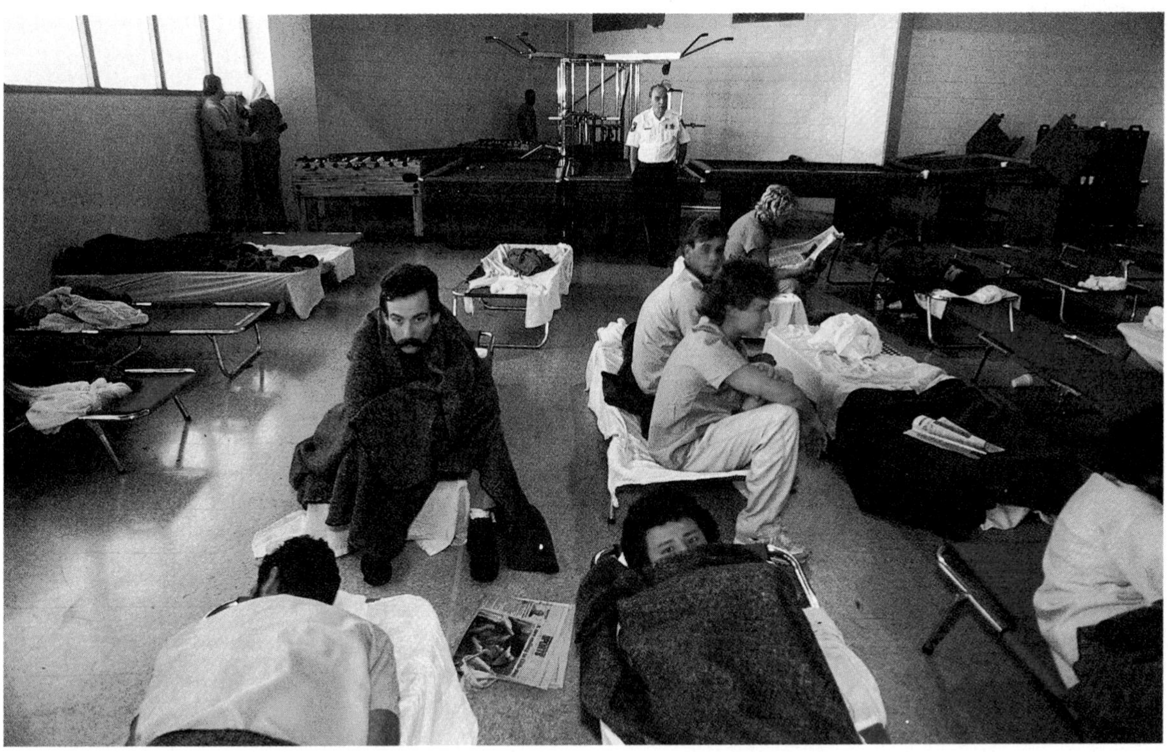

The growing number of prisoners puts a great strain on already overcrowded jails and prisons.

serious crimes, such as murder and robbery, are usually sent to prisons. In prison they are called inmates.

An inmate's time in prison may be lowered for good behavior. Letting an inmate go free to serve the rest of his or her sentence outside of prison is called ***parole.*** A group called a parole board decides whether to let inmates go before their sentences are over.

At the present time over 540,000 Americans are in state and federal prisons. Over 270,000 are in jails. Our society spends a large amount of money running jails and prisons. For example, there are over 900 state prisons with a yearly cost of over $4 billion.

Problems in the Criminal Justice System

One of the biggest problems facing our criminal justice system is overcrowding. Courts and prisons are bursting at the seams in most states. In the courts, there are more cases than ever, but not enough judges. Larger and larger numbers of people are waiting for trial. In many states, the constitutional right to a speedy trial cannot be guaranteed.

Prisons, too, are overcrowded. The number of people in our prisons continues to rise as the public demands that criminals be locked up longer. Prisons, however, cost a great deal to build and to run. Most states do not have the money to build new ones. As a result, too many inmates are crowded together, increasing the chance of riots and prison violence.

A serious problem is that the American public is losing confidence in the criminal justice system. In a recent survey, 73 percent of those who were asked said they had little or no confidence in our criminal courts, while

Teaching Note: For information on lengths of criminal jury trials and lengths of civil and criminal trials, see page 588.

Teaching Note: For a discussion/activity on the issue of outlawing the death penalty, see "Taking a Stand" on page 451.

83 percent said the courts are too easy on criminals.

You can see, however, that the public's desire for tougher treatment of criminals will only make the problem of prison overcrowding worse. Crime presents our society with difficult challenges.

Proposals for Fighting Crime

Because of public pressure, Presidents, governors, and mayors have been giving top priority to fighting crime. These leaders have many ideas about how to solve our crime problem. However, few of them agree. What a person thinks is the best solution to crime often depends on what he or she sees as the major cause.

Preventing crime. Many people think we should work hardest at keeping crimes from taking place, rather than at dealing with people after they have broken the law. There are several ways to help prevent crime.

A growing number of communities are using the "Neighborhood Watch." In this program, people who live on the same block get to know each other and agree to look out for each other's property. They are ready to report problems quickly to the police. Signs are put up to let criminals know they are more likely to get caught in that neighborhood. Police officers say that Neighborhood Watch can cut crime in half.

Meanwhile, many people favor broader ways of fighting crime. They want to attack what they see as the root causes of crime: poverty and other social problems. This approach has wide support. In a recent national poll, 61 percent of Americans agreed that the best way to reduce crime is to "attack social problems."

Being tougher on criminals. Another view of the best way to fight crime is to be harder on criminals. For example, people have called for mandatory sentences—punishments that are set by law and that a judge must give no matter who the defendant is or the reason for the crime. Many states have passed mandatory sentencing laws. In some states anyone who uses a gun while carrying out a crime must be sent to prison.

Some people also favor the death penalty, or capital punishment, as a sentence for serious crimes such as murder. The death penalty, however, is controversial.

Those who favor the death penalty believe that it helps keep people from committing murder. Those opposed to the death penalty see it as "cruel and unusual punishment," which the Bill of Rights forbids. Opponents also point to the many studies showing that the death penalty does not discourage people from committing murder. Nevertheless, the Supreme Court has upheld state laws allowing the death penalty.

Rehabilitation. Rehabilitation is the process of trying to teach prisoners how to live useful lives when they get out. Unfortunately, rehabilitation is not working very well. A large number of inmates break laws again after they are released. Many people, however, say that rehabilitation programs can be improved and become an important way of fighting crime.

AMERICAN NOTEBOOK

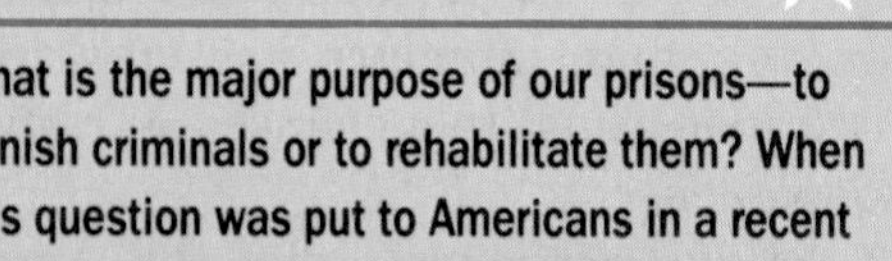

What is the major purpose of our prisons—to punish criminals or to rehabilitate them? When this question was put to Americans in a recent national poll, 48 percent said prisons should rehabilitate criminals. Thirty-eight percent said punishment is a prison's major job. What do you think?

A study of jail inmates by the United States Bureau of Justice Statistics found that 56 percent were white and 41 percent were black; 61 percent had not completed high school; and 43 percent were unemployed at the time of arrest. Inmates' average annual income before arrest was $3,714.

Teaching Note: Use Teaching Activity 2, page T 142, as a culminating activity after students have read the material in Section 19-2.

Some rehabilitation programs go on within prison. Inmates, for example, may get counseling that helps them understand and change the way they act. Educational and job-training programs are also a part of prison rehabilitation. Inmates usually have a chance to obtain a high school diploma and take college-level courses.

Rehabilitation may continue after the time in prison is over. Some ex-prisoners live in halfway houses for people who are returning to life outside prison. There they get support and help. They can test new skills in a job that brings in a steady income. Studies have shown that skills training and help in finding a job can reduce the number of former inmates who commit crimes again and return to prison.

Our serious crime problem and our overcrowded prisons call out for new solutions. The more you know about about the purpose and problems of the criminal justice system, the better you will be able to work with other citizens to solve these problems.

Answers will be found on T 144.

Section Review

1. Define *probable cause, warrant, bail, indictment, arraignment, plea bargaining,* and *parole.*
2. Why is a police officer's job challenging?
3. What must the prosecutor prove during the preliminary hearing?
4. What must a jury decide in order to return a verdict of guilty?
5. List three possible ways of fighting crime.

Analysis. What are the ways in which the criminal justice system tries to make sure that an innocent person is not mistakenly found guilty of a crime?

Data Search. Look at the pie graphs on page 417. What percentage of the people arrested for serious crimes in 1989 were under age 18?

19-3 THE JUVENILE JUSTICE SYSTEM

Read to Find Out

- what the terms *delinquent, status offender,* and *probation* mean.
- how juveniles are treated differently than adults in the courts.
- what programs exist to help juvenile offenders.

In the early part of our country's history, children accused of crimes were treated like adults. They were thrown in jails with hardened criminals and given long prison terms if they were found guilty.

Some people objected to this harsh treatment of young offenders in courts and prisons. They argued that children need special treatment. Finally, about 100 years ago, a group of reformers set out to create a separate justice system for juveniles, or children.

Juvenile Courts

Juvenile courts are state courts set aside for children. Their goal is to help children in trouble, not to punish them. These courts are meant to work in the "best interests of the child."

The first juvenile court was opened in Illinois in 1899. Its purpose was to give personal attention to each child. An understanding judge and social workers and psychologists worked with each child who got in trouble with the law. The Illinois juvenile court has served as a model for similar courts set up in other states.

Who enters the juvenile justice system? Most states say that a juvenile is a person under the age of 18, although a few states set the

One of the goals of the juvenile justice system is to provide counseling to help young offenders and their families.

age at 16 or 17. A youth thought to have broken a criminal law is brought before a juvenile court. A juvenile who is found guilty of a crime is called a ***delinquent.***

Children may also have to appear in juvenile court if they are charged with truancy, disobedience, or running away. These acts are not crimes. They are against the law only for young people. A youth who is found guilty of one of these acts is called a status offender. A ***status offender*** is a youth who is judged to be beyond the control of his or her parents or guardian.

Juvenile Court Procedure

What happens when Jenna Williams, a sixteen-year-old girl, is arrested for shoplifting makeup in a department store? As you will see in the following paragraphs, the steps she goes through are different from the ones for an adult charged with a crime.

Arrest and intake. When Jenna is arrested, the police now have the power to decide what to do with her. They might return her to her parents or give her case to a social service agency, an organization that helps children and families.

In Jenna's case the police do not send her home. Jenna has been charged with shoplifting before, and she has a history of running away from home. For these reasons, the police take her to a county detention home, or juvenile hall.

Next, Jenna goes through an informal court process called "intake," to decide if her case should be sent to juvenile court. A social worker asks Jenna questions and looks at her past record and family situation. At this point almost half of all cases are dismissed and the juvenile is sent home or directed to a social service agency. Because of Jenna's past record, however, the social worker sends her case to the next step in juvenile court.

The initial hearing. At the first—or initial—hearing the judge must be convinced that a law was broken and that there is good evidence that the young person was the one who did it. If there is not enough evidence, the juvenile is sent home.

The judge hearing Jenna's case decides that there is probable cause to believe that Jenna stole the makeup. The judge then sends Jenna

Challenge (Evaluation): In June 1989, the Supreme Court ruled that the death penalty can be used in cases of murder committed by youths at the age of 16 or 17. Have students discuss the pros and cons of this ruling. They should provide reasons for their opinions.

PEOPLE MAKE A DIFFERENCE

Teen Court Shows Both Sides of the Law

The first time Bobby Gonzales entered a courtroom as a defense attorney, he was only 17 years old. Of course he was nervous. The prosecutor and the members of the jury, however, were all just as young. They were all part of Teen Court, a new approach to juvenile justice in Odessa, Texas.

Teen Court hears the cases of young people who have pleaded guilty to a misdemeanor in regular juvenile court. Teen Court holds a "trial" to determine the circumstances of the crime. Based on what is discovered, the teen jury hands out a sentence.

Sentences usually include doing community service and being on the Teen Court jury. After a person serves the Teen Court sentence, the charge is taken off his or her record.

"It gives people a second chance," says Gonzales. "It [also] opens your eyes to how the law works—and that you have to abide by the law."

Students in Odessa who are interested in participating become part of the jury first. They can then become a bailiff, defense attorney, or prosecutor. A retired district court judge presides over the court.

Many students who are active in Teen Court started out on the other side. Eric Burke, for example, got a speeding ticket when he was 16. He chose to go through Teen Court.

"It was scary to face a panel of peers," he remembers. "But it came out fine. It was very educational." Eric stayed with Teen Court for two years.

"The process of going through Teen Court, of being judged by your peers, can change a person," says Chris Vore. Heather Coe agrees. "Often kids have no idea that what they are doing is wrong," she says. "They need to understand the law more. Teen Court gets kids associated with the law at an early age. I think it helps them later."

back to juvenile hall, so that she will not run away before her case is settled. As a juvenile, Jenna has no right to bail.

The adjudicatory hearing. The third step, the adjudicatory hearing, takes the place of a trial. It is not public, and there is no jury. The young person, however, may have an attorney. About half of all youths who are arrested and brought to court reach this "trial" phase.

Jenna has an attorney appointed by the court. The prosecutor presents the facts of the case. Jenna's attorney questions witnesses and asks Jenna to tell her side of the story. After the hearing, the judge makes a decision. In this case the judge finds Jenna to be delinquent under the juvenile law of her state.

The dispositional hearing. At the next step, the dispositional hearing, the judge decides on the sentence. Usually, a report has been prepared that recommends a sentence. This

Discussion: Have students discuss the qualities necessary to be a fair and impartial member of the jury of Teen Court.

The Juvenile Court Process

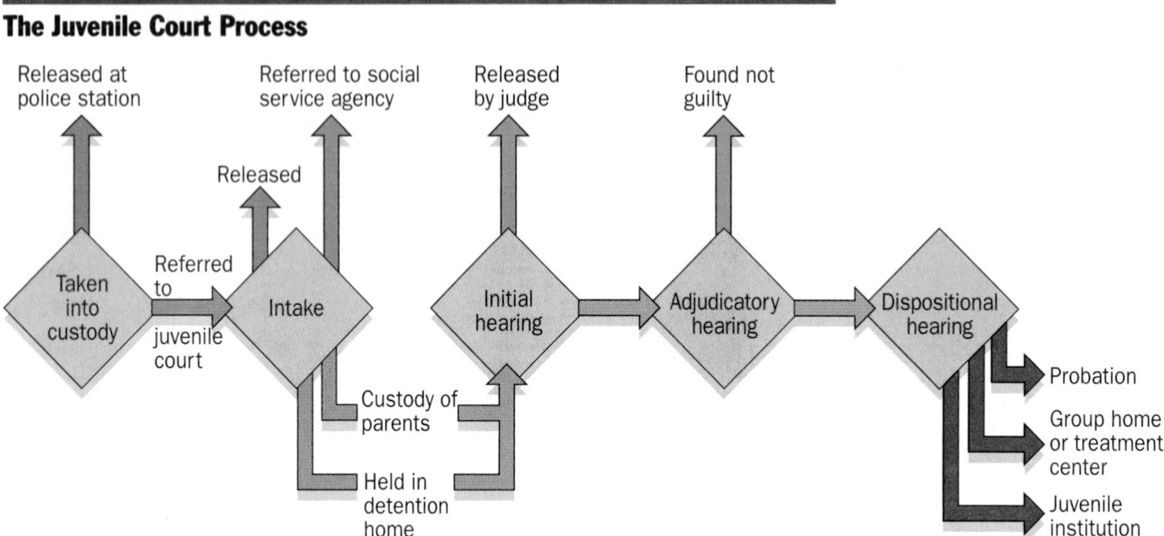

report is based on information about the youth's school situation, family, and past behavior.

The judge uses the probation report to decide on a sentence. Shall the youth be sent to a state institution for juveniles, placed in a group home or community treatment program, or put on probation? ***Probation*** is a kind of sentence in which a person goes free but must be under the supervision of a court official called a probation officer.

Like many delinquents, Jenna is put on probation and given a probation officer to whom she must report regularly. She is also ordered to take part in individual and family counseling.

Aftercare. The purpose of juvenile aftercare is to help young people, after they have been released from an institution. Each youth is given a parole officer who can give advice and information about school, jobs, and other needed services.

Strengthening Juvenile Justice

Some people think that the juvenile justice system has been a big disappointment. Instead of warm, understanding judges who are specially trained to deal with young people, they see overworked judges who make quick decisions without much knowledge of children or families. They see crowded courts and overworked staffs. They see far too little money being spent on giving the help that troubled young people need to straighten out their lives.

Others say that the system is too easy on young criminals. They point to an increase in violent crimes committed by young people, including arson, murder, armed robbery, and rape. In fact, about 30 percent of all people arrested for serious crimes are under eighteen. These critics want young offenders to be tried in regular criminal courts.

Other people have argued that juvenile courts should be done away with altogether. It is in the best interests of a young defendant, they say, to go to trial in a criminal court. There the defendant's rights to due process have much stronger protections.

Community-based programs. Even though the juvenile justice system has in many ways failed to carry out its goals, there are many successful programs for juvenile offenders.

Juvenile records cannot be released to the public without a court order. This regulation prevents a child from being stigmatized for life by a criminal record. Adults do not have to report their juvenile offenses to prospective employers.

Teaching Note: Use the Enrichment Activity, page T 144, and accompanying worksheet in the Activity Book after students have read the material in this section.

One is the community residential treatment center. Youths live in small group homes instead of being locked up in a large state institution.

In a group home, counseling helps young people feel better about themselves and their future. Psychologists and social workers help them learn to get along better with other people in their lives.

Wilderness programs. Some delinquent youths take part in tough outdoor programs. The purpose is to get them away from their neighborhood and the influences that brought them trouble.

At the Hurricane Island Outward Bound School in Maine, for example, delinquent youths go out into the wilderness. The idea of this school is that your self-esteem grows as you find that you can do difficult tasks. In the wilderness, youths discover that they have the power within them to change the way they act and to affect the world around them in positive ways. Studies have shown that programs such as these work very well for about half of all delinquent youths.

Keeping kids from becoming criminals. A large percentage of adults convicted of crimes were youths when they first got in trouble with the law. Therefore, the better our society is at preventing juvenile crime, the fewer adults the criminal justice system will have to deal with.

To fight our crime problem, it is important that all children have the chance to succeed in life within the law. In addition, those who do break the law must be given a chance to become law-abiding adults.

Answers will be found on T 144.

Section Review

1. Define *delinquent, status offender,* and *probation.*
2. How does the adjudicatory hearing differ from an adult criminal trial? How is it similar?
3. How do wilderness programs help juvenile delinquents?

Evaluation. Do you think the juvenile justice system protects the rights of the accused as well as the criminal justice system? Explain.

A BROADER VIEW

Many societies in the past have given very harsh treatment to people accused of crimes. These people had little chance to challenge the charges or to gain help in defending themselves. Punishment was often painful and swift. In some ancient societies, for example, a person caught stealing would have a hand cut off. Only a few hundred years ago, European and American women who were thought to be witches were burned alive or drowned.

In the United States today, the accused have some of the most complete rights and safeguards in history. The rights of due process, as well as the many steps that police and courts must follow, help make sure that innocent people are not punished for crimes they did not commit. In addition, people who are convicted of crimes cannot be given cruel or unusual punishments, and they are generally given the chance to return to society as normal citizens.

Teaching Note: The Evaluating Progress activity, page T 143, can be used to assess students' understanding of the chapter.

CHAPTER SURVEY

Answers to Survey and Workshop will be found on page T 145.

UNDERSTANDING NEW VOCABULARY

Seeing Relationships

The vocabulary terms in each pair listed below are related to each other. For each pair, explain what the terms have in common. Also explain how they are different.

1. *arraignment* and *indictment*
2. *probable cause* and *warrant*
3. *probation* and *parole*
4. *delinquent* and *status offender*

Putting It in Writing

Based on what you have learned about a preliminary hearing, write a short fictional conversation, or dialogue, between a judge and a district attorney during such a hearing. The district attorney is trying to convince the judge that there is enough evidence to charge the suspect with burglary. Be sure your dialogue uses the term *probable cause* and shows what it means.

LOOKING BACK AT THE CHAPTER

1. In what kind of community is the crime rate most likely to be high?
2. Why is robbery considered both a crime against a person and a crime against property?
3. Why is embezzlement a white-collar crime?
4. Why do people believe that some "victimless" crimes really do hurt innocent people?
5. What are the two responsibilities that the criminal justice system must balance?
6. What is the job of a grand jury?
7. What are some of the factors a judge considers when deciding the sentence of a lawbreaker?
8. Why do some people think that evidence obtained illegally should *not* be suppressed in court?
9. What is the difference between a preliminary hearing and a trial?
10. What is the goal of the juvenile justice system?
11. *Analysis*. How do juvenile courts differ from regular criminal courts?
12. *Synthesis*. Imagine that a city with a high crime rate suddenly receives enough money to hire as many police officers as it wishes. As the police force grows, do you think that the crime rate will drop? Why or why not?
13. *Evaluation*. Do you agree or disagree with the use of plea bargaining as a method of settling criminal cases quickly? Support your argument.
14. *Application*. How might a child's upbringing make him or her more likely to commit crimes as an adult?
15. *Evaluation*. Do you think juveniles who commit serious crimes should be treated as adults? If so, for which crimes? Explain your reasons.

WORKING TOGETHER

1. Look at different television shows for several nights in a row. Count the number of violent acts in each show. Keep track of the kinds of violence you see. As a class discuss the effect this violence might have on people.
2. Contact your local police department to find out if the crime rate in your community has increased or decreased over the last ten years. Which of the factors discussed in this chapter are most likely to have affected the crime rate?
3. In a small group, design your own community treatment program for juvenile offenders. Your goal is to help youths in trouble with the law increase their self esteem and learn how to settle conflicts peacefully. Describe what you would have participants do, and how you would measure their success.

Teaching Note: For reinforcement of decision-making skills, use Decision-Making Worksheet Chapter 19.

SOCIAL STUDIES SKILLS

Analyzing Area Graphs

You are already familiar with line, circle, and bar graphs. Each provides a good way to show a certain kind of information. What kind of graph would you use to show how many people now in your class will graduate from high school, and how many of those will graduate from college?

This kind of information can be shown on an area graph, which is good at showing smaller and smaller parts of the same original whole. Look at the area graph below. Each circle represents a percentage of the largest circle. The questions will help you analyze this area graph to find information about crime and punishment in a recent year.

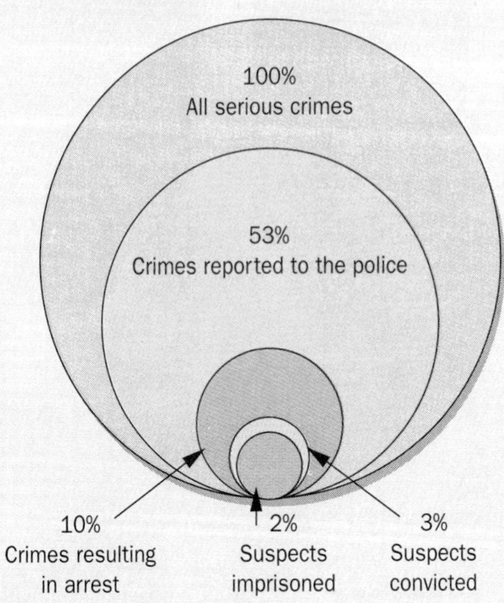

1. What percent of serious crimes in that year resulted in the suspect being convicted?

2. In that year about 13,500,000 serious crimes were reported. About how many serious crimes were probably committed?

3. For every person imprisoned for a crime, how many serious crimes are committed?

DECISION-MAKING SKILLS

Which Statements are True?

Suppose that you are taking part in a national survey on how to improve the juvenile justice system. Before you can decide what to recommend, you need accurate information. How you would check the accuracy of each of the following pieces of information? If necessary, refer to the guidelines on pages 258–259. Then answer the questions that follow.

A. A study released this year by the Office of Juvenile Justice and Delinquency Prevention shows that half of the juveniles in state detention facilities committed their offenses under the influence of drugs or alcohol.

B. During lunch you talked to a student who had spent time in the juvenile detention center. He said, "The first time in detention was only 24 hours. It was supposed to scare me straight. But it didn't work. No one can be scared into obeying the law."

C. A graph in the FBI Uniform Crime Reports for the years 1983 to 1985 shows that sixteen-year-olds committed more property crimes than any other age group.

D. A police officer told you, "Juvenile courts focus mostly on minor offenders, while the real killers get away with murder."

1. Look at the source of each statement. Which source would you consider most reliable? Explain why. Which one would you consider least reliable? Explain why.

2. What questions would you want to ask the police officer? The student?

3. What types of information would you need in order to check the accuracy of the statements made by the student and the police officer? Where might you find that information?

4. Why is it important to use accurate information when making a decision?

WINDHAM COUNTY COURT HOUSE

Chapter Themes: The main purpose of civil law is to settle disagreements fairly, based on the principles of compensation and equity. A wide range of cases are tried in civil trials. Court delays and expenses have created the need for other methods of settling civil disputes.

CHAPTER 20

Civil Justice

First you hear it—the tinkling of bells. Soon a familiar scene is taking place. Children are forming a crooked line next to a brightly colored ice cream truck. The pictures of the frozen treats look mouth-watering, and excitement fills the air.

Whenever children gather near a busy street, though, accidents are likely to happen. A recent incident in Ohio illustrates this fact.

On a summer afternoon, five-year-old Tommy heard the sounds of an ice cream truck. Clutching a handful of change, Tommy dashed out of the house. He quickly spotted the truck, which was parked near the corner on the other side of the street. His mind was busy deciding which kind of ice cream he would buy, and his eyes were fixed on the shortest route to his destination. Instead of using the crosswalk, he ran out into the street. Just then a car turned the corner and struck him.

Fortunately Tommy was not killed. However, he was badly injured. The question of who should pay his medical bills became the subject of a serious dispute. Tommy's parents blamed the driver of the car, as well as the truck driver for parking in a dangerous location. Neither driver, however, would accept responsibility for the accident. Both of them said that Tommy should have used the crosswalk. How could this disagreement be settled? Tommy's parents realized that they might have to go to court.

In this chapter you will learn about the American civil justice system, which provides a way for people to settle conflicts in a fair, orderly manner. You will read about some types of cases that are decided in civil courts, how the civil justice system works, and what problems the system is facing.

Teaching Note: Use the Introducing the Chapter activity, page T 148.

20-1

THE ROLE OF CIVIL LAW

Read to Find Out

- what the terms *lawsuits, compensation, damages, equity, injunction,* and *contracts* mean.
- what are the main principles of civil law.
- what are some kinds of civil cases.

Our civil justice system includes the judges, juries, and lawyers who help people settle conflicts according to the rules of civil law. In a typical year Americans file more than a million ***lawsuits***, or cases in which a court is asked to settle a dispute. Some people who file lawsuits believe that someone has injured them physically. Others believe that someone owes them money. Some think that their rights have been violated.

All of the people who file lawsuits have two things in common. They believe that they have been harmed, and they want the courts to do something about it. Our civil justice system is based on the idea of responsibility. Civil trials are one way to make people take responsibility for the harm they have caused others. In short, the civil justice system makes it possible for each of us to "have our day in court" if we believe that we have been wronged.

A civil case, like a criminal case, always has a plaintiff and a defendant. In a criminal case, the plaintiff is always the government. The defendant is the person or persons accused of a crime. In a civil case, however, the plaintiff is most often an individual. The defendant may be an individual, a group, a business, or even a government body. For instance, a person may sue the maker of a product that does not work. Someone may also sue the government to try to make it do or stop doing something.

Principles of Civil Law

As you already know, civil law has different purposes than criminal law. Criminal law protects society by punishing people who break the law. The main purpose of civil law, however, is not to punish wrongdoers but to settle disagreements fairly. Civil courts depend on two main principles for settling conflicts: the principle of compensation and the principle of equity.

Compensation. Under civil law a person has a right to ***compensation***, or being "made whole" for harm caused by another person's acts. Suppose someone breaks your bicycle, and you have to pay $15 to get it repaired. The person refuses to pay you back, so you decide to take him or her to court. The judge rules that the person must give you $15. This money is not a fine because it is not meant to be a punishment. Instead it is called ***damages***, money that is paid in an effort to compensate, or make up for, a loss.

Sometimes the payment of damages completely makes up for a loss. For instance, if you get the $15 you paid to repair your bike, you are back in the same place you were before the bike was broken.

In many cases, though, the payment of damages cannot completely make up for the harm done. An example would be money a court gives to a person left paralyzed by an auto accident. The money will not make the person able to walk again. Instead, it is an effort to soften the effects of the injury.

Equity. Not every problem can be settled by the payment of money. Sometimes courts rely on ***equity***, the use of general rules of fairness to settle conflicts. Suppose, for example, that

The majority of cases heard in American courtrooms today are civil cases. For a discussion of how people in other countries settle disagreements, see "A Broader View" on page 445.

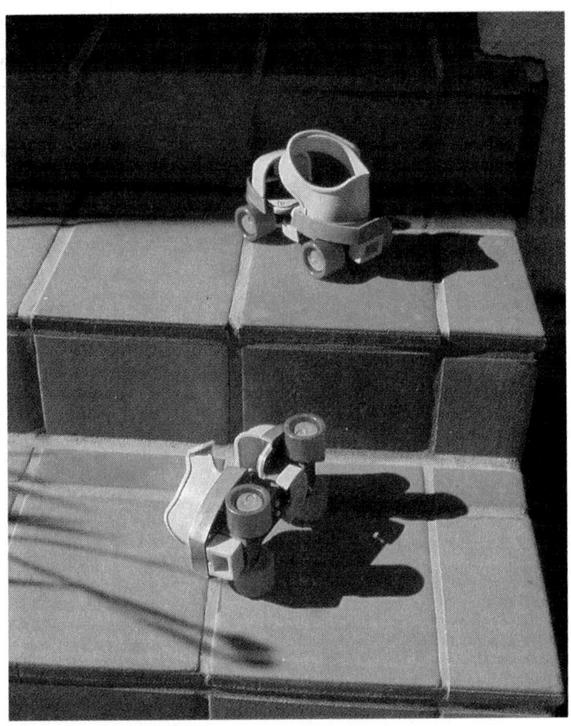

Suppose a visitor is injured by slipping on skates that a child left in a dangerous spot. The next step could be a lawsuit against the parents.

Teaching Note: For a discussion of a personal injury suit involving the New York Mets, see "Issues That Affect You: A Case Study" on pages 446–447.

bad-smelling fumes are coming from a nearby factory. Forcing the factory owners to pay money to everyone in town will not stop the smell. The dispute between the owners and the community has to be settled in a different way.

Under the rules of equity, a court may issue an ***injunction***, an order to do or not do a certain act. For instance, a court could order the factory to keep the fumes from escaping. Unlike damages, which make up for past injuries, an injunction prevents future harm.

Some Types of Civil Cases

In almost every area of our lives, problems come up that can be settled in court through compensation or equity. Many civil cases, such as Tommy's, are personal injury cases. Personal injury cases can involve both physical and mental suffering. In some cases, such as those involving plane crashes, survivors may seek compensation for emotional stress. Also, relatives of a person killed in an accident may receive payments for mental suffering if the death was caused by someone else's carelessness.

In addition to personal injury cases, there are many other types of civil cases. Some kinds that you are most likely to hear about are property cases, consumer cases, housing cases, domestic relations cases, and probate cases.

Property cases. People often want payment for damage to their property. For instance, a car owner might sue a repair shop if the car comes back with a new dent. A homeowner might sue party guests who refuse to pay for damage they did to some furniture.

Before going to court, however, a person should carefully consider whether it is fair to blame someone else for the damage. If the case comes to trial, the plaintiff must prove that the defendant did the damage either on purpose or out of carelessness.

Another common type of property case involves charges of trespassing. In many trespassing cases, a plaintiff is trying to prove that the defendant knowingly and wrongfully crossed over his or her land. Property owners do have rights, of course, and signs saying "Private Property—Keep Out" are quite common. However, laws also protect people who have good reasons for crossing someone's property. For example, the person who reads your gas meter is not trespassing. As another example, consider the following case.

For years students had been using a path through a vacant lot as a shortcut to school. José and his friends had used the path regularly, and José knew that his parents had used the path when they were students. The owners of the lot had never minded children crossing

In the 1800s and early 1900s, an employer could obtain an injunction to stop any union activities that hurt his or her business in any way. The Norris-La Guardia Act, passed in 1932, restricted federal courts from issuing injunctions to stop strikes, boycotts, and picketing that involved no violence.

In order to claim compensation for damage caused by a neighbor's fallen tree, the homeowner must prove that the tree's owner was guilty of carelessness.

their property. However, when a new owner bought the land, he decided to go to court to prevent students from using the path.

Unfortunately for the new owner, the judge ruled that the students had a right to use the path, as long as they did not damage the property. The judge's decision was based on a state law. The law said that if people have been allowed to cross a certain piece of property for 21 years in a row, the property may be crossed forever. Since no owners had objected during all that time, it was reasonable and fair for the public to expect to continue crossing the property.

Property cases may be settled through compensation or through equity. Payment of money, for instance, may make up for damage to a person's furniture. However, courts usually settle trespassing cases through equity. A court may issue an injunction ordering a defendant to stay off the plaintiff's land in the future.

Consumer cases. "This computer you sold me broke down just one week after I took it home," declared Sharon. "I want my money back."

What happens if a product does not work as it was supposed to? What can consumers do if they are misled by an advertisement or by a salesperson? What guarantees must come with products you buy?

These questions and many others related to consumers' rights are covered in a collection of laws called the Uniform Commercial Code. Many of these laws set basic rules for ***contracts***, legal agreements between buyers and sellers. The buyer promises to pay for a product or service, and the seller agrees that it will meet certain standards. Conflicts arise when either a buyer or a seller says that the other has not lived up to the contract.

In Sharon's situation, for instance, if the computer store does not settle the problem, she may decide to sue the store. If the court finds that Sharon is not to blame, it may order the store to repair or replace the computer for free. In this way, Sharon's rights as a consumer are protected by law.

Housing cases. Suppose that you live in an apartment building where the landlord refuses to repair some broken stairs. Do you have a legal right to do something about it?

Housing cases involve relationships between landlords and tenants. When you rent an apartment or a house, you usually sign a lease, an agreement stating the rights and responsibilities of the landlord and the tenant. The tenant agrees to pay rent every month, and the landlord agrees to keep the rental unit safe and in good repair.

Under civil law, a tenant and a landlord may take certain steps if either one believes that the other has not lived up to the lease. In some situations tenants can pay for needed repairs and take the cost out of the rent. If living conditions get too bad, tenants have the right to end their leases and move out without paying rent.

On the other hand, landlords who meet their responsibilities can force tenants to leave for not paying rent or violating other terms of the lease. In cases of housing law, the courts must consider the rights and responsibilities of both landlords and tenants.

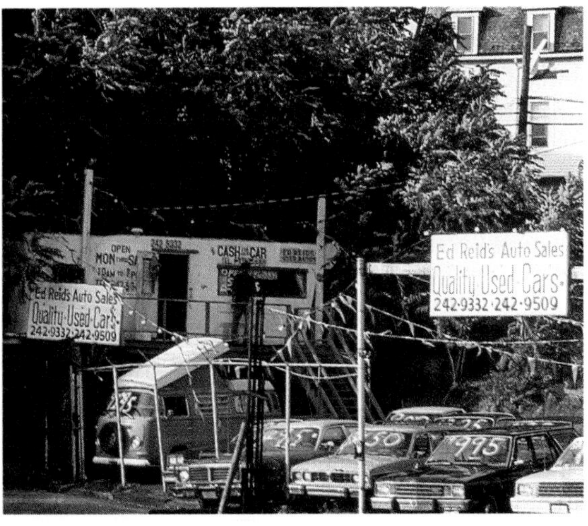

When buying a car, a customer signs a contract with the dealer. If either party breaks the terms of that contract, the other party may sue.

Domestic relations cases. Cases that concern family relationships are called domestic relations cases. Most domestic relations cases relate to divorce. The problems in divorce cases are often complicated and emotional. How will the couple divide up their property? Who will have custody of the children? Who will support them? In a divorce case, there are seldom easy answers.

In divorce cases people are not usually asking for money to make up for harm caused. Instead, they simply want to make sure that the property and the responsibilities are divided fairly.

Probate cases. Disagreements can also arise over how to divide up the property of a friend or relative who has died. Such cases are called probate cases.

Sometimes there is no will, a document that tells what is to be done with the dead person's money and other property. Usually, however, probate cases involve questions about whether the will can be trusted. Is the signature real? Was the person who made the will unfairly influenced or not thinking clearly? In probate cases, it may take years for the court to decide how to divide the property.

The Wide Range of Civil Cases

You have looked at just a few of the many types of civil cases. In fact, cases can arise over just about any area of people's lives—family relationships, school, jobs, recreation activities, and so on.

Civil courts can find ways to settle any type of disagreement. In some cases, such as property damage, the courts use compensation. Others, such as probate cases, are usually settled through equity. Sometimes courts use a combination of compensation and equity. For instance, a person who dumps trash on your land may have to pay you back for the cost of removing it. In addition, the court may issue an injunction ordering the person never to dump trash there again.

Regardless of how civil cases are settled, they all have something in common. Their goal is to make a fair settlement and to place the responsibility where it belongs.

Challenge (Synthesis): A lease is a legal agreement, or contract. Have students generate a list of precautions and actions a person should take before signing a lease.

Teaching Note: Use Teaching Activity 1, page T 148, as a culminating activity after students have read the material in Section 20-1.

Answers will be found on page T 150.

Section Review

1. Define *lawsuits, compensation, damages, equity, injunction,* and *contracts.*
2. Compare the two main principles of civil law.
3. What are the main types of civil cases?

Analysis. How does our civil justice system help to make people responsible for their actions?

20-2 CIVIL PROCEDURE

Read to Find Out

- what the terms *complaint, answer, discovery, subpoena,* and *deposition* mean.
- what steps are needed to prepare for a trial.
- how civil trials differ from criminal trials.
- why civil trials can take a long time to settle.

Civil procedure is the process followed in taking a case through the civil justice system. The federal courts and many state courts have rules about how a disagreement must be brought to trial. The purpose of these rules is to settle disputes in a fair and orderly way.

Preparing for a Civil Trial

Think back to the accident described at the beginning of this chapter. Tommy's parents thought that one or both of the drivers were responsible. The parents hired a lawyer. The lawyer tried to get either of the two drivers to pay the medical bills. When that failed, she advised the parents to go to court.

Court filings. A civil lawsuit begins with a *complaint*, a legal document that charges someone with having caused harm. The complaint, which is filed with a court, describes the problem and suggests a possible solution—damages, equity, or both. By filing a complaint against each driver, Tommy and his parents became the plaintiffs in the case.

The defendant learns about the civil lawsuit when he or she receives a copy of the complaint and a summons, an order to appear in court. Next, the defendant is permitted to tell the court his or her side of the story.

The defendant's written response to a complaint is called an ***answer.*** In the answer the defendant will either admit or deny responsibility. For example, the driver whose car hit Tommy may blame Tommy for not using the crosswalk and the ice cream truck driver for parking in a dangerous place. The driver of the ice cream truck, meanwhile, may blame both Tommy and the driver of the car.

Obtaining evidence. The next step is for the parties—the two sides in the lawsuit—to

AMERICAN NOTEBOOK

Language used by trial lawyers often confuses people who do not know legal terms. The following memo written by a defense attorney might even baffle other lawyers:

> **The appellee [plaintiff] initially filed a motion to strike appendices to Brief for Appellant [defendant] on July 22. Appellant filed a brief in response, which appellee replied to. Appellant has subsequently filed another brief on this motion, Appellant's Reply to Appellee's Reply to Appellant's Brief in Response to Appellee's Motion to Strike Appendices to Brief for Appellant (appellant's most recent brief), to which the appellee herein responds.**

Teaching Note: You may wish to use the Unit 6 Activity, "A Mock Trial," in the Activity Book after students have read the discussion of civil trials.

gather evidence. Each party has a right to know any relevant information, including information held by the other party. The process of gathering evidence before a trial is known as ***discovery.***

The purpose of discovery is to make sure that the plaintiff, defendant, and lawyers know of any evidence that might be presented at the trial. You may hear about "surprise witnesses" in movie or television courtroom dramas, but they have no place in a real civil or criminal trial.

One method of discovery is a ***subpoena*** (suh-PEE-nuh), a court order to produce a witness or document. A plaintiff who was injured when her car's brakes failed might ask for a subpoena ordering the car maker to provide written records of factory brake tests.

Information may also be gathered by asking questions. The record of answers to questions asked of a witness in person before a trial is called a ***deposition*** (dep-uh-ZISH-uhn). A court reporter is present at the interview and writes down the answers. Lawyers often use depositions to find out what witnesses will say in court. The lawyer representing Tommy and his parents, for instance, might get depositions from both drivers and from any neighbors who saw the accident.

Questions can also be mailed to a person, who must then answer them in writing. Written questions are often used to get detailed or technical information. Both depositions and written answers must be truthful. They are given under oath, just like testimony during the trial itself.

Juries and Verdicts in Civil Trials

Once the evidence has been gathered, the parties are ready for the trial to begin. As in criminal trials, witnesses are questioned, evidence is presented, and a judge makes sure that the trial proceeds in an orderly manner.

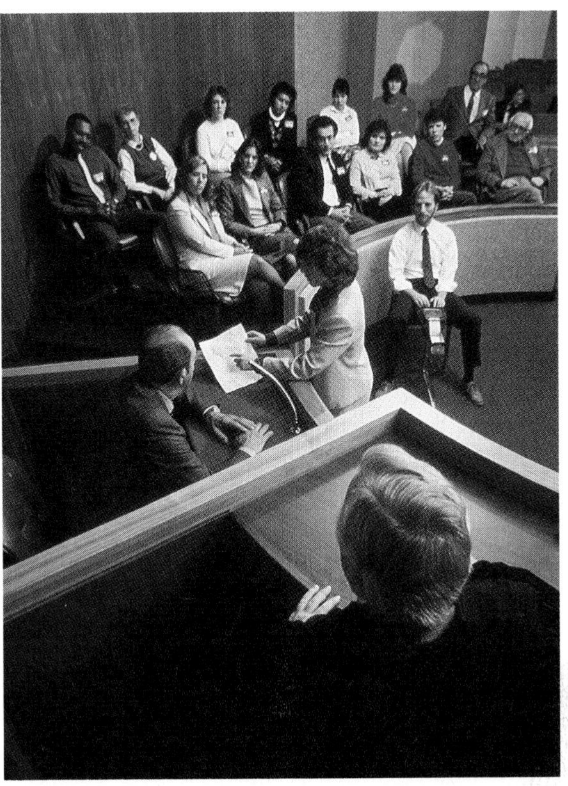

In a civil trial, as in a criminal trial, lawyers present pieces of evidence, called "exhibits," to support their arguments.

However, there are some important differences between criminal and civil trials.

First of all, there is usually more at risk in a criminal trial. Someone convicted of a crime can be sentenced to jail or prison and may even be sentenced to death. Therefore, the defendant has the right to a jury. The verdict must be based on the unanimous vote of a group of citizens rather than on the judgment of one person. A criminal case may be tried without a jury only if both parties agree.

Parties in a civil case, who run less risk, do not always have the right to a jury. Under the Constitution, federal courts must allow juries in civil cases that involve more than $20. However, over 90 percent of all civil cases are heard in state and local courts, where the

Differentiate between a summons and a subpoena. A summons notifies a defendant that he or she is being sued and will need to appear in court. A subpoena compels a witness to go to a judicial proceeding.

Challenge (Analysis): The right to a jury in civil cases is exercised mostly in compensation cases. Have students discuss reasons why juries are often preferred in these cases.

minimum amount is usually over $2,000. Furthermore, juries are used mostly for compensation cases. They are rarely used in equity cases. In any civil trial, both parties may agree to have a judge decide the case without a jury.

A jury in a civil trial is often made up of twelve people. In some states, though, there can be as few as six jurors, if both parties agree. Also, the jury does not always have to reach a unanimous decision. Agreement by three fourths of the jury is enough for a verdict in many states.

The burden of proof. Verdicts in civil cases are based on a less difficult burden of proof than in criminal cases. In a criminal case, the government must prove the defendant's guilt "beyond a reasonable doubt." In civil cases the plaintiff must prove the case only "with a preponderance [greater weight] of the evidence." The difference is like that between "probably so" and "without a doubt."

The expression "preponderance of the evidence" does not mean a greater amount of evidence. It refers to the "weight" of the evidence. In other words, the courts look at which side presents evidence that is more convincing and reasonable. You may recall that the symbol of justice holds scales, showing each side's evidence weighed on the scales of justice. The side whose evidence has the greatest "weight" should win the case.

Because of overcrowding and delays, it may be months before the courtroom door finally opens for a trial to begin.

Problems in the Civil Courts

Tommy and his parents were very happy when their trial was over. The jury decided that the ice cream truck driver was at fault because his truck had blocked the view of oncoming traffic. The jury awarded the family enough money to pay Tommy's medical bills. Still, the whole process had taken nearly two years and had been very expensive.

In 1988, lawyers and judges throughout the nation were asked what they believed were the biggest problems in the civil justice system today. A vast majority answered that lawsuits take too long and cost too much.

Court delays. Why do lawsuits often take a long time to settle? First of all, there are not enough judges and courtrooms to handle the growing number of cases being filed. In 1940, for example, the average federal judge was assigned only 190 cases a year. By 1988, however, the average number of cases was well over 400. Someone filing a lawsuit can expect to wait weeks or months before a judge has time to hear the case.

Once the trial finally starts, it can take weeks, months, or even years to settle. The average federal lawsuit takes around nine months from start to finish. However, at present there are over 20,000 federal cases that

Teaching Note: For information on lengths of civil and criminal trials, see page 588.

Civil Cases in U.S. District Courts 1945–1989

Year	Cases Begun	Non-jury Trials	Jury Trials
1945	60,965	3,561	1,704
1950	54,622	4,276	2,263
1955	59,375	4,110	2,939
1960	59,284	3,453	3,035
1965	67,678	4,459	3,154
1970	87,321	6,078	3,371
1975	117,300	7,903	3,700
1980	168,800	9,254	3,937
1985	273,700	8,817	5,437
1989	233,500	6,878	5,207

Sources: *Historical Statistics of the United States: Colonial Times to 1970; Statistical Abstract of the United States, 1991,* U.S. Bureau of the Census.

are more than three years old. Delays in state courts are sometimes much longer.

One cause of delay is the time it takes to gather evidence, especially in complicated cases. Also, selecting a jury can take a long time because both sides have to approve the members. In addition, court rules make it possible for lawyers to delay trials in ways that will help their side.

High costs. Why are trials often expensive? For many civil trials people need the help of lawyers, who understand the law and know how to prepare the case. Lawyers' fees make up much of the cost of most civil cases.

In some cases, the lawyers are paid by the hour. When there is a great deal of evidence to gather and study, and many hours to spend in court, the fees can add up. In personal injury cases, like Tommy's, the lawyer's fee is often a large percentage of the money awarded by the judge or jury. Other costs include filing fees for court papers and payments for expert witnesses, such as doctors. Of course, there is also the cost in time and inconvenience to the parties themselves.

The Need for Alternatives

Many Americans know that trials are often long and costly, but few know that most lawsuits never make it to trial. As the chart on this page shows, few cases actually get heard by a judge or jury. Plaintiffs often drop cases if they think they have little chance of winning. Sometimes what a trial will cost causes parties to settle out of court.

Also, the judge and lawyers involved in a case may strongly encourage the parties to find other ways of settling the conflict. In some states, courts will not even hear certain types of cases, such as those involving child custody, unless the parties have already tried to settle the conflict out of court.

In recent years, more and more people have been looking for ways of settling conflicts more quickly and cheaply. In the next section, you will explore some of the methods they have used.

Answers will be found on page T 150.

Section Review

1. Define *complaint, answer, discovery, subpoena,* and *deposition.*
2. How is evidence gathered for a trial?
3. How does the burden of proof in a civil trial differ from that in a criminal trial?
4. Why are civil trials often long and costly?

Analysis. Why do you think that many states do not use juries in cases involving fairly small amounts of money?

Data Search. How does the information in the chart on this page help explain why delay has become an increasing problem in our civil courts over the years?

Teaching Note: Use the Evaluating Progress activity, page T 149, and the Reinforcement Activity, page T 149, and accompanying worksheet in the Activity Book after sudents have read the material in this section.

Teaching Note: For one judge's suggestions for how people can avoid having to go to court, see "In Their Own Words" on page 450.

20-3

CHOICES IN CIVIL JUSTICE

Read to Find Out

- what the terms *mediation, arbitration,* and *small claims court* mean.
- what are some alternatives to civil trials.
- how the cost of civil trials can be reduced.
- what are some arguments for and against large awards in civil cases.

Many people go to court without being aware of the time and cost involved in a civil trial. Often they do not know about other ways to settle conflicts peacefully. In this section, you will look at some methods of settling disagreements without a civil trial. You will also see that even when people do have to go to court they can find ways to save time and money.

Avoiding Civil Trials

There are a number of ways to keep from going to trial. One possibility, of course, is for the people to discuss the problem themselves and come to an agreement. However, what happens if people cannot reach an agreement but still want to avoid a regular trial? Often they can bring in a third person to help them settle the conflict. There are three main methods for doing this: mediation, arbitration, and "rent-a-judge" programs.

Mediation. In 1981, major league baseball players went on strike. Months of discussions had failed to settle their contract dispute with club owners. The season was saved when the owners and the players agreed to settle their differences through the use of mediation.

Mediation is a process by which people agree to use a third party to help them settle a conflict. The third party, called a mediator, does not make a decision. Instead, mediation is a way to bring people together so that they can settle their own disagreement. When people ask for mediation, they are saying to the mediator, in effect, "Listen to each of us and help us reach a compromise."

In many states there are programs that train people to be mediators. Many mediation programs are sponsored by city or county courts, while others are run as private businesses. Mediation programs handle a variety of problems, including child custody, housing, and consumer problems. Mediation helps people solve their problems in an inexpensive and convenient way.

One successful program, the Community Boards Program in San Francisco, California, works mostly with problems between neighbors. It operates in over 20 different San Francisco neighborhoods. The courts and police often advise people to use the Community Boards program instead of filing a lawsuit.

Mediation can also be used to settle conflicts between students. Schools in California, Hawaii, and New York, for example, have successful mediation programs. Students in elementary schools as well as in junior and senior high schools act as official "conflict managers," helping their fellow students end disputes. In one program, a student must have 15 hours of special training before wearing a "Conflict Manager" T-shirt and formally acting as a mediator.

Arbitration. For mediation to work, both sides must be willing to compromise. No one is legally required to obey an agreement reached by mediation. Therefore, people who want a conflict settled "once and for all" often turn to ***arbitration***, the use of a third person to make a legal decision that is binding on all parties. In effect both sides are saying to the

Mediation can play an important role in relations between governments. In 1987, President Oscar Arias Sánchez of Costa Rica won the Nobel Prize for Peace for his efforts in mediating conflicts between Latin American countries.

Teaching Note: You may want to use Teaching Activity 2, page T 149, as a culminating activity after students have read the material on mediation.

third person, or arbitrator, "Listen to each of us. Then we will obey whatever decision you make."

Arbitration almost always costs less than a civil trial and is considerably faster. One reason is that the arbitrator is usually an expert on the subject in dispute. Therefore, it takes less time to hear a case and come to a decision. Another reason is that the parties save the expense of filing court papers. Also, people who choose arbitration are less likely to have cases that need lawyers.

Arbitration has become so successful that today the federal government and more than forty states have laws requiring that arbitrators' decisions be obeyed. Many courts will make arrangements for people to use arbitration. In certain conflicts involving public employees, such as firefighters or police officers, federal and state laws actually require arbitration.

Rent-a-judge programs. People can also settle conflicts through rent-a-judge programs, in which the two sides hire a retired judge to hear the case. Each side presents witnesses and evidence. After the evidence has been heard, the judge—who is known as a "referee"—gives the verdict. Many states have passed laws requiring people to obey referees' decisions.

As you can see, a rent-a-judge trial is similar in some ways to a regular trial. However, rent-a-judge trials take less time because the process of gathering evidence is less formal and therefore faster. Also, they help protect people's privacy because they are not open to the public.

Mediation, which helps people avoid going to court, also provides students with a way to settle conflicts peacefully at school.

PEOPLE MAKE A DIFFERENCE

Mediation Centers Provide Missing Links

Your neighbors' dog has been waking you up with loud barking every night. Every time you try to talk with your neighbors about the problem, they get angry. If possible, though, you want to avoid taking them to court. You decide to seek the help of a mediator.

If you lived in Albuquerque, New Mexico, chances are you would take your problem to the Metropolitan Court Mediation Center. "We don't try to determine who's right and wrong," says Cynthia Olson, director of the center. "We work on how not to make the conflict happen again."

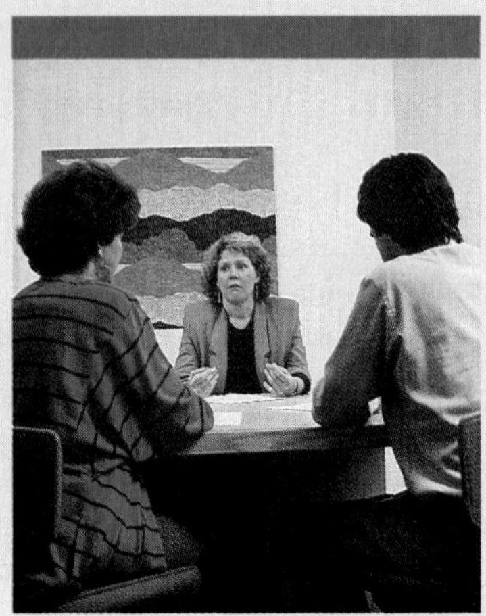

At the center, a mediator begins by listening to both sides and asking questions to get a clearer picture of the conflict. He or she then helps both parties piece together an agreeable solution. Often the parties write and sign a contract that they agree to follow.

Founded in 1986, the Metropolitan Court Mediation Center now has over 70 mediators. Volunteer mediators receive special training. These mediators make a real difference to the court in Albuquerque. They handle about 10 percent of the civil cases, which helps save both time and money. Mediators commonly handle family and neighborhood disputes, as well as conflicts involving contracts, cars, landlords and tenants, and consumer issues.

Whatever the conflict, mediators help to keep both sides talking to each other. As Cynthia Olson says, "Mediation is healthy communication."

Mock trials. Even after both sides in a conflict have filed court papers, they may change their minds and decide not to go to trial. In some cases this change of mind comes as a result of a "mock trial," a preview of how the case would probably be settled if a civil trial were held.

A mock trial has been described as a "trial on fast-forward" because there are no witnesses, and no evidence is presented. Instead, the lawyers for each side summarize their case before a jury, which then gives an unofficial verdict. The two sides do not have to follow the jury's verdict. However, they get a very good idea of what the result would be if a real trial were held. With this in mind, the parties are often able to reach a compromise without having to spend months in court.

One such mock trial involved 29 people who were suing a company for injuries. There were thousands of pages of evidence and over 160 witnesses. The judge estimated that it would take at least 18 months to settle the case. However, after a three-day mock trial and eight hours of negotiation, a $3.5 million settlement was awarded to the plaintiffs.

Cutting the Cost of Civil Trials

Although conflicts can often be settled out of court, there are still good reasons for having

Activity: Have students use the yellow pages of the local telephone directory to find out if mediation services are offered in your community.

civil trials. Sometimes one or both sides are unwilling to compromise or to accept an arbitrator or referee. Perhaps they want to make sure that the verdict or settlement can be legally enforced in any state. Often a plaintiff thinks that he or she can get a better settlement by going to trial. In such situations, a civil trial may be the only solution. A trial, however, does not always have to involve a lot of time and money.

Small claims court. When people have a conflict over a fairly small amount of money, they have a good chance of getting a quick, inexpensive trial if they use a special kind of court. ***Small claims court*** is a civil court that people may use when the amount of money they want to recover is small, usually not more than $1,000 or $2,000.

Most small claims courts are part of larger city or county courts. They are one answer to the question of how to cut the high costs of taking a case to court.

In small claims court, the whole trial may take less than five minutes, and the costs are not much more than the $5 to $10 filing fee. Usually there are no lawyers. Instead, both parties tell their stories directly to the judge. Either side can bring witnesses, but there are no formal rules for questioning them. The judge either decides the case on the spot or mails the decision to the parties in a day or two.

Prepaid legal plans. Even when a dispute involves too much money to qualify for small claims court, the costs of going to trial can still be reduced. One method is prepaid legal plans, which are like insurance policies. For a fixed yearly fee, these plans cover almost all of the costs of going to court, no matter how high. Presently, more than 12 million Americans have prepaid legal plans, and the number is growing daily.

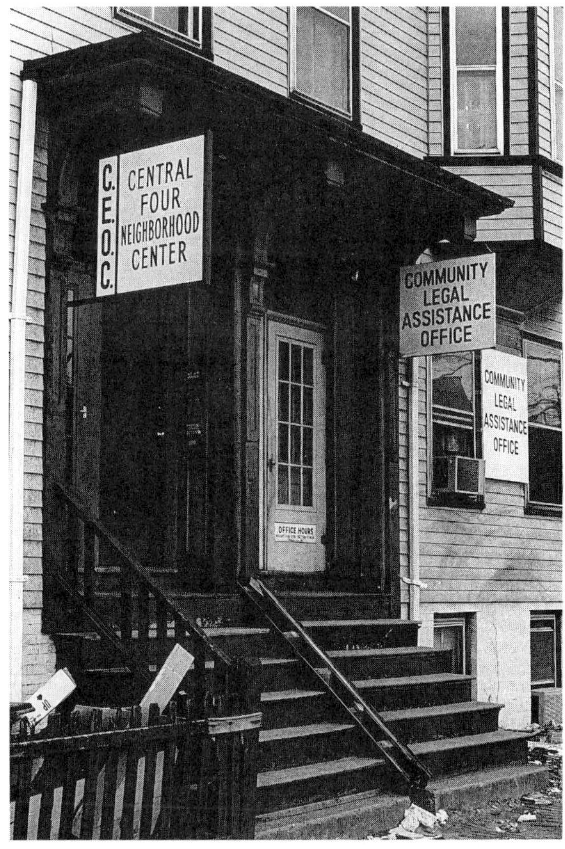

Low-cost legal services help people who otherwise could not afford lawyers' fees and the other costs of going to court.

Storefront law offices. Another trend in low-cost legal services is the "storefront law office." Storefront law offices provide legal services for low prices. These offices are usually located in convenient places such as shopping malls. They often advertise on television. One organization has more than 200 offices and a total staff of over 600 lawyers nationwide.

Traditional lawyers generally charge their clients by the hour at rates that can range from $75 to $275 per hour. Storefront offices, however, usually have a printed "menu" of set prices for specific services, such as preparing legal papers. For example, the cost to prepare a will might be $100. Because customers are

Challenge (Analysis): One reason for civil trials is to make sure verdicts or settlements can be legally enforced in any state. Have students identify kinds of cases that might require enforcement in more than one state.

In this cartoon the artist is making fun of the idea that every kind of dispute can be settled by bringing a lawsuit.

"If I make you drink your milk you'll sue me?"

Drawing by W. Miller; © 1978 *The New Yorker Magazine.*

told the total fee for services ahead of time, they are able to shop around and compare prices before selecting a lawyer.

Of course, when choosing a lawyer a person should not simply look for the least expensive one. A better guide is the advice of trusted friends who have had experience with various lawyers. A person should also look for a lawyer who is an expert in the kind of problem he or she has.

The Debate over Large Awards

In a recent civil lawsuit, a jury ordered a large company to pay $85 million in damages to several plaintiffs for accidentally spilling a dangerous chemical in their Missouri town. In 1987, a jury awarded an eight-year-old boy $95 million in damages for birth defects caused by a prescription drug his mother took while she was pregnant. When a waste-disposal business used illegal pricing to drive a competitor out of business, a jury in Vermont ordered the company to pay the competitor $6.5 million.

The large awards in these cases and in many others are the subject of a major public debate. Some people argue that such awards are needed to make up for serious losses. They also argue that the largest awards are usually paid by those who can afford to pay them, especially insurance companies representing large businesses.

Other people argue, however, that in the long run the average American consumer bears the burden of large awards. To cover their costs, businesses raise prices and insurance companies raise the rates that everyone who owns insurance must pay.

Also, some services are no longer provided because the cost of insurance is too high. For instance, many public swimming pools no longer have diving boards. Some schools do not allow certain "high-risk" sports, such as pole vaulting. Others no longer take students on field trips.

Both sides in the debate think that awards should be fair and reasonable. However, the question of what is fair and reasonable is often hard to answer. As the debate continues, a number of efforts have been made to limit the size of awards.

First of all, judges usually have the power to reduce the amount of an award made by a jury. In addition, laws have been passed that limit awards in certain types of cases. Under

Decision Making: Have students discuss how they would go about deciding whether to settle a dispute in court or out of court.

Teaching Note: Use the Enrichment Activity, page T 150, and accompanying worksheet in the Activity Book after students have read the material in this section.

federal law, for example, airlines do not have to pay more than $1,250 per person for lost baggage, no matter how much it was worth. Another federal law limits the amount of damages a person may collect when injured by an accident at a nuclear power plant.

"No-fault" auto insurance plans are another way to avoid large awards. Under these plans, people hurt in auto accidents do not sue the person responsible for their injuries. Instead, their medical bills are paid directly by their own insurance companies. In many cases, this means that the parties do not have to go to court.

To Sue or Not to Sue?

As you have seen, the civil justice system is burdened with many cases. Civil trials are often long and costly. People may have to wait months before their trial can start. Once the trial has begun, months or even years may pass before the case is finally settled.

In short, people involved in a conflict should think carefully about what is the best way to settle it. Going to court may be the best solution in some cases. However, many judges and lawyers agree that people should first explore whether other methods might work, such as mediation, arbitration, or other alternatives. In many cases, going to court may be the last, not the first, resort.

Answers will be found on page T 150.

Section Review

1. Define *mediation, arbitration,* and *small claims court.*
2. Describe two of the ways in which people can settle conflicts without going to trial.
3. When people have to go to court, how might they reduce the cost?
4. Why do some people criticize large awards in civil cases?

Evaluation. Give an example of a conflict that you think would be best settled in court. Give an example of one that you think would be best settled out of court. Give reasons to support your opinion.

A BROADER VIEW

Americans often turn to the courts to make people take responsibility for the harm they have caused. In many countries, however, conflicts are usually settled in more informal ways, such as mediation and arbitration.

In some countries, such as China and Japan, it is considered shameful to sue someone. In this view, public trials disrupt the harmony of society. Recently, for instance, a Japanese couple collected $24,000 in damages from a babysitter who carelessly allowed their three-year-old daughter to drown. The lawsuit got much attention, and the couple received angry letters from thousands of Japanese. Finally, in disgrace, the couple returned the money to the babysitter.

In other nations civil trials may not be thought disgraceful. However, many countries, including France, West Germany, and Italy, depend on trials less than we do. Legal experts have studied why different countries have different attitudes toward civil trials. However, there are no clear-cut explanations. The reasons are rooted deep in the different cultures and in different traditions of how to best maintain justice and order in society.

Under traditional insurance principles, the right to be compensated for injuries in an automobile accident is based on clear evidence of negligence by a specific party or parties. Many experts consider this principle to be slow, expensive, and impractical.

Personal Injury Suits

The batter swung, getting a piece of the fastball. The ball, however, flew back into the stands, hitting Mrs. Uzdavines on the side of the face.

Later, Mrs. Uzdavines explained that she had just at that instant turned to say something to her husband, who was sitting beside her. "It happened so fast," she said.

Mr. Uzdavines recalled counting at least six holes in the screen.

Getting hit by a foul ball was the last thing Mrs. Uzdavines had expected that evening. She and her family had looked forward to an exciting baseball game at Shea Stadium in New York between the New York Mets and the Philadelphia Phillies.

They had really good seats, too—right behind home plate. They were less than forty feet from the batter. Fans in this area of the ballpark were supposed to be protected from any foul tips by a huge protective screen.

As it turned out, however, the screen had holes in it. Mr. Uzdavines recalled counting at least six holes in the screen when he returned to his seat after taking his wife to the first aid station. Aware of the holes, the entire family moved to safer seats for the rest of the game.

Mrs. Uzdavines's injury was emotionally as well as physically painful. She believed that the accident would not have occurred if the protective screen had been kept in good repair. She claimed it was the responsibility of the New York Mets management to see to it that the facilities at Shea Stadium were safe and in good condition for the baseball season. Therefore, Mrs. Uzdavines decided to file a civil lawsuit against the Mets for being careless in carrying out their responsibility.

The Mets, however, did not believe that their carelessness had caused the accident. In court, they argued that when people attend a

sporting event, they "assume the risk" that an object such as a baseball could fly into the crowd. It would be impossible, they said, for the operators of a baseball park to construct safety screens which could protect every person in every seat from such harm. Moreover, said the Mets, the fans are aware of this fact when they attend a game.

The court, however, ruled in favor of Mrs. Uzdavines. It said the Mets would have to pay her damages. The size of this sum of money would be determined later.

The legal concept of "assumption of risk" is often used to avoid a finding of negligence on a wrongdoer's part when the person injured has put himself or herself in "an inherently dangerous" situation. Have students give examples of "assumption of risk" situations.

Answers will be found on page T 151.

Explaining its decision, the court said that the Mets did have the responsibility to keep the safety net in good repair. The fans who were watching the game from behind home plate, it said, normally would have thought that they were seated in a safe place.

To reach this conclusion, the court looked to see how other courts in New York had decided this same kind of question. The court paid particular attention to a similar case, *Akins* v. *Glenn Falls School District*, that had been decided just the year before.

In that case, Robin Akins had gone with some friends to watch a baseball game at her high school. The field was equipped with a backstop 24 feet high and 50 feet wide. Behind the backstop were bleachers which could seat about 120 people. In addition, two three-foot-high chain link fences ran from each end of the backstop along the base lines of the field.

Robin and her friends chose to watch the game from seats behind the chain link fence near third base. During the game, a foul ball struck Robin in the eye. She filed a civil suit against the school for failing to provide safe and proper screening along the base lines to protect spectators.

The court deciding the *Akins* case said that the owner of a baseball field must provide a safety screen only in the most dangerous place—the area behind home plate. Because Robin chose not to sit behind the backstop, she had "assumed the risk" that she could be hit by a stray ball. Therefore, she could not hold the school responsible for her injury.

The Mets argued that when people attend a sporting event, they "assume the risk."

However, the court also said that any safety screen must be in good repair so that people sitting behind it are protected. The court deciding Mrs. Uzdavines's case took careful note of this part of the earlier decision.

The New York Mets had not kept their safety screen in good repair. The court reasoned that while some fans want to watch a baseball game without a screen or net in front of them, those who choose to sit behind a screen have the right to expect that their seats are in a completely safe location.

Analyzing the Case

1. Why did the Mets believe that they were not responsible for Mrs. Uzdavines's injury?
2. What was the ruling in the Akins case that the court followed as precedent?
3. Do you think that the court made the correct decision in this case? Why or why not?
4. Do you think that the court would have decided the case differently if the net had been in good repair but the foul ball had torn a hole in the net before it hit Mrs. Uzdavines? Explain your answer.

Activity: Ask students to walk around the school to look for activities and/or structures that put people at risk and to find precautions that keep people safe. Notify the administration of any safety concerns students identify.

CHAPTER SURVEY

Answers to Survey and Workshop will be found on page T 151.

UNDERSTANDING NEW VOCABULARY

Seeing Relationships

The vocabulary terms in each pair listed below are related to each other. For each pair, explain what the two terms have in common. Also explain how they are different.

1. *damages* and *injunction*

2. *complaint* and *answer*

3. *arbitration* and *mediation*

Putting It in Writing

Think of a case that could be settled through both compensation and equity. Imagine that you are a lawyer. Write a complaint to be filed with the civil court in your city or town. Be sure to describe what happened, why you think the other person was responsible, and what settlement you are seeking. Use the following terms in your complaint: *compensation, damages, equity, injunction.*

LOOKING BACK AT THE CHAPTER

1. Explain how both equity and compensation are ways of making people take responsibility for their actions.

2. How does compensation differ from equity?

3. Pick three types of civil cases and name some of the types of conflicts that they deal with.

4. Explain what discovery is and why it is important.

5. How is a civil trial similar to and different from a criminal trial?

6. Why are civil courts overcrowded?

7. Pick two alternatives to regular civil trials and explain how they can be used to settle conflicts in a quicker, less costly way.

8. How can people save time and money when they have to go to trial?

9. *Application.* Give your own example of each of the following:
(a) a case settled by compensation
(b) a case settled by equity
(c) a case settled by both compensation and equity
Your examples can be real cases or ones that you make up.

10. *Analysis.* How are mediation, arbitration, and "rent-a-judge" programs similar and different?

11. *Synthesis.* What additional steps do you think might be taken to solve the problem of overcrowded courts? Explain how these steps would help.

12. *Evaluation.* Do you think that large awards in civil cases are fair? Support your opinion with reasons.

WORKING TOGETHER

1. Look through recent newspapers and magazines to find articles about three civil cases that you find interesting. Prepare a report on the cases. Tell what the main issues were in each case and how you think each case should be decided. For any case that was already decided, explain why you agree or disagree with the verdict.

2. Working in groups of eight, prepare and act out a civil trial in front of the class. Decide who should play the roles of judge, plaintiff, defendant, the plaintiff's lawyer, the defendant's lawyer, a witness for the plaintiff, and a witness for the defendant. You might have the rest of the class act as a jury.

3. In groups of three or four, plan a mediation program for your school. Decide how it would be started, how mediators would be trained, and what would been done if a student refused to cooperate with a mediator. Then compare your plan with those of other groups.

SKILLS WORKSHOP

Teaching Note: For reinforcement of decision-making skills, use Decision-Making Worksheet Chapter 20.

SOCIAL STUDIES SKILLS

Interpreting Comic Strips

Many cartoonists use humor to make observations or comments about life and politics in the United States and in other nations. In the comic strip below, cartoonist Jim Unger pokes fun at how some Americans use the civil justice system.

1. Comic strips tell a story or create a situation with just a few words and pictures. What situation does the cartoonist create here?

2. Cartoonists often make a situation funny by taking it to extremes. What is extreme about this situation?

3. In the cartoonist's view, who is the innocent victim in this situation? How does the cartoonist show this?

4. What do you think is the main message the cartoonist is trying to get across?

DECISION-MAKING SKILLS

Which Sources Can You Trust?

Suppose that your class is staging a mock trial and that you are the judge. It is a civil case in which parents are having a conflict with their fourteen-year-old son over the money the son is earning through a part-time job. The parents claim that they have the right to use all of their son's earnings to cover family expenses. They want their son's employer to send the wages directly to them. The son claims that the money belongs to him.

Before you can give your verdict, you need information about the laws that relate to this type of case. Determine which of the following sources would be most reliable on the issue of parents' rights to their children's earnings. If necessary, review page 146.

A. A book titled *You and the Law: A Practical Guide to Everyday Law and How It Affects You and Your Family*. The book was written by a dean of one of the top law schools in the nation. Now in its tenth edition, the book was first published in 1971.

B. A conversation you had with your boss, the manager of a fast-food restaurant. She has taken a course in business law at the local community college. Also, she has been in charge of the restaurant's payroll for five years.

C. A friend who says that his cousin had a similar conflict. The cousin read a magazine article which stated that children have a right to keep their wages.

1. Which one of the sources described above would be most reliable on the issue of parents' rights to their children's earnings? Explain why.

2. Explain in your own words how to determine the reliability of a source.

3. When making a decision, why is it helpful to determine the reliability of the sources you use for your information?

IN THEIR OWN WORDS

Justice Richard Neely: Court As the Last Resort

Answers will be found on page T 153.

No one in the United States is more aware of the problem of overcrowded courts than the people who actually hear the cases—the judges. Often judges have suggestions for how people can avoid having to go to court.

The following advice is from Richard Neely, who worked as a lawyer before becoming a judge and later Chief Justice of the West Virginia Court of Appeals.

> To the maximum extent possible, people should rely on their own private systems for self-preservation rather than courts. . . . While the ideal of conflict avoidance and self-reliance cannot always be realized, it can be realized more often than is currently the case. . . .
>
> Starting with simple things, a cheap burglar alarm is better protection against thieves than the police. The object of a burglar alarm is not to alert the neighbors or the police but to frighten the burglar . . . before he does any damage. The ringing of a loud bell has a chilling effect on a burglar's incentive [desire] to browse through the bureaus and closets of a house. It is a more effective deterrent than the cop on the beat.
>
> In many communities, volunteer neighborhood watches seem to be successful in deterring crime. . . .

> Where people must live in a high-crime area, a little community initiative can bring substantial returns. . . .
>
> On the civil side, it is very difficult to avoid domestic-relations courts, although a majority of divorcing couples more or less settle their differences [in a friendly way]. . . . Yet it is possible to avoid being a plaintiff in court by being careful with whom one does business. No one should rely on a written contract as a guarantee of satisfactory performance. A personal relationship with the people with whom one does business, the reputation of the company for satisfying its customers, and the [hope] of a profitable business relationship in the future are what good business relations depend upon. . . .
>
> [Former Supreme Court Justice] Felix Frankfurter once observed that the best way of resolving conflict is to avoid it. That is the type of remark that any judge will make after a few years on the bench. . . . Going to court should always be the last, not the first, resort.

From Richard Neely, Why Courts Don't Work. *New York: McGraw-Hill, 1983.*

Analyzing Primary Sources

1. Justice Neely says that people should depend on "their own private systems for self-preservation rather than courts." What does he mean by this?
2. What are two examples that Justice Neely gives of methods of "self-preservation" against crime? Explain why each of these methods can help in preventing crimes from being committed.
3. Do you agree with Justice Neely that going to court should always be the last resort in settling a conflict? Support your opinion with reasons.
4. If more people followed Justice Neely's advice, what do you think would be the effect on the court system?
5. Now that you have read Justice Neely's account, what is one question you would want to ask him about what he has written? Explain why you would want to ask this question.

Activity: Have students draw a series of cartoons to show behaviors and beliefs that will keep them out of court if they follow Justice Neely's advice.

UNIT SURVEY

Answers will be found on page T 153.

LOOKING BACK AT THE UNIT

1. Name two purposes of laws and explain how those purposes relate to both criminal law and civil law.

2. How do the purposes of criminal and civil law differ?

3. Describe some problems facing the criminal and juvenile justice systems.

4. Describe some problems facing the civil justice system.

TAKING A STAND

The Issue

Should the death penalty be outlawed?

It is called death row. In prison cells across the nation, over 1,200 people wait to be executed for committing murder and other serious crimes. They have been sentenced to die in the gas chamber, by electrocution, or by drug injection. Many have been on death row for months or years as their lawyers appeal the death sentences. Meanwhile, the public debate continues over whether the death penalty, also called capital punishment, should be allowed at all.

Opponents of the death penalty argue that putting someone to death for a crime is "cruel and unusual punishment," which is forbidden by the Eighth Amendment to the Constitution. Opponents also argue that using violence to punish criminals is not the right way to discourage violent behavior such as murder. They point out that many nations, including Canada and most European and Latin American countries, have outlawed the death penalty as being uncivilized. The United States urges other countries to respect "human rights," they say. What is more basic than the right to life?

In response, supporters of the death penalty say that it actually protects life by making people think twice about committing murder. They also argue that criminals sentenced to death are simply getting what they deserve. A person must respect the right of others to live. Those who kill deserve to be killed.

Supporters of capital punishment also note that the Supreme Court has ruled in favor of the death penalty as long as it is applied fairly. Furthermore, they say, the methods of execution are quick and relatively painless and are therefore not cruel.

Supporters admit that there is no clear proof that capital punishment reduces the number of murders. After all, murder rates in states with the death penalty are the same as in states that have outlawed it. Nevertheless, they point out, punishment is the only threat the government has, and most people fear death more than any other punishment. Furthermore, murderers who have served their prison terms sometimes go out and kill again. The death penalty, supporters argue, is the best way to protect the public.

Opponents reply that even if the death penalty were to discourage some people from committing murder, it is not being applied fairly. Criminals who are executed are mostly poor and non-white. Opponents also point out the risk that an innocent person could be executed. Obviously, an innocent person who has been imprisoned can later be freed. The same is not true for a person who has been put to death.

Expressing Your Opinion

Find out what your state's law is on capital punishment. Then write a one-page letter to your representative in the state legislature explaining why you support or oppose the law. Include not only reasons to support your position but also arguments against the opposing side. Close your letter by urging your representative to either support the current law or to work to have it changed.

UNIT 7

Unit Quotations: Like eighteenth-century French philosopher Rousseau, President Kennedy thought a great deal about the vital role that citizens play in a democracy. Kennedy knew this quotation from Rousseau and made its message part of his inaugural address in 1961.

PEOPLE MAKE A DIFFERENCE

Participating in Our Democracy

As soon as any[one] says of the affairs of the state, What does it matter to me? the state may be given up as lost.

—Jean-Jacques Rousseau

And so, my fellow Americans, ask not what your country can do for you; ask what you can do for your country.

—President John F. Kennedy

As you read these words, can you think of ways to participate in our democracy? You have seen that our government is built on the belief that people should govern themselves. As Rousseau said, a society cannot work well unless its citizens care about the "affairs of the state." What did he mean? How would you respond to President Kennedy's statement?

In Unit 7 you will take a look at ways in which Americans, as a group and as individuals, make a difference in government. You will see how people can play their citizen roles through political parties, through voting and running for public office, and through helping solve the problems that face our society.

NORTH CAROLINA
IDAHO
BUSH '88
BUSH QUAYLE
BUSH QUAYLE
GEORGE BUSH '88
GEORGE BUSH '88
GEORGE BUSH '88

Chapter Themes: Political parties help make our government work. Parties also help citizens fulfill their responsibilities in our democracy. The most important role of political parties is selecting the candidates who will run for office.

CHAPTER 21

Political Parties in Our Democracy

"Hey, isn't your eighteenth birthday next week?" Marta asked Tony.

"That's right," Tony replied.

"Great. That means you can vote in the next election if you register soon enough."

"I hadn't thought of that. Gosh, I don't even know how to register. And how am I supposed to know who to vote for?"

"I don't know exactly how you register either,"said Marta, "but I'm pretty sure you'll have to decide whether you're going to be a Democrat or a Republican. I think I'll probably register as a Republican."

"How come?"

"Well, my parents are Republicans and I kind of liked the Republicans who ran in the last election. My dad even helped out with one candidate's campaign for representative."

"Hmm. My mom's a Democrat, but she voted for several Republicans in the last election," Tony said. "Do I really have to register one way or the other?"

"I'm not sure. I think what's most important is to register so that you can vote."

"Well," said Tony, "I guess I need to find out more about what the parties stand for and what they do. I think I'd like to register with a party so that I could learn more about its candidates."

"It's up to you," replied Marta. "Let me know what you decide."

In this chapter, you will learn what a political party is and how parties help government and citizens. You will read about the two-party system in the United States and the similarites and differences between the two parties. Finally, you will study how we nominate candidates for public office.

Teaching Note: Use the Introducing the Chapter activity, page T 155.

21-1

THE ROLE OF POLITICAL PARTIES

Read to Find Out

- what the terms *political party, nominate, platform, planks,* and *canvass* mean.
- how political parties help government.
- how political parties link citizens to government.

People want many things from government. They want their rights protected. They want to feel secure against poverty and unemployment. They want to be treated fairly in business, at work, and in the courts. They want a clean environment. Many want government to pass laws or to pay for specific programs that they believe are important, such as education for the handicapped, product safety, gun control, or finding a cure for cancer.

Alone, an individual may feel powerless to make his or her wants, needs, and ideas known. Acting together, however, groups of people can often have a greater effect than individuals acting alone. You saw in Chapter 3 how Peter Ky was able to convince the school board to take action on recycling. He formed a group. On page 175 you read about David and Reba Saks, who formed OUT in order to be heard.

On a larger scale, people form groups called political parties in order to influence government. A ***political party*** is an organization of citizens who wish to influence and control government by getting their members elected to office. Party members share similar ideas about what they want government to do. If a party can put enough of its members into office, that party can have a major effect on the policies and programs of the government.

It has been said that parties are the oil that makes the machinery of American democracy work. Indeed, parties play a key role in government and provide opportunities for citizens to take part in the political process.

How Parties Help Government

You are probably aware of the active competition between the two main political parties in the United States, the Republican party and the Democratic party. You may even have heard Republicans criticizing Democrats or Democrats complaining about Republicans. Even Thomas Jefferson, who helped start the Democratic party, said, "If I could not get to heaven except with a political party, I would not go there at all." Are parties really useful? The answer is yes.

Parties help government at the local, state, and national levels in a number of ways. As you will see, they select candidates for many public offices. They set goals for the government and provide leadership to reach those goals. Political parties also keep an eye on each other, a function much like the checks and balances you learned about earlier.

Selecting candidates. A major way in which political parties help govern is to ***nominate***, or name candidates to run for public office. Parties take the responsibility for finding and nominating qualified candidates.

There are over half a million elected positions in the local, state, and national governments of the United States. Some public offices, especially in local government, are nonpartisan, which means that the candidates do not declare themselves to be members of a political party when running for office. For example, judgeships and seats on school boards and city councils are often nonpartisan offices. However, most offices are partisan. The candidates for these offices run as

In the 1980s, part of the Republican party platform was a commitment to a "drug-free America." The Just Say No to Drugs program was one way the party backed up this position.

members of political parties. If elected, they try to carry out the party's programs.

Parties try to choose candidates who have the ability and experience to lead well and who can gain enough public support to get elected. Later you will take a closer look at the actual process by which parties nominate candidates.

Setting goals. A political party establishes positions on issues and sets goals for government. Each party has a ***platform***, a statement of a party's official stand on major public issues. The platform is made up of ***planks***, position statements on each specific issue in a party's platform. These planks are often turned into government programs by party members who are elected to office.

Providing leadership. Parties help provide day-to-day leadership in government. Leadership is necessary to make the laws and carry out the programs that citizens want. You saw in Chapter 8 that party members in Congress select majority and minority floor leaders and whips to provide leadership in making laws. Parties work in much the same way in state legislatures, too.

Political parties also provide leadership in the executive branch of government. The political party of the executive—the President or governor—is referred to as the party "in office." The executive often appoints loyal members of the party in office to high government posts. They are then in a position to help shape government programs and policies.

Parties as "watchdogs." Political parties also play an important "watchdog" role in government. After an election, the party not in power (the party "out of office" or the minority party in a legislature) makes sure that the public knows when the party in power is not living up to its promises.

Parties keep tabs on the behavior of members of the other party and are eager to report any wrongdoing. The watchdog function of parties helps government by making sure that

The platform represents the party's official stand on major public issues. Because individuals within the party may disagree on issues, there is always the potential for the party to become divided over particular planks.

members of the party in power are honest and hard-working.

How Parties Help Citizens

You have seen the ways in which political parties help make our government work. Parties also help citizens fulfill their responsibilities in our democracy. Parties link citizens to their government by making their voices heard and providing ways for them to participate. Parties also inform citizens and can help make political decision making easier.

Giving citizens a voice in government. One reason why people form political parties is that parties provide a way for citizens to be heard.

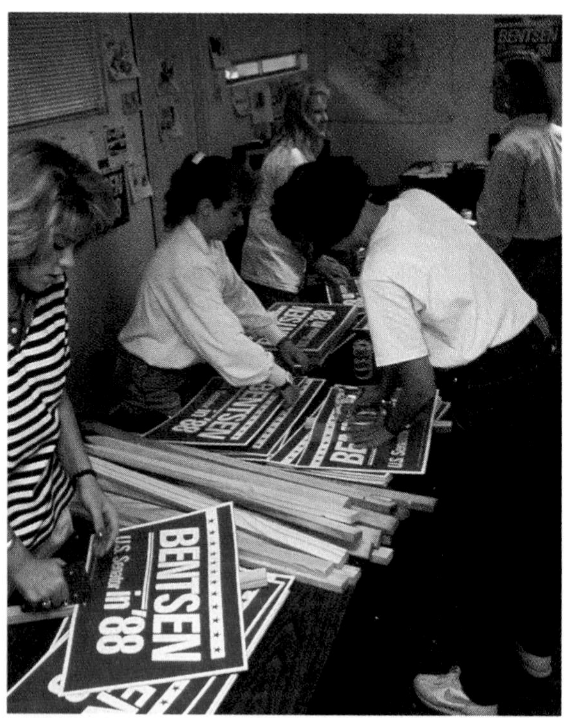

Volunteers of all ages are needed to run a successful campaign. These workers are helping out at campaign headquarters.

Edie Stevenson, the county chairperson of her political party, describes her experience:

> When I accepted the job as county chair, few people in our county were aware of what the party stood for. So we wrote short statements of our policies on such topics as education and the environment. Then we held a series of community meetings. The people who came really spoke up about what was most important to them. We rewrote some of our statements based on what we learned about people's concerns. Our candidates discovered that the meetings were a good way to keep up on what people around here want from government.

Do political parties really reflect what citizens want? Edie's experience shows that at the local level parties can help give citizens a voice in government. At the state and national levels, party members help hammer out the party platform, debating and deciding on the issues.

Informing citizens. By writing policy statements, Edie's party was helping to provide citizens in her county with information—facts, figures, and party stands on various important issues. Some other ways parties inform citizens are by sending out mailings and giving information to newspapers, radio, and television.

A more personal way in which parties inform citizens is by arranging meetings with candidates. Party members and volunteers also ***canvass***, or go door-to-door handing out information and asking people which candidates they support.

Parties canvass and provide information in order to encourage people to vote for their candidates. However, by making information available to voters, parties can also help simplify political decision making. If a voter agrees with a party's point of view or its stand on a particular issue, he or she can vote on the

Challenge (Application): Have students discuss the following question: How can students who are not yet of voting age fulfill the role of citizen by involvement in a political party?

Teaching Note: Use Teaching Activity 1, page T 155, as a culminating activity after students have read the material in Section 21-1.

basis of the party. At election time Edie's party published "Voters' Tip Sheets"—the collection of statements they had prepared. They found that people who agreed with what the party stood for felt comfortable supporting most of the party's candidates.

Involving citizens. Political parties provide citizens with a variety of ways to get involved in the political process. To be successful, a party needs the help of many people, especially at election time. Campaign volunteers write letters and pamphlets and send them to voters. They raise money and hold picnics and other events at which candidates can meet voters. They make phone calls and canvass neighborhoods. On election day, volunteers remind people to vote and may even drive them to the polls.

You are free to choose how active a role you want to play in a political party. Your level of involvement will depend on many factors, including how important the party is to you and how strongly you feel about a candidate or issue.

As a citizen, it is both your right and responsibility to participate in government. Working through a party is one way to play your citizen role.

Answers will be found on page T 157.

Section Review

1. Define *political party, nominate, platform, planks*, and *canvass.*
2. List four ways in which political parties help government.
3. What are some ways in which political parties help citizens get involved in government?

Analysis. How can political parties be seen as the oil that makes the machinery of American democracy work?

21-2
OUR TWO-PARTY SYSTEM

Read to Find Out

- what the terms *precincts, patronage, straight ticket, split ticket*, and *independent voters* mean.
- how our two-party system developed.
- how the two major parties are different and similar.
- how party strength has changed.

Even though political parties are an important part of American government, they are not mentioned in the United States Constitution. In fact, George Washington feared that conflict between political parties might destroy the new democracy. He warned against "the baneful [harmful] effects of the spirit of party" in his farewell address in 1796.

However, even at the birth of our nation, Americans were banding together in groups, each with different ideas about the role of government. There were those who supported a strong central government (Federalists) and those who feared it (Anti-Federalists). The first political parties arose out of these different views of the role of government.

A Brief History

Alexander Hamilton, President Washington's Secretary of the Treasury, led the first political party, the Federalist party. The Federalists, who wanted a strong national government, had the support of merchants and bankers. The party's power declined in the early 1800s.

The rival of the Federalists was the Democratic-Republican party, led by Thomas Jefferson. This party opposed a strong national government and supported the power of the

During his first administration, Washington tried to bring Hamilton and Secretary of State Jefferson into agreement and prevent the growth of political parties. However, Washington's support of Hamilton's fiscal policies led to Jefferson's resignation in 1793 and increasing political divisions.

AMERICAN NOTEBOOK

You might recognize the donkey and the elephant as the symbols of the Democratic and Republican parties. Where do these symbols come from? They were first used by cartoonist Thomas Nast in 1874.

Nast got the idea for the donkey from Populist Ignatius Donnelly's comment, "The Democratic party is like a mule—without pride of ancestry nor hope of posterity [future generations]."

Nast first used the elephant to represent the Republican vote. Later it came to stand for the party itself. Why the elephant? Democrat Adlai Stevenson's opinion was that "the elephant has a thick skin, a head full of ivory, and . . . [it] proceeds best by grasping the tail of its predecessor."

individual states. The Democratic-Republican party had the support of farmers and frontier settlers. In 1828, under the leadership of Andrew Jackson, the party took the name the Democratic party. The Democrats gained support from immigrant workers as well as farmers.

The Whig party, organized in 1834, opposed the Democrats. The Whigs believed in a strong legislative branch of government. With the support of business leaders, the Whigs were successful in getting their candidate, William Henry Harrison, elected president in 1840. The Whigs and the Democrats remained rivals until the early 1850s.

Democrats and Republicans. Our current two-party system emerged in 1854. In that year the Republican party was born, replacing the Whigs as a major party. It was formed by groups opposed to slavery. It supported business interests and at first was purely a party of the North.

In 1860, Abraham Lincoln became the first Republican President. The Republican party remained the majority party from the Civil War until the Great Depression of the 1930s. It dominated both the presidency and the Congress during those years.

A major shift in party power began in 1932 when Franklin D. Roosevelt, a Democrat, was elected President. Roosevelt's New Deal programs were designed to bring the country out of the depression. The Democrats had the support of farmers, laborers, immigrants, and much of the educated middle class. Except for the years 1953 to 1961, Democrats held the presidency until 1969. They have also dominated Congress.

The timeline on this page shows the five major political parties and the years they held the presidency. In spite of Washington's warn-

Major Political Parties in the United States

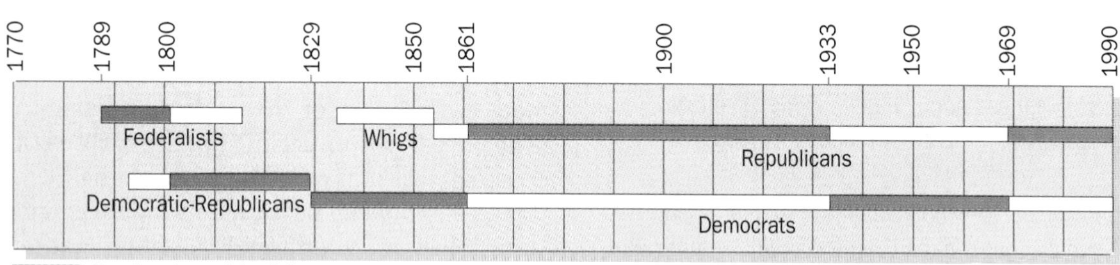

ing, political parties are an important part of the way our government works. For more than 130 years the two major parties have been the Democrats and the Republicans.

The Role of Third Parties

Even though ours is a two-party system, third parties do arise, especially during presidential election years. Sometimes a third party forms to support a cause or idea. When the Republican party formed in opposition to slavery, it was actually a third party to the Democrats and the Whigs. Another example of a third party formed around ideas was the Populist party. Active in the late 1800s and early 1900s, the Populist party favored social and government reforms.

A second reason why a third party forms is to back a candidate, often one who splits from a main party. In 1912, former President Theodore Roosevelt failed to win the Republican nomination for President. With a strong following, Roosevelt formed the Progressive, or "Bull Moose," party. The Bull Moose party disappeared after Roosevelt lost the election.

Third party candidates face many problems. It may be difficult to get on the ballot because election laws in many states favor the two major parties. People often hold back from giving money because they doubt that a third party candidate can win. Also, even people who agree with the third party's ideas often decide that voting for its candidate would be wasting their vote.

The importance of third parties. Even though third parties rarely win many votes, they still play an important role in American politics. A third party candidate can change the outcome of an election by drawing votes away from one of the main parties. In 1912 Theodore Roosevelt won many votes that would otherwise have gone to the Republican candidate, President William Howard Taft. As a result, Woodrow Wilson, a Democrat, won the 1912 election.

Senator Robert La Follette, the Progressive party's candidate for President in 1924, addresses women voters from the steps of his home.

Third parties can also play a key role by bringing up new ideas or pressing for action on certain issues. If these ideas gain enough popular support, major parties might adopt them in a campaign or as a part of public policy. For example, the Seventeenth Amendment to the Constitution, which provides for the direct election of senators, grew out of ideas of the Populist party.

Characteristics of Today's Parties

If you asked several Democrats what their party stands for today, you would probably get several different answers. The same thing would happen if you asked Republicans. Some people would describe strong party values and beliefs. Others would tell you about

There have been three major types of third parties in the United States: single-issue parties like the Prohibition party; total-change parties like the Socialist Worker party; and personality parties such as Teddy Roosevelt's Bull Moose party.

Selected 1988 Party Platform Statements

Democratic Party 	Republican Party 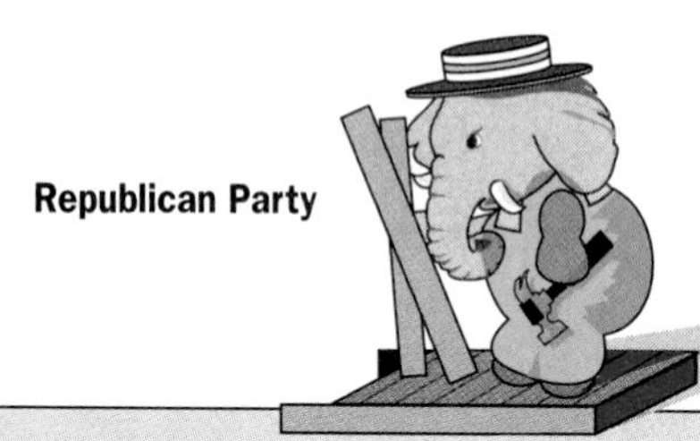
The Economy	
We believe that the time has come for America to take charge once again of its economic future, to reverse seven years of "voodoo economics," "trickle down" policies, fiscal irresponsibility, and economic violence against poor and working people. . . .	Our nation of communities is prosperous and free. in the sixth year of unprecedented economic expansion, more people are working than ever before; real family income has risen; inflation is tamed. By almost any measure, Americans are better off than they were eight years ago. The Reagan Revolution has become a Republican renaissance.
The Family	
We believe it is time for America to change and move forward again in the interest of all its families—to turn away from an era in which too many of America's children have been homeless or hungry and invest in a new era of hope and progress, an era of secure families in a secure America in a secure world.	Strong families build strong communities. They make us a confident, caring society by fostering the values and character—integrity, responsibility, sharing and altruism—essential for the survival of democracy.
Education	
We believe that the education of our citizens, from Head Start to institutions of higher learning, deserves our highest priority; and that history will judge the next administration less by its success in building new weapons of war than by its success in improving young minds.	Republican leadership has launched a new era in American education. Our vision of excellence has brought education back to parents, back to basics, and back on a track of excellence leading to a brighter and stronger future for America.
America in the World	
We believe in an America that will promote human rights, human dignity and human opportunity in every country on earth; that will fight discrimination, encourage free speech and association and decry oppression in nations friendly and unfriendly. . . .	Republicans know that free nations are peace loving and do not threaten other democracies. To the extent, therefore, that democracies are established in the world, America will be safer. Consequently, our nation has a compelling interest to encourage and help actively to build the conditions of democracy wherever people strive for freedom.

government programs that the party supports. Still others might tell you what a party leader has said the party is. Why all these different answers? What do parties really stand for?

One way to answer this question is to look at a party's platform. Generally, the Democratic party believes that the federal government should take responsibility for many social programs, such as aid to the poor. Democrats are more likely than Republicans to support tax increases, if needed, to pay for these programs. Over the years the Democratic party has also been more likely to support labor unions.

In recent years, the Republican party has supported a strong military and has opposed tax increases. In general, Republicans tend to believe that state and local governments, as well as non-government organizations, should take more responsibility for social programs.

Political parties are similar. When you look at the two parties you can see differences. However, when the party in office or the majority party in the legislature changes, we do not usually have a radical change in government policies. Why not? The answer lies in the fact that, in many ways, our two major political parties are similar.

In Chapter 1 you learned about the American belief in equal respect and our values of freedom, justice, and equality for all. The two political parties have different historical traditions and see the role of government differently. However, the parties, like the American people they represent, hold the same basic beliefs and values.

Furthermore, in order to win elections, both parties need broad support. Each party tries to attract members from a broad spectrum of people—rich and poor, white collar and blue collar, rural and urban. To keep the support of all these different groups, both parties avoid taking extreme stands on issues. Each party also tries to attract the votes of the large number of voters who are not strongly committed to either party.

Party organization. The Democratic and Republican parties are also similar in the way they are set up. Both parties have local, state, and national organizations. These organizations work independently of each other. In other words, there is no single authority making decisions for the whole party.

The most important part of a party is the individual members at the local level. These members do the job of getting the party's candidates elected. Each community is divided into ***precincts***, or voting districts. Precincts are made up of anywhere from 200 to 1,000 voters who all vote at the same polling place. In each precinct, each party has a chairperson or captain who organizes volunteers to try

Political Party Organization

Political Party Organization
National Committee
State Committees
Green County — County and Local Committees
Vote for Smith — Precinct Organization
Party Members

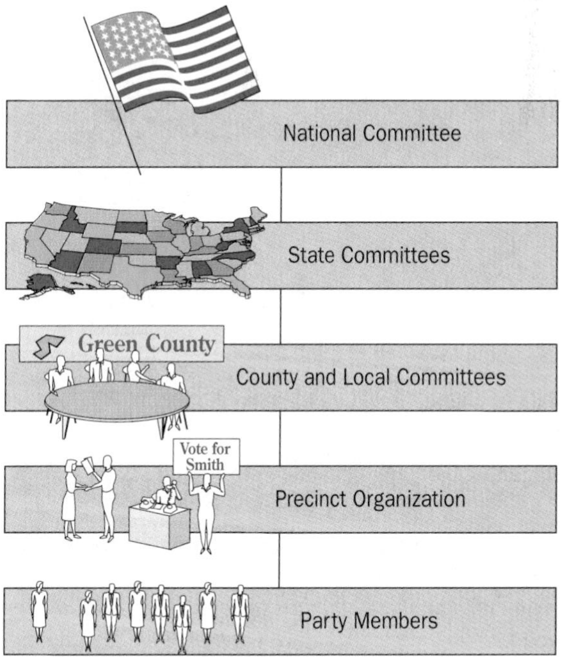

Challenge (Analysis): Have students discuss the cost to democracy of political parties avoiding extreme stands.

to get as many party members as possible to vote.

Parties at the local level elect members to city and county committees. These committees may recommend candidates for office and are responsible for running local campaigns.

Each party is also organized at the state level. Most states have party committees, each with a chairperson. At state conventions, party leaders write the state party platform and nominate candidates for office. Party leaders also raise money and help with candidates' campaigns.

Once every four years, each party holds a national convention. At the convention, delegates write the national party platform and nominate the candidates for President and Vice-President.

Between national conventions, the national committee keeps the party running. The national committee is made up of representatives from each state, each territory, and the District of Columbia. It is headed by the national chairperson, who is usually chosen by the party's presidential candidate. During election years, the national committee helps the candidates for President and Vice-President run their campaigns. It also works to elect members of Congress and to raise funds for the party.

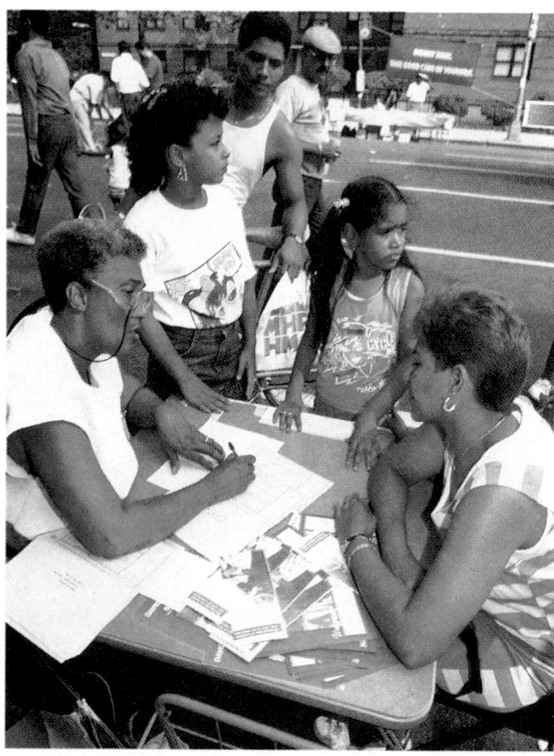

Voter registration tables like this one are a common sight around election time. Most states allow people to declare their party when they register.

Supporting a Party

Membership in a political party is not like membership in a club. You do not need to pay dues or attend meetings. All you need to do is think of yourself as a member. In most states, you can officially declare your party when you register to vote. Even so, you are free to vote for any party's candidates in general elections and to change your party registration whenever you wish.

How do you decide what party to support, or whether to support a party at all? One influence is your family. An individual often develops political attitudes and opinions close to those of his or her parents. If you grow up listening to your parents talk about politics, you may come to share their views. The views of friends, co-workers, and teachers may also influence you. If people you respect support a party, you, too, may choose to back that party.

Your views on issues may also influence which political party you support. If you take a strong stand on an issue, you are more likely to back a party that shares your view. You may even work actively in the party to make that view heard. Also, if you like certain candidates and agree with their opinions, you

Decision Making: Have students discuss in small groups how they would go about deciding which political party to support.

may be attracted to their party. Reading a party's platform or a candidate's position statements on issues is a way to help you decide whether you will support a party.

Changes in Party Strength

Parties depend for their strength on their ability to elect their candidates. In order to be successful in elections, parties must have dedicated members to work on campaigns. Parties also need loyal voters whom they can count on to vote for the party's candidates.

The strength of parties seems to be declining. Historically, political parties have maintained their strength through a combination of three elements: (1) a system of patronage, (2) a central role in election campaigns, and (3) voter loyalty. Each of these elements has changed in recent years.

Patronage. The system in which party leaders do favors for loyal supporters of the party is called ***patronage***. Today, some patronage is still possible, especially at high levels. For example, the President often appoints loyal party members to cabinet positions. However, as you have learned, most people now get government jobs through the civil service system. As a result, the patronage system has largely disappeared. Thus one source of party strength—a loyal group of workers at the local level—has declined.

Parties in campaigns. Another way in which party strength has changed is in the parties' role in campaigns. In earlier times, candidates for office worked within the party and depended on party support in their campaigns.

Today, candidates can more easily strike out on their own and run a campaign apart from the party. They can raise their own campaign funds, buy television ads, and print their own pamphlets. When candidates are less dependent on party help, they may be less bound to support the party's programs.

Voter loyalty. A third change that has weakened political parties is a change in voter loyalty. Few people now vote a ***straight ticket***, the practice of voting for the candidates of only one party. Voters now tend to base their decisions on the appeal of a particular candidate or issue rather than on party loyalty. Many people now vote a ***split ticket***, the practice of voting for candidates of more than one party on the same ballot.

As a result of split-ticket voting, parties can no longer count on a certain core of party votes in an election. In 1988, for example, Republican presidential candidate George Bush won 60 percent of the popular vote in Virginia. However, Virginia voters elected a Democrat, Charles Robb, to the Senate in the same election.

The core of "strong" or committed supporters for each party—people likely to vote a straight ticket—is quite small. In 1986, the number of people who called themselves "strong Democrats" made up about 18 percent of voters, and "strong Republicans" about 10 percent. Other people were more loosely linked to a party. "Weak Democrats" made up about 22 percent of voters, and "weak Republicans" about 15 percent.

How do the rest of the voters think of themselves? Recent studies show that more than 30 percent are ***independent voters***, people who say they do not support a political party. This number has been growing, especially among young voters. However, a certain percentage of independent voters "leans" toward one party or the other.

Some observers claim that the influence of political parties is weakening—that "the party is over." Others believe that our two-party system will stay in place, but that the parties will change in response to changing times.

For most of the nineteenth century, patronage was powerful in urban political machines. However, in 1883 Congress passed the Pendleton Act (also called the Civil Service Act) to control the inefficiency and dishonesty created by patronage.

Teaching Note: Use Teaching Activity 2, page T 155, and the Enrichment Activity, page T 156, and accompanying worksheet in the Activity Book after students have read the material in Section 21-2.

Answers will be found on page T 157.

Section Review

1. Define *precincts, patronage, straight ticket, split ticket,* and *independent voters.*
2. Describe how third parties have played an important role in our political system.
3. In what ways are our two major political parties similar?
4. What effect has the decrease in patronage had on political parties?

Evaluation. Could you choose which party to support based on the excerpts on page 462? Why or why not?

Data Search. Look at the graphs on pages 590 and 591. In which years shown were the majority in Congress and the President of the same party? What was the trend in the 1980s?

21-3

CHOOSING CANDIDATES

Read to Find Out

- what the terms *self-nomination, write-in candidate, caucus, direct primary, closed primary,* and *open primary* mean.
- how candidates for office are nominated.
- what role political parties play in nominating presidential candidates.

The most important role of political parties is selecting, or nominating, the candidates who will run for office. Political parties are the only organizations that play this role in our political system.

Not all offices require party nominations. You will see that individuals can also nominate candidates. However, taking a look at the nominating process for candidates in general, and for presidential candidates in particular, is a good way to see parties in action.

Nominating Candidates

Suppose you want to run for office. The first step is to declare that you intend to run, or "throw your hat in the ring." After that, the nominating process ranges from simple to complex, depending on the office.

The simplest way to become a candidate is ***self-nomination***, which means declaring that you are running for office. Self-nomination is still possible for many local offices. A self-nominee usually pays a small fee called a filing fee. Another type of self-nominated candidate is a ***write-in candidate***, one who asks voters to write his or her name on the ballot.

For some offices, a candidate may need to file a nominating petition. A number of voters must sign the petition saying that they support the nomination. Then the candidate pays the filing fee and begins the campaign. Candidates for local offices and candidates who are not running as members of a major party are often nominated by petition. For other offices, candidates are chosen by delegates at party meetings called conventions. Parties hold local, state, and national conventions.

A few states select candidates or choose delegates to conventions at a caucus. A ***caucus*** is a meeting of party leaders to discuss issues or choose candidates. In earlier days, caucuses put great power in the hands of a few party leaders because the meetings were closed to ordinary members. Today a few state and local caucuses are still held, but they are very different. Most caucuses are open meetings.

Primaries. Most candidates for state and federal office are now chosen in a direct primary. A ***direct primary*** is an election in which members of a political party choose candidates to run for office in the name of the party. The

Between 1800 and 1824, secret congressional caucuses, made up of party leaders, nominated presidential and vice-presidential candidates. In the 1820s, people began to condemn this undemocratic system, and by 1832, party delegates met in open, national conventions to nominate candidates.

PEOPLE MAKE A DIFFERENCE

Party Commitment Begins Early

Catherine Bertini's political activities began at thirteen. She helped her father campaign for city council by handing out flyers. At fifteen, she spent several days at the Teen-Age Republicans' School of Politics. After that, she was hooked.

"I came back committed to a political career," says Bertini. "I saw that in government and politics there is much you can do. You really can make a difference—and enjoy doing it."

Catherine Bertini was born in Syracuse, New York. Because of her interest in politics, Bertini started the Teen-Age Republican Club at her high school. In college she studied government and politics while working part time as a legislative aide for a senator.

Although Bertini first joined the Republican Party because of her father, she later chose it on her own. She thinks parties do a good job of bringing people of similar viewpoints together to influence public policy.

Bertini believes that youth should get involved in politics early. In 1972, she headed the same Teen-Age Republicans' School of Politics that she had attended. She became the National Youth Director for the Republican party in 1975 and continues to promote youth participation in politics.

In 1982 Bertini ran for Congress. Although she did not win the election, her commitment to serving in government remains high. Today she works in Washington, D.C., as an assistant secretary in the Department of Agriculture. One reason Bertini was asked to take her current position was her long involvement with the Republican party.

About her political party experience in her teen-age years Bertini says, "You never know when what you did in the past will influence what you do in the future. What I did years ago has brought me to where I am today."

candidate with the most votes is then that party's nominee in the general election.

Most states use one of two kinds of direct primary: closed or open. A ***closed primary*** is a primary in which a voter must be registered as a party member and may vote only for candidates of that party. Only Democrats may vote in the Democratic primary to choose Democratic candidates, and the same is true for Republicans. Voters registered as independent cannot vote in a closed primary. An ***open primary*** is a primary in which voters do not need to declare a party before voting, but may vote in only one party's primary.

Choosing Presidential Candidates

The primaries that receive the most attention take place once every four years to select the parties' candidates for President. Who runs for President? As you know, anyone over 35 years old and born in the United States may run for President. In fact, however, a candidate needs to be well known, to have experience in government, and to be able to raise enough money for the campaign.

Most presidential candidates from the major parties have held elected office before seeking the nomination for President. Since World

Discussion: Have students discuss ways that youth can participate in government and politics.

Governor Michael Dukakis accepts his party's nomination for President at the 1988 Democratic national convention.

War II, 80 percent of Republican and Democratic candidates for President have been senators or governors. Also since 1900, every President who has wanted to run for re-election has gained his party's nomination.

Paying for a primary campaign. In the presidential primaries, candidates raise much of their money from individuals. Federal laws, however, say that individuals may give only $1,000 to each candidate per election. Once candidates have raised at least $5,000 in each of 20 states, they can receive an equal amount from the federal government, up to a total of $5 million.

Choosing delegates. Delegates to the national nominating conventions are chosen in one of two ways: through a presidential preference primary election or through a state-wide caucus or convention process. Each state has different rules for choosing delegates.

In a preference primary, voters show which candidates they prefer by voting either for the candidates themselves or for the delegates who support that candidate. In most primary states, delegates must promise to support a certain candidate at the national convention. In states without primaries, delegates are chosen by caucus or state convention.

In February or March of a presidential election year, candidates traditionally begin the race in New Hampshire, a primary state, and Iowa, a caucus state. How well a candidate does in these early tests will affect his or her ability to raise money and attract voters in later primaries and caucuses. As the process continues through June, some candidates drop out and others gain strength.

National conventions. In July or August of an election year, the parties hold their national conventions. Perhaps you have watched one on television. You have seen a large hall filled with people waving signs and banners and wearing campaign hats and buttons. Bands play, flags wave, and thousands of balloons fill the air. For four days the delegates debate and discuss the candidates, listen to speeches, vote on the nominations, and hammer out the party platform.

At conventions in the early 1900s, several votes had to be taken before the delegates could decide a presidential nominee. Today, because of the primaries, almost all delegates are "pledged" to a candidate before the con-

Challenge (Evaluation): Have students discuss whether the United States should have a national primary rather than separate state primaries in order to reduce campaigning time and costs. Students should provide reasons for their opinions.

Teaching Note: Use the Evaluating Progress activity, page T 156, to assess students' understanding of this section.

vention begins. Usually only one vote is needed to choose the candidate. Once the candidate for President has been chosen, the delegates most often approve that candidate's choice for Vice-President.

Another task of the national convention is to approve the party platform. A committee writes the platform with advice from party leaders, including the candidates. Each plank is carefully worded to appeal to the widest possible audience. The delegates debate and finally approve a platform.

The convention winds up with acceptance speeches from the presidential and vice-presidential candidates. These speeches are meant to bring the party together after months of primaries and four grueling days of discussions and—often—disagreements. The next step to gaining office will be the election campaign, leading up to the presidential election in November.

Answers will be found on page T 157.

Section Review

1. Define the terms *self-nomination, write-in candidate, caucus, direct primary, closed primary,* and *open primary.*
2. Describe four ways in which candidates can be nominated.
3. Explain in your own words how presidential candidates are nominated.

Evaluation. "The amount of money candidates spend on a campaign should not be limited." Do you agree or disagree? Why?

A BROADER VIEW

The United States has had two political parties for so long that many Americans cannot imagine another system. However, two-party systems are rare. They are found only in Great Britain, the United States, and a few other former British colonies. In the rest of the world, multi-party or single-party systems are more common.

In most democratic countries, several political parties compete for power. Each party represents a different set of interests or ideas that are usually better defined than in a two-party system. Voters in Israel choose from more than 20 political parties in national elections. In Italy, more than 10 parties compete for votes. In both of these countries, voters have a wide range of choices.

A problem in some multi-party countries has been frequent changes in government. When no one party receives a majority of votes, two or more parties must join together to form a government that represents a majority of voters. If these parties cannot work together, the government soon falls apart. Italy, for example, went through 49 changes of government from 1946 to 1989.

Single-party systems are typical of communist countries and many of the world's poorer nations. In many single-party countries only the ruling party is allowed. Opposition parties are outlawed. Supporters of single-party government argue that it builds national unity. Opponents say that single party governments grow corrupt and lazy without an opposition party to keep them honest and hard-working.

Most Americans see their two-party system as a good compromise between multi- and single-party systems. A two-party system is more stable than a multi-party system. Also, having two parties means that there is always one party playing the watchdog role.

Teaching Note: Use the Reinforcement Activity, page T 156, and accompanying worksheet in the Activity Book.

CHAPTER SURVEY

Answers to Survey and Workshop will be found on page T 157.

UNDERSTANDING NEW VOCABULARY

Seeing Relationships

The vocabulary terms in each pair listed below are related to each other. For each pair, explain what the terms have in common. Also explain how they are different.

Example: A *caucus* and a *direct primary* are similar because they both are ways in which parties nominate candidates. They are different because a caucus is a meeting of party members, and a direct primary is an election to choose candidates to run for office.

1. *platform* and *plank*

2. *straight ticket* and *split ticket*

3. *closed primary* and *open primary*

Putting It in Writing

Write a paragraph describing how candidates are chosen by a political party to run against another party's candidate in an election. Use the terms *political party*, *nominate*, *caucus*, *direct primary*, *open primary*, and *closed primary*.

LOOKING BACK AT THE CHAPTER

1. What is the difference between a partisan and a nonpartisan election?

2. How does a political party establish positions on issues and set goals for what the government should accomplish?

3. How can the party out of power act as a watchdog over the party in power?

4. In what ways do political parties inform citizens about various political issues?

5. Give two reasons why third parties form.

6. Why is there more split-ticket voting than there used to be?

7. How are direct primaries more democratic than the party caucuses of earlier days?

8. What tasks are accomplished at party national conventions?

9. *Evaluation.* Do you think it is a good idea that political parties recommend to their members how to vote on issues and candidates? Why or why not?

10. *Application.* If you were to write a platform for a third party you were forming, what would some of the main planks be?

11. *Synthesis.* Imagine the American political system without political parties. How might candidates for President be chosen?

12. *Evaluation.* Do you think that having only two major parties makes our political system stronger or weaker? Explain your answer.

WORKING TOGETHER

1. Find out about the local political parties in your city or town. Invite representatives from these parties to your classroom to debate key local issues. How do the parties differ in their views of these issues?

2. Hold a mock national convention in your classroom. Divide the class into different delegate groups. Each group should choose one person to be a candidate. Develop a party platform that all the delegate groups can agree on, and select the final presidential and vice-presidential nominees.

3. In a group of three or four, find out about an actual third party, either past or present. Why was this party formed? What were some of its key platform issues? Give a brief oral report to the rest of the class.

4. Observe the elections for student government at your own school. What issues do candidates focus on? In your opinion, what makes for a strong candidate? If possible, have the candidates come to your classroom to give their campaign speeches and to answer questions.

Teaching Note: For reinforcement of decision-making skills, use Decision-Making Worksheet Chapter 21.

SOCIAL STUDIES SKILLS

Analyzing Election Results

In the last 150 years, only ten third parties have been able to win more than 5 percent of the votes in a presidential election. This table of election results shows what happened to these major third parties in the next election.

Major Third Party Election Results

Party	Year	Vote	Next Election
Anti-Masonic	1832	7.8%	Supported Whig candidate
Free Soil	1848	10.1%	4.9%
American ("Know-Nothing")	1856	21.5%	Disappeared
Southern Democrat	1860	18.1%	Disappeared
Constitutional Union	1860	12.6%	Disappeared
Populist	1892	8.5%	Supported Democrats
Progressive ("Bull Moose")	1912	27.4%	.02%
Socialist	1912	6.0%	3.2%
Progressive	1924	16.6%	Disappeared
American Independent	1968	13.5%	1.4%

1. How many of these parties ran candidates in the election that followed their first impressive showing?

2. What happened to the parties that did not run candidates in the next election?

3. How many of these third parties were able to win at least 5 percent of the vote in more than one election?

4. In one sentence, summarize the pattern you see in these election results.

DECISION-MAKING SKILLS

What Relates to Your Subject?

Suppose that you are trying to decide which political party to support. Examine each of the following statements to determine which ones give information that might be relevant to your decision. Be prepared to explain why some of the statements are irrelevant. If you need to review how to identify relevant information, refer to the lesson on page 190.

A. The candidates of a political party try to appeal to as many different types of voters as possible in order to win an election.

B. There are some differences and similarities between political parties in the United States and political parties in Great Britain.

C. A political party's stand on major issues can be found in the party platform.

D. Each political party is organized at the local, state, and national levels.

E. Republicans and Democrats generally differ in their views of how the minimum wage affects workers, including teenagers.

1. Which statements might be relevant to deciding which political party to support? Explain how they are relevant.

2. Which statements are irrelevant to deciding which political party to support? Explain.

3. What are some other kinds of relevant information that would help you decide which political party to support? Explain.

4. Why is the skill of identifying relevant information important to good decision making?

5. Name a decision that you might have to make in the near future. Give an example of information that would be relevant to your decision. Give an example of information that would be irrelevant to your decision.

TE HERE
NOV. 2

Chapter Themes: Americans perform an important civic duty when they vote on candidates and ballot measures. Candidates and interest groups use a variety of methods to try to influence voters. Campaigns, which are often professionally managed, inform voters about candidates and issues.

CHAPTER 22

Voting and Elections

Ian was cooking dinner when his mother arrived home from work. She had a funny smile on her face, and he knew she had some good news. "What's up, Mom?" he asked.

"I've decided to run for city council," she said.

"Really? Gee, Mom, that's great!" exclaimed Ian. "I can tell all my friends that my mother holds a government office!"

"Now wait a minute, Ian," she replied. "I haven't won the election yet. I'm just going to run. There are six other candidates, at least."

"Yeah, I know," said Ian. "What I meant to say is that I'm proud of you. It's a lot of work to run for office."

"Thanks. It's good to hear I have some support already," said Ian's mother. "By the way, you'll turn eighteen before the election. That means you can vote for the first time. May I count on your vote?"

"Well. . . ," he said teasingly, "I haven't decided yet if you're the best candidate." His mother smiled and they both burst out laughing.

This chapter is about elections. As you read, you will first learn what it means to be a voter—sorting out messages from candidates, deciding how to vote, and finally marking your ballot. Then you will learn about how political candidates go about organizing and running their campaigns.

Teaching Note: Use the Introducing the Chapter activity, page T 160.

22-1

BEING A VOTER

Read to Find Out

- what the terms *general election* and *registration* mean.
- what we vote for in general elections.
- how and when elections are held, and who may vote in them.
- how to become an informed voter.

At your age, you have the chance to play several citizen roles. You go to school, you obey laws, and you may do volunteer work. Soon, you will be old enough to play the most important citizen role in a democracy: the role of voter.

General Elections

You will have a chance to vote in two kinds of elections: primary elections and general elections. In Chapter 21 you learned that in a primary election members of political parties nominate candidates. That is, they vote to choose who will run for office in the name of their party. A ***general election*** is an election in which voters make final decisions about candidates and issues.

More than half a million federal, state, and local offices are filled in general elections. These offices include everything from President of the United States to member of a town council. When people vote in general elections, they are choosing people to represent them in government.

A general election may also offer citizens a chance to play a more direct part in government. Voters in many states, counties, and cities are asked to vote on certain ballot measures in a general election. Measures include initiatives, referendums, and recalls. They give each voter a voice in deciding what laws should be passed, how the government should raise money, and who should be removed from office.

In the general elections of 1988, a total of 230 proposals for new laws, constitutional amendments, and new taxes or other ways of raising money appeared on the ballots of 41 states. Voters in California alone were asked to vote on 29 measures, including one to cut insurance rates and one to put a new tax on cigarettes.

In addition to deciding about state-wide measures, many voters across the country were asked to vote on local ballot measures. These measures involved new laws, public building projects, new taxes, and other government issues.

The Basics of Voting

Who may vote in a general election? The Constitution states that in order to vote you must be at least 18 years of age and a citizen of the United States. In addition, you must be a resident of the state in which you will vote. However, not everybody who meets these qualifications has the right to vote. Prison inmates and people who are mentally incompetent are not allowed to vote.

Registration. In every state except North Dakota you must register before you vote. ***Registration*** is the process of signing up to be a voter. Registration was introduced in the late 1800s to keep noncitizens from voting. It was also meant to stop voter fraud, such as the same person voting more than once.

In a few states, voters are allowed to register at the polling place when they go to vote. In most states, however, you must register several weeks ahead of time. To make it easier, many cities and towns set up registration

By the early 1900s, political machines had gained power in many American cities. (See Chapter 12.) Sometimes the machines resorted to voter fraud to get their candidates elected. Voting lists often included the names of dogs, children, and nonexistent persons.

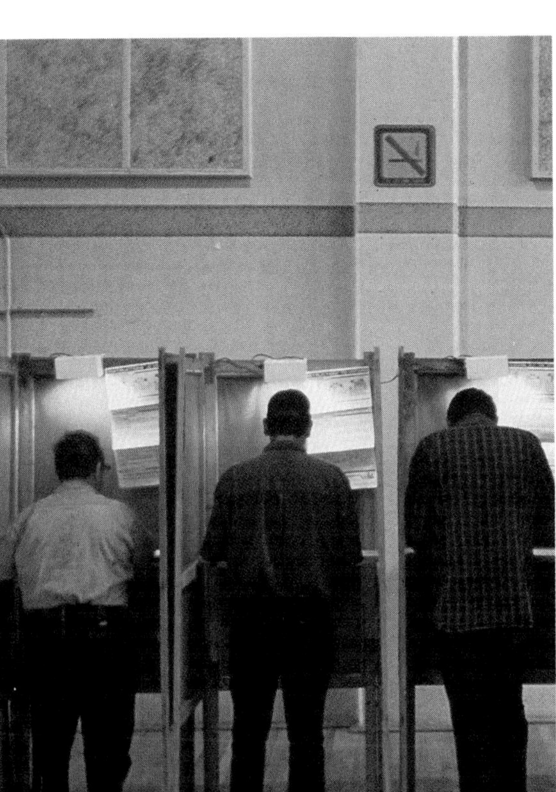

While voting laws and procedures vary slightly from state to state, local polling places all try to ensure privacy to voters.

tables in libraries, church basements, and even shopping centers.

In some states, once you are registered you are permanently on the list of voters. Other states use what is called periodic registration. To be able to vote in these states, you have to re-register every two or four years. In still other states, you stay registered only if you vote in every election. In these states, people who do not vote are removed from the list and must re-register for the next election.

Voting—when and where. With over 500,000 offices to fill, general elections in the United States are many and frequent. We vote for members of Congress every two years in even-numbered years, and for President every four years in even-numbered years. An act of Congress set the Tuesday after the first Monday in November as the day for these federal elections, and most elections for state offices take place at the same time.

Primary elections and elections for local governments may take place at any time during the year, but most are set for the spring. Usually these local and primary elections are held on the same day. Special elections to choose candidates to finish the terms of officeholders who have died, resigned, or been recalled also may be held at any time.

Voting takes place in what are called polling places. As a registered voter, you are assigned to a polling place near where you live. Each polling place serves a voting district or precinct—an area with between 200 and 1,000 voters. Before election day you must find out where you vote. In some states you get this information in the mail. Your polling place may be a nearby school or church, or even a neighbor's garage. In most states, polling places are open for 12 hours.

How to cast a vote. On entering the polling place, you check in with an election official, who looks up your name to see that you are registered to vote there. In some places the official will give you a printed ballot or punch card that lists the candidates and measures on which you will vote. You will then go into a booth and mark or punch the ballot to make your choices in secret. Many polling places now have voting machines. In that case, you simply pull levers to make your choices, and the machine records your vote.

If you know that you will not be able to get to the polling place on election day—you will be on vacation, for example—you can ask for an absentee ballot. It will be mailed to

Challenge (Analysis): Some observers believe that voter turnout would improve if local, state, and national elections were consolidated into one or two elections per year. Have students discuss the implications of such a plan.

your home shortly before the election. After marking your ballot, you return it by mail. Thus you can vote even if you are out of town.

Becoming an Informed Voter

Going to your polling place and casting your vote is relatively easy. To vote wisely, however, you must become an informed voter. To prepare to vote on candidates for public office, you should find out all you can about them. What are their qualifications? Where do they stand on important issues? If they have held public office before, how good a job did they do?

You can get the answers to these questions from many sources. The candidates themselves can tell you how they stand on the issues. Public service organizations with no ties to political parties, such as the League of Women Voters, often put out excellent information. You can also count on newspapers to write stories on the candidates' records, backgrounds, and stands on the issues.

You can also learn a great deal about the candidates by watching them in action. By going to hear them speak or watching news on television, you can see what the candidates are doing and saying. If you have a chance to watch candidates debate each other, you can see how they answer questions and handle themselves in a tough situation.

You should also learn about initiatives and other ballot measures. Find out why a measure was proposed and what the outcomes might be if it is passed or turned down.

Having a complete picture of a ballot measure is very important. For example, at first glance you might vote against a 25-cent-per-gallon rise in the tax on gasoline because it would make driving your car cost more. However, if you learned that the money raised by the tax would go to building a highway that would shorten your drive to work by 10 miles, you might change your mind. Most states provide information on ballot measures, often in a voters' handbook sent to all registered voters.

Average Voter Turnout by Age Group Presidential Election Years 1972–1988

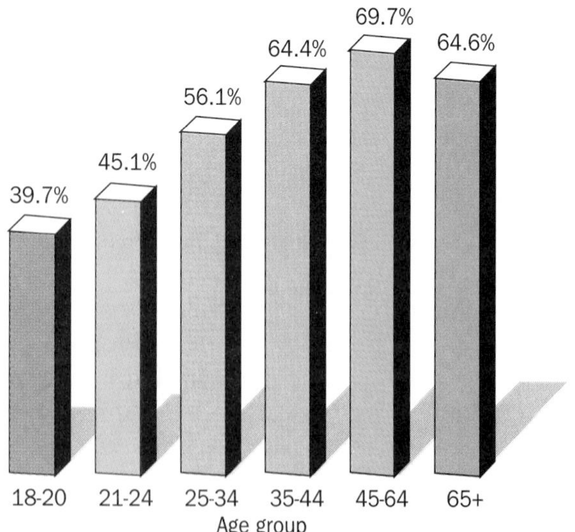

Source: *Statistical Abstract of the United States, 1989*

Why vote? In recent years, only about half of all eligible citizens have actually voted in presidential elections. Even fewer have voted in most state and local elections.

Why have so many people chosen not to use their right to vote? Some people say they do not vote because the candidates are all pretty much the same. The government will follow the same policies no matter who wins, they say, so why bother to vote? Others choose not to vote because they think that no candidate truly represents them or understands their problems.

Sometimes people do not participate in elections because they think their vote cannot possibly affect the final outcome. How, they

The most significant factor in predicting voting behavior is level of education. The higher an individual's education, the more likely the person is to vote. The second most significant factor is age, with the voting rate highest among people in the mid-forties to mid-sixties.

VIEWS OF NOTED AMERICANS

Curtis Gans

Curtis Gans likes to tell people that he first became politically active in the seventh grade when he was assigned to attend an all-white school. Gans believed strongly in the American value of equality, so he took action by refusing to go to that school. He says that his plan worked—he was sent to an integrated school.

Today, the kind of political activity that Gans cares about most is voting. As director of the Committee for the Study of the American Electorate (CSAE), he has dedicated his career to studying why so few Americans make use of their most basic political right—the right to vote.

"I always found both politics and public affairs interesting," says Gans. "I never kept my opinions bottled up, but expressed them."

Gans wonders why so few Americans feel the same way. When he was working in politics, he was particularly bothered by the fact that the United States has one of the lowest rates of voter participation of any democracy in the world. In order to find out why so many Americans fail to vote, Gans founded CSAE in 1976.

CSAE is not connected to any political party. Under Gans's direction, it has become the best source of information about voter participation in the United States.

According to Gans, one of the major causes of low voter turnout in elections is the way television presents politics. He claims that TV helps strengthen the attitude that average citizens have no influence on politics.

Gans has proposed several solutions to the problem of low voter participation. He would like to see changes in the way television covers political campaigns and changes in voter registration laws.

Gans also thinks that the schools should provide better civic education for youth. "There have to be changes made in early childhood," says Gans. "We need a commitment to civic education and to stressing participation in schools and the community."

ask, can my one vote make a difference in a presidential race in which more than 90 million people cast ballots?

It is true that elections are almost never won by 1 or by even 100 votes. However, if thousands of voters all stayed home on election day, you can see that it might affect the outcome.

Furthermore, even if your candidate loses, your vote still matters. Through the ballot box you announce where you stand on the issues and what kind of representatives you want. By casting your vote you perform an important civic duty. You take part in the process of deciding who will lead our government and what policies those leaders will follow.

Discussion: Have students discuss other reasons why people do not vote. What can be done to turn nonvoters into voters?

Teaching Note: Use Teaching Activity 1, page T 160, as a culminating activity after students have read the material in Section 22-1.

Answers will be found on page T 162.

Section Review

1. Define *general election* and *registration*.
2. Besides the names of candidates, what may be on the ballot in a general election?
3. What are the qualifications for voting in most states?
4. What should you find out about the candidates in order to become an informed voter?

Evaluation. "Bad officials are elected by good citizens who do not vote." Do you agree or disagree? Explain your answer.

22-2

HOW CANDIDATES AND GROUPS TRY TO INFLUENCE YOUR VOTE

Read to Find Out

- what the terms *direct mail, media, propaganda,* and *bias* mean.
- how candidates get their election messages to the voters.
- how interest groups try to influence your vote.
- what propaganda methods are used in election messages.
- how the media report election campaigns.

The television screen shows a man walking down a quiet, tree-lined street holding the hands of his two young children. You hear an announcer saying, "Bob Kane has lived in our city all his life. He graduated from our public schools. His children attend those schools. He knows your problems and he knows what you want." Another television ad shows an empty jail cell. A frightened voice says, "What Bob Kane has done puts criminals back in our neighborhoods—not here, where they belong."

Before an election, you will see and hear many campaign messages. Each will try to influence how you vote. Some will give you information. Others, like these TV ads, will try to play on your fears and other feelings. In evaluating such messages, you should be aware that you cannot always trust what they say.

Messages from the Candidates

Candidates have many different methods to try to get you, the voter, to vote for them. Depending on the office for which they are running and the number of votes they must win, they may shake your hand in person or buy thousands of dollars' worth of television advertising time. As a voter, you will want to know about the many ways candidates try to get their messages to you.

Posters, bumper stickers, and leaflets. In the months before election day, you will see posters and stickers plastered on lampposts, billboards, windows, and car bumpers. You will also see people wearing buttons, pins, and caps with candidates' names on them. People running for office want to make their names known to the voters.

To give voters a better picture of the person behind the name, candidates use leaflets and flyers. Volunteers hand them out at shopping centers and put them under your door. Such leaflets give short biographical sketches of the candidates and tell where they stand on the major issues. All this information is written to appeal to as many voters as possible.

Personal appearances. Candidates running for a town council usually campaign in a personal way. The numbers of people who vote

Teaching Note: For Davy Crockett's advice to politicians on how to win elections, see "In Their Own Words" on page 516.

David Dinkins made personal appearances a key part of his successful 1989 campaign for mayor of New York City.

in such elections are so small—often fewer than 1,000—that candidates can meet most voters in person. They ring doorbells and hold neighborhood meetings, bringing their messages to citizens through conversations and speeches to small groups.

Even in elections for state and national offices, candidates appear in person to spread their messages among the voters. Your chance to "meet" someone running for state or national office usually comes at huge political rallies in public parks or auditoriums or at neighborhood political meetings. At these events, the candidates make speeches telling you why you should elect them and not the people running against them.

Direct mail. One of the best ways to get the attention of voters is by mail. With the help of computers, candidates can use ***direct mail,*** a way of sending messages to large groups of people through the mail. Direct mail allows candidates to target voters who have special interests. A candidate can send a message to senior citizens promising to support higher social security payments. That candidate can also send a message about ideas on education to members of teachers' unions.

Advertisements in the media. Candidates for state and national office must reach very large numbers of voters. They have found that one of the best ways to get their messages out is through advertisements in the ***media***—television, radio, newspapers, and magazines.

However, using the media can be very expensive. A full-page advertisement in a major newspaper costs thousands of dollars. The cost of a few minutes on television can run into hundreds of thousands of dollars.

Since television time and newspaper space are so expensive, political advertisements are usually short and simple. They often give very little in the way of information. Instead, they

Challenge (Analysis): Have students discuss the advantages and disadvantages of providing equal television time and newspaper space free of charge to all candidates.

These members of a special interest group, the American Association of Retired Persons, are helping "get out the vote" on issues that affect them.

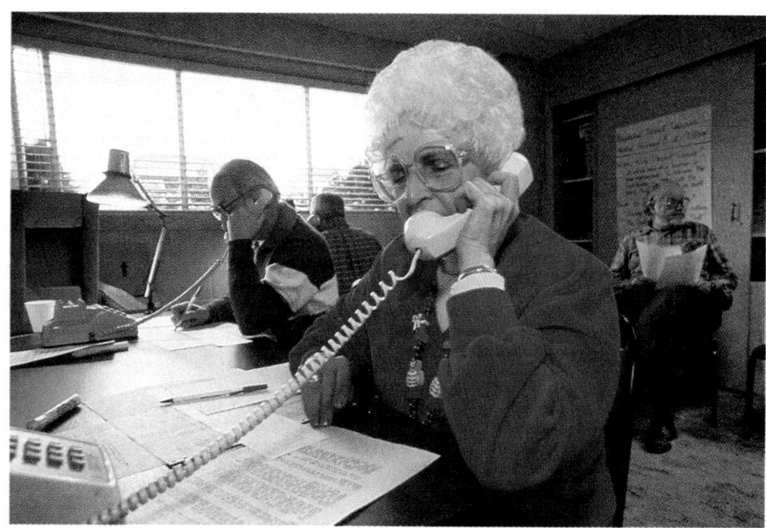

try to grab your attention and to focus on a candidate's personality rather than qualifications and abilities. Many media ads depend on slogans, such as "Building a Better Tomorrow" or "It's Morning in America."

For these reasons, TV and newspaper ads are not a good source of information about what a candidate would do if elected. They rarely say much, for example, about how a candidate plans to fight the drug problem or improve the economy. However, some of these ads do tell voters what stands the candidates have taken on major issues.

Messages from Interest Groups

Candidates are not the only people trying to get your vote. Interest groups, too, put out their share of direct mail and media ads. Interest groups want to help elect candidates who agree with their views and to defeat candidates who have taken stands against them. Interest groups also work to pass or defeat ballot measures.

Interest groups try to achieve their election goals in two other ways. They endorse, or lend their names in support of, candidates and ballot measures. They also give money to campaigns.

The largest interest groups have political action committees (PACs) whose job is to carry out these election activities. PACs often work very hard for and against ballot measures. In 1988 the National Rifle Association spent more than $5 million in a campaign to overturn Maryland state laws that banned some handguns.

PACs also give large sums of money to campaigns for state and national office. United States senators running for re-election in 1990 received an average of almost $1 million each from PACs.

Since the early 1970s, the number of PACs in the United States has grown from just over 600 to about 4,700. Some PACs get their money from the people they represent—union members, employees of businesses, and corporation stockholders. Others use direct mail to find people who agree with their views and will send them large sums of money. The success of both methods of raising money has given PACs a large voice in campaigns.

Federal law limits the amount that PACs may give to each candidate. However, there

The Federal Election Campaign Act of 1971 limited the amount an individual or group could contribute to any one candidate. The Federal Election Commission, created to enforce the act, collects data on PACs and their contributions to candidates.

Teaching Note: For information on top PAC contributors and PAC contributions to congressional campaigns, see page 590.

are few rules for how much PACs may spend on running their own campaigns. In the 1990 federal elections, PACs spent more than $20 million on these independent campaigns.

Many people believe that PACs have too much influence on the outcome of elections. They charge that the "special interests" that PACs represent are gaining too much power in government. Each interest group represents only a small percentage of Americans, or cares about only one issue, they say. Through PACs, however, interest groups can have a voice in who will hold office and make decisions on issues that affect everyone.

Although some people want limits placed on what PACs can do, other people are opposed to such limits. They argue that PACs are simply using their First Amendment right of free speech.

Recognizing Propaganda Techniques

Why do candidates and interest groups work so hard to get their messages across to voters? They all have the same goal: to influence the way you think and act. A message that is meant to influence people's ideas, opinions, or actions in a certain way is called ***propaganda.***

Do you think of propaganda as lies or false information? Although propaganda can includes lies, it can also contain truthful—or mostly truthful—information. A message is

Propaganda Techniques

Glittering Generalities
Use words and phrases that sound appealing and that everyone agrees with.
Example: "I stand for freedom and the American way."

Card Stacking
Use only those facts that support your argument.
Example: "My opponent voted against raising social security benefits." (You do not mention that she voted no because the proposed increase was too small.)

Just Plain Folks
Tell voters that you are just like them—an ordinary person with similar needs and ideas.
Example: "I've lived in this city all my life. My children go to the same schools as your children."

Name Calling
Attach negative labels to your opponent.
Example: "He's soft on crime."

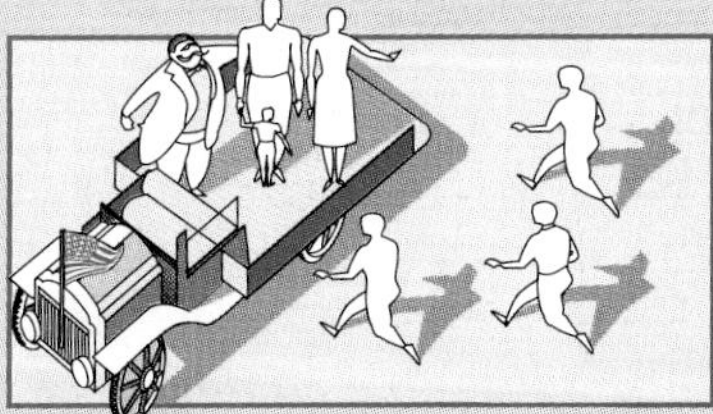

Bandwagon
Play on the fear of voters that they are being left out of something.
Example: "Polls show that more than 80 percent of voters support me."

Transfer
Connect yourself to a respected person, group, or symbol.
Example: "Remember what Abraham Lincoln said..."

Decision Making: Have students evaluate campaign material on a candidate or ballot measure and discuss how they would judge that information when deciding how to vote.

called propaganda when it tells only one side of the story, distorts the truth, or appeals mostly to people's feelings.

Messages from candidates and PACs make use of many different kinds of propaganda. Six of the most common propaganda techniques used by candidates are described in the box on page 481.

When reading and listening to political messages, be aware of the kinds of propaganda techniques that might be at work. Recognizing them will help you decide how to act on the messages.

How News Media Report the Elections

In addition to running ads paid for by the candidates and interest groups, the media put out their own information about candidates and issues. This information comes in two forms: editorials and news reporting.

In their editorials, the media give their opinions on ballot measures and candidates. News reporting, on the other hand, is supposed to stick to the facts.

Election news. Election news reports give information about what a candidate says and does. They tell what a candidate said in last night's speech, for example, or what the candidate has promised to do for the schools.

Even though news reports give facts, not opinions, they can present these facts in ways that favor one candidate over another. In other words, ***bias***, which means favoring one point of view, may show in the way the media report on elections.

For the most part, the news media usually try not to show bias. They do not want to be accused of favoring one candidate over another. However, reporters, news directors, and editors have their opinions, likes, and dislikes. Sometimes their feelings affect their work.

How can you spot bias in news reporting? Bias can show when stories about one candidate are given more time or space or better placement than stories about other candidates. If you were running for class president, how would you feel if a story about you got 10 lines on page 6 of the school newspaper, while your opponent was given half of the front page?

Another sign of bias is when the media play up the negative side of one candidate's personality or behavior. They may run stories, for example, about a candidate's bad temper or a divorce that took place years ago. Such stories, though they may not be lies, can give voters a bad impression of the candidate and influence the way they vote.

Opinion polls. Along with reporting on what candidates are doing and saying, the news media also present the results of opinion polls. Polls can show which candidate people favor at a certain time, why they like that candidate, and what issues they think are most important.

The basic idea behind a poll is that you do not have to talk to every person in a group to find out what the outcome of that group's vote will be. A poll asks questions of a sample, or small part, of the group. The answers given by the people in the sample are then taken to stand for how the whole group would answer if everyone were asked.

Polling, however, works only if the people are chosen at random, that is, by chance. Choosing a poll's sample by chance helps make sure that the views of the people in the sample will stand for those of the whole group.

Most of the major national polls use random sampling and ask fair questions. You can count on these polls to show what the public thinks about such issues as choice of presidential candidate.

Sherwood Anderson, an American short-story writer and novelist, once wrote, "There is something terrible to me in the thought of the art of writing being bent and twisted to serve the ends of propaganda."

"That's the worst set of opinions I've heard in my entire life."

However, not all polls reported in the news are good ones. A poll that gets answers from only certain kinds of people may not be very accurate. Such polls include those in which people send in answers to lists of questions in magazines or call in their answers by telephone.

Some people think that polls should not be used. They believe that polls can change the results of elections. They point to voters who say they will vote for a certain candidate mainly because that candidate is leading in the polls. In other words, those voters will jump on the candidate's "bandwagon."

Also, some voters may decide whether to vote or not based on the results of opinion polls. Studies suggest that if the polls show a huge gap between candidates, some people believe that the leading candidate will win, and they do not bother to vote.

The impact of television. Today, many voters receive most of their information by watching the television news. For this reason, television has had a big impact on the way people see the candidates, understand the issues, and cast their votes.

Critics charge that television has made election issues seem unimportant because it covers the more exciting activities of the candidates, rather than paying attention to the major issues. These people also say that to make election news exciting and appealing, television tries to reduce campaign stories to 20-second "sound-bites" that catch viewers' attention but give little or no information.

Television has also had a powerful impact on the way candidates run their campaigns. They make their messages short and simple to fit easily on the television news. They also plan campaign activities that will look good on TV.

Overall, television has created a new kind of political candidate. A person running for high office today must come across well on the screen. This "television" candidate, by and large, must be good looking, have a nice personality, and be at ease in front of the camera. Otherwise, he or she may face a tough time in an election. As Walter Mondale noted after he lost the 1984 presidential election, "I never warmed up to television and television never warmed up to me."

Even though network news is not always the best source of facts about the candidates and issues, good sources do exist. Public television, special network programs, newspapers, and magazines all provide fuller coverage. It may take more work to seek out good information. However, if being an informed voter is important to you, the effort will be worth it.

Election results based on voter exit interviews are projected on television before polls in the western states close. Some observers believe these early projections sway votes or discourage people from voting and propose a news blackout in national elections until all polls are closed.

Teaching Note: Use Teaching Activity 2, page T 160, as a culminating activity after students have read the material in Section 22-2.

Answers will be found on page T 162.

Section Review

1. Define *direct mail, media, propaganda,* and *bias.*
2. List four methods candidates use to get their messages to voters.
3. What are the election aims of interest groups?
4. List the major propaganda techniques that might be used in campaign messages.
5. How may opinion polls affect the outcome of an election?

Evaluation. Abraham Lincoln was one of our greatest Presidents. He was also awkward and tired-eyed. Do you think that Lincoln could become President today? Explain.

Data Search. Look on page 590 in the Data Bank. What happened to the amount of money that PACs contributed to candidates running for the House?

22-3 CAMPAIGNING FOR OFFICE

Read to Find Out

- what the term *incumbent* means.
- how a major campaign is organized.
- how a major campaign is paid for.
- what role the Electoral College plays in the election of the President.

In the movie *The Candidate*, actor Robert Redford plays a man running for Congress. At one point the candidate says that he wants to "go where I want, say what I want, do what I want." His campaign advisor then writes a message on a matchbook and pushes it toward the candidate. The message reads, "You lose."

Campaigning for a major office is not something a person does alone. It is a highly organized, tightly controlled activity. To learn about how a campaign for a major office works, you will read about the way candidates run for the presidency. Keep in mind as you read that not all campaigns take as much planning and money as a presidential campaign. All of them, however, share a common goal—to get the candidate elected, and most use the same techniques to work toward that goal.

Planning and Running a Campaign

A person who is running for President in the November general election has already passed several major hurdles. After winning primary elections and caucuses in many states, the candidate has been nominated by his or her party at its national convention. He or she has chosen a running mate, raised a large amount of money, and built up an organization. Much work, however, still lies ahead.

A great deal of thought, planning, and hard work by many people goes into a presi-

AMERICAN NOTEBOOK 

Early in our country's history, people noticed that race horses and candidates had a lot in common. They borrowed the vocabulary of horse racing to describe political campaigns and elections. To this day, we still call an election a "race" in which the candidates "run." A "dark horse" is a relatively unknown candidate who gets the nomination unexpectedly. The probable winner is called the "front runner." In a close race, as the votes are tallied, two candidates may be said to be "neck and neck."

Teaching Note: Use the Enrichment Activity, page T 161, and accompanying worksheet in the Activity Book after students have read Section 22-2.

As a campaign manager for Michael Dukakis when he ran for President in 1988, Susan Estrich was responsible for the overall conduct of the campaign.

dential campaign. Paid staff members work with the candidate to plan and carry out the campaign. Thousands of workers put in long hours stuffing envelopes, making telephone calls, and ringing doorbells. The candidate's party contributes money, people, and other kinds of support. The final success or failure of the campaign depends not just on the candidate but also on the organization as a whole.

Campaign organization. Besides the candidate, the most important person in a campaign is the campaign manager. Along with a small group of assistants and advisors, the manager helps plan the broad outlines of the campaign: where to go, what issues to talk about, what image of the candidate to put forth. The manager also guides the work of other important members of the staff: fundraisers, speech writers, media advisors, and so on.

The manager also keeps in touch with the people who run the campaign in different parts of the country. These lower-level managers are in charge of the thousands of volunteers who work "in the field," handling the day-to-day campaign work that is needed to win the election.

Finally, the manager is in charge of the workers who plan for the candidate to appear at meetings, picnics, and rallies. These "advance people" make sure that the candidate is in the right place at the right time, and that a big crowd is on hand.

Finding out what the public thinks. A successful campaign must keep its finger on the pulse of the American public. How do people think things are going? What issues should the candidate be talking about? A presidential campaign usually has its own opinion poll taker who finds the answers to such questions.

The poll taker is able to find out which issues the voters think are important. Polls can also show what impact the campaign is

Challenge (Synthesis): Have students discuss what professional, organizational, and communication skills are necessary for campaign managers to have. Then ask students to write a job description for a campaign manager.

having in different parts of the country and among different groups of voters.

Managing and using the media. Wherever they go, people who run for President are followed by planeloads and busloads of people from the media. Making certain that the news shows the candidate in the best light is the job of the campaign press secretary. The press secretary tells reporters about public appearances and gives them copies of speeches and policy positions.

The press secretary also helps make sure that the media is on hand when the candidate is "making news." A television news report on a candidate's visit to a children's hospital will be seen by thousands of people. Such media coverage is a good source of free publicity for the candidate.

The best way for national candidates to get their message across to the public is by advertising in newspapers and on radio and television. A campaign hires media advisors to create these advertisements. Television ads, especially, can have a major impact on a campaign.

Media people have learned that saying bad things about the other candidate can sometimes work better than saying nice things about their own. They also know that it is often best to focus on image and style rather than issues and ideas.

Some critics say that this approach amounts to little more than "packaging and selling" the candidates. It is up to you, the voter, to view these ads carefully and to pay attention to the propaganda techniques being used.

Cross-country travel is a major campaign expense. Here Jesse Jackson makes a stop on his campaign for the Democratic nomination in 1988.

Financing a Campaign

People who run for President and for other national and state offices have one thing in common—they need a lot of money. As former Speaker of the House Tip O'Neill once said, "There are four parts to any campaign. The candidate, the issues of the candidate, the campaign organization, and the money to run the campaign with. Without money you can forget the other three."

Where do people get the money to run for office? Candidates for local, state, and national office get most of their money from individuals. Many candidates, especially those for national and high state office, also get money from political parties and PACs.

In the early 1970s, the high costs of running for office began to worry people. They began to think that individuals, businesses, and interest groups that gave large sums of money might have too much influence on candidates.

Studies show that people are more likely to believe information they hear on television than information they read in newspapers or hear on radio. Television is the single most important source of news for most Americans.

In response, Congress passed several laws making rules for how campaigns for federal office can be paid for. The law now says that no one person may give more than $1,000 to a candidate. The law also says that candidates must report the name of anyone who has given them more than $200. As a result, the public can know where the money is coming from. Congress set up the Federal Election Commission (FEC) to carry out these and other rules.

Changes were also made in the way presidential campaigns are paid for. Citizens may now give $1 of their taxes each year to a presidential campaign fund. Every election year, the FEC offers money from this fund to each of the major candidates for the presidency. This system was first used in 1976. Once presidential candidates accept these public funds, they cannot accept or spend money from any other sources.

FEC rules allow a PAC to give up to $5,000 to a presidential candidate in the primary elections. However, in the general election, candidates who have accepted public tax money may not take money from PACs. Of course, as you have learned, this rule does not keep PACs from spending as much as they like on their own campaigns in support of certain candidates.

Many people complain that elections cost too much money. The high cost of running for even a local office, they say, keeps many good people from running at all. If costs continue to rise, people ask, will only the wealthy—and candidates backed by wealthy individuals and groups—be able to run and win?

Questions like these were behind the laws that limit contributions for federal elections. Some groups, however, would like to go further. They want to have all campaigns paid for entirely with public funds so that candidates do not have to raise funds privately.

How much should campaigns cost? Who should pay for them? The debate over these issues raises questions that by now should be familiar to you. Does our belief in equality mean that all candidates should have an equal opportunity to run and to get their messages across to the public? On the other hand, does our belief in freedom mean that every citizen should be free to give as much money to a candidate as he or she wishes?

Who Wins an Election?

It is a goal of our democracy to elect people who will be our best leaders and decision makers. Being a good leader and being able to make good decisions, however, are not all it takes to win an election. As you have seen, it is also important to look good on television, have a good organization, and be able to raise a lot of money, especially if you are running for national office. It also helps to have the backing of either the Democratic or Republican party.

One other factor is also very important. An ***incumbent***, someone who already holds the office for which he or she is running, has a very good chance of winning. Incumbents win re-election far more often than they lose. In 1988, only 7 out of 408 incumbents who ran for re-election to the House of Representatives were defeated.

An incumbent has a name that voters know and a record to point to. Unless an incumbent has made major mistakes, a challenger usually faces a hard battle with only a small chance of winning.

The Electoral College

In the presidential election of 1988, more than 47 million people voted for George Bush. Did 47,645,225 people elect George Bush? No. Instead, they really elected people

Incumbents in an election also have a financial advantage. Primary campaigns are less costly for incumbents because they are already well known, and incumbents often have no opposition in the primaries.

Electoral Votes by State

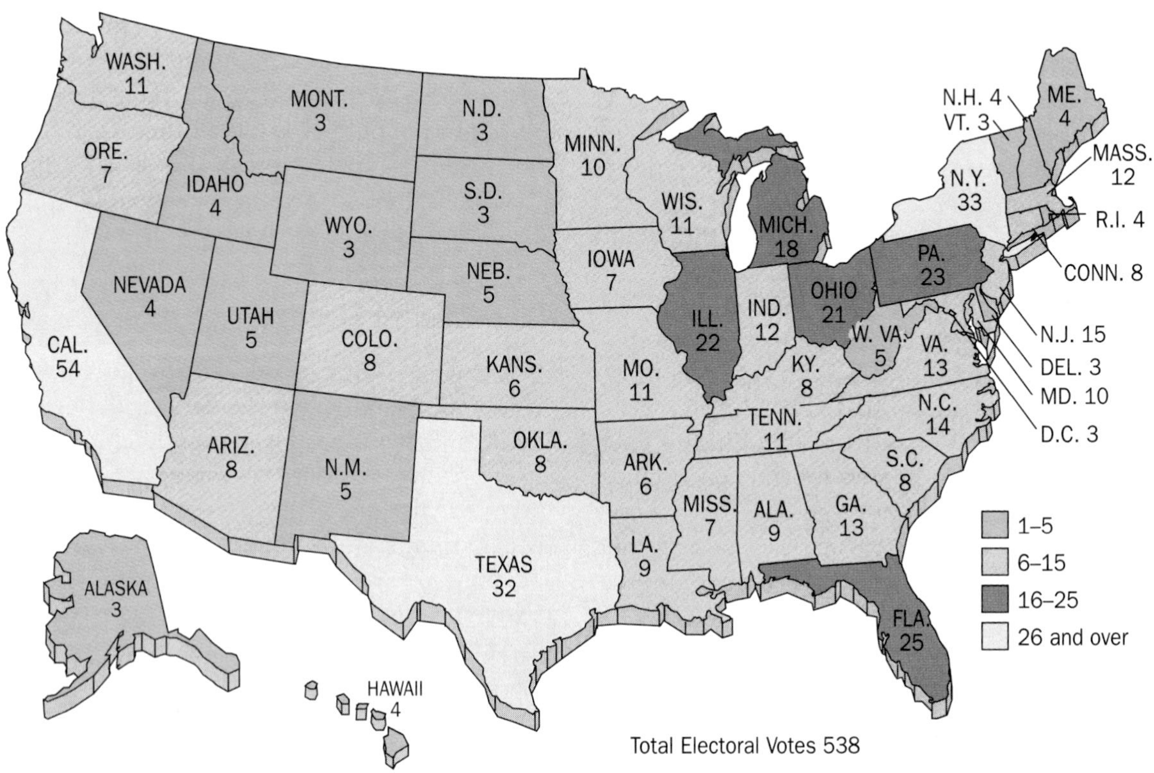

from their states, called electors, who promised to cast votes for Bush. As set down in the Constitution, the President is chosen not by a vote of the people, but by electoral votes in what is called the Electoral College.

How does the Electoral College work? Each state has the same number of electors as it has members of Congress. Indiana, for example, with 10 representatives and 2 senators, has 12 electors. The District of Columbia has three electors. The Electoral College is made up of 538 electors, each with one vote.

Before the presidential election, each political party in every state draws up a list of electors who promise to vote for the party's presidential candidate. In other words, each candidate has a "team" of electors in every state. On election day, when you vote for a certain candidate, you are really voting for that candidate's team of electors.

On election night, the whole nation waits to find out which states each candidate has "won." "Winning" a state, means that a candidate's whole team of electors has won in that state. That winning team then has the right to cast their electoral votes in the Electoral College.

A few weeks after the election, the official electoral voting takes place in each state. An elector is not required by law to vote for the candidate to whom he or she is pledged, but nearly all do. The votes are then counted in Congress. To win, a candidate needs an absolute majority of electoral votes—270 or more.

Teaching Note: Use the Evaluating Progress activity, page T 161, to assess students' understanding of the chapter.

Over the years, many people have charged that the "winner-take-all" method of awarding electoral votes from each state is not fair. They point out that a candidate can get less than a majority of the votes nationwide but, by winning enough large states, can still be elected President. Presidents were chosen this way in 1824, 1876, and 1888. In most cases, however, the person who gets the majority of popular votes also gets the majority of electoral votes.

Choosing a President every four years is an important process in our democracy. Citizen participation, however, is just as necessary in other elections, including those in states, counties, cities, and towns. Only by voting can Americans claim to live in a country where the government truly represents the will of the people.

Answers will be found on page T 162.

Section Review

1. Define *incumbent.*
2. Who is in charge of the overall organization of a presidential candidate's election campaign?
3. Where do presidential candidates get most of their campaign money for the general election?
4. Explain how presidential candidates win electoral votes.

Evaluation. Do you think campaigns should be paid for entirely with public funds? Explain.

Data Search. Look on page 590 in the Data Bank. What evidence can you find that incumbents have an advantage over challengers in congressional elections?

A BROADER VIEW

On November 9, 1988, newspaper headlines splashed the news. George Bush would be the new President. Hidden in the news, however, was an upsetting fact: of the Americans who could have voted, barely half had gone to the polls.

This rate of voting is much lower than that in almost every other democratic country. More than 90 percent of voters went to the polls in recent elections in Australia, Austria, and Belgium. The figure was well over 80 percent in Denmark, France, Italy, the Netherlands, New Zealand, Norway, Sweden, and West Germany. Only Switzerland had a lower voting rate than that in the United States.

Why is voter turnout higher in other democracies? To begin with, voting is required in some countries, such as Australia and Italy. People who do not vote must pay a fine.

Another important reason is that countries with high rates of voting hold their elections less often than we do. Perhaps people in those countries are more likely to vote because they do not have to do it as often.

Finally, when voters in many countries reach a certain age, they automatically have the right to vote. Unlike Americans, they do not have to take that extra step of registering.

Many Americans have looked at the voting laws in other countries and proposed similar ones for the United States. These proposals include requiring people to vote, dropping registration, and holding elections on Sunday. In the long run, however, the major responsibility for increasing our voter turnout lies with individual citizens. It is up to each citizen to decide how seriously to take the right to vote.

Teaching Note: Use the Reinforcement Activity, page T 161, and accompanying worksheet in the Activity Book.

The Process

Teaching Note: For reinforcement of decision-making skills, use Decision-Making Worksheet Chapter 22.

Taking Action

Remember your first day at school? Maybe you were worried about not being able to find your way around. Perhaps you set yourself a goal: "I am going to make sure that I don't get lost." However, a goal will not do you much good unless you take steps to make sure you reach it. In decision making, you need to plan how to reach your goal, and then you must carry out that plan.

For carrying out everyday decisions, such as doing what you decided to do first after you get home from school, you can make a quick plan in your head. However, more difficult action plans often involve writing down the steps you must take to reach your goal. In previous lessons, you have concentrated on how to set a goal and how to choose from a number of options. In this lesson you can take a closer look at what to do after you have chosen an option.

EXPLAINING THE PROCESS

The following guidelines can help you make a plan for carrying out a decision. Notice how the guidelines would apply if you decided to try to get elected to your school's student council.

1. State your action goal. Your action goal is to carry out the decision you just made. [If your decision was to run for student council, your action goal now is to get elected.]

2. Identify resources (what will help you) and obstacles (what you will have to overcome). Knowing what you can use and what problems you might face will help you decide what has to be done. Be sure to check the accuracy of any information you gather about possible resources and obstacles. [One resource, or strength, might be that most students in your class know you well. Being a member of some school clubs might also help you gather voter support. Some possible obstacles are not being well-known outside of your class or running against a former student council member. What other resources and obstacles can you think of?]

3. List what you have to do to achieve your goal. Think about what needs to be done, who will do it, and when it will be done. [As a student council candidate, you might list such tasks as thinking up campaign slogans and making posters. What are some other tasks involved in a campaign? In what order would the campaign tasks need to be done?]

4. As you carry out your plan, check how well it is working and change it if necessary. Make sure that what you planned to do is getting done. Check each item on your schedule to make sure it is getting done well and on time. Identify any problems with the plan, as well as any new resources and obstacles. Then make changes in your plan if necessary. [You and the friends helping you might use checklists, staff meetings, and opinion polls to keep track of the campaign's progress. Perhaps you might change your plan to account for new resources, such as more students volunteering to help, or new obstacles, such as a popular student entering the race.]

5. Judge how well your plan worked. Identify the results of what you did, including any unexpected results. Determine what you might do differently if you found yourself in a similar situation in the future. [After a campaign you might find out that posters with both your name and a campaign slogan on them were more effective than posters with just your name. Therefore, in any future campaign you might include slogans on all posters.]

You may wish to have students work in groups when doing "Applying the Process."

Action Goal:	To get elected to the student council.
Resources I Have:	I am well-known within my class. My friend Jim will help.
Resources Needed:	more volunteer campaign workers, poster materials (paper, cardboard, paint, brushes)

Obstacles:	Ways to Overcome Obstacles:
1. not well known outside of class	1. have friends introduce me to other students
2. running against former council member	2. campaign theme: "new member—new ideas"

What to Do?	Who Does It?	By When?	Checked	Did It Work?
1. Recruit 10 volunteers.	Jim and I	9/20	☑ (9/18)	Yes
2. Schedule staff meeting.	Jim and I	9/25	☑ (9/24)	Yes
3. Campaign slogans	campaign staff	9/28	☑ (9/28)	Yes
4, Posters	campaign staff	9/30	☑ (10/1)	No

Answers will be found on page T 162.

APPLYING THE PROCESS

Suppose there is a large open area near your school. Over the years, people have made it an unofficial park. You learn that the city council will vote next week on a plan to build houses there. You and your friends want to keep the land as a park. After considering many ways to do this, you decide to launch a campaign to make the area an official city park.

Now it is time to take action. What will you do to carry out this decision? Use a chart like the one above to make an action plan for saving the park.

CHECKING YOUR UNDERSTANDING

After you have completed your action plan, answer the following questions.

1. What was your action goal?

2. What resources did you identify that might help you achieve your goal? How did you plan to make use of those resources?

3. What were some obstacles that you expected? How did you plan to overcome them?

4. In what order did you put the steps of your plan? Explain why.

5. Pick three steps you listed and explain why each was important. Tell how you and your friends would complete each step.

6. What would be some good ways of checking how your plan was working? Explain.

7. Suppose the proposal was changed so that a youth recreation center would be built in addition to houses. Would you stay with your plan, change it, or drop it? Explain.

REVIEWING THE PROCESS

8. Why are planning and taking action important parts of decision making?

9. How would you explain the process of making and carrying out a plan to a seventh-grade student?

10. Think of a decision you have made recently. How close did you come to your goal? What happened that you had not planned on and how did you deal with it? What would you do in a similar situation in the future?

Instead of answering questions 1–6 in writing, students might compare their action plans by discussing the answers in groups.

CHAPTER SURVEY

Answers to Survey and Workshop will be found on page T 163.

UNDERSTANDING NEW VOCABULARY

Seeing Relationships

The vocabulary terms in each pair listed below are related to each other. For each pair, explain how the two terms are related.

1. *general election* and *registration*
2. *media* and *direct mail*
3. *propaganda* and *bias*

Putting It in Writing

Suppose someone asked you, "Why is it important to be an informed voter?" Write an answer to this question. Use the following terms, making sure that your meaning is clear: *direct mail, media, propaganda, bias.*

LOOKING BACK AT THE CHAPTER

1. What is the difference between voting for officeholders and voting on initiatives and referendums?
2. Why was voter registration introduced in the United States?
3. What reasons do people give for not voting?
4. Why has direct mail become a popular campaign method?
5. Why does PAC involvement in elections worry some people?
6. What does it mean to use the bandwagon propaganda technique?
7. Describe the difference between an editorial and a news report.
8. In order for an opinion poll to be accurate, what must be true of its sample?
9. What effect has television had on candidates running for election?
10. Describe the job of a campaign manager.
11. Why does a presidential campaign hire its own opinion poll takers?
12. Why is it important for a candidate to have the media on hand when he or she is "making news"?
13. Why were laws passed that limited the amount of money that can be given to candidates running for federal office?
14. *Evaluation.* Should voting in the United States be required by law? Why or why not?
15. *Analysis.* Five hundred people in each of four cities were approached on busy downtown streets by poll takers. Each person was asked which presidential candidate he or she favored. How reliable a measure of American public opinion would the results of this poll be? Explain.
16. *Application.* Refer to the propaganda chart on page 481. Write a political advertisement that includes at least two propaganda techniques. Name the techniques you have used and explain the aim of each one.
17. *Evaluation.* "The Electoral College is undemocratic and should be given up." Do you agree or disagree? Explain your answer.

WORKING TOGETHER

1. With a group, conduct an opinion poll among the students in your school to discover what they think about an issue affecting your school or community. Be sure your questions are unbiased. Determine how you will select a random sample of students who represent the student population as a whole.
2. Collect materials and prepare a collage that shows the different kinds of media advertisements used by political candidates.
3. Together with a number of other students, organize a campaign committee for someone who is running for student body president. Each person should be assigned a position—campaign manager, fund-raiser, press secretary, speech writer, and so on. Develop a plan to get your candidate elected.

SOCIAL STUDIES SKILLS

Evaluating Public Opinion Polls

Public opinion polls are used to measure what Americans think about nearly everything, from toothpaste brands to presidential candidates. How reliable are they?

The table below shows the results of two polls taken by the National Opinion Research Center in 1985. The first poll asked people if the amount the federal government was spending on "welfare" was too little, about right, or too much. The second poll was exactly the same, except that the wording of the question was changed. The word *welfare* was replaced with the phrase *assistance to the poor.* Since welfare is another word for assistance to the poor, both polls were asking the same thing.

	Poll A "Welfare"	Poll B "Assistance to the poor"
Too little is spent	19%	63%
Right amount is spent	45%	10%
Too much is spent	33%	25%
No opinion	4%	2%

1. What percentage of people polled thought too little was spent on welfare? On assistance to the poor?

2. What conclusion can you make about the influence of the wording of questions in a public opinion poll?

3. If you were President and wished to increase welfare spending, which results would you include in a televised speech to the American public?

4. What have you learned about how you should evaluate the results of a poll?

DECISION-MAKING SKILLS

Taking Action

In reaction to rising vandalism and drug abuse, your city council has set a curfew. Under the curfew, any person under eighteen is not permitted in a public place after 10:00 P.M. unless accompanied by an adult. A referendum on the curfew is to be held a month from now. Even though you cannot vote, you have a strong interest in the issue. You want the voters to reject the curfew.

You know that less than 50 percent of eligible voters actually cast ballots in most elections, and that voting turnout is often lower in most local elections. Therefore, you decide to organize a "get out the vote" campaign in your community. Working individually, or with two or three classmates, develop an action plan. Use a chart like the one on page 491. After you have completed your action plan, answer the following questions.

1. What was your action goal?

2. What steps did you plan to take to reach your goal? Explain why you think each of these steps was important.

3. What resources did you identify that might help you achieve your goal? How did you plan to use those resources?

4. What were some obstacles that you expected? What would you do in order to deal with each of these obstacles?

5. In what ways could you check how well your plan was working? Explain.

6. In decision making, why is it important to judge your action plan both while you are carrying it out and after it has been completed?

7. In making an action plan, you need to judge the information available to you. Name at least two critical-thinking skills that can help you judge this information. Explain why these skills are important in decision making.

142025
VE IT YOURSELF WITH
RYDER
The Custom Shop

Chapter Themes: It is the responsibility of citizens to help government find solutions to public problems. While government has the power to make public policy, concerned citizens can make their opinions known and participate actively in bringing about change.

CHAPTER 23

Confronting Society's Problems

The year: 1633. The place: Dorchester, Massachusetts, now part of Boston. The trouble: cows and goats had broken through the fences and were wrecking the village green.

John Maverick, a Dorchester minister, began to worry that the village green would be destroyed. He knew that he could not take care of the matter by himself. Furthermore, in 1633 Dorchester had no local government, no elected or appointed government officers to turn to. John Maverick decided to put the problem to members of the community. He asked them to come together to talk about it.

When the citizens of Dorchester met to discuss the problem of their village green, they were holding our country's first town meeting. Then, as today, citizens agreed to talk with one another and work together to solve shared problems.

Every society faces problems. The citizens of Dorchester faced the problem of cows and goats on the village green. Today Americans face problems such as poverty, homelessness, drugs, and pollution. Like the citizens of Dorchester, we have to work together to confront our problems and seek solutions.

It would be impossible in one chapter to study all the problems our society faces. Instead, you will take a close look at two problems that affect people in almost every community in the country. The first is the problem of AIDS, a deadly disease with which thousands of Americans are being infected. The second is the problem of how to dispose of trash and garbage from households and industries.

By looking at these two problems and how people are trying to solve them, you will get a better idea of the role citizens play in our democracy. You will see that even while we debate the actions government can take, we can find ways to make a difference as individuals.

The story about John Maverick was adapted from David Mathews, The Promise of Democracy, A Source Book for Use With the National Issues Forums, *June 1987.*

Teaching Note: Use the Introducing the Chapter activity, page T 166.

Teaching Note: You may wish to use the Unit 7 Activity, "Petitioning the School Board," in the Activity Book after students have read the material in Chapter 23.

23-1

PROBLEMS AND PUBLIC ISSUES

Read to Find Out

- what the terms *issue* and *public policy* mean.
- what private and public problems are.
- how issues arise in trying to solve problems.
- how people go about solving public problems.

You have learned about the formal institutions in American politics—political parties, campaigns, and elections. Through these institutions we choose the people who speak for us in government. Some citizens think that once they have voted, they are "off the hook" and do not have to deal with the problems of society.

Just electing someone to public office, however, does not allow citizens to give up their responsibility to care, to be informed, and to face problems. As citizens, it is our right to call attention to problems that we see around us. It is also our duty as citizens in a democracy to take part in finding solutions.

Of course, when people think about a problem they do not always come up with "right" solutions. As people offer solutions, many questions may occur to you and to others. What should be done? Is this solution the best one? Are there other solutions that might work? Understanding the problem and why people have different ideas about solutions will help you decide which solution to support.

Private or Public Problems?

What is a problem? It is an event or situation that troubles someone. A problem causes a person, or people, to feel uncomfortable or uncertain and to look for a solution. Here are three examples:

- You have homework due tomorrow and your favorite TV show is on tonight.
- Teachers at a local school say that too many students are wearing sloppy clothes to school.
- Automobile drivers age 16 to 21 have a much higher accident rate than do other groups of drivers.

What is your reaction to these situations? Would any of them trouble you? Why or why not?

The first situation might be troubling for you alone. In this sense, it is a private problem. You are the person who must decide to do or not do your homework. You must decide to watch or not watch the TV show. You make your decisions based on what you think is more important.

The second and third situations affect many people. Therefore, they are public—or social—problems. In these cases, people are troubled, annoyed, or upset by the situation. The teachers think that sloppy dress gets in the way of learning. People fear that young drivers make the roads unsafe.

A situation becomes a problem when it does not "fit" with a person's values. If the situation does not fit the accepted values of the community, it is a social problem. If enough people believe a situation needs to change, they will begin to take action.

How Issues Arise

Many people may agree that a certain situation is a problem. However, once someone offers a solution, people may not agree about whether it is a good—or the best—solution. Then issues arise. An ***issue*** is a point of conflict or a matter to be debated. Think about the issues that might arise from the following proposals.

Challenge (Analysis): Have students discuss how private problems become public problems. When do personal freedoms create public problems?

A major public problem is that a growing number of American families and individuals cannot find housing they can afford.

- To solve the problem of sloppy dress, the school district ought to make a rule that students must wear uniforms.
- To cut the accident rate of teenage drivers, all cars driven by this age group should have mechanical governors, which limit speed to 55 mph.

What do you think about these proposals? Would you support or oppose them? What reasons would you give for your opinion?

Each proposed solution raises issues. The issues come up because people's values are different. Notice the key words *ought* and *should*. Those words are a sign that values are involved. In the first proposal, being neat is given a high value. Neatness becomes an issue, or point of conflict, when someone else gives a higher value to people's freedom to dress as they wish. In the second proposal, equal treatment of all drivers is given a lower value than safety.

When people ask government to help solve a problem, the issues that arise are known as public issues. In the first case, the principal might ask the school board to make a rule that students must wear uniforms. In the second case, the state legislature might consider a bill to put governors on cars driven by young people.

Once government action is called for as part of a solution to a public problem, the issues then become the subject of public debate. Government response to public issues is known as ***public policy***.

Federal agencies make key decisions about many public policy issues. The importance of these decisions in our nation today has prompted some analysts to refer to the federal bureaucracy as the "fourth branch of government."

PEOPLE MAKE A DIFFERENCE

Youth Helps the Homeless

Many people are concerned about problems in society but do nothing about them. Trevor Ferrell is not such a person.

One winter night when he was eleven, Trevor saw a news program about the homeless in nearby Philadelphia. He was upset that people were living on the streets in the cold.

Trevor asked his parents to drive him to the city that night. He gave a blanket and pillow to the first homeless person he saw. Trevor did not know it then, but he had started his "campaign."

Trevor and his parents began making the trip to the city every night to give food and clothing to people on the streets. His father put up a sign at his electronics store, asking for donations.

His mother cooked the food.

At first, his school friends teased him. However, these friends were soon volunteering to help.

In a few years, "Trevor's Campaign for the Homeless" grew into a large organization. It had three vans, a thrift shop, and a 33-room shelter called Trevor's Place. Every night, local volunteers served meals to nearly 300 people. Trevor was honored by President Reagan and asked to make a speech at the United Nations.

Trevor says that before he started his campaign, he was just an ordinary kid. He struggled with his schoolwork. He played video games and watched television.

"I lived in the suburbs and never knew about the homeless," Trevor says. "I was just eleven years old. You don't think about these things when you're eleven. You think about yourself."

Trevor, however, made an important discovery. "One person can make a difference," he says. "Just do what you can and follow your heart."

Issues and Choices

Each proposal on page 497 presents just one solution. Of course, social problems often have more than one possible solution. Public debate over a given problem involves looking at several possibilities. In making public policy, government officials must make choices and trade-offs. You, too, must make choices when you are deciding which solution to support.

Take, for example, two other possible solutions to the accident rate problem:

- Raise the minimum age of drivers to 22.
- Take away the licenses of young drivers who are in accidents. Do not allow them to drive until age 22.

What conflicts of values might come up when citizens debate these possible solutions?

Raising the driving age may seem to be a simple solution, and it might satisfy people who want to see equal treatment for all drivers. However, is this policy fair to careful young drivers who are unlikely to cause an accident? Does it cause unfair hardship to youth

Activity: Have students find out what programs of community service or volunteer work are available for teens in their community. Have them write articles for the school newspaper or find other ways to inform other students of these opportunities.

Teaching Note: For a discussion of citizen action for clean air in New York City, see "Issues that Affect You: A Case Study" on pages 512–513.

who need to drive in order to get to school or to work?

In the case of the other solution, taking away a driver's license no matter who caused the accident may make young drivers more careful, but does the policy treat people equally? Would it be fair if you lost your license because someone else rear-ended your car?

Think about the three possible solutions to the accident rate problem. Which solution do you favor? What values influenced your decision? Can you think of any better solutions?

In the rest of this chapter you will be reading about two public problems. Ask yourself the following questions about each of the problems:

- What makes each situation a public problem? Who is troubled or upset? Why?
- What issues arise from proposed solutions to the problem? In other words, why do people disagree? What values are involved?
- Do you favor some solutions over others? Why?

These questions will help you to understand the problem and why people do not agree on how to solve it.

Also keep in mind how you might help solve each problem. Chapter 3 presented the idea that in our democracy, the office of citizen is the highest office in the land. In holding this office, American citizens are never "off the hook" when it comes to governing themselves.

Solving public problems requires the effort of the people we elect to public office. It also requires that individual citizens take responsibility. The key to finding and carrying out solutions to the public problems that face us lies in government, community, and individuals working together.

As American cities and their surrounding areas continue to grow, traffic becomes a more and more pressing problem.

Answers will be found on page T 168.

Section Review

1. Define the terms *issue* and *public policy.*
2. How does a situation become a problem?
3. Why do issues come up when people are trying to solve problems?
4. What process is involved in solving a public problem?

Application. Tell about a private problem and a public problem that you are aware of. What makes them problems?

Data Search. Look at the Data Bank, page 591, to see the national concerns of youth. What concerns young people most? What percentage of young people are "very concerned" about AIDS? How concerned are you about the seven topics in the bar graph?

Teaching Note: Use Teaching Activity 1, page T 166, as a culminating activity after students have read the material in this section.

23-2

AIDS: A CRISIS FOR ALL AMERICANS

Read to Find Out

- why AIDS is both a public and a private problem.
- what some public policy issues that arise from the problem of AIDS are.
- how individuals are making a difference in the AIDS crisis.

AIDS, which stands for acquired immune deficiency syndrome, is a relatively new problem in the United States. AIDS was first identified in the United States in 1981. Since then, cases have been found in all 50 states and in more than three quarters of the countries of the world. By early 1990, more than 85,000 Americans had been found to have AIDS, and over 48,500 of them had died.

AIDS is caused by the human immune deficiency virus, or HIV. Some people with HIV become ill in just a few months; others show no signs of being ill for up to ten years. The first signs of AIDS can include swollen glands, fever, skin rashes, diarrhea, and loss of weight for no clear reason.

The AIDS virus destroys the body's power to fight off sickness. As a result, a person with AIDS has no protection against an illness such as cancer or pneumonia. These two diseases are the leading causes of death among AIDS patients.

Currently, there is no cure for AIDS. Doctors and scientists around the world are now finding some ways to treat the symptoms of HIV. In addition, experts are working hard to try to come up with a vaccine that will help prevent AIDS. However, scientists think it could be more than ten years before such a vaccine is found.

The Problem

Most Americans believe that AIDS is a problem—a very serious problem. Thousands of people who have AIDS are dying each year. People of both sexes and all ages are getting AIDS.

Because symptoms often do not appear for many years, it is hard to tell how many people have AIDS now. Scientists at the federal government's Centers for Disease Control (CDC) estimated that at the end of 1989 around 1.5 million Americans had the AIDS virus. In the year 1992 alone, they say, doctors will find about 80,000 cases, and 65,000 people with AIDS will die. Knowing that thousands will die, and not knowing who may already have the virus, is upsetting and frightening to many people.

People also worry about the high cost of AIDS to both individuals and society. According to Dr. C. Everett Koop, the former Surgeon General of the United States, "The expenses associated with caring for the sick, finding a cure, and preventing the disease . . . can have a serious effect on the economic fabric of the United States." Like Dr. Koop, many Americans think that cost will be a major part of the AIDS problem.

How AIDS spreads. Many people are worried that they can get AIDS just by being near a person with the virus at work, at school, or in a public place. However, there is no evidence for such fears. According to the World Health Organization, "HIV is not spread through casual contact, routine social contact in schools, the workplace or public places, nor through water or food, eating utensils, coughing or sneezing, insect bites, toilets or swimming pools."

The AIDS virus spreads in only a few ways. It spreads by an exchange of body fluids between a person who has the virus and a

AZT is a drug that blocks the reproduction of the HIV virus. It controls the disease but does not get rid of the virus. It costs patients some $10,000 per year. New, less toxic drugs which can be tolerated by more people are currently being researched.

AIDS Cases Reported in the U. S. as of July 1991

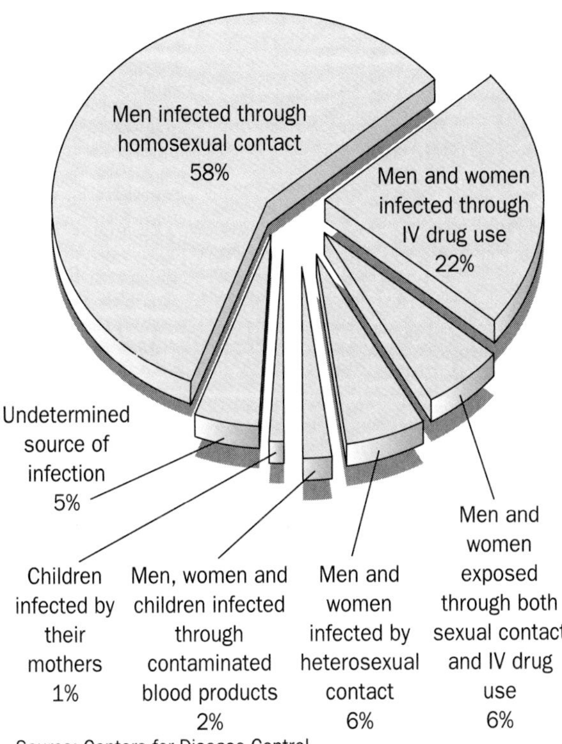

Source: Centers for Disease Control

person who does not. It also spreads when the virus enters the bloodstream by some other means. Specifically, AIDS can be spread through sexual intercourse and through sharing of needles among intravenous (IV) drug users. AIDS can also spread from mother to child during pregnancy, birth, or breast-feeding. People have also gotten AIDS through blood transfusions. However, since 1985 all blood for transfusions has been checked for the virus.

After the first cases of AIDS were found in 1981, homosexuals were thought to be the major high-risk group. Next, IV drug users were shown to be a group with a high chance of getting AIDS. Between 1985 and 1986, reports showed that the virus was spreading quickly among heterosexuals, particularly those who use IV drugs or have many sex partners.

In 1991, basketball star Magic Johnson announced that he had become infected with the AIDS virus. He noted his past carelessness in sexual relationships with women and pledged to devote himself to helping educate young people about the danger of AIDS. Clearly, AIDS has touched, and will continue to touch, a wide range of Americans.

A private and public problem. AIDS is both a private and a public problem. It is a private problem for people who have the virus. They must make choices about their own behavior with their friends and families. For example, a woman with AIDS has a one in four chance of spreading it to her child through pregnancy. Thus, she must choose whether or not to have children.

AIDS patients and their families also face the private problem of how to deal with a long, terrible illness and high medical costs. Further, people with AIDS often suffer the hardship of being rejected by those who fear the disease.

AIDS is also a public problem. The Surgeon General has called AIDS this country's number-one health problem. Until a vaccine is found, many people who take part in high-risk behavior will continue to get AIDS. People who do not yet know they have the virus could continue to spread it. Babies will be born to mothers with AIDS. Babies who have the virus have little hope of leading healthy lives.

AIDS is also a public problem because it puts a financial strain not only on individuals and families, but also on hospitals and other medical facilities for both adults and children. Who will pay the medical costs, which will be in the billions of dollars each year?

This quilt bearing the names of more than 1,900 people who have died of AIDS was unfurled in Washington, D.C., in 1987.

Finally, because AIDS frightens people, they sometimes discriminate against persons with AIDS. People are looking for ways to protect themselves. In some cases, they are looking for someone to blame for this public problem.

The Public Policy Issues

There is no question that AIDS affects many people, that it is costly, and that it can be frightening. What is the public response?

Scientists are responding by trying to learn more about AIDS. Individuals and groups are looking for ways to help AIDS patients and their families. Many people are calling for the government to take action. As ideas are put forth and solutions are offered, issues arise, and public debate grows heated.

Finding out more about AIDS. One important step in finding a solution to a social problem is to understand the problem better. In 1981, doctors and researchers knew almost nothing about AIDS. Today, hundreds of public and private medical research projects are aimed at finding out more about who has HIV, how to stop its spread, and how it can be treated. Citizens are putting pressure on government to direct and pay for this research. In 1989, the federal government spent $841 million on AIDS research, and federal and state spending has continued to rise in the 1990s.

It may seem important to find out who has

the virus, how to stop its spread, and how to cure it. However, this kind of research raises at least two issues. One issue is whether the government should have a testing program to find out who has the HIV virus. Some people think that nationwide testing, even if only high-risk people had to be tested, would be an invasion of privacy. They fear that people who test positive would be discriminated against at work or at school.

Another issue is how much government money should be spent on AIDS research. People who support large-scale government spending believe that stopping AIDS must be a major goal of our government. Other people's values tell them there are more important social problems to attend to. They worry that spending more for AIDS means spending less for solving other medical problems, such as finding a cure for cancer or heart disease.

Preventing the spread of AIDS. While scientists seek medical solutions to the AIDS crisis, debates rage over how to stop the disease from spreading. One idea is to isolate—or quarantine—people with AIDS. A few communities have kept children with AIDS out of school. Some employers have fired or refused to hire workers who have the virus.

These measures raise different issues. If victims are kept separate, what about their civil rights and their right to human dignity? People who support quarantines are willing to set limits on individual freedom, when it comes to AIDS, because they think that such freedom might put others at risk.

Those who argue against quarantines say that it is not fair to assume that a person with AIDS will spread the virus. This view is supported by the Centers for Disease Control, which recommends that children with AIDS be allowed to attend school. When people have asked the courts to decide, in almost all cases the courts have supported the individual's right to hold the job or attend the school.

Most communities see education as the key to preventing the spread of AIDS. More and more state governments are either requiring schools to teach about AIDS or are strongly recommending AIDS education.

Requiring AIDS education in the schools raises issues that people feel strongly about. Many people worry about how it will affect students. Some fear that talking about how AIDS is spread will encourage young people to take part in high-risk behavior.

Others do not agree. They believe that knowledge is very important in stopping the

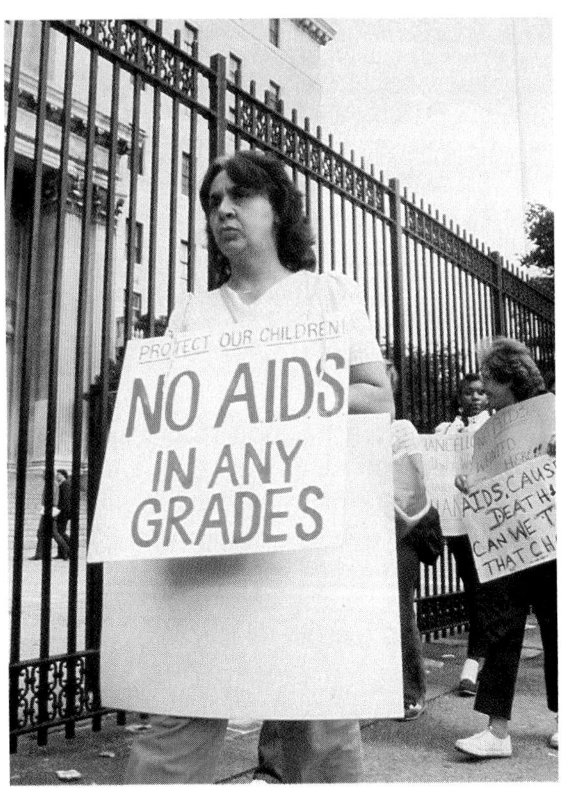

In spite of protests and demonstrations, courts have repeatedly ruled that children with AIDS have the right to attend school.

Challenge (Evaluation): Some communities give out clean IV needles to drug users to help prevent the spread of AIDS. Opponents argue that such action promotes drug use. Have students support or oppose this policy, providing reasons for their opinions.

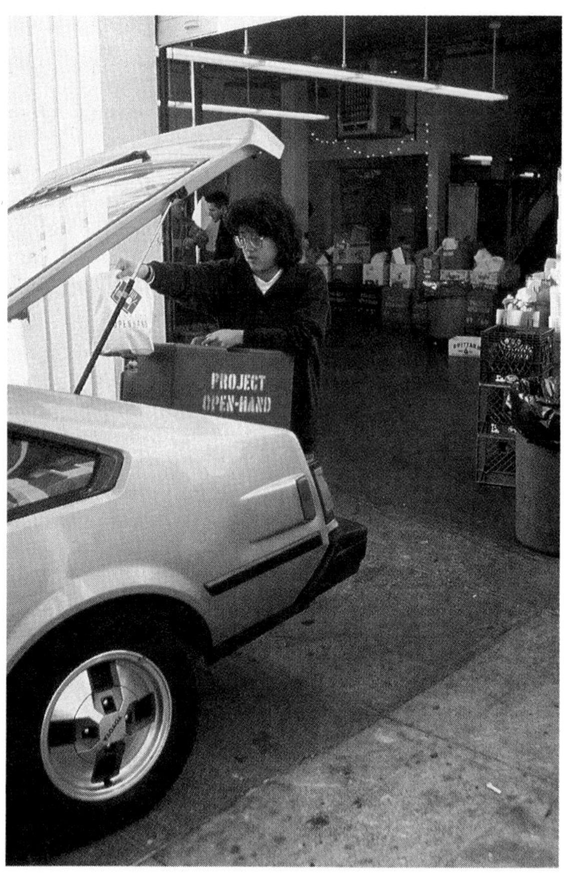

One of the organizations helping people with AIDS is Project Open Hand in San Francisco, whose volunteers deliver meals to patients.

spread of the disease. A person who knows how AIDS is spread, they say, will avoid high-risk behavior. Further, that person will be better able to help solve the problem—for example, by warning others.

Caring for AIDS patients. Thousands of people are now suffering with AIDS. A person with AIDS often goes through a series of serious illnesses. At those times the AIDS patient often cannot work and needs hospitalization and much care, at great cost.

In 1991, for example, an estimated 172,000 AIDS patients needed medical care costing between $8 and $16 billion. Many organizations are now raising money for AIDS care. As the number of patients grows, though, people worry about the strain on American hospitals. Who will pay the cost?

Some people believe that government should make caring for AIDS patients a top budget priority. Others believe that taxpayers should not have to bear the financial burden of AIDS. These public policy debates continue at both the federal and state levels.

Making a Difference

You have seen some of the public policy issues that have arisen from the AIDS crisis. How much time and money should be put into AIDS research? What about testing to see who is carrying AIDS? Should children and adults with AIDS be quarantined? Should the schools be teaching children about AIDS? Who should bear the cost of caring for the sick and dying?

While citizens and government officials study and debate these issues, Americans are not simply waiting for solutions. Every day, people in thousands of communities are taking action on their own, helping to meet needs and make a difference in the battle against AIDS.

Consider the example of Stacy Green. When Stacy was eighteen, she became a "buddy" for a forty-year-old AIDS patient. She visited him regularly, building a friendship so that as his health got worse she could be a support to him. Stacy explained her reasons:

> I was terrified of AIDS. My way of getting over that was to learn as much as I could. There's so much to be gained from helping in the fight against AIDS, especially for young people. We're less fearful, are often more understanding, and have so much to look forward to. Sharing that optimism with someone can make a big difference.

In 1991 the cost of treating AIDS surpassed the medical costs of treating the leading forms of cancer. Each patient's care costs $80,000 to $150,000, depending on how long he or she lives.

Teaching Note: Use the Enrichment Activity, page T 167, and accompanying worksheet in the Activity Book after students have read Section 23-2.

A crisis like AIDS can tear a community apart because of the value conflicts and fear it raises. A crisis like AIDS can also bring a community together. In news reports we learn that young children with AIDS are being kept out of schools. We also learn about people who are providing a safe and supportive environment for AIDS patients. We hear of young people like Stacy Green making friends with AIDS patients and thus getting over their own fears. We learn of social workers who work with at-risk, runaway youth on the streets of our cities, teaching them about the threat of AIDS and how to protect themselves.

Action against the crisis of AIDS is just beginning. This crisis is likely to go on for many years, both in the United States and throughout the world. As with any public problem, AIDS will also continue to stir up controversy—controversy that cuts to the very core of people's value systems.

On a personal level, you can make a difference both in your citizen role and in your own behavior. On the public policy level, many plans will be tried and given up in favor of other, more promising solutions. The crisis of AIDS will be a challenge to citizens and to our government for years to come.

Answers will be found on page T 168.

Section Review

1. In what ways is AIDS both a public and a private problem?
2. Describe some of the ways in which people's values are affecting the public debate over AIDS.
3. What are some ways that people can make a difference in the AIDS crisis?

Evaluation. "AIDS education should be required in every state." Do you agree or disagree? Why?

23-3

WASTE: MANAGING OUR GARBAGE AND TRASH

Read to Find Out

- why the problem of waste is both a space problem and a people problem.
- what issues have arisen from proposed solutions to the problem of waste in our country.
- how people can make a difference in solving the problem of waste.

In March 1987, a barge left Islip, New York, loaded with more than 3,000 tons of garbage and trash. For almost two months the huge barge traveled along the eastern coast of the United States, but no state would allow it to unload. Neither would Mexico, Belize, nor the Bahamas.

Finally, the barge returned to Islip, swarming with flies and smelling rotten. After much bargaining, the garbage was finally burned over a period of twelve days in Brooklyn, New York.

Why was garbage sent to sea, only to come home to be burned? This story illustrates a situation facing Americans today—what to do with the huge amounts of garbage we produce.

Each day, the average American throws away four pounds of trash and garbage. This amounts to tons of trash and garbage per person over an average lifetime. Where does this waste all go? Most of us stuff our trash into plastic bags that we put out on the curb. From time to time, a truck comes by to collect the bags. As the truck drives away, a large metal blade compacts the bags into small bale-like chunks. Our trash and garbage are out of sight—and out of mind. So what is the problem?

Much of the trash in American landfill sites consists of materials that could be recycled.

The Problem

Technically, garbage is kitchen waste. Trash is all other household waste, from gum wrappers to disposable diapers. Both terms, *garbage* and *trash*, are commonly used for all kinds of household waste. No matter what you call such waste, the problem of how to dispose of it is becoming staggering.

A space problem. Every year, United States households throw away nearly 200 million tons of trash and garbage—enough to cover the state of Rhode Island with six inches of waste each year. In addition, industries put out close to 7 billion tons of waste a year. Much of our trash, especially plastics, is not biodegradable, which means that over time it does not break down into natural substances. Such items do not just go away. They can last for hundreds of years.

For much of its history, the United States did not have to worry about what to do with its waste. Our country had a small population and lots of empty space. There was always plenty of extra land where waste could be put. Today, we do not have such new frontiers. Yet 90 percent of our trash and garbage is still put in landfill sites, commonly called dumps. Using dumps has been inexpensive, and people have become used to paying very little for waste disposal.

Dumps across the nation are filling up, though. Experts estimate that we now have about 6,500 landfill sites in the United States, down from 10,000 in 1980. Almost one third of our dumps are due to close in the early 1990s. Few new sites are planned because finding space for them is getting more difficult.

Cities are especially affected by the problem. For example, Philadelphia, which has run out of dump space, must send its trash and garbage to Ohio and Virginia. Thus the cost of disposing of Philadephia's waste has increased from $20 per ton in 1980 to more than $100 per ton today.

A people problem. The problem of waste in the United States is as much a people problem as it is a space problem. Not only does our population continue to grow, but many Americans have a "purchase-consume-dispose" way of looking at things. We often value convenience more highly than the safety of the environment, which can seem far away from our daily lives.

Out of every $10 we spend on food and drinks, Americans are willing to pay $1 for packaging. We then consume the product and throw away the paper, glass, metal, or plastic it came in. Think of a fast-food restaurant, for example. The package your food comes in goes from counter to table to trash in a matter of minutes.

Another people-related problem is called the NIMBY attitude. NIMBY stands for Not in My Back Yard. People want to continue to pay low rates for trash collection. They also want to buy products in handy packages. However, when a city proposes opening a new dump site, the people who live in that area storm city hall in protest. They do not want the dump near where they live.

The same NIMBY attitude has kept cities from building new kinds of waste disposal plants, such as large incinerators to burn trash. The NIMBY view was largely responsible for keeping the Islip garbage barge from dumping its load.

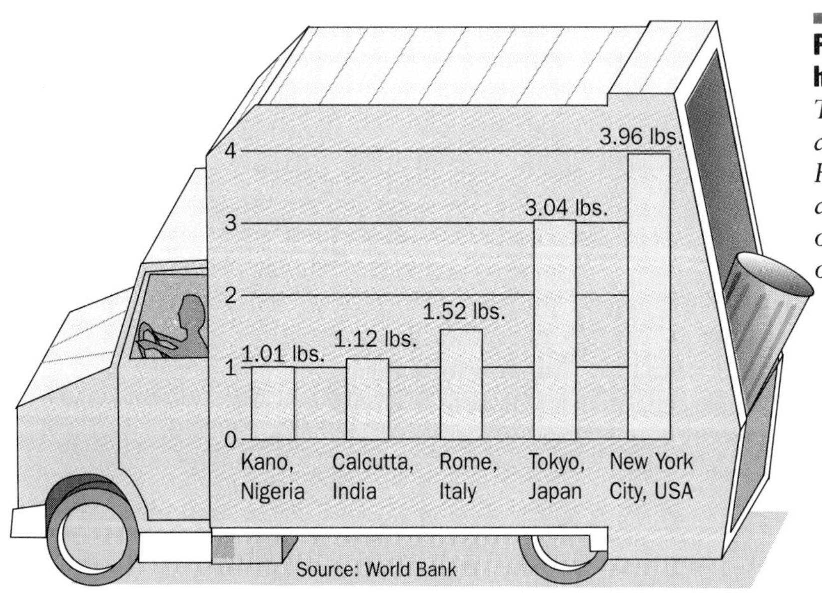

Per-Person, Per-Day Household Waste (in pounds), 1989. *The United States has been called a "throw-away society." Here is how one American city compares with cities in four other countries in the amount of waste generated.*

NIMBY is accompanied by other attitudes: GOOBY (Get Out of My Backyard); LULU (Locally Undesirable Land Use); and NIMEY (Not in My Election Year).

What Happens to Recycled Trash. *This chart shows some of the new products that can be made from recycled plastic, paper, glass, and aluminum trash.*

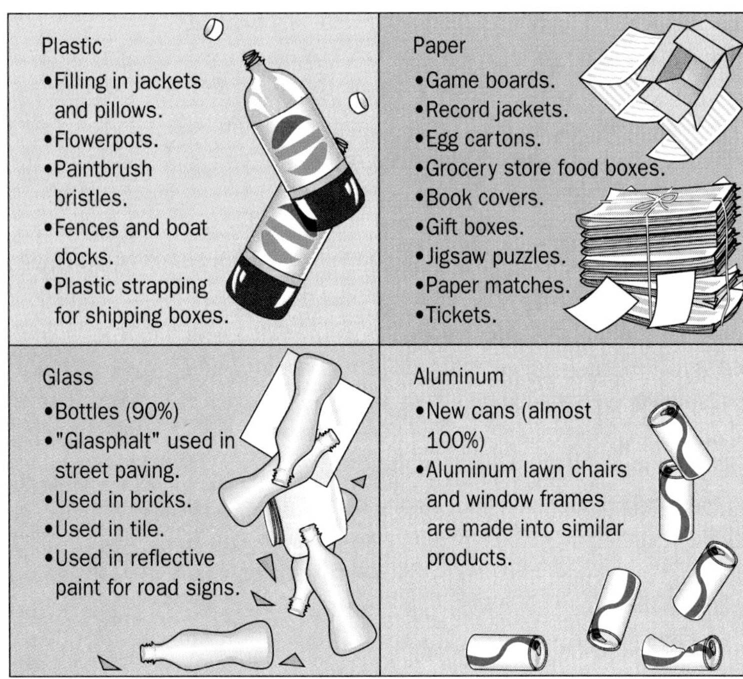

Plastic
•Filling in jackets and pillows.
•Flowerpots.
•Paintbrush bristles.
•Fences and boat docks.
•Plastic strapping for shipping boxes.
Paper
•Game boards.
•Record jackets.
•Egg cartons.
•Grocery store food boxes.
•Book covers.
•Gift boxes.
•Jigsaw puzzles.
•Paper matches.
•Tickets.
Glass
•Bottles (90%)
•"Glasphalt" used in street paving.
•Used in bricks.
•Used in tile.
•Used in reflective paint for road signs.
Aluminum
•New cans (almost 100%)
•Aluminum lawn chairs and window frames are made into similar products.

The Public Policy Issues

As you have seen, the "frontier days" of being able just to toss things away are over. Local authorities, environmental experts, and concerned citizens agree that managing waste is becoming a crisis situation. Public issues center around three kinds of proposals: (1) recycling waste, (2) reducing the amounts of waste we put out, and (3) finding alternative means of disposal.

Recycling waste. Recycling, or returning trash to a form that can be used again, can help cut down the waste problem. In Japan, individuals and industries recycle 50 percent of the paper and 95 percent of the glass. In many European countries, recycling efforts have had similar results. In contrast, the United States recycles only 25 percent of its paper and 7 percent of its glass.

The major recycling issue is freedom of choice. Should states or local communities—and perhaps the federal government—pass laws that require recycling, or should individuals and businesses be free to choose whether or not they will recycle?

People who support recycling believe that the only way to solve the waste problem is for government to get involved. In some towns, there are laws that require people to recycle. People who do not must pay high fines. Other towns have raised the fee charged for garbage pick up. The idea is that if people must pay more, they are likely to try to cut down on the amount of their waste.

People against recycling laws claim that waste disposal is a matter of choice and should not be regulated. They believe that government should not get involved in ways that limit people's freedom and affect their daily habits.

Decision Making: Have students prepare possible action plans for reducing the amount of waste in their community or school. If necessary, have them review the steps on page 490.

Although some people think that recycling laws are the only way to make real progress in solving the waste problem, other solutions have helped, too. Nine states now have laws under which people are paid to return used glass bottles. Some states provide funds to help cities set up recycling programs. Further, many people are starting new businesses that are beginning to earn profits by recycling glass, metals, and tires.

Reducing waste. A major cause of the waste problem is packaging. In the United States, packaging accounts for about one third of the weight of trash and one half of the volume. The packaging we throw away amounts to about 600 pounds per person per year. New technology is producing new packaging that is not biodegradable and cannot be recycled. Some packages keep products safe and fresh for consumers. In other cases, however, packaging is merely used to attract the attention of consumers.

Adding to the difficulty of reducing waste is America's love affair with convenience. It seems so much easier to use disposable diapers, disposable razors, and cheap ball-point pens than to wash diapers and buy razor blades and pen refills. Until recently, few consumers have thought about the effects of such convenience on our waste problem.

When it comes to reducing waste, free enterprise is a major issue. Should government be able to decide what products a business can make or how much and what kind of packaging it can use? For example, should government make a law that all packaging materials must be biodegradable?

Some businesses argue that such a law would raise their costs, and then they would have to raise the prices of their goods. Another argument is that in a market economy, businesses respond to what consumers want. If consumers want disposable goods and fancy packages, businesses must make them or lose out on sales.

Alternative means of disposal. As individuals and government are debating ways to cut down on the amount of waste, they are also looking for new means of waste disposal. One way is through waste-to-energy plants that burn garbage to produce electricity or steam. These plants are attractive to governments of large cities, where the dump shortage is at a crisis stage. However, the cost of building and running these plants is very high, and citizens are not eager to pay for them.

Public health and safety are also major issues in waste-to-energy plant development.

AMERICAN NOTEBOOK

Here are some facts about American trash.

- **Recycling all copies of just one Sunday edition of *The New York Times* could leave 75,000 trees standing.**
- **The aluminum that Americans throw away would be enough to rebuild all our commercial airplanes every three months.**
- **Americans use 18 billion disposable diapers each year, making up about 3.5 to 4.5 percent of all household solid waste. Landfill disposal of these diapers costs at least $300 million a year.**
- **The glass bottles and jars that Americans throw away would fill the 1,350-foot twin towers of New York's World Trade Center every two weeks.**

Packaging makes up one third of solid waste, but throw-away items like plastic utensils account for even more. Each year Americans throw away 1.6 billion disposable pens, 2 billion disposable razors, and 16 billion disposable diapers.

Paper, cardboard, and other materials are being recycled at this facility in Seattle, one of many city-run programs across the nation.

Should communities go ahead and build plants in the face of possible health and safety hazards? Such plants can cut down on the amount of waste by 90 percent. However, some people worry that burning waste can create dioxins. Dioxins are chemicals that weaken the body's power to fight off sickness, increasing the chance of getting cancer. Critics also warn that the ash left over from burning is often poisonous and needs to be carefully disposed of so that it does not leak into water systems.

When people discuss a public problem like waste disposal, the solution almost always involves a trade-off. Is a proposed solution good enough, or will it create more problems than it solves?

Making a Difference

Government has always played a major role in waste disposal in the United States. However, while we are debating what further action government should take, citizens—on their own and working together—have already begun to make a difference in solving this nationwide problem.

Schools have put on recycling and cleanup programs. These programs have not only cut down on waste. They have also taught students about their duties. Students who have taken part in such projects often go on to help their families begin recycling at home.

Entrepreneurs have seen opportunities to make "money out of garbage" by setting up

Challenge (Evaluation): During wars, Americans have been willing to make individual sacrifices for the common good. Ask students if they think Americans are willing to trade the convenience of disposable goods for a cleaner environment. Students should provide reasons for their opinions.

Teaching Note: Use Teaching Activity 2, page T 166, as a culminating activity after students have read the material in this section.

recycling businesses. Meanwhile, consumers have begun putting pressure on producers by not buying goods in expensive, wasteful packages. One environmentalist went so far as to express his view by sending his packaging trash back to the producer.

As long as Americans think in terms of "purchase-consume-dispose" and NIMBY, overcoming the problem of waste disposal in the United States will not be easy. Local, state, and national government can pass laws to help manage and control waste. However, many citizens believe that the problem will only be solved when people take on a new way of thinking and change their behavior.

Answers will be found on page T 168.

Section Review

1. Explain how the problem of waste is a people problem.
2. Why is free enterprise an issue in the debate over how to reduce the amount of waste?
3. What are some ways in which people are making a difference in solving the problem of waste?

Evaluation. "All households should be allowed only one trash can full of waste each week." Do you agree or disagree with this statement? Why?

A BROADER VIEW

United States citizens and industries are the largest waste producers in the world, with Australians, Canadians, and New Zealanders not far behind. Although the countries of Western Europe produce only half the trash and garbage per person that Americans do, they have much less space for landfills. Thus, they, too, face a serious problem of how to get rid of their waste.

Industrialized countries have tried several solutions to the problem of disposing of waste. Many countries burn much of their waste. In Denmark, Japan, Sweden, and Switzerland, half of household waste is burned, compared with the United States figure of 3 percent. Now, however, there is growing concern about the pollution and poisonous ash that burning causes.

A more recent strategy is to export waste. Cities and industries have made contracts with entrepreneurs to remove their waste. Then where does it go? These entrepreneurs pay other countries—especially poor ones—to take the waste. A problem is that the chemicals in the waste threaten to pollute soil and water where the waste is dumped.

The export of waste alarms governments and environmentalists. The United States Environmental Protection Agency has ruled against exporting poisonous waste. The Organization of African Unity has spoken out against dumping poisonous waste on African soil. Several African countries have passed laws against importing waste. Still, the pressure on the industrial countries to get rid of their waste is very great.

Should there be a law against exporting waste? The people who support such a law say that it would force industrial countries to look for their own solutions at home instead of causing more problems around the world. One thing is clear: the problem of waste disposal is a global problem.

Teaching Note: Use the Evaluating Progress activity, page T 167, to assess students' understanding of the chapter and the Reinforcement Activity, page T 167, and accompanying worksheet in the Activity Book.

Cleaning up the Air

Everyone knew that New York City's air was dirty. By 1974, New Yorkers were choking on air that contained over five times the amount of carbon monoxide allowed by federal health standards.

This situation might have been accepted as normal if it had not been for one fact. Four years before, the federal government had ordered that the air be cleaned up.

Congress had passed the Clean Air Act in 1970 to protect the public's health from the harmful effects of air pollution. Under this law, the federal government had created national air quality standards.

The law required each of the 50 states to submit a clean air plan to the Environmental Protection Agency (EPA). Each plan outlined the steps the state would take to clean up the air in its cities so that they would meet the federal air quality standards. After submitting its plan, each state was given a deadline—a date by which it had to meet the federal standards.

The clean air plan that New York State had submitted to the EPA described 32 steps which it would take to clean up the air of its most polluted city—New York City. This plan was meant to drastically reduce levels of pollutants in New York City's air by April 1975. Carbon monoxide levels, for example, had to be cut by 78 percent.

By 1974, however, nothing had been done to clean up New York City's air. In fact, the air was more polluted than ever.

Nothing had been done to clean up New York City's air. In fact, the air was more polluted than ever.

The blame for this situation fell on New York City officials. They had failed to take any action to reach the goals of the state plan or to go along with the Clean Air Act.

The Friends of the Earth, a citizen group concerned about the environment, decided to take action. They filed a civil lawsuit against the state and city of New York to force them to clean up the city's air.

In court, the defendants argued that Friends of the Earth should not be allowed to bring a lawsuit against the city at that time. They explained that they and the EPA were currently working together to create a new, less strict clean air plan. Until that matter was settled, they said, the court should not force the city to follow its original plan. The defendants claimed that Friends of the Earth was being a troublemaker by getting involved

In addition to carbon monoxide, sulfur oxide emissions pollute the air of New York City. After the EPA required that low-level sulfur fuels be used, in factories for example, the quantity of sulfur oxides in the air of New York City descreased by 25 percent.

Answers will be found on page T 169.

in a matter that governments were trying to settle.

The court ruled, however, that the city of New York must immediately begin to clean up its air under the original plan. Its ongoing discussions with the EPA made no difference, said the court.

"The record before us cries out for prompt and effective relief," the court declared. The city must be forced to act if the desire for clean air is "to have any meaning and effect in New York City."

The court explained that the Clean Air Act provides two methods to enforce the law if a city is not meeting safe air quality standards. First, the EPA may bring a lawsuit against the city to force it to clean up the air. Second, any person or group may bring a "citizen suit" against the city if the EPA fails to act.

When Congress passed the Clean Air Act, the court said, it showed that in the fight for clean air, citizen groups are "welcome participants." Congress gave citizens and citizen groups the right to file suit as a way to "stir slumbering agencies" into action.

In bringing legal action against cities, citizens or citizen groups would be "performing a public service," said the court. It also noted that to encourage citizen suits, the Clean Air Act specifically allows the plaintiffs to demand that their legal expenses be paid by the city if they win their suit.

The court admitted that enforcement of New York's clean air plan might well be inconvenient and costly to both the government and private parties.

In the fight for clean air, citizen groups are "welcome participants."

"But Congress decreed," said the court, "that whatever time and money otherwise might be saved should not be gained at the expense of the lungs and health of the community's citizens. . . ."

"The protection of the public health," the court made clear, "will require major action throughout the nation. Many facilities will require major investments in new technology and new processes. Some facilities will need altered operating procedures or a change of fuels. Some facilities will be closed." In spite of the possible costs and difficulties, the court concluded, government must not ignore the need for healthy, pollution-free air.

Analyzing the Case

1. What are the two ways that the Clean Air Act can be enforced?
2. Why did the City of New York want the court to delay taking any action at the time Friends of the Earth brought its case to court?
3. The court stated that "many facilities will need major investments" and that "some facilities will be closed" because they cannot afford the expense of pollution-control equipment. Do you think that this is fair? Support your opinion with reasons.

Discussion: Members of the Friends of the Earth citizen group were called troublemakers because they got involved in a matter that governments were trying to settle. Have students discuss the meaning of *troublemaker.* Is it acceptable to be a troublemaker? Why or why not?

CHAPTER SURVEY

Answers to Survey and Workshop will be found on page T 169.

UNDERSTANDING NEW VOCABULARY

Seeing Relationships

The terms in each pair listed below are related to each other. For each pair, explain what the vocabulary term from the chapter has in common with the other term. Also explain how they are different.

1. *issue* and *problem*

2. *public policy* and *public issues*

Putting It in Writing

Using the terms *issue* and *public policy*, write a paragraph describing the waste problem. Tell about efforts being made by the government and private citizens to solve the problem.

LOOKING BACK AT THE CHAPTER

1. What is the difference between a private problem and a public problem?

2. Why does solving public problems involve making choices?

3. What are two major problems created by the AIDS crisis?

4. Tell about two proposed ways to help control the spread of AIDS. What issues do they raise?

5. How could a nationwide HIV testing program lead to discrimination against individuals at work and at school?

6. Why does the Centers for Disease Control say that it is safe for people with AIDS to go to work and school?

7. Explain the NIMBY attitude. How does it contribute to the waste problem?

8. Explain the main issue in the debate over recycling laws.

9. What are some solutions that have worked to get consumers and businesses to recycle their waste?

10. Explain why packaging is a part of the problem of waste that the United States is facing.

11. What are some of the trade-offs that might be involved in using alternative means of waste disposal?

12. *Application.* What issues might arise from the following proposed school rules?

- To help students improve their grades, study halls should be required for all students.
- To prevent alcohol use at school dances, all students should be searched at the door.

13. *Analysis.* For someone not infected with the AIDS virus, is AIDS a public or a private issue?

14. *Evaluation.* Should the government be able to prevent businesses from using certain kinds of packaging? Why or why not?

WORKING TOGETHER

1. Interview ten other students at your school to find out what five problems they think are the most serious concerns today. Make a chart showing the results of your survey.

2. Watch a local or national news program or check the newspaper to find a pressing public problem. Then answer the following questions.

- What is the problem? What are some proposed solutions?
- What issues do these solutions raise? What values are involved?
- What public policy and/or citizen action would you support?

3. Keep a list of everything you throw away for one day. How much of it could have been recycled? Would the amount of waste have been less if things had been packaged differently? Share your results with the class.

SKILLS WORKSHOP

SOCIAL STUDIES SKILLS

Using a Magazine Index

The most up-to-date information on social problems often appears in magazine articles. How do you find an article on a certain topic among the thousands of magazines published every month?

Magazine indexes will help you find the articles you want. Indexes list articles alphabetically by subject as well as by author, and sometimes by title. The most widely used of these indexes is the *Readers' Guide to Periodical Literature*, found in most libraries.

Each month, a new *Readers' Guide* comes out with listings of articles published the month before. At the end of every year, the listings for that whole year are collected in a yearly volume of the *Readers' Guide*.

To use the *Readers' Guide*, first choose the volumes that cover the dates of interest to you. Then look up the subject you want to know more about. Under each subject heading you will find listings like the one below.

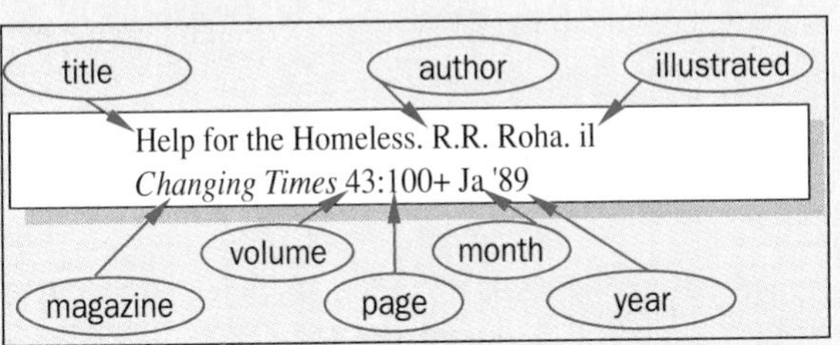

Copy the listings of articles you want to read and then ask your librarian for help in locating the magazines you want.

1. When was the article listed above published?

2. What subject might you have looked under to find this listing?

3. What information from a listing would a librarian need in order to find the magazine you want to read?

Teaching Note: For reinforcement of decision-making skills, use Decision-Making Worksheet Chapter 23.

DECISION-MAKING SKILLS

Opinion or Statement of Fact?

Suppose you are trying to decide which type of organization to donate money to first—one that does AIDS research, one that does heart disease research, or one that does cancer research. Determine which of the following pieces of information are opinions and which are statements of fact. If you need to review how to tell the difference, refer to page 212.

A. Only 1 percent of AIDS cases have occurred among persons younger than age 20.

B. In the next ten years, cancer will pose a far greater health threat than AIDS.

C. Cancer research organizations need less money than heart research organizations do.

D. The federal government is not spending enough money on heart disease research.

E. There are 27 more cancer deaths than AIDS deaths every half hour.

F. Estimates of the size of the AIDS epidemic are much too low.

G. AIDS is the most terrifying disease ever to threaten the human race.

H. More federal funding goes for AIDS research than for research on heart disease.

1. Identify which pieces of information are statements of fact. Then pick two and tell how they could be proved or disproved.

2. Identify which pieces of information are opinions. Explain how you can tell.

3. Pick two of the opinions. For each one, tell two questions you would ask to get more information about it.

4. Explain how distinguishing statements of fact from opinions will help you judge the accuracy of the information.

IN THEIR OWN WORDS

Davy Crockett: "Promises cost nothing"

Answers will be found on page T 170.

Davy Crockett did not have much education, or "book larnin'," as he would have called it. In the backwoods of Tennessee it was more important to be able to shoot straight, track a bear for miles, and tell a good story.

Crockett's backwoods wit helped him win election to three terms in the House of Representatives. That same wit shines through here in Davy Crockett's advice to politicians.

> When the day of election approaches, visit your constituents far and wide. Treat [generously] . . . in order to rise in their estimation, though you fall in your own. True, you may be [criticized] by some of the clean-shirt and silk-stocking gentry, but the real roughnecks will style you a jovial fellow. Their votes are certain, and frequently count double.
>
> Do all you can to appear to advantage in the eyes of women. That's easily done. You have but to kiss and [slobber over] their children, wipe their noses, and pat them on the head. This cannot fail to please their mothers, and you may rely on your business being done in that quarter.
>
> Promise all that is asked . . . and more if you can think of anything. Offer to build a bridge or a church, to divide a county, to create a batch of new offices, make a turnpike, or anything they like. Promises cost nothing; therefore, deny nobody who has a vote or sufficient influence to obtain one.
>
> Get up on all occasions, and sometimes on no occasion at all, and make long-winded speeches, though composed of nothing else but wind. Talk of your devotion to your country, your modesty and disinterestedness [unselfishness], or on any such fanciful subject. Rail against taxes of all kinds, officeholders, and bad harvest weather; and wind up with a flourish about the heroes who fought and bled for our liberties in the times that tried men's souls. . . .
>
> If any charity be going forward, be at the top of it, provided it is to be advertised publicly. If not, it isn't worth your while. None but a fool would place his candle under a bushel on such an occasion.
>
> These few directions, . . . if properly attended to, will do your business. And when once elected—why a fig for the dirty children, the promises, the bridges, the churches, the taxes, the offices, and the [charities]. For it is absolutely necessary to forget all these before you can become a . . . politician and a patriot of the first water.
>
> *From David Crockett,* Exploits and Adventures in Texas, *1836.*

Davy Crockett left Congress in 1835 and moved to Texas the following year. There he died as one of the heroes he joked about, defending the Alamo in the Texas war for independence from Mexico.

Analyzing Primary Sources

1. List at least five campaign strategies Crockett advised politicians to follow.
2. Which of the strategies you listed are still used by politicians today?
3. What advice do you think Crockett might give politicians today?

Discussion: Have students discuss the various campaign methods suggested by Davy Crockett. Why did Crockett advise appealing to women even though they could not vote at the time? How have changing values affected campaign methods, at least on the surface?

UNIT SURVEY

Answers will be found on page T 170.

LOOKING BACK AT THE UNIT

1. You have decided to run for President. Arrange the campaign events listed below in the order in which they must happen.

(a) Receive 52.7% of the popular vote.
(b) Accept federal campaign money.
(c) Win the Illinois primary.
(d) Receive 290 electoral college votes.
(e) Accept your party's nomination at its national convention.

2. Suppose that there is a measure on the state ballot to ban the use of styrofoam containers by take-out restaurants. What role might each of the following play in the campaign?

(a) An environmental interest group.
(b) A candidate for governor.
(c) You as a citizen.
(d) A political party.

TAKING A STAND

The Issue

Should laws be passed to encourage consumers to return bottles to the store instead of throwing them away?

"Solid waste"? "Landfill"? Or just plain "trash"? Call it what you like, America's waste is getting out of hand, growing from 87.5 million tons in 1960, to an estimated 192.7 million in the year 2000.

To help solve this problem, some states have passed laws putting deposit fees on drink containers, such as soda bottles. Consumers must pay 5 to 10 cents per bottle—money that is given back when the buyer returns the container. Such laws are intended to encourage people to recycle bottles instead of throwing them out.

Deposits sound like a good idea. However, bottle makers object. They say that their businesses will be hurt and employees lose jobs if bottles are used again and again. They also say that dumping the waste problem on their industry is unfair. Why single out bottles when old newspapers, which could also be recycled, fill up much more dump space?

The protests are equally loud from grocery store owners. To them, collecting and sorting bottles means finding added storage room and paying higher labor costs. Smelly, unwashed bottles attract bugs, forcing owners to pay the high price of pest control. Few customers, they claim, will bother to wash their bottles even if the law requires it.

The store owners may have a point. Many Americans do not want to put time and energy into recycling. To them, a deposit fee added to the price of bottles they never intend to return to the store is a "tax" aimed at people who drink bottled drinks. Others say that the fees are a burden on the poor and elderly, who often must lug their used bottles back to the store on public transportation, or else lose their deposit money.

Very well, say supporters of bottle-return laws, but the alternative to such laws may be to watch the waste pile up at our curbs. As dumps continue to fill up and close down, supporters of bottle-return laws argue that every little bit of recycling helps. A law in New York State, they point out, reduced drink containers in dumps by 72 percent.

Expressing Your Opinion

You have taken a job writing speeches for a candidate you support. Your boss is running for state office, and the state legislature is currently considering a law that would require deposits on bottles. Your boss needs a statement on the issue to deliver at a press conference. Decide what stand you and your candidate will take. Then write a two-minute statement supporting or opposing the law. Make your argument as persuasive and powerful as possible.

UNIT 8

Unit Quotation: Eight years after leading the Allies to victory in Europe in World War II, Dwight D. Eisenhower became President of the United States. As President, Eisenhower dedicated himself to making the world a place where all people could live in peace.

THE UNITED STATES AND THE WORLD

Citizenship Means Caring About the World

What we call foreign affairs is no longer foreign affairs. It's a local affair. Whatever happens in Indonesia is important in Indiana. We cannot escape each other. As long as any [nation] cannot enjoy the blessings of peace with justice, then indeed there is no peace anywhere.

—President Dwight D. Eisenhower

In this book, you have been learning what it means to be a citizen of the United States. As former President Eisenhower suggests, however, being a responsible citizen also means being a citizen of the world.

This unit will introduce you to the world beyond the borders of the United States. First you will learn about nations and how they relate to each other. Then you will study our nation's foreign policy and role in world affairs. Finally, you will read about some of the serious problems that face all nations and that challenge Americans to act as citizens of both our nation and our world.

Sri Lanka
Sweden
Lesotho
Luxembourg
Malawi
Mauritania
Madagascar
Malaysia
Salvador
Fiji
France
Australia
Austria

Chapter Themes: The world is made up of nations at different levels of political, military, and economic development. Each nation attempts to promote and protect the best interests of its citizens in its international relations.

CHAPTER 24

One Nation Among Many

Julie Lambert had a great idea. She would interview her grandfather for a report on how the world has changed in the twentieth century. "After all," Julie said, "he lived through most of it."

Julie's grandfather was pleased by the idea. "I was born in 1923," he told Julie, "and grew up on a farm in Wisconsin. During my teen years, we all worked hard. That was the time of the Great Depression, and we farmed mostly just to eat.

"People live better now than when I was your age. We have better houses, cars, and phones. We also have better health care. We can fly to almost anywhere in the world. And television, which I didn't have until 1960, brings us news from all over the world just about as fast as it happens.

"I really didn't know much about what was going on in the world when I was a kid. Oh, I'd heard about Hitler, but I didn't pay much attention. But after the Japanese bombed Pearl Harbor in 1941, I signed up with the Navy. My knowledge of the world changed in a hurry. Probably the biggest event in my lifetime was when the atomic bomb was dropped on Japan. Since then I don't think our world has really been safe from nuclear war.

"There have been so many changes, and they have happened so fast since World War II, that it's hard to keep track. Just think of all the new technology—computers, supersonic jets, and satellites in space. And the political picture has changed, too. I don't know how many countries we have in the world now, but there have been a lot of new ones since the war.

"How's that for once-over-lightly? Now, Julie, ask me some questions. So much has happened that I'm sure I have forgotten something."

The major purpose of this chapter is to expand your horizons—to help you see the United States as one nation among many. You will learn some key ideas about nations in our world. You will find out how nations differ from each other and how they interact. Finally, you will read about changes that are bringing the nations of the world closer together into an interdependent world system.

Teaching Note: Use the Introducing the Chapter activity, page T 172.

24-1

THE NATIONS OF THE WORLD

Read to Find Out

- what the terms *sovereignty, nationalism, colony,* and *standard of living* mean.
- what the characteristics of nations are.
- how developed and developing nations differ.

Imagine that you are an astronaut looking back at the earth from far out in space. You see a beautiful blue sphere covered with oceans. In places the blue is broken by green and brown areas, the continents. Clouds swirl over both land and sea.

From space, you see the earth as a small globe, the shared home of more than five billion human beings. Now, look at the map of the world on page 594 of this book. How is that map different from an astronaut's view of our planet? In addition to being flat, the map shows the nations of the world and the borders that divide them. An astronaut cannot see these nations. Nevertheless, they are of great importance to the people living inside their borders.

The Characteristics of Nations

What is a nation? One way to describe a nation is as a group of people who share a language, a history, and an identity. People use the word *nation* in this way when they speak of a people such as the Navaho Indians as the Navaho nation.

More often we use the word *nation* to mean a political unit with a well-defined territory and a government that has authority over the people living there. Usually the citizens of a nation have a shared history. They also share an identity. That is, they think of themselves as Canadians, Italians, and so on.

Every nation has three basic characteristics. First, it has a territory with borders—shown by those lines that you see on the world map. Geographers call this defined territory a country.

Second, a nation has a government. There are many kinds of national governments. For example, Mexico's government is a federal republic. The government of Japan is a parliamentary monarchy.

Third, a nation has ***sovereignty***, the power to make and carry out laws within the nation's borders. The government also has the power to deal with other nations. Having sovereignty means, for example, that a nation can control who may enter its territory.

National interest. Another characteristic of a nation is a duty to try to protect the interests of the nation as a whole. Each nation has an interest in protecting itself from outside attack. It is also in each nation's interest to build a strong economy that will provide for the well-being of its citizens.

To look after its national interests, a nation must have power. National power takes many forms. Some nations gain power because they have valuable resources. Saudi Arabia, for example, has power because it is the world's largest producer of oil.

Some nations gain power through military strength. Israel is an example of a strong military power. Some become powerful by building strong economies and becoming leaders in the use of new technology. Japan is an example of a nation with great economic power.

Nationalism. A final characteristic of most nations is ***nationalism***, a feeling of loyalty to a nation, which is shared by its citizens. Nationalism can come from having the same language, religion, or set of political beliefs. A sense of having a shared history is also an important basis of nationalism.

Challenge (Analysis): Issues of sovereignty often hinder the development of international cooperation. Have students discuss why nations are wary of giving up some of their sovereignty. Would students relinquish some sovereignty in order to assure greater world security? Why or why not?

People show nationalism in many ways. Being proud of your country's beauty or history is one form of nationalism. So is the feeling that "we're the best." Nationalism can also mean feeling loyal to your country even when you do not like what its government is doing at the moment.

Nationalism is important if a nation is to remain strong. For this reason, governments often try to stir feelings of nationalism through holidays, slogans, songs, and pledges.

Gates at a border crossing are a sign that every nation has the power to decide who may enter or leave its territory.

The Different Histories of Nations

While nations share many characteristics, they are also different from one another in many ways. Some nations are rich, while others are poor. Nations have different climates, landscapes, languages, and religions.

One of the most important ways in which nations differ is in their histories. Some nations, such as China, have existed for thousands of years. Others, such as some of the nations in Africa, are less than 50 years old. Some have histories filled with fighting. Others have known more peace than war.

Colonies and colonial powers. In the past, many nations in the Americas, Africa, and Asia were colonies. A ***colony*** is a territory ruled by a more powerful nation called a colonial power. Why did colonial powers want colonies? The reason is that colonies could supply crops such as rubber and coffee, and natural resources such as oil and copper. They were also a source of cheap labor for the colonial power.

A few colonies, such as the 13 American colonies and Australia, were settled by large numbers of people from the colonial power. In their rush to get land, the newcomers killed or pushed aside the native peoples. In time, these people became a small minority in their own lands.

In most colonies, by contrast, the native peoples remained in the majority. Under colonial rule, however, their traditional ways of life were upset. A colonial power often forced its own language and laws on its colonies. It forced native peoples to leave their villages to work as miners, laborers, and plantation workers.

Independence. Since 1776, when the 13 American colonies declared their independence, people in colonies all over the world have fought to free themselves. Most colonies in Latin America gained independence in the early 1800s. More than 80 colonies in Africa, Asia, and the Middle East became independent after World War II.

Some former colonies, such as the United States, have become strong and wealthy nations. However, many have not had that good fortune. Often the colonial powers left their colonies poorly prepared for nationhood.

Developed and Developing Nations

When people describe the nations of the world today, they often divide them into two groups: the "developed nations" and the "developing nations." These two groups of nations differ mainly in their ***standard of living***, or the number and kinds of goods and services people can have.

The developed world. The developed nations have much in common. They are all heavily industrialized. They depend on factories and modern technology to turn out a wide range of goods and services. Most of their citizens live in towns and cities, and many of them work in service jobs. While the developed nations have only about a quarter of the world's population, they have more than three quarters of the world's annual income.

The developed world has a relatively high standard of living. Most people have decent medical care. They have telephones, running water, and electricity in their homes. Most people also own many consumer goods, ranging from cars to VCRs. While there is poverty, hunger, and homelessness in nearly all developed nations, the poor are a minority of the population.

Rich Nations and Poor Nations

The world's nations have very different standards of living. One way to measure a nation's standard of living is to calculate its per capita gross national product—its GNP divided by its total population. This number is a rough estimate of how much the average person in a nation contributes to that nation's GNP. Here are estimates of the per capita GNP of some of the world's nations in 1989.

Nation	Per capita GNP, in dollars
Norway	22,290
United States	20,910
Italy	15,120
Australia	14,360
Israel	9,790
South Korea	4,400
Iran	3,200
El Salvador	1,070
Indonesia	500
Kenya	360
China	350

Source: World Bank

The developing world. In contrast, the majority of people in the developing world are poor. Many are also hungry. In the time it takes you to read this page, 24 people will die of hunger. Of these, 18 will be children.

People in developing nations are poor and hungry for many reasons. In some places poor soil and lack of rain make it hard for people to grow food. In Africa, for example, the Sahara Desert is expanding southward. Land that was once farmed in the nations of Mali or Chad is now covered by desert sand.

Some developing nations, such as India, grow enough food to feed their people. Like most developing nations, however, India does not have enough jobs for those who need work. Therefore, many Indians are too poor to buy the food.

One reason people in developing nations are poor is that it is hard for them to get an education. Many poor nations, such as Kenya and Haiti, do not have enough schools for their children. Furthermore, they do not have enough teachers to teach adults how to improve their lives through better food, health care, and farming methods.

The annual income of a great proportion of people living in developing nations is $500 or less. By contrast, annual income in the United States averages more than $12,000 per person.

The results of having been colonies. People in developing nations are poor for another reason. Most developing nations were once colonies. Their resources were used to increase the wealth of colonial powers rather than to improve the standard of living of their people.

When colonies won their independence, they had little money. They had few people trained in engineering, banking, business, or government service. In addition, the new nations were left with economies that had been set up to export resources to the developed world. Changing those economies to meet the basic needs of their own people proved very difficult.

Many new countries also faced political problems. The colonial powers had created some colonies that included groups of people with different languages, religions, and histories. Once such colonies won their independence, these groups fought among themselves for power. In the African nation of Nigeria, conflict between the Ibo and Hausa peoples led to a bloody civil war in the 1960s. More recently, the Middle Eastern nation of Lebanon has been torn apart by fighting between Muslims and Christians.

Economic development. As the word *developing* suggests, the poorer nations are working to develop their economies. They have been aided in this huge task by the developed nations and by international organizations such as the United Nations, which you will learn about in Chapter 26. While many nations are still poor, the gap between rich and poor nations has slowly narrowed.

Some nations have had great success. One of them is South Korea. In 1963 the per capita gross national product (GNP) of South Korea was just $82. In other words, if the value of the goods and services produced in South Korea in 1963 had been divided among all South Koreans, each person would have received $82. By 1980, South Korea was becoming a worldwide exporter of manufactured goods, from cars and steel to shoes and clothing. Its GNP had risen to $1,500 per person. Since then the per capita GNP has nearly tripled again.

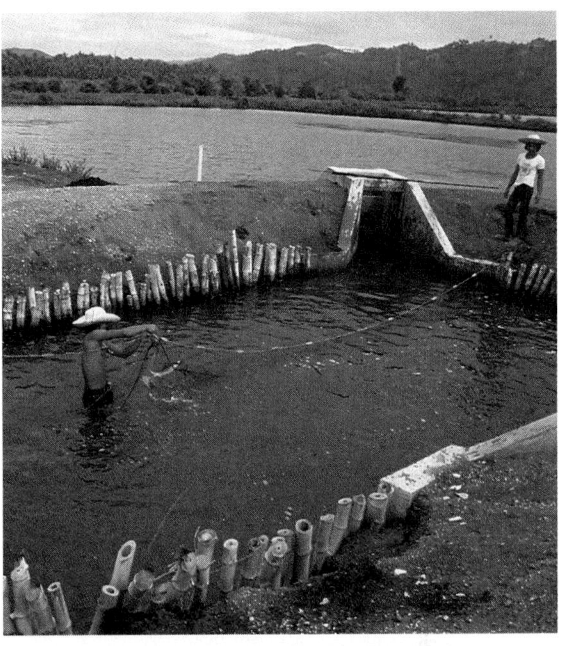

Local efforts, like this project started by a fishing community in the Philippines, help the economies of developing nations to grow.

There are other success stories, as well. In the African nation of Zimbabwe, villagers have formed cooperatives to work together to improve their lives. In just a few years, harvests by village farmers have increased fourfold. Sri Lanka, an island nation in the Indian Ocean, has made education an important part of its development plan. As a result, 87 percent of Sri Lankans can read and write.

Economic development has improved life for many people in developing nations. Even so, a billion people in the world, or about one person in five, go to bed hungry every night. One challenge facing us in the years ahead is to help the developing nations meet the basic needs of their people.

Teaching Note: Use Teaching Activity 1, page T 172, as a culminating activity after students have read the material in Section 24-1.

Answers will be found on page T 174.

Section Review

1. Define *sovereignty, nationalism, colony,* and *standard of living.*
2. What are the characteristics shared by most nations?
3. Why have the developing nations found it difficult to meet the needs of their people?

Analysis. Compare nationalism with "school spirit."

Data Search. Look on page 586 in the Data Bank and at the table on page 524. Compare the economic performance of some of the world's nations. At what level of per capita GNP would you draw the line between the developed and developing nations? Explain why.

24-2 RELATIONS BETWEEN NATIONS

Read to Find Out

- what the terms *communism, cold war, alliance,* and *détente* mean.
- why conflict occurs between nations.
- how the United States and the Soviet Union came into conflict after World War II.
- how tensions have relaxed between the superpowers.

Like people, nations come into conflict, compete, and cooperate. Unfortunately, conflict and competition have shaped human history far more than has cooperation.

In this century alone, there have been two terrible world wars and dozens of smaller ones. Many of these "small wars" have been civil wars, while others have been conflicts between nations.

Conflict and Competition

If you look in any daily newspaper, you will surely find a story about conflict or competition between nations somewhere in the world. Both conflict and competition set nations against each other. However, they are different in important ways. Conflict is a struggle for something that two or more groups each want for themselves, such as land or power. Conflict can take many forms, from a war of words to a shooting war.

In competition, groups are trying to be the best at something. Nations compete in many areas, from sports to trade. Unlike conflict, competition seldom leads to war.

Causes of conflict. Why do nations and groups come into conflict? At the root of most conflicts is the belief held by one group that its interests are opposed by another group. In other words, if one group gets what it wants, the other group is likely to lose out.

A study of past wars suggests that there are four basic causes of war. The first is a long-standing quarrel between peoples. It might be over the desire of a people to be free to rule themselves, or it might be over a piece of land. In 1982, for example, Argentina began a war with Great Britain to settle an old quarrel over which country owned the Falkland, or Malvinas, Islands.

A second cause of war is unrest or disorder within a country. In the 1960s, law and order began to break down in the Central American nation of El Salvador. Death squads and terrorist groups roamed the country. Bitter fighting, sometimes neighbor against neighbor, has continued for years.

A third cause of war is one nation's belief that it is stronger than another. Such a belief can make leaders think that they can get what they want by force. An example was Germany's invasion of Poland in 1939. The

Teaching Note: Use the Reinforcement Activity, page T 174, and accompanying worksheet in the Activity Book after students have read Section 24-1.

Missile launchers and troops on parade in Moscow displayed the Soviet military power that helped fuel the arms race for more than forty years.

German leaders had decided to attack that neighboring country in order to gain more territory. By invading Poland, Germany triggered a long and bloody world war.

A fourth cause of war is fear of being attacked. One way to deal with this fear is to attack first. In 1982 Israel sent its army into neighboring Lebanon. The Israelis attacked because they feared that Arabs living in Lebanon would soon attack Israel.

Competition between nations. Competition, like conflict, is a normal part of the way nations interact. Countries that compete economically may even gain from that competition. Companies in both the United States and Japan have improved the way they do business by studying their rivals across the Pacific.

However, competition may lead to conflict when one nation believes that another nation is not being fair. At one time France decided to help its lamb growers. It refused to let Great Britain sell lamb in France. In response, the British threatened to hurt the French economy by keeping French products out of Great Britain.

Nations also compete for military power. After World War II, the United States and the Soviet Union competed in the most dangerous arms buildup in history. The competition between these two "superpowers" was known as the arms race. During the arms race, each of the superpowers spent billions of dollars trying to build up a more powerful force of planes, tanks, ships, submarines, and nuclear missiles.

Both Arabs and Jews have lived in Palestine for thousands of years and claim the land is theirs. With the creation of Israel in 1948 and the Arab-Israeli war of 1948–1949, about 700,000 Palestinian Arabs fled to other Middle Eastern countries. From there they launched raids against Israel.

Condoleezza Rice

Until halfway through college, Condoleezza Rice had followed in her mother's footsteps. She was going to be a classical pianist. Then she took her first course in political science, or government, and her career goals changed.

Rice became fascinated by the competition between the United States and the Soviet Union, and how each side built up its military strength. After college she studied international relations at the University of Denver, earning a doctorate degree in 1981.

As an expert on the United States' relations with the Soviet Union and Eastern Europe, Rice then accepted a position at Stanford University. There she taught classes and was assistant director of

Stanford's Arms Control and Disarmament Program. Her research into weapons and national security led her, in 1986, to serve as an advisor to military officials at the Defense Department in Washington, D.C. Rice welcomed the opportunity to help influence the government's policy on nuclear weapons.

Recognized as brilliant and tough-minded, Rice was asked by President Bush to join the National Security Council in 1989. She advised the President on military and national security issues. Her job was to determine how best to protect American interests while avoiding military conflict.

As a member of this top-level group of advisors to the President, Rice was in a good position to carry on her commitment to protect our system of government. "If there has to be a great power in the international system," said Rice, "I would choose democracy and the United States."

The Cold War: A Case Study in Conflict

Conflict and competition between the United States and the Soviet Union had a great impact on the world. The superpower rivalry created tensions that no nation could escape. It also forced people to live with the fear of a nuclear war that could destroy the world.

The beginnings of conflict. How did this conflict come about? In 1917 a revolution ended the rule of the tsar, or emperor, of Russia. The leaders of the revolution turned Russia into a communist nation called the Soviet Union. As practiced in the Soviet Union, ***communism*** was a system under which the government owned all land, businesses, and resources. The communist economy in the Soviet Union was created to be a command economy, with the government making all important economic decisions.

During World War II, the United States and the Soviet Union fought on the same side. Together, they helped to defeat Germany and its allies. By 1945 the United States and the Soviet Union were the two most powerful nations in the world.

Discussion: Advisors like Condoleezza Rice help influence government policy on nuclear weapons. Have students discuss other ways that policymaking in the government is influenced.

Decision Making: Have students discuss consequences that a nation might consider when deciding whether to take military action against another nation.

After the war, conflict arose between the former allies. They could not agree on the future of Germany and Eastern Europe. By 1948 the Soviet Union had set up communist governments in Poland, Hungary, Bulgaria, Romania, Czechoslovakia, and East Germany. These nations, which were all on or near the Soviet border, were known as "satellites" of the Soviet Union.

Americans opposed Soviet expansion. Aided by France and Britain, the United States worked to help West Germany, Austria, Italy, Greece, and Turkey form democratic governments. It also began to circle the Soviet Union with American military bases.

The growing conflict between the United States and the Soviet Union was over more than territory. It was a conflict between two ideas about what was good for the world: Soviet communism or American free market and democracy. It was also a conflict between two superpowers, each of which viewed the other as a danger to its national interests and even its survival.

The Soviet view. The Soviet view of the West—the United States and the nations of Western Europe—was shaped by history. Many times in the past Russia had been invaded by armies from the West. In the early 1800s, the French emperor Napoleon almost conquered Russia. During World War I, Russia suffered more losses than any other nation. During World War II, the Soviet Union was invaded again, this time by Germany. More than 20 million Soviets died in the fight to defeat the Germans.

Fear of invasions was a major reason why the Soviets wanted power over the nations of Eastern Europe. These nations provided the Soviet Union with a "territorial cushion" against any future invasion from the West. They became the Soviets' first line of defense against attack.

The Soviets had other reasons to fear the United States. The United States was the world's most powerful nation. For a few years, it was also the only country with the atomic bomb, the most powerful weapon ever built. Airplanes armed with atomic bombs could reach almost any Soviet city from an American base near the Soviet Union.

The American view. History had also taught Americans to fear the Soviet Union. During the 1920s and 1930s, Soviet leaders under Joseph Stalin had crushed anyone who opposed communism. Millions of Soviet citizens were killed or thrown into prison. As a result, Americans saw communism as a cruel system.

Americans also saw communism as a danger to their way of life. Soviet leaders preached that communism was the best economic system. They said that it would soon overtake and replace market economies. To help that day come about, the Soviets aided communist revolutions in other countries. Americans feared that the spread of communism might eventually destroy the free market economy of the United States.

Americans feared the Soviet Union for another reason. Soviet citizens had none of the basic political, economic, and religious freedoms Americans treasure. When the Soviets set up communist governments in Eastern Europe, most freedoms were crushed in those countries, as well. Americans did not want that to happen in the United States.

The cold war. The growing conflict between the United States and the Soviet Union became known as the ***cold war***, a struggle between the superpowers, much like a real war but with no armed battles. Instead, this war was fought with words and warnings.

In order to protect the interests they shared, the United States and the nations of Western Europe formed the North Atlantic

In March 1946, British Prime Minister Winston Churchill described the separation of Eastern and Western Europe: "An iron curtain has descended across the continent." The Soviet Union controlled almost every nation east of that "iron curtain."

Treaty Organization (NATO) in 1949. NATO is an ***alliance***, a group of nations that have agreed to help or protect each other. A few years later the Soviet Union and the Eastern European nations formed the Warsaw Pact alliance. Each alliance built up its military power.

Several times the cold war led the superpowers to the brink of nuclear war. In 1962, for example, the Soviets began to put nuclear missiles in Cuba, which had become a communist country in 1959. Because Cuba is an island in the Caribbean Sea, just 80 miles from the United States, our government felt threatened by the Soviet action. For a few days, the United States stood "eyeball to eyeball" with the Soviet Union. Then the Soviets agreed to withdraw their missiles. Tensions eased.

"Hot" wars. Several times the cold war also broke into "hot" wars between Soviet and American allies. In 1950, the government of North Korea, backed by the Soviets, invaded South Korea. The United States and its allies helped South Korea fight off the attack.

Europe in 1955

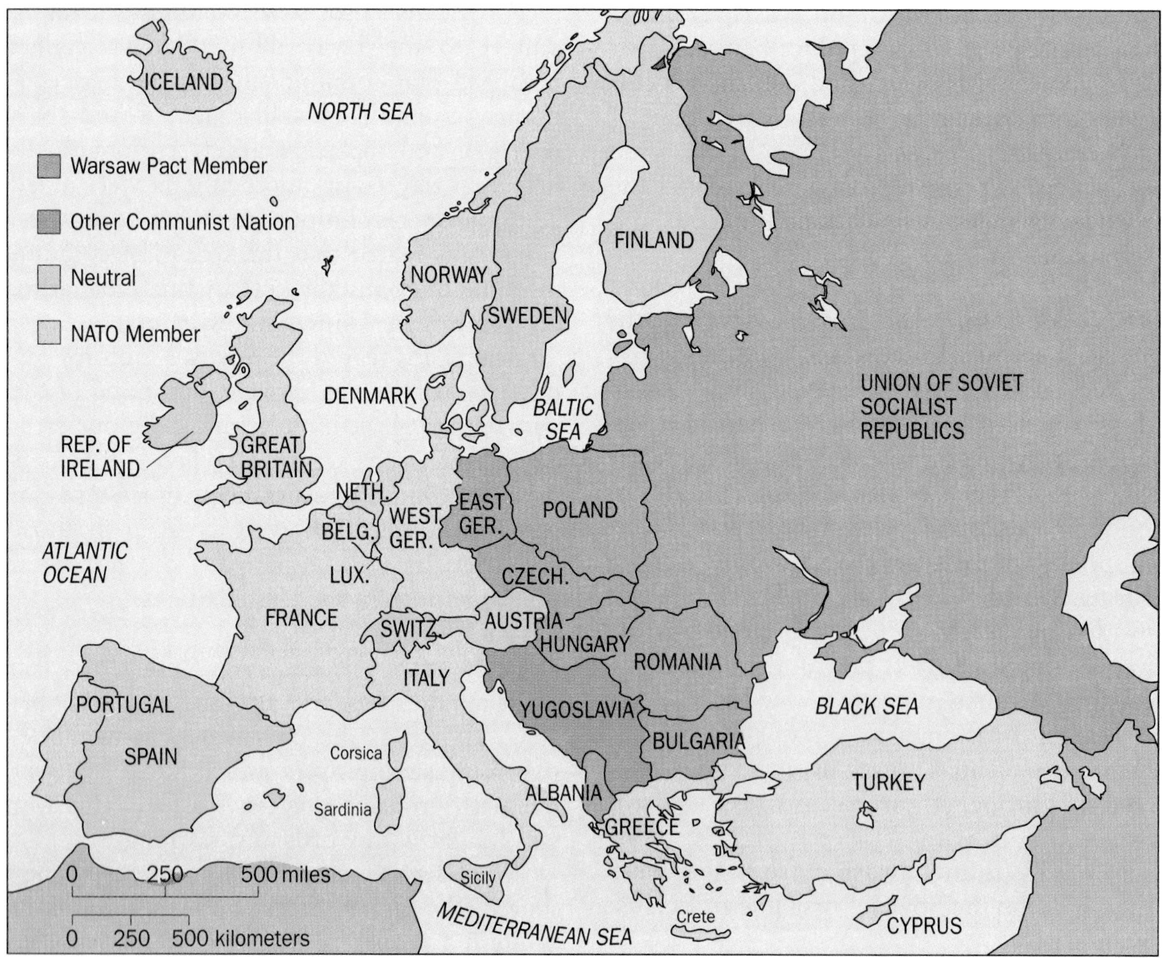

The cold war turned hot again in Vietnam. Between 1964 and 1973 the United States sent hundreds of thousands of American troops to South Vietnam to prevent communists from taking over its government. Despite American efforts, the communist government of North Vietnam took over all of Vietnam in 1975.

The United States and the Soviet Union also supported conflicts in Ethiopia, Afghanistan, and Nicaragua. However, at no time did Americans and Soviets fight each other, nor were nuclear weapons used.

Cooperation Between Nations

In spite of the cold war, nations found ways to cooperate with each other, working together for common goals. In recent years, nations have joined together to promote trade and economic growth. They have also worked together to improve the environment and protect wildlife.

Countries have also shown that they can cooperate militarily to stop aggression. Such was the case in the Persian Gulf War of 1991, in which troops from twenty-eight nations joined forces to defeat Iraq's army, which had invaded the country of Kuwait.

Regional cooperation. Shared interests have led nations in many areas to form regional organizations. The nations of Western Europe, some of them enemies in World War II, have formed the European Community (EC). They are now working together to break down all barriers to trade and travel within Western Europe.

The Association of Southeast Asian Nations (ASEAN), the Organization of American States (OAS), and the Organization of African Unity (OAU) are other examples of regional organizations. Each of these groups works for economic and political cooperation in its part of the world.

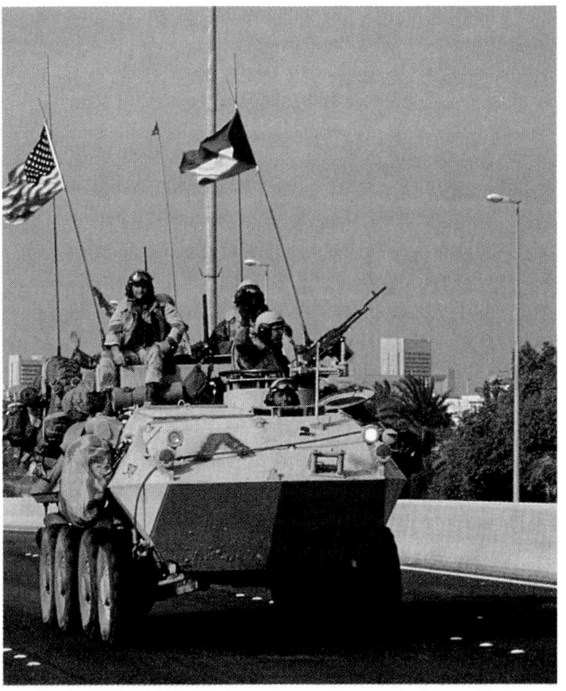

In Operation Desert Storm, many nations cooperated to force Iraq to withdraw its troops from Kuwait in 1991.

The end of the cold war. In the 1970s the United States and the Soviet Union also found ways to cooperate. The new relationship was called ***détente*** (day-TAHNT), which means a lessening of tensions. During this period, the two superpowers signed treaties to slow down the arms race. Trade increased. In the spirit of détente, Soviet and American astronauts linked their spaceships together while orbiting the earth.

Despite periods of tension in the early 1980s and renewed arms buildups on both sides, détente had helped erode the distrust that had caused the cold war. By the middle of the 1980s, the superpowers had begun to work together again in the area of arms control. "The fact that neither of us likes the other system," said President Ronald Reagan, "is no reason to refuse to talk." Mikhail Gorbachev, who had become leader of the Soviet Union in 1985, agreed.

Challenge (Analysis): Have students consider how the end of the cold war has led to better relations between the nations.

Teaching Note: Use Teaching Activity 2, page T 173, as a culminating activity after students have read the material in Section 24-2.

In 1987 the superpowers signed a landmark agreement known as the Intermediate Nuclear Force (INF) treaty. It marked the first time that both sides had agreed to reduce the actual number of nuclear weapons. After the signing of the INF treaty, Soviet and American relations improved further.

Then, in late 1989, stunning political changes began to unfold in the Soviet Union and Eastern Europe. Very rapidly, these countries became less of a threat to the security of the United States. As you will read in Chapter 25, these explosive changes were set off by President Gorbachev's policy of openness and fueled by citizens' demands for greater political and economic freedom.

One by one, the nations of Eastern Europe rid themselves of one-party rule and began to switch to free-market economies. The Warsaw Pact dissolved. Then the Soviet Union itself began to unravel as its republics called for independence and its economy sputtered.

By the end of 1991 the Soviet Union had ceased to exist and its Communist system had been rejected. There was no longer a powerful enemy for the United States to oppose. The cold war, world leaders agreed, was over. And one major barrier to increased global cooperation had been overcome.

Answers will be found on page T 175.

Section Review

1. Define *communism, cold war, alliance,* and *détente.*
2. What causes conflict within and between nations?
3. Why did Soviets fear the United States after World War II?
4. How did the superpowers ease tensions?

Synthesis. What do you think nations should do to cooperate with each other more?

24-3 THE CHALLENGE OF INTERDEPENDENCE

Read to Find Out

- how nations today are interdependent.
- what changes have led to increased interdependence.
- what it means to think of the world as a system.

You are an independent person. You make your own decisions about what to eat and what to wear. You decide whom you want to be friends with. However, you are also dependent on other people. You depend on your friends for advice, favors, and a friendly ear. Your friends, of course, depend on you for the same things. You are *inter*dependent. You depend on each other.

Nations are much the same. They are independent, but they also depend on each other for some of what they need and want. Nations today are interdependent in many ways. They rely on each other for help in dealing with earthquakes and floods. They share data about the world's weather. They use the same satellites for sending messages around the world. Nations also rely on each other to try to settle conflicts peacefully.

The Global Economy

Perhaps the most important way in which nations are dependent on each other is through world trade. As you learned in Chapter 14, connections among the economies of the world's nations have created a global economy.

In the global economy, nations depend on each other for products they cannot make or

Teaching Note: You may wish to use the Unit 8 Activity, "Economic Interdependence: A Visual Presentation," in the Activity Book after students have read the discussion of the global economy.

grow themselves. They also depend on each other for natural resources not found within their own borders. Although nations have traded for hundreds of years, in the last 20 years there has a been a rapid increase in trade. Also, there are a growing number of multinational corporations, companies with factories and offices in many countries.

If you had been a European farmer 800 years ago, nearly all your food and clothing would have been produced within walking distance of your home. Today, in contrast, much of what you consume comes from other countries. For example, the beef in your hamburger may have come from Brazil. Your banana probably grew in Honduras or Mexico. Your bicycle was very likely made in Japan. People in other nations, in turn, depend on us for goods and services they want.

Once economic links have been made between nations, there can be problems if they are broken. For example, when Arab nations cut off the supply of oil to many countries in 1973, it seriously hurt the ones whose economies depended on Arab oil.

Local decisions may have far-reaching effects on our global economy. Consider what could happen if a multinational corporation based in Austin, Texas, decided to open a new factory in Thailand. This decision could give a boost to Thailand's economy and provide more of the company's products to people in

In a global economy a company like McDonald's, which is based in one nation, may do business in many others.

Nations with single-product economies are at the mercy of the world marketplace. Guatemala, dependent on coffee exports, could be economically devastated by a small drop in world coffee prices. Nations with more diverse resources are cushioned against such economic disasters.

Japan. However, it could also result in the company closing one of its older American factories and laying off those workers.

The Role of Technology

Interdependence is a result of improvements in the technologies of communication and transportation. Satellites, computers, planes, and fax machines have linked nations in ways that were wild dreams only 100 years ago.

Advances in technology have linked people, too. Americans with cable television can watch news broadcasts from the Soviet Union. People in Asian villages can hear news from around the world on radios.

A smaller world. Technology has made the world seem like a smaller place by creating better connections between people and nations. When Chinese students demonstrated for democracy in Beijing's Tiananmen Square in 1989, the world watched each day's events on television. The Chinese government tried to cut China off from the world news media. However, news continued to flow into and out of China by long distance telephone links, fax machines, and satellite broadcasts.

A view of our planet from space helps us see that the many nations and peoples of the world are really interconnected parts of one whole.

As technology has shrunk time and distance, nations and people have become less separated from each other. We now have a better chance of understanding what humans share in common and of focusing on common goals rather than on opposing interests.

AMERICAN NOTEBOOK

As an industrial nation the United States plays an important role in the global economy. However, you might be surprised to learn that one of our biggest exports is food.

In fact, the United States is the world's leading producer and exporter of many important food products. In 1987, for example, 70 percent of the corn and 72 percent of the soybeans traded on the world market were grown in the United States. The United States is also the world's leading exporter of wheat and the second largest exporter of rice.

Our Shared Environment

The global economy and improvements in communication create connections between the world's nations. These connections are made up mostly of exchanges of goods, services, money, information, and know-how.

We are also connected simply because we all live on the same planet. We are interdependent because we share the same air and water. Pollution in one nation can affect every person and living thing on earth. As a result, the nations of the world are dependent on

Challenge (Analysis): In June 1989, the student leaders of a protest against government policies in the People's Republic of China had easy access to worldwide telecommunications. Have students discuss how such access helped or hindered the protesters' cause.

Teaching Note: Use the Enrichment Activity, page T 174, and accompanying worksheet in the Activity Book after students have read the chapter. Use the Evaluating Progress Activity, page T 173, to assess students' understanding of the chapter.

each other to protect an environment that knows no national boundaries. Later, in Chapter 26, you will read about some global pollution problems.

The World as a System

Interdependence and warnings about global pollution have caused many people to conclude that "we're all in the same boat." They have begun to see the world not as a collection of independent nations, but as a system.

A system is any whole made up of interconnected parts. The most important characteristic of a system is that a change in any one part will affect every other part because the parts are all connected. In the case of the world, the "whole" is the planet on which we live, and the "parts" are nations, organizations, and individuals.

Physically, the earth has always been a system. Our planet has one atmosphere and interconnected oceans.

People and nations, however, have not always been aware that they, too, are important parts of the global system. One reason is that the world used to seem so big. People and nations could not easily see how their actions affected other people and nations far away.

Today it is easier to see how the parts of our system are connected. At the same time, we are continuing to create new links. The result is a closely interconnected, interdependent world—a world that is a system.

Answers will be found on page T 175.

Section Review

1. How has the global economy made nations more interdependent?
2. What role has technology played in increasing international interdependence?
3. How is the world an example of a system?

Application. Give an example of how your own actions might affect people in other nations.

A BROADER VIEW

During the 1960s, the first space flights carrying humans and television cameras into orbit gave people a new way of looking at our planet. They also suggested a comparison to Buckminster Fuller, an inventor and college professor. He compared the earth to a spaceship.

Like a spaceship, the earth is a closed system. Its living passengers depend completely on the system for what they need to live. Furthermore, everything the passengers create that is dangerous to life—such as toxic chemicals and air pollution—stays in the system. Social problems, such as poverty, hunger, and war, are also a danger to the system.

Fuller described "Spaceship Earth" as a very complex system that needs care and maintenance. He said that since we humans are able to understand our spaceship, it is up to us to help protect it.

Buckminster Fuller had special faith in young people. He said that since they are not confined by old ways of thinking, they can come up with new ideas and ways of doing things to keep our planet in good condition. Over 25 years ago he wrote a message to everyone who wants to preserve our spaceship's ability to support life: "Go to work, and above all cooperate and don't . . . try to gain at the expense of another."

Inventor Buckminster Fuller described the nature of systems as synergistic, meaning that a system has greater power than the sum of its individual parts. The power of the human intellect increases the potential for synergy.

DECISION MAKING

The Process

Teaching Note: For reinforcement of decision-making skills, use Decision-Making Worksheet Chapter 24.

Choosing and Taking Action

"Perform without fail what you resolve." These words of advice from Benjamin Franklin apply to anyone who has made a decision. Another way of putting this advice is, "After you decide what to do, *do* it."

You already know that decision making involves choosing and taking action. The lesson in Chapter 17 helped you set clear goals, and Chapter 18 provided tips on how to choose the best option. In Chapter 22 you looked at how to make an action plan. Here you will have an opportunity to put the whole process together.

EXPLAINING THE PROCESS

When making an important decision, how can you keep track of all the things you have to do? One way is to make a checklist.

In the lesson on page 302 you saw a short checklist. Now that you know more about decision making, you can make a more detailed list. Copy the partial checklist that appears on page 537 and add items to complete it. If necessary, review previous lessons on the decision-making process and on critical-thinking skills helpful in decision making.

APPLYING THE PROCESS

After you have completed your checklist, you are ready to use it as a guide in making a decision. In this chapter you have read about competition between nations. One kind of competition between the United States and other nations is economic competition, which can lead to difficult decisions for American consumers. When comparing products, an American consumer might wonder whether to buy an American product or one made by a foreign company.

Suppose your family is deciding which car to buy. After comparing the comfort of various cars, you narrow the options to one American model and one foreign model. Now you have to decide which car to buy.

Choosing. Make a chart like the one on page 405 and fill it in as you move through the process of choosing. Use your critical-thinking skills to judge the following pieces of information that might relate to your decision:

A. The foreign car sells for $19,990, and the dealer offers a loan at 11% interest. The American car sells for $19,720, and the dealer offers a loan at 11.5%. Local banks offer 10%.

B. A consumer magazine says both cars have an "average" predicted reliability, which refers to how often repairs are needed.

C. Both cars get 15 miles per gallon in city driving. On the expressway, the foreign car gets 34 miles per gallon, and the American car gets 30 miles per gallon.

D. The American car is available now, but not in the color you want. The foreign car will be available in a month in the color you want.

E. A Department of Commerce official declared that "American businesses must be protected from too much competition from foreign imports." The official noted that "limits on foreign imports are fair because many nations severely limit American imports."

F. A trade official from a foreign country declared that many American cars are not selling well because they are not as well made as leading foreign cars. The official also said that stricter limits on imports make it easier for American companies to raise prices and therefore hurt American consumers.

If necessary, have students review the steps for choosing (pages 404–406) and taking action (page 490).

Decision-Making Checklist

Choosing	Critical Thinking	Taking Action
✓ Do I have a clear goal?	✓ Have I checked how reliable my sources of information are?	✓ Is my action goal clearly stated?
✓ Do I know what my standards are?	✓ Do I know which kinds of information relate to my subject?	✓ Do I know what resources I can use?
✓ Have I brainstormed all my options?	✓ Do I know which pieces of information are statements of fact and which are opinions?	✓ Do I know what problems I might face?
✓ Have I identified which types of information I need about each option?		✓ Do I know what needs to be done to reach my action goal?

Answers will be found on page T 175.

G. An American labor union leader states that limits on imports are necessary to boost sales of American products and protect American jobs.

H. Neighbors and friends are worried about the possible closing of a nearby factory that makes American cars. They urge you to "buy American."

I. Some foreign car companies have factories in the United States, which provide jobs for Americans.

Taking Action. After you have made your choice, use a chart like the one on page 491 to make an action plan for buying the car. State your action goal, the resources and obstacles, what steps have to be taken to achieve the goal, and who will take those steps.

CHECKING YOUR UNDERSTANDING

After making your choice and completing your action plan, answer these questions.

1. What goal or goals did you set?

2. What were two of your standards?

3. What types of information did you collect about each car?

4. Pick one of the cars and tell what characteristics and consequences you listed.

5. Pick two critical-thinking skills and explain how they helped you evaluate the pieces of information that you listed.

6. Which car did you choose? Explain why.

7. What resources might help you achieve your action goal? What obstacles might you face, and how might you overcome those obstacles?

8. In what order did you put the steps of your plan for buying the car? Explain why.

9. Suppose that your family picks what seems to be a reasonable amount of money to offer for the car. However, after talking with the sales manager, the salesperson says that the offer is too low. Describe what you would do and explain why.

REVIEWING THE PROCESS

10. Explain how to judge options.

11. Why should you check how well your action plan is working while you are carrying it out?

12. Explain why critical thinking is important in making good decisions.

You may wish to have students make group decisions, working together in small groups to fill out the charts for choosing and taking action.

CHAPTER SURVEY

Answers to Survey and Workshop will be found on page T 176.

UNDERSTANDING NEW VOCABULARY

Seeing Relationships

The vocabulary terms in each pair listed below are related to each other. For each pair, explain how the two terms are related.

1. *sovereignty* and *nationalism*
2. *cold war* and *détente*

Putting It in Writing

Using the terms *communism, cold war, alliance,* and *détente,* write a paragraph explaining how the relationship between the Soviet Union and the United States changed after World War II.

LOOKING BACK AT THE CHAPTER

1. In what ways can a nation build its power in order to protect its national interest?

2. What shared characteristics can be the basis for a feeling of nationalism among a nation's people?

3. How did colonial powers benefit from having colonies? How did the colonies suffer?

4. What might it be like to live in a typical developing nation today?

5. When may competition between nations lead to conflict?

6. What was one reason the Soviet Union wanted control of nations on its western border?

7. Explain some of the reasons why the United States and the Soviet Union came into conflict after World War II.

8. In what ways do the world's nations cooperate with one another?

9. Explain what it means for two nations to be interdependent. Give an example.

10. In what ways is the world a "smaller" place than it was before?

11. How does the environment make nations interdependent?

12. *Analysis.* Could a nation be a nation if it lacked sovereignty? Explain.

13. *Application.* Suppose you heard someone argue that the people in developing nations are poor because they are lazy and stupid. How would you respond?

14. *Analysis.* Compare developing and developed nations according to the following characteristics.

(a) standard of living
(b) level of education
(c) level of industrialization

15. *Analysis.* Why do you think open warfare between the United States and the Soviet Union has not occurred?

16. *Application.* In what ways are the members of your family like the nations of the world? Give examples of conflict, competition, cooperation, and interdependence among your family members.

17. *Evaluation.* "The United States should not rely on other nations for its energy needs." Do you agree or disagree? Explain.

WORKING TOGETHER

1. With a small group, present a report on the United States' relationship over the past ten years with a country other than the Soviet Union. Tell why we have cooperated with, competed with, or perhaps come into conflict with that nation. Discuss what should be done to ensure good relations in the future.

2. Check the labels on your clothes. Make a list of the clothes you own that were made in the United States and in other nations. Be sure to write down which nation each article of clothing came from. As a class, compare your results. What can you say about where clothes are made in the world?

SKILLS WORKSHOP

SOCIAL STUDIES SKILLS

Analyzing Systems Diagrams

Systems diagrams show how the parts of a system are related to each other. The system shown in such a diagram might be anything from an electrical system for a building to a complex ecological system involving plants, animals, soil, and weather.

The diagram below shows how two nations and two world regions are connected to one another in the global economy. The numbers indicate the value of goods traded in billions of dollars in a recent year.

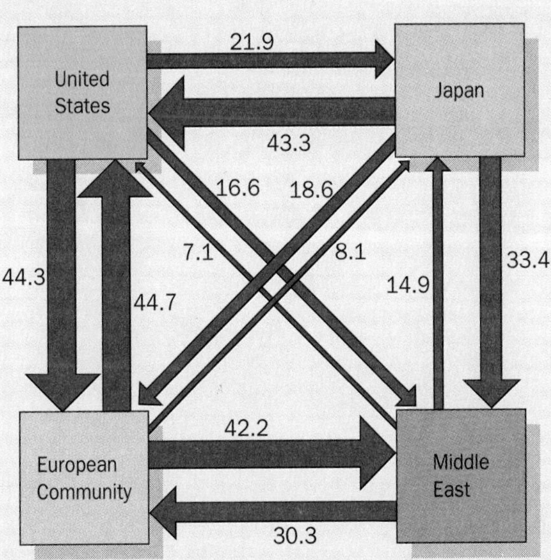

1. Which nations are shown on this diagram? Which regions?

2. What does the width of the lines between nations or regions indicate?

3. Which nation or region is the major trading partner of the United States?

4. What do you notice about trade between the United States and Japan?

5. Between which two nations or regions is trade most balanced?

DECISION-MAKING SKILLS

Choosing and Taking Action

Decisions the President makes can affect the future of our nation and even the entire world. In October 1962, for instance, President Kennedy faced a crisis that brought the United States to the brink of war with the Soviet Union. The Soviets had secretly installed nuclear missiles in Cuba, and Soviet ships carrying more missiles were making their way toward the island. President Kennedy decided to order American ships to set up a blockade around Cuba. After several tense days the Soviet ships returned home, and the Soviets agreed to remove the missiles from Cuba.

Put yourself in President Kennedy's position and think about how he might have made his decision. Then answer these questions.

1. What goal or goals do you suppose Kennedy had when dealing with the crisis?

2. Name two standards that President Kennedy might have used to judge his options.

3. In addition to a blockade, what other options do you think President Kennedy might have considered?

4. List the possible consequences of each option, including the blockade.

5. What resources might President Kennedy have identified for making his blockade plan successful? What might have been some obstacles he faced? Explain.

6. How might President Kennedy and his staff have checked to see how well the blockade plan was working?

7. If you were in his position, what would you have done if the Soviet ships had tried to pass through the blockade? Explain why.

8. If a similar situation were to occur today, what do you think the President should do? Explain why.

Port of Seattle
HITACHI
PORT OF SEATTLE
Y.S. LINE
3

Chapter Themes: Foreign policy is a plan that determines how a country will act toward another nation. Our government's foreign policy is influenced by public and private groups and individuals. United States foreign policy has changed with the nation's changing role in the world.

CHAPTER 25

American Foreign Policy

One by one they enter the room and take seats around the huge table. Several of them are wearing military uniforms hung with medals. Finally the President arrives. He greets the people gathered in the room—the members of the National Security Council.

The President begins by listing the topics they will discuss. He needs advice about how much to request for the military budget next year and whether to seek money to develop a new fighter-bomber. He also wants to make a decision about whether to give more military aid to an ally of the United States in Central America. First, however, he would like to talk about ways to stop the flow of illegal drugs from certain South American countries.

The President says that attempts to keep drugs from being smuggled into the United States have not worked well enough. Action must be taken, he says, to stop the flow of drugs at its source. He asks members of the group for ideas about how to solve the problem.

One member suggests using United States military forces to find and destroy drug-making factories in those countries. Another says it would be better to give the countries more money so that their own armies and police forces can do the job. Other suggestions are made. Then the members discuss each plan's strengths and weaknesses.

The President gives careful thought to each idea. Before the end of the day he must have a plan worked out. Tomorrow he is going to give a speech in Congress, setting out a program for fighting the drug problem beyond the borders of the United States.

The President is in the middle of an important process—the making of foreign policy. In this chapter you will learn what foreign policy is and how it is made. You will also read about how our foreign policy has changed over time to reflect the changing role of the United States in the world.

Teaching Note: Use the Introducing the Chapter activity, page T 179.

25-1
WHAT IS FOREIGN POLICY?

Read to Find Out

- what the terms *aggression, deterrence, diplomacy, summit meeting, foreign aid,* and *intelligence* mean.
- what the goals of American foreign policy are.
- what tools the United States uses to achieve its foreign policy goals.

The United States is one nation among many in the world. Other nations may hurt us or help us. They may buy our products or sell us goods. Some nations may need our help. We have to find ways to work with other nations, and sometimes to defend ourselves against them.

One of the main duties of any government is making a plan for relating to other nations. A government's foreign policy is a plan that outlines the goals it hopes to meet in its relations with other countries. Foreign policy also sets forth the ways these goals are to be met.

Goals of Foreign Policy

What do Americans hope for in relations with other countries? To think about that question, you might ask yourself what we, as individual Americans, want in our relations with the people around us.

First of all, we want to be respected. We want others to treat us as equals. We would like to live in a safe place, free from the fear of harm. As adults, we would like to be able to earn a living.

These goals are like the goals we have as a nation. In general, the foreign policy goals of the United States are to protect citizens' safety, to promote prosperity, and to work for peace and democracy in other countries.

National security. You learned in Chapter 24 that government leaders naturally try to protect the interests of their country. Acting in the national interest involves making sure the nation is safe. National security, or the ability to keep the nation safe from attack or harm, is the chief goal of American foreign policy. Because war is the greatest danger to any nation, national security mainly focuses on the threat of war.

World peace. A second goal of American foreign policy is to get countries to work together as a way to keep out of war. In today's world, wars anywhere can be a threat to people everywhere. People fear that other countries may be drawn into the fighting. They fear that nuclear weapons may be used and the world destroyed.

Polls show that most Americans think world peace should be the most important foreign policy goal. They want the United States to work with other countries to find peaceful solutions to conflicts.

Trade. Increasing trade is a third goal of United States foreign policy. Trade is good for the United States economy. Trade creates markets for American goods and services, earning profits for our businesses. It also brings us goods from other countries.

Trade also brings greater interdependence and therefore cooperation. Maintaining good trading relations helps the United States meet its goals of national security and world peace. The profit and products nations gain from trade give them a good reason to avoid war with their trading partners.

Human rights and democracy. Another goal of American foreign policy is to encourage all countries to respect the human rights of freedom, justice, and equality. Americans believe that democracy, in which citizens have the

During his administration from 1977 to 1981, President Jimmy Carter made concern about human rights a key consideration in his foreign policy decisions. He limited or completely banned American aid to some nations whose governments he believed were violating human rights.

In 1978 President Jimmy Carter worked for world peace by helping the leaders of Egypt and Israel settle some of their differences.

final say in their government, is the best way to protect human rights. Thus, they want to help people in other countries who are trying to form or keep democratic governments.

History shows that countries in which human rights are denied can be a threat to world peace. When citizens do not have the right to take part in their own government, revolutions and civil wars are likely to break out, and other countries are likely to be drawn in. Therefore, encouraging human rights and democracy is also a way to meet our foreign policy goals of peace and security.

Tools of Foreign Policy

How does a country go about meeting its foreign policy goals? The United States uses several tools, such as defense, alliances, diplomacy, trade measures, and intelligence, in its relations with other nations.

Defense. Defense is an important tool of American foreign policy. It helps the government maintain national security. American armed forces, with modern weapons, aircraft, and ships, are the means by which we defend ourselves against ***aggression***, an attack or threat of attack by another country.

A key part of United States foreign policy has been ***deterrence***, keeping a strong defense to discourage aggression by other nations. In Chapter 24 you read about the arms race between the United States and the Soviet Union. Both sides claimed that they were building weapons as deterrence against aggression.

Sometimes it is not clear whether a nation is using its armed forces for defense or aggression. When the Soviets sent their army into Afghanistan in 1979, they said they were just helping the Afghan government defend against anti-communist forces. The United States accused the Soviets of aggression—

Teaching Note: For a discussion of American policy toward political refugees, see "Issues that Affect You: A Case Study" on pages 558–559.

Challenge (Evaluation): Approximately 26 percent of our federal budget is spent on defense. Have students discuss whether that amount is appropriate for the existing world situation. Students should provide reasons for their opinions.

of using its military power to take over an independent nation.

In 1989, when American forces overthrew Panama's dictator, Manuel Noriega, Latin American leaders accused the United States of aggression. President Bush said the invasion's purpose was to protect American interests, especially the Panama Canal, and to help Panama get rid of a corrupt leader.

Alliances. The United States also meets its foreign policy goals by forming military, political, or economic alliances with other countries. In Chapter 24 you read about NATO, a military alliance created to protect Western Europe from Soviet aggression. NATO members pooled military forces into one army in order to better defend themselves if attacked.

An example of a political alliance is the Organization of American States (OAS), made up of countries in North, Central, and South America. The OAS helps its members work together peacefully, trying to settle disputes before they become violent. The OAS also reports on human rights in its member countries and helps to keep elections fair and honest.

The United States is a member of several economic alliances. One is the Organization for Economic Cooperation and Development (OECD). The 24 members of the OECD, mostly Western European countries, agree to help each other's economic well-being through trade. They also work together in giving aid to developing nations.

Diplomacy. Can you remember settling a disagreement with someone by talking it out? In a similar way, the American government tries to settle disagreements with other countries peacefully. To do so, it depends mostly on a third tool of foreign policy, diplomacy. ***Diplomacy*** is the relations and communications carried out between countries. When countries disagree, they send representatives called diplomats to talk about the issues.

The United States uses diplomacy not only to settle disagreements but also to accomplish tasks such as building a canal or space station. Alliances and trade agreements are also made through diplomacy. Diplomacy often results in formal agreements known as treaties.

Usually, diplomacy is carried out by members of the Department of State. Sometimes, however, there is a ***summit meeting***, a meeting at which the President talks about important issues with heads of other governments. The number of summit meetings has increased in recent years. The 1988 meeting at which President Ronald Reagan and Soviet leader Mikhail Gorbachev agreed to the INF treaty is an example of a summit meeting.

Foreign aid. Another tool used to meet foreign policy goals is ***foreign aid***, a program of giving military and economic help to other countries. After World War II the United States gave aid to European countries to help them rebuild factories, farms, cities, and homes destroyed in the war. Since the end of World War II, the United States has given or loaned almost $350 billion in foreign aid to over 100 countries.

Foreign aid can support American policy goals by strengthening governments and political groups that are friendly to the United States. In some cases this military aid has helped countries that are trying to put down rebellions within their borders. Sometimes the United States has sent weapons to rebels who are struggling against governments considered unfriendly to American interests.

Economic aid takes many forms. The United States might help pay for a hospital, or a dam to control floods or produce electricity. Aid might be loans or grants to help a country start a new industry.

Sending experts and teachers to work in

The United States government spends less than 1 percent of its annual budget on foreign aid. This percentage is one of the lowest among major economic powers.

Teaching Note: For a discussion/activity on the issue of limiting imports, see "Taking a Stand" on page 581.

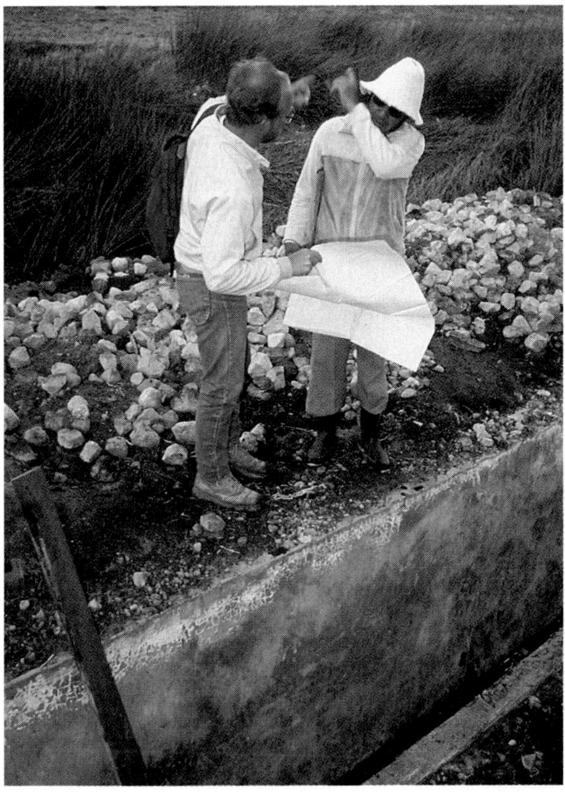

Money and equipment are not the only forms of foreign aid. Peace Corps volunteers like this one in Ecuador give help to developing nations.

Sending experts and teachers to work in developing countries is also a form of aid. The United States also sends aid in a crisis such as a flood or earthquake. Aid helps nations' economies to grow and is seen as a way to reduce the chance of revolution and war.

Foreign aid has caused bitter debates in Congress and the nation. Americans disagree over how much and what kind of aid to give. Some say that giving help to other countries is our duty as a rich and powerful country. They say that if we do not give aid, poorer nations will turn to communist governments for help. Another argument for economic aid is that it helps the United States. Countries that receive our aid can then buy American products.

Those who oppose aid do so for two main reasons. Some say that we should solve problems at home first and not send so much money out of the country.

Other critics say that the kind of aid we give does more harm than good. They charge that our military aid has sometimes helped governments that violate human rights. Just because a group is friendly to the United States, they say, is not a good reason to give it money and weapons. Critics also believe that some kinds of economic aid give the United States too much control over how other countries develop.

Trade measures. The terms under which the United States trades with other countries are another tool of foreign policy. Trade measures include agreements about how much of a foreign product may be sold in the United States and whether the product will be subject to a tariff, or tax. Measures also include the terms under which the United States sells to other countries.

The United States has two main aims in offering good trade terms to another country. One aim is to get other countries to buy American goods, which helps meet the goal of economic prosperity.

Another aim is to get our trading partners to support us in other foreign policy goals. During the cold war, for example, the United States sold weapons on favorable terms to encourage developing nations to resist Soviet influence.

Sometimes the United States tries to meet foreign policy goals by punishing a nation with which it trades. For example, to show its disapproval of racial segregation in South Africa, the United States in 1986 made it illegal for American companies to invest in that country. Boycotting goods and setting limits on the amount of a product that can be sold in the United States are also methods our government uses to try to make other countries change their behavior.

Some American trade agreements have a "most favored nation" clause. This clause ensures that any reduction in import tariffs granted to one nation will automatically be given to all countries with most favored nation status. This provision is a powerful negotiating tool for the United States.

Teaching Note: Use Teaching Activity 1, page T 179, after students have read the material in Section 25-1.

Intelligence. Information about another country and what its government plans to do is called ***intelligence.*** Most countries work hard to gather intelligence in order to help them meet the goal of national security.

The Central Intelligence Agency (CIA) and other agencies gather information for the United States government. The CIA focuses mostly on countries it thinks might be unfriendly, and tries to learn what the governments of these countries intend to do. It also tries to predict how these governments will react to what the United States does.

Much of intelligence is secret. Information is sometimes gathered by spying. Sometimes intelligence agencies have helped overturn the government of a country. In Chile in 1973, for example, the CIA took part in overthrowing the government of Salvador Allende. The United States government thought Allende was not favorable to our national interest. Like defense, diplomacy, foreign aid, and trade measures, intelligence is an important tool of foreign policy.

Answers will be found on page T 181.

Section Review

1. Define the terms *aggression, deterrence, diplomacy, summit meeting, foreign aid,* and *intelligence.*
2. Why is world peace a goal of American foreign policy?
3. How does the United States use diplomacy as a tool of foreign policy?

Synthesis. Explain how the foreign policy goal of promoting trade relates to the goals of national security and world peace.

Data Search. Look at the chart on page 591 in the Data Bank and the world map on page 594. Then explain whether they support the following statement: The United States gives most of its aid to nations near its borders.

25-2 MAKING FOREIGN POLICY

Read to Find Out

- what role the President and the various departments of the executive branch play in making foreign policy.
- what powers Congress has over foreign policy.
- how private groups and citizens help shape foreign policy.

Sarah was upset. She had learned that whales might become extinct because they were being hunted. Every year there were fewer and fewer whales left. "There must be something we can do," she thought.

Sarah found out that in 1946 all the countries that hunted whales, including the United States, had formed the International Whaling Commission (IWC). The goal of the IWC was to protect whales.

Each year the IWC had set a limit on the number of whales that could be killed. Even so, by the 1980s there were so few whales left that the IWC decided to ban whaling for a while. However, Iceland, whose economy depended on whaling, refused to go along with the ban.

"How can we stop Iceland from hunting whales?" asked Sarah. She wondered if people in the government could help.

"Why don't you start by writing our representative in Congress?" suggested Sarah's father. So she did.

Sarah is one person hoping to affect American foreign policy. Like Sarah, many people and organizations have ideas about America's relations with other countries. They want the government to take action to help achieve their goals.

Who decides how the United States should behave toward other countries? Who decides what action to take? As you will see, many people both inside and outside of government play a role in foreign policy.

The Executive Branch

Sarah was only one of many people who spoke out against whaling. The issue came to the attention of the President. The Constitution gives the President the major responsibility for making foreign policy. Since most foreign policy issues touch many parts of American life, from jobs to the environment, many departments and agencies of the executive branch get involved in foreign policy decisions.

The President. The President shapes foreign policy both as commander in chief of the armed forces and as the nation's chief diplomat. The President sets defense policies, meets with leaders of other countries, and makes treaties and executive agreements. The President also appoints ambassadors to represent the United States in other countries and makes budget proposals to Congress for defense spending and foreign aid.

The President does not make foreign policy decisions alone, however. In the case of Iceland and whaling, the President might begin by asking the chief of staff to look into the matter. The chief of staff would then raise the question at a meeting with other members of the White House staff. Here are some of the members who would be likely to take part in the meeting.

- The assistant for legislative affairs keeps track of issues that Congress is interested in. Sarah's letter, and thousands like it, may have brought whaling to the attention of Congress. This assistant can provide information on how most members of Congress are likely to view the issue.
- The assistant for policy development may have to come up with new policies toward Iceland.
- The National Security Advisor has to think about how policies might affect the country's safety. Iceland is a member of NATO and an ally of the United States.
- The assistant for political and intergovernmental affairs makes sure that other departments know about the whaling issue.

President Nixon renewed U.S. relations with China during a historic visit in 1972. Here, officials and photographers greet the Nixons.

Once the White House staff has talked over the problem, the chief of staff might send a letter to the Secretary of State, asking for information and perhaps some recommendations.

Becoming an American foreign service officer is very competitive. Each year 10,000 to 15,000 applicants take examinations to fill fewer than 200 positions. Those who succeed receive training in diplomacy, political and economic analysis, and foreign languages.

The Department of State. The Department of State advises the President on foreign policy. It also carries out foreign policy once that policy has been made. The Secretary of State works closely with the President and represents the United States in many diplomatic meetings. The Secretary is assisted by experts on different parts of the world, such as the Middle East or Europe, and by experts on foreign policy.

The Department of State also has nearly 16,000 officials working in other countries. These officials are known as foreign service officers. They include ambassadors, who represent our country in embassies, or diplomatic offices, around the world. They also include consuls, who help American business people and travelers abroad.

Members of the foreign service carry out our foreign policy. They also give the State Department information about the countries in which they serve.

When the President asked the Secretary of State to look into the whaling issue, here are some of the State Department offices and officials who took part.

- The Bureau of Northern European Affairs has an Icelandic "desk" that keeps track of our relations with Iceland. The desk officer gave reports from our ambassador in Iceland. The Prime Minister of Iceland claimed that his country would take only a few whales each year for a scientific study.
- The Bureau of Oceans and International Environmental and Scientific Affairs gave evidence that Iceland's "study" is really an excuse to keep whaling.
- The Policy Planning Staff makes suggestions to the Secretary of State on what the United States should do. Their suggestions on Iceland gave the pros and cons of each course of action.
- The Congressional Liaison Office of the State Department tells the Secretary of State what actions are allowed by Congress. This office informed the Secretary that Congress had given the President power to use trade measures in this case.

AMERICAN NOTEBOOK

To help foreign relations run smoothly, nations have agreed on certain ways to treat diplomats. Some of these are:

- **A diplomat cannot be arrested by the country in which he or she serves.**
- **An embassy is treated as part of the diplomat's home country. Soldiers or police cannot enter unless invited.**
- **Packages sent home by diplomats cannot be seized or searched.**
- **At ceremonies, diplomats are seated according to strict rules of rank.**

The Department of Defense. The Department of Defense also plays a part in making foreign policy. It advises the President on matters such as what weapons to make and where to place bases and troops. The President and the Secretary of Defense work closely with the Joint Chiefs of Staff—the heads of the Army, Navy, Air Force, and Marines.

The United States Navy has bases in Iceland to track Soviet nuclear submarines that enter the Atlantic Ocean from Soviet bases in the Arctic. The Secretary of Defense could warn the President that if trade were cut off, Iceland might threaten to close these bases.

The National Security Council. The National Security Council (NSC) advises the President

Challenge (Evaluation): Under the War Powers Act, the President can send American forces into action for 90 days without congressional approval. Do students think this is a necessary presidential power? Why or why not?

The Department of Defense, with headquarters in the vast Pentagon building, has an important role in making and carrying out American foreign policy.

on the country's safety. The NSC includes the President and Vice-President and the secretaries of state and defense. The director of the CIA and the head of the Joint Chiefs of Staff, as well as other experts, also attend NSC meetings. The President calls a meeting of the NSC when a crisis comes up somewhere and American security seems in danger.

The President's National Security Advisor is the director of the NSC. Like the Secretary of Defense, he or she would consider how changing our trade policy with Iceland could affect NATO and our bases.

Other executive departments and agencies. Depending on the problem, the President may seek help from other executive departments and agencies. In the whaling case, for instance, the Department of Commerce played an important role.

One division of the Department of Commerce is responsible for protecting marine mammals and representing the United States on the International Whaling Commission. The Secretary of Commerce is required by law to tell the President when a nation violates the IWC's whaling ban. The Secretary advised the President to take steps to force Iceland to go along with the ban.

Congress

Although the President plays the major role in making and carrying out foreign policy, Congress also has some power over foreign policy. The Senate has the power to approve or reject treaties. The President's choices for the diplomatic corps must also be approved by the Senate. Furthermore, only Congress can declare war.

Congress has power over foreign policy through the budget, too. It must approve all spending, such as for defense and foreign aid. Often the executive and legislative branches have conflicts over such spending. In 1982, the House turned down President Reagan's request for money to help anti-communist rebels fighting the Nicaraguan government.

Several congressional committees are important in making foreign policy. Those most directly involved are the Senate Foreign Relations Committee, the House Foreign Affairs Committee, and the Armed Services committees in both houses.

These committees hold hearings and write and study bills that affect our relations with other countries. The Secretary of State and other executive branch officials are often asked to come before these committees to answer questions.

Beginning with John Adams, American Presidents have sent troops into battle more than forty times without the approval of Congress. These undeclared wars include American involvement in the war in Vietnam from 1961 to 1974 and the invasion of Panama in 1989.

PEOPLE MAKE A DIFFERENCE

Youth Gain Understanding

In Belle Fouche, South Dakota, Susan Olson is an only child. In Sakshaug, Norway, she has two brothers, a sister, and another mom and dad. She gained her new "family" while on a summer exchange with Youth For Understanding, an organization which arranges for high school students to go to school in foreign countries.

Susan's time in Norway gave her the chance to see another culture. "I didn't know much about other countries," she said. "You learn stuff in school, but you learn much more by being there."

Susan traveled with the Stokkes family around Norway. She learned about their lives and values and saw how their schools and government work. She made many new friends. Susan came home believing that other countries are just as important as the United States and that "it is not just us in the world, but it's important to think of other people, too."

Learning about another country helps keep world peace, Susan says. "You try harder to get along when you know the people. It's not just the government's job but up to everyone. We all need to be concerned about other people."

Because Susan's summer was such a good experience, the Olson family decided to have a foreign student stay with them. They wanted to continue to learn about the world through others.

Thomas Bjerregaard from Oslo, Norway, came to live with the Olsons for a year. Used to living in a city, he now lived on a farm, ten miles from the nearest town. He went to school with Susan, joined the football team, and took classes with American students. Most important, he got to know Americans as friends.

Thomas says that young people ought to learn about other countries personally because they will someday be in charge. Living in another country "gives people the chance to understand each other," says Thomas. "You gain a lot—and grow."

Private Groups

Private organizations and individuals can also shape foreign policy. Sarah had read about the whaling problem in a magazine put out by an environmental protection group. Many groups have special interests that are affected by foreign policy. These groups want to have a voice in what that policy will be.

Business groups. You saw in Chapter 24 that countries around the world are linked by trade. Businesses that trade with other nations have a direct interest in foreign policy. Restaurant owners, for example, might want to buy Icelandic fish because of its low cost. They would complain to the President and Congress about a foreign policy that made it impossible for them to get Icelandic fish.

Some businesses form groups, such as the National Association of Manufacturers. They hire lobbyists to present their foreign policy views to Congress and to policymakers of the executive branch.

Activity: Organize a panel of students who have lived outside the United States to speak about their experiences. Invite them to bring pictures and mementos of their travels.

Labor groups. Today, Americans are buying more foreign-made goods than we are selling to other countries. The result has been the loss of many jobs in the United States. Labor groups, therefore, try to get executive branch policymakers and members of Congress to protect jobs by limiting or taxing certain imports and by putting pressure on our trading partners to buy more American products.

Political groups. Many other organizations, such as the environmental group that got Sarah interested in the whaling issue, try to affect foreign policy. Anti-nuclear groups want the United States to stop sending nuclear weapons to support NATO forces in Europe. Church groups and human rights groups also get involved.

The United States is home to people of diverse backgrounds, some of whom try to shape policy toward areas of the world they care about. American Jews who support Israel are active in pushing for policies that help that nation. Some Irish-Americans have tried to get the United States to support groups in Northern Ireland that want independence from Great Britain.

Individuals. Individuals can also play a role in foreign policy. Americans who keep up with international news, and who study, travel, or work abroad, learn about foreign countries and our government's policies toward them. Being better informed helps citizens make better decisions on foreign policy.

There are many ways that citizens who care about foreign policy can make a difference. Running for office or voting for a candidate who shares your views are two important ways. Letting your senator or representative know what you think about the issues is another way. Strong opposition by many citizens is a major reason why Congress did not pass President Reagan's plan for aid to the Nicaraguan contras in 1982.

In the whaling matter, Iceland agreed to go along with the IWC ban. It decided not to risk losing the American market for its fish. In this case, citizens' groups and individuals played an important role in getting our government to put pressure on Iceland.

Answers will be found on page T 181.

Section Review

1. Briefly tell what responsibilities the President has in foreign policy.
2. In what ways does Congress help shape foreign policy?
3. Why do business and labor groups take a special interest in foreign policy?

Synthesis. Why do you think so many government groups and private groups try to affect foreign policy?

25-3
FOREIGN POLICY IN ACTION

Read to Find Out

- what the terms *isolationism*, *neutrality*, and *containment* mean.
- how American foreign policy has changed over the nation's history.
- what foreign policy challenges face the United States.

You have read about the goals of American foreign policy and the tools our leaders use to meet these goals. Although the goals have stayed largely the same over the years, the role that the United States plays in the world is continually changing. At times we have followed ***isolationism***, a foreign policy that seeks

Teaching Note: Use Teaching Activity 2, page T 180, after students have read the material in Section 25-2. Use the Evaluating Progress activity, page T 180, to assess students' understanding of Section 25-2.

to limit our relations with other countries as much as possible. During other periods, the United States has tried to meet its goals by taking an active part in affairs around the world.

Early Isolationism

In its early years, the United States had a mostly isolationist foreign policy. A farming country with very little industry, we had just fought a costly war for independence. President George Washington believed that the young country could not afford to take part in European alliances and wars. He chose a position of ***neutrality***, a policy of not taking sides in wars between other countries.

This neutrality served two foreign policy aims. It kept the United States out of war. It also allowed America to continue to trade with both sides in a war.

Staying isolated was not easy to do. European countries were expanding into Latin America, competing with our economic interests and threatening American security. In 1823 President James Monroe responded to the threat with the Monroe Doctrine. He warned European nations not to create more colonies in the Western Hemisphere. Monroe promised that in return, America would stay out of European affairs. Monroe saw this position as a way to protect American interests and still stay isolated from Europe.

Foreign Policy and Expansion

The policy of isolationism was again tested as Americans began to move west, seeking more land. Expansion forced the United States into contact—and sometimes conflict—with France, Spain, Great Britain, and Russia, which held claims to these lands.

The United States used several foreign policy tools to help it grow in size. Sometimes it gained land through purchase or treaty. At other times, it used its armed forces to win land in war or by threat of war.

Meanwhile, American businesses were expanding across the Pacific, beginning to trade with Japan, China, and other Asian countries. The United States built military bases in Hawaii and the Far East to protect this trade and prevent European countries from setting up colonies.

American business also expanded into Central and South America. The policy of isolationism did not apply to that part of the world, which the United States, still following the Monroe Doctrine, viewed as being in its own backyard. Many times, the United States sent its armed forces into Latin America. Most often, the goal was to protect economic interests or national security.

World War I and Return to Isolationism

World War I forced the United States to change its policy of isolationism toward Europe. Although at first President Woodrow Wilson took a position of neutrality, German aggression caused Congress to declare war in 1917. President Wilson said that the goal in entering the war was to make the world "safe for democracy." He believed that this would be the "war to end all wars," leading to lasting world peace.

After the war, Wilson helped found the League of Nations, a new organization intended to help keep peace. However, Congress was eager to withdraw from European affairs and return to isolationism. It refused to approve American membership in the League.

World War II: The End of Isolationism

The efforts of the League of Nations failed to keep peace, and within 20 years the world was again at war. When World War II began in Eu-

In 1904, President Theodore Roosevelt expanded the Monroe Doctrine by declaring that the United States could intervene in disputes between Latin American nations and European powers. The "Roosevelt Corollary" was used to justify American intervention in Latin America until 1930.

rope, the United States tried to stay out of the conflict. However, when the Japanese bombed the American Navy at Pearl Harbor, Hawaii, in 1941, the United States declared war.

When the war ended in 1945, the United States was the richest and most powerful country in the world. It believed it could play a key part in keeping world peace. American leaders met with Soviet and European leaders to make a peace plan. The United States also helped to found the United Nations, an international organization you will learn more about in the next chapter.

As part of its policy of containment, the United States provided weapons to Afghan rebels fighting the Soviet takeover of their country in 1979.

From Containment to Cooperation

The end of World War II marked the end of the belief that the United States should try to stay out of conflicts between other nations. American leaders saw that our own national security went hand-in-hand with global security. Trouble anywhere in the world could mean trouble for the United States. Therefore, the goal of world peace took center stage in foreign policy.

As you read in Chapter 24, many Americans thought that the Soviet Union and the spread of communism were the main dangers to the goal of peace. Already the Soviets had taken control of several Eastern European countries. When the communists, backed by the Soviets, tried to take over Greece and Turkey, President Harry Truman sent American military aid to help those countries defend themselves.

Truman's action was the beginning of a new foreign policy of ***containment***, a policy of using military power and money to prevent the spread of communism. At first, the government's main tool of containment was economic aid. By giving economic aid, the United States hoped to strengthen the economies of European countries so that they could hold out against Soviet aggression.

Later, the United States came to depend more and more on military strength and deterrence to support the policy of containment. As you saw, the cold war was fought with words and warnings, and sometimes confrontation. The Cuban missile crisis and the wars in Korea and Vietnam are examples of confrontations that grew out of the effort to contain communism.

By the mid-1960s, it was clear the Soviet Union was gaining nuclear strength nearly equal to that of the United States. In Chapter 24 you read about détente in the 1970s, when the superpowers turned to treaties and diplomacy to ease the tensions caused by the military buildup. Through the 1980s, leaders continued to see that depending on military strength alone would not guarantee national

George F. Kennan, a State Department expert on the Soviet Union, was largely responsible for development of the containment policy. Although Kennan left the State Department in 1947, this policy guided American relations with the Soviet Union for the next 40 years.

As the communist government of East Germany crumbled in late 1989, the hated Berlin Wall could no longer keep East and West apart.

security. Even though both the United States and the Soviet Union continued building up arms, the spirit of cooperation grew.

A Collapse of Communist States

As the 1980s gave way to the 1990s, the improving relationship between the superpowers was overshadowed by some breathtaking events. First, communist governments fell in Poland and other Eastern European countries. Then the Soviet Union itself began to fall apart. Suddenly, the ground on which almost forty years of American foreign policy had been built had shifted greatly. No longer could Americans picture the world as a cold-war battleground, with communist nations united against democracies.

The breakup of the Soviet Union. Changes had begun to take place in the Soviet Union in the mid-1980s. Mikhail Gorbachev, the new head of the Soviet Communist party, undertook reforms, known as *perestroika*, aimed at improving the economy. *Perestroika* loosened some government controls over the economy and encouraged some private business. Gorbachev also announced a policy of *glasnost*, or "openness" between government and citizens.

Gorbachev's policies gave the people of the Soviet Union a taste of freedom—and they wanted more. Citizens grew impatient with the slow pace of change, and nationalist feelings erupted among the diverse peoples of the fifteen Soviet republics.

While liberals criticized Gorbachev for not making reforms fast enough, conservatives feared the changes. In August 1991, a group of conservative leaders arrested Gorbachev and seized power. The coup, however, lacked support among the people and the military. Within several days it had collapsed.

The coup's failure sped the breakup of the Soviet Union. By the end of 1991, every Soviet republic had declared its independence, the communist central government had been dissolved, and the Soviet Union had ceased to exist. As independent nations, the former Soviet republics could decide what form a new union would take—or whether any union would survive at all.

Eastern Europe. When *glasnost* first took hold in the Soviet Union, demands for greater openness and economic freedom were heard in many communist Eastern European countries. By the fall of 1989, pressure on the old systems of rule had reached the breaking point.

Hungary declared itself a democratic republic. Voters in Poland elected the first noncommunist government in the region since World War II. In Czechoslovakia, after masses of citizens marched in the streets, communist

In late 1991, amid rallies like this one in Ukraine, Soviet republics declared themselves independent states. A paint-splattered poster of Lenin represents rejection of Soviet communism. By the end of that year the Soviet Union ceased to exist—a startling development that raised new foreign policy issues for the United States.

leaders gave up power. The Romanian people overthrew a hated dictator. In November 1989, the Berlin Wall, symbol of the cold war, was torn down. Eleven months later, East and West Germany were united as a single democratic nation.

These stunning changes have challenged American policymakers. Although the communist threat is gone, Europe remains unstable. Also, Europeans have questioned their relationship with the United States.

The end of the Warsaw Pact means that Western Europeans do not have to rely so much on the United States for their security. Many want a defense alliance separate from NATO. As NATO's role changes, so too does American influence in Europe.

The United States, therefore, faces serious questions. What principles should guide its foreign policy without the old East-West standoff? How should tools of foreign policy be used to influence further changes in Eastern Europe? What does greater European unity mean for the United States?

Relations with China. Some observers of the startling events in Eastern Europe and the Soviet Union spoke of the "death of communism." However, the world's most populous country—China—was still ruled by a communist government.

Trade has increased between China and the United States, but China's treatment of its own citizens has hurt relations between the two countries. Americans were outraged when Chinese troops crushed a student-led democratic movement in June 1989, killing thousands of protestors in Beijing's Tiananmen Square.

There is debate over how to react to these human rights violations. Should we punish China by cutting off diplomatic relations and trade? Or should we maintain such contacts as ways of influencing Chinese leaders?

Challenge (Evaluation): Given the potential of China as a trading partner, have students discuss how forceful the United States should be in its demands that the human rights of Chinese protesters be protected. Students should provide reasons for their opinions.

Decision Making: Have students analyze a recent foreign policy decision or one that is being considered, discussing the possible positive and negative consequences of each option.

Changes in Economic Power

The United States also faces changes in economic power around the world. We are no longer the leader in world trade. As other countries have gained strength, American leaders have had to rethink policies.

Japan, in particular, has become a great economic power. While the United States buys many Japanese products, Japan buys far fewer American goods and services. An important goal of American foreign policy is to try to balance this trade.

The countries of Western Europe have also gained economic strength. You have read about the European Community (EC) and its efforts to break down trade barriers between its member nations. This alliance gives the countries of the EC power that could affect the United States.

Another source of economic power outside the United States is the oil-rich countries. United States foreign policy toward the Middle East has been greatly affected by our need to buy oil. The oil-producing countries have sometimes used oil as a trade weapon. In 1973, Arab nations cut off oil to the United States and its allies as a punishment for their support of Israel. This action touched the daily lives of Americans and also showed the power that oil-rich countries could have.

Clearly the United States will have to make new policies to deal with changes in economic power. Neither isolationism nor military strength can meet the challenges posed by the changing world economy.

Challenges in Developing Nations

In Chapter 24 you read about some of the problems facing developing nations. Two developing areas that have posed many problems for United States foreign policy are Latin America and the Middle East.

Latin America. As you have seen, the United States has long played an active role in events in Latin America. In recent decades, the United States has used aid, diplomacy, and military intervention to protect its economic interests and try to stop the spread of communism in Latin America. The goal of supporting human rights and democracy has also caused the United States to act in the internal affairs of many Latin American countries.

Our government gave money and weapons to groups fighting the communist government of Nicaragua. It supported efforts by leaders in Honduras and El Salvador to put down rebellions in their countries. In each of these cases, many American citizens, including some of the members of Congress, have disagreed with our government's actions.

American policy in Latin America will continue to be the subject of much debate. In forming that policy, the United States will have to settle many questions. What is the best way to help democracy? How can we protect our interests and still let Latin American countries decide their own futures?

The Middle East. The Middle East, a group of countries where Europe, Asia, and Africa meet, has been troubled by a long history of religious and political conflicts. One conflict that has been a major concern of the United States is the struggle between Israel and its Arab neighbors. American policy has been to support Israel but at the same time to maintain our supply of Arab oil.

For decades, the involvement of the United States in the Middle East was limited to diplomatic pressure and foreign aid. In 1991, however, thousands of American troops fought in the Persian Gulf War.

Shortly after Iraq invaded its neighbor Kuwait, the United States sent soldiers to Saudia Arabia and ships to the Persian Gulf. Iraq refused to withdraw. After many tense months,

Teaching Note: Use the Reinforcement Activity, page T 180, and accompanying worksheet in the Activity Book after students have read the material in this section.

the United Nations authorized the use of military action against Iraq. Forces from the United States and many other countries attacked Iraq in what was called Operation Desert Storm. In a few weeks of fighting, Iraq suffered many deaths and much damage. As a result, it withdrew from Kuwait.

The United States achieved its goal of stopping Iraq's aggression, but its use of massive military force added a new variable to the complicated situation in the Middle East. It is not clear what the long-term effects of this action will be.

Looking to the Future

For much of its history, the nation stayed as isolated as possible in order to meet foreign policy goals. More recently, we have depended on being the strongest power. Today, neither isolation nor absolute strength are workable options for foreign policy.

Looking to the future, we Americans have to ask ourselves new questions about foreign policy. Can we make major cuts in arms without leaving ourselves unprotected? What is the best way to aid developing countries without interfering in their choice of leaders and policies? Should the United States act—as it did in the Persian Gulf War—as "the world's policeman"?

As citizens we have the opportunity—and the responsibility—to think about these questions. We also have the responsibility to help our government develop a foreign policy to meet the challenges of our "smaller world."

Answers will be found on page T 182.

Section Review

1. Define *isolationism*, *neutrality*, and *containment*.
2. Why did the United States choose a policy of isolationism early in its history?
3. What challenges do the shifts in global economic power pose for the United States?

Evaluation. "The United States should return to an isolationist foreign policy." Do you agree or disagree? Why?

A BROADER VIEW

From the dawn of civilization, a key role of any government has been to carry out foreign policy. Ancient rulers all had their ambassadors and spies to help them deal with foreign powers.

Foreign policy has often meant conflict. Wars are caused not only by competition for land and resources but also by the attitudes that different countries have toward each other. The ancient Greeks, for example, saw all non-Greeks as uncivilized barbarians. Until recent times the Chinese viewed foreigners as "devils."

Often it seems that people's sense of belonging to a group is strengthened by having an "enemy" to oppose. However, nationalism—pride in one's country—does not have to mean viewing other countries as bad. Indeed, in an interdependent world threatened with nuclear war, everyone's survival may depend on understanding and respecting the differences between nations.

The ending of the cold war, unthinkable just a few years ago, may well be one of the greatest opportunities the world has seen for turning fear and distrust into cooperation. In the words of Mikhail Gorbachev, "Long-held dislikes have been weakened and enemy images have been shaken loose."

Teaching Note: Use the Enrichment Activity, page T 181, and accompanying worksheet in the Activity Book after students have read the chapter.

Becoming a Political Refugee

Beatrice Ananeh-Firempong feared for her life. A student at an American college, she had received terrifying reports from her family back in the African nation of Ghana. Her parents' bank account had been seized by the government, and the entire family had been arrested.

Beatrice could no longer communicate with her family by letter or by phone. She heard from a friend in Ghana, however, that government soldiers had beaten and seriously injured her nephew, who was staying at her parents' home.

The problems had begun a year before, when the constitutional government in Ghana was overthrown by armed forces led by a former military officer named Jerry Rawlings. Beatrice had known then that this was not good news for her or her family.

Her father had been an active member of the former government. In fact, he was a close friend of the founder of that government, Dr. Hilla Limann. Beatrice knew that Rawlings would be suspicious of anyone who had been connected with the former government.

Her father was also well-educated and worked as Headmaster of Schools. Beatrice guessed that educated and professional people would be in danger of persecution, or mistreatment, by the government. To make matters worse, she and her family were members of the Ashanti people, and Rawlings belonged to a group in Ghana that hated the Ashanti.

Soldiers had beaten and seriously injured her nephew.

Sure enough, the Rawlings government soon began attacking those groups Beatrice had guessed were in danger: people connected to the former government, educated people, and the Ashanti. Recently, Beatrice had heard that the Rawlings government had killed hundreds of such people.

For the moment, Beatrice herself was safe in the United States. However, she was about to graduate from college, and under the terms of her student visa, she was required to return home right after graduation.

Because of the situation in Ghana, Beatrice feared that if she returned home her life would be in danger. Therefore, she asked the Immigration and Naturalization Service (INS) to allow her to remain in the United States.

The INS, however, said that she could not stay in the United States. Beatrice decided to appeal her case to the United States Court of Appeals.

Beatrice's lawyer knew that a federal law gave Beatrice the legal basis for staying in the country. This law

Activity: Have students find out if a local church, synagogue, or private group has provided sanctuary for political refugees seeking asylum. You may want to invite a refugee and/or member of the organization to class to be interviewed.

Answers will be found on page T 182.

is the Immigration and Nationality Act. It says that the United States government shall not send an alien back to his or her native country if that person's "life or freedom would be threatened in such country on account of race, religion, nationality, membership in a particular social group, or political opinion."

This law was passed by Congress in response to what it saw as a need to protect those threatened by persecution in their homelands. Congress had written into the law that its purpose is to support the traditional role of the United States as a safe place for "the oppressed of other nations."

The law says that for an alien to be allowed to stay in the United States, he or she must first be classified as a "refugee." A refugee is someone who lives outside of his or her native country and is unable to return to that country because of "a well-founded fear of persecution."

For a person to be called a refugee, the law says that the person must be able to offer "reasonably specific information" that shows a real threat of personal harm. The person's fear of harm cannot be based on just a general concern for his or her safety.

The reason for this strict definition of "refugee" is to limit the number of people who would qualify as refugees. The strict definition is in keeping with Congress's general policy of limiting the number of aliens who are allowed to enter the United States each year.

Beatrice feared that if she returned home her life would be in danger.

The Court of Appeals had to take all these aspects of the Immigration and Nationality Act into account in Beatrice's case. The main question it had to decide was whether Beatrice fit the strict definition of a "refugee."

In court, Beatrice presented her own sworn statement. She told how she feared harm if she returned to Ghana, based on what had happened to members of her family there. She also presented a sworn statement by an expert on African politics, as well as newspaper and magazine articles about events in Ghana.

The court concluded that the evidence Beatrice presented put her "squarely within" the definition of "refugee." It ruled that the INS should not send her back to Ghana.

Analyzing the Case

1. What law did Beatrice depend on to allow her to remain in the United States?
2. Why does the law say that an alien requesting refugee status must provide "reasonably specific information" showing a real threat of personal harm?
3. Do you think the INS should always make it difficult for an alien to remain in the United States as a refugee, as it did in Beatrice's case? Explain your view.

The United States has granted special status to more than 2 million refugees seeking asylum. Since the late 1970s, however, fewer refugees have been granted asylum, due to overcrowding of immigration centers and the inability of local governments to provide adequate services.

CHAPTER SURVEY

Answers to Survey and Workshop will be found on page T 182.

UNDERSTANDING NEW VOCABULARY

Seeing Relationships

The terms in each pair listed below are related to each other. For each pair, explain what the terms have in common and how they are different.

1. *aggression* and *deterrence*
2. *diplomacy* and *summit meeting*
3. *isolationism* and *neutrality*
4. *containment* and *deterrence*

Putting It in Writing

Using the terms *deterrence*, *diplomacy*, and *foreign aid*, write one or two paragraphs about the different ways the United States tries to meet its foreign policy goals.

LOOKING BACK AT THE CHAPTER

1. How does trading with foreign countries benefit the United States economy?

2. How does the United States use deterrence as a part of its defense against foreign aggression?

3. How do alliances help the United States meet its foreign policy goals?

4. How does foreign aid support United States foreign policy goals?

5. What are some criticisms of United States foreign aid programs?

6. Why do countries work so hard to gather intelligence about one another?

7. What is the Department of State's role in United States foreign policy?

8. How do the powers of Congress over foreign policy check the powers of the executive branch?

9. What role do private groups play in foreign policy?

10. Why did George Washington decide on a foreign policy position of neutrality toward European conflicts?

11. How did America's territorial expansion challenge its foreign policy of isolationism?

12. How has global economic power shifted in recent years?

13. *Evaluation.* Of all the United States' foreign policy goals, which do you think is the most important?

14. *Analysis.* Is it possible to tell whether a country is using its military force for aggression or defense? Why or why not?

15. *Analysis.* Why are powers over the budget important in making foreign policy?

16. *Application.* What are three ways the United States might use trade measures to help meet its foreign policy goals?

17. *Synthesis.* How do you think international relations would be different today if the former Soviet Union had not adopted *perestroika* and *glasnost*?

WORKING TOGETHER

1. In groups of three or four, choose a foreign country with which the United States has ongoing foreign relations. Collect newspaper and magazine articles about our relations with this country. What do the articles tell you about United States foreign policies toward this country? Do you agree with the policies? What tools is the United States using to fulfill its foreign policy goals? Prepare a short report to give to the class.

2. Working with a group, choose two or three countries and write or call their embassies in Washington, D.C., or their consulates in the nearest big city. Request information about the services they provide for their citizens in this country. Make a presentation to the class about your findings.

Teaching Note: For reinforcement of decision-making skills, use Decision-Making Worksheet Chapter 25.

SOCIAL STUDIES SKILLS

Interpreting Graphics

A graphic is a visual way of showing an object, idea, or relationship. We see graphics all around us—maps, logos, posters, advertising art, and illustrations. Graphics communicate in a vivid way without words.

The graphic below shows the destructive power of nuclear weapons. The dot in the center square represents all of the weapon power used in World War II, including the two atomic bombs dropped on Japan. The other dots represent the weapon power of all nuclear weapons in the 1980s. The weapon power in two squares could destroy all medium and large cities on earth.

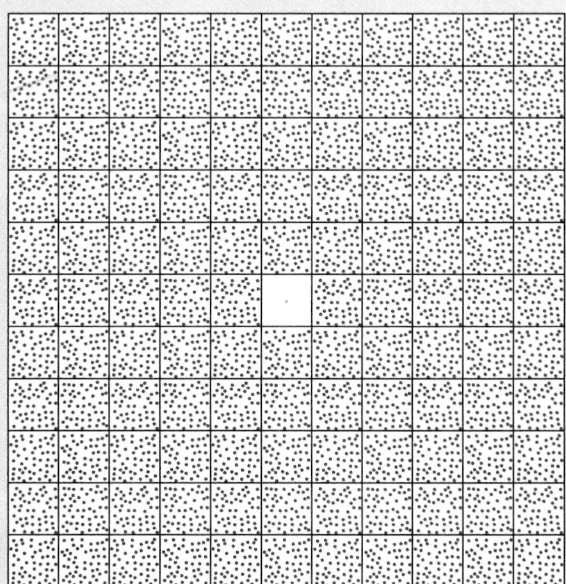

1. What does the dot in the center square of this graphic represent?

2. What do the other 6,000 dots represent?

3. What does this graphic say to you?

4. Write a title for this graphic.

5. How does this graphic relate to the policy goals of national security and world peace?

DECISION-MAKING SKILLS

What Relates to Your Subject?

Imagine that you are a voter trying to decide which presidential candidate to vote for. You want to find out each candidate's views on foreign policy issues. Determine which of the following statements are relevant to the subject of the candidates' views on foreign policy. If necessary, review page 190.

A. One of the candidates believes that the United States should protect American businesses by increasing tariffs on imports.

B. Each of the candidates was drafted to serve in the Korean War during the 1950s.

C. As a member of Congress, one of the candidates voted to increase military spending.

D. One of the candidates favors selling fighter planes to Saudi Arabia.

E. Each candidate favors cutting the income tax rate for middle-class people.

F. One of the candidates opposes banning oil drilling off the California coast.

G. The candidates believe that the United States should provide more help to nations struggling to stop illegal drug trade.

1. Which statements are relevant to the candidates' views on foreign policy? Pick two and explain why they are relevant.

2. Which statements are irrelevant to the candidates' views on foreign policy? Pick two and explain why they are irrelevant.

3. Name two other kinds of information that would be relevant to the candidates' views on foreign policy.

4. Name a decision that you might have to make. What types of information would be relevant to your decision? What types would be irrelevant?

Chapter Themes: All the world's people are threatened by pollution, shortages of resources, the arms buildup, terrorism, and violations of human rights. International organizations, nations, and individuals can combine their skills, ideas, and resources to help solve such global problems.

CHAPTER 26

Making a Difference in the World

At the Johnson house, the television was switched on to the six o'clock news. The screen filled with the image of a huge American cargo plane being unloaded at an airport in the Sudan. As workers carried bags of food to waiting trucks, a reporter stood on the runway speaking to viewers thousands of miles away.

"Shipments of food from the United States and other countries," said the reporter, "are desperately needed to help people survive the terrible famine in this part of Africa." The scene then shifted to a Red Cross camp that had been set up for famine victims.

The Johnsons hardly had time to take in the sight of dusty tents and starving children before they were transported back to the network news center in New York. "In other news today," the anchorwoman was saying, "scientists at an international conference in Toronto, Canada, discussed the possibility that air pollution is heating up the earth's atmosphere. Changes in climate could threaten not only human health but also food and water supplies throughout the world. The scientists urged all nations to take action against pollution."

The anchorwoman moved on to another subject: "At a special session of the United Nations today, representatives of 159 nations failed to agree on a proposal to reduce the number of nuclear and nonnuclear weapons. Discussions will continue, but clearly many countries are not seeing eye-to-eye on arms control."

Mrs. Johnson turned toward her husband and their children. "You know," she said, "sometimes I feel like tuning out the news and escaping from the world's problems. The more I learn, though, the more I see that we can't escape. They are our problems, too, and we have to face them. We can't afford not to."

In this chapter you will explore some of the problems facing our world. You will also be looking at how organizations and individuals are making a difference in dealing with those problems. After reading this chapter, you will have a better sense of why we and the citizens of other nations must work together to meet the challenges that face us all.

Teaching Note: Use the "Introducing the Chapter" activity, page T 185.

26-1

GLOBAL PROBLEMS FOR SPACESHIP EARTH

Read to Find Out

- what the terms *renewable resource, nonrenewable resource, deforestation,* and *terrorism* mean.
- why the world faces a shortage of resources.
- why pollution is a global problem.
- how an arms buildup, terrorism, and human rights violations threaten the world.
- how nations can cooperate in solving global problems.

The world is getting used to warnings. Scientists and government officials point to a "population explosion" that is straining the earth's supply of fresh water and food. "Acid rain" pollutes lakes and rivers. Many scientists think that air pollution will cause a dangerous rise in the earth's temperature. Meanwhile, we must continue to slow down the arms race and try to keep a nuclear war from happening.

How are limited resources, pollution, and the arms race alike? They are all global problems—problems that affect the whole world and that can be solved only by countries working together. It is becoming clear to people everywhere that decisions made in one country can have effects on other countries. Sometimes those effects are good, and sometimes they cause great harm.

As you read about some of the major problems facing all of us who live on the earth, you will see why no one person or country can solve them alone. You will see why we Americans cannot afford to say, "Those are your problems, not ours." As you read, think about your duty to life on our planet. How might you help to make a difference?

Limited Natural Resources

How much longer will the world's oil last? What can be done about the lack of water in many places? Questions like these point to one of the major problems facing the world: the earth has limited natural resources.

Our main natural resources are water, air, soil, trees and other plants, animals, sunlight, and minerals. To understand why we are running short, you first need to know the difference between renewable and nonrenewable resources.

A ***renewable resource*** is a resource that can be replaced after being used. Trees are a renewable resource because new ones can be planted to replace those cut down. However, just because some resources are renewable does not mean that there will always be enough of them. Often it takes a long time to replace a resource. You can cut down a tree in minutes, but it takes years to grow a new one. If people do not plant new trees, the world may run out of wood.

A ***nonrenewable resource*** is a resource that cannot be replaced once it has been used. Metals, coal, and oil are nonrenewable resources. At some point they may all be used up. The metals in some products may be used again. The same is not true of fossil fuels such as coal and oil. Once they are burned up, they are gone forever. You can plant a new tree, but you cannot "grow" more coal, oil, or metals.

Another problem is that resources are not spread evenly around the world. Some countries are "water-rich" because they get plenty of rainfall. Countries in dry parts of the world are "water-poor." Some countries have enough oil or coal, but others must buy most of the oil and coal they need.

Population growth also puts pressure on resources. The number of people in the world is growing, but the supply of many resources

Making aluminum from bauxite (the principal natural source of aluminum) is ten times more expensive than recycling old cans. Today, half of the aluminum cans used in our country are recycled, yet Americans toss out enough aluminum every three months to rebuild the entire American airline fleet.

Challenge (Application): Have students report on a situation in their community that involves a conflict between protection of the environment and industrial or economic growth.

World Population 1950–2050

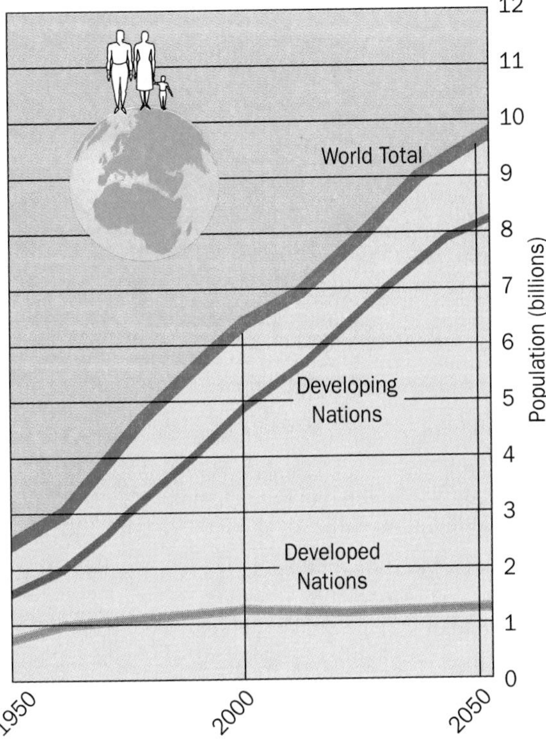

Source: United Nations

is staying the same or shrinking. For instance, there are three times as many people in the world today as in 1900, but the amount of fresh water has stayed about the same.

People's life-styles also put a strain on resources. Developed nations use up oil and coal to make gasoline and electric power for factories and houses. The average person in a developed nation uses 80 times as much energy as the average person in a developing nation, who lives without electricity or a car.

Meanwhile, people in developing nations want to improve their standard of living. To meet their needs, as well as our own, we must try to find new resources and not waste the ones we have, or else learn to do without.

Pollution

Human beings can live on the earth because it has land, water, and air. Too often, people are careless with these resources. We are polluting the environment. That is, we are making it unclean and unhealthy.

Pollution is a hard problem to tackle. One reason is that we do not know enough about its causes. When the first factories and cars were built, people did not know how they would affect the land, water, and air. Even today scientists do not know the effects of many new products, such as pesticides. Also, after a product is found to be harmful, months or years may be needed to undo the damage it has caused.

Perhaps an even greater roadblock to reducing pollution is the fact that most people think that the effort is too hard or costs too much. For instance, everyone knows that carpooling or taking a bus helps to cut down air pollution, but people still like to drive their own cars. Farmers are finding that using pesticides is the easiest way of killing bugs and protecting their crops. Meanwhile, companies say it costs them too much to try to limit the amount of smoke coming from their factories.

However, scientists fear for the earth. They warn that problems such as toxic chemicals, acid rain, the greenhouse effect, and the weakening of the ozone layer are threatening the world.

Toxic chemicals. Millions of tons of chemicals are produced each year throughout the world. There are over 70,000 different ones in everyday use. They are found in many products—from household cleansers to weed killers. Many are helpful in households, farming, and industry, but some can also be toxic, or poisonous, to people and the environment. Chemicals can get into rivers, lakes, and wells.

Industry can reduce the use of toxic chemicals in five ways: change the raw materials used, produce different products, modify or modernize production lines, improve monitoring and cleanup methods, and recycle materials within the production process.

The burning of Amazon rain forests, like air pollution from cars and factories, releases large amounts of carbon dioxide, which may cause a dangerous warming of the earth's atmosphere.

Toxic chemicals are a global problem because rivers polluted by chemicals often flow from one country to another. Also, multinational corporations have factories in many countries around the world. In India, for example, gas leaking from an American factory killed over 2,000 people in 1984.

Acid rain. Perhaps you have heard news reports about acid rain. When coal and oil are burned, they give off chemicals that mix with water in the air to form acids. These acids fall to the ground as acid rain—polluted fog, rain, and snow. Scientists have found that acid rain falling into lakes kills fish. Many believe that it is the main reason why whole forests are dying in Europe and Canada.

Acid rain is a global problem because the wind blows pollution from factory smokestacks across borders. Canada says that half of the acid rain falling on its lakes, farms, and forests comes from American factories. In short, the problem cannot be solved unless countries work together.

The greenhouse effect. Many scientists believe that the earth is slowly getting warmer. They say one cause of this warming is that factories and cars burn fossil fuels. Another possible cause is ***deforestation***, cutting and burning forests to clear land for farms and cattle grazing. Deforestation is taking place in many parts of the world, including the huge Amazon River Basin in South America.

Burning fossil fuels and forests is said to cause global warming by adding to the blanket of carbon dioxide in the air. Carbon dioxide traps the sun's heat, much as a garden greenhouse does. Many scientists believe that too much carbon dioxide will dangerously increase this "greenhouse effect." Rising temperatures could cause droughts. They might also melt glaciers and ice caps, raising the sea level and flooding coastal cities.

Some scientists do not think that the earth is getting warmer. However, most believe that we must take steps to cut down the amount of carbon dioxide in the air. If we do nothing now, we may find later that it is too late.

The weakened ozone layer. High in the air a layer of ozone gas protects the earth against most of the sun's ultraviolet rays, which can cause skin cancer and eye damage. Without this layer, most plants and animals probably could not live.

Scientists have discovered that the layer of ozone is getting thinner, and holes are open-

Deforestation is occurring at the rate of 27 million acres a year. At this rate, the Environmental Defense Fund predicts, all the world's rain forests will be gone by the year 2032. Scientists say average carbon dioxide growth can be offset by planting 1 million acres of new forest a year.

ing in it. The main cause is chlorofluorocarbons (CFCs) used in refrigerators and air conditioners, spray cans, and many take-out food packages. In the air, CFCs cause a chemical reaction that cuts down the amount of ozone. For this reason, more and more countries have banned the use of certain CFCs.

The Arms Buildup

Nations must also face the challenge of preventing war, especially nuclear war. The end of the cold war has not removed the need for arms control. Indeed, a recent poll reports that 60 percent of the American people believe that limiting arms is still our most important challenge. People in many other countries share that belief.

A number of countries now have the power to wage a nuclear war that could destroy life on earth as we know it. Also, some countries have large amounts of nerve gas and other chemical weapons. Some are testing biological weapons such as deadly viruses. The arms race even reaches outer space, as industrial countries do research on space-to-earth weapons.

Terrorism

Arab gunmen killed two Israeli athletes at the Olympic Games in Munich in 1972 and took nine other people hostage. In 1988, eleven people were killed when a bomb exploded in a town center in Northern Ireland. Violent acts like these are signs of a growing world problem: terrorism.

Terrorism is the use or threat of violence to spread fear, usually for the purpose of reaching political goals. The terrorists who attacked the athletes hoped to pressure the government of Israel into giving independence to Palestinian Arabs. The Irish Republican Army, a group that wants Northern Ireland free of British control, carried out the bomb attack. Terrorists are often people who think there is no peaceful way to get governments to make changes they want.

Terrorists have made use of technology, such as air travel and television. By hijacking planes and having their demands reported over radio and television, they can gain worldwide attention. Terrorists can strike anywhere, in any country. Their attacks are hard to prevent.

Violations of Human Rights

Human rights has also become a global issue. One reason is that violations of human rights in one country affect other countries when refugees flee across borders. Perhaps more important is the fact that more and more people

AMERICAN NOTEBOOK

Imagine how circling the Earth in a spacecraft might change the way you see our home planet. Here is how some astronauts described their reactions to that unforgettable experience:

> **For those who have seen the Earth from space, and for the thousands more who will, the experience most certainly changes your perspective. The things that we share in our world are far more valuable than those which divide us.**
>
> **—Donald Williams, USA**

> **It does not matter what country you look at. We are all Earth's children.**
>
> **—Aleksandr Aleksandrov, USSR**

> **The first day or so we all pointed to our countries. The third or fourth day we were pointing to our continents. By the fifth day we were aware of only one Earth.**
>
> **—Sultan Bin Salman al-Saud, Saudi Arabia**

Spending trade-offs between military and social or environmental priorities are constantly necessary. For example, the cost of the Trident II submarine and F-18 jet fighter programs equals the estimated cost of cleaning up the nation's 10,000 worst hazardous waste dumps.

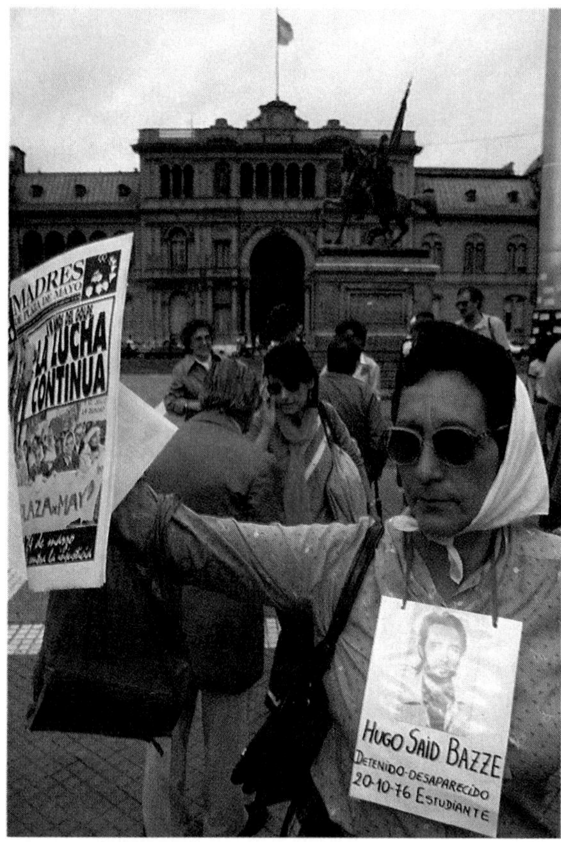

One way governments violate human rights is by secretly jailing or executing people. This woman protests her son's disappearance.

are beginning to believe that every person in the world has certain basic rights.

Many countries have accepted an agreement called the Universal Declaration of Human Rights, which lists political rights such as the right to vote and the right of free speech. It also lists economic rights such as freedom from hunger, and social rights such as the right to marry and start a family.

In spite of the declaration, some governments continue to violate the human rights of their citizens. To stay in power, their leaders arrest citizens who speak out against the government. They keep them in prison or put them to death without a trial. Prisoners are often tortured, either by order of the government or because the police are not well supervised.

One nation whose violations of human rights have received worldwide attention is the Union of South Africa. The South African government has laws creating *apartheid* [ah-PAHRT-hayt], a policy of keeping people of different races separate. Under apartheid, nonwhite people have been denied such basic rights as the right to vote and the right to live and travel where they wish.

People who seek to protect human rights face two challenges. One is to find out where the violations are taking place. The other is to find ways to make governments stop the violations.

Working Toward Solutions

What needs to be done to solve global problems? First, we need more information about the causes and effects of the problems, especially pollution problems such as acid rain and the greenhouse effect. As American inventor Buckminster Fuller noted, "The most important fact about Spaceship Earth [is that] an instruction book didn't come with it."

Secondly, we need to work together in looking for solutions. Getting cooperation, however, is a problem in itself. Nations must first respect each other's sovereignty. No country wants others telling it what to do with its money or natural resources.

Countries must also share the blame for the problems that face the world, instead of pointing fingers at each other. They must look beyond their own short-term goals to see the "big picture." Each country must see that in the long run, what is best for the world is also best for that country.

Developing resources and reducing pollution. It is not easy to get people to think in terms of what is best for the world in the long run. One

Demonstrations in Argentina in the late 1970s (photo above) protested human rights violations by the military government and eventually contributed to the return of civilian rule in 1983.

Challenge (Analysis): Have students discuss the kinds of attitudes and actions that prevent nations from working together to solve global problems.

reason is that developing nations are in a hurry to "catch up." They want to improve their economies by building factories and clearing land for farming and other uses.

People in developing nations are angry when other people try to tell them what they should and should not do. They point out that the developed nations wasted resources and polluted the environment when their own economies were growing. Besides, they say, many scientists think that factories and cars in the developed world are still the major cause of pollution.

World reactions to deforestation in the Amazon are a good example of conflicting views on the use of resources. In the 1970s, Brazil allowed people to clear rain forests for farming and cattle ranching. Since then, more than 8 percent of the Amazon forests have been destroyed. Environmentalists have blamed Brazil for letting this happen. However, as one rancher put it, "We do not call it deforestation. We call it development."

If Brazil does not protect its forests, though, its economy may be hurt in the long run. The soil of the cleared land is poor and will be good for farming for only a few years. Furthermore, the economy could benefit from the many animals and plants that grow naturally in the rain forests and which can be used for foods, medicines, and other products.

Meanwhile, the burning sends carbon dioxide into the air, which may add to the greenhouse effect. Brazil's government is now trying to limit deforestation because it sees that the rain forests are more valuable to the country and to the world if most of them are left standing.

Nations must share responsibility for solving problems related to pollution and limited resources. Instead of blaming each other, they must help each other grow and prosper in ways that protect the environment and use the earth's resources wisely.

Facing threats to security. People in every country fear nuclear war, but governments are not rushing into arms control agreements. Since each country wants to protect its own security, it is careful about reducing its military power or trusting other countries. During the 1980s the United States and the Soviet Union each sent inspectors to check whether the other side was following the terms of arms control treaties.

Countries must try to weigh the need for security against the danger of an uncontrolled arms race. Also, governments must think about the risks of selling arms to other countries. Another thing they should do is weigh the need for more military spending against the need for spending in other areas, such as improving their economies and protecting the environment.

Terrorism, of course, is another threat to security. Facing this threat means more than adding guards and security devices at airports. Governments must also try to deal with some of the causes of terrorism, such as poverty, injustice, and racism.

Protecting human rights. In dealing with human rights issues, we must accept the fact that not everyone agrees about what human rights are. Different countries have different views about which rights belong to every person and which ones are most important. For example, some countries stress economic rights, while in the United States we think that political rights are most important.

People must also try to understand the pressures that can lead to human rights violations. For example, a government that is struggling to stay in power may ban free speech and freedom of the press to silence opponents. All nations must work together to make sure that respect for human rights can go hand-in-hand with national security and economic growth.

Decision Making: Have students discuss options for dealing with a particular global problem, such as toxic waste, violations of human rights, or terrorism.

Teaching Note: Use Teaching Activity 1, page T 185, as a culminating activity after students have read the material in Section 26-1.

Answers will be found on page T 187.

Section Review

1. Define *renewable resource, nonrenewable resource, deforestation,* and *terrorism.*
2. What are some reasons why the world may run out of natural resources?
3. Describe three types of pollution and explain why they are global problems.
4. Why have the arms buildup, terrorism, and human rights become international issues?
5. Why is it sometimes hard for nations to cooperate with each other? What can be done to encourage cooperation?

Evaluation. Do you think the developed nations have a greater responsibility to deal with global problems than the developing nations? Explain.

Data Search. Look on page 591 in the Data Bank to answer these questions. What are two resources that are likely to run out within your lifetime? What are two that are not likely to run out during your lifetime?

26-2

ORGANIZATIONS FACING THE PROBLEMS

Read to Find Out

- how the United Nations is organized to deal with global problems.
- how nongovernmental organizations are helping to solve global problems.
- what can weaken and strengthen the impact of international organizations.

How do people from different countries work together to solve problems facing the world? In many cases, representatives from two or more countries meet to talk about problems. International economic conferences and summit meetings of world leaders are examples of such meetings. However, as nations have grown more interdependent, permanent organizations have also been set up to deal with the world's problems.

Some organizations are formed by governments. You have read about NATO, the European Community, and the Organization of American States. Others, such as the International Red Cross, are private. In this section you will look at the role of the largest organization of governments, the United Nations. You will also see how private groups are helping to solve global problems.

The United Nations

The United Nations, or UN, has 159 member nations—almost every nation in the world. Its constitution, the United Nations Charter, sets forth the rules and purposes of the UN. The UN was created in 1945, at the end of World War II. Its goals are to preserve world peace, to promote justice, and to encourage international cooperation. Since 1952, the headquarters of the UN has been New York City.

The UN has six main parts: the Security Council, the General Assembly, the Secretariat, the Economic and Social Council, the International Court of Justice, and the Trusteeship Council. As you will see, in some ways the UN is like a national government. However, it is not a "super-government." It does not have sovereignty over its member nations.

The Security Council. The most powerful arm of the UN is the Security Council. It has power to take action to keep the peace and help settle conflicts that break out.

The Security Council was created with five permanent members: the United States, the Soviet Union, Great Britain, China, and France.

Teaching Note: Use the Evaluating Progress activity, page T 186, to assess students' understanding of Section 26-1.

The Secretariat is headed by the Secretary-General, who is appointed to a five-year term by the General Assembly. The Secretary manages the staff of the Secretariat and reports on UN activities to the General Assembly.

They were the five most powerful countries at the end of World War II. Russia now holds the Soviet seat. Ten other members are elected to two-year terms by the General Assembly. For an action to be approved, nine votes out of fifteen are needed.

When the UN was created, none of the "Big Five" countries wanted to give up any of its power. Therefore, each has veto power in the Security Council. If a proposal is vetoed by one of the "Big Five," it is defeated, no matter how many members voted for it.

When a war breaks out, the Security Council may send a peace-keeping force to the trouble spot. The job of these UN soldiers is usually not to fight, but to help settle the conflict and make sure that both sides go along with the agreement. The Security Council may also ask member nations to stop trading with the warring countries or perhaps to break diplomatic relations with them.

The General Assembly. Every member nation has a vote in the General Assembly. Problems anywhere in the world can be discussed there. The General Assembly also decides how the UN will spend its money.

The General Assembly cannot make laws that must be obeyed. It can only make resolutions, or recommendations. However, General Assembly resolutions can lead to international agreements. In 1987, for instance, 24 countries signed an agreement to cut back on production of CFCs.

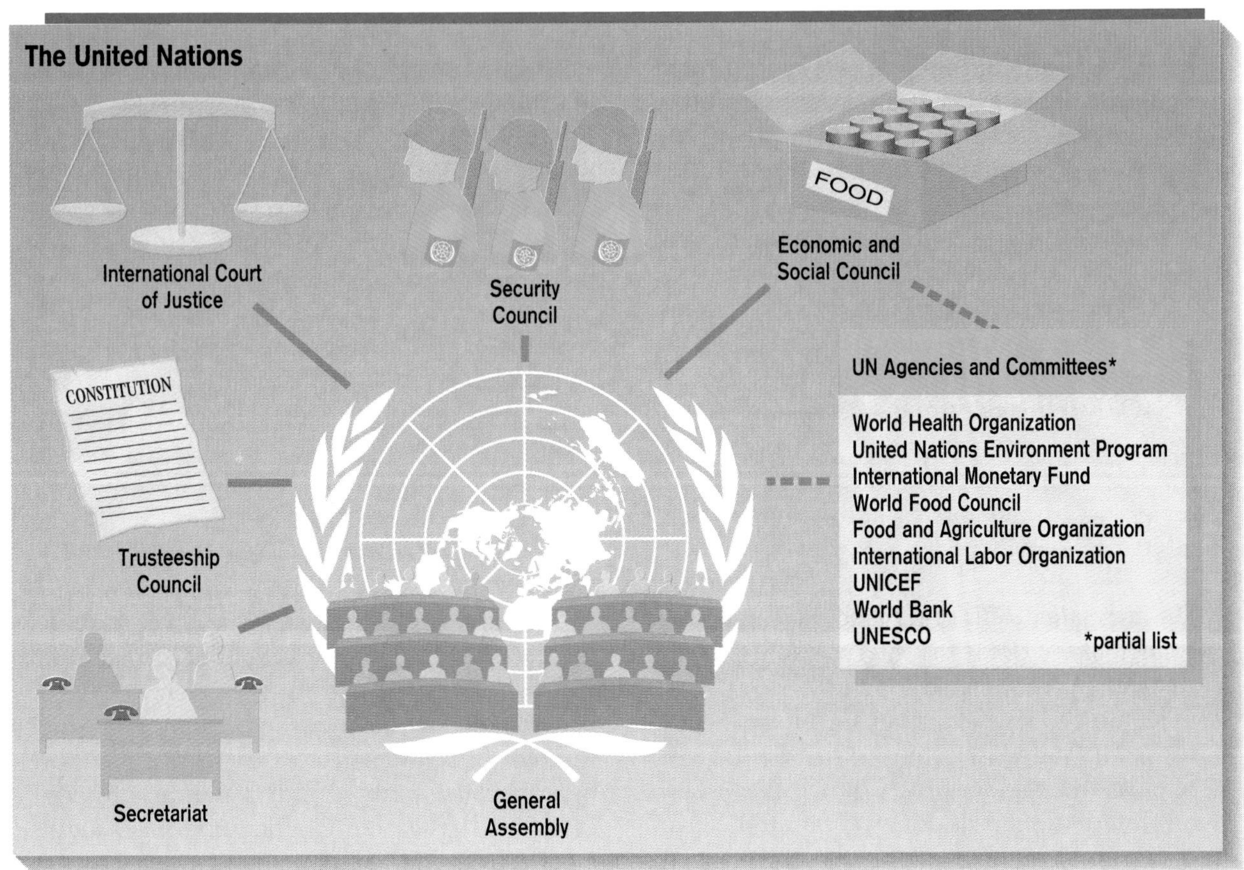

The Secretariat. Like any government, the UN needs a bureaucracy to carry out its daily tasks. People from 150 countries work in the UN bureaucracy, called the Secretariat. They translate documents, prepare reports, and provide services to UN councils and agencies. There are 5,000 workers in New York and 10,000 more in UN offices in Geneva, Vienna, Nairobi, Rome, and The Hague in the Netherlands.

The Economic and Social Council. The Economic and Social Council works to improve standards of living. The Council has representatives from 54 countries and works closely with a number of UN agencies, such as the United Nations Educational, Scientific, and Cultural Organization (UNESCO).

UNESCO supports education, science, art and culture, and communications. It has helped developing nations set up radio stations and newspapers. It has scientific projects to study the earth's crust, atmosphere, and water supply. UNESCO also sets up exchanges of teachers and students between countries so that people of different nationalities can learn about each other's cultures.

In addition to agencies, the Council works with UN committees, like the United Nations Children's Fund (UNICEF). The goal of UNICEF is to give food and health care to needy children throughout the world. The fund is supported by money from governments and individuals, and from sales of UNICEF holiday cards.

The International Court of Justice. The judicial branch of the UN is the International Court of Justice. Often called the World Court, it is made up of 15 judges from 15 different countries. The judges, elected by the General Assembly and the Security Council, hear cases on international disputes. The "Big Five" countries have permanent seats on the Court.

One purpose of the UN is to provide relief during emergencies. Here, UN trucks deliver bags of rice to a refugee camp in Thailand.

World Court judges work with a growing body of international law. Like common law, it is made up of long-standing customs, such as allowing freedom of travel on the seas. Treaties, UN declarations, and World Court decisions are also part of international law.

The judges' decisions are by majority vote. However, a country does not have to accept what the Court decides. Only 44 countries have agreed to accept all Court rulings. Neither the United States nor the Soviet Union accepts all the Court's decisions as binding. As countries become more interdependent, though, the Court may play a growing role in getting them to settle conflicts peacefully.

The Trusteeship Council. When the UN was formed after World War II, there were still some territories that did not have governments. The job of the Trusteeship Council was to help govern them until they were ready to become independent nations. Today 10 of the original 11 trust territories are independent or have become parts of other nations. Therefore, the Trusteeship Council no longer plays a major role in the UN.

Ginetta Sagan

It was February 1945. After five years of helping political prisoners escape from Nazi prisons in Italy, Ginetta Sagan was caught, taken to prison, and tortured by the Nazis. She escaped two months later, but she has never forgotten her time in prison. She has dedicated her life to working with Amnesty International to free political prisoners anywhere in the world.

Ginetta Sagan was born June 1, 1925, in Milan, Italy. A teenager when World War II broke out, Sagan began handing out leaflets supporting democracy and protesting the fascist government. Nicknamed "Little Mouse," she was soon working to free people who were in prison for resisting the Nazis. "Our responsibility is to help innocent victims of all repressive regimes," she says. "But I am completely committed to pacifism [acting peacefully]. I was never a part of the shooting."

Sagan came to the United States in 1951. She joined Amnesty International in 1967 while living in Washington, D.C. After moving to California in 1968, Sagan began organizing chapters of Amnesty International throughout the western states.

Sagan's entire family has supported her work. Her three sons even volunteered to move into the garage so that their bedrooms could be used as office space.

Each chapter of Amnesty International "adopts" political prisoners in certain countries and begins working for their release. The groups write letters, hold rallies, and raise money to support the prisoners they have adopted.

"I used to call Amnesty International the voice of the voiceless," Ginetta Sagan says. "It's hard to believe that governments kill people just for expressing ideas. Yet it happens so often."

Ginetta Sagan firmly believes that her work does more than help individual prisoners. She knows she is working for world peace. "Repression of any kind leads to instability, internal conflict, and war," Sagan says. "In order to have peace, we must protect and respect human rights. Each individual can make a difference by protecting the life of one person who can then make a difference in his or her own country."

Nongovernmental Organizations

The UN and other organizations of governments are not the only groups working on global problems. There are also private nongovernmental organizations, or NGOs. They meet many challenges—from protecting human rights to working for arms control.

Some NGOs protect political and economic rights. Amnesty International, for instance, calls attention to violations of the rights of political prisoners. CARE and the Red Cross help victims of war and natural disasters.

Among the religious groups working to protect human rights is the World Council

Activity: Have students write letters to a country requesting the release of a political prisoner. The letters should cite principles of basic human rights and give reasons for the release. The country can be fictitious, or students can get information on violations from Amnesty International.

Teaching Note: Use Teaching Activity 2, page T 186, as a culminating activity after students have completed Section 26-2. Use the Reinforcement Activity, page T 186, and accompanying worksheet in the Activity Book.

of Churches, with members from Christian churches in over 100 countries. Each country also has its own council. In the United States, the National Council of Churches brought apartheid to the attention of Americans and asked companies to stop doing business in South Africa. The Catholic Church works with the World Council and also has its own programs to protect human rights.

Private groups deal with other global problems, as well. Greenpeace, an environmental group, takes on many challenges—from preventing pollution of the oceans to stopping the unnecessary killing of whales and other animals. A group called Physicians Against Nuclear War works to achieve control of nuclear weapons.

Some large organizations, such as the Ford Foundation in the United States, give millions of dollars to fight hunger and other global problems. However, small groups also play a role. The Noyes Foundation of New York is spending $20,000 in Chile to help farmers grow crops without harmful pesticides.

Many Americans have become involved in groups that are trying to solve world problems. What these people share is an awareness that "global issues" and "local issues" are becoming one and the same.

The Impact of Organizations

For organizations to be successful in facing global problems, countries have to be willing to work together. There has to be some "give and take." However, there is a limit to what each country is willing to give up. Nations are not likely to give up any of their political power. When a country's security is at stake, it usually wants to make its own decisions.

It is not surprising, then, that the UN has had trouble stopping conflicts. When a war breaks out, UN peace-keeping forces are sent only if both sides agree. Also, a dispute can come before the World Court only if the parties involved agree.

Countries are most willing to work together when it does not mean giving up power. For this reason, the UN and other worldwide organizations have had some of their greatest success dealing with economic, rather than political, problems. Teams of experts teach farmers better ways of preparing fields and raising crops. International agencies help countries build dams and railroads, start businesses, and enter into world trade. Groups help victims of famines, earthquakes, and other disasters.

Countries tend to cooperate best in smaller, regional organizations, such as NATO and the Organization of African Unity. Members of such groups usually have more in common than do members of worldwide organizations like the UN.

As countries gain more experience in working together, though, and as people's awareness of the world's problems increases, we will see more clearly that we are "all on the same spaceship." As that happens, the countries of the world may become more willing to turn to worldwide organizations to help them solve global problems.

Answers will be found on page T 188.

Section Review

1. Explain what roles the United Nations plays in dealing with global problems.
2. Give two examples of how nongovernmental organizations play an important role in solving global problems.
3. What encourages governments to work together? What can get in the way of cooperation between governments?

Evaluation. Do you think that all UN members should have to follow resolutions passed by the General Assembly? Explain.

Challenge (Analysis): Have students discuss why it is difficult for the UN to maintain world peace. What could be done to strengthen the UN's peace-keeping ability?

26-3

HOW INDIVIDUALS CAN MAKE A DIFFERENCE

Read to Find Out

- how people can use their skills to deal with global problems.
- how people have used their connections to help other people and nations.
- how one person's time and effort can make a difference in facing global problems.

"The world has so many problems. I don't see how I can make a difference." Many people have this feeling. Yet every day, in every country, individuals are taking steps to help solve the world's problems.

The organizations you have just read about are simply groups of people putting their skills together. The world's future really depends on individuals—working within groups and on their own. In the following pages you will see some ways in which individuals have made a difference in the world.

Using Skills

In 1985, some of the world's best rock musicians and bands put on a huge concert called Live Aid. They wanted the world to know that because of a long drought in East Africa, millions of people were starving to death.

Over a billion people around the world saw the concert and heard its message on television and radio. They gave more than $71 million to send food to East Africa. Like the performers at the Live Aid concert, writers, actors, and news reporters can use their skills to bring problems to the attention of millions of people.

Skills can be used not only to inform people about problems but also to find solutions. Scientists, for instance, play a key role in finding ways to control pollution and save resources. At international meetings, they share what they have learned about ozone, acid rain, and other important subjects. Scientists are also helping farmers in developing nations. They are studying ways to raise crops without hurting the environment.

Medical workers can also use their skills to meet international needs. For example,

In 1985 performers from many nations helped starving people in Africa by staging "Live Aid" benefit concerts in Philadelphia and London.

Challenge (Application): Have students identify other benefit concerts, books or authors, and individual efforts that have made a difference in solving global problems.

Have students discuss how the saying "Think globally, act locally" might apply to their lives.

after the earthquake in Soviet Armenia in 1988, medical teams from the United States and other countries rushed to the Soviet Union to treat injured people.

Of course, you do not have to be a musician, writer, scientist, or medical worker. Almost any skill you have or learn you can use to make a difference in the world.

Making Connections

In 1944 a Swedish businessman named Raoul Wallenberg risked his life by entering Hungary to save Jews there from being sent to Nazi death camps. He talked the Swedish government into giving Jews official-looking "passports" and helped pay for shelters where escaping Jews could stay. In this way, he helped save the lives of more than 100,000 Jews.

Wallenberg's story shows that people with connections to businesses and governments can use those resources to do good. Another example is the American businessman Armand Hammer, whose business contacts helped the United States improve relations with the Soviet Union and China.

Hammer was also able to use his money and connections to give aid in times of crisis. He sent medical teams to help victims of the earthquake in Armenia and radiation accidents in the Soviet Union and Brazil. He also helped pay for art and education projects around the world.

Volunteering Time

Obviously, you do not need to be a business leader with worldwide connections in order to make a difference. Any time and effort you give can be important. Your commitment might be a few hours of volunteer work, or it might be a lifetime, as in the case of Mother Teresa.

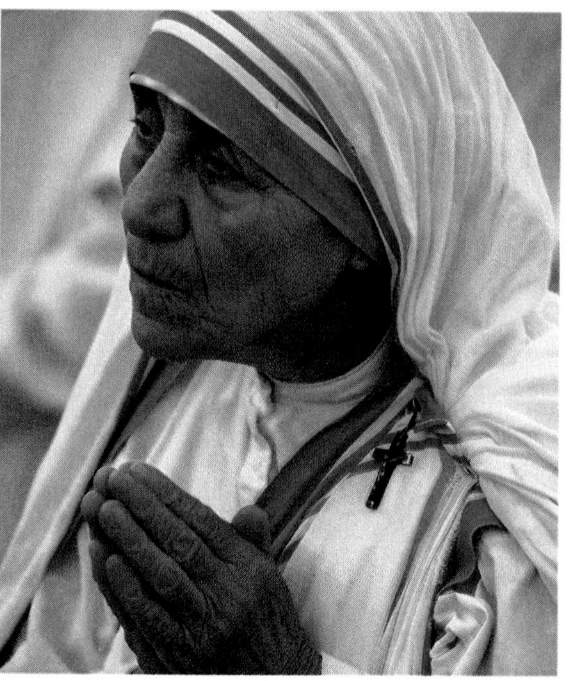

By serving the poor, Mother Teresa has shown how one person can help solve problems facing people throughout the world.

A tireless Roman Catholic nun, Mother Teresa began her work in the slums of Calcutta, India. With other nuns who came to work with her, she provided shelter and schooling for children and gave food and medicine to sick and needy people. She also picked up dying people off the streets to give them a place to die in dignity.

Mother Teresa's struggle to help poor people received worldwide attention. In 1979 she won the Nobel Peace Prize. However, Mother Teresa was humble, always seeing herself as just one person working together with many others. She inspired millions of people who used to think they were not "important enough" to make a difference.

Taking Everyday Steps

Using skills, donating money, and volunteering time are not the only ways to make a dif-

People who personally bring about change must be willing to accept certain risks. For example, Mikhail Gorbachev took a political risk when he encouraged reform in the Soviet Union and allowed changes in the communist governments of Eastern Europe.

Teaching Note: For astronomer Carl Sagan's views on how to ensure the survival of humankind and our planet, see "In Their Own Words" on page 580.

ference. Every day you can take small but important steps to help solve the large problems facing the world. One obvious step, for example, is to make use of daily opportunities to save resources and reduce pollution.

One way you can save resources is by recycling or reusing glass, cans, newspapers, cardboard, and grocery bags. You can save energy by turning off the house lights and heater when they are not being used. Installing a low-flow shower head saves water. Carpooling and using public transportation not only save oil but also reduce pollution. Small steps like these can make a big difference when many people take them together.

You Can Make A Difference

In this book you have studied citizenship and what citizens have done to help their communities, their country, and the world. You have learned something about making decisions and taking action to carry them out. You can use these skills to work on problems facing the whole world, from pollution to hunger to war.

Americans are free to make their own decisions. While visiting a church in the United States, a Soviet citizen once asked, "Who tells people to come here?" This person was surprised at the freedom that Americans have. As an American, you have the right and the opportunity to join with others in making this world a better place.

Answers will be found on page T 188.

Section Review

1. How have people used their skills to deal with global problems?
2. How did both Raoul Wallenberg and Armand Hammer help other people?
3. Why is Mother Teresa a good example of how one person can make a difference?

Analysis. Which global problem or problems did Mother Teresa face? Which did Armand Hammer face? Explain.

A BROADER VIEW

You will be taking on many responsibilities as a citizen in the twenty-first century. Perhaps you are wondering, "What will life be like in the future?" Researchers known as "futurists" are exploring that question by looking at where trends might lead us.

Some futurists are hopeful. They think that space colonies and new supplies of energy will solve the problems of hunger, poverty, and pollution. Others, however, warn that pollution will get worse and that many more people will starve as populations grow and resources run out.

Many futurists think that life styles will change over the next hundred years. They say that people will be less interested in making and buying goods and services and will try harder to protect the environment. Perhaps computers will allow most people to work at home. As the cost of housing rises, people may have to live in large groups of up to a dozen people.

Futurists also make political predictions. Some think that a nuclear war will break out, while others believe that countries will form a worldwide democratic government.

What do you think about these views? Think about which ones are likely to happen. Then ask yourself what you hope the future will be and what steps we might take to reach that future.

Teaching Note: Use the Enrichment Activity, page T 187, and accompanying worksheet in the Activity Book as a culminating activity for this chapter.

CHAPTER SURVEY

Answers to Survey and Workshop will be found on page T 188.

UNDERSTANDING NEW VOCABULARY

Seeing Relationships

The vocabulary terms in each pair listed below are related to each other. For each pair, explain what the terms have in common. Also explain how they are different.

1. *renewable resource* and *nonrenewable resource*

2. *terrorism* and *deforestation*

Putting It in Writing

Using the terms *renewable resource, nonrenewable resource,* and *deforestation,* write a paragraph describing how our use of natural resources has led to pollution and environmental destruction.

LOOKING BACK AT THE CHAPTER

1. Why do people in developed nations use so much more energy resources than those living in developing nations?

2. Describe two of the roadblocks to solving the pollution problem.

3. Why is it difficult for nations such as the United States and the Soviet Union to reach arms agreements?

4. Give two examples of how human rights are being violated.

5. Of the six main parts of the United Nations, which one is best suited for open debate among representatives from the world's nations? Explain.

6. Why is the UN not always successful in settling international disputes and stopping armed conflicts between nations?

7. Why are nations more willing to cooperate with the UN when dealing with economic problems than with political disputes?

8. How does the UN differ from organizations such as the Red Cross and CARE?

9. Describe some ways in which individuals can help solve global problems.

10. *Application.* Think of three things you have thrown away recently. Which were made from renewable and which from nonrenewable resources? Could any parts be recycled?

11. *Evaluation.* Explain why you agree or disagree with the following statement: "The pollution problem is due more to people's attitudes and life styles than to their machines and chemicals."

12. *Synthesis.* How can developed nations help developing nations improve their economies without hurting the environment?

13. *Evaluation.* Only large, organized groups can hope to make any difference at all with issues such as hunger, poverty, war, and pollution." Do you agree or disagree? Give reasons for your answer.

WORKING TOGETHER

1. What kinds of human rights should all people throughout the world be entitled to? In a group of three or four, develop a list of basic human rights that you think everyone in the world should have. Present your ideas to the entire class for debate. Then, as a class, write your own Declaration of Human Rights. You might want to compare your list with the Universal Declaration of Human Rights.

2. Collect newspaper and magazine clippings on a global problem. Report on progress made by groups and individuals to solve the problem and discuss challenges to be faced in dealing with the problem.

3. Organize a mock UN session to discuss a global problem, with students representing major developed and developing nations. Think about possible conflicts between the nations and how they might compromise to solve this global problem.

SKILLS WORKSHOP

Teaching Note: For reinforcement of decision-making skills, use Decision-Making Worksheet Chapter 26.

SOCIAL STUDIES SKILLS

Interpreting Maps

It is almost impossible to study global problems without maps. Maps can show not only geographic and political features but also information on such topics as population growth, economic development, resource use, and global pollution.

Most maps of the world have the North Pole at the top and the South Pole at the bottom. The two maps below are drawn from a different point of view. They show what the world would look like if seen from above the South Pole. The large continent near the center of each map is Antarctica. The continent near the top edge is Australia.

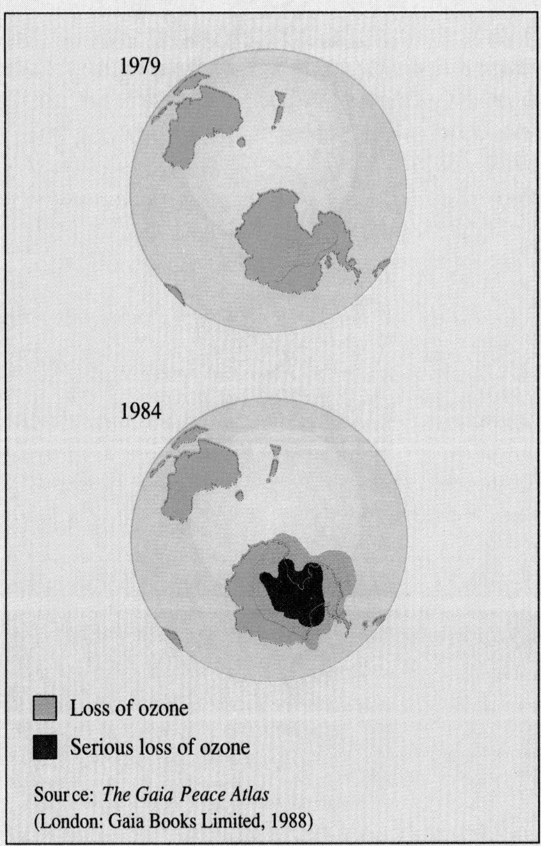

Source: *The Gaia Peace Atlas* (London: Gaia Books Limited, 1988)

1. What time span do the maps cover?

2. What is the subject of the two maps?

3. In one sentence tell what these maps show about the subject. Be sure to tell what happened, where it happened, and when.

DECISION-MAKING SKILLS

Choosing and Taking Action

The founding of the United Nations is a good example of the decision-making process in action. Review the information on the UN in this chapter. Then imagine yourself as one of the representatives to the conference at which the UN was created. Think about how those representatives might have decided to create an international organization and how their plan was carried out. Then answer the following questions.

1. What goals did the representatives have that probably led them to create an international organization?

2. You already know the kind of organization that the representatives decided on. What other ways of organizing the UN do you think they might have considered?

3. What positive consequences do you think they saw in the kind of organization they eventually chose? What negative consequences do you think they saw?

4. What resources do you think were needed to set up the UN organization? Explain how they might have been helpful.

5. What are some obstacles that might have made it hard to form the UN organization? Explain your answer.

6. What do you think were some of the steps that had to be taken to form the UN?

7. Suppose that representatives of the world's nations were to discuss possible changes in the way the UN is organized. What changes would you recommend they make and why?

Carl Sagan: "One more step is needed now"

Answers will be found on page T 190.

Astronomer Carl Sagan studies stars and galaxies. However, in the following excerpt from his essay "Planetary Perspective," he looks at the future of humankind and of our planet.

We stand today at a great branch point in human history. During the million years or so that humans have inhabited the Earth, there have been many points at which our ancestors turned toward one of many possible futures: What we in this century must decide is whether we will have a future at all.

It is difficult to be an optimist in a century so burdened with dangerous evolutionary baggage. Shortsightedness, greed, blind submission to leaders, [fear and hatred of] outsiders—when combined with modern technology, raise grave doubts about our capacity to survive.

But we have also acquired compassion for others, a love for our children and our children's children, a desire to learn from history and a great, soaring, passionate intelligence. This is why it is also a mistake to surrender to pessimism. We have been gathering, across [thousands of years], an awareness that we are members of a larger group. [At first], our loyalties were to ourselves and our immediate family; next, to bands of wandering hunter-gatherers; then to tribes, small settlements, city-states, nations, continental and transcontinental empires. At every stage, we have broadened a little the circle of those we love.

The consequences of that broadening are written in modern history. . . . Slavery has virtually been eliminated. Women, traditionally denied real economic and political power, are [making up for] ancient injustices. For the first time, major wars of aggression have been stopped partly because of [opposition] by citizens of the aggressor nations. The consciousness that we are one species increasingly permeates our lives. One more step is needed now. . . .

If we are willing to contemplate nuclear war and the wholesale destruction of our emerging global society, should not we also be willing to contemplate a [complete reorganization] of our societies? . . . Should we not then be willing to explore vigorously, in every nation, major changes in the traditional ways of doing things, a redesign of economic, political, social, and religious institutions? No nation, no religion, no economic system is likely to have all the answers for our survival. There must be many social systems better than any now in existence. In the scientific tradition, our task is to find them.

From Carl Sagan, "Planetary Perspective," in The International Herald Tribune Centennial Magazine, *September 1987.*

Analyzing Primary Sources

1. According to Sagan, what key question must we decide in this century?
2. Why is Sagan optimistic about our chances?
3. In Sagan's view, what is the "one more step" that we must take now?
4. What goals do you think should guide our search for better social and economic institutions? Explain why.

Activity: Have students work in groups to list the changes that have taken place in their community in recent years. Then ask students to predict what changes will occur in the future. How will these changes affect their lives?

UNIT SURVEY

Answers will be found on page T 190.

LOOKING BACK AT THE UNIT

1. Explain how developed nations differ from developing nations. Why does this difference often make it hard for nations to cooperate in solving global problems?

2. Describe some common types of foreign policy issues. In making foreign policy, why should our government consider the needs of other nations rather than just our own needs?

3. Choose one global problem. Discuss how American foreign policy could help solve it.

4. Explain how the UN is both similar to and different from national governments.

TAKING A STAND

The Issue

Should the United States protect its steel industry from foreign competition?

In 1950, United States furnaces blasted out 46 percent of the world's steel. Thirty years later that figure had taken a chilling drop, to 16 percent.

What had happened? One after another, foreign steelmakers fired up new plants with the help of money from their governments. With this government aid, the foreign companies could make steel more cheaply and sell it at lower prices than American companies could. Foreign nations greatly increased their steel production, both to fill their own needs and to sell steel to other countries.

Steel users, here and abroad, began buying the cheaper steel made by foreign companies. American steelmakers could not compete. Plants closed, and thousands of workers were laid off. American steel industry representatives and government leaders warned that our steel companies might go out of business. We would be at the mercy of foreign steelmakers, who could raise their prices.

In 1984 our government almost closed the door on foreign steel. It made a rule that only 20 percent of the steel sold in the United States could come from abroad. The result: our steel industry, which had lost almost $3 billion a year in the early 1980s, was making a profit of $2 billion a year by 1988.

Many Americans, however, are not happy with the 20 percent import limit. They think it is harmful, and they want it scrapped. An industry that takes in $2 billion a year, they say, needs no protection.

Furthermore, without foreign competition, American steelmakers can charge higher prices, hurting companies that need steel to make their products. In fact, between 1986 and 1989, steel prices rose 19 percent. Also, the limit is causing American workers to lose their jobs. One study found that although 17,000 steelmaking jobs were saved, over 52,000 jobs were lost in steel-using industries.

Those who want the United States to open its markets to more foreign steel also point out that free competition is the American way. They say it works best for the world. Trade barriers between nations cause bitterness, destroying the international good will that is our best defense against war.

Supporters of the import limit, though, point out that other countries do not always play by the rules of free trade. Other large steel-producing countries, they say, keep their own import limits well below 20 percent. When overseas buyers close their doors to us, they argue, we must do the same to them.

Expressing Your Opinion

Write a one-page letter to the President of the United States, taking a stand either for a protected steel industry or for free trade in steel. Begin your letter, "Dear Mr. President:" and address it to "The President, The White House, Washington, D.C., 20500."

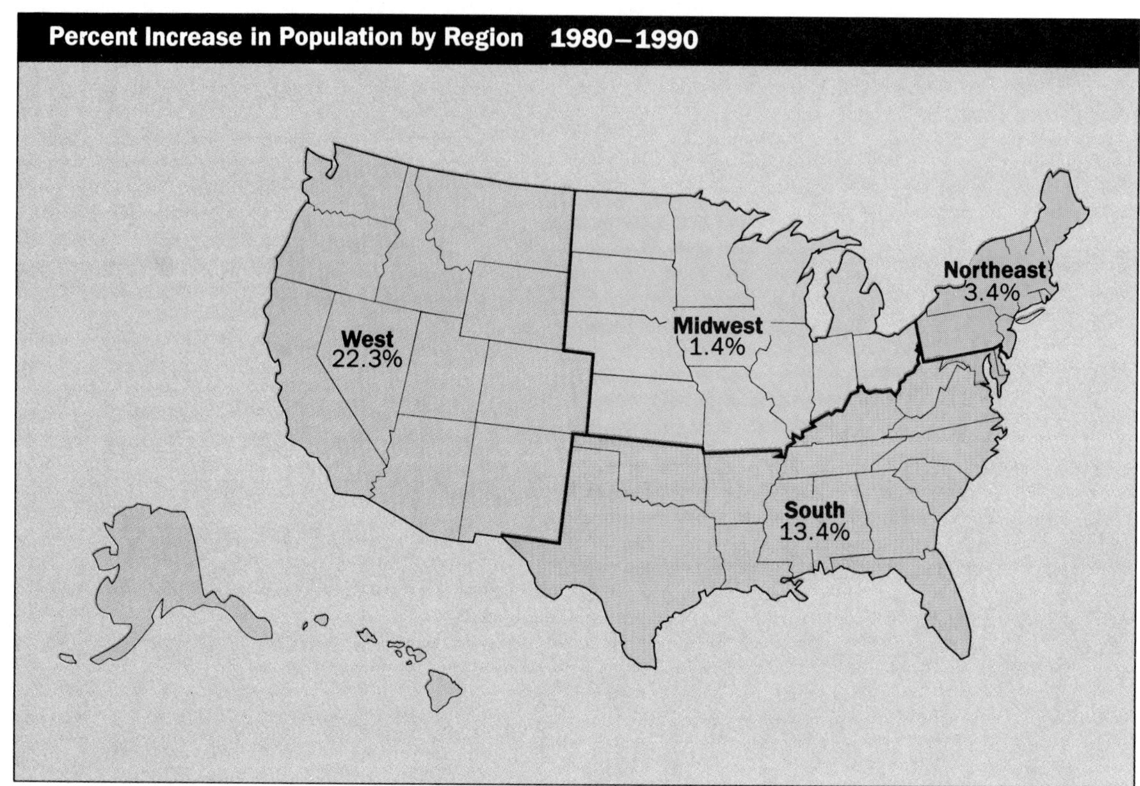

Source: Bureau of the Census

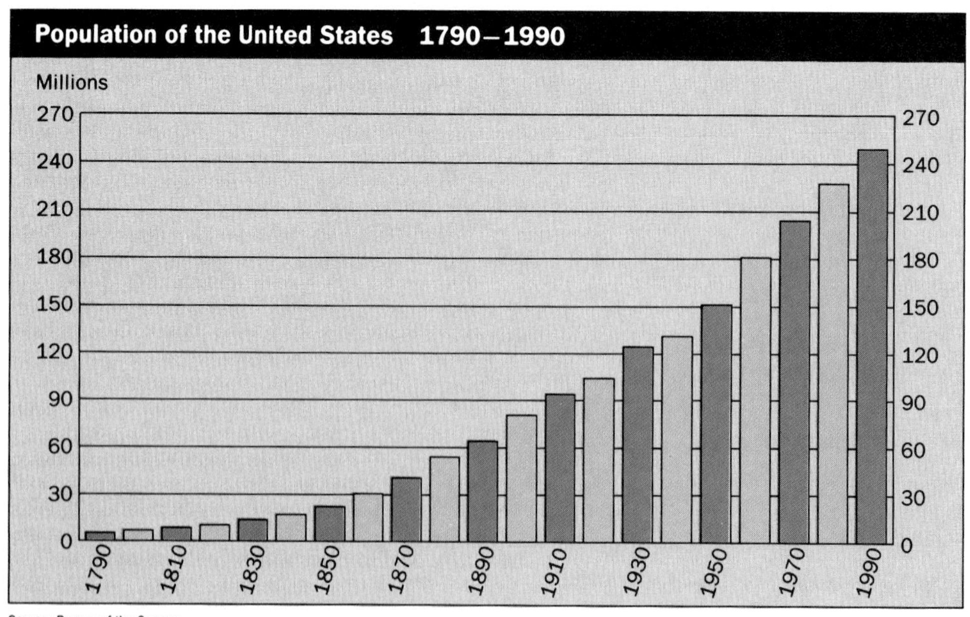

Source: Bureau of the Census

Level of Education Completed 1940–1989

Percent of persons
25 years and over
High school only
Four or more years of college
100
75
50
25
0
1940
1950
1960
1970
1980
1989

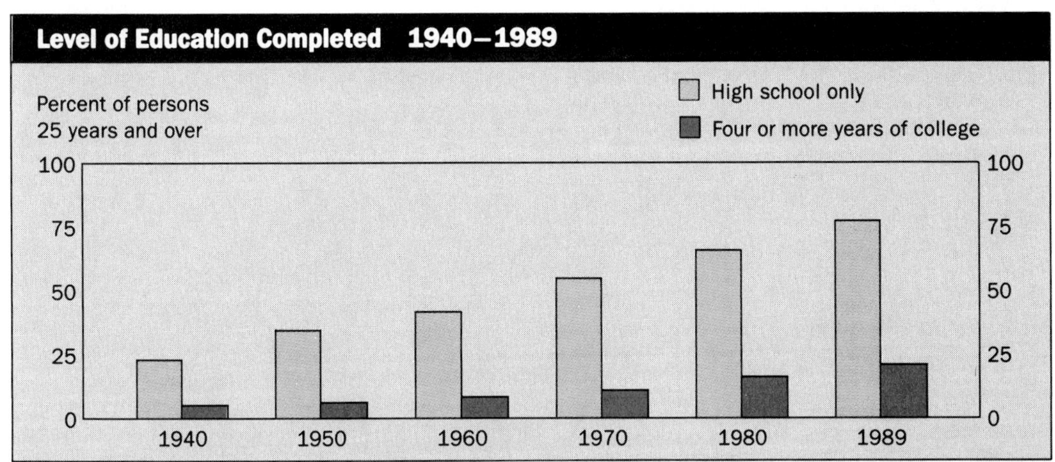

Source: National Center for Educational Statistics; U.S. Bureau of the Census, 1991

Immigration 1820–1990

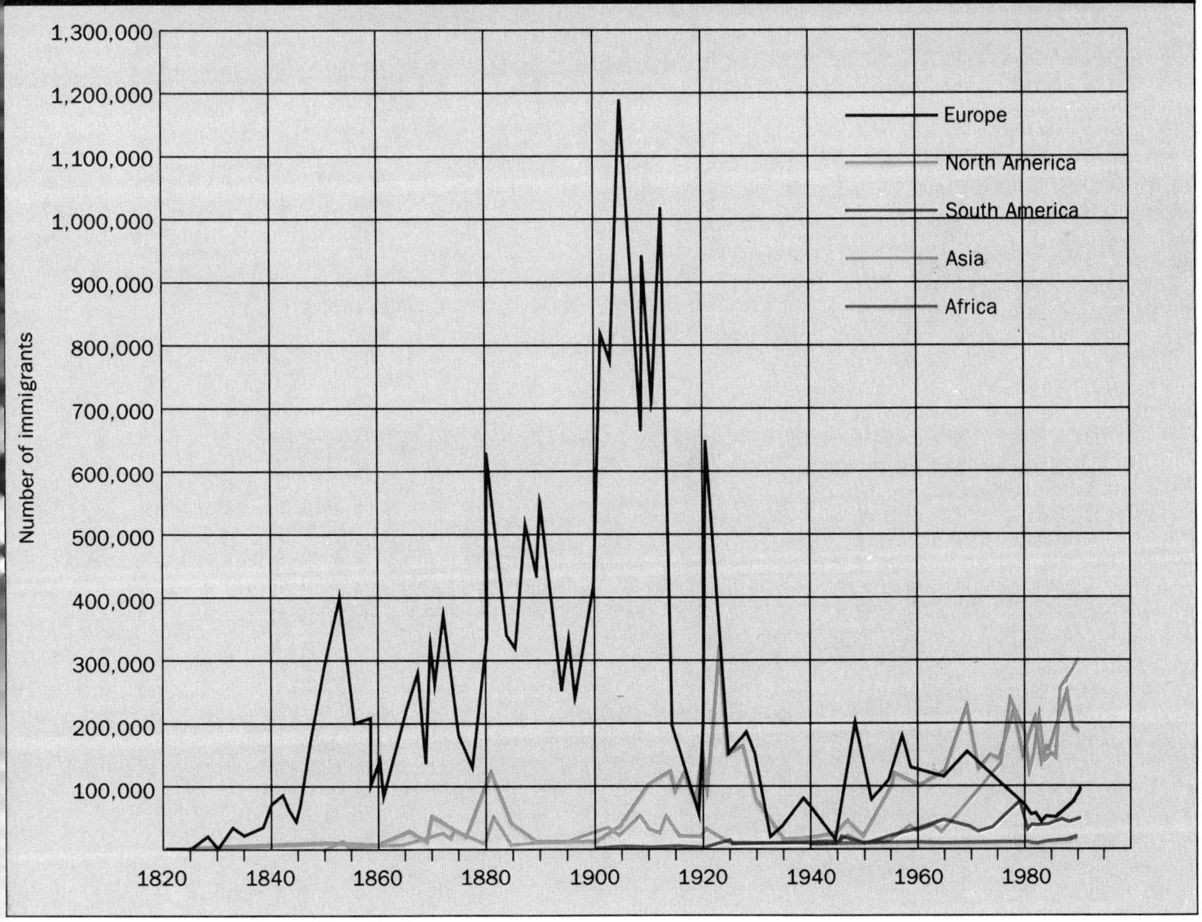

Number of immigrants
1,300,000
1,200,000
1,100,000
1,000,000
900,000
800,000
700,000
600,000
500,000
400,000
300,000
200,000
100,000
Europe
North America
South America
Asia
Africa
1820
1840
1860
1880
1900
1920
1940
1960
1980

Source: *Historical Statistics of the United States;* U.S. Bureau of the Census

Naturalizations 1910–1990

Year	Total number of people naturalized
1910	39,448
1915	91,848
1920	177,683
1925	152,457
1930	169,377
1935	118,945
1940	235,260
1945	231,402
1950	66,346
1955	209,526
1960	119,442
1965	104,299
1970	110,399
1975	141,537
1980	157,938
1985	244,717
1990	270,101

Source: *Historical Statistics of the United States*, Bureau of the Census

Colonial Population by Nationality

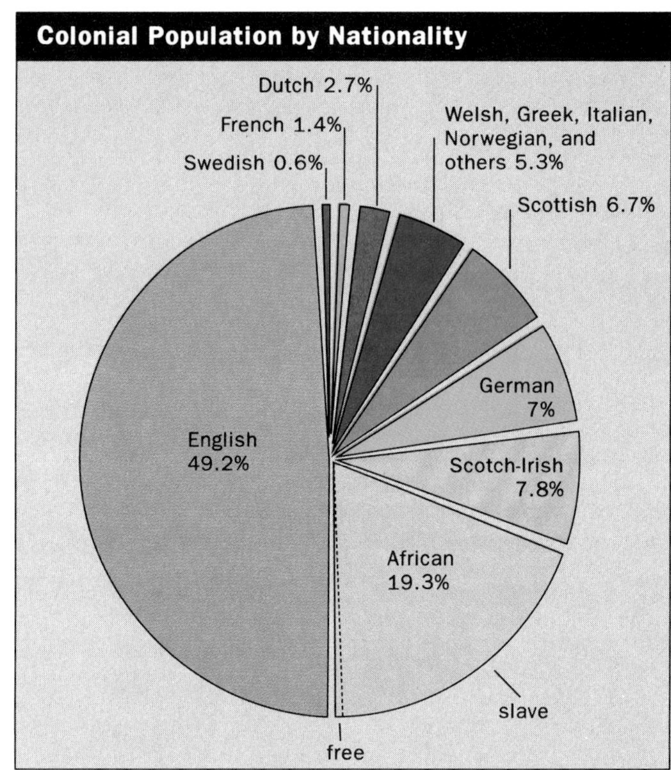

Estimates about the number of non-English colonists were made from names in the 1790 census. Many non-English colonists had changed their names and thus may have been counted as English.

Population of the States 1790

State	Population	State	Population
Connecticut *	238,000	New York *	340,000
Delaware *	59,000	North Carolina *	394,000
Georgia *	83,000	Pennsylvania *	434,000
Kentucky	74,000	Rhode Island *	69,000
Maine	97,000	South Carolina *	249,000
Maryland *	320,000	Tennessee	36,000
Massachusetts *	379,000	Vermont	85,000
New Hampshire *	142,000	Virginia *	692,000
New Jersey *	184,000		

*Original 13 states
Source: Bureau of the Census

Foundations of American Rights

Rights	The Magna Carta (1215)	The English Bill of Rights (1689)	The Virginia Declaration of Rights (1776)	The Bill of Rights (1791)
Trial by jury		•		•
Due process	•	•		•
Private property	•			•
No unreasonable searches or seizures			•	•
No cruel punishment		•	•	•
No excessive bail or fines		•		•
Right to bear arms		•		•
Right to petition		•		•
Freedom of speech			•	•
Freedom of the press			•	•
Freedom of religion			•	•

Standing Committees of Congress

Senate	House of Representatives
Agriculture, Nutrition, and Forestry	Agriculture
Appropriations	Appropriations
Armed Services	Armed Services
Banking, Housing, and Urban Affairs	Banking, Finance, and Urban Affairs
Budget	Budget
Commerce, Science, and Transportation	District of Columbia
Energy and Natural Resources	Education and Labor
Environment and Public Works	Energy and Commerce
Finance	Foreign Affairs
Foreign Relations	Government Operations
Governmental Affairs	House Administration
Judiciary	Interior and Insular Affairs
Labor and Human Resources	Judiciary
Rules and Administration	Merchant Marine and Fisheries
Small Business	Post Office and Civil Service
Veterans' Affairs	Public Works and Transportation
	Rules
	Science, Space, and Technology
	Small Business
	Standards of Official Conduct
	Veterans' Affairs
	Ways and Means

Changes in the House of Representatives After the 1990 Census

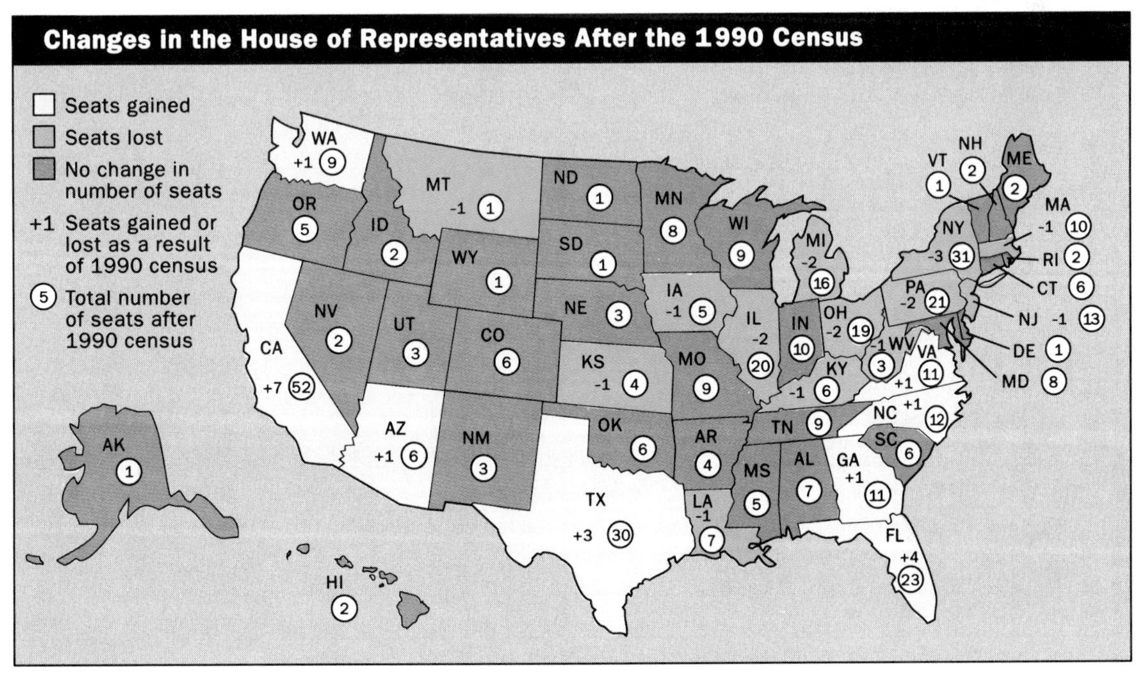

The Budgets of Federal Executive Departments (in billions of dollars)

Department	1980	1990
Agriculture	34.8	48.2
Commerce	3.1	3.9
Defense	146.1	311.5
Education	14.8	22.3
Energy	6.5	12.3
Health and Human Services	194.2	435.8
Housing and Urban Development	12.7	22.8
Interior	4.5	5.8
Justice	2.6	6.9
Labor	29.7	24.9
State	1.9	3.8
Transportation	19.8	28.3
Treasury	76.5	247.2
Veterans Affairs	21.1	28.7

Source: U.S. Office of Management and Budget; Statistical Abstract of the United States

Governments in the United States

Type of government	Number of governments	Number of elected officials	Average number of officials per government
Federal	1	542	542
State	50	18,171	363
Local			
County	3,042	59,932	20
Municipality	19,200	137,688	7
Township	16,691	120,790	7
School district	14,721	86,772	6
Other special district	29,532	80,509	3
Total	83,237	504,404	6

Source: Bureau of the Census, 1991

Quality of Life Measures in Ten Selected Countries 1990

	Brazil	Egypt	France	India	Japan
Population	150.4 mill.	53.2 mill.	56.7 mill.	853.4 mill.	123.6 mill.
Gross national product (GNP)	$375 bill.	$33 bill.	$1,001 bill.	$287 bill.	$2,920 bill.
Per capita GNP	$2,540	$640	$17,820	$340	$23,810
Imports	$16.6 bill.	$23.3 bill.	$177.2 bill.	$15.7 bill.	$210.8 bill.
Exports	$26.2 bill.	$5.7 bill.	$162.1 bill.	$9.7 bill.	$275.2 bill.
Telephones (per 1000 people)	100	29	667	5.3	556
Cars (per 1000 people)	115	26	500	4.4	435
Population with safe water	78%	73%	100%	57%	98%
Literacy rate	79%	45%	99%	44%	100%
Child deaths (per 1000 children under 5)	86	124	10	148	8
Life expectancy at birth	66	60	77	59	79

Sources: *World Development Report*, The World Bank, 1991 *Encyclopaedia Britannica, 1991 Yearbook*

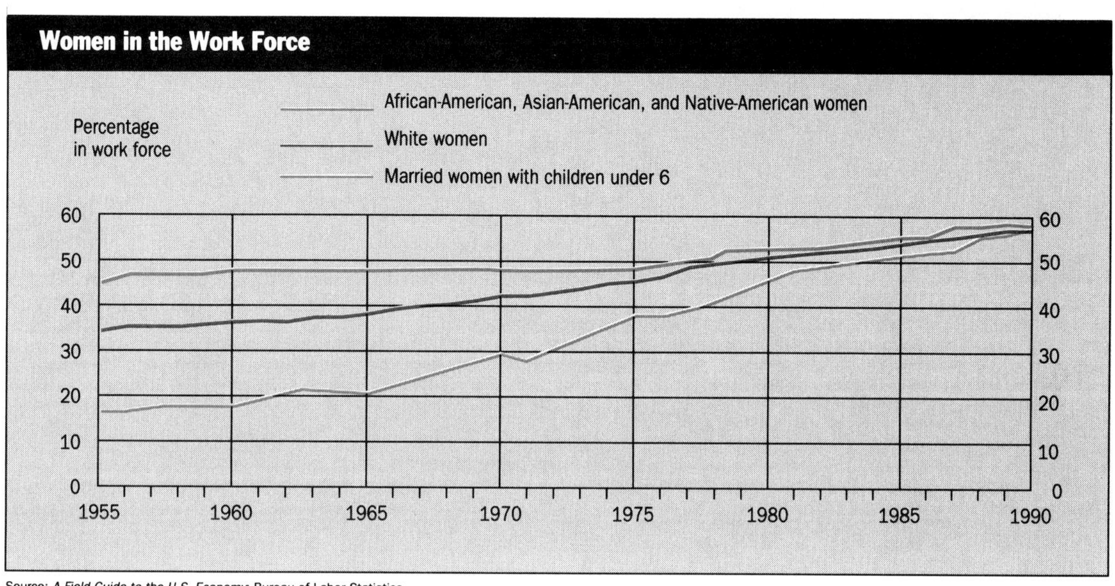

Source: *A Field Guide to the U.S. Economy*; Bureau of Labor Statistics

Mexico	United Kingdom	United States	Vietnam	Zaire	
81.9 mill.	57.4 mill.	248.7 mill.	66.1 mill.	34.1 mill.	Population
$170 bill.	$834 bill.	$5,238 bill.	$12.6 bill.	$8.8 bill.	Gross national product (GNP)
$2,010	$14,610	$20,910	$200	$260	Per capita GNP
$19.6 bill.	$198.1 bill.	$493.4 bill.	$3.25 bill.	$756 mill.	Imports
$20.8 bill.	$152.9 bill.	$363.8 bill.	$1.27 bill.	$98 mill.	Exports
109	520	769	1.9	1.0	Telephones (per 1000 people)
101	385	770	n/a	2.9	Cars (per 1000 people)
77%	100%	100%	46%	33%	Population with safe water
90%	100%	96%	94%	61%	Literacy rate
68	11	12	91	161	Child deaths (per 1000 children under 5)
69	76	76	66	53	Life expectancy at birth

Unpaid Consumer Credit 1980–1990		
Year	Billions of dollars	Percent of disposable income
1980	$350.3	18.3
1981	366.9	17.2
1982	383.1	16.9
1983	431.2	17.8
1984	511.3	19.2
1985	592.1	20.9
1986	649.1	21.5
1987	681.9	21.3
1988	731.5	21.0
1989	778.0	20.6
1990	808.9	20.5

Source: *Statistical Abstract of the United States*, 1991; *The World Almanac*, 1992

Education and Median Annual Income	
Education completed	Median income in 1989
8 years or less	12,696
1–3 yrs high school	17,767
4 yrs high school	28,060
1–3 yrs college	35,083
4 yrs or more of college	49,180

Source: *Statistical Abstract of the United States*, 1991

Typical Lengths of Parts of Some Criminal Jury Trials* (in hours and minutes)

	Narcotics	Assault	Robbery	Rape	Homicide
Jury Selection	2:00	2:11	3:00	4:15	8:14
Prosecutor's Case	2:49	4:06	3:41	6:14	13:43
Defense Case	1:30	1:47	1:40	2:08	4:38
Jury Deliberation	2:12	2:38	1:50	3:40	5:30

*Based on data gathered from over 1,500 trials in New Jersey, Colorado, and California.

Source: *On Trial: The Length of Civil and Criminal Trials*. Williamsburg, VA: National Center for State Courts, 1988

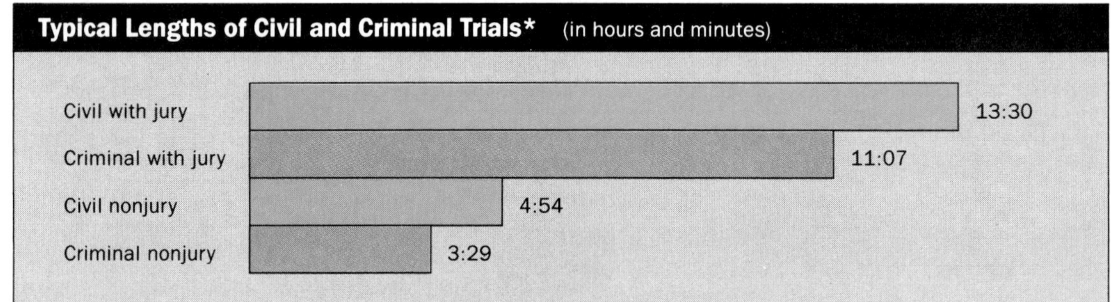

*Based on data gathered from over 1,500 trials in New Jersey, Colorado, and California.

Source: *On Trial: The Length of Civil and Criminal Trials*. Williamsburg, VA: National Center for State Courts, 1988

Some Types of Crimes

Felonies in all or most states	Misdemeanors in all or most states	Felonies or misdemeanors (depending on circumstances)
arson	contempt of court	assault and battery
burglary	disorderly conduct	blackmail
counterfeiting	littering	embezzlement
grand larceny	minor traffic violations	forgery
kidnapping	petty larceny	perjury
murder	prostitution	possession of illegal drugs
rape	public drunkenness	smuggling
robbery	vagrancy	tax evasion
sale of illegal drugs	vandalism	

Crime in the United States

(reported to the police)

Year	Violent crimes	Property crimes	Total
1980	1,345,000	12,064,000	13,408,000
1981	1,362,000	12,062,000	13,424,000
1982	1,322,000	11,652,000	12,974,000
1983	1,258,000	10,851,000	12,109,000
1984	1,273,000	10,609,000	11,882,000
1985	1,329,000	11,103,000	12,431,000
1986	1,489,000	11,723,000	13,212,000
1987	1,484,000	12,025,000	13,509,000
1988	1,566,000	12,357,000	13,923,000
1989	1,646,000	12,605,000	14,251,000

Source: Federal Bureau of Investigation

The Crime Clock

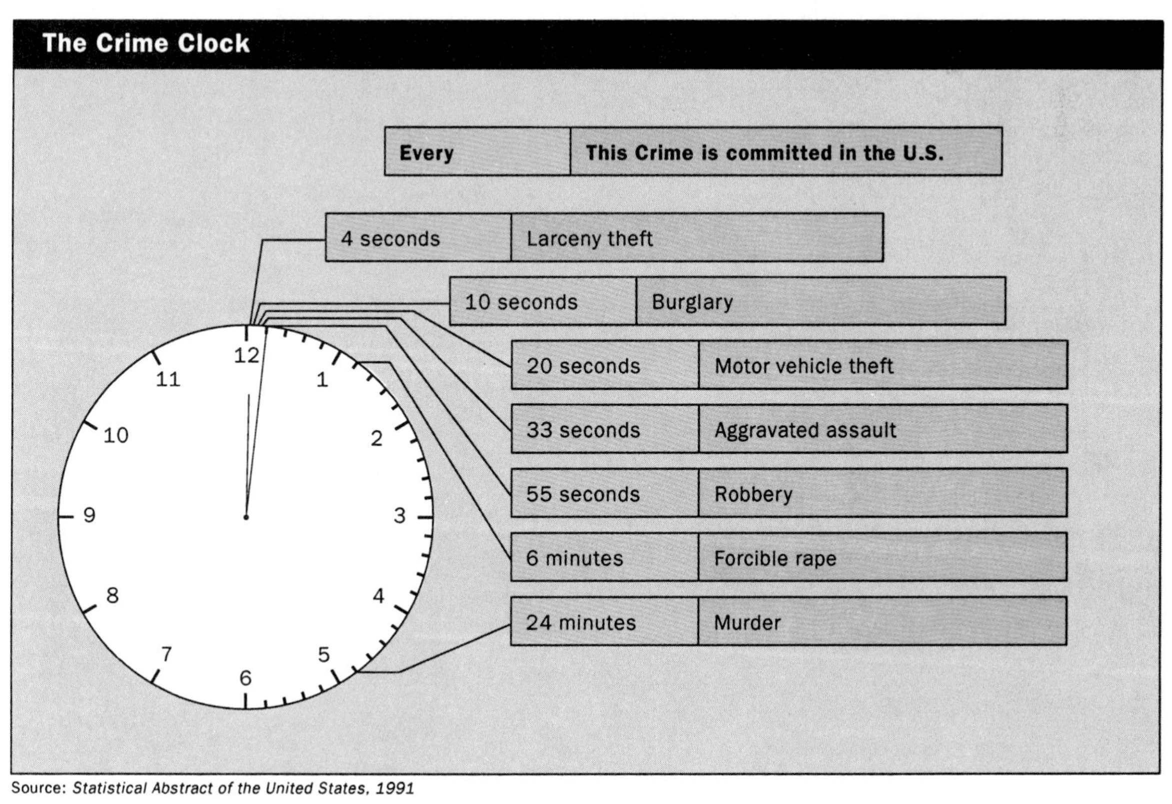

Every	This Crime is committed in the U.S.
4 seconds	Larceny theft
10 seconds	Burglary
20 seconds	Motor vehicle theft
33 seconds	Aggravated assault
55 seconds	Robbery
6 minutes	Forcible rape
24 minutes	Murder

Source: *Statistical Abstract of the United States, 1991*

Composition of Congress by Political Party in Selected Years

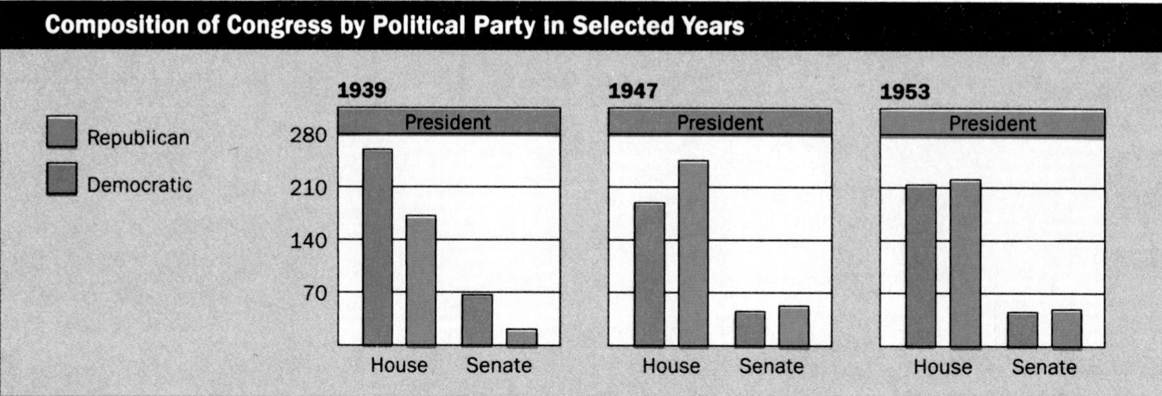

Source: *Statistical Abstract of the United States*, 1989; *Time*, November 19, 1990

Political Action Committee (PAC) Contributions to Congressional Campaigns 1979–1990

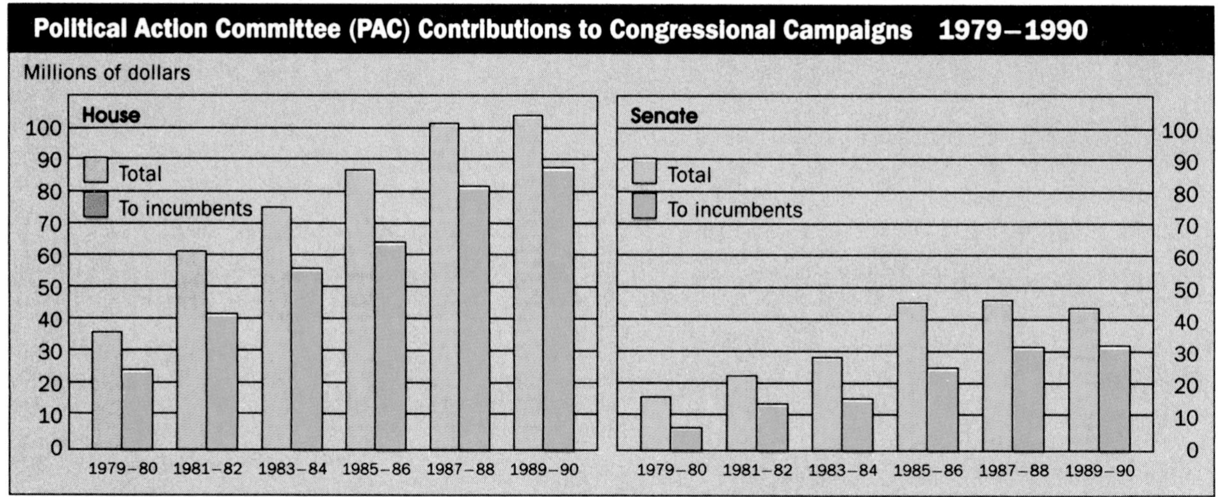

Source: U.S. Bureau of the Census; Federal Election Commission; Common Cause

Top PAC Contributors to Candidates for Federal Office in the 1988 Elections

Contributor	Amount
National Association of Realtors	$3,094,228
American Medical Association	2,375,992
Democratic Republican Independent Voter Education Committee	2,349,575
National Educational Association	2,320,155
United Auto Workers	1,790,912
National Association of Letter Carriers	1,731,050
American Federation of State, County, and Municipal Employees	1,553,970
National Association of Retired Federal Employees	1,553,000
Association of Trial Lawyers of America	1,526,600
United Brotherhood of Carpenters and Joiners of America	1,491,020

Source: Federal Election Commission

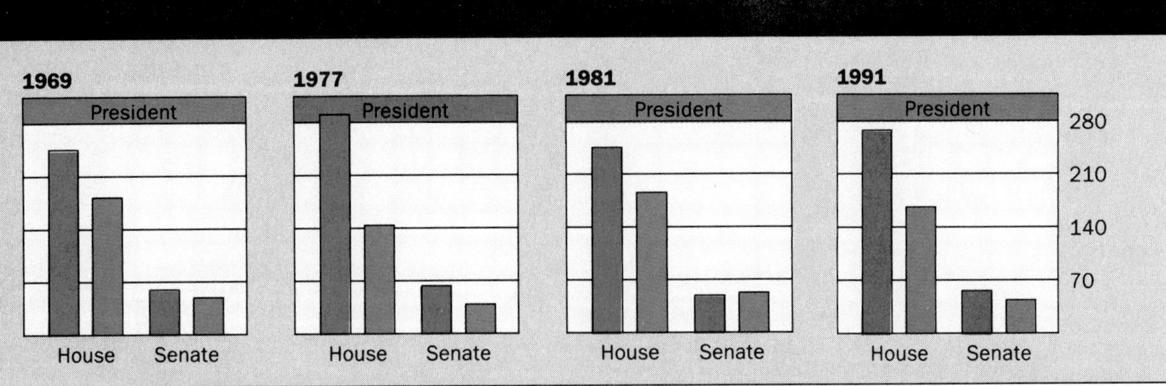

Concerns of American Youth Ages 8–17

	Very concerned	Sort of concerned	Not really concerned
Kidnapping	76%	16%	8%
Possibility of nuclear war	65%	20%	12%
Spread of AIDS	65%	20%	10%
Drug use by pro athletes	52%	25%	20%
Having to fight a war	47%	26%	25%
Air and water pollution	47%	38%	13%
Increasing divorce among parents	39%	33%	25%

Source: The American Chicle Youth Poll, 1987

Foreign Nations Receiving the Most United States Aid 1990

Nation	Amount of aid*
Egypt	$9,907,000,000
Israel	4,641,000,000
Philippines	381,000,000
Turkey	379,000,000
El Salvador	273,000,000
Poland	265,000,000
Pakistan	264,000,000
Bangladesh	228,000,000
Honduras	222,000,000
Sudan	144,000,000
Kenya	140,000,000
Bolivia	97,000,000
Panama	97,000,000
Nicaragua	97,000,000

*net grants of economic and military aid

Source: *The World Almanac 1992*

Known Global Reserves of Nonrenewable Resources

Nonrenewable resource	Estimated number of years until resource is used up, at present consumption rate
Aluminum	31
Coal	111
Copper	21
Gold	9
Iron	93
Lead	21
Natural gas	22
Petroleum	20
Silver	13
Tin	15

Source: *Global Issues*, SSEC & CTIR, Boulder/Denver, CO

MAP OF THE UNITED STATES

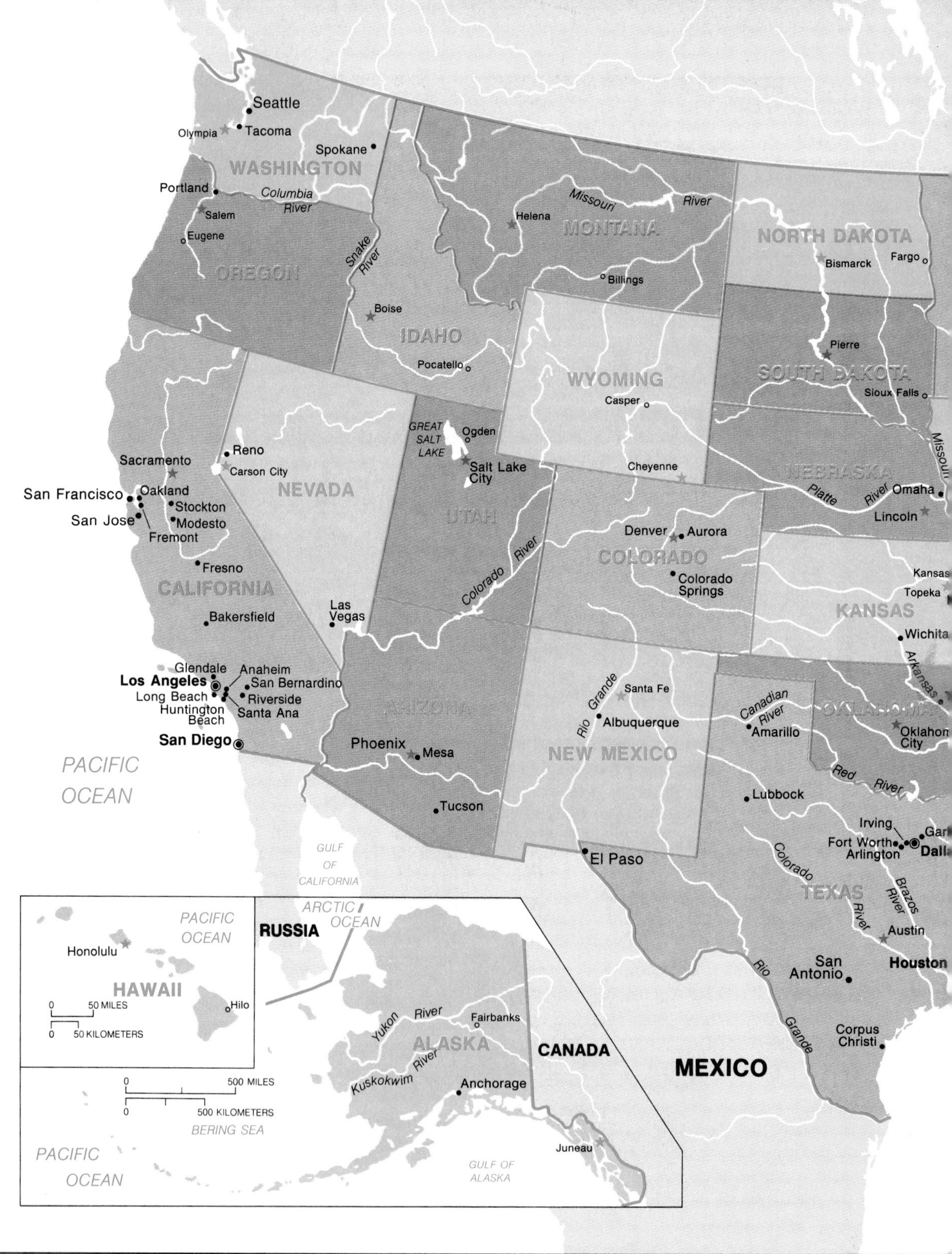

Seattle
Olympia
Tacoma
Spokane
WASHINGTON
Portland
Columbia River
Salem
Eugene
OREGON
Snake River
Helena
Missouri River
MONTANA
NORTH DAKOTA
Bismarck
Fargo
Billings
Boise
IDAHO
Pocatello
WYOMING
Casper
Pierre
SOUTH DAKOTA
Sioux Falls
GREAT SALT LAKE
Ogden
Reno
Carson City
Sacramento
NEVADA
Salt Lake City
Cheyenne
NEBRASKA
Platte River
Omaha
Lincoln
Missouri
San Francisco
Oakland
Stockton
San Jose
Modesto
Fremont
UTAH
Colorado River
Denver
Aurora
COLORADO
Colorado Springs
Fresno
CALIFORNIA
Kansas
Topeka
KANSAS
Wichita
Las Vegas
Bakersfield
Glendale
Anaheim
Los Angeles
San Bernardino
Long Beach
Riverside
Huntington Beach
Santa Ana
ARIZONA
Rio Grande
Santa Fe
Albuquerque
NEW MEXICO
Canadian River
Amarillo
OKLAHOMA
Oklahoma City
Arkansas
San Diego
Phoenix
Mesa
Tucson
PACIFIC OCEAN
Red River
Lubbock
Irving
Fort Worth
Arlington
Dallas
El Paso
GULF OF CALIFORNIA
Colorado
TEXAS
Brazos River
River
Austin
San Antonio
Houston
Rio Grande
Corpus Christi
MEXICO
PACIFIC OCEAN
Honolulu
HAWAII
Hilo
0 50 MILES
0 50 KILOMETERS
RUSSIA
ARCTIC OCEAN
Yukon River
Fairbanks
ALASKA
Kuskokwim River
Anchorage
CANADA
0 500 MILES
0 500 KILOMETERS
BERING SEA
PACIFIC OCEAN
Juneau
GULF OF ALASKA

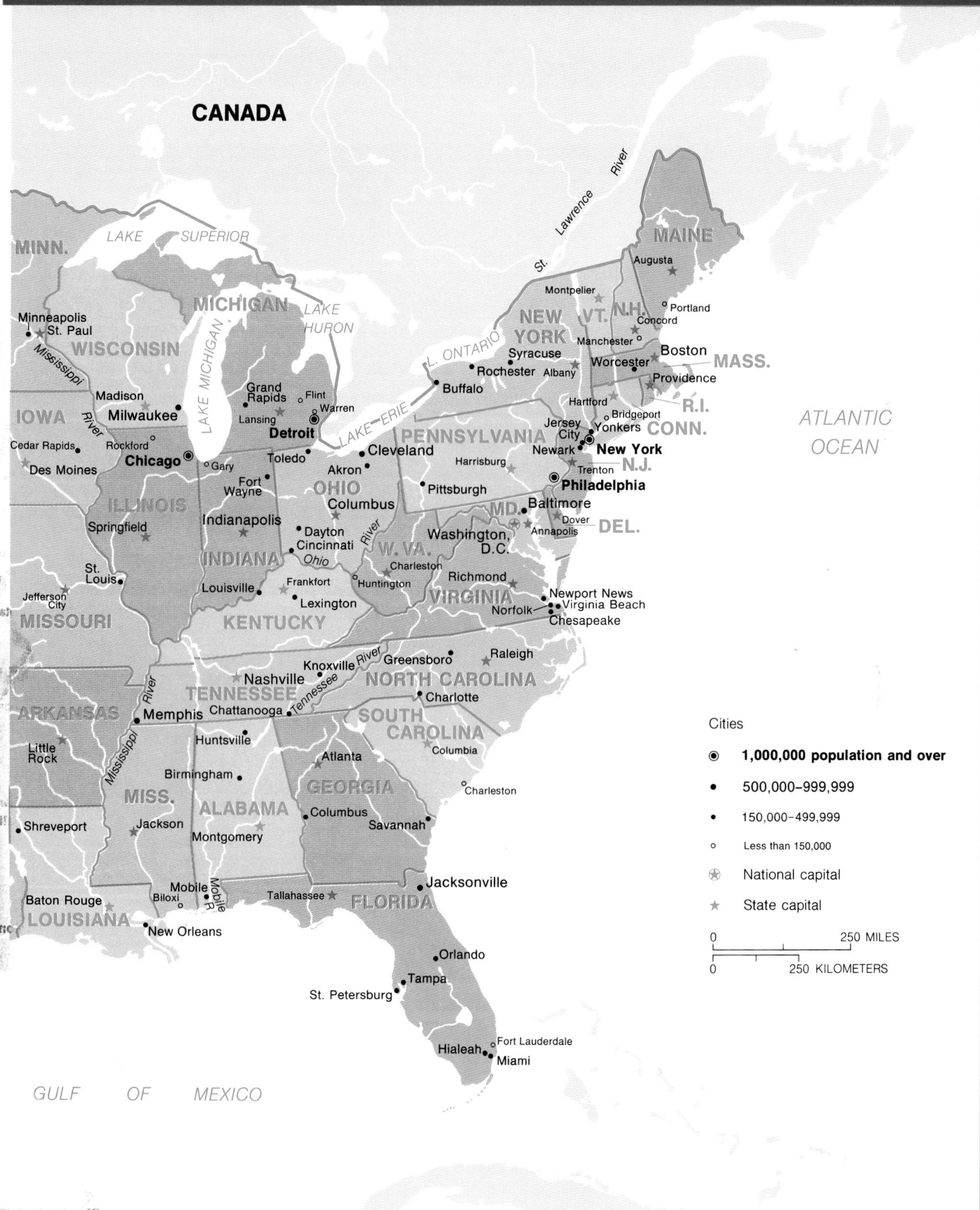
CANADA
LAKE SUPERIOR
LAKE HURON
LAKE MICHIGAN
L. ONTARIO
LAKE ERIE
St. Lawrence River
MINN.
MICHIGAN
WISCONSIN
IOWA
ILLINOIS
INDIANA
OHIO
PENNSYLVANIA
NEW YORK
VT.
N.H.
MAINE
MASS.
R.I.
CONN.
N.J.
DEL.
MD.
W. VA.
VIRGINIA
KENTUCKY
MISSOURI
TENNESSEE
NORTH CAROLINA
SOUTH CAROLINA
GEORGIA
ALABAMA
MISS.
ARKANSAS
LOUISIANA
FLORIDA
ATLANTIC OCEAN
GULF OF MEXICO
Mississippi River
Ohio River
Tennessee River
Mobile R.
Minneapolis
St. Paul
Madison
Milwaukee
Cedar Rapids
Des Moines
Rockford
Chicago
Gary
Grand Rapids
Flint
Warren
Lansing
Detroit
Toledo
Fort Wayne
Indianapolis
Springfield
St. Louis
Jefferson City
Dayton
Cincinnati
Louisville
Frankfort
Lexington
Cleveland
Akron
Columbus
Pittsburgh
Harrisburg
Buffalo
Rochester
Syracuse
Albany
Montpelier
Augusta
Portland
Concord
Manchester
Boston
Worcester
Providence
Hartford
Bridgeport
Yonkers
Jersey City
Newark
New York
Trenton
Philadelphia
Baltimore
Dover
Annapolis
Washington, D.C.
Charleston
Huntington
Richmond
Newport News
Virginia Beach
Norfolk
Chesapeake
Raleigh
Greensboro
Knoxville
Nashville
Charlotte
Memphis
Chattanooga
Columbia
Little Rock
Huntsville
Atlanta
Birmingham
Charleston
Columbus
Savannah
Shreveport
Jackson
Montgomery
Jacksonville
Mobile
Biloxi
Tallahassee
Baton Rouge
New Orleans
Orlando
Tampa
St. Petersburg
Fort Lauderdale
Hialeah
Miami
Cities
1,000,000 population and over
500,000–999,999
150,000–499,999
Less than 150,000
National capital
State capital
0 250 MILES
0 250 KILOMETERS

MAP OF THE WORLD

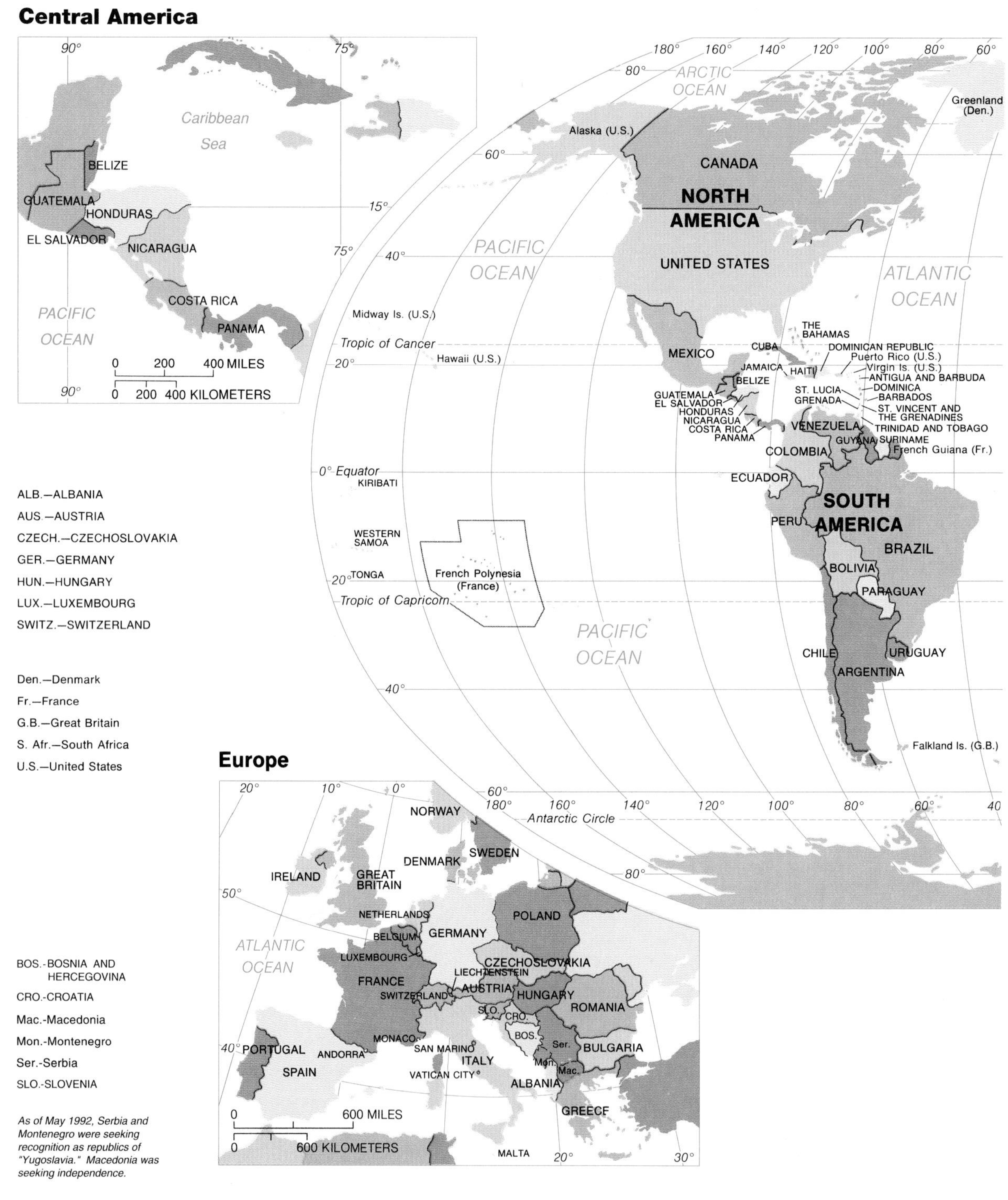
Central America
Caribbean Sea
BELIZE
GUATEMALA
HONDURAS
EL SALVADOR
NICARAGUA
COSTA RICA
PANAMA
PACIFIC OCEAN
0 200 400 MILES
0 200 400 KILOMETERS
ARCTIC OCEAN
Alaska (U.S.)
Greenland (Den.)
CANADA
NORTH AMERICA
UNITED STATES
PACIFIC OCEAN
ATLANTIC OCEAN
Midway Is. (U.S.)
Tropic of Cancer
Hawaii (U.S.)
MEXICO
THE BAHAMAS
CUBA
DOMINICAN REPUBLIC
Puerto Rico (U.S.)
Virgin Is. (U.S.)
ANTIGUA AND BARBUDA
DOMINICA
BARBADOS
ST. VINCENT AND THE GRENADINES
TRINIDAD AND TOBAGO
JAMAICA
HAITI
BELIZE
GUATEMALA
EL SALVADOR
HONDURAS
NICARAGUA
COSTA RICA
PANAMA
ST. LUCIA
GRENADA
VENEZUELA
GUYANA
SURINAME
French Guiana (Fr.)
COLOMBIA
0° Equator
KIRIBATI
ECUADOR
SOUTH AMERICA
PERU
BRAZIL
WESTERN SAMOA
TONGA
French Polynesia (France)
Tropic of Capricorn
BOLIVIA
PARAGUAY
PACIFIC OCEAN
CHILE
URUGUAY
ARGENTINA
Falkland Is. (G.B.)
Antarctic Circle
ALB.—ALBANIA
AUS.—AUSTRIA
CZECH.—CZECHOSLOVAKIA
GER.—GERMANY
HUN.—HUNGARY
LUX.—LUXEMBOURG
SWITZ.—SWITZERLAND
Den.—Denmark
Fr.—France
G.B.—Great Britain
S. Afr.—South Africa
U.S.—United States
Europe
NORWAY
SWEDEN
DENMARK
IRELAND
GREAT BRITAIN
NETHERLANDS
POLAND
BELGIUM
GERMANY
LUXEMBOURG
CZECHOSLOVAKIA
ATLANTIC OCEAN
FRANCE
LIECHTENSTEIN
AUSTRIA
SWITZERLAND
HUNGARY
SLO.
CRO.
ROMANIA
BOS.
Ser.
BULGARIA
MONACO
SAN MARINO
PORTUGAL
ANDORRA
ITALY
Mon.
Mac.
SPAIN
VATICAN CITY
ALBANIA
GREECE
0 600 MILES
0 600 KILOMETERS
MALTA
BOS.-BOSNIA AND HERCEGOVINA
CRO.-CROATIA
Mac.-Macedonia
Mon.-Montenegro
Ser.-Serbia
SLO.-SLOVENIA
As of May 1992, Serbia and Montenegro were seeking recognition as republics of "Yugoslavia." Macedonia was seeking independence.

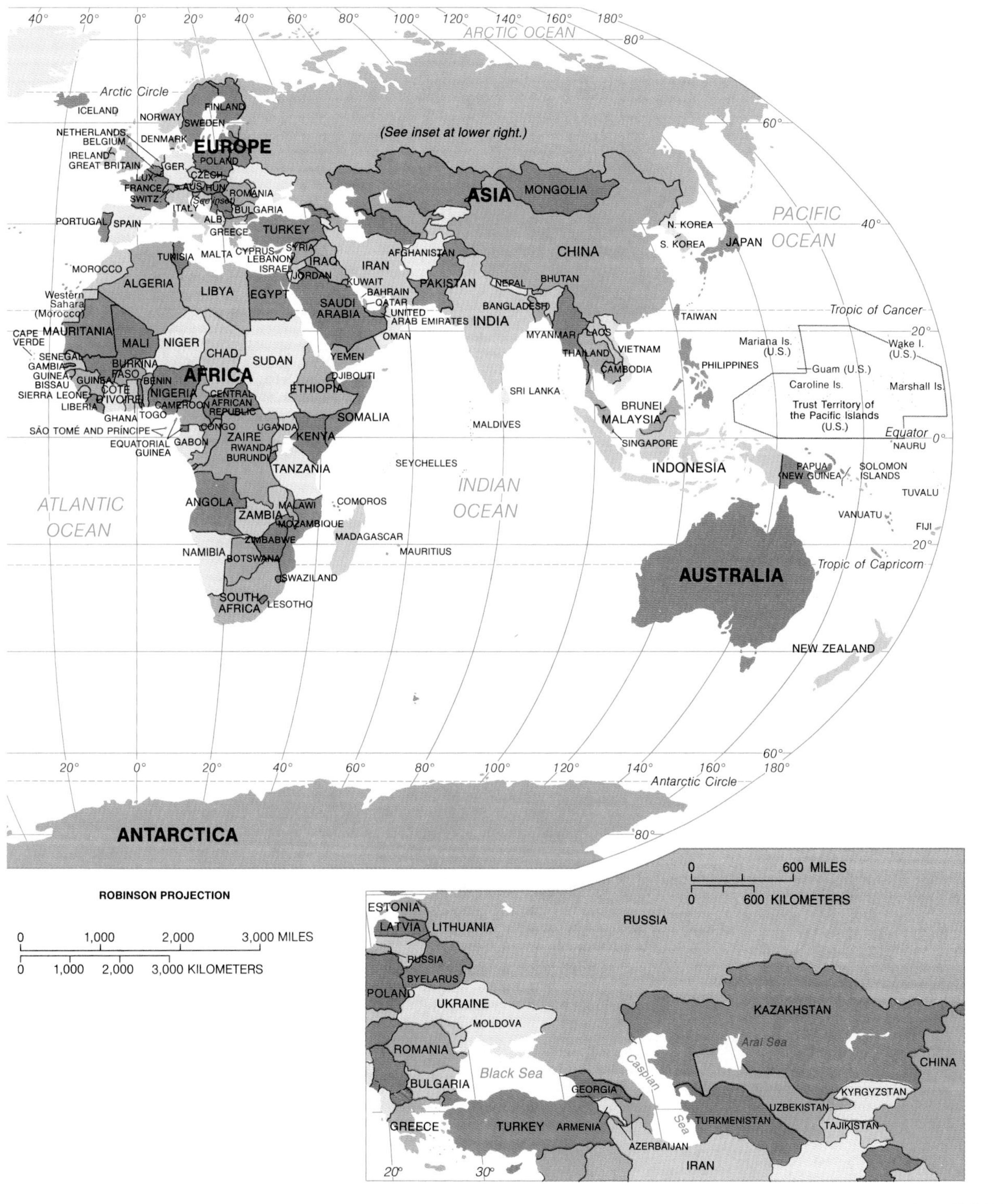

ARCTIC OCEAN
Arctic Circle
ICELAND
NORWAY
SWEDEN
FINLAND
NETHERLANDS
BELGIUM
DENMARK
IRELAND
GREAT BRITAIN
EUROPE
GER.
POLAND
CZECH.
LUX.
FRANCE
AUS.
HUN.
SWITZ.
ROMANIA
ITALY
(See inset)
BULGARIA
ALB.
GREECE
PORTUGAL
SPAIN
TURKEY
(See inset at lower right.)
ASIA
MONGOLIA
CHINA
N. KOREA
S. KOREA
JAPAN
PACIFIC OCEAN
MOROCCO
TUNISIA
MALTA
CYPRUS
LEBANON
ISRAEL
SYRIA
IRAQ
JORDAN
IRAN
AFGHANISTAN
PAKISTAN
NEPAL
BHUTAN
ALGERIA
LIBYA
EGYPT
KUWAIT
BAHRAIN
QATAR
UNITED ARAB EMIRATES
SAUDI ARABIA
OMAN
INDIA
BANGLADESH
Western Sahara (Morocco)
CAPE VERDE
MAURITANIA
MALI
NIGER
CHAD
SUDAN
YEMEN
Tropic of Cancer
TAIWAN
MYANMAR
LAOS
THAILAND
VIETNAM
CAMBODIA
PHILIPPINES
Mariana Is. (U.S.)
Guam (U.S.)
Wake I. (U.S.)
Caroline Is.
Marshall Is.
Trust Territory of the Pacific Islands (U.S.)
SENEGAL
GAMBIA
GUINEA-BISSAU
GUINEA
SIERRA LEONE
LIBERIA
BURKINA FASO
CÔTE D'IVOIRE
GHANA
TOGO
BENIN
NIGERIA
CAMEROON
AFRICA
CENTRAL AFRICAN REPUBLIC
ETHIOPIA
DJIBOUTI
SOMALIA
SRI LANKA
MALDIVES
BRUNEI
MALAYSIA
SINGAPORE
Equator
NAURU
SÃO TOMÉ AND PRÍNCIPE
EQUATORIAL GUINEA
GABON
CONGO
ZAIRE
UGANDA
KENYA
RWANDA
BURUNDI
TANZANIA
SEYCHELLES
INDONESIA
PAPUA NEW GUINEA
SOLOMON ISLANDS
TUVALU
ATLANTIC OCEAN
ANGOLA
ZAMBIA
MALAWI
COMOROS
MOZAMBIQUE
INDIAN OCEAN
VANUATU
FIJI
ZIMBABWE
MADAGASCAR
NAMIBIA
BOTSWANA
MAURITIUS
Tropic of Capricorn
AUSTRALIA
SWAZILAND
SOUTH AFRICA
LESOTHO
NEW ZEALAND
Antarctic Circle
ANTARCTICA
ROBINSON PROJECTION
0 1,000 2,000 3,000 MILES
0 1,000 2,000 3,000 KILOMETERS
0 600 MILES
0 600 KILOMETERS
ESTONIA
LATVIA
LITHUANIA
RUSSIA
BYELARUS
POLAND
UKRAINE
MOLDOVA
KAZAKHSTAN
Aral Sea
ROMANIA
Black Sea
Caspian Sea
CHINA
BULGARIA
GEORGIA
KYRGYZSTAN
UZBEKISTAN
GREECE
TURKEY
ARMENIA
TURKMENISTAN
TAJIKISTAN
AZERBAIJAN
IRAN

PRESIDENTS AND VICE-PRESIDENTS

	President	Born-Died	Party	Years in Office	State*	Vice-President
1	George Washington	1732–1799	Federalist	1789–1797	Virginia	John Adams
2	John Adams	1735–1826	Federalist	1797–1801	Massachusetts	Thomas Jefferson
3	Thomas Jefferson	1743–1826	Democratic-Republican	1801–1809	Virginia	Aaron Burr George Clinton
4	James Madison	1751–1836	Democratic-Republican	1809–1817	Virginia	George Clinton Elbridge Gerry
5	James Monroe	1758–1831	Democratic-Republican	1817–1825	Virginia	Daniel D. Tompkins
6	John Quincy Adams	1767–1848	National-Republican	1825–1829	Massachusetts	John C. Calhoun
7	Andrew Jackson	1767–1845	Democratic	1829–1837	Tennessee	John C. Calhoun Martin Van Buren
8	Martin Van Buren	1782–1862	Democratic	1837–1841	New York	Richard M. Johnson
9	William H. Harrison	1773–1841	Whig	1841	Ohio	John Tyler
10	John Tyler	1790–1862	Whig	1841–1845	Virginia	
11	James K. Polk	1795–1849	Democratic	1845–1849	Tennessee	George M. Dallas
12	Zachary Taylor	1784–1850	Whig	1849–1850	Louisiana	Millard Fillmore
13	Millard Fillmore	1800–1874	Whig	1850–1853	New York	
14	Franklin Pierce	1804–1869	Democratic	1853–1857	New Hampshire	William R. King
15	James Buchanan	1791–1868	Democratic	1857–1861	Pennsylvania	John C. Breckinridge
16	Abraham Lincoln	1809–1865	Republican	1861–1865	Illinois	Hannibal Hamlin Andrew Johnson
17	Andrew Johnson	1808–1875	Democratic	1865–1869	Tennessee	
18	Ulysses S. Grant	1822–1885	Republican	1869–1877	Illinois	Schuyler Colfax Henry Wilson
19	Rutherford B. Hayes	1822–1893	Republican	1877–1881	Ohio	William A. Wheeler
20	James Garfield	1831–1881	Republican	1881	Ohio	Chester A. Arthur
21	Chester A. Arthur	1830–1886	Republican	1881–1885	New York	
22	Grover Cleveland	1837–1908	Democratic	1885–1889	New York	Thomas Hendricks
23	Benjamin Harrison	1833–1901	Republican	1889–1893	Indiana	Levi P. Morton
24	Grover Cleveland	1837–1908	Democratic	1893–1897	New York	Adlai E. Stevenson
25	William McKinley	1843–1901	Republican	1897–1901	Ohio	Garret A. Hobart Theodore Roosevelt
26	Theodore Roosevelt	1858–1919	Republican	1901–1909	New York	Charles Fairbanks
27	William H. Taft	1857–1930	Republican	1909–1913	Ohio	James S. Sherman
28	Woodrow Wilson	1856–1924	Democratic	1913–1921	New Jersey	Thomas R. Marshall
29	Warren G. Harding	1865–1923	Republican	1921–1923	Ohio	Calvin Coolidge
30	Calvin Coolidge	1872–1933	Republican	1923–1929	Massachusetts	Charles G. Dawes
31	Herbert Hoover	1874–1964	Republican	1929–1933	California	Charles Curtis
32	Franklin D. Roosevelt	1882–1945	Democratic	1933–1945	New York	John Garner Henry Wallace Harry S Truman
33	Harry S Truman	1884–1972	Democratic	1945–1953	Missouri	Alben Barkley
34	Dwight Eisenhower	1890–1969	Republican	1953–1961	New York	Richard Nixon
35	John F. Kennedy	1917–1963	Democratic	1961–1963	Massachusetts	Lyndon Johnson
36	Lyndon Johnson	1908–1973	Democratic	1963–1969	Texas	Hubert Humphrey
37	Richard Nixon	1913–	Republican	1969–1974	New York	Spiro Agnew Gerald Ford
38	Gerald Ford	1913–	Republican	1974–1977	Michigan	Nelson Rockefeller
39	Jimmy Carter	1924–	Democratic	1977–1981	Georgia	Walter Mondale
40	Ronald Reagan	1911–	Republican	1981–1989	California	George Bush
41	George Bush	1924–	Republican	1989–	Texas	J. Danforth Quayle

*State of residence when elected

FACTS ABOUT THE STATES

State	Year of Admission	Capital	Estimated 1995 Population (Rank)	Area in Square Miles (Rank)	Nickname
Alabama	1819	Montgomery	4,307,000 (22)	51,609 (29)	Yellowhammer State
Alaska	1959	Juneau	636,000 (48)	586,412 (1)	The Last Frontier
Arizona	1912	Phoenix	4,218,000 (23)	113,909 (6)	Grand Canyon State
Arkansas	1836	Little Rock	2,482,000 (33)	53,104 (27)	Land of Opportunity
California	1850	Sacramento	31,463,000 (1)	158,693 (3)	Golden State
Colorado	1876	Denver	3,637,000 (26)	104,247 (8)	Centennial State
Connecticut	1788	Hartford	3,376,000 (27)	5,009 (48)	Constitution State
Delaware	1787	Dover	702,000 (46)	2,057 (49)	First State
Florida	1845	Tallahassee	14,189,000 (4)	58,560 (22)	Sunshine State
Georgia	1788	Atlanta	7,338,000 (10)	58,876 (21)	Peach State
Hawaii	1959	Honolulu	1,243,000 (40)	6,450 (47)	Aloha State
Idaho	1890	Boise	1,034,000 (42)	83,557 (13)	Gem State
Illinois	1818	Springfield	11,625,000 (6)	56,400 (24)	Prairie State
Indiana	1816	Indianapolis	5,545,000 (14)	36,291 (38)	Hoosier State
Iowa	1846	Des Moines	2,652,000 (31)	56,290 (25)	Hawkeye State
Kansas	1861	Topeka	2,515,000 (32)	82,264 (14)	Sunflower State
Kentucky	1792	Frankfort	3,745,000 (24)	40,395 (37)	Bluegrass State
Louisiana	1812	Baton Rouge	4,517,000 (20)	48,523 (31)	Pelican State
Maine	1820	Augusta	1,247,000 (39)	33,215 (39)	Pine Tree State
Maryland	1788	Annapolis	5,025,000 (17)	10,577 (42)	Old Line State
Massachusetts	1788	Boston	5,985,000 (13)	8,257 (45)	Bay State
Michigan	1837	Lansing	9,318,000 (8)	58,216 (23)	Wolverine State
Minnesota	1858	St. Paul	4,426,000 (21)	84,068 (12)	North Star State
Mississippi	1817	Jackson	2,792,000 (30)	47,716 (32)	Magnolia State
Missouri	1821	Jefferson City	5,304,000 (15)	69,686 (19)	Show Me State
Montana	1889	Helena	798,000 (44)	147,138 (4)	Treasure State
Nebraska	1867	Lincoln	1,574,000 (37)	77,227 (15)	Cornhusker State
Nevada	1864	Carson City	1,198,000 (41)	110,540 (7)	Sagebrush State
New Hampshire	1788	Concord	1,251,000 (38)	9,304 (44)	Granite State
New Jersey	1787	Trenton	8,252,000 (9)	7,836 (46)	Garden State
New Mexico	1912	Santa Fe	1,809,000 (35)	121,666 (5)	Land of Enchantment
New York	1788	Albany	17,886,000 (3)	49,576 (30)	Empire State
North Carolina	1789	Raleigh	7,106,000 (11)	52,586 (28)	Tar Heel State
North Dakota	1889	Bismarck	643,000 (47)	70,665 (17)	Flickertail State
Ohio	1803	Columbus	10,742,000 (7)	41,222 (35)	Buckeye State
Oklahoma	1907	Oklahoma City	3,318,000 (28)	69,919 (18)	Sooner State
Oregon	1859	Salem	2,828,000 (29)	96,981 (10)	Beaver State
Pennsylvania	1787	Harrisburg	11,689,000 (5)	45,333 (33)	Keystone State
Rhode Island	1790	Providence	1,029,000 (43)	1,214 (50)	Ocean State
South Carolina	1788	Columbia	3,740,000 (25)	31,055 (40)	Palmetto State
South Dakota	1889	Pierre	711,000 (45)	77,047 (16)	Coyote State
Tennessee	1796	Nashville	5,135,000 (16)	42,244 (34)	Volunteer State
Texas	1845	Austin	19,012,000 (2)	267,339 (2)	Lone Star State
Utah	1896	Salt Lake City	1,893,000 (34)	84,916 (11)	Beehive State
Vermont	1791	Montpelier	579,000 (49)	9,609 (43)	Green Mountain State
Virginia	1788	Richmond	6,551,000 (12)	40,817 (36)	Old Dominion
Washington	1889	Olympia	4,841,000 (18)	68,192 (20)	Evergreen State
West Virginia	1863	Charleston	1,786,000 (36)	24,181 (41)	Mountain State
Wisconsin	1848	Madison	4,811,000 (19)	56,153 (26)	Badger State
Wyoming	1890	Cheyenne	495,000 (50)	97,914 (9)	Equality State
District of Columbia			620,000	67	

The words in the Glossary are defined to clarify their meaning in the text. The page numbers given after each definition refer to the places in the text where the words first appear.

Pronunciation Key

Certain glossary terms and other words have been respelled in the text as an aid to pronunication. The term *entrepreneur,* for example, has been respelled: AHN-truh-preh-NOOR. The small capital letters mean that the first syllable should be spoken with a minor stress. The large capital letters mean that the last syllable should be spoken with a major stress. The vowel sounds shown by the letters *ah, uh, eh,* and *oo* in the respelling correspond to the vowel sounds in the pronunciation key below.

Pronounce	as in	Pronounce	as in
a	hat	j	jet
ah	father	ng	ring
ar	tar	o	frog
ay	say	ō, oh	no
ayr	air	oo	soon
e, eh	hen	or	for
ee	bee	ow	plow
eer	deer	oy	boy
er	her	sh	she
ew	new	th	thick
g	go	u, uh	sun
i, ih	him	z	zebra
ī	kite	zh	measure

administration: a team of executive branch officials appointed by each President (page 201)
affirmative action: steps to counteract effects of past racial discrimination and discrimination against women (page 161)
aggression: an attack or threat of attack by another country (page 543)
alien: a citizen of one country who lives in another country (page 46)
alliance: a group of nations that have agreed to help or protect each other (page 530)
ambassadors: official representatives to foreign countries (page 198)
amendments: changes to the Constitution (p. 103)
answer: the defendant's written response to a complaint (page 436)
appeal: to ask a higher court to review a decision and determine if justice was done (page 221)
appellate jurisdiction: a court's authority to hear an appeal of a decision by another court (page 221)
apportioned: divided among districts (page 248)
arbitration: the use of a third person to make a legal decision that is binding on all parties (page 440)
arraignment: a court hearing in which the defendant is formally charged with a crime and enters a plea of guilty or not guilty (page 418)

bail: money that a defendant gives the court as a kind of promise that he or she will return for trial (page 418)
beliefs: certain ideas that people trust are true (page 16)
bias: a favoring of one point of view (page 482)
bicameral: two-house, as in a legislature with two houses (page 93)
bill: a proposed law (page 174)
board: a group of people who manage the business of an organization (page 264)
bonds: certificates that people buy from the government, which agrees to pay back the cost of the bond, plus interest, after a set period of time (page 250)
boycott: to refuse to buy a certain company's products (page 320)
budget: a plan for raising and spending money (page 180)
bureaucracy: an organization of government departments, agencies, and offices (page 201)
business cycle: a repeated series of "ups" of growth and "downs" of recession (page 354)

Cabinet: an important group of policy advisors to the President, made up of the executive department heads and a few other officials (page 203)
candidate: a person running for office (page 53)
canvass: to go door-to-door handing out political information and asking people which candidate they support (page 458)

capital: anything produced in an economy that is saved to be used to produce other goods and services (page 289)
capitalism: another name for market economy; a system in which people make their own decisions about how to save resources as capital and how to use their capital to produce goods and services (page 300)
caucus: a meeting of party leaders to discuss issues or choose candidates (page 466)
census: an official count of the population made every ten years to find out how many representatives each state should have (page 177)
charter: a document giving permission to create a government (page 70)
checks and balances: the system that gives each of the three branches of government ways to limit the powers of the other two (page 105)
citizen: a person with certain rights and duties under a government; a person who by birth or by choice owes allegiance, or loyalty, to a nation (page 46)
civil disobedience: breaking a law because it goes against personal morals (page 394)
civil law: the group of laws that help settle disagreements between people (page 400)
closed primary: a primary election in which a voter must be registered as a member of a party and may vote only for candidates of that party (page 467)
cloture: agreement to end the debate on a bill in the Senate (page 188)
cold war: a struggle between the superpowers, much like a real war but with no armed battles (page 529)
collective bargaining: the process by which representatives of a union and of a business discuss and reach agreement about wages and working conditions (page 320)
colony: a territory ruled by a more powerful nation called a colonial power (page 523)
command economy: an economic system in which the government or a central authority owns or controls the factors of production and makes the basic economic decisions (page 297)
common good, the: the well-being of all members of society (page 51)
common law: a body of law based on judges' decisions (page 396)
communism: a system under which the government owns all land, businesses, and resources (page 528)
compact: a written agreement to make and obey laws for the welfare of the group (page 80)
compensation: being "made whole" for harm caused by another person's acts (page 432)
complaint: a legal document that charges someone with having caused harm (page 436)
concurrent powers: the powers shared by the federal and state governments (page 104)
congressional district: the area that a member of the House represents (page 177)
constituents: the people a member of Congress represents (page 174)
constitution: a plan of government (page 80)
constitutional initiative: a process in which citizens can propose an amendment by gathering a required number of signatures on a petition (page 244)
consumer: a person who uses, or consumes, goods and services to satisfy his or her wants (page 35)
consumption: the act of buying or using goods or services (page 290)
containment: a policy of using military power and money to prevent the spread of communism (page 553)
contracts: legal agreements between buyers and sellers (page 434)
corporation: a business that is separate from the people who own it and legally acts as a single person (page 315)
crime: any behavior that is illegal because the government considers it harmful to society (page 399)
criminal law: the group of laws that tell which acts are crimes, how accused persons should be tried in court, and how crimes should be punished (page 399)
currency: the coins and paper bills used as money in an economy (page 328)

damages: money that is paid in an effort to compensate, or make up, for a loss (page 432)
defendant: the party who answers a complaint and defends against it in a court case (page 219)

deficit: the amount by which government spending is greater than government income (page 359)
deforestation: cutting and burning forests to clear land for farms and cattle grazing (page 566)
delegated powers: the powers given to Congress rather than to the states (page 101)
delinquent: a juvenile who is found guilty of a crime (page 424)
demand: the amounts of a product or service buyers are willing and able to buy at different prices (page 310)
demand deposit: the money in a checking account (page 332)
democracy: a system of government in which the power is shared by all the people (page 38)
deposition: the record of answers to questions asked of a witness in person before a trial (page 437)
détente: a lessening of tensions between the superpowers (page 531)
deterrence: keeping a strong defense to discourage aggression by other nations (page 543)
dictatorship: a government controlled by one person, called a dictator, who usually takes power by force, rather than by inheriting it (page 38)
diplomacy: the relations and communications carried out between countries (page 544)
direct democracy: a form of government in which laws are made directly by the citizens (page 75)
direct mail: a way of sending messages to large groups of people through the mail (page 479)
direct primary: an election in which members of a political party choose candidates to run for office in the name of the party (page 466)
discovery: the process of gathering evidence before a trial (page 437)
discrimination: the unfair treatment of a group of people compared with another group (page 11)
disposable income: the amount of money left after taxes have been paid (page 369)
diversity: differences (page 7)
dividends: payments from the profits of companies in which a person owns stock (page 369)
domestic policy: plans for dealing with national problems (page 199)
double jeopardy: being placed on trial twice for the same crime (page 138)
due process of law: a process by which the government must treat accused persons fairly according to rules established by law (page 137)

economy: a system for producing and distributing goods and services to fulfill people's wants (page 35)
eminent domain: the power of the government to take private property for public use (page 137)
entrepreneur: a person who starts a business (page 312)
equality: the condition of everyone having the same rights and opportunities (page 16)
equity: the use of general rules of fairness to settle conflicts in a civil court case (page 432)
excise tax: a charge on certain goods, such as alcoholic beverages, gasoline, and tobacco (page 249)
executive agreements: agreements with other countries that do not need Senate approval (page 198)
executive branch: the branch of government responsible for executing or enforcing the laws (page 196)
executive orders: rules or regulations that executive branch employees must follow (page 198)
executive privilege: the President's right to keep some information secret from Congress and the courts (page 209)

factors of production: the resources people have for producing goods and services to satisfy their wants (page 289)
federalism: the division of power between the states and the federal, or national, government (page 104)
felony: a crime for which the penalty is imprisonment for more than one year, a fine, or a combination of both. Felonies include crimes such as kidnapping and murder. (page 400)
filibuster: the use of long speeches to prevent a vote on a bill in the Senate (page 188)
fiscal policy: a government's decisions about the amount of money it spends and the amount it collects in taxes (page 355)
fixed expenses: expenses that remain the same from month to month (page 370)

floor leaders: officers who guide through Congress the bills that their party supports (page 183)
foreign aid: a program of giving military and economic help to other nations (page 544)
foreign policy: plans for guiding our nation's relationships with other countries (page 198)
free enterprise: the system in which individuals in a market economy are free to undertake economic activities with little or no control by the government (page 300)
freedom: the ability to say what you want, go where you want, and do you want (page 17)
fringe benefits: indirect payments for work (page 369)

general election: an election in which voters make final decisions about candidates and issues (page 474)
goods: physical products, such as food and clothing (page 35)
gross national product (GNP): the total dollar value of all final goods and services produced in a country in a year (page 357)

heritage: the traditions passed down from generation to generation (page 70)
home rule: the right of a city or county to choose its own form of government (page 276)

immigrants: people who move from one country to make their homes in another (page 8)
impeach: to accuse the President or other high government officials of serious wrongdoing (page 105)
income tax: a tax on what individuals and businesses earn (page 249)
incumbent: someone who already holds the office for which he or she is running (page 487)
independent voters: people who say they do not support a political party (page 465)
indictment: a formal charge against a person accused of a crime (page 418)
inflation: a general rise in the prices of goods and services throughout the economy (page 341)
initiative: the process by which citizens can propose laws (page 248)
injunction: a civil court order to do or not do a certain act (page 433)
insurance: a plan by which a company gives protection from the cost of injury or loss (page 376)
intelligence: information about another nation and what its government plans to do (page 546)
interest: payment for the use of capital (page 309)
interest groups: groups of people who work together for similar interests or goals (page 175)
intergovernmental revenue: money given by one level of government to another (page 273)
invest: to use money to help a business get started or grow, with the hope that the business will earn a profit (page 299)
isolationism: a foreign policy that seeks to limit our relations with other countries as much as possible (page 551)
issue: a point of conflict or a matter to be debated (page 496)
item veto: a state governor's power to reject particular parts, or items, of a bill (page 252)

judicial activism: an effort by judges to take an active role in policymaking by overturning laws relatively often (page 229)
judicial restraint: an effort by judges to avoid overturning laws and to leave policymaking up to the other two branches of government (page 230)
judicial review: the Supreme Court's power to overturn any law that it decides is in conflict with the Constitution (page 225)
jury of peers: a group of ordinary citizens who hear a court case and decide whether the accused person is innocent or guilty (page 50)
justice: fairness; the idea that every person deserves to be treated fairly (page 18)

labor unions: organizations of workers that seek to improve wages and working conditions and to protect members' rights (page 319)
laws: rules of society that are enforced by governments (page 392)
lawsuits: cases in which a court is asked to settle a dispute (page 432)
legal code: a written collection of laws, often organized by subject (page 397)

legislature: a group of people chosen to make laws (page 70)
liability insurance: insurance that protects a person from the costs of damage or injury to others (page 377)
liquidity: the ability to turn savings back into cash (page 375)
loan: an amount of money borrowed for a certain time period (page 333)
lobbyists: people who represent interest groups (page 175)

majority party: the political party with more members in the House or Senate (page 183)
market: a place or situation in which an exchange of goods or services takes place, such as stores, shops, or stock exchanges (page 35)
market economy: an economic system in which private individuals own the factors of production and are free to make their own choices about production, distribution, and consumption (page 298)
market price: the price at which buyers and sellers agree to trade (page 311)
media: television, radio, newspapers and magazines (page 479)
mediation: a process by which people agree to use a third party to help them settle a conflict out of court (page 440)
minority party: the political party with fewer members in the House or Senate (page 183)
misdemeanor: a crime for which the penalty is a jail sentence of not more than one year, a fine, or a combination of both. Littering and driving without a license are examples of misdemeanors. (page 400)
mixed economy: an economy that is a mixture of the characteristics of two or more of the three basic systems (page 300)
monarchy: a form of government in which all or most of the power is in the hands of one individual, the monarch. The monarch's authority is hereditary. (page 38)
monetary policy: regulation of the money supply by the Federal Reserve System (page 354)
money: anything that is generally accepted as payment for a good or service (page 36)
monopoly: a single business with the power to control prices in a market (page 350)
morals: beliefs about what is fair and what is right or wrong (page 394)
municipality: a government that serves people who live in an urban area (page 266)

national debt: the total amount of money the government owes to lenders (page 360)
nationalism: a feeling of loyalty to a nation, which is shared by its citizens (page 522)
natural rights: rights that people are born with and that no government can take away, such as the rights to life, liberty, and property (page 76)
naturalized: to have gone through the process of becoming a citizen. Naturalization is a process which applies to a person not born a citizen of the United States. (page 46)
neutrality: a policy of not taking sides in wars between other nations (page 552)
nominate: to name candidates to run for public office (page 456)
nonrenewable resource: a resource that cannot be replaced once it has been used (page 564)

open primary: a primary election in which voters do not need to declare a party before voting, but may vote for the candidates of only one party (page 467)
opportunity cost: the benefit given up when scarce resources are used for one purpose instead of the next best purpose (page 291)
ordinances: local laws (page 264)
original jurisdiction: a court's authority to hear a case first (page 221)

parole: letting an inmate go free to serve the rest of his or her sentence outside of prison (page 421)
partnership: a type of business in which two or more people share ownership (page 315)
patronage: the system in which party leaders do favors for loyal supporters of the party (page 465)

plaintiff: an individual or a group of people who bring a complaint against another party in a civil case (page 219)
planks: position statements on each specific issue in a party's platform (page 457)
platform: a statement of a party's official stand on major public issues (page 457)
plea bargaining: agreeing to plead guilty in exchange for a lesser charge or a lighter sentence (page 419)
pocket veto: a way in which the President can veto a bill by pocketing, or keeping, the bill for ten days, during which Congress ends its session (page 186)
policy: a plan of action designed to achieve a certain goal (page 174)
political party: an organization of citizens who wish to influence and control government by getting their members elected to office (page 456)
precedent: a guideline for how all similar court cases should be decided in the future (page 220)
precincts: voting districts (page 463)
president pro tempore: an officer who presides over the Senate when the Vice-President is absent. [Also known as president pro tem.] (page 183)
price: the amount a person must pay for a good or service (page 35)
probable cause: a good reason to believe that a suspect has been involved in a crime (page 417)
probation: a kind of sentence in which a person goes free but must be under the supervision of a court official called a probation officer (page 426)
profit: the difference between what it costs to produce something and the price the buyer pays for it (page 299)
propaganda: a message that is meant to influence people's ideas, opinions, or actions in a certain way (page 481)
property tax: a tax on land and buildings (page 272)
prosecution: a government body that brings a charge against a defendant who is accused of breaking one of its laws (page 219)
public assistance: government programs that give help to people in need (page 242)
public policy: government response to public issues (page 497)
racism: the belief that members of one's own race are superior to those of other races (page 11)
ratification: approval, as in approval of an amendment to the Constitution (page 82)
recall: a process for removing elected officials from office (page 248)
recession: a slowdown in economic activity and production (page 341)
referendum: the process by which a law proposed or passed by a state legislature is referred to the voters to approve or reject (page 248)
registration: the process of signing up to be a voter (page 474)
renewable resource: a resource that can be replaced after being used (page 564)
rent: payment for the use of land (page 309)
representatives: people who are chosen to speak and act for their fellow citizens in government (page 47)
republic: a government in which citizens elect representatives to make laws (page 75)
reserved powers: those powers that the Constitution neither gives to Congress nor denies to the states (page 104)
revenue: income (page 249)
rules: specific expectations about what our behavior should be (page 26)

sales taxes: charges made on purchases of goods and services, usually a percentage of the price of a product (page 249)
scarcity: the problem that resources are always limited in comparison with the number and variety of wants people have (page 291)
segregation: separation, as in separation of one racial group from another (page 159)
self-nomination: declaring that you are running for office (page 466)
separation of church and state: the situation in which government may not favor any religion or establish an official state religion (page 134)
separation of powers: dividing government power among legislative, executive, and judicial branches (page 77)
services: work that you will pay to have done, such as cleaning or repair work (page 35)

small claims court: a civil court that people may use when the amount of money they want to recover is small, usually not more than $1,000 or $2,000 (page 443)
social institutions: systems of values and rules that determine how our society is organized. Five major institutions in our society are the family, religion, education, the economy, and government. (page 28)
social roles: roles people play in real life, such as mother, husband, worker, friend, or consumer (page 55)
socialization: the process of learning how to participate in a group; learning to accept the values in a group and learning the rules for behavior within it (page 27)
sole proprietorship: a business owned by an individual (page 314)
sovereignty: a nation's power to make and carry out laws within its borders (page 522)
Speaker of the House: the presiding officer of the House of Representatives (page 183)
split ticket: the practice of voting for candidates of more than one party on the same ballot (page 465)
standard of living: the number and kinds of goods and services people can have (page 524)
status offender: a youth who is judged to be beyond the control of his or her parents or guardian (page 424)
statutes: written laws made by legislatures (page 395)
stock: shares of ownership in a corporation (page 315)
straight ticket: the practice of voting for the candidates of only one party (page 465)
strike: the situation in which workers refuse to work unless employers meet certain demands (page 320)
subpoena: a court order to produce a witness or document (page 437)
suffrage: the right to vote (page 155)
summit meeting: a meeting at which the President talks about important issues with heads of other governments (page 544)
supply: amounts of a product that producers are willing to offer at different prices (page 310)

terrorism: the use or threat of violence to spread fear, usually for the purpose of reaching political goals (page 567)
time deposit: a savings plan with a set length of time that money must be kept in the account and a penalty for withdrawing the money early (page 375)
traditional economy: an economic system in which the basic economic decisions are made according to long-established ways of behaving that are unlikely to change (page 296)
treaties: formal agreements with other countries (page 198)
trust: a group of several companies organized to benefit from the high prices they all agree to charge (page 350)

utilities: services needed by the public, such as water, gas, and electricity (page 268)

values: standards of behavior; guidelines for how people should treat each other (page 16)
variable expenses: expenses that change from month to month (page 371)
veto: to reject, as in to reject a bill (page 101)

wants: desires for goods and services (page 35)
warrant: a legal paper, issued by a court, giving police permission to make an arrest, seizure, or search (page 417)
warranty: a manufacturer's promise to repair a product if it breaks within a certain time from the date of purchase (page 373)
whips: assistant floor leaders in each house of Congress (page 183)
witnesses: people who have seen events or heard conversations related to a court case, or who have special information that may help settle a case (page 50)
write-in candidate: a candidate who asks voters to write his or her name on the ballot (page 466)

zoning: local rules that divide a community into areas and tell how the land in each area can be used (page 270)

Italicized page numbers preceded by an *f* indicate a special feature. ***Boldface*** page numbers indicate pages on which glossary terms first appear.

ILLUSTRATION CREDITS

Cover Photograph: Alex Bee*/Erickson Photography Inc.

Cover Illustration: Russell Leong

Table of Contents: i Curt Fischer*; **iii** Carlye Calvin; **iv** Tim Davis*; Curt Fischer*; **vii** Bohdan Hrynewych/Stock, Boston; **viii** Lynn Johnson/Black Star, Curt Fischer*; **x** Pete Silva/Picture Group

Unit 1: **xvi** Terry Ashe/TIME Magazine; **1** "Goddess of Liberty": New York State Historical Association, Cooperstown; Daguerreotype of Frederick Douglas: The National Portrait Gallery, Smithsonian Institution; photography by Curt Fischer*.

Chapter 1: **2** Bob Daemmrich/Stock, Boston; **6** Gabe Palmer/The Stock Market; **7** Larry Manning/Woodfin Camp & Associates; **9** The Bettman Archive; **10** Danny Lyon/Magnum Photos; **13** Jeanne M. Shutes; **14** Scala/Art Resource; **17** David Madison; **18** Tim Davis*.

Chapter 2: **24** Tom Sobolik/Black Star; **27** Tim Davis*; **30** Tim Davis*; **31** Courtesy The Rev. Henry Vellinga; **32** Pamela Price/Picture Group; **37** Chuck Fishman/Woodfin Camp & Associates.

Chapter 3: **44** Peter Yates/Picture Group; **49** Lionel Delevingne/Stock, Boston; **50** Chuck Feil/Stock, Boston; **52** Nancy Rica Schiff/Black Star; **57** Lester Sloan/Woodfin Camp & Associates; **64** Fred Ward/Black Star.

Unit 2: **66** Robert Rathe/Stock, Boston; **67** TIME cover of March 19, 1965: Time Inc. Magazines cover illustration by Ben Shahn; photography by Curt Fischer*.

Chapter 4: **68** Cary Wolinsky/Stock, Boston; **72** The Granger Collection; **73 L** Rare Book Division, The New York Public Library, Aster, Lenox and Tilden Foundations; **73 R** Culver Pictures, Inc.; **75** Bibliotheque Nationale, Paris; **76** The Bettman Archive; **77** By permission of the Houghton Library, Harvard University; **78** Library of Congress; **79** The Historical Society of Pennsylvania; **81** Cindy Charles*; **82** Culver Pictures, Inc.; **85** The Historical Society of Pennsylvania.

Chapter 5: **88** Michael O'Neill; **91** Commissioned by the PA, DE, NJ State Societies, Daughters of the American Revolution. Independence National Historic Park Collection. Copyright Louis Glanzman.; **92** The Thomas Gilcrease Institute of American History and Art, Tulsa, Oklahoma; **93** Henry E. Huntington Library and Art Gallery; **96** The Bettman Archive; **97** Library of Congress; **99** New York Historical Society, New York City; **100** Cary Wolinsky/Stock, Boston; **103** Sal DiMarco/Black Star.

Chapter 6: **130** Simon Nathan/The Stock Market; **133** The Bettman Archive; **138** Flip Schulke/Black Star; **141** UPI/Bettmann Newsphotos; **143** Arnold Zann/Black Star; **144** Elliott Smith*; **147** John Coletti/Stock, Boston.

Chapter 7: **150** Sylvia Johnson/Woodfin Camp & Associates; **154** Steve Schapiro/Black Star; **156** AP/Wide World Photos; **157** Vernon Merritt/Black Star; **160** Collection of the Supreme Court of the United States; **161** Carl Iwasaki/Life Magazine (c) 1953 Time Inc.; **162** Ellis Herwig/Stock, Boston; **164** Dennis Brack/Black Star; **167** Tim Davis*; **168** Independence National Historical Park Collection, painting by C.W. Peale.

Unit 3: **170** Catherine Karnow/Woodfin Camp & Associates; **171** East, Route 66 sign: Terry Moore/Woodfin Camp & Associates; Photography by Curt Fischer*.

Chapter 8: **172** Steve Weber/Stock, Boston; **175** Courtesy David and Reba Saks; **176** Cindy Charles*; **177** Al Stephenson/Picture Group; **179** Jon Feingersh/The Stock Market; **187** Mark Reinstein/Photoreporters.

Chapter 9: **194** Stacy Pick/Stock, Boston; **197** Brad Markel/Gamma-Liaison; **199** Dennis Brack/Black Star; **200** James Colburn/Photo Reporters; **202** Ken Regan/Camera 5; **205** Michael Sargent/The White House; **207** Webb/Magnum; **209** From the collection of the Louisiana State Museum; **210** Nixon Project/National Archives.

Chapter 10: **216** Steve Elmore/The Stock Market; **218** Michael Heron/Woodfin Camp & Associates; **219** Comstock; **226** The Supreme Court Historical Society; **227** Wally McNamee/Woodfin Camp & Associates; **229** UPI/Bettman Newsphotos; **230** Shepard Sherbell/Picture Group; **232** Tim Davis*; **236** The Bettman Archive.

Unit 4: **238** Donald Dietz/Stock, Boston; **239** photography by Curt Fischer*.

Chapter 11: **240** Bob Daemmrich/Stock, Boston; **243** By permission of Honolulu Star Bulletin; **245** Al Grillo/Picture Group; **247** Stacy Pick/Stock, Boston; **251** Shelly Katz/Black Star; **253** Harry Langdon Photography; **255** Luis Villota/The Stock Market.

Chapter 12: **262** John M. Roberts/The Stock Market; **265** Reprinted by permission: Tribune Media Services; **266** Andrew Holbrooke/Black Star; **270** Leo Touchet/Woodfin Camp & Associates; **271** Tim Davis*; **273** Barbara Docktor; **275** Marv Wolf/After-Image; **276** Bohdan Hrynewych/Stock, Boston; **278** Tim Davis*; **282** New York Historical Society, New York City.

Unit 5: **284** James R. Holland/Stock, Boston; **285** Toy bank: Strong Museum, Rochester, New York; Daguerreotype of man posing with tools of goldminer: Minnesota Historical Society; photography by Curt Fischer*.

Chapter 13: **286** Craig Aurness/West Light; **288** Billy E. Barnes/Stock, Boston; **289** Charles Gupton/Stock, Boston; **291** William Strode/Woodfin Camp & Associates; **293** Herb Snitzer/Stock, Boston; **294** Ted Horowitz/The Stock Market; **295** (c) Bradford F. Herzog; **297** Terry E. Eiler/Stock, Boston; **298** Wendy Stone/Bruce Coleman Inc.; **299** Martine Franck/Magnum; **300** Ricki Rosen/Picture Group.

Chapter 14: **306** Julie Houck/Stock, Boston; **308** Peter L. Chapman/Stock, Boston; **311** Tim Davis*; **313** James McGoon; **314** Tim Davis*; **315** Nubar Alexanian/Woodfin Camp & Associates; **316** Courtesy NCR Corporation; **317** Cotton Coulson/Woodfin Camp & Associates; **318** International Museum of Photography at George Eastman House; **322** Bob Abraham, Hawaii.

Chapter 15: **326** Erich Hartmann/Magnum Photos, Inc.; **329** Rare Book Division, New York Public Library; Astor, Lenox and Tilden Foundations; **331** Culver Pictures; **333** Bill Ross/West Light; **335** Palmer & Brillant*.

Chapter 16: **344** Bill Gillette/Stock, Boston; **347** Library of Congress—Lewis W. Hine photograph; **348** Ron Watts/Black Star; **350** The Granger Collection; **351** Tim Davis*; **352** Pam Price/Picture Group; **353** D.B. Owen/Black Star; **355** Fred Ward/Black Star; **360** Chuck Brooks; **362** Tim Davis*.

Chapter 17: **366** Leonard Freed/Magnum Photos, Inc.; **368** Chris Jones/The Stock Market; **370** Brian Smith/Stock, Boston; **371** Tim Davis*; **372** Lawrence Migdale/Stock, Boston; **373** (c) 1990 Sidney Harris; **375** Chris Jones/The Stock Market; **377** John Coletti/Stock, Boston; **379** Tim Davis*; **386** Chuck Nacke/Picture Group.

Unit 6: **388** Tim Davis; **389** "Nevada Sheriff's Department": Butler's Uniforms, San Francisco, CA; "Judge Jack Puffenberger, Toledo Municipal Court": Hart Associates; "Warning, Member Neighborhood Crime Watch": (c) The Sign Center, San Diego, CA; photography by Curt Fischer*.

Chapter 18: **390** Jennie Jones/Comstock; **393** NHTSA/U.S. Department of Transporation; **394** Jeff Zaruba/The Stock Market; **397** Lynn Johnson/Black Star; **398** Charles Feil/Stock, Boston; **400** Frank Siteman/Stock, Boston; **401** Harvard Law Art Collection; **402** Elliott Smith*.

Chapter 19: **410** James Marshall/The Stock Market; **412** Tim Davis*; **413** R.P. Kingston/Stock, Boston; **415** Cary Wolinsky/Stock, Boston; **418** Tim Davis*; **419** Stephanie Maze; **421** James Kamp/Black Star; **424** Steve Chenn/West Light; **425** The Odessa American.

Chapter 20: **430** Anne Heimann/The Stock Market; **433** Tim Davis*; **434** Nik Kleinberg/Stock, Boston; **435** Frank Siteman/Stock, Boston; **437** Jim Pickerall/Black Star; **438** Bob Daemmrich/Stock, Boston; **441** Keith Marcum/San Francisco Community Board Program; **442** Dick Ruddy*; **443** Daniel S. Brody/Stock, Boston; **446** Jeffrey E. Blackman/ The Stock Market; **450** Courtesy Justice Richard Neely.

Unit 7: **452** Berenholtz/The Stock Market; **453** photography by Curt Fischer*.

Chapter 21: **454** Dennis Brack/Black Star; **457** Charlie Archambault/ Picture Group; **458** Pete Silva/Picture Group; **461** UPI/Bettmann Newsphotos; **464** Lisa Quinones/Black Star; **467** Tom Haskell; **468** Rick Friedman/Black Star.

Chapter 22: **472** David Ryan/Photo 20–20; **475** Mark Richards/Picture Group; **477** Courtesy Curtis Gans; **479** Peter Morgan/Picture Group; **480** Kenneth Jarecke/Woodfin Camp & Associates; **485** Christopher Brown/Stock, Boston; **486** Jacques Chenet/Woodfin Camp & Associates.

Chapter 23: **494** Bill Wassman/The Stock Market; **497** Andrew Holbrooke/Black Star; **498** Trevor's Campaign for the Homeless; **499** Richard Howard/Black Star; **502** (c) 1987 Matt Herron; **503** Charles Steiner/Picture Group; **504** Elliott Smith*; **506** Peter Menzel/Stock, Boston; **510** David Sears/Gamma-Liaison; **512** Daniel S. Brody/Stock, Boston; **516** Culver Pictures.

Unit 8: **518** Roy Morsh/The Stock Market; **519** photography by Curt Fischer*.

Chapter 24: **520** Allsport Photography, USA; **523** Cary Wolinsky/ Stock, Boston; **525** Joe Viesti/Viesti Associates, Inc.; **527** Sebastiao Salgado/Magnum; **528** David Madison; **531** Delahaye/Sipa Press; **533** Jason Laure/Woodfin Camp & Associates; **534** NASA.

Chapter 25: **540** Charles Krebs/The Stock Market; **543** D.B. Owen/ Black Star; **545** Pedro Meyer/Black Star; **547** Tashi/Black Star; **549** Dennis Brack/Black Star; **550** Courtesy Susan Olson; **553** Steve McCurry/ Magnum; **554** Robert Wallis/SIPA Press; **555** A.F.P. Photo; **558** Elliott Smith*.

Chapter 26: **562** Peter Morgan/Picture Group; **566** Claus Meyer/ Black Star; **568** Owen Franken/Stock, Boston; **572** Joe Urban/Picture Group; **573** Tim Davis*; **575** Jacques Chenet/Woodfin Camp & Associates; **576** Susan Meiselas/Magnum; **580** Cynthia Johnson/Gamma-Liaison.

* Photos provided expressly for the publisher

Special thanks to The Paper Pile of San Anselmo, California, for their help in finding memorabilia for the Table of Contents and unit opener pages.

Information graphics by Glasgow and Associates.

TEACHER'S EDITION PHOTO ACKNOWLEDGMENTS

T2–3 Bob Daemmrich/Stock, Boston; **T4** Mark Antman/The Image Works; **T4–5** Spencer Grant/Stock, Boston; **T6** Bob Daemmrich/ Stock, Boston; **T7** Brian Parker/Tom Stack & Associates; **T8 B** Larry Kolvoord/The Image Works; **T8 T** Miriam White/The Stock Market; **T10 BL** Bob Daemmrich/Stock, Boston; **T10 BR** John Lei/Stock, Boston; **T10 T** Bob Daemmrich/Stock, Boston; **T12 L** Mark Sherman/ Bruce Coleman Inc.; **T12 T** Bob Daemmrich/The Image Works; **T12–13** Charles Gupton/Stock, Boston; **T14** Bob Daemmrich/Stock, Boston.